THE PAINTINGS OF BENJAMIN WEST

Benjamin West
by Sir Thomas Lawrence
1818–21. Oil on canvas
Wadsworth Atheneum
Hartford, Connecticut.
(detail)

The Paintings of
BENJAMIN WEST

Helmut von Erffa and Allen Staley

A BARRA FOUNDATION BOOK

Yale University Press · New Haven & London 1986

Designed by Gillian Greenwood

Filmset in Monophoto Baskerville in Great Britain by
BAS Printers Limited, Over Wallop, Hampshire
Printed in Italy by Amilcare Pizzi s.p.a., Milan

99696

Library of Congress Cataloging-in-Publication Data

Staley, Allen.
  The Paintings of Benjamin West.
  Bibliography : p.
  Includes index.
1. West, Benjamin, 1738–1820—Catalogs.   I. Title.
ND237. W45A4 1986   759.13   85–22500
ISBN 0–300–03355–9

Contents

Preface

This book contains a catalogue of the paintings and more ambitious drawings of Benjamin West, preceded by a brief overview of the course of West's art during a working career of approximately seventy years. Nothing comparable devoted to the artist now exists. West was an artist who had an immense reputation during his lifetime, and he remains one whose pivotal historical significance is widely acknowledged, but he is a figure whose contributions to the history of art have usually been seen separately and somewhat one-dimensionally, owing to the virtual impossibility heretofore of taking a comprehensive view of his very large *oeuvre*. Quite simply, the main purpose of the present volume is to rectify that situation by presenting all his paintings, together with the available documentation, thus allowing West's art to be seen and considered as a whole. It stems from a project that has been underway for over forty years. The genesis and history of that project, as well as the roles of the two authors, the late Helmut von Erffa and myself, call for a few words of explanation.

Helmut von Erffa was born in Luneburg, Germany, in 1900. He studied for a period at the Bauhaus before coming to the United States in 1923. In America he continued his education as an undergraduate at Harvard and as a graduate student at Harvard and at Princeton, where he received a Master of Fine Arts degree in 1938. During the early 1940s, he was on the faculty of Swarthmore College in Swarthmore, Pennsylvania, and there was responsible for a collection of drawings by Benjamin West that had been presented to the college by alumni and friends. The presence of that collection at Swarthmore, and of a Benjamin West Society inaugurated in 1931, is a reflection of the fact that Swarthmore College is a product of the Quaker community into which West was born in 1738. Indeed, the very house in which West is traditionally said to have been born still stands on the Swarthmore campus.

Professor von Erffa's initial study of West centered on identifying and explaining the subject matter of some of the drawings at Swarthmore. The earliest letters that I have found in the files upon which the catalogue entries in this volume are based date from 1944 and, it is perhaps interesting to note, were written by Agnes Mongan and C. H. Collins Baker, in response to queries about related drawings in their charges, and by Erwin Panofsky, about a Latin inscription and Anacreon. In 1946 von Erffa left Swarthmore for Rutgers University in New Brunswick, New Jersey, where he remained until his retirement in 1964, serving during most of his tenure there as chairman of the department of Art History. By 1951, his interest in Swarthmore's holdings had evolved into a comprehensive catalogue of West's drawings, and that, in response to the need to identify the finished works for which many of the draw-

Self portrait c. 1776 (Cat. No. 526)

ings were preparatory studies, rapidly turned into a catalogue of West's entire *oeuvre*. This proved to be an immense undertaking, but by 1976, some twenty-five years after the catalogue's commencement, it had reached a sufficient degree of completion for questions about when, where, and how it should be published to take on considerable urgency. Professor von Erffa's health and strength were then starting to fail, and it had become apparent to him that, on his own, he would not be able to bring the vast body of material that he had collected into final publishable form.

In 1976 I was invited by the Barra Foundation to assume the task of completing von Erffa's catalogue. I accepted the invitation, hoping and expecting to work in close consultation with Professor von Erffa, but with the understanding that I would take complete responsibility for the final work. Sadly, Professor von Erffa's health continued to deteriorate, and he died in February 1979. I have, therefore, carried on without the benefit of his participation and guidance, and I have written the entire catalogue as it now appears. I have also added the six introductory chapters providing a chronological perspective on West's artistic evolution. These chapters had not initially been envisioned as part of the book, but they came to seem necessary as I worked on thematically organized entries, which deal with problems raised by the specific works. Thus, the shortcomings, oversights, omissions, errors, and instances of dubious judgement in the following pages are solely due to me. Nonetheless, Professor von Erffa's name stands properly first on the title page. He began this undertaking, devoted over thirty years to it, provided the basic organizational framework that I have continued to follow, and collected a corpus of photographs and a huge amount of documentary material, which together constitute the essential core of the catalogue. Moreover, I have imbibed so much from his notes and correspondence that I have felt it only appropriate and proper to use the plural pronoun, "we", or variations thereof, whenever opinions are expressed. In the very few cases where I disagree with him, I have noted his opinion, in accordance with our initial agreement about how we would deal with any potential conflicts.

Like von Erffa's, my interest in West commenced as a result of curatorial responsibility in the artist's native state. In 1965, Evan H. Turner, the director of the Philadelphia Museum of Art, where I had recently been hired as an assistant curator of paintings, suggested that I write an article for the museum's bulletin about West's sketch (No. 36 in this catalogue) for *Agrippina Landing at Brundisium with the Ashes of Germanicus*, which had been given to the museum earlier that year by the Robert L. McNeil, Jr., Trusts. In 1975, the impetus to do more extended work on West was provided by sight of *Lot and His Daughters Conducted by Two Angels* (No. 238), which had been acquired by the Detroit Institute of Arts a few years before. This splendid late work (painted in 1810), which initially had belonged to a patron of Turner's, made me realize that there were dimensions to West's art and his place in the history of art that I had never suspected. In 1976–77 a grant from the National Endowment for the Humanities allowed me to spend a sabbatical year in London, where I planned to investigate West's later career and his significance for developments in English art of the nineteenth century. During the course of that year, with the approval of the authorities at the National Endowment, I redirected my activities in response to the invitation to take over responsibility for the present catalogue.

As mentioned above, that invitation came from the Barra Foundation. This publication would not exist if it had not been for the Foundation's recognition of the catalogue's importance, its willingness to make a large and nebulously open-ended investment, and its continuing commitment to a project that has stretched on beyond even the direst predictions of what would be required. The Foundation provided Professor von Erffa the assurance that the catalogue upon which he had been laboring would be published. It also guaranteed to him that the material which he had collected would be preserved after completion of the catalogue and made available to future scholars by being deposited in the Yale Center for British Art in New Haven. Since 1976, the Foundation has provided me a team of research assistants, photographs and other research tools, funds for travel, and funding for a sabbatical leave in 1982–83 that allowed me to devote a year's full-time work to the book. It has also made a significant subvention to underwrite the costs of its publication. I am deeply indebted to Robert L. McNeil, Jr., the Barra Foundation's president, for his whole-hearted, generous, and patient support. I should also point out that long before the Barra Foundation undertook responsibility for this project, his beneficence to the Philadelphia Museum in 1965 set in motion a chain of events that led to my participation. Professor Jules Prown, as an advisor to the Foundation, had an instrumental role in its decision to take on the catalogue, and, as a scholar and friend, he has given advice and assistance to both authors. Gail H. Fahrner, the Foundations's program officer, has tended to the innumerable day-to-day problems with efficiency and grace.

Columbia University, where I have been employed since 1969, has provided me facilities and support, and my colleagues and students have stimulated and helped me in an infinite number of ways. Seven present or former graduate students at Columbia—Barbara Coffey Bryant, Michael Fitzgerald, Lewis Andrews, Janet Boyd, Nancy Heiner, William Kennon, and Marjorie Wieseman—have played major roles in the preparation and completion of the book, the three first named as research assistants employed by the Barra Foundation, the latter four working under the auspices of the University. Mrs Bryant recorded and measured all the prints after West's paintings in the Department of Prints and Drawings of the British Museum; she transcribed the titles and frequently appended texts from the catalogues of Royal Academy and other exhibitions, allowing us to give them in full in this catalogue; she went through the typescript of Joseph Farington's diary to find and transcribe all passages pertinent to West, which constitute a major component of many entries; and she performed the same task with the collections of newspaper cuttings in the libraries of the Victoria and Albert Museum and the Courtauld Institute of Art. Michael Fitzgerald sought out and transcribed documentary material in the microfilm holdings of the Archives of American Art and in other repositories in New York. Lewis Andrews is responsible for Appendix

II of this volume and for the Index of Subjects and Titles. All seven have shared the Herculean job of checking the data for every entry, tracking down obscure, incomplete, and incorrect references, finding others, and guaranteeing the completeness and accuracy of what is presented here. With enterprise, ingenuity, and hard work, they have found solutions to problems which I considered impenetrable, and, in many ways, their contributions, which lie behind every word of this book, are of as fundamental importance to the catalogue's ultimate value as a work of reference as those of the co-authors whose names appear on the title page.

A surprisingly large number of West's paintings still belong to descendants of the patrons for which they were painted. First among those patrons, not only because of rank, but because of the sixty-odd pictures which the artist painted for him, was West's monarch, King George III, described by the painter as "the best friend I ever had in my life." The largest gathering, by far, of West's paintings remains that in the English Royal Collection. We are grateful to Her Majesty the Queen for her gracious permission to reproduce no less than thirty paintings by West, as well as several related drawings, and to quote extensively from the Farington Diary, which is in the Royal Library at Windsor Castle. It is also a pleasure to point out that West served for almost thirty years as Surveyor of the King's Pictures, and to acknowledge the significant assistance provided to us by Sir Oliver Millar, the present holder of that position. In addition to the help that he has given us directly for almost the entire span of time that this catalogue has been underway, Sir Oliver has provided a model of scholarship in his catalogue of *Later Georgian Pictures in the Collection of Her Majesty the Queen*, and our debts to it in our entries for pictures from the Royal Collection are manifest.

Among West's other original patrons, Chief Justice William Allen of Philadelphia more than any one else made it possible for the artist to leave the American colonies, study in Italy, and pursue a career in England. His descendant, the late Anthony Barnes, did considerable research for the sake of this catalogue into the history of his forebear's acquisitions, and Anthony Barnes's widow (now also deceased) and daughters have continued a tradition which began when West took passage to Leghorn on William Allen's ship, the *Betty Sally*, in 1760.

The authors have received much help and hospitality from descendants of the artist, particularly Mrs. F. C. W. Howard, Mrs. Leänore Murray, the late Mrs. Eleanor Rule, the late Herbert G. Margary, Aubyn Raphael Margary, and Aubyn de Margary, to whom I express our gratitude.

For a catalogue of this sort, we have inevitably drawn on the facilities of many libraries and other repositories of archival material. Helmut von Erffa's study of West began at Swarthmore College, and the Friends Historical Library at Swarthmore contains a major collection of material related to West, which we have used extensively. The Archives of American Art in Washington and New York have provided us access to much manuscript material via microfilm; we have also consulted the important possessions of the Historical Society of Pennsylvania and the American Philosophical Society directly. We have made heavy use of the photographic collections and other holdings of the Witt Library, The Frick Art Reference Library, the Paul Mellon Centre for Studies in British Art, the National Portrait Gallery in London, and of the major auction houses, Christie's and Sotheby's. The Department of Prints and Drawings of the British Museum has been a resource to which we have turned constantly. Additionally, we have worked extensively in the British Library, the library of the Victoria and Albert Museum, the New York Public Library, and, of course, the libraries of Rutgers University and Columbia University. To the librarians and staffs of all these institutions, and of others which we have used less frequently, we are indebted for permission to use, reproduce, or quote from materials in their possessions, and for countless acts of assistance.

To the owners of works by the artist, we are indebted for permission to include them in this catalogue, for hospitality to both of the the authors on visits to see works in their possession, and for much information that has found its way into the following pages. We are equally indebted to the curators of museums that possess works included in this catalogue, to the proprietors of galleries that own or have owned works by West, and to the auction houses through which works by the artist have passed. I have tried to acknowledge specific debts in the individual entries, although I have undoubtedly overlooked many. Over the years, both authors have also benefitted more generally from long-standing interest in and encouragement for our labor on the part of many colleagues and friends. The list that follows is an attempt to name some of those people, past and present, who have given significant, frequent, and much-appreciated aid either to Helmut von Erffa or to me, or, in many instances, to both of us in our work on the catalogue: Boyd Alexander, Brian Allen, Mortimer Brandt, Martin Butlin, Robert Carlen, Professor Eric Carlson, T. A. Carter, Charles D. Childs, Margaret Christian, Ronald Cohen, Malcolm Cormack, Mary Bartlett Cowdrey, Edward Croft-Murrary, Gillian Darley, Jane Dillenberger, Professor John Dillenberger, William Drummond, Professor Donald Drew Egbert, Professor Dorinda Evans, Stuart Feld, Kathleen Foster, Henry Francis, Charlotte Frank, Robert Frank, Professor William Gerdts, Charles Gibbs-Smith, Jack Goodison, St. John Gore, Professor Lawrence Gowing, Janet Green, Robin Hamlyn, Norman Hirschl, Graham Hood, Mrs. Henry W. Howell, Jr., Heidi Jackson, John Kerslake, Jan Klein, Nancy Little, Richard Lloyd, Professor Thomas J. McCormick, Professor Edward A. Maser, James Miller, Professor Charles Mitchell, David Moore-Gwyn, Owen Morshead, Edward Morris, Morton Morris, Charles M. Mount, Professor Kathleen J. Nicholson, Lucy Oakley, Richard Ormond, William Plomer, Nancy Pressly, Professor William Pressly, M. S. Robinson, Joseph Rishel, Oswaldo Rodriguez, Professor Robert Rosenblum, Francis Russell, Anna Wells Rutledge, Sidney Sabin, Helen Sanger, Charles Coleman Sellers, Theodore Siegl, Professor Theodore Sizer, Victor Spark, Professor Wolfgang Stechow, Mildred Steinbach, John Sunderland, Paul Thomson, Robert C. Vose, Jr., S. Morton Vose, II, R. J. B. Walker, Professor Robert Walker, André Wauters, Mr. and Mrs. Robert Weatherall, Julius Weitzner, Anne Somerville Wiegert, Clare Wilkins, and Michael Wynne. Without their contributions, others that are acknowledged in individual entries, and many others that go unacknowledged, this book would be far less complete.

Helmut von Erffa started to accumulate material destined to be reproduced in this book when he started to work on West. His collection of photographs (which will eventually go to Yale) is the basic tool with which this catalogue has been built. Many were made for him by the firms of A. C. Cooper Ltd. and Fleming and Co. in London. He and I have also benefited enormously from the kind generosity with which the staff of Sotheby's and many individual dealers have sent us photographs of works when they have appeared on the market. Before the Barra Foundation assumed the burden, the Photograph Collection of the Department of Art History and Archaeology of Columbia University acquired numerous photographs on my behalf, and it has provided many of those reproduced in this book. The Witt Library and the Paul Mellon Centre for the Study of British Art have also been important sources. We are indebted to Christopher White, the former director of the Mellon Centre, and to Mrs. Evelyn Newby of the Centre's Photo Archive for undertaking to make many photographs for us in London and vicinity, and to Darrel Sewell, Curator of American Art at the Philadelphia Museum of Art, for assistance in obtaining photographs of works in and around Philadelphia. At the Yale University Press, Celia Jones has gathered together the many photographs that remained outstanding as the book went to press with professional aplomb, and she has obtained most of the transparencies used for the color reproductions.

To all of the people responsible for producing this large and complicated work, my gratitude is heartfelt. John Nicoll, the Managing Director of the Yale University Press in London, has been part of the plans for the book as long as I have. Gillian Greenwood has carried out the complex job of mixing together text and image, with results that seem to me both brilliant and sympathetic to the material. Susan Haskins has been a model editor, who has devoted long hours, arduous work, and a great deal of herself to the undertaking, and in a ridiculously short time has brought a leavening of consistency, propriety, and discipline to the huge mass of material presented to her. Marjorie Wieseman and Della Sperling corrected the galley proofs with dispatch, exemplary care, and thoroughness. Tracie Felker has assisted with the indices and numerous other final details.

For help in a variety of ways and for good-natured tolerance of a project that has dominated my life and has substantially affected theirs over the last decade, I thank my wife Etheleen and our sons, Oliver and Peter Staley. Helmut von Erffa's wife, Eleanor, and their daughter, Julie Gregg, have also lived with West as part of their lives for a considerably longer span of time. I am grateful to Eleanor von Erffa for her continuing support and good will and for her judicious balance of concern and forebearance as her husband's life work has proceeded towards publication. I hope that she finds this book a worthy fulfillment of the venture she saw begun over forty years ago.

Allen Staley

1 America 1738–1760

President of the Royal Academy, Historical Painter to the King of England, teacher and shining example to three generations of American artists, Benjamin West during the years prior to his death at the age of eighty-one in 1820 was the most prominent artist in the English-speaking world. In France, according to a visitor to Paris in 1814, "the French artists held Mr. West in the highest esteem as an Artist, and . . . when David spoke of him . . . He was quite moved to tears. For other British Artists they have no applause."[1] Works by him were in the collections of the czars of Russia (Nos. 132, 537, and 565) and of several German courts (Nos. 18, 25, 95, 212, and 217). Well before his death, however, his reputation had started to plummet among younger artists and critics, and it eventually declined to depths from which it has not yet fully recovered. As a consequence, West has probably been less attended to by scholars and is less appreciated by larger audiences than any other artist of comparable stature, but for over half a century, loved or scorned, he was one of the most conspicuous landmarks in the English and indeed the international artistic milieu.

As West approached his eightieth birthday, although mention of his name in the press was invariably accompanied by the adjective "venerable," he in no way withdrew into honored retirement, but rather produced a sequence of extraordinarily ambitious works, which kept him in the public eye more firmly than ever. His fame inevitably made him an object of attention, and hence we are well supplied with countless bits of information about his latter years from contemporary letters and diaries, particularly the voluminous diaries kept by his fellow artist and Royal Academician Joseph Farington, in which West as the Academy's leader and chief ornament plays the central role. His stature at the end of a successful and eventful career also explains the numerous catalogues of his works and reverential accounts of his life that appeared in a variety of English and American publications. A brief notice and a partial list of his exhibited pictures appeared in the *European Magazine* in 1794, and in 1804 came the first of several "complete catalogues" of his *oeuvre* accompanied by more substantial biographical accounts.[2] In 1816 the Scottish novelist John Galt published *The Life and Studies of Benjamin West, Esq. President of the Royal Academy of London, Prior to his Arrival in England; Compiled from Materials Furnished by Himself*, to which in the year of West's death Galt added a second volume devoted to the artist's English years. As their titles indicate, the main source of information for these two volumes was West, and, according to Galt, West read, or was read, the texts of both and approved them.[3] The first is full of wonderful tales of an instinctive genius, who made his first paintbrush by stealing hairs from the tail and back of the family cat, who was taught by the Indians to prepare colors, and who later astonished the *cognoscenti* of Rome by comparing the *Apollo Belvedere* to a Mohawk warrior. These stories are told "in a spirit which we are more accustomed to find applied to South Italian Saints than to a Quaker Academician who lived into the last century,"[4] and few modern scholars take them seriously. Nevertheless, since the stories evidently came from the aging artist, they either record what he genuinely thought had occurred in his early life, or what he wanted Galt and Galt's readers to believe about it. Although some details may be suspect, the main outlines of that life as presented by Galt are confirmed by an essentially similar account based on interviews with West in 1818 and published in 1820 by William Carey, who in 1817 had devoted a book-length treatise to one of West's paintings (No. 401), and they fit with what we can deduce from the extant early works and from the contemporary documentation that is here and there available.[5] One brief phase of West's early life, his visit to Italy from 1760 to 1763, is remarkably well recorded in two long letters by West[6] and by a number of other sources (including even a Florentine surgeon's description of an operation on the artist's ankle);[7] otherwise, however, we must rely primarily upon Galt to track West's progress to that point where he had achieved sufficient prominence to claim notice in the letters, diaries, and memoirs of his contemporaries.

West was born in Springfield, Pennsylvania, near Philadelphia, on 10 October 1738. Although he grew up in a Quaker community, he does not seem ever to have been a member of the Society of Friends,[8] despite occasional statements to the contrary (see No. 524). Nevertheless, the contrast between West's humble beginnings in a rural Quaker village in what was still a remote and relatively recently settled colony and his subsequent role as a famous artist, favorite of the King of England and President of the Royal Academy, was sufficient to give mythic dimensions to Galt's presentation of his life's story. After setting the picturesque anecdotes aside, what we can distill from Galt and from other sources is that West from an early age was encouraged by a family friend in the pursuit of his future career and was given paints and engravings to copy. An obscure, somewhat mysterious, and definitely minor painter named William Williams, whom West met in Philadelphia around 1747, gave the boy advice and also lent him books on painting by Charles Alphonse du Fresnoy and Jonathan Richardson. We do not know much about West's early education but his uncertain command of spelling and grammar in later life suggests that it was slim. In 1804 his wife told Joseph Farington, "He was so devoted to drawing while a Child and a Youth, that every other part of his education was neglected."[9] Around 1756 he attracted the attention of the Reverend William Smith, the first Provost of the newly formed College of Philadelphia, which later was to become the University of Pennsylvania. Smith invited West to study with him in Philadelphia and there provided him the rudiments of a classical education specially designed to serve his needs as an artist.[10]

The earliest paintings by West now known are probably two small paintings of the Morris children (Nos. 667 and 668, ill. p. 4), which according to tradi-

Self-Portrait, c. 1758–59 (Cat. No. 524)

Self-Portrait, 1793 (Cat. No. 529)

Jane Morris, c. 1752 (Cat. No. 668)

tion were painted about 1752. Modest in scale and full of naïve charm that seems entirely appropriate to the tender years of the subjects, they reveal not only the inexperience of the artist (who would have been fourteen years old in 1752), but also the provincial limitations of art in the American colonies at the middle of the eighteenth century. West's technical competence progressed rapidly in the following few years, and he undoubtedly profited by studying what works he could by older artists such as William Williams, Gustavus Hesselius, who had been working in Philadelphia on and off since 1712, and John Hesselius, Gustavus's son, who became active as a portraitist around 1750. Several paintings which West probably painted in 1755 or 1756 during a visit to Lancaster, Pennsylvania, show a considerable advance over the portraits of the Morris children, and the most ambitious of them, the portraits of the attorney George Ross and his wife (Nos. 691 and 692 *opposite*), have a dignity that is truly remarkable for an artist still no more than eighteen years old.

In the Lancaster paintings West does not appear to have been trying to imitate the work of any one artist, but there can be little doubt that in Philadelphia subsequently he did deliberately adopt the style and mannerisms of the peripatetic English-born painter John Wollaston, who had first visited the city

John Hesselius, *Lynford Lardner*, 1749. Oil on canvas, 39¼ × 32 in. Private collection

Mrs. George Ross,
c. 1755–56 (Cat. No. 692)

in 1752 and reappeared there in 1757 or 1758.[11] The close similarity of West's portraits of Elizabeth Peel (No. 681) and Mrs. William Smith (No. 701) to pictures by Wollaston was pointed out by William Sawitzky in his fundamental article about West's American work, published in 1938,[12] and it is worth mentioning that three paintings included in this catalogue (Nos. 642, 663, ill. p. 8, and 717) at one time or another have born attributions to Wollaston. Although an artist of modest abilities and ambitions, Wollaston was probably the most technically proficient painter yet to be active in the colonies. He brought with him a style of portraiture formed in England in the 1730s and 1740s and reminiscent of artists such as Joseph Highmore or Thomas Hudson, which appeared sufficiently sophisticated and advanced in Philadelphia in 1758 to inspire an effusive "Verses inscribed to Mr. Wollaston" in the twelfth number of the recently established *American Magazine and Monthly Chronicle for the British Colonies*. The author of these verses, Francis Hopkinson, praised "famed Wollaston" at considerable length:

John Wollaston, *Margaret Oswald, c.* 1758. Oil on canvas, 50 × 40 in. The National Trust, Cliveden, Germantown, Pennsylvannia

> Ofttimes with wonder and delight I stand
> To view th'amazing conduct of your hand.

He then turned from Wollaston to devote his last ten lines to West:

> Nor let the muse forget thy name O West,
> Lov'd youth, with virtue as by nature blest!
> If such the radiance of thy *early Morn*,
> What bright effulgence must thy Noon adorn?
> Hail sacred Genius! may'st thou ever tread,
> The pleasing path your Wollaston has lead.
> Let his just precepts all your works refine,
> Copy each grace, and learn like him to shine,
> So shall some future muse her sweeter lays,
> Swell with your name, and give you all *his* praise.[13]

In urging emulation of Wollaston as the appropriate path for West to follow, these lines suggest that West had already taken Wollaston as his model. They also demonstrate the degree of public visibility achieved in Philadelphia by the younger artist before he had yet reached his twentieth birthday. Indeed, as pointed out in a footnote to the "Verses inscribed to Mr. Wollaston," the reference there to West was the second time he had been noticed in the *American Magazine*. In the previous February one of his own paintings had inspired a poem by an anonymous author, "Upon seeing the Portrait of Miss **—** by Mr. West," and that poem was preceded by a prefatory note identifying the artist:

> We are glad of this opportunity of making known to the world, the name of
> so extraordinary a genius as Mr. West. He was born in Chester county in this
> province, and without the assistance of any master, has acquired such a
> delicacy and correctness of expression in his paintings, joined to such a laudable
> thirst of improvement, that we are persuaded, when he shall have obtained
> more experience and proper opportunities of viewing the productions of able
> masters, he will become truly eminent in his profession.[14]

Jane Galloway (Mrs. Joseph Shippen), c. 1757
(Cat. No. 622)

The author of the poem (which says nothing of significance about West's painting) and the subject of the painting have not been certainly identified, although there has been speculation about both (see Nos. 622 *above* and 701), but the writer of the prefatory note was almost certainly West's mentor, the Reverend William Smith, the founder and editor of the *American Magazine*. Francis Hopkinson, who wrote the verses on Wollaston and may have written

Thomas Mifflin, c. 1758–59 (Cat. No. 663)

those about the "Portrait of Miss **—**," was one of four students of Smith at the College of Philadelphia whom, according to John Galt, the Provost recommended to West "as possessing endowments of mind greatly superior to the common standard of mankind."[15] Thus the attention paid to West in the *American Magazine* must be seen as a product of the interest taken in the artist by Smith, and as part of Smith's program of promoting and directing his early career. Because of Smith, West was propelled into an intellectually precocious milieu in Philadelphia, and it would be due to Smith's subsequent efforts on his behalf that he would leave that milieu in 1760 to view "the productions of able masters" in Italy.

Smith had initially taken an interest in West because of one work, which he had seen on a visit to Lancaster, the *Death of Socrates* (No. 4, ill. p. 10), West's first venture in painting a historical subject. Even more than the portraits which West executed in Lancaster contemporaneously, this painting reveals all the awkwardness and naïveté of an untutored provincial artist, but at the same time it is an extraordinarily prophetic work, whose subject anticipates not only the paintings with which West in subsequent years would make his reputation in England but indeed the entire Neo-Classical movement. The aspirations embodied in the attempt to paint such a subject were undoubtedly what led Smith to take the artist under his wing, but those aspirations would seem not to have stemmed from West himself but from an earlier patron of the young artist, the Lancaster gunsmith and inventor William Henry (see No. 637). At a time when the professional painters in America were to a man portrait painters, Henry had sufficiently advanced ideas to tell West that he was wasting his time painting portraits and to urge him to devote himself to historical subjects "illustrating the moral effect of the art of painting." West knew nothing of the subject that Henry proposed for him to paint, and the undertaking was commenced by Henry's reading to West the story of the death of Socrates. Henry also provided West a compositional model to imitate in the form of an engraved illustration of the same subject after a drawing by Hubert Gravelot, which served as frontispiece to the volume from which he had read, and he had a worker in his factory pose for the half-naked figure standing above Socrates at the center of the composition.

It would be unrealistic to think that an eighteen-year-old boy of West's background would have had sufficient familiarity with the details of Socrates' death to have been able to compose a picture of the subject without consulting a historical text, so we cannot take the fact that he was read the story as evidence in itself of the inadequacies of his education. Nevertheless, Galt's account of the genesis of the work foretells his descriptions of the circumstances under which West undertook his two most important paintings of classical subjects from the following decade: *Agrippina Landing at Brundisium with the Ashes of Germanicus* (No. 33), for which the Archbishop of York, or one of his sons, read to West from Tacitus, and the *Departure of Regulus* (No. 10), for which George III read to him from Livy. These repeated anecdotes do provide some confirmation of what Mrs. West told Farington about West's neglect of proper study, for which Provost Smith's tutorials could have compensated only so

far. Although West was a painter of learned subjects, he was not himself a
learned man. The anecdotes also underscore the important roles that West's
patrons played in giving shape to his career. In his most ambitious departures
in America in the 1750s West carried out programs that had been prescribed
for him by Henry and Smith, as subsequently in England in the 1760s he would
be directed by the Archbishop and the King. Nevertheless, to attract such
enlightened patrons in his native land and such exalted ones in his adopted
home, West must have had extraordinary qualities of personality, and he must
have shown extraordinary signs of promise. And despite its manifest inadequacies, the early *Death of Socrates* was certainly the most ambitious and interesting
painting that had been produced in the American colonies to date.[16] It is not
a copy of the Gravelot illustration, but an original composition in which West
has rearranged and rethought every detail. In studying a semi-nude figure

The Death of Socrates, c. 1756 (Cat. No. 4)

Hubert Gravelot and J. P. Le Bas, *The Death of Socrates*, 1739.
Engraving (see catalogue entry No. 4, note 4)

from the life he sought to impart to the work an element of actuality that the illustration did not provide, and the expression on each face and the gesture of every limb, however awkwardly expressed, do embody a carefully worked out variety of responses to the solemn central event. The crude gestures and expressions accompany a simplification of Gravelot's spatially-conceived asymmetrical vertical composition into a symmetrically balanced and planar horizontal arrangement. All these qualities and changes can and should be interpreted as reflections of a young artist's limited competence, but, in turning a sophisticated, if conventional, late Baroque design into a work of primitive directness, West imbued his painting with thought and feeling to give it greater narrative clarity and expressive power than his model. This small painting is an isolated anomaly in West's *oeuvre*, separated from all his known subsequent history paintings by a considerable span of years, by education, and by experience. West's later career was born in Italy, not America. Nevertheless, the *Death of Socrates* was not forgotten. West's son Raphael went to see it on a trip to America around 1800; West discussed it with an American visitor in 1807; and Galt's extended account of it in 1816 must reflect the artist's own view of its importance in his early advancement as an artist.

The one other historical composition that West is known to have painted in America has evidently been destroyed (see No. 290), and a genre painting of a man reading by candlelight, which had been inspired by the sight of a Flemish picture, had been lost to sight by the time Galt wrote in 1816 (see No. 454). An early seascape, probably copied from an unidentified Dutch or

Landscape with Cow, (?)*c.*1752–53 (Cat. No. 481)

Flemish source (No. 480), and what is probably a landscape composition of West's own invention (No. 481 *above*) belong to the Pennsylvania Hospital in Philadelphia. Galt mentions two copies done in America, one after an engraving of the well-known *Belisarius* of Salvator Rosa (No. 517), the other after an unidentified *St. Ignatius* in the manner of Murillo (No. 512), but neither is now known. The latter is dimly reflected in a portrait of Provost Smith (No. 699), which Smith induced West to paint, as an experiment, in the style and attitude of the *St. Ignatius*, but that portrait is now such a complete ruin that we can only guess at its original appearance. It was probably West's most adventurous and complex American portrait, and the only one in which he treated a portrait as a composition showing the sitter in a characteristic act or situation rather than merely posing for the artist, but we have no way of knowing how closely West modelled his likeness of the Protestant clergyman and teacher on the earlier painting of the founder of the Jesuit order. Otherwise

West's American portraits, which constituted the preponderant part of his work done prior to 1760, do not depart radically in kind from the pattern of the painters active around West in Philadelphia such as Wollaston and John Hesselius. At their best, however, as for example in the portrait of the future Governor Mifflin (No. 663, ill. p. 8), which was probably one of the last portraits painted by West before his departure from Philadelphia, they do have a freshness and vitality that makes them memorable in a way that paintings by Wollaston and Hesselius rarely, if ever, are. By the end of the 1750s, comparable or superior portraits were being painted in Boston by West's exact contemporary, John Singleton Copley, but in Philadelphia West had outstripped his competition and learned all that he was going to learn locally. He required stimulus, experience, and opportunities that colonial Pennsylvania could no longer provide him.

Galt reports that West felt he had to leave Philadelphia for three reasons: he could not raise his prices if he stayed constantly in one place; he needed to see life in various lights; and "he was profoundly sensible, by this time, that he could not hope to attain eminence in his profession, without inspecting the great master-pieces of art in Europe, and comparing them with his own works in order to ascertain the extent of his own powers."[17] To fulfill the first of these goals and to help pay for the second and third, West travelled to New York, probably in 1759. There, according to Galt, he remained eleven months, had "much employment in taking likenesses," and doubled his prices.[18] Yet not a single work painted by West in New York is now known, and this lacuna has led to questions of whether he stayed as long or did as much in New York as Galt claims.[19] It also leaves questions about a significant phase in West's progress, since the New York paintings were presumably the last executed by him in the western hemisphere. While there he heard from Provost Smith of a merchant ship about to leave Philadelphia for Italy, upon which Smith had arranged for him to take passage. West returned to Philadelphia and sailed on 12 April 1760. He arrived at the port of Leghorn (or Livorno) on 16 June, and was in Rome by 10 July.

II Italy and England

His Italian sojourn was to last three years. Upon arriving in Rome he was almost immediately plagued by ill health, and after less than six weeks he was forced to return to Leghorn to recuperate. A return to Rome precipitated a relapse at the end of seven months, a second return to Leghorn in the summer of 1761, and a further stay there of four months. On this occasion, after the fever that had driven him from Rome had subsided, he was found to have a dangerous infection in his left ankle that required specialized attention, for which he went to Florence in November 1761. There the eminent surgeon Angelo Nannoni performed four operations, the last on 2 February 1762. West was then confined to bed until May and after that had a slow recovery which severely restricted what he could do. In August 1762 he left Florence for a tour of Bologna, Parma, and Venice, where he evidently stayed for much of the autumn (see No. 676). After a brief second stay in Florence during which he completed a copy of the *Venus of Urbino* by Titian that he had left unfinished in August (No. 520), he returned in January 1763 to Rome, which he had last seen in the summer of 1761. He was in Florence and Leghorn again at the beginning of June, subsequently revisited Parma, where he completed a copy of the *Madonna of St. Jerome* by Correggio that he had begun in 1762 (No. 505), and then proceeded on to Genoa and Turin, to France, and to England, where he arrived in August 1763.

This recitation of dates of confinements and travels establishes that the time West spent in Rome itself was relatively short, probably only slightly over twelve months in all, divided into three different visits. Yet it was his exposure to current artistic developments in Rome, enhanced by the sight and study of classical antiquities and of Renaissance and Baroque paintings in Rome and elsewhere, that set the course that his art was to follow for the rest of his life. He arrived in Rome armed with letters of introduction, and literally within hours of his arrival (if Galt is to be believed) he met Cardinal Alessandro Albani and many of the other leading *cognoscenti* in the city. Among artists, we know from a story later told by West that he visited the most prominent Italian painter in Rome, Pompeo Batoni, and saw him paint,[20] while Galt's account of West's first few weeks in Rome mentions encounters with the foreign-born painters Anton Raphael Mengs, Gavin Hamilton, and Nathaniel Dance (German, Scottish, and English respectively), who at precisely the moment of West's arrival were producing what are generally recognized as the first monuments of Neo-Classical painting. Of these artists, Mengs had by far the strongest impact on West. In a letter written shortly after his arrival in London, West described the German as his favorite master.[21] He painted two copies after Mengs while in Italy (Nos. 510 and 511). His trip to Bologna, Parma, and Venice was taken in accordance with Mengs's advice, and his greatest triumph in Rome, as reported by Galt, was when a portrait he had

The Cricketers (Cat. No. 726), detail

(*left*) Anton Raphael Mengs, *Lord Grey*, *c*. 1760. Oil on canvas, 38 × 29 in. National Trust, Dunham Massey

(*right*) Angelica Kauffmann, *Benjamin West*, 1763. Chalk, 16½ × 12½ in. National Portrait Gallery, London

John Allen, *c*. 1760 (Cat. No. 582)

painted of Thomas Robinson, a *milord inglese* who had taken West under his wing (No. 689), was thought by the *cognoscenti* to be the work of Mengs.

Four portraits painted by West in Italy are now known (Nos. 582, 658, 676, and 730).[22] The portrait of Robinson cannot be identified with certainty, but it may possibly be identical with the portrait of an unidentified sitter traditionally called "The Prince of Savoy" (No. 730). According to Galt, it was painted before West's first departure from Rome on 20 August 1760, that is, within six weeks of his arrival. West probably painted the portrait of John Allen, with whom he had travelled to Italy (No. 582 *opposite*), in Leghorn a few months later, and that of Captain Medows, a British naval officer he met in 1760 (No. 658), bears an old inscription stating that it was painted in Leghorn in 1761. All three demonstrate how rapidly West learned to make his portraits look like those currently being painted in Rome by Batoni and Mengs, and the story of one of his pictures being confused for a work by Mengs is a contemporary testimonial to his success. In two of the portraits, the sitters wear Van Dyck costume, an affectation which had started to appear in English painting around 1730 and was adopted by Batoni for several portraits of British sitters painted in the 1750s. West himself soon owned or had access to such an outfit, and when the Swiss painter Angelica Kauffmann drew him in Rome in 1763, she showed him similarly garbed. In the one earlier likeness of West now known, a self-portrait miniature done in Philadelphia (No. 524, ill. p. 2), he wears modest Quaker attire and presents himself as a prim young man for whom the conceit of fancy costume would have been inconceivable.

Anne, Countess of Northampton, and Her Daughter, Lady Elizabeth Compton,
1762 (Cat. No. 676)

Mrs West and Raphael West , (?)*c.* 1770 (Cat. No. 538)

Raphael, *Madonna della Sedia*. Oil on panel, $27\frac{7}{10}$ in. diameter. Pitti Palace, Florence

The remaining portrait painted by West in Italy that can now be identified is that of the Countess of Northampton and her daughter done in Venice in the autumn of 1762 (No. 676 *opposite*), and this picture demonstrates another facet of West's Italian education. In this instance, his inspiration did not come from contemporary art but from Renaissance painting, specifically the Madonnas of Raphael with which he had become familiar in Florence a few months before. As a patently derivative work, the portrait echoes the earlier portrait of Provost Smith, which West based on a painting he had copied in Philadelphia, but after two years in Italy the artist could draw upon a vastly expanded knowledge of earlier painting. The Northampton portrait is not a modified copy, as the Smith portrait evidently was, and it depends on more than one source, but the dependence is nonetheless recognizable, and that recognizability must have been intended by the artist. Equally recognizable adaptations of earlier paintings appear in many of West's later portraits (see Nos. 535–38 and 629–30), and slightly less overt borrowings can be readily found throughout his mature *oeuvre*, as they can be also in the works of many of his English colleagues active in the second half of the eighteenth century. Reynolds provides the great example of such practice, and Reynolds's *Discourses* repeatedly insist upon the necessity of the study and imitation of earlier masters as the most fundamental ingredient of an artist's education.[23]

As Reynolds's successor as President of the Royal Academy, West in his official addresses said much the same thing, as he did also on other occasions when he gave advice to younger artists.[24] Thus the eclectic dependence on earlier painting that the *Countess of Northampton* so conspicuously displays anticipates a central tenet of English academic theory as well as West's own later orientation. By the end of his life, he had a reputation not only as a painter, but also as a knowledgeable connoisseur, who was instrumental in shaping several important collections, and who had accumulated a considerable collection of his own.[25] Following the dispersal of many continental collections in the aftermath of the French Revolution and the consequent importation of large numbers of paintings into England, he was even accused by George III of being "an encourager of those who looked only to works of Old Masters," rather than patronizing English artists. In reply, West asserted that he "really did think the introduction of fine works of art to be of great Consequence, as they raised the minds of Artists, & without seeing them Artists cd. not be expected merely by the force of their own conceptions to carry their practice as far as with fine models before them."[26] Since he had started his own practice in colonial America with no fine models before him, West knew whereof he spoke, and the process of raising his mind began with the study and imitation of contemporary and older masters whose works he saw in Italy.

Yet, rewarding as West's experiences in Italy must have been, they did not correct all the deficiencies in his early training. When he first met Mengs in 1760 and was asked by the German artist to show a specimen of his drawing, he could not comply. Instead, he told Thomas Robinson that he had never learned to draw, and he painted rather than drew the portrait of Robinson that was to pass for a Mengs. Having acknowledged his inability to draw, he does not seem to have done much about it; nor was he encouraged to. When Mengs saw the painted portrait, he assured West that he already had the "mechanical part" of his art and recommended the course of study of the Carracci, Correggio, Tintoretto, Titian, and Veronese that West followed during the rest of his stay in Italy.[28] Thus his Italian education was primarily art-historical. He does seem to have devoted some attention to the study of anatomy and to drawing from antique statues and the human figure,[29] but, in the midst of illness and travel, the time he could have allowed to these pursuits was hardly sufficient to provide the technical mastery required by a painter of ambitious historical compositions. Despite West's later role as President of the Royal Academy, he did not have a thorough academic training but was essentially a self-taught artist. His control of anatomy, although advancing manifestly from that displayed in the early *Death of Socrates*, remained shaky at best, and throughout his career he lacked the assurance as a draughtsman that comes from long and assiduous application to the fundamentals. To some extent West's knowledge of art history, his ability to make an apt quotation,

William Allen, c. 1763 (Cat. No. 581)

Thomas Gainsborough, *Thomas Coward, c.* 1760–64. Oil on canvas, 50 × 40 in. Birmingham City Art Gallery

became a crutch which he could substitute for more fundamental technical proficiency.

The concomitant of studying the works of the masters was painting copies after them, which West did primarily for two wealthy Philadelphians, Chief Justice William Allen (see No. 581) and his brother-in-law Lieutenant-Governor James Hamilton (see No. 633). West travelled to Italy on a ship carrying a cargo of sugar sent by Allen. One of his fellow passengers was John Allen, the eldest son of the Chief Justice, whose portrait West painted in Italy (No. 582, ill. p. 16), and a second was Colonel Joseph Shippen, a relative who seems to have acted as Allen's agent. Governor Hamilton owned the *St. Ignatius* which West had copied in Philadelphia and had emulated in his portrait of Provost Smith (see Nos. 512 and 699), but there is no other record of any connection between the artist and these two patrons prior to the voyage. West's passage was arranged for him by Smith while he was in New York, and accounts of the trip do not suggest that he expected to receive any financial support from Justice Allen and Governor Hamilton. Evidently John Allen's and Joseph Shippen's glowing reports of West's first reception in Italy inspired them to commission a collection of copies, and the idea may have been prompted in the minds of artist and patrons by the example of established artists in Rome such as Batoni and Mengs, both of whom during the 1750s had painted copies after Raphael for a gallery of copies planned for Northumberland House in London.[30] A letter from West to Shippen dated 11 May 1762 thanks him and John Allen for bringing the commission about. This and a second letter from West to Shippen and two letters to Shippen from Robert Rutherford, Allen's agent in Leghorn, all of which are primarily about the copies, are our main contemporary sources of information about West's activities in Italy. Documentation of Chief Justice Allen's support of West is also provided by two letters from Allen to David Barclay, his banker in London.[31] The first, dated 19 August 1761, approves an advance of sixty pounds made by John Allen to West and authorizes a second advance of 100 more. The second, dated 10 October 1762, explains that Allen and Hamilton were employing West to make copies; mentions that Allen had already supplied West £150 (presumably the advances totalling £160 referred to in the preceding letter somehow reduced by £10); and announces that Governor Hamilton has promised to give a like sum: "We have such an extraordinary Account of Mr. West's Genius in the painting way, that we venture to afford him these Supplies, and for his Incouragement to take it out in Copies."

In return for his Philadelphia patrons' £300 or £310, West painted six copies (Nos. 504, 506, 510, 511, 516, and 520), of which four are now known. Two other copies painted by West in Italy, which did not go to Philadelphia, are also recorded (Nos. 505 and 507). The four known copies do not show much individual character, but they are remarkably competent works to have been produced by an artist of West's limited training. He evidently undertook the first two (Nos. 506 and 510) before receiving any actual commission from Justice Allen, although probably with the encouragement of Shippen and John Allen. He was subsequently sent a list of desired works to copy, to one of which (the *St. Michael* by Guido Reni) he took exception as requiring too much work for the proposed price,[32] and it would seem that he did not take this list too seriously but instead chose what he thought would be agreeable to his patrons. He painted one copy for them after a painting ascribed to Annibale Carracci; others after Domenichino, Guido Reni and Titian; and two after contemporary or near contemporary paintings by Mengs. The copies that he kept for himself were after Correggio and Van Dyck. This list embodies fairly conventional, even conservative eighteenth-century taste. The most surprising name on it is that of Mengs, but it reflects Mengs's great reputation as well as West's respect for him. The paintings by Mengs which West copied were not the celebrated *Parnassus* in the Villa Albani or other comparable essays in early Neo-Classicism, but rather a *Sibyl* modelled on Guercino and a *Holy Family* that looks back to sixteenth- and seventeenth-century prototypes.[33] Absent from the artists whose works West copied in Italy are Raphael and Poussin, both of whom were to have an important influence on him as he turned to classical subjects and a more classicizing style in England some years later. He was not yet the Neo-Classical artist he would soon become.

Before West left America in 1760 he had become engaged to Elizabeth Shewell in Philadelphia, and, according to what he told William Carey in 1818, when he left he promised her that he would not prolong his absence beyond three years.[34] Nevertheless, in the spring of 1763, Robert Rutherford, the agent in Leghorn, reported to Joseph Shippen that West was planning to visit Britain at the invitation of Richard Dalton, George III's librarian, whom West had met in Venice in 1762.[35] West had even received a royal commission from Dalton (see No. 195), who was in Italy buying pictures for the King, and West's English acquaintances in Rome agreed that he should not lose the opportunity presented by the invitation. As things worked out, Dalton's and West's plan to travel together foundered, due to Dalton's failure to rejoin West in Rome, but West found another travelling companion, a Mr. Patoun, and proceeded on anyway in the summer of 1763. The Seven Years' War having come to an end a few months before, they were able to travel through France, and they stopped briefly in Paris to see the French royal collections and works by French artists. On 20 August they reached London, and on 1 September West wrote to Joseph Shippen: "I am at last arrived at the mother country, which we Americans are all so desirous to see, and which I could not but desire as much, or more than Italy itself."[36]

Galt and Carey both tell us that West intended to remain in England for only a short visit,[37] but the question of whether or not he would return to America had already surfaced while he was in Italy. Robert Rutherford, writing to Shippen in April 1763, offered the opinion that attachment, gratitude to benefactors, and love of friends would lead West to return to his native land, but this prediction followed not only Rutherford's report of Dalton's proposal to conduct West to England, but also mention of two commissions for portraits of English sitters that West had successfully carried out in Venice (Nos. 673 and 676). Dalton seems to have promised West royal support, and Rutherford expected that he would also have the favor of "Several English Noblemen who during their stay in Italy seemed to be very fond of his performance." West did eventually gain royal patronage, but not until 1768, long after he had made his decision to stay in England. He exhibited three paintings at the Society of Artists in London in the spring of 1764, and their success there seems to have been the chief factor that encouraged him to remain.[38] His two most important benefactors from Philadelphia, Provost Smith and Chief Justice Allen, both happened to be in London in 1763–64. They evidently acquiesced in the decision,[39] and Smith, who returned to America at the end of April 1764, even seems to have played a role in straightening things out with West's fiancée and arranging that she join him in London (see No. 700). Accompanied by West's widowed father and by her cousin, the painter Matthew Pratt, she sailed from Philadelphia in June and married West in London on 2 September 1764. West, who was twenty-four years old when he arrived in England in the summer of 1763, never returned to America, and, apart from one brief visit to Paris in 1802, was never to leave the British Isles during the remaining fifty-seven years of his life.

Since West's primary professional activity prior to 1763 had been as a portrait painter, it was perhaps inevitable that he would continue to paint portraits when he arrived in England, where there was little tradition of patronage for painting of any other kind. For the first twenty years of his residence in England he maintained a steady output of likenesses, and they undoubtedly accounted for a substantial part of his income. Then in the mid-1780s, as other commissions monopolized his time, he almost entirely ceased painting portraits. He took them up again in the 1790s, but only occasionally and then often of family or personal friends. During the earlier period, a substantial part of his portrait practice was devoted to Americans. The first pictures he painted in England were probably portraits of Chief Justice Allen,

The Cricketers, (?)1763 (Cat. No. 726)

General Robert Monckton, c. 1764 (Cat. No. 665)

General Honble Robert Monckton.

Nathaniel Dance, *James Grant, John Mytton, Thomas Robinson, and Thomas Wynne,* 1760–61. Oil on canvas, 38 × 48½ in. Philadelphia Museum of Art

Sir Joshua Reynolds, *Sir John Molesworth,* 1755. Oil on canvas, 50 × 40 in. Private collection

with whom West spent a month at Bath shortly after his arrival (No. 581, ill. p. 21), and of Anne Allen, the Chief Justice's daughter (No. 584). Other early subjects included a group portrait of two Allen sons and three of their friends usually called *The Cricketers* (Nos. 726 *opposite* and 727; see also No. 583), a second portrait of Provost Smith (No. 700), Governor Hamilton, who visited London between 1765 and 1767 (No. 633), and Francis Hopkinson's mother (No. 641). In 1772, West's early patrons in Lancaster, Pennsylvania, commissioned him to paint the benefactress of their library, Lady

John Sawrey Morritt, 1765 (Cat. No. 669)

Juliana Penn (No. 682), and various other portrait commissions stemmed in one way or another from Pennsylvania. The only other significant American patronage that West received came from the Middleton family of South Carolina, for whom he painted four portraits (Nos. 659–62), following his inclusion of Arthur Middleton in *The Cricketers* along with two sons of Chief

Mrs. John Sawrey Morritt, c. 1765 (Cat. No. 670)

Justice Allen. His English sitters cannot be easily categorized. A few sat to him because of connections either from America (see Nos. 606, 635, and 665) or from Italy (Nos. 625 and 677). Purchasers of West's history paintings or other types of pictures in some cases also commissioned portraits, and he painted a relatively large number of clerical portraits and numerous portraits of

27

members of the royal family. But despite such august patronage, West's portraiture never stood on the same plane as that of the professional portrait painters, such as Reynolds, Gainsborough, or Romney, and the total number of portraits he painted was tiny compared to theirs. As his reputation as a history painter grew, it seems likely that he was chosen for portrait commissions where some kind of emblematic or iconographic statement about the sitter was sought, and, from the portraits of Alderman Sawbridge as a Roman senator of 1772 (No. 694) and Joseph Banks wearing a Maori cloak of 1773 (No. 586 *opposite*), to John Eardley Wilmot seated before an allegorical *Reception of the American Loyalists*, of 1812 (No. 718), a considerable number do present quirkily distinctive likenesses of their distinguished subjects, who evidently preferred to be painted in a less conventional, if also less polished, manner than that offered by the established portrait painters.

Although West's most characteristic portraits do not show much resemblance to portraits by Reynolds or Gainsborough or Romney, and hence suffer

Sir William Young, Bt., with His Wife Elizabeth and a Child, 1767 (Cat. No. 723)

Sir Joseph Banks, c. 1771–73, mezzotint by J. R. Smith after No. 586

by comparison when expected to look like them, they were nonetheless strongly influenced by such models. When he arrived in England West sought to emulate the practice of the English portraitists in the same manner that he had imitated Batoni and Mengs upon his arrival in Rome. The portraits of Chief Justice Allen and Anne Allen, which he probably painted at Bath, both suggest that he had looked at works by Gainsborough, who was practicing in Bath at the time. The group portrait, *The Cricketers*, is a conversation piece in an English vein, entirely without precedent in West's own art, but undoubtedly modelled on the group portraits of Englishmen on the Grand Tour which Nathaniel Dance painted in Rome and which West certainly knew from there.

The influence of Reynolds is evident in West's first full-length portrait, that of General Robert Monckton (No. 665, ill. p. 25), which, at the urging of Reynolds and of Richard Wilson, was one of the first three pictures that West exhibited in London in the spring of 1764. It not only echoes Reynolds's pictures of military officers thematically and compositionally, but also displays a boldness of handling that was probably inspired by the same source. In subsequent portraits of the 1760s, West's manner of painting was to become drier and more linear, and when he began to use a freer brushstroke after 1770 it showed greater affinity to Copley than Reynolds.[40] Nevertheless, West advised students who wished to learn portraiture to go to Reynolds,[41] and Reynolds's influence is palpably evident in much of West's portraiture from the 1770s, when he was most active in the genre. It is most obvious in pictures of sitters in antique dress and participating in Greco-Roman rituals such as Nos. 694, 591, and 607 (*below*), but Reynolds's endless invention and his adaptations from an enormous variety of sources, which he used to enliven his pictures and characterize his subjects, must have been generally important for West, whose portraiture during the 1770s was to take on a similarly eclectic

Mr. and Mrs. John Custance, 1778 (Cat. No. 607)

Mr. and Mrs. Robert Crafton, 1773 (Cat. No. 606)

quality. As we have seen, West had already experimented in this vein before leaving Philadelphia as well as in Venice in 1762, and Galt described his portrait of Provost Smith in the attitude of a Spanish St. Ignatius (No. 699) as an independent anticipation of Reynolds's discovery.[42] In England, West, like Reynolds, looked frequently to sixteenth- and seventeenth-century prototypes, sometimes quoting them explicitly as in No. 630, but unlike Reynolds he also experimented in the different manners of his contemporaries, moving readily from the grand style of Reynolds in formal portraits of dukes (No. 683) and portraits of the royal family (Nos. 547–78), to domestic scenes on a small scale reminiscent of Zoffany in portraits of friends (No. 606 *above*) or of his own family (No. 546). Where he went beyond his English contemporaries and virtually created a new mode of painting was in the combination of portraiture and contemporary history in paintings such as the *Death of General Wolfe* (No. 93) and *Lord Clive Receiving the Grant of the Duanney* (No. 101), works which must be discussed in the context of West's evolution as a history painter.

III History Painting, Neo-Classicism, George III, and the Royal Academy

In 1760, when Mengs told West that he should travel to Bologna, Parma, and Venice to see works by painters such as the Carracci and Correggio, he followed that advice with the direction that West should then return to Rome, "and paint an historical composition to be exhibited to the Roman public."[43] West did as he was told and painted a composition depicting *Cymon and Iphigenia* in Rome during the winter and spring of 1763. In Leghorn in June he showed it to Robert Rutherford, who reported that it had been "much admired by the Judges at Rome." West then took it to England and exhibited it in London in the spring of 1764 along with a companion picture of *Angelica and Medoro* and his portrait of General Monckton. In the following year he exhibited pictures of *Jupiter and Europa* and *Venus and Cupid* and two further portraits.

The *Cymon and Iphigenia* painted in 1763 is now lost (see No. 195), but the *Angelica and Medoro*, which West possibly painted or began in Rome as well, may perhaps be identified as No. 188 (ill. p. 34). The *Venus and Cupid* of 1765 is known (No. 128, ill. p. 35), and a second *Cymon and Iphigenia*, which West exhibited in 1766 (No. 196), may give some notion of the earlier painting of 1763. Although West painted the first of these works in accordance with Mengs's instruction that he paint "an historical composition," none of them showed a subject drawn from actual history, but subjects drawn from literature (*The Decameron* and *Orlando Furioso*) or myth instead. This distinction is probably not one that would have seemed of great moment to West in Rome in 1763, but it would take on significance as he came to define his position as a history painter in England in subsequent years. These subjects painted from 1763 to 1765 reflect conventional mid-eighteenth-century taste for scenes of amorous dalliance in rustic or Olympian settings, of the sort that we associate with François Boucher and other painters of the French Rococo. The *Angelica and Medoro* (No. 188) is particularly suggestive of Boucher, but, nevertheless, the main contemporary inspiration must have come from artists to whom West had been exposed in Italy, most prominently Pompeo Batoni. Mengs left Rome for Spain in August of 1761, and West had no further contact with him after his own departure for Leghorn in the summer of 1761, but Batoni remained and stood unchallenged as the leading artist in Rome when West returned there in the winter of 1763. Batoni's historical pictures from this period are relatively rare, but the *Diana and Cupid* in the Metropolitan Museum of Art, dated *1761*, which was bought by a British patron in 1762 and subsequently described as "thought at Rome to be the best picture he ever made,"[44] repre-

Pompeo Batoni, *Diana and Cupid*, 1761. Oil on canvas, 49 × 68 in. Metropolitan Museum of Art, New York

Angelica and Medoro, c. 1763–64 (Cat. No. 188)

Venus and Cupid, c. 1765 (Cat. No. 128)

sents the type of quasi-Rococo painting, both in subject and in style, which West undertook to paint in 1763 and continued to produce in the following few years. Angelica Kauffmann, who arrived in Rome in 1763, painted a *Bacchus and Ariadne* in much the same Batonian vein in the following year (Vorarlberger Landesmuseum, Bregenz),[45] and Nathaniel Dance, who was an avowed disciple of Batoni, was probably working in a similar manner, although his chief history painting from this period, the *Meeting of Aeneas and Achates with Venus*, has disappeared. The *Cymon and Iphigenia* which West painted in Rome was supposed to fulfill the commission for a picture for George III given him by Richard Dalton, and it is worth noting that Dance, writing from Rome on 6 February 1763, announced that Dalton was expected there every day, "and I am told by a friend of his that . . . he talked of getting me perhaps a commission to do a picture for His Majesty." In an earlier letter of 4 December 1762, Dance mentioned that he was keeping the *Meeting of Aeneas and Achates with Venus* to show to Dalton; so it was presumably on hand to be seen by West also as an example of what a potentially munificent patron was expected to admire.[46]

The earlier artists whose influence we can discern in West's imaginative paintings from 1763 to 1766 or 1767 are chiefly the artists whose works he had copied and studied in Italy: the Carracci, Guido Reni, Domenichino, Correggio, and Titian. These were the artists who had the greatest influence on painting in the early and middle years of the eighteenth century in general, and it would be an idle exercise to attempt to sort out the mix of ingredients as they were absorbed and reflected in West's paintings. West later told Joseph Farington that "his mind was full of Correggio" when he painted the *Venus and Cupid* exhibited in 1765 (No. 128), and Correggio was probably the artist that West most consciously and consistently attempted to emulate, but his most obvious imitations were two mythological pictures echoing Titian, which he exhibited in 1767 (Nos. 112 and 155). Both Correggio and Titian represent tastes and aspirations that West would never abandon, but that would be temporarily set aside as he turned to a more radical Neo-Classical style of history painting in the second half of the 1760s.

The first inkling of a new orientation came as early as 1764 in the *Choice of Hercules*, which West did not exhibit, but which is signed and dated (No. 143 *opposite*). This painting depends compositionally upon a picture of the same subject by Poussin, which West had seen on a visit to Stourhead in Wiltshire in the autumn of 1763, and it thus constitutes his earliest display of interest in the artist who was to have a pervasive influence on much Neo-Classical painting. It also quotes Reynolds's parody of the subject, *Garrick between Comedy and Tragedy*, painted two years earlier and showing a witty and creative transformation of traditional motifs that must have come as a revelation to West. Although the *Choice of Hercules* is not much more than a pastiche of its sources (and West may not have exhibited it because of reservations about its too-derivative nature), those sources, an English painting and a Poussin in an English collection, symbolize the new stimuli which England provided and which West was prepared to absorb. His continuing growth in England dis-

Nicolas Poussin, *The Choice of Hercules*. Oil on canvas, 35¾ × 28¼ in. National Trust, Stourhead

The Choice of Hercules, 1764 (Cat. No. 143)

Sir Joshua Reynolds, *Garrick Between Comedy and Tragedy* 1762.
Oil on canvas, $58\frac{1}{4} \times 72$ in. Private collection

tinguishes him from Angelica Kauffmann and Nathaniel Dance, both of whom came to England in 1766 sharing much the same background, but who, as history painters, never went significantly beyond what they brought with them from Rome.

Ironically, the most substantial steps that West took towards a new style in England also were steps back toward artists he had known in Rome and whose paintings in one case we have seen he had admired: Mengs and Gavin Hamilton. Their most adventurous works had probably been too advanced for West to appreciate fully when he was in Italy, but after three further years in England, he seems to have been ready for them. The painting which perhaps more than any other signalizes the commencement of West's Neo-Classicism is the small *Paetus and Arria* in the Yale Center for British Art, which is signed and dated *1766* (No. 38 *opposite*). Although not such an obvious pastiche as the *Choice of Hercules* of 1764, this picture does appear to reflect awareness of two paintings: in the placement of the figures and their relation to the architecture it suggests the *Octavius and Cleopatra* by Mengs which, like the Poussin *Choice of Hercules*, West had seen at Stourhead, where it remains; and in the figure of Arria dying from a self-inflicted wound, it recalls the figure of Lucretia in the *Oath of Brutus* by Hamilton (versions at the Yale Center for British Art and elsewhere), which West had probably seen in some form before leaving Rome in 1763.[47] The picture also suggests a reawakening of the concerns embodied in West's own *Death of Socrates* painted in Lancaster a decade earlier.

Like the *Death of Socrates* and like the paintings by Mengs and Hamilton, but unlike all West's known subject paintings from the preceding few years,

Anton Raphael Mengs, *Octavius and Cleopatra*, 1760. Oil on canvas, National Trust, Stourhead

Paetus and Arria, 1766 (Cat. No. 38)

(*left*) Gavin Hamilton, *The Oath of Brutus*, c. 1763–67. Oil on canvas, 84 × 104 in. Yale Center for British Art, New Haven

(?)*Octavius and Cleopatra*, (?)drawing by West (see p. 156, note 47). Pen, 10½ × 7⅝ in. Historical Society of Pennsylvania, Philadelphia

the *Paetus and Arria* shows figures in an interior setting. The architectural discipline of pilasters, niche, moldings, and tiles on the floor not only gives a geometrical order to the composition, but also confines the two figures in a shallow, enclosed space that is the antithesis of the bucolic landscape of the amorous couple in West's *Rinaldo and Armida* of 1763–64. Like Mengs's Octavius and Cleopatra, West's Paetus and Arria are set side by side in a confrontation on one plane in their limited space. They do not touch each other, nor do their figures overlap (except for one foot). They are drawn with clear, simple outlines, and their actions are readily legible. Although the colors are delicate pinks and greens of a Rococo prettiness, the handling of paint is dry to the point of seeming amateurish. Combined with the stiff rhetorical drawing of the figures, it suggests that in 1766 West still had not overcome the inadequacies of his early training to achieve the assurance of handling that we might expect from a professionally accomplished master. However, such an assessment is probably wrong. Although West never overcame substantial technical limitations, the dryness of handling and the compositional stiffness of the *Paetus and Arria* certainly represent a deliberate formal sobriety and severity in keeping with the sober and severe message of the picture's subject. West had earlier demonstrated himself capable of painting with much greater vigor in works such as the portrait of General Monckton exhibited in 1764, and he had striven to master the painterly styles of Correggio and Titian. In rejecting fluency and richness of handling in the *Paetus and Arria* (and in his most ambitious works of the next few years), West was following the lead of Mengs in works such as the *Octavius and Cleopatra*. The stylistic redirection in the work of both artists, as in the later work of Jacques-Louis David and other Neo-Classical artists, accompanied and was in keeping with a fundamental redirection in the nature of the subjects they chose to paint.

Apart from portraits, West's exhibited pictures in 1764 and 1765 were compositions formed in each case of two figures, or two main figures, one male and one female, as the two proper names in each of their titles indicate (*Angelica and Medoro*, *Cymon and Iphigenia*, etc.), and he continued this pattern in two pictures he exhibited in 1766 and two in 1767. The *Paetus and Arria* of 1766 also shows one male and one female figure, but unlike all those other paintings, it does not depict a relationship whose interest is fundamentally erotic. And, unlike all the others, the source of the subject is neither literature nor myth but Roman history, as recorded by Pliny. Along with a painting of the *Continence of Scipio*, which he exhibited in 1766 (No. 18), it is the first painting since the *Death of Socrates* that West had painted of an actual historical event. These three works, unlike his paintings of rustic idylls from Boccaccio and Ariosto or of the loves of the gods from Ovidian myth, present scenes of self-sacrifice and moral behavior. Arria is not a fictional creation, but supposedly someone who actually lived and who chose to take her own life to set an example of courage for her hesitant husband. Like her act, West's painting depicting it teaches a lesson in virtue. Its purpose is to instruct rather than to please, and it is one of many similarly didactic works produced by numerous artists during the second half of the eighteenth century.[48]

Such paintings provide the visual equivalents to contemporary Enlightenment thought, the rejection of the decorative frivolities of the Rococo in painting paralleling the rejection of the injustices, excesses, and privileges of the *ancien régime* and its English equivalent that would engender revolutions in America in 1776 and France in 1789. Throughout this period, in life as in art, classical antiquity provided models of behavior that were to inspire devotion to ideals of self-sacrifice for the sake of justice, honor, duty, and country, and one of the salient features of much Neo-Classical art is the studious attention with which artists or patrons sought appropriately elevating subjects in the writings of the Greek and Roman historians. West had been started on this route by William Henry in Lancaster and by Provost Smith in Philadelphia before 1760, but during the middle years of the eighteenth century a belief that artists should be thoroughly educated in classical history and literature was so widespread among critics and theorists, who deplored what they considered the vacuity of much contemporary art, that it would be wrong to assign West's early mentors undue credit for his interests in mature life. As a painting of a subject from Roman history, West's *Paetus and Arria* followed the paintings by Mengs and Hamilton which we have proposed as its chief stylistic sources. Nevertheless, it does not repeat the subject of either, and the subject of Paetus and Arria is sufficiently rare to assure us that its choice was not due to convention or tradition as the choice of time-honored themes such as the Choice of Hercules or the Continence of Scipio might well have been. The painting has a clarity and a directness of message, reinforced by its almost primitive formal simplicity, that set it apart from Mengs and Hamilton. The role of the female Arria as the participant who acts heroically is the reverse of that of Mengs's Cleopatra, who humbles herself at the feet of Octavius, or even of Hamilton's Lucretia, whose death is not heroic but provokes Brutus and his companions to heroic action. While displaying little kinship with West's earlier and contemporary Angelica, Iphigenia, Europa, and Venus, whose roles are entirely sexual, Arria anticipates the Agrippina of No. 33 of 1768 and the Epponina of No. 41 of 1795, and forceful heroines from more modern history or from literary sources in West's later paintings: Queen Philippa in Nos. 61 and 64, Cordelia in Nos. 212–15, and Euphrasia in No. 204.

West also returned to the subject of Paetus and Arria in two later and distinctly different compositions: in No. 39 of 1770, which shows a pathetic Arria, eyes rolled to heaven; and No. 40 of 1781, which shows a more aggressive Arria turning and seizing the arm of the horrified Paetus. In both works, the psychological dimensions are more complex than in the painting of 1766, and so is the formal language. The Arria of No. 39 of 1770 recalls Gavin Hamilton's Lucretia even more than does her predecessor in No. 38 and the position of Paetus behind her, which West repeated with some modification in No. 40, was apparently inspired by the position of Lucretia's husband behind her in Hamilton's painting. The change in the placement of Paetus in West's two later pictures creates more unified compositions, which demonstrate by contrast the primitivistic compositional severity of the painting of 1766, and also how short-lived West's devotion to such formal severity was to be, since he

Pylades and Orestes, 1766 (Cat. No. 186)

abandoned it when he returned to the subject in 1770. Nevertheless, in the few years from 1766 to 1769 West established himself not only as the most advanced proponent of the Neo-Classical style, but also as the foremost history painter in England.

He achieved this position on the basis of five works exhibited during those years: the *Continence of Scipio* (No. 18) and *Pylades and Orestes* (No. 186 *above*) exhibited in 1766; *Pyrrus when a Child Brought before Glaucias* (No. 8) in 1767; *Agrippina Landing at Brundisium with the Ashes of Germanicus* (No. 33, ill. p. 46) in 1768; and the *Departure of Regulus* (No. 10, ill. p. 48) in 1769 (he did not exhibit the paintings of *Paetus and Arria* of 1766 and 1770). These five paintings constitute only a small part of West's exhibited *oeuvre* during this period, and they appeared side by side each year with pictures such as the *Diana and*

Raphael, *The Sacrifice at Lystra*. Gouache on paper, 136 × 213 in. Her Majesty the Queen (on loan to the Victoria and Albert Museum, London)

Orestes Sacrophagus formerly in the Villa Ridolfi, Rome. Marble, 2nd century AD. Glyptothek, Munich

Figures from the Orestes Sarcophagus formerly in the Villa Ridolfi, drawings utilized by West for No. 186. Swarthmore College, Swarthmore, Pennsylvania

Endymion (No. 137), *Venus and Adonis* (Nos. 112 and 116) and *Venus and Europa* (No. 141), which often must have seemed to contemporary viewers the more attractive and successful works, as indeed they still may today. The *Venus and Adonis* shown in 1769 (No. 116 *opposite*) has a fair claim to being considered West's most beautiful painting. But West was not to build a reputation as a painter of beautiful pictures. He aspired to a serious and dignified history painting to which beauty was an incidental irrelevancy. Four of the five paintings listed above showed subjects drawn from Greek or Roman history, and the fifth, *Pylades and Orestes*, was based on Greek tragedy, *Iphigenia in Tauris* by Euripides, which describes events in the aftermath of the Trojan war. Its companion in 1766, the *Continence of Scipio*, echoes a painting by Poussin of the same subject (Pushkin Museum, Moscow),[49] and further echoes, both compositional and iconographic, establish that throughout this group of works Poussin had replaced Correggio and Titian as West's chief model. The degree to which Poussin was in his mind is indicated by the comment reported by Galt, which West made about the subject of *Agrippina Landing at Brundisium with the Ashes of Germanicus* when he showed the picture to George III: "it was, indeed, surprising it should have been neglected by Poussin, who was so well qualified to have done it justice, and to whose genius it was in so many respects so well adapted."[50] In fact, West had probably been partly led to Germanicus as a subject and also to Pyrrhus in his painting of the previous year by well-known works by Poussin showing different moments in the lives (or deaths) of both protagonists: the *Death of Germanicus* (Minneapolis) and the *Saving of Pyrrhus* (Musée du Louvre, Paris). The other pervasive influence on these paintings is that of Raphael: on the earlier three it is primarily the Raphael of the tapestry cartoons, which we know that West went to see at Hampton Court in 1763,[51] while in the more spatially conceived *Agrippina* and *Regulus* we can also discern consciousness of the compositions of the *Disputa* and *School of Athens* in the Stanza della Segnatura in the Vatican. There are also quotations from classical antiquity. The most obvious are the adoptions in Nos. 33 and 186 of figures from sculptural reliefs which West had sketched in Italy, and the most scholarly is the background view of Brundisium in No. 33, based on a plate from Robert Adam's *Ruins of the Palace of the Emperor Diocletian at Spalatro* published four years previously.

West's *Agrippina Landing at Brundisium with the Ashes of Germanicus* (ill. p. 46) depicts a subject also painted by Gavin Hamilton (Tate Gallery, London), and there is an interesting but unclear relationship between the paintings by the two men. West's was completed and exhibited four years before Hamilton's, but Hamilton's picture was commissioned in 1765,[52] before West began his, and it is possible that Hamilton painted a *modello* for the composition well before then, before West left Rome in 1763. We can only speculate on this point, but the compositions are similar enough to make some awareness on the part of one artist of the other's work seem certain. If West was inspired by memory of a sketch that he had seen in Rome in 1763, it is significant that it took him five years to use it, and when he did, he was able to produce very different results despite the underlying compositional similarities. His sophisticated use

Venus Lamenting the Death of Adonis, 1768–1819 (Cat. No. 116)

of sculptural prototypes contemporary with the event for his main figures and of Robert Adam's reconstruction of a façade facing on the Adriatic for his view of Brundisium demonstrates a concern with historical propriety of a kind that does not seem to have troubled Hamilton, and the balanced and measured composition focussing on and framing the frieze-like procession of Agrippina, her children, and their attendants has an iconic simplicity and a dignified *gravitas* that makes Hamilton's picture look like an exercise in late Baroque theatricality. The contrast demonstrates that West had absorbed what he could from Mengs and Hamilton, his predecessors in this type of painting, and had gone on to develop a consistent, compelling, and convincing Neo-Classical language distinct from that of either.

Nevertheless, *Agrippina Landing at Brundisium with the Ashes of Germanicus* is not a work free from powerful, if non-visual, contemporary influences. It was commissioned by Robert Hay Drummond, Archbishop of York. As mentioned earlier (p. 9), Drummond dictated the subject and read (or had one of his sons read) the relevant passage from Tacitus to West. According to Galt: "Having read the passage he commented on it at some length, in order to convey to Mr. West an idea of the manner in which he was desirous the subject should be treated."[53] We can surmise that Archbishop Drummond brought Adam's *Ruins of the Palace of the Emperor Diocletian at Spalatro* to West's attention, since he was one of the original subscribers to the publication,[54] and we can interpret Galt's words to indicate that the Archbishop's desires about how the subject should be treated were of no slight significance in determining how it was treated. We are told by one of the Archbishop's sons, "his knowledge of history, ancient and modern, was most accurate, extensive, and profound.

Gavin Hamilton, *Agrippina Landing at Brundisium with the Ashes of Germanicus*, exhibited 1772. Oil on canvas, Tate Gallery, London

Agrippina Landing at Brundisium with the Ashes of Germanicus, 1768 (Cat. No. 33)

Detail of the frieze from the Ara Pacis Augustae, drawing by West
(cf. No. 33). Black chalk, heightened with white, 8 × 10½ in.
Philadelphia Museum of Art

It was the favourite of his familiar hours of instruction with his children," and
he deduced from history, "the most useful remarks on government, manners,
morals, and religion."[55] Drummond's belief in the value of examples of ancient
virtue for modern imitation is made manifest in West's portrait of his two eldest
sons (No. 608 *below*), which was exhibited together with the *Agrippina* in 1768.
In this double portrait of the two boys wearing academic robes, the older
brother holds a scroll on which can be read the name *Regulus*, and he points
to a Temple of Virtue in the upper left background, while a statue of Athena
balances it on the right. A father who would want his sons portrayed in such
a manner might be expected to have strong feelings about how a historical
composition that he had commissioned should appear, and his knowledge and
interest are probably more directly reflected in the painting of *Agrippina* than
those of the artist, who was still sufficiently unformed to have the requisite
malleability and flexibility to respond to the demands of a well-informed and
committed patron. Upon the Archbishop's recommendation, West was invited
to show the completed *Agrippina* to King George III. Galt reports that the
King commented on the rarity of the subject, proposed "another noble Roman

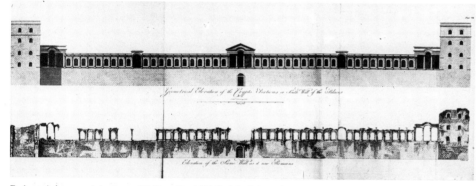

Robert Adam and Anthony Walker, *South Wall of the Palace of
Diocletian.* (cf. No. 33). Plate VIII of *The Ruins of
the Palace of the Emperor Diocletian at Spalatro*, London, 1764

The Drummond Brothers, 1767 (Cat. No. 608)

subject which corresponds to this one, and I believe it also has never been well painted: I mean the final departure of Regulus from Rome," and then, not to be outdone by Archbishop Drummond, commenced the royal patronage that would support West for the next forty years by himself reading to the artist from Livy (see No. 10). Whether or not this story is accurate, we know from West's portrait of the Drummond brothers that Regulus was a noble Roman whom the Archbishop instructed his sons to admire. It is, therefore, difficult not to see in George III's choice of subject a continuation of the Archbishop's interests, and the activities of arriving in one painting and departing in the other raise a suspicion that the *Agrippina* and the *Regulus* were conceived by the Archbishop as thematically related works. Galt's report of Archbishop Drummond's delight in learning that George III had commissioned a picture from West,[56] and his subsequent report of Drummond's concern over West's plans to paint the *Death of General Wolfe* (No. 93) in modern dress demonstrate that the prelate continued to concern himself with forwarding West's career in a manner not unlike Provost Smith in Philadelphia a decade earlier, albeit

The Departure of Regulus from Rome, 1769 (Cat. No. 10)

now on a much larger stage and with higher stakes. At the time West completed the *Agrippina* and received his first royal commission he had not yet reached his thirtieth birthday.

George III was an exact contemporary of West. He came to the throne in 1760, the year that West left America for Italy, and by 1762 his librarian Richard Dalton was in Italy buying paintings and dispensing royal commissions or the promise of royal commissions. The great collection of paintings by Canaletto et al. in the Royal Collection, which was purchased from Consul Smith in Venice, was the richest prize of Dalton's trip, but in addition, Dalton and the promise of royal patronage seem to have been responsible for luring at least two Italian artists, the landscape painter Francesco Zuccarelli and the engraver Francesco Bartolozzi, to England in 1764. Dalton was also responsible for George III's first commissions of historical paintings from British artists. As we have seen, West expected his *Cymon and Iphigenia* painted in Rome in 1763 to fulfill a commission from Dalton, and his coming to England was at least partly due to Dalton. Nathaniel Dance in Rome also hoped for patronage from the same quarter, and George III did buy from Dance a painting of *Timon of Athens*, which although completed and exhibited only in 1767, may have been commissioned by Dalton.[57] West's *Cymon and Iphigenia* did not enter the Royal Collection and, as far as we know, Dalton had nothing to do with George III's commission of the *Departure of Regulus* in 1768 or with any of West's subsequent dealings with George III. It seems, however, that West suppressed all references to Dalton in the accounts of his life that he gave to Galt and other biographers, as none of them mentions the royal librarian at all; so Dalton may have had more to do with the King's patronage of West in 1768 than the available evidence indicates. On the other hand, since by 1768 West had attracted support from patrons as highly placed as the Archbishop of York, and since George III was himself beginning to play a central role in the arts in England, they probably no longer required an intermediary such as Dalton.

West had the good fortune to arrive in England at precisely the time when the artists were about to form an organization that had among its goals the creation of a distinguished native school of history painting that would attempt to rival the great schools of the past, and at a time when England had its first monarch who was ready and eager to support such a goal. When Archbishop Drummond sent West to the King in 1768, George III discovered the artist who promised to fulfill widespread aspirations for British art. Whether George III actually enjoyed West's pictures does not seem to have mattered. According to John Galt:

> For the fine arts he [the King] had not, perhaps, any natural taste; . . . he was fully aware of the lustre which the arts have, in all ages, reflected on the different countries in which the cultivation of them has been encouraged to perpetuate the memory of great events. His employment of Mr. West, although altogether in his private capacity, was therefore not wholly without a view to the public advantage, and it is the more deserving of applause, as it was rather the result of principle than of personal predilection.[58]

Annual exhibitions of works of art commenced in England only in 1760. When West arrived in 1763 they were still a novelty, but they provided a place where he could publicly show his works, which he did from 1764 onwards. In 1765 he became a member of the Society of Artists, which organized the exhibitions, and by 1768 he was a director. However, the Society of Artists was plagued by schisms and rivalries, and in 1768 machinations were underway to replace it with a more ambitious organization, the Royal Academy of Arts, which would both sponsor exhibitions and be the chief school in England for young artists. The support of the King was enlisted for the new Academy, and his patronage was undoubtedly of paramount importance to its success. George III's involvement in the formation of the Royal Academy and his patronage of West began at almost exactly the same time and were closely intertwined. West evidently received the commission for the *Departure of Regulus* before the discussions that led to the founding of the Royal Academy had begun, and while he was at work on the painting he was frequently invited to spend the evening at Buckingham House, where he conversed with the King "on topics connected with the best means of promoting the study of the fine arts in the kingdom. It was in these conversations that the plan of the Royal Academy was digested."[59] Galt describes the two audiences when West showed George III the sketch for the *Departure of Regulus* and when he later showed the finished picture as pregnant moments for the Academy's early history, during which decisions and disclosures about its future were made.[60] At the King's instruction, the picture appeared in the first exhibition of the Royal Academy in the spring of 1769 and, of the 136 works in that opening exhibition, it most completely represented the high-minded art which the Academy was intended to encourage, but which would be produced with any frequency only by West, because only West managed to attract and to keep the all-important patronage of the King.

Between 1768 and 1801, West was to paint some sixty pictures for George III, for which, together with a few sketches for decorative schemes, he was paid a total of £34,187.[61] From 1772 onwards he identified himself in the catalogues of Royal Academy exhibitions as "Historical Painter to the King," and from 1780 he received an annual stipend from the King of £1,000. During these years West effectively monopolized all royal patronage except for portraiture, and during some of them he was painting portraits of the royal family as well. Since he also succeeded in obtaining a large share of whatever non-royal commissions there were to be had, he left few crumbs for potential rivals in the field.[62] Thus, the aims of George III and the founders of the Royal Academy to encourage and support a school of history painting in England led to all the support going to one man, while others who were encouraged to aspire to similar heights were either doomed to squalid poverty, as in the case of James Barry, or forced to follow more humble paths where they had a better chance of making a living.

Leonidas and Cleombrutus, 1768 (Cat. No. 13)

OPPOSITE *The Death of Hyacinthus*, 1771 (Cat. No. 145)

IV *The Death of General Wolfe* and New Directions in the 1770s

George III undoubtedly expected West to continue to paint pictures of classical history similar to the *Departure of Regulus*, and West's second painting for the King, the *Oath of Hannibal* (No. 17), is similar in many respects. Yet the subject shows a shift of emphasis from the theme of self-sacrifice in the earlier work to one of paternal instruction and filial obedience, which was probably seen by the King as in some way corresponding to his own role in relation to his son, the future George IV. Two further paintings of ancient subjects, the *Family of the King of Armenia before Cyrus* and *Segestes and His Daughter before Germanicus* (Nos. 2 and 32), which West painted for George III to hang together with the *Regulus* and the *Hannibal*, also center on the relations of parents and children in princely families, and the latter shows purported ancestors of the English royal family. Subjects from classical history were therefore evidently sought and selected in response to the personal and parochial concerns of George III, who, as the father of a growing family, would understandably have found images of familial loyalty more sympathetic than the exhortations to duty at the expense of family of the *Departure of Regulus* and other works, such as *Leonidas and Cleombrutus* (No. 13, ill. p. 53), which did not enter the Royal Collection. For a non-royal customer during the same period, West painted at least one picture whose subject, Julius Caesar's envy of Alexander the Great, by most estimations embodies the opposite of virtue, but which presumably reflected the ambitions of the military officer who commissioned it (No. 26). Such works demonstrate West's development of the Neo-Classical style into an increasingly flexible language, but they also reflect a slackening of the belief in the moral superiority of classical antiquity, which ultimately was the mainspring of the Neo-Classical style. Except for a hiatus between 1781 and 1794, West continued to paint classical subjects throughout his career, but after 1769, his most original, his most ambitious, and his most influential works showed other types of subjects. He painted the most original, ambitious and influential of them all, the *Death of General Wolfe* (No. 93, ill. p. 58), in 1770, one year after the *Departure of Regulus*.

The *Death of General Wolfe* shows an event that had taken place on the North American continent only ten years prior to the first exhibition of the Royal Academy. The participants wear contemporary military dress, and, with the exception of the main figure, they were all still alive when West painted the picture. While it was in progress, reports of this radical departure from the subjects West had been painting began to circulate and were not well received. According to Galt, George III told West that he had heard that the modern military costume impaired the dignity of the subject, "that it was thought very ridiculous to exhibit heroes in coats, breeches, and cock'd hats."[63] The King

Chryses Invoking the Vengeance of Apollo against the Greeks,
1773 (Cat. No. 159)

consequently did not buy the painting, although he later commissioned a replica (No. 94). Archbishop Drummond feared that West would lose the reputation established by the *Agrippina* and the *Regulus*, and he enlisted Sir Joshua Reynolds to dissuade the artist from running such a risk. Reynolds's chief concern, as summarized by West and quoted by Galt, was that the employment of modern dress would incur ridicule, "and he concluded with urging me earnestly to adopt the classic costume of antiquity, as much more becoming the inherent greatness of my subject than the modern garb of war." West dismissed Reynolds's concern as a prejudice and argued in response,

> The same truth that guides the pen of the historian should govern the pencil of the artist. I consider myself as undertaking to tell this great event to the eye of the world; but if, instead of the facts of the transaction, I represent classical fictions, how shall I be understood by posterity![64]

Despite this argument, West did not attempt to paint the subject with the "same truth that guides the pen of the historian," but deliberately took extraordinary liberties with the known historical facts (discussed in the entry for the painting) in order to give the subject an appropriately epic treatment (for which see the discussion under No. 108). He used contemporary costume and other detail to create a convincing rather than accurate representation of the event.

For Reynolds, the subject had "inherent greatness," and West in replying to him called it "a topic that history will proudly record." Wolfe's death for his country as part of the price of a great victory was a modern martyrdom as inspiring as that of Regulus, and the worthiness or propriety of the subject never seems to have been questioned on the grounds of its modernity. Reynolds's rather odd proposal that West cloak it in the costume of antiquity suggests that he expected West to treat Wolfe's death more in the allegorical manner of a funereal monument than as a depiction of the event as it might have happened.[65] Such a proposal was consistent with Reynolds's own use of classical dress in allegorical portraits such as *A portrait of a lady and her son, whole lengths, in the character of Diana, disarming love* and *A portrait of a lady in the character of Juno, receiving the cestus from Venus*, both of which appeared in the Royal Academy exhibition of 1769.[66] West's *Agrippina* and *Regulus* were, however, very different paintings, more fundamentally different than Reynolds perhaps recognized, and West's attempts to present plausible reconstructions of remote historical events in these pictures anticipated his insistence upon "the facts of the transaction" in a more recent subject.

The American subject of the *Death of General Wolfe*, complete with an American Indian in the foreground, must have been one which West, because of his origins in that remote and unfamiliar continent, felt that he was uniquely equipped to paint. He had previously depicted American subjects on several occasions. As early as September 1760, within months of his arrival in Italy, he was asked to paint a picture of *A Savage Warrior Taking Leave of His Family* (No. 452) to be utilized by an Italian artist as a model for one of a series of paintings of the four continents. In England, probably in 1765, he produced a pair of drawings to illustrate a book written by his old teacher Provost Smith

Savage Warrior Taking Leave of His Family, engraving by Francesco Bartolozzi after No. 452

The Death of General Wolfe, 1770 (Cat. No. 93)

describing the expedition of a battalion of British soldiers into the Indian territory of Ohio in the autumn of 1764.[67] At about the same time he also painted
a picture in oil showing a celebrated act of kindness by the American General
William Johnson toward the captured Baron Ludwig von Dieskau, which
accompanied a British-American victory over the French on the shores of Lake
George in upstate New York in 1755 (No. 92). Although West did not exhibit
this picture (and may not have completed it at this time), it demonstrates
his interest before 1769 in painting stirring and elevating moments from the
history of his native colonies, and many elements from it—the pointing hand
of General Johnson, the position of the lower half of Baron von Dieskau's body,
the Indian, the two soldiers looking on from the right—found their way into
the *Death of General Wolfe*. But whereas the earlier painting does not transcend
illustration of what took place, and to be understood requires our prior knowledge of the story, West carefully organized the components of the *Death of
General Wolfe* to give it the monumental dignity of traditional history painting
and to convey a message about martyrdom by making Wolfe's death recall
scenes of the death of heroes and the lamentation over the dead Christ in such
painting.

Sir Anthony Van Dyck, *The Lamentation.* Oil on canvas, Alte
Pinakothek, Munich

In addition to the dying Wolfe, six of the figures in the painting were identified in a key published in 1776. One of them, General Robert Monckton, West had painted previously in No. 665 (ill. p. 25), and the *Death of General Wolfe* repeats the military uniform and related imagery of that painting and at least one other portrait from the 1760s (No. 647 *below*). It is not primarily a group portrait, but its interest to the public was certainly enhanced by recognizable likenesses of contemporary figures as participants in the great

[?] *Sir William Johnson, Bt., c. 1767–70 (Cat. No. 647)*

Lord Clive Receiving from the Mogul the Grant of the Duanney,
c. 1774–95 (Cat. No. 101), detail

event. West painted replicas of the picture for members of the families of two of the officers shown, and these purchasers must have thought of the work as rather like a grand conversation piece, which artists often multiplied by producing versions for all the different sitters. After West's death, he was accused of soliciting payments from officers to include their portraits, but this seems unlikely. The reason for including actual portraits was to enhance the picture's illusion of actuality and authenticity, in the same manner that dressing the participants in correct uniforms or including a convincing view of the place where the event occurred enhanced that illusion. Nevertheless, in West's subsequent pictures of contemporary events the portrait element played an increasingly prominent role. In the key (ill. p. 221) to the *Death of Lord Nelson* of 1806 (No. 108, ill. p. 130), fifty-eight participants are identified. Other pictures of recent historical events such as *Lord Clive Receiving from the Mogul the Grant of the Duanney* (No. 101) and the *Signing of the Preliminary Treaty of Peace in 1782* (No. 105 *below*) are commemorative group portraits whose interest lies almost entirely within the realm of portraiture.

Signing of the Preliminary Treaty of Peace in 1782, 1783–84.
(Cat. No. 105)

The *Death of General Wolfe,* on the other hand, effectively combined different genres—topical illustration, portraiture, history painting—in a manner which, if not entirely novel, did have far-reaching consequences. Upon seeing the completed picture, Reynolds is reported to have withdrawn his earlier objections, telling West, "I foresee that this picture will not only become one of the most popular, but occasion a revolution in the art."[68] Testimony to the painting's popularity is provided by the number of replicas painted by West or in his studio (Nos. 94–98) and by countless copies after it by other hands. The revolution Reynolds predicted it would bring about did come, and by the end of the eighteenth century leading artists everywhere were devoting their highest efforts to ambitious paintings monumentalizing recent historical events. Two artists who were to make a specialty of such subjects, John Singleton Copley and John Trumbull, as well as many lesser figures, felt West's influence at first hand. Outside of England, the *Death of General Wolfe* and West's other historical compositions, like those of Gavin Hamilton before him, became widely familiar through the medium of reproductive prints.[69]

The first print known to be after a work by West seems to be an engraving by Francesco Bartolozzi after the *Savage Warrior Taking Leave of His Family,* which appeared in an Italian translation of Edmund Burke's *Account of the European Settlements in America* published in Venice in 1763.[70] The two illustrations to Provost Smith's *Account of the Expedition against the Ohio Indians* were published in the second edition of that book in 1766. The earliest dated reproductive print after one of West's paintings published as an independent print rather than as a book illustration was a mezzotint after a portrait of Thomas Newton, the Bishop of Bristol (No. 675, and see No. 163), published on 1 December 1767.[71] This print was issued by John Boydell, the dominant figure in the eighteenth-century print trade, who the following year published a print after the *Angelica and Medoro* exhibited in 1764 and in 1769 published prints after two paintings of classical subjects that West had exhibited in 1767 (Nos. 8 and 112). Of the five paintings exhibited from 1766 to 1769 which we have cited as establishing West's reputation as a history painter (p. 42), all but the *Continence of Scipio* of 1766 were reproduced in prints published by Boydell in 1769, 1771, and 1776. These works, in which the nobility of subject conveyed by an appropriately noble composition was all important, and in which the painterly charms of color and handling were deliberately minimized, were particularly suited for reproduction through the black-and-white medium of mezzotint engraving, and the prints after them have an inherent dignity which must have been all the more impressive to those viewers who knew the works only in this form.

Through the rest of the eighteenth century, reproductive prints after West's major paintings continued to appear regularly, giving his compositions an international circulation and allowing him to expand his income by appealing to a public far larger and more diffuse than the tiny fraction of it that could afford to buy large paintings. In expanding the market for works of art, the flourishing print industry encouraged and responded to popular taste, and so did painters such as West, particularly West. He seems to have painted several relatively modest works such as Nos. 296 and 425 specifically to be reproduced as popular prints, and he undertook a major late work, the *Death of Lord Nelson* as a speculative venture in partnership with the engraver James Heath. At times, like many other artists, he painted directly on commission from Boydell (see Nos. 207 and 210) and other print publishers (see Nos. 50, 52, and 325), who in the 1780s and 1790s became the most munificent and adventurous patrons of contemporary British art. West also played a role in the popularization of new graphic and reproductive processes. In 1801, three years after Aloys Senefelder had invented the technique of lithography, West seems to have been the first artist of significance anywhere to produce a work in the new medium, the lithograph of the *Angel of the Resurrection*, which appeared in the *Specimens of Polyautography* published by Philipp André in 1803 (see No. 375).[72] Some twenty years earlier, when the entrepreneur Joseph Booth devised a "Polygraphic" method of reproducing pictures in oil on canvas, West (in Booth's words), "with a mind much superior to professional prejudices, indulged the artist with the use of one of his pictures, from which he has taken the first piece he dares submit to the approval of the public."[73]

Boydell was able to become a patron on a princely scale partly because of the money he made from William Woollett's engraving after the *Death of General Wolfe*, published in 1776. For this print and a companion print by John Hall after *Penn's Treaty with the Indians* (No. 85), Boydell chose the medium of line engraving rather than mezzotint, as it would allow much larger editions, and for the same reason later prints after West's most popular compositions, the *Battle of La Hogue* (No. 90), the *Battle of the Boyne* (No. 88), the *Death of Lord Nelson*, and others, are also in line. Of these prints, that after the *Death of General Wolfe* had the most phenomenal sales, which made it one of the most commercially successful engravings in history and earned Boydell (who had only a one-third interest in the profits) a sum of £15,000 by 1785.[74] Such success represents genuine and widespread popularity, earned in part by the work's merits as a work of art, but won more by what Reynolds termed "the inherent greatness of the subject," its powerful appeal to patriotic sentiments, an appeal that as an icon of British, Canadian and American history it has not yet entirely lost.

The *Death of General Wolfe* instantly occasioned a revolution in West's career, and several later works can be considered in different ways as sequels to it. The most obvious is the *Death of Lord Nelson* (ill. p. 130), which shows the similar death of an immensely popular hero at the moment of a glorious victory. In this instance there was no time lag at all between the event depicted and the creation of the painting commemorating it, West having started the undertaking as soon as the news of the Battle of Trafalgar reached England. Such haste was not only generated by contemporary excitement about the event, but also had the purpose of putting the first painting and (more important) engraving of what everyone expected to be a lucrative subject into the market-place. This competitive situation was in itself a consequence of the popular and commercial success of the *Death of General Wolfe*.[75] West had waited for over thirty years to paint such an auspicious sequel to the earlier painting, and he

The Angel of the Resurrection, lithograph by West, 1801 (see No. 375, note 4)

John Singleton Copley, *The Death of the Earl of Chatham*, 1779–1781. Oil on canvas, 90 × 121 in. Tate Gallery, London

OPPOSITE
The Death of Nelson (Cat. No. 108), detail

The Death of the Earl of Chatham, c. 1778–86 (Cat. No. 104)

reputedly told Lord Nelson himself some time before the Battle of Trafalgar that he had painted no more pictures like the *Death of General Wolfe* because there were no more such subjects to paint. He had sketched another contemporary death scene, the *Death of the Earl of Chatham* (No. 104 *below*), but gave it up so as not to compete with his compatriot Copley, and Copley rather than West made a specialty of such subjects, following his *Death of Chatham* of 1779–81 with the *Death of Major Peirson* in 1782–84 (both Tate Gallery, the former on extended loan to the National Portrait Gallery).

For George III, West painted a repetition of the *Death of General Wolfe* (No. 94) and two further paintings conceived and commissioned as appropriate companions: the *Death of Epaminondas* (No. 5, ill. p. 66) showing a death that took place in 326 B.C., and the *Death of the Chevalier Bayard* (No. 77, ill. p. 67) showing one in A.D. 1524. This commission is an example of the late eighteenth-century proclivity to equate past and present, a proclivity which

The Death of Epaminondas, 1773 (Cat. No. 5)

The Death of the Chevalier Bayard, 1772 (Cat. No. 77)

explains to us the commitment of West and other artists to historical subjects, and which justified to the artists' public the new fashion of contemporary history painting. The equation of Wolfe and Epaminondas was the invention of neither West nor George III; the analogy seems to have come automatically to eighteenth-century minds and was drawn in at least two contemporary accounts of the Battle of Quebec.[76]

West proposed to Lord Grosvenor, the purchaser of the original *Death of General Wolfe*, that he paint for him another event that had taken place in America during his youth, the discovery of the bones of the army of General Edward Braddock, which had been annihilated by the French in western Pennsylvania in 1755, but the subject was rejected as too obscure.[77] Nevertheless, West did follow the exhibition of the *Death of General Wolfe* at the Royal Academy in 1771 with a painting in 1772 showing a confrontation in seventeenth-century Pennsylvania, *William Penn's Treaty with the Indians (right)*. Although painted for another patron, William Penn's son, it was perceived as closely enough related to the *Death of General Wolfe* for Boydell to commission his prints after the two works as companions, which were announced together in a broadside published in January 1773. For Lord Grosvenor, West eventually painted four further historical paintings of subjects drawn from seventeenth-century England (Nos. 83, 84, 88, and 90, ill. pp. 70 and 71). These four pictures were evidently intended as companions to the *Death of General Wolfe* (they are approximately the same size, and the five pictures hung together in the nineteenth century), and following the picture of a medieval subject that West painted along with an ancient one as companions to George III's version, they demonstrate the displacement of the classical past by other periods in West's choice of historical subjects, which was to be characteristic of his art from the 1770s onwards. By the end of his life he had painted more paintings depicting the history of Britain than historical subjects drawn from ancient Greece and Rome.

West was not the first artist, or even one of the first, to paint subjects from British history. From 1759 to 1777, the Society of Arts sponsored an annual competition for "the best original Historical Picture, the subject to be taken from the English [changed in 1763 to 'British or Irish'] History only."[78] In 1763, the year of West's arrival in England, the premium of 100 guineas went to Robert Edge Pine for *Canute the Great Reproving His Courtiers for Their Impious Flattery*. John Hamilton Mortimer, an erstwhile student of Pine, won second prize for *Edward the Confessor Stripping His Mother of Her Effects*, and a special premium went to George Romney for a painting of the *Death of General Wolfe*. Pine and Mortimer both produced pictures of medieval England with some frequency and Pine, an artist whose career curiously reversed that of West,[79] also won a premium from the Society of Arts in 1760 for a *Surrender of Calais to Edward III*, a subject that West was later to paint (No. 64). Other artists who preceded West were Samuel Wale, an illustrator and the first Professor of Perspective in the Royal Academy, who exhibited scenes from medieval England (often identified as sketches or stained drawings) at the Society of Artists between 1760 and 1767 and at the Academy regularly from 1769 to

William Penn's Treaty with the Indians, 1771–72 (Cat. No. 85)

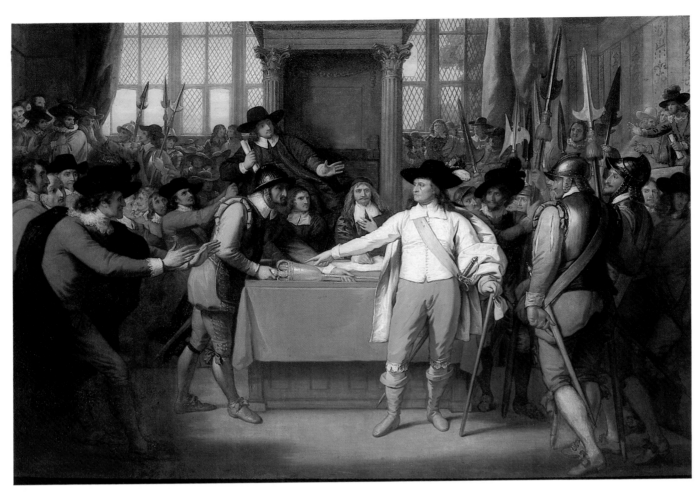

Oliver Cromwell Dissolving the Long
Parliament, 1782 (Cat. No. 83)

General Monk Receiving Charles II
on the Beach at Dover, 1782 (Cat. No. 84)

The Battle of the Boyne, 1778
(Cat. No. 88)

The Battle of La Hogue, c. 1775–80
(Cat. No. 90), detail over page

1776, and Angelica Kauffmann, who exhibited paintings of similar subjects in 1770 and 1771. These paintings and West's slightly later ones were products of a growing interest in national history and an antiquarian enthusiasm, which were to touch other aspects of British life in the later eighteenth century. Many of West's paintings were based on David Hume's *History of England* published from 1754 to 1762, and he incorporated details of dress and other features from the antiquarian studies of Joseph Strutt, which began to appear in 1773.[80] Much of his activity from 1779 to 1801 was connected with the restoration of Windsor Castle, a genuine medieval structure, and between 1796 and 1799 he was engaged upon decorations for Fonthill Abbey, an imitation one.

As implied in the Epaminondas-Bayard-Wolfe linkage of the three paintings commissioned together by George III, themes from more recent history were expected to convey many of the same elevating messages as subjects from classical antiquity. Those painted by West are full of examples of self-sacrifice, charity, generosity, patriotism, courage, and so on, paralleling the admirable conduct of the Greeks and Romans. Yet differences do appear. Whereas his paintings of classical subjects extolled virtue in the manner of a detached philosophical dialogue, in keeping with the chronological and geographical distance of the events shown, themes from the more recent history of England inevitably appealed to feelings of patriotism and a host of more local and immediate interests. Historical accuracy, based on scholarly research into details of arms, architecture, heraldry, the appearance of participants, etc., is a much more conspicuous concern in these works than in scenes from antiquity. Whereas there was general familiarity with classical antiquity among educated men, the Middle Ages were largely *terra incognita*, and several sources emphasize the hours West devoted to study to accumulate the necessary information.[81] Such research into what happened, who participated, and how things looked, tended to become an end in itself, leading to illustrations of significant historical events simply as elaborate reconstructions of those events, chosen perhaps because they fit the artist's and patron's ideas of what was important in history, and thus reinforcing in most instances a monarchical view of history, but not to teach moral lessons. Works such as *General Monk Receiving Charles II on the Beach at Dover* of 1782 (No. 84, ill. p. 70) or the *Institution of the Order of the Garter* of 1787 (No. 67, ill. p. 95) are examples. In other subjects, virtues may be celebrated incidentally in works that are really about something else. The *Battle of La Hogue* (No. 90, ill. p. 71) and *Edward III Crossing the Somme* (No. 56, ill. p. 96) show acts of bravery and patriotism, but they are basically animated scenes of stirring victories, which elicit quite different responses than do the resolute self-sacrifices of an Arria or a Regulus.

To paint such subjects, West had to adopt an appropriate formal language. Already in 1770 in the *Death of General Wolfe* he seems to have based the central figures on a painting of the *Lamentation* by Anthony Van Dyck (ill. p. 58)[82] and the borrowing, both in evoking parallels between the Union Jack and the Cross and between Wolfe and Christ, and in providing a pattern for uniting the men supporting Wolfe into a compact group of mourners, is responsible for much of the painting's emotive resonance. In the language of the debates

The Battle of the Boyne (Cat. No. 88), detail

75

Alexander III of Scotland Saved from a Stag by Colin Fitzgerald (The Death of the Stag), 1786 (Cat. No. 54), detail

of the French Académie Royale a century earlier, it also marks a shift from *Poussinisme* to *Rubénisme*, since the style of Van Dyck is much closer to Rubens, his master, than to Poussin, West's chief inspiration of the previous few years. Such a shift does not represent an absolute stylistic commitment, but rather a growing stylistic flexibility on West's part in accord with his growing flexibility in choice of subjects. Thus in the Royal Academy exhibition of 1773 he exhibited a *Holy Family in Imitation of Correggio's Manner* (No. 303) and a painting illustrating *The Faerie Queene* (No. 220, ill. p. 82) that was obviously and deeply indebted to Salvator Rosa. Among the works he sent to the exhibition of 1780 were a design of a Roman subject, *Cornelia, Mother of the Gracchi* (No. 20), in the most delicate Neo-Classical manner, and a painting of a seventeenth-century battle, the *Battle of La Hogue*, shown as a turbulent scene of confused activity, in which painterly handling obscures detail, and emphatic

diagonals create a powerful sense of movement in the manner of seventeenth-century battle paintings. Nevertheless, from the mid-1770s to the mid-1790s, as classical subjects constituted an ever-shrinking part of West's output (he exhibited none at all from 1782 through 1793), his stylistic orientation became increasingly neo-Baroque rather than Neo-Classical. This development culminated in the huge Rubensian *Alexander III of Scotland Saved from a Stag* of 1786 (No. 54) and in other large-scale works from the next few years such as Nos. 210 and 397 (ill. pp. 88 and 100).

The redirection of West's art in the 1770s reflected in his move from Greek and Roman to British history is even more emphatically displayed in his paintings of religious and literary subjects. He had painted and exhibited pictures of both types prior to 1770; as we have seen, two of the three paintings he exhibited in 1764 were based on Ariosto and Boccaccio (Nos. 188 and 195), and he exhibited paintings of Old Testament subjects in 1767 and 1768

Jacob Blesseth Joseph's Two Sons (?) 1766 (Cat. No. 250)

Rinaldo and Armida, 1773 (Cat. No. 228)

(ill. p. 77). But in 1772, 1773, and 1777 he exhibited paintings which for the first time were based on an English poet, Spenser, and of these three works the second, the *Cave of Despair*, painted in 1772 and exhibited in 1773 (ill. p. 82) is dramatically unlike anything that he had painted heretofore. It is, however, echoed both in comparable subject and in style by an Old Testament subject, *Saul and the Witch of Endor*, which he painted in 1777 but did not exhibit (No. 275, ill. p. 83). Both paintings depict protagonists who do not act, but respond as spectators to terrifying figures or apparitions, which they encounter or see conjured up before them. The paintings are about responses, and they provide textbook demonstrations of "the sublime," a concept given currency in England by Edmund Burke's *Philosophical Enquiry into the Origin of Our Ideas of the Sublime and Beautiful*, published in 1757. This immensely influential treatise defined sublimity as an aesthetic category equal to beauty but of an opposite nature, growing out of our psychological responses to what we perceive as threatening. It thus legitimized and popularized the evocation of terror and related responses as a goal of a work of art, and led a generation

Isaac's Servant Tying the Bracelet on Rebecca's Arm, 1775
(Cat. No. 243)

of artists to an obsession with awe, horror, and terror. West's *Cave of Despair* and *Saul and the Witch of Endor* are products of this obsession and should be seen in relation to contemporary and earlier works by John Hamilton Mortimer, Joseph Wright of Derby, Henry Fuseli, and others.[83] Fuseli made drawings of both subjects, that of the *Cave of Despair* (Art Institute of Chicago) probably in 1769, before West, that of *Saul and the Witch of Endor* (Victoria and Albert Museum) in 1777, the same year as West's painting; and Mortimer also treated both subjects in works that have since disappeared. The chief stylistic influence on all these artists in such works was Salvator Rosa, whose painting (and life) came to be seen by the late eighteenth century as the ultimate embodiment of sublimity. Salvator was the source of the grisly details in the *Cave of Despair*, and West's *Saul and the Witch of Endor* is a reworking, which repeats all the main features, of Salvator's *Saul and the Witch of Endor* in the Louvre.

Awe and terror remained components of much of West's subsequent painting, as they remained major elements of much painting of the Romantic period

The Golden Age, 1776 (Cat. No. 419)

Isaac's Servant Tying the Bracelet on Rebecca's Arm (Cat. No. 243), detail

The Cave of Despair, 1772 (Cat. No. 220)

OPPOSITE *Saul and the Witch of Endor*, 1777 (Cat. No. 275)

in general for half of the nineteenth century. West, however, did not continue to paint such overtly sublime paintings.[84] The two works from 1772 and 1777, neither of which is very large, should perhaps be thought of as exercises in a currently fashionable mode rather than as profoundly personal creations. Yet they are more than just exercises in describing and evoking terror, and they differ from the *Agrippina* and the *Regulus* not only in rejecting the contemplative dignity of those paintings. Instead of depicting heroes such as Regulus, who control their destinies, acting philosophically on the basis of their convictions and thus becoming models of virtuous behavior, both paintings show weak and emotional figures. The threat of death lies before them, but, unlike Regulus, they face it with terror, rather than philosophically or heroically. Both works are images of human frailty and inadequacy before forces outside the realm of the rational and the comprehensible, and the world they show is one in which men's destinies are determined by powers that they cannot control. This view of man's lot is the prevailing one in West's later works,

Salvator Rosa, *Saul and the Witch of Endor*. Oil on canvas, 107 × 76 in. Musée du Louvre, Paris

and, explicitly or implicitly, it is the main message of the biblical subjects which were to constitute the largest part of his *oeuvre* from the 1770s onward.

Such pessimism, in contrast to the hortatory tone of much Neo-Classical painting, is also a message of countless works by other artists active at the end of the eighteenth century and the beginning of the nineteenth. It is often described as a consequence of the warfare and chaos engendered by the American and French revolutions, which led to rejection of the rational Enlightenment thought of many mid-eighteenth-century thinkers whose utopian belief in human perfectibility lay behind those revolutions. An argument of this nature can be made in relation to West. As a courtier and as an artist bearing an appointment from the King of England, he had to be circumspect in what he said, but as an American he was not untouched by the conflict in his native land before and after the Declaration of Independence in 1776.[85] The changing nature of his protagonists from a Regulus in 1769 to a Saul in 1777, and of the manner in which he depicted them, must have been given some impetus by contemporary events. He painted *Saul and the Witch of Endor*, in which an evil king learns of his impending defeat, death, and loss of his kingdom, in the same year as the Battle of Saratoga, which was widely interpreted at the time not only as a humiliating defeat for the British forces but as a prophetic turning point in the American war. The parallel may have been coincidental, and it almost certainly was not consciously intended by West, since public expression of its implied message would have been professionally suicidal. Nonetheless, one cannot help interpreting *Saul and the Witch of Endor* and many other works—the heath scene from *King Lear* painted at the time of George III's first attack of apparent insanity (No. 210, ill. p. 100), various Apocalyptic subjects such as *Death on the Pale Horse* (Nos. 401–3, ill. pp. 146 and 148)—as embodying, probably unconsciously, his responses to things happening around him, responses which were all the more disturbing because West's position forbade their open expression and perhaps even their acknowledgment to himself. It is no coincidence that formally these paintings are West's least Neo-Classical, most precociously neo-Baroque, and hence that they are his works that seem most prophetic of the stylistic language of much Romantic painting of the early nineteenth century.

Daniel Interpreting to Belshazzar the Writing on the Wall, 1775 (Cat. No. 288)

v Patronage and Major Commissions 1773–1801

Prior to 1770, West had been patronized by the Archbishop of York, the Bishop of Bristol, and other dignitaries of the Church. Their purchases were made in their private capacities, rather than for the Church, and were of pictures of both secular (Nos. 33 and 163) and religious (Nos. 281 and 320) subjects. Archbishop Drummond's pivotal importance in West's career has been noted. His commissions after 1768 were confined to portraits, but the Bishop of Bristol, Thomas Newton (see No. 675), who was also Dean of St. Paul's Cathedral, played a part in a scheme to decorate St. Paul's with paintings. This project was put forth by several members of the Royal Academy, including West, in 1773 and immediately vetoed by the Bishop of London (see No. 705) on the grounds of popery.[86] Before that, West had received a commission for an altarpiece for Rochester Cathedral from an acquaintance he had known from Rome (see No. 714), and he appeared in the Royal Academy exhibition of 1774 solely as a painter of religious works, his three entries consisting of the completed Rochester altarpiece (No. 304), a design for the aborted St. Paul's project (No. 257), and a design for a large painting for the church of St. Stephen Walbrook in London, which he completed and exhibited two years later (Nos. 388 and 389). He followed them with large altarpieces for the chapel of Trinity College, Cambridge, in 1777 (No. 406) and for Winchester Cathedral in 1780 (No. 339), and probably in 1782 he received the commission for the most ambitious altarpiece of all, for the chapel at Greenwich Hospital (No. 397, ill. p. 88). This huge work was not completed until 1789 and, presumably because of its size, it was installed in the chapel (where it remains as the most important painting by West still in the spot for which it was intended) without being exhibited at the Royal Academy; but a sketch for it (No. 398) did appear there in 1787. West's other chief religious works from the 1780s and 1790s were painted for George III and destined for two chapels at Windsor Castle.

Although West described himself in Royal Academy catalogues from 1772 onward as Historical Painter to the King, after 1773 he painted no historical pictures for the King for a period of six or seven years. The *Departure of Regulus*, the second version of the *Death of General Wolfe*, and all his other early paintings for George III were destined for one room in Buckingham Palace, the Warm Room, and when the walls of the Warm Room were filled, George III evidently had no need or desire for further paintings of similar subjects. However, after a short interval, he found employment for West as a portrait painter. Six group portraits of members of the royal family bear dates from 1776 through 1779, and West continued to paint portraits of the same sitters, or related pictures such as the *Apotheosis of Prince Alfred and Prince Octavius* (No. 575) through 1783.

Death on the Pale Horse (Cat. No. 403), detail

Interior of the Chapel of Sts. Peter and Paul, Royal Naval College, Greenwich

St. Paul Shaking the Viper from His Hand after the Shipwreck, 1789 (Cat. No. 397), detail

His commissions to paint portraits of the royal family followed those given to Zoffany, who painted numerous royal portraits before 1772, and preceded the portraits commissioned by George III from Gainsborough in the early 1780s.[87] Zoffany was in Italy from 1772 to 1779, and his extended absence from England partly explains why the King turned to his Historical Painter for likenesses of his growing family.

The circumstance that led George III to commission further historical pictures from West seems to have been a decision made around 1778 to restore and refurbish Windsor Castle and to make Windsor the chief royal residence. Apart from portraits, all West's work for George III after 1778 was connected with Windsor, and views of Windsor also appear prominently in the backgrounds of several portraits (Nos. 556, 558, 571, and 575). West himself bought a house in Park Street in Windsor, and he was given a room in the castle

Six Children of George III, 1776 (Cat. No. 570)

in which to work. There and in London he devoted himself to a series of paintings of biblical subjects for the Royal Chapel and to a series of historical subjects for the Audience Chamber, both in the state apartments in the Upper Ward of the castle; an altarpiece and designs for stained glass windows for St. George's Chapel in the Lower Ward; designs for a ceiling in the Queen's Lodge built by Sir William Chambers between 1778 and 1782 on the south terrace outside the castle proper (Nos. 435–39); and three large paintings in watercolors which served as decorations for celebrations at the castle in 1789 (Nos. 432–34). All this added up to a vast amount of work, and it was with the beginning of his work at Windsor that West started to receive an annual stipend of £1,000 from the King.

The first of the Windsor projects begun, and by far the largest, which remained unfinished when West's royal patronage came to a halt in 1801, was the series of paintings intended for the Royal Chapel, upon which he had started to work by October 1779. A painting for the chapel (No. 334) appeared at the Royal Academy in 1781, and it was followed during the course of the next twenty years by a steady stream of companion works (see Appendix I). These were paintings on a large scale; the largest of them (No. 258) is eighteen feet high by over twelve feet wide, and twelve of the nineteen works which West actually painted for the chapel were over twelve feet high. Despite the magnitude of this undertaking, in 1782 or 1783 West also began to work on designs and cartoons for stained glass windows in St. George's Chapel. By 1796 four windows after his designs had been installed, and in 1797 he exhibited a design for a fifth, showing the *Crucifixion*, which would have filled the edifice's west end, balancing his earlier *Resurrection* on the east (see Nos. 356 and 360 *opposite*). The *Crucifixion* window was never completed, due to the death in 1807 of the glass-maker after more than ten years of work upon it. Although West did not execute the windows himself, he did prepare full-size cartoons, of which one still exists (No. 298). The windows were on an even grander scale than the paintings for the chapel in the state apartments, and West was paid correspondingly more (2,000 guineas each for the designs and cartoons for the east and west windows, versus 1,200 guineas for the largest chapel picture). These were the highest prices he received for any work until the last decade of his life. The largest cartoon, that of the *Crucifixion* (No. 357), measured thirty-six by twenty-eight feet and was described in 1807 as the largest picture in the world. These windows, which were already considered by many of West's contemporaries as a desecration of the medieval structure,[88] were removed and destroyed in the mid-nineteenth century. However, a large tripartite window designed during the same period and installed in 1789 in the recently built church of St. Paul's in Birmingham remains in situ (see No. 392, ill. p. 92) and is powerfully and dramatically impressive, in a Baroque style consistent with West's other works of the late 1780s.

The watercolor decorations made for Windsor in 1789 have disappeared and have probably long been destroyed. The Queen's Lodge ceiling was destroyed in 1823 along with the lodge itself, but sketches for it exist (Nos. 435 [ill. p. 93]–439) and are of considerable interest as allegorical celebrations of

Anon. *St. George's Chapel, Windsor, c.* 1820. Watercolor, St. George's Chapel, Windsor

The Call of the Prophet Jeremiah, c. 1784 (Cat. No. 286)

The Resurrection, c. 1782 (Cat. No. 360)

Interior of St. Paul's Church, Birmingham

The Conversion of St. Paul, 1786 (Cat. No. 392)

Genius Calling Forth Arts and Sciences, 1789 (Cat. No. 435)

up-to-date scientific, technological, and commercial concerns. On a modest scale and with a frankly decorative purpose, the program echoes aspects of James Barry's slightly earlier series of huge paintings devoted to the *Progress of Human Culture* in the Society of Arts. Although allegorical, West's sketches demonstrate how alien the traditional vocabulary of allegory had become for artists of his generation, and two of them, for *Agriculture* and *Manufactory* (Nos. 436 and 437), are essentially genre scenes, which are given further significance only by the over-all iconographic program. West made designs for the ceiling in 1787 and 1788. The actual decorations were carried out in the novel medium of colored marble dust and installed in 1789.

At the same time, between 1786 and 1789, West also painted eight paintings for the Audience Chamber at Windsor. These paintings, which are on a scale corresponding to those for the Royal Chapel (the three largest are each approximately nine by fifteen feet and commanded prices of 1,300 guineas), are West's only paintings of all those intended for Windsor Castle that remain in the Royal Collection. They are no longer together, or in their original location, but we do know how they originally looked in the Audience Chamber from a watercolor by Charles Wild. This shows a sumptuous setting which pays not the least heed to the castle's medieval origins; nor is there anything medieval in the style of West's paintings. The most generally admired of them, the *Institution of the Order of the Garter* (*opposite*), has a composition taken from Rubens's *Coronation of Marie de Médicis*, in this respect anticipating Jacques-Louis David's use of the same prototype for the composition of his *Coronation of Napoleon* of 1805–7. Nevertheless, in subject the paintings, which show events from the fourteenth-century reign of Edward III, were completely appropriate for Windsor.

Prior to George III and George IV, Edward III had been the English monarch most closely associated with Windsor Castle, and George III commissioned the paintings because of that association.[89] In painting the series, one of which even shows an event that took place in St. George's Chapel in 1348 (see No. 67), West anticipated George III's Gothic Revival restorations at Windsor carried out by the architect James Wyatt after 1796 (see Appendix I). He also painted the most ambitious and important group of pictures of subjects from the Middle Ages produced during the eighteenth century. As such, they prefigured the efflorescence of medieval subject matter in the nineteenth century, from the French *style troubadour* at the beginning of the century, to the Arthurian medievalism of Rossetti and Burne-Jones and the historical costume

Charles Wild, *The Audience Chamber, Windsor Castle*. Watercolor, Her Majesty the Queen

The Institution of the Order of the Garter, 1787 (Cat. No. 67)

Peter Paul Rubens, *Coronation of Marie de Medicis*. Oil on canvas. Musée du Louvre, Paris

Edward III Crossing the Somme, 1788 (Cat. No. 56)

pieces of Seymour Lucas and others at the end. As a sequence of scenes from British history commissioned to decorate a state apartment intended for official and public functions, they look forward to the paintings commissioned for the new Houses of Parliament in the 1840s and 1850s, and, appropriately, the three largest paintings from the series (Nos. 58, 67, and 74) now hang on extended loan in the Houses of Parliament.[90] The Audience Chamber paintings, as depictions either of the Middle Ages or of English history, were not unprecedented in West's *oeuvre* (see above, pp. 65–75), but, in scale, and as a group of thematically connected works, they constituted his most monumental undertaking as a painter of historical subjects, as well as an early landmark in the development of a tradition of painting English history. After 1789 West continued to contribute to that tradition by painting pictures for two series illustrating English history commissioned by Robert Bowyer in 1792 (Nos. 50 and 52) and by Alexander Davison in 1806 (No. 80).

Although West worked on his paintings for the Royal Chapel until 1801 and produced his last design for a window for St. George's Chapel in 1796, he received no royal commissions for new projects after 1789. In 1791 he succeeded Richard Dalton as Surveyor of the King's Pictures, but on 23 November 1793, Joseph Farington recorded in his diary that remarks were being made at Windsor that West no longer went there as usual.[91] On 17 December 1797, West told Farington that the bulk of the money owed him by the Crown had not been paid and that he had not resided in his house at Windsor since May of 1796.[91] Then, on 15 August 1801, he received instructions from James Wyatt to stop work on the paintings for the Royal Chapel, the one commission from the King upon which he was still engaged. The reasons for West's fall from royal favor were multiple. One was probably the rivalry of Wyatt, who insinuated himself in the King's confidence in West's place.[93] Another certainly was George III's growing distrust of West's political loyalties. On 6 December 1794, Farington recorded West's distress about the King's "having been informed of his holding democratic principles."[94] But the most central reason was the

Edward, the Black Prince, Receiving John, King of France, Prisoner, after the Battle of Poitiers (Cat. No. 75)

Noah Sacrificing, c. 1801 (Cat. No. 236)

deterioration of George III's health and mental stability following his first breakdown in the autumn of 1788. West's watercolor decorations of 1789 were made for festivities at Windsor celebrating the King's return to health,[95] but the return did not prove permanent, and when the King's behavior became erratic, decisions were made on his behalf by the Queen. According to Galt, the order to tell West to stop work in August 1801 was given to Wyatt by Queen Charlotte, and Galt adds, "What was the state of His Majesty's health at that time is now a matter of historical curiosity."[96] The King did have a severe attack in February 1801, which led to his being forcibly detained at the Queen's behest, and West on 26 September 1801, replying to the order to suspend work, wrote to the King at Weymouth, where he was still convalescing. In 1803 West told Farington that during the King's first illness in the winter of 1788–89, the Queen ordered his ceiling in the Queen's Lodge taken down, only for it to be installed again when the King recovered, and that he "continued to feel coldness on the part of Her Majesty."[97] Although he long since had been told to stop work, he continued to receive £1,000 a year from the Crown until the onset of the King's final illness, which led to the establishment of a regency in 1811. His payments stopped at Christmas 1810. West told Farington, "The Queen is considered to be at the bottom of this business," and he attempted without success to get the Prince Regent to reinstate the stipend.[98] He did keep his position as Surveyor of the King's Pictures until his death.

As suggested above (p. 50), purely aesthetic appreciation does not seem to have been an important reason for the King's support of West, but lack of such appreciation may have played a role in the waning of that support, espe-

Pharaoh and His Host Lost in the Red Sea, c. 1792 (Cat. No. 255)

cially to the extent that West's fall from favor was due to parties other than the King. By 1789 reservations about the quality of his painting were becoming unavoidable. Between 1786 and 1789, West produced a huge volume of work for his royal patron, including all the pictures for the Audience Chamber and all the designs for the Queen's Lodge. During those same years, he also painted the very large *Alexander III of Scotland Saved from a Stag* for the future Lord Seaforth, the first of two large Shakespearean paintings for Boydell (*above*), and the still larger Greenwich altarpiece. His output of smaller pictures virtually dried up; nonetheless, it is obvious that he spread himself thin. To cover so many square feet of canvas, he had to rely upon studio assistants, five of whom—John Trumbull, Gilbert Stuart, Richard Livesay, and his two sons, Raphael and Benjamin, Jr.—are portrayed with him as part of the audience watching the Garter ceremonies in No. 67 of 1787 (*right*), and he must have delegated a substantial part of the execution of such works to them. Furthermore, his own technical limitations in draughtsmanship and anatomy

King Lear : Act III, Scene IV (King Lear in the Storm), 1788
(Cat. No. 210)

OPPOSITE
King Lear : Act III, Scene IV (King Lear in the Storm) c. 1788
(Cat. No. 211)

Detail from the *Institution of the Order of the Garter* (No. 67, ill. p. 95): West, Mrs. West, their sons Raphael and Benjamin, John Trumbull, Gilbert Stuart, and Richard Livesay

became magnified on canvases ten or twenty feet in height with over life-size figures. For all his largest pictures he painted oil sketches, which in many instances he also exhibited, and to his contemporaries the superiority of these sketches to the large finished pictures seems to have been universally apparent. Their preference was articulated in a conversation that took place after West's death between William Beckford and an anonymous visitor, a conversation prompted by the sketch, which Beckford owned (No. 211 *above*), for the Boydell *Lear* of 1788:

> I have seen . . . most of West's great pictures, but there is more genius in that sketch than in anything I ever saw of his. I think he took too much pain with his sketches [i.e. in developing them into large pictures]. The consequence was that the original spirit evaporated long before the completion of the great tame painting, where his men and women too often look like wooden lay figures covered with drapery.[99]

This opinion was anticipated by the negative comments which West's large paintings for the Royal Chapel attracted with increasing frequency as he exhibited them in the 1780s and 1790s. In 1796, for example, *Moses and Aaron before Pharaoh* (No. 252) was described and dismissed as a "three-acred piece," and every critic expressed preference for the sketches in the same exhibition, notably that of *Death on the Pale Horse* (No. 403, ill. p. 146), which, in the words of one, "we hope never to see dilated into one of his immense pieces of Moor-cloth manufactory." (It was; see No. 401, ill. p. 148.)

Wooden figures were certainly not absent from West's work prior to the large paintings of the 1790s, but in the earlier Neo-Classical pictures, they could be interpreted as embodying an appropriate rigor consistent with the formal and thematic discipline of these basically static tableaux. As West's images became more active, an increasingly pronounced brush stroke and a relatively small figural scale obviated the problem in works of moderate size such as the *Battle of La Hogue*, while the freer and bolder brush stroke in sketches such as No. 211, which seems to be an extension of their now fully Baroque compositions, enlivens everything in them. But this lively handling disappeared when the sketches were worked up into large finished pictures. West's inability to translate the consistency and the quality of the small sketches onto a public scale was one that he shared with many other artists, and the widespread critical preference for his preparatory sketches over the finished products which he based on them anticipates judgments frequently made of the work of nineteenth-century painters such as Constable and Corot. Nevertheless, that preference was undoubtedly a factor in the virtual disappearance of new commissions for very large paintings after 1789.

As West's royal commissions were beginning to dwindle, the most significant new patron he acquired in the 1790s was the immensely wealthy and eccentric William Beckford, the author of *Vathek* and builder of the most spectacular of all Gothic Revival monuments, Fonthill Abbey in Wiltshire. The architect of Fonthill Abbey, which was begun in 1796 to replace a Palladian mansion built by Beckford's father, was James Wyatt. Wyatt, as we have seen, was the royal architect at Windsor, and he suggested to Farington that the socially ostracized Beckford, who had ambitions for a peerage, was attracted to West and presumably to Wyatt himself because of their positions at court.[100] But we know from various sources, including the conversation quoted above, that Beckford genuinely admired West's sketches, and it seems likely that what prompted him to approach West was the sight at the Royal Academy exhibition of 1796 of West's sketch of *Death on the Pale Horse* (No. 403) intended for one of the paintings of subjects from Revelation planned for the Royal Chapel at Windsor. West was soon receiving £1,000 a year from Beckford (while still receiving the same amount from the King), for which he was to paint pictures for a Revelation Chamber in Fonthill Abbey. In the catalogues of the Royal Academy exhibitions of 1797–99 West identified nine works either as pictures or as sketches for pictures or stained glass windows intended for the new abbey at Fonthill. Beckford eventually came to own eighteen paintings by West, a number surpassed only by the works commissioned by George III.

St Thomas à Becket, 1797 (Cat. No. 415)

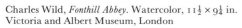

Charles Wild, *Fonthill Abbey*. Watercolor, $11\frac{1}{2} \times 9\frac{1}{4}$ in.
Victoria and Albert Museum, London

OPPOSITE
Moses Shown the Promised Land,
1801 (Cat. No. 269)

OPPOSITE
*Joshua Passing the River Jordan
with the Ark of the Covenant,* 1800
(Cat. No. 270)

The Ascension, c. 1801
(Cat. No. 383)

Beckford's Wests included four portraits of Beckford's mother, aunt, and grandparents or great-grandparents, one landscape, and a variety of other subjects, as well as scenes from Revelation. He acquired at least one painting (No. 211) after he left Fonthill and after West's death, but the works he commissioned were intended for Fonthill and were concentrated in the years from 1796 to 1799. The annual stipend probably lasted only two or three years at the most, and Beckford's last purchase of a work directly from West seems to have been in 1801 (No. 242). The Revelation Chamber was never completed, and we do not know the number of pictures planned for it, their intended sizes, or even whether it was to be decorated with paintings or with stained glass after West's designs. We can only speculate whether dissatisfaction with West's work was a reason for dropping the project, but we do know that four proposed paintings from Revelation, which Beckford had commissioned, were still unpainted in September 1799 and were to remain unpainted. Beckford subsequently owned the oil sketches, an outcome which may have been an accidental result of his changing plans and cancellation of the commissions, but one which probably did not displease him. On 1 November 1797, a year before Farington knew about the intended Revelation Chamber, Wyatt told him that Beckford liked West's sketches, "but not his pictures, and wishes him to make them like his sketches as He can."[101] Thus, West's inability to make his finished pictures sufficiently like his sketches may have been a reason that the Revelation Chamber never came about. Despite the huge scale of Fonthill Abbey and the large sums paid to the artist, none of the works which we can identify from among those Beckford owned is very large (the four family portraits, each measuring fifty-seven by forty-five inches, are the largest), but the Revelation sketches do embody greater ambitions than their actual dimensions imply and they have a visionary vitality that almost certainly would not have survived the process of turning them into large finished pictures. Iconographically, they were preceded and inspired by West's planned Apocalyptic subjects for the Royal Chapel. In turn, they anticipated William Blake's designs from Revelation made between 1800 and 1805, and the later grandiose paintings of Apocalyptic subjects by Francis Danby and John Martin. There is a direct historical link between West's and Danby's paintings based on Revelation through Beckford, who was a patron of both.[102] In a painting such as *An Attempt to Illustrate the Opening of the Sixth Seal* of 1828, which Beckford bought (National Gallery of Ireland, Dublin), Danby was primarily influenced by Martin, with whom he was trying to compete, but both artists owed substantial debts to West, either directly or indirectly. Their immediate points of departure, however, were the large and highly visible paintings of biblical subjects which West painted in the last decade of his life, not the small paintings and sketches for Beckford from the 1790s, which they probably had no opportunity to see prior to the Fonthill sales of 1822 and 1823.[103]

Blake, on the other hand, was born in London in 1757 and did see the paintings of biblical subjects which West exhibited with regularity at the Academy from 1771 onwards. Simply by dint of being the most prominent painter of such works, West probably did have an influence on Blake's immature draw-

King Lear: Act III, Scene IV
(King Lear in the Storm)
(Cat. No. 211), detail

William Blake, *The Great Red Dragon and the Beast from the Sea.*
c. 1803–5. Watercolor, 16¼ × 14 in. National Gallery of Art,
Washington, D.C.

ings of the early 1780s,[104] and Blake must have taken keen interest in West's paintings of Apocalyptic subjects of the following decade. Since the Middle Ages, illustrations of the Book of Revelation had been exceedingly rare and, therefore, West's paintings inevitably provided useful guide posts for younger artists, although the guide posts used by West remain something of a mystery. Blake's first Apocalyptic watercolor was of *Death on the Pale Horse*, drawn *c.* 1800, four years after West exhibited No. 403, and every one of the pictures from Revelation which West exhibited between 1796 and 1798 found an echo in a drawing by Blake a few years later.[105] The most striking similarity is between West's depiction of the angel from the tenth chapter of Revelation (No. 404) and Blake's drawing of the same subject (Metropolitan Museum of Art, New York),[106] but even Blake's fantastic multi-headed monsters of the *Great Red Dragon and the Beast from the Sea* (National Gallery of Art, Washington) followed West's monstrous beasts in what the miniature painter Ozias Humphry called the "finest conception ever come from mind of man" (No. 409 *opposite*). Humphry was an old friend of Blake, and he may have drawn Blake's attention to works such as this painting, as well as bringing work by the still obscure Blake to West's. On 19 February 1796, Farington recorded a conversation at the Royal Academy Club in which West, Humphry, and Richard Cosway (another miniature painter and also a friend of Blake) "spoke warmly in favour of the designs of Blake the Engraver, as works of extraordinary genius and imagination."[107] At that date, when West may have been working on the version of his *Death on the Pale Horse* that he exhibited the following May, he could have seen some of Blake's large color prints of 1795 and several of the prophetic books. Blake is said to have given him a copy of *America, A Prophecy* of 1793.[108] Thus, there does seem to have been some common ground between the two artists at a time when it would have been most useful to them, despite vast differences in temperament and in their positions in English artistic life.

The Beast Riseth out of the Sea, 1797
(Cat. No. 409)

VI The Venerable West 1792–1820

In 1792 West succeeded Sir Joshua Reynolds as second President of the Royal Academy. As a surviving founding member of the Academy, as the member closest to the Academy's royal patron, and as the artist who most completely devoted himself to the high-minded art the Academy was supposed to foster, West was the most obvious candidate, if not the ideal person, for the position. The diary which Joseph Farington started to keep in 1793 records in great detail the tribulations of the Academy during West's tenure of office. In 1805, due to a series of squabbles with a faction led by his compatriot and erstwhile friend, Copley, his position became so difficult that he resigned the presidency, to be replaced by James Wyatt, but he resumed it again the following year and retained the office until his death, serving for a total of twenty-seven years. Unlike his predecessor and unlike Sir Thomas Lawrence, his successor in 1820, and all subsequent presidents, he was not knighted. Although offered a knighthood, he declined it on the grounds, as quoted by Galt, "that he really thought he had already earned by his pencil more eminence than could be conferred on him by that rank." In declining, he proposed that a hereditary title, accompanied by an independent fortune, would be more appropriate, but that was not forthcoming.[109]

His election as President of the Academy came at a time when West's art was starting to undergo a significant redirection. The slackening (and in 1801 the end) of his royal commissions for large-scale paintings of religious and historical subjects provided him the time and the need to paint other, smaller, and more marketable pictures. In 1786 and 1787, he exhibited only two pictures each year at the Academy, and in 1788 and 1789 only one, and all of these paintings were either commissioned works or related studies, but in the following twelve years from 1790 to 1801 he sent ninety-nine pictures to exhibition, for an average of over eight entries each year. Many of these pictures were still commissioned. For example, in 1798, West exhibited fourteen works, including one for the Royal Chapel at Windsor, and five for Fonthill. The remaining entries included portraits (Nos. 650, 698, and 702), genre (No. 450), landscapes (Nos. 487 and 488), and two paintings of classical subjects (Nos. 123 and 127).

Of the portraits that West exhibited in 1798, at least one, that of General Tadeusz Kosciuszko (No. 650, ill. p. 133), was certainly not commissioned but undertaken by West because of the historical interest of the subject, and a second, showing Sir John Sinclair (No. 698), was evidently not commissioned either, as it remained in West's possession. The third (No. 702) showed the son of the engraver Sir Robert Strange, who had been a personal friend. West

Lot and His Daughters Conducted by Two Angels (Cat. No. 238), detail

111

Henry Singleton, *The Royal Academicians*, 1795. Oil on canvas, 78 × 102 in. Royal Academy, London. West, wearing a hat, is seated in the president's chair, slightly to the left of center. Joseph Farington is the tall balding man standing before the *Laocoon*. The shorter man standing with him and holding a walking stick is John Singleton Copley

Sir Francis Baring, Bt., 1804 (Cat. No. 587)

did not sell the genre subject (No. 450) either, and that was probably by choice. In 1797 he told Joseph Farington that he could have sold a genre painting that he exhibited that year, *A Drayman Drinking* (No. 443, ill. p. 114), "but wd. not sell any of his small pictures; can live witht. it and is desirous of making up in the course of 8 or 10 years more a collection to sell at once which may contribute to make an independence for others."

West first exhibited a painting of a genre subject in 1793 and, if we have correctly identified that work as No. 444, it suggests that this departure was inspired by the paintings of *The Cries of London* by Francis Wheatley, the first six of which had appeared at the Royal Academy in the previous year. The *Drayman Drinking* of 1797 recalls pictures of draymen and their horses that the animal painter George Garrard painted between 1784 and 1796 for the brewer Samuel Whitbread,[110] and, along with works such as Nos. 451 and 453, showing agricultural laborers, it also brings to mind pictures by George Morland.[111] This type of painting was widely popular and certainly more salable than history painting, something of which West was undoubtedly mindful as he tried "to make an independence for others." Nevertheless, he was probably not lured from the narrow path of history painting strictly by such a crassly practical consideration. He must have been attracted to these humble subjects by many of the same feelings that prompted collectors to buy pictures by Wheatley and Morland. By the 1790s, such paintings were seen as belonging to an English tradition stemming from Hogarth, and after war broke out with revolutionary France in 1793 their celebration of native English ways took on a pronounced patriotic appeal.

All told, West painted less than a dozen genre pictures of this character, and he exhibited only eight, all between 1793 and 1801. We have catalogued a few other odd works such as the ethnographic *Savage Warrior* painted in Italy

*The Sun Setting Behind a Group of Trees
on the Banks of The Thames at Twickenham
(Landscape-Evening)*, (Cat. No. 470), detail

in 1762 as genre paintings, *faute de mieux*, but they stand apart from the subjects West painted between 1793 and 1801. On the other hand, there is no distinct line between his genre and landscape paintings. The picture which we have catalogued and referred to as the genre picture exhibited in 1798 (No. 450) was exhibited under the title "A Landscape with women and children," and several other pictures from this period could be categorized either as genre or landscape. A few works that we have catalogued as Biblical, Historical, Mythological, and Homeric are also primarily landscapes, and some were exhibited with the word "landscape" as part of their titles, but they belong to a tradition of so-called historical landscape, in which biblical, historical, or mythological figures are depicted on a small scale in an extensive and usually invented landscape setting.

Landscapes comprise only a small part of West's total output, but they are more numerous than his genre paintings. He painted them occasionally throughout his career, starting in America before he was twenty years old (see Nos. 480–83 and ill. p. 12), and frequently between 1794 and 1812. They

A Drayman Drinking, 1796 (Cat. No. 443)

The Sun Setting Behind a Group of Trees on the Banks of The Thames at Twickenham (Landscape-Evening), (?)1799 (Cat. No. 470)

Illustrated pp 118, 119
View of Snow Hill, Windsor Great Park (Cat. No. 476), detail

View from the East Terrace of Windsor Castle Looking over Datchet, (?)1792 (Cat. No. 477)

Richard Wilson, *Ceyx and Alcyone*, 1768. Oil on canvas, 40 × 50 in. National Museum of Wales, Cardiff

The First Interview of Telemachus with Calypso, 1801 (Cat. No. 181)

include views of recognizable places as well as historical landscapes, the former painted chiefly for relaxation or as a diversion while relaxing. A significant number show views at or near Windsor, where he owned a house, and in 1808 he exhibited four landscape views painted in the vicinity of Bath, which he had visited the previous summer and autumn for the sake of his wife's health. His first picture identified as a landscape in a Royal Academy catalogue was a view of Windsor Great Park shown in 1785 (No. 473). His next landscapes identified as such by their titles appeared at the Academy in 1794. Prior to 1785, he had exhibited one historical landscape, the *First Interview of Telemachus and Calypso* (No. 180) as early as 1773, although without calling it a landscape. His other known historical landscapes, which include later versions of No. 180 (*below*), all date from between 1790 and 1812.

The historical landscape, inspired by the example of seventeenth-century paintings by Poussin and Claude, was looked upon in England in the eighteenth and early nineteenth centuries as a way of elevating the lesser art

Cicero Discovering the Tomb of Archimedes, 1797 (Cat. No. 22)

of landscape to the dignity of history painting, and as the highest type of painting to which landscape artists could and should aspire. Richard Wilson was
the first distinguished native painter of historical landscapes, and West's *First
Interview of Telemachus and Calypso* of 1772 was modelled on pictures by Wilson
such as *Ceyx and Alcyone*, exhibited in 1768 and engraved in 1769, and *Apollo
and the Seasons*, engraved in 1772.[112] The subject of a subsequent historical
landscape, *Cicero Discovering the Tomb of Archimedes* of 1796–97 (Nos. 22 *above*
and 24), was suggested to West by the distinguished connoisseur and champion
of Wilson, Sir George Beaumont, who owned Wilson's best-known historical
landscape, the *Destruction of Niobe's Children* (destroyed, formerly National Gallery, London). That painting, in Beaumont's words, established Wilson's reputation for "elevation of thought and dignity of composition,"[113] that is, a
reputation not unlike West's. In proposing a subject from the life of Cicero
to West, Beaumont must have had in mind Wilson's *Cicero and His Friends at
His Villa at Arpinum*,[114] although he may have been conscious as well of a work
showing the specific subject painted by the French artist Pierre-Henri de
Valenciennes in 1787 (Toulouse). In April 1797, before West sent the painting
to the Royal Academy, Beaumont pronounced it superior even to Poussin,
and one can understand why the picture, combining a classical landscape and

celebration of such a distinguished example of antiquarian enthusiasm, would have appealed to a learned and serious patron such as Beaumont. Indeed, the overgrown monument, which Cicero is having uncovered, looks forward to the monument to Sir Joshua Reynolds, which Beaumont was to erect on his own estate in Leicestershire in 1812, and which would later be the subject of a well-known picture by Constable.

West seems to have taken a paternal interest in Constable, possibly because of Beaumont, with whom Constable had connections stemming from his native East Anglia. Charles Robert Leslie's *Life* of Constable records several instances of assistance, encouragement, and advice proffered by the President of the Academy to the younger man, including the memorable dictum: "Always remember, sir, that light and shadow *never stand still*."[115] In turn, Constable genuinely admired West's landscapes, and West was one of five English land-

John Constable, *The Cenotaph*, 1836. Oil on canvas, 52 × 42¾ in. National Gallery, London

The Deluge, 1790–1803 (Cat. No. 235)

scape painters praised by Constable in a lecture given in 1833 (the others were Wilson, Gainsborough, Cozens, and Girtin).[116] West also gave instruction to John Linnell at the beginning of Linnell's career, but neither Constable nor Linnell seems to have taken much from West, and the pictures by West which we know Constable admired, the *First Interview of Telemachus and Calypso* and *Saul before Samuel and the Prophets*, were of a type which he himself did not aspire to paint. We can find more in common between West and Turner, although there is little record of actual exchanges between them equivalent to those between West and Constable.

In 1801 Joseph Farington recorded in his diary that West had spoken "in the highest manner" of a picture by Turner, but in 1804 came the comment that Turner's recent pictures were inferior to his former production, and in 1805 he was "tending to imbecility."[117] This *volte-face*, which paralleled many other contemporary views of Turner, most notably that of Sir George Beaumont, reflects initial recognition of Turner's great abilities and approval of his art as long as it appeared directed toward the old-masterly qualities to which West aspired, but subsequent distrust of the ambitions that soon led Turner to go beyond the implicit limitations established by earlier painting. West's *Cicero Discovering the Tomb of Archimedes* exhibited in 1797 and the *Bath of Venus: a poetic landscape* exhibited in 1799 (see No. 113), and some of his biblical subjects

J. M. W. Turner, *The Fifth Plague of Egypt*, 1800. Oil on canvas, 49 × 72 in. Indianapolis, Museum of Art, Indianapolis

Philip James de Loutherbourg, *Coalbrookdale by Night*, 1801.
Oil on canvas, 26¾ × 42 in. Science Museum, London

painted for George III, notably the *Deluge* exhibited in 1791 (see Nos. 234 and 235 *opposite*), were the most prominent historical landscapes to be seen at the Royal Academy between 1790 and 1800, and Turner could not have been unaware of them when he first turned to this type of painting in the *Fifth Plague of Egypt* of 1800 which, not incidentally, was purchased by West's patron William Beckford. After 1800, however, Turner set the pace in historical landscape, and West's *Lot and His Daughters* of 1810 (No. 238 *below*), which was bought by Turner's patron Sir John Fleming Leicester, is inconceivable without the prior example of paintings of similar subjects exhibited by Turner between 1800 and 1810. Not only does the subject shift to an Old Testament one, in place of the classical themes of West's historical landscapes of 1797 and 1799, but the conflagration in the background echoes the various biblical disasters that provide the main *raison d'être* of many of Turner's most spectacular pictures, including one of the same subject painted *c.* 1805 (Tate Gallery, London).[118] Nevertheless, in 1810 West was seventy-two years old, and, although his ability to respond to a much younger artist at such an advanced stage in his career is in itself remarkable, he inevitably painted a much more conservative picture than the models he was imitating. The flames destroying his Sodom stay well in the distance, and stylistically they have more in common with the theatrical effects of Philip James de Loutherbourg, a near contemporary of West's, than with Turner's more naturalistic and, at the same time, more imaginative treatment of conflagrations.[119]

Lot and His Daughters Conducted by Two Angels, 1810
(Cat. No. 238)

Historical Landscape : Saul before Samuel and the Prophets,
1812 (Cat. No. 274)

West's last landscape, *Saul before Samuel and the Prophets* of 1812 (No. 274 *above*) is also based on the Old Testament, but unlike *Lot and His Daughters*, and unlike most of Turner's Old Testament subjects, it does not show a cataclysmic disaster, and it is entirely Poussinesque in composition. It is West's largest and most complex landscape composition, as well as a remarkably large landscape by any measure, and it seems to have been universally admired when exhibited at the Royal Academy, albeit in terms that acknowledged the fundamental eclecticism of West's art. One critic managed to find in it "the strength and fidelity" of Raphael, "the grand style" of the Carracci, and the "classic fancy" of Poussin, while another declared that it would not suffer in competition with Rubens. After almost fifty years in England, pursuing a career that embodied the most extraordinary flexibility and receptiveness to new developments, West had not strayed far from the path upon which he had embarked when he arrived in Italy in 1760.

As previously mentioned, classical subject matter disappeared from West's exhibited *oeuvre* between 1781 and 1794. Its reappearance in the latter year can be seen as part of the growing diffuseness of West's art in the 1790s occasioned by the slackening of commissions for major pictures, but a more specific impetus for his renewed interest in classical antiquity was probably provided by sight of the outline designs of John Flaxman, particularly those illustrating

Thetis Bringing the Armor to Achilles, 1805, stipple engraving by William Bond after No. 170

the *Iliad* and the *Odyssey* published in 1793. His election to the presidency of the Royal Academy may also have encouraged him to return to the type of subject with which he had established his reputation at the time of the Academy's founding, as probably did as well his election in the same year to the Society of Dilettanti, an organization devoted to "Grecian Taste and Roman Spirit" and the principal sponsor of archaeological investigations of classical Greece and Rome during the late eighteenth century (see No. 529). In 1805 Thomas Hope, the champion of the Greek Revival style in architecture, commissioned three pictures "from the Greek History" from West, but this commission came over a decade after the artist had started to paint classical subjects again, and patronage in itself does not seem to have been a significant factor prompting West's rekindled interest in such subjects. Nevertheless, the pictures West painted for Hope, particularly the large *Thetis Bringing the Armor to Achilles* (No. 170 *opposite*), epitomize his use in this later period of an emphatically archaeological and Grecian style for classical subjects, in place of the style based primarily on Raphael and Poussin which he had employed in the *Agrippina* and the *Regulus* of 1768 and 1769. The exaggerated profiles, pronounced outlines, and two-dimensionality of the *Thetis* recall Greek vase painting, but Greek vase painting modulated through Flaxman's designs, which were certainly of more immediate importance for West.

By 1805, West had also seen French paintings of a similar archaizing bent while visiting Paris during the brief Peace of Amiens of 1802. There, we know that he had seen Jacques-Louis David's great effort in the "Greek style," the *Sabines* (Musée du Louvre), which he discussed with Farington, Fuseli, and John Opie on 4 September 1802,[120] but his prime admiration went to the more mannered painting of Pierre-Narcisse Guérin, who "had carried the art

Pierre-Narcisse Guérin, *Phaedra and Hippolytus*, 1802. Oil on canvas, 101 × 132 in. Musée du Louvre, Paris

further than David or any other of their Artists."[121] Guérin's most recently completed picture, shown in the Salon of 1802 and much commented upon by English visitors,[122] was the *Phaedra and Hippolytus* now in the Louvre, a work which, in precise archaeological style, melodramatic poses and expressions, and in many details, closely prefigures West's *Thetis* of three years later. The impact of the Paris trip on West's art can perhaps first be seen in his *Venus Lamenting the Death of Adonis* of 1803 (No. 118 *above*), and comparison of this small painting with his previous treatment of the same subject from 1768 (No. 116, ill. p. 45) demonstrates the radical redirection of his later paintings.

Venus Lamenting the Death of Adonis, 1803 (Cat. No. 118)

Cupid Stung by a Bee, (?)c. 1796–1802 (Cat. No. 133)

Despite West's admiration for Guérin, and despite the echoes of the *Phaedra and Hippolytus* and other works that he had seen in Paris discernible in his pictures from the years following 1802, he was not overly sympathetic toward contemporary French art. While in Paris, he told Farington that the French "paint Statutes,"[123] and a year later he told a party dining at Sir George Beaumont's that the French artists' "Studies of the Grecian statues, and their whole practice seemed to qualify them for executing everything that relates to Ornament, but they do not pursue their studies with the true minds of Painters, feeling scarcely at all some of the highest requisites of the Art."[124] Ornament, however, was a main interest of Thomas Hope, and in the works by West which he commissioned, as well as in other works by the artist from the same period (see for example No. 178), the decorative and revivalistic use of classical motifs makes these paintings seem ornamental and stylized in a manner that distinguishes them markedly from West's treatments of classical subjects of the 1760s and 1770s. Because the visualizations of the subjects are also intensely theatrical (recalling Guérin), the paintings often seem highly artificial, in contrast to the earlier works in which a convincing reconstruction of "the facts of the transaction" was always a prime goal. In this respect, it is significant that in this later period West rarely chose to depict actual events from Greek and Roman history in the manner of his *Agrippina* and *Regulus* (*Cicero Discovering the Tomb of Archimedes* is the closest approximation) but devoted himself primarily to Homeric and mythological subjects. Historical verisimilitude appears instead in works showing more recent events, such as the *Death of Lord Nelson* (No. 108 *right*), which West began on his own initiative in the same year that he received his commission for Greek subjects from Thomas Hope. Nevertheless, if the paintings of mythological subjects, such as the several treatments of *Cupid Stung by a Bee* (Nos. 131–36, ill. pp. 129, 132) often seem as unrelated to actuality and as frivolous as mid-century Rococo paintings of similar subjects, the same cannot be said of the pictures of Homeric subjects, in which we cannot help but feel reverberations of contemporary warfare between England and revolutionary and Napoleonic France. *Thetis Bringing the Armor to Achilles*, for example, which shows the goddess urging her son to return to battle, was painted in the spring of 1805 at the moment when the English were returning to war after the Peace of Amiens amidst universal expectation of a French invasion, the threat of which would be ended by the Battle of Trafalgar later in the year. When the Polish hero Tadeusz Kosciuszko visited London in 1797, West painted him in a moving portrait and also presented him an equally moving drawing of *Hector Parting from Andromache* (No. 165, both ill. p. 133), which translated into a Homeric vocabulary Kosciuszko's own role as a warrior in the doomed cause of his country's independence from Russian domination.

In the winter of 1807–8 West first saw the sculptures from the Parthenon which the Earl of Elgin had brought to England in the previous few years. He seems to have recognized instantly the importance of the sculptures, and he became eventually one of the chief proponents of their acquisition by the state. In the summer of 1808 he received permission from Lord Elgin to paint

The Death of Lord Nelson, 1806 (Cat. No. 108)

Cupid Stung by a Bee, 1802 (Cat. No. 134)

copies from the Marbles, and he produced six large paintings based on them (Nos. 498–503), all of which have sadly disappeared. This activity constituted his closest study of Greek art, or of any ancient art, but it served to lead him away from the archaeological style of the *Thetis* and related compositions rather than to reinforce it. In a letter to Lord Elgin, West wrote in 1811 that if he had seen the sculptures earlier, "more character, and expression, and life would have pervaded all my humble attempts in Historical Paintings," and the works which he claimed they did influence were the late paintings of biblical subjects, *Christ Healing the Sick* and *Christ Rejected* (Nos. 336 and 353, ill. pp. 143, 145), which show none of the archaism of his painting of the previous decade.

In 1808 West worked side by side from the Elgin Marbles with Benjamin Robert Haydon, who was to assume the self-appointed role of public champion of the sculptures' merits. Haydon had nothing but scorn for West's ensuing paintings, but he was twenty-two years old in 1808, whereas West was seventy, and the two inevitably approached the sculptures from vastly different vantage points. West must have been as incapable of comprehending those principles which Haydon purported to find in the sculptures as he was uninterested in talking scientifically about them, much to the younger man's annoyance. Although West did not find the same things in the sculptures as Haydon, he was sufficiently moved by them to tell Joseph Farington that he wished he could "be again only 20 years of age that he might labour to profit by them,"

Archibald Archer, *The Temporary Elgin Room in the British Museum in 1819* (cf. No. 498). Oil on canvas, British Museum, London. West and the Museum's Principal Librarian, Sir Joseph Planta, are seated in the foreground. Benjamin Robert Haydon is on the extreme left in the background

*The Fright of Astyanax
(Hector Taking Leave of
Andromache)*, 1797
(Cat. No. 165)

General Tadeusz Kosciuszko,
1797 (Cat. No. 650)

Raphael West and Benjamin West, Jr., 1796 (Cat. No. 543)

and his discovery of character, expression, and life in the Marbles, and thus something quite unlike the increasingly frozen rigidity of Neo-Classicism as it evolved after 1800, was not violently at odds with Haydon's claims for the sculptures' superior naturalism.

West's devotion to the Elgin Marbles may have been misunderstood by Haydon, and it was viciously caricatured by Haydon's contemporary, Lord Byron (quoted under No. 498), but it was a manifestation of a receptiveness to new experiences and an eagerness to learn from them that characterized his entire career, and that became more and more of an animating force as he advanced in years. Like many of his contemporaries, he was obsessed by technical nostrums and attempts to discover the methods of the masters. In 1767 Charles Willson Peale reported that West was using "a Different Manner from Common Oil Paintings which gives great luster & strength to the Colouring—a method of art no Painter here Else knows any thing of."[125] In 1796 a father and daughter named Provis approached West with a formula that they claimed to have found in an old book brought from Italy. West painted several pictures according to their prescription, the so-called Venetian Secret (see Nos. 22, 133 (ill. pp. 120, 129), 356, and 543 *opposite*), before realizing that the purplish tonality it produced was not that of Titian. In doing so, he managed to alienate not only the Provises, who accused him of trying to cheat them, but also his fellow artists, who suspected him of trying to monopolize the Secret for his own advantage.[126] A decade later, in 1806, he copied paintings by Van Dyck and Rembrandt at the newly founded British Institution alongside Academy students who were his junior by half a century (Nos. 508 and 515). In the following year, when Rembrandt's *Woman Taken in Adultery* came up for sale at Christie's, West pronounced it "in its way the finest piece of Art in the world," and immediately set about repainting one of his earlier compositions with a technique he learned from examination of the picture (see No. 68).

Rembrandt van Rijn, *The Woman Taken in Adultery*. Oil on canvas. National Gallery, London

Cupid Releasing Two Doves, 1798–1808 (Cat. No. 127)

It is worth noting that in 1807 West chose to repaint an earlier picture in Rembrandt's manner rather than undertake a new composition. After 1800 repainting earlier works became one of his main activities, and many of his pictures bear two (and sometimes three) dates recording when he worked upon them.[127] In 1803 he got into trouble with his colleagues at the Royal Academy by submitting for exhibition a painting of *Hagar and Ishmael* that he had previously exhibited in 1776 (No. 239 *opposite*). When criticized for violating the Academy's rule against exhibiting the same work more than once, he argued that the painting was so completely repainted that it was in every respect a

Hagar and Ishmael, 1776–1803 (Cat. No. 239)

Omnia Vincit Amor, 1809 (Cat. No. 422)

new painting, and he went on to assert that the two dates to be found on many of his pictures would prove to posterity "how anxious I have been to leave the few works I have done as perfect as was in my power to make them." Undoubtedly he was sincere in believing that his early works would be improved by being repainted in his latest style, but the contrast between the early and late manners in many of these works is now often conspicuous and disturbing (and it presents horrendous problems to conservators).[128] By the last year of his life, it was disturbing to his friends, and on 3 September 1819, Joseph Farington, speaking at the behest of Lawrence and of West's son, attempted to point out to him "the injury he does to his pictures long since

Benjamin Franklin, c. 1816–17 (Cat. No. 618)

painted by touching upon them with fresh colours which would not assimilate with the old colour."[129] Five months previously, in April 1819, Farington recorded that the eighty-year-old artist was working daily in his studio from eight a.m. to six p.m. on a painting of the *Stolen Kiss*, which he exhibited at the Royal Academy that May, and which he had almost certainly begun long before, probably in the 1770s (No. 202). The painting which his sons described as his last work and which is signed and dated *October 10th 1819* (his eighty-first birthday), was also almost certainly a repainted earlier one (No. 124), and as far as we can tell, all the paintings that West exhibited during the last five years of his life were either works that he had painted or begun at an earlier date or reworkings of earlier compositions. In some cases, however, notably

The Messiah, 1814 (Cat. No. 399)

Nos. 103, 338, and 401, those reworkings were on a very ambitious scale, and as late as 22 May 1817, West told Farington that he had a painting of the *Crucifixion* (presumably based on his design for a window intended for St. George's Chapel [No. 356]) drawn in on a canvas thirty-six feet high by twenty-eight wide (No. 358).

If West had completed the *Crucifixion* he described to Farington in 1817, it would have been the fourth in a sequence of huge religious paintings produced during the last decade of his life. As he became "the venerable West," a survivor from the era of Reynolds and Gainsborough living twenty years into the nineteenth century, he not only devoted an increasing amount of time to the customary old-age activities of retouching earlier works and looking back over a long career,[130] but, more significantly, he also produced a final group of large, highly visible, and much publicized paintings, which had the greatest public and popular success of anything he had done during that career. The paintings were *Christ Healing the Sick*, completed in 1811 (*right*), *Christ Rejected*, completed in 1814 (ill. p. 145), and *Death on the Pale Horse*, completed in 1817 (ill. p. 148).

West painted the first of these works at the invitation of the officers of the Pennsylvania Hospital in Philadelphia, who wrote to him in 1800 soliciting the gift of a painting. West consented to their request, and in 1801 he exhibited a sketch of *Christ Healing the Sick* (No. 337) at the Royal Academy, identifying it in the catalogue as for a large picture to be painted for the hospital. Despite this prompt and positive response, it took him a full decade to produce the large painting, doubtlessly because a work for which he did not expect to be paid had low priority among his commitments. Ironically, however, when he finally completed it in 1811, he was paid and paid well, accepting an offer of 3,000 guineas for the picture from the directors of the British Institution. This meant that the Pennsylvanians still did not receive the painting they had asked for in 1800, but West did promise to paint a second version, and he eventually did complete a slightly larger and modified replica in 1815 (No. 338, ill. p. 144). After two more years of delay, it went off to Philadelphia in August 1817.

The sum of 3,000 guineas that West received in 1811 was not only more than he had previously received for any other single work, but at the time the highest price known ever to have been paid to any artist for any work and, coming from a public institution, which intended the purchase to be the commencement of a national gallery, it provided concrete recognition of West's stature in the profession. The price, which was not kept secret, guaranteed the painting's public success when it went on view in April 1811 at the British Institution, which made a profit on its investment from paid admissions, and it inevitably led the artist to think of appropriate sequels. By July 1811 he had prepared an oil sketch (No. 354) for the even larger *Christ Rejected*, which he completed three years later, to be followed in its turn after three more years by *Death on the Pale Horse*, his last major work. These two paintings he did not sell, although he was reported to have declined staggering offers for *Christ Rejected*, and he exhibited them himself in special exhibitions at 125 Pall Mall,

Christ Healing the Sick, 1811, engraving by Charles Heath after No. 336

a former home of the Royal Academy. In this he followed the lead of Copley, who had successfully exhibited privately his *Death of the Earl of Chatham* in 1781 as well as several subsequent pictures. In 1806, following his temporary resignation of the presidency of the Royal Academy, when he exhibited no work there for the only time between 1769 and 1819, West exhibited his *Death of Lord Nelson* privately, but in his own studio and evidently without charging admission. For *Christ Rejected* the price of admission was one shilling, and it was claimed in 1829 that 240,000 people had come to see it.

Although it took West another ten years to complete *Christ Healing the Sick*, he promised to paint it and exhibited a sketch for the picture in 1801, the year that his work on the paintings for the Royal Chapel in Windsor Castle was stopped. He sold the completed picture to the British Institution at precisely the moment that his stipend from the Crown came to an end. These conjunctions of dates do not entirely explain West's motives in undertaking the picture and its sequels, but the dates are relevant, since West's late religious paintings not only constituted a return to the public scale of the paintings for the chapel, but two of them also grew directly out of compositions initially conceived for the chapel. In 1811, *Christ Healing the Sick* was the largest work that West had painted since 1801. Its subject repeated that of his first painting for the Windsor chapel (No. 334), and the composition was developed from still earlier sketches, which West made *c.* 1779–80 in conjunction with the chapel and then modified in the large No. 334 completed in 1781. The larger and later *Death on the Pale Horse* similarly was based on two sketches of its subject for the chapel (Nos. 402 and 403), which West had exhibited in 1784 and 1796, but had not worked up into a large painting. Thus, on his own at the end of his life, having lost the support of the King, West continued to paint pictures of the kind that he had painted for George III's chapel, but now as a truly public art, paid for by the public with shillings at the door, rather than by the largesse of a public-spirited royal patron.

Christ Healing the Sick, 1815 (Cat. No. 338)

We know from numerous sources that during the last decade of West's life he was plagued with the ailments and infirmities that accompanied his advancing years. On 5 November 1816, for example, a friend of Farington's called on West and found him working on *Death on the Pale Horse* with his left hand, "His right hand being wrapped up with Gout."[131] His wife died in December 1814, and in the following year his younger son, Benjamin, with his wife and son came to reside with him and to take care of him. His older son, Raphael, meanwhile spent alternate weeks working in West's studio, and he told Farington that he painted the outlines in the large canvases, leaving the rest for his father "to fill up agreeably to His own ideas."[132] How much more Raphael, and possibly his brother as well, may have done is a matter for speculation, but it seems likely that they played an increasingly important role as time went on. The late paintings present many of the same problems as the large paintings of the 1780s and 1790s, compounded by their even larger sizes (*Christ Rejected* is almost twenty feet across, *Death on the Pale Horse* is twenty-five) and the state of West's health when they were painted. Hence, the contrast between the large paintings and the oil sketches upon which they were based (Nos. 337, 354, and 403) is even more marked than it had been in the earlier years. The sketch of *Christ Healing the Sick* had been painted at least ten years before the large painting, that of *Death on the Pale Horse* twenty, and the time lags did

not serve to the advantage of the final products. Even in the case of *Christ Rejected*, for which West painted the sketch immediately prior to starting to work on the large canvas, the sketch seems to have attracted high praise from the critics and connoisseurs such as Sir George Beaumont, when West sent it to the Royal Academy in 1815, in stated or implied preference to the large painting which was on view in Pall Mall at the same time.

It is difficult for modern viewers not to share that preference. The sketch of *Death on the Pale Horse* (ill. p. 146) in particular is one of West's masterpieces, which was recognized as such during his lifetime; the artist himself thought highly enough of it to choose it as the one work he took to Paris to exhibit in the Salon of 1802 during the Peace of Amiens, and its admirers ranged from Washington Allston and George IV to Jacques-Louis David and Napoleon Bonaparte. In expanding a composition approximately two feet high and four feet across into one six times as wide and seven times as high, West

Christ Rejected, 1814 (Cat. No. 353)

Death on the Pale Horse, 1796 (Cat. No. 403)

could not help dissipating and coarsening the sketch's concentrated imagery of unleashed horror. Nevertheless, the sheer magnitude of the late works is in itself impressive, and the scale was necessary for the paintings to fulfill their intended public roles, whereas purely aesthetic quality was more or less irrelevant. Accompanied by explanatory catalogues and treatises which themselves took on monumental proportions (William Carey's tract devoted to *Death on the Pale Horse* was 172 pages long), the paintings were elaborate visual sermons aimed at a different audience than that tiny percentage of affluent and relatively sophisticated members of the population who had hitherto supported the arts by buying paintings. To succeed as commercial speculations, these works had to succeed at the box office. Their public exhibitions were

popular entertainments, not unlike the painted panoramas which had their greatest vogue during the same period,[133] and, although shocking, it was not out of keeping that Benjamin Robert Haydon, who followed West's example in staging his own exhibitions of large pictures deeply indebted to *Christ Healing the Sick* and *Christ Rejected*, eventually found himself defeated in competition with P. T. Barnum's presentation of General Tom Thumb. West more successfully merged art and entertainment, or at least managed to blur the distinctions between the two. Early on in his career, with the far-reaching popular success of the engravings after the *Death of General Wolfe*, he started to appeal to a large public outside the world of collectors and connoisseurs, and it was to that public that he directed his last ambitious works.

Death on the Pale Horse, 1817 (Cat. No. 401)

Death on the Pale Horse (Cat. No. 403), detail

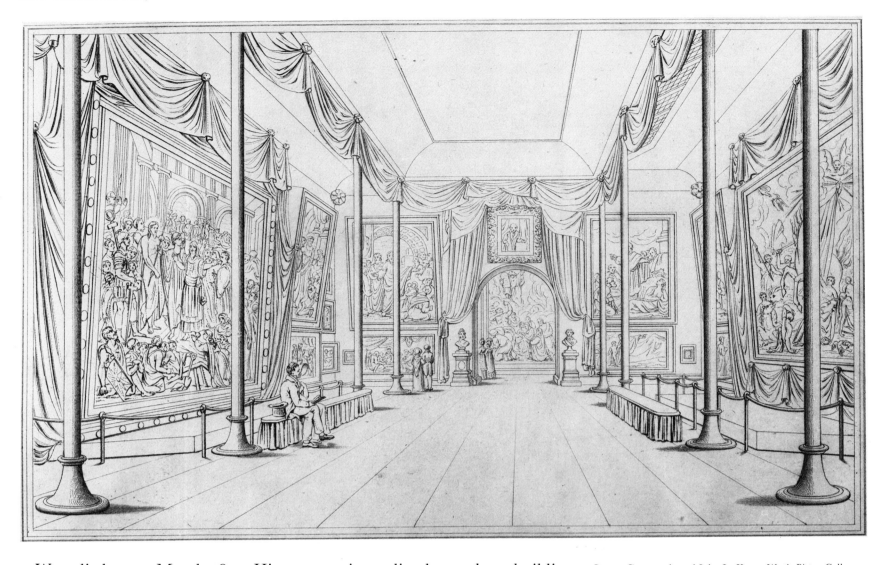

George Cattermole and John Le Keux, *West's Picture Gallery.* Engraving, 1821

West died on 11 March 1820. His two sons immediately set about building a large gallery in the garden of his home and studio in Newman Street, and in 1821 they opened there an exhibition of the works that remained on their hands, dominated by the two huge paintings of *Christ Rejected* and *Death on the Pale Horse.* This posthumous exhibition at first had some success as a popular attraction. In 1854 Thackeray, describing sightseeing in London in the early 1820s, included a visit to West's gallery along with the tombs in Westminster Abbey and St. Paul's, the Tower of London, a waxwork display in Fleet Street, and Miss Linwood's gallery of needlework pictures among the delights most enjoyed by a young child.[134] However, the novelty soon paled, and, as attendance dropped, Raphael and Benjamin West, Jr., tried in 1826 to sell their inheritance to the government of the United States as the foundation of an American national gallery. Their proposal was rejected, and, after continuing the exhibition in Newman Street for three more years, they dispersed the collection by auction in 1829.

Writing to the Speaker of the House of Representatives about the pictures in 1826, Raphael and Benjamin argued, "They are the productions of American-born genius, and let them be deposited in whatever quarter of the globe destiny may place them, the honor of having produced them belongs to the United States of America."[135] Despite the fact that West was born and always remained a British subject, despite the fact that he left his native shores when he was twenty-one years old to spend his entire mature life in England, and despite the fact that as President of the Royal Academy he stood at the head of the British artistic establishment, his sons' claims for his Americanness would have seemed plausible to his contemporaries. In 1806 Joseph Farington told a friend, who was distressed by West's partiality to Bonaparte, "West certainly has not an *English mind* & is kept to this Country only by the Income He receives from the King, & by His Sons having married here."[136] Two years previously, West had told Farington,

That were He 10 years younger *He wd. go to America*, where he was sure that much might be done as the people had a strong disposition to the Arts, & it would be easy to encourage a Spirit of rivalry in that respect between the Cities of Philadelphia and New York.—Trumbull, He sd, shd, settle at the latter place & He at the former, & raise the spirit as High as it could be.[137]

John Pasmore, *West's Gallery*, c. 1821. Oil on canvas, 29½ × 24¼ in. Wadsworth Atheneum, Hartford, Connecticut

From Matthew Pratt in 1764, to Charles Robert Leslie, who came in 1811, virtually every young American artist who could manage to cross the Atlantic became West's pupil, retaining in most cases a devotion to West as a man and as an artist long after personal contact had come to an end.[138] West's reputation in America was such that at the first meeting of the board of the newly founded Pennsylvania Academy of the Fine Arts in Philadelphia in 1805, one of its first acts was to elect him the Academy's first honorary member. In the same year, when the Boydell Shakespeare Gallery was dispersed, Robert Fulton, a former pupil who was to distinguish himself in other realms than painting (see No. 620 and *opposite*), bought two large paintings of scenes from *Hamlet* and *King Lear* that Boydell had commissioned from West. Fulton took them back to America and placed them on loan in the Pennsylvania Academy, where they became the first important works painted by West after his departure from America to be seen in his native land.[139] Fulton, as a consequence, was made the Academy's second honorary member. He subsequently put forth two schemes for the Academy to buy collections of West's works, neither of which came to anything, but in 1817 the second version of *Christ Healing the Sick* arrived in Philadelphia and was installed by the Pennsylvania Hospital in a new building constructed specially for it. In 1829, following the auctions of the pictures from West's estate, where both *Christ Rejected* and *Death on the Pale Horse* were bought in by West's sons, Benjamin West, Jr. sent the former to America on a two-year tour. *Death on the Pale Horse* was purchased in 1835 by the Pennsylvania Academy as a speculative venture, and it was immediately also sent off on a tour that lasted until 1837. It then remained as a permanent attraction at the Academy. *Christ Rejected* returned to Philadelphia by 1857 as the property of a private collector, and in 1878 it was given to the Pennsylvania Academy, reuniting the great works that terminated West's career in the city where it had begun.

View of the interior of the Pennsylvania Academy of the Fine Arts, Philadelphia, 1985

Notes

For citations given in abbreviated form, see the list of abbreviations at the end of the catalogue, pp. 585–9. Where material pertaining to a specific work is quoted or cited, see the entry for that work for citation of the source.

1. Farington Diary, 1 June 1814 (Farington 1978—, XIII, p. 4530).

2. See pp. 161–2 for a brief discussion of these publications.

3. Galt 1820, p. 3.

4. Waterhouse 1953, p. 190.

5. For a fuller discussion of the question of Galt's reliability, see Alberts 1978, pp. 409–12 ("Appendix I: John Galt's Biography of West as a Source"). It is perhaps worth pointing out here that Galt's account of West's comparison of the *Apollo Belvedere* to a Mohawk warrior (Galt 1816, p. 105), which is the most frequently cited of his anecdotes, is given some substantiation by the fact that West himself had told the same story over twenty years earlier, in a discourse to the students of the Royal Academy in 1794 (quoted in the *True Briton* for 11 December 1794). That does not prove the truth of Galt's anecdote, but it does establish that he did not invent it.

6. For these letters and other correspondence related to West's Italian trip, see Richardson 1978.

7. Adrian W. Zorgniotti, M.D., "Benjamin West's Osteomyelitis: a Translation," *Bulletin of the New York Academy of Medicine*, XLIX, 1973, pp. 702–7. The surgeon who performed the operation and wrote the original report was Angelo Nannoni (1715–90).

8. Hart 1908, pp. 1–3.

9. Farington Diary, 26 Dec. 1804 (Farington 1978—, VI, p. 2480). In the words of Leigh Hunt (1784–1859), whose mother was the niece of Mrs. West: the artist, "so well bred, and so indisputably clever in his art (whatever might be the amount of his genius), had received so careless, or so homely an education when a boy, that he could hardly read." (*The Autobiography of Leigh Hunt*, London, 1850, pp. 148–9). For accounts of West's earliest activity as an artist, see Nos. 482 and 509.

10. Galt 1816, pp. 37–38.

11. For Wollaston's movements in America, see Carolyn J. Weekley, "The Early Years, 1564 to 1790," in *Paintings in the South: 1564–1980* (exhibition catalogue), Virginia Museum, Richmond, 1983, pp. 25–26.

12. Sawitzky 1938, pp. 443–44.

13. *The American Magazine and Monthly Chronicle for the British Colonies*, I, no. 12, Sept. 1758, pp. 607–8.

14. Ibid., I, no. 5, Feb. 1758, pp. 237–38.

15. Galt 1816, pp. 38–43. The other three students mentioned by Galt were Thomas Godfrey (1736–1763), Joseph Reed (1741–1785), and Jacob Duché (1737/8–1798). Francis Hopkinson (1737–1791) had been the first student to enroll in the Academy of Philadelphia in 1751, and in 1757 he received the first degree granted by the College of Philadelphia. In addition to writing poetry, he was a composer, lawyer, and public servant, and, as a member of the Continental Congress in 1776, he was a signatory of the Declaration of Independence. He visited England in 1766–67 and resided with West for part of his stay, during which West painted a portrait of his mother (No. 641). Godfrey was a poet and playwright, whose *Prince of Parthia*, written in 1759, was the first drama written by an American to be produced upon the professional stage. Reed was to become a close friend and associate of George Washington, a member of the Continental Congress, and a general in the revolutionary army. Duché became an Anglican clergyman, who served as chaplain of the Continental Congress, but had a change of heart in 1777 and lived in England from 1777 to 1792. A two-volume collection of his sermons published in London in 1779 contained frontispieces engraved after pictures by West (Nos. 304 and 351), and his son, Thomas Spence Duché (1763–1790), studied briefly under West in the 1780s. Galt calls Hopkinson "Hopkins"; Reed "Reid"; and Duché "Duchey."

16. For a comparison with a roughly contemporary work by Copley, see Flexner 1952, p. 28.

17. Galt 1816, pp. 75–76.

18. Ibid., pp. 70, 81–82, and 84–85. See also Carey 1820, p. 515.

19. Sawitzky 1938, p. 440, and Wayne Craven, "Painting in New York City, 1750–1775," in Ian M. G. Quimby, ed., *American Painting to 1776: A Reappraisal*, Winterthur, Delaware, 1971, pp. 274–76.

20. Farington Diary, 18 [19] Dec. 1795 (Farington 1978—, II, p. 449).

21. Richardson 1978, p. 21. In 1807, in a conversation with Nicholas Biddle, West praised Mengs while disparaging Johann Winckelmann, the great theorist of early Neo-Classicism whose name is often linked with that of Mengs. Although the conventional art-historical view is that Mengs carried Winckelmann's ideas into practice, West agreed with Biddle's suggestion that "the best part of Winckelmann's book was made by Mengs" (Wainwright 1978, p. 112).

22. One other (No. 714) is known via an engraving.

23. See in particular Reynolds's Sixth Discourse (10 December 1774). See also Edgar Wind, "Borrowed Attitudes in Reynolds and Hogarth," *Journal of the Warburg and Courtauld Institutes*, II, 1938, pp. 182–85, and E. H. Gombrich, "Reynolds' Theory and Practice of Imitation," *Burlington Magazine*, LXXX, 1942, pp. 40–45.

24. West's presidential addresses were never collected and published in the manner of Reynolds's, but

Agrippina Landing at Brundisium with the Ashes of Germanicus (Cat. No. 33), detail

155

substantial excerpts from them are quoted in Galt 1820, pp. 77–176. For other advice and instruction given by him to younger artists, see Forster-Hahn 1967 and Evans 1980.

25. West's numerous involvements with collectors and dealers are referred to throughout Farington's diary. The dealer William Buchanan's assessment of his position is summarized in Francis Haskell, *Rediscoveries in Art*, London, 1976, p. 29. West's own collection is recorded in sales of the drawings and prints, Christie's, London, 9 June and 1 July 1820 and Sotheby's, London, 11 May 1836; and of the paintings, Christie's, London, 23–24 June 1820 and 28 May 1824. See also Hugh Brigstocke, *William Buchanan and the 19th century Art Trade*, privately printed, 1982.

26. Farington Diary, 8 Aug. 1803 (Farington 1978–, VI, p. 2101).

27. Galt 1816, p. 119.

28. Ibid., p. 122.

29. Carey 1820, p. 516.

30. See Thomas Pelzel, *Anton Raphael Mengs and Neoclassicism*, New York and London, 1979, pp. 56–60. Lorenzo Masucci and Placidio Costanzi also painted copies for the gallery in Northumberland House.

31. West's letters to Shippen and Allen's to Barclay are published in Richardson 1978. Robert Rutherford's letters to Shippen are in the American Philosophical Society in Philadelphia.

32. Richardson 1978, p. 19.

33. It is worth noting that West's copy of Mengs's *Holy Family* (No. 511) was thought to be a copy after Carlo Maratta before documentation linking it to Mengs came to light.

34. Carey 1820, p. 515.

35. Galt (1816, p. 143) and Carey (1820, p. 517) tell a slightly different story in which there is no mention of Dalton, and West's decision to visit England is prompted instead by a letter from his father.

36. Richardson 1978, p. 23.

37. Galt 1820, pp. 1–2, and Carey 1820, pp. 517–18.

38. Carey 1820, p. 518.

39. Galt 1820, p. 10.

40. See Prown 1966, II p. 274, where the affinities of Nos. 590 and 610 to portraits by Copley are pointed out.

41. Dunlap 1918, I, p. 220. See also West's negative comment about Reynolds, quoted in note 66 below.

42. Galt 1816, pp. 71–72.

43. Ibid., p. 122.

44. Letter from Richard Bull to Lord Ashburnham, 15 Feb. 1787, quoted by Edgar Peters Bowron in *Pompeo Batoni 1708–1787: A Loan Exhibition of Paintings*, Colnaghi, New York, 1982, no. 19. For Batoni's purported praise of West's *Cymon and Iphigenia*, see Carey 1820, p. 517; however, since Carey also cites the response of Mengs, who could not have seen the painting, his testimony is somewhat suspect.

45. See Bregenz 1968 (exhibition catalogue), pp. 8 and 48 (no. 48).

46. Letters of 4 December 1762 and 6 February 1763, quoted by David Goodreau in *Nathaniel Dance 1735–1811* (exhibition catalogue), the Iveagh Bequest, Kenwood, 1977, introduction. It is possible that West was the unnamed friend of Dalton's referred to by Dance.

47. For the Mengs, see Pelzel, op. cit., pp. 91–102; for the Hamilton, see Robert Rosenblum, "Gavin Hamilton's 'Brutus' and Its Aftermath," *Burlington Magazine*, CIII, 1961, pp. 8–11, and letters from Basil Skinner and Robert Rosenblum, ibid., p. 146. An interesting drawing belonging to the Historical Society of Pennsylvania (ill. p. 38) appears to combine the subject of Mengs's painting, complete with pyramid in the background, and a figure of Cleopatra derived from the expiring Lucretia in Hamilton's *Oath of Brutus*. It may be, however, that the drawing shows Joseph and Potiphar's wife, for whom an Egyptian setting would be equally appropriate. Helmut von Erffa, who believed that the drawing showed the latter subject, questioned its attribution to West. It is certainly not characteristic of West's mature drawings and, if by him, it must be from early in his career, viz. from before the *Paetus and Arria* of 1766.

48. See Rosenblum 1967, pp. 50–106 ("Chapter II: The *Exemplum Virtutis*").

49. This painting belonged to Sir Robert Walpole by 1741 and remained in England until 1779.

50. Galt 1820, p. 25.

51. Ibid., p. 5.

52. Ellis K. Waterhouse, "The British Contribution to the Neo-Classical Style in Painting," *Proceedings of the British Academy*, XL, 1954, pp. 72–73.

53. Galt 1820, p. 12.

54. West also owned a copy by the time of his death in 1820 (sold, Christie's, London, 9 June 1820, 4th day, lot 113), but he was not one of the subscribers listed in the publication of 1764, and it seems unlikely that he would have possessed a copy at such an early date.

55. *Sermons on Public Occasions, and a Letter on Theological Study by Robert Late Archbishop of York to Which are prefixed Memoirs of His Life by George Robert Hay Drummond, A.M., Prebendary of York*, Edinburgh, 1803, p. xxvi.

56. Galt 1820, p. 26.

57. Millar 1969, I, pp. 23–24.

58. Galt 1820, pp. 32–33.

59. Ibid., pp. 33–34.

60. Ibid., pp. 36–41. See also Sidney C. Hutchison, *The History of the Royal Academy 1768–1968*, London, 1968, pp. 34–50.

61. Galt 1820, pp. 207–15.

62. One such rival, Henry Fuseli, wrote to his friend William Roscoe in 1790: "'There are' says Mr. West, 'but two ways of working successfully, that is lastingly, in this country, for an artist—the one is, to paint for the King; the other to mediate a scheme of your own.' The first he has monopolized; in the second he is not idle." (quoted in David Irwin, "Fuseli's Milton Gallery: Unpublished Letters," *Burlington Magazine*, CI, 1959, p. 436). Fuseli responded to the situation by undertaking his Milton Gallery, which opened in 1799 and was not a success.

63. Galt 1820, p. 46.

64. Ibid., p. 48.

65. In the actual monument to Wolfe in Westminster Abbey by Joseph Wilton, probably begun before West's painting but completed after, the dying hero is nude, but his attendants wear contemporary military uniform. See Margaret Whinney, *Sculpture in Britain 1530–1830*, Harmondsworth, 1964, p. 139 and pl. 109.

66. See Ellis K. Waterhouse, *Reynolds*, London, 1941, pls. 125 and 126. In 1795, discussing a proposed statue of Lord Cornwallis, West told the Council of the Royal Academy: "that the prejudice in favor of representing Moderns in Ancient dresses was an absurdity. —That Sir Joshua Reynolds in his opinion had judged ill in accustoming himself to dress his women in fancied drapery and wd. have rendered them more interesting to posterity had He followed their fancies and described them in the fashion of their day with all the taste he was master of." (Farington Diary, 24 July 1795 [Farington 1978–, II, pp. 369–70].)

67. The drawings are in the Yale Center for British Art. For the engravings based on them, see Abrams 1982, pp. 66–68, figs. 7 and 8.

68. Galt 1820, p. 50.

69. See David Alexander and Richard T. Godfrey, *Painters and Engraving: The Reproductive Print from Hogarth to Wilkie* (exhibition catalogue), Yale Center for British Art, New Haven, 1980, pp. 32–35 ("VI: Benjamin West and the Market for Prints after History Paintings").

70. It is possible that earlier prints after designs by West were published anonymously. Ann Uhry Abrams has plausibly suggested that West may have been responsible for the cover illustration of Provost Smith's *American Magazine* published in Philadelphia in 1757 and 1758 (Abrams 1982, pp. 63–64, fig. 2).

71. An undated engraving by James Watson after the *General Robert Monckton* of 1764 (No. 665) may be earlier.

72. Felix H. Man, *Artist's Lithographs: A World History from Senefelder to the Present Day*, New York, 1970, p. 16. West made two further lithographs dated 1801 and 1802 after details of the *Baptism* (No. 316).

73. Whitley 1928a, II, pp. 25–26. For the painting used by Booth see No. 139.

74. Winifred H. Friedman, *Boydell's Shakespeare Gallery*, New York and London, 1976, pp. 39–40.

75. For the rival *Death of Lord Nelson* by Arthur William Devis (National Maritime Museum, Greenwich), which, not incidentally, was sponsored by Boydell, see Marks 1965 and Mitchell 1967.

76. In "J.P.," *The Life of General James Wolfe, the Conqueror of Canada*, London, 1760 (quoted in Irwin 1966, p. 148), and in Captain John Knox, *An Historical Journal of the Campaigns in North America*, London, 1769 (reprint edition, 1968, pp. 114–16; kindly pointed out to us by Alan D. McNairn). In February 1759, before Wolfe's death in Quebec, the "Death of Epaminondas" was proposed as a subject for a competition sponsored by the Society of Arts. "Regulus taking leave of his Friends when he departed on his return to Carthage" was another (John Sunderland, "Mortimer, Pine and Some Political Aspects of English History Painting," *Burlington Magazine*, CXVI, 1974, p. 325).

77. Galt 1816, pp. 61–68.

78. Sunderland, op. cit., p. 325, note 34.

79. Pine (1730–1788) was born in London, the son of an engraver, and had an early success as a painter of historical subjects, winning premiums from the Society of Arts in 1760 and 1763. In 1783 he went to America to paint portraits of the leading figures in the American Revolution, and he died in Philadelphia. His first American painting was of West's old friend Francis Hopkinson.

80. Strong 1978, pp. 47–58 and 78–85.

81. Brayley and Britton 1801, p. 224; Galt 1820, pp. 72–73; Angelo 1830, I, pp. 152–53.

82. Mitchell 1944, p. 31.

83. See Rosenblum 1967, pp. 11–12.

84. West's paintings based on the Book of Revelation (Nos. 399–411) might be considered exceptions to this statement (the opening words of John Galt's text in the catalogue published in 1817 to accompany No. 401, the final version of *Death on the Pale Horse*, are: "the general effect proposed to be excited by this Picture is the terrible sublime and its various manifestations"), but they are works of such ambition and complexity that to explain them solely or primarily as exercises in the sublime does not do them justice. For further discussion of *Death on the Pale Horse* see Staley 1980.

85. See Alberts 1978, pp. 113–26 ("Chapter 10: The American War").

86. Galt 1820, p. 15.

87. See Millar 1969, I, pp. xiii–xvii.

88. Farington Diary, 6 Nov. 1797 (Farington 1978–, III, p. 916).

89. Galt 1820, pp. 51–52.

90. A tenuous link between West and the Parliament paintings is provided by John Partridge's group portrait of the commissioners responsible for the decoration of the new building (National Portrait Gallery, London), which includes the *Battle of La Hogue* (No. 90) among "the works of our principal deceased artists" in the background (Richard Ormond, "John Partridge and the Fine Arts Commissioners," *Burlington Magazine*, CIX, 1967, pp. 397–401).

91. Farington 1978–, I, p. 99.

92. Ibid., III, p. 948; see also the entry of 28 Dec. 1797 (ibid., p. 956).

93. Farington Diary, 2 Oct. 1803 (ibid., VI, p. 2136). See also Appendix I.

94. Ibid., I, p. 270; see also the entry for 26 Jan. 1806 (ibid., VII, p. 2675).

95. See also No. 107, *The Recovery of His Majesty in the Year 1789*.

96. Galt 1820, p. 192.

97. Farington Diary, 27 Nov. 1803 (Farington 1978–, VI, p. 2173).

98. Farington Diary, 3 Feb. 1812 (ibid., XI, p. 4075).

99. Lansdown 1893, p. 13.

100. Farington Diary, 1 Nov. 1797 (Farington 1978–, III, p. 912).

101. Ibid.

102. See No. 404.

103. Martin, born in Newcastle in 1789, only came to London in 1806, and Danby, born in Ireland in 1793, first visited London in 1813. Danby did come armed with a letter of introduction to West (from Chris. Park, Dublin, dated 27 May 1813 [Historical Society of Pennsylvania, Philadelphia]).

104. See David Bindman, *Blake as an Artist*, Oxford and New York, 1977, pp. 29–34.

105. See Nos. 400, 403–5, 408–9; and compare Martin Butlin, *The Paintings and Drawings of William Blake*, New Haven and London, 1981, I, pp. 367–70, nos. 514, 517–21, and 524.

106. Danby also produced a very similar painting of this subject for William Beckford (collection of Robert Rosenblum).

107. Farington 1978–, II, p. 497.

108. Bindman, op. cit., p. 99.

109. Galt 1820, pp. 189–90. See also Farington Diary, 22 Dec. 1799 (Farington 1978–, IV, p. 1330).

110. See Stephen Deuchar, *Paintings, Politics, & Porter: Samuel Whitbread and British Art* (exhibition catalogue), Museum of London, 1984, nos. 5, 6, 20, and 21.

111. We should also note that Morland's brother-in-law James Ward, who painted similar pictures at the beginning of his career, was to have a close personal association with West as his neighbor in Newman Street, but Ward evidently moved to Newman Street only in 1799.

112. See David H. Solkin, *Richard Wilson* (exhibition catalogue), Tate Gallery, London, 1982, nos. 128 and 131.

113. Ibid., no. 87.

114. This composition exists in several versions, one of which appeared at the Royal Academy in 1770 (ibid., no. 130). Farington referred to a later version of West's painting (No. 23) as "Cicero's Villa."

115. C. R. Leslie, *Memoirs of the Life of John Constable* (first published 1843), London, 1951, p. 14.

116. Ibid., p. 322; and see No. 180.

117. Farington Diary, 18 April 1801, 10 April 1804, and 11 May 1805 (Farington 1978–, IV, p. 1539; VI, p. 2295; and VII, p. 2555). In 1807 West told Nicholas Biddle that Turner had been a promising artist, "but has fallen off much." He made this remark after calling Turner's *Bridgewater Seapiece* of 1801 the best work in the Stafford Gallery (Wainwright 1978, p. 110).

118. See Martin Butlin and Evelyn Joll, *The Paintings of J. M. W. Turner*, New Haven and London, 1977, I, p. 37, no. 56.

119. The similarity of this painting to pictures by de Loutherbourg was pointed out by Michael Fitzgerald in a seminar report at Columbia University in 1978.

120. Farington 1978–, V, p. 1826.

121. Farington Diary, 19 Nov. 1802 and 13 Jan. 1803 (ibid., pp. 1935 and 1961).

122. Ibid., p. 1836.

123. Farington Diary, 1 Sept. 1802 (ibid., p. 1820).

124. Farington Diary, 2 June 1803 (ibid., VI, p. 2045).

125. See No. 112.

126. For the "Venetian Secret," in addition to the catalogue entries cited, see John Gage, "Magilphs and Mysteries,") *Apollo*, LXXX, 1964, pp. 38–41, and

Farington's diary entries from 25 Nov. 1796 to 25 June 1797 (Farington 1978–, III, pp. 702–859).

127. No. 127 *Cupid Releasing Two Doves* (ill. p. 136), for example, is signed *B. West 1798, retouched 1803 and 1808*.

128. No. 280 *Elisha Raising the Shunamite's Son*, which is signed *Begun 1765 and finished 1814 Oct. 10th*, is an example of a picture that is not currently exhibitable, owing to problems created by West's two periods of work upon it almost fifty years apart. We are indebted to Richard Muhlberger, the Director of the George Walter Vincent Smith Museum, for pointing out some of the issues raised by these repainted works.

129. Farington 1978–, XV, p. 5403 (3 Sept. 1819).

130. On 26 January 1808, Farington reported West had told him: "that He had been for sometime employed in cleaning & putting into the best condition He could several of His pictures & should proceed to do so, till He shall have restored all those that He wishes should be preserved, & He would employ the Brush & White Paint to cover all those which He wd. not wish to have His name attached to. He sd. this He wd. now do, that in case He *should drop*, His House may not be found like those of Romney & Opie full of rubbish that it was disgraceful to them to have brought forward to a sale. I told Him I perfectly agreed with Him in this opinion, thinking that in this respect a man should be what might be called His Own Executor." (Farington 1978–, IX, p. 3208).

131. Ibid., XIII, p. 4729. (6 Nov. 1815).

132. Farington Diary, 8 Sept. 1815 (ibid., XIII, pp. 4703–4).

133. For West's interest in panoramas, see Richard D. Altick, *The Shows of London*, Cambridge, Mass., and London, 1978, pp. 132 and 135.

134. Ibid., pp. 221–22.

135. See p. 160.

136. Farington Diary, 16 Nov. 1806 (Farington 1978–, VIII, p. 2908).

137. Farington Diary, 31 May 1804 (ibid., VI, p. 2339).

138. Their relations with West are all documented and discussed in Evans 1980.

139. Fulton also bought and sent to the Pennsylvania Academy one painting by Raphael West of *Orlando and Oliver* from *As You Like It* (location unknown). Following Fulton's death in 1815, the paintings were transferred by his widow to the American Academy of Fine Arts in New York, which opened its first exhibition in 1816, and they stayed there until 1828, when they were sold by the Fulton heirs. John Trumbull was the dominant figure in the American Academy, and he was undoubtedly responsible for obtaining the extended loan of his old teacher's works as its star attraction. In 1828 the *King Lear* was bought by the Boston Athenaeum and it has subsequently passed from the Athenaeum to the Museum of Fine Arts in the same city. Thus it has been in public institutions in each of the three chief urban centers of the eastern United States continuously since 1807.

Introduction to the catalogue

This catalogue of the paintings of Benjamin West includes all known or recorded paintings in oil, including oil sketches on a variety of supports. It also includes those drawings which West exhibited or which are known to have left the artist's possession during his lifetime (i.e., drawings whose histories suggest that they were thought of as complete works in themselves, not as studies). Other drawings are discussed, where relevant, in entries for the paintings to which they correspond. The catalogue includes paintings seen by the compilers and believed by them to be by West, paintings known indirectly via prints or photographs, and works known only from records. We have included entries for all paintings for which there is reliable documentation dating from West's lifetime and for all paintings included in the posthumous sales of his estate. We have excluded other works known to us only from printed sources subsequent to 1820. In doing so, we have undoubtedly left out paintings that may be genuine, but over the years West's name has been attached to so many works that patently are not by him that entries for all such works would significantly extend the length of an already long catalogue and confuse rather than clarify the outlines of his *oeuvre*. Similarly, we have not included entries for known works that have been ascribed to West but whose attributions we reject. Copies of genuine works and rejected works that show the same or similar subjects as works whose authenticity we accept are referred to in the appropriate entries.

The catalogue is organized thematically rather than chronologically. Historical subjects appear in approximate chronological sequence by event shown, Homeric and biblical subjects in narrative sequence. Works illustrating subjects from Renaissance and post-Renaissance literature are organized alphabetically by author, and in other categories the arrangement is also generally alphabetical. For abbreviations see pp. 585–9.

Dimensions are recorded with height preceding width. In entries where the first set of measurements (in inches) is enclosed within parentheses, they have been taken from a source, usually nineteenth-century, whose accuracy we cannot confirm.

A question mark immediately preceding the headings of PROVENANCE, EXHIBITIONS, LISTED, and LITERATURE indicates that there is some question about whether the entire body of documentation which follows pertains to that work. In most cases, the problems of identification are discussed in the accompanying text. Question marks preceding individual citations pertain, of course, only to those specific references.

Under PROVENANCE, certain frequently repeated references require explanation:

In 1797 and 1801 West drew up accounts of the works that he had painted for George III. The account of 1797 exists in a manuscript dated 20 June

1797 in the possession of the Historical Society of Pennsylvania. It contains only works painted between 1780 and 1797. The account of 1801 is printed as the first Appendix (pp. 207–15) in *The Life Studies and Works of Benjamin West, Esq.* by John Galt, published in 1820, the second of Galt's two volumes devoted to West (Galt 1820, *under* LITERATURE). According to Galt it is a "True Copy from Mr. West's Account Books," but the actual account books have evidently disappeared. It repeats, with slight differences, the account of 1797, but additionally includes works painted for the King before 1780 and after 1797 as well as a few that were planned but not yet painted (they never were). We have included all the information provided in these accounts, omitting the repetitive elements in the account of 1801. The page numbers accompanying the references to the account of 1801 are those of Galt's pages.

In 1809 West made a list of twenty-five paintings, accompanied by prices, which he sent to Robert Fulton, who in turn submitted it in 1810 to the Pennsylvania Academy of the Fine Arts in Philadelphia with a proposal that the Academy purchase the paintings for a total price of £7,500 or $32,888. The Academy declined. West's list, dated 3 May 1809, and Fulton's letter, dated 12 April 1810, are in the archives of the Pennsylvania Academy. Although Fulton acknowledged that not all twenty-five works were yet completed, and some may not even have been begun (this was one reason cited by the Academy in declining the offer), we have included entries, or references in the relevant entries, for all twenty-five.

In 1826, six years after West's death, his two sons, Raphael and Benjamin, proposed to sell to the government of the United States some 150 paintings. Their letter, dated 12 April 1826, addressed to J. W. Taylor, the Speaker of the House of Representatives, and the list of works were published as *Letter from the Sons of Benjamin West, Deceased, Late President of the Royal Academy of London, Offering to Sell to the Government of the United States Sundry Paintings of that Artist*, in an official government document: *Doc. No. 8, 19th Congress, 2d Session, Ho. of Reps., ... Read, and laid upon the table. December 11, 1826.* Virtually all of these works reappeared in the main sale of 181 paintings from West's estate conducted by George Robins at West's former home in Newman Street, London, on 22–25 May 1829. Therefore, we have included citations of the offer made in 1826 in all cases but have provided further information from this list only in the few instances where titles or dimensions differ from those in the more substantial sale catalogue of 1829. In all entries we have included complete catalogue information from the Robins sale of 22–25 May 1829. The catalogue of that sale also contained discussions of every work (written, according to W. T. Whitley, by W. H. Pyne); for the most part these consist of little more than extravagant praise intended to boost prices, rather than inform, and we have quoted from them only sparingly. A second and larger Robins sale, devoted to sketches, unfinished pictures, some portraits, and other items, took place the following month on 20–22 June 1829, but references to the "Robins sale," if they do not specify which, refer always in this catalogue to the sale of 22–25 May.

Under EXHIBITIONS we have included the title under which a work first appeared if exhibited during West's lifetime, but we have omitted the titles used subsequently except where they differ significantly from the original title or where they add further information. We have printed accompanying quotations and explanatory notes in full. The abbreviations RA and BI are used to indicate both the regular annual exhibitions of the works of living artists at the Royal Academy and the British Institution during West's lifetime and the loan exhibitions of the works of old masters in years following his death in 1820. The most important loan exhibition took place at the British Institution in 1833 and included fifty-one paintings by West, together with similar groups of works by Reynolds and Lawrence. For the exhibitions at 125 Pall Mall between 1814 and 1818 see the entries for Nos. 353, 338, and 401. These exhibitions all included from ten to fifteen sketches or smaller paintings of biblical subjects in addition to the large works which provided their *raison d'être*. The catalogues published in 1814, 1816, and 1818 we have recorded as separate exhibitions.

Following West's death in 1820, his sons constructed a gallery in the garden of his former home and studio at 14 Newman Street and presented there from 1821 through 1828 a more or less continuous exhibition of the paintings in their possession. Their catalogue published in 1821 included ninety-four paintings. In 1822 they expanded the number of paintings on view to 142. This exhibition then continued without significant change until they sold most of the works in the estate in 1829. The catalogues published between 1822 and 1828 repeat each other with so little change that we have recorded the activity in West's gallery from 1822 onwards as a single exhibition, noting in the entries for the works affected the very few changes (some of them handwritten) appearing in the later catalogues. The appearance of the Great Room of West's gallery in 1821 is recorded in an engraving by G. Cattermole and J. Le Keux published in 1824 (ill. p. 150 and see Gardner 1966 under LITERATURE). A painting by John Pasmore (ill. p. 151, and see Cunningham 1956) also shows the same interior, but with less precision so that we cannot be certain if it depicts the gallery before or after the reinstallation of 1822.

In entries where an exhibition is recorded, we have not listed the catalogue again under LITERATURE, although in recent years, beginning with the West exhibition in Philadelphia in 1938, exhibition catalogues have often included substantial and significant discussion of the works. A few catalogues also present information about works not actually included in the exhibition; these we have treated both as exhibitions (New York 1975, Washington and Philadelphia 1980, San Antonio 1983) for the works exhibited, and as books (Kraemer 1975, Evans 1980, and Pressly 1983, respectively) for other references.

Under LISTED are four catalogues of West's works published during his lifetime (abbreviated as *PC*, *UM*, Barlow, and *BA*), a fifth published in the year of his death (Galt), a more limited list of major works chiefly painted for George III (*AA*), and one modern publication that incorporates a concordance of earlier lists and a separate check-list of West's religious paintings (Dillenberger). These lists all present essentially the same information. Accordingly, we have given full titles, etc., as first published (usually in *Public Characters of 1805* [*PC*]) and have only recorded significant variations from the later lists. Although the forms vary, the majority of entries in *Public Characters* begin with the words "The picture of" or with a "Do." (for ditto) indicating the same thing. In most entries we have omitted these constantly repeated words, but we retain them or their equivalents if they provide further information (i.e., in describing a work as a sketch, small picture, or drawing). West seems to have thought of the list of his works in *Public Characters of 1805* as the fundamental account of his *oeuvre*. In a letter to Joseph Farington dated 13 February 1813, replying to an enquiry made by Farington on behalf of the publishers Cadell & Davies, he recommended it as "a list of my paintings— as they stood at that time, all but fifteen in number—which not having been exhibited, and not in catalogues, had escaped their notice." That list accompanied an account of West's life, which West told Farington on 17 November 1804 (when it appeared) had been written by one of West's sons and one other person. The list published in *Academic Annals* in 1805 (*AA*) was provided by West himself, and that published by Joel Barlow in 1807 as a footnote to Barlow's *Columbiad* was stated by Barlow to have been given him by West in 1802. West and Barlow had contact in the summer of 1802 in Paris, where Barlow was then living, and it seems likely that West drew up the list from memory on that occasion. Whereas the lists in the *Universal Magazine*, *La Belle Assemblée*, and Galt's life of West all repeat the one in *Public Characters* with only slight modifications in details here and there, Barlow's shows numerous discrepancies, which can be accounted for by the circumstances under which it was evidently produced. A few further early lists of West's works are also known. A short biographical article published in the *European Magazine* in 1794 (vol. XXVI, pp. 163–67) included an incomplete list of exhibited pictures. An American periodical, the *Port Folio*, republished in 1811 (vol. VI, pp. 542–45) the list that had previously appeared in *La Belle Assemblée*. A manuscript list of some forty major pictures, probably drawn up between 1802 and 1804 to accompany a draft of a biography of the artist, is in the Fordham University Library. None of these lists adds anything to what we know from other sources, and we have not included references to them in this catalogue.

Under LITERATURE we have included in approximate chronological order all significant references except those previously given under the headings PROVENANCE, EXHIBITED, and LISTED. Citations of publications that appear only once or twice are given in full in the individual entries; all others are in abbreviated form. Publication of the most important single contemporary source of information for the later part of West's career, the diary of Joseph Farington, has been in progress during the period final preparation of this catalogue has been underway. It had previously been available to students (and still is) in the form of a typed transcription in the Department of Prints and Drawings of the British Museum, and all our references to Farington were initially taken from that source. We have included indication both of date of entry and published volume and page number for all references to the diary. Because of William Dunlap's various roles as student of West, artist who tried to emulate him, and historian who at an early date collected information about his works and activities, we have also included double entries for his diary (by date and by published page numbers) and for the first edition of 1834 and the standard critical edition of 1918 of his *History of the Rise and Progress of the Arts of Design*. We have distinguished the two volumes of John Galt's life of West by the years in which they initially appeared, 1816 and 1820.

Contemporary journalistic reviews we have consulted chiefly through the collections of press cuttings in the libraries of the Victoria and Albert Museum and the Courtauld Institute of Art. Since both collections contain numerous cuttings from unidentified sources, our references are to the repositories (abbreviated as V and A Cuttings and Courtauld Cuttings), to which we have added identification of origins when possible. We have quoted the contemporary critical writing only infrequently. West was an artist who promoted his works by encouraging the most shameless puffing. A vigorous search for further criticism would undoubtedly turn up some interesting and informative commentary, but the corpus of West criticism that we have seen consists of writing that, apart from the invective of William Hazlitt (which we do quote), is remarkable chiefly for its vacuity.

HISTORICAL SUBJECTS

1 Sappho

LOCATION UNKNOWN (POSSIBLY NEVER PAINTED)

(96 × 72 in.) (244 × 183 cm.)

PROV: Offered by West to the Pennsylvania Academy of the Fine Arts in 1809 ("The painting, life[-sized], of Sappho precipitating herself from a rock," 8 ft. × 6, £250)

This work is known only from its inclusion in a group of paintings that West proposed to sell to the new Pennsylvania Academy in 1809. We know from Robert Fulton's letter to the President of the Academy,[1] which accompanied West's list, that only about half of the proposed works had been painted; the absence of any further record of the existence of a painting of the subject suggests that No. 1 belonged to the unpainted half. West may have intended to paint it as a companion to the *Bard* (No. 198) of 1809, which it immediately follows on his list with identical measurements and price. Like No. 198, it would have shown not only a poetic or quasi-poetic subject, but probably a similar composition of a single figure in a precipitous situation.

The poetess Sappho was a historical figure, born on the island of Lesbos around 640 B.C. The story of her throwing herself into the sea in despair because of her unrequited love for the boatman Phaon is now usually dismissed as romance, but it had considerable currency in the eighteenth and early nineteenth centuries. In undertaking or contemplating a painting of the subject, West may have had in mind the *Sappho* of 1801 by Baron Gros (Musée Baron Gérard, Bayeux), which he would have known from his visit to Paris in 1802.[2]

[1] Robert Fulton to George Clymer, New York, 12 April 1810 (Pennsylvania Academy of the Fine Arts, Philadelphia).

[2] See Rosenblum 1967, pp. 21–22, where other paintings of the subject are also cited, and fig. 18.

2 The Family of the King of Armenia before Cyrus 1773

HER MAJESTY THE QUEEN

Oil on canvas: 41¼ × 54 in. (104.8 × 137.2 cm.)

Signed lower right: *B. West/1773*

PROV: Painted for George III (1801 account, p. 207: 6, "Cyrus receiving the King of Armenia and family prisoners," 1772, £157.10.0.)

EXH: BI 1833 (26 or 32) both catalogued as "A Subject from the History of Cyrus," lent by William IV; *American Painting from the Eighteenth Century to the Present Day*, Tate Gallery, London, 1946 (238); *English Taste in the Eighteenth Century*, Royal Academy, London, 1955–56 (383) as "Cyrus Liberating the Family of Astyages," 1770; *British Painting in the Eighteenth Century*, Montreal Museum of Fine Arts, etc., 1957–58 (71)

ENGR: Engraving (16¹⁵⁄₁₆ × 23¼ in.) by James Fittler, pub. 25 March 1788, by John and Josiah Boydell (as "The Distress of Tigranes, before Cyrus, on finding his Father the King of Armenia, Mother, Wife, and Children, Prisoners," painted in 1769)

2

LISTED: *PC*, p. 559 ("Cyrus and the King of Armenia with his family, captives," George III, Queen's House); *UM*, p. 527; *AA*, p. 67 ("The King of Armenia and his Family before Cyrus," 5 ft. × 7); Barlow, p. 431; *BA*, p. 13; Galt, p. 216; Dillenberger, p. 136 (7)

LIT: Galt 1820, p. 50; Evans 1959, pp. 43 and 118, note 42, p. 22; Irwin 1966, pl. 51, pl. 43; Millar 1969, i, p. 131 (1154), ii, pl. 119

Oliver Millar has identified the source of this painting as Xenophon's *Cyropaedia* (III, i, 1–37). The Persian ruler Cyrus has captured the King of Armenia and his family. The King's elder son, Tigranes, who had once been a hunting companion of Cyrus, at this juncture returns from a journey abroad to find all his family prisoners, and he observes the trial of his father conducted by Cyrus. When the King concedes that he deserves to be put to death for his sins against Cyrus, Tigranes intervenes, and successfully pleads his father's cause. The painting shows Cyrus seated on the right, the captured Armenian royal family in carriages on the left, and the aged King and Tigranes in between. The moment is when the King has evidently condemned himself: "Then his son, when he heard this, stripped off his turban and rent his garments, and the women cried aloud and tore their cheeks, as if it were all over with their father and they were already lost."[1]

West painted No. 2 together with a companion depiction of the family of the German chieftain Segestes in an analogous situation before Germanicus (No. 32). Both works show the conquerors, Cyrus and Germanicus, sitting in judgment, before responding graciously and generously to appeals made on behalf of the captured families by one of their members. The two paintings are the smallest of the group of seven works that West painted for George III between 1769 and 1773 and that hung together in the Warm Room in Buckingham House (the others were Nos. 5, 10, 17, 77, and 94). According to Galt, Nos. 2 and 32 were commissioned last of the group, to fill two panels that remained empty, and West proposed the subjects. The engraving by James Fittler after No. 2, published in 1788, describes the original as painted in 1769, but that date seems palpably wrong. The date on the canvas has been variously read as *1770* and *1773*; the latter reading appears to be correct and fits with Galt's description of Nos. 2 and 32 as the last works painted for the Warm Room.

[1] Xenophon, *Cyropaedia*, III, i, 13 (trans. by Walter Miller; Loeb Classical Library, I, pp. 225–27).

3 The Departure of Leonidas

LOCATION UNKNOWN

PROV: Sold by West's sons, Robins, London, 20–22 June 1829, lot 74 ("Departure of Leonidas . . . a coloured sketch")

(?) LISTED: *PC*, p. 565 ("The picture of Leonidas taking Leave of his Family on his going to Thermopylae," West, Painting-room); *UM*, p. 530; Barlow, p. 434; *BA*, p. 17; Galt, p. 227; Dillenberger, p. 171 (317)

The subject of this work was evidently the fifth-century Leonidas I, who fought heroically against the Persian invasion at Thermopylae, rather than the third-century Leonidas II, depicted by West in No. 13. No. 3 is known only from the early lists of West's works and the inclusion of a *Departure of Leonidas* in one of the sales following West's death. There is a slight discrepancy between the work described as a picture in the lists and the colored sketch in the sale, but it seems probable that both entries referred to the same work.

4 The Death of Socrates *c.* 1756
See color illustration, p. 10

PRIVATE COLLECTION

Oil on canvas: 34 × 41 in. (86.4 × 104.1 cm.)

Signed lower left: *B. West . . . xit*, and also inscribed with the name *Henry*

PROV: Painted for William Henry (1729–1786), Lancaster, Pennsylvania; by family descent to the present owner

EXH: Allentown 1962 (2); *Philadelphia: Three Centuries of American Art*, Philadelphia Museum of Art, 1976 (52)

LIT: Galt 1816, pp. 35–38; Carey 1820, p. 514; Francis Jordan, Jr., *The Life of William Henry of Lancaster Pennsylvania 1729–1786*, Lancaster, 1910, pp. 29–33, ill. opp. p. 30; Landis 1925; Sawitzky 1938, p. 461; Tinkcom 1951, p. 382 (Sir Augustus Foster); Flexner 1952, pp. 5–41; Evans 1959, p. 13, pl. 13; Rosenblum 1967, p. 73; Peter S. Walch, "Charles Rollin and Early Neoclassicism," *Art Bulletin*, XLIX, 1967, p. 123, fig. 1; Ann C. Van Devanter, "Benjamin West's Death of Socrates," *Antiques*, CIV, 1973, pp. 436–39; Alberts 1978, pp. 18–19; Wainwright 1978, p. 111 (Nicholas Biddle, 1807)

The *Death of Socrates* was West's first historical painting, and it is the only one now known dating from before his departure from America in 1760. A slightly later *Trial of Susannah* (No. 290), which is mentioned in the early literature on West, was reportedly destroyed in a fire before 1840.

The earliest biographies of West report that in Lancaster, Philadelphia, and New York, "he painted many portraits, and several historical pictures, with considerable success,"[1] but give no further detail. The first specific reference to No. 4 seems to be in an entry in the diary of Nicholas Biddle (1786–1844) who, while serving in London in 1807 as secretary to the American envoy James Monroe, recorded several conversations with West:

On another occasion, when I dined at Mr. Monroe's with West & Dr. Jenner, happening to sit next to the former I took occasion to question him on his art.

When he was a boy he had a passion for painting which was much encouraged by a Mr. William Henry a gunsmith near Lancaster (now dead) who might have made a great man. He once suggested to West the death of Socrates which they were reading together. Henry made one of his workmen stand up that West might design his fine nervous arm, & it was from this that W took the disposition to copy nature. His piece (the death of S.) is now at Lancaster, & according to Fulton & West's son, the composition is admirable. He was then about 13 or 14.[2]

An account of the picture in the first volume of John Galt's biography of West, published in 1816, does not significantly contradict what West told Biddle, but gives more detail. West had gone to Lancaster, Pennsylvania, to paint portraits, and there, according to Galt, William Henry told him that he should not waste his time on portraits, but should devote himself to historical subjects:

and he mentioned the Death of Socrates as affording one of the best topics for illustrating the moral effect of the art of painting. The painter knew nothing of the history of the Philosopher; and, upon confessing his ignorance, Mr. Henry went to his library and taking down a volume of the English translation of Plutarch, read to him the account given by that writer of this affecting story.

Galt states that West then made a drawing of the subject before undertaking the painting for Henry, and he repeats the story of one of Henry's workmen posing for West.

Although West told Nicholas Biddle that he painted No. 4 when he was about thirteen or fourteen years old, that is, in 1751 or 1752, it seems likely that he made the trip to Lancaster at a somewhat later date, in 1755 or 1756.[3] Among other products of his visit are portraits of Mr. and Mrs. Henry (Nos. 637 and 638). No. 4 still remains in the possession of William Henry's descendants. William Sawitzky in 1938 listed it in his article on the American works of West on the basis of written sources, but described the painting itself as unlocated. It had, however, earlier been reproduced by Francis Jordan, Jr., in a biography of William Henry published in 1910, and was discussed in 1925 in a paper by Charles Landis, who led a delegation from the Lancaster Historical Society to see it. It was subsequently rediscovered by James Thomas Flexner, who wrote his fundamental article on West's American Neo-Classicism largely about it. After the Allentown exhibition of 1962, the *Death of Socrates* underwent conservation by Bruce Etchison during which the signature was brought to light. The article by Ann C. Van Devanter published in 1973 reports on Etchison's findings.

In 1910 William Henry's descendant, Francis Jordan, Jr., pointed out that West had based the composition of No. 4 on the engraved frontispiece to a volume of Charles Rollin's *Ancient History* (ill. p. 10), and that the volume of Rollin, like the painting itself, still remained in the possession of the Henry family. Hence, although Galt states that Henry read to West from Plutarch, the text which West utilized for the painting must have been that of Rollin instead. The illustration upon which West based his composition is by Hubert Gravelot.[4] West added numerous figures, transformed Gravelot's vertical composition into a horizontal one, and changed almost every detail, but the dependence is nonetheless obvious.

Galt states that the completed painting attracted much attention in Lancaster and that among those who saw it there was Dr. Smith, the Provost of the College at Philadelphia, who, after seeing the picture and conversing with West, invited the young artist to come study with him in Philadelphia (see No. 699). Robert Fulton (for whom see No. 620), whose opinion of the painting Nicholas Biddle cited, grew up in Lancaster, and he was certainly familiar with William Henry's paintings by West from before his departure from America in 1786.[5] West's son Raphael visited America between 1798 and 1802 and must have seen the *Death of Socrates* then. Another visitor to Lancaster who saw the painting at an early date was Sir Augustus Foster, a British diplomat who served in America from 1804 to 1807 and again in 1811–12. He described it as a historical picture, "in which Socrates looks like a Dunker, and is sitting down drinking Poison while his Friends stand round him with very rueful faces." Foster also implied, somewhat ambiguously, that all the works by West that he had seen in William Henry's son's possession were signed and dated *1756* (see No. 637).

The early lists of West's works include one drawing of the *Death of Socrates* belonging to the artist.[6] Whether or not that drawing was the one that he had shown to William Henry before painting No. 4 is impossible to say.

See also pp. 9–11 above.

[1] *Public Characters* 1805, p. 525.
[2] Quoted from Wainwright 1978, p. 111. The date of Biddle's entry is 24 June 1807, but the conversation had obviously taken place earlier. Jenner is Dr. Edward Jenner (1749–1823), the inventor of the vaccination.
[3] For the date of this trip, see the arguments put forward by Flexner, pp. 22–24.
[4] The actual engraving is reproduced by Jordan, opp. p. 28. The engraving is by J. P. Le Bas and is dated 1 June 1739. It appeared as the frontispiece of volume four of the second English edition of Rollin's *History*, the full title of which is

The Ancient History of the Egyptians, Carthaginians, Assyrians, Babylonians, Medes and Persians, Macedonians, and Grecians, published in ten volumes between 1738 and 1740. The original French edition was published from 1730 to 1738.
[5] See Jordan p. 51. The subject of Fulton's acquaintance with Henry has received considerable attention because of Fulton's possible debts to Henry in the development of the steamboat.
[6] *PC*, p. 568 ("The Drawing of the Death of Socrates," under "Drawings and Sketches on Paper, in the Gallery"); *UM*, p. 532; *BA*, p. 19; Galt, p. 233; Dillenberger, p. 184 (461).

5 The Death of Epaminondas 1773
See color illustration, p. 66

HER MAJESTY THE QUEEN

Oil on canvas: $87\frac{1}{2} \times 70\frac{5}{8}$ in. (222.2 × 179.4 cm.)

Signed lower right: *B. West/1773*

PROV: Painted for George III (1801 account, p. 207: 4, "The Death of Epaminondas," 1771, £315)

EXH: RA 1773 (304) "The Death of Epaminondas"; BI 1833 (144) lent by William IV; *Bicentenary Exhibition*, Royal Academy, London, 1968–69 (57)

ENGR: Mezzotint ($24\frac{3}{4} \times 20\frac{1}{8}$ in.) by Valentine Green, pub. 21 Feb. 1774 by J. Boydell; engraving ($19\frac{3}{8} \times 15\frac{7}{16}$ in.) by P. Bernard, (with explanatory text in French); engraving ($18 \times 24\frac{11}{16}$ in.) by Jazet, pub. by Ostervald *l'aîné*, Paris (with explanatory text in French) and the composition modified by additional figures on either side, etc., to become horizontal; outline engraving ($3\frac{15}{16} \times 3\frac{3}{4}$ in.) by Normand *fils*, pub. in Hamilton 1831

LISTED: *PC*, p. 559 ("Epaminondas," George III, Queen's House); *UM*, p. 527; *AA*, p. 67 (10 ft. × 7); Barlow, p. 431; *BA*, p. 13; Galt, p. 216; Dillenberger, p. 136 (4)

LIT: Farington Diary, 21 Feb. 1799 (Farington 1978–, IV, p. 1163); Hamilton 1831 (77); Locquin 1912, p. 154; Evans 1959, p. 44, pl. 27; Irwin 1966, p. 148; Peter S. Walch, "Charles Rollin and Early Neoclassicism," *Art Bulletin*, XCIX, 1967, p. 123, fig. 3; Millar 1969, I, p. 132 (1156), and II, pl. 123.

Epaminondas, a Theban general, was mortally wounded in the Battle of Mantinea in 326 B.C. Told that he would die when the point of the spear that had broken off in his chest was removed, he asked if his shield had been saved. No. 5 shows the moment when Epaminondas, assured of the Theban victory and being shown the shield, declares, "It is time to die," and directs that the spear point be removed. The story is told by various ancient historians, including Xenophon and Diodurus Siculus, but West's source was probably the *Ancient History* of Charles Rollin. Peter Walch has noted that the composition of this painting is based upon the frontispiece by Hubert Gravelot to the fifth volume of Rollin's *History*.[1]

George III commissioned No. 5 along with the *Death of the Chevalier Bayard* (No. 77), and a second version of the *Death of General Wolfe* (No. 94) to hang in the Warm Room in Buckingham House, where they had been preceded by the *Departure of Regulus* and the *Oath of Hannibal* (Nos. 10 and 17). He also apparently commissioned the *Family of the King of Armenia before Cyrus* and *Segestes and His Daughter before Germanicus* (Nos. 2 and 32), on this occasion to complete the decoration of the room. According to Galt, West proposed the *Death of Epaminondas* "as a classic subject, and with Grecian circumstances," to make "a suitable contrast" with the *Death of Wolfe*. As David Irwin has observed, the earliest biography of Wolfe, published in 1760, compared his death in battle to that of Epaminondas.

A cryptic passage on a sheet of notes by Joseph Farington intended for his diary entry for 21 February 1799, contains the comment "Epaminondas, clever composition, but Epam: a common soldier." The passage is part of a summary of a description by the painter Sawrey Gilpin of a visit to Buckingham House, so although West did exhibit another *Epaminondas* in 1799 (No. 6), the remark seems to have been about No. 5. The previous sentences in Farington's notes are: "West pointed to 2 door pieces—'these not mine' yet they have hung many years. Feet of Gaul come below frame." What West meant by this is not clear; it is possible that the reference was to two otherwise unidentified paintings, which were in fact not by him, but which hung as part of the group of his works in the Warm Room.

The early lists of West's works include one drawing of the *Death of Epaminondas*.[2] A small and rough sketch in the Pierpont Morgan Library may show the subject, but has only slight similarity with No. 5.[3]

[1]Gravelot's frontispiece is reproduced by Walch, fig. 4. For West's earlier reliance upon Gravelot's illustrations to Rollin see No. 4.
[2]*PC*, p. 568 (among "Drawings and Sketches on Paper, in the Gallery"); *UM*, p. 531; *BA*, p. 19; Galt, p. 233; Dillenberger, p. 183 (445).
[3]Black chalk, $3\frac{13}{16} \times 5\frac{3}{8}$ in., Kraemer 1975, p. 7 (7) and pl. 4. A further drawing mentioned by Kraemer does not appear to show this subject.

6 The Death of Epaminondas *c.* 1799

CITY ART GALLERY, WAKEFIELD, YORKSHIRE

Oil on canvas, mounted on board: $9\frac{3}{4} \times 11\frac{1}{8}$ in. (25 × 28.5 cm.)

PROV: Offered by West's sons to the United States in 1826 (101, "The Death of Sir Philip Sydney—Epaminondas, and the Chevalier Bayard," in one frame, each 10 × 11 in.) and sold by them, Robins, London, 22–25 May 1829, lot 97 ("The Death of Sir Philip Sydney, Epaminondas, And Chevalier Bayard, in One Frame," 12 in. × 3 ft.), bt. by Shippery for £52.10.0.; purchased by the Wakefield City Art Gallery in 1942 together with the companion pictures, Nos. 78 and 79

EXH: RA 1799 (191) "A frame containing the deaths of Sir Philip Sidney, Epaminondas, and the Chevalier Bayard"; West's Gallery 1821 (4), 1822–28 (91)

LISTED: *PC*, p. 567 ("The Death of Epaminondas," West, Gallery); *UM*, p. 531; Barlow, p. 435; *BA*, p. 18; Galt, p. 231; Dillenberger, p. 179 (401)

6

7

Three small paintings of the *Death of Epaminondas* (No. 6), the *Death of Bayard* (No. 78), and the *Death of Sir Philip Sidney* (No. 79) are uniform in size and scale and originally shared one frame, although they are now framed separately. No. 79 is signed and dated *1799*, and in that year the three pictures appeared at the Royal Academy. Nos. 6 and 78 repeat subjects that West had painted in 1772 and 1773 as companion pictures for George III (see Nos. 5 and 77) but are in no way reminiscent of the earlier works.

7 Alexander's Confidence in His Physician Philip *c.* 1771

WELLCOME INSTITUTE FOR THE HISTORY OF MEDICINE, LONDON

Oil on canvas: $37\frac{3}{4} \times 40\frac{3}{4}$ in. (96 × 103.5 cm.)

PROV: Painted for Giles Stibbert (died 1809); probably in West's possession again by 1811; purchased by the Marquess of Stafford from West in 1819; by family descent to the fourth Duke of Sutherland (1851–1913); sold from his estate, Christie's, London, 11 July 1913 (23), bt. by Tooth for 63s.

EXH: RA 1819 (345) "Alexander's confidence in his physician Philip"; BI 1833 (19, lent by the Duke of Sutherland); BI 1850 (170)

ENGR: Mezzotint ($16\frac{3}{4} \times 20\frac{13}{16}$ in.) by Valentine Green, pub. by John Boydell, 1 Jan. 1772, as from the picture in the collection of G. Stibbert, Esq.; outline engraving (7 × 8 in.) drawn by Henry Corbould,

engraved by Henry Moses, pub. 2 Dec. 1811 as pl. VII in Moses 1811; etching ($3\frac{7}{16} \times 4$ in.) by John Young, pub. 1825 in *A Catalogue of the Collection of Pictures of the Most Noble the Marquess of Stafford*, vol. II, no. 256

LISTED: *PC*, p. 563 ("Alexander and his Physician," for General Stibert); *UM*, p. 529; Barlow, p. 433; *BA*, p. 15; Galt, p. 223; Dillenberger, p. 159 (211)

LIT: Moses 1811 (VII); Farington Diary, 10 May 1819 (Farington 1978—, XV, p. 5363); John Young, *A Catalogue of the Collection of Pictures of the Most Noble the Marquess of Stafford, at Cleveland House, London*, London, 1825, II, pp. 183–84 (256); Passavant 1836, I, p. 146; Waagen 1854, II, p. 72

The subject of No. 7 is from Plutarch's life of Alexander the Great. Alexander had fallen ill while on campaign in Cilicia. The physician Philip, an Acarnian, undertook to cure him by preparing a strong medicine that Alexander was to drink. Meanwhile, however, Alexander received a letter warning him that Philip had been bribed by Darius to poison him. Alexander hid the letter, took the medicine brought him by Philip, then showed Philip the letter while continuing to drink the medicine.

It was an amazing sight, then, and one well worthy of the stage,—the one reading the letter, the other drinking the medicine, and then both together turning their eyes upon one another, but not with the same expression; for Alexander by his glad and open countenance, showed his good will towards Philip and his trust in him, while Philip was beside himself at the calumny, now lifting up his hands toward heaven and calling upon the gods to witness his innocence, and now falling upon the couch on which Alexander lay and beseeching him to be of good courage and obey his physician.[1]

The figure standing on the left is Alexander's friend Hephestion.

West first exhibited this painting only in 1819 (the last occasion that he sent works to the Royal Academy before his death in March 1820), but he must have painted it by 1771, since the mezzotint by Valentine Green was published on 1 January 1772. Farington wrote in 1819 that it had been painted about 1770. It formed a pair with *Caesar Reading the History of Alexander's Exploits* (No. 26), which the Robins catalogue of 22–25 May 1829 states was painted in 1771. The G. Stibbert, who is recorded on the Green mezzotint as the owner of No. 7, was apparently Giles Stibbert, an officer in the Bengal Army. He was promoted to general in 1777: hence the "General Stibert" on the various lists of West's works. Stibbert was on furlough in England *c.* 1769–72 and had a son born in London in 1771.[2] He entered the Bengal Army under the patronage of Lord Clive, and it is perhaps not a coincidence that the first records of Clive's patronage of West begin at about the same time that West painted Nos. 7 and 26. These two paintings were probably back in West's possession by 1811, when they were engraved by Henry Moses without indication of an owner. After sending both pictures to the Academy in 1819, West broke up the pair by selling No. 7. According to Farington, Charles Long had seen it in the Academy exhibition, suggested its purchase to the Marquess of Stafford, and approached West on Stafford's behalf. Although West initially declined to name a price, John Young states that he was paid "a considerable sum."

Comparison with prints after them indicates that both Nos. 7 and 26 have had their original dimensions reduced. In the case of *Alexander's Confidence in His Physician Philip*, this evidently happened before 1811, as the Moses engraving published in that year shows the composition essentially the same as the painting, whereas the Green engraving of 1772 records what would have been several further inches of canvas behind Hephestion and Philip on either side of the composition. There are fairly evident signs of later retouching, particularly in the curtain in the upper left, probably done by West after the painting had returned to his possession.

[1] Plutarch, *Life of Alexander*, XIX (trans. by Bernadotte Perrin; Loeb Classical Library, VII, p. 277).
[2] V. C. P. Hodson, *List of the Officers of the Bengal Army 1758–1834*, London, 1927–47, V, pp. 194–95.

8 Pyrrhus when a Child, Brought before Glaucias *c.* 1767

LOCATION UNKNOWN

PROV: (?) Robert Hay Drummond, Archbishop of York (1711–1776); (?) Lord Hardwicke

EXH: SA 1767 (173) "Pyrrhus when a child, brought to Glaucias, King of Illyria, for protection," with no. 174 "The Fright of Astyanax" (No. 163) described as its companion

ENGR: Engraving ($17\frac{1}{4} \times 22\frac{7}{16}$ in.), drawn by Richard Earlom and engraved by John Hall, pub. 1 June 1769 by J. Boydell; anonymous outline engraving ($3\frac{1}{8} \times 4\frac{1}{8}$ in.), pub. in Hamilton 1831 (4)

LIT: V and A Cuttings, I, p. 75 (*Public Advertiser*, May 1767); Carey 1820, p. 690; *Annual Register* 1820, p. 1169; Graves 1907, p. 275 (Horace Walpole, 1767); Gatty 1938–39, p. 8 (Walpole, 1767); von Erffa 1973, pp. 11–12

Pyrrhus (318–272 B.C.) is the subject of one of Plutarch's *Lives*. The son of the deposed ruler of Epirus, he was brought as a fugitive, while a small child, to the court of Glaucias in Illyria. Upon arriving there and being set on the floor before the ruler, "Pyrrhus, of his own accord, crept along the floor, on to his feet at the knees of Glaucias, who was moved at first to laughter, then to pity, as he saw the child clinging to his knees and weeping like a formal suppliant."[1] Pyrrhus was thereupon raised by Glaucias, who eventually set him upon the throne of Epirus. He became a famous soldier, who carried on campaigns against Rome, and whose name has become immortalized in our term for a victory gained at too great a cost.

No. 8 is not on any of the early lists of West's works, but a sketch (No. 9) is. G. Hamilton's *English School*, published in 1831, states that West painted No. 8 for Archbishop Drummond, but this assertion is not substantiated by any other source. According to Galt, West was introduced to Archbishop Drummond in 1765 by Dr. Markham, the Master of Westminster School (see No. 655), who also in the same year introduced the artist to Dr. Newton, Bishop of Bristol (see No. 675). West painted the *Fright of Astyanax* (No. 163) for Dr. Newton, and, since he exhibited No. 163 in 1767 as the companion of No. 8, it seems plausible that he may have painted the two works in response to a pair of related commissions from the two clerics. On the other hand, William Carey, whose account was based on conversations with West, stated that Dr. Drummond saw the picture of the young Pyrrhus when it was exhibited at the Society of Artists in 1767, "and was so struck with its merits, that he called on the painter at his house, took him home in his carriage to dine with him, and, after dinner, gave him a commission to paint the *Landing of Agrippina with the ashes of Germanicus at Brundisium.*" That Drummond commission is No. 33, which

West completed and exhibited the following year. Carey continues, "This, according to our notes, taken from Mr. West's recollections, was the first commission for an historical picture that he received in England." Carey does not indicate that Dr. Drummond acquired No. 8, and Galt does not mention the painting at all. The equally questionable inclusion of Lord Hardwicke in the provenance is due to a nineteenth-century identification of the Earlom-Hall engraving after No. 8 as "nach dem Bilde aus dem Kabinett Hardwicke."[2] Present members of the Hardwicke family have no knowledge of the painting.[3]

A drawing showing the composition in reverse from the engravings and with a colonnade running across the background is at Swarthmore,[4] and a very slight sketch, which may represent an early idea for the disposition of the figures and architecture, is in one of West's sketchbooks belonging to the Royal Academy.

Two sets of catalogues of the exhibition of the Society of Artists contain different comments by (or supposedly by) Horace Walpole about No. 8. One, recorded by Graves, is: "The colouring, expression and attitude very fine." The other, recorded by Gatty, is less wholehearted: "Design good, colouring heavy." The assessment in the *Public Advertiser* was also mixed:

In the Picture of *Glaucias* there is Expression in the Countenances, the Figures are well grouped, none of them tame or unmeaning, and the Light and Shade is well managed, but the Manner is harder than in the Other Pictures, the Drapery heavy, and every would-be Critic calls little Pyrrus's Head of Hair a Mop.

[1] Plutarch, *Life of Pyrrhus*, III, 2 (trans. by Bernadotte Perrin; Loeb Classical Library, IX, pp. 351–53).
[2] *Naglers Künstler-Lexikon*, 1835–52, XXIV, p. 169.
[3] Letter from Lady Annabel Lindsay, 4 May 1983.
[4] Chalk, 12 × 17 in.

Pyrrhus when a Child, Brought before Glaucias, engraving by Richard Earlom and John Hall after No. 8

9 Pyrrhus when a Child, Brought before Glaucias

LOCATION UNKNOWN

PROV: Sold by West's sons, Robins, London, 20–22 June 1829, lot 49 ("Pyrrhus, when a Child, brought before Glaucias")

LISTED: *PC*, p. 567 ("The Sketch of Pyrrhus, when a Child, before King Glaucus," West, Gallery); *UM*, p. 531; Barlow, p. 435; *BA*, p. 18; Galt, p. 230; Dillenberger, p. 177 (388)

10 The Departure of Regulus from Rome 1769

See color illustrations, pp. 48, 49

HER MAJESTY THE QUEEN

Oil on canvas: 88½ × 120 in. (229.9 × 304.8 cm.)

Signed lower left on block of stone: *BENJAMIN WEST/PINXIT/LONDINI 1769*

PROV: Painted for George III (1801 account, p. 207: 1, "Regulus, his Departure from Rome," 1769, £420)

EXH: RA 1769 (120) "The departure of Regulus from Rome"; BI 1824 (143); BI 1833 (15); Manchester 1857 (113); *International Exhibition*, South Kensington, 1862 (92); *The First Hundred Years of the Royal Academy*, Royal Academy, London, 1951 (395)

ENGR: Mezzotint (24¹³⁄₁₆ × 34⅝ in.) by Valentine Green, pub. 14 Nov. 1771 by J. Boydell; outline engraving (3½ × 4¹¹⁄₁₆ in.) by "Br.," pub. in Hamilton 1831 (40)

LISTED: *PC*, p. 559 ("Regulus," George III, Queen's House); *UM*, p. 527; *AA*, p. 67 ("The departure of Regulus from Rome, on his return to Carthage," 10 ft. × 7); Barlow, p. 431; *BA*, p. 13; Galt, p. 216; Dillenberger, p. 136 (2)

LIT: *Public Characters* 1805, pp. 533–34, 551; Galt 1820, pp. 20–26, 33–41, 45–46; Carey 1820, pp. 690, 692, 694; Angelo 1830, I, p. 280; Hamilton 1831 (40); Copley-Pelham 1914, p. 339 (letter from Copley to Henry Pelham, 25 June 1775); Locquin 1922, pp. 277–80; Waterhouse 1954, p. 191, pl. 170a; Evans 1959, pp. 21, 43–44, 48, pl. 19; Millar 1969, I, p. 131 (1152), II, pl. 121; Charles Coleman Sellers, *Charles Willson Peale*, New York, 1969, p. 64; Burke 1976, pp. 243–45, pl. 68B; Alberts 1978, pp. 89–90, 94–95, 101–2

Marcus Atilius Regulus was a Roman consul in 267 and 256 B.C. In the first Punic War he was taken prisoner by the Carthaginians. His captors sent him to Rome as part of an embassy to negotiate peace and the return of Carthaginian prisoners held by the Romans in exchange for himself, under the condition that if the Carthaginian proposals were not successful he would return to captivity. In Rome he persuaded the Senate to reject the Carthaginian terms as dishonorable and disadvantageous to Rome and then returned to Carthage where death by torture awaited him. The story is frequently cited, by Cicero and Horace among others, as a distinguished example of virtuous and heroic Roman behavior, but modern scholars have questioned how true it is. John Galt states that George III suggested the subject to the artist and that the King himself read to West from "the volume of Livy in which the event is related," but, as Oliver Millar has pointed out, the story is only summarized by Livy in the epitome of the lost Book XVIII of *Ab Urbe Condita*, whereas it appears in much greater detail in the *Punica* by Silius Italicus.[1] The abbreviated account of the event in Livy does not mention Regulus' wife, Marcia, and her two children, who form a group on the left side of this painting, but Silius Italicus describes Marcia fainting at the sight of Regulus in Carthaginian dress. That incident, however, occurs at the moment of Regulus' arrival in Rome, rather than that of his departure, which No. 10 otherwise appears to show, and which most early sources indicate that it does.

No. 10 was the first painting by West to enter the Royal Collection (but see No. 195), and it marked the commencement of over thirty years' sustained patronage of the artist by George III. After West had painted the *Landing of Agrippina at Brundisium* (No. 33) for Archbishop Drummond, the artist was invited at the Archbishop's instigation to show that picture to George III. According to William Carey this happened in February 1768, before West sent the *Agrippina* to that year's exhibition at the Society of Artists. Galt gives a lengthy description of the interview: George III admired the *Agrippina*, summoned Queen Charlotte to see it, described to her the sketch that West had made of that subject for the Archbishop of York (No. 36), then turned and said to West:

There is another noble Roman subject which corresponds to this one, and I believe it also has never been well painted; I mean the final departure of Regulus from Rome. Don't you think it would make a fine picture?

When West agreed, the King announced, "You shall paint it for me," called for his Livy, which he read to the artist, and ordered West "to come with the sketch as soon as possible." When that sketch (No. 11) was made and shown to the King, West's new patron chose a wall in one of his principal apartments and directed the artist to paint the picture "of a size sufficient to fill the whole space." While West was at work on the painting, negotiations leading to the formation of the Royal Academy were underway, and his new intimacy with George III made him the chief conduit between the artists and the King.[2] Galt claims that George III first heard about the resignation in November 1768 of West and several other artists as directors of the Society of Artists on the very day West brought his sketch of No. 10 to show him, which seems like an inexplicably long time after the King's initial commission in February, and that when West brought the finished picture to Buckingham House, the King instructed him to exhibit it at the new Royal Academy, much to the discomfiture of the President of the Society of Artists, Joshua Kirby, who chanced to be present at the time. This encounter, according to Galt, took place the day before the artists elected Joshua Reynolds president of the planned Academy, which must have been on or before 14 December 1768, when the first general assembly of the Academy took place, but this date seems too early for completion of the picture, impossibly early if we accept Galt's account of when George III first saw the sketch. William Carey does not state when West showed George III the sketch, but he does say that West "speedily executed a design for the picture," after his royal patron gave him the initial commission in February. Carey also indicates that West took the *Regulus* for the King's inspection before Reynolds accepted the presidency of the Academy, some time between 28 November and 10 December 1768, but he describes the painting as "nearly finished" at the time, rather than finished, as in Galt.

No. 10 is signed and dated *1769*, and it did appear at the first exhibition of the Royal Academy, which opened on 25 April 1769, together with *Venus Lamenting the Death of Adonis* (No. 116), which is signed and dated *1768*. After George III saw the approbation which the painting received at the Royal Academy, both Galt and Carey state that he summoned West yet again and commissioned a companion picture of Hamilcar making his son Hannibal swear implacable enmity against the Romans (No. 17).

Although Galt claims that George III proposed the subject of Regulus to West, it seems likely that the Archbishop of York may have suggested it to the King. In West's portrait of the Archbishop's two eldest sons (No. 608) which is dated *1767* and which he exhibited together with the *Agrippina* in 1768, Robert, the elder, holds a scroll with the name *REGULUS* inscribed upon it, and in a later group portrait of members of the Drummond family (No. 611), the brothers' sister (?) holds a book in which *REGULUS* is again legible.

Charles Willson Peale, who was in London from 1767 to 1769, is said to have posed for the figure of Regulus in No. 10, and the features of the central figure are similar to those in West's portrait of Peale (No. 680), albeit affected by the addition of a beard.

The sketch mentioned by Galt and Carey (No. 11) has disappeared. The early lists of West's works include one drawing of the subject, in the artist's possession.[3] West told John Singleton Copley that he believed he had made at least fifty drawings for the painting, but the only drawing known to the compilers of this catalogue is a tiny compositional sketch in one of the artist's sketchbooks now belonging to the Royal Academy.

Henry Angelo records David Garrick's admiration for No. 10, and in the same paragraph an exchange about West between Francesco Zuccarelli and Johann Zoffany, which may have been inspired by No. 10 as well. To Zuccarelli's "Here is a painter who promises to rival Nicolas Poussin," Zoffany replied, "a figo for Poussin, West has already beaten him out of the field."

See also pp. 46–55 above.

[1] Book VI, lines 62–551.
[2] See Sidney C. Hutchison, *The History of the Royal Academy 1768–1968*, London, 1968, pp. 40–50.
[3] *PC*, p. 568 ("The Drawing of Regulus," West, Gallery); *UM*, p. 531; *BA*, p. 19 ("The Drawing of Regulus, his departure from Rome"); Galt, p. 232; Dillenberger, p. 181 (432).

11 The Departure of Regulus from Rome

LOCATION UNKNOWN

LIT: Galt 1820, pp. 25–26, 33, 35–36; Carey 1820, p. 690

Both Galt and Carey refer to a preliminary sketch for No. 10, which West was requested to paint and show to George III before painting the large picture, but nothing further is known about that sketch. It was probably comparable to No. 36, the oil-sketch for *Agrippina Landing at Brundisium*, which figures prominently in Galt's account of the genesis of No. 10.

12 The Departure of Regulus from Rome

LOCATION UNKNOWN (PROBABLY NEVER PAINTED)

PROV: Offered by West to the Pennsylvania Academy of the Fine Arts in 1809 ("The Departure of Regulus from Rome," 7 ft. × 10 ft., £500)

In a letter to the President of the Pennsylvania Academy, accompanying West's list of paintings he was offering to sell to the Academy, Robert Fulton described half the works on the list as copies of West's own works, which would probably be superior to the originals, but which would not be "finished and ready to ship in less than two or three years."[1] No. 12 belonged almost certainly to this half of the list, and it may never have even been begun.

[1] Letter from Robert Fulton to George Clymer, 12 April 1810, in the archives of the Pennsylvania Academy of the Fine Arts, Philadelphia.

13 Leonidas and Cleombrutus 1768

See color illustration, p. 53

TATE GALLERY, LONDON

Oil on canvas: $54\frac{1}{2} \times 73$ in. (138.5×185.5 cm.)

Signed lower right: *B. West PINXIT/1768*

PROV: (?) William Locke of Norbury: William Smith, MP, by 1797; William Wilkins, RA, by whom presented to the British Museum in 1827; transferred to the National Gallery before 1836, and to the Tate Gallery in 1929

EXH: SA 1768 (special exhibition in honor of the King of Denmark) (122) "Leonidas ordering into banishment Cleombrutus"; RA 1770 (197) "Leonidas and Cleombrutus"

ENGR: Mezzotint ($23\frac{5}{16} \times 17\frac{7}{16}$ in.) by Charles Howard Hodges, pub. 1 May 1789 by John and Josiah Boydell; steel engraving ($4\frac{9}{16} \times 6\frac{7}{16}$ in.) by Thomas Garner, pub. as no. 8 in series *The National Gallery*

LISTED: *PC*, p. 563 ("Leonidas ordering Cleombrotas into Banishment with his Wife and Children," for W. Smith, Esq.); *UM*, p. 529; Barlow, p. 433; *BA*, p. 15 (... W. Smith, Esq., first painted for W. Locke, Esq.); Galt, p. 223; Dillenberger, p. 159 (209)

LIT: Farington Diary, 17 May 1797 (Farington 1978–, III, p. 840); Passavant 1836, I, pp. 55–56; Waagen 1854, I, p. 366; Graves 1906, VIII, p. 212 (Horace Walpole, 1770); Locquin 1912, p. 154; Rosenblum 1967, p. 66, fig. 66

The subject of No. 13 is from Plutarch's *Life of Agis* (XVI–XVIII). Cleombrutus, who had briefly deposed his father-in-law Leonidas II as King of Sparta, has taken refuge in the Temple of Poseidon. There his wife Chilonis, with her two children at her side, pleads with her father to spare the life of Cleombrutus. In response to this display of fidelity and devotion, Leonidas does spare Cleombrutus, but orders him into exile, while begging Chilonis to remain. She had previously shared exile with her father during Cleombrutus' usurpation of the throne, but she now chooses to follow her husband into banishment: "Both as a wife and mother I was born to share only the misfortune and dishonor of the men nearest and dearest to me."[1]

West completed No. 13 by 30 September 1768, when it was included in a private two-day exhibition at the Society of Artists held on the occasion of a visit to England by the King of Denmark. Although the Royal Academy had a policy against including previously exhibited works in its exhibitions,[2] this private exhibition evidently did not count, and West re-exhibited No. 13 in the second exhibition of the new Academy in 1770. He presumably did so because extended bad health had prevented his finishing either of his two major works, the *Oath of Hannibal* and the *Death of General Wolfe* (Nos. 17 and 93), before the opening of the exhibition, although he did complete both before the end of the year.

No. 13 was in the collection of William Smith (1756–1835) by May 1797, when Joseph Farington saw the painting in his house. Although the early lists of West's works describe No. 13 as painted for Smith, this seems highly unlikely, since Smith was only twelve years old in 1768, and one list, that in *La Belle Assemblée*, describes the painting as originally painted for W. Locke, presumably a reference to William Lock (or Locke) of Norbury Park (1732–1810). One other work by West (No. 371) may have shared the same early history. William Wilkins, RA (1778–1839), who presented No. 13 to the British Museum in 1827, was a leading Greek Revival architect, best known for designing the National Gallery in Trafalgar Square. His acquisition

of a work such as No. 13 certainly must have had something to do with his tastes as an architect. Wilkins was a protégé of Thomas Hope (1769–1831), who was also a purchaser of paintings of classical subjects by West (see No. 170).

A sketch is No. 14 below. A drawing for the figure of Leonidas is in the Victoria and Albert Museum.[3] A drawing of a male figure in the Philadelphia Museum of Art, which was described as Leonidas when the drawing was sold in 1967, has no evident relation to No. 13.[4] See also No. 3.

Horace Walpole's opinion of No. 13 in 1770 was: "Solemn and good, tho' hard and heavy."

[1] Plutarch, *Life of Agis*, XVII (trans. by Bernadotte Perrin; Loeb Classical Library, X, p. 39).

[2] See Nos. 116 and 239. We have not been able to establish if this prohibition had become a firm policy of the Academy as early as 1770; it is not among the rules promulgated for the Academy's exhibition in January 1769 (see Sidney Hutchison, *The History of the Royal Academy 1768–1968*, London, 1968, pp. 54–55).

[3] Chalk, $16\frac{1}{2} \times 10\frac{5}{8}$ in. Although this drawing bears a false signature, it appears to be by West.

[4] Pen, $15\frac{1}{2} \times 11\frac{1}{8}$ in.; sold by Mrs. Claire Francis, Christie's, London, 14 March 1967, lot 46.

14 Leonidas and Cleombrutus

LOCATION UNKNOWN

(Oil on paper)

LISTED: *PC*, p. 568 ("The Sketch, in oil, of Leonidas ordering Cleombrutus into Banishment, on paper," West, Gallery); *UM*, p. 531; *BA*, p. 19; Galt, p. 232; Dillenberger, p. 182 (444)

In all the lists, No. 14 follows No. 36, the oil sketch for *Agrippina Landing at Brundisium*, and is described identically (by a ditto). The two finished pictures of the subjects (Nos. 13 and 33) were both completed and exhibited in 1768.

15 Antiochus and Stratonice 1772

PRIVATE COLLECTION

Oil on canvas: 50×72 in. (127×183 cm.)

Signed lower right: *B. West 1772*

PROV: Richard, Lord Grosvenor (later the first Earl Grosvenor) by 1776; in West's possession again by 1809, when it was among the pictures he proposed to sell to the Pennsylvania Academy of the Fine Arts ("Antiocus and Stratonica," 6 ft. × 4 ft. 2 in., £200); offered by West's sons to the United States in 1826 (no. 23) and sold by them, Robins, London, 22–25 May 1829, lot 177 ("Antiochus and Stratonice," 4 ft. 1 in. × 6 ft.), bt. by Hayes for £54.12.0.; (?) John Allnutt sale, Christie's, London, 20 June 1863, lot 368; (?) Miss E. Cowan, Kensington, in 1938; sold anonymously, Christie's, London, 18 Feb. 1944, lot 143, bt. by James; H. M. Calmann, London, 1950; Ray L. Murphy, New York

EXH: RA 1775 (333) "Erasistratus, the physician, discovers the love of Antiochus for Stratonice"

ENGR: Mezzotint ($18\frac{3}{8} \times 25\frac{3}{4}$ in.) by Valentine Green, pub. 27 May 1776 by John Boydell, "From the Original Picture in the Possession of Lord Grosvenor"; stipple engraving ($10\frac{9}{16} \times 14\frac{1}{2}$ in.) by George Graham, pub. 24 June 1793 by J. and J. Boydell

LIT: Locquin 1922, pp. 477–81; Wolfgang Stechow, "The Love of Antiochus with Faire Stratonica in

Art," *Art Bulletin*, XXVII, 1945, pp. 222, 232–33; H. Stewart Leonard, "Benjamin West's Antiochus and Stratonice," *Bulletin of the City Art Museum of St. Louis*, XXXVI, 1951, pp. 48–50; Wolfgang Stechow, "Addenda to The Love of Antiochus with Faire Stratonica," *Bulletin du Musée National de Varsovie*, V, 1964; William L. Pressly, "Antiochus and Stratonice: A Copy after a Lost Painting by James Barry," *Worcester Art Museum Journal*, IV, 1980–81, pp. 12–27

The prostrate figure at the center of No. 15 is Antiochus, the son of Seleucus, the Hellenistic King of Syria, who is shown seated in a melancholy pose supporting his son's head. Bending over Antiochus is the physician Erasistratus, who has been summoned to diagnose a mysterious disease from which Antiochus is suffering. He identifies its cause as Antiochus' repressed passion for his young and beautiful stepmother Stratonice. When told of this, Seleucus cedes his wife to his son to save the latter's life. The story is told by many antique sources, and its various depictions in painting, including West's, are discussed in the article by Wolfgang Stechow published in 1945. No. 15 appears to depend upon *De Dea Syria* once attributed to Lucian (cap. 17–18). This account describes Erasistratus placing his left hand upon the patient's heart, while feeling his pulse with the other, as he does in No. 15. While he does this, all the beautiful young people of the court enter the room upon his command, and the quickening of Antiochus' heartbeat at the sight of Stratonice, who is shown standing at the foot of the bed in No. 15, provides the clue that allows the physician to identify the malady. The story had a considerable vogue in the second half of the eighteenth century and was the subject set both for the English Royal Academy's gold medal competition for 1773–74 and the French Academy's Prix de Rome competition of 1774.

West's exhibition of No. 15 at the Royal Academy in 1775 followed not only the competition for Academy students but also the exhibition of a painting of the same subject by James Barry at the Academy in 1774. Barry's painting is lost, but William Pressly has identified a painting in the Worcester Art Museum, which was acquired by the museum as a work by West,[1] as an early copy after it. Whether Barry actually painted the subject before West is uncertain. No. 15 is signed and dated *1772*, but Barry also was at work on the subject as early as 1772. Whoever had precedence, West must have been well aware of Barry's painting when he exhibited No. 15 in 1775, and there are significant similarities in the two compositions, notably in the position of Stratonice standing on the left in both. As Pressly points out, Barry's Stratonice echoes the Helen of Troy in the engraving by Domenico Cunego after Gavin Hamilton's *Andromache Bewailing the Death of Hector* of 1764, and West's painting also recalls Hamilton's composition. West's Stratonice, however, repeats a female figure from the left side of his own *Oath of Hannibal* of 1770 (No. 17) more closely than she does the figures of either Hamilton or Barry. A drawing of the subject by West in the St. Louis Art Museum, which appears to be later than No. 15, shows a similar Stratonice but a substantially modified composition otherwise, with Antiochus depicted seated rather than lying down as in No. 15. This is probably the drawing included in the early lists of West's works.[2]

No. 15 itself does not appear on the early lists, although the drawing and a small version (No. 16) do. It belonged to Lord Grosvenor in 1776, when the mezzotint by Valentine Green was published, but later returned to West's possession, probably before 1809 when the artist offered to sell a painting of the subject to the Pennsylvania Academy of the Fine Arts. Lord Grosvenor may have sent No. 15 back in exchange or part payment for other work subsequently acquired by

15

him from the artist (such as Nos. 83, 84, 88 or 90). What appears to have been a copy after No. 15 went through Christie's in 1979.[4]

[1]This painting probably was sold at Christie's, London, 31 July 1919, lot 107, as by West. It was purchased by the Worcester Art Museum in 1920, and was exhibited as a work by West several times subsequently: Brooklyn 1922 (27) as *Historical Theme*; Philadelphia 1938 (58); Amherst 1950 (8). Stechow questioned the attribution to West in 1945.

[2]Pen and ink, with blue wash and some body-color: $17\frac{1}{2} \times 23\frac{3}{8}$ in. This drawing is faintly signed and dated, bottom left of center; the date has been read both as *1773* and *1777*. It is also dated *1773* on the mount by another hand, but the date of 1773 seems improbably early.

[3]*PC*, p. 568 ("The Drawing of Antinous and Stratonice," West, Gallery); *UM*, p. 532; *BA*, p. 16 ("Antiochus"); Galt, p. 233; Dillenberger, p. 183 (452).

[4]Christie's, London, 27 June 1979, lot 161, 31 × 43 in., as by "B. West."

16 Antiochus and Stratonice

LOCATION UNKNOWN

EXH: BI 1806 (North Room, no. 57) "Antiochus and Stratonice," 4 ft. 7 in. × 5 ft. 5 in. (including frame)

LISTED: *PC*, p. 565 ("The small picture of Antiochus and Stratonice," West, Painting-room); *UM*, p. 530; Barlow, p. 434; *BA*, p. 16; Galt, p. 226; Dillenberger, p. 167 (286).

See No. 15. That painting is too large to have been called "the small picture" in the lists of West's works, and too large to have been the painting of the subject which West exhibited in 1805. It is conceivable that the painting that went through the market in 1979 is identical with No. 16, but from a photograph, that work (a close copy of No. 15) gives little evidence of being by West's hand.

17 The Oath of Hannibal 1770

HER MAJESTY THE QUEEN

Oil on canvas: $88\frac{1}{4} \times 119\frac{3}{4}$ in. (229.1 × 304.1 cm.)

Signed: *B. West PINXIT/1770*

PROV: Painted for George III (1801 account, p. 207: 2. "Hamilcar swearing his Son Hannibal at the Altar," 1769, £420

EXH: RA 1771 (209) "Hannibal brought, when nine years old, by his father, Hamilchar, to the altar of Jupiter, where he swears eternal enmity to the Romans"; BI 1824 (149); BI 1833 (18); *International Exhibition*, South Kensington, 1862 (161); *English Taste in the Eighteenth Century*, Royal Academy, London, 1955–56 (385)

ENGR: Mezzotint ($24\frac{3}{4} \times 34\frac{3}{4}$ in.) by Valentine Green, pub. 1 Nov. 1773 by J. Boydell; outline engraving ($3\frac{1}{2} \times 4\frac{13}{16}$ in.) by Normand *fils*, pub. in Hamilton 1831 (17)

LISTED: *PC*, p. 559 ("Hannibal," George III, Queen's House); *UM*, p. 527; *AA*, p. 67 ("Hannibal when nine years old, swearing eternal enmity to Rome," 10 ft. × 7); Barlow, p. 431 ("Hannibal sworn when a child"); *BA*, p. 13; Galt, p. 216; Dillenberger, p. 136 (3)

LIT: Galt 1820, pp. 45–46; Carey 1820, p. 694; Hamilton 1831 (17); Graves 1906, VII, p. 212 (Horace Walpole, 1771); Locquin 1912, pp. 154, 156, note; Irwin 1966, pp. 50, 122, pl. 40; Rosenblum 1967, p. 69, fig. 71; Millar 1969, I, p. 131 (1153), II, pl. 122

No. 17 shows an incident described at the opening of Book XXI of the *Ab Urbe Condita* of Livy. As Hamilcar, the Carthaginian leader, was sacrificing before setting off for a campaign in Spain, his nine-year-old son Hannibal asked to go with him. Hamilcar took the boy to the altar, made him touch the offerings and swear that he would be the declared enemy of Rome. Silius Italicus, who was the probable source for West's companion picture of *Regulus* (No. 10), also tells the story and gives a description of the temple where the sacrifice supposedly took place. The statues in No. 17 may owe something to this account, which mentions statues of Belus, Agenor, Phoenix, and Dido and Sychaeus, but

West instead has included a colossal statue of Jupiter, based partly on the *Belvedere Torso*, seated behind the altar, and figures seemingly based on the *Farnese Hercules* and the *Belvedere Faun* in the two most prominent niches.

George III commissioned No. 17 as a companion to the *Departure of Regulus* (No. 10) following the success of that picture at the Royal Academy in 1769. According to Galt, when West delivered No. 17 to Buckingham House, the King was so pleased that he decided to commission West to paint additional pictures of suitable subjects to fill the remaining panels of the room in which the two paintings had been placed. Although West exhibited No. 10 in 1769, he did not exhibit the *Oath of Hannibal* until 1771, the same year that he exhibited the *Death of General Wolfe* (No. 93), and a replica of the *Death of General Wolfe* (No. 94) was one of the works that George III commissioned to accompany Nos. 10 and 17. The others were Nos. 2, 5, 32 and 77. A letter from West to Charles Willson Peale dated 21 June 1770 (after the opening of that year's Royal Academy exhibition) states that he has been commissioned by George III to paint two more pictures the same size as the *Regulus* and that he is now at work on the *Hannibal*; and a letter from West to Francis Hopkinson dated 20 July 1770, also mentions that he is at work on the *Hannibal*.[1] Both letters refer to No. 17 as his second painting for the King. Contrary to his statement to Peale, West did not paint a third picture the same size for George III, and no further documentation of such a commission has come to light. As No. 17 is signed and dated 1770 West evidently completed it in that year, but after the first version of the *Death of Wolfe* (No. 93), which he had finished by the time he wrote to Peale on 21 June. West also reported to Peale that he had had much sickness since Peale left London (in March 1769), depriving him of more than six months of work. That sickness undoubtedly explains why he did not complete No. 17 in time to exhibit it in 1770, but exhibited as his major work a picture he had completed two years before (No. 13) instead.

No oil sketch for the *Oath of Hannibal* is known or recorded, although the artist probably would have painted one before undertaking such an ambitious work. A drawing showing a substantially different composition is at Swarthmore,[2] and the early catalogues of West's works list one drawing of the subject.[3]

Horace Walpole's comment about the painting in 1771 was: "Very bricky colouring and the Amilcar very ill drawn."

See also p. 55 above.

[1] Both letters are in the Historical Society of Pennsylvania.
[2] Charcoal, $7\frac{1}{4} \times 11\frac{1}{8}$ in.
[3] *PC*, p. 568 ("The Drawing of the Swearing of Hannibal," West, Gallery); *UM*, p. 531; Galt, p. 232; Dillenberger, p. 182 (440).

18 The Continence of Scipio *c.* 1766

FITZWILLIAM MUSEUM, CAMBRIDGE, ENGLAND

Oil on panel: $39\frac{1}{2} \times 52\frac{1}{2}$ in. (100.5 × 133.5 cm.)

PROV: (?) Alexander Geddes; (?) Gerard Vandergucht (died 1778); sold Christie and Ansell, London, 14–15 March 1777, lot 95 (the property of a gentleman deceased, companion to lot 94, "Pylades and Orestes"), bt. by Graves for 105 gns.; John Knight, Portland Place, London; his sale, Phillips, London, 23–24 March 1819, lot 37, bt. by Sir T. Hesketh (probably Sir Thomas Dalrymple Hesketh, [1777–1842] of Rufford Hall, Lancashire); given by Charles Fairfax Murray to the Fitzwilliam Museum in 1908

17

18

EXH: SA 1766 (179) "The Continence of Scipio," with no. 180 "Pylades and Orestes" (No. 186) listed as its companion

LISTED: *PC*, p. 563 ("The Continence of Scipio," Knight, Esq., Portland-place); *UM*, p. 529; Barlow, p. 433; *BA*, p. 15; Galt, p. 223; Dillenberger, p. 160 (215)

LIT: Galt 1820, pp. 16–17; Carey 1820, p. 689; *Annual Register* 1820, p. 1169; Locquin 1912, p. 154; Goodison 1977, pp. 227–28 (655), pl. 21; Alberts 1978, pp. 73–74

No. 18 depicts the young Scipio Africanus virtuously refusing to exercise his rights as a conqueror and not only returning a captive Carthaginian maiden to her parents and fiancé, but also presenting to her fiancé as an addition to her dowry the gold which had been brought for her ransom. Although the story is told by Livy and Valerius Maximus, among others, the subject was so frequently depicted in the eighteenth century that West probably depended more upon pictorial tradition than upon written sources.

Although there is no serious reason to doubt that No. 18 is the *Continence of Scipio* which West exhibited at the Society of Artists in 1766 with *Pylades and Orestes* (No. 186) as its companion, No. 18 is on panel whereas No. 186 is on canvas. Both works are in considerably deteriorated condition, but they are consistent with one another in style, size, and scale of figures. *Pylades and Orestes* became one of West's most celebrated early works, but the *Continence of Scipio* never attracted as much attention. Because the two were sold together in 1777, we can assume that they shared the same history until that date, although the published accounts of the early fortunes of No. 186 in the marketplace do not mention No. 18.

The early lists of West's works include one drawing of the subject.[1] This may be the large drawing showing the same composition as No. 18 in the National Gallery of Scotland, Edinburgh.[2] Another drawing of the subject, which has no compositional similarity to No. 18, but may have some connection with the picture exhibited by West in 1771 (see No. 19) is in the Historical Society of Pennsylvania.[3] Two further drawings, which seem to show the subject, are similar to one another but not to No. 18.[4] Paintings of the *Continence of Scipio* which were sold in 1924 and 1961 as works by West are not by him.[5]

[1]*PC*, p. 569 ("The Drawing of the Continence of Scipio," West, Gallery); *UM*, p. 532; *BA*, p. 19; Galt, p. 234; Dillenberger, p. 185 (476).
[2]Pen, black chalk and brown wash, varnished, $18\frac{1}{8} \times 21\frac{3}{4}$ in.
[3]Pen and wash, $9 \times 7\frac{3}{8}$ in. This may be the drawing in pen and ink, washed with bistre, sold by Benjamin West, Jr., S. Leigh Sotheby, London, 1 June 1839, lot 52.
[4]Pen and pencil, $11\frac{5}{8} \times 17$ in. (Victoria and Albert Museum, London); and pen $3\frac{5}{8} \times 5\frac{1}{16}$ in. (*Exhibition of English Watercolours*, Leger Galleries, London, 1976, no. 72, ill.).
[5]Christie's, London, 28 March 1924, lot 64; and Christie's, London, 15 Dec. 1961, lot 158.

19 The Continence of Scipio c. 1771

EXH: RA 1771 (213) "The continence of Scipio," companion to no. 212 "Hector Taking Leave of Andromache" (for which see Nos. 164 and 179)

Both No. 19 and the "Hector taking leave of Andromache" listed as its companion in 1771 (see No. 164) seem to have disappeared without a trace. Since the early lists of West's works include only one version of each subject by him, it may be that the two pictures exhibited in 1771 were both works that, contrary to the policy of the Academy, he had exhibited previously at the Society of Artists: the *Continence of Scipio* in 1766 (No. 18), and "Hector Taking Leave of Andromache" in 1767, under the title "The Fright of Astyanax" (No. 163). If so, pictures previously exhibited separately, each with another companion (No. 18 with No. 186 *Pylades and Orestes*, and No. 163 with No. 8 *Pyrrhus when a Child, Brought before Glaucias*), must have been sufficiently similar that they could be presented as companions. Another possibility, which seems more likely, is that the two pictures exhibited in 1771 are two pictures now in the New-York Historical Society showing *Chryseis Returned to Her Father Chryses* and *Aeneas and Creusa* (Nos. 160 and 179), which for unknown reasons were exhibited at the Royal Academy under incorrect titles. For discussion of this question, see under Nos. 160 and 179. A drawing in the Historical Society of Pennsylvania, which evidently depicts the *Continence of Scipio* and has been thought to show the composition of the picture exhibited in 1771, also has significant similarities with Nos. 160 and 179 and appears to be a companion drawing to one of *Chryseis Returned to Her Father*.[1]

[1] See No. 18, note 3; and No. 160, note 1.

20

20 The Mother of the Gracchi Displays Her Children as Her Only Jewels 1780

PRIVATE COLLECTION

(?) Tempera on panel: oval, $4\frac{1}{2} \times 5\frac{7}{8}$ in. (11.5 × 15 cm.)

Signed lower left: *B. West 1780*

PROV: By descent in the family of the artist

EXH: RA 1780 (322) "The mother of the Gracchi displays her children as her only jewels; a design for a fan" by B. West, RA and [Anthony] Poggi

ENGR: Stipple engraving ($4\frac{1}{4} \times 5\frac{7}{8}$ in.) by Francesco Bartolozzi, pub. by A. Poggi, 10 Nov. 1783

Anthony (or Antonio di) Poggi, who was listed together with West in the Royal Academy catalogue of 1780, and who published an engraving after No. 20 in 1783, held an exhibition of fan painting in 1781.[1] In 1791, the exhibition of the European Museum included a "Cornelia the mother of the Gracchi, rebuking the vanity of another Roman Matron" (187) by Poggi, "from a design of Mr. West's." The catalogue does not specify that it was a fan. During the 1780s Poggi became active as a publisher of engravings, and he was responsible for the engravings after the first two paintings from the series of subjects from the American Revolution by John Trumbull, to whom he had been introduced by West.[2]

No. 20 appears to have been West's only venture in the field of designing for fans. The story of Cornelia, the virtuous widow who presents her children when asked by a visitor to be shown her jewels, is from Valerius Maximus.

[1] Whitley 1928a, II, pp. 111-12.
[2] Trumbull 1953, p. 91.

21 Marius on the Ruins of Carthage 1796
Illustrated over page

GRAPHISCHE SAMMLUNG ALBERTINA, VIENNA

Pen and ink, wash, and body-color: $18\frac{1}{8} \times 28\frac{3}{8}$ in. (46 × 72 cm.)

Signed bottom center: *Benjⁿ West 1796*

PROV: The Archduke Joseph of Austria (1776–1847) by 1804

LISTED: *PC*, p. 565 ("The Drawing of Marius on the Ruins of Carthage" . . . in the possession of the Archduke Joseph, but included among works in West's Painting-room); *UM*, p. 530; Barlow, p. 434; *BA*, p. 17 (. . . duplicate with Mr. West); Galt, p. 226; Dillenberger, p. 168 (295)

No. 21 and a companion drawing of *Cato Giving His Daughter in Marriage* (No. 25) were listed together as in the collection of the Archduke Joseph in the early lists of West's works. The duplicates in West's possession, recorded in *La Belle Assemblée*, have disappeared.

Caius Marius, the Roman general who had been six times consul, was driven from Rome by Sulla in 88 B.C. Fleeing to Africa, he landed at Carthage, where a servant sent by the Roman governor, Sextilius, immediately gave him an order to leave. To this order, Marius made the famous reply: "Tell the praetor that you have seen Caius Marius a fugitive, seated amid the ruins of Carthage." The story, from Plutarch (*Lives of Pyrrhus and Caius Marius*, XL), was the basis of a sixteenth-century tragedy by William Otway, *The*

History and Fall of Caius Marius, where this scene (act IV, scene 2) takes place in "the Country" rather than Carthage.

At Radburne Hall in Derbyshire there is a large painting of the subject by John Hamilton Mortimer, which Mortimer exhibited along with a drawing of *Caius Marius* at the Society of Artists in 1774, accompanying the former with a quotation from Otway. An engraving by Robert Blyth after Mortimer's drawing was published in 1782. Mortimer also painted a *Belisarius* as a companion to his *Caius Marius*.[1] West drew a Belisarius recalling Mortimer's as early as 1784, and a drawing of *Belisarius Brought to His Family* which is now lost (No. 45) appears on the lists immediately after Nos. 21 and 25. Although the *Belisarius Brought to His Family* did not go to Vienna with Nos. 21 and 25, it may have been drawn as a companion piece as well, in a juxtaposition probably inspired by Mortimer's.

A slighter drawing of *Marius on the Ruins of Carthage*, showing Marius alone and differing considerably in composition from No. 21 but reminiscent in pose of Mortimer's Marius, is in the collection of Richard G. Carrott.[2] West also drew the related subject of the slave sent to murder Marius in prison dropping his sword when confronted by his intended victim (Museum of Fine Arts, Boston).[3]

[1] Exhibited 1772, engraved 1780; both paintings are reproduced by E. K. Waterhouse, *Three Decades of British Art 1740–1770*, Philadelphia, 1965, figs. 19 and 20.
[2] Pen, $6\frac{1}{16} \times 4\frac{13}{16}$ in.
[3] Pen and wash, $8\frac{1}{2} \times 12\frac{11}{16}$ in.; sold by Benjamin West, Jr., S. Leigh Sotheby, London, 1 June 1839, lot 92.

21

22 Cicero Discovering the Tomb of Archimedes
1797
See color illustration, p. 120

PRIVATE COLLECTION

Oil on canvas: 49 × 71 in. (124.5 × 180.5 cm.)

Signed lower right: *Benjn West 1797*

PROV: Henry Hope, Cavendish Square, London (died 1811); possibly in his sale, Christie's, London, 27–29 June 1816 (not included in the catalogue, but in the copy in the Victoria and Albert Museum at the bottom of the page where three pictures by West are listed there is an addition written in pencil: "Mr. West Picture 95/11"); James Wadmore, 1834; Mrs. Robert Frank, London; Ray L. Murphy, New York

EXH: RA 1797 (247) "Cicero, with the magistrates of Syracuse, discovers the Tomb of Archimedes; an historical picture"; SA 1834 (124) lent by Jas. Wadmore

LISTED: *PC*, p. 562 ("Cicero at the Tomb of Archimedes," in the collection of Henry Hope, Esq., first painted for the late Bishop of Bristol); *UM*, p. 528; Barlow, p. 433; Galt, p. 221; Dillenberger, p. 155 (172)

LIT: Farington Diary, 25 June 1796, 6 and 17 January, 6, 9, 25, 27, and 28 April, and 3 June 1797 (Farington 1978–, II, p. 590, and III, pp. 739, 750, 816, 818–19,

827, 828, and 848); V and A Cuttings, III, p. 785 (*True Briton*, 6 May 1797); *Public Characters* 1805, p. 554; Hall 1962, p. 101

The painting is based on a passage in Book v of Cicero's *Tusculan Disputations* written in 45 B.C., in which the author recalls his discovery some thirty years earlier of the grave of the great Syracusan mathematician Archimedes (287–212 B.C.). Although the grave was unknown to the Syracusans, Cicero was able to identify it because he remembered some doggerel lines stating that on top of it were set a sphere and a cylinder. One of the extant treatises by Archimedes is *De Sphaera et Cylindro*. The volcano in the background of No. 22 presumably represents Mount Etna, which is some fifty miles north of Syracuse. According to a review of the Royal Academy exhibition of 1797 in the *True Briton* the subject was suggested to West by Sir George Beaumont, to whom West had presented the oil sketch (No. 24) in 1796. Beaumont may have taken the idea from Pierre-Henri de Valenciennes who presented a painting of the same subject to the French Académie Royale as his *morceau de réception* in 1787 (Musée des Augustins, Toulouse, on loan from the Louvre).

Joseph Farington reported on 25 June 1796 that West had given to Beaumont the sketch, which he had just finished. In 1796 West learned the nostrum of the "Venetian Secret" from Thomas Provis and his daughter, and No. 22 was one of the works upon which he used it. The entries in Farington's diary indicate that

West had Provis prepare a canvas for this painting sometime in the autumn of 1796 (after 31 October), but on 6 January 1797, West still only proposed to paint the picture for that year's exhibition. By 6 April 1797 it was sufficiently far along for the Provises to call on West to see it; West described it then as, "executed in a mixed manner, partly Venetian, partly with body colours." Three days later, on 9 April, Sir George Beaumont had also been to see it, and, according to Farington:

He is delighted with the large Landscape of "Cicero at the Tomb of Archimedes" painted by West— 6 feet by 4.—It is superior He thinks even to the Landscapes of N. Poussin.—For grandeur and variety, and entertainment it is remarkable,—and on the whole the best of West's performances. West works upon it every night, & sometimes till two o'Clock in the morning.

Because of widespread interest in the Venetian Secret, *Cicero Discovering the Tomb of Archimedes* attracted considerable comment. As early as 6 April 1797, West claimed, "Much had been talked of the Picture, but the Artists will be astonished when they see it." At the Royal Academy at the end of the month, Hoppner hated it, Lawrence liked it, and Richard Westall told West, "it appeared *black*." To this West replied, "it was very odd,—it looked bright at home," and he added (in Farington's words) "the process is excellent but is not yet fully understood." In June the engraver Nathaniel Marchant echoed Westall, telling Farington that "Wests Cicero was a *moonlight Landscape* with figures in *Sun*." The lengthy discussion of No. 22 in the *True Briton* also said much the same; "There is a vividness in the drapery of the figures, and a chilling coldness in the whole of the scenery. The first are in open day. The last seems to be in moon-light."

For the Venetian Secret, see also Nos. 133, 543, and 356. Although we might consider the nocturnal effect, which several writers ascribed to No. 22, a possible result of West's work on it at night by artificial light, his other paintings exhibited in 1797 in which he employed the Venetian technique drew similar criticisms. The contrast between figures and setting noted by Marchant and the *True Briton*'s critic may have been the result of the "mixed manner" which West reported he was using.

A replica with numerous slight differences is No. 23 below, and the oil sketch is No. 24. A drawing for the composition with many differences in detail belongs to the Royal Academy.

The lists of West's works include No. 22 among a group of paintings described as "painted for the late Bishop of Bristol," before belonging to Henry Hope. Since the late Bishop of Bristol who patronized West was Dr. Thomas Newton, who died in 1782 (see No. 675), the claim is impossible for No. 22. Henry Hope (for whom see No. 640) settled in England in 1794 and probably bought No. 22 directly from the artist in 1797 or shortly thereafter.

See also pp. 120–1 above.

23 Cicero Discovering the Tomb of Archimedes
1804

YALE UNIVERSITY ART GALLERY, NEW HAVEN

Oil on canvas: $49\frac{1}{2} \times 71\frac{3}{4}$ in. (125.7 × 182.2 cm.)

Signed lower right: *B. West/1804*

PROV: Probably the picture referred to by Farington as "Cicero's Villa" which West tried to sell to John Julius Angerstein in September 1804; offered by West to the Pennsylvania Academy of the Fine Arts in 1809 ("Cicero and the Magistrates of Coracuse at the Tomb of Archimedes," 6 ft. × 4 ft. 2 in., £350); offered by his sons to the United States in 1826 (12) and sold by them, Robins, London, 22–25 May 1829, lot 35 ("Cicero Discovering the Tomb of Archimedes," 4 ft. 1 in. × 6 ft.), bt. by H. P. Bone for £315, on behalf of Joseph Neeld, MP, Grittleton House, Wilts.; by descent in the Neeld family until sold by Miss C. K. M. Neeld, Christie's, London, 16 Nov. 1962, lot 96, bt. by Weitzner; Mrs. M. H. Drey, London; bt. by the Yale University Art Gallery in 1963 (John Hill Morgan Fund 1963.49)

EXH: RA 1804 (72) "Cicero and the Magistrates of Syracuse Ordering the Tomb of Archimedes to be freed from the bushes that had obscured it"; BI 1806 (22 North Room); West's Gallery 1822–28 (61); BI 1833 (31) lent by Joseph Neeld

LISTED: *PC*, p. 565 ("The second picture of Cicero at the Tomb of Archimedes," West, Painting-room); *UM*, p. 530; Barlow, p. 434; *BA*, p. 17; Galt, p. 227; Dillenberger, p. 171 (321)

LIT: Farington Diary, 6 Sept. 1804 (Farington 1978—, VI, p. 2405); *Yale University Art Gallery Bulletin*, XXX, 1964, p. 23

No. 23 is a replica of No. 22, corresponding to it in size and in composition. There are, nevertheless, many differences in detail, of which the most conspicuous are thicker foliage, partly concealing the tomb, on the right, and the addition of a column with an urn upon it, breaking the horizon at the point where the silhouette of the background volcano meets the rocky hillside, on the left of the painting. There are also several more background figures, chiefly near the left edge of the composition, possibly added by the artist in response to a criticism of No. 22 by the *True Briton* in 1797 that he had not included enough of the "common file."

23

24 Cicero Discovering the Tomb of Archimedes
c. 1796

LOCATION UNKNOWN

PROV: Presented by West to Sir George Beaumont in
June 1796

LISTED: *PC*, p. 563 ("The original Sketch of Cicero at
the Tomb of Archimedes" for Sir George
Beaumont); *UM*, p. 529; *BA*, p. 15; Galt, p. 223;
Dillenberger, p. 159 (208)

LIT: Farington Diary, 25 June 1796 (Farington
1978—, II, p. 590)

See No. 22.

**25 Cato Giving His Daughter in Marriage at His
Death** 1797

GRAPHISCHE SAMMLUNG ALBERTINA, VIENNA

Pen and ink, wash, and body-color: $18\frac{3}{16} \times 28\frac{3}{4}$ in.
$(46 \times 73$ cm.)

Signed bottom left: *Benjⁿ West 1797*

PROV: Archduke Joseph of Austria (1776–1847) by
1804

LISTED: *PC*, p. 565 ("The Drawing of Cato giving his
Daughter in Marriage on his Death . . ." in the possession of the Archduke Joseph, but included among

the works in West's Painting-room); *UM*, p. 530;
BA, p. 17 (. . . duplicate with Mr. West); Galt,
p. 226; Dillenberger, p. 168 (296)

Marcus Porcius Cato (known as Cato the Younger or
Cato of Utica) was a republican who, rather than flee
from or surrender to Caesar, took his own life in 46 B.C.,
while besieged in Utica on the African coast near Carthage. No. 25 is based on Joseph Addison's tragedy
Cato, first performed in 1713, and shows the closing
scene, when Cato, who has already stabbed himself,
gives his daughter Marcia in marriage to the Numidian
prince Juba, an incident that does not take place in
Plutarch's life of Cato. (The historical Marcia became
the wife of Caesar's assassin Brutus.) The other figures
are Cato's son Portius, Lucius, a Roman senator, and
Lucia, Lucius's daughter, whom Cato has just decreed
should marry Portius. On a table to the left are Cato's
sword and a copy of Plato's *Phaedo*, which Cato read
prior to taking his life. In the background are the ships
in which, at Cato's orders, his followers are escaping
Caesar's approaching troops.

No. 25 was clearly intended as a companion to
Marius on the Ruins of Carthage (No. 21), which West had
drawn in the previous year. See also *Belisarius Brought
to His Family* (No. 45).

Benjamin West, Jr. sold a drawing of *Cato* in 1839.[1]
This drawing may have been the duplicate of No. 25,
listed in *La Belle Assemblée* as belonging to West.

[1]S. Leigh Sotheby, 1 June 1839, lot 51, outline in pen and
ink, washed with bistre.

**26 Caesar Reading the History of Alexander's
Exploits** *c.* 1771

VIRGINIA MUSEUM OF FINE ARTS, RICHMOND,
VIRGINIA

Oil on canvas: $37 \times 39\frac{1}{2}$ in. $(94 \times 100.5$ cm.)

Signed lower left: *B. West/pinxit/17[??]*

PROV: Painted for Giles Stibbert (died 1809); probably
in West's possession again by 1811; sold by his sons,
Robins, London, 22–25 May 1829, lot 1 ("Julius
Caesar's Regret on Reading the Life of Alexander,"
3 ft. 2 in. × 3 ft. 5 in.), bt. by Hopkinson for £27.6.0.;
Mortimer Brandt, New York, from whom purchased
by the Virginia Museum in 1964

EXH: RA 1819 (337) "Caesar reading the History of
Alexander's exploits"; West's Gallery 1822–28 (79)
"Julius Caesar's Regret on reading the Life of
Alexander"

ENGR: Outline engraving $(7\frac{1}{16} \times 8$ in.) by Henry
Moses, pub. 2 Dec. 1811 by Moses as pl. VIII of Moses
1811

LISTED: *PC*, 1805, p. 563 ("Julius Caesar reading the
Life of Alexander," for General Stibert); *UM*,
p. 529; Barlow, p. 433; *BA*, p. 15; Galt, p. 222; Dillenberger, p. 159 (212)

LIT: Moses 1811 (VIII)

No. 26 is a companion to *Alexander's Confidence in His
Physician Philip* (No. 7). It shows Caesar at the age of

25

26

intended companion to the "Mark Anthony" sold by West's sons in 1829 must be the same painting, since many of the works offered by West to the Academy in 1809 had not been finished, or in some cases even begun. West exhibited No. 28 in 1775, and he may have begun No. 27 around then. Two drawings of men in togas holding daggers, which West may have made in connection with No. 27, are at Swarthmore and appear to date from relatively early in his career.[1]

The indication in Joel Barlow's catalogue of West's works that a painting of the *Death of Caesar* had left West's possession is confirmed by no other source. Other early lists include a drawing of the subject, but no painting.[2]

No. 27 may have been the *Death of Caesar* by West which John Sellers tried to sell to John Sartain in 1877 for $750 (with no mention of its being unfinished),[3] but we should note that a painting of the subject appeared at the Pennsylvania Academy in 1813 catalogued as a copy after West by Jeremiah Paul. A painting of the *Murder of Caesar* sold at Christie's in 1963 as by West is not by him and appears from a photograph to be French rather than English.[4]

[1]Both pen and wash, $16\frac{1}{4} \times 9\frac{3}{4}$ in.
[2]*PC*, p. 568 ("The Drawing of the Death of Caesar," West, Gallery); *UM*, p. 531; Galt, p. 232; Dillenberger, p. 182 (439).
[3]Letter in the archives of the Pennsylvania Academy of the Fine Arts, dated 9 May 1877.
[4]Christie's, London, 29 March 1963, lot 106.

28 Mark Antony Showing the Robe and the Will of Julius Caesar to the People of Rome

LOCATION UNKNOWN

(72×111 in.) (183×282 cm.)

PROV: Offered by West to the Pennsylvania Academy of the Fine Arts in 1809 (9 ft. 6 in. × 6 ft. 6 in., £450); offered by his sons to the United States in 1826 (3), and sold by them, Robins, London, 22–25 May 1829, lot 42 (6 ft. × 9 ft. 3 in.), bt. by W. Ward for £283.10.0., apparently on behalf of Raphael West; sold by Raphael West, Robins, London, 16 July 1831, lot 38

EXH: RA 1775 (332) "Mark Anthony showing the robe and the will of Julius Caesar to the people of Rome"; BI 1816 (187); West's Gallery 1822–28 (83)

ENGR: Mezzotint ($24\frac{3}{4} \times 34\frac{13}{16}$ in.) by Valentine Green, pub. by J. Boydell, 17 Sept. 1781; mezzotint ($23\frac{3}{4} \times 35$ in.) by John Murphy, pub. by John and Josiah Boydell, 1 March 1787; aquatint ($18 \times 24\frac{7}{8}$ in.) by Jazet, pub. by Ostervald *l'aîné*, Paris

LISTED: *PC*, p. 565 ("Mark Antony shewing the Robe and Will of Julius Caesar to the People," West, Painting-room); *UM*, p. 530; Barlow, p. 434; *BA*, p. 17; Galt, p. 227; Dillenberger, p. 170 (308)

LIT: V and A Cuttings, I, p. 117 (*Public Advertiser*, 1775) and IV, p. 1011 (1816)

Although No. 28 has been lost since 1831, its appearance is known from engravings and from a copy made by Jacob Eicholtz (1776–1842), now at Franklin and Marshall College. It attracted a long and glowing review in the *Public Advertiser* when exhibited in 1775, and, when re-exhibited in 1816, a less enthusiastic one in an unidentified journal, which cited it as an example of the failure of the British in painting elevated subjects.

thirty-three, while on campaign in Spain in 67 B.C. He is reading the life of Alexander, who had died at thirty-three, and commenting (in the words of Plutarch), "Do you not think it is a matter for sorrow that while Alexander, at my age, was already King of so many peoples, I have as yet achieved no brilliant success?"[1] West evidently based No. 26 on Plutarch's *Life of Caesar*, in which Caesar reads about Alexander; in Suetonius' account of the incident, his regret is inspired by the sight of a statue of Alexander. The text by Robert Hunt, which accompanied Henry Moses's engraving after No. 26 describes the subject as an execrable "desire of celebrity" and Caesar as an odious monster, whose baldness even is seen as the result of his "licentious excesses." Whether West intended No. 26 to convey such condemnation is questionable. It seems likely that the subjects of No. 26 and its companion, No. 7, were chosen by West's patron, who was himself a military officer and was probably sympathetic to Caesar's ambitions.

No. 26 is signed and dated but the date is no longer legible. The Robins sale catalogue states that it was painted in 1771. Its companion, No. 7, must have been painted by 1771 as well, since an engraving after it was published on 1 January 1772. Both pictures shared the same early history until West sold No. 7 in 1819. Like No. 7, No. 26 appears to have been cut down at some time, but at a date later than the former since the Moses engraving of 1811 shows a composition which extends further on each side than the present painting. There are also numerous differences in detail between No. 26

and the engraving, which should probably be explained as liberties taken by Moses. It is also possible that West worked on the painting after it was engraved in 1811, but, unlike No. 7, No. 26 does not show obvious signs of late repainting.

[1]Plutarch, *Life of Caesar*, XI (trans. by Bernadotte Perrin; Loeb Classical Library, VII, p. 469).

27 The Death of Caesar (?)*c.* 1775

LOCATION UNKNOWN

(78×114 in.) (198×289.5 cm.)

PROV: Offered by West to the Pennsylvania Academy of the Fine Arts in 1809 ("The Death of Caesar," 9 ft. 6 in. × 6 ft. 6 in., £450); sold by his sons, Robins, London, 20–22 June 1829, lot 111 ("The Death of Caesar, intended as a companion to the celebrated Picture of Mark Antony . . . not finished"); (?) John Sellers, New York, 1877

LISTED: Barlow, p. 433 ("Death of Caesar," under "In Various Collections"); Dillenberger, p. 164 (257)

This painting immediately precedes *Mark Antony Showing the Will and Robe of Caesar* (No. 28) on the list of works West wanted to sell to the Pennsylvania Academy in 1809 and is listed with the same dimensions, which were shared by no other works on that list. The unfinished

The early lists include one drawing of the subject.[1] West began the *Death of Caesar* (No. 27) as a companion.

[1] *PC*, p. 568 ("The Drawing of Mark Antony shewing the Robe and Will of Caesar," West, Gallery); *UM*, p. 530; *BA*, p. 19; Galt, p. 232; Dillenberger, p. 182 (433).

29 Agrippina with Her Children Going through the Roman Camp 1785

PRIVATE COLLECTION

Pen and ink, wash, and body-color: $16\frac{1}{2} \times 23$ in. (42×58.5 cm.)

Signed lower right: *B. West 1785*

PROV: Traditionally said to have been given by West to Charles Willson Peale; Sophonisba Peale Sellers and then by descent to the late Charles Coleman Sellers

LIT: Kraemer 1975, p. 19; Lillian B. Miller, "Charles Willson Peale as History Painter: *The Exhumation of the Mastodon,*" *American Art Journal*, XIII, 1981, pp. 48, 49, fig. 2

No. 29 is the first in narrative sequence but the last in order of date of execution of several works by West based on the *Annals* of Tacitus (Books I–III) and devoted to Germanicus Caesar (15 B.C.–A.D. 19), the nephew and adopted son of the Emperor Tiberius, and his wife Agrippina, the daughter of Agrippa and grand-daughter of Augustus. With her children, Agrippina accompanied Germanicus on campaign in Germany, but when a mutiny broke out among the Roman troops, she was forced to flee to the Gallic tribe of the Treviri for protection. No. 29 shows Agrippina, carrying her infant son Caligula and pregnant with another child, at the head of a procession of women and children leaving the Roman camp, while the troops, moved by the sight, implore her to stay, and eventually abandon their revolt.

A tradition in the Sellers family that West gave this work to Charles Willson Peale (for whom see No. 680) in return for uniforms and other historical material pro-

Mark Antony Showing the Robe and the Will of Julius Caesar to the People of Rome, mezzotint by Valentine Green, after No. 28

vided to West by Peale would suggest that West sent the drawing to America soon after he made it, since the uniforms in question were presumably those requested from Peale by West in 1783.[1] Another drawing of the subject went through auction in London in 1790 (No. 30) and a further version is recorded in the early lists of West's works (No. 31). That work was described as a sketch in oil on paper, and hence cannot be identified with a drawing the same size as No. 29 and virtually identical in all details which was formerly in the collection of Mrs. F. Howard, a descendant of the artist.[2] A vertical drawing of the subject with a dif-

ferent composition, showing Agrippina in profile, belongs to the Historical Society of Pennsylvania,[3] and a slighter drawing, showing her in profile but in a horizontal composition, is in the Pierpont Morgan Library.[4]

[1] See Marks 1974, pp. 15–16.
[2] Pen, $16\frac{5}{8} \times 22\frac{3}{4}$ in., and signed identically. This drawing may have been partly traced from No. 29, or vice versa.
[3] Pen, $12\frac{7}{16} \times 9$ in. (ill. Kraemer 1975, p. 19, fig. 15).
[4] Black chalk, $4\frac{13}{16} \times 7$ in. (Kraemer 1975, p. 19, no. 25 and pl. 16).

30 Agrippina in the Roman Camp

LOCATION UNKNOWN

PROV: Sold anonymously, Greenwood, London, 22 April 1790, lot 110 ("Agrippina attended, passing the mutinous army of Germanicus, drawing, very capital [not engraved]")

31 Agrippina in the Roman Camp

LOCATION UNKNOWN

PROV: In West's possession in 1804

LISTED: *PC*, p. 568 ("The Sketch, in oil, on paper, of the Procession of Agrippina with her Children and the Roman Ladies through the Roman Camp, when in Mutiny," West, Gallery); *UM*, p. 532; *BA*, p. 19; Galt, p. 233; Dillenberger, p. 184 (464)

32 Segestes and His Daughter before Germanicus 1773

HER MAJESTY THE QUEEN

Oil on canvas: $41 \times 53\frac{3}{4}$ in. (104.1×136.5 cm.)

Signed lower left: *B. West./1773*

PROV: Painted for George III (1801 account, p. 207: 7, "Germanicus receiving Sagastis and his Daughter prisoners," 1772, £157.10.0.)

29

EXH: BI 1833 (26 or 32) both catalogued as "A Subject from the History of Cyrus," lent by William IV; *American Painting from the Eighteenth Century to the Present Day*, Tate Gallery, London, 1946 (239); *English Taste in the Eighteenth Century*, Royal Academy, London, 1955–56 (395); *Il Settecento a Roma*, l'Associazone Amici dei Musei di Roma e l'Istituto di Studi Romani, Rome, 1959 (663)

LISTED: *PC*, p. 559 ("Germanicus and Segestus with his daughter, captives," George III, Queen's House); *UM*, p. 527; *AA*, p. 67 ("Segestus and his Daughter [the wife of Arminius] before Germanicus," 5 ft. by 7); Barlow, p. 431; *BA*, p. 13; Galt, p. 216; Dillenberger, p. 137 (8)

LIT: Galt 1820, pp. 50–51; Millar 1969, I, pp. 131–32 (1155), II, pl. 120

In his German campaign, subsequent to the mutiny of his own troops depicted in No. 29, Germanicus intervened in a conflict between two German chieftains, Arminius, a foe of the Romans, and Segestes, a friend. In rescuing Segestes from his enemies, Germanicus also captured a numerous band of kinsfolk and dependants, including Segestes' pregnant daughter, the wife of Arminius. No. 32 shows Germanicus enthroned on the left; Segestes addressing him; Segestes' son, Segimundus, who had gone over to the enemy, looking over his father's shoulder while Segestes asks for his forgiveness; and Segestes' daughter, who remains defiant, but for whom Segestes also pleads:

> As for my daughter, I admit that it is by compulsion she has been brought here. It will be for you to consider which fact weighs most with you, that she is with child by Arminius or that she owes her being to me.[1]

Germanicus replies by promising safety for Segestes' kinsfolk. The subject comes from the *Annals* of Tacitus, but Oliver Millar has pointed out the scene is described in greater detail in the *Geography* of Strabo (Book VII, I, 4), which West may have consulted as well.

See No. 2, to which No. 32 is a companion. West painted both works for George III and, according to Galt, the King was much pleased with the subject of the latter because of a belief that the Hanoverian family was descended from the daughter of Segestes.

A drawing for this painting, showing a vertical composition rather than horizontal but otherwise similar in main details is in the Historical Society of Pennsylvania.[2] Other drawings that show, or seem to show the same subject, but with considerably different compositions, belong to the Royal Academy[3] and Swarthmore College.[4] Benjamin West, Jr. and Mrs. Albert F. West sold drawings of the subject in 1839[5] and 1898[6] respectively.

[1] Tacitus, *Annals*, I, 58 (trans. by Alfred John Church and William Jackson Brodribb, New York, 1942, p. 39).
[2] Pen and wash, $7\frac{1}{2} \times 6\frac{1}{2}$ in.
[3] Pencil, $7\frac{7}{8} \times 6\frac{7}{8}$ in.
[4] Three drawings: pen, $6 \times 12\frac{3}{8}$ in.; pen, $5\frac{3}{4} \times 8\frac{1}{8}$ in.; and pen and wash, 17×19 in.
[5] S. Leigh Sotheby, London, 1 June 1839, lot 118 ("Sejestes and his Daughter before Germanicus," pen and bistre, and colored in oil; framed and glazed).
[6] Christie's, London, 18 March 1898, lot 120 ("Segestes and His Daughter before Germanicus," sepia).

33 Agrippina Landing at Brundisium with the Ashes of Germanicus 1768

See color illustrations, pp. 46, 154

YALE UNIVERSITY ART GALLERY, NEW HAVEN

Oil on canvas: $64\frac{1}{2} \times 94\frac{1}{2}$ in. (164 × 240 cm.)

Signed lower center: *B. West PINXIT. 1768*

32

PROV: Commissioned by Robert Hay Drummond (1711–1776), Archbishop of York; his son, Robert Auriol Hay-Drummond, tenth Earl of Kinnoull (died 1804); (?) sold by W. Keith Rous, Christie's, London, 29 June 1934, lot 65 (64 × 94 in., with provenance listed as "presented by the Nabob of Arcot to Sir Edward Hughes"), bt. by Morris; purchased from E. and A. Silberman Galleries, New York, and presented to the Yale University Art Gallery in 1947 by Louis M. Rabinowitz

EXH: SA 1768 (175) "Agrippina Lands at Brundisium, with the Ashes of Germanicus"; SA 1768 (special exhibition in honor of the King of Denmark) (120); *European and American Masterpieces*, High Museum of Art, Atlanta, 1947 (1); *The Colonial Americas*, Columbus Gallery of Fine Arts, 1947 (23); *Neo-Classicism: Style and Motif*, Cleveland Museum of Art, 1964 (76); *American Art 1750–1800: Towards Independence*, Yale University Art Gallery, New Haven, and Victoria and Albert Museum, London, 1976 (19)

ENGR: Mezzotint ($19\frac{5}{8} \times 28\frac{1}{16}$ in.) by Richard Earlom, pub. by John Boydell, 1 July 1776, as from the picture in the collection of the Archbishop of York

LISTED: *PC*, p. 564 ("Agrippina landing at Brundisium" [the first picture]—painted for Drummond, Archbishop of York, in the possession of Lord Kinnoul); *UM*, p. 529; Barlow, p. 434; *BA*, p. 16; Galt, p. 225; Dillenberger, p. 164 (249)

LIT: *Public Characters* 1805, pp. 533, 551; Galt 1820, pp. 11–13, 21–26; Carey 1820, p. 690; Locquin 1912, pp. 154, 156, pl. XVI; Gatty 1938–39, p. 81 (Horace Walpole, 1768); Flexner 1939, pp. 57–61; James Thomas Flexner, "The American School in London," *Metropolitan Museum of Art Bulletin*, VII, 1948, pp. 64–67; Flexner 1952, pp. 32–33; Evans 1959, pp. 5 et passim, pl. I; Allen Staley, "The Landing of Agrippina at Brundisium with the Ashes of Germanicus," *Philadelphia Museum of Art Bulletin*,

LXI, 1965–66, pp. 10–19; Irwin 1966, pp. 50, 80, pl. 38; Rosenblum 1967, pp. 42–43; Cummings 1968, pp. 98–99; Kraemer 1975, p. 5; Alberts 1978, pp. 84–89

No. 33 shows the widowed Agrippina bearing back to Rome the cremated remains of her husband Germanicus, who died under mysterious circumstances in Syria in A.D. 19. According to Tacitus (*Annals*, III, 1–2), it was widely believed that Germanicus had been poisoned by the governor of Syria, Gnaeus Piso, with the approval of the Emperor Tiberius, the uncle of Germanicus who feared him as a potential rival. When Agrippina disembarked at Brundisium (the modern Brindisi) at the end of her voyage she was met by large crowds of sympathizers. In this painting she is shown accompanied by her two young children, Caligula, the future emperor, and Agrippina the younger, who was to be the mother of the Emperor Nero.

William Carey states that Dr. Drummond, the Archbishop of York, commissioned No. 33 after seeing and admiring *Pyrrhus when a Child, Brought before Glaucias* (No. 8), exhibited at the Society of Artists in 1767. According to Galt's fuller account, the commission originated during a conversation about enlightened patronage of the arts while West was dining with the Archbishop. The Archbishop sent one of his sons (for whom see Nos. 608–11) to the library for the appropriate volume of Tacitus, then read the passage and "commented on it at some length in order to convey to Mr. West an idea of the manner in which he was desirous the subject should be treated." Upon returning home, West immediately composed and painted a sketch of the subject, probably No. 36. He showed it to the Archbishop the next day, whereupon the prelate requested him to proceed without delay in the execution of the picture. West told Carey in 1818 that this had been the first commission for a historical picture that he received in England. The painting was completed by February 1768, when Archbishop Drummond arranged to have West invited to take it to show to King

George III. The King admired it and commissioned the artist to paint the *Departure of Regulus from Rome* (No. 10), thus beginning the royal patronage that was to sustain West through much of his career. According to Horace Walpole, the price the Archbishop paid for No. 33 was £300. Walpole's full comment, made when he saw No. 33 at the Society of Artists in 1768, was, "not very fine, but the Archbp of York gave 300£ for it!" West also exhibited a double portrait of the Archbishop's two eldest sons (No. 608) in the same exhibition.

No. 33 was evidently in the possession of Archbishop Drummond's eldest son, the tenth Earl of Kinnoull, when the list of West's works published in *Public Characters of 1805* was drawn up, but the subsequent history of the work between 1804 and 1947 is opaque. We have tentatively included a sale in 1934, and further indication of the painting's history from the 1934 catalogue, in the provenance above, but it is possible that the painting sold then was a replica, No. 35, rather than No. 33. We can, however, identify No. 33 as the picture painted for Archbishop Drummond because of the date of 1768 on the canvas[1] and the correspondence in all details to the mezzotint by Richard Earlom, which bears a legend identifying its source as the Archbishop's painting.

The arcaded structure in the background is based on a reconstruction in Robert Adam's *Ruins of the Palace of the Emperor Diocletian at Spalatro*, published in 1764 (ill. p. 47), to which Archbishop Drummond had been a subscriber. A copy of this book was included in a sale of works from West's collection in 1820, but it is impossible to know if he owned it as early as 1768. The main group of figures is based loosely upon the frieze from the *Ara Pacis Augustae*, and drawings after the *Ara Pacis* by West are in the Philadelphia Museum of Art (ill. p. 47) and in the Pierpont Morgan Library.[2] A drawing of Agrippina and her two children is at Swarthmore.[3] A faint drawing of a hooded woman with two companions in the Philadelphia Museum has also been associated with No. 33, but, as Jerry Meyer has pointed out, is more closely related to the *Three Marys at the Sepulchre* (No. 367) of 1782–83.

The late Theodore Siegl of the Philadelphia Museum, who cleaned and relined No. 33 in 1975, dis-

covered a half inch of painted canvas, which had been tucked over the top of the stretcher, and further indications along the bottom of the picture to suggest that the painting had been restretched at some time so as to increase slightly the area of foreground along the bottom, while concealing a corresponding area along the top. Mr. Siegl found analogous adjustments to the visible size of No. 34, the replica of No. 33 belonging to the Philadelphia Museum, and he concluded that the changes in both cases were probably due to West himself, made possibly in 1770 at the time West completed No. 34. In No. 33 the change allows us to see the foot of the boatman in the lower right, which initially must have been partially hidden by the frame.

See also pp. 42–50 above.

[1] According to a conservation report by Theodore Siegl, dated 31 July 1975, the signature is worn and had at some time been reinforced, but it appears nonetheless genuine.
[2] Black chalk heightened with white, $8 \times 10\frac{1}{2}$ in. (Kraemer 1975, p. 5, no. 2, and pl. 2).
[3] Pen, $7 \times 5\frac{1}{8}$ in. Helmut von Erffa questioned whether this drawing is in West's hand.

34 Agrippina Landing at Brundisium with the Ashes of Germanicus 1770

PHILADELPHIA MUSEUM OF ART

Oil on canvas: 65×94 in. (165×239 cm.)

Signed lower center: *B. West. PINXIT./1770*

PROV: Painted for the ninth Earl of Exeter, Burghley House, Lincolnshire; at Burghley House until 1972 when purchased by the Philadelphia Museum of Art

LISTED: *PC*, p. 564 ("Agrippina landing at Brundisium," for the Earl of Exeter at Burleigh [second picture]); *UM*, p. 529; Barlow, p. 434; *BA*, p. 16; Galt, p. 225; Dillenberger, p. 164 (250)

LIT: Waagen 1854, III, p. 407; Rosenblum 1967, pp. 42–43, pl. 39

No. 34 is a full-size replica of No. 33. The most notable differences between the two are that in the former Agrippina's head is partly uncovered, and Caligula has

a fillet around his head. The urns which Agrippina carries are also of somewhat different designs, and she holds the one in No. 34 in a more upright position.

Theodore Siegl noted comparable adjustments to the visible areas of Nos. 33 and 34, evidently made in both cases by West himself, but through different means. The lowest half inch of No. 34 is painted on a strip of wood which has been tacked to the edge of the stretcher, and at the top, the rabbet of the frame, which is the original one, has been gouged out to an exceptionally deep $1\frac{1}{4}$ in., thus concealing an area of painted canvas corresponding to that folded over the top of No. 33.

35 Agrippina Landing at Brundisium with the Ashes of Germanicus

LOCATION UNKNOWN

PROV: Painted for a Mr. Joyce; (?) Gerard Vandergucht (died 1776); sold, Christie and Ansell, London, 14–15 March 1777, lot 96 (the property of a gentleman deceased), bt. by Pierce for 110 gns.; Hatch, Esq., Essex

LISTED: *PC*, p. 564 ("Agrippina landing at Brundisium," for Mr. Joyce, [third picture] now in the possession of Hatch, Esq. in Essex); *UM*, p. 529; Barlow, p. 434; *BA*, p. 16; Galt, p. 225; Dillenberger, p. 164 (251)

Nothing is known of this version other than its appearance on the early lists of West's works, and in a sale in 1777. It is also possible that the *Agrippina* sold in 1934 (see the provenance under No. 33) was No. 35 rather than No. 33. Since No. 35 was explicitly described as the third version of the subject on the lists, West probably painted it after No. 34, the second version, which is dated 1770.

36 Agrippina Landing at Brundisium with the Ashes of Germanicus (?)c. 1767

PHILADELPHIA MUSEUM OF ART

Oil on paper mounted on canvas: $13\frac{3}{8} \times 18\frac{7}{8}$ in. (34×48 cm.)

Inscribed bottom left: *B. West/1766*

PROV: (?) Sold by West's sons, Robins, London, 20–22 June 1829, lot 101 ("Agrippina mourning over the Ashes of Germanicus, a sketch"); sold anonymously, Christie's, London, 19 July 1963, lot 121 (as "A Roman Funeral"), bt. by Jones; given by Robert L. McNeil, Jr., Trusts to the Philadelphia Museum of Art in 1965

EXH: *Romantic Art in Britain: Paintings and Drawings 1760–1860*, Detroit Institute of Arts and Philadelphia Museum of Art, 1968 (49)

LISTED: *PC*, p. 568 ("The sketch, in oil, of the Landing of Agrippina, on paper," West, Gallery); *UM*, p. 534; *BA*, p. 19; Galt, p. 232; Dillenberger, p. 182 (443)

LIT: Galt 1820, pp. 12–13; Allen Staley, "The Landing of Agrippina at Brundisium with the Ashes of Germanicus," *Philadelphia Museum of Art Bulletin*, LXI, 1965–66, pp. 10–19; Cummings 1968, pp. 98–99

No. 36 is probably the first sketch for No. 33, which John Galt describes West painting immediately after receiving the commission from Archbishop Drummond, and which the artist supposedly showed to his patron on the following day. If Galt's and Carey's accounts of the genesis of No. 33 are to be believed, this would have occurred in 1767, after the Archbishop had visited that year's exhibition of the Society of Artists.

34

36

For the subject of this painting, see No. 33. No. 37 does not illustrate a specific passage from Tacitus, and in painting a more generalized picture of Agrippina as a devoted widow West may have been imitating the example of Gavin Hamilton, who exhibited an *Agrippina Weeping over the Ashes of Germanicus* at the Royal Academy in 1770 (location unknown), as well as an *Agrippina Landing at Brundisium, with the Ashes of Germanicus* in 1772 (Tate Gallery, London). The urn upon which Agrippina rests her head in No. 37 is inscribed, *OSSA/GERMANICI/C. AUG.* The semi-nude youth at her feet must represent the future Emperor Caligula.

Horace Walpole's comment about No. 37 in 1773 was "Her head fine" (he had dismissed Gavin Hamilton's painting of the subject in 1770 as "Bad").

The "Vesey, Esq. in Ireland" in the catalogues of West's *oeuvre*, who was described as "A. Vesey" on the mezzotint by Valentine Green, also owned *Cupid Stung by a Bee* (No. 131) of 1774. He was evidently Agmondisham Vesey, who rebuilt his house, Lucan, near Dublin, in the Grecian taste at about the time he patronized West. Agmondisham Vesey was the husband of the famous "blue-stocking" Elizabeth Vesey, and both were related to Thomas Vesey, the first Viscount de Vesci, whose portrait with *his* wife West painted in 1776 (No. 708).

A drawing dated *1771* in the Historical Society of Pennsylvania shows the basic composition of No. 37 but with significant differences in details; it includes only two children, and Caligula is a baby who sprawls on

A date of 1767, although consistent with the appearance of the finished No. 33 at the following year's exhibition, contradicts the date of *1766* on the lower left of No. 36 itself. That date, however, and the accompanying signature do not appear to be in West's hand, and they may well have been added to the sketch long after it was painted.

The composition of No. 33 follows that of No. 36 closely, but there are numerous differences in detail. Most prominent are the different position of the boatman in the lower right, the addition of masts and riggings in the area above him, and the addition of a large number of lamenting spectators in the background. This last change is in accordance with Tacitus' description of crowds of mourners filling the city walls and roofs of Brundisium.

37 Agrippina, Surrounded by Her Children, Weeping over the Ashes of Germanicus *c.* 1773

JOHN AND MABLE RINGLING MUSEUM OF ART, SARASOTA, FLORIDA

Oil on canvas: $80 \times 56\frac{1}{2}$ in. (203 × 143.5 cm.)

PROV: Agmondisham Vesey (died 1785), Lucan, County Dublin, Ireland, by 1774

EXH: RA 1773 (303) "Agrippina, surrounded by her children, weeping over the ashes of Germanicus"

ENGR: Mezzotint ($23\frac{7}{8} \times 17$ in.) by Valentine Green, pub. by J. Boydell, 25 July 1774, as from the picture in the possession of A. Vesey, Esq., painted in 1773

LISTED: *PC*, p. 563 ("Agrippina surrounded by her Children, and reclining her head on the Urn containing the Ashes of Germanicus," Vesey, Esq. in Ireland); *UM*, p. 529; Barlow, p. 434 ("Agrippina leaning on the urn of Germanicus"); *BA*, pp. 15–16; Galt, p. 223; Dillenberger, p. 160 (221)

LIT: Graves 1906, VIII, p. 213 (Horace Walpole, 1773); Wilhelm E. Suida, *A Catalogue of Paintings in the John and Mable Ringling Museum of Art*, Sarasota, 1949, p. 331 (403); Evans 1959, p. 44 and pl. 25

37

his mother's lap instead of a boy who stands at her feet.[1] A drawing in the Museum of Fine Arts, Boston, showing a seated woman holding an urn on her lap may also represent Agrippina, but has no visible relation to No. 37.[2] West's sons and descendants sold drawings of Agrippina and her children in 1839[3] and 1898[4] and an oil sketch of *Agrippina Mourning over the Ashes of Germanicus* in 1829.[5] An oil sketch for No. 37 is not otherwise known or recorded, and we have, therefore, tentatively equated that sketch with No. 36 rather than No. 37.

[1]Black and white chalk, $12\frac{5}{8} \times 9\frac{3}{4}$ in., ill. in Evans 1959, pl. 24.
[2]Black and white chalk, $11\frac{7}{8} \times 8\frac{3}{8}$ in.
[3]S. Leigh Sotheby, London, 1 June 1839, lot 71.
[4]Christie's, London, 18 March 1898, lot 104.
[5]Robins, London, 20–22 June 1829, lot 101.

38 Paetus and Arria 1766

See color illustration, p. 39

YALE CENTER FOR BRITISH ART, NEW HAVEN, PAUL MELLON COLLECTION

Oil on canvas: 36×28 in. (91.5 × 71 cm.)

Signed lower left: *B. West 1766*

PROV: Colonel Matthew Smith (1739–1812), the Tower, London; his sale, Christie's, London, 1 May 1812, lot 51; George Silvertop (1775–1849), Minsteracres Hall, Northumberland, by July 1812;[1] at Minsteracres until sold, Anderson and Garland, Newcastle-upon-Tyne, 22 Jan. 1957, lot 33, where bt. by Professor Lawrence Gowing; Mr. and Mrs. Paul Mellon

LISTED: *PC*, p. 564 ("Paetus and Arria," Col. Smith— at the Tower); *UM*, p. 529; Barlow, p. 434; *BA*, p. 16; Galt, p. 224; Dillenberger, p. 163 (240)

The engraving after a later version of the subject (No. 39) bears the following explanatory text:

Paetus, a Noble Roman, being, upon a false accusation, doomed to death by the Emperor Claudius was gratified with the choice of the manner in which he would put an end to his life.—As he was trembling and hesitating about it, Arria his wife, a woman of as much resolution as beauty, seized a dagger, plunged it into her breast, and then offering it to him spoke these words.—Here Paetus, this gives no pain.

The story is told by Pliny (*Letters*, III, 16), and is also known by Arria's words "non dolet" (it does not hurt), which Pliny, writing within a century of her death, already cited as widely famous.

West painted at least three distinct versions of the subject, only one of which (presumably No. 38) appears on the lists of his works, and only one of which (presumably No. 40) was exhibited in his lifetime. The two later paintings (Nos. 39 and 40) were both engraved. The composition of No. 38, the earliest, and indeed, with the *Continence of Scipio* (No. 18), one of the first of West's subjects from Roman history, is closely related to that of the large *Octavius and Cleopatra* (ill. p. 38) by Anton Raphael Mengs of 1759–60 at Stourhead, where West had visited in 1763.[2]

See also pp. 38–42 above.

[1]An invoice for £21 for a picture of *Paetus and Arria* by B. West, plus additional charges for regilding the frame, shipping, etc., dated 14 July 1812 and made out to Silvertop, Esq., is in the Day Books of Smith and Successors, I, p. 52, in the Library of the Victoria and Albert Museum.
[2]Galt 1820, p. 5.

39

39 Paetus and Arria 1770

PRIVATE COLLECTION

Oil on canvas: $36 \times 30\frac{1}{8}$ in. (91.5 × 76.5 cm.)

Signed upper right: *Benj.—West 1770*

PROV: Offered by West's sons to the United States in 1826 (123), and sold by them, Robins, London, 22–25 May 1829, lot 161 (36 × 30 in.), bt. by Rothchild for £73.10.0.; Appleby Brothers, London; Charles D. Childs, Boston, 1956; purchased in London before 1960 by Simon Stone, MD, Manchester, New Hampshire; Wildenstein & Co., New York

EXH: (?) West's Gallery 1821 (92), 1822–28 (104 or 140)

ENGR: Mezzotint ($18 \times 13\frac{7}{8}$ in.) by Robert Dunkarton, pub. by John Boydell, 1 Mar. 1773, with explanatory text (quoted under No. 38 above)

LIT: Locquin 1912, p. 154

An X-ray of No. 39 made by Wildenstein in 1969 indicated that the head of Paetus was originally looking up and to his left.[1] This is Paetus' position in a drawing for this painting in the Historical Society of Pennsylvania.[2] The pose of Arria in this drawing is basically the same as in No. 39 but shows the full length of her left arm and seems to be derived from that of the dying Lucretia in Gavin Hamilton's *Oath of Brutus* (ill. p. 38), which had been engraved by Domenico Cunego in 1768. There is also a related drawing at Swarthmore, showing only the figure of Arria.[3]

[1]Letter from Peter H. Davidson to Helmut von Erffa, 17 Nov. 1969.
[2]Pen and wash, $9\frac{11}{16} \times 5\frac{5}{8}$ in.
[3]Black chalk, $5\frac{7}{16} \times 4\frac{5}{8}$ in.

40 Paetus and Arria *c.*1781

LOCATION UNKNOWN

(?) 84 × 57 in. (213.5 × 145 cm.)

PROV: Offered by West to the Pennsylvania Academy of the Fine Arts in 1809 (The picture, life[-sized] of "Patus and Aria," 7 ft. × 4 ft. 6 in., £150); offered by his sons to the United States in 1826 (14, "Paetus and Arria," 8 ft. × 6), and sold by them, Robins, London, 22–25 May 1829, lot 108 (7 ft. × 4 ft. 9 in.), bt. by Burland for £63

EXH: RA 1781 (266) "Paetus and Arria"; (?) West's Gallery 1821 (92), 1822–28 (104 or 140)

ENGR: Mezzotint (24⅝ × 16 in.) by Valentine Green, pub. by Green, 1 May 1781, with a dedication to the Princess Daschkan

Despite the discrepancies in the measurements cited in the provenance, it seems more likely that the measurements given in 1826 were wrong than that yet another large version of the subject was in West's estate. A drawing of the composition is in the Historical Society of Pennsylvania.[1] There is also a circular drawing at Swarthmore, apparently by a hand other than West's, which shows bust-length figures and a visualization of the subject halfway between Nos. 39 and 40.[2]

[1] Pen and wash, 22 × 15½ in.
[2] Brown wash, 5½ × 5 in.

41 Epponina *c.* 1794

LOCATION UNKNOWN

EXH: RA 1795 (160) "Eponina giving bread to her husband in concealment"

ENGR: Stipple engraving (17¹³⁄₁₆ × 13⅝ in.) by Charles Wilkin, pub. 1 May 1794, with accompanying text (quoted below)

LISTED: *PC*, p. 567 ("Eponina with her children giving Bread to her Husband when in Concealment," West, Gallery); *UM*, p. 531; Barlow, p. 435; *BA*, p. 18; Galt, p. 231; Dillenberger, p. 180 (411)

LIT: *Notes and Queries*, 13th series, vol. 1, 14 July 1923, pp. 34–35

The print by Charles Wilkin after the lost No. 41 bears the following explanatory text:

Sabinus commanded a small army in Gaul, and declared himself Emperor on the death of Vitellius; he was soon defeated by Vespasian's general, and compelled to seek safety in caverns. In this situation he remained nine years, attended by his faithful wife Epponina, who supplied him with provisions. She was at length discovered in the performance of that pious office, and Sabinus taken and carried to Rome. Epponina accompanied him, and appeared before the Emperor, with her two children, to implore her husband's pardon; but neither her tears nor intreaties could prevail and Sabinus suffered by the executioners.

This account seems to follow most closely that in Dio Cassius (*Roman History*, epitome of Book LXV, 3 and 16) where, however, the heroine is named Peponilla. The story is also told, with some discrepancies, by Plutarch (*Amatorius*, 25), where she is Empona. In Tacitus (*Histories*, IV, 67), where she is Epponina, her noble example is referred to, but not described.

Although the early lists of West's works suggest that the picture was in his possession at the beginning of the nineteenth century, it may have been sold before 1820, as it does not appear in any of his sons' posthumous exhibitions or sales of their father's works.

42 Belisarius and the Boy 1802

DETROIT INSTITUTE OF ARTS

Oil on canvas: 26½ × 18¾ in. (67.5 × 47.5 cm.)

Signed lower right: *B. West/1802*

PROV: Sir Francis Baring, Bt. (died 1810); his son Sir Thomas Baring, Bt. (1772–1848); his sale, Christie's, London, 2–3 June 1848, lot 26, bt. by Fuller for £16.5.6.; A. Leonard Nicolson, London, by whom presented to the Detroit Institute of Arts in 1913

Paetus and Arria, mezzotint by Valentine Green after No. 40

Epponina, stipple engraving by Charles Wilkin after No. 41

42

the Emperor and was briefly imprisoned, but the story that he was deprived of his sight and reduced to beg his bread was a fabrication of the Middle Ages. The text accompanying the Moses engraving after No. 44 cites Gibbon's dismissal of the story as a fiction. Nonetheless, the tradition was widely accepted, and there are numerous seventeenth- and eighteenth-century paintings of the subject, including one by Salvator Rosa, an engraving of which West had copied before the publication of Marmontel's *Bélisaire* (No. 517). The inscription *DATE OBOLUM BELISARIO* (Give a penny to Belisarius), which appears in Nos. 42 and 44, and which was quoted in the Royal Academy catalogue of 1802, is traditional and is quoted (in English) by Gibbon as part of the false legend. It is not quoted by Marmontel, but the same Latin wording as subsequently used by West is inscribed on a block of stone in the foreground of the most celebrated eighteenth-century painting of the subject, the *Belisarius* by Jacques-Louis David of 1781 (Musée des Beaux-Arts, Lille), which suggests that West may have been inspired by the Morel engraving of 1799 after the David. The inscription on the wall behind Belisarius in No. 42, *MOENIA URBIS REPARATA SUB IUSTINIANO A BELISARIO* (the fortifications of the city restored under Justinian by Belisarius) seems to refer to Belisarius' rebuilding of the walls of Rome in A.D. 537, although, in fact, he ended his days in Constantinople. The block of stone upon which Belisarius sits is carved with a relief showing a Victory holding a wreath over the head of a triumphant general riding in a chariot.

No. 42 is signed and dated *1802* and hence can be equated with the *Belisarius and the Boy* exhibited by West in that year. It must also be the painting of the subject included under "In Various Collections" in Joel Barlow's list of West's works which, according to Barlow, West gave him in 1802. On that list No. 42 immediately precedes West's portrait of *Sir Francis Baring and Family* (see No. 587), and this pattern is repeated on all the other early lists of West's works, where the owner of both paintings is identified as Sir Francis Baring.

A drawing of the related subject of "Belisarius Recognized by His Soldiers," which Ruth Kraemer suggests may contain the first idea for No. 42, is in the Pierpont Morgan Library.[1]

[1]Pen, $6\frac{5}{16} \times 7\frac{1}{8}$ in. (Kraemer 1975, pp. 40–42, no. 67, pl. 40).

43 Belisarius and the Boy 1804

ALEXANDER GALLERY, NEW YORK

Oil on canvas: 22×16 in. (56×40.5 cm.)

Signed lower left: *B. West/1804*

PROV: Sold anonymously, Sotheby's, London, 11 July 1984, lot 75

(?) LISTED: *PC*, p. 565 ("The small picture of Belisarius and the Boy—different from that in the possession of Sir Francis Baring," West, Painting-room); *UM*, p. 530; *BA*, p. 17; Galt, p. 227; Dillenberger, p. 171 (322)

Nos. 43 and 44 have essentially the same composition. The backgrounds are different, and the placard, which is tucked under the boy's arm and bears no writing in the former, hangs above the head of Belisarius and is inscribed *DATE OBOLUM BELISARIO* in No. 44. Both paintings show the same subject as No. 42, but differ from it not only in the reversed positions of the two figures, but in numerous details. Belisarius is differently garbed; his head is bare, rather than hooded; and the boy's gesture in Nos. 43 and 44 is more overtly rhetorical.

EXH: RA 1802 (139) "Bellisarius and the boy: Date Obolum Bellisario"; BI 1824 (157); BI 1833 (21); BI 1845 (99); *From El Greco to Pollock: Early and Late Works*, Baltimore Museum of Art, 1968 (48)

LISTED: *PC*, p. 563 ("Belisarius and the Boy," Sir Francis Baring); *UM*, p. 529; Barlow, p. 434; *BA*, p. 16; Galt, p. 224; Dillenberger, p. 161 (227)

LIT: *Bulletin of the Detroit Museum of Art*, VII, 1913, pp. 21, 45–46, ill. p. 47; Evans 1959, pp. 90–91, pl. 68; Cummings 1968, pp. 99–100; Kraemer 1975, pp. 40–42

For West's various depictions of *Belisarius* see Nos. 517 and 42–45. He exhibited paintings entitled *Belisarius*

and the Boy at the Royal Academy in 1802 and 1805. In the latter year, the title in the catalogue also bore the words *vide Marmontel*, referring to the short novel *Bélisaire* published in 1767 by the French author François Marmontel. No known painting of Belisarius by West illustrates a specific passage in the novel, but Nos. 42, 43, and 44 all depict the blind and aged Belisarius reduced to beggary and accompanied by a young boy as a guide, as described by Marmontel. This was a historical fiction, as Marmontel admitted in his preface and as was subsequently pointed out by Edward Gibbon in chapter XLIII of *The Decline and Fall of the Roman Empire* (1776–88). At the end of his life, in A.D. 563, Belisarius, the great general under the Emperor Justinian, was accused of conspiring against

43

44

Since No. 43 is dated *1804*, it, rather than No. 44 which is dated *1805*, must be the "small picture of Belisarius and the Boy—different from that in the possession of Sir Francis Baring" listed among the works in West's Painting-room in *Public Characters of 1805*, which appeared in October of 1804. Nonetheless, it seems somewhat more likely that No. 44 was the version of the subject that West exhibited in 1805 and 1806. This is the version engraved in Henry Moses's *Gallery of Pictures Painted by Benjamin West* in 1811, which suggests that it still belonged to West then, and, hence, No. 44 was probably the version that remained in West's possession and was sold by his sons in 1829. The history of No. 43 after 1804 is a blank. It was sent in to Sotheby's in London in 1972 with the subject identified as "Tobias standing by his Blind Father".[1] It was photographed then, but not put up for sale. In 1984 it reappeared on the market under its proper title.[2]

[1] Letter from Janet Green to Helmut von Erffa, 18 Jan. 1972.
[2] Letter from David Moore-Gwyn, 30 April 1984.

44 Belisarius and the Boy 1805

ANTHONY BURTON CAPEL PHILIPS

Oil on canvas: $24\frac{1}{4} \times 18$ in. (61.5 × 45.5 cm.)

Signed lower right: *B. West/1805*

(?) PROV: Offered by West's sons to the United States in 1826 (58, "Belisarius and the Boy," 2 ft. × 1 ft. 6 in.), and sold by them, Robins, London, 22–25 May 1829, lot 54 ("Belisarius," 24 × 14½ in.), bt. by Sir O. Mosley (Sir Oswald Mosley, 1785–1871, 2nd Baronet), for £26.5.0.

EXH: (?) RA 1805 (145) "Belisarius and the boy. Vide Marmontel"; (?) BI 1806 (Middle Room, 46) "Belisarius and the boy, begging alms"; (?) West's Gallery 1821 (84), 1822–28 (8); Liverpool 1976 (71)

ENGR: Outline engraving ($7\frac{5}{16} \times 5\frac{9}{16}$ in.), drawn by Henry Corbould, engraved by Henry Moses, pub. by Moses, 1 May 1811, as pl. III of Moses 1811.

LIT: Moses 1811 (III)

See No. 43, with which No. 44 is virtually identical in composition, although differing in some details.

A copy after this painting passed through the market in 1982.[1]

[1] Christie's, London, 29 Jan. 1982, lot 69 ($23\frac{1}{2} \times 17\frac{1}{2}$ in.).

45 Belisarius Brought to His Family

LOCATION UNKNOWN

PROV: Mr. Mier, Hamburg (? Johann Valentin Meyer, 1745–1811)

LISTED: *BA*, p. 17 ("The drawing of Belisarius brought to his family"; for Mr. Mier, at Hamburgh—duplicate with Mr. West); Dillenberger, p. 168 (297)

In addition to two versions of *Belisarius and the Boy* (see Nos. 42 and 43), the list of West's works published in the supplement to *La Belle Assemblée* in 1808 includes a *Belisarius Brought to His Family*, which West evidently drew for a German collector in Hamburg, and a duplicate of that drawing in his own possession. The other early lists include only the version belonging to West himself.[1] According to the suggestion of Dr. Hanna Hohl of the Hamburger Kunsthalle, "Mr. Mier, at Hamburgh" may have been Johann Valentin Meyer (1745–1811), who had an extensive collection of eighteenth-century drawings.[2]

No. 45 has disappeared, but a drawing in the Philadelphia Museum of Art may be the "duplicate with Mr. West."[3] This drawing has an inscription on the back indicating that it belonged to West's descendants until 1850, so it would not have been the version sent to Hamburg. It does not show Belisarius' family, but it does show the aged and blind general being led by a boy. The drawing is signed and dated *1784*, eighteen years earlier than the date on No. 42, West's first painted version of *Belisarius and the Boy*, and shows a distinctly different composition from that work and from Nos. 43 and 44.

In the list of West's works in *La Belle Assemblée*, No. 45 follows immediately after drawings of *Marius on the Ruins of Carthage* (No. 21) and *Cato Giving His Daughter in Marriage* (No. 25), with duplicates belonging to West in each case. Although No. 45 had a different purchaser from the other two drawings, it is possible that West thought of the three as a group. All show ancient heroes brought low at the ends of their lives, and all apparently were based on modern literary sources: Marmontel, Otway, and Addison respectively. Nos. 21 and 25 demonstrably form a pair, have been together since they were drawn, and were probably thought of together additionally because of the geographic proximity of Utica and Carthage. Thematically, however, the stories of Marius and Belisarius form even closer parallels. The two subjects had been painted together in a pair of large paintings by John Hamilton Mortimer for Radburne Hall in Derbyshire, which were exhibited at the Society of Artists in 1772 and 1774.[4] Both subjects by Mortimer were engraved, *Belisarius*, in 1780. The striding pose of Belisarius in the Philadelphia drawing of 1784 is close, though in reverse, to that in Mortimer's painting and, as Frederick Cummings has pointed out, the style of draughtsmanship in that drawing is very close to that of Mortimer's drawings.[5] The date of the Philadelphia drawing is considerably earlier than the dates of *1796* and *1797* on Nos. 21 and 25, but it is possible that the duplicates of those drawings belonging to West had been drawn earlier. We do not know the date of No. 45 itself.

[1] *PC*, p. 565; *UM*, p. 530; Galt, p. 226. Further drawings of "Belisarius and his family" are also recorded in West's possession: *PC*, p. 569; *UM*, p. 532; *BA*, p. 19; Galt, p. 234; Dillenberger, p. 186 (479).
[2] Letter to Michael C. Fitzgerald, 11 May 1979.
[3] Pen $16\frac{3}{8} \times 18\frac{3}{4}$ in., signed lower left: *B. West 1784*; inscribed, verso: *Doct.—Chepmell/with Mrs. West's and Mrs. Margary's Kind regards/July 1850*. (Mrs. West was the wife of Raphael West, and Mrs. Margary was her daughter.)
[4] Reproduced in E. K. Waterhouse, *Three Decades of British Art 1740–1770*, Philadelphia, 1965, figs. 19 and 20.
[5] Cummings 1968, p. 100.

46 Prince Bladud Contemplating the Medicinal Virtues of the Bath Waters by Observing their Effect on Swine 1807

ROYAL ACADEMY OF ARTS, LONDON

Colored chalk and wash, heightened with white, on tinted paper: $28 \times 41\frac{1}{2}$ in. (71 × 105.5 cm.)

Signed lower left: *B. West Bath Sep 20 1807*

PROV: In the possession of West's heirs in 1823

EXH: RA 1808 (431) "Prince Bladud, eldest son of Lud Hudibras, King of Britain; he first discovered the medicinal virtues of the Bath springs by observing the salutary effect those waters produced on swine"; West's Gallery 1823 (Room of Drawings, no. 37)

LISTED: *BA*, p. 20 ("The drawing of Prince Bladud contemplating the medicinal virtues of the Bath waters by observing their effect on Swine," West); Dillenberger, p. 189 (504)

LIT: Farington Diary, 10 Nov., 19 Nov., and 4 Dec. 1807 (Farington, 1978—, VIII, pp. 3139, 3144, and

3157); Paul Hulton, "A Little Known Cache of English Drawings," *Apollo*, LXXXIX, 1969, p. 54, ill.; Alberts 1978, p. 337

Bladud was the legendary founder of Bath in 863 B.C. According to a long-standing local tradition, which was recorded by John Wood the Elder, Bladud contracted leprosy and was banished from the court of his father, King Hudibras.[1] He became a swineherd, whereupon the pigs in his charge caught leprosy from him. After they wallowed in the warm ooze of the hot springs that subsequently became the site of Bath, Bladud discovered that they had been cured. He then followed their example and was himself cured.

West visited Bath from July until November 1807 for the sake of his wife's health, and at the Royal Academy in 1808, in addition to No. 46, he exhibited four views of the vicinity of Bath and Bristol (Nos. 458–61). He must have begun No. 46 while there, as it is dated 20 September 1807, but Joseph Farington saw him touching on it with white chalk on 19 November, after his return to London. It is pieced together from several sheets of paper, and it is possible that some of these represent additions or revisions made in London.

[1] John Wood, *An Essay Towards the Description of Bath*, Bath, 1742, pp. 6–8 (and repeated in numerous later editions).

47 William de Albanac Presents His Three Daughters to Alfred III, King of Mercia c. 1778

DESTROYED

(58 × 82 in.) (147.5 × 208.5 cm.)

PROV: Painted for Charles Manners (1754–87), fourth Duke of Rutland; destroyed by fire at Belvoir Castle on 26 October 1816.
EXH: RA 1778 (331) "William de Albanac presents his three daughters (naked) to Alfred, the third, King of Mercia, with the following words, 'Here be my three daughters, chuse to wife which you list; but, rather than you should have one of them to your concubine, I would slay her with mine own hand.' *Leland's Itin.*, vol. VIII, p. 58"
ENGR: Engraving ($16\frac{15}{16} \times 23\frac{1}{4}$ in.) by J. B. Michel, pub. by John Boydell, 9 Nov. 1782; outline engraving ($4\frac{1}{8} \times 4\frac{3}{8}$ in.), pub. in Hamilton 1831
LISTED: *UM*, p. 528 ("Wm. Dalbeny presenting his three Daughters to Alfred the 3rd.," in the possession of the Duke of Rutland); Barlow, p. 435 ("Ubald brings his three daughters to Alfred for him to choose one for his wife"); *BA*, p. 19 ("William of Dolbeny presenting his three daughters to King Alfred III to make choice of one for his wife," painted for the late Duke of Rutland, and now at Belvoir Castle); Dillenberger, pp. 181 (425) and 187 (493)
LIT: *General Advertiser* May 1778 (V and A Cuttings); Hamilton 1831 (286); the Revd. Irvin Eller, *The History of Belvoir Castle*, London, 1846, p. 132; Marc Rosenberg, *Von Paris von Troja bis zum König von Mercia: Die Geschichte einer Schönheitskonkurrenz*, Darmstadt, 1930, pp. 93–96; Gert Schiff, *Zeichnungen von Johann Heinrich Füssli: 1741–1825*, Zurich, 1959, pp. 28–29, ill.; Irwin 1966, p. 96; Rosenblum 1967, p. 22, n. 62; Gert Schiff, *Johann Heinrich Füssli 1741–1825*, Zurich and Munich, 1973, I, pp. 138, 502–3; Kraemer 1975, p. 14; Alberts 1978, p. 132; Strong 1978, p. 26

As the quotation accompanying the title of this painting in the Royal Academy catalogue for 1778 indicated, the subject is from the antiquarian notes compiled by John Leland between 1534 and 1543 and first published as *Leland's Itinerary* in nine volumes in 1710. The relevant passage illustrated by West is:

Belisarius Brought to His Family, drawing by West, (?) after No. 45. Philadelphia Museum of Art

46

William de Albanac Presents His Three Daughters to Alfred III, King of Mercia, engraving by J. B. Michel after No. 47

Owt of an old boke that the Erles of Rutland hathe. In the yere of owr Lorde 734. *Alfredus tertius Merc. rex* in the . . . yere of his reigne cam to the stronge castell of Albanac nere Grantham, and there desyryd to have for wyfe one of the 3. dowghtars of Guliam de Albanac, wherapon Gul. desired him to tary all night at his castle, and in the morninge Gul. brought his eldist dowghtar namyd Adeline starke naked in one hand, and a swerde draune in the othar. His wyffe led the 2. caullyd Etheldred. Guliam, sone to William, led in one hand the 3. dowghtar caullid Maude, and a swerde in the othar.

Guliam the father then said to the Kynge Alfrid:

Sir, heire be my 3. doughters, chese to wyfe which ye liste; but rather then he shuld have any of them to your concubine I wold sle her with my owne hands. The kynge answerid that he ment to take one of them to wife, and chose Etheldrede that had fat bottoks, and of her he had Alurede that wan first all the Saxons the monarchy of England.

The Dukes of Rutland trace their ancestry to a medieval William de Albanac (or Albini), hence the commission. There was, however, no Alfred III of Mercia, and even the *Itinerary* bears the marginal comment, "*Leland* thinkithe all this to be a lye."[1]

No. 47 was apparently not included in the original

manuscript that provided the basis for the published lists of West's works. It does not appear at all in *Public Characters* or Galt, and it is at the very end of the lists in Joel Barlow's *Columbiad* and *La Belle Assemblée* under differing titles (hence the two listings in Dillenberger).

Ruth Kraemer identifies a drawing in the Morgan Library as preparatory for the central daughter.[2] A copy was at one time in the collection of the Princes Hohenzollern-Hechingen, Löwenberg, Silesia.[3] A drawing by Fuseli of the subject, probably inspired by the Michel engraving after No. 47 is in the Stiftung Oskar Reinhart, Winterthur.[4]

[1] Quoted from *The Itinerary of John Leland in or About the Years 1535–1543,* Lucy Toulmin Smith, ed., London, 1964, v, p. 149. West probably used the third edition of the *Itinerary,* published in 1769–70, where the passage and the marginal disclaimer are in vol. VIII, p. 26.
[2] Black chalk, $6\frac{3}{8} \times 4\frac{1}{2}$ in. (Kraemer 1975, p. 14, no. 19 and pl. 6).
[3] Oil on canvas, 42×57 in. (Gustav Parthey, *Deutscher bildersaal,* Berlin, 1864, II, p. 778).
[4] Gert Schiff, *Johann Heinrich Füssli 1741–1825,* Zurich and Munich, 1973, I, pp. 138, 502–3 (810), II, ill. p. 212.

48 Alfred the Great Dividing His Loaf with a Pilgrim 1779

WORSHIPFUL COMPANY OF STATIONERS AND
NEWSPAPER MAKERS, LONDON

Oil on canvas: 90×110 in. (228.5×279 cm.)

Inscribed lower left: *Painted by Benj West Historical Painter to His Majesty & presented to the Stationers Company by Mr. John Boydell AD 1779*

PROV: Presented to the Worshipful Company of Stationers by John Boydell in 1779 or 1780

EXH: RA 1779 (341) "Alfred the Great divides his loaf with a pilgrim"

ENGR: Engraving ($17 \times 23\frac{1}{2}$ in.) by William Sharp, pub. by John Boydell, 9 Nov. 1782, with a dedication to the Master, Wardens, Assistants & Livery of the Worshipful Company of Stationers, and identification of the source as the picture in Stationer's Hall presented by John Boydell in 1780; steel engraving ($4\frac{1}{2} \times 6\frac{3}{8}$ in.) by W. H. Egleton, pub. by Fisher, Son & Co.

LISTED: *PC*, p. 563 ("Alfred dividing his Loaf," presented to Stationer's Hall by Alderman Boydell); *UM,* p. 529; Barlow, p. 433; *BA*, p. 15; Galt, p. 223; Dillenberger, pp. 154 (163) and 160 (217) (listed twice)

LIT: Frederick Hilles and Philip B. Daghian, eds., *Anecdotes of Paintings in England (1760–1795) . . . Collected by Horace Walpole,* v, New Haven, 1937, p. 115; Strong 1978, pp. 26 and 116

Alfred and his followers, wintering in the fortress of Athelney in Somerset before their final struggle with the Danes in A.D. 878, ran out of food. While the entire population of the fortress except the King and Queen and their children were out fishing and foraging, a pilgrim arrived and asked for something to eat. The Queen found only one loaf of bread and showed it to Alfred to demonstrate their inability to give the pilgrim anything, but the King nonetheless gave half of it to the pilgrim and consoled the Queen with the biblical story of the loaves and fishes. No. 48 is a straightforward depiction of the incident as described in *The Life of Alfred the Great* by A. Bicknell, published in 1777 (pp. 149–51). Alfred's crown is on the table, and the books next to it give evidence of his studious habits. According to Bicknell, Alfred, as was his custom, was reading a book when the pilgrim arrived, and returned to it when the visitor departed.

48

A drawing for the Queen and children, with Alfred roughly blocked in, is at Swarthmore.[1] An oil sketch is No. 49 below.

The engraving by William Sharp after No. 48 shows a composition that is slightly more extended on both sides, so that there is space between the pilgrim and the edge of the picture on the left, and between the Queen and the edge on the right. However, the relations of these two figures to the edges of the canvas are virtually identical in Nos. 48 and 49, suggesting that the differences between No. 48 and the print may be due to liberties taken by Sharp, rather than that No. 48 has been cut down.

[1] Black and white chalks, on blue paper: $5\frac{3}{4} \times 9\frac{1}{8}$ in.

49 Alfred the Great Dividing His Loaf with a Pilgrim 1778

JAMES RICAU

49

Oil on canvas: $19\frac{7}{8} \times 25\frac{3}{8}$ in. (50.5×64.5 cm.)

Signed lower left: *B. West*/[. . .]8

PROV: Offered by West's sons to the United States in 1826 (149), and sold by them, Robins, London, 22–25 May 1829, lot 116 ("King Alfred Dividing His Loaf with the Pilgrim," the original study for the well known and much admired great picture, placed in Stationers' Hall, 1 ft. 7 in. × 2 ft. 2 in.), bt. by Cook for £33.12.0.; sold by Joseph J. Flack & Co., London, to a Mr. Manton, 24 Feb. 1872 (label on verso); James Ricau by 1962; currently on extended loan to the Brooklyn Museum

EXH: Allentown 1962 (12)

LISTED: *PC*, p. 568 ("The Sketch, in oil, of King Alfred dividing his Loaf with a Pilgrim," West, Gallery); *UM*, p. 532; *BA*, p. 19; Galt, p. 233; Dillenberger, p. 185 (467)

No. 49 is a monochromatic sketch for No. 48, differing only in minor details (i.e., there is no crown on the table) from the large picture. The date accompanying West's signature on No. 49 is very faint and only partially legible, but since the last digit appears to be an *8*, he evidently painted it in 1778, the year before he exhibited No. 48.

50 The Citizens of London Offering the Crown to William the Conqueror *c.* 1792–97

WALKER ART GALLERY, LIVERPOOL

Oil on canvas: 78×60 in. (198×152.5 cm.)

PROV: Painted for Robert Bowyer (1758–1834); his sale, Peter Coxe, London, 29–30 May 1807, lot 56; Liverpool Royal Institution; Liverpool University; presented to the Walker Art Gallery in 1969

EXH: Historic Gallery, Pall Mall

ENGR: Engraving ($11\frac{3}{16} \times 8\frac{1}{4}$ in.) by George Noble, pub. 1 Dec. 1797 by R. Bowyer, Historic Gallery, Pall Mall, and included in Bowyer's edition of *The History of England* by David Hume, London, 1805–6, I, between pp. 222 and 223; engraving by J. Rogers, pub. by J. & F. Tallis, London, Edinburgh, and Dublin

LISTED: *PC*, p. 563 ("The Citizens of London offering the Crown to William the Conqueror," Historical Gallery, Pall-mall); Barlow, p. 433; *BA*, p. 15; Galt, p. 222; Dillenberger, p. 157 (193)

LIT: Irwin 1966, pp. 96–97; Strong 1978, p. 26

This work, which is in extremely deteriorated condition, is one of two pictures painted by West for the miniature painter and publisher Robert Bowyer. The other is No. 52 below. Both were engraved in Bowyer's edition of David Hume's *History of England* and exhibited as part of the Historic Gallery that Bowyer established in his house in Pall Mall. A press clipping dated 2 January 1792, mentions West among the artists contributing to the illustrated edition of Hume,[1] so he may have begun one or both of his works for Bowyer by then. He must have completed No. 50 by 1797, when it was engraved.

The event shown took place in 1066 after William the Conqueror's defeat of Harold at the Battle of Hastings. William is on the left. The kneeling figure presenting him the crown is Edgar Atheling, who had been named king upon the death of Harold but yielded the crown as soon as William approached London. The more prominent prelate on the right probably is Stigand, Archbishop of Canterbury. In Hume's account Stigand, Edgar, and all the chief nobility met William before he came in sight of London. The edifice in the background may have been intended by West to represent either Canterbury Cathedral or Westminster Abbey, where William's coronation subsequently took place but, as David Irwin has pointed out, the Gothic details, such as flying buttresses, are anachronisms for an event occurring in A.D. 1066.

[1] V and A Cuttings, III, p. 617. See also Boase 1963, pp. 169–71.

50

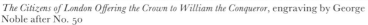

The Citizens of London Offering the Crown to William the Conqueror, engraving by George Noble after No. 50

52

51 The Citizens of London Offering the Crown to William the Conqueror

LOCATION UNKNOWN

(19½ × 14½ in.) (49.5 × 37 cm.)

PROV: Offered by West's sons to the United States in 1826 (91) and sold by them, Robins, London, 22–25 May 1829, lot 11 ("Presentation of the Crown to William the Conqueror," 1 ft. 7½ in. × 1 ft. 2½ in.), bt. by Smith for £27.6.0.

EXH: RA 1808 (592) "The Citizens of London presenting the crown to William; a sketch"; West's Gallery 1822–28 (64)

LISTED: *PC*, p. 567 ("The Presentation of the Crown to William the Conqueror," West, Gallery); *UM*, p. 531; Barlow, p. 435; *BA*, p. 18; Galt, p. 231; Dillenberger, p. 180 (415)

No. 51 was evidently a sketch for No. 50. West exhibited it at the Royal Academy together with a sketch of his other Bowyer subject, the *Intercession of the Queen Mother with Richard I* (see Nos. 52 and 53), in 1808, over a decade after he had painted the larger pictures.

52 The Intercession of the Queen Mother with Richard I to Pardon His Brother John *c.* 1792–94

WASHINGTON UNIVERSITY, ST. LOUIS, MISSOURI

Oil on canvas: 86 × 60 in. (218.5 × 152.5 cm.)

Signed lower left: *B. West* [?]*79*[?]

PROV: Painted for Robert Bowyer (1758–1834); his sale, Peter Coxe, London, 29–30 May 1807, lot 57; (?) John Nussey, 1857; acquired by Washington University through the William K. Bixby American Art Acquisition Fund prior to 1927

EXH: Historic Gallery, Pall Mall; (?) BI 1857 (99) "Queen Eleanor Suing Richard I," lent by John Nussey

ENGR: Engraving (11$\frac{3}{16}$ × 8$\frac{3}{16}$ in.) by James Stow, pub. 15 Jan. 1795 by R. Bowyer, Historic Gallery, and included in Bowyer's edition of *The History of England* by David Hume, London, 1805–6, II, between pp. 480 and 481

LISTED: *PC*, p. 563 ("The Queen soliciting the King to pardon her Son John," Historical Gallery, Pall-mall); *UM*, p. 528; Barlow, p. 433 ("The Queen soliciting king Henry to pardon her son John"); *BA*, p. 15 ("The Queen-Mother soliciting the King to pardon her son John"); Galt, p. 222; Dillenberger, p. 157 (194)

LIT: Irwin 1966, pp. 96–97; Strong 1978, p. 26

The painting shows Eleanor of Guienne, the widow of Henry II, and two of her sons, Richard I and John. When Richard was imprisoned by the Emperor Henry VI while returning from the Third Crusade, he was treacherously betrayed by John, who allied himself with Richard's enemy, Philip of France, and attempted to claim Richard's throne. Nonetheless, following Richard's return to England in 1194, John deserted the French and, in Hume's words, "threw himself at his brother's feet, craved pardon for his offences, and by the intercession of Queen Eleanor was received into favor. 'I forgive him,' said the king, 'and hope I shall as easily forget his injuries as he will my pardon.'"

See No. 50 for Bowyer's Historic Gallery. No. 52 was completed before January 1795, when it was engraved. The *79*, which on the canvas accompanies West's very faint signature, must be the two middle digits of the date, the first and last having disappeared.

53 The Intercession of the Queen Mother with Richard I to Pardon His Brother John

LOCATION UNKNOWN

Oil on board: 18 × 14 in. (45.5 × 35.5 cm.)

PROV: Offered by West's sons to the United States in 1826 (78) and sold by them, Robins, London, 22–25 May 1829, lot 66 ("King Richard Pardoning His Brother John," 18½ × 14 in.), bt. by Ablet for £22.1.0.; sold anonymously, Christie's, London, 12–13 Oct. 1972, lot 195

EXH: RA 1808 (593) "The intercession of the Queen Mother with Richard the First to pardon his brother

53

John; a sketch"; West's Gallery 1821 (12), 1822–28 (36)

LISTED: *PC*, p. 567 (listed twice: as "The Sketch of the pardoning of John by his Brother King Henry, at the Solicitation of his Mother" and as "The picture of the pardoning of John, at his Mother's Solicitation," both in West's Gallery); *UM*, p. 531 (listed twice); Barlow, p. 435 (listed once, as "King Henry pardoning his brother John at the prayer of his mother"); *BA*, p. 18 (listed twice, with "King Henry" changed to "King Richard the First"); Galt, p. 231 (listed twice, "King Henry" again); Dillenberger, pp. 179 (409) and 180 (413)

No. 53 is a sketch for No. 52; see also No. 51, which was evidently a corresponding sketch for No. 50 and which West exhibited together with No. 53 in 1808.

The list of West's pictures in *Public Characters of 1805* includes a "Sketch of the pardoning of John by his Brother King Henry, at the solicitation of his Mother," which we have interpreted as an accidental and erroneous second listing of No. 53, which also appears under its correct title elsewhere on the same page. The two listings are repeated in most of the subsequent lists (with "Henry" corrected to "Richard" in *La Belle Assemblée*), but we have found no corroborative evidence to indicate that West painted two small versions of the subject in addition to the larger picture for Robert Bowyer.

54 Alexander III of Scotland Saved from a Stag by Colin Fitzgerald (The Death of the Stag) 1786
See color detail, p. 76

TOWN HALL, FORTROSE, ROSS AND CROMARTY, SCOTLAND

Oil on canvas: 144 × 205¼ in. (366 × 521 cm.)

Signed lower left: *B. West/1786*

PROV: Painted for Francis Humberston MacKenzie (1754–1815, created Lord Seaforth and Baron MacKenzie of Kintail in 1797) for 800 guineas; still in West's studio in 1821, but the property of Lord Seaforth's oldest daughter and heir, Mary (1783–1862), the wife of James Alexander Stewart Mac-Kenzie; subsequently at the MacKenzie family seat, Brahan Castle, until Brahan Castle was demolished

in 1952, when presented to the Fortrose Town Council by Madeleine, Countess of Midleton (the great-great-granddaughter of Lord Seaforth)

EXH: RA 1786 (148) "Alexander, the third King of Scotland, rescued from the fury of a stag, by the intrepidity of Colin Fitzgerald, the ancestor of the present Mackenzie family"; West's Gallery 1821 (87)

ENGR: Stipple engraving (19⅞ × 26⁹⁄₁₆ in.) by Francesco Bartolozzi, commissioned by West, but apparently never published

LISTED: *PC*, p. 565 ("The large picture of the Death of the Stag, or the rescuing of Alexander III," 12 ft. × 18, for Lord Seaforth, listed as in West's Painting-room); *UM*, p. 530; Barlow, p. 434; *BA*, p. 17 (. . ., the drawing and painted sketch with Mr. West); Galt, p. 226; Dillenberger, p. 168 (298)

LIT: V and A Cuttings, I, pp. 279, 285, 290 (all 1786) and II, p. 370; Farington Diary, 26 May 1799, 4 July 1801, and 3 March 1804 (Farington 1978–, IV, pp. 1228, 1573, and VI, p. 2260); *Public Characters* 1805, p. 552; Angelo 1830, p. 281; Adams 1874, III, p. 433; H.M.C. (Henry Manners Chichester), *DNB*, X, p. 205; Alexander MacKenzie, *History of the MacKenzies*, Inverness, 1894, p. 12; Kraemer 1975, pp. 81–83; Alberts 1978, p. 301; Strong 1978, p. 26

This painting illustrates a legendary anecdote from the history of the Clan MacKenzie. Colin Fitzgerald, traditionally said to have been the founder of the clan, had been driven out of Ireland and sought refuge at the court of Alexander III of Scotland, who had succeeded to the throne in 1249. While hunting near Kincardine, the King was attacked by a stag and saved by Fitzgerald, who shot the beast with an arrow in the forehead. In gratitude, the monarch granted Colin Fitzgerald the lands of Kintail in Ross and the Mac-Kenzie armorial bearings showing a stag bleeding in the forehead. The entire story is probably apocryphal.

Francis Humberston MacKenzie, later Lord Seaforth, who commissioned the painting, had succeeded to the family estates and to the chieftainship of the Clan MacKenzie in 1783, the year before West exhibited a study for No. 54 (see No. 55). West evidently never delivered the picture to his patron. The early lists of his works describe it as in his studio, and John Quincy Adams saw it there in 1816. According to the life of Lord Seaforth in the *Dictionary of National Biography* West bought the painting back for the price he had originally been paid for it, but a letter written two years after Lord Seaforth's death by his daughter's husband tells the artist that she has no intention of selling it.[1] The *History of the MacKenzies* published in 1894, which describes the painting as at Brahan Castle, states that West "in his old age" wished to buy it "in order to have it exhibited in his own collection." Following West's death, his sons did exhibit it in Newman Street in 1821, but withdrew it in the following year.

No. 54 is a huge painting, and the 800 guineas which West received for it constituted a conspicuously high price. In 1804 when a dispute arose between John Singleton Copley and Sir Edward Knatchbull over the £1,800 Copley was asking for his large *Knatchbull Family*, West was called to testify against his fellow artist and, according to Joseph Farington's diary, stated that he "thought himself very handsomely paid" for No. 54, and "that there was as much work in it as in Copleys picture."[2]

West's, or his patron's, choice of subject, a supposedly historical event in which a man is saved from a savage beast, was probably partly inspired by Copley's *Watson and the Shark*, exhibited at the Royal Academy in 1778. No. 54 also shows an obvious debt to Rubens's hunting scenes and the positions of the two most prominent horses, in the upper left and lower right

corners, suggest that West was aware of Rubens's *Wolf and Fox Hunt* (opposite). He had seen the version of this composition at Corsham Court, which he had visited in 1763.[3]

An oil sketch is No. 55 below. Three drawings by West of the composition are known; the largest of these is signed and dated *1784*.[4] A drawing showing all the horses in No. 54, but with none of the figures, is in a private collection in England,[5] and a drawing of a stag, which West may have utilized for No. 54, is at Swarthmore.[6] An outline drawing of the composition in the Pierpont Morgan Library does not appear to be by West's hand, and Ruth Kraemer has suggested that it may have been made by Francesco Bartolozzi in connection with his print after this work, to which it corresponds in size.[7] A copy in oils by Charles Robert Leslie, which is signed and dated *1814*, is in the Athenaeum of Philadelphia.[8]

West himself commissioned the print after No. 54 by Bartolozzi, but the venture was not a success. In 1799, Farington recorded that the print was "very bad" and that West was "much disappointed." In 1801 when Copley was sued by the engraver Jean-Marie Delattre because Copley had rejected the Delattre engraving after his *Death of Chatham* on the grounds of poor quality West, testifying this time on Copley's behalf, stated that he had paid Bartolozzi 500 guineas for the plate of No. 54, "yet it is so badly done that He cannot publish it." No lettered proofs of the print are recorded in the standard catalogue of Bartolozzi's *oeuvre*[9] or are known to the authors of this catalogue.

No. 54 attracted considerable comment when first exhibited in 1786. Most of the criticism was enthusiastic, one writer describing it as "by far the most capital work of Mr. West, and superior even to the *Death of Wolfe* [No. 93], or the *Battle of La Hogue* [No. 90]." Another critic, while praising the subject— "Men, horses and dogs, in action; a stag pressed hard, and the life of a King at stake—A romantic country too—what a field for Painting to effect magic in!"— found fault with most of West's figures: the King was "a veteran old tar" rather than an august sovereign; Colin Fitzgerald was too "statue-like"; and, "Of the other figures, we must remark, the artist appears to have mounted the Patriarchs and Angels of his other pictures on horseback and treated them with a stag hunt." Henry Angelo in his *Reminiscences* records the joint admiration of his father (a riding master) and George III for the action of the horse in the lower right corner:

I recalled the rapture with which he [Angelo's father] spoke of the action of the prostrate horse, as curbed down by the Scottish peasant, in his grand picture of Alexander, King of Scotland, being rescued, by Fitzgerald, from the fury of a stag. "It is motion—it is alive, and please your Majesty," said my father to his munificent patron, the King. "I think with you, Mr. Angelo," replied his Majesty; adding "This is the more admirable, for though painters and sculptors have given a noble and pictorial air to the horse, it would seem that they did not understand his action."

Angelo then implies that West had benefited from George Stubbs's studies of horses and thus had been saved from the errors of those who had gone before.

[1]Letter dated 1 December 1817 (Historical Society of Pennsylvania), cited in Kraemer 1975, p. 82.

[2]West did receive considerably higher prices for numerous pictures painted for George III in the 1780s, but when Copley's son, the future Lord Lyndhurst, who was acting as his father's lawyer, attempted to ask about them, the question was considered improper. West did testify also about the prices of Nos. 397 (£1,200) and 640 (500 guineas). See Farington 1978–, VI, pp. 2257–60, and Prown 1966, pp. 360–71.

[3]Galt 1820, p. 5. The better-known version of the *Wolf and Fox Hunt* now in the Metropolitan Museum (opposite) was

54

Peter Paul Rubens, *Wolf and Fox Hunt*. Oil on canvas,
96 × 148¼ in. Metropolitan Museum of Art, New York

in Spain in the eighteenth century. See also Nos. 401, 402,
and 412.

⁴Pen, brown ink, and brown wash, 13¾ × 20¼ in., signed lower
left *B. West 1784* (sold by Mrs. P. M. Smith, Sotheby's,
London, 20 July 1978, lot 123, ill. in the catalogue); black
and white chalk on blue paper, 10⅝ × 9 9/16 in. (formerly in
the collection of Mrs. Claire Francis); pencil, pen and
brown ink, and brown washes, 5¾ × 10 in. (sold by Mrs. F.
Howard, Sotheby's, London, 22 March 1979, lot 15, ill. in
the catalogue). Drawings of the subject are listed in *PC*,
p. 568 (two drawings, both in West's Gallery; *UM*, p. 532;
BA, p. 19 (and see also under LISTED above); Galt, pp. 233

and 234; Dillenberger, pp. 184 (465) and 185 (471).
⁵Pen, 18¾ × 20 in. Inscribed (not by West's hand) lower left:
Sketches/by B. West for the painting/of Death on the/Pale Horse.
⁶Black chalk, 17½ × 10 in.
⁷Pencil, 19⅞ × 26½ in. (Kraemer 1975, pp. 81–83, no. 204 and
pl. 108). Another drawing of a stag hunt in the Morgan
Library (Kraemer p. 60, no. 109 and pl. 104) has no
evident connection with No. 54.
⁸Oil on canvas, 60 × 77 in., signed lower left: *C. R. Leslie 1814/
after B. West*
⁹A. De Vesme, *Francesco Bartolozzi*, Milan, 1928, p. 135 (517).

55 Alexander III of Scotland Saved from a Stag by Colin Fitzgerald (The Death of the Stag) *c.* 1784

LORD EGREMONT AND LECONFIELD, PETWORTH
HOUSE, SUSSEX

Oil on canvas: 20 × 27 in. (51 × 68.5 cm.)

Signed lower left: *B. West*

PROV: Probably purchased from Raphael West by the
third Earl of Egremont after 25 Feb. 1824; by family
descent to the present owner

EXH: (?) RA 1784 (402) "Alexander III of Scotland
saved from the fury of a stag by Colin Fitzgerald."

LISTED: *PC*, p. 568 ("The small picture of the Death
of the Stag," West, Gallery, listed with Drawings and
Sketches on Paper); *UM*, p. 532; *BA*, p. 19 (see also

No. 54, under LISTED); Galt, p. 234; Dillenberger,
p. 185

LIT: Collins Baker 1920, p. 133 (160); Hall 1962,
p. 108, no. 276 (letter from John Young to Sir John
Fleming Leicester, 25 Feb. 1824)

This painting is a small version of No. 54, corresponding closely to the large picture in all details. Its early
history is not entirely clear. It was presumably the oil
study for the large stag hunt, "painted for a noble
family in Scotland about forty years since," which John
Young saw at Raphael West's home at Staines in 1824,
and, as Raphael was then ready to sell it, it was presumably bought by the third Earl of Egremont soon thereafter. Since it still belonged to a member of the family
in 1824, it can be equated with the small painting of
the *Death of the Stag* described by *Public Characters* and
other early lists as in West's gallery, and with the painted sketch for the large picture additionally listed in
La Belle Assemblée.

We have also tentatively identified No. 55 as the version of the subject which West exhibited at the Royal
Academy in 1784. That work, however, was displayed
in the Exhibition Room of Sculpture and Drawings,
rather than in a gallery devoted to paintings and,
hence, may have been a drawing. The argument
against identifying the exhibited work as a drawing is
that West usually identified drawings with the word

55

"design" in the Academy catalogues; in 1784 he did exhibit three drawings (Nos. 256, 345, and 402), each distinguished in the catalogue as a design, in the same room with the exhibited version of *Alexander III Saved from a Stag*. That work was not so described and accordingly there is reason to question if it was a drawing, especially since No. 55 is sufficiently small (smaller indeed than any of the three drawings exhibited by West) that it would not have struck a discordant note in a room of drawings. If West had completed No. 55 by April of 1784, he certainly would have sent it to the Academy, rather than any of the known drawings of the composition (see No. 54, note 4), none of which seems sufficiently large or finished to have been the exhibited work.

56 Edward III Crossing the Somme 1788
See color illustration, p. 96

HER MAJESTY THE QUEEN

Oil on canvas: 54 × 59 in. (137.2 × 149.9 cm.)

Signed lower left: *B. West 1788*

PROV: Painted for George III (1797 account: "Edward III forcing the Passage of the River Somme," 1788, £630; 1801 account, p. 214, for His Majesty's State Rooms in Windsor Castle, 7, . . .)

EXH: RA 1792 (66) "Edward III^d passing the river Soame, painted for the audience chamber, in Windsor Castle"; Bregenz 1968 (479) as *Die Schlacht bei Crecy*

LISTED: *PC*, p. 560 ("Edward III. crossing the Somme," George III, In the King's Audience-room at Windsor Castle); *UM*, p. 527; *AA*, p. 68 ("Edward the III^d crossing the river Soane in France," 6 ft. × 5); Barlow, p. 431; *BA*, p. 13 (5 ft. × 6); Galt, p. 217; Dillenberger, p. 140 (33)

LIT: Brayley and Britton 1801, pp. 224–25; *Windsor Guide* 1807, p. 49; Pyne 1819, I, pp. 166–67; Evans 1959, pl. 52; Irwin 1966, pp. 95–96, pl. 116; Millar

1969, I, pp. 132–33 (1158), II, pl. 125; Strong 1978, pp. 79, 83, 85, fig. 92

Between 1786 and 1789 West painted a series of eight paintings for the King's Audience Chamber at Windsor Castle. The series consists of three very large paintings measuring approximately 113 × 177 in. each (Nos. 58, 67, and 74); three modestly sized pictures each measuring approximately 39 × 60 in., which in at least one case served as an overdoor (Nos. 61, 64, and 72); one painting of *St. George and the Dragon* measuring 77 × 86 in., which hung over a mantel (No. 412); and No. 56, whose size was dictated by its position adjacent to the throne, balancing a door, with one of the smaller pictures above it. In addition to these works, which form a coherent group, the chamber contained one further work by West: a double portrait of George III and Queen Charlotte (No. 560), incorporated as a medallion in the canopy over the throne. The arrangement of the room at the beginning of the nineteenth century can be seen in a watercolor by Charles Wild (ill. p. 94).[1] The chamber was rebuilt under George IV, and the paintings no longer hang together. Nos. 58, 67, and 74 have been on loan in the Palace of Westminster since 1968.

According to Galt, West in conversation with the King had expressed disapproval of the base use of the talents of Italian painters

to illustrate monkish legends, in which no one took any interest, while the great events in the history of their country were but seldom touched. This led to some further reflections; and the King, recollecting that Windsor-Castle had, in its present form, been erected by Edward the Third, said, that he thought the achievements of his splendid reign were well calculated for pictures, and would prove very suitable ornaments to the halls and chambers of that venerable edifice.

The royal commission may also have been inspired by the exhibition in 1786 of the large *Alexander III of Scotland Saved from a Stag* (No. 54), which we know from Henry Angelo that George III admired. A sketch for one painting in the Audience Chamber series (No. 413)

is signed and dated *1786*, and in the following year West exhibited another sketch for one of the paintings (probably No. 68) at the Royal Academy. He exhibited other works intended for or related to the series in 1788 (No. 65), 1792 (Nos. 56 and 67), 1793 (No. 58 and probably No. 61), and 1794 (No. 74). He first identified works as painted for the Audience Chamber in the Academy catalogue of 1792, but the latest date on any of the actual paintings is *1789*, and they must have been in place by 9 October 1791, when Horace Walpole described the room in a letter to Mary Berry.[2]

The historical significance of West's attempt in this series of works to give an accurate picture of the Middle Ages has been pointed out by Roy Strong in *Recreating the Past* and by Mark Girouard in *The Return to Camelot*. Girouard discusses the importance for the growth of interest in the Middle Ages of the *Letters on Chivalry and Romance* published in 1762 by Bishop Richard Hurd (1720–1808), and he has suggested that Hurd, who was a favorite of George III and preceptor to the Prince of Wales and Duke of York, was probably in some way behind George III's commission of the paintings for the Audience Chamber. We know from Galt that George III consulted Hurd about the religious works West painted for Windsor. In Galt's account the projects for the Audience Chamber and for the Royal Chapel are described in reverse order chronologically from that in which we know West actually began these two overlapping sets of commissions (i.e., West started to work on the chapel series in 1779 and exhibited a painting for the chapel [No. 334] as early as 1781), but they are so closely linked that the King's enthusiasm for the paintings devoted to Edward III leads to the growth of the idea for the chapel and the consultation with Hurd, all in one paragraph. Nonetheless, Galt does not explicitly associate Hurd with the Audience Chamber paintings, and he indicates that West himself did most of the requisite research for the series:

The historical pictures for Windsor Castle cost him many a patient hour of midnight research; for the means to assist his composition, especially in architecture, and the costume of the time, were then far from being so easy of access as they are at present. A long period of preference for classic literature, and the illustration of the Greek and Roman story, had withdrawn the public taste from the no less glorious events of our own annals.

Henry Angelo states that West partly executed the series in an apartment at Windsor, and that the King, who frequently visited him, inevitably noted and commented upon the changes West made in his small studies for the paintings as he obtained new historical facts. For the subject matter, West seems to have relied chiefly on David Hume's *History of England*, published between 1754 and 1762, although he may also have employed the earlier history by Paul de Rapin, published in the 1720s, and the fourteenth-century *Chronicles* of Jean Froissart, which had been translated into English in the sixteenth century. His dependence on *The Regal and Ecclesiastical Antiquities of England* (1773) and *Honda Angel-cynnan or, A compleat View of the Manners, Customs, Arms, Habits, etc. of the Inhabitants of England* (1774–76) by Joseph Strutt for many details throughout the series is demonstrated by Strong. Extended explanations of West's subjects in the series were published in 1801 in the first volume of *The Beauties of England and Wales* by Edward Wedlake Brayley and John Britton. This source states that West not only "diligently investigated the history of each event," but also "introduced portraits of as many distinguished characters as the subjects and spaces would admit." Heraldic insignia, most frequently in the form of crests on the participants' helmets, provide the basis for identifying these figures and, according to Brayley and Britton, West provided George III a list of persons together with descriptions of their insignia for each of the paintings. The original copy of this key has evidently disappeared, but West gave Brayley and Britton a "correct copy" for inclusion in their book, where the long lists of distinguished names and descriptions of the heraldic devices are printed as footnotes to the discussion of each work.

Apart from *St. George Slaying the Dragon* (No. 412), No. 56 depicts the earliest subject in historical sequence of the eight pictures painted by West for the chamber. Nos. 56 and 58, *Edward III with the Black Prince after the Battle of Crécy*, show closely related events from Edward's brilliantly successful campaign in northern France in the summer of 1346. Pursued by the French King and an army of 100,000 men, Edward and his much smaller army found the bridges over the Somme either destroyed or heavily defended. A peasant showed him a ford near Abbeville where, however, Edward found a French army under Godemar de Faye awaiting him on the opposite bank. According to Hume, Edward threw himself into the river at the head of the troops, but according to Froissart's fuller account, the King was preceded by the most doughty and best mounted

of his marshals, as shown in this painting, with men from both sides being unhorsed in the water. The English archers, who in No. 56 are visible over the heads of Edward and his knights, were credited by Froissart with forcing the French to give way.

West's key lists the King's companions, riding behind him, as from left to right: Lord Chandos, the Earl of Arundel, the Earl of Warwick, Lord Godfrey Harcourt, Sir Hugh Courtenay, the Earl of Salisbury, the Prince of Wales, and Lord Roos. The key does not identify any of the struggling figures in the lower left part of the composition.

An oil sketch is No. 57 below. A drawing of the head of a caparisoned horse, which Ruth Kraemer has identified as a study for No. 56, is in the Pierpont Morgan Library.[3]

[1]Reproduced in Millar 1969, I, pl. VIII; for discussion of the series as a whole, see ibid., pp. xviii–xix; also Brayley and Britton 1801, pp. 223–41; Galt 1820, pp. 51–52 and 72–73; Angelo 1830, I, pp. 152–53; Strong 1978, pp. 78–85 et passim, and Girouard 1981, pp. 19–24. We are indebted to Miss Heidi Jackson for bringing to our attention the

fundamental discussion of these works by Brayley and Britton.
[2]W. S. Lewis, ed., *Horace Walpole's Correspondence*, XI, New Haven, 1944, p. 363.
[3]Black chalk, heightened with white, on gray paper: $5\frac{7}{8} \times 8\frac{7}{8}$ in. (Kraemer 1975, p. 29, no. 42, and pl. 25).

57 Edward III Crossing the Somme 1788

SANTA BARBARA MUSEUM OF ART, PRESTON MORTON COLLECTION

Oil on canvas: $17\frac{1}{4} \times 22$ in.

Signed lower left: *B. West/1788*

PROV: Offered by West's sons to the United States in 1826 (106) and sold by them, Robins, London, 22–25 May 1829, lot 103 (1 ft. 5 in. × 1 ft. 9 in.), bt. by Pickering for £52.10.0.; Spink and Son, London, by 1951; M. Knoedler and Co., New York, from whom purchased by Preston Morton in 1960

57

EXH: West's Gallery 1822–28 (100)

LISTED: *PC*, p. 564 ("Edward III. crossing the River Somme," West's House at Windsor); *UM*, p. 529; Barlow, p. 434; *BA*, p. 16; Galt, p. 225; Dillenberger, p. 165 (268)

58 Edward III with the Black Prince after the Battle of Crécy 1788

HER MAJESTY THE QUEEN

Oil on canvas: 113 × 176 in. (287 × 447 cm.)

Signed: *B. West. 1788*

PROV: Painted for George III (1797 account: "The picture of Edward the 3rd embracing his son the Black Prince after the Battle at Cressy" for the Audience Chamber in Windsor castle, 1787, £1,365; 1801 account: p. 213, . . . no. 1, "Edward III. embracing his Son on the field of battle at Cressy" . . .)

EXH: RA 1793 (16) "King Edward III embracing his son, Edward the Black Prince, after the battle of Cressy, painted for His Majesty's Audience Chamber in Windsor Castle."

LISTED: *PC*, p. 559 ("The Battle of Cressy, when Edward III. embraced his son," George III, In the King's Audience-room at Windsor Castle); *UM*, p. 527; *AA*, p. 68 ("Edward the IIId embracing his Son on the field of battle at Cressy," 9 ft. × 15); Barlow, p. 431; *BA*, p. 13 (9 ft. × 16); Galt, p. 216; Dillenberger, p. 139 (28)

LIT: Brayley and Britton 1801, pp. 225–28; *Public Characters* 1805, p. 552; *Windsor Guide* 1807, p. 49; Pyne 1819, I, p. 167; Millar 1969, I, p. 134 (1164); Strong 1978, pp. 79–85, fig. 89; Girouard 1981, pp. 19, 21, pl. III

See No. 56 for the Audience Chamber at Windsor. No. 58 is visible in Wild's view of the chamber (ill. p. 94).

The Battle of Crécy took place in August 1346 immediately after Edward III's successful crossing of the Somme shown in No. 56. Crécy is situated a few miles to the north of Abbeville. During the battle, in which the English army overwhelmed a French force three times its size, the fifteen-year-old Prince of Wales (or Black Prince) particularly distinguished himself. This painting shows the evening after the battle when, in Hume's words,

The king, on his return to the camp, flew into the arms of the prince of Wales, and exclaimed, "My brave son, persevere in your honorable course: you are my son! for valiantly have you acquitted yourself to-day; you have shown yourself worthy of empire."

In the foreground are the bodies of the King of Bohemia and his companions, who had fought on the side of France. The King of Bohemia, who was blind, had ordered his horse tied to the horses of two gentlemen of his train, and after the battle their bodies were found together. By his head lies his coronet inscribed with the words *ICH DIN* (properly *Ich dien*—I serve), which, along with the ostrich feathers seen decorating the coronet, is traditionally said to have been adopted by the

Prince of Wales in memory of the great victory. West's notes on the painting, published by Brayley and Britton, identify some twenty-five further figures and some forty-five additional unseen participants in the battle.

An oil sketch and a small replica are Nos. 59 and 60 below. Ruth Kraemer has identified a small drawing in the Pierpont Morgan Library as showing the two principal figures in No. 58 in reversed position.[1]

The prices of £1,365 (or 1,300 guineas) recorded for Nos. 58, 67, and 74, constituted the highest payment received by West for any individual works for George III and indeed for any paintings prior to the 3,000 guineas he was to receive from the directors of the British Institution for *Christ Healing the Sick* (No. 336) in 1811.[2]

[1] Pen and brown ink, $3\frac{1}{2} \times 5\frac{3}{8}$ in. (Kraemer 1975, p. 29, no. 43).
[2] He did receive higher total amounts for Nos. 356 and 357 and for Nos. 360 and 361, the designs and cartoons for the *Crucifixion* and *Resurrection* windows for the west and east ends of St. George's Chapel.

59 Edward III with the Black Prince after the Battle of Crécy

HER MAJESTY THE QUEEN

Oil on canvas: 15 × 20½ in. (38.1 × 52.1 cm.)

PROV: Sold by West's sons, Robins, London, 20–22 June 1829, lot 91 ("King Edward embracing his Son after the Battle of Cressy"); sold by the executors of

58

59

Mrs. T. Natt, Christie's, London, 12 June 1886, lot 33; bought by Queen Victoria in 1887

(?) EXH: See No. 60

LISTED: *PC*, p. 565 ("First Sketch of the Battle of Cressy," West, Painting-room); *UM*, p. 530; *BA*, p. 17; Galt, p. 227; Dillenberger, p. 171 (319)

LIT: Millar 1969, I, pp. 134–35 (1165)

It is possible that there is some confusion in the histories of Nos. 59 and 60, both of which are now in the Royal Collection along with No. 58. The lists, however, do make a distinction between a "first sketch" and a "small picture" of the subject. The present work is clearly a preliminary sketch with much less detail than either Nos. 58 or 60, and there are several compositional differences from the large painting, most notably in the positions of the horses.

60 Edward III with the Black Prince after the Battle of Crécy 1789

HER MAJESTY THE QUEEN

Oil on canvas, mounted on panel: $16\frac{1}{2} \times 25\frac{3}{4}$ in. (41.9 × 65.4 cm.)

Signed lower right: *B. West 1789*

PROV: Offered by West's sons to the United States in 1826 (108 . . . 1 ft. $2\frac{1}{2}$ in. × 2 ft. 1 in.), and sold by them, Robins, London, 22–25 May 1829, lot 105 ("Edward the Third Embracing His Son after the Battle of Cressy," 1 ft. $2\frac{1}{2}$ in. × 2 ft.), bt. for £105 by Robert Vernon (died 1850); sold by his heirs, Christie's, London, 21 April 1877, lot 124; bought by Queen Victoria in 1887

EXH: (?) West's Gallery 1821 (16), 1822–28 (102); SBA 1832 (125) "The Battle of Cressy," lent by Robert Vernon

LISTED: *PC*, p. 565 ("Small picture of the Battle of Cressy," West, Painting-room); *UM*, p. 530; Barlow, p. 434; *BA*, p. 17; Galt, p. 226; Dillenberger, p. 169 (301)

LIT: Millar 1969, I, p. 135 (1166), II, pl. 126

This painting is a reduced replica dated a year later than the large picture (No. 58) and repeating it in all

significant details. See also No. 75, which West may have intended as a companion picture.

61 Queen Philippa at the Battle of Neville's Cross 1789

HER MAJESTY THE QUEEN

Oil on canvas: $38\frac{3}{4} \times 59\frac{3}{4}$ in. (98.4 × 151.8 cm.)

Signed lower right: *B. West 1789*

PROV: Painted for George III (1797 account: "The Battle of Nevills Cross," for the Audience Chamber in Windsor Castle, 1787, £525; 1801 account, p. 213, . . ., no. 5 "Queen Philippa defeats David King of Scotland, at Nevil's Cross, and takes him prisoner," . . .)

EXH: (?) RA 1793 (74) "Philippa, Queen Consort to Edward III, at the battle of Nevill's Cross, near Durham where David, King of Scotland, was made prisoner"

LISTED: *PC*, p. 559 ("The Battle of Nevil's Cross," George III, In the King's Audience-room at Wind-

61

sor Castle); *UM*, p. 527; *AA*, p. 68 ("Queen Philippa taking David King of Scotland Prisoner at the Battle of Durham," 4 ft. × 6); Barlow, p. 431 ("Battle of Nevilcross"); *BA*, p. 13 (6 ft. × 4); Galt, p. 217; Dillenberger, p. 139 (31)

LIT: Brayley and Britton 1801, pp. 228–29; *Windsor Guide* 1807, p. 49; Pyne 1819, I, pp. 167–68; Millar 1969, I, p. 133 (1160), II, pl. 127; Strong 1978, pp. 79, 85, fig. 85

See No. 56 for the Audience Chamber at Windsor.

While Edward III was engaged in France in 1346, the Scottish King, David II (or David Bruce), who was allied with France, invaded England. On 17 October 1346, he was met by an army raised by Philippa, Edward's Queen, at Neville's Cross, near Durham, where the Scots were soundly defeated and David himself was taken prisoner. This painting appears to show a synoptic view of the battle. According to Hume and Froissart, the Queen was not present during the battle itself, but prior to the battle, in Hume's words, "riding through the ranks of her army, [she] exhorted every man to do his duty, and to take revenge on these barbarous ravagers. Nor could she be persuaded to leave the field, till the armies were on the point of engaging." According to Froissart, after she heard of the victory she mounted her palfrey and returned to the field of battle, but while it was being fought she remained in Newcastle. The painting shows the Queen present while the battle rages. The figure to her left, according to West's key, is Lord Percy, the commander of the English forces, and the figure on the extreme right, who wears a mitre and clerical robes as well as armor, is the Archbishop of Canterbury. The mitred heads of the Archbishop of York and of the Bishops of Durham and Lincoln are also discernible in the intervening group. Lying dead in the foreground is Lord Hay. Millar identifies the figure on foot in the left background as the Scottish King about to be made prisoner. He also suggests that the prominence of the axes on the left reflects Froissart's account of the battle, in which mention is made of the sharp and hard Scottish axes.

Two further versions of the subject by West are known or recorded (Nos. 62 and 63). The present work was probably the version that West exhibited at the Royal Academy in 1793, but unlike other paintings for the Audience Chamber that he exhibited in 1792, 1793, and 1794 (Nos. 67, 56, 58, and 74), it was not identified as for the Audience Chamber in the Academy catalogue.

62 Queen Philippa at the Battle of Neville's Cross

ART INSTITUTE OF CHICAGO

Oil on canvas: $14\frac{7}{8} \times 20\frac{3}{8}$ in. (38 × 52 cm.)

PROV: Offered by West's sons to the United States in 1826 (112) and sold by them, Robins, London, 22–25 May 1829, lot 110 (1 ft. 3 in. × 1 ft. 8½ in.) bt. by Ward (W. J. Ward) for £68; purchased by Vincent Carney, Rochelle, Illinois, at a house sale in Dubuque, Iowa, in 1971, and given by him to the Art Institute of Chicago in 1972

EXH: West's Gallery 1822–28 (112); BI 1833 (3) lent by W. J. Ward

LISTED: *PC*, p. 565 ("The small Sketch of the Battle of Nevil's Cross," West, Painting-room); *UM*, p. 530; *BA*, p. 17; Galt, p. 227; Dillenberger, p. 170 (311)

LIT: *The Art Institute of Chicago: Annual Report 1972–73*, p. 13, ill. p. 127

The brief text accompanying the entry for this work in the Robins sale catalogue of 22–25 May 1829, described it as "not only one of the most interesting, but finest coloured of the studies *for the large pictures at Windsor.*" No. 62 is essentially the same in composition as No. 61, but differs in numerous details, such as the heraldry on Queen Philippa's saddle cloth. Most of the banners, which form a conspicuous part of the finished picture, are here only sketchily finished, without heraldic detail.

62

63 Queen Philippa at the Battle of Neville's Cross

LOCATION UNKNOWN

LISTED: *PC*, p. 564 ("Queen Philippa at the Battle of Nevil's Cross," West's House at Windsor); *UM*, p. 529; Barlow, p. 434; *BA*, p. 16; Galt, p. 225; Dillenberger, p. 165 (269)

This work is known only through its appearance on the lists. Since the available evidence indicates that the sketch now in Chicago (No. 62) was the only version of the subject in West's heirs' possession in the 1820s, No. 63 may have been sold before the artist's death.

64 The Burghers of Calais 1789

HER MAJESTY THE QUEEN

Oil on canvas: $39\frac{3}{8} \times 60\frac{3}{8}$ in. (100 × 153.3 cm.)

Signed lower left: *B. West 1789*

PROV: Painted for George III (1797 account: "Queen Philippa interceding for the brave Burghers of Calais" for the Audience Chamber in Windsor castle, 1787, £525; 1801 account, p. 214, . . . no. 6. "Queen Philippa soliciting Edward III to save St. Pierre and the brave burgesses of Calais," £525)

64

65

LISTED: *PC*, p. 559 ("The Burgesses of Calais before Edward III," George III, In the King's Audience-room at Windsor Castle); *UM*, p. 527; *AA*, p. 68 ("Queen Philippa interceding with Edward III to pardon the Burghers of Calais," 4 ft. × 6); Barlow, p. 431; *BA*, p. 13 (6 ft. × 4); Galt, p. 217; Dillenberger, p. 139 (32)

LIT: Brayley and Britton 1801, pp. 229–31; *Windsor Guide* 1807, p. 48; Pyne 1819, I, p. 168; Millar 1969, I, p. 133 (1161), II, pl. 128; Strong 1978, pp. 26, 79, 84, pl. 14

For the Audience Chamber at Windsor Castle see No. 56. No. 64 is visible over the door to the right of the throne in Charles Wild's view of the chamber (ill. p. 94).

Following his victory at Crécy in August 1346, Edward III laid siege to Calais, where he was joined by Queen Philippa after her triumph over the Scots at Neville's Cross. Calais surrendered on 3 August 1347, and Edward agreed to spare its inhabitants on the condition that six of the town's most considerable citizens

should be sent to him bare-headed, bare-footed, with ropes around their necks, and carrying the keys of the city. Edward ordered them to be led to execution, but finally yielded when the Queen begged him to spare their lives. The St. Pierre who is mentioned in some variations of the picture's title was Eustace de St. Pierre, the wealthiest citizen of Calais and the first to volunteer to sacrifice himself for the sake of his neighbors. The keys of the city are on the ground before Edward along with swords and a French flag. The strange-looking object in the lower right is identified by Strong as a cannon, derived from an illustration in Joseph Strutt's *Honda Angel-cynnan*. Strong also points out that the palisading behind the King and Queen comes from Strutt's book. West's notes published by Brayley and Britton identify the three figures standing behind the King on the left as the Prince of Wales, the Earl of Warwick, and Lord Stafford.

If West had illustrated Froissart exactly, the Queen, very big with child, would have been on her knees before the King, and so would have been the six bare-headed burghers of Calais, pleading with upraised hands for their lives. West's treatment of the subject

as a dignified confrontation between proud adversaries, with nobody on his or her knees, probably reflects eighteenth-century distaste for such a scene of cruelly authoritarian behavior on the part of an otherwise admirable monarch. Hume devotes a footnote to questioning the truth of the story, attacking the reliability of Froissart, and asserting how barbarous Edward's determination to execute his prisoners seems in contrast to his usual generosity and humanity.

West exhibited a painting of the subject at the Royal Academy in 1788, but that work can be identified as No. 65, which is signed and dated *1788*, rather than this painting, which is dated *1789*. A smaller oil sketch dated *1787*, which is closer to No. 64 than to No. 65, is No. 66 below. A related drawing is in the Delaware Art Museum,[1] and a drawing, which Ruth Kraemer has associated with the present work and which she identifies as a copy from a fourteenth-century manuscript belonging to George III, is in the Pierpont Morgan Library.[2]

[1] Pencil, 10 × 14¾ in.
[2] Pen and brown ink on oatmeal paper, 4¹³⁄₁₆ × 7 in. (Kraemer 1975, pp. 29–30, no. 44, pl. 28).

65 The Burghers of Calais 1788

DETROIT INSTITUTE OF ARTS

Oil on canvas: $39\frac{1}{2} \times 52\frac{1}{4}$ in. (100.5×132.5 cm.)

Signed lower left: *B. West/1788*

PROV: Sold as "the property of Thomas Hankey, deceased, collected during the course of a number of years by John Bernard, Esq.," Christie's, London, 7–8 June 1799, lot 20 ("The Surrender of Calais," the admired model for the large picture in St. George's Hall at Windsor), bt. by Willett for £89.5.0.; sold by John Willett, Peter Coxe, London, 1 June 1813, lot 79, for £73.10.0.; given to the Detroit Institute of Arts in 1889 by James E. Scripps

EXH: RA 1788 (89) "Queen Philippa soliciting her husband Edward the third, to save the lives of the brave burghers of Calais"; Allentown 1962 (17)

LISTED: *PC*, p. 563 ("The second picture of Philippa soliciting of Edward III. the Pardon of the Burgesses of Calais"—in the possession of Willet, Esq.); *UM*, p. 529; Barlow, p. 433; *BA*, p. 16; Galt, p. 224; Dillenberger, p. 162 (231)

LIT: V and A Cuttings, II, pp. 368, 411, 423; Evans 1959, p. 69, pl. 50

This painting shows basically the same composition as the previous one, but in reverse and differing considerably in detail. Although approximately the same height, it is eight inches narrower than No. 64 and does not have figures corresponding to the three women, one with a child in her arms, at the extreme right of No. 64. Since No. 65 is signed and dated a year earlier than No. 64, the description of it in the lists as West's second picture of the subject is misleading. On the other hand, it is a finished picture, and was the painting of the subject West exhibited as such at the Royal Academy in 1788; so to describe it as a model for the picture in the Royal Collection, as was done in 1799, seems equally misleading. West quite possibly originally intended No. 65 for the Audience Chamber at Windsor but replaced it with No. 64 for some unknown reason.

No. 65 was the only work that West exhibited at the Royal Academy in 1788. In Johann Heinrich Ramberg's view of the royal family at the private view of that year's exhibition, it is visible at the center of the far wall, immediately above the head of the King.[1]

[1] Ill. in Evans 1982, p. 78, fig. 62.

66 The Burghers of Calais 1787

MRS. JOHN DAVENPORT

Oil on canvas: $14\frac{1}{2} \times 20\frac{1}{4}$ in. (37×51.5 cm.)

Signed lower left: *B. West 1787*

PROV: Offered by West's sons to the United States in 1826 (105), and sold by them, Robins, London, 22–25 May 1829, lot 102 ("Surrender of Calais," 1 ft. 3 in. × 1 ft. 8½ in.), bt. by Bone for £115.10.0. on behalf of Joseph Neeld, MP, Grittleton House, Wilts.; by descent in the Neeld family until sold, Christie's, London, 13 July 1945, lot 174 as a pair with No. 73; sold anonymously, Knight, Frank, & Rutley, London, 26 Nov. 1958, lot 15, as a pair with No. 73; Nicholson Gallery, New York; Vose Galleries, Boston by 1962; purchased by the present owner in 1965

EXH: West's Gallery 1821 (11), 1822–28 (99); BI 1833 (24) lent by Joseph Neeld

LISTED: *PC*, p. 565 ("The Sketch of Edward III. with his Queen, and the Citizens of Calais," West, Painting-room); *UM*, p. 530; *BA*, p. 17; Galt, p. 227; Dillenberger, p. 169 (304)

When sold in 1829, this work was described as "the original study" for West's painting of the subject in the Audience Chamber at Windsor (that is, for No. 64), and in most respects it is closer to No. 64 than to the version of the subject now in Detroit (No. 65). It does not, however, include the group of women at the right of the composition of No. 64, and there are numerous differences in minor details.

66

67 The Institution of the Order of the Garter 1787

See color illustration , p. 95

HER MAJESTY THE QUEEN

Oil on canvas: $113 \times 176\frac{1}{2}$ in. (287×448.3 cm.)

Signed lower left: *B. West 1787*

PROV: Painted for George III (1797 account: "The Institution of the most Noble Order of the Garter" for the Audience Chamber in Windsor castle, 1787, £1,365; 1801 account: p. 213, no. 2 . . .)

EXH: RA 1792 (8) "The first ceremony, when Edward the Third, with the original Knights, instituted the most noble order of the Garter, painted for the Audience Chamber in Windsor Castle"

ENGR: See No. 68

LISTED: *PC*, p. 559 ("The Institution of the Order of the Garter," George III, In the King's Audience-room at Windsor Castle); *UM*, p. 527; *AA*, p. 68 ("Edward the III[d] establishing the Order of the Garter," 9 ft. × 15); Barlow, p. 431; *BA*, p. 13 (9 ft. × 16); Galt, p. 216; Dillenberger, p. 139 (30)

LIT: *Public Advertiser* 3 Aug. 1787; Brayley and Britton 1801, pp. 233–35; *Windsor Guide* 1807, p. 49; Pyne 1819, I, p. 169; Galt 1820, pp. 72–73; Tuckerman 1867, p. 104; Mason 1879, p. 277; William T. Whitley, *Gilbert Stuart*, Cambridge, Mass., 1932, p. 64; Martin Davies, *National Gallery Catalogues: British School*, London, 1946, pp. 170–71; Millar 1969, I, pp. 133–34 (1162); Strong 1978, pp. 78–79, 82–83, fig. 85

For the Audience Chamber at Windsor see No. 56. No. 67 is one of the three very large paintings executed by West for the chamber, and it seems to have been viewed by the artist as the central piece of the undertaking. More studies or replicas (Nos. 68–71) are recorded for it than for any other painting in the series. Nos. 67 and 412 were the first works in the series to be completed; both bear the date *1787*, whereas all the other dated works are from either 1788 or 1789, and a press notice in the *Public Advertiser* indicates that West had completed this painting by August 1787. A "finished sketch" of the subject, which West exhibited at the Royal Academy in that year (probably No. 68), was the first composition related to the chamber to be seen publicly, and Nos. 67 and 56, when sent to the Royal Academy in 1792, were the first of the actual pictures for the room to be exhibited and to be identified in the catalogue as for the Audience Chamber at Windsor.

The event shown in No. 67 is taking place at Windsor, where Edward III established the Order of the Knights of the Garter in 1348 and also founded the College of St. George, under the Dean and Canons of Windsor, to serve as the spiritual center for the Order. The setting, appropriately enough, appears to be the nave of St. George's Chapel, although in fact the Gothic nave was not erected until around 1500. Above the arches, across the top of the painting, are the arms of the original Knights of the Garter. The shields and banners hanging from the pillars are trophies of war and are identified in West's notes printed by Brayley and Britton. Edward III and the Prince of Wales, attended by the other original knights, kneel on either side of the altar, where the Bishops of Winchester and Salisbury perform mass. Queen Philippa kneels facing the altar slightly to the left of the picture's center. Her attendants standing behind her include, according to West's list, the Princess Royal, the Fair Maid of Kent, the Duchess of Norfolk, the Countess of Ulster, Lady Mowbray, and Lady Mortimer. Before them in the lower left corner are two kneeling almoners of poor knights and the standing ambassadors from Gascony and Normandy. On a balcony above the altar are the

King of Scotland, who had been taken prisoner at Neville's Cross in 1346 (see No. 61), and the Bishop of St. Andrews. The group under the arch furthest to the right of the three background arches includes the Queen of Scotland and several of the younger children of Edward III, among them the ten-year-old Duke of Clarence and his wife, the daughter of the Countess of Ulster, whom he had married when four years old. The group under the central arch evidently consists of "several French prisoners of noble birth, whom Edward had permitted to witness the magnificence of the institution,"[1] but West's key identifies only the seated man wearing a coronet and resting upon his elbow. He is Charles of Blois, the nephew of Philip VI of France, who was a prisoner from 1347 until 1356. In the Robins catalogue of 20–22 June 1829, where a sketch for No. 67 was lot 68 (No. 70 below), the model for the corresponding figure is identified as the art dealer Noël Desenfans (1745–1807).

The same source identifies the seven figures under the arch on the extreme left (who are not mentioned in West's key) as West himself, his wife and two sons, and the painters John Trumbull, Gilbert Stuart, and Richard Livesay, all of whom worked as West's assistants in the 1780s (ill. p. 101). The *Public Advertiser* of 3 August 1787 (quoted by Whitley) states that West's portrait was included by the King's desire, and that West, "properly studious of identity," had asked Stuart to paint the portrait for him. It may be that Stuart painted the entire group, although Stuart's early biographer George Mason says that West painted Stuart's head. The reason for West's inclusion is given by Galt:

> In the composition for the Institution of the Garter, the late Marquis of Buckingham offered several suggestions, which were adopted; and on His Lordship mentioning to the King that Mr. West was descended of the Delawarre family, the head of which bore a distinguished part in the great events of that time, His Majesty ordered Mr. West to insert his own portrait among the spectators represented in the gallery, and immediately over the shield bearing the arms of the Earl of Delawarre. Mr. West himself was not, at that period, acquainted with the descent of his pedigree; but it happened in a conversation one day with Lord Buckingham, that His Lordship enquired from what part of England his family had been originally, and upon Mr. West telling him, His Lordship said that the land which his ancestors has possessed was become his by purchase; and that the Wests of Long Crandon were sprung from the ancient Earls of Delawarre.

The creation of the Order of the Garter is mentioned by Hume and briefly described by Froissart. Another, more important source for West was probably *The Institution, Laws & Ceremonies of the Most Noble Order of the Garter* by Elias Ashmole (London, 1672), but Strong points out that the embroidered robes of the knights are derived from *The Regal and Ecclesiastical Antiquities of England* published by Joseph Strutt in 1773. The composition as a whole appears to have been based on Rubens's *Coronation of Marie de Médicis* (ill. p. 95).

[1]Brayley and Britton, p. 234.

68 The Institution of the Order of the Garter
c. 1787

TATE GALLERY, LONDON

Oil on canvas: 16 × 22 in. (40.5 × 56 cm.)

PROV: Offered by West's sons to the United States in 1826 (107) and sold by them, Robins, London, 22–25 May 1829, lot 100 ("The Institution of the Order of the Garter," 1 ft. 4 in. × 1 ft. 10 in., described as the original study for one of the series of large pictures, recording memorable events of the reign of Edward the Third), bt. by Robert Vernon for

68

£131.5.0.; presented by Vernon to the National Gallery, London, in 1847; transferred to the Tate Gallery in 1954

EXH: (?) RA 1787 (19) "The original institution of the most noble order of the Garter by Edward III[d], a finished sketch"; (?) West's Gallery 1821 (9), 1822–28 (101); BI 1833 (23) "A Study of one of the series of Pictures recording memorable events in the reign of Edward the Third", lent by Robert Vernon

ENGR: Steel engraving (8 × 10⅝ in.) by W. Taylor, pub. by G. Virtue as "The Installation" in the series *The Vernon Gallery* in the *Art Journal*, 1852, p. 361

(?) LISTED: *PC*, p. 565 ("Small sketch of the Order of the Garter," West, Painting-room); *UM*, p. 530; *BA*, p. 17; Galt, p. 226; Dillenberger, p. 169 (302)

LIT: V and A Cuttings, II, pp. 337–38; Farington Diary, 10 June 1807 (Farington 1978—, VIII, p. 3064); Martin Davies, *National Gallery Catalogues: British School*, London, 1946, pp. 170–71 (315)

There are four recorded smaller sketches or versions of No. 67 and sorting them out is necessarily somewhat speculative. No. 68 is the only one of them now known. It was the version of the subject included in the Robins sale of 22–25 May 1829, where it was bought by Robert Vernon; hence West's sons probably considered it more important or more saleable than the two other versions remaining in their possession (Nos. 69 and 70), which appeared in the lesser sale the following month; and it would seem, therefore, to have been the version exhibited in West's gallery in the 1820s and offered to the United States in 1826. Since No. 68 was described in 1829 as the "original study," it also was quite possibly the "finished sketch" of the subject exhibited at the Royal Academy in 1787; there is, however, no way of proving this. No. 68 does show basically the same composition as No. 67, but with some significant differences in, for example, the placing of the foreground steps, the treatment of the Prince of Wales, the omission of the arms above the arches, and the omission of the last bay on the left, eliminating thus the group of West

and his associates as well as the two ambassadors who stand before them in No. 67.

On 10 June 1807, Joseph Farington recorded that West had seen and admired Rembrandt's *Woman Taken in Adultery* at Christie's (ill. p. 135) and, in response to Farington's recommendation that he paint a subject in the same manner, West declared that he intended to do so and that he "had fixed upon His Sketch of the Institution of the Order of the Garter which would afford Him an opportunity to introduce much in imitation of the Altar in Rembrandt's picture." Whether West intended to paint a new Rembrandtesque picture on the basis of one of his sketches or to repaint a sketch is unclear, and we have no certain confirmation that he ever carried out his intention. But the sketch that he mentioned to Farington must have been one of the three (Nos. 68, 69, or 70) remaining in his possession. Conservation of the present work in 1983 indicates that it did undergo substantial repainting at an early date, quite possibly by West himself.[1] Hence there is a reasonable likelihood that this painting was the work in question. Farington summarized West's description of Rembrandt's technique in the *Woman Taken in Adultery* as follows:

> He said He had examined it carefully & saw that it was painted upon a ground originally *White* & that passed over with a wash of *Burnt Umber* to which was added some yellow colour to make it more luminous. Upon this rich toned ground the whole subject was washed in with *Black only*, the ground giving warmth sufficient to that cool colour. The next proceeding was to wash in with thin colours the colour of each object and gradually to increase the colour of the *light parts* till the whole effect was produced.

No. 68 is unfortunately too deteriorated to allow a determination of whether or how precisely West followed this method. Extensive cracking of the paint in the central portion of the composition does not itself appear to have resulted from the experiment in technique applied to a sketch painted twenty years previously, but rather to have occurred soon after the picture was painted, but the cracking possibly prompted West to utilize the sketch for his attempt at imitation. Subsequent overcleaning of the same area may have been the result of a mistaken interpretation of West's later additions as the work of another hand, since they presumably would not have been in his usual manner. It should be noted that one other sketch or small version of the *Institution of the Garter* (No. 71) was described as not in West's usual hard manner but painted in a "free and juicy" manner; however, this work had left West's possession by 1801 and so could not have been the sketch he proposed to repaint in 1807. Also the earlier masters that it was said to recall were Rubens, Van Dyck, and Veronese, rather than Rembrandt.

¹This work was done by William MacKinnon of the Tate Gallery's conservation department. We are indebted to Mr. MacKinnon and to Heidi Jackson for an informative discussion of the problems raised by No. 68.

69 The Institution of the Order of the Garter

LOCATION UNKNOWN

PROV: Sold by West's sons, Robins, London, 20–22 June 1829, lot 89 ("Institution of the Order of the Garter, a very masterly Sketch")

LISTED: *PC*, p. 565 ("The second small sketch of the Order of the Garter," West, Painting-room); *UM*, p. 530; *BA*, p. 17; Galt, p. 227; Dillenberger, p. 174 (354)

70 The Institution of the Order of the Garter

LOCATION UNKNOWN

PROV: Sold by West's sons, Robins, London, 20–22 June 1829, lot 68 ("The Institution of the Order of the Garter. Under the Gothic arch to the right are seven portraits, representing the painter and his family; also portraits of Mr. Trumbull; Mr. Stewart, the American portrait painter, and Mr. Livesay, the artist. In the front of the second arch is the late Noel Desenfans, Esq., the Original Collector of the Dulwich Gallery")

(?) LISTED: *PC*, p. 566 ("The Order of the Garter," West, Gallery); *UM*, p. 530; Barlow, p. 435; *BA*, p. 17; Galt, p. 229; Dillenberger, p. 174 (354)

As noted under No. 68, the documentation of the four smaller versions of No. 67 is not entirely clear. The sale catalogue of June 1829 describes this version as carefully finished and refers to it as an "elaborate cabinet picture," rather than as a sketch. Hence, it may have been the version of the subject in West's collection listed in the early catalogues without being described as a small sketch, as were Nos. 68 and 69. If the 1829 catalogue described the present work accurately, the composition was reversed from that in Nos. 67 and 68, the group of West et al. on the left side of No. 67 being here on the right.

71 The Institution of the Order of the Garter

LOCATION UNKNOWN

(16 × 22 in.) (40.5 × 56 cm.)

PROV: William Beckford (1760–1844), Fonthill Abbey, Wilts., by 1801; in the Fonthill sale catalogue, Christie's, 17 Sept. 1822, lot 97 ("A Grand Mass in the Interior of St. George's Chapel at Windsor, in which are introduced the Kings of France and Scotland, when Prisoners at Windsor." Cabinet size), but not in the subsequent Fonthill sale of 10–14 October 1823; sold, English and Son, Bath, 25 Nov. 1845, lot 319 ("A Grand Mass . . .," 16 × 22 in.) for £113.8.0.

LISTED: *PC*, p. 561 ("The small picture of the Order of the Garter, differing in composition from the great picture at Windsor," for Wm. Beckford, Fonthill); *UM*, p. 528; Barlow, p. 432; *BA*, p. 14; Galt, p. 220; Dillenberger, p. 151 (136)

LIT: Brayley and Britton 1801, p. 234; Willes Maddox, *Views of Lansdown Tower, Bath: The Favorite Edifice of the Late William Beckford Esq.*, London, 1844, p. 7; *The Bath and Cheltenham Gazette*, 26 Nov. 1845; Lansdown 1893, pp. 30–31

No. 71 is referred to as the "original sketch" for No. 67 in Brayley and Britton's *Beauties of England and Wales*, where the following remarks provided by William Beckford are quoted:

> Above 100 figures are grouped together, with such effect, and painted with so much spirit, as to raise this beautiful performance almost to a level with the happiest effusions of the pencils of Rubens and Vandyck. The coloring, for richness and transparency, equals the best works of the Flemish school. To the utmost power of execution, it joins the historical interest of the subject; and the curiosity of displaying portraits of Edward the Third, the Black Prince, Queen Philippa, all the Royal Children, the Fair Maid of Kent, and the beautiful Countess of Kildare; with the King of Scots, and Charles of Blois, then prisoners in the castle.

A letter written by a visitor to Beckford in 1838, who had seen the painting in Lansdown Tower, built by Beckford behind his home in Bath, also reports that the painting had nothing of West's usual hard manner, but was touched "in the free and juicy manner of the sketches of Rubens or Paolo Veronese."

A description of Lansdown Tower published in 1844 describes No. 71 as "Picture of a Coronation, introducing the Ancestry of Mr. Beckford" and, according to a local newspaper account of the Beckford sale in the following year:

> It is well known that Mr. Beckford claimed descent from both the Royal families of France and Scotland, and kindred with many illustrious knights of the order of the Garter, whose portraits are here introduced, which induced the artist to designate this a family picture.

At Fonthill Abbey Beckford had devoted a gallery, 127 feet long, to Edward III, from whom he was descended or believed himself descended, and he included in it a series of portraits of his claimed gartered ancestors. Hence the subject of No. 71 must have appealed to his genealogical and Gothicizing interests. West may have modified details of the composition of No. 67 to introduce more of Beckford's purported ancestry, since *Public Characters* and the other early lists described No. 71 as "differing in composition from the great picture"; nevertheless, of the historical figures specifically mentioned by Beckford in his remarks quoted above, all but one (the Countess of Kildare) can be readily identified in the large picture.

A manuscript inventory of Beckford's collections, drawn up after his death in 1844, lists No. 71 under the title "Interior of Old Westminster Hall."¹

¹Sold in the Beckford Papers, Sotheby's, London, 6 July 1977, lot 272 (catalogue, p. 148).

72 Edward III Entertaining His Prisoners 1788

HER MAJESTY THE QUEEN

Oil on canvas: 39⅜ × 60⅛ in. (100 × 152.7 cm.)

Signed lower left: *B. West 1788*

PROV: Painted for George III (1797 account: "Edward the 3rd crowning Ribemon at Calais," 1788, £525; 1801 account: p. 214, for His Majesty's State Rooms in Windsor Castle, 8, "Edward III. crowning Ribemont at Calais" . . .)

LISTED: *PC*, p. 560 ("Edward III. crowning Ribemont at Calais," George III, in the King's Audience-room at Windsor Castle); *UM*, p. 527; *AA*, p. 68 ("Edward the IIId crowning Ribaumont at the Banquet in Calais," 4 ft. × 6); Barlow, p. 418; *BA*, p. 13 (5 ft. × 4); Galt, p. 217; Dillenberger, p. 140 (34)

LIT: Brayley and Britton 1801, pp. 231–32; *Windsor Guide* 1807, pp. 47–48; Pyne 1819, 1, pp. 168–69; Evans 1959, pp. 69–70, pl. 51; Millar 1969, 1, p. 133 (1159); Strong 1978, pp. 79, 81–82, fig. 91

For the Audience Chamber, see No. 56.

72

After the English conquest of Calais in 1347, the French attempted by stealth to retake the town in December 1348. The English, however, learned of their plans, were prepared, and defeated the French once again. In the battle, Edward III, fighting incognito, engaged in single-handed combat against a French knight named Eustace de Ribeaumont, who twice forced the English King to his knees before at last surrendering. That evening, which was New Year's Eve, Edward entertained his French prisoners at supper in the castle of Calais. After they had dined, while conversing with them, he placed on Eustace de Ribeaumont's head a chaplet of pearls which he himself had been wearing, as a compliment for being the best combatant of the day and, in addition, he released Ribeaumont from ransom and set him free. The chief source for the story is Froissart, but Hume's comment on the incident is worth noting:

Nothing proves more evidently the vast superiority assumed by the nobility and gentry above all other orders of men, during those ages, than the extreme difference which Edward made in his treatment of these French knights, and that of the six citizens of Calais who had exerted more signal bravery in a cause more justifiable and more honorable.

In West's key, the only figure in this painting to be identified, apart from Edward III, is Sir Walter Manny, standing behind and to the left of the King.

An oil sketch is No. 73 below. A slight drawing formerly in the collection of A. Paul Oppé, which is signed *B. West 1788 / Windsor*, shows the head and shoulders of a bearded, bare-headed man wearing armor and may be a study for either Edward III or Sir Walter Manny in this painting.[1]

[1]Pen, $5\frac{3}{4} \times 5\frac{1}{4}$ in.

73 Edward III Entertaining His Prisoners

MRS. JOHN DAVENPORT

Oil on canvas: $14\frac{1}{2} \times 20\frac{1}{4}$ in. (37×51.5 cm.)

PROV: Offered by West's sons to the United States in

1826 (110, "Edward 3d Crowning Ribemond," 1 ft. 8 in. × 1 ft. $8\frac{1}{2}$ in.) and sold by them, Robins, London, 22–25 May 1829, lot 107 ("King Edward the Third Crowning Ribemond at Calais," 1 ft. 3 in. × 1 ft. $8\frac{1}{2}$ in.), bt. by Bone for £42 on behalf of Joseph Neeld, MP, Grittleton House, Wilts.; by descent in the Neeld family until sold at Christie's, London, 13 July 1945, lot 174 as a pair with No. 66; sold anonymously, Knight, Frank, & Rutley, London, 26 Nov. 1958, lot 15, as a pair with No. 66; Nicholson Gallery, New York; Vose Galleries, Boston, by 1962; purchased by the present owner in 1965

EXH: West's Gallery 1821 (10), 1822–28 (109); BI 1833 (33) lent by Joseph Neeld

LISTED: *PC* p. 565 ("The small picture of Edward III. crowning Ribemont at Calais—a sketch," West, Painting-room); *UM*, p. 530; *BA*, p. 17; Galt, p. 227; Dillenberger, p. 170 (316)

74 Edward, the Black Prince, Receiving John, King of France, Prisoner, after the Battle of Poitiers 1788

HER MAJESTY THE QUEEN

Oil on canvas: 113×177 in. (287×449.6 cm.)

Signed lower left: *B. West 1788*

PROV: Painted for George III (1797 account: "John King of France brought Prisoner to the Black Prince," for the Audience Chamber in Windsor castle, 1787, £1,365; 1801 account: p. 213, no. 3, "Edward the Black Prince receiving John King of France and his son as prisoners," . . .)

EXH: RA 1794 (8) "Edward, the Black Prince receiving John, King of France, prisoner, after the battle of Poitiers, painted for His Majesty's Audience Chamber in Windsor Castle"

LISTED: *PC*, p. 559 ("The Battle of Poitiers, when John

King of France is brought prisoner to the Prince," George III, in the King's Audience-room at Windsor Castle); *UM*, p. 527; *AA*, p. 68 ("Edward Prince of Wales receiving John King of France as Prisoner after the Battle of Poitiers," 9 ft. × 15); Barlow, p. 431; *BA*, p. 13 (9 ft. × 16); Galt, p. 216; Dillenberger, p. 139 (29)

LIT: V and A Cuttings, III, pp. 671 and 698; Brayley and Britton 1801, pp. 235–38; *Public Characters* 1805, pp. 552–53; *Windsor Guide* 1807, p. 49; Pyne 1819, I, pp. 169–70; Millar 1969, I p. 134 (1163); Strong 1978, pp. 80–81, fig. 88

For the Audience Chamber see No. 56.

In the Battle of Poitiers, on 19 September 1356, the English under the Prince of Wales routed a much larger French army and even succeeded in capturing the French King. This painting shows the captured King and his son Philip conducted to the Prince of Wales's tent, where they were greeted with courtesy, sympathy, and respect. Hume describes the moderation and humanity shown by the twenty-seven-year-old Prince on this occasion as his real and truly admirable heroism, to which, in comparison, victories are vulgar things.

In West's list of portraits in No. 74, published by Brayley and Britton, he points out that the plume of ostrich feathers in a coronet worn by the Prince of Wales is that worn by the King of Bohemia at the Battle of Crécy (see No. 58). A helmet adorned with a chaplet of pearls lying among the trophies in the foreground he identifies as belonging to Eustace de Ribeaumont (see No. 72), who was slain at the Battle of Poitiers. In addition to the three principal participants, the key identifies twenty-two further figures.

One smaller version of the composition is known (No. 75), and a second is recorded (No. 76). A drawing in the Philadelphia Museum of Art shows the composition in a preliminary stage, with the Prince and King shaking hands, and numerous other differences from the finished painting.[1]

[1]Pen and blue wash, $9\frac{1}{2} \times 18\frac{1}{4}$ in., signed lower right: *B. West*.

73

75 Edward, the Black Prince, Receiving John, King of France, Prisoner, after the Battle of Poitiers

See color illustration, p. 97

GEORGE E. DOTY

Oil on canvas: $16\frac{1}{2} \times 25\frac{1}{2}$ in. (42×65 cm.)

PROV: Offered by West's sons to the United States in 1826 (111), and sold by them, Robins, London, 22–25 May 1829, lot 109 (1 ft. $4\frac{1}{2}$ in. × 2 ft. $1\frac{1}{2}$ in.), bt. for £173.5.0 by W. J. Ward, who still owned it in 1833; sold by Francis Duroveray, Christie's, London, 2 March 1850, lot 195; W. Jackson, Parliament Row, Sussex; sold anonymously, Christie's, London, 18 June 1976, lot 47, where bought by the present owner

EXH: West's Gallery 1821 (17), 1822–28 (111); BI 1833 (4) lent by W. J. Ward

LISTED: *PC*, p. 564 ("The small picture of John King of France brought to the Black Prince," West, Painting-room); *UM*, p. 530; Barlow, p. 434; *BA*, p. 16; Galt, p. 226; Dillenberger, p. 167 (285)

Parts of the histories of this painting and No. 76 may be confused. The early lists of West's works include only one version of the subject in his possession, in addition to No. 74 in the Royal Collection. Nonetheless, two versions were sold by West's sons in 1829. We have equated No. 75 with the painting sold in May 1829 because of the exact correspondence in size with the measurements

74

wounded on 30 April 1524, during the French army's retreat from the forces of the Emperor Charles V near the River Sesia in Lombardy. He refused to be taken away and was left by his soldiers propped against a tree to await the enemy. In the painting he is shown calmly reciting the Miserere and holding the hilt of his sword up to form a cross. Paying him homage are his adversaries, led by the Marquis of Pescara and the Constable of Bourbon, Bayard's former companion in arms, who had deserted to the imperial cause and to whom Bayard addressed his last words. The figures on the lower left are raising a tent, which the Marquis had ordered to shelter the dying knight.

Eulogistic biographies of Bayard were published in France in 1760 and 1769,[1] and No. 77 may have been inspired indirectly by one of them. It appears to have been the first picture by any artist, English or French, to depict Bayard's death, but another English artist, Edward Penny, who also anticipated West in painting the death of Wolfe, had exhibited a picture of an incident from Bayard's life, the *Generous Behavior of the Chevalier Bayard*, at the Society of Artists in 1768 (121).

There is what appears to be an early and slight sketch for the composition of No. 77 in one of West's sketchbooks belonging to the Royal Academy.

[1] See Rosenblum 1967, p. 58, notes 29 and 30.

listed in the Robins catalogue. No. 75 is a replica rather than a preparatory sketch. It corresponds closely to the large painting in all details, and unlike several other smaller versions of paintings for the Audience Chamber (Nos. 62, 66, 68, and 413) it was not described in the Robins catalogue as a sketch or study. In that sale, it received the highest price, by a considerable margin, of any of this group of works. An analogous replica is No. 60, after *Edward III with the Black Prince after the Battle of Crécy* (No. 58). Nos. 60 and 75 are the same size, and both were described in the early lists as small pictures of the subjects, without being qualified as sketches.

76 Edward, the Black Prince, Receiving John, King of France, Prisoner, after the Battle of Poitiers

LOCATION UNKNOWN

PROV: Sold by West's sons, Robins, London, 20–22 June 1829, lot 90 ("The Black Prince receiving John, King of France, prisoner"); owned by E. Wyndham in 1834

EXH: SBA 1834 (134) lent by E. Wyndham

In the sale of 20–22 June 1829, No. 76 followed immediately after No. 69, which was described as a "very masterly sketch" of the *Institution of the Order of the Garter* (No. 67), and it preceded a painting of "King Edward embracing his Son after the Battle of Cressy," which was not identified as a sketch in the sale catalogue, but which we identify as No. 59 (now in the Royal Collection), an oil sketch for No. 58, the large painting of the same subject. Hence it seems probable that No. 76 was also a preparatory sketch, possibly corresponding in size to No. 59.

77 The Death of the Chevalier Bayard 1772
See color illustration, p. 67.

HER MAJESTY THE QUEEN

Oil on canvas: $87\frac{1}{4} \times 70\frac{1}{2}$ in. (221.6 × 179.1 cm.)

Signed lower left (on a mallet lying on the ground): *B. West/1772*

PROV: Painted for George III (1801 account: p. 207,

no. 3, "Bayard at the moment of his death receiving the Constable Bourbon," 1771, £315)

EXH: RA 1773 (305) "The death of the Chevalier Bayard"; BI 1833 (39); *American Painting from the Eighteenth Century to the Present Day*, Tate Gallery, London, 1946 (240); *Bicentenary Exhibition*, Royal Academy, London, 1968–69 (52)

ENGR: Mezzotint ($24\frac{3}{4} \times 20\frac{1}{4}$ in.) by Valentine Green, pub. 1 Feb. 1774 by J. Boydell; engraving ($19\frac{5}{16} \times 15\frac{1}{2}$ in.) by P. Bernard (with explanatory text in French); outline engraving ($4 \times 3\frac{1}{4}$ in.) by Normand *fils*, pub. in Hamilton 1831

LISTED: *PC*, p. 559 ("Bayard", George III, Queen's House); *UM*, p. 527; *AA*, p. 67 ("The Death of Bayard," 10 ft. × 7); Barlow, p. 431; *BA*, p. 13; Galt, p. 216; Dillenberger, p. 136 (5)

LIT: Galt 1820, p. 50; Hamilton 1831 (97); Locquin 1912, pp. 154, 157; Waterhouse 1953, p. 192; Evans 1959, p. 44, pl. 26; Irwin 1966, p. 148; Rosenblum 1967, p. 34, note 107; Millar 1969, I, p. 132 (1157), II, pl. 124

According to John Galt, West proposed No. 77 along with the *Death of Epaminondas* (No. 5), as suitable companions to the replica of the *Death of Wolfe* commissioned by George III (No. 94). Each of the pictures shows the death of a hero on the field of battle in a different historical period. Whereas the *Death of Epaminondas*, in Galt's words, "would, as a classic subject, and with Grecian circumstances, make a suitable contrast with *The Death of Wolfe*," the *Death of the Chevalier Bayard* "would serve to illustrate the heroism and peculiarities of the middle ages." No. 77 was West's first painting of a medieval subject, anticipating his paintings from the life of Edward III (Nos. 56–76) for the Audience Chamber at Windsor by some fifteen years. Nos. 77 and 5 are the same size. Both were exhibited at the Royal Academy in 1773, but No. 77 was apparently completed before No. 5, which is signed and dated *1773*. There is no correspondence in size between these two paintings and the version of the *Death of Wolfe* which they were painted to accompany, although there is correspondence in subject.

Pierre Terrail, Seigneur de Bayard (1473–1524), "chevalier sans peur et sans reproche," was mortally

78

78 The Death of the Chevalier Bayard *c.* 1799

CITY ART GALLERY, WAKEFIELD, YORKSHIRE

Oil on canvas, mounted on board: $9\frac{3}{4} \times 11\frac{1}{8}$ in. (25 × 28.5 cm.)

PROV: As for No. 6

EXH: As for No. 6

LISTED: *PC*, p. 567 ("The Death of Bayard," West, Gallery); *UM*, p. 531; Barlow, p. 435 ("Death of the Chevalier Bayard"); *BA*, p. 18; Galt, p. 231; Dillenberger, p. 179 (402)

See Nos. 6 and 79, together with which this work was initially framed.

79 The Death of Sir Philip Sidney 1799

CITY ART GALLERY, WAKEFIELD, YORKSHIRE

Oil on canvas, mounted on board: $9\frac{3}{4} \times 11\frac{1}{8}$ in. (25 × 28.5 cm.)

Signed lower left: *B. West 1799*

PROV: As for No. 6

EXH: As for No. 6

LISTED: *PC*, p. 567 ("The Death of Sir Philip Sydney,"

79

West, Gallery); *UM*, p. 531; Barlow, p. 435; *BA*, p. 18; Galt, p. 231; Dillenberger, p. 178 (400)

See Nos. 6 and 78, together with which No. 79 was originally framed. Unlike those pictures, the present work does not repeat a subject that West had previously painted. The artist subsequently did paint a larger painting of the same incident in 1806 (No. 80). His interest in Sidney may have been inspired by John Francis Rigaud's painting of the same subject dated 1793.[1] Rigaud's picture was intended for Robert Bowyer's Historic Gallery, to which West also contributed (see Nos. 50 and 52).

Sir Philip Sidney (1554–1586), soldier, statesman, and poet, was wounded by a bullet in his left thigh at the Battle of Zutphen in the Netherlands, in which he had fought as a volunteer. After suffering from extreme thirst, he was finally brought a drink, but, seeing a dying foot-soldier nearby, he handed the water to him with the words "Thy necessity is yet greater than mine." Although No. 79 was exhibited in 1799 as "the death of Sir Philip Sidney," the painting, unlike Nos. 6 and 78, its companions, does not show an actual scene of death. Sidney was wounded on 22 September 1586, when the incident shown took place, but he lived on for twenty-six days, dying on 17 October.

In Hume's words, Sidney "was the most perfect model of an accomplished gentleman that could be formed even by the wanton imagination of poetry or fiction. Virtuous conduct, polite conversation, heroic valor, and elegant erudition all concurred to render him the ornament and delight of the English court."

[1]With Sabin Galleries, London, 1969. We are indebted to William Pressly for information about this work.

80 The Death of Sir Philip Sidney 1806

WOODMERE ART GALLERY, PHILADELPHIA

Oil on canvas: 78 × 62 in. (198 × 157.5 cm.)

Signed lower left: *B. West 1806*

PROV: Commissioned in 1806 by Alexander Davison, St. James's Square, London; his sale, Stanley, London, 28 June 1823, lot 25; Joseph Harrison, Philadelphia, by 1867; Sarah Harrison, Philadelphia; purchased in 1912 by Charles Knox Smith, Chestnut Hill, Philadelphia, and left by him to the Woodmere Art Gallery, which he founded.

LIT: *A Descriptive Catalogue of Paintings by British Artists, executed for A. Davison, Esq. of subjects selected from the History of England, as arranged in his house in St. James's Square*, privately printed, 1806; *A Catalogue of a Splendid Collection of Pictures by British Artists, the Subjects taken from English History. Painted expressly for Alexander Davison, Esq. which will be Sold by Auction by Mr. Stanley at His Great Room, Maddox-Street, Hanover Square, on Saturday the 28th of June 1823*, pp. 16–17; Tuckerman 1867, pp. 101 and 630

In 1806 Alexander Davison (1750–1829), a ship-owner and government contractor, commissioned eight pictures by as many artists of subjects from English history. The choice of specific subject was left to each artist, the only condition being that he include a self-portrait in the work. The artists were West, Copley, James Northcote, Henry Tresham, Robert Smirke, Richard Westall, Arthur William Devis, and David Wilkie. The artists provided descriptions of their works which were printed in Davison's catalogue published in 1806 and reprinted in the catalogue of the sale of the collection in 1823. In No. 80 West is the balding man on the extreme right who leans on a horse and contemplates the scene. The figure in dark armor on horseback directly above the wounded Sidney, according to West's description, represents the Earl of Leicester, who was Sidney's uncle as well as commander of the English forces at Zutphen. Next to him Sidney's servant tries to control his master's "still restive and ungovernable" horse.

No. 80 does not appear to be based in any way on No. 79, West's earlier painting of the same subject. West, however, seems to have been working on the composition of this painting before receiving Davison's commission in 1806 for a picture from English history. Two drawings of Sidney are included in the list of West's works published in *Public Characters of 1805*,[1] and one or the other may have been the drawing in West's gallery mentioned by the artist in a letter to the first Earl of Lonsdale, dated 18 March 1808: "From that drawing I painted a picture for Alex Davison Esq.—it is one of my best works; and in the catalogue of his pictures there is a description of it."[2]

In a letter to a Mr. T. Smith (probably John Thomas Smith), dated 18 December 1806,[3] West announced that he was painting the subject and asked for assistance in obtaining likenesses of Sir Philip and the Earl of Leicester. The source which he seems to have used for Sidney was George Vertue's engraving after the well-known miniature at Windsor Castle by Isaac Oliver of a young man seated under a tree, which was published as a portrait of Sidney in 1745, and which West recommended to Lord Lonsdale as the most authentic likeness. The miniature is no longer believed to represent Sidney:[4] it nonetheless probably accounts for Sidney's very different appearance in No. 80 from that in No. 79, West's earlier small painting of the same subject, where the mustache and beard recall the likeness of Sidney in John Francis Rigaud's painting of 1793.

[1]*PC*, pp. 568 and 569 ("The Drawing of the Death of Sir Philip Sydney" and "The Drawing of Sir Philip Sydney ordering the Water to be given to the wounded Soldier," both West, Gallery); *UM*, pp. 531 and 532; *BA*, p. 19; Galt, pp. 233 and 234; Dillenberger, pp. 183 (447) and 186 (482).

[2]Pierpont Morgan Library.

[3]Archives of American Art, microfilm roll D10, frames 1692–93.

[4]Roy Strong, *National Portrait Gallery: Tudor and Jacobean Portraits*, London, 1969, I, p. 293.

81 The Destruction of the Spanish Armada

LOCATION UNKNOWN

PROV: Sold by West's sons, Robins, London, 20–22 June 1829, lot 40 ("Defeat of the Spanish Armada, a sketch")

LISTED: *PC*, p. 567 ("The Sketch of the Destruction of the Spanish Armada," West, Gallery); *UM*, p. 531; Barlow, p. 433 (under "Various Collections" and not described as a sketch); *BA*, p. 18; Galt, p. 232; Dillenberger, pp. 164 and 180 (256 and 420)

This mysterious work, which we know only from a title in the early lists of West's *oeuvre* and from an entry in the sale catalogue of 20–22 June 1829, may have been related in some way to No. 82, showing Queen Elizabeth after the defeat of the Armada. Nos. 81 and 82 could not have been the same work masquerading under two titles, since both appear on the early lists of West's works and they were sold separately in 1829, but No. 81 may have been a preparatory sketch for No. 82.

82

82 Queen Elizabeth Going in Procession to St. Paul's Cathedral after the Destruction of the Spanish Armada 1792

LOCATION UNKNOWN

Oil on canvas: 17 × 26 in. (43 × 66 cm.)

Signed and dated *1792*

PROV: Offered by West's sons to the United States in 1826 (118) and sold by them, Robins, London, 22–25 May 1829, lot 70 ("Procession of Queen Elizabeth to St. Paul's after the Defeat of the Spanish Armada," 1 ft. 5 in. × 2 ft. 2 in.); bt. by Bone for £63 on behalf of Joseph Neeld, MP, Grittleton House, Wilts.; by descent in the Neeld family until sold, Christie's, London, 13 July 1945, lot 172; Vose Galleries, Boston, by whom sold in 1964 to the late L. Gerard Paine, Boston

EXH: RA 1794 (20) "Queen Elizabeth going in procession to St. Paul's Cathedral after the destruction of the Spanish Armada"; West's Gallery 1821 (13); BI 1833 (48) lent by Joseph Neeld

LISTED: *PC*, p. 566 ("Queen Elizabeth's Procession to St. Paul's," West, Gallery); *UM*, p. 530; Barlow, p. 435; *BA*, p. 18; Galt, p. 229; Dillenberger, p. 174 (358)

LIT: Strong 1978, pp. 26–27, fig. 17

The defeat of the Spanish Armada took place in 1588. Roy Strong proposes that the likeness of Queen Elizabeth is based on Francis Delaram's engraving of c. 1617–19 after a portrait by Nicholas Hilliard (British Museum) and that the likeness of Lord Burghley, who bows reverently to her, is based on the portrait attributed to Marcus Gheeraerts in the National Portrait Gallery, showing Burghley as a Garter Knight.

83 Oliver Cromwell Dissolving the Long Parliament 1782
See color illustration, p. 70

MONTCLAIR ART MUSEUM, MONTCLAIR, NEW JERSEY

Oil on canvas: 60¼ × 84¼ in. (153 × 214 cm.)

Signed lower left: *B. West 1782*

PROV: Probably commissioned by Richard, Lord

80

Grosvenor (later the first Earl Grosvenor) and certainly in his possession by 1789; by family descent to the second Duke of Westminster (died 1953); sold in a local sale near Chester in 1959; sold anonymously, Sotheby's, London, 2 Dec. 1959, lot 127, bt. by Appleby; purchased by the Montclair Art Museum in 1960

EXH: RA 1783 (62) "Oliver Cromwell ordering the mace to be taken away when he expelled the long parliament"; Allentown 1962 (14); Washington and Philadelphia 1980

ENGR: Engraving (17 × 23¼ in.) by John Hall, pub. 5 April 1789 by B. West, J. Hall, and E. Woollett, from the picture in the possession of the Earl Grosvenor; engraved key identifying the main figures in Nos. 83 and 84; engraving (8⅝ × 11⅝ in.) by B. Baling (?); outline engraving (3¼ × 4⅞ in.) by Normand *fils*, pub. in Hamilton 1831 (195)

LISTED: *PC*, p. 561 ("Cromwell dissolving the long Parliament," the Earl of Grosvenor); *UM*, p. 528; Barlow, p. 432; *BA*, p. 14; Galt, p. 220; Dillenberger, p. 152 (144)

LIT: V and A Cuttings, I, p. 232 (*Morning Herald*), and II, p. 340; Buckler 1826, p. 3; Hamilton 1831 (195); Morris 1889, pp. 34–35; Kraemer 1975, pp. 24–25, fig. 18; Strong 1978, pp. 26, 148–49, fig. 170

This painting is one of five pictures of approximately the same size and showing subjects from English history which Lord Grosvenor purchased from West. The others are *General Monk Receiving Charles II on the Beach at Dover* (No. 84), the *Battle of the Boyne* (No. 88), *The Battle of La Hogue* (No. 90), and the *Death of General Wolfe* (No. 93). It has occasionally been stated that the five paintings were commissioned by Lord Grosvenor, but this was certainly not true of the *Death of General Wolfe*, which West undertook on his own initiative. The catalogue of the collection at Grosvenor House published by John Young in 1821 states that Nos. 88 and 90 were painted for Lord Grosvenor, but does not mention Nos. 83 and 84, and the earliest evidence found by the authors of this catalogue indicating that West painted No. 83 for Lord Grosvenor is a remark to that effect in G. Hamilton's *English School* of 1831, which is not an absolutely reliable source. Nonetheless, because of the uniformity of size (a size which West rarely used otherwise), there is an evident connection among the five works, and it does seem likely that Lord Grosvenor, who had purchased the *Death of General Wolfe* in 1771, subsequently commissioned the other four paintings to hang with it. Two of them (Nos. 88 and 90) appeared together at the Royal Academy in 1780 and were engraved in 1781; the other two (Nos. 83 and 84) were exhibited in 1783 and engraved in 1789. Unlike the *Death of General Wolfe*, the later four paintings all show subjects from the seventeenth century. In the 1820s the pictures were divided. Nos. 88, 90, and 93 were at Grosvenor House in London, according to Young's catalogue published in 1821, while five years later the Bucklers' *Views of Eaton Hall* described Nos. 83 and 84 as in the Ante-Dining-room of the Grosvenor seat in Cheshire. In the later nineteenth century all five paintings hung together above the book cases in the library at Eaton Hall.

No. 83 shows the moment on 20 April 1653, when Oliver Cromwell dissolved and forcibly expelled the Long Parliament, which had been sitting since 1640. Cromwell stands slightly to the right of center ordering one of his soldiers to remove the mace ("take away that shining bauble"). The figure in the left corner with outstretched arms and wearing a hat is Sir Henry Vane, whose protest against Cromwell's action provoked the reply: "O Sir Henry Vane, Sir Henry Vane, the Lord deliver me from Sir Henry Vane!" Behind Cromwell

sits Henry Scobell, the Clerk of the Parliament, and above and behind him is the Speaker, William Lenthall, being roughly pulled from his place by Colonel Thomas Harrison. A key, presumably published to accompany John Hall's engraving after No. 83 (and the companion engraving after No. 84) identifies several further figures in the composition, including Generals Fairfax, Lambert, and Fleetwood. It also includes Cromwell's son-in-law Henry Ireton (bareheaded and behind the soldiers on the right), although Ireton had been dead since November 1651.

West evidently owned a drawing of Cromwell by or ascribed to Samuel Cooper, which he may have used for the likeness in No. 83.[1] A drawing at Swarthmore contains profiles of two heads possibly intended for figures in No. 83 and a sketch of the central group with Lenthall seated undisturbed in his chair and Cromwell hatless and in a different position.[2] A drawing in the Pierpont Morgan Library shows Cromwell pointing with both hands toward the mace while looking in the opposite direction.[3]

A large painting, which was sold in New York in 1912, and which is now in a private collection in California, appears from a photograph to be a copy of No. 83.[4] There is no documentary evidence to suggest that West ever painted a second version of the subject.

[1] Sold Sotheby's, London, 11 May 1836, lot 18, Cooper, "The Portrait of Oliver Cromwell, supposed to be the first design for his celebrated miniature, framed."
[2] Black chalk on blue paper: 9⅜ × 11½ in. (ill. in Kraemer 1975, fig. 19).
[3] Black chalk on blue paper: 6 × 5⅜ in. (Kraemer 1975, pp. 24–25, no. 37, and pl. 23).
[4] Oil on canvas, 60 × 84 in., Forrest sale, Anderson Galleries, New York, 5–7 Feb. 1912, lot 572 (with dimensions listed as 75 × 104 in.).

84 General Monk Receiving Charles II on the Beach at Dover 1782
See color illustration, p. 70

MILWAUKEE ART CENTER, LAYTON ART GALLERY COLLECTION

Oil on canvas: 59½ × 84½ in. (151 × 214.5 cm.)

Signed lower right: *B. West 1782*

PROV: Probably commissioned by Richard, Lord Grosvenor (later the first Earl Grosvenor) and certainly in his possession by 1789; by family descent to the second Duke of Westminster (died 1953); sold by the executors of his estate, Sotheby's, London, 15 July 1959, lot 126, bt. by Weitzner; Lawrence A. Fleischman, Detroit; Kennedy Galleries, New York; purchased by the Milwaukee Art Center in 1964

EXH: RA 1783 (91) "General Monk receiving King Charles II on the beach at Dover"; *American Painting 1760–1960*, Milwaukee Art Center, 1960

ENGR: Engraving (16⅞ × 23⅜ in.) by William Sharp, etched by William Woollett, pub. 5 April 1789 by B. West, E. Woollett, and J. Hall, from the picture in the possession of the Earl Grosvenor; engraved key identifying the main figures in Nos. 83 and 84; engraving by Alois Kessler; outline engraving (3¼ × 4½ in.) by Normand *fils*, pub. in Hamilton 1831 (177)

LISTED: *PC*, p. 561 ("The Restoration of Charles II," the Earl of Grosvenor); *UM*, p. 528; Barlow, p. 432; *BA*, p. 14; Galt, p. 220; Dillenberger, p. 152 (143)

LIT: V and A Cuttings, I, p. 232 (*Morning Herald*); Buckler 1826, p. 3; Hamilton 1831 (177); Morris 1889, pp. 34–35; Strong 1978, p. 26

For the group of paintings of scenes from British History

which belonged to Lord Grosvenor, see the preceding entry.

In 1660, after nine years of exile, Charles II returned to England and to the throne, at the invitation of Parliament, but largely because of the efforts of General George Monk (or Monck, later created first Duke of Albemarle). This painting shows General Monk on his knees greeting the King on his arrival at Dover on 25 May 1660. The King's brothers, the Dukes of Gloucester and York, who accompanied him, stand behind him, and in the crowd behind them are the Earl of Clarendon and Sir John Grenville, who had served as chief intermediary between Monk and Charles II. In the background is Dover Castle.

A drawing for the composition, which differs considerably from the finished painting, is in the British Museum,[1] and a slight sketch of two heads, which West may have drawn for the two principal figures, is in a sketchbook used by the artist *c.* 1782–85, now in the Yale Center for British Art.[2]

William Woollett, the engraver, died in 1785, and accordingly the print after No. 84, which he commenced, was completed by William Sharp. That print must be the one referred to by Joseph Farington in 1796 under the wrong title, since neither Woollett nor Sharp worked on the plate after No. 83:

> Boydell said that though West had joined in attacking his Uncle for continuing Woolletts name to the retouched Plate of Wolfe, He himself had gone much farther, for He had published the Print of "Oliver Cromwell ordering the Mace to be taken from the House of Commons", with Woolletts name as having etched it, though Sharp told Boydell, "Woollett only etched one head and one Hand."[3]

The Boydell quoted by Farington was Josiah Boydell, the nephew and partner of Alderman John Boydell, who was one of the initial publishers, along with Woollett himself, of Woollett's engraving of the *Death of General Wolfe* (No. 93). His criticism of West's use of Woollett's name reflects some commercial rivalry, since West and the two engravers Woollett and John Hall (who had engraved *William Penn's Treaty with the Indians* [No. 85] for Boydell) were themselves the publishers of the prints after the four sequels to the *Death of General Wolfe* belonging to Lord Grosvenor, thus excluding the Boydells from the market for companions to their earlier prints.[4]

[1] Pencil and black chalk, 6⅜ × 9½ in. (1920-6-15-19).
[2] Pencil, sheet size 6⅜ × 4⅛ in.
[3] *Farington Diary*, 16 Dec. 1796 (Farington 1978–, III, p. 720).
[4] The engravings after Nos. 83 and 84, published after William Woollett's death, list E. Woollett, rather than W. Woollett, as one of the three publishers.

85 William Penn's Treaty with the Indians
1771–72
See color illustrations, pp. 68, 158

PENNSYLVANIA ACADEMY OF THE FINE ARTS, PHILADELPHIA

Oil on canvas: 75½ × 107¾ in. (192 × 273 cm.)

Signed lower left: *B. West | 1771*

PROV: Painted for Thomas Penn (1702–1775), Stoke Court, Bucks.; by family descent to Granville John Penn (1803–1867) by whom offered for sale, Christie's, London, 10 July 1851, lot 72, and bt. in for £441; subsequently purchased privately from Granville Penn in 1851 or 1852 by Joseph Harrison, Philadelphia; placed on loan by him in the National Museum, Independence Hall, Philadelphia, in 1873, and bequeathed by him in 1874 to the Pennsylvania Academy to be left on deposit in Independence Hall, where it remained until 1961

EXH: RA 1772 (270) "William Penn's treaty with the Indians, when he founded the province of Pennsylvania in North America"; BI 1833 (42) lent by John Penn; PAFA 1853 (23) lent by Joseph Harrison; PAFA 1864 (513); *William Penn Parlor*, Great Central Fair, Logan Square, Philadelphia, 1864 (1); *World's Columbian Exposition*, Chicago, 1893; Philadelphia 1938 (24); *Life in America*, Metropolitan Museum, New York, 1939–40 (26); *Survey of American Painting*, Carnegie Institute, Pittsburgh, 1940 (82); *American Processional*, Corcoran Gallery, Washington, 1950 (2); Philadelphia 1976 (2)

ENGR: Engraving (16¾ × 23¼ in.) by John Hall, pub. 12 June 1775, by John Boydell, from the painting belonging to the late Thomas Penn, and dedicated to the Proprietors of the Province of Pennsylvania; numerous later prints of the picture, most of which seem to have derived from the Hall engraving, are listed in Brinton 1941, pp. 146–66

LISTED: Barlow, p. 433 ("William Penn treating with the Savages," under "Various Collections"); Dillenberger p. 164 (255)

LIT: Farington Diary, 2 April 1804 (Farington 1978–, VI, p. 2288); *Public Characters* 1805, pp. 538–39, 552; Roberts Vaux, "A Memoir on the Locality of the Great Treaty between William Penn and the Indian Natives in 1682," *Memoirs of the Historical Society of Pennsylvania*, I, 1826 (reprinted 1864), pp. 104–6; Dunlap 1834, I, pp. 41, 57–58, 91–92 (Dunlap 1918, I, pp. 40–41, 60–61, 101–2); Peter S. Du Ponceau and J. Francis Fisher, "A Memoir on the History of the Celebrated Treaty made by William Penn with the Indians under the Elm Tree at Shackamaxon in the Year 1682," *Memoirs of the Historical Society of Pennsylvania*, III, pt. II, 1836, pp. 162–64; Tuckerman 1867, p. 101; John Hall and Samuel Clarkson, *Memoirs of Matthew Clarkson of Philadelphia 1735–1800 and of His Brother Gerardus Clarkson 1737–1790*, privately printed, 1890, p. 24; Graves 1906, VIII, pp. 212–13 (Horace Walpole, 1772); Hart 1908, pp. 14–15, 17; Landis 1926, pp. 247–48; Neumeyer 1938, p. 165; Wind 1938, p. 121; Brinton 1941, pp. 99–189; Evans 1959, pp. 51, 54, 120, note 60, pl. 35; Irwin 1966, pp. 145–46; *Symbols of Peace: William Penn's Treaty with the Indians*, Pennsylvania Academy of the Fine Arts, Philadelphia, 1976 (exhibition catalogue with essays by Charles Coleman Sellers and Anthony N. B. Garvan); Dillenberger 1977, pp. 22–24, fig. 12; Alberts 1978, pp. 110–11; Ann Uhry Abrams, "Benjamin West's Documentation of Colonial History: *William Penn's Treaty with the Indians*," *Art Bulletin*, LXIV, 1982, pp. 59–75

The painting shows William Penn (1644–1718), the founder of the colony of Pennsylvania, making a treaty of peace with the local Lenape Indians shortly after his arrival in America in 1682. This event is traditionally said to have taken place under the "Great Elm" at Shackamaxon (later Kensington, and now part of Philadelphia) on the Delaware River. The area is to the north-east of downtown Philadelphia, and there is a small Penn Treaty Park on the site.

Although Penn certainly made various agreements with Indians, particularly in regard to purchase of land, whether the specific event depicted in No. 85 actually took place has been questioned by many biographers of Penn and by Ellen Starr Brinton in her fundamental article about the painting. No written treaty is known to exist, and the first published account, in *Memoirs of the Private and Public Life of William Penn* by Thomas Clarkson, dates only from 1813. Clarkson consulted West in writing his biography of Penn, and his description of the ceremony reads suspiciously like a description of West's painting, which, indeed, seems to be the earliest known document of any sort indicating that such an event took place at all. Nonetheless, West seems firmly to have believed, probably on the basis of family and local tradition in his native Pennsylvania, that the meeting did take place, and in a letter apparently written to John Penn, Thomas Penn's son, some time after 1810, he referred to the elm tree "which was held in the highest veneration by the original inhabitants of my native country, by the first settlers, and by their descendants, and to which I well remember, about the year 1755, when a boy, often resorting with my school-fellows."[1]

The most important document we have concerning No. 85 is a letter written by West in 1805 in response to a request for information about the painting:

Indisposition for several days last deprived me the satisfaction of answer your enquiries respecting the portraits in the picture of the Treaty between Wm. Penn and the American Indians. When I painted the picture of that Treaty for the late Thos. Penn, every enquire was made to obtain portraits of those who accompanied his distinguished Father into the wilderness of North America; but without effect, except in the portrait of Wm. Penn—and for that I am indebted to the Medalion made in wax by Silvinius Bevan and the description given to me by my father of Wm. Penn's person.

The great object I had in forming that composition was to express savages brought into harmony and peace by justice and benevolence, by not withholding from them what was their reight, and giving to them what they were in want of, as well as a wish to give by that art a conquest made over native people without sward or Dagder.

The leading characters which make that composition are the Friends and Indians—the characteristicks of both have been known to me from my early life—but to give that Identity which was necessary in such a noval subject, I had recourse to many persons then living for that Identity—and among that number was my honoured Father and his eldest son, my half Brother, Thos. West, and by possessing the real dresses of the Indians, I was able to give that truth in representing their costumes which is so evident in the picture of the Treaty. Those were the principles and my reasons in giving that picture of the Wm. Penn Treaty to the civilized world.

The object in composing that picture and the materials to give it truth I have above presented, and if they should be found by you to any way contribute to that information you are about to give in a Biographical History on Portraits, they are much at your service.[2]

A portrait (in ivory, rather than wax) by Silvinius (or Sylvanus) Bevan, a London Quaker apothecary, was carved from memory shortly after Penn's death and depicted him in old age.[3] West's depiction of Penn as a portly man who appears considerably older than thirty-eight, his age in 1682, does seem to have been based on it. The description of Penn's person given to West by his father was presumably derived from reminiscences of the artist's grandparents. Thomas Pearson, West's mother's father, was, according to Thomas Clarkson's account, one of Penn's companions in the ceremony shown in No. 85.

West also mentioned the inclusion of his father and his half-brother, Thomas West, in a letter dated 12 July 1775, to his brother William accompanying an engraving of the picture, which had been published the previous month.[4] There he identified Thomas as resting on his cane, standing immediately behind Penn. Their father, John West, is the elderly man in the group to the left (see No. 545 for a very similar portrait of West's father and No. 546 for slightly later portraits of both men). West's possession of "the real dresses of Indians" is confirmed by a letter to Matthew Clarkson of Philadelphia, dated 23 January 1772, asking Clarkson's instructions about what to do with the Indian dresses when the picture is completed.[5] The dresses referred to may have been acquired by Clarkson in a trip to the Ohio valley in 1766–67.

Despite, or because of, West's efforts for the sake of accuracy, the painting is full of inaccuracies. In addition to Penn's being made to appear too old, the dress of all the Quakers is that of the eighteenth rather than the seventeenth century, and the building activity at Shackamaxon would hardly have been so advanced in 1682. An unpublished study of the dress of the Indians by Carol K. Rachlin reveals a mixture of authenticity in some details and gross inauthenticity in others.[6] Her conclusion is that "West used authentic Indian specimens of mixed Lenape, Iroquois and northern Algonquian origin, which he modified and combined, in terms of his knowledge, to achieve what he considered a more artistic presentation."

Although No. 85 is signed and dated *1771*, West wrote to Matthew Clarkson on 23 January 1772, that he was making progress with the picture and expected to have it done early in the spring. On 9 April 1772, Henry Merchant visited West's studio and reported that West was "just finishing" the picture.[7] The Royal Academy exhibition of 1772, in which it was included, opened in early May. Horace Walpole in marginal comments in his Royal Academy exhibition catalogue wrote that it had been painted in three weeks.

The painting does not appear on any of the early lists of West's works except on that of Joel Barlow. A drawing included in the other lists as in West's possession[8] may have been the large drawing sold by the Baroness Burdett-Coutts in 1922.[9] A small and faint drawing for the composition, showing some differences in detail, is in the Cooper-Hewitt Museum, New York.[10] Two versions in oil, whose authenticity is supported by contemporary documentation are Nos. 86 and 87 below. Copies and variants, which are numerous because of the image's adoption as an icon both of Quakerism and of American history, are recorded by Brinton and in the catalogue of the exhibition *Symbols of Peace*.

Gilbert Stuart's portrait of the engraver John Hall (*below*) includes a detail of No. 85, or, more appropriately, of Hall's engraving after the painting, in the background. This corresponds to the inclusion of the

Gilbert Stuart, *John Hall*. Oil on canvas, 35½ × 27⅝ in. National Portrait Gallery, London

Death of General Wolfe (No. 93) in the background of Stuart's portrait of William Woollett in the Tate Gallery (ill. p. 213).

Horace Walpole's full comment about this painting in 1772 was:

> This picture, which contains many figures, was painted in three weeks, has good drawing and great merit. The contrast of simplicity between the Quakers and Indians has great effect. The colouring, like all his pictures in his second manner, is heavy, brickish, and void of clearness. . . . His first manner was in changeable colours like Baroccio.
>
> The best of his works in the Exhibition.[11]

In 1804 Joseph Farington recorded the opinions of four of his colleagues about the work. Henry Fuseli and James Northcote thought "very lightly" of it, but Robert Smirke and John Opie "approved it highly." Opie, at whose home the discussion took place, "said it was a consistent and good prose picture.—It was narrative painting."

Alfred Neumeyer suggested in 1938 that the composition of No. 85 was derived from the *Tribute Money* by Masaccio, via an engraving by Thomas Patch published in 1772. This was immediately challenged by Edgar Wind, who argued instead that the gestures are typical of the English conversation-piece. In a major article published in 1982 and devoted to No. 85, Ann Abrams has proposed a number of additional stylistic and iconographic sources and has provided an assessment of the painting's message as understood in the context of the contemporary political developments in Pennsylvania.

[1] Quoted by Roberts Vaux in 1826.
[2] Landis 1926, p. 248, and Brinton 1941, pp. 114–15. The exact date of the letter is 2 Feb. 1805. Landis gives the name of the recipient as H. Darton, Brinton as W. Darton. He was evidently William Darton (1747–1819), who had published a *Biographical sketches of eminent British characters, c.* 1800. The "Biographical History" mentioned by West must have been an intended sequel.
[3] See William J. Hall, *William Penn: Topical Biography,* London, etc., 1937, pp. 300–301, ill. opp. p. 304. Bevan's likeness of Penn was carved in the round, but it served as the basis for further portraits on medals. There is a version in wax of one of these in the Historical Society of Pennsylvania (see Nicholas B. Wainwright, *One Hundred and Fifty Years of Collecting by the Historical Society of Pennsylvania 1824–1974,* Philadelphia, 1974, p. 3).
[4] Pennsylvania Academy of the Fine Arts, quoted in Brinton 1941, p. 114.
[5] Quoted in Hall and Clarkson, p. 24.
[6] "Report on the Identification and Authenticity of the Indian Costumes Portrayed in the Painting *Penn's Treaty with the Indians* by Benjamin West," sent to Helmut von Erffa in 1955.
[7] Quoted in *Symbols of Peace.*
[8] *PC,* p. 568 ("The Drawing of Kenn's [*sic*] Treaty," West, Gallery); *UM,* p. 531; *BA,* p. 19 ("Penn's"); Galt, p. 232; Dillenberger, p. 181 (431).
[9] Christie's, London. 4–5 May 1922, lot 11 (sepia, 16½ × 23½ in.).
[10] Pen and wash, 5$\frac{11}{32}$ × 8$\frac{1}{8}$ in. (Brinton 1941, p. 134, no. 3, and Philadelphia 1976, no. 1).
[11] Graves, from whom these remarks are quoted, gives them in slightly different order, the sentence about West's first manner accompanying another work two entries later (see No. 169). It, nonetheless, clearly continues the discussion of West's color begun by Walpole in relation to No. 85.

86

86 William Penn's Treaty with the Indians

THOMAS GILCREASE INSTITUTE OF AMERICAN
HISTORY AND ART, TULSA, OKLAHOMA

Oil on canvas: 75 × 108 in. (190.5 × 274 cm.)

PROV: Offered by West to the Pennsylvania Academy of the Fine Arts in 1809 ("Wm. Penns treaty with the Indians," 6 ft. × 9 ft. 6 in., £400); sold by his sons, Robins, London, 20–22 June 1829, lot 180 ("Penn's Treaty with the Indians, duplicate on large canvas, unfinished"); Joseph Strutt, Derby, by 1835; presented by him to the Mechanics Institute, Derby, *c.* 1844; Robert Carlen Gallery, Phildelphia, 1953; Hirschl & Adler Galleries, New York, 1954; purchased by Thomas Gilcrease from Knoedler Galleries, New York, in Nov. 1958

LIT: *A Catalogue of Paintings and Drawings . . . in the Collection of Joseph Strutt, Derby, Derby,* 1835 (250); Brinton 1941, pp. 109–10, 134–35 (4)

The Tulsa painting's provenance can be traced back to 1835, when it was described in Joseph Strutt's catalogue as "The original Sketch of the great Picture in the possession of Mr. Penn, Spring Gardens." It is unfinished in many areas and, hence, appears to be identical with the large unfinished picture sold by West's sons in 1829. It was possibly commenced *c.* 1809 to be one of the works West hoped to sell to the Pennsylvania Academy. Many of the works on West's list of 1809 were not finished (indeed, not begun), so the appearance of a work on that list is consistent with its being unfinished. Because of the subject matter No. 86 would have been a particularly suitable work for the new academy in Philadelphia, and it is appropriate that West's original treatment of the subject now hangs there.

87 William Penn's Treaty with the Indians

CHICAGO HISTORICAL SOCIETY

Oil on panel: 17$\frac{1}{8}$ × 23$\frac{7}{8}$ in. (43.5 × 60.5 cm.)

PROV: (?) John Boydell, London, by 1773; sold by the estate of Richard Price Jones, Christie's, London, 26 Feb. 1791, lot 40 ("Penn's treaty, small, painted for the plate—engraved") for £25.4.0; sold by Sir Edmund Charles Nugent, Bt., Puttick & Simpson, London, 2 May 1929, lot 96, bt. by De Casseres; Percy A. Rockefeller; Emily Crane Chadbourne

EXH: J. Boydell's, 90 Cheapside, London, 1773

ENGR: Engraving (16$\frac{3}{4}$ × 23$\frac{1}{4}$ in.) by John Hall, as under No. 85

LIT: Brinton 1941, pp. 109, 134 (2)

No. 87 is an exact but reduced replica of No. 85. It apparently was sold during West's lifetime along with a small version of the *Death of Wolfe* (No. 100) as a copy made by the artist for the engraver to work from. The engravings of *Penn's Treaty* by John Hall and *The Death of Wolfe* by William Woollett seem to have been undertaken as a pair, and Boydell's advertisement of the two, dated 1 Jan. 1773, stated that "Two Pictures, the same size as the Prints" could be seen at his establishment in Cheapside;[1] so the appearance together in 1791 of the two small paintings fits with their having been painted for the engravers. West's engravers usually do not seem to have worked from reduced copies, but it is possible that, because of the special interest of West's first exhibited paintings of modern subjects, both showing events set in America, the artist took special pains to ensure the success of the engravings. Those pains were justified by the extraordinary commercial success of the engravings, particularly that of the *Death of Wolfe.* Nonetheless, although West may have taken responsibility for the small versions, and although No. 87 appears to be of high quality, it is reasonable to question to what extent they would have been painted by his own hand.

A drawing which is inscribed "Orig¹: plate drg. by J. Hall / Penn & the Indians after West" is in the Historical Society of Pennsylvania.[2]

[1] Reproduced in Brinton 1941, opp. p. 118.
[2] Pencil, ink, and red chalk, 17$\frac{1}{4}$ × 23$\frac{3}{4}$ in., squared for transfer (Philadelphia, 1976, no. 3).

88 The Battle of the Boyne 1778
See color illustrations, pp. 71, 74

HIS GRACE THE DUKE OF WESTMINSTER

Oil on canvas: 60 × 83 in. (152.5 × 211 cm.)

Signed lower left: *Benj. West, 1778*

PROV: Painted for Richard, Lord Grosvenor (later the

first Earl Grosvenor); by family descent to the present owner

EXH: RA 1780 (58) "The battle of the Boyne"; BI 1851 (112); Manchester 1857 (116)

ENGR: Engraving (16$\frac{15}{16}$ × 23$\frac{3}{8}$ in.) by John Hall, pub. 18 Oct. 1781, by B. West, J. Hall, and W. Woollett, from the picture in the collection of Lord Grosvenor, and dedicated to the Prince of Wales; engraved key identifying the main figures in Nos. 88 and 90; mezzotint (7$\frac{1}{2}$ × 10$\frac{11}{16}$ in.) by J. Grozier, dated 1771 (the date is within the image and is certainly incorrect); engraving by J. Rogers; etching (4$\frac{1}{2}$ × 6$\frac{1}{4}$ in.) by John Young, pub. in Young 1821, pl. 6 (14)

LISTED: *PC*, p. 561 ("The Boyne," the Earl of Grosvenor); *UM*, p. 528; Barlow, p. 432; *BA*, p. 14; Galt, p. 220; Dillenberger, p. 152 (142)

LIT: V and A Cuttings, I, p. 185 (*London Courant*, 6 May 1780); Young 1821, p. 6 (14), pl. 6; Angelo 1830, I, pp. 27–28, II, p. 106; Passavant 1836, I, p. 158; Waagen 1854, II, p. 174; Morris 1889, pp. 34–35; William T. Whitley, *Gilbert Stuart*, Cambridge, Mass., 1932, pp. 190–91; Strong 1978, p. 26

In the Battle of the Boyne, which took place on 1 July 1690, on the banks of the River Boyne in Ireland, William III defeated James II, who, after he was replaced on the throne of England by William and Mary in the revolution of 1689, had established himself in Ireland. In the painting, William, who personally had led a wing of his army into battle, is the central figure on a white horse. Prince George of Denmark and the Duke of Ormond are behind the King on the extreme left of the painting, and in the right foreground, the eighty-two-year-old Duke of Schomberg is being carried from the field of battle, mortally wounded. A small figure falling from his horse in the distance at the center of the picture is the Reverend George Walker, the Protestant rector of Donaghmore, who had previously fought valiantly against James II at Londonderry, and who was also killed at the Boyne. James II remained aloof from the fighting and is not depicted in the painting.

No. 88 is one of the group of historical pictures bought from West by Lord Grosvenor, for which see No. 83. In 1821 it was at Grosvenor House and in 1889 at Eaton Hall.

Gilbert Stuart claimed to have posed in armor for the fallen Duke of Schomberg and on horseback for King William III. According to Stuart, the horse belonged to George III, but according to Henry Angelo, William's steed was a horse named Monarch belonging to Angelo's father, "the finest horseman in the world," who himself posed for William III at the suggestion of George III. Angelo implies that this happened in 1766, a date that is impossibly early, as is also the date of 1771, which appears on the Grozier mezzotint of No. 88. Nevertheless, No. 88 may have been begun several years before it was first exhibited in 1780; it is signed and dated *1778*, two years before.

One drawing of the subject appears on the early lists of West's works.[1] A drawing in the British Museum, showing numerous differences in detail, bears a false signature and does not appear to be by West.[2] A version in oil of the subject, which belonged to Jane Teller of New York in *c.* 1921 appears to be a copy by another hand.[3]

[1] *PC*, p. 568 ("The Drawing of the Boyne," West, Gallery); *UM*, p. 532; *BA*, p. 19; Galt, p. 233; Dillenberger, p. 184 (462). This was probably the drawing sold, S. Leigh Sotheby, London, 1 June 1839, lot 50 ("The Battle of the Boyne, a design for a picture painted for Earl Grosvenor, as a Companion to the Battle at La Hogue," pen and ink washed).
[2] Pen and sepia ink and wash, 7$\frac{1}{4}$ × 10$\frac{1}{2}$ in. (1871-6-10-756).
[3] Ill. in Jaffe 1975, p. 153, fig. 122.

89 The Battle of the Boyne

LOCATION UNKNOWN

(72 × 96 in.) (183 × 244 cm.)

PROV: Offered by West to the Pennsylvania Academy in 1809 ("The Battle of the Boyne," 6 ft. × 8, £400); sold by his sons, Robins, London, 20–22 June 1829, lot 151 ("Two large canvases—The Commencement of the Battle of the Boyne, and Christ with a Child" [see No. 324])

If the word "Commencement" in the sale catalogue of 1829 referred to the state of the painting, rather than the state of the battle, it suggests that this version was not even far enough along to be described as "unfinished". It was possibly begun, like No. 86, as part of West's project to paint a group of works for the Pennsylvania Academy.

90 The Battle of La Hogue *c.* 1775–1780
See color illustrations, pp. 71–73

NATIONAL GALLERY OF ART, WASHINGTON, D.C.

Oil on canvas: 60$\frac{1}{8}$ × 84$\frac{3}{8}$ in. (152.5 × 214.5 cm.)

PROV: Painted for Richard, Lord Grosvenor (later the first Earl Grosvenor); by family descent to the second Duke of Westminster (died 1953) and sold by the executors of his estate, Sotheby's, London, 15 July 1959, lot 125, bt. by Nicholson; acquired by the National Gallery in 1959 (Andrew W. Mellon Fund)

EXH: RA 1780 (73) "The destruction of the French fleet at La Hogue, 1692"; BI 1851 (117); Manchester, 1857 (109)

ENGR: Engraving (16$\frac{13}{16}$ × 23$\frac{1}{2}$ in.) by William Woollett, pub. 18 Oct. 1781 by B. West, W. Woollett, and J. Hall, from the picture in the collection of Lord Grosvenor, to whom the plate is dedicated; engraved key identifying the main figures in Nos. 88 and 90; engraving (8$\frac{7}{16}$ × 11$\frac{5}{16}$ in.) by Voysard, pub. by Isabey, Paris, dedicated to the Comte de Briassac, and accompanied by a text in French; etching (4$\frac{7}{16}$ × 6$\frac{5}{16}$ in.) by John Young, pub. in Young 1821, pl. 7 (18); outline engraving (4$\frac{9}{16}$ × 4$\frac{15}{16}$ in.), pub. in Hamilton 1831 (280)

LISTED: *PC*, p. 561 ("The Battle of La Hogue," the Earl of Grosvenor); *UM*, p. 528; Barlow, p. 432; *BA*, p. 14; Galt, p. 220; Dillenberger, p. 152 (141)

LIT: *Morning Post*, 4 May 1780; *London Courant*, 6 May 1780 (V and A Cuttings, I, p. 185); Farington Diary, 2 and 8 July 1806 and 1 July 1808 (Farington 1978–, VIII, pp. 2803 and 2806, and IX, p. 3307); *Public Characters* 1805, p. 553; Young 1821, p. 7 (18), pl. 7; Hamilton 1831 (280); Dunlap 1834, I, pp. 65, 88–91 (Dunlap 1918, I, pp. 69–70, 98–101); Passavant 1836, I, p. 158: Waagen 1854, II, p. 173; Morris 1889, pp. 34–35; Flexner 1939, p. 71; Gardner and Feld 1965, pp. 29–34; Dickason 1970, p. 132 (letter from West to Thomas Eagles, 10 Oct. 1810); Kraemer 1975, pp. 13–14; Strong 1978, p. 26

The Battle of La Hogue was fought by the combined English and Dutch fleets against the French in the English Channel from 19 May to 24 May 1692.[1] Having sustained heavy losses, the French admiral, the Comte de Tourville, took a dozen ships into the Bay of La Hogue, near Cherbourg, to gain the protection provided by the guns of two overlooking fortresses. The English sent in a flotilla of small boats under Admiral George Rooke, who succeeded in burning not only the French warships but also transport ships intended to carry a mixed French and Irish army to England. This disaster ended Louis XIV's plans to invade England

in order to restore James II to the throne. The key to Nos. 88 and 90 identifies the standing figure holding a sword in the small boat left of center as Admiral Rooke and a tiny figure on the distant cliff to the right of center as James II. The exiled King, as he watched the destruction of the fleet that was to return him to his throne, is said to have exclaimed, "None but my brave English tars could have performed so gallant an action."

See No. 83 for the group of historical pictures by West belonging to Lord Grosvenor. No. 90 was probably commissioned by Lord Grosvenor as a pair with the *Battle of the Boyne* (No. 88). The two appeared together at the Royal Academy in 1780; engravings after them were published on the same day in 1781; they share a key; and they shared the same history until No. 90 was sold in 1959. In July 1806 West cleaned No. 90 and the *Death of Wolfe* (No. 93), for his patron's son in his own studio, where they were seen by Joseph Farington.

No. 90 is not signed or dated. It was first exhibited in 1780, but may have been painted some years earlier. Its companion (No. 88), together with which it appeared at the Royal Academy in 1780, is signed and dated *1778*. and a second version (No. 91), which West is unlikely to have begun before No. 90, is inscribed *B. West 1778. Retouched 1806*. William Dunlap variously described No. 90 as probably painted five or more years before the publication of William Woollett's engraving in October 1781 and as probably painted in 1774 or 1775. Despite the imprecision of these dates, Dunlap almost certainly had seen No. 90 in West's studio in the summer of 1785, when John Trumbull was copying it (see No. 91) and when Dunlap was himself copying West's *Choice of Hercules* (No. 143), so he may well have known something of its earlier history. Dunlap, who called No. 90 one of West's best paintings and devoted several pages to it, also reported that when West was painting No. 90, "an admiral took him to Spithead and to give him a lesson on the effect of smoke in a naval battle, ordered several ships of the fleet to manoeuvre as in action and fire broadsides, while the painter made notes."

In 1810 West wrote to Thomas Eagles that he had included a likeness of William Williams in the painting, "in one of the Boats, next in the rear of Sir George Rook." Williams (1727–1791), West's early mentor and friend in Philadelphia, had returned to England during the American revolutionary war and lived for a while in London. Although West's wording is slightly ambiguous, Williams can probably be identified as the prominent figure with his hand on a cannon and wearing a feathered hat on the extreme left of the composition (*below*).[2]

The Battle of La Hogue (Cat. No. 90), detail

One drawing of the subject is included in the lists of West's works.[3] Two drawings of naval subjects in the Morgan Library may have been made in conjunction with West's preparatory researches, although they are not reflected either compositionally or in details in No. 90.[4] A drawing in the British Museum does not appear to be by West;[5] it bears a false signature similar to that on a drawing by another hand also in the British Museum of the *Battle of the Boyne*, also ascribed to West.

The second version, partly painted by John Trumbull, is No. 91 below. A copy by George Chambers (1803–40), which is signed and dated 1836, is in the National Maritime Museum at Greenwich.[6] Another copy by an unknown artist is now at Swarthmore,[7] and several other copies are recorded in private collections. A drawing by Dirk Langendijk (1748–1805), which appears to be a free copy after the Woollett engraving of No. 90 transformed into the destruction of the English Fleet by the Dutch at Chatham in 1667, is in the Teylers Museum in Haarlem, and was engraved in 1783.[8]

No. 90 is one of ten paintings by ten British painters included in an "imaginary collection of our principal deceased Artists" in the background of *The Fine Arts Commission* of 1846 by John Partridge (National Portrait Gallery, London).[9]

[1] For a recent detailed account, see Philip Aubrey, *The Defeat of James Stuart's Armada*, Leicester University Press, 1979.
[2] Compare Williams's *Self-Portrait* of *c.* 1781 or later, reproduced in Dickason 1970, fig. 1. For a different identification, see Flexner 1952, p. 41.
[3] *PC*, p. 568 ("The Drawing of La Hogue," West, Gallery); *UM*, p. 532; *BA*, p. 19; Galt, p. 233; Dillenberger, p. 183 (456).
[4] See Kraemer 1975, pp. 13–14, Nos. 17 and 18, and pl. 9.
[5] Pen and sepia ink and wash, $6\frac{1}{2} \times 9\frac{7}{8}$ in. (1860-6-9-1).
[6] 60 × 85 in.
[7] 27 × $23\frac{1}{2}$ in.; exhibited in Philadelphia 1921 (11) and Brooklyn 1922 (11) lent by Richard W. Lehne.
[8] See Dunlap 1918, I, pp. 70 and 98–101; and the entry for Langendijk by A. Staring in Thieme-Becker, XXI, p. 331.
[9] See Richard Ormond, "John Partridge and the Fine Arts Commissioners," *Burlington Magazine*, CIX, 1967, pp. 397–402.

91 The Battle of La Hogue

METROPOLITAN MUSEUM OF ART, NEW YORK

Oil on canvas: $64\frac{1}{2} \times 96$ in. (164 × 244 cm.)

Signed on the stern of Admiral Rooke's boat: *B. West 1778. Retouched 1806*

PROV: Offered by West to the Pennsylvania Academy in 1809 ("The Battle of La Hogue," 6 ft. × 8, £400); offered by his sons to the United States in 1826 (8), and sold by them, Robins, London, 22–25 May 1829, lot 101 ("Battle of La Hogue," 5 ft. 5 in. × 8 ft.), bt. by Monckton for £388.10.0; Edward P. Monckton, Fineshade Abbey, Northants., by 1888; sold by George Edward Monckton, Sotheby's, London, 10 Feb. 1921, lot 3; Sigmund Samuel, Toronto; Leslie W. Lewis, Toronto; Will Bradley Chapoton, Leamington, Ontario, by 1952; Victor D. Spark, New York; Graham Gallery, New York; purchased by the Metropolitan Museum in 1964 (Harris Brisbane Dick Fund).

EXH: West's studio, 1806; West's Gallery 1822–28 (69); RA 1888 winter (154) lent by Edward P. Monckton; New York 1962 (5)

LISTED: *PC*, p. 564 ("The second picture of the Battle of La Hogue," West, Painting-room); *UM*, p. 530; Barlow, p. 434; *BA*, p. 16 ("The second picture of the Battle of La Hogue, with alterations"); Galt, p. 225 ("The first and second picture of the Battle of La Hogue"); Dillenberger, p. 166 (279)

91

LIT: Farington Diary, 11 May 1806 (Farington 1978—, VII, p. 2757); Trumbull 1953, p. 87; Gardner and Feld 1965, pp. 29–32; Jaffe 1975, pp. 70, 316, fig. 44

This painting was begun as a companion to a version of the *Death of Wolfe* (No. 98), which has the same dimensions and is inscribed *B. West 1776—Retouched 1806*. The artist probably retouched both pictures in 1806 in order to display them in his studio along with the freshly completed *Death of Nelson* (No. 108). Joseph Farington saw the three pictures together there on 11 May 1806. At that time West told him that No. 91 had been painted twenty-five years earlier, i.e., in 1781. That date seems reasonable for a second version of No. 90, which had been exhibited in 1780 and of which the engraving was published in 1781, but it contradicts the *1778* on the canvas. The earlier date is plausible if we accept William Dunlap's statement that No. 90 was painted as early as 1774 or 1775.

If No. 91 was begun in 1778, it seems in fact to have been painted largely in 1785 by John Trumbull. In his *Autobiography* Trumbull mentions completing a copy of *La Hogue*, larger on every side than the original, in the summer of 1785, and there is a fuller entry in his account book:[1]

> *The Battle of La Hogue.* Copied for Mr. West, from his original picture.—the same size, but on a Cloth—12 inches longer, & 6 inches higher:—this extra size is left equally on every side, with a view to enlarge the Composition for a Companion to the Copy of Wolfe:—This Copy was painted up entirely at once, and will only be retouched and harmonized by Mr. West:—the universal Shadow was blue black prepared by Jenkins, by means of which the union & silvery tone were obtained—this picture was begun by Mr. Raphael West, who was soon fatigued and gave it up:—it was finished by me in less than Sixty days and given to Mr. West—it now (1813) hangs in his painting Room, having been continued to the whole surface of the Cloth by him, and is valued at Guineas 600.

No. 91 is $4\frac{3}{4}$ in. higher and $11\frac{5}{8}$ in. wider than No. 90, and the additions along the top and on both sides are evident. There are additional figures on the left, and

the man clinging to a mast on the right, who is bald in No. 90, has hair in No. 91.

[1] Quoted in Jaffe 1975, p. 316.

92 General Johnson Saving a Wounded French Officer from the Tomahawk of a North American Indian *c.* 1764–68

DERBY MUSEUM AND ART GALLERY

Oil on canvas: 51 × 42 in. (129.5 × 106.5 cm.)

PROV: Offered by West's sons to the United States in 1826 (30), and sold by them, Robins, London, 22–25 May 1829, lot 171 ("General Johnson Saving a Wounded French Officer from the Tomahawk of a North American Indian," 4 ft. 2 in. × 3 ft. 4 in.) bt. by Caspar for £50.8.0; given by Miss Eleanor Tennant, Spofforth Grange, near Harrogate, Yorks., to the Derby Art Gallery in 1937

EXH: West's Gallery 1822–28 (95)

This little-known picture is not signed or dated. It does not appear on any of the lists of West's works published during his lifetime, nor is there any other documentation of its existence until 1822, two years after his death, when it was exhibited along with other pictures in his estate. Although there is a substantial gap in its history prior to 1937, size and subject correspond so closely that there can be little doubt that it was the painting in West's sons' possession in the 1820s and sold by them in 1829. It appears to have been begun soon after West's arrival in England in 1763, the most obvious stylistic affinities being with his portrait of *General Monckton* (No. 665) and *Angelica and Medoro* (No. 188), both of which were exhibited in 1764, but it may have been completed or substantially repainted at a later date, possibly by another hand after West's death. It has suffered somewhat over the years, and its present condition does not encourage more precise attempts at dating or discrimination of hands.

The Robins sale catalogue of 1829 describes the subject thus:

> In the old American war, in the days of General Wolfe, the intrepid General Johnson, in the midst

of a skirmishing party, saw one of his confederate Indians about to kill a French officer, and according to their savage mode of warfare, by way of trophy, to take his *scalp*. The General flew to the rescue of the victim, and admonished the Indian thus. "If you want a trophy, go to the woods and collect scalps from the brave who have fallen in the fight."

General Johnson was Sir William Johnson (1715–1774), an American from New York State who served as Superintendent of Indian Affairs.[1] In 1755 he was commissioned major-general to lead a force of Mohawks and New England militia against the French at Crown Point on Lake Champlain. Before arriving there, while encamped at the southern end of Lake George, he was attacked by the French under Baron Ludwig August von Dieskau. Johnson's forces successfully repelled the French, and Dieskau was wounded and taken prisoner. He was brought to Johnson's tent and there treated with great courtesy by his captor,

who himself had been wounded earlier in the day. Thereupon Indians also came to the tent, intending, as Johnson explained to his captive, to kill Dieskau in revenge for Indians killed by the French. Johnson protected him, ordering the Indians away.

The victory at Lake George was immediately famous; Johnson was made a baronet because of it, and West as a young man of seventeen in the American colonies would certainly have known about it. But it is worth noting that Johnson's courtesy and particularly his protection of Dieskau were well known in Europe at the time this work was painted. A main source for the story as told by later historians such as Francis Parkman is Diderot's account in his *Memoirs* of what Dieskau had told him in 1760 about the incident.[2] Dieskau lived in England for several years after his return from America, and it is possible that West met him before painting No. 92.

For Johnson, see also Nos. 93 and 647. For other and

earlier depictions of American Indians by West see No. 452. See also p. 58 above.

[1] See Arthur Pound and Richard E. Day, *Johnson of the Mohawks*, New York, 1930. The incident depicted in No. 92 is described on pp. 212–13. See also James Thoma Flexner, *Lord of the Mohawks*, Boston, 1979, pp. 147–60.
[2] Francis Parkman, *Montcalm and Wolfe*, Boston, 1907, I, pp. 319–22.

92

93 The Death of General Wolfe 1770
See color illustrations, pp. 54, 58

NATIONAL GALLERY OF CANADA, OTTAWA

Oil on canvas: $59\frac{1}{2} \times 84$ in. (151 × 213.5 cm.)

Signed lower right: *B. West PINXIT.| 1770*

PROV: Purchased from West by Richard, Lord Grosvenor (later the first Earl Grosvenor); by family descent to the second Duke of Westminster, by whom presented to the Canadian War Memorials, through Lord Beaverbrook, in 1918

EXH: RA 1771 (210) "The death of General Wolfe"; BI 1843 (150); RA 1870 winter (85); *Canadian War Memorials*, Royal Academy, London, and Anderson Galleries, New York, 1919 (353); *American Colonial and Early Federal Art*, Detroit Institute of Arts, 1930 (88); Philadelphia 1938 (20); *Survey of American Painting*, Carnegie Institute, Pittsburgh, 1940 (83); *Old and New England*, Rhode Island School of Design, Providence, 1945 (64); *American Painting*, Tate Gallery, London, 1946 (227); *From Colony to Nation*, Art Institute of Chicago, 1949 (127); *Likeness of America*, Fine Arts Center, Colorado Springs, Colorado, 1949 (16); *American Processional*, Corcoran Gallery, Washington, 1950 (34); *American Painting*, Vancouver Art Gallery, 1955 (6); *British Painting in the Eighteenth Century*, Montreal Museum of Fine Arts, etc., 1957–58 (70); *A Pageant of Canada*, National Gallery of Canada, Ottawa, 1967 (115); *The Age of Neo-Classicism*, Royal Academy, London, 1972 (271)

ENGR: Engraving ($16\frac{7}{8} \times 23\frac{5}{16}$ in.) by William Woollett, pub. 1 Jan. 1776 by Messrs. Woollett, Boydell, and Ryland, from the picture in the collection of Lord Grosvenor, dedicated to George III; engraved key ($5\frac{1}{2} \times 7\frac{1}{8}$ in.) identifying the main figures, pub. 4 March 1776, by Messrs. Woollett, Boydell, and Ryland; engraving ($16\frac{9}{16} \times 23\frac{1}{8}$ in.) by Theodore Falkeysen, pub. in Basle and Augsburg; engraving ($16\frac{5}{8} \times 23$ in.) by Augustin le Grand; engraving ($8\frac{7}{16} \times 11\frac{5}{8}$ in.) by Carl Guttenberg, pub. in Nuremberg and Paris; outline engraving ($4\frac{1}{2} \times 6\frac{1}{4}$ in.) by J. Mitan, pub. by John Bell in *La Belle Assemblée*, IV, 1808, opp. p. 10 and in *The Portfolio*, VI, 1811, p. 254; etching ($4\frac{3}{4} \times 6\frac{1}{4}$ in.) by John Young, pub. in Young 1821, pl. 2; outline engraving ($3\frac{1}{8} \times 4\frac{5}{16}$ in.) by AR (monogram), pub. in Hamilton 1831 (285)

LISTED: *PC*, p. 561 ("The Death of Wolfe, the first picture," the Earl of Grosvenor); *UM*, p. 528; Barlow, p. 432; *BA*, p. 14; Galt, p. 220 ("the third picture"); Dillenberger, p. 152 (140)

LIT: Farington Diary, 2 and 8 July 1806, 1 July 1808, and 14 Feb. 1810 (Farington—, VIII, pp. 2803 and 2806, IX, p. 3307, and X, p. 3599); *Public Characters*, 1805, pp. 538–39, 552; Galt 1816, p. 67; Galt 1820, pp. 46–50; Carey 1820, pp. 694–95; Young 1821, p. 2 (4), pl. 2; Hamilton 1831 (285); Dunlap 1834, I, pp. 62–64 (Dunlap 1918, I, pp. 66–68); Passavant 1836, I, p. 158; Curwen 1842, p. 52; Waagen 1854, II, p. 173; Morris 1889, pp. 34–36; A. Doughty and G. W. Parmelee, *The Siege of Quebec and the Battle of the Plains of Abraham*, Quebec, 1901, I, p. 67, II, p. 314,

III, pp. 221–22; Graves 1906, VIII, p. 212 (Horace Walpole, 1771); Locquin 1912, pp. 154–57; The Marquess of Sligo, "Some Notes on the Death of Wolfe," *Canadian Historical Review*, III, 1922, pp. 272–78; A. E. Wolfe-Aylward, *The Pictorial Life of Wolfe*, Plymouth, [1927]; Webster 1930; Wind 1938; Neumeyer 1938; Flexner 1939, pp. 65–67; Mitchell 1944; Agnes Addison, "The Legend of West's Death of Wolfe," *College Art Journal*, V, 1945, pp. 23–25; Wind 1947; Waterhouse 1953, pp. 190–92; Kerslake 1959; R. H. Hubbard, *The National Gallery of Canada : Catalogue of Paintings and Sculpture : 1 Older Schools*, Ottawa, 1961, pp. 132–33 (8007); Stacey 1966; Irwin 1966, pp. 147–50; Millar 1969, I, p. 135; Burke 1976, pp. 245–48; Strong 1978, pp. 24–26; Alberts 1978, pp. 103–10 and 410–16; Montagna 1981

Major-General James Wolfe (1727–1759) was mortally wounded while commanding the British forces against the French at Quebec on 13 September 1759. He survived long enough to hear that the French were giving way, and his dying words supposedly were "Now, God be praised, I will die in peace." The painting shows the dying General in the foreground, while on the left a running soldier bearing a captured French standard brings the news of victory. It has been suggested that a figure falling from a horse in the background, faintly visible above the head of the running soldier, represents Wolfe's adversary, the Marquis de Montcalm, who also died in the battle.[1] The setting is the Plains of Abraham outside Quebec, and the St. Lawrence River is on the right. A church tower in the distance evidently represents the steeple of the cathedral in the city of Quebec. As Dennis Montagna has pointed out in his article about No. 93 published in 1981, this view is remarkably true to the actual topography of the Plains of Abraham. Montagna also shows that the activity in the background of the painting presents a synoptic narrative of the day's action, progressing from the British troops unloading ships and ascending the cliff on the right, through scenes of battle, to announcement of victory on the left.

A key published in 1776 to accompany the Woollett engraving identifies six figures in addition to Wolfe. They are Brigadier-General Robert Monckton, second in command (standing with his arm in a sling and holding his chest in the group to the left); Colonel George Williamson, commanding the artillery (the older officer, next to the officer holding the flag above Wolfe); Major Isaac Barré, adjutant-general (immediately behind Wolfe and below Williamson); Captain Hugh Debbieg, engineer (behind and to the left of Monckton and helping to support him); Captain Hervey Smyth, *aide-de-camp* to General Wolfe (kneeling to the left of Wolfe and holding his arm); and Mr. Adair, director and first surgeon of the hospital (kneeling to the right of Wolfe holding a dressing to the dying general's chest). With one exception, all these officers are known to have served at Quebec. They wear uniforms appropriate to their branch of service, and the likenesses generally correspond with those in known portraits. For Wolfe, West evidently made use of a portrait given to him by the Wolfe family.[2] He subsequently painted two imaginary portraits of Wolfe as a boy (Nos. 719 and 720). For General Monckton, see No. 665. Monckton is shown bandaged and supported by two officers because he was wounded at Quebec. The only slightly questionable identification among those provided by the key is that of Mr. Adair, since two surgeons named Adair served in the British Army during the Seven Years' War. The better-known of the two, however, Robert (or "Robin") Adair, was never in North America. According to an article by Colonel C. P. Stacey, the other, John Adair, was at Crown Point serving in General Amherst's army at the time, but if

he was not at Quebec on 13 September 1759, he later claimed that he had been, although not in fact present at the moment of Wolfe's death. A note written in 1775 by James Barry, who was then preparing to paint his version of the subject, states: "Mr. Adair the Surgeon told me that he was not present at the Death of General Wolfe, that when he arrived he found him lying under a tree, where Mr. Browne related to him tho[se] memorable words with which Wolfe expired."[3]

In 1821 John Young described the two soldiers standing on the right as "a Grenadier of the General's own regiment, and his servant, lamenting his fate." Young also identified the officer on the left wearing moccasins and other Indian trappings as Sir William Howe, and this identification has been accepted and repeated in most subsequent accounts of the picture until challenged by Colonel Stacey in 1966. Howe (1729–1814) had served with distinction at Quebec, leading the detachment that first scaled the Heights of Abraham and made the British victory possible, and he supposedly was a friend of West's.[4] Nonetheless, the identification of Howe, made in 1821, and later identifications of other figures in the painting, mentioned below, all seem fundamentally questionable; if West had intended further recognizable portraits in the picture, why were those portraits not identified in the original key published in 1776? Howe had the conspicuous and important appointment as commander of the British army in North America at the time the key appeared, and it is difficult to believe that he could have been omitted from it by oversight. Furthermore, Colonel Stacey argues that the uniform worn by this officer in the painting is that of an American ranger, which would have been inappropriate for Howe. The uniform is evidently that of Rogers Rangers, some of whom served with Wolfe's army at Quebec. Robert Rogers himself was not at Quebec, but he was in London in 1769 and 1770, when West was at work on No. 93, and it has been suggested that he may have lent West a uniform to be copied into the picture.[5]

Detail from the *Death of General Wolfe* (No. 93)

Colonel Stacey points out that the ranger's powder horn has a crude map inscribed on it and the words *Sr. Wm. Johnson* | *MOHAWK RIVER* (*above*). These words clearly refer to the Sir William Johnson (1715–1774), whom West depicted in No. 92 and possibly in No. 647, but whether or not they were intended to identify the possessor of the horn in this painting as Johnson is a question. Johnson was not a ranger, and he was not at Quebec in 1759. He did participate in Amherst's campaign against Montreal in the following year, and West may have either mistakenly believed that he was at Quebec as well, or thought that Johnson's role in the Seven Years' War as Superintendent of Indian Affairs justified his inclusion. Such a hypothesis is supported by the juxtaposition of this figure with an American Indian, who would have served under Johnson's command, although in fact no Indians

served with the British at Quebec either, but it is also possible that, despite the inscription on the powder horn, neither the American ranger nor the American Indian was intended as a specific portrait.

A few other identifications have been put forward in this century. The figure behind the ranger wears kilts, which the Marquess of Sligo described in 1922 as Fraser tartans, thus identifying the wearer as Simon Fraser, Master of Lovat, who commanded a battalion at Quebec. Sligo, citing family tradition, also identified the officer holding the British colors above Wolfe as his ancestor, Lieutenant Henry Browne of the Louisbourg Grenadiers.[6] The thin-faced man looking over Monckton's left shoulder and helping to support him has been called Colonel George Napier on the basis of physical resemblance, but Napier was not in America in 1759, and the degree of resemblance has been questioned by members of the Napier family.[7]

Stories that West solicited payment from officers to include their portraits in the painting are not convincing. The earliest and chief of these dates from over seventy years after the picture was painted and is a rather confused explanation by the daughter of General John Hale as to why her father does not appear in engravings of the painting.[8] West did sell versions of the painting (Nos. 96 and 97) to officers he had represented or to members of their families.

All commentators have pointed out that the scene as portrayed by West is a fabrication. Of Wolfe's companions named above, only Lieutenant Browne, whose identification in the picture is not at all certain, seems likely to have been with him when he died. Monckton and Barré are both known to have been wounded and elsewhere at the moment of Wolfe's death. What is still accepted as the most reliable account of Wolfe's death, in *An Historical Journal of the Campaigns in North America* by Captain John Knox, was published in 1769. West must have known it and utilized it, and he certainly could have painted a more accurate picture if he had chosen to. That he did not suggests that he was already developing his ideas of Epic Composition, which he later expressed in his explanation of the equally inaccurate *Death of Lord Nelson* (No. 108). The most obvious prototype for No. 93 was the painting of the same subject by Edward Penny shown at the Society of Artists in 1764 (versions at Petworth [*see opposite*] and in the Ashmolean Museum), which is a reasonably straightforward depiction of what was reported to have happened, and West must have known that in departing from Penny he was departing from strict truth. His idealization of the subject by modelling the main group on seventeenth-century paintings of the *Deposition* (see ill. p. 58) and by numerous other borrowings is brilliantly discussed in Charles Mitchell's fundamental article about the picture published in 1944. The death of Wolfe was also painted before West by George Romney in 1763 (location unknown) and after him by James Barry in 1776 (New Brunswick Museum, Saint John, New Brunswick).

The novelty, or lack thereof, of showing the figures in modern costume has been extensively discussed by Wind, Mitchell, Addison, Alberts, and others. According to Galt's account, Sir Joshua Reynolds and Archbishop Drummond, who had been West's most important patron prior to 1769 (see No. 33), tried to dissuade the artist from painting the scene in modern costume. West persevered, arguing that "the same truth that guides the pen of the historian should govern the pencil of the artist," and that the event to be commemorated took place "in a region of the world unknown to the Greeks and Romans, and at a period of time when no such nations, nor heroes in their costume, any longer existed." After the picture was finished Drummond and Reynolds came to see it. As quoted by Galt, Reynolds retracted his objections and announced: "I foresee that this picture will not only

Edward Penny, *The Death of General Wolfe*, 1764. Oil on canvas, 24½ × 29 in. National Trust, Petworth House, Sussex

Gilbert Stuart, *William Woollett*. Oil on canvas, 35½ × 27¾ in. Tate Gallery, London

become one of the most popular, but occasion a revolution in the art."

Although No. 93 was first exhibited in 1771, it is dated *1770*, and a letter from West to Charles Willson Peale, dated 21 June 1770, in the Historical Society of Pennsylvania, indicates that it was finished by then and had already "procured me great honour." Galt states that George III declined to buy the picture because the dignity of the subject had been impaired by showing "heroes in coats, breeches, and cock'd hats," and consequently Lord Grosvenor purchased it. George III subsequently commissioned the first of several replicas West made of the subject (No. 94). West proposed that Lord Grosvenor commission a painting of the *Finding of the Bones of Braddock's Army* as a companion, but his lordship objected that because of the obscurity of the subject it would not be interesting to the public. He did, however, purchase from West four pictures of subjects from English history (Nos. 83, 84, 88, and 90), which are the same size as the present painting, and which in the later nineteenth century hung in a group with it in the library at Eaton Hall.

Horace Walpole's comment about No. 93 in 1771 was "Fine picture, tho' there is too little concern in many of the principal figures, and the granadier on the right too tall." Walpole wrote that Lord Grosvenor had paid £400 for the painting, but Samuel Curwen was told in 1776 that the price paid by Lord Grosvenor had been 600 guineas. Curwen saw No. 93 in April 1776 in West's studio, to which it probably had been returned so that it could be copied. Two later versions (Nos. 95 and 98) both bear the date *1776*. According to Farington, No. 93 was again in West's studio in July 1806 to be cleaned, along with the *Battle of La Hogue* (No. 90). This was apparently to prepare them to hang in a room in Grosvenor House devoted to English pictures. Two years later West told John Constable, who reported it to Farington, that the then Lord Grosvenor (the son of the original purchaser) had hung West's pictures so badly, "It was a national concern." In 1821, Nos. 93, 90, and 88, *The Battle of the Boyne*, hung in the Ante-room at Grosvenor House.

The engraving of No. 93 by William Woollett was one of the most commercially successful prints ever published, and the income from it provided the cornerstone of the fortune made by Alderman Boydell as a print publisher. No. 93 is visible in the background of the portrait of Woollett by Gilbert Stuart in the Tate Gallery (*above right*).

A preliminary sketch of the composition is No. 99 below. In West's portrait of himself in Baltimore (No. 526) he holds a drawing of the two standing soldiers on the right.

In addition to the versions listed below, there exist innumerable copies by other hands. No. 93, or Woollett's engraving after it, was also the basis of a caricature

James Gillray, *The Death of the Great Wolf*. Etching, 1795

of Pitt by James Gillray, *The Death of the Great Wolf*, published 17 December 1795 and dedicated to West (*below*).[9]

See also pp. 55–76 above.

[1] Stacey 1966, p. 5.
[2] Sold by West's sons, Robins, London, 20–22 June 1829, lot 194 ("Portrait of the illustrious General Wolfe when a Boy. This most interesting study was presented to the late Mr. West by the General's family, to assist him in forming the likeness of the hero as represented in the celebrated picture of the Death of General Wolfe. Said to be unique.") See also Kerslake 1959 and Kerslake 1977, I, pp. 314–20, and II, pls. 901–14, for portraits of Wolfe.
[3] David Irwin "James Barry and the Death of Wolfe in 1759," *Art Bulletin*, XLI, 1959, p. 351.
[4] See No. 647, note 10.
[5] Burt Garfield Loescher, *The History of Rogers Rangers*, San Francisco, 1946, pp. 280–84.
[6] This identification is questioned in A. G. Doughty, "A New Account of the Death of Wolfe," *Canadian Historical Review*, IV, 1923, pp. 45–55.
[7] See Webster 1930, p. 68.
[8] Quoted by Doughty and Parmelee, III, p. 222.
[9] Hill 1965, pp. 59–60.

94

94 The Death of General Wolfe 1771

HER MAJESTY THE QUEEN

Oil on canvas: $60\frac{1}{2} \times 96\frac{1}{2}$ in. (153.7×245.1 cm.)

PROV: Painted for George III (1801 account, p. 207, no. 5, "The Death of General Wolfe," 1771, £315)

EXH: BI 1833 (17); Manchester 1857 (115); *International Exhibition*, South Kensington, 1862 (123); *Centennial Exhibition*, Philadelphia, 1876 (184); *American Art 1750–1800: Towards Independence*, Yale University Art Gallery, New Haven, and Victoria and Albert Museum, London, 1976 (20); Washington and Philadelphia 1980

LISTED: *PC*, p. 559 ("Wolfe, the second picture," George III, Queen's House); *UM*, p. 527; *AA*, p. 67 (5 ft. 6 in. × 8 ft.); Barlow, p. 431; *BA*, p. 13; Galt, p. 216 ("Wolfe, the first and second"); Dillenberger, p. 136 (6)

LIT: Galt 1820, pp. 46, 50; Webster 1930, p. 65; Evans 1959, pl. 5; Theodore Crombie, "The Death of Wolfe in Paintings: a Bicentenary Review," *Connoisseur*, CXLIV, 1959, p. 57, fig. 2; Irwin 1966, pp. 147–48, pl. 144; Stacey 1966, p. 1, fig. 2; Millar 1969, I, p. 135 (1167); Montagna 1981, p. 80, fig. 11

George III commissioned No. 94 after No. 93 had been purchased by Lord Grosvenor. West proposed the subjects of two companion pictures, the *Death of Epaminondas* (No. 5), which "would, as a classic subject, and with Grecian circumstances, make a suitable contrast with the *Death of Wolfe*," and the *Death of the Chevalier Bayard* (No. 77), "which would serve to illustrate the heroism and peculiarities of the middle ages." As David Irwin has pointed out, within a year of Wolfe's death at the moment of victory at Quebec, Wolfe was compared to Epaminondas.[1] Bayard also died in battle, but not in victory. When West painted later versions of the deaths of Epaminondas and Bayard (Nos. 6 and 78), he replaced the *Death of Wolfe* with the *Death of Sir Philip Sidney* (No. 79) as their companion. The *Death of Wolfe* and its two companions painted for George III hung together in the same room at Buckingham House with the *Departure of Regulus* (No. 10) and the *Oath of Hannibal* (No. 17), which had been commissioned earlier, and with the *Family of the*

King of Armenia before Cyrus (No. 2) and *Segestes and His Daughter before Germanicus* (No. 32) which, according to Galt, were also commissioned at the same time as No. 94.

The canvas of No. 94 has additions of approximately six inches along each side, and the picture as a whole is approximately a foot wider than No. 93. In the addition on the right there are further details of ships in the river and figures disembarking that are not included in No. 93. On the left, the running soldier who brings news of victory is larger and thus brought closer to the foreground group than the corresponding figure in No. 93. The French flag he carries is also at a different angle and more prominent. The increase in size may have been dictated by the space in Buckingham House for which No. 94 was intended; the proportions, however, do not correspond with those of any of the other pictures by West in the Royal Collection with which No. 94 hung. The artist anticipated the wider format in an early sketch for the composition (No. 99) and repeated it in two later versions of the subject (Nos. 95 and 98).

[1] Irwin cites *The Life of General James Wolfe, the Conqueror of Canada*, by J.P., London, 1760. A parallel between Wolfe and Epaminondas was also drawn by Captain John Knox in *An Historical Journal of the Campaigns in North America*, published in 1769 (1968 reprint, pp. 114–16); kindly brought to our attention by Alan McNairn (letter of 18 Nov. 1977) and also cited and discussed in Montagna 1981, p. 81.

95 The Death of General Wolfe 1776

WILLIAM L. CLEMENTS LIBRARY, UNIVERSITY OF MICHIGAN, ANN ARBOR, MICHIGAN

Oil on canvas: $60\frac{1}{2} \times 96\frac{3}{8}$ in. (153.7×244.8 cm.)

Signed lower right: *Painted by B. West | London 1776*

PROV: Bought for £250 by Friedrich, Prince of Waldeck (1743–1813) in 1776; in the Waldeck collection, Arolsen, Germany, until *c.* 1927; bought from the Paul Bottenweiser Galleries, New York, by William L. Clements and presented to the University of Michigan in April 1928

LISTED: *PC*, p. 563 ("The Death of Wolfe, the third

picture," in the possession of the Prince of Waldeck); *UM*, p. 529; Barlow, p. 434; *BA*, p. 16; Galt, p. 223 ("the fourth picture"); Dillenberger, p. 161 (222 and 223)

LIT: *Public Characters* 1805, p. 546; "Notes of the Month," *International Studio*, CX, June 1928, p. 66, ill.; [Edna Vosper], *Benjamin West's the Death of Wolfe*, Ann Arbor, 1928; Webster 1930, pp. 65–67; Stacey 1966, p. 1, fig. 4

In size and background detail this work corresponds to the second version of the subject (No. 94) rather than the original picture of 1770 (No. 93). The most significant addition is a pair of moccasins in the lower left corner. These were apparently added by the artist in response to a criticism by Henry Laurens that the Indian in the foreground should not have been shown with bare feet, since an Indian warrior was never known to go into battle without his moccasins.[1] Laurens (see No. 105) visited London in 1771.

The Prince of Waldeck travelled to England in the summer of 1775 and in the following April he agreed to provide a regiment of troops from Waldeck to fight on behalf of England in America.[2] He must have commissioned No. 95, which appropriately shows a scene of English military victory in America, during his visit. A letter in the archives of Waldeck, dated 3 Sept. 1776 from C. H. Hinuber to the Prince's private secretary, accompanying West's receipt for £250, and asking if the Prince was pleased with the painting, was published by Webster in 1930. The Prince apparently was pleased as he presented West a picture of himself showing No. 95 to his principal historical painter.[3] This painting may be reflected in either one of a pair of drawings owned by Mortimer Brandt in 1963, each of which shows two men examining a painting. One of them has an inscription on the stretcher of the picture within the drawing, *la mort du gen. Wolf par West*. The painter to whom the Prince showed No. 95 was possibly either Johann Heinrich Tischbein the Elder (1722–1789) or Johann Friedrich August Tischbein (1750–1812), both of whom worked extensively for the Prince's court at Arolsen.

[1] Dunlap 1834, I, p. 64 (Dunlap 1918, I, p. 689).
[2] L. Curtze, *Geschichte und Beschreibung des Fürstenthums Waldeck*, Arolsen, 1850, pp. 564–66.
[3] Sold by West's sons, Robins, London, 20–22 June 1829, lot 162 ("Portrait of the Prince Waldeck, exhibiting Mr. West's Wolfe, to his principal Historical Painter, the Picture presented to the late Mr. West by the Prince"). See also *Public Characters* 1805, p. 546.

96 The Death of General Wolfe 1779

NATIONAL TRUST, ICKWORTH, SUFFOLK

Oil on canvas: 60×85 in. (152.5×216 cm.)

Signed lower left: *B. West | 1779*

PROV: In the possession of Frederick William Hervey, fifth Earl and first Marquess of Bristol (1769–1859) by 1804; by family descent to the fourth Marquess (died 1951); accepted along with the house and other contents in lieu of death duties in 1956 by the Treasury and given to the National Trust

LISTED: *PC*, p. 563 ("The Death of Wolfe, the fourth picture"—Lord Bristol); *UM*, p. 529; *BA*, p. 16; Galt, p. 223 ("the fourth picture"); Dillenberger, p. 161 (222 and 223)

LIT: Gervase Jackson-Stops, *Ickworth, Suffolk*, The National Trust, 1976, p. 17, ill. opp. p. 17

It is not known which member of the Hervey family acquired the painting, or when. Captain Hervey Smyth, Wolfe's *aide-de-camp* who kneels at his side in the painting, was a nephew of the first Earl of Bristol.

No. 96 is approximately the same size as No. 93, the first version of the subject. It does not have the additional ships and men which are visible on the right in Nos. 94, 95, and 98, but the running figure on the left corresponds to the figure in these versions rather than the one in No. 93.

97 The Death of General Wolfe

PRIVATE COLLECTION, ENGLAND

Oil on panel: $17\frac{3}{8} \times 25$ in. (44×63.5 cm.)

PROV: The Monckton family by c. 1804 and by family descent to the present owner

LISTED: PC, p. 563 ("A small picture of the Death of Wolfe, the fifth picture," Monckton Family); UM, p. 529; Barlow, p. 434 ("smaller size"); BA, p. 16; Galt, p. 223; Dillenberger, p. 161 (223 and 224)

This small painting corresponds with No. 93 in all significant details. Because of its provenance, it would seem to be the small fifth version of the *Death of General Wolfe*, which by 1804 was recorded in *Public Characters* as belonging to the Monckton family. For a second painting with a Monckton provenance, see the following entry.

98 The Death of General Wolfe 1776–1806

ROYAL ONTARIO MUSEUM, TORONTO

Oil on canvas: $65 \times 96\frac{1}{4}$ in. (165×244.5 cm.)

Signed lower right: *B. West—1776—Retouched 1806*

PROV: Offered by West to the Pennsylvania Academy of the Fine Arts in 1809 ("The Death of Wolfe," 6 ft. × 8, £400); offered by his sons to the United States in 1826 (7, "Death of General Wolfe," 5 ft. 5 in. × 8 ft.); and sold by them, Robins, London, 22–25 May 1829, lot 94 ("Death of General Wolfe," 5 ft. 4 in. × 8 ft.), bt. by Monckton for £577.10.0; Edward P. Monckton, Fineshade Abbey, Northants., 1888; sold by George Edward Monckton, Sotheby's, London, 10 Feb. 1921, lot 2; Sigmund Samuel, Toronto, by whom presented to the Royal Ontario Museum as part of the Sigmund Samuel Canadiana Building

EXH: West's studio, 1806; West's Gallery 1822–28 (76); RA 1888 winter (156) lent by Edward P. Monckton; *Return to Albion: Americans in England, 1760–1940*, National Portrait Gallery, Washington 1979 (7)

LISTED: PC, p. 564 ("The sixth picture of the Death of Wolfe," West, Painting-room); UM, p. 530; Barlow, p. 434; BA, p. 16 ("The Sixth picture of the Death of Wolfe, with alterations"); Galt, p. 225; Dillenberger, p. 166 (278)

LIT: Farington Diary, 11 May 1806 (Farington 1978—, VII, p. 2757); Webster 1930, p. 65; Stacey 1966, p. 1, fig. 3; Jaffe 1975, pp. 69–70, 316; Kenin 1979, ill. p. 9

This painting and a second version of the *Battle of La Hogue* (No. 91), which is the same size, seem to have been commenced as a pair. According to Irma Jaffe's biography of John Trumbull, West initially asked Trumbull to make both copies, but if the dates on the canvases are to be trusted, they were commenced before Trumbull entered West's studio. Raphael West started the copy of the *Battle of La Hogue*, and Trumbull subsequently took it over. He evidently did not work on No. 98, but it seems probable that the picture was largely the work of a studio assistant rather than of West's own hand. West retouched the two pictures in

1806 before exhibiting them in his studio as companions to the *Death of Nelson* (No. 108). This retouching explains the "with alterations," which accompanies the listing of each work in *La Belle Assemblée* published in 1808, but not that in *Public Characters* published in 1804. The most obvious alterations in No. 98 from earlier versions of the subject consist of the addition of sails to the ships on the right side. Otherwise it is basically similar to the versions in the Royal Collection and at Ann Arbor (Nos. 94 and 95). There are moccasins in the lower left corner as in No. 95.

In several publications No. 98 has been erroneously identified as the version included in the early lists of West's works as in the possession of the Monckton family (No. 97). No. 98 did belong to members of the Monckton family from 1829 to 1921, but it was purchased only in 1829, long after the lists were published. After 1829 two versions of the *Death of Wolfe* belonged to Moncktons, whose interest in the subject is explained by the prominent position of General Robert Monckton (for whom see also No. 665) in the composition.

No. 98 is visible in the painting by H. Jamyn Brooks of *The Private View of the Old Masters Exhibition, 1888, Royal Academy of Arts, Burlington House* (National Portrait Gallery, London).

99 The Death of General Wolfe

NATIONAL GALLERY OF CANADA, OTTAWA

Pencil, pen, watercolor, body-color, and oil paint on paper, mounted on masonite board: $16\frac{7}{8} \times 24\frac{1}{8}$ in. (43×61 cm.)

Signed lower left: *Benjn West 1765*

PROV: Offered for sale by Benjamin West, Jr., S. Leigh Sotheby, London, 1 June 1839, lot 120 ("The original drawing of the Death of General Wolf, In pen and umber, and touched upon in oil colour, framed and glazed"); sold by Mrs. Albert F. West, Christie's, London, 19 March 1898, lot 139 ("The Death of General Wolfe, Sketch for the large picture," $17\frac{1}{2} \times 27$ in.), bt. by Obach, together with lot 138 *The Last Supper* (No. 345) for £5.15.0.; Samuel W. Pennypacker, Philadelphia, by October 1899;

99

sold anonymously, Sotheby Parke Bernet, New York, 30 May 1984, lot 1

LISTED: PC, p. 568 ("Drawing of the Death of Wolfe," West, Gallery); UM, p. 532; BA, p. 19; Galt, p. 233; Dillenberger, p. 184 (466)

No. 99 has a note attached to the back of the frame signed by Samuel W. Pennypacker and dated 4 Oct. 1899, which states that it had been preserved by West's family until within the last year. Thus it appears to have been the *Death of General Wolfe* sold by Mrs. Albert F. West in 1898 and identified at that time as a sketch for the large picture. It must also have been the "original drawing" included as the last lot in the sale of West's drawings in 1839, where it was evidently bought in. That drawing was described in the catalogue as in pen and umber but touched upon in oil color, a description which fits No. 99. It is in the monochromatic browns, heightened with white, characteristic of West's early compositional studies (see, for example, No. 36). The date of 1765 accompanying West's signature is improbably early, and it seems likely that the signature and date were added later, or that the original signature was tampered with. Nevertheless, the 1765 was probably on No. 99 by 1839, since the discussion accompanying it in the catalogue of the drawing sale of that year gives 1765 as the date of the finished composition (No. 93), an error which must have been prompted by the date on the drawing.

No. 99 shows basically the same composition as No. 93, but there are numerous and significant differences throughout. The most conspicuous change between the two works is in the positions and dress of the two standing figures on the right. The Indian's legs are reversed, and the arms and hands of the two officers pointing to the captured French flag on the left are parallel to one another in No. 99, crossed in No. 93. West altered the features of almost all the participants in the completed painting, and he changed most of the uniforms, recording the distinguishing markings with much greater precision. The activities of the figures immediately behind the foreground group in the center and right side of the composition are similar, but there are numerous additional figures in the further background of No. 93. The small figure falling from a horse

101

in the left background of No. 93 is not present in No. 99. The church tower is lightly sketched in in pencil, but the hillside where it is situated does not appear at all. On the right there is more space behind the standing grenadier than there is in No. 93, and in this respect the sketch anticipates the expanded composition of the second finished version (No. 94).

100 The Death of General Wolfe

LOCATION UNKNOWN

Oil on panel: $17 \times 23\frac{1}{2}$ in. $(43 \times 59.5$ cm.)

PROV: (?) John Boydell, London, by 1773; sold by the estate of Richard Price Jones, Christie's, London, 26 Feb. 1791, lot 39 ("The death of General Wolfe, small, painted for the plate engraved"), for £29.8.0.; sold by Sir Edmund Charles Nugent, Bt., Puttick and Simpson, London, 2 May 1929, lot 97, bt. by Gooden & Fox

EXH: J. Boydell's, 90 Cheapside, London, 1773

ENGR: Engraving $(16\frac{7}{8} \times 23\frac{5}{16}$ in.) by W. Woollett, as under No. 93

See the entry for No. 87, a comparable small version of *William Penn's Treaty with the Indians*, with which No. 100 seems to have shared the same history until the two pictures were sold in 1929.

101 Lord Clive Receiving from the Mogul the Grant of the Duanney *c.* 1774–95
See color detail, p. 61

THE EARL OF PLYMOUTH

Oil on canvas: *c.* 115×180 in. $(292 \times 457$ cm.)

PROV: Commissioned by Robert Clive, first Lord Clive ("Clive of India," 1725–1774); by family descent to the present owner

EXH: RA 1795 (28) "Lord Clive receiving from the Mogul the grant of the Duanney"

ENGR: Lithographic key identifying the main figures, drawn by J. Baker and printed by D. Redman

LISTED: *PC*, p. 563 ("The late Lord Clive receiving the Duannie from the Great Mogul," for Lord Clive); *UM*, p. 529; Barlow, p. 433; *BA*, p. 15; Galt, p. 222; Dillenberger, p. 158 (205)

LIT: Farington Diary, 28 and 29 April 1795 and 25 Feb. 1818 (Farington 1978–, II, pp. 331, 332, and XV, pp. 5162–63); V and A Cuttings, III, pp. 716, 720, 744, and 745 (*Morning Chronicle*, 6 May 1795); Curwen 1842, p. 52; Croft-Murray 1970, pp. 69 and 291; Mark Bence-Jones, "Clive of India as Builder and Collector II: A Nabob's Choice of Art," *Country Life*, CL, 1971, p. 1448

On 12 August 1765, in a meeting at Allahabad between the Mogul Emperor Shah Alam II and Lord Clive, who

was then Governor of Bengal, the Emperor granted to the East India Company the fiscal administration, known as the *diwani* (or *duanney, dewannee,* etc.), of Bengal, Behar, and Orissa. The grant was the culminating achievement of Clive's activity in India, and is the event that is usually seen as the formal beginning of the British Raj in India.

Like most of West's paintings of recent historical events, No. 101 is not an accurate reconstruction. The ceremony did not take place in the palatial setting shown in No. 101, but in Clive's tent, with an armchair placed on Clive's dining-table serving as throne.[1] Whereas a key to No. 101 identifies six Englishmen in addition to Clive: General John Carnac, Captain Archibald Swinton, Major Pearson, Sir Henry Strachey, Thomas Kelsall, and Anselm Beaumont, Mark Bence-Jones claims that two of them, Kelsall and Beaumont, were certainly not with Clive at Allahabad in 1765.[2]

Around 1771, Clive began to seek West's advice when buying pictures by old masters. For the Eating Room at Claremont, the house in Surrey which Clive had purchased in 1769 and immediately began to rebuild, he commissioned from West a series of large canvases depicting the chief events of his Indian career. One drawing by Capability Brown, the architect at Claremont, shows a design for one of the walls of the room with No. 101 in place, and other drawings, which have not been published, reportedly establish that there would have been a second, equally large, painting on the opposite wall, two vertical canvases on either side of the fireplace, and four roundels over the doors.[3] The scheme was cut short by Clive's suicide in 1774, and No. 101 seems to have been the only one of West's paintings for Claremont which was actually begun. Samuel Curwen saw it in West's studio in 1776, but the artist may not have finished it until 1795. An unidentified review of that year's Royal Academy exhibition states, "This picture, we understand, has long been upon his hands, though touched up for the present exhibition." Joseph Farington saw West "touching on His pictures" at the Academy on 29 April 1795, before the opening of the exhibition. A later diary entry by Farington (quoted under No. 103) implies that No. 101 was still in West's possession in 1818 and that West intended to give it further work.

Apart from the drawing by Brown mentioned above, there is a drawing of the composition in the British Museum, signed and dated 1774.[4] Another drawing in the British Museum, showing figures in European and Indian dress meeting in a tent, may represent an earlier and more historically accurate visualization of the event.[5] The lists of West's works include a small drawing and a large drawing of the subject.[6]

For a further version, or versions, of the subject see the following two entries. The documentation of Nos. 102 and 103 is hopelessly entangled, and it seems likely that only one of these works, the latter, was actually painted. Despite the indication on the lists of West's works that No. 102 was painted for Madras, we have been unable to confirm that a painting of the subject ever went there. In 1818 Joseph Farington was aware of two versions of the subject, and two are now known. He was also told that West was to paint yet another, but since West was by then eighty years old, it is unlikely that this still uncommenced painting was ever carried out. It is likely, however, that West painted the second version of No. 101 and planned to paint a third in fulfillment of commissions originally given him and paid for by the first Lord Clive before his death in 1774. The repetitions may have been requested by Clive's son in place of the further works intended for the Eating Room at Claremont, since the scheme of decoration to which they belonged had been abandoned. Although we have no record of the actual commissions, No. 101 is a very large painting, in 1774 the most ambitious work in size yet undertaken by the artist; so if West had received payment in advance for the entire series of paintings, the sums involved must have been substantial.

[1] See Mark Bence-Jones, *Clive of India*, London, 1974, p. 219.
[2] Ibid., p. 297.
[3] Dorothy Stroud, "A Capability Brown Discovery: Designs of Claremont for Lord Clive," *Country Life*, CVIII, 1950, p. 63, fig. 6.
[4] Sepia wash, $4\frac{5}{8} \times 7\frac{5}{8}$ in. (1895-2-25-1).
[5] Black and white chalk on blue paper, $8\frac{1}{4} \times 7\frac{1}{2}$ in. (1920-6-15-20).
[6] *PC*, p. 569 ("The Drawing, in small, of the Duannie received by Lord Clive," and "The large Drawing of the giving the Duannie to Lord Clive," both West, Gallery); *UM*, p. 532; *BA*, p. 19; Galt, p. 234 (lists only the small drawing); Dillenberger, pp. 185 (475) and 186 (483).

102 Lord Clive Receiving from the Mogul the Grant of the Duanney

LOCATION UNKNOWN (POSSIBLY NEVER PAINTED)

LISTED: *PC*, p. 563 ("The late Lord Clive receiving the Duannie from the Great Mogul, a second picture,"—for Madras); *UM*, p. 529; *BA*, p. 16; Galt, p. 224; Dillenberger, p. 161 (230)

See No. 101.

103 Lord Clive Receiving from the Mogul the Grant of the Duanney *c.* 1802–18

INDIA OFFICE LIBRARY AND RECORDS, LONDON

Oil on canvas: 114 × 159 in. (290 × 404 cm.)

PROV: Presented by the first Earl of Powis to the East India Company in October 1820

EXH: RA 1818 (106) "The Great Mogul presenting to the late Lord Clive the Grant of the Dewannee for the India Company."

LISTED: Galt, p. 234 ("The third great picture of Lord Clive receiving the Duannic"); Dillenberger, p. 190 (514)

LIT: Farington Diary, 25 Feb., 25 March, and 13 April 1818 (Farington 1978–, XV pp. 5162, 5180, and 5187); Courtauld Cuttings, II, p. 125; William Foster, *A Descriptive Catalogue of the Paintings, Statues, etc. in the India Office*, London, 1924, p. 15; Paul R. Weidner, ed., "The Journal of John Blake White," *South Carolina Historical and Genealogical Magazine*, XLII, 1941, p. 99; Mark Bence-Jones, "Clive of India as Builder and Collector II: A Nabob's Choice of Art," *Country Life*, CL, 1971, p. 1448, ill.; Mark Bence-

Jones, *Clive of India*, London, 1974, ill. opp. p. 254 and color frontispiece; Alberts 1978, p. 380

On 24 February 1818, Joseph Farington recorded in his diary:

Before dinner Mr. West took me into His great Painting room & shewed me a large picture, abt. 18 feet wide of Lord Clive, accompanied by Genl. Carnack &c, receiving a paper of agreement from a Nabob. This picture He sd., is for the *India House*. The original picture of this subject He sd. is to be completed and sent to Powis Castle near Welsh pool, & He is to paint another for *Lord Clive*, to be placed in his house in Shropshire.

The picture that Farington was shown in February must be the one that West exhibited at the Royal Academy the following May. West told Farington that it was for India House, and it went there in 1820, presented by Clive of India's son, the Earl of Powis. West apparently did not paint the third picture for Lord Clive (the son of the Earl of Powis), to be placed in his house (Oakly Park) in Shropshire. Instead, the original picture (No. 101) went to Oakly Park and is still there. No painting of the subject is at or is recorded to have been at Powis Castle.

When presented to the East India Company by the Earl of Powis, No. 103 was described as "a copy by Mr. West of his original painting."[1] Nonetheless, No. 103 may be in part by a student of West's from South Carolina, John Blake White, who recorded in his diary that in October 1802 he commenced copying "a very large picture for Mr. West, the subject being Lord Clive's Embassy to the Court of the Mogul." No. 103 is slightly less wide than No. 101 and lacks one figure on the right side and two on the left, as well as open spaces visible beyond the framing columns on either edge of the original painting.

[1] Minutes of the Court of Directors, 25 October 1820 (letter from L. C. Everard, Commonwealth Relations Office, London, to Helmut von Erffa, 25 March 1952).

103

104 The Death of the Earl of Chatham *c.* 1778–86
See color illustration, p. 65

KIMBELL ART MUSEUM, FORT WORTH, TEXAS

Oil on canvas: 28 × 35¾ in. (71 × 90.8 cm.)

PROV: Sold by West's sons, Robins, London, 22–25 May 1829, lot 71 ("The Death of the Earl of Chatham," 2 ft. 3 in. × 2 ft. 11 in.), bt. for £48.6.0. by Charles Morgan, Caeforgan, Llanrhidian, Glamorganshire; by descent in the Morgan family until 1977; Trafalgar Galleries, London; Hirschl & Adler Galleries, New York, from whom purchased by the Kimbell Art Museum in 1980

EXH: *A Gallery Collects*, Hirschl & Adler Galleries, New York, 1977 (6)

LISTED: *PC*, p. 567 ("The Death of Lord Chatham," West, Gallery); *UM*, p. 531; Barlow, p. 435; *BA*, p. 18; Galt, p. 231; Dillenberger, p. 180 (414)

LIT: Whitley 1928, I, pp. 355–56; *Sophie in London 1786: being the Diary of Sophie v. la Roche*, trans. by Clare Williams, London, 1933, p. 153; Flexner 1939, p. 154; Prown 1966, II, pp. 280–81; Kraemer 1975, pp. 14–15; Edmund Pillsbury, "Recent Painting Acquisitions; The Kimbell Art Museum," *Burlington Magazine*, CXXIV, Jan. 1982, supplement, pp. v–vi, fig. 8

William Pitt, first Earl of Chatham (1708–1778), collapsed in the House of Lords on 7 April 1778, while speaking in a debate on American Independence (which he opposed). He died at his home at Hayes, outside of London, a few weeks later. West apparently began the painting soon after as a sketch for a larger picture. The Robins sale catalogue of May 1829 states that he had "already found a generous patron in his Sovereign," but that he never painted the large picture in order not to compete with John Singleton Copley, who independently had begun his own version of the subject (completed in 1781; see ill. p. 65). Substantiating the information from the Robins catalogue is a notation by Horace Walpole, probably written *c.* 1785:

> Mr. West made a small Sketch of the death of Lord Chatham, much better expressed & disposed than Copley's. It has none but the principal person's present; Copley's almost the whole peerage, of whom seldom so many are there at once, & in Copleys most are meer [*sic*] spectators. but the great merit of West is the principal Figure which has his crutch & gouty stockings, which express his feebleness & account for his death. West wd not finish it not to interfere with his friend Copley.[1]

In No. 104 Chatham, who did suffer from gout, is shown wearing "gouty stockings" with his crutch at his side.

A drawing in the Pierpont Morgan Library,[2] which although considerably different from the present work in composition seems to be preparatory for it, is inscribed with names identifying some seventeen figures. From this drawing, we can identify the peer standing at the center of the painting as the Duke of Richmond, to whose address Chatham was attempting to reply when he collapsed. To the left of Richmond and wearing a black broad-brimmed hat is the Earl Bathurst, the Lord Chancellor. The group around Chatham in the drawing includes the Dukes of Cumberland, Manchester, and Portland, the Earl Temple, and Viscount Mahon, Chatham's son-in-law. The man holding a cloth to Chatham's head probably represents Richard Brocklesby, the physician to the House of Lords who, in the drawing, is on his knees at his patient's side. The boyish head looking over Brocklesby's shoulder is probably that of one of Chatham's three sons who accompanied him to the House of Lords on 7 April, perhaps James Pitt (1761–1780); a similar

figure in the drawing is identified there only as "Mr. Pitt." Other figures identified in the Morgan Library's drawing are the Archbishops of Canterbury and York, the Duke of Grafton, the Marquess of Rockingham, the Earls of Abingdon, Mansfield, and Shelburne, and Lord Camden. There is also a drawing in the Huntington Library showing the central group of Bathurst, Richmond, and the figures around Chatham in approximately the same positions as in No. 104.[3]

Two further drawings of the entire composition, each with some variations, are in the British Museum,[4] and in the National Gallery of Art in Washington.[5] The authors of this catalogue do not believe that these two drawings are by West. They were published by Jules Prown in 1966 with tentative attributions to Copley, which the subsequent reappearance of No. 104 in 1977 would seem to sustain. They appear to be free copies after this picture, rather than studies for it, and if they are indeed by Copley, they suggest that Copley began to shape the composition of his picture by copying West's and introducing slight modifications into the composition. Despite Walpole's emphasis on the differences between the works and the Robins catalogue's statement that the two artists were not initially aware of each other's undertaking, the compositions of No. 104 and of Copley's picture are sufficiently alike to make Copley's dependence upon West seem probable.

Although the two artists soon became bitter rivals, West looked benevolently enough upon Copley's undertaking for the latter to show him the finished picture when, according to what West later told Joseph Farington, it was still in a crude state, and "It was under the eye of West that Copley harmonized it with mummy etc."[6] Copley is known to have been at work on his painting by May of 1779.[7] If the foregoing suggestion about his dependence upon West is valid, West must have commenced No. 104 before then, but he may not have completed it until considerably later, since Sophie von la Roche, who visited West's studio in 1786, described his latest work as showing "Lord Chatham swooning in Parliament, and all the Lords gathered round him."[8] In its present state the painting is in no way sketchy or incomplete. It is a finished picture in its own right, and it may be that West, having earlier abandoned the canvas, took it up again and brought it to its present state of completion after Copley had finished his picture. If so, the painting may not only have been Copley's source but also, as we now see it, incorporate hints taken by West from Copley.

The two men standing above the other peers and looking down on the scene from the right side of No. 104 echo two observers hanging from the side of a boat in the upper right of the *Battle of La Hogue* (No. 90), upon which West was probably engaged by 1778.

[1] Quoted by Prown from Horace Walpole's "Book of Materials," p. 113, Lewis-Walpole Library, Farmington, Conn.
[2] Black chalk on blue paper, 7 7/16 × 11 in. (Kraemer 1975, pp. 14–15, no. 20, and pl. 10).
[3] Red and white chalks on blue paper, 5¼ × 6½ in.
[4] Black and white chalk, 20 × 26¾ in. (ill. Prown 1966, II, pl. 400).
[5] Black chalk, 12 × 19¼ in. (ill. Prown 1966, II, pl. 399).
[6] Farington Diary, 2 July 1806 (Farington 1978–, VIII, p. 2803).
[7] Prown 1966, II, pp. 278 and 282.
[8] Although this description must be of No. 104, Sophie (if correctly transcribed and translated) also referred to the painting as "on copper." She may have been misled by the copper-colored spandrels over the arches in the upper right and left corners.

105 Signing of the Preliminary Treaty of Peace in 1782 1783–84
See color illustration, p. 60

HENRY FRANCIS DU PONT WINTERTHUR MUSEUM, WINTERTHUR, DELAWARE

Oil on canvas: 28½ × 36½ in. (72.5 × 92.5 cm.)

PROV: Sold by West's sons, Robins, London, 20–22 June 1829, lot 75 ("Portraits of Dr. Benjamin Franklin, Mr. Adams, Mr. Jay, Mr. Laurens, and Mr. Temple Franklin, in consultation at the memorable Treaty of Paris, painted from the life"); Joseph Strutt, Derby (1765–1844); by family descent to Algernon Henry Strutt, 3rd Baron Belper (1883–1956), from whom acquired in 1916 by J. Pierpont Morgan, New York (1867–1943); sold by M. Knoedler and Co., New York, as agents of the Morgan Estate, to Henry Francis du Pont in 1943

EXH: *Early American Paintings*, Brooklyn Museum, 1917 (133); *Franklin and His Circle*, Metropolitan Museum of Art, New York, 1936 (100); *Masterpieces of American Historical Portraiture*, M. Knoedler and Co., New York, 1936 (22); *Two Hundred Years of American Painting*, Baltimore Museum of Art, 1938 (7); Philadelphia 1938 (35); *Life in America*, Metropolitan Museum of Art, New York, 1939 (35); *Survey of American Painting*, Carnegie Institute, Pittsburgh, 1940 (80)

LIT: Adams 1874, III, p. 559; John Jay Ide, *The Portraits of John Jay*, New York, 1938, p. 52 (17); Sellers 1962, pp. 398–401, 420–21, pl. 27; Andrew Oliver, *Portraits of John and Abigail Adams*, Cambridge, Mass., 1967, pp. 39–45, 244 (35); Marks 1974, pp. 15–35; Alberts 1978, pp. 149–53

West began this painting sometime in 1783 but never completed it. The reason it was not finished can be found in a passage from John Quincy Adams's diary, which is quoted below. Probably because of being left unfinished, it does not appear on any of the early lists of West's works. It may have been conceived originally as part of a series of paintings depicting the great events of the American revolutionary war, which West mentioned in letters to Charles Willson Peale in June and August 1783, but which, apart from No. 105, he never carried out. For a thoroughgoing discussion of that project, as well as of No. 105, see the article by Arthur S. Marks published in 1974. The painting shows the American participants in the signing of the preliminary treaty of peace between America and Britain, which took place in Paris on 30 November 1782. From left to right, they are: John Jay, John Adams, Benjamin Franklin, Henry Laurens, and William Temple Franklin, Benjamin Franklin's grandson, who served as secretary to the American commissioners. On the unfinished right side of the painting would have been the British representative, Richard Oswald, and his secretary, Caleb Whitefoord. The final peace treaty was signed the following year with a somewhat different cast of characters.

The first recorded mention of the painting is in a letter from Caleb Whitefoord in London to William Temple Franklin in Paris, dated 30 June 1784:

> Sometime ago, our friend Mr. West, having the opportunity of seeing three of the American Plenipos' here & whishing to transmit their Portraits to Posterity in some Historical picture, made a sketch of the signing of the Preliminary Treaty, to which I contributed a material part by lending him the Portrait of your grandfather by Mr. Joseph Wright, which I brought with me from Paris.[1]

The portrait by Joseph Wright (Royal Society, London) was copied from a portrait of Franklin painted in 1778 by the French artist Joseph Siffred Duplessis (versions in the Metropolitan Museum, and New York Public

Library). William Temple Franklin visited London in the autumn of 1784 and posed then for his portrait in the composition. At that time he reported to his grandfather in Paris that West was doing the latter's head from a miniature portrait that Franklin had sent to Georgiana Shipley, the daughter of the Bishop of St. Asaph. That miniature, according to Sellers and Marks, was also a copy of the portrait by Duplessis (see also No. 618). The other three "Plenipos'" all visited London in 1783 or 1784, and Whiteford's letter implies that West was able to paint them from life. That he painted John Adams from life is confirmed by Adams's son, John Quincy Adams, who accompanied his father to London in the autumn of 1783.

In June 1817, when John Quincy Adams was concluding his service as American ambassador to London and about to return to America, West called on him and also sent No. 105 for him to see. According to Adams's diary:

I then recollected having seen it before, at the time when my father was sitting to him for his likeness in it. The most striking likeness in the picture is that of Mr. Jay. Those of Dr. Franklin, and his grandson, W.T., who was secretary to the American Commission, are also excellent. Mr. Laurens and my father, though less perfect resemblances, are yet very good. Mr. Oswald, the British Plenipotentiary, was an ugly-looking man, blind in one eye, and he died without leaving any picture of him extant. This Mr. West alleged as the cause which prevented him from finishing the picture many years ago. Caleb Whiteford, the Secretary of the British Commission, is also dead, but his portrait exists, from which a likeness may be taken. As I very strongly expressed my regret that this picture should be left unfinished, Mr. West said he thought he could finish it, and I must not be surprised if some day or other it should be received at Washington. I understand his intention to be to make a present of it to Congress.

Evidently the problem of obtaining a likeness of Oswald was still as insurmountable in 1817 as it had been in the 1780s, and the painting remained unfinished in West's estate until sold in 1829.

There are copies, which have histories tracing back to the nineteenth century, in the Department of State in Washington and in the John Jay Homestead in Katonah, New York. A copy made when the picture belonged to J. Pierpont Morgan is in the Adams Historic Site in Quincy, Massachusetts.

[1] Franklin Papers, American Philosophical Society, Philadelphia, quoted by Sellers, pp. 420–21, and by Marks, p. 26. We have followed Marks's transcription, which varies slightly from that of Sellers. Whiteford's Joseph Wright was not the English painter Joseph Wright of Derby, but an American artist of the same name born in 1756.

106 Reception of the American Loyalists by Great Britain in the Year 1783 c. 1812

LOCATION UNKNOWN

ENGR: Outline engraving ($7\frac{7}{16} \times 9\frac{5}{8}$ in.) by Henry Moses, published in 1815 as the frontispiece to *Historical View of the Commission for Enquiring into the Losses, Services, and Claims of the American Loyalists at the close of the War between Great Britain and her Colonies in 1783: with an Account of the Compensation granted to them by Parliament in 1785 and 1788*, by John Eardley-Wilmot

LIT: Lorenzo Sabine, *The American Loyalists, or Biographical Sketches of Adherents to the British Crown in the War of Revolution*, Boston, 1847, pp. 301, 527–28; Lewis Einstein, *Divided Loyalties: Americans in England during the War of Independence*, Boston and New York, 1933, pp. 240–42; Helmut von Erffa, "West's

Portrait of John Eardley-Wilmot," *Auction*, IV, Nov. 1970, pp. 49–50; Kraemer 1975, pp. 52–53; Linda Landis, *Benjamin West's Portrait of John Eardley-Wilmot* (exhibition catalogue), Yale Center for British Art, New Haven, 1983

The outline engraving by Henry Moses of the *Reception of the American Loyalists* reproduces a painting which appears, framed, in the background of West's *Portrait of John Eardley Wilmot* now in the Yale Center for British Art (No. 718). The portrait is signed and dated *1812* and it appeared at the Royal Academy in that year. The Moses engraving was published three years later in Wilmot's account of his activity from 1783 to 1788 as a commissioner to inquire into the claims of the American loyalists for compensation for their losses suffered during the American revolutionary war. The engraving was accompanied by the following explanatory text:

Religion and Justice are represented extending the mantle of Britannia, whilst she herself is holding out her arm and shield to receive the Loyalists. Under the shield is the crown of Great Britain, surrounded by Loyalists. This group of figures consists of various characters, representing the Law, the Church, and the Government, with other inhabitants of North America; and, as a marked characteristic of that quarter of the globe, an Indian chief extending one hand to Britannia, and pointing the other to a Widow and Orphans, rendered so by the civil war: also a Negro and Children looking up to Britannia in grateful remembrance of their emancipation from Slavery.

In a cloud, on which Religion and Justice rest, are seen in an opening glory the Genii of Great Britain and of America, binding up the broken fasces of the two countries, as emblematical of the treaty of peace and friendship between them. At the head of the group of Loyalists are likenesses of Sir William Pepperell, Bart. one of the Chairmen of their Agents to the Crown and Parliament of Great Britain; and

William Franklin, Esq., son of Dr. Benjamin Franklin, who, having His Majesty's commission of Governor of New Jersey, preserved his fidelity and Loyalty to his Sovereign from the commencement to the conclusion of the contest, notwithstanding powerful incitements to the contrary.

The two figures on the right are the painter, Mr. West the President of the Royal Academy, and his Lady, both natives of Pennsylvania.

In 1933 Lewis Einstein asserted that West drew an allegorical sketch of this subject in 1788, when Wilmot's commission had finished its work, but the only evidence there is to substantiate this claim is a drawing in the British Museum, which is signed and dated *1788*, of an American Indian, Britannia, and a third figure binding a fasces.[1] This is a motif related to two *putti* binding a fasces in the background of the Moses engraving, but there is no further similarity. It seems more likely that the composition of No. 106 dates from 1812, the year of No. 718, West's portrait of Eardley Wilmot, and it is quite possible that No. 106 never existed as an independent painting but only as a picture within a picture, in the background of No. 718. A date of 1812, when West was seventy-four years old, is consistent with his appearance, leaning on a cane, in No. 106.

Ruth Kraemer has connected with No. 106 a sketchy drawing in the Morgan Library showing a seated Britannia holding out her hand to a group of vaguely gesticulating figures.[2] That drawing is on the verso of a more elaborate sketch of a frontally enthroned Britannia surrounded by Religion and other figures, which is related to a finished pen drawing in the Huntington Library, signed and dated *1812*,[3] and to two further sketches.[4] These drawings are quite distinct compositionally from No. 106, but the Huntington drawing does nonetheless appear to represent the same subject. A drawing formerly in the collection of Mrs. F. Howard, showing a figure wearing a helmet similar to that worn by Britannia in No. 106, and bending over a group of prostrate figures, may also be related.[5]

The Reception of the American Loyalists by Great Britain in the Year 1783, outline engraving by Henry Moses after No. 106

[1] Pen, sepia ink, and wash, $8\frac{1}{4} \times 10\frac{1}{2}$ in., $6\frac{3}{4} \times 9\frac{1}{4}$ in. (1920-6-15-17).

[2] Pen and brown ink, $5\frac{5}{8} \times 5\frac{5}{8}$ in. (Kraemer 1975, pp. 52–53, no. 93 and pl. 61).

[3] Pen, $9 \times 5\frac{9}{16}$ in. (ill. in Kraemer 1975, p. 52, fig. 35).

[4] Both in pen and ink: $6\frac{3}{4} \times 3\frac{3}{4}$ in. and $6 \times 5\frac{5}{8}$ in. (exhibited New York 1968, nos. 19 and 21).

[5] Black chalk, $6 \times 8\frac{5}{8}$ in. (? sold Sotheby's, London, 22 March 1979, as part of lot 5, "Study of a Prostrate Figure, possibly Saul before the Witch of Endor").

107 The Recovery of His Majesty in the Year 1789 *c* 1789

TRAFALGAR GALLERIES, LONDON, AND HIRSCHL & ADLER GALLERIES, NEW YORK

Oil on canvas: $20\frac{7}{16} \times 30\frac{1}{4}$ in. (52×77 cm.)

PROV: Sold by West's sons, Robins, London, 22–25 May 1829, lot 81 ("His Late Majesty Resuming Royal Power in 1789," 1 ft. 8 in. × 2 ft. 6 in.), bt. for £42 by Charles Morgan, Caeforgan, Llanrhidian, Glamorganshire; by descent in the Morgan family until 1977; Trafalgar Galleries, London

EXH: *A Gallery Collects*, Hirschl & Adler Galleries, New York, 1977 (7); *American Art From the Colonial and Federal Periods*, Hirschl & Adler Galleries, 1982 (23)

LISTED: *PC*, p. 565 ("The small picture of the Recovery of his Majesty in the Year 1789," West, Painting-room); *UM*, p. 530; Barlow, p. 434; *BA*, p. 17; Galt, p. 227; Dillenberger, p. 170 (314)

No. 107 is an emblematic representation of the resumption of power by George III in March 1789 following his recovery from his first attack of apparent insanity (now generally diagnosed as a congenital disease named porphyria), which had completely incapacitated him the previous autumn. The King, under a burst of light from heaven and accompanied by Queen Charlotte, approaches a throne upon which lie a crown and sceptre. Standing to the left of the throne are the President of the Privy Council, Lord Camden, and the Lord Chancellor, Lord Thurlow. To the right of it is the Prime Minister, William Pitt. Immediately behind the main figures are three columns upon which hang shields bearing inscriptions. The column furthest to the

left, behind Thurlow, has the word *HONOR* inscribed on the abacus of its Corinthian capital and, on the shield, *THE XCIX | PEERS who nobly supported in the HOUSE OF LORDS | the KING and | CONSTITUTION | on the XXVI | of D*. Behind Pitt, the abacus of the second column, which is Doric, bears the word *VIRTUE*, and the shield is inscribed *THE CCLXVII | WORTHY Members | of the HONBLE HOUSE | of COMONS who nobly supported the | KING | [an]d CONSTITUTION | on the XVI | of Decbr. | MDCCLXXXVIII*. These inscriptions refer to the voting in the two houses of Parliament, led respectively by Thurlow and Pitt, which supported the interests of George III during his incapacity by limiting the powers of the Prince of Wales during a regency. The third column, also Doric, which is above three academically-robed figures standing behind the King on the right side of the painting, has the word *SCIENCE* on the abacus, and *THE KING | being restored to | HEALTH opened | the PARLIAMENT on | the X of March | MDCCLXXXIX*. In an unpublished seminar report at Columbia University, Marie Busco has proposed that the figures standing immediately below these words represent the men of science who were generally credited with bringing about the King's recovery, and she identifies the two closest to the King as Dr. Francis Willis (1717–1807) and his son John Willis, in whose care George III had been placed the previous December.[1] Appropriately, their patient strides away from them towards the leaders of the government on the opposite side of the picture. Windsor Castle, to which the King triumphantly returned on 14 March, is visible in the background.

A drawing for the composition is in the collection of John Davis Hatch, Lenox, Massachusetts.[2] Another drawing, less close compositionally and in which Queen Charlotte plays a more important role, is in the Royal Collection at Windsor.[3] The shields on the columns in the Hatch drawing are blank. In the drawing in the Royal Collection, which has two columns rather than three, as in No. 107, that on the left has *VIRTUTI* inscribed on the abacus, and *THE MAJORITY OF LXXV IN PARLMT 1788* on the shield; that on the right has *HONORIS* and *THE MAJORITY OF XXXIII IN THE LORDS 1788*. A. Paul Oppé, who first published the Windsor drawing, suggested that it may

have been intended for a transparency. At the time Oppé wrote he was unaware of the drawing's relation to this painting, which following the West sale in 1829 had disappeared from sight until it turned up on the market in 1977; nonetheless, both drawings, as well as No. 107, do indeed seem to have some connection with a transparency displayed by West before his house in Windsor to celebrate the King's return on 14 March 1789. According to a contemporary description of West's transparency:

> In the centre was a striking likeness of the King, the eye of Providence was seen above, diffusing a light over the features. On one side was the plain column of Virtue, with an inscription to the praise of the Right Hon. W. Pitt, and the 266 who supported the King and Constitution, Dec. 16, 1788. On the other was the ornamental column of Honour, inscribed to the Lord Chancellor, and the Peers who voted with him.[4]

The distinction between a simple column of Virtue and an ornate column of Honor is observed in both the Windsor drawing and No. 107, and the burst of light over the head of George III in the painting would appear to be the light-diffusing eye of Providence of the transparency rendered in slightly more naturalistic terms. In the Hatch drawing the burst of light comes from what is quite clearly an eye, and in the painting, at the point where the light originates, the iris and outline of an eye are unobtrusively but unmistakably delineated. See also No. 432, another work from 1789 celebrating the King's return to health.

For further portraits of the King and Queen painted by West in 1789 see No. 560.

[1] For reproductions of portraits of both men by John Russell, see Charles Chenevix Trench, *The Royal Malady*, London, 1964, ill. opp. p. 148.

[2] Sepia ink and wash, $6\frac{1}{4} \times 8\frac{3}{4}$ in. (*100 American Drawings from the J.D. Hatch Collection*, Heim Gallery, London, 1976, no. 5 and pl. 7).

[3] Pen and brown wash, $13\frac{1}{8} \times 18$ in. (Oppé 1950, p. 99, no. 641, and fig. 54).

[4] V and A Cuttings, II, p. 495a, "Extract of a letter from Windsor, 23 March."

107

108 The Death of Lord Nelson 1806
See color illustration, pp. 64, 130

WALKER ART GALLERY, LIVERPOOL

Oil on canvas: 70×96 in. (178×244 cm.)

Signed bottom center: *B. West 1806*

PROV: According to Joseph Farington, West gave No. 108 to Mrs. West (died 1814), and she in turn gave or left it to Maria, the daughter of Raphael West, who approached Farington in July 1820 for assistance in attempting to sell it to the Greenwich Hospital for a price of £1,000 to £1,500; sold by West's sons, Robins, London, 22–25 May 1829, lot 91 ("The Death of Lord Nelson," 5 ft. 10 in. × 8 ft.), bt. by Henry Sandby for £892.10.0.; presented by Bristow H. Hughes to the Walker Art Gallery in 1866

EXH: West's studio, 1806; RA 1811 (116):

> The Death of Lord Nelson, or the Naval Victory off Trafalgar; being one of the most distinguished that ever occurred in the annals of Great Britain, for heroism and national importance. Mr. West, conceiving that such an event demanded a composition every way appropriate to its dignity and high importance, formed it into an Epic Composition. This enabled him to give it that character and interest which the subject demanded. Avail-

ing himself of that character in composition, he laid the heroic Nelson wounded on the quarterdeck of his ship, The Victory, with his Captain (now Sir Thomas Hardy) holding the dying Hero by the hand, and from a paper in the other, announcing to him the number of ships taken from the enemy's Combined Fleet. The surrounding groups of gallant officers and men are sympathizing with each other in the sufferings of their wounded Friend and expiring Commander: and the dead and wounded in the several groups are introduced as episodes, to commemorate these with honour, who fell on board the Hero's ship in that distinguished action. The ships in the distance display the flags and signals of the other triumphant British Admirals, as well as those of the vanquished enemy, which are marked with all the wrack of battle, and that defeat which took place on the 21st of October, 1805;

West's Gallery 1822–28 (131) (in the catalogue for 1828, No. 108 is scratched out and replaced by *The Deluge* [No. 234]); Liverpool 1976 (73)

ENGR: Engraving (17⅛ × 23⅝ in.) by James Heath, pub. 1 May 1811 by Benjamin West and James Heath and dedicated to George III; key to the Heath engraving.

LISTED: *BA*, p. 20 ("The Victory off Trafalgar, or the death of Lord Nelson, a large composition; in the possession of Mr. West"); Dillenberger, p. 188 (500)

LIT: Farington Diary, 29 Nov. 1805, 16 March, 11 May, 2 and 8 July 1806, 21 April, 10 June and 12 Dec. 1807, 23 March and 20 May 1811, and 6 and 14 July 1820 (Farington 1978–, VII, pp. 2652, 2694, and 2757, VIII, pp. 2802–3, 2806, 3029, 3064, and 3162–63, XI, pp. 3898 and 3933, and XVI, pp. 5534 and 5537); "Mr. West's Grand Historical Picture of the Death of Lord Nelson," *La Belle Assemblée*, I, May 1806, pp. 217–18; *Monthly Magazine*, XXVII, 1809, p. 325; George S. Hilliard, ed., *Life Letters and Journals of George Ticknor*, Boston, 1876, I, p. 63; Whitley *1800–1820*, 1928, pp. 98, 104; Evans 1959, pl. 64; Marks 1965, pp. 27–35; Mitchell 1967, passim; Alberts 1978, pp. 324–27; Montagna 1981, p. 87 and fig. 12

The British naval victory off Cape Trafalgar, on the coast of Spain, over the combined French and Spanish fleets occurred on 21 October 1805. During the battle Viscount Horatio Nelson, commanding the British fleet, was struck by a sniper's bullet while on the deck of his flagship the *Victory*; he died of his wound several hours later below deck, in the ship's cockpit. The news of the English victory and of Nelson's death in the moment of his greatest triumph reached London sixteen days later on 6 November. Approximately three weeks after that, on 29 November, West told Joseph Farington that he had begun the design of a painting

at the instigation of the engraver James Heath. West and Heath were to be partners in the publication of an engraving after the picture, which would serve as a companion to William Woollett's engraving of the *Death of General Wolfe* (No. 93). On 16 March 1806, when Farington dined at West's, the picture was "all painted in & would employ him a month more to harmonize and give effect to it," and on 11 May 1806, Farington found West seated before the "new finished picture." The engraving was published five years later.

A long description and explanation of what is shown in No. 108 appeared in *La Belle Assemblée* in May 1806, and a key identifying fifty-eight figures, ships in the background, and other details was published to accompany Heath's plate in 1811 (*below*). The picture shows the dying Nelson, in full dress, on the quarterdeck of the *Victory*. He is supported by the chaplain, purser, and surgeon of the *Victory*. Next to the dying hero and clasping his hand, the ship's captain, Thomas Hardy, holds a paper from which he reads the number of enemy ships taken. Kneeling before Nelson and laying a Spanish flag at his feet is a seaman named Saunders. Behind Saunders an officer, named Wynn, carries a captured French flag. In the lower left corner, head downward, is the body of Captain Charles Adair, his arm held by his grief-stricken servant, Charles Chappel. The latter came to London from Chatham on 17 February 1806 to pose and was paid one guinea by West to defray his expenses, as apparently were also numerous other

Key to the *Death of Lord Nelson* (No. 108). Engraving, 1811

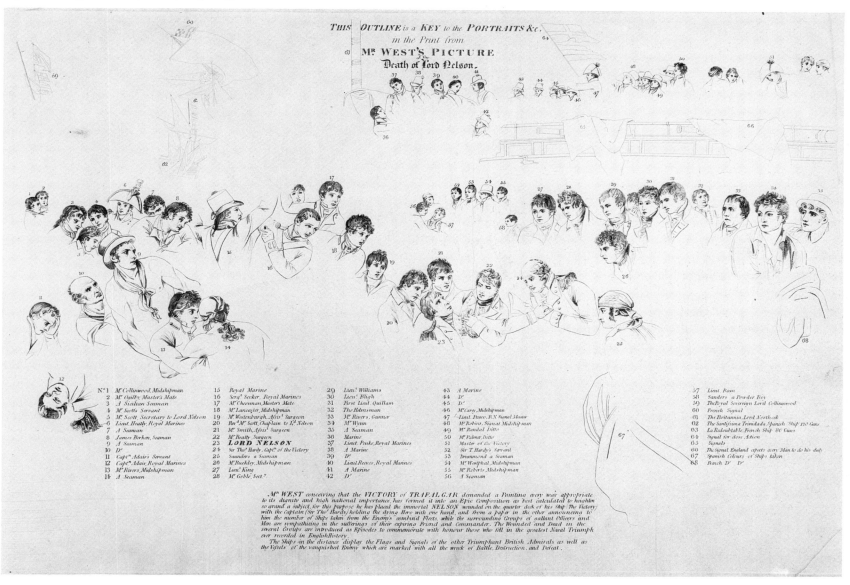

seamen who came from Chatham to sit for the picture.[1]

Saunders, the seaman who kneels before Nelson, visited West's studio on 8 July 1806, and there told Farington that he had not seen Nelson after he was wounded, as Nelson had been carried below deck immediately: "West has made a picture of what might have been, not of the circumstances as they happened." West was well aware that No. 108 was an inaccurate depiction of Nelson's death. Although he himself two years later did paint a picture of Nelson dying below deck (No. 109), he told Farington in 1807:

> there was no other way of representing the death of a Hero but by an Epic representation of it. It must exhibit the event in a way to excite awe & veneration & that which may be required to give superior interest to the representation must be introduced, all that can shew the importance of the Hero. Wolfe must not die like a common soldier under a Bush, neither should Nelson be represented dying in the gloomy hold of a ship, like a sick man in a Prison Hole. To move the mind there should be a spectacle presented to raise & warm the mind, & all shd. be proportioned to the highest idea conceived of the Hero. No Boy, sd. West, wd. be animated by a representation of Nelson dying like an ordinary man, His feelings must be roused & His mind inflamed by a scene great & extraordinary. A mere matter of fact will never produce this effect.

West also explained his ideas about Epic Composition in statements accompanying the painting in the catalogue of the Royal Academy exhibition of 1811 (quoted above) and accompanying the key to Heath's engraving. In a fundamental essay about the painting published in 1967, Charles Mitchell has argued persuasively that West imbibed those ideas from his friend the Reverend Robert Anthony Bromley, whose two-volume *Philosophical and Critical History of the Fine Arts*, published in 1793 and 1795, defined epic history painting in similar terms.

West exhibited the picture in his own studio in 1806 rather than send it to the Royal Academy, the presidency of which he had resigned the previous December and at which in 1806, for the first and only time from its opening exhibition in 1769 until his death in 1820, he exhibited nothing. On 11 May 1806 he told Farington that "it had been a great motive to induce him to paint that picture *The Death of Nelson*, to shew the Academy what they had done to cause the Author of it to withdraw himself, and an Architect to be placed in his room." On 2 July, Farington recorded that West had issued 6,500 cards for admittance and believed that 30,000 people had been to his house to see it. With the painting, West displayed versions of the *Battle of La Hogue* (No. 91) and the *Death of General Wolfe* (No. 98). He finally sent No. 108 to the Royal Academy in 1811 to coincide with the publication of Heath's engraving, a proof of which was exhibited at the same time.

In 1815 West showed No. 108 to an American visitor, George Ticknor from Boston, and told him the following story:

> Just before he [Nelson] went to sea for the last time, West sat next to him at a large entertainment given to him here, and in the course of the dinner Nelson expressed to Sir William Hamilton his regret, that in his youth he had not acquired some taste for art and some power of discrimination. "But," said he, turning to West, "there is one picture whose power I do feel. I never pass a printshop where your 'Death of Wolfe' is in the window, without being stopped by it." West, of course, made his acknowledgements, and Nelson went on to ask why he had painted no more like it. "Because, my Lord, there are no more subjects." "D—n it," said the sailor, "I didn't think of that," and asked him to take a glass of champagne. "But, my lord, I fear your intrepidity will yet furnish

me such another scene; and, if it should, I shall certainly avail myself of it." "Will you?" said Nelson, pouring out bumpers, and touching his glass violently against West's,—"will you, Mr. West? then I hope that I shall die in the next battle." He sailed a few days after, and the result was on the canvas before us.

This story sounds almost too good to be true, and Charles Mitchell has pointed out that Sir William Hamilton, who is mentioned in the anecdote, had died in 1803, so the dinner could not have taken place "just before" Nelson went to sea for the last time. West had met Nelson and Hamilton at a dinner given by William Beckford at Fonthill on 23 December 1800, and that may have been the "large entertainment" referred to in Ticknor's account. In any case, a Wolfe–Nelson parallel was something West was clearly conscious of, and it is reflected in the composition of No. 108. Heath's engraving is approximately the same size as William Woollett's engraving of the *Death of Wolfe*.

The relation of No. 108 to the numerous contemporary paintings and prints by other artists depicting the death of Nelson is discussed by Arthur Marks in his unpublished thesis, and more summarily by Charles Mitchell.

A drawing of the deck of the *Victory* with only the dying Nelson and three other figures, instead of the crowd in No. 108, is on the verso of a drawing for a monument to Nelson in the Yale Center for British Art (see No. 110). The Yale drawing is dated *1806*, but it is on several sheets of paper joined together, and one of those sheets is the reverse side of the sketch for Nelson's death[2] which West may well have drawn directly from the actual deck of the *Victory* when it returned from Trafalgar in December 1805. A drawing of Nelson and the three officers supporting him was with the Bernard Black Gallery in 1968,[3] and two studies of costume for figures on the upper deck in the background were formerly in the collection of Mrs. F. Howard.[4]

[1] Letter from West to Watkins Trench, 17 Feb. 1806 (Historical Society of Pennsylvania).
[2] Pencil, $7\frac{5}{8} \times 8\frac{7}{8}$ in.
[3] Black chalk, $7\frac{1}{8} \times 7\frac{1}{4}$ in. (New York 1968, no. 18).
[4] Both in black and white chalk on grey paper, $15\frac{1}{4} \times 10\frac{1}{4}$ in. (sold Sotheby's, London, 22 March 1979, lot 1).

109 The Death of Lord Nelson in the Cockpit of the Victory 1808

NATIONAL MARITIME MUSEUM, GREENWICH

Oil on canvas: $34\frac{1}{2} \times 28\frac{1}{2}$ in. (87.5 × 72.5 cm.)

Signed lower right: *B. West | 1808*

PROV: Commissioned by John M'Arthur; presented by Jasper de St. Croix and others to the Greenwich Hospital in 1849

EXH: RA 1808 (119) "The death of Lord Nelson in the cockpit of the ship Victory."

ENGR: Engraving ($8\frac{7}{16} \times 6\frac{15}{16}$ in.) by R. Golding, pub. 1809, opp. p. 453 of Vol. II of *The Life of Admiral Lord Nelson, K.B.*, by James Stanier Clarke and John M'Arthur, as "Nelson in the Victory's Cockpit, Mortally Wounded, October 21st 1805."

LISTED: *BA*, p. 20 ("The death of Lord Nelson in the cockpit of the ship Victory," painted for John M'Arthur); Dillenberger, p. 188 (501)

LIT: James Stanier Clarke and John M'Arthur, *The Life of Admiral Lord Nelson, K.B.*, London, 1809, I, pp. xliii–xliv; *National Maritime Museum Catalogue*, Greenwich, 1937, p. 216 (18); Evans 1959, pl. 65; Marks 1965, pp. 95–99; Mitchell 1967, p. 272; Kraemer 1975, p. 50

Nos. 109, 111, and groups of canvases by Richard Westall and Nicholas Pocock served as the basis of engravings in the monumental two-volume life of Nelson by Clarke and M'Arthur published in 1809. In the book, the illustrations were described as "Expressly Painted for the Work, and the Originals in the Possession of John M'Arthur, Esq." The paintings are all now in the National Maritime Museum. The engraving of No. 109 was accompanied by the following explanatory text, which was probably provided by West himself:

> The point of view is taken from the cable tier before the Cockpit. The wounded Admiral is represented laid on a pallet, on the larboard side of the Cockpit, with pious resignation in his dying moments, his hand in Captain Hardy's. Mr. Burke, the purser in a reclining posture in front, is supporting him with pillows. The Rev. Dr. Scott, the chaplain, is behind supporting his head. Mr. Beatty, the surgeon, having his right hand with a handkerchief placed on the wound, expresses in his countenance that the vital spark is almost extinguished. Next to him stands Mr. Smith, the assistant surgeon, apparently listening to the last words articulated by the dying Hero, namely, 'I HAVE DONE MY DUTY———I PRAISE GOD FOR IT.' The carpenters mate is represented in the foreground to the left of the picture in a stooping attitude, stepping over the coil of cables. The masses of the chiara-scuro, which fall on this figure and the quoil of cables from the lights of the two lanterns, contribute to give harmony and effect to the body of light thrown on the predominant group. Mr. Bunce, the carpenter, is represented standing near the cockpit ladder, with a mallet in his hand, and a bundle consisting of plugs and oakam suspended from his shoulder. His attention appears to be arrested to the principal figure of the group, whilst he was returning aft, with his mate to ascend the Cockpit ladder, from the duty of plugging shot holes. Henry Chevailler, Nelson's faithful servant is represented, in a dejected attitude looking on, and holding his master's hat and coat. Next to him, on his left, stands Gaetano Spedillo, another servant. At a distance descending the ladder to the cockpit, is represented in aerial perspective a wounded Officer, carrying down to the Cockpit by two sailors.
>
> The principal Portraits of this Picture were painted by Mr. West from life; those of Captain Hardy, the Rev. Dr. Scott, Mr. Burke, and Mr. Beatty, as well as that of the dying Admiral, are such characteristic Likenesses, as to add no small degree of interest and sympathy to the affecting scene of historical composition.

No. 109 appears to contradict what West had told Farington in 1807 (quoted under No. 108) that Nelson should not "be represented dying in the gloomy hold of a ship, like a sick man in a prison hole." That statement had been provoked by West's seeing a painting of the death of Nelson by Arthur Devis (also National Maritime Museum),[1] which showed the hero dying in the hold in a visualization not unlike West's in No. 109. West may have realized that the historical inaccuracy of his "epic" treatment in No. 108 would have been conspicuously inappropriate for an illustration to a text describing how Nelson actually died, and he probably felt that the epic treatment was not necessarily called for in the modest scale of book illustration. Placing the scene in a lantern-lit hold also allowed him to indulge in the "masses of chiara-scuro" mentioned in the explanatory text. His interest in such effects was probably stimulated by his admiration of Rembrandt's *Woman taken in Adultery* (ill. p. 135), which he had seen at Christie's in June 1807 and had praised to Farington in the highest terms, citing among other things its extraordinary effect of instilling such reverence in the spectator that all who approached it instinctively removed

109

His Majesty, on the 10th of December, 1805, having signified his commands to the Royal Academy, by his Secretary of State, the Rt. Hon. Lord Hawkesbury, for the members of that body to consider the best mode of perpetuating the memory of Lord Nelson; in obedience to that command this design was made, composed of three branches of art which constitute the Academy: Painting, being best calculated, by its power of combining imagery, to give allegorical figures their full effect, and to form a composition expressive of Lord Nelson's nautical achievements, and the immortality of his greatness. The leading point in the picture represents Victory presenting the dead body of the hero to Britannia, after the battle of Trafalgar, from the arms of Neptune, with the trident of his dominions. Britannia sits in shaded gloom, as expressive of that deep regret which overwhelmed the united kingdom at the loss of so distinguished a character. In the other parts of the picture are seen the concomitant events of his life, and the sons and daughters of the union preparing the mournful sable to his memory. The winged boys around his body are figurative that the influence of his genius still exists. The sculptured part of this design is best calculated to give the sepulchre its appropriate character; it is a plain stone of considerable magnitude, and of a double cube in form, without ornaments or inscription, except the honoured name of Nelson encircled with the emblem of Eternity. The supporters of this honoured stone, on the right, are a group of British seamen, as seen when opposed to the enemy in battle, inspired by the genius of Nelson and ready to defend their country's cause; on the left, another group, composed of marines from the three nations which now form the united kingdom, reflecting, and participating with their country, in the loss of so great a commander. Architecture, ever denoting civilization, has inscribed on its frize the honours which Parliament decreed to the family of Nelson: over which is the tablet containing the number of battles he had been in, and terminated by his crest, surrounding which are the insignia of Victory and Virtue, and the spoils of the vanquished enemy, with the hulks of the San Josef and San Nicolas, which Nelson boarded and captured. The columns rising from the base, on which are the prows of British men-of-war, are figurative of that glorious immortality which the general design of this sketch of a monument exhibits.

The model for the monument, which is to be executed for perpetuating the memory of Lord Nelson, having been decided on by the Committee of Taste, Mr. West, after making this design, painted this picture, to accompany his other works on the subject of Lord Nelson's victories.

their hats.[2] He told Farington that he had seen such an effect produced by a picture once previously, in his own studio during the exhibition of No. 108, and he followed that remark with his comments about Devis's picture and the impropriety of showing Nelson dying in the hold.

Ruth Kraemer has proposed that a drawing in the Pierpont Morgan Library, which is inscribed *Midshipman's Berth & Cockpit Ladder as seen from the Cable tiers*, is a preparatory sketch for No. 109.[3] As she acknowledges, however, there is not a very direct connection between the details of the drawing and those of the ship's interior shown in No. 109.

[1] Ill. in Mitchell 1967, fig. 2.
[2] Farington Diary, 10 June 1807 (Farington 1978—, VIII, p. 3064); see also No. 68.
[3] Ink and grey wash, 9 × 12⅛ in. (Kraemer 1975, p. 50, no. 87, and pl. 57).

110 Sketch for a Monument to Lord Nelson 1807

YALE CENTER FOR BRITISH ART, NEW HAVEN, PAUL MELLON COLLECTION

Oil on canvas: 39⅝ × 29¼ in. (100.5 × 74.5 cm.)

Signed lower left: *B. West 1807*

PROV: Offered by West's sons to the United States in 1826 (120), and sold by them, Robins, London, 22–25 May 1829, lot 158 ("A Design for a Monument for the Late Lord Nelson," 3 ft. 4 in. × 2 ft. 3 in.), bt. by Gerard for £47.5.0.; Cooper Union Museum, New York, by 1900; sold by the museum, Sotheby's, London, 24 Feb. 1960, lot 99, bt. by Patch for £290; M. Bernard, London; Mr. and Mrs. Paul Mellon, Upperville, Va., by 1961

EXH: RA 1807 (194) "The sketch of a monument for perpetuating the memory of the late Lord Nelson":

West's Gallery 1822–28 (130); *Painting in England 1700–1850: Collection of Mr. and Mrs. Paul Mellon*, Virginia Museum of Fine Arts, Richmond, Va., 1963 (374), Royal Academy, London, 1964–65 (248), and Yale University Art Gallery, New Haven, 1965 (218); New Haven 1983 (4)

LIT: Evans 1959, pp. 90, 100, pl. 67; Marks 1965, pp. 66–70; Mitchell 1967, pp. 266, 272; George T. Noszlopy, "A Note on West's Apotheosis of Nelson," *Burlington Magazine*, CXII, 1970, pp. 813–17; Alberts 1978, pp. 326–27

Only a few words need be added to West's remarkably complete explanation which appeared in the Royal Academy catalogue of 1807 and which is printed above. As West's statement implies, George III's request to the Royal Academy for consideration of the best way to perpetuate the memory of Nelson developed into a competition conducted by the Committee

223

110

Courtyard and portico of the King William Block, Royal Naval College, Greenwich

the British lions holding inscribed plaques in Nos. 110 and 111 and for the almost identical lion, representing earth, in *Omnia Vincit Amor* (No. 422) of 1809.[7]

[1] See Marks 1965, pp. 54–70.
[2] Alison Kelly, "A Camouflage Queen by the River: Mrs. Coade at Greenwich," *Country Life*, CLXV, 1979, pp. 244–45; see also J. Cooke and J. Maule, *A Description of the Royal Hospital for Seamen at Greenwich*, Greenwich, 1813, pp. 8–9.
[3] Both in ink with extensive body-color, $13\frac{5}{8} \times 68\frac{7}{8}$ in., and $14\frac{7}{8} \times 67\frac{7}{8}$ in. The Howe drawing is dated *1812*. In Cooke and Maule's guide to Greenwich a description of the pediment devoted to Nelson is followed by a note, "This is the first of a series of compositions, commemorative of the great Naval Actions that have occurred in the present reign, that are to be fixed in the several vacant pediments in various parts of the Hospital." A slighter design for the Howe pediment is in the Huntington Library (pen and graphite, $8 \times 12\frac{1}{2}$ in.), and a drawing for a pediment possibly devoted to Lord Rodney is in the Pierpont Morgan Library (graphite, $7\frac{3}{8} \times 9$ in.; see Kraemer 1975, pp. 39–40, no. 66). See also No. 497.
[4] Pen and ink, $9\frac{1}{2} \times 8\frac{3}{8}$ in.
[5] Pen and ink, $11\frac{3}{4} \times 7\frac{5}{8}$ in. (1920-6-15-18).
[6] Pen and ink, $23\frac{1}{2} \times 12\frac{5}{8}$ in.
[7] Black and white chalk, $12\frac{1}{4} \times 16\frac{1}{2}$ in.

111 The Immortality of Nelson 1807

NATIONAL MARITIME MUSEUM, GREENWICH

Oil on canvas: $35\frac{1}{2} \times 29\frac{1}{2}$ in. (90 × 75 cm.)

Signed: *B. West 1807*

PROV: As for No. 109

EXH: RA 1807 (217) "The Immortality of Nelson. Vide No. 194" (i.e., No. 110 above); *La peinture romantique et les préraphaélites*, Petit Palais, Paris, 1972 (326); *The Age of Neo-Classicism*, Royal Academy, London, 1972 (273)

ENGR: Line engraving ($8\frac{15}{16} \times 7\frac{7}{16}$ in.) by Charles Heath, pub. in 1809 as the frontispiece to vol. I of *The Life of Admiral Lord Nelson, K.B.*, by James Stanier Clarke and John M'Arthur

LISTED: *BA*, p. 20 ("Victory bearing the body of Lord Nelson to the arms of Britannia," painted for John M'Arthur); Dillenberger, p. 189 (502)

LIT: *Farington Diary*, 16 March 1807 (Farington 1978–, VIII, p. 2990); James Stanier Clarke and John M'Arthur, *The Life of Admiral Lord Nelson, K.B.*,

of Taste, a group of amateurs whose responsibility was to advise on national monuments. In March 1807, the Committee awarded to John Flaxman the commission for a monument to be erected in St. Paul's.[1] West subsequently secured for himself the commission for an even grander sculptural monument to Nelson: a pediment, measuring ten feet high by forty feet across, for the King William Block of the Greenwich Hospital (*above* and *opposite*). The composition of this huge work is essentially that of the painted portion of the monument shown in No. 110 modified to fit the pedimental shape. It was modelled by West and Joseph Panzetta and executed in artificial stone by the firm of Coade and Sealy (of which Panzetta was an employee) between 1810 and 1813.[2] A large drawing for it dated *1810* is in the National Maritime Museum along with a second drawing of a pediment devoted to Lord Howe,

which must have been intended as a companion.[3]

Stylistic and iconographic sources for Nos. 110 and 111 are discussed by Marks and Noszlopy. The arguments of the latter should be treated with caution, since they were put forth without reference to West's statement in the Royal Academy catalogue.

At the Royal Academy in 1807 West also exhibited a separate painting (No. 111) showing, with only slight variations, the painting depicted within No. 110. Drawings of the subject, varying considerably from these two paintings are at Swarthmore College[4] and in the British Museum.[5] A third related drawing, which is signed and dated *1806*, and which shows a sculptural grouping of similar allegorical figures around a column dedicated to Nelson, is in the Yale Center for British Art.[6] A drawing of a lion now in the Delaware Art Museum was probably used by West for

Detail of previous illustration: pedimental sculpture by West and Joseph Panzetta

111

London, 1809, I, p. xxxvii; "Lives of Nelson," *Quarterly Review*, III, 1810, pp. 223–24; *National Maritime Museum Catalogue*, Greenwich, 1937, p. 217 (20); Evans 1959, pl. 66; Marks 1965, pp. 96–97 and 102–4; Irwin 1966, pp. 149–50, pl. 146; Mitchell 1967, p. 272; George T. Noszlopy, "A Note on West's *Apotheosis of Nelson*," *Burlington Magazine*, CXII, 1970, pp. 813–17

No. 111 repeats with only slight variations the painting included as the central feature in West's sketch for a proposed monument to Nelson (No. 110). The most evident changes are in the wording on the scroll held by Britannia, which in No. 110 is faintly inscribed *VOTES . . . PARLIAMENT . . . THE FAMILY OF NELSON* and in No. 111 bears the words inscribed on the monument above the painting in No. 110: *THE ROYAL ASSENT TO EARL NELSONS ANNUITY BILL OF FIVE THOUSAND POUNDS—ONE HUNDRED AND TWENTY THOUSAND FOR THE PURCHASE OF A SPLENDID DOMAIN FOR THE FAMILY*. In addition, on the right the words *NILE* and *COPENHAGEN* (for two of Nelson's great victories) which are on separate tablets held by a lion in No. 110, are combined on one tablet in No. 111, and on the second is an inscription, *CXXII BATTLES*, which in No. 110 appears on a block at the top of the monument. The composition is also slightly cropped on the left in No. 111 so that fewer figures are visible in the water in the lower left corner, and the flags above them are cut by the edge of the canvas.

Joseph Farington saw West at work on No. 111 on 16 March 1807. Like No. 109 it was painted for and engraved in Clarke and M'Arthur's life of Nelson published in 1809. The engraving there was accompanied by a gloss based on the statement which accompanied No. 110 in the Royal Academy catalogue of 1807.

A review of Clarke and M'Arthur's book, which appeared in the *Quarterly Review* the following year, singled out the engraving after No. 111 for caricaturing attack. Declaring that the "famous situation of Dr. Burney with his harpsicord in the Thames [in James Barry's much-lampooned *Triumph of the Thames* in the Society of Arts] appears perfectly reasonable when compared with this accumulation of incongruities," the critic expressed hope that there would come a time when "such gross allegories" would be deemed repugnant to true taste. "The invisible world is not within the artist's province."

MYTHOLOGICAL SUBJECTS

112

112 Venus Relating to Adonis the Story of Hippomenes and Atalanta c. 1767

PRIVATE COLLECTION

Oil on canvas: 65 × 86 in. (165 × 218.5 cm.)

PROV: Offered by West's sons to the United States in 1826 (20, "Venus and Adonis," 5 ft. 8 in. × 7 ft.), and sold by them, Robins, London, 22–25 May 1829, lot 157 ("Venus Relating to Adonis the Story of Hippomenes and Atalanta," 5 ft. 4 in. × 7 ft. 2 in.), bt. by Bone for £294 on behalf of Joseph Neeld, MP, Grittleton House, Wilts.; by family descent to Miss C. K. M. Neeld, by whom sold, Christie's, London, 16 Nov. 1962, lot 101; Graham Gallery, New York; Peter Rose Gallery, New York, from whom acquired by the present owner in 1983

EXH: SA 1767 (171) "Venus relating to Adonis the story of Hippomenes and Atalanta"; BI 1833 (43), lent by Joseph Neeld

ENGR: Engraving (14¾ × 19⅝ in.) in reverse, drawn by Richard Earlom, engraved by John Hall, pub. by J. Boydell, 1 Sept. 1769

LISTED: PC, p. 564 ("Venus and Adonis, large as Life," West, Painting-room); UM, p. 530; Barlow, p. 434; BA, p. 16; Galt, p. 225; Dillenberger, p. 166 (277)

LIT: V and A Cuttings (Public Advertiser, May 1767); Passavant 1836, I, p. 187; Graves 1907, p. 275 (Horace Walpole, 1767); Locquin 1912, p. 154; Gatty 1938–39, p. 8 (Walpole 1767); Sellers 1939, I, p. 75 (Charles Willson Peale, 1767); von Erffa 1973, pp. 12, 14

The story of Venus and Adonis is told in the *Metamorphoses* of Ovid (10, 519–739). The goddess has fallen in love with Adonis because of an accidental prick from Cupid's arrow and, as a warning to avoid savage beasts, she tells him the story of Atalanta and Hippomenes, who were turned into lions by Cybele. Ovid describes Venus telling her story while lying on the ground and resting her head on Adonis' breast, as shown by West in this painting. Adonis disregards the warning, and, as soon as Venus leaves him, he goes hunting and is killed by a wild boar. Venus in her grief thereupon transforms him into the anemone.

No. 112 is the first of a series of works depicting different moments from the story of Venus and Adonis (Nos. 112–18), which West exhibited at intervals through his career. It was probably preceded by an unexhibited small painting of Venus grieving over the dead Adonis (No. 117). The artist had earlier, while in Italy, painted a copy of a *Venus Lamenting Adonis* by or supposedly by Annibale Carracci, which he sent back to Philadelphia (see No. 504), and at some time he acquired and copied a version of the *Venus and Adonis* by Titian, which shows the moment before Adonis sets off for his fatal hunt (see No. 521). He probably only came into possession of his Titian after he had painted No. 112, but he must have been well aware of the type, which is not only one of Titian's most frequently repeated compositions, but also the best-known rendering of the subject by any artist.

The painting was one of five pictures exhibited by West at the Society of Artists in 1767. Although not listed as companions, Nos. 112 and 155 *Jupiter and Semele*, which follows it in the catalogue, seem to have been regarded as related works by all contemporary observers. Horace Walpole described the two together in one copy of his exhibition catalogue as "Indifferent," and in a second copy, in a remark perhaps intended only for No. 112, he wrote "Figures not very fine." A writer signing himself "X.W." in the *Public Advertiser* praised No. 112 as "fine: the Figures have the true antique Grace," adding that Venus was not equal to Semele in No. 155, while Adonis was "much superior to Jupiter." Charles Willson Peale saw the two pictures together ready for exhibition shortly after his arrival in London in February 1767 and wrote to his patron and friend John Beale Bordley: "They are Painted in a Masterly Style and in a Different Manner from Common Oil Paintg. which gives great luster & strength to the Colouring—a method of art no Painter here Else knows any thing of." The method admired by Peale was probably that based primarily on Correggio, which West was much later to describe to Joseph Farington (see Nos. 186 and 128).

West repeated the motif of a cupid holding or releasing two doves on a string, which appears in the left background of the painting, as an independent picture in 1798 (No. 127).

113 Venus and Adonis, with Cupids Bathing (The Bath of Venus) c. 1799

ALEXANDER GALLERY, NEW YORK

Oil on canvas, mounted on panel: 28¾ × 39¼ in. (73 × 99.5 cm.)

PROV: Offered by West's sons to the United States in 1826 (10) and sold by them, Robins, London, 22–25 May 1829, lot 95 ("Venus and Adonis, with Cupids Bathing," 28 × 39 in.), bt. by Holloway for £65.2.0; sold anonymously, Sotheby's, London, 5 July 1984, lot 277

EXH: (?) RA 1799 (156) "The Bath of Venus; a poetic landscape"

LISTED: PC, p. 566 ("Venus and Adonis looking at Cupids bathing," West, Gallery); UM, p. 530; Barlow, p. 434 ("Venus and Adonis seeing the Cupids bathe"); BA, p. 17; Galt, p. 228; Dillenberger, p. 173 (345)

LIT: (?) V and A Cuttings, II, p. 791 (1799)

The Ovidian version of the story of Venus and Adonis does not mention bathing cupids. In the *Idyllium* of Bion, "On the Death of Adonis," which West quoted in 1804 in connection with No. 118, cupids bathe the dead Adonis (lines 114–20), but there is no scene corresponding to that shown in this painting.

Stylistically No. 113 appears to date from around 1800, when West was repeatedly attempting to emulate the qualities of Venetian art. The importance of the landscape in the composition and the fact that it shows a scene of bathing lead us to equate it with the work that West exhibited at the Royal Academy in 1799 under the title "The Bath of Venus; a poetic landscape," which is otherwise unrecorded in the early documentation of West's art. The exhibited picture was discussed at some length in a review from an unidentified periodical in the collection of clippings in the Victoria and Albert Museum Library:

This landscape, which is very luxuriant, is painted according to what is called the revived principle of the Venetian School. Mr. West has certainly improved in the practice of this principle, for the Landscape before us has none of the coldness that marked his Pictures painted in the same manner last year. In a picture that professes to represent Poetical Nature, and that introduced ideal characters, it would be absurd to expect the scenery that pleases the more vulgar spectator. The figures are well-disposed, and there is a richness and splendour in the whole which induce us to wish that Mr. West would oftener employ his pencil on such subjects.

For "the revived principle of the Venetian School," see

113

Nos. 22, 133, 356, and 543. West's chief experiments painted in the manner did not appear at the Royal Academy the year before, but two years before, in 1797.

114 Adonis with His Dogs 1800–6

DAYTON ART INSTITUTE, DAYTON, OHIO

Oil on canvas: 20 × 14 in. (51 × 35.5 cm.)

(Signed right side: *B. West 1800/Retouched 1806*)

PROV: Offered by West's sons to the United States in 1826 (126 *Adonis*, 1 ft. 8 in. × 1 ft. 2 in.), and possibly sold privately by them between 1826 and 1829 since No. 114 was not included in either of the sales of works from West's estate in 1829 or any later sale by members of the West family; given by Abraham Adler and Norman Hirschl to Morgan State College, Baltimore, in 1968; Ira Spanierman, Inc., New York, 1980

EXH: RA 1800 (136) "Adonis with his dogs conducted to the chase by Love"

ENGR: Outline engraving ($7\frac{1}{2} × 5\frac{9}{16}$ in.) by Henry Moses, pub. by Joseph Thomas, and included in some later issues of Moses 1811

LISTED: *PC*, p. 567 ("Adonis and his Dog going to the Chase," West, Gallery); *UM*, p. 531; Barlow, p. 435; *BA*, p. 18; Galt, p. 230; Dillenberger, p. 177 (381)

LIT: Moses 1811 (only in later editions), text signed *GMB*

Only very faint and illegible traces of a signature are visible on No. 114 itself, but the outline engraving by Henry Moses shows the full signature in the corresponding place above the heads of the two dogs on the right. The print also shows the head of an additional, fifth dog emerging from behind the rock upon which Adonis rests his left foot.

A small and very sketchy drawing of the composition belongs to a descendant of the artist.[1] What may have

been a second version is discussed in the following entry. See also No. 521, West's copy of a *Venus and Adonis* by Titian.

[1] Pen, $2\frac{13}{16} × 2\frac{5}{16}$ in.

115 Adonis and His Dog

LOCATION UNKNOWN

LISTED: *BA*, p. 17 ("The small picture [?] of the Death of Adonis, from Anacreon—Its companion Adonis and his Dog," West, Painting-room); Dillenberger, p. 171 (324)

This work, evidently a second version of No. 114, is recorded only in the catalogue of West's works published in *La Belle Assemblée* in 1808. If that source is to be trusted, West presumably painted No. 115 between 1804, the date of the publication of the list in *Public Characters*, and 1808. It should be noted that, according to the engraving after No. 114, he retouched that work in 1806, and it is possible that for the sake of retouching it he moved No. 114 from his gallery, where it is listed in *Public Characters*, to the painting-room, where this version is listed in *La Belle Assemblée*, and consequently the same work is inadvertently listed twice in the later publication. On the other hand, *La Belle Assemblée* describes No. 115, the *Adonis and His Dog* in the Painting-room, as a companion to a *Death of Adonis*, which we can identify as No. 118. That work measures $15\frac{1}{2} × 16\frac{1}{2}$ in., and it is reasonable to think that its companion would have been approximately the same size, rather than having the considerably different dimensions of No. 114.

114

116 Venus Lamenting the Death of Adonis
1768–1819

See color illustration, p. 45

MUSEUM OF ART, CARNEGIE INSTITUTE, PITTSBURGH

Oil on canvas: 62 × 68 in. (157.5 × 172.5 cm.)

Signed lower right: *B West PINXIT/1768*; and lower left: *B. West 1772/Retouched 1819*

PROV: Sir William Young, Bt. (1725–1788), by 1771; the fifth Earl Ferrers (died 1778); his sale, Christie and Ansell, London, 3 June 1779, lot 112 ("The Death of Adonis"), bt. in for £29.8.0; the sixth Earl Ferrers (died 1787); his sale, Christie's, Staunton Harold, Leicestershire, 25 June 1787, lot 55, bt. by Porter for £30.9.0.; sold by Porter, Christie's, London, 3–4 April 1789, lot 98, bt. by Knight for £51.9.0; John Knight, Portland Place, London; his sale, Phillips, London, 23–24 March 1819, lot 5; (?) N. Ogle, 1819; Vose Galleries, Boston

EXH: RA 1769 (121) "Venus Lamenting the Death of Adonis"; Philadelphia 1938 (23); Allentown 1962 (9)

ENGR: Engraving (13¼ × 16¼ in. reversed) by Matthew Liart, pub. 13 Dec. 1771 by Liart, *From the Original Picture in the Collection of Sir William Young, Bart.*

LISTED: *PC*, p. 563 ("The Death of Adonis," Knight, Esq., Portland-place); *UM*, p. 529; Barlow, p. 433; *BA*, p. 15; Galt, p. 223; Dillenberger, p. 159 (214)

LIT: Farington Diary, 3 April 1819 (Farington 1978–, xv, p. 5346); Evans 1959, p. 45, pl. 31

This work shows the moment in the story of Venus and Adonis, following the death of Adonis, when the goddess has returned to grieve over her dead lover. The swans that pull the chariot in which she had departed and returned are in the right background, and in the left Adonis' hounds pursue the boar that had been responsible for his death. While in Italy, West had copied a painting attributed to Annibale Carracci showing the same subject (see No. 504). A small painting which still belongs to a descendant of the artist (No. 117) also probably pre-dates No. 116 and seems to show a concept of the scene intermediary between that of the copy and the present work.

The signature and date of *1768* on the right side of No. 116 were only revealed in 1969, when Bernard Rabin of Rutgers University cleaned the picture. Prior to 1969, the date of *1772* on the lower left had been generally accepted as the proper date, thus precluding the possibility of identifying No. 116 as the painting of the subject which West exhibited at the first exhibition of the Royal Academy in 1769. The earlier date on the canvas establishes that No. 116 was the exhibited work. Confirmation that West painted No. 116 before 1772 is provided by Matthew Liart's engraving published in 1771. The conservation work in 1969 also uncovered an inscription *Retouched 1819* accompanying the signature and date of *1772*. Hence, it seems probable that West only added the second signature and the *1772* after retouching the picture in the final year of his life, when he had evidently forgotten the original date (and when the earlier signature on the right must have already been covered over). We know that he had forgotten if and when he had exhibited it, because on 3 April 1819 his son and daughter-in-law called on Joseph Farington to consult Farington's collection of catalogues to see if No. 116 had ever been exhibited.

The attention to No. 116 in 1819 was due to its having been sold at auction on 23 March of that year. It evidently appeared at the auction house in a somewhat neglected state, as two days later, on 25 March, West wrote to the purchaser congratulating him but also complaining that the picture had been placed in a bad

situation at the sale and without a frame.[1] The reappearance of the painting, which had left the artist's hands soon after it had been painted, over fifty years previously, led not only to investigations about its earlier exhibitions (doubtlessly in the vain hope that it could be exhibited at the Academy in 1819) but also to West's retouching it. He evidently cut several inches off both sides at this time, so that the painting is now almost square while the engraving of 1771 shows a composition that would have been some eight to ten inches wider. This may have been because the edges of the painting had suffered damage during its previously unframed state. West seems to have made no other significant compositional changes while retouching the painting, but Bernard Rabin did find in 1969 that parts had been heavily overpainted; that overpainting presumably was the fruit of West's labors in 1819.

Matthew Liart published his engraving after No. 116 with a companion print after the *Death of Procris* (No. 150). The prints, which were published on the same day and are the same size, also have identical illusionistic frames around the images.[2] The subjects of grief following deaths by hunting accidents are similar, and the compositions of Nos. 116 and 150 do balance one another. Nonetheless, the paintings do not form a pair. No. 116 is much larger than No. 150; it was painted two years before the latter; and by 1771 it had left West's hands, whereas No. 150 remained the property of West and his descendants until 1898. The owner of No. 116 recorded on the Liart engraving, Sir William Young, was painted together with his wife and daughter by West in 1767 (No. 723) and West also painted two portraits of his son at approximately the same time (Nos. 724 and 725).

A carefully finished drawing, probably not made as a study for No. 116 but possibly copied after it for Liart to work from, went through the market in 1972.[3]

[1] Manuscript letter to a Mr. Ogel or Ogle, 25 March 1819 (University of Michigan Library, Ann Arbor). The recipient (and owner of No. 116) was presumably the Mr. Ogle who, according to Joseph Farington's diary, visited West in his bedroom on 8 September 1819 and bought some works from him (Farington 1978–, xv, p. 5404), and he may have been the N. Ogle recorded among the mourners at West's funeral in 1820 (Galt 1820, p. 248). West had earlier been patronized by the Very Rev.d Newton Ogle (1726–1804) who, as Dean of Winchester, had been responsible for the commission for No. 339, and subsequently one of West's great-grandsons was to be named Herbert West Ogle Margary.

[2] With the frames each measures 15⅜ × 19 in.

[3] Pencil, heightened with white, 13½ × 17 in. (sold, Sotheby's, London, 17 Dec. 1972, lot 146).

117 Venus Lamenting the Death of Adonis
c. 1763–67

PRIVATE COLLECTION

Oil on board: 9¼ × 9⅝ in. (23.5 × 24.5 cm.)

PROV: (?) Offered by West's sons to the United States in 1826 (86) and sold by them Robins, London, 22–25 May 1829, lot 33 ("Venus weeping over the Body of Adonis," 11 × 12 in.), bt. by Smith for £35.14.0. presumably on behalf of Raphael West; by descent in the family of Raphael West to the present owner

(?) EXH: West's Gallery 1822–28 (56) "Venus weeping over the Body of Adonis"

(?) LISTED: *PC*, p. 564 ("The small picture of the Death of Adonis," West, Painting-room); *UM*, p. 530; Barlow, p. 434; *BA*, p. 16; Galt, p. 226; Dillenberger, p. 167 (284)

On stylistic grounds this small painting appears to have been painted soon after West's arrival in England,

117

probably preceding *Venus Relating to Adonis the Story of Hippomenes and Atalanta* (No. 112) exhibited in 1767, as well as the larger *Venus Lamenting the Death of Adonis* (No. 116), exhibited in 1769. Venus, with one breast bare, and Adonis in her arms are distinctly reminiscent of the corresponding figures in the painting of the subject ascribed to Annibale Carracci, which West had copied in Florence (see No. 504). The figures in No. 117 are, however, not copied from the earlier painting, and they are seen whole-length, albeit on a small scale, in an extensive landscape setting, thus anticipating No. 116.

Although there is a discrepancy between the measurements of the present panel and those listed in 1826 and 1829, the provenance, exhibition history, etc., listed above with question marks, are probably correct, unless West painted yet another lost *Venus Lamenting Adonis*, while No. 117 went unrecorded. If properly identified, No. 117 seems to have been tacitly thought of as the companion to the lost *Ariadne on the Sea-shore* (No. 121), which it immediately follows in all the early lists of West's works and in the Robins sale catalogue of 22–25 May 1829. The brief discussion of No. 117 in the latter publication states, "In style, it assimilates with the feeling of the old masters, and in size, character, and expression, *is a suitable companion to the preceding lot, the Weeping Ariadne.*"

118 Venus Lamenting the Death of Adonis 1803
See color illustration, p. 128

RUTGERS UNIVERSITY ART GALLERY, NEW BRUNSWICK, NEW JERSEY

Oil on panel: 15½ × 16½ in. (39.5 × 42 cm.)

Signed lower left: *B. West 1803*

PROV: Sold by West's sons, Robins, London, 22–25 May 1829, lot 89 ("Venus Lamenting the Death of Adonis," 1 ft. 3½ in. × 1 ft. 4½ in.), bt. by Ward for £115.10.0.; Paul Magriel, New York; Victor Spark, New York, from whom purchased by the Rutgers University Art Gallery in 1953

EXH: RA 1804 (131) "Venus lamenting the death of Adonis":

The death of fair Adonis I deplore;
The lovely youth, Adonis, is no more:
The cruel fates have cut his vital thread,
And all the loves lament Adonis dead.
Ah Venus! Never more in purple rest;
For mournful sable change thy flowery vest;

Thy beauteous bosom beat, thy loss deplore
Aloud with sighs—Adonis is no more!
For the lov'd youth these copious tears I shed,
And all the cupids mourn Adonis dead.

Vide Idylliums of Bion

BI 1806 (North Room, 10); (?) West's Gallery, 1822–23 (14) "The Death of Adonis" (replaced in later catalogues by a "Last Supper"); *The Great American Nude*, New York Cultural Center, New York, 1975

ENGR: Outline engraving ($7\frac{1}{16} \times 7\frac{1}{2}$ in.) drawn by Henry Corbould and engraved by Henry Moses, pub. by Moses, 2 Dec. 1811, as pl. IX in Moses 1811

LISTED: *PC*, p. 565 ("The small picture of the Death of Adonis, from Anacreon," West, Painting-room); *UM*, p. 530; *BA*, p. 17 ("The Death of Adonis, from Anacreon—Its companion Adonis and his Dog"); Galt, p. 228; Dillenberger, p. 171 (324)

LIT: Moses 1811 (IX); Gerdts 1974, p. 31, ill. 2–3; Kraemer 1975, p. 42

The passage quoted in the Royal Academy catalogue of 1804 to accompany the painting is from the first ten lines of the *Idyllium*, "On the Death of Adonis," by the Greek pastoral poet Bion. The translation is that of Francis Fawkes (1720–1777) published in 1760. The citation of Anacreon rather than Bion in the lists of West's works is evidently an error, which can be explained by the fact that Fawkes's translations from Anacreon, which West cited on several occasions (see Nos. 125, 133, and 134) were published in the same volume together with those from Bion.

Since No. 118 was painted only in 1803, it was not included in the list of West's works given by the artist to Joel Barlow in 1802 and published in *The Columbiad*. The companion *Adonis and his Dog*, mentioned in *La Belle Assemblée*, is discussed in entry No. 115.

Ruth Kraemer has identified a sketch in the Pierpont Morgan Library as possibly a preparatory drawing for Venus in No. 118.[1]

[1]Pen and black ink on grey paper, $6\frac{3}{8} \times 4\frac{1}{4}$ in. (Kraemer 1975, no. 69).

119 Arethusa *c.* 1802

LOCATION UNKNOWN

(21 × 15 in.) (53.5 × 38 cm.)

PROV: Offered by West's sons to the United States in 1826 (128), and sold by them, Robins, London, 22–25 May 1829, lot 84 ("Arethusa," 1 ft. 9 in. × 1 ft. 3 in.), bt. by Ward for £63

EXH: RA 1802 (134) "Arethusa. Vide Ovid's Metamorphoses, i, 5"

LISTED: *PC*, p. 567 ("Arethusa bathing," West, Gallery); *UM*, p. 531; Barlow, p. 435; *BA*, p. 18; Galt, p. 232; Dillenberger, p. 181 (421)

LIT: Leslie 1860, II, p. 10

The story of Arethusa appears in the fifth book of Ovid's *Metamorphoses*. The nymph Arethusa undresses and bathes in a stream where she is observed and then pursued by the river god Alpheus. She ultimately escapes him by becoming a fountain in the island of Ortygia near Syracuse.

This work has been lost since 1829, but we have some idea of its appearance due to its having been copied by Charles Robert Leslie. On 12 May 1812, Leslie wrote to his sister in Philadelphia: "I have just begun to copy a small picture of Mr. West's of Arethusa Bathing; it is a most beautiful thing; when it is finished I shall endeavor to send it over . . ." That copy must

Thomas Sully, *Musidora c.* 1813. Oil on panel, 22 × 17½ in. Private collection

Thomas Sully, *Musidora* 1815–35. Oil on panel, 28⅛ × 22½ in. Metropolitan Museum of Art, New York

have been the *Musidora Bathing after West*, which Leslie exhibited at the Pennsylvania Academy in Philadelphia in the following year, and of which the young Thomas Sully in turn began two copies while it was at the Academy. One of these copies by Leslie or Sully was probably the *Musidora* exhibited as a work by West at the Peale Museum in Baltimore in 1820.

Despite the different title, the story of Musidora from James Thomson's *Seasons* is, like that of Arethusa, about a girl discovered while bathing in a stream; hence, a painting of a nude female figure out of doors in or near a body of water could, unless elaborated by further details, bear either title. West did, in fact, paint a picture of Musidora based on Thomson (No. 231), but based on an early edition of the *Seasons* in which she has two companions. No. 231 was not the source of Leslie's copy exhibited in 1813, as we have at least partial knowledge of that picture from Thomas Sully's two copies. One of those, which is signed with Sully's monogram and also inscribed *B. West*, is in a private collection in Baltimore (*above left*).[1] The other, which Sully did not complete until 1835, and which is signed and dated *1835*, is in the Metropolitan Museum of Art (*above right*).[2] They both clearly derive from the same source, but the composition of one reverses that of the other, and while the bather in the Baltimore painting gazes out at the spectator, her counterpart in the painting in the Metropolitan Museum turns away. In general, the Baltimore painting looks more like a composition by West, and, since it bears his name, it probably does reproduce Leslie's copy after No. 119 without radical change. In the Metropolitan Museum's painting, the pose is more coy or modest, and the twist of the bather's neck seems unlike anything painted by West. Thus this painting probably represents Sully's independent modification of his source in the twenty-year interval after his initial sight of the composition.

What was evidently a second version is No. 120 below. For a consideration of the possibility that West exhibited No. 119 or 120 at the British Institution in 1806 under a different title see the entry for *Salmacis and Hermaphroditus* (No. 154).

[1]Oil on panel, 22 × 17½ in. We are indebted to Wilbur H. Hunter, Director of the Peale Museum, who brought this

painting to our attention and provided information about the exhibition at the Peale Museum in 1820, and to Sona Johnston and Margaret Ash of the Baltimore Museum of Art, who found Sully's monogram. Prior to this discovery the picture had been ascribed to West.
[2]Oil on panel, 28½ × 22½ in. In addition to being dated *1835* on the front, the painting is also inscribed on the back: *Begun in 1815—finished in 1835*. See Gardner and Feld 1965, pp. 161–62.

120 Arethusa

LOCATION UNKNOWN

PROV: Sold by West's sons, Robins, London, 20–22 June 1829, lot 103 ("Arethusa")

Although the appearance of "Arethusas" in separate sales of paintings from West's estate in May and June of 1829 would seem to indicate the existence of a second version of the subject, it is also possible that No. 119 was bought in in May and resold in June. The Ward who is recorded as purchasing No. 119 at the earlier sale seems to have made purchases there on behalf of West's sons.

121 Ariadne on the Sea-shore

LOCATION UNKNOWN

(11 × 12 in.) (28 × 30.5 cm.)

PROV: Offered by West's sons to the United States in 1826 (84) and sold by them, Robins, London, 22–25 May 1829, lot 32 ("Ariadne on the Sea-shore," 11 × 12 in.), bt. by Smith for £34.13.0.

EXH: West's Gallery 1822–28. (53)

LISTED: *PC*, p. 564 ("The small picture of Ariadne on the Sea-shore," West, Painting-room); *UM*, p. 530; Barlow, p. 434; *BA*, p. 16; Galt, p. 226; Dillenberger, p. 167 (283)

This painting has been lost since the Robins sale of 22–25 May 1829, but it is described in some detail in the catalogue of that sale:

A small cabinet picture worthy the old Italian school. The disconsolate daughter of Minos, thus left deserted on the shore of the island Naxos, by the faithless Theseus, is herein depicted wrapped in the silent agony of grief which is inconsolable. In vain are the little loves, seated near, ministering comfort—their infantile sadness is unheeded, and the distant barque to which one points, seems about to awaken her to despair.

The entry in the same catalogue for the following lot, 33, "Venus Weeping over the Body of Adonis" (see No. 117), describes that work as "in size, character, and expression" to be "a suitable companion to the preceding lot, the Weeping Ariadne." If we have properly identified the companion lot as the very early No. 117, then No. 121 was also probably an early work.

Two sketches of female figures looking out to sea on a sheet of sketches in the Historical Society of Pennsylvania may be related to the subject of Ariadne, but they suggest little of the grief that seems to have been so prominently displayed in the painting.[1] A drawing of what appears to be this subject in the Detroit Institute of Arts, although bearing an old inscription with West's name on the mount, is not by him and is related to paintings of Ariadne by Angelica Kauffmann.[2]

[1] Pen and ink, $10\frac{1}{4} \times 6$ in.

[2] Ink and sepia wash, $5\frac{1}{4} \times 5\frac{3}{4}$ in. For *Ariadne* by Angelica Kauffmann, see Rosenblum 1967, p. 20, and fig. 17. The Detroit drawing also bears an inscription on the mount identifying its subject as *Dido surprised at the Departure of Aeneas.*

122 Arion *c.* 1802

LOCATION UNKNOWN

$(9 \times 12$ in.$)$ $(23 \times 30.5$ cm.$)$

PROV: Offered by West's sons to the United States in 1826 (75, "Arion on the Dolphin," 9 in. × 1 ft.), and sold by them, Robins, London, 22–25 May 1829, lot 69 ("Arion," 9 × 12 in.), bt. by Ward for £17.17.0.

EXH: RA 1802 (133) "Orion cast into the sea, carried safe to land on the back of a dolphin":

> He on his crouching back sits all at ease,
> With harp in hand, by which he calms the seas,
> And for his passage with a song he pays.
> *Vide Ovid's Fast. ii.*

West's Gallery 1828 (31) "Arion."

LISTED: *PC*, p. 566 ("Orion on the Dolphin's Back," West, Gallery); *UM*, p. 530; Barlow, p. 435; *BA*, p. 17; Galt, p. 229; Dillenberger, p. 174 (355)

Although printed "Orion" in the Royal Academy catalogue of 1802 and in the early lists of West's works, the subject of this lost painting is *Arion*, a legendary musician. Returning to Corinth from a musical contest, Arion was threatened with murder by the sailors of his ship. He leapt overboard and was saved by a dolphin who had been charmed by his music.

The Robins sale catalogue of May 1829 described this picture as "an emanation of splendor worthy the mind of Correggio."

123 A Bacchante 1797

MR. AND MRS. PHILIP I. BERMAN, ALLENTOWN, PENNSYLVANIA

Oil on canvas: 50 × 40 in. (127 × 101.5 cm.)

Signed lower left: *B. West 1797*

123

PROV: Purchased from the artist in 1808 for 150 guineas by Sir John Fleming Leicester (later Lord de Tabley); his sale, Christie's, London, 7 July 1827, lot 43, bt. by Watts Russell for 115 guineas; Jesse Watts Russell, Ilam Hall, Staffordshire; his sale, Christie's, London, 3 July 1875, lot 13, bt. by Agnew; sold by Agnew to D. Brossilow in 1876; purchased from the Brossilow estate by Julius Weitzner in 1961 and sold by him to the present owners in 1962

EXH: RA 1798 (181) "A Bacchante"; Allentown 1962 (23)

ENGR: Etching ($3\frac{5}{16} \times 2\frac{11}{16}$ in.) by John Young, pub. in 1821, opp. p. 13 of Young's *Catalogue of Pictures by British artists, in the possession of Sir John Fleming Leicester, Bart.*

LISTED: *PC*, p. 565 ("A Bacchanté, as large as Life, half length," West, Painting-room); *UM*, p. 530; *BA*,

p. 17, ("now in the possession of Sir John Leicester"); Galt, p. 227; Dillenberger, p. 171 (318)

LIT: Farington Diary, 26 Aug. 1797 (Farington 1978–, III, p. 889); V and A Cuttings, II, p. 456 (1827), IV p. 1142, and v, p. 1269 (1822); William Carey, *A Descriptive Catalogue of a Collection of Paintings by British Artists in the Possession of Sir John Fleming Leicester, Bart.*, London, 1819, pp. 86–89 (29); John Young, *A Catalogue of Pictures by British Artists in the possession of Sir John Fleming Leicester, Bart.*, London, 1821, p. 13 (29), ill.; Hall 1962, pp. 100 and 121 (109)

On 26 August 1797, after calling on West, Joseph Farington wrote in his diary:

> West has painted a Bacchante on a Buff-Col'd. ground, adhering *to the process* except in Flesh which in the body colour becomes a contrast which He thinks luminous—He says 'twas the way of Titian—

the other *process that* of Bassan. Said He made this objection to Provis formerly—vide "see" Wests declaration.

The "process" referred to by Farington was that of the "Venetian Secret," which West had learned from Thomas Provis and his daughter during the previous year, and with which he had experimented in several works (see Nos. 22, 133, 356, and particularly 543). By 6 June 1797 West had misgivings about the method, and told Farington that Provis's grounds were "too *cold and purple*," possibly in response to criticism of his pictures in the new method exhibited at the Royal Academy in 1797 as "remarkable for a dark and purpurine hue." On 6 June Farington had looked at the grounds of paintings by Titian in West's collection and decided that they were much warmer than Provis's.[1] West's agreement with this opinion is indicated by his reference in August to the ways of Titian and Bassano and his use of a buff ground in No. 123.

In an attempt to encourage Sir John Fleming Leicester to buy another, more expensive, picture (No. 420), rather than this picture, West described No. 123 in a letter dated 25 March 1808, as "not of that class in composition by which my works are known; but one of those in the corse of my practice, I paint, to diversify my professional pursuits." Since Leicester was assembling a representative collection of modern British paintings, West's argument was as legitimate as self-serving. Nonetheless, Leicester acquired No. 123. He may have thought of it as a possible companion to a painting the same size of *Lady Hamilton as a Bacchante* by George Romney, which he had purchased the year before.[2]

Paintings of *bacchanti* were exhibited at the Royal Academy by Reynolds in 1784 and by John Hoppner in 1789. If the latter's exhibited *Bacchante* can properly be identified as the picture now in the Nelson-Atkins Museum in Kansas City usually known as the *Tambourine Girl*,[3] the scenes of bacchanalian revel in the backgrounds of that work and of No. 123 are sufficiently similar to suggest that it may have been an inspiration to West in undertaking the same subject. However, as noted by Carey, Young, and other commentators while No. 123 was in the Leicester collection, the chief inspiration for the work came from a painting by Titian of a girl holding a tray of fruit, traditionally identified as a portrait of Titian's daughter Lavinia. The Titian exists in several versions, and Young identified West's model as that in the possession of the Countess de Grey, which had come to England in the Orléans collection. This painting is now generally considered a workshop copy of the original in Berlin and shows the subject in a green costume rather than brown and holding a casket rather than a tray of fruit.[4] West had seen the Orléans collection (then in the possession of Monsieur Laborde de Mereville) by 6 June 1797.[5]

A second version of No. 123 of good quality, but nonetheless, in the opinion of the compilers, a copy, belongs to the English-Speaking Union in London.[6] Essentially the same compositionally, this version is less assured in handling and eliminates several of the figures from the scene of bacchanalia in the right background. It may have been the *Girl with Cymbals* included in the sale of pictures from Turner's collection in 1874, which John Gage has tentatively identified as a version of West's *Bacchante*.[7]

[1] Farington refers specifically to the *Hunting piece* (also identified as a *Death of Actaeon*) and the *Last Supper*. West also owned a version of Titian's *Venus and Adonis* (see No. 521). None of his Titians are now accepted as works by the master's hand.

[2] Hall 1962, p. 119 (nos. 80 and 82); Leicester owned two paintings by Romney of *Lady Hamilton as a Bacchante*, whose histories are somewhat confused. See also *Lady Hamilton*, exh. cat., Arts Council of Great Britain, 1972, no. 54.

[3] Ill. in *Handbook of the Collections in the William Rockhill Nelson Gallery of Art and Mary Atkins Museum of Fine Arts*, Kansas City, 1959, p. 131.

[4] Harold E. Wethey, *The Paintings of Titian II: The Portraits*, London, 1971, p. 115 (60, variant 1) and fig. 193.

[5] Farington Diary, 6 June 1797 (Farington 1978—, III, p. 850).

[6] This painting, which is approximately the same size as No. 123, was acquired in Vienna prior to 1929 by a relative of Mr. and Mrs. F. J. MacGarvey, who presented it to the English-Speaking Union in 1949.

[7] Christie's, London, 25 July 1874, lot 12, bt. by Eyre for £15.4.6. as cited in John Gage, *Colour in Turner*, London and New York, 1969, p. 244, note 101.

124 Bacchanté Boys (Boys and Grapes) 1819

DR. AND MRS. J. B. CHASTAIN

Oil on canvas: 26 × 35 in. (66 × 89 cm.)

Signed bottom left: *Benjamin West October 10th 1819*

PROV: Offered by West's sons to the United States in 1826 (139) and sold by them, Robins, London, 22–25 May 1829, lot 181 ("Boys and Grapes," 2 ft. 4 in. × 3 ft.), bt. by Shearman for £38.17.0.; sold anonymously, Christie's, London, 23 June 1972, lot 27 (as "Infant Bacchanals"); Old Hall Gallery, Iden, Rye, Sussex, from whom purchased by the present owners in 1973

EXH: West's Gallery 1821 (65), 1822–28 (125) "The Boys and Grapes: The Last Picture painted by Mr. West"

(?) LISTED: *PC*, p. 366 ("The Bacchanté Boys," West, Painting-room); *UM*, p. 530; *BA*, p. 17; Galt, p. 228; Dillenberger, p. 172 (337)

The date of 10 October 1819 on this painting, five months before West's death on 11 March 1820, confirms that it was the *Boys and Grapes* exhibited and sold by West's sons during the following decade with the claim that it was the artist's last picture. In the Robins sale of May 1829, where it was the last entry in the catalogue, it was immediately preceded by a work described as West's first picture (see No. 509), and the dis-

cussion accompanying No. 124 described the two as the "Alpha" and the "Omega" of his art.

We have tentatively equated No. 124 with the "Bacchanté Boys" included in the list of West's works published in 1804 in *Public Characters* and in other early catalogues, because it patently fits that title. To have been included on the lists the painting would have had to have been in existence long before 1819, in contradiction to the signature and date on the canvas, as well as to the claims made for the picture. Nonetheless, 10 October 1819, was West's eighty-first birthday, and by that date he was in failing health. In the diary of Joseph Farington, who kept a close eye on West during his last years, there is no indication that West commenced any new pictures in 1819, but there is a mention on 3 September 1819, slightly over a month before the date on No. 124, of his retouching earlier pictures. In its present state the painting does appear to be the product of such retouching. The reddish flesh tones and flaccid modelling of the boys belong to West's last years, whereas the much more vigorously painted still-life details on the left are consistent with his art of some twenty years earlier. Furthermore, it should be noted that if the painting is not the retouched "Bacchanté Boys" from the lists, then that work evidently disappeared without a trace sometime before the 1820s.

125 Sleeping Cupid (Cupid Sleeping on a Bed of Roses) (Cupids) *c*. 1802

LOCATION UNKNOWN

(11 × 14½ in.) (28 × 37 cm.)

PROV: Offered by West's sons to the United States in 1826 (74) and sold by them, Robins, London, 22–25 May 1829, lot 62 ("Cupid Sleeping on a Bed of Roses," 11 × 14½ in.), bt. by Smith for £16.16.0.

EXH: RA 1803 (135) "Cupid sleeping on a bed of Roses: from Anacreon"; West's Gallery 1821 (14), 1822–28 (30) "Cupid sleeping on a Bed of Roses"

124

LISTED: *PC*, p. 567 ("Cupid Asleep," West, Gallery); *UM*, p. 531; Barlow, p. 435; *BA*, p. 18, Galt, p. 230; Dillenberger, p. 178 (392)

The citation of Anacreon which accompanied the picture in the catalogue of the Royal Academy exhibition of 1803 refers to the opening lines of the ode "Cupid Wounded," which West had quoted in the previous year's catalogue in conjunction with a version (? No. 133) of *Cupid Stung by a Bee*:

> Once as Cupid, tir'd with play
> On a bed of roses lay

Although first exhibited in 1803, No. 125 must have been in existence by the summer of 1802, since it appears on the list of works given by West to Joel Barlow at that time. A second painting of the same or a similar subject is No. 126 below.

126 Sleeping Cupid

LOCATION UNKNOWN

(11½ × 16 in.) (29 × 40.5 cm.)

PROV: Sold by West's sons, Robins, London, 22–25 May 1829, lot 2 ("Cupids," 11½ × 16 in.), bt. by Nash for 14 guineas; John Nash (1752–1835); his sale, Christie's, London, 11 July 1835, lot 80 ("Cupid—a sketch")

EXH: (?) RA 1818 (111) "Sleeping Cupid"; West's Gallery, 1822–28 (84) "Cupids"

This painting was exhibited by West's sons in the 1820s and sold in 1829 under the plural title "Cupids" but, since it was purchased in 1829 by the architect John Nash, it must have been the same work sold six years later in Nash's sale as "Cupid—a sketch," in the singular. Hence, although we know from the discussion of the picture in the sale catalogue of 1829 that it showed two figures of boys, one presumably was considerably more prominent than the other. We also know from the catalogue of 1829 that the two figures were depicted as being of different ages and that one of them was asleep:

> Woe to those who waken the one, or trip the other off his reverie. These destructive archers differ in age; the major is almost old enough for Hymen; but the minor is not too young to pierce the bosom of an approaching Alexander.

Since No. 126 does not appear on any of the early lists of West's works, it was probably painted after 1804, and it can reasonably be equated with the otherwise unrecorded *Sleeping Cupid* that the artist exhibited at the Royal Academy in 1818. Both Nos. 125 and 126 have disappeared, so it is impossible to determine whether the latter was fundamentally a replica of the former. The comments in the Robins catalogue imply that it was not; whereas No. 125 was, "Chaste in colour, and painted with effective breadth," No. 126 was "original in design, and painted with spirit." The "spirit" combined with the work's small size would account for its being described as a sketch in the catalogue of the Nash sale.

127 Cupid Releasing Two Doves 1798–1808
See color illustration, p. 136

PRIVATE COLLECTION

Oil on panel: 56 × 39 in. (142 × 99 cm.)

Signed lower left: *B. West 1798, retouched 1803/and 1808*

PROV: Acquired by Mr. (or Captain) Agar in 1808 (? George Charles Agar, 1780–1856); DeLancey Kountze, New York; sold anonymously, Parke-Bernet, New York, 28 Feb.–1 March 1945, lot 73;

sold anonymously, Sotheby's, London, 23 Nov. 1966, lot 52; M. Bernard Galleries, London, 1967; The Sporting Gallery, Middleburg, Va.; Robert Scott Wiles, Washington, D.C., 1969, from whom purchased by the Norfolk Museum of Arts and Sciences, Norfolk, Va., in 1970; Hirschl & Adler Galleries, New York, 1980

EXH: RA 1798 (145) "Cupid"; *American Art from the Colonial and Federal Periods*, Hirschl & Adler Galleries, New York, 1982 (25)

LISTED: *PC*, p. 567 ("Cupid letting loose two Pigeons," West, Gallery); *UM*, p. 531; Barlow, p. 435 ("Cupid letting loose two Doves"); *BA*, p. 18 ("now in possession of Captain Agar"); Galt, p. 230; Dillenberger, p. 178 (391)

LIT: Hall 1962, p. 100; *Art Quarterly*, XXXIII, 1970, p. 193

On 25 March 1808, West wrote to Sir John Fleming Leicester attempting to dissuade him from buying *A Bacchante* (No. 123) and to interest him in another work in its stead: "I am at present painting a picture expressive of the harmony of love over creation—the figures are the size of the cupid in the picture I parted with to Mr. Agar." No. 127 is clearly the picture referred to as having gone to Mr. Agar and, as it was retouched by West in 1808, it could not have gone long before 25 March. The painting expressing the harmony of love over creation (No. 420) appeared at the Royal Academy in May 1808 and evidently showed a subject closely related to that of *Omnia Vincit Amor, or the Power of Love in the Three Elements* (No. 422), which is signed and dated *1809*. In the latter work not only is the size of the central figure approximately the same as that of the Cupid in No. 127, but the subject seems to be an extension of that of No. 127. The motif of Cupid holding two harnessed pigeons or doves appears earlier in West's art in *Venus Relating to Adonis the Story of Hippomenes and Atalanta* (No. 112).

The Agar who purchased No. 127 may have been the Hon. George Charles Agar, the second son of the first Earl of Normanton, who held a commission in the Foot Guards in 1808. The list of West's works published in *La Belle Assemblée* in 1808 refers to the painting's new owner as Captain Agar.

128 Venus and Cupid *c.* 1765
See color illustration, p. 35

THE PARTHENON, NASHVILLE, TENNESSEE

Oil on canvas: oval, 37½ × 32¼ in. (95 × 82 cm.)

PROV: John William Steers, London, *c.* 1804; Acermans, Bristol (? W. Acraman, Clifton), *c.* 1808; (?) sold by Daniel Wade, Clifton, 1842; sold by Captain R. A. Ogilvy, Bellipar House, County Londonderry, Christie's, London, 28 April 1922, lot 115, bt. by Leger; Arthur Tooth and Sons, London, by whom sold, American Art Galleries, New York, 19 Feb. 1925 (71); M. A. Newhouse & Son, St. Louis; James M. Cowan, Aurora, Illinois, by whom presented to the city of Nashville in 1929

EXH: SA 1765 (152) "Venus and Cupid"

LISTED: *PC*, p. 563 ("Venus and Cupid," oval, Mr. Steers, Temple); *UM*, p. 529; Barlow, p. 433; *BA*, p. 15 (... Mr. Steers, Temple, now Mr. Acermans, Bristol); Galt, p. 233; Dillenberger, p. 160 (216)

LIT: Farington Diary 26 Jan. 1808 (Farington 1978–, IX, pp. 3207–8); (?) Passavant 1836, I, pp. 320–21; *Art News*, XXIII, 11 April 1925, p. 5, ill.; Gatty 1938–39, p. 81 (Horace Walpole, 1765); Lee Minton, MD., and A. Averette James Jr., MD., "The James M.

Cowan Collection of American Paintings in the Parthenon, Nashville, Tennessee," *Antiques*, CXVIII, 1980, pp. 988, 994, and pl. I

Our chief source of information about this early work is Joseph Farington, who wrote in his diary on 26 January 1808:

> West I called upon, & found Him much pleased with a picture which He had just cleaned & varnished. It was painted by Himself in 1765 & was the first commission He recd. in England, the subject, *Venus & Cupid*, which He exhibited that year. He said it was painted while His mind was full of Corregio, as was that of *Pylades and Orestes* belonging to Sir George Beaumont. He said that having long considered in what manner Corregio obtained that purity of Colouring in His flesh, He at last determined that it was by mixing *Ultramarine with his White* so that it should make a part of every tint & by using Indian Red only to give warmth, & black in His shadows. With these colours only He painted His flesh & *when finished*, made use of warm glazing Colours which cool, pure colours produced the most charming effect. He would never use yellow in painting His flesh.

Although No. 128 may have been West's first commission in England, he evidently did not consider the fact sufficiently significant to tell it to his biographers, none of whom mentioned the painting. Mr. Steers, the owner as of 1804, was probably not the patron who commissioned the work, but a subsequent purchaser. Between 1804 and July 1808, when the list of West's works in *La Belle Assemblée* appeared, the painting changed hands again, and West presumably cleaned and varnished it in January 1808 for its new owner. The dark outline of the profile of Cupid, which looks more like West's later work than that of the mid-1760s, suggests that the artist took advantage of having the painting in his hands again to retouch at least that part of it as well.

West exhibited *Pylades and Orestes* (No. 186), which he mentioned to Farington along with No. 128, in 1766, a year after the *Venus and Cupid*. Although there is no reason to doubt his statement about his mind being "full of Corregio" while painting the two, it is unclear whether he intended his subsequent description of Correggio's methods to describe his own methods in painting Nos. 128 and 186. Prior to his arrival in Italy in the summer of 1760, West had never seen a Correggio and, although he did paint a copy of the *Madonna of St. Jerome* in 1762 and 1763 (No. 505), he hardly had had the time to have "long considered" Correggio's manner when he undertook No. 128. Additionally, we know that West's concern with Correggio lasted well beyond the period when he painted Nos. 128 and 186. In 1773 he sent to the Royal Academy a painting with the title "A Holy Family, in imitation of Correggio's manner" (No. 303), and it is in that lost work rather more than in No. 128 that we might expect to find the techniques that West described to Farington in 1808. Nevertheless, the painting does give ample evidence of West's awareness of Correggio. There are obvious thematic affinities with the *Mercury Instructing Cupid* or *School of Love* (National Gallery, London), and West's curly-haired and bewinged Cupid appears to be based upon his counterpart in that work, which West would have known through a copy or engraving.[1] The inclined profile of Venus' head also echoes Correggio.

Venus and Cupid also appear either alone together or with additional subordinate figures in several other paintings by West showing variations of the subject of *Cupid Stung by a Bee* (Nos. 131–36). Although this type of subject is comparable to the many quasi-erotic mythological scenes painted in France in the eighteenth century by artists such as François Boucher, it was relatively rare in England. No. 128 and *Jupiter and Europa*

(? No. 140), which appeared with it at the Society of Artists in 1765 were not only West's first exhibited paintings of mythological subjects, but also constituted the virtual introduction of such themes into English art; the former in particular anticipates Reynolds's earliest exhibited subject pictures such as *Hope Nursing Love* (Bowood House, Calne, Wiltshire), which appeared at the first Royal Academy exhibition in 1769, and *Venus Chastising Cupid* (Iveagh Bequest, Kenwood), which he exhibited two years later.

The "Mr. Acermans, Bristol" listed in *La Belle Assemblée* as the owner of No. 128 is almost certainly identical with a W. Acraman, Esq., whom Johann David Passavant visited in Clifton in 1831, and a painting in his collection which Passavant described under the title "Cupid and Psyche" as showing half-length figures in an oval form, and as having been painted by West shortly after his return from Italy, is probably identical with No. 128 (see also No. 151).

West's heirs sold two smaller paintings of the same or a similar subject in 1829 and 1898 (Nos. 129 and 130). A copy of No. 128, in which some details are simplified or eliminated (i.e., Venus does not hold a ribbon in her right hand), is in the William Benton Museum of Art, Storrs, Connecticut.[2] West's first American pupil, Matthew Pratt, who was in London from 1764 to 1766, painted a copy of No. 128, and it was probably also copied by a second American, Abraham Delanoy, who was in London at approximately the same time.[3] It is possible that one of these copies is the painting now at Storrs.

See also pp. 33–6 above.

[1] The *School of Love* was in Spain in the eighteenth century and came to England only in 1815, but it was a famous painting and numerous early copies are recorded; see Cecil Gould, *The Paintings of Correggio*, Ithaca, New York, 1976, pp. 213–16.
[2] Oil on canvas: $37\frac{1}{2} \times 32\frac{1}{2}$ in.
[3] See Evans 1980, pp. 24 and 33.

129 Venus and Cupid

LOCATION UNKNOWN

(12×16 in.) (30.5×40.5 cm.)

PROV: Offered by West's sons to the United States in 1826 (96) and sold by them, Robins, London, 22–25 May 1829, lot 73 ("Venus and Cupid," 12×16 in.), bt. by Smith for £23.2.0.

EXH: West's Gallery 1822–28 (71) "Venus and Cupid"

130 Venus Admonishing Cupid

LOCATION UNKNOWN

($5\frac{1}{2} \times 8$ in.) (14×20.5 cm.)

PROV: Sold by Mrs. Albert F. West, Christie's, London, 19 March 1898, lot 136 ("Venus Admonishing Cupid," $5\frac{1}{2} \times 8$ in.), bt. by Ruston for 4s.

131 Cupid Stung by a Bee 1774

CORCORAN GALLERY OF ART, WASHINGTON, D.C.

Oil on canvas: round, $47\frac{3}{4} \times 48\frac{7}{8}$ in. (121.5×124 cm.)

Signed lower left: *B. West/1774*

PROV: Agmondisham Vesey (died 1785), Lucan, County Dublin, Ireland, by 1776; sold anonymously, Christie's, London, 3 Dec. 1926, lot 92, bt. by Walton, and again 25 March 1927, lot 95, bt. by Barclay; Mortimer Brandt, New York, from

131

whom acquired by Mrs. E. Lovette West, Bronxville, New York; her daughter, Bernice West Beyers, by whom given to the Corcoran Gallery in 1963

EXH: RA 1775 (335) "Cupid, stung by a bee, is cherished by his Mother."

ENGR: Mezzotint ($16\frac{15}{16}$ in. in diameter) by Valentine Green, pub. 25 March 1776 by John Boydell, *From the Original Picture in the Possession of A. Vesey, Esq*; stipple engraving ($8\frac{3}{4}$ in. in diameter, reversed) by I. B. Michel, pub. by Boydell, 1 March 1779

LISTED: *PC*, p. 563 ("Cupid stung by a Bee, oval," Vesey, Esq. in Ireland); *UM*, p. 529; Barlow, p. 433; *BA*, p. 15; Galt, p. 223; Dillenberger, p. 160 (220)

No. 131 is the first of several paintings (Nos. 131–36) showing Cupid being comforted by Venus after a bee has stung his finger. West's chief source for all of them appears to have been the fortieth ode, "Cupid Wounded," by Anacreon (or pseudo-Anacreon, as the author is now usually identified). In 1802, to accompany two later versions of the subject, West quoted separate passages from this ode, both from the translation by Francis Fawkes published in 1760 (see Nos. 133 and 134). In addition to these works, West also exhibited a *Cupid Sleeping on a Bed of Roses* in 1803, based on the opening lines of the same ode (No. 125).

In No. 131 the cause of Cupid's grief is visible on a rose petal lying in front of his left foot. In the background, a swarm of bees attack three *putti* near a hive. This little scene has nothing to do with the ode by Anacreon but may have been inspired by the nineteenth idyllium of Theocritus, "The Honey-Stealer," also translated by Fawkes, in which Cupid is stung while stealing honey from a hive, but in which there is no mention of a rose.

For Agmondisham Vesey, the first owner of No. 131, see No. 37.

132 Cupid Stung by a Bee c. 1786

THE HERMITAGE, LENINGRAD

Oil on canvas: $30\frac{1}{4} \times 25\frac{1}{4}$ in. (77×64 cm.)

PROV: Painted for Empress Catherine II

LIT: Sophie von la Roche, *Sophie in London 1786*, trans. by Clare Williams, London, 1933, pp. 152–53; [Alexandra Kroll], *The State Hermitage: English Paintings: Catalogue* (in Russian), Leningrad, 1969, p. 113, ill. p. 114

Sophie von la Roche, a German visitor to London who was taken to West's studio in 1786, saw and admired No. 132 there, and reported in her diary that it was intended for Catherine II. The painting is otherwise unrecorded in the early West literature, presumably

132

because it went unexhibited and left the artist's possession as soon as it was completed.

Although the composition of No. 132 is quite different from that of No. 131, painted some twelve years earlier, the subject is the same. Sophie described it as a "very attractive composition from an ode by Anacreon." A replica, with slight differences in detail is No. 133 below.

133 Cupid Stung by a Bee (?)c. 1796–1802
See color illustration, p. 129

NELSON-ATKINS MUSEUM OF ART, KANSAS CITY, MISSOURI

Oil on canvas: $29\frac{1}{2} \times 24\frac{1}{4}$ in. (75 × 61.5 cm.)

PROV: Sold anonymously, Christie's, London, 21 Dec. 1923, lot 44, bt. by Tooth; sold by Arthur Tooth, American Art Galleries, New York, 19 Feb. 1925, lot 42; Ehrich Galleries, New York, from whom purchased by the present owner in 1933

EXH: (?) RA 1802 (135) "Cupid wounded by a bee in the finger: Venus thus replied, and smiled":

Dry———
Dry thy tears—for shame, my child!
If a bee can wound so deep,
Causing Cupid thus to weep,
Think, o think! What cruel pains
He that's stung by thee sustains.

Philadelphia 1938 (46)

(?) LISTED: *PC*, p. 566 ("Cupid complaining to Venus of a Bee having stung his Finger," West, Gallery); *UM*, p. 530; Barlow, p. 435; *BA*, p. 18; Galt, p. 229; Dillenberger, p. 174 (356)

LIT: (?) Farington Diary, 25 and 28 Nov., 19 and 30 Dec. 1796, 11, 17, and 18 Jan. 1797 (Farington 1978—, III, pp. 702, 703, 722, 732, 744, 750, and 751); John Gage, "Magilphs and Mysteries," *Apollo*, LXXX, 1964, pp. 38–41, ill. p. 40

No. 133 is essentially a replica of the previous entry. The compositions are similar but there are differences in the details of Venus' dress and hair, and in the draperies that fall over Cupid's right wrist. In No. 132 there is only one quiver in the lower left corner, which

reappears in this painting, but there is also a second quiver above Cupid's arm in No. 133; and in addition to the single rose with a bee upon it in No. 132, there are two further roses above Venus' arm in No. 133. A further copy of the composition, which repeats No. 133 rather than No. 132 in details, is in a private collection in Pittsburgh.[1] This may be the copy after West's *Cupid Stung by a Bee* painted by Edward Savage and exhibited in the Columbian Gallery in New York in 1802.[2]

The documentation of the two paintings of *Cupid Stung by a Bee* that West exhibited at the Royal Academy in 1802 and of a version or versions of the subject upon which he is known to have painted in 1796 is extremely opaque, and linking those recorded works with currently known ones is to some extent a matter of guess-work. Because No. 133 is unsigned and its history prior to 1923 is unknown, it is the version of the subject about which we know least; nonetheless, for want of evidence to the contrary, we have tentatively identified No. 133 not only as one of the two paintings of the subject that West exhibited in 1802, but also as one that we can associate with his activity in 1796.

That activity was the affair or fiasco of the "Venetian Secret" (for which see also Nos. 22, 356, and particularly 543). On 25 November 1796, the first hint recorded by Joseph Farington in his diary that something was afoot is a mention, "West told me He had just finished a small picture coloured in the manner of the Venetians." A few more brief references to this small picture in the Venetian manner follow in entries from November and December. Then in January 1797 a scandal developed, when the sources of the secret, Thomas Provis and his daughter, claimed that West was cheating them. According to Provis's statement, recorded by Farington on 11 January when West first learned about the secret he attempted to use it in his *Crucifixion* (No. 356), but had difficulties. He then applied to Provis for assistance:

> In consequence experiments recommenced & West painted his "Cupid stung by a Bee" from Anacreon, that is with the assistance of Miss Provis, who, Provis said, painted several parts of it though West put his own name only at the bottom.

On 17 January Farington heard West's side of the story. On 31 October 1796, after he completed his *Crucifixion*, it was agreed that he should make an experiment, and on the following day he began to paint under Miss Provis's direction upon a small canvas that had been prepared by Provis. He also at this time painted a double portrait of his sons (No. 543).

> After the small picture was finished West proposed to Provis to paint large pictures to prove that the process would equally answer whether in large or in small pictures. He had accordingly a large canvas prepared for the subject of "Cupid stung by a Bee" from Anacreon,—another for the subject of "Cicero discovering the Tomb of Archimedes" [No. 22], and these with the portraits of his Sons, would be sufficient proofs.

On the following day Farington, together with Robert Smirke, called on West,

> and saw his two pictures painted agreeable to Provis's process—One Cupid Stung by a Bee, the other portraits of His Sons—On comparing the effect of the Colours particularly of the Small picture, (Cupid &c) with West's other pictures we thought they had a manifest advantage.

These references seem to indicate that the small picture painted by West under Miss Provis's direction and perhaps partly with her assistance was the *Cupid Stung by a Bee* which Farington saw in January 1797, and that it was to be the basis for a large painting of the subject, about which we only know that the canvas was prepared.

Nos. 543, 356, and 22 all appeared at the Royal Academy in 1797, but no *Cupid Stung by a Bee* was with them. We can only speculate why, but it is reasonable to assume that West did not complete the large painting in time to submit it. He may not have exhibited the smaller canvas, which he had completed by 25 November 1796, because of the controversy with the Provises and Miss Provis's claim to have painted parts of it.

John Gage initially proposed an identification of No. 133 painting as the smaller *Cupid Stung by a Bee* painted by West under Miss Provis's guidance. If that identification is valid, then the large canvas may have become No. 135, which West only completed in 1813 and exhibited in 1814, but in which the similar pose of Venus does suggest that it had its beginnings in an attempt to expand the composition of No. 133 (and of No. 132) onto a larger canvas. It is alternatively possible that West never completed the larger picture because of dissatisfaction with the technique he was testing. "The Cupid stung by a Bee, composition unfinished" sold by his sons in 1829 would probably then have been that work, but in that case the composition of No. 135 may still reflect what he had set out to do on the larger picture in 1796.

The chief reason for equating No. 133 with the small painting completed in November 1796 is that there is no other likely candidate. No. 134, which is a more overtly Venetian painting, is eliminated because it is on panel, while, according to what West told Farington, he conducted his experiments on a canvas prepared by Provis. For the sake of an experiment in technique, West probably would have chosen to repeat a pre-existing composition rather than complicate his labors by inventing a new one, and the nature of the composition established in No. 132 allowed the main emphasis of the experiment to be on the flesh tones, which seem to have been West's abiding interest in his concern with the techniques of earlier masters.[3]

The reason for suggesting that West exhibited No. 133 in 1802 is also the lack of alternative candidates. By 1802 he may have felt that the Provis controversies were sufficiently in the past to be forgotten, and it is likely that he reworked the painting again before exhibiting it. The handling in No. 133 is consistent with that in other works by West from around 1800, but the picture is not very similar to No. 543, which now hangs in the same museum, and which can be identified with certainty as one of the works painted by West in 1796. While No. 543 displays the purplish, moonlit quality that contemporary critics saw as the chief results of the technique (at least, as utilized by West), No. 133 does not.

Since No. 133 did not appear in any of the posthumous exhibitions or sales of West's works, he evidently sold it during his lifetime.

[1] Oil on canvas: 26 × 26 in. This copy does not include the lower 4 in. of No. 133 and the lower of Cupid's two quivers. Helmut von Erffa accepted this picture as a work by West repainted in some details (letter of 18 January 1974).

[2] See Rita Susswein Gottesman, *The Arts and Crafts in New York: 1800–1804*, New York, 1965, p. 27. Edward Savage (1761–1817), had been in London for several years in the 1790s.

[3] See for example his remarks to Farington about Correggio made in 1808, quoted in entry No. 128.

134 Cupid Stung by a Bee 1802

See color illustration, p. 132

PRIVATE COLLECTION

Oil on panel: $12\frac{3}{4} \times 21$ in. (32.5×53.5 cm.)

Signed lower left: *B. West 1802*

PROV: John Joshua Proby (1751–1828), first Earl of Carysfort: his sale, Christie's, London, 14 June 1828, lot 22 ("Venus reposing with Cupid and the Graces"); Edward W. Lake, by 1833; his sale, Christie's, London, 11 July 1845, lot 17 ("The Couch of Venus;

Cupid stung by a bee," 12 × 20 in., from the collection of Lord Carysfort), bt. by Eden for £15.4.6.; Mortimer Brandt, New York, from whom acquired by Mrs. E. Lovette West, Bronxville, New York; by descent to the present owner

EXH: (?) RA 1802 (140) "Cupid stung by a bee, complains to his mother":

> Once, as Cupid, tir'd with play,
> On a bed of roses lay,
> A rude bee, that slept unseen
> The sweet-breathing buds between,
> Stung his finger–cruel chance!
> With its little pointed lance.
> *Vide Fawkes's translation of Anacreon, ver. 40.*

BI 1833 (34) "The Couch of Venus, Cupid stung by a Bee," lent by Edward W. Lake

(?) LISTED: *PC*, p. 567 ("The small sketch of Cupid shewing Venus his Finger stung by a Bee," West, Gallery); *UM*, p. 531; Barlow, p. 435; *BA*, p. 19; Galt, p. 232; Dillenberger, p. 181 (424)

Since this painting is signed and dated *1802*, it almost certainly is one of the two pictures of *Cupid Stung by a Bee* which West exhibited at the Royal Academy in that year. The two were accompanied in the catalogue with quotations of separate lines from Francis Fawkes's translation of the same ode, but neither the passages quoted nor the actions shown in Nos. 134 and 133, which was probably its companion in 1802, allow us to determine with any certainty which quotation belongs to which work.

The three dancing figures in the right background evidently represent the Hesperides, the daughters of Hesperus; the golden apples which they guard hang on a tree on the extreme right edge of the painting. The Hesperides do not appear in any of West's other paintings of this subject and are not mentioned in the ode quoted by him in 1802.

135 Cupid Stung by a Bee (?) 1796–1813

NORWICH CASTLE MUSEUM, NORWICH

Oil on canvas: $40\frac{1}{8} \times 51$ in. (102×129.5 cm.)

Signed lower right, on the quiver: *B. West 1813*

PROV: Offered by West's sons to the United States in 1826 (26) and sold by them, Robins, London, 22–25 May 1829, lot 9 ("Cupid Complaining to Venus of Being Stung by a Bee," 3 ft. 4 in. × 4 ft. 3 in.), bt. by W. Ward for £57.15.0.; bequeathed by Mrs. S. A. Bridgeman to the Norwich Castle Museum in 1916

EXH: RA 1814 (16) "Cupid stung by a bee, complains to his mother.—Anacreon"; West's Gallery 1822–28 (39); Liverpool 1976 (75)

LIT: V and A Cuttings, III, p. 886 (4 May 1814); Hazlitt 1930–34, XVIII, p. 18 (1814)

Although signed and dated *1813*, and exhibited in 1814, No. 135 must have been commenced at an earlier date. Between January 1812 and March 1814 West was hard at work on the huge painting of *Christ Rejected* (No. 353), and he hardly would have taken the time away to paint from scratch a new and good-sized picture of an entirely unrelated mythological subject, nor, at the age of seventy-five, would he have had the energy to do so. West's other work exhibited at the Royal Academy in 1814, although signed and dated *1814*, must also have been begun well before, since it was a portrait of the third Duke of Portland, who had died in 1809 (No. 684). In 1813 and 1814 at both the Royal Academy and the British Institution West otherwise only exhibited works that he had painted earlier (Nos. 274, 253, and 238).

As proposed in entry No. 133, this work may be the large painting of *Cupid Stung by a Bee* which West began, or for which he had a canvas prepared, in the winter of 1796–97. The figure of Venus in No. 135 repeats with slight modification the Venus in No. 133, and the composition of this version can be seen as an extension onto

135

a larger format of that of No. 133. The position of Cupid, the additional figures, and the landscape background also echo to some extent No. 134, dated *1802*, and it is possible that, though West may have begun No. 135 in 1796–97, he did little work on it until after 1802. He may have painted No. 134 as a sketch (it is evidently the work listed as a sketch in *Public Characters* and other early lists) in anticipation of his work on the larger canvas. The handling in parts of the painting, notably the Cupid, who differs considerably from the Cupid in No. 133, suggests that West probably did not complete it until 1813, the date on the canvas.

When exhibited in 1814, No. 135 elicited William Hazlitt's oft-quoted comment about West: "He is only great by the acre."

136 Cupid Stung by a Bee

LOCATION UNKNOWN

PROV: Sold by West's sons, Robins, London, 20–22 June 1829, lot 147 ("Cupid stung by a Bee, composition unfinished")

See No. 133.

137 Diana and Endymion *c.* 1766

PRIVATE COLLECTION

33 × 26¼ in. (84 × 66.5 cm.)

PROV: Probably commissioned or purchased by the second Marquess of Rockingham (1730–1782), Wentworth Woodhouse, Yorkshire; his nephew and heir, the fourth Earl Fitzwilliam (1748–1833); by descent to the eighth Earl Fitzwilliam (1910–1948); his sale, Christie's, London, 11 June 1948, lot 67, bt. by Walsh; sold anonymously, Christie's, London, 25 July 1952, lot 52; Frost and Reed, London; Vose

137

Galleries, Boston, by whom sold to the present owner in 1953

EXH: SA 1766 (182) "Diana and Endymion," companion to no. 181 "Cymon and Iphigenia" (No. 196)

LISTED: *PC*, p. 565 ("Cymon and Iphigenia, and Endymion and Diana," at Wentworth Castle, Yorkshire [listed with pictures in West's Painting-room]); *UM*, p. 530; Barlow, p. 434; *BA*, p. 17; Galt, p. 226; Dillenberger, pp. 165 (260) and 168–69 (299)

LIT: V and A Cuttings, I, pp. 68–69 (*Public Advertiser*, April 1766); Gatty 1938–39, p. 81 (Horace Walpole, 1766)

See *Cymon and Iphigenia* (No. 196), which appeared together with No. 137 at the Society of Artists in 1766 and shared the same history until 1948.

The subject of Endymion, the beautiful shepherd, with whom Diana falls in love, and whom she visits as he sleeps on Mount Latmos, has its origins in numerous ancient sources. The story was frequently retold by various writers from the sixteenth to the nineteenth centuries and also depicted by numerous post-Renaissance artists, particularly in the eighteenth century, so it seems unlikely that in painting No. 137 West necessarily depended on any specific written or visual source.[1] Although he had probably seen the well-known Hellenistic relief of the sleeping Endymion in the Capitoline Museum in Rome, there is no significant similarity between it and No. 137.[2]

A second version is No. 138 below. A small drawing of the subject at Swarthmore may embody an early idea for No. 137.[3] This drawing is round and shows the central figure in a different position, but the compositions and many details are similar.

No. 137 is the most ambitious painting of a nighttime subject by West now known (for other recorded works, see Nos. 454 and 205). It appeared in the same exhibition of the Society of Artists as Joseph Wright of Derby's *Philosopher Giving a Lecture on the Orrery* (Derby Museum and Art Gallery), and a year after Wright's first exhibited nocturnal painting, *Three Persons Viewing the Gladiator by Candle-light* (private collection).

[1] See Edward Semple LeComte, *Endymion in England: The Literary History of a Greek Myth*, New York, 1944.
[2] This relief was of seminal importance for other visitors to Rome, such as James Barry (see Pressly 1981, pp. 50–52).
[3] Brown ink, round, 5¼ in. in diameter.

138 Diana and Endymion

LOCATION UNKNOWN

PROV: Sold by West's sons, Robins, London, 20–22 June 1829, lot 80 ("Diana and Endymion, an early picture")

LISTED: *BA*, p. 17 ("Cymon and Iphigenia, and Endymion and Diana;" at Wentworth Castle, Yorkshire—duplicate with Mr. West); Dillenberger, pp. 168–69 (299)

139 Europa Crowning the Bull with Flowers

SABIN GALLERIES, LONDON

Oil on canvas: 25 × 30 in. (63.5 × 76 cm.)

PROV: (?) Sold by Mrs. Albert F. West, Christie's, London, 18–19 March 1898, lot 141 ("Europa and the Bull," on panel, 24½ × 30 in.), bt. by Misell for £1.1.0.

EXH: Polygraphic Society, London, *c.* 1788 (18) *Rape of Europa*, 30 × 35 in. (including frame); (?) RA 1816 (64) "Europa"

139

LISTED: *PC*, p. 567 ("Europa crowning the Bull with Flowers," West, Gallery); *UM*, p. 531; Barlow, p. 435; *BA*, p. 18; Galt, p. 231; Dillenberger, p. 180 (416)

LIT: (?) V and A Cuttings, IV, pp. 1005 and 1059 (1816); Whitley 1928, II, pp. 25–26

The subject of No. 139 is the opening incident in the story of the rape of Europa. As told by Ovid (*Metamorphoses*, II, lines 831–75), Jupiter in the form of a white bull joins a herd of cattle and with them approaches the shore where Europa, daughter of Agenor, King of Phoenicia, is playing with the young girls of Tyre. She admires the bull, loses her fear, offers him flowers and, when he lies down, climbs upon his back; whereupon he carries her off to sea and eventually to Crete.

The painting appears to be a work that is at least partly by West and, therefore, we have equated it with the *Europa Crowning the Bull with Flowers* included in all the early published lists of his works. It appears also to have been substantially painted or repainted by another hand, possibly by one of West's students or studio assistants during his lifetime, and probably at a more recent date as well. If, as the correspondence in measurements suggests, it was the "Europa and the Bull" sold by descendants of the artist in 1898, the low price it fetched then (one guinea) may have been a reflection not only of its quality, but also of its bad condition. Since the picture sold in 1898 was described as on panel, while No. 139 is on canvas, it may have been transferred from one support to the other, as well as undergoing other restoration, between that date and its reappearance on the market in 1979.

The *Europa* that West exhibited at the Royal Academy in 1816 was described in one contemporary review as a small picture, which appeared "to have been removed from the easel a considerable time, though recently retouched and varnished." Although the title

used by West in 1816 does not tell us very much, No. 139 probably was the exhibited picture. It is the smallest of West's known treatments of the story of Europa (cf. Nos. 140–42). It must have been in existence in some form long before 1816 to have been included in the list West gave Joel Barlow in 1802. And it is a work whose present appearance suggests that it may well have undergone some repainting by the time it was exhibited. The *Europa* was the only work West sent to the Royal Academy in 1816, and a second reviewer speculated rather bluntly upon why it was there:

We have seen so many masterly specimens from the pencil of this venerable artist, that we can only account for a picture of this description appearing in the Exhibition by supposing that it was placed here rather for the purpose of Mr. West's name appearing in the catalogue, than with the idea of making any addition to his well-merited fame.

On 26 March 1816, West had written to the portrait painter James Green that, indisposition and gout having so restricted his activities during the past month, he feared he would not be able to send anything to that year's exhibition.[1]

In its present condition No. 139 does not provide much evidence to indicate when West initially undertook the composition. It is possible that he may have begun it as early as the 1770s. Since No. 139 remained in West's possession it probably was the work that the painter and entrepreneur Joseph Booth borrowed from West and used as the basis of his first "Polygraphic" copy, published in 1784. The polygraphic process, which was invented by Booth, was a method of mechanically reproducing pictures in oil paint. In a pamphlet about his invention, Booth acknowledged the assistance of Sir Joshua Reynolds, then continued, "Mr. West, too, with a mind much superior to professional prejudices, indulged the artist with the use of

one of his pictures, from which he has taken the first piece he dares to submit to the approval of the public."[2] According to W. T. Whitley, the picture in question was of *Jupiter and Europa*, and the reproductions were offered at three guineas each, frame included. In subsequent exhibitions of the Polygraphic Society, it was entitled *Rape of Europa* and the price went up to four guineas. The measurements of 30 × 35 in. including frame, listed in the Society's catalogue, fit the dimensions of No. 139 perfectly and are too small to allow any of West's other known or recorded paintings of Europa (Nos. 140–42) to be identified as the exhibited work. Two additional paintings by West were also reproduced polygraphically and included in exhibitions of the Society (see Nos. 248 and 321). No polygraphic copies after West are known as such to the authors of this catalogue but, until we know more, we should not preclude the possibility that the painting reproduced and discussed here as No. 139 is itself a copy made by this process rather than the original painting by West.

[1] Collection of Colin Sanderson and kindly brought to our attention by Elizabeth Childs. James Green exhibited a portrait of West at the Royal Academy in 1817.

[2] This passage is quoted from W. T. Whitley's account of Booth's first pamphlet published in 1784, which we have been unable to locate. Later catalogues of the Polygraphic Society are in the Library of the Victoria and Albert Museum and the Frick Art Reference Library. These are undated but probably were published *c.* 1786–88.

140 Europa on the Back of the Bull (?)*c.* 1765

LOCATION UNKNOWN

(?) (43 × 34 in.) (109 × 86.5 cm.)

PROV: (?) Sold anonymously (the property of an Engt. [?] Nobleman), Skinner, London, 1794 ("Europa", 43 × 34 in.); in Calcutta by 1804

EXH: (?) SA 1765 (151) "Jupiter and Europa"

LISTED: *PC*, p. 563 ("Europa on the Back of the Bull," at Calcutta); *UM*, p. 529; Barlow, p. 433; *BA*, p. 16 ("Europa on the back of the Bull," at Calcutta—8 feet by 11); Galt, p. 224; Dillenberger, p. 162 (232)

LIT: V and A Cuttings, I, p. 64 (*Public Advertiser*, 1767); Whitley 1928, I, p. 373 (Horace Walpole, 1765); Gatty 1938–39, p. 81 (Walpole, 1765)

The "Jupiter and Europa" exhibited by West at the Society of Artists in 1765 presumably is or was the "Europa on the Back of the Bull" described by *Public Characters* as in Calcutta. The alternative possibility that the exhibited work might have been No. 139 is improbable on stylistic grounds, and, if we are right in identifying that painting as the "Europa" exhibited by West in 1816, then, according to the Academy's regulations, it could or should not have been previously exhibited. On the other hand, the "Europa on the Back of Bull" could not have been the "Europa" exhibited in 1816, since by then it was already in India. Neither No. 141 nor No. 142 seems likely to have been exhibited under the title "Jupiter and Europa," since in both Venus plays a more active and more prominent role than Jupiter.[1]

The dimensions of 8 × 11 ft. (96 × 132 in.) ascribed to *Europa on the Back of the Bull* only in *La Belle Assemblée* seem improbable and may have been intended to accompany a version of *Lord Clive Receiving the Grant of the Duanney* (No. 102) listed two lines above No. 140. Whereas the two known versions of the Clive painting (Nos. 101 and 103) are larger still, West never painted any mythological subject on such a scale or, indeed, prior to his late religious pictures, any work that was not a commission. The dimensions of 43 × 34 in. (or possibly vice versa) ascribed to a "Europa" sold in 1794

141

Of the two paintings, No. 141 seems clearly to be the earlier. Although it is signed and dated *1770*, it is probably the painting of *Venus and Europa* that West exhibited two years earlier in 1768. It certainly must have been painted before 1770, since an engraving after it was published on 1 February of that year,[1] and the dryness of handling and less fluid composition suggest the earlier date as well. The *1770* on the canvas may reflect a subsequent retouching, or it may have been added erroneously from memory at some later date.

Helmut von Erffa has pointed out the similarity not only in Europa's pose but also in details of her robes and sandalled feet to the well-known *Sleeping Ariadne* (or *Cleopatra*) in the Vatican. The pose of head on hand is traditional in images of Melancholy, and West used variants of it to convey similar meanings in three pictures that he exhibited in 1768 (Nos. 141, 13, and 33).

Benjamin West, Jr. sold a drawing of the subject in 1839.[2]

[1] The Darling edition of 1770 of Sharp's print is not recorded in W. S. Baker, *William Sharp: Engraver*, Philadelphia, 1875 (see p. 82, no. 112), and the first dated print in Baker's chronological table of Sharp's works is 1775 (p. 113). Nonetheless, the publication date on the print is clearly 1770, and Sharp (born in 1749) was presumably old enough at the time to have made it.

[2] S. Leigh Sotheby, London, 1 June 1839, lot 117 ("Venus and Europa," pen and bistre, washed with the same).

142 Venus and Europa 1772

WILLIAM BENTON MUSEUM OF ART, UNIVERSITY OF CONNECTICUT, STORRS, CONNECTICUT

Oil on canvas: 65 × 85 in. (165 × 216 cm.)

Signed bottom right: *B. West/1772*

PROV: (?) Sold by Noël Desenfans (1745–1807), Skinner and Dyke, London, 24–28 Feb. 1795, lot 83 ("Venus appearing to Europa"); sold anonymously, Christie's, London, 7 May 1943, lot 144 (as "Reverie," 65 × 85 in.), bt. by Vokins; W. Duff Murdoch; Leger Galleries, London, 1952; Mrs. Robert Frank, London, 1953; Robert Osborne, New York, 1967; Tillou Gallery, Litchfield, Conn.; purchased by the William Benton Museum in 1970

ENGR: Engraving ($15\frac{5}{8} \times 20\frac{5}{8}$ in., reversed), by T. Cook and R. Pollard, pub. 30 Jan. 1797 by R. Pollard, as "Jupiter & Europa"; engraving ($3\frac{1}{16} \times 2\frac{7}{16}$ in., with the composition squeezed into a vertical format), by Lewis Schiavonetti, pub. 31 July 1810 by Suttaby & Co., over the title "Moschus":

> Once Venus to Agenor's royal maid
> A vision's airy portraiture display'd
>
> *Europa, Idyll II*

as the frontispiece to vol. II of *The Idyllia, Epigrams, and Fragments of Theocritus, Bion and Moschus*, trans. by the Revd. Richard Polwhele

LISTED: Barlow, p. 434 ("Venus and Cupid smiling at Europa when Jupiter had left her," under "In Various Collections"); Dillenberger, p. 165 (259)

LIT: Helmut von Erffa, "Benjamin West's *Venus and Europa*," *North Carolina Museum of Art Bulletin*, VIII, June 1969, pp. 25–26; Frederick Den Broeder, "Notes on Works by Benjamin West in the Collection," *Bulletin, Museum of Art, The University of Connecticut, Storrs*, I, 1972, pp. 8–10, fig. 1

For a discussion of the relationship of Nos. 141 and 142 see the previous entry. Frederick Den Broeder has proposed that No. 142 might have been a commission inspired by the smaller and earlier No. 141. The modifications in composition in No. 142 may reflect West's patron's taste, but they also are in harmony with his

seem much more appropriate for a work painted by West as early as 1765, and, since those dimensions do not fit any known "Europa" by West, we have tentatively equated No. 140 with that painting.[2] If that is correct, No. 140 went to India between 1794 and 1804.

Two publications of Horace Walpole's marginal comments about the exhibition of 1765 taken from separate sets of marked catalogues record different but equally pithy assessments of No. 140: it is "abominably bad" in one, "abominably gaudy" in the other. In the *Public Advertiser* a discussion of all West's works exhibited in 1765 (Nos. 128, 140 and two portraits, Nos. 735 and 736) praised the artist for "great dexterity both in the Idea and Execution," but worried that his figures were too much the same and too delicate. The review concluded: "It is dangerous to attempt to exhibit forms more beautiful than those of nature."

[1] It should be acknowledged, however, that No. 142 was engraved in 1797 under the title "Jupiter & Europa."

[2] Redford 1888, II, p. 128. We have not been able to consult a catalogue of this sale.

141 Venus and Europa c. 1768–70

NORTH CAROLINA MUSEUM OF ART, RALEIGH, NORTH CAROLINA

Oil on canvas: $28\frac{1}{4} \times 36\frac{1}{4}$ in. (72 × 92 cm.)

Signed lower left: *B. West/1770*

PROV: Sold anonymously, Christie's, London, 31 July 1931 (114), bt. by Gooden & Fox; Cornelius F. Kelley, Manhasset, New York, 1933–57; Thomas J. Gannon, Inc., New York, 1958; given by Mr. and Mrs. L. Y. Balentine, Varina, North Carolina, to the North Carolina Museum of Art in 1960

EXH: (?) SA 1768 (178) "Venus and Europa, taken from Horace, Ode 27, book 3"

ENGR: Engraving ($5\frac{1}{4} \times 6\frac{1}{2}$ in., reversed), by William

Sharp, pub. by W. Darling, 1 Feb. 1770, and again by John Boydell, 24 June 1783

(?) LISTED: *PC*, p. 565 ("Venus and Europa," West, Painting-room); *UM*, p. 530; Barlow, p. 434; *BA*, p. 16; Galt, p. 226; Dillenberger, p. 168 (292)

LIT: Helmut von Erffa, "Benjamin West's *Venus and Europa*," *North Carolina Museum of Art Bulletin*, VIII, June 1969, pp. 22–26; Gerdts 1974, p. 31

Nos. 141 and 142, which show the same subject, are not based on the Ovidian story of the rape of Europa, but on Horace. Ode 27 of Book III by Horace, which is cited in the Society of Artists' exhibition catalogue of 1768 and also on the engraving by William Sharp after No. 141, is entitled "To Galatea," but the second half of the ode is devoted to Europa after she has been raped. As she grieves over her fate, Venus and Cupid come to cheer her, and Venus tells her that she is the wife of Jove and will give her name to a continent.

In both paintings, Europa sits to the left in an identical pose and almost identical dress, and in both Jupiter is relegated to a subordinate position in the right middle distance, where he is represented as a bull accompanied by an eagle. In No. 141 the landscape, which according to the myth should be Crete, is more extensive, and Venus and Cupid stand on the ground, whereas in No. 142 they ride on a cloud, Venus reclining, Cupid seated before her. Venus with one finger raised to her chin could best be described as thoughtful in both works, and in neither does she appear to smile, but the impassive expression of the Cupid in No. 141, who is shown in strict profile, has given way to a more relaxed, smiling one on the part of his successor in No. 142. This change would seem to indicate that No. 142 is the "Venus and Cupid smiling at Europa when Jupiter had left her" included under the heading "In Various Collections" in Joel Barlow's list of West's works published in *The Columbiad*, while No. 141 is the less precisely titled "Venus and Europa" described in all the early lists as belonging to West.

142

and his painting does not include the emblematic bridle, helmet, and vases, etc., called for by Shaftesbury and depicted by de Matteis.[1] The subject is one that has been frequently painted in post-Renaissance art, and No. 143 certainly depends more upon pictorial tradition than upon written sources.

The earliest published comment about the painting, presumably written by Leigh Hunt in 1817, includes the statement that West seems to have had in his eye an engraving by Sir Robert Strange after a painting by Pietro da Cortona. There is not much similarity, however, between No. 143 and treatments of the subject by Pietro da Cortona,[2] and it seems likely that what Hunt had in mind was the engraving by Strange published in 1759 after a painting by Nicolas Poussin, which our painting does definitely recall.[3] The Poussin *Choice of Hercules* (ill. p. 36) was and is at Stourhead where, according to Galt, West inspected the collections in the autumn of 1763.[4] In addition to Poussin, West also seems to have been aware of Reynolds's *Garrick between Comedy and Tragedy* (ill. p. 36), which had been exhibited at the Society of Artists in 1762, the year before West's arrival in England. Thus while the general configuration of No. 143 and the pose of Hercules appear to be based on Strange's engraving (which reverses the composition of Poussin's original), the strict profile and upraised arm of Virtue on the right are closer to the figure of Tragedy in the corresponding position in the Reynolds. It has also been suggested at various times that the seated figure of Vice owes something to the engraving by Simon Gribelin after the painting by de Matteis, which served as an illustration in collected editions of Lord Shaftesbury's writings, and that the figure of Hercules reveals debts to the antique statue of Meleager in the Vatican, to the *Farnese Hercules* (which is now in Naples, but stood in the courtyard of Palazzo Farnese in Rome when West was there), and to the figure of Apollo in Anton Raphael Mengs's ceiling fresco of *Parnassus* in the Villa Albani.

What appears to be an early drawing of the subject by West is at Swarthmore.[5] In this drawing Hercules leans on his club, which is being tugged at by a cupid, Virtue stands on the left, and there are numerous other differences from No. 143. A drawing of the subject was with the Bernard Black Gallery in 1968,[6] but since that drawing is on a note addressed to West at 14 Newman Street, where he moved only in 1774, it must be considerably later than the painting.

See also p. 36 above.

[1] Anthony Ashley Cooper, 3rd Earl of Shaftesbury, *Characteristicks of Men, Manners, Opinions, Times*, 2nd ed., 1714, p. 386. The "Notion . . ," which had been published separately in 1713, is reprinted as pp. 345–91 of this edition of Shaftesbury's works, and an engraving by Simon Gribelin after the painting by de Matteis appears on p. 345. The painting itself is now in the Ashmolean Museum (see *Burlington Magazine*, CXXIII, 1981, p. 626 and fig. 30).
[2] Erwin Panofsky, *Hercules am Scheidewege*, Leipzig and Berlin, 1930, pls. XLIX, LVIII, and LIX.
[3] Ibid., pl. LXIII, and also Saxl and Wittkower, pls. 64 and 65, where the dependence upon Poussin was first pointed out.
[4] Galt 1820, p. 5.
[5] Pen, $6\frac{1}{8} \times 5\frac{1}{4}$ in.
[6] Black crayon, $4\frac{4}{4} \times 5\frac{1}{8}$ in. (New York 1968, no.1).

own progression in the 1770s to a more fluent and, ultimately, less classical, more Baroque style.

The two engravings published after No. 142 in 1797 and 1810 both bear misleading titles. Although the composition of the painting could be interpreted as showing Venus and Cupid appearing to Europa in a vision or dream, Europa's dream in the second Idyll of Moschus (which is cited and partly quoted on the print published in 1810) is about a war between personifications of Europe and Asia, and the Idyll contains nothing about the visit of Venus and Cupid to Europa after the rape. The title on the earlier print seems to be no more than a careless error, due perhaps to the fact that West painted No. 142 a quarter of a century before the print appeared.

A copy of the painting was sold in London in 1980.[1]

[1] Christie's, London, 30 July 1980, lot 124 (as "Cupid and Psyche Approaching Venus," $27\frac{3}{4} \times 36$ in.).

143 The Choice of Hercules 1764
See color illustration, p. 37

VICTORIA AND ALBERT MUSEUM, LONDON

Oil on canvas: 40 × 48 in. (101.5 × 122 cm.)

Signed bottom center: *B. West. 1764*

PROV: Raphael West, 1824; bequest of Mrs. Harrison to the Victoria and Albert Museum in 1886

ENGR: Outline engraving ($7\frac{1}{8} \times 8\frac{1}{2}$ in.) by Henry Moses, pub. 1817 by Moses and included in some later editions of Moses 1811

LISTED: *PC*, p. 565 ("The Choice of Hercules," West, Painting-room); *UM*, p. 530; Barlow, p. 434; *BA*, p. 16; Galt, p. 226; Dillenberger, p. 167 (291)

LIT: Moses 1811 (with accompanying text signed L. H. [Leigh Hunt]; only included in later editions); Dunlap 1834, I, p. 258 (Dunlap 1918, I, p. 305); F.

Saxl and R. Wittkower, *British Art and the Mediterranean*, Oxford, 1948, pl. 64, fig. 4; Evans 1959, pp. 41–42, pl. 20; Hall 1962, p. 108, no. 276 (letter from John Young to Sir John Fleming Leicester, 25 Feb. 1824); von Erffa 1962, p. 633, fig. 8; Irwin 1966, p. 50; von Erffa 1973, pp. 9–10, fig. 4; Gerdts 1974, pp. 21–24, ill. 1–10; Kraemer 1975, p. 61; Pressly 1981, p. 18, pl. 7

This good-sized and important early painting, which figures prominently in the recent literature, has a curiously obscure early history. It appears on the early lists of West's works, but it was never publicly exhibited prior to entering the Victoria and Albert Museum in 1886, and it was only engraved in 1817, fifty-three years after it was painted, and then in outline on a small scale as a late addition to Henry Moses's book published six years before. William Dunlap copied it in the summer of 1785. William Pressly has suggested that James Barry saw No. 143 before painting his *Temptation of Adam* of 1767–70 (National Gallery of Ireland, Dublin) and, if that is so, Barry must have seen it in West's studio prior to his departure from London for Rome in October 1765. In 1824 John Young reported to Sir John Fleming Leicester that the painting belonged to Raphael West, who was willing to sell it. No. 143 was then at Raphael's house at Staines and was not included in the posthumous exhibitions of their father's works presented by Raphael and his brother in West's former home in Newman Street.

The story of the choice of Hercules between Virtue or Vice (or Hercules at the crossroads) derives from Xenophon's *Memorabilia*. In 1711 the third Earl of Shaftesbury wrote "a Notion of the Historical Draught or Tablature of the Judgment of Hercules," based on Xenophon and embodying Shaftesbury's instructions to the Neapolitan painter Paolo de Matteis, whom he had commissioned to paint a picture of the subject. West may have been aware of Shaftesbury's essay, but, contrary to several recent assertions, it seems unlikely that he was significantly inspired or influenced by it,

144 The Death of Hippolytus

LOCATION UNKNOWN

PROV: Sold by West's sons, Robins, London, 20–22 June 1829, lot 172 ("Hypollitus's Horses Frightened by the Monster of the Sea, a spirited sketch")

LISTED: (?) *PC*, p. 568 ("The Large Drawing of the Death of Hippolytus," West, Gallery); *UM*, p. 531; *BA*, p. 19; Galt, p. 232; Dillenberger, p. 182 (437)

LIT: Kraemer 1975, p. 38

The "spirited sketch" sold by West's sons in 1829 was not described in the sale catalogue as a drawing, and hence we have included it here. Nonetheless, it seems quite likely that it was the large drawing of the subject described by *Public Characters* in the early catalogues of West's works as belonging to the artist. Possibly, as in the case of several other works, West's heavy use of body-color may have led to some confusion over the medium (see No. 256).

In Ovid (*Metamorphoses*, XV, 494–545), Hippolytus, who has been banished from Athens by Theseus because of Phaedra's accusations, is killed when the horses pulling his chariot along the shores of the Corinthian gulf are frightened by a monstrous horned bull emerging from the sea. As they run away, Hippolytus is thrown from the chariot, and his body, becoming entangled in the reins, is pulled apart.

Ruth Kraemer has identified two drawings in the Pierpoint Morgan Library as showing this subject.[1] One of them is on paper watermarked *1799*; thus, if they were sketches for No. 144, as seems likely, it was probably done between 1799 and 1804. In 1802, in Paris, West admired a drawing of the subject by Carle Vernet.[2] He also saw the celebrated *Phaedra and Hippolytus* (ill. p. 127) by Pierre-Narcisse Guérin during the same trip.

[1]Both in pen and brown ink, $7\frac{3}{8} \times 9\frac{1}{8}$ in., and $6\frac{5}{8} \times 8$ in. (Kraemer 1975, nos. 61 and 62).
[2]Farington Diary, 28 Sept. 1802 (Farington 1978–, V, p. 1882).

145 The Death of Hyacinthus 1771
See illustration, p. 52

SWARTHMORE COLLEGE, SWARTHMORE, PENNSYLVANIA

Oil on canvas: $90\frac{1}{2} \times 75$ in. (230 × 190.5 cm.)

Signed lower left: *B. West PINXIT/1771*

PROV: Francis Thomas Fitzmaurice, third Earl of Kerry (1740–1818), by whom sold, Christie & Ansell, London, 25 Feb. 1778, lot 2, bt. by Hickey; T. J. Blakeslee, New York, by whom sold, American Art Galleries, New York, 21–23 April 1915, lot 163; Vose Galleries, Boston; given by Arthur J. Secor to the Toledo Museum of Art in 1922; withdrawn from the museum and given by Arthur Secor to Swarthmore College in 1936; presently on extended loan to the Philadelphia Museum of Art

EXH: RA 1772 (273) "The Death of Hyacinthus," companion to no. 272 "Juno receiving the Cestus from Venus" (No. 169); (?) exhibited in Paris in or before 1804

ENGR: Engraving ($19\frac{7}{8} \times 17\frac{5}{16}$ in., reversed), by Robert Pollard, pub. by Pollard, 1 Jan. 1793

LISTED: *PC*, p. 563 ("The Death of Hyacinthus," painted for Lord Kerry, but now in the National Gallery at Paris, . . . figures as large as life); *UM*, p. 529; Barlow, p. 433; *BA*, p. 16; Galt, p. 224; Dillenberger, p. 162 (233)

LIT: *Middlesex Journal*, 481, 28–30 April 1772; *Museum News*, Toledo Museum of Art, Oct. 1922, ill. on cover; Gerdts 1974, p. 31, ill. 2–2

The painting illustrates lines 162–219 of Book X of Ovid's *Metamorphoses*. While Apollo and the beautiful boy Hyacinthus, whom the god loves, are playing with a discus, the discus thrown by Apollo strikes Hyacinthus on the head and kills him. Apollo in his grief turns Hyacinthus into a flower the color of blood. In No. 145 the fatal discus lies on the ground, and a flower can be seen where Apollo touches the forehead of his dead companion.

The subject, and to some extent the composition of the painting, were probably inspired by an engraving by Domenico Cunego after a fresco of the same subject by Domenichino in the Palazzo Farnese. The engraving was published in 1771, the same year as the date on West's painting.

Domenichino, *Death of Hyacinthus*, engraving by Domenico Cunego

No. 145 and its companion No. 169 seem to have shared the same history until early in this century when they were sold separately by the New York dealer T. J. Blakeslee. There is, however, a gap in their provenances following 1778, and for part of the time, according to entries for the two pictures in *Public Characters* and the other early lists, they may have been in Paris. There was a national gallery (the Louvre) in Paris by 1804, but we have been unable to confirm that Nos. 145 and 169 were there, and, if so, in what fashion. One of the few other known paintings of the subject of the death of Hyacinthus was exhibited by the French artist Jean Broc (1771–1850) at the Salon of 1801.[1] The proximity of that date to the indication in *Public Characters* that No. 145 was in Paris suggests the possibility that the painting was in Paris before 1801 and that Broc had seen it before undertaking his own more mannered but not dissimilar treatment of the subject. Broc also could have seen Pollard's engraving after No. 145 published in 1793.

A drawing for the two grieving cherubs in the upper left of No. 145, which is signed and dated *1771*, belongs to a descendant of the artist.[2]

[1]See *French Painting 1774–1830: The Age of Revolution*, Réunion des Musées Nationaux, Paris, Detroit Institute of Arts, and Metropolitan Museum of Art, New York, 1974–75, pp. 339–41 (16) (entry by Robert Rosenblum), and ill. p. 180.
[2]Black and white chalks, $6\frac{3}{8} \times 6\frac{5}{8}$ in., signed lower left: *B. West 1771*.

146 Narcissus 1805

ALEXANDER GALLERY, NEW YORK

$23 \times 36\frac{1}{4}$ in. (58.5 × 92 cm.)

Signed lower right: *B. West 1805*

PROV: Commissioned by Thomas Hope (1769–1831); by descent to Lord Francis Hope (later eighth Duke of Newcastle), by whom sold, Christie's, London, 20 July 1917, lot 71 ("Narcissus and Cupids," $23 \times 36\frac{1}{4}$ in.); Scott and Fowles, New York; John Gans, Jr., 1922; Alexander Gallery, New York, 1984

EXH: Brooklyn 1922 (26) "Narcissus" lent by John Gans, Jr

LIT: David Watkin, *Thomas Hope 1769–1831 and the Neo-Classical Idea*, London, 1968, pp. 45 and 177

The story of Narcissus, who falls in love with his own reflection, is from Ovid's *Metamorphoses* (III, 338–511).

West painted the subject twice (Nos. 146 and 147). No. 146 was sold in 1917 by a descendant of the great collector Thomas Hope. Hence it can be identified as one of the three "pictures from the Greek History," which on 17 March 1805, Joseph Farington recorded that Thomas Hope ordered from West.[1] Two of the paintings commissioned by Hope are listed in *La Belle Assemblée* (*Thetis Bringing the Armor to Achilles* [No. 170] and *Iris Delivering Jove's Command to Priam* [No. 176]). The third is not, but David Watkin has identified it as depicting "Adonis contemplating Cupid, watched by Venus." Watkin also mentions a "Narcissus" by West which hung in the drawing-room of Hope's country house, The Deepdene, in Surrey. No. 146 was sold as "Narcissus and Cupids" in 1917, and it clearly does show that self-absorbed figure seated by the pool, with Echo partly concealed by a tree in the background. Yet it does not have as close a dependence upon the Ovidian story of Narcissus as that in No. 147, and the title "Adonis contemplating Cupid[s], watched by Venus" (which has no literary basis), could easily and understandably, though erroneously, be used to describe what is shown. No further record of a work with that title is known to the compilers of this catalogue, so it would seem that Thomas Hope's *Adonis* and his *Narcissus* were one and the same.

One drawing of Narcissus appears on the early lists of West's works.[2] Since it was included in the list published in *Public Characters of 1805* in the autumn of 1804, it must have been made by then, several months before Farington's reference to Thomas Hope's ordering pictures from West, but it nonetheless may have served as the basis for No. 146 or the still later No. 147.

[1]Farington 1978–, VII, p. 2532.
[2]*PC*, p. 569 ("The Drawing of Narcissus in the Fountain," West, Gallery); *UM*, p. 532; *BA*, p. 19; Galt, p. 234; Dillenberger, p. 185 (474).

147 Narcissus 1808

BOSCOBEL RESTORATION, GARRISON, NEW YORK

Oil on canvas: $23\frac{3}{4} \times 36\frac{1}{2}$ in. (60.5 × 92.5 cm.)

Signed bottom center: *B. West 1808*

PROV: Offered by West's sons to the United States in 1826 (42) and sold by them, Robins, London, 22–25 May 1829, lot 45 ("Narcissus," 2 ft. × 3), bt. by H. P. Bone for £231 on behalf of Joseph Neeld, MP, Grittleton House, Wilts.; by descent in the Neeld family until sold, Christie's, London, 13 July 1945, lot 168; Vose Galleries, Boston, 1957; Hirschl & Adler Galleries, New York, by whom sold to the present owner

EXH: RA 1809 (502) "Narcissus in love with his own image, which he sees in the fountain"; West's Gallery 1821 (70), 1822–28 (92); BI 1833 (40) lent by Joseph Neeld; *250 Years of Art in Pennsylvania*, Westmoreland County Museum of Art, Greensburg, Pennsylvania, 1959 (132); *Selections from the Collection*, Hirschl & Adler Galleries, New York, 1962 (27)

In accordance with the Ovidian story, No. 147 shows Narcissus, wearied with hunting, lying on the ground and gazing at his reflection in the pool. His hounds rest near him, and the nets into which Ovid describes him driving deer are visible under the background trees. Echo, who out of love for Narcissus has wasted away into a disembodied voice, is the floating female figure on the left, and the nymphs who will mourn his death are on the right.

West evidently painted No. 147 too late in 1808 for it to be added to the list of his works published in *La Belle Assemblée* in that year, and he first exhibited it in the following May.

146

147

rich produce of grapes; and icy winter, rough with hoary hair.——Lo, Aurora opens the purple gates of the east, and her courts strewed with roses. The stars disappear; Lucifer drives them before him in troops, and moves the last from his station in the heavens. Soon as the father saw the earth and sky covered with a rosy blush, and the blunted horns of the moon just ready to vanish, he commands the nimble hours to join the horses to the chariot. The swift goddesses instantly obey, and lead from the high stalls the glowing steeds, snorting fire, and satiated with the juice of Ambrosia.——I am called; Aurora having dispersed the darkness, shines out. Haste, snatch the reins; or, if you have a mind that can be moved by advice, take my council, not my chariot, while it is yet in your power, and you stand securely on the earth,—While, I say, you are not yet mounted upon the axle-tree so rashly wished for, suffer me to give light to the world, which you may enjoy, in full security.

Vide Ovid's Metam.

BI 1806 (North Room, 6) "Phaeton soliciting the chariot of the Sun"; BI 1816 (188) "The Hours bringing out the horses of the chariot of the sun at the Solicitations of Young Phaeton"; the European Museum, London, 1819 (495) "Phaeton obtains permission to conduct the Chariot of the Sun, the Hours bringing forth the horses"; West's Gallery 1822–28 (46); BI 1833 (6) lent by J. Smith; Egyptian Hall, Piccadilly, 1839

LISTED: *PC*, p. 565 ("Phaeton soliciting Apollo for the Chariot of the Sun," West, Painting-room); *UM*, p. 530; Barlow, p. 434 ("Phaeton reciving from Apollo the chariot of the Sun"); *BA*, p. 17; Galt, p. 227; Dillenberger, p. 171 (320)

LIT: Farington Diary, 7 Feb., 17 April, and 6 Sept. 1804 (Farington 1978–, vi, pp. 2235, 2299, and 2405); *Public Characters* 1805, p. 555; Hall 1962, p. 101

Although this major work has disappeared, we can get some idea of its appearance from a small copy in gou-

Phaeton Soliciting Apollo for the Chariot of the Sun, copy by Daniel Pasmore after No. 148). Professor H. A. D. Miles

148 Phaeton Soliciting Apollo for the Chariot of the Sun *c.* 1802–4

LOCATION UNKNOWN

(56 × 84 in.) (142 × 213.5 cm.)

PROV: Offered by West to John Julius Angerstein in 1804 and to the Pennsylvania Academy in 1809 ("Phaeton soliciting the chariot of the Sun with the Hours bringing the Horses," 7 ft. × 4 ft. 6 in., £350); the European Museum, London, 1819, where bought or bought back by West for £600; offered by West's sons to the United States in 1826 (11) and

sold by them, Robins, London, 22–25 May 1829, lot 31 ("Phaeton Soliciting Apollo for the Chariot of the Sun," 4 ft. 8 in. × 7 ft.), bt. by Lt. Geraud de St. Peray (or L. Girarde) for £446.5.0.; J. Smith, 1833; offered for sale by Benjamin West, Jr. in a notice in the catalogue of a sale of drawings by West, S. Leigh Sotheby, London, 1 June 1839

EXH: RA 1804 (192) "Phaeton solicits, and obtains leave of his father Phoebus to conduct the chariot of the sun":

Here the spring, crowned with chaplets of flowers; here the summer, naked and adorned with garlands made of ears of corn; autumn too, with the

ache made by Daniel Pasmore in 1829 (*above*).[1] A drawing in the British Museum corresponds to the Pasmore copy in composition; it thus would seem to be a preparatory study for No. 148 and in some ways may reflect it more adequately than Pasmore's rather clumsy copy.[2] In addition, a description of No. 148 was published in *Public Characters of 1805*:

In the picture of Phaeton receiving from Apollo his last commands how to govern the chariot of the Sun, the boldness of the ambitious youth is sublimely contrasted with the parental solicitude of Apollo. All the images of the poet are upon the canvas; the swift Hours harnessing the horses, and leading the fiery steeds with their silken reins; the palace, the chariot, the four seasons, the zodiac, all have their place, their characters, and attributes: in one place we behold the rosy-fingered morn unbarring the gates of light . . .; in another the hoary, shivering winter, the green spring, the plenteous summer, and the autumn . . .

According to the sale catalogue of 1829, a flood of celestial light bathed the upper part of the composition, while beneath, "the stars astronomically personified," faded into the shade.

The source of all this and of the quotation that accompanied No. 148 in the catalogue of the Royal Academy exhibition of 1804 is the second book of Ovid's *Metamorphoses*, lines 1–149.

Although first exhibited in 1804, No. 148 must have existed in some form by 1802, since it appears on the list of works West gave to Joel Barlow in that year. On 7 February 1804, Joseph Farington reported that West put the picture in a frame for the first time and saw many things that it required. On 17 April, before the opening of the Academy exhibition, Turner commented to Farington about the "extraordinary incorrectness in the detail of West's figures viz: His heads & extremities. This particularly in His picture of Phaeton."

West seems to have made great efforts to sell No. 148. According to Farington, reporting in September 1804 what he had been told by Lawrence, West wrote to the collector John Julius Angerstein proposing to sell him No. 148 and a picture of *Cicero's Villa* (probably No. 23). West offered it to the Pennsylvania Academy in 1809 along with a companion work depicting Phaeton's fall, which he evidently never painted (No. 149). He exhibited it twice at the British Institution, and its appearance at the European Museum in 1819 was probably due to West's having sent it there himself in a further attempt to sell it. West's heirs had little more success; although No. 148 appears to have been sold in 1829, both the purchaser in 1829 and the different lender to the British Institution four years later may have been agents acting for West's younger son, in whose possession No. 148 once again found itself in 1839.

[1] Watercolor and gouache, $9\frac{1}{2} \times 14\frac{1}{4}$ in., signed lower right: *D. Pasmore / 1829 / after / B. West P.R.A.*, in the collection of Professor Hamish Miles, to whom we are indebted for information about this work and for a photograph.
[2] Pen, $5\frac{7}{8} \times 10\frac{1}{2}$ in. (1920-6-15-13).

149 The Fall of Phaeton

LOCATION UNKNOWN (PROBABLY NEVER PAINTED)

(84×54 in., or vice versa) (213.5×137 cm.)

PROV: Offered by West to the Pennsylvania Academy in 1809 ("The Fall of Phaeton," 7 ft. × 4 ft. 6 in., £350)

Since no record of the *Fall of Phaeton* is known apart from its inclusion among the works West proposed to sell to the Pennsylvania Academy, it seems probable that West never painted it, like a number of works in that group. He evidently intended it as a companion to No. 148, which it immediately follows on his list. Both works there have the same dimensions and the same price. Although the sizes as given imply that they were vertical compositions, we know from other sources that No. 148 was the opposite, and No. 149 probably was, or was intended to be, as well.

150 The Death of Procris 1770

ART INSTITUTE OF CHICAGO

Oil on panel: $13\frac{3}{8} \times 16\frac{7}{8}$ in. (34×42.9 cm.)

Signed lower left: *B. West/1770*

PROV: Offered by West's sons to the United States in 1826 (77) and sold by them, Robins, London, 22–25 May 1829, lot 63 ("Cephalus Lamenting the Death of Procris," 13×16 in.), bt. by W. Ward for £35.14.0., evidently on behalf of West's sons; sold by Mrs. Albert F. West, Christie's, London, 19 March 1898, lot 133 ("Cephalus and Procris," on panel, $12\frac{1}{2} \times 16$ in.), bt. by Cohen; given to the Art Institute of Chicago in 1900 by William O. Cole

EXH: RA 1771 (214) "The Death of Procris"; West's Gallery, 1822–28 (35) "Cephalus lamenting the Death of Procris"; *Century of Progress*, Chicago, 1933 (429, as "Troilus and Cressida"); *American . . . Colonial and Provincial Painting*, University Art Gallery, University of Minnesota, Minneapolis, 1939 (42, as "Troilus and Cressida") *American Paintings from Colonial Times until Today*, Saginaw Museum, Saginaw, Michigan, 1948 (67 as "Troilus and Cressida")

ENGR: Engraving ($13\frac{1}{16} \times 16\frac{3}{16}$ in., reversed), by Matthew Liart, 13 Dec. 1771, as "Cephalus Lamenting the Death of Procris," inscribed: *From an original Picture the same size in the Possession of B. West Esqr*

LISTED: *PC*, p. 567 ("Death of Cephalus," West, Gallery); *UM*, p. 531; Barlow, p. 435; *BA*, p. 18; Galt, p. 231; Dillenberger, p. 179 (406)

LIT: Kraemer 1975, pp. 65–66 and 83

The subject of No. 150 comes from Book VII, lines 785–862 of Ovid's *Metamorphoses*. Cephalus, while hunting, accidentally kills his wife Procris, who while spying on him had made a noise that he mistakenly believed to have been made by a wild animal. The gold-tipped javelin lying prominently in the foreground, with which Cephalus has killed Procris, had earlier been given to him by Procris, and the story of his wife's death, which Cephalus tells, is part of a longer narrative devoted to this weapon.

150

The engraving by Matthew Liart was published with a companion print after *Venus Lamenting the Death of Adonis* (No. 116). The paintings themselves are of radically different sizes, but it may be that West intended No. 150 as a sketch for a larger work that would have been the same size as No. 116.

A tracing of part of the composition of No. 150, which Ruth Kraemer suggests may have been made by Liart, is in the Pierpont Morgan Library.[1]

[1] Tracing, $14\frac{1}{8} \times 10\frac{3}{4}$ in. (Kraemer 1975, p. 83, no. 205).

151 Cupid and Psyche

LOCATION UNKNOWN

(14×12 in.) (35.5×30.5 cm.)

PROV: Offered by West's sons to the United States in 1826 (93) and sold by them, Robins, London, 22–25 May 1829, lot 112 ("Cupid and Psyche," 14×12 in.); (?) W. Acraman, Clifton (near Bristol) 1831

EXH: West's Gallery 1822–28 (73 or 132)

LISTED: See No. 153

LIT: (?) Passavant 1836, I, pp. 320–21

This small painting was described in 1829 as, "an early effort of the artist's pencil, the thought obviously supplied by the celebrated antique group, sculptured in marble." West had probably seen two versions of the well-known antique sculpture, in Rome and in Florence, while he was in Italy.[1]

In 1831 Johann David Passavant saw in the collections of W. Acraman a painting by West which he described as: "Cupid and Psyche; one of his best pictures, painted shortly after his return from Italy. Half-length figures, in an oval form." This may refer to No. 151, but W. Acraman of Clifton must surely be the same as "Mr. Acermans, Bristol," who appears in the list of West's works in *La Belle Assemblée* as the owner of *Venus and Cupid* (No. 128), and it seems likely that Passavant saw that work, which is early and oval and shows half-length figures, rather than No. 151.

[1] For the sculpture, see Haskell and Penny 1981, pp. 189–91 (26).

152 Cupid and Psyche 1808

CORCORAN GALLERY OF ART, WASHINGTON, D.C.

Oil on canvas: 53 × 56 in. (134.5 × 142 cm.)

Signed lower right: *B. West 1808*

PROV: Offered by West's sons to the United States in 1826 (25) and sold by them, Robins, London, 22–25 May 1829, lot 75 ("Cupid and Psyche," 4 ft. 8 in. × 4 ft. 8 in.), bt. by Hick for £89.5.0.; John Hick, Mytton Hall, Whalley, Lancashire; his sale, Christie's, London, 18 June 1909, lot 80, bt. by Permain; T. J. Blakeslee, New York, by whom sold to the Corcoran Gallery in 1910

EXH: West's Gallery 1822–28 (73 or 132); Manchester 1857 (114) lent by John Hick; *National Exhibition of Works of Art*, Leeds, 1868 (1268) lent by Hick; *Early American Paintings*, National Gallery, Washington, 1925–26 (87); *The Greek Tradition in Painting and Sculpture*, Walters Art Gallery, Baltimore and the Baltimore Museum of Art, 1939; *The Nude in American Painting*, Brooklyn Museum, 1961 (4)

LIT: Evans 1959, pp. 91–92 and pl. 69; Gerdts 1974, p. 32, ill. 2–4.

The story of Cupid and Psyche has been a common theme in western art since the Renaissance. The literary source is *The Golden Ass* written by Lucius Apuleius in the second century A.D. West based his *Eagle Bringing the Cup of Water to Psyche* (No. 153) exhibited in 1805 on a specific passage from a new adaptation by Hudson Gurney of the Cupid and Psyche portion of *The Golden Ass* published in 1799, but No. 152 does not display such a close relation to the text. The only lines in Gurney's *Cupid and Psyche* that it could be said to illustrate describe the embracing pair:

> With honied words, around his form
> With fond devotion now she twines,
> With rapt'rous kisses pressed and warm
> Each soothing, witching art combines.
>
> Forgetting his celestial race
> Unconscious of his own misdeeds
> He yields to her resistless grace—
> Who can resist when woman pleads?

Like this passage, No. 152 presents a generalized picture of an amorous couple with little specific narrative detail. The same can also be said of other well-known treatments of the subject of which West was probably aware, such as the painting by François Gérard of 1798 and the sculpture by Antonio Canova completed in 1793 (both now in the Louvre).

The emphatic profiles in No. 152 suggest a lingering awareness of the French Neo-Classical paintings that West had seen in Paris in 1802, but there is not much further affinity between this painting and the painting by Gérard. On the other hand, the *Cupid and Psyche* by Canova, which West had seen in the collection of Murat in 1802 and which four years later he recalled seeing,[1] was probably a source of inspiration for No. 152, particularly for the positions of the two heads and for Psyche's arms upraised around Cupid's neck. The pose of the figure of Psyche comes even more directly from an engraving after a painting showing an embracing faun and bacchante published in the English edition of the *Antiquities of Herculaneum* in 1773, of which West was one of the original subscribers.[2] It

152

is perhaps worth noting that the same ancient painting was identified by C. F. Fernow in 1806 as the inspiration for Canova's composition. If West was aware of this, which is not unlikely, it might well have provoked him to paint No. 152 to demonstrate that he could make better use of the motif than Canova. His recollection in 1806 of seeing the celebrated works of Canova in 1802 occurred while he was sitting at the dinner table next to Henry Hope (see No. 640), who at one time had owned Canova's *Cupid and Psyche*.

The detail in the upper right corner of two doves being attacked by a darker bird does not correspond directly to anything in the text, but corresponds symbolically to the treatment of Cupid and Psyche in the story. The motif echoes analogous scenes of aerial conflict in versions of *Death on the Pale Horse* (Nos. 401, 402, and the engraving after No. 403, published in the same year West painted No. 152).

West painted No. 152 too late for it to appear in the early lists of his works, and he did not exhibit it during his lifetime, probably because of the erotic content.

There are conspicuous *pentimenti*, showing trees, behind Cupid's back in the sky, left of center.

A drawing catalogued as "Cupid and Psyche," which has no relation to No. 152 and no relation to the sculpture which No. 151 was said to resemble, was sold by a descendant of the artist in 1979.[3]

[1] See Farington Diary, 3 Oct. 1802 and 25 June 1806 (Farington 1978—, v, p. 1899 and vii p. 2796. For the early history of Canova's *Cupid and Psyche*, see Mario Praz and Giuseppe Pavanello, *L'Opera Completa del Canova*, Milan, 1976, p. 68 (65).

[2] *The Antiquities of Herculaneum: Translated from the Italian by Thomas Martyn and John Lettice*, London, 1773, pl. xv (West is listed as a subscriber on p. xi; his copy was sold by his heirs, Christie's, London, 1 July 1820 and following days, 5th day, lot 42). This is an abbreviated English edition of the first volumes of *L'Antichita de Ercolano esposti*, 8 vols., 1757–92. West's borrowing was first noted by William Gerdts.

[3] Pencil, $6\frac{1}{4} \times 7\frac{3}{4}$ in., sold Sotheby's, London, 22 March 1979, lot 14.

153 The Eagle Bringing the Cup of Water to Psyche *c*. 1802–5

PRINCETON UNIVERSITY ART MUSEUM, PRINCETON, NEW JERSEY

Oil on panel: $11\frac{3}{4} \times 16\frac{3}{4}$ in. (29.8 × 42.6 cm.)

PROV: Offered by West's sons to the United States in 1826 (117) and sold by them, Robins, London, 22–25 May 1829, lot 79 ("Psyche Obtaining the Guarded Water," 12 × 16½ in.), bt. by Cooke (Richard Cook, RA, 1784–1857) for £32.11.0.; Vose Galleries, Boston; John F. Braun, Merion, Pennsylvania, by 1921; John Levy Galleries, New York, from whom acquired by the Princeton University Art Museum in 1952

EXH: RA 1805 (153) "The Eagle bringing the cup of water to Psyche"; BI 1806 (24, North Room) "Psyche"; West's Gallery 1821 (1), 1822–28 (116)

153

"Psyche obtaining the Guarded Water"; Philadelphia 1921 (22) lent by John F. Braun, Brooklyn 1922 (17); Philadelphia 1938 (57)

LISTED: *PC*, pp. 565 ("The small picture of the Eagle giving the Vase of Water to Psyche," West, Painting-room) and 567 ("The small picture of the Eagle bringing the Cup to Psyche," West, Gallery); *UM*, pp. 530 and 531; Barlow, p. 434; *BA*, pp. 17 and 18; Galt, pp. 228 and 230; Dillenberger, pp. 171 (323) and 178 (395)

LIT: Robert Rosenblum, "Benjamin West's 'Eagle Bringing the Cup of Water to Psyche': a Document of Romantic Classicism," *Record of the Art Museum: Princeton University*, XIX, 1960, pp. 66–75

The painting shows the eagle of Jupiter coming to the aid of Psyche, who has been ordered by Venus to fetch a goblet of water from the River Styx. Robert Rosenblum has pointed out that this infrequently painted scene was probably inspired by Hudson Gurney's verse adaptation of the story of Cupid and Psyche first published in 1799. The mountainous setting, cataract on the right, and dragons on either side are all described in Gurney's verse.

West exhibited the subject at the Royal Academy in 1805, but he must have painted it earlier since the title is included in the list of his works he gave to Joel Barlow in 1802. It is possible that he painted two depictions of the subject since it appears twice (with slightly different titles) on the other early lists. However, only one version of the subject appeared in the posthumous exhibitions and sales of his works, whereas those same exhibitions and sales contained two paintings of the related subject of Cupid and Psyche. Therefore, it seems perhaps more likely that one of the entries for a small "Eagle bringing the Cup (or Vase) to Psyche" was a mistake for the small *Cupid and Psyche* (No. 151), which certainly had been painted long before 1804, and which otherwise went unrecorded in the lists.

Several drawings by West of eagles or hawks are known,[1] but none of them seems to have much connection with the eagle in this painting, which, on the other hand, does resemble his equally long-necked counterpart accompanying Mrs. Worrell in West's portrait of that lady as Hebe (No. 721).

[1] Black and white chalk on blue paper $5\frac{1}{4} \times 6\frac{1}{2}$ in. (private collection); black chalk on blue paper, $5\frac{3}{4} \times 5\frac{1}{4}$ in. (sold by Mrs. F. Howard, Sotheby's, London, 22 March 1979, lot 11); a sheet of studies of heads and claws, etc., of an eagle or falcon was also at one time in the collection of Herbert G. Margary.

154 Salmacis and Hermaphroditus

LOCATION UNKNOWN

EXH: BI 1806 (Middle Room, 47) "Salmacis and Hermaphroditus (from Ovid)"

The only record of this work is the catalogue of the first exhibition of the British Institution in 1806. West was represented there by no less than fifteen works, many of which he had exhibited previously at the Royal Academy, and it is possible that *Salmacis and Hermaphroditus* was also an earlier work, most probably *Arethusa* (No. 119), reappearing under a different title. Like the story of Arethusa, that of Hermaphroditus (from Ovid's *Metamorphoses* IV, 285–388) is about voyeurism followed by pursuit, with the pursued party in each case being observed while swimming. The most conspicuous difference is that the sexual roles are reversed; Salmacis, the aggressor, is a naiad, and her victim, Hermaphroditus, to whom she clings so tightly that their bodies become one, is the son of Mercury and Venus (or Hermes and Aphrodite, hence his name). One might expect this myth to demand an illustration rather different from No. 119, which shows or showed a beautiful bathing nymph, but since West would not have depicted the male sexual organs (he never did), the usual distinguishing feature of an hermaphrodite would not have been visible. Thus the painting, if it showed its two protagonists in their united state in the manner of the well-known antique *Hermaphrodite* in the Louvre,[1] could well have looked like and have been identical with No. 119.

[1] See Haskell and Penny 1981, pp. 234–36 (48).

155 Jupiter and Semele *c.* 1767

DESTROYED

PROV: (?) T. Bradford, 1771; (?) Gerard Vandergucht, London (died 1776); sold anonymously ("The Property of a Gentleman deceased"), Christie and Ansell, London, 14–15 March 1777, lot 93, bt. by Pierce for 63 guineas; lost at sea before 1804

EXH: SA 1767 (172) "Jupiter and Semele"

(?) ENGR: Engraving ($15\frac{5}{16} \times 20\frac{1}{2}$ in., reversed [?]), by Thomas Cook, pub. by T. Bradford, 25 Feb. 1771, after the *original Picture in the Possession of Mr. Bradford*

LISTED: *PC*, p. 564 ("The large picture lost at Sea," following the entry for "A small picture of Jupiter and Semele"—in the possession of Mr. Mitchel [see No. 156]); *UM*, p. 529; Barlow, p. 434; *BA*, p. 16; Galt, p. 225; Dillenberger, p. 164 (252)

LIT: V and A Cuttings (*Public Advertiser*, May 1767); Gatty 1938–39 (Horace Walpole, 1767); Sellers 1939; I, p. 75 (Charles Willson Peale, 1767); von Erffa 1973, pp. 12–14

The story of Jupiter and Semele is from Ovid's *Metamorphoses*, III, lines 295–315. Juno, having learned that Semele, the daughter of Cadmus, is pregnant with Jupiter's child, entices her to extract a promise from Jupiter that he will show himself to her as he appears to Juno. When Jupiter reluctantly fills his promise, accompanied by mists, clouds, and thunderbolts, Semele is instantly burned to ashes. Their child, whom Jupiter saves, becomes Bacchus.

Charles Willson Peale saw No. 155, which he called "Jupiter coming to Celemna in thunder," and *Venus Relating to Adonis the Story of Hippomenes and Atalanta* (No. 112) in West's studio in February 1767. The two appeared together at the Society of Artists' exhibition in the spring of 1767, and were compared to one another in a review in the *Public Advertiser*, which described the figure of Semele as a masterpiece. Horace Walpole dismissed both paintings as "Indifferent."

The early lists of West's works describe this painting as lost at sea, but its probable appearance is known from an engraving published in 1771 and from a small version of the subject (No. 156), which shows the same composition as the engraving but in reverse. We have assumed that the engraving was made from No. 155 rather than No. 156; nevertheless, it shows no significant differences from No. 156 and hence may well be after that painting rather than the lost larger one. The *Jupiter and Semele* that may have belonged to the dealer Gerard Vandergucht and that was included in a sale in 1777 listed under PROV. above (and for which see also No. 186) could have been either No. 155 or No. 156.

If No. 155 was truly a companion to No. 112, its

Jupiter and Semele, engraving by Thomas Cook, probably after No. 155

dimensions would have been 65 × 86 in. The compositions of both works reflect the powerful impact upon West of paintings by Titian that he had seen and, in one instance (see No. 520), copied in Italy. For the technique and color of No. 155 see the description by Charles Willson Peale quoted under No. 112.

156

156 Jupiter and Semele

MRS. DOUGLAS H. GORDON

Oil on canvas: 28 × 36 in. (71 × 91.5 cm.)

PROV: Mr. Mitchel, *c.* 1804; Mr. Gritton, 1832; Benjamin Harwood, Annapolis, Maryland, from whom acquired by the grandfather of the present owner *c.* 1850

EXH: SBA 1832 (311) lent by Mr. Gritton

LISTED: PC, p. 564 ("A small picture of Jupiter and Semele"—in the possession of Mr. Mitchel); *UM*, p. 529; *BA*, p. 16; Galt, p. 225; Dillenberger, p. 164 (252)

This painting is in extremely deteriorated condition, and much of it was clumsily repainted at some time in the past. Nonetheless, it appears to be a work by West himself and, hence, can be identified as the "small picture of Jupiter and Semele" included in the early lists of his works. As noted in the preceding entry, the recorded histories of Nos. 155 and 156 may be partly confused, and the engraving listed there as after the lost No. 155 could have been made after No. 156 intead.

157 Venus at Her Birth Attired by the Graces
(?)1799–1806

PRIVATE COLLECTION

Oil on canvas laid on panel: 19½ × 14 in. (49.5 × 35.6 cm.)

Signed lower right: *B. West (?)1799/Retouched 1806*

PROV: Offered by West's sons to the United States in 1826 (131) and sold by them, Robins, London, 22–25 May 1829, lot 78 ("Venus Attired by the Graces," 1 ft. 8 in. × 1 ft. 2½ ins.), bt. by Hayes for £29; John Allnutt (1773–1863); his sale, Christie's, London, 20 June 1863, lot 437; sold anonymously, Christie's, London, 18 Dec. 1959, lot 100; Mrs. Robert Frank, London; Mr. and Mrs. Charles Handley-Read, London

EXH: RA 1800 (130) "Venus at her birth attired by the Graces"; *Paintings, Water-colours and Drawings from the Handley-Read Collection,* Fine Art Society, London, 1974 (97)

ENGR: Outline engraving (7⅝ × 5¹¹⁄₁₆ in.) by Henry Moses, pub. 1 May 1811 as pl. II of Moses 1811, under the title "Venus Rising from the Sea"

LISTED: PC, p. 567 ("Venus attended by the Graces," West, Gallery); *UM*, p. 531; Barlow, p. 435; *BA*, p. 18; Galt, p. 230; Dillenberger, p. 176 (377)

LIT: Moses 1811 (II); Kraemer 1975, pp. 33–34, 64, 77

The date on this painting is slightly unclear. It has been recorded as *1793* but appears more probably to be *1799*.

The pose of Venus seems to be a composite based on three antique statues of Venus, all of which stood in the Tribune of the Uffizi when West was in Florence in the 1760s.[1] The position of Venus' right arm holding her hair above her head, which derives ultimately from descriptions of a painting by Apelles, also recalls James Barry's *Venus Rising from the Sea,* exhibited at the Royal Academy in 1772 (Municipal Gallery of Modern Art, Dublin).[2]

Ruth Kraemer has identified three sketches on one sheet in the Morgan Library as studies for No. 157,[3] and she has more loosely associated two further drawings in the same collection with it as well.[4]

What was evidently a second version is No. 158 below.

[1]Haskell and Penny 1981, pp. 320–33 (nos. 85, 88, and 91).
[2]Pressly 1981, pp. 32–35, and pl. 21.
[3]Black chalk, 9¹¹⁄₁₆ × 5¹³⁄₁₆ in. (Kraemer 1975, pp. 33–34, no. 53).
[4]Black chalk, 6½ × 4⁹⁄₁₆ in., and black chalk, 12¾ × 8¹⁄₁₆ in. (Kraemer 1975, p. 64, no. 124 and p. 77, no. 182).

158 Venus at Her Birth Attired by the Graces

LOCATION UNKNOWN

PROV: Sold by West's sons, Robins, London, 20–22 June 1829, lot 81 ("Venus attired by the Graces . . . a very elegant composition".)

157

HOMERIC AND RELATED SUBJECTS

159 Chryses Invoking the Vengeance of Apollo against the Greeks 1773

See color illustration, p. 56

MOUNT HOLYOKE COLLEGE ART MUSEUM, SOUTH HADLEY, MASSACHUSETTS

Oil on canvas: 50 × 40 in. (127 × 101.5 cm.)

Signed lower left: *B. West/1773*

PROV: Offered by West's sons to the United States in 1826 (33) and sold by them, Robins, London, 22–25 May 1829, lot 113 ("Chryses Invoking the Vengeance of Apollo Against the Greeks," 4 ft.2 in. × 3 ft. 4 in.), bt. by J. Taylor for £28.7.0.; Hackney Town Hall; sold Christie's, London, 6 April 1882, lot 9, bt. by Burgh; acquired by the Trafalgar Galleries, London, in 1979 and sold by them to the Mount Holyoke College Art Museum in 1982 (Warbeke Museum Fund)

EXH: RA 1773 (308) "Chryses, priest of Apollo, invoking his God to revenge the injuries done him by Agamemnon"; West's Gallery 1822–28 (78) "Chryses invoking the vengeance of Apollo against the Greeks":

> God of the silver bow, thy shafts employ,
> Avenge thy servant, and the Greeks destroy;
> Thus Chryses pray'd, the fav'ring pow'r attends,
> And from Olympus' lofty tops descends.
> *Pope's Homer's Iliad, B. i*

Trafalgar Galleries at the Royal Academy, Royal Academy, London, 1979 (25); Washington and Philadelphia 1980

ENGR: Mezzotint (17$\frac{13}{16}$ × 13$\frac{15}{16}$ in.) by J. R. Smith

LISTED: *PC*, p. 565 ("Chrysus on the Seashore," West, Painting-room); *UM*, p. 530; Barlow, p. 434; *BA*, p. 16; Galt, p. 226; Dillenberger, p. 167 (288)

LIT: Graves 1906, VIII, p. 213 (Horace Walpole, 1773)

No. 159 is based upon the opening narrative in the first book of the *Iliad*. Chryses, priest of Apollo in Chryse near Troy, is seen praying to Apollo to avenge Agamemnon's refusal to restore to Chryses his daughter Chryseis, who had been captured by the Greeks. Apollo, who is visible in his chariot in the upper right of the painting, responds to Chryses' plea by inflicting a plague upon the Greeks. This eventually leads Agamemnon to return Chryseis to her father (see No. 160), but he takes Briseis from Achilles to fill her place and thus provokes Achilles to withdraw himself and his men from the war. The relevant lines (47 ff.) describe Chryses praying to Apollo as he walks alone by the seaside after being rebuffed by Agamemnon. On the ground at his feet are the rejected gifts he had offered as his daughter's ransom.

Both in features and expression Chryses in No. 159 recalls the figure of Simeon in No. 312, which West had exhibited at the Royal Academy the previous year. The same model probably posed for both works as well as for *Chryseis Returned to Her Father* (No. 160), which West painted in 1771 and which shows the narrative sequel to No. 159, and for several other paintings from the early 1770s (Nos. 278, 292, 321).

A drawing in pencil of the subject, which is close to No. 159 in all details and is perhaps more likely to have been made as a copy after the painting than as a study for it, was formerly in the possession of Herbert Margary, a descendent of the artist.

160 Chryseis Returned to Her Father (?)1771

THE NEW-YORK HISTORICAL SOCIETY

Oil on canvas: 73$\frac{1}{4}$ × 55$\frac{1}{4}$ in. (186 × 140.5 cm.)

Signed lower left: *B. West/[?]1771*

PROV: Francis Thomas Fitzmaurice, third Earl of Kerry (1740–1818), by whom sold, Christie & Ansell, London, 25 Feb. 1778, lot 12 ("Chryseis returned to her father," 72 × 54 in., companion to lot 11 "Eneas and Creusa" [No. 179]), bt. by Hickey for 130 guineas for the pair; presented by William H. Webb to the New-York Historical Society, 3 January 1865

EXH: (?) RA 1771 (312) as "The Continence of Scipio," companion to no. 212 "Hector Taking Leave of Andromache" (for which see Nos. 164 and 179)

LIT: Tuckerman 1867, p. 101; Kraemer 1975, pp. 12–13

The painting shows Odysseus returning Chryseis to her father, Chryses, the priest of Apollo, as described in Book I of the *Iliad*. A statue of Apollo is in the upper left, and the altar at which the text describes the reunion taking place is in the left foreground. The oxen in the right foreground and in the background, which Odysseus will sacrifice to propitiate Apollo on behalf of the Greeks, and the ship in the background, which has brought Odysseus and Chryseis to Chryse, are also mentioned in the text.

A painting of this subject appears on the early lists of West's works, but that picture is more likely to be No. 161, a small sketch sold by West's sons in 1829, rather than the present painting. It may be that No. 160 was exhibited at the Royal Academy in 1771 as "The Continence of Scipio" rather than under its correct title. The painting itself clearly illustrates the passage from the *Iliad* rather than Scipio, but the subjects in both stories of a daughter being returned to her parent or parents are sufficiently similar to make past confusion over what No. 160 depicts seem distinctly possible. The date of *1771* on the picture, if correctly read, also supports the likelihood of its having been exhibited in that year, but it should be noted that the date is difficult to read, and has been recorded by other observers as *1777*. Alternative possibilities for the identification of the exhibited "Continence of Scipio" are discussed in the entry for No. 19. The exhibited picture was described in the Academy catalogue as the com-

panion of a painting of "Hector Taking Leave of Andromache," and No. 160 does have a companion picture, the same size and in the same collection (No. 179), which although it does not show that subject has always been believed to. These two paintings were sold under their proper titles in 1778 by Lord Kerry, along with three further paintings that had been exhibited at the Royal Academy in 1772 (Nos. 145, 169, and 312). Finally, it should be said that if Nos. 160 and 179 were not the companion pictures exhibited in 1771, then the subsequent histories of the exhibited pictures are completely blank, which seems as unlikely as the possibility of West having painted two such large and ambitious works as Nos. 160 and 179 but never exhibiting them. A hypothetical explanation of why both were catalogued under incorrect titles is that West may have sent them to the Academy without indicating their subjects, and that consequently the titles in the catalogue were provided by someone else on the basis of what the pictures evidently seemed to show. We might expect that such flagrant errors in the titles would have been detected and corrected, but it should be observed that No. 179, a scene from the *Aeneid*, subsequently masqueraded under the wrong title for well over a century in a public collection in New York, without the error being detected.

The model for Chryses in No. 160 was evidently the same model who was to pose for Chryses in No. 159 of 1773, and who also seems to have posed for the fathers in two paintings of biblical familial reunions which West also exhibited in 1771, *The Prodigal Son Received by His Father* (No. 321) and *Tobias Curing His Father's Blindness* (No. 291).

A closely related drawing of the subject is in the Historical Society of Pennsylvania.[1] A somewhat smaller and freer drawing in the Pierpont Morgan Library shows less similarity with No. 160;[2] it has a horizontal composition and appears more closely related to the oil sketch discussed under No. 161 than to No. 160. A third drawing, which appears to represent an intermediary stage in the development of the composition, belongs to the Art Gallery of New South Wales in Sydney.[3]

[1] Ink and wash, 8$\frac{13}{16}$ × 6$\frac{3}{4}$ in. (Kraemer 1975, pp. 12–13, fig. 8). Kraemer suggests that this is probably the drawing of the subject sold, S. Leigh Sotheby, London, June 1839, lot 14.

[2] Ink on grey paper, 4$\frac{3}{4}$ × 6$\frac{15}{16}$ in. (Kraemer 1975, pp. 12–13, no. 16 and pl. 8).

[3] Ink and wash, 16 × 13$\frac{7}{8}$ in.

161 Chryseis Returned to Her Father

LYMAN ALLYN MUSEUM, NEW LONDON, CONNECTICUT

Oil on canvas: 16 × 40 in. (40.5 × 101.5 cm.)

PROV: Offered by West's sons to the United States in

161

162

1826 (121) and sold by them, Robins, London, 22–25 May 1829, lot 178 ("Chryseis Restored to Her Father", 1 ft. 4 in. × 3 ft. 3 in.), bt. by Dunlop for £23.2.0.; gift of James Coats to the Lyman Allyn Museum in 1962

EXH: West's Gallery 1821 (88), 1822–28 (137)

LISTED: *PC*, p. 564 ("Chrysus returned to her Father Chyrus", West's House at Windsor); *UM*, p. 529; Barlow, p. 434 ("Chryseis restored to her Father"); *BA*, p. 16; Galt, p. 225; Dillenberger, p. 166 (275)

Helmut von Erffa rejected the ascription of No. 161 to West. It does, however, correspond in size to the version of the subject sold by West's sons in 1829. That work was described in the catalogue as a "masterly sketch" showing the "empassioned meeting of the father and his beloved daughter." Certain details such as the figure seen from the rear in the lower left corner and the highlights on the candelabrum in the upper right look sufficiently like West's work to justify accepting No. 161 as the picture sold in 1829, and there is also a similarity in the grouping of the three central figures with that in the drawing in the Pierpont Morgan Library cited under No. 160. On the other hand, in detail and in handling, most of the picture looks very unlike a painting by West, and it would seem that, even if No. 161 was sold as a sketch by West, it was largely painted, or repainted, by another hand.

162 Helen Brought to Paris 1776

NATIONAL MUSEUM OF AMERICAN ART, WASHINGTON, D.C.

Oil on canvas: 56½ × 75 in. (143.5 × 190.5 cm.)

Signed lower right: *B. West/1776*

PROV: A family in Kent; John Morant, Brockenhurst Park, Hampshire; Mrs. Robert Frank, London, 1958; Graham Gallery, New York, from whom purchased by the National Collection of Fine Arts (now National Museum of American Art) in 1969

EXH: New York 1962 (2)

LISTED: *PC*, p. 563 ("Helen brought to Paris, in the possession of a Family in Kent, name not ascertained"); *UM*, p. 529; Barlow, p. 433; *BA*, p. 15; Galt, p. 223; Dillenberger, p. 160 (218)

This painting illustrates lines from Book III of the *Iliad*. A reluctant Helen, averting her eyes, is urged by Aphrodite into the arms of Paris, whom the goddess has just saved from death at the hand of Menelaus, Helen's rightful husband.

No. 162 was not exhibited during West's lifetime, but it does appear on all the early lists of his works. The curious indication that the name of the owner had not been ascertained suggests that West probably sold the painting at a sufficiently early date to have lost contact with its possessor by the time the lists were made up shortly after 1800.

163 The Fright of Astyanax (Hector Taking Leave of Andromache) *c.* 1766

LOCATION UNKNOWN

(48 × 57 in., including frame) (122 × 145 cm.)

PROV: Painted for Thomas Newton (1704–1782), Bishop of Bristol; his sale, 125 Pall Mall, London, 8 April 1788, lot 132 ("Hector and Andromache," 4 ft. × 4 ft. 9 in., including frame); evidently reacquired by West before 1804; (?) offered by his sons to the United States in 1826 (69, "Hector parting from his wife and Child," 1 ft. 2 in. × 1 ft. 4¼ in.), and (?) sold by them, Robins, London, 22–25 May 1829, lot 61 ("Hector parting with his Wife and Child," 2 ft. 3 in. × 1 ft. 8 in.), bt. by Smith for £26.5.0.

EXH: SA 1767 (174) "The Fright of Astyanax," companion to no. 173 "Pyrrhus when a child, brought to Glaucias, King of Illyria, for protection" (No. 8); 125 Pall Mall 1788 (special exhibition of Bishop Newton's collection in conjunction with the sale of

his pictures); (?) West's Gallery, 1822–28 (23) "Hector parting with his Wife and Child"

ENGR: No. 163 appears in the background of the mezzotint by Richard Earlom, pub. 1 Dec. 1767, after West's portrait of Bishop Newton (No. 675)

(?) LISTED: *PC*, p. 564 ("Hector parting with his Wife and Child at the Sun Gate," West's House at Windsor); *UM*, p. 529; Barlow, p. 434; *BA*, p. 16 ("Hector parting with his Wife and Child at the Scaean Gate"; painted for Dr. Newton, late Bishop of Bristol, Mr. West's House at Windsor); Galt, p. 225; Dillenberger, p. 165 (265)

LIT: V and A Cuttings, I, p. 75 (*Public Advertiser*, May 1767) and II, p. 423 (29 March 1788); Galt 1820, p. 9; Carey 1820, p. 694; Graves 1907, p. 275 (Horace Walpole, 1767); von Erffa 1973, p. 9

No. 163 and West's other treatments of the same subject variously known as the "Fright of Astyanax," "Hector and Andromache," "Hector Parting with His Wife and Child," etc., are based on the sixth book of the *Iliad*. No. 163 has disappeared, but the composition showing Astyanax, who has been frightened by Hector's helmet, in the arms of his nurse is known from the inclusion of No. 163 in the background of West's portrait of the Bishop of Bristol (No. 675).

According to Galt, West was introduced in 1765 to Bishop Newton, who engaged the artist to paint No. 163 and subsequently No. 675. When Newton's paintings were sold in 1788, a notice described West's "Departure of Hector" as having been painted twenty-two years earlier, that is, in 1766. It is probable, therefore, that No. 163 was the *Fright of Astyanax* which West exhibited at the Society of Artists in 1767.[1] Its companion picture, *Pyrrhus when a Child, Brought to Glaucias* (No. 8), may have been painted for Robert Hay Drummond, the Archbishop of York, to whom, according to Galt, West was introduced at the same time he met Bishop Newton. Both paintings seem to have been well received when exhibited, and Horace Walpole (if accurately recorded by Graves) gave each an identical note in the margin of his catalogue: "the colouring, expression and attitude very fine."

What happened to No. 163 following Newton's sale in 1788 is unclear. The early lists of West's works all include a "Hector parting with his Wife and Child" as a painting in West's possession, and one of those lists, that in *La Belle Assemblée*, which is the most authoritative, indicates that West's "Hector" was the picture that had previously belonged to Newton. If that is correct, West presumably bought the painting back either at or following the Newton sale, and No. 163 was most likely the "Hector parting with his Wife and Child" in the posthumous exhibitions in West's gallery. However, there are significant discrepancies in measurements between those recorded for No. 163 and those of the version, or versions, of the subject offered by West's sons to the United States in 1826 and sold in the main Robins sale in May 1829. A version of the subject also appeared in the secondary Robins sale in June 1829 (No. 167), but No. 163 was presumably too significant a picture in West's career to have been relegated there. The measurements of 48 × 57 in., including frame, in the Newton sale catalogue of 1788 seem consistent with the image in the background of Newton's portrait, whereas the dimensions listed in 1826 and 1829 both seem too small. We can also tell from the engraving and the catalogue of 1788 that No. 163, like No. 8, its companion in 1767, was a horizontal composition, whereas the painting sold in May 1829 was supposedly vertical. It is possible, of course, that incorrect measurements were recorded for the same work on one or more occasions, and it is also possible that the different sets of dimensions record the different sizes of separate paintings. In that case, the version offered to the United States in 1826 may have been identical with the version of the subject sold in June 1829 (No. 167), for which no dimensions are recorded. Yet another possibility is that West altered the size of No. 163 after the Newton sale of 1788. One bit of evidence encouraging such speculation about the "Hector parting with His Wife and Child" sold in May 1829 is provided by a brief comment in the sale catalogue: "It will be observed, that this picture is incomplete. It was the intention of the painter to add to the expression of the nurse, and the suggested alteration is marked in outline." The words "add" and "alteration" suggest that the incompleteness of the work was not due to its having been left unfinished, which would preclude identifying it with a previously exhibited picture, but rather resulted from West's repainting or beginning to repaint an earlier work, a practice which he indulged in sufficiently frequently in the year preceding his death to cause distress among his family and friends.[2] If No. 163 was the retouched picture, then it is also possible that the discrepancy in the proportions of the canvas between the sales in 1788 and 1829 was caused by West's cutting down the original, presumably by eliminating the two soldiers visible on the right in No. 675, who have no immediate relevance to the Homeric narrative, and thus changing a horizontal composition into a vertical one. It is noteworthy that the nurse's expression, the feature marked for change in 1829, was the one aspect of Bishop Newton's picture mentioned in 1767 in a review in the *Public Advertiser*, which noted a strong resemblance to David Garrick, and either West or his patron may have been unhappy about her expression by the time West painted No. 675, as the upper part of her body seems to have been deliberately hidden in that work.

The two soldiers on the right side of the composition are echoed by two analogous figures in Gavin Hamilton's picture of the same subject painted around 1775 (collection of the Duke of Hamilton).[3]

In addition to the work or works so far discussed, other versions, proposed versions, or pictures exhibited as versions of the subject are Nos. 164, 165, and 166 below. Two sketches of the subject, both with vertical compositions, are known: one, in watercolor, showing the nurse standing on the left was formerly in the collection of Mrs. F. Howard;[4] the other, a slighter drawing in chalks, showing the nurse kneeling, as in No. 163 (and the later No. 165), but on the right, is in the Historical Society of Pennsylvania.

A painting of the *Fright of Astyanax* sold in 1974 as a work by West is not by him and has subsequently been ascribed to the French artist Charles de la Fosse.[5]

[1] William Carey, writing in 1820, included the "Hector taking leave of Andromache, painted on a commission for Dr. Newton, Bishop of Bristol," in a list of works exhibited by West at the Royal Academy in 1770. West exhibited a picture under that title at the Academy in 1771 (see Nos. 164 and 179), along with the other works on Carey's list, but not in 1770, and it seems improbable, for reasons discussed under No. 179, that the "Hector" exhibited in 1771 was Newton's picture.
[2] Farington Diary, 3 Sept. 1819 (Farington 1978–, xv, p. 5403).
[3] Irwin 1966, pl. 12.
[4] Watercolor, $9\frac{1}{2} \times 7\frac{1}{2}$ in.; sold, Sotheby's, London, 22 March 1979, lot 12.
[5] Sotheby's, London, 17 July 1974, lot 93.

164 The Fright of Astyanax (Hector Taking Leave of Andromache) *c.* 1771

EXH: RA 1771 (212) "Hector taking Leave of Andromache," with no. 213 "The Continence of Scipio" listed as its companion (see Nos. 19 and 160)

A painting in the New-York Historical Society showing a subject from the *Aeneid* (No. 179) has always been

The Fright of Astyanax, detail showing No. 163, from the background of the mezzotint by Richard Earlom after No. 675

identified as a picture of "Hector Taking Leave of Andromache" and has generally been assumed to be the picture exhibited by West at the Royal Academy in 1771. No. 179 does not show that subject, although it may still have been exhibited at the Academy under the wrong title. For a fuller discussion see the entries for Nos. 160 and 179.

165 The Fright of Astyanax (Hector Taking Leave of Andromache) 1797
See color illustration, p. 133

J. PAUL GETTY MUSEUM, MALIBU, CALIFORNIA

Pencil, pen and ink, watercolor and body-color on brown paper: $12\frac{1}{2} \times 18$ in. (31.5×45.5 cm.)

Signed upper left: *From Benj[n] West Esq./to/Gen[l] Kosciuszko/London June 10th/1797*

PROV: Given by West to Tadeusz Kosciuszko, in June 1797; given by Kosciuszko to Thomas Jefferson prior to May 1798; at Monticello until Jefferson's death in 1826; sold anonymously, Christie's, New York, 7 Jan. 1981, lot 55; Paul Magriel, New York; Hirsch & Adler Galleries, New York, from whom acquired by the present owner in 1984

LIT: Marie G. Kimball, *The Furnishings of Monticello*, Charlottesville, Va., 1927, pp. 10 and 12; Marie Kimball, "Jefferson's Works of Art at Monticello," *Antiques*, LIX, 1951, pp. 297 and 308; Seymour Howard, "Thomas Jefferson's Art Gallery for Monticello," *Art Bulletin*, LIX, 1977, p. 599; Alberts 1978, pp. 221–22

West presented this drawing to General Tadeusz Kosciuszko on 10 June 1797, shortly after his visit to the General described by Joseph Farington in his diary on 8 June and discussed in the entry for No. 650, West's portrait of Kosciuszko begun at the same time. Kosciuszko was in London in 1797 en route to America. He took No. 165 with him, and before he left America

on 4 May 1798, he in turn gave the drawing to Thomas Jefferson, whom he had met and become friendly with while both were living in Philadelphia (Jefferson as vice-president of the United States) in the autumn and winter of 1797–98. The drawing is mentioned in descriptions of Monticello (cited by Marie Kimball) and is included in a manuscript "catalogue of Paintings etc. at Monticello," presumably made by Jefferson himself some time after 1808 (University of Virginia, Charlottesville, transcribed by Kimball and Howard): "57. Hector and Andromache in water colours. an original by West. The scene is their meeting in Homer 6.494 etc. given by West to Gen[l]. Kosciuzko, and by him to Th.J."

Lines 494 ff. of Book VI of the *Iliad* cited by Jefferson come at the commencement of the scene between Hector and Andromache at the Scaean Gate (in Pope's translation). However, it seems likely that Jefferson's "494" was a mistake for "594," the first line of the frequently quoted passage in which Astyanax is frightened by Hector's helmet.

Although the date in the inscription on No. 165 clearly indicates when West presented the drawing to Kosciuszko, rather than when it was done, the style of the drawing is consistent with a date of 1797, and it is likely that West made the drawing specifically as an appropriate gift for Kosciuszko.

166 The Fright of Astyanax (Hector Taking Leave of Andromache)

LOCATION UNKNOWN

(96×72 in.) (244×183 cm.)

PROV: Offered by West to the Pennsylvania Academy of the Fine Arts in 1809 ("Hector taking Leave of his Wife and Child," 8 ft. × 6, life [–sized figures], £300)

Like several of the paintings offered by West to the

Pennsylvania Academy in 1809–10, No. 166 may have been a work that the artist proposed to paint, not one he had actually painted. No painting of these dimensions is otherwise known or recorded.

167 The Fright of Astyanax (Hector Taking Leave of Andromache)

LOCATION UNKNOWN

PROV: Sold by West's sons, Robins, London, 20–22 June 1829, lot 58 ("The Parting of Hector and Andromache and Christ Blessing Little Children")

See No. 163.

168 Diomedes and his Horses Stopped by the Lightning of Jupiter 1793

LOCATION UNKNOWN

$(20\frac{1}{2} \times 27\frac{1}{2}$ in.) $(52 \times 70$ cm.)

Signed bottom left: *B. West 1793*

PROV: Offered by West's sons to the United States in 1829 (50) and sold by them, Robins, London, 22–25 May 1829, lot 19 ("The Combat Between Hector and Diomede Prevented by the Lightning of Jupiter," 1 ft. $8\frac{1}{2}$ in. × 2 ft. $3\frac{1}{2}$ in.), bt. by W. Ward for £73.10.0., evidently on behalf of Benjamin West, Jr.; Benjamin West, Jr., 1833; J. Leger and Son, London and New York, 1930

EXH: RA 1794 (80) "Diomed and his horses stopped by the lightning of Jupiter;" West's Gallery 1822–28 (9) "The Combat between Hector and Diomede prevented by the Lightning of Jupiter"; BI 1833 (8) lent by B. West, Jr.; *American Paintings of the Eighteenth and Nineteenth Centuries*, J. Leger & Son, New York, 1930 (4)

ENGR: Outline engraving $(7 \times 9\frac{5}{16}$ in.), drawn by Henry Corbould and engraved by Henry Moses, pub. 1 Dec. 1811 by Henry Moses as "The Alarm

of Nestor at the Lightning which Precedes Hector" in Moses 1811, pl. XI

LISTED: *PC*, p. 566 ("Diomed and his Chariot-Horses struck by the Lightning of Jupiter," West, Gallery); *UM*, p. 530; Barlow, p. 435; *BA*, p. 17; Galt, p. 229; Dillenberger, p. 174 (350)

LIT: Moses 1811 (XI); Evans 1959, pp. 77–78, pl. 58; Rosenblum 1960, p. 78; Kraemer 1975, p. 54

The subject of No. 168 comes from the eighth book of the *Iliad*. At the climactic moment of the combat between Diomedes and Hector, who is visible in his chariot in the lower right, Zeus sends a bolt of lightning to the ground before Diomedes' horses in order to stop the fighting. The horses rear; Nestor, whom Diomedes has invited into his chariot, drops the reins in fear; and the two withdraw. The figure on the ground on the lower right is presumably Eniopeus, Hector's charioteer, whom Diomedes has killed.

A drawing in the Museum of Fine Arts, Boston, which is signed and dated *1788* shows most of the ingredients of No. 168 in a more extended and elaborate composition.[1] Ruth Kraemer has also related a drawing in the Morgan Library of a Greek soldier wearing a helmet and holding a large shield to the figure of Diomedes in No. 168.[2] That drawing is on the verso of a letter to West from Henry Howard dated 31 July 1813, and Kraemer suggests that West copied it from No. 168 preparatory to undertaking a later version of the subject (evidently never carried out).

As noted by Grose Evans, the horses, and to some extent the composition as a whole, appear to be derived from an engraving after the *Defeat of Sennacherib* by Rubens.[3] Robert Rosenblum has also pointed out the dependence of No. 168 on Gavin Hamilton's similarly composed *Achilles Venting His Rage on Hector*, now known through an engraving by Domenico Cunego published in 1766.[4]

[1] Sepia ink, $10\frac{3}{8} \times 15\frac{7}{8}$ in.; signed lower right: *B. West 1788*.
[2] Black chalk, $8\frac{1}{2} \times 11$ in. (Kraemer 1975, p. 54, no. 95).
[3] The engraving by P. Soutman is ill. in Evans, pl. 59.
[4] Ill. in Irwin 1966, pl. 14.

168

169 Juno Receiving the Cestus from Venus 1771

UNIVERSITY OF VIRGINIA ART MUSEUM, CHARLOTTESVILLE, VIRGINIA

Oil on canvas: $90\frac{5}{8} \times 75\frac{3}{8}$ in. $(230 \times 191.5$ cm.)

Signed lower left: *B. West Pinxit/1771*

PROV: Francis Thomas Fitzmaurice, third Earl of Kerry (1740–1818), by whom sold, Christie & Ansell, London, 25 Feb. 1778, lot 3, bt. by Hickey for 70 gns.; S. J. Smith and Son, London, from whom bought by T. J. Blakeslee, New York; bought from Blakeslee by Vose Galleries, Boston, 1912; sold by them, American Art Association, New York, 11 March 1929, lot 180; Joseph Richter; Daniel M. Richter, Palm Beach, Florida; Hirschl & Adler Galleries, New York, from whom acquired by the University of Virginia Art Museum in 1981

EXH: RA 1772 (272) "Juno receiving the cestus from Venus," with no. 273 "The Death of Hyacinthus" (No. 145) listed as its companion; (?) exhibited in Paris in or before 1804; Brooklyn 1922 (28) lent by Vose and Company; *A Gallery Collects*, Hirschl & Adler Galleries, New York, 1977 (5)

LISTED: *PC*, p. 564 ("Venus presenting her Girdle to Juno," painted for Lord Kerry, and in the National Gallery; Figures as large as Life in both pictures [i.e., in No. 169 and in No. 145, "The Death of Hyacinthus," which immediately preceded No. 169 in all lists but that of Joel Barlow and is described as painted for Lord Kerry, but now in the National Gallery at Paris]); *UM*, p. 529; Barlow, p. 433; *BA*, p. 16; Galt, p. 224; Dillenberger, p. 162 (234)

LIT: *Middlesex Journal*, 481, 28–30 April 1772; Graves 1906, VIII, p. 213 (Horace Walpole, 1772); Evans 1959, pp. 45, 119, note 48, and pl. 29

In Book XIV of the *Iliad* Hera (or Juno) borrows the cestus of Aphrodite (Venus) to enhance her own charms so that she can seduce and distract Zeus. No. 169 shows Aphrodite handing the cestus, or girdle, to Hera. The three Graces in the background and Cupid standing at Aphrodite's feet are not mentioned in the text. A long discussion of No. 169 that appeared in the *Middlesex Journal* describes Cupid's expression as seeming to say: "Indeed, Juno, you may take the Cestus, but with that and every other ornament of dress, you will never be so lovely as my mother."[1]

Horace Walpole's comment about this painting in his Royal Academy catalogue in 1772 was, "the head of Juno has dignity, and that of Venus grace, but too many straight lines like the foregoing." The foregoing was presumably *Simeon with the Child Jesus in His Arms* (No. 312), which immediately preceded No. 169 in the Academy catalogue and about which Walpole otherwise said nothing. Walpole's next sentence, "His first manner was in changeable colours like Baroccio," does not seem to be about No. 169, except in implying that it is not in West's first manner, but to be an extension of his criticism of *William Penn's Treaty with the Indians* (No. 85), two entries before in the catalogue, in which Walpole described the color as "heavy, brickish, and void of clearness," like that in all of West's pictures "in his second manner."

We have been unable to confirm that either No. 169 or No. 145 was in Paris, as stated in the entries for the latter in *Public Characters of 1805* and other lists and implied in those for the former, either before or at the time the lists of West's works were compiled.

West may have been attracted to this subject by the example of Reynolds, who exhibited a *Portrait of a Lady in the Character of Juno, Receiving the Cestus from Venus* at the Royal Academy in 1769, but there is no significant visual similarity between the works.[2] Grose Evans's suggestion that the figure types in No. 169 were

inspired by the *Townley Venus*, now in the British Museum, is invalidated by the fact that the sculpture was discovered at Ostia only in 1775, four years after the date on No. 169.[3]

[1]We are indebted to Brian Allen for a transcription of this review.

[2]See Ellis K. Waterhouse, *Reynolds*, London, 1941, pl. 126. The Reynolds belonged to the same dealer in New York, T. J. Blakeslee, early in this century as did Nos. 169 and 145. The subject of the portrait was Annabella, wife of Sir Patrick Blake, first Baronet.

[3]Haskell and Penny 1981, p. 68.

170 Thetis Bringing the Armor to Achilles 1805
See illustration, p. 126

LOCATION UNKNOWN

(96 × 70 in.) (244 × 178 cm.)

PROV: Commissioned by Thomas Hope (1769–1831) in 1805; by descent to Lord Francis Hope (1866–1941, later eighth Duke of Newcastle), by whom sold, Christie's, London, 20 July 1917, lot 70

EXH: RA 1805 (139) "Thetis Bringing armour to her son":

Soon as Aurora heav'd her orient head
Above the waves that blush'd with early red,
(With new-born day to gladden mortal sight,
And gild the courts of heaven with sacred light),
Th' immortal arms the goddess mother bears
Swift to her son: her son she finds in tears,
Stretch'd o'er Patroclus' corse; while all the rest
Their sov'reign's sorrows in their own exprest;
A ray divine her heav'nly presence shed,
And thus, his hand soft touching, Thetis said:
Suppress, my son, this rage of grief, and know
It was not man, but heav'n, that gave the blow;
Behold what arms by Vulcan are bestow'd,
Arms worthy thee, or fit to grace a god.
Vide Homer's Iliad, book xix. to ver. 14

BI 1833 (30) lent by Henry Thomas Hope

ENGR: Stipple engraving ($8\frac{7}{8} \times 6\frac{9}{16}$ in.) by William Bond, pub. by John Britton 1 Nov. 1809 with a dedication to Thomas Hope, and also included in Britton's *Fine Arts of the English School*, London, 1812; outline engraving ($7\frac{1}{2} \times 5\frac{5}{8}$ in.) by Henry Moses, pub. 1 May 1811 as pl. 1 in Moses 1811; outline engraving ($4\frac{5}{8} \times 3\frac{3}{8}$ in.) by Normand *fils*, pub. in Hamilton 1831 (20)

LISTED: *UM*, p. 529 ("Thetis bringing the Armour to Achilles, and three Sketches preparative to painting that picture", Thomas Hope, Esq.); *BA*, p. 19 ("Thetis bringing the armour from Vulcan to her son Achilles"; painted for Thomas Hope, Esq.); Dillenberger, p. 187 (491)

LIT: Farington Diary, 17 March and 4 April 1805 and 4 May 1806 (Farington 1978—, VII, pp. 2532, 2538, and 2746); Moses 1811 (1); John Britton, *The Fine Arts of the English School*, London, 1812, p. 17; Hamilton 1831 (20); David Watkin, *Thomas Hope and the Neo-Classical Idea*, London, 1968, p. 45; Kraemer 1975, pp. 43–50

This painting and a related group of works (Nos. 171–75) all illustrate, or illustrated, the opening lines of the nineteenth book of the *Iliad*, in which Thetis brings to Achilles, who has been grieving over the body of Patroclus, new armor made by Hephaistos (or Vulcan) to replace that belonging to Achilles, which Patroclus had been wearing when he was slain. West exhibited two versions of the subject at the Royal Academy in 1805 under similar titles, but with different quotations, both from Alexander Pope's translation. The quotation accompanying no. 139 in the catalogue in 1805 (see above under EXH.) is from lines 1–14 and describes Thetis' arrival and her address to her tearful son, while that accompanying no. 151 (see under No. 173) is from lines 25–38 and opens with the words Achilles addresses to Thetis expressing his intention to return to the battle. These different lines allow us to distinguish the two main variants of subject (Nos. 170 and 173). The third exhibited work, which appeared at the Royal Academy in 1808 without an accompanying quotation may be No. 175, which is basically a repetition of No. 170 but altered by the addition of a group of Achilles' Myrmidons on the left. Significantly, neither of the quotations that appeared in the Academy catalogue in 1805 mention the Myrmidons, although their fear at the sight of the armor is described in the *Iliad* in the lines (15–18) immediately following those accompanying No. 170 in the catalogue. Of the other versions, Nos. 171 and 172 are studies for, or copies after No. 170, while No. 174 contains elements of both main compositions. No. 174 is signed and dated *1804* and may have been West's first treatment of the subject, which he subsequently divided into different scenes showing separate moments in the narrative. A group of drawings showing Achilles wearing the armor suggests that West contemplated painting yet a third scene based on the same book of the *Iliad*, but no further painting related to those drawings is known or recorded.[1]

Although No. 170 has disappeared, its appearance is known from the engravings by Bond and Moses and from No. 171, the sketch belonging to the Royal Academy, which when sold in 1829 was described as "the same size as the picture . . . in the collection of T. Hope, Esq.". Thomas Hope's commission to West for three pictures from Greek history is mentioned in Joseph Farington's diary entry for 17 March 1805,[2] and John Britton in 1812 also described No. 170 as having been commissioned by Hope in 1805. Thomas Hope, the second cousin of Henry Hope, whose family West painted in 1802 (No. 640), played a conspicuous role as a tastemaker in England in the first two decades of the nineteenth century, and Henry Moses's volume of outline engravings after paintings by West (Moses 1811), in which an engraving of No. 170 is the first plate, is dedicated to him.

Probably as a reflection of Hope's interests, the archaeological details of helmet, shield, sword, etc., in No. 170 are more prominent than are the corresponding components of West's earlier paintings of classical subjects, and, according to John Britton, West drew them "with scrupulous regard to the best specimens of Greek costume." Achilles' shield in No. 170 is based on Homer's description in Book XVIII of the *Iliad*. Recognizable on it are scenes of a marriage procession; elders in session on benches of polished stone; oxen being attacked by lions; sheep in a fold; the earth, sun, moon, stars, and signs of the zodiac at the center; and the waves of the ocean around the rim.

Ruth Kraemer has suggested that some of the details of ornament and West's representation of Thetis are based on John Flaxman's illustrations to the *Iliad*, first published in 1793. However, apart from the similarly inclined head of Thetis, there is no compositional similarity between No. 170 and Flaxman's treatment of the same subject, and West's shield is much more elaborate than Flaxman's, anticipating the sculptor's later attempt to recreate Homer's description in an actual shield to be presented to the Duke of Wellington.[3] The severe profiles, linear patterns, emphatic anatomy, and melodramatic air of No. 170 suggest that West may have been influenced not only by Flaxman, but also by the French Neo-Classical painting that he had seen in Paris in 1802 during the Peace of Amiens.

A small painting, which appears to be a copy after No. 170, not by West, is in the Vassar College Art Gallery.[4] Numerous drawings related to Nos. 170–75 are known and are discussed at length by Ruth Kraemer. Among these, three figural studies in the Pierpont Morgan Library are for Achilles in No. 170.[5] A drawing of a helmet in the same collection shows the helmet brought by Thetis in the painting, and, as Kraemer has pointed out, appears to be inspired by the helmet worn by Mars in plate 32 of Flaxman's *Iliad* illustrations.[6]

See also pp. 127–132 above.

[1]See Kraemer 1975, pp. 48–50 (82–86) and pls. 51–55.

[2]The other two pictures were presumably *Iris Delivering Jove's Command to Priam* (No. 176) and *Narcissus* (No. 146). Hope evidently never received the former.

[3]See *John Flaxman, R.A.*, Royal Academy, London, 1979, pp. 91 (99) and 145–47 (187).

[4]Oil on canvas: 16 × 12 in.

[5]Black chalk, $9\frac{5}{8} \times 7\frac{1}{8}$ in. (Kraemer 1975, pp. 44–46, no. 75, pl. 48); black chalk heightened with white, $8\frac{3}{4} \times 11\frac{1}{4}$ in. (Kraemer, p. 47, no. 78, pl. 49); and black chalk, $9\frac{1}{4} \times 6\frac{7}{8}$ in. (Kraemer, p. 47, no. 79, pl. 49).

[6]Pen and brown ink, $8\frac{1}{4} \times 6\frac{3}{4}$ in. (Kraemer p. 48, no. 80, pl. 50).

171 Thetis Bringing the Armor to Achilles 1805

ROYAL ACADEMY OF ARTS, LONDON

Oil on canvas: 97 × 71 in. (246.5 × 180.5 cm.)

Signed lower right: *B. West 1805*

PROV: (?) Offered by West to the Pennsylvania Academy of the Fine Arts in 1809 ("Thetis bringing the Armour to Achilles," 8 ft. by 6, life [-sized figures], £300); sold by his sons, Robins, London, 20–22 June 1829, lot 84 ("Thetis bringing the Armour to Achilles, sketch on canvas, the same size as the picture of the late B. West . . . in the collection of T. Hope, Esq.")

LISTED: (?) *UM*, p. 529 (as one of three sketches for No. 170); *BA*, p. 20 (. . . "Two sketches of the same subject [as No. 175] without the Myrmidons"—one in colours the other in claro-scuro; in the possession of Mr. West); Dillenberger, p. 188 (499)

LIT: Kraemer 1975, p. 45 (fig. 29)

This full-sized work corresponds to No. 170 in composition and in most details, although it shows much less detail than the prints after No. 170. It is here equated with the chiaroscuro sketch listed in *La Belle Assemblée* and with the sketch on canvas sold by West's sons in 1829. However, it was more likely to have been undertaken as a copy of No. 170, as the commencement of a second version, and hence we have also equated it with the work of the same size which West offered to the Pennsylvania Academy in 1809. West presumably never finished that picture after the Academy failed to accept his offer.

172 Thetis Bringing the Armor to Achilles 1805

THE NEW-YORK HISTORICAL SOCIETY

Oil on paper, mounted on canvas: $17\frac{1}{2} \times 14$ in. (44.5 × 35.5 cm.)

Signed lower left: *B. West 1805*

PROV: (?) Sold by West's sons, Robins, London, 20–22 June 1829, lot 193 ("The Angel at the Tomb, large sketch on canvas, and study for Achilles"); Thomas

171

172

J. Bryan, New York, by whom presented to the New-York Historical Society in 1867

EXH: Allentown 1962 (29)

LISTED: (?) *UM*, p. 529 (as one of three sketches for No. 170)

LIT: Kraemer 1975, p. 45

No. 172 differs from Nos. 170 and 171 in several details. The body of Patroclus is covered. Achilles' head is uncovered, and his legs are in a different position. The helmet and shield carried by Thetis are also in different positions. There is considerably less detail than in No. 170 and the handling is much broader and sketchier than in any of West's other treatments of the subject. The painting would thus seem to be an early and somewhat tentative sketch, intermediary between No. 174 and the final composition shown in Nos. 170 and 171.

Because of discrepancies in dimensions, No. 172 cannot be equated with either of the versions of the subject sold by West's heirs in the Robins sale of 22–25 May 1829; it may, however, have been the "study for Achilles" sold without further identification in the following month.

173 Thetis Bringing the Armor to Achilles *c.* 1805

LOCATION UNKNOWN

EXH: RA 1805 (151) "Thetis brings to her son the armour made by Vulcan":

> Goddess (he cry'd), these glorious arms that shine
> With matchless art, confess the hand divine.
> Now to the bloody battle let me bend;
> But ah! the relicks of my slaughter'd friend:
> In those wide wounds thro' which his spirit fled,
> Shall flies and worms obscene pollute the dead?
> That unavailing care be laid aside,
> (The azure goddess to her son reply'd):
> Whole years untouch'd, uninjur'd, shall remain,
> Fresh as in life, the carcass of the slain.
> But go, Achilles (as affairs require),
> Before the Grecian peers renounce thine ire:
> Then uncontroll'd in boundless war engage,
> And heaven with strength supply the mighty rage!
> *Vide Homer's Iliad, book xix. to ver. 40*

ENGR: Lithograph (12 × 8⅞ in.) by Henry Corbould, pub. by F. Moser, 1 March 1820

LIT: Kraemer 1975, p. 46, fig. 31

Thetis Bringing the Armor to Achilles, lithograph by Henry Corbould after No. 173

As discussed in the entry No. 170 West exhibited two paintings of Thetis and Achilles at the Royal Academy in 1805. The titles of the two, although phrased with slight variation in wording, are too similar to provide any help in differentiating between them, but the quotations accompanying them in the catalogue are of different lines, indicating that the two paintings illustrated successive moments in the narrative. That accompanying the second of the two entries (quoted above) commences with Achilles crying that he will bend to the battle and closes with Thetis referring to his mighty rage. Thus, it would appear to belong to the image of an active Achilles who has taken the armor as shown in No. 173, rather than the brooding figure in Nos. 170–72 and 175. Also, this painting is the only known version of the subject sufficiently unlike No. 170 for West to have shown the two together in the same exhibition. Whereas it provides a sequel and an appropriate companion, all the other versions would have appeared as redundant repetitions.

No. 173 is now known only through a lithograph by Henry Corbould published in 1820. The inscription on that print, *B. West P. R. A. pinxit*, indicates that it was made after a painting rather than a drawing.

Ruth Kraemer has pointed out that a slight sketch in the Morgan Library, which is on the reverse of a study for No. 174, shows Achilles in the same pose as No. 173.[1] That drawing shows the composition in reverse from the lithograph, but it may be that Corbould reversed the composition of the painting in making his print.

[1]Black chalk, $9\frac{1}{4} \times 6\frac{7}{8}$ in. (Kraemer 1975, p. 46, no. 76 and pl. 47).

174 Thetis Bringing the Armor to Achilles 1804

PRIVATE COLLECTION

Oil on canvas: 27 × 20 in. (68.5 × 51 cm.)

Signed lower left: *B. West 1804*

(?) PROV: Offered by West's sons to the United States in 1826 (79 . . . 1 ft. 8 in. × 2 ft. 2 in.), and sold by them, Robins, London, 22–25 May 1829, lot 151 ("Thetis Bringing the Armour to Achilles," 2 ft. 2 in. × 1 ft.), bt. by J. R. Smith for £52.10.0.

174

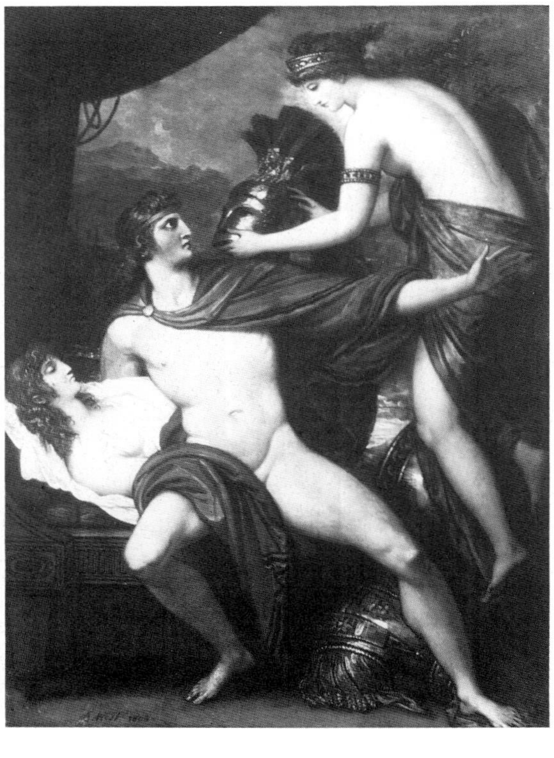

EXH: (?) West's Gallery 1821 (18), 1822–28 (13 or 37)

(?) LISTED: *UM*, p. 529 (as one of three sketches for No. 170); *BA*, p. 20 (. . . "Two sketches of the same subject [as No. 175] without the Myrmidons—one in colours the other in claro-scuro," in the possession of Mr. West); Dillenberger p. 188 (499)

LIT: Kraemer 1975, pp. 43–44, fig. 27

No. 174 shows a different composition and a different moment in the story from either No. 170 or No. 173. Achilles looks up to Thetis, with an arm outstretched in her direction, but he has not yet taken the armor from her. The date of *1804* is a year earlier than that known or recorded for any of West's other versions of the subject, and, hence, it appears that No. 174 embodies the artist's earliest conception of his treatment, which he subsequently put aside, painting instead two separate contrasting scenes. Nonetheless, both Nos. 170 and 173 are closely related to this painting, and it can be looked on as preparatory for both. Since it is closer to No. 170 than is No. 173 it seems less likely to have been exhibited along with No. 170 in 1805, but if it remained in West's possession, it quite probably could have been one of the two versions, along with No. 175, exhibited in West's gallery following his death.

No. 174 could only have been one of the works offered by West's sons to the United States in 1826 and sold in May 1829 if there were mistakes in the dimensions published for it on both occasions. That, however, is not out of the question, and it may be that in correcting the erroneous indication in the earlier lists that No. 174 was a horizontal picture, West's sons accidently omitted the inches from the horizontal dimensions in their sale catalogue three years later. No likely candidate for either listing is otherwise known.

Drawings more or less related to No. 174 are in the Pierpont Morgan Library,[1] at Swarthmore,[2] in the Vassar College Art Gallery,[3] in the New Britain Museum of American Art,[4] and in the collection of Paul Magriel.[5] One of the drawings in the Morgan Library (Kraemer no. 76) also has a sketch for No. 173 on the reverse, and the drawing at Swarthmore is on a sheet with several studies for *Iris Delivering Jove's Command to Priam* (No. 176), which, like No. 170, was supposedly commissioned by Thomas Hope.

[1]Black chalk, $4\frac{1}{2} \times 3\frac{1}{2}$ in. (Kraemer 1975, pp. 43–44, no. 74, pl. 45); black chalk, $9\frac{1}{4} \times 6\frac{7}{8}$ in. (Kraemer, p. 46, no. 76, pl. 46); black chalk, $5\frac{1}{4} \times 6$ in. (Kraemer, p. 48, no. 81, pl. 56).
[2]Pen and brown ink, $6\frac{15}{16} \times 11\frac{1}{4}$ in., (Kraemer, p. 45, fig. 30).
[3]Black chalk, $6 \times 9\frac{3}{4}$ in. (Kraemer, p. 47, fig. 33).
[4]Pen and ink, $7\frac{3}{4} \times 7$ in. (Kraemer, p. 44, fig. 28).
[5]Pen and brown ink over pencil, $9 \times 7\frac{1}{4}$ in.

175 Thetis Bringing the Armor to Achilles (?)1806

NEW BRITAIN MUSEUM OF AMERICAN ART, NEW BRITAIN, CONNECTICUT

Oil on canvas: $19\frac{1}{2} \times 26\frac{1}{2}$ in. (49.5 × 67.5 cm.)

Signed lower right: *B. West* [?] *1806*

PROV: Offered by West's sons to the United States in 1826 (49) and sold by them, Robins, London, 22–25 May 1829, lot 20 ("Thetis Bringing the Armour to Achilles," 1 ft. 8 in. × 2 ft. 3 in.), bt. by W. Ward for £147; sold anonymously, Christie's, London, 9 July 1926, lot 58, bt. by Carroll; Vose Galleries, Boston, from whom purchased in 1942 by the New Britain Museum of American Art (Charles F. Smith Fund)

EXH: (?) RA 1808 (73) "Thetis presenting the armour made by Vulcan to her son Achilles"; (?) West's Gallery, 1821 (18), 1822–28 (13 or 37); *The Great American Nude*, New York Cultural Center, New York, 1975

LISTED: *BA*, p. 20 ("The small picture of Thetis bringing the armour to Achilles in which the Myrmidons are introduced" . . . in the possession of Mr. West); Dillenberger, p. 188 (498)

LIT: Gerdts 1974, pp. 32–33, pl. 3; Kraemer 1975, pp. 46–47, fig. 32

The main figures of Thetis, Achilles, and Patroclus in No. 175 repeat those in No. 170 with only slight differences in detail, but the composition has been added to on both sides so that No. 175 is a horizontal picture, and in the additional space are some ten awestruck spectators. These are Achilles' Myrmidons, whose fear of the armor brought by Thetis is described on lines 15–18 of Book XIX of Pope's translation of the *Iliad*. Their inclusion makes No. 175 a substantially different composition from No. 170, West's prime earlier treatment of the subject, and No. 175, therefore, seems most likely to have been the version which West exhibited at the Royal Academy in 1808. It does not appear in the earlier lists of West's works but is explicitly described in *La Belle Assemblée*, published in 1808. The date on the canvas is difficult to read and could be either *1806* or *1808*.

176 Iris Delivering Jove's Command to Priam 1808

WESTMORELAND COUNTY MUSEUM OF ART, GREENSBURG, PENNSYLVANIA

Oil on canvas: $47\frac{7}{8} \times 69\frac{3}{4}$ in. (121.5 × 177 cm.)

Signed lower right: *B. West 1808*

PROV: Possibly commissioned by Thomas Hope, but evidently never delivered to him; offered by West to the Pennsylvania Academy in 1809 ("Iris Delivering to Priam the Command of Jove," 6 ft. × 4 ft. 2 in., £300); offered by his sons to the United States in 1826 (22) and sold by them, Robins, London, 22–25 May 1829, lot 74 ("Iris Coming to Priam," 4 ft. × 5 ft. $10\frac{1}{2}$ in.), bt. by Leigh for £52.10.0.; Robert Frank, London, 1952; French and Company, New York, from whom purchased by the Westmoreland County Museum in 1967

EXH: RA 1808 (63) "Iris communicating to King Priam Jove's commands, that he should go in person to solicit from Achilles the dead body of his son Hector":

> Then down her bow the winged Iris drives,
> And swift at Priam's mournful court arrives;
> Where the sad sons beside their father's throne
> Sat bath'd in tears, and answered'd groan
> with groan;
> And all amidst them lay the hoary sire,
> (Sad scene of woe!) his face, his wrapt attire
> Conceal'd from sight; with frantic hands he
> spread, &c.
>
> *Pope's Homer's Iliad, book xxiv, v. 195*

BI 1809 (170) "Iris delivering Jove's Command to Priam, for him to go and solicit the body of his son Hector, in the tent of Achilles," 5 ft. 9 in. × 7 ft. 7 in. (including frame); BI 1816 (186) "Iris conveying Jove's commands to King Priam, surrounded by his sons, who are in grief at the loss of Hector"; West's Gallery 1822–28 (122) "Iris coming to Priam"; New York 1962 (15)

LISTED: *BA*, p. 19 ("Iris bearing Jove's command to King Priam, to go and solicit the body of his son Hector," painted for Thomas Hope, Esq.); Dillenberger, p. 187 (492)

175

[2]Whitley 1928b, p. 255, citing a letter from Charles Robert
Leslie to Samuel F. B. Morse, 30 January 1816.
[3]Pen and brown ink, $5\frac{15}{16} \times 11\frac{1}{4}$ in.; the verso of this drawing
is ill. in Kraemer 1975, p. 45, fig. 30. See also No. 174.
[4]Pen, $8\frac{1}{4} \times 8\frac{1}{4}$ in.
[5]Pen and wash, $5\frac{7}{8} \times 4\frac{7}{8}$ in.

177 Iris Delivering Jove's Command to Priam

LOCATION UNKNOWN

PROV: Sold by West's sons, Robins, London, 20–22
June 1829, lot 56 ("Iris coming to Priam, and the
Nativity, sketches . . .")

178 Priam Soliciting of Achilles the Body of Hector

LOCATION UNKNOWN

PROV: In West's possession *c.* 1804.

ENGR: Outline engraving ($7\frac{15}{16} \times 8\frac{7}{8}$ in.) by Henry
Moses, pub. 2 Dec. 1811 as pl. XII of Moses 1811

LISTED: *PC*, p. 567 ("The Sketch of Priam soliciting
of Achilles the Body of Hector," West, Gallery); *UM*,
p. 531; *BA*, p. 18; Galt, p. 232; Dillenberger, p. 181
(422)

LIT: Moses 1811 (XII)

The appearance of this work is known only through
the outline engraving by Henry Moses published in
1811 in *The Gallery of Pictures Painted by Benjamin West*.
It is listed as a sketch in the early lists but West may
have turned it into a more finished picture between the
time the lists were drawn up, in or before 1804, and
the publication of Moses's engraving.

The subject comes from Book XXIV of the *Iliad*. In
narrative sequence it follows *Iris Delivering Jove's Command to Priam* (No. 176), but since No. 178 was recorded

LIT: James Thomas Flexner, *America's Old Masters*,
revised edition, New York, 1967, ill. opp. p. 92

As indicated by the quotation that appeared in the
Royal Academy catalogue in 1808, the subject of
No. 176 comes from the twenty-fourth (and last) book
of the *Iliad*. In the left background can be seen Achilles
in his chariot dragging the body of Hector, while
Aphrodite anoints the body with oil to protect it from
harm.

The catalogue of West's works published in *La Belle
Assemblée* in 1808 describes a painting of the subject as
painted for Thomas Hope, who, as we know from
Joseph Farington's diary, had commissioned three
works from West in 1805.[1] Two of them (Nos. 146 and
170) were sold by a descendant of Hope in 1917.
No. 176 was not sold with them and is recorded as
painted for Hope only in *La Belle Assemblée*
Nevertheless, it was presumably the third picture commissioned by him in 1805, which for some reason was
never delivered.

Since No. 176 is signed and dated *1808*, it seems
reasonable to identify it as the picture exhibited at the
Royal Academy in that year, and since in size it corresponds to the painting of the subject that West
exhibited at the British Institution the following year,
to the painting he offered to the Pennsylvania Academy
in 1809, and to the work sold by his sons in 1829, it
seems probable that the various early listings and references are all for the same painting rather than that
West painted one version for Hope and retained
another large painting of the subject in his own possession. That he would have exhibited No. 176 at the
Royal Academy in 1808 and at the British Institution
in 1809 was consistent with his practice and with the
tolerant rules of the British Institution. Its reappearance at the British Institution in 1816 is explained by
the fact that submissions there were so poor that year
that West had to come to the rescue by providing works
to fill its walls.[2]

A sketch for No. 176 is No. 177 below. A sheet of
studies for No. 176 and for one or more versions of

Thetis Bringing the Armor to Achilles is at Swarthmore.[3]
A drawing for the figure of Priam, in a slightly different
position, was formerly in the possession of a descendant
of the artist,[4] and another drawing evidently also for
Priam, but looking heavenwards with arms upraised,
is at Swarthmore.[5]

[1]Farington Diary, 17 March 1805 (Farington 1978–, VII,
p. 2532).

176

Priam Soliciting of Achilles the Body of Hector, outline engraving by Henry Moses after No. 178

in the lists of West's works as early as 1804, it was evidently painted before No. 176, which is dated *1808*. The composition recalls that of Gavin Hamilton's painting of the same subject.[1] On the left is the shield brought to Achilles by Thetis in No. 170 of 1805, as seen in Henry Moses's outline engraving after that work. The details on the two shields correspond exactly, but it may be that the decoration on the shield in the engraving of No. 178 may have been copied by Moses from that in No. 170 rather than that West himself would have devoted such effort to what is a minor part of the composition. Also conspicuous in the engraving are several vases of different shapes, each depicted in precise and minute detail. Although West may have included these *objets d'art* in the painting to represent the goblet, cauldrons, etc., that Priam brought as ransom for the body of Hector, their prominence in the print also suggests the importance that such decorative objects have as the subjects of many of Moses's engravings, reflecting not only his own interests, but also, and more significantly, those of his patron Thomas Hope, who had commissioned No. 170 and to whom Moses's volume of prints of West's works was dedicated.[2] Their combined enthusiasms probably explain why Moses included No. 178, which had never been exhibited and seems to have been a relatively minor work, as one of the twelve prints in his series of engravings after West. It is worth noting that three of the twelve engravings published in 1811 were of subjects from the *Iliad* (Nos. 168, 170, and 178) and five additional prints also showed classical subjects (Nos. 7, 26, 44, 118, and 157), providing in the first book devoted to the artist a very one-sided view of his *oeuvre*.

[1] Location unknown; oil sketch in the Tate Gallery; engraved by Domenico Cunego, 1778; see Cummings 1968, pp. 46–47 (11).
[2] See David Watkin, *Thomas Hope and the Neo-Classical Idea*, London, 1964, passim.

179 Aeneas and Creusa *c.* 1771

THE NEW-YORK HISTORICAL SOCIETY

Oil on canvas: 73 × 55 in. (185.5 × 139.5 cm.)

PROV: Francis Thomas Fitzmaurice, third Earl of Kerry (1740–1818), by whom sold, Christie & Ansell, London, 25 Feb. 1778, lot 11 ("Eneas and Creusa," 72 × 54 in., with lot 12 "Chryseis returned to her father" [No. 160] listed as its companion), bt. by Hickey for 130 guineas for the pair; presented by William H. Webb to the New-York Historical Society, 3 January 1865

EXH: (?) RA 1771 (212) as "Hector Taking Leave of Andromache," with no. 213 "The Continence of Scipio" listed as its companion (see Nos. 19 and 160)

LIT: Tuckerman 1867, pp. 101 and 622 (as "Hector Parting with his Wife"); Evans 1959, p. 44, pl. 28 (as "Hector Parting with his Wife and Child at the Scaen Gate," 1771); Rosenblum 1960, p. 76

We are indebted to William Lasher for identifying the subject of this picture. Since at least 1867, No. 179 has always been called "Hector Parting with His Wife," but, as Mr. Lasher has pointed out, that is incorrect.[1] The child is too old to be Astyanax, who should be held by his nurse while Hector converses with Andromache; in the Homeric account there is mention neither of an old man, corresponding to the prominent figure on the right of No. 179, nor of a meteor in the sky; and finally the child in No. 179 has a flame above his head, which is the object of his father's attention. Hence, as observed by Mr. Lasher, the painting is clearly not based on the *Iliad*, but illustrates the passage in the *Aeneid* describing the omens which persuade Aeneas and his family to flee Troy. The relevant lines from Dryden's translation, which may well have been West's source, are:

> Arm'd once again, my glitt'ring Sword I wield,
> While th' other hand sustains my weighty Shield,
> And forth I rush to seek th' abandon'd Field.
> I went; but sad Creusa stopp'd my Way,
> And cross the Threshold in my Passage lay,
> Embrac'd my Knees, and, when I would have gone,
> Shew'd me my feeble Sire and tender Son:
> 'If death be your design, at least,' said She,
> 'Take us along to share your destiny.
> If any farther hopes in Arms remain,
> This Place, these Pledges of your Love, maintain.
> To whom do you expose your Father's Life,
> Your Sons's, and mine, your now forgotten Wife!'
> While thus she fills the House with clam'rous Cries,
> Our Hearing is diverted by our Eyes;
> For, while I held my Son, in the short Space
> Betwixt our Kisses and our last Embrace:
> Strange to relate, from young Iulus' Head
> A lambent Flame arose, which gently spread
> Around his Brows, and on his Temples fed.
> Amaz'd, with running water we prepare
> To quench the sacred Fire, and slake his Hair;
> But old Anchises, vers'd in Omens rear'd
> His hands to Heav'n, and this request preferr'd:
> 'If any Vows, almighty Jove, can bend
> Thy Will; if Piety can Pray'rs commend,
> Confirm the glad presage which thou art pleas'd to
>   send.'
> Scarce had he said, when, on our left, we hear
> A peal of rattling Thunder roll in air:
> There shot a streaming Lamp along the Sky,
> Which on the winged Lightning seem'd to fly'
> From o'er the Roof the blaze began to move,
> And trailing, vanish'd in th' Idaen Grove.
> It swept a path in Heav'n, and shone a Guide,
> Then in a steaming stench of Sulphur dy'd.
>
> *Book II, 915–45*

Apart form a drawing, recorded in the early lists of West's works as "The Death of Dido,"[2] No. 179 is the artist's only known subject from Virgil. It was sold as "Eneas and Creusa" in 1778, but that title does not appear on the early lists of West's works or in any catalogues of exhibitions. It is possible that the picture appeared at the Royal Academy in 1771 as "Hector Taking Leave of Andromache," the title by which (with slight variations in wording) it has been known since the mid-nineteenth century. The picture exhibited in 1771 had a companion showing the *Continence of Scipio*, and No. 179 presently has a companion in the same collection showing *Chryseis Returned to Her Father* (see Nos. 19 and 160). As discussed in the entry for No. 160, that picture shows a subject that could be mistaken for the *Continence of Scipio*. Ambivalent evidence indicating either that No. 179 or a very similar picture was shown at the Academy in 1771 is provided

by a drawing of that year's exhibition by Charles Brandoin (H. E. Huntington Library and Art Gallery, San Marino, California), which was subsequently engraved by Richard Earlom.[3] Drawing and engraving show a painting hanging high on the right-hand wall, which does seem to show *Hector Taking Leave of Andromache* with Astyanax in his nurse's arms, but which also shows a composition dominated by an arch similar to that in No. 179. Brandoin's rendering of other works seems to have been pretty careless (the *Compassion of Pharoah's Daughter for the Infant Moses* [No. 251] by West and *Venus Chiding Cupid* by Reynolds [Kenwood] are recognizable on the left), so whether his view includes an inaccurate record of No. 179 (presumably drawn from memory and unconsciously altered to conform to traditional treatments of *Hector Taking Leave of Andromache*) or a lost, closely related, painting of *Hector Taking Leave*, cannot be absolutely determined, but the former alternative seems somewhat more likely. For further discussion, see the entry for No. 160.

A drawing for No. 179 is in the Art Gallery of Ontario.[4]

[1] In oral communications and an unpublished paper written in 1978. We are also indebted to Professor Robert Rosenblum for first informing us of Mr. Lasher's discoveries and to Richard Koke of the New-York Historical Society.
[2] *PC*, p. 568 (in West's Gallery); *UM*, p. 531; Galt, p. 232; Dillenberger, p. 182 (435).
[3] Reproduced in Sidney C. Hutchison, *The History of the Royal Academy*, London, 1968, pl. 4. We are indebted to John Sunderland for helpful correspondence about this drawing and the problems it presents.
[4] Pen and ink and watercolor, $4\frac{3}{4} \times 3\frac{5}{8}$ in.

180 The First Interview of Telemachus with Calypso *c.* 1772

LOCATION UNKNOWN

PROV: (?) Thomas Newton (1704–82), Bishop of Bristol; Henry Hope, London, by 1797; his sale, Christie's, London, 27–29 June 1816, lot 74; James Dunlop, by 1824 and still in his possession in 1833

EXH: RA 1773 (306) "The first interview of Telemachus with Calypso"; BI 1833 (7) lent by James Dunlop

ENGR: Engraving ($17\frac{3}{16} \times 22\frac{7}{8}$ in.), inscribed: *Painted by Benjamin West, Esqr 1772.|Etched by William Woollett & Engraved by S. Middiman.|The figures by J. H. Robinson, pub. 12 April 1824 by Hurst, Robinson & Co., From the original Picture in the possession of James Dunlop Esqr to whom this Print is most respectfully dedicated.* (There is also a proof of the etched state of this print in the British Museum, inscribed: *Painted by B. West 1772|Etched by W. Woollett 1783*)

LISTED: *PC*, p. 562 ("The picture of Telemachus and Calypso," in the collection of Henry Hope, Esq., First painted for the late Bishop of Bristol); *UM*, p. 528; Barlow, p. 433; Galt, p. 221; Dillenberger, p. 155 (169)

LIT: Farington Diary, 8 March 1797 (Farington 1978–, III, p. 789); *Public Characters* 1805, pp. 553–54; Dunlap Diary, 25 April 1811 (Dunlap 1930, II, p. 447); Graves 1906, VIII, p. 213 (Horace Walpole, 1773); John Constable, *Discourses*, R. B. Beckett, ed., Ipswich, 1970, p. 68

Because of the subject's obvious relation to that of the *Odyssey*, we have included No. 180 and related works in this part of the catalogue, although the specific source is not Homer but *Les aventures de Télémaque, fils d'Ulysse* of 1699 by François de Salignac de La Mothe-Fénelon (1651–1715). West presumably used the translation by John Hawkesworth published in 1768.

The First Interview of Telemachus with Calypso, engraving by William Woollett, S. Middiman and J. H. Robinson after No. 180

tion of the subject is in the University of Kansas Museum of Art.[2] Although differing in almost every detail and showing considerably less emphasis on the landscape setting, this drawing is basically similar in composition to No. 180. There is also a slighter sketch on the verso, which shows smaller figures and a more extensive landscape but is less evidently related to No. 180.[3]

Thomas Sully and Charles Bird King painted copies after West's *Telemachus and Calypso* during the winter of 1809–10.[4] Since No. 180 was at that time in the possession of Henry Hope, they probably copied one of the later versions still belonging to West, most probably No. 181. What appears to be yet another copy, this time after No. 180 and corresponding closely in detail to the engraving by Woollett et al., is in the Witte Memorial Museum in San Antonio, Texas.[5]

See also pp. 117–120 above.

[1]David Watkin, *Thomas Hope and the Neo-Classical Idea*, London, 1968, p. 3.
[2]Pen and ink, 12¼ × 19⅛ in.; see *American Drawings and Water-colors from the University of Kansas Museum of Art*, University of Kansas Museum of Art, Lawrence, Kansas, 1973 (15).
[3]The view has some similarity to No. 467, *The Bathing Place at Ramsgate*.
[4]Location unknown and in a private collection; see Andrew J. Cosentino, *The Paintings of Charles Bird King*, Washington, 1977, pp. 20 and 200 (601), and Edward Biddle and Mantle Fielding, *The Life and Works of Thomas Sully*, Philadelphia, 1921, pp. 19 and 388 (2599). According to these sources, King's copy measured 43 × 56 in., Sully's 56 × 33 in. (or more likely vice versa). King's copy appeared at the Pennsylvannia Academy in 1813; Sully showed his there in 1811.
[5]Oil on canvas, 26 × 37 in.; said to have been purchased in Philadelphia in 1820 and to have passed by family descent to Boyer Gonzales, San Antonio, whose son presented it to the museum.

The shipwreck of Telemachus and his companion Mentor (or more properly Minerva in the guise of Mentor) and their meeting with Calypso are described in the opening paragraphs of the book.

No. 180 is the first of several versions, either known or recorded, of the subject of Telemachus and Calypso (for the others see Nos. 181–84). It has disappeared, but its composition is known through the engraving by William Woollett (*above*) et al., as well as from West's other, later treatments of the subject, which repeat the composition shown in the engraving in reverse, each with only slight modifications of detail. According to the inscription on the engraving, West painted No. 180 in 1772, a date consistent with the picture's appearing at the Royal Academy in 1773. The long gestation of the print from 1783, when it was etched by Woollett, to 1824, when it was finally published, can partly be explained by the death of Woollett in 1785. Even after the print had finally appeared, the entry in the Robins sale catalogue of 22–25 May 1829 for West's second version of the subject (No. 181) contained the lament, "It is to be regretted that the engraving of this finely composed scene had not been finished by a hand that could as congenially have felt the spirit of West's pencil, as did that of Woollett."

In No. 180 the landscape is considerably more prominent and the figures in it are smaller than in any of West's previous works exhibited since his arrival in England. It is not a pure landscape, a genre that he practised at intervals throughout his career, but the combination of literary subject and extensive landscape setting makes it his first venture into so-called historical landscape. West subsequently painted several other paintings of this type between 1796 (Nos. 22 and 24) and 1812 (No. 274), and he exhibited later versions of *Telemachus and Calypso* (Nos. 181 and 182) in 1801 and 1806, but No. 180 is separated from all these later pictures by more than twenty years. The painting was undoubtedly at least partly inspired by the historical landscapes exhibited by Richard Wilson during the preceding dozen years, and it is noteworthy that William Woollett, who commenced the engraving of No. 180, had initially made his reputation as an engraver of landscapes after Wilson, although his most famous single print was that after West's *Death of General Wolfe* (No. 93).

In 1773 Horace Walpole described No. 180 as "all good but the trees." In 1836, in a lecture entitled "The Decline and Revival of Landscape," John Constable praised West for "great ability in the composition of landscape, which he sometimes practised for itself, with figures entirely subordinate," and, using the engraving by Woollett et al. as an illustration, he described No. 180 as "an extremely beautiful combination of landscape and figures."

In the catalogues of West's works published in *Public Characters of 1805* and the *Universal Magazine*, six works are listed together as "In the Collection of Henry Hope, Esq./First painted for the late Bishop of Bristol." That these paintings did belong to Hope is confirmed by the fact that all except one, a family portrait (No. 640), appeared in Hope's sale in 1816, but their connection to the Bishop of Bristol is less certain. Presumably the bishop referred to was Thomas Newton (1704–82), who was an important early patron of West's. Newton could not have owned at least three of the works in the group (Nos. 22, 392, and 640) which were painted well after his death, but it is possible that he was the first owner of No. 180, which is the first work listed immediately after the reference to the late Bishop. It is worth noting that the date of *1783* on Woollett's etching follows that of Newton's death by one year; by then No. 180 may have returned to West's studio, where William Dunlap, who arrived in England in 1784, was later to recollect having seen a painting of the subject. Joseph Farington subsequently saw it in Henry Hope's house in Hanover Square in March 1797, but it could not have been there for too long a time previously, as Hope had only moved to London from the Netherlands in 1794.[1]

A drawing which may represent an earlier visualiza-

181 The First Interview of Telemachus with Calypso 1801
See color illustration, p. 117

ARDEN COLLECTION, NEW YORK

Oil on canvas: 40 × 56¼ in. (101.5 × 143 cm.)

Signed lower right: *B. West/1801*

(?) PROV: The European Museum, London, 1819, where bought (or bought back) by West for £300; offered by West's sons to the United States in 1826 (13) and sold by them, Robins, London, 22–25 May 1829, lot 40 ("Telemachus and Mentor on the Island of Calypso," 40 × 52 in.), bt. by W. Ward for £294 presumably on behalf of West's heirs; offered for sale by Benjamin West, Jr., in a notice in the catalogue of a sale of drawings by West, S. Leigh Sotheby, 1 June 1839; sold by Mrs. Albert F. West, Christie's, London, 18–19 March 1898, lot 145 (40 × 56 in.), bt. by Sampson for £11.11.0.; James J. Hill, Saint Paul, Minnesota; given by the family of Louis W. Hill to the Saint Paul Gallery and School of Art (subsequently Minnesota Museum of Art) in 1958; Myron Kunin, Minneapolis, 1979; sold anonymously, Sotheby Parke Bernet, New York, 25 April 1980, lot 2

(?) EXH: RA 1801 (198) "Mentor and Telemachus; their first interview with Calypso"; The European Museum, London, 1819 (498) "Calypso with her nymphs receiving Telemachus and Mentor after their shipwreck"; West's Gallery 1822–28 (54); Egyptian Hall, London, 1839; *Dedicatory Exhibition*,

Tweed Gallery, University of Minnesota, Duluth, 1965 (5)

(?) LISTED: 1826 offer, no. 13 (40 × 52 in.); *PC*, p. 566 ("Calypso and Telemachus on the Sea-shore—second picture", West, Gallery); *UM*, p. 531; Barlow, p. 435; *BA*, p. 18; Galt, p. 229; Dillenberger, p. 175 (368)

(?) LIT: Hall 1962, p. 101

The histories of the later versions of No. 180 are hopelessly confused, and the entries for Nos. 181–84 can only be described as tentative attempts, based on insufficient evidence, to sort them out. No. 181 was at one time badly overcleaned and repainted, and it was cleaned and substantially repainted once again by the late Theodore Siegl in 1961. It could easily be a picture that West had left unfinished and thus be identical with one of the two unfinished pictures of the subject sold by West's sons in June 1829 (see the provenances for Nos. 183 and 184). Nonetheless, the picture does bear a signature and date of *1801*, which Mr. Siegl believed to be original, not a later addition,[1] and, therefore, it seems logical to equate No. 181 with the painting of the subject that West exhibited at the Royal Academy in 1801.

This painting and No. 183, which is very similar to it, differ from the engraving after No. 180 in showing the composition in reverse and in a number of details. Calypso wears a coronet whereas her hair is more loosely bound in No. 180, and her right breast, which is bare in the engraving after No. 180, is covered in Nos. 181 and 183. There are also numerous changes in details of the ship, the configuration of the waves, and in the distant landscape, and a pile of large rocks has been added behind Telemachus and Mentor at the edge of the composition.

If correctly identified here, No. 181 would have been the "Telemachus and Calypso" included in the early lists of West's works as the second picture of the subject, belonging to the artist, and No. 181 is the strongest candidate for identification as the version exhibited in West's gallery following his death and sold in the main sale of his works in May 1829.[2] A "Calypso with her nymphs receiving Telemachus and Mentor after their shipwreck" was for sale at the European Museum in 1819, but it was evidently bought by West himself, so presumably it was the same picture as well. Three paintings by West were listed in the European Museum catalogue for 1819 (Nos. 148, 181, and 410); he probably sent two of them there (Nos. 148 and 181), and he bought back all three.[3]

No. 181, since it remained in West's possession, was probably the version of the subject copied by Thomas Sully and Charles Bird King in 1809–10.

[1] Letter to Helmut von Erffa, 9 November 1960.
[2] There is a slight discrepancy between the measurements for work given in 1826 and 1829 and those of No. 181, but these may be due to an error in the 1826 list, perpetuated in 1829, and, in any case, the difference of 4 in. does not seem sufficient to suggest that there was yet another version of the picture.
[3] We are indebted to Mr. R. J. Lloyd, a descendant of John Wilson, the museum's proprietor, for this information.

182 The First Interview of Telemachus with Calypso

LOCATION UNKNOWN

(50 × 72 in.) (127 × 183 cm.)

PROV: Offered by West to the Pennsylvania Academy of the Fine Arts in 1809 ("The picture of Telemachus and Calypso—their first interview; a Poetical Landscape," 6 ft × 4 ft 2 in., £350)

(?) EXH: BI 1806 (North Room, 63) "Telemachus and Calypso, their first interview," 70 × 92 in. (including frame)

Although it would have been possible as well as consistent with West's practice for him to have sent the same picture that he had exhibited at the Royal Academy in 1801 (see No. 181) to the British Institution in 1806, it is difficult to reconcile the measurements listed in the British Institution catalogue (70 × 92 in., including frame) with those of No. 181, as they suggest a work of different proportions. These measurements are, however, consistent with the dimensions of 4 ft. 2 in. × 6 ft. given by West (in reverse) for a version of the subject that he offered to the Pennsylvania Academy in 1809.[1] Thus it seems likely that he did paint a picture of the subject, larger than No. 181, which he exhibited in 1806 and offered for sale in 1809, but which subsequently disappeared. Since it was sufficiently finished to be exhibited in 1806, it would not have been one of the unfinished pictures of the subject sold by West's heirs in June of 1829.

[1] Subtracting the measurements listed in 1809 from those in the British Institution catalogue leaves differences of 20 in. for both the vertical and horizontal dimensions, corresponding to a frame of 10 in. all around.

183 The First Interview of Telemachus with Calypso

CORCORAN GALLERY OF ART, WASHINGTON, D.C.

Oil on canvas: 41¼ × 58¾ in. (105 × 149 cm.)

183

PROV: (?) Sold by West's sons, Robins, London, 20–22 June 1829, lot 132 ("Telemachus in the Island of Calypso, unfinished"); (?) Henry Corbould (1787–1844), 1833; Mortimer Brandt, New York, from whom acquired by Mrs. E. Lovette West, Bronxville, New York; her daughter, Bernice West Beyers, by whom given to the Corcoran Gallery in 1963

EXH: (?) SBA 1832 (266) "Mentor and Telemachus at the Island of Calypso— unfinished," lent by H. Corbould, Esq.; *Seascape and the American Imagination*, Whitney Museum of American Art, New York, 1975 (120); Washington and Philadelphia 1980

This painting corresponds with No. 181 in all significant details, but there are some slight differences in the plants in the immediate foreground, in the foliage of the trees in the upper right, and in the distant landscape. In handling, particularly in the figures, No. 183 does not look entirely like the work of West,[1] and, as it is not signed, unlike No. 181, it seems proper to identify it as one of the unfinished pictures sold by West's sons in June 1829. If it was the unfinished version of the subject lent to an exhibition by Henry Corbould in 1832, then it may have been completed either by him or by his son, Edward Henry Corbould (1815–1905), as both were artists.

[1] Dorinda Evans in the catalogue of the Washington-Philadelphia exhibition of West and his American students held in 1980 suggested that the figures of Calypso and her companions in No. 183 appear to be by one of West's students (p. 187, note 46).

184 The First Interview of Telemachus with Calypso

LOCATION UNKNOWN

PROV: Sold by West's sons, Robins, London, 20–22 June 1829, lot 153 ("The Captive from Sterne, a study, by the late B. West ...—beginning of Telemachus in the Island of Calypso, by ditto—View from Greenwich Hill, by ditto")

Aegisthus Discovering the Body of Clytemnestra, mezzotint by Valentine Green after No. 185

185 Aegisthus Discovering the Body of Clytemnestra *c.* 1780

LOCATION UNKNOWN

(41 × 53 in.) (104 × 134.5 cm.)

PROV: Offered by West's sons to the United States in 1826 (92) and sold by them, Robins, London, 22–25 May 1829, lot 13 ("Aegisthus Viewing the Body of Clytemnestra," 3 ft. 5 in. × 4 ft. 5 in.), bt. by Erskine for £28.7.0.

EXH: RA 1780 (59) "Ægistus, raising the veil, discovers the body of Clytemnestra.—Franklin's Sophocles"; West's Gallery 1822–28 (67) "Aegisthus viewing the Body of Clytemnestra"

ENGR: Mezzotint (19$\frac{13}{16}$ × 25$\frac{3}{8}$ in.) by Valentine Green, pub. 25 March 1786, by V. and R. Green

LISTED: *PC*, p. 565 ("Ægistus viewing the Body of Clytemnestra," West, Painting-room); *UM*, p. 530; Barlow, p. 434; *BA*, p. 17; Galt, p. 227; Dillenberger, p. 170 (309)

LIT: von Erffa 1969, p. 30; Kraemer 1975, pp. 84–85

No. 185 has been lost since the West sale of 22–25 May 1829, but its appearance is known through the mezzotint by Valentine Green (*above*) published in 1786. The subject comes from the final scene of the *Electra* by Sophocles (lines 1290 ff. in the Francklin translation). The central figure is, of course, Aegisthus, shown starting back upon the discovery of the body of Clytemnestra. Electra stands to the left, Orestes to the right. One of the figures standing behind Orestes presumably represents his companion Pylades. In the sequence of the lives of Orestes and Pylades, No. 185 precedes *Pylades and Orestes* (No. 186), although West painted the former some fifteen years later.

Thomas Francklin (1721–1784), whose translation of Sophocles West cited in the Royal Academy cata-

logue in 1780, was Professor of Ancient History in the Academy from 1774 to 1784. His translation of the tragedies of Sophocles was published in 1759.

Related drawings are at Swarthmore,[1] in the Museum of Fine Arts, Boston,[2] and in the Pierpont Morgan Library.[3] A drawing of the "Discovery of Clytemnestra's Body" was exhibited in West's Gallery in 1823,[4] and one of "Egisthus viewing the body of Clytemnestra" was sold by Benjamin West, Jr. in 1839.[5]

[1]Sepia ink, 5$\frac{3}{4}$ × 7$\frac{3}{8}$ in.
[2]Sepia ink and wash over pencil, 8$\frac{1}{4}$ × 12$\frac{1}{16}$ in.
[3]Tracing, 14$\frac{3}{8}$ × 22 in. (Kraemer 1975, p. 84, no. 207).
[4]Room of Drawings, no. 45.
[5]S. Leigh Sotheby, London, 1 June 1839, lot 90, pen and ink, washed with bistre.

186 Pylades and Orestes 1766
See color illustration, p. 42

TATE GALLERY, LONDON

Oil on canvas: 39$\frac{1}{2}$ × 49$\frac{3}{4}$ in. (100.5 × 126.5 cm.)

Signed lower left: *B. West 1766*

PROV: Bought from the artist by Alexander Geddes, in 1766 for 100 guineas and still in his possession in 1771; (?) Gerard Vandergucht, London (died 1776); sold anonymously (The property of a Gentleman, deceased), Christie & Ansell, London, 14–15 March 1777, lot 94, bt. by Graves for 105 guineas; West; acquired from West probably between 1802 and 1804 by Sir George Beaumont, Bt. (1753–1827); presented by Beaumont to the National Gallery in 1826; transferred to the Tate Gallery in 1929

EXH: SA 1766 (180) "Pylades and Orestes," companion to no. 179 "The Continence of Scipio" (No. 18); Bregenz 1968 (474)

ENGR: Engraving (18 × 22$\frac{5}{16}$ in., reversed) by James Basire, pub. 1 July 1771 by John Boydell, *From the original picture . . . in the collection of Alex^r. Geddes, Esqr.| Size of the picture 3 F 3 $\frac{1}{2}$ I by 4 F 4 $\frac{1}{2}$ I*"; two outline engravings of details of the heads of Iphigenia and her companions (oval, 4$\frac{1}{4}$ × 6$\frac{1}{4}$ in.) and of the heads of Pylades, Orestes, and the soldier immediately to their left (oval, 4$\frac{1}{8}$ × 6$\frac{3}{8}$ in.), pub. in *Physiognomische Fragmente* by Johann Caspar Lavater, Leipzig and Winterthur, 1775, I, opp. p. 110; outline engraving (5$\frac{7}{8}$ × 7$\frac{1}{2}$ in.) by Henry Moses, pub. by Moses, 11 Jan. 1816 and included in later editions of Moses 1811; outline engraving (3$\frac{1}{4}$ × 4$\frac{1}{4}$ in.) by Normand *fils*, pub. in Hamilton 1831 (156); steel engraving (4$\frac{15}{16}$ × 6$\frac{1}{16}$ in., reversed) by J. Kennerley, pub. by Jones & Co., in series *The National Gallery* (13)

LISTED: *PC*, p. 563 ("Pylades and Orestes," Sir George Beaumont); *UM*, p. 529; Barlow, p. 435 (in West's own collection); *BA*, p. 15; Galt, p. 222; Dillenberger, pp. 159 (207) and 181 (426)

LIT: V and A Cuttings, I, p. 69 (*Public Advertiser*, April 1766); Johann Caspar Lavater, *Physiognomische Fragmente, zur Beförderung der Menschenkenntnis und Menschenliebe*, Leipzig and Winterthur, 1775, I, pp. 110–11; Farington Diary, 7 Nov. 1806, 26 Jan. 1808, and 3 Feb. 1812 (Farington 1978—, VIII, p. 2898, IX, p. 3207, and XI, p. 4075); Moses 1811 (only in later editions); James Northcote, *The Life of Sir Joshua Reynolds*, (2nd ed.), London, 1819, I, pp. 42–43; Galt 1820, pp. 16–17; Carey 1820, pp. 689–90; *Annual Register* 1820, p. 1169; Hamilton 1831 (176); Passavant 1836, I, pp. 55–56; Tom Taylor, ed., *Life of Benjamin Robert Haydon* (2nd. ed.), London, 1853, I, p. 176; Waagen 1854, I, p. 366; Locquin 1912, pp. 154, 156; Locquin 1922, pp. 477, 479; Gatty 1938–39, p. 81 (Horace Walpole, 1766); Walter Muschg, ed., *Heinrich Füssli: Briefe*, Basel 1942, pp. 175–77 (Fuseli to Lavater, 14 June 1777); Evans 1959, pp. 9–10, 47–48, 119, notes 54–56, and pl. 9; Irwin 1966, pp. 50–51, pl. 37; von Erffa 1973, pp. 10–12 and fig. 5; Alberts 1978, pp. 73–74

No. 186 is based upon *Iphigenia in Tauris* by Euripides, presumably via the translation by Gilbert West (1703–1756), first published in 1749 and with numerous later editions, including one published in 1766. The action of the play takes place in Scythia (or Tauris), where Iphigenia, the sister of Orestes, is a priestess of Diana. The moment shown is from the third act, when Orestes and his companion Pylades have been brought onto the stage as prisoners, but have not yet been released from their bonds. They are led by the shepherd who had reported their capture in the previous act and are accompanied by priests and guards, who proceed into the temple on the left. Before the temple, standing behind a sacrificial altar, are Iphigenia and a chorus of captive Greek women. In the background is the statue of the goddess which the oracle at Delphi has told Orestes to seize and bring to Athens in expiation for the murder of Clytemnestra. In the ensuing scene Orestes and Iphigenia recognize one another as brother and sister. The animated group in the right background does not seem to be based upon anything that happens in the play.

Exhibited in 1766, along with the *Continence of Scipio* (No. 18) as its companion, and subsequently the first work by West to enter a public museum or gallery, this picture is the best known and most extensively discussed of the works painted by the artist during the first few years of his first residence in England.

According to several sources, No. 186 created a sensation while still in West's studio, even before being sent to exhibition at the Society of Artists in April 1766. The account of its popular success was first reported by James Northcote in 1819, in the second edition of his life of Reynolds, to illustrate a story about the reluctance of the English to purchase pictures of historical subjects; according to Northcote, not one of West's wealthy and aristocratic visitors, who had come to his studio to admire the painting, even asked about the price. William Carey, who quotes Northcote, states additionally that in 1818 West told him that after No. 186 had been returned to him from the Society of Artists, still unsold, the steward of an unidentified nobleman, a Mr. Geddes, purchased it for one hundred guineas, "with expressions of honest indignation against his superiors in rank and fortune." This story is partly confirmed by the Basire engraving published in 1771, which identifies Alexander Geddes as the picture's owner, but Carey's subsequent statement that West purchased No. 186 back at the sale of Geddes's estate seems unlikely, unless Geddes was a much more substantial collector than Carey implies. No. 186 was one of a group of four pictures by West (the others were No. 18, its companion, *Jupiter and Semele* [No. 155], and No. 35, a version of *Agrippina with the Ashes of Germanicus*) sold as "The Property of a Gentlemen, deceased" in March 1777; that gentleman was probably the engraver and dealer Gerard Vandergucht, whose pictures by earlier masters had been sold at the same auction house a week earlier. Graves, the purchaser in 1777, may have been acting as West's agent, or he may subsequently have sold the painting to him. West was evidently the owner in 1802, the date of the compilation of the list of his works in Joel Barlow's *Columbiad*, but by 1804, when the list in *Public Characters* appeared, No. 186 belonged to Sir George Beaumont. That eminent collector, who eventually presented No. 186 to the British Nation as one of the foundation gifts forming the National Gallery, admired the painting sufficiently in 1806 to compare to it his recently acquired Wilkie, the *Blind Fiddler* (now also Tate Gallery),[1] and in 1812 to ask Benjamin Robert Haydon to paint a companion to it. Haydon declined the request.[2]

Despite the reports of the attention the painting supposedly received in 1766, we have seen no contemporary praise or criticism specifically devoted to it. Horace Walpole tersely dismissed four of the five pictures exhibited by West at the Society of Artists with "hard & gaudy, & little expression." A correspondent signing himself Smirk also wrote in the *Public Advertiser* about West's pictures in general rather than about individual ones:

Mr. West's Colouring is rich and yet not delicate, his Drawing good, but not graceful, his Designs original yet not pleasing; when a few years have lost these Luxuriances and Imperfections in each other, we may expect to see something great indeed.

In 1775 Johann Caspar Lavater published outline engravings of two details from No. 186, showing the heads of the principal groups, as illustrations to the first volume of his *Physiognomische Fragmente*. The prints were probably made after the engraving by Basire (Lavater's discussion describes them as copied after a copy), although they show the heads in the same direction as the original, whereas Basire's engraving is reversed. The illustrations are among some twenty-one accompanying Lavater's ninth *Fragment*, or chapter, "Von der Harmonie der moralischen und körperlichen Schönheit," the others encompassing a range of artistic sources from Raphael to Hogarth. Apart from the Polish-German painter Daniel Chodowiecki (1726–1801), West was the only living artist represented in this *Fragment*, and Lavater praised No. 186 not only as the embodiment of the harmony between physical and moral beauty, but as "eins des schönsten Stücke die ich Kenne." West evidently appreciated this sufficiently to give Lavater a painting (No. 323), which itself became an illustration to the fourth volume of the *Physiognomische Fragmente*, published in 1778. On the other hand, Lavater's boyhood friend Henry Fuseli, in a letter to

Lavater from Rome dated 14 June 1777, vigorously objected to the praise of West:

Was du mit Wests Pylades und Orestes meinest, weiss Gott. Ist es denn möglich dass der, welcher die Kartone von Raphael gesehen und den Antinous und Apollo zu kennen denkt, das der sich mit Beschreibung und Zergliederung dieser zahmen, ausdruckslosen, uncharakteristischen Marionette abgebe und Köpfe kopiere, von denen er endlich selber gesteht, dass sie nichts taugen?

(God knows what you mean with West's Pylades and Orestes. Is it possible that someone, who has seen the Cartoons of Raphael and believes that he understands the Antinous and Apollo, can concern himself with describing and analyzing these tame, inexpressive, and characterless marionettes and copy heads, which he finally admits to himself are worthless?)

Probably because of Fuseli's disapproval, the engravings after No. 186 disappeared from the later French and English editions of the *Physiognomische Fragmente*, although engravings after No. 323 remained and were even joined by portraits of West (the one in the English edition of 1789–98 is after No. 527).

West told Joseph Farington in January 1808 that "his mind was full of Correggio," while he had been painting No. 186. His following remarks, as reported by Farington, indicate that the reference to Correggio, which had been prompted by the sight of another early work, *Venus and Cupid* (No. 128) of 1765, related primarily to the coloring of flesh. Fuseli's comments in 1777 point to further sources for No. 186: there are echoes of the *Apollo Belvedere* in the legs of both Pylades and Orestes, and of an Antinous figure (specifically the *Capitoline Antinous*)[3] in the pose and type of Orestes, while the composition is equally reminiscent of the Tapestry Cartoons by Raphael, among which the *Sacrifice at Lystra* (ill. p. 43), which shows analogous subject, is the most relevant, as Grose Evans has pointed out. Even more relevant are the reliefs showing the same subject on antique sarcophagi. Evans illustrates his discussion of No. 186 with an engraving from Winckelmann's *Monumenti antichi inediti*, which he acknowledges West could not have known, since that book appeared only in 1767. But the sarcophagus reproduced by Winckelmann, which is now in the Glyptothek in Munich (ill. p. 43), was in the Villa Ridolfi in Rome in the eighteenth century,[4] and West had probably seen and copied it there. Two drawings at Swarthmore (p. 43) appear to be free copies from the figures of Orestes and Pylades on the Munich sarcophagus, with drapery sketched over them by West.[5] These two figures reappear in the painting in reversed relationship from that on the sarcophagus, but with the figure of Pylades, on the right in No. 186, in a virtually identical pose and with draperies added, as they are also in the drawing at Swarthmore. Orestes in No. 186 is altered by his right arm being moved from behind his back, as in the relief and the drawing, to hang by his side in a position reminiscent of the *Capitoline Antinous*, and his drapery is slung over the opposite shoulder from that shown in the corresponding drawing at Swarthmore. A similar Orestes relief also appears in the background of the portrait of *Goethe in the Campagna* (Staedel Institute, Frankfurt) painted by J. H. W. Tischbein in 1786–87 while Goethe was at work on his *Iphigenia*.

A "duplicate" of No. 186 (No. 187) was sold by West's sons in June 1829. A copy made by Thomas Sully in 1809 is in the collection of James Ricau (on extended loan to the Brooklyn Museum).[6] Charles Bird King also painted a copy (unlocated) at the same time. Sully's journal entry for 14 September 1809 records returning West's "original" to the artist after he and King had completed their copies.[7] In 1809 No. 186 belonged to Sir George Beaumont, so it is possible that King and Sully did not copy it, but rather the duplicate in West's possession.

[1] Farington Diary, 7 Nov. 1806.
[2] Farington Diary, 3 Feb. 1812.
[3] See Haskell and Penny 1981, pp. 143–44 and 148–51. Jean Locquin and David Irwin have also suggested the dependence of the figures in No. 186 on a classical Antinous.
[4] Adolf Furtwängler, *Beschreibung der Glyptothek König Ludwigs I zu München*, Munich, 1900, pp. 340–42 (363). The sarcophagus dates from the second century A.D., and went to Munich in 1817.
[5] Both in charcoal: $6\frac{1}{4} \times 3\frac{3}{4}$ in.
[6] Oil on canvas: 39×50 in.; exhibited Pennsylvania Academy, 1811.
[7] Andrew J. Cosentino, *The Paintings of Charles Bird King*, Washington, 1977, p. 199.

187 Pylades and Orestes

LOCATION UNKNOWN

PROV: Sold by West's sons, Robins, London, 20–22 June 1829, lot 65 ("Pylades and Orestes, duplicate by the late B. West ... of the picture by the same Master, in the National Gallery"); (?) L. A. Wates, Catford, London, 1953

The only documentation for a second version of No. 186 is the catalogue of the sale of lesser works from West's estate in June 1829. The fact that it was not in the main sale the preceding month, and not in the early catalogues of his paintings suggests that it may not have been by West, contrary to the statement in the sale catalogue, or that something else may have been amiss.

A version of No. 186 was in a private collection in 1953, but a photograph sent by its owner to Helmut von Erffa at that time is inadequate to allow any opinion about its authorship.

SUBJECTS FROM RENAISSANCE AND MODERN LITERATURE

188 Angelica and Medoro *c.* 1763–64

See color illustration, p. 34

UNIVERSITY ART GALLERY, STATE UNIVERSITY OF
NEW YORK AT BINGHAMTON, NEW YORK

Oil on canvas: 36¼ × 28¼ in. (92.1 × 71.8 cm.)

PROV: (?) Mr. Mitten, Shropshire (? John Mytton, Halston, Shropshire, 1737–1783) by or before 1804; Vose Galleries, Boston, 1920; Mr. and Mrs. George P. Douglas, Minneapolis, 1920–55; bequeathed by Mrs. Douglas to the Minneapolis Institute of Arts; Victor D. Spark, New York, by 1956; Graham Galleries, New York, from whom acquired by the present owner in 1969

EXH: (?) SA 1764 (131) "Angelica and Medoro, an historical picture," with the following entry, no. 132, "Cymon and Iphigenia," listed as its companion (see No. 195); New York 1962 (10); Washington and Philadelphia 1980

ENGR: Mezzotint (21¼ × 14¹⁵⁄₁₆ in., reversed), by Richard Earlom, pub. by John Boydell, 1768; stipple engraving (oval, 11¹³⁄₁₆ × 9½ in., reversed and with some detail omitted) by George Sigmund Facius and/or John Gotlieb Facius, pub. 1 January 1778 by John Boydell; mezzotint (18⁷⁄₁₆ × 13⅞ in.) by C. Corbutt

(?) LISTED: *PC*, p. 565 ("Cymon and Iphigenia, and Angelica and Madora—in the possession of Mr. Mitten, of Shropshire, painted at Rome" [listed with pictures in West's Painting-room]); *UM*, p. 530; *BA*, p. 17; Galt, p. 226; Dillenberger p. 169 (300)

LIT: *Public Characters* 1805, pp. 529 and 532; Galt 1816, p. 142; Galt 1820, p. 6; Carey, 1820, pp. 517–18; Gatty 1938–39, p. 81 (Horace Walpole, 1764); von Erffa 1963, pp. 631–33, and fig. 7; von Erffa 1973, pp. 5–7, and fig. 1; Rensselaer W. Lee, *Names on Trees: Ariosto into Art*, Princeton, 1977, pp. 65–70, 109–10, note 136, and fig. 48; Alberts 1978, pp. 54, 59, 63

No. 188 depicts a subject from the nineteenth canto of *Orlando Furioso* by Ariosto, in which, following the marriage of Angelica and Medoro, the newly-wed lovers inscribe their names on every stone and tree. This is by far the most frequently illustrated passage in *Orlando Furioso*, and its treatment by various artists from the sixteenth to the nineteenth centuries is the subject of an exemplary book by Rensselaer Lee, appropriately titled *Names on Trees*. Lee includes a brief discussion of No. 188, suggesting that West may have undertaken it as a compliment to Angelica Kauffmann, whom he had met in Florence in 1762.

West painted four, or possibly five, pictures of Angelica and Medoro, but No. 188 is the only one currently known. Since its acquisition by Binghamton it has generally been described as West's first treatment of the subject, begun probably in 1763. In style it does appear to have been painted in the first half of the 1760s, and it is reproduced (in reverse) in an engraving

by Richard Earlom published in 1768, so it must have been completed before then. However, no firm evidence establishes it as the first version, and until the other recorded versions come to light considerable uncertainty about the picture and its relation to West's other treatments of the theme must remain.

West's first version of the subject is one of two compositions, apart from portraits and copies, which his early biographers mention as having been painted in Rome. The companion picture of *Cymon and Iphigenia* (No. 195) is now lost. The brief account of West's life in *Public Characters of 1805* states that West painted the two during his final residence in Rome (to which he had returned in January 1763, after a long stay in Florence and a trip to Bologna, Parma, and Venice). The first volume of Galt's biography, published in 1816, describes *Cymon and Iphigenia* as preceding the *Angelica and Medoro* and states that both were well received in Rome, justifying the high opinion Anton Mengs had earlier expressed of West's talent (see No. 689). The memoir of West by William Carey published in the *New Monthly Magazine* in 1820 gives essentially the same information, but the second volume of Galt's biography, published in the same year, contradicts Galt's own earlier statement, asserting that *Angelica and Medoro* was the first picture West executed in England, and that he exhibited it together with the *Cymon and Iphigenia* painted in Rome and a portrait of General Monckton (No. 665), at the Society of Artists in 1764. Galt further states that Dr. Markham (for whom see No. 655) called on West while the artist was at work on the *Angelica and Medoro*.

Since the majority of sources, including Galt writing in West's lifetime, state that West painted the *Angelica and Medoro* in Rome, it is tempting to dismiss the differing account in Galt's second volume. There may, however, be some truth in it. While there is contemporary documentation which confirms that West painted *Cymon and Iphigenia* in Italy, notably two letters written by Robert Rutherford in 1763 (quoted under No. 195), none seems to exist for the *Angelica and Medoro*. West, writing to Joseph Shippen on 1 September 1763, stated explicitly that he painted only two pictures during his final stay in Rome: a copy of Guido's *Herodias* (No. 516), "and another picture which I composed as a study of my own." That picture must have been the *Cymon and Iphigenia*, but it is possible that West was not entirely honest to Shippen. He may have felt that he had to report the one independent composition he had shown to Rutherford, who in turn described it to Shippen, but that he should not let his patrons in Philadelphia know that he had taken further time away from making the copies for which they were paying him. It is also possible, as proposed by Rensselaer Lee, that West began an *Angelica and Medoro* in Rome, but completed it later. If we accept No. 188 as his first version of the subject, the background does sustain Lee's suggestion that West painted that part of the picture after he had seen the rolling downs and grazing sheep of the English countryside.

West did exhibit pictures of *Cymon and Iphigenia* and *Angelica and Medoro* as companions at the Society of Artists in 1764, and, according to the early lists of his works, which describe the two as painted in Rome, they were subsequently together in the collection of a Mr. Mitten who was presumably the Mr. Mytton included in a group portrait painted in Rome in 1760 or 1761 by Nathaniel Dance (ill. p. 25), which also included West's early patron in Rome, Thomas Robinson (see No. 689). Mytton must have been back in England in 1764, when he was elected to membership of the Society of Dilettanti. The other recorded versions of the subject are discussed in the following entries (Nos. 189–92). One of them was lent to the British Institution in 1833 (no. 10) by James Dunlop, but without further evidence it is impossible to say which it was.

The three works that West sent to the Society of Artists in 1764 were his first publicly exhibited works. According to both Carey and Galt, West exhibited them at the express request of Joshua Reynolds and Richard Wilson and, according to Carey, the praise they received was one of the factors that induced West to remain in England rather than return to America. That the *Cymon and Iphigenia* and *Angelica and Medoro* were generally well received is indicated by Horace Walpole's unenthusiastic comment in the margin of his catalogue: "These are much admired, but are very tawdry in the manner of Baroccio." An anonymous writer in the *Public Advertiser* signing himself Crito also questioned the praises West was attracting: "Until Mr. West exhibits some more striking Performances than those he has already done, surely the glorious title of the American Raphael can never be, without Irony, bestowed on him."[1]

See also pp. 33–36 above.

[1] V and A Cuttings, I, pp. 39–40 (*Public Advertiser*, 5 May 1764). West's paintings are not mentioned specifically by name, but the discussion of West appears in a review of the Society of Artists' exhibition.

189 Angelica and Medoro

LOCATION UNKNOWN

PROV: (?) Thomas Newton, Bishop of Bristol (1704–1782); Henry Hope, London (died 1811); his sale, Christie's, London, 27–29 June 1816, lot 83 ("Angelica and Medoro") sold for £106.1.0.

LISTED: *PC*, p. 562 ("Angelica and Madora," in the collection of Henry Hope, Esq.: First painted for the late Bishop of Bristol); *UM*, p. 528; Barlow, p. 433; Galt, p. 221; Dillenberger, p. 155 (170)

In *Public Characters* the list of works owned by Henry Hope is prefaced by the words "First painted for the late Bishop of Bristol."[1] The late bishop referred to was presumably Thomas Newton (1704–1782), who was Bishop of Bristol from 1761 until his death and an important early patron of West (see No. 675). If West did paint No. 189 for Newton, then the picture might well date from as early as 1765, and could even be identical with the painting now in Binghamton (No. 188), which we know was painted before 1768, when it was engraved. According to the second volume of Galt's biography of West, the artist was working on a painting of *Angelica and Medoro* when Dr. Markham, the Master of Westminster School, called on him, and it was Markham who introduced West to Newton; so it does not seem out of the question that Newton might either have purchased the painting upon which West was engaged or have commissioned another version. Also, if the *Damsel and Orlando* (No. 193) is properly identified (in the entry for No. 193) as the painting described in the catalogue of the Hope sale as the companion of No. 189, then No. 189 presumably had dimensions of approximately 36 × 28 in., corresponding to the size of No. 193. That is also the size of No. 188, the Binghamton picture, which again suggests the possibility of that work's being the Hope picture rather than the painting listed in *Public Characters* as painted in Rome and belonging to Mr. Mitten.

On the other hand, it is clear that all the works in Hope's collection were not originally painted for Newton, although the organization of the lists in *Public Characters* and the *Universal Magazine* implies that they were. (No. 193, for example, is dated *1793*, eleven years after Newton's death, and another work in the group is No. 640, the group portrait of the Hope family painted in 1802). Thus it is not certain what work or works in Hope's collection had previously belonged to Newton, or indeed if any one of them had. Also, Galt gives no indication that Newton purchased an *Angelica and*

Medoro from West, although he both states that West was at work on the subject when Dr. Markham visited him and mentions two works that Newton did commission from the artist following Markham's introduction.[2] And finally, if Nos. 189 and 193 were companion pictures, as there seems little reason to doubt, it is more likely that the two would have been painted at approximately the same time, rather than one some thirty years after the other, and that the time would have been in or near 1793, the date on No. 193.

[1]The phrase is repeated in the *Universal Magazine* and in *La Belle Assemblée*, but in the latter the titles of Hope's pictures do not appear, having been left out evidently by a printer's error. Barlow lists the pictures as in Hope's collection without indication of any earlier owner, while Galt omits all indication of their owners.

[2]Galt 1820, pp. 6 and 9.

190 Angelica and Medoro

LOCATION UNKNOWN

PROV: Painted for General Lawrence (? Stringer Lawrence, 1697–1775); Park or Pauch Esq., by 1804 (? Sir Robert Palk, 1717–1798)

LISTED: *PC*, p. 564 ("Angelica and Madora," painted for General Lawrence, and in the possession of Park, Esq.); *UM*, p. 529; Barlow, p. 433; *BA*, p. 16 (. . . Pauch, Esq., originally painted for General Lawrence); Galt, p. 224; Dillenberger, p. 163 (238)

No. 190 is one of four pictures described in the early lists of West's works as painted for General Lawrence and subsequently in the possession of Park or Pauch. For discussion, see No. 251. The one datable work in this group, which may give some indication of when Lawrence patronized West, is No. 251, which appeared at the Royal Academy in 1771.

191 Angelica and Medoro

LOCATION UNKNOWN

(36 × 28 in.) (91.5 × 71 cm.)

PROV: Offered by West's sons to the United States in 1826 (44) and sold by them, Robins, London, 22–25 May 1829, lot 172 ("Angelica and Medora," 3 ft. × 2 ft. 4 in.) bt. by Meek for £45.5.0.

EXH: West's Gallery 1822–28 (12)

LISTED: *PC*, p. 566 ("The second picture of Angelica and Madora," West, Painting-room); *UM*, p. 530; Barlow, p. 434; *BA*, p. 17; Galt, p. 228; Dillenberger, p. 172 (330)

In *Public Characters* and all the other early lists of West's works, the entry following that for No. 191 is for a painting listed (by a ditto) as "The second picture of the [or a] Damsel and Orlando." Although the two works were not sold at the same time following West's death and were never explicitly described as companion pictures, it seems likely that West intended them as a pair, replicating the pair of paintings of the same subjects in the collection of Henry Hope (Nos. 189 and 193). The second *Damsel and Orlando* is No. 194 below; its dimensions correspond to those given in 1826 and 1829 for No. 191.

192 Madora

LOCATION UNKNOWN

LISTED: *PC*, p. 563 ("A picture of Madora"); *UM*, p. 529; *BA*, p. 15; Galt, p. 222; Dillenberger, p. 158 (203)

Madora is the spelling of Medoro in the entries for the paintings of *Angelica and Medoro* (Nos. 188–91) in all the early lists of West's works. The title of No. 192 implies that it showed only the single figure of Medoro, but it is possible that it was yet another version of the subject of Nos. 188–91.

193 The Damsel and Orlando 1793

TOLEDO MUSEUM OF ART, TOLEDO, OHIO

Oil on canvas: $35\frac{7}{8} \times 27\frac{15}{16}$ (91.1 × 71 cm.)

Signed lower left: *B. West/1793*

PROV: Henry Hope, London (died 1811); his sale Christie's, London, 27 June 1816, lot 84 ("Historical, the companion" [to lot 83, "Angelica and Medoro", see No. 189 above]), for £64.1.0; purchased in 1912 from Cooper and Griffith, New York, by Florence Scott Libbey and given by her to the Toledo Museum of Art in the same year

LISTED: *PC*, p. 562 ("The Damsel and Orlando," in the collection of Henry Hope, Esq.); *UM*, p. 528; Barlow, p. 433; Galt, p. 221; Dillenberger, p. 155 (170)

LIT: Gardner and Feld, 1965, p. 32

The Toledo Museum of Art acquired No. 193 in 1912 as a painting of an unidentified subject and until 1965 catalogued it as "The Hero Returned" without specification of a literary or historical source. A second, unfinished, version of the composition in the Metropolitan Museum (No. 194), which corresponds to No. 193 in all significant details, had also long eluded correct identification and for many years was called a scene from *The Tempest* by Shakespeare.

193

In 1965 Albert Ten Eyck Gardner and Stuart Feld identified the source of the paintings as the twenty-third canto of *Orlando Furioso* by Ariosto. Orlando had given to Angelica a golden bracelet adorned with rich jewels. She, in turn, following her marriage to Medoro and their idyllic honeymoon (see Nos. 188–92), presented it to a shepherd and his wife in recompense for their hospitality. Orlando, coming later to the shepherd's house and already grieving for the loss of Angelica, is told about the lovers' stay there by the shepherd, who concludes his story by having the bracelet shown to Orlando. This blow so affects Orlando that it drives him to madness, the "Furioso" of the poem's title. The moment when Orlando sees the bracelet seems clearly to be the subject of Nos. 193 and 194. Orlando's horse, Brigliadoro, upon whom he has just arrived at the shepherd's house, is on the right, and his golden spurs and armor, which he removes before the shepherd tells him the story, are prominently displayed in the upper right and lower left. Gardner and Feld state the shepherd's wife shows Orlando the bracelet, and this may be what West intended, but Ariosto's text only says that the shepherd had the bracelet brought in, without mentioning the shepherd's wife; hence, the prominent role of the female figure holding the bracelet in the paintings and her even greater prominence in the title, "The Damsel and Orlando," which appears in the lists of West's works is somewhat at odds with his source.[1]

The painting is signed and dated and is more highly finished than No. 194, which is not signed. No. 193 would, therefore, seem almost certainly to be the version of the picture which belonged to Henry Hope, while No. 194 would have remained in West's Painting-room. Hope's picture was described in 1816 as a companion to his painting of *Angelica and Medoro* (No. 189) and it also appears immediately following No. 189 in *Public Characters* and the other early lists of West's works, although without being described as a companion. Which of the four or five recorded versions of *Angelica and Medoro* was the one in Hope's collection is discussed in the entry for No. 189. No. 193 is approximately the same size as the one version of *Angelica and Medoro* now known (No. 188).

[1] Neither of the two translations of *Orlando Furioso* that West could have known, that by Sir John Harington of 1591 or that by John Hoole of 1783, refers either to the shepherd's wife or to a damsel in relation to the encounter between Orlando and the shepherd.

194

194 The Damsel and Orlando

METROPOLITAN MUSEUM OF ART, NEW YORK

Oil on canvas: 36 × 28 in. (91.5 × 71 cm.)

PROV: Sold by West's sons, Robins, London, 20–22 June 1829, lot 64 ("Composition from Ariosto"); Arthur E. S. Seguin (1809–52) by 1851; by descent to Mrs. E. S. R. Seguin; on deposit in the Pennsylvania Academy, Philadelphia, from *c.* 1851 to *c.* 1864, and at the Metropolitan Museum from 1881 to 1923, when purchased by the museum from Mrs. Seguin

EXH: PAFA 1851 (249) "Scene from The Tempest," lent by S. Seguin, and again in most subsequent years through 1856; *The Painter and the New World*, Montreal Museum of Fine Arts, 1967 (209)

LISTED: *PC*, p. 566 ("The second picture of a Damsel and Orlando," West, Painting-room); *UM*, p. 530; Barlow, p. 434 ("The Damsel and Orlando"); *BA*, p. 17 ("The second picture of the Damsel and Orlando"); Galt, p. 228; Dillenberger, p. 172 (331)

LIT: Gardner and Feld 1965, pp. 32–33

No. 194 corresponds closely to No. 193 in all significant details, but it is more roughly painted, and significant parts, such as Orlando's garments, are unfinished. Also, unlike No. 193, it is not signed. Hence, it probably was the version of the subject that remained unsold in West's possession. No. 193 which belonged to Henry Hope, was a companion to the *Angelica and Medoro* in the same collection (No. 189), and No. 194 seems to have been the companion of another *Angelica and Medoro* (No. 191), which also remained West's property and which immediately precedes it in all the early lists of the artist's works. The two paintings were, however, sold separately in 1829: No. 191 was in the main sale of paintings from West's estate on 22–25 May, while No. 194, perhaps because of its unfinished state, was in the sale of lesser works on 20–22 June.

195 Cymon and Iphigenia 1763

LOCATION UNKNOWN

PROV: (?) Commissioned in 1762 by Richard Dalton for George III; Mr. Mitten, Shropshire (? John Mytton, Halston, Shropshire, 1737–1783) by or before 1804

EXH: SA 1764 (132) "Cymon and Iphigenia," companion to no. 131, "Angelica and Medoro" (see No. 188)

LISTED: *PC*, p. 565 ("Cymon and Iphigenia, and Angelica and Madora—in the possession of Mr. Mitten, of Shropshire, painted at Rome" [listed with pictures in West's Painting-room]); *UM*, p. 530; Barlow, p. 434; *BA*, p. 17; Galt, p. 226; Dillenberger, p. 169 (300)

LIT: *Public Characters* 1805, pp. 529 and 532; Galt 1816, p. 142; Galt 1820, p. 6; Carey 1820, pp. 517–18; Gatty 1938–39, p. 81 (Horace Walpole, 1764); von Erffa 1973, pp. 5, 6, 11; Alberts 1978, pp. 51–54, 56, 63

West painted this painting in Rome in the winter and spring of 1763. Robert Rutherford, the Leghorn merchant who had taken an almost parental interest in West since his arrival in Italy, described it in a letter to Joseph Shippen, written after West had visited Leghorn during his trip from Rome to London in the summer of 1763:

His figures are half life. Iphigenia has two female attendants who sleep as Soundly as herself, and in the background at a proper and respectfull distance, lies Stretched her drowsy Squire: Cymon and two Little Loves are the waking figures. He fixed in Stupid amaze on the Beauties of Iphigenia, and they looking like two Little Rogues who in spight of their tender age begin to know what's what. I am assured by good authority that this performance has been much admired by the Judges at Rome.[1]

The subject comes from the opening paragraphs of the first story, told by Pamfilo, on the fifth day of the *Decameron* by Giovanni Boccaccio. The story is also retold in English verse in the *Fables* of John Dryden. In both, Cymon is the doltish son of a wealthy family who, because he is so backward, has been sent to the country to live with the peasants. There he comes upon Iphigenia and her companions asleep, and the sight of Iphigenia's beauty, not only kindles admiration and love but also works a radical transformation of Cymon's hitherto (in Dryden's words) "heavy, dull, degenerate mind." The remainder of the story describes Cymon's adventurous pursuit and courtship of Iphigenia, concluding with their marriage, but the moment shown in No. 195 (and most paintings of the story) is Cymon's first sight of Iphigenia, when,

The fool of nature stood with stupid eyes,
And gaping mouth that testified surprise.
(*Dryden*)

West painted at least three versions of the subject (Nos. 195–97 and see also No. 228). According to Rutherford, Richard Dalton, the royal librarian who was in Italy making purchases for George III and who met West in Venice in the autumn of 1762, commissioned No. 195 from West for the King. However, there is no evidence to indicate that any painting of *Cymon and Iphigenia* by West ever entered the Royal Collection, the first recorded contact between West and George III otherwise, as well as West's first certain commission from the King, coming only in 1768 (see Nos. 10 and 33). The probable explanation of why No. 195 never reached the King is that West and Dalton did not follow the travel plans that they had intended at the time Dalton gave West the commission. Rutherford's letters indicate that Dalton originally suggested that West travel to England with him in 1763 but subsequently wrote to West breaking the arrangement, leaving West to travel on his own. Hence, Dalton did not meet West again and had no opportunity to see the completed painting until his own return to England, after West had exhibited No. 195, and after West probably had given up on him and found another purchaser.[2]

Whatever the circumstances of the commission, West painted No. 195 in Rome. On 22 April 1763, Rutherford passed on to Shippen a report from Rome that West was then at work on it, but was uncertain if he would be able to finish it before his departure. It was evidently the picture "composed as a study of my own" mentioned by West to Joseph Shippen in a letter dated 1 September 1763, describing his activities during the latter part of his stay in Italy,[3] and, as we have seen, it was described by Robert Rutherford, to whom West must have shown it on a visit to Leghorn in June 1763

immediately before his departure for England. Several early biographical accounts describe it and an *Angelica and Medoro* (see No. 188) as having been painted in Italy, but all of them give precedence to *Cymon and Iphigenia*, and, as discussed in the entry for No. 188, there is some question if the *Angelica and Medoro* was indeed painted in Italy. William Carey quotes the praises of both Anton Mengs and Pompeo Batoni for No. 195, but his report should be taken with more than a grain of salt, since Mengs had left Rome in August 1761, long before West commenced No. 195, and he did not return until 1771.[4]

West exhibited this painting and the companion *Angelica and Medoro* at the Society of Artists in 1764, where they received considerable, but not entirely enthusiastic, attention (see No. 188), and they appear together in the early lists of West's works as being in the same collection. If the companion is properly identified as the painting now in Binghamton (No. 188), No. 195 presumably had the same dimensions of 36 × 28 in. This is in keeping with Rutherford's description of Dalton's commission to West "to paint a small composition for his Majesty," but perhaps less so with Rutherford's subsequent description of the figures in the actual painting as "half life."

In addition to West's later paintings of the subject (Nos. 196, 197 and possibly 228) several drawings are also recorded.[5] The one drawing known to the compilers of this catalogue (Historical Society of Pennsylvania)[6] is clearly much later in date than the 1760s and has little resemblance either to Rutherford's des-

cription of No. 195 or to West's second painting of the subject (No. 196).

[1] American Philosophical Society, Philadelphia (quoted in Alberts 1978, pp. 53–54). The letter dated 21 June 1763 is on the same sheet as another letter from Rutherford to Joseph Shippen dated 22 April 1763, which is also quoted in this entry. The letter of 21 June opens by acknowledging that the preceding letter is a copy of what Rutherford had written in April.

[2] Michael Levey (in *The Later Italian Pictures in the Collection of Her Majesty the Queen*, London, 1964, p. 29) implies that Dalton remained in Italy through at least part of 1764; more precise information about Dalton's movements is difficult to come by. Rutherford, in writing to Joseph Shippen on 21 June 1763, stated that West had received a letter in Rome from Dalton telling him that Dalton would be unable to meet him in Rome or fix another meeting place because of the uncertainty of his own plans. Rutherford's previous letter in April had reported West's intention of travelling with Dalton.

[3] Richardson 1978, p. 23.

[4] Thomas Pelzel, *Anton Raphael Mengs and Neoclassicism*, New York and London, 1979, pp. 127 and 147–48.

[5] S. Leigh Sotheby, London, 1 June 1839, lot 77 (pen and ink, washed with bistre); and Christie's, London, 18 March 1898, lots 102 and 112.

[6] Pen and ink, $12\frac{1}{2} \times 18\frac{3}{4}$ in.

196 Cymon and Iphigenia *c.* 1766

PRIVATE COLLECTION

Oil on panel: 32 × 24 in. (81.5 × 61 cm.)

196

PROV: Probably commissioned or purchased by the second Marquess of Rockingham (1730–1782), Wentworth Woodhouse, Yorkshire; his nephew and heir, the fourth Earl Fitzwilliam (1748–1833); by descent to the eighth Earl Fitzwilliam (1910–1948); his sale, Christie's, London, 11 June 1948, lot 35; Antiques and Old Masters Limited, London, by 1952; purchased in London before 1958 by the late Herman H. Stone, Scarsdale, New York

EXH: SA 1766 (181) "Cymon and Iphigenia", with no. 182 "Diana and Endymion" (No. 137) as its companion; New York 1962 (6)

LISTED: PC, p. 565 ("Cymon and Iphigenia, and Endymion and Diana, at Wentworth Castle, Yorkshire" [listed with pictures in West's Painting-room]; UM, p. 530; BA, p. 17; Galt, p. 226; Dillenberger, pp. 168–69 (299)

LIT: V and A Cuttings, I, pp. 68–69 (Public Advertiser, April 1766); Gatty 1938–39, p. 81 (Horace Walpole, 1766)

In the concluding paragraph of the first chapter of his volume devoted to West's life in London, Galt states that in 1765 Dr. Markham (for whom see No. 655) introduced West to the Bishops of Bristol and Worcester and to the Archbishop of York, all of whom commissioned works from the artist. He contrasts this encouragement to the negligence of the fine arts by the nobility and opulent gentry, but then cites one "illustrious exception" to the bad behavior of the latter groups: "Lord Rockingham offered Mr. West a regular, permanent engagement of £700 per annum to paint historical subjects for his mansion in Yorkshire." West declined the offer, but No. 196 and its companion, Diana and Endymion (No. 137), were recorded in Public Characters and the other lists, as being at Rockingham's vast Yorkshire seat, Wentworth Woodhouse (called Wentworth Castle in the lists), and they remained there until 1948.

West's introduction to Rockingham must have been via Markham, either directly, or possibly through Edmund Burke, to whom he was introduced by Markham, but when that occurred is not clear. Galt implies that it was in 1765, but since he misdates West's marriage, placing it in September 1765, rather than 1764, while stating that it followed Rockingham's offer, his account is not a reliable indication. Nos. 196 and 137, however, must have been completed by April 1766, when West sent them to exhibition at the Society of Artists.

The relation of No. 196 to the lost Cymon and Iphigenia that West had exhibited two years earlier (No. 195) is a matter for speculation. The two putti in No. 196 would seem to correspond to the "two Little Loves" which figure prominently in Robert Rutherford's description of No. 195, but Rutherford's drowsy squire in the background is not visible in No. 196, and the full-length figures in a painting only 32 in. high are at odds with Rutherford's description of the figures in No. 195 as "half life."

For critical reaction to the pictures West exhibited in 1766, see Pylades and Orestes (No. 186).

197 Cymon and Iphigenia

LOCATION UNKNOWN

PROV: Sold by West's sons, Robins, London, 20–22 June 1829, lot 96 ("Cimon and Iphigenia, an early picture")

LISTED: BA, p. 17 ("Cymon and Iphigenia, and Endymion and Diana; at Wentworth Castle, Yorkshire—duplicate with Mr. West"); Dillenberger, pp. 168–69 (299)

198 The Bard 1809

PRIVATE COLLECTION

Oil on canvas: 96 × 72 in. (244 × 183 cm.)

Signed bottom center: B. West/1809

PROV: Offered by West to the Pennsylvania Academy in 1809 ("The picture, life [-sized] of Gray's Bard—now exhibited at the Academy," 8 ft. × 6, £250); offered by his sons to the United States in 1826 (15) and sold by them, Robins, London, 22–25 May 1829, lot 43 ("The Bard," 8 ft. × 6 ft.), bt. by Ward, presumably on behalf of Raphael West, for £178.10.0.; sold by Raphael West, Robins, London, 16 July 1831, lot 42; H. A. J. Munro of Novar; his sale, Christie's, London, 11 May 1867, lot 25; James O'Byrne (1835–1897)

EXH: RA 1809 (119) "The Bard, from Gray's Pindaric ode":

> On a rock whose haughty brow
> Frowns o'er Conway's foaming flood,
> Rob'd in the sable garb of woe,
> With haggard eyes the poet stood;
> (Loose his beard, and hoary hair
> Stream'd, like a meteor to the
>   troubled air,)
> And with a master's hand, and
>   prophet's fire,
> Struck the deep sorrow of his lyre.

BI 1811 (29) "The Bard, from Gray," 9 ft. 7 in. × 7 ft. 8 in. (including frame); West's Gallery 1822–28 (87); Liverpool 1976 (74)

ENGR: Engraving (16 3/16 × 11 7/8 in.) by John Charles Bromley, Jr., not dated, but executed c. 1815[1]

LIT: Kraemer 1975, pp. 50–51 and fig. 34 (the Bromley engraving); The Tate Gallery 1974–6: Illustrated Catalogue of Acquisitions, London, 1978, pp. 41–42

Thomas Gray's "Bard" was composed between 1754 and 1757 and published in the latter year by Horace Walpole. The poet explained the subject in a preface to the poem: "The following Ode is founded on a tradition current in Wales, that Edward the First, when he compleated the Conquest of that country, ordered all the Bards, that fell into his hands, to be put to death." The lines that accompanied No. 198 in the Royal Academy catalogue of 1809 (quoted above) come from the second stanza (or first Antistrophe) of the poem and are preceded by a description of the setting and of

Edward's army, upon whom the Bard calls down his curses. The opening words of the poem are "Ruin seize thee, ruthless King!," and according to the Robins sale catalogue of 1829, the sight of No. 198 prompted the actress Mrs. Siddons to exclaim them, "with the poetic fervor of sudden inspiration."

Gray in a note to "The Bard" stated that the image of his protagonist was taken from Raphael's figure of God in the Vision of Ezekiel (Pitti Palace, Florence), but in 1775 William Mason quoted Gray as saying that the figure of Moses Breaking the Law by Parmigianino (Chiesa della Steccata, Parma) "came still nearer to his meaning than the picture of Raphael."[2] West was probably well aware of both references, as they appeared in Mason's edition of Gray's poems published in 1775. In 1790 Reynolds cited Gray's indebtedness to Parmigianino's Moses in his final Discourse.[3] There are notable similarities between West's Bard and both his own and Parmigianino's depictions of Moses, and these may be the result of West's consciousness of Gray's visual sources. An earlier oil sketch of the subject (No. 199), although recognizable as the Bard because of the lyre and the armies in the lower left, seems so like an image of Moses, that it is tempting to think that West may have conceived it initially as a figure of Moses. The sketch is dated 1778, three years after Mason's comments were published, and they may have given West the idea of transforming one subject into the other. Conversely, a much later drawing showing Moses either receiving or breaking the tables of the law (discussed under No. 257) has affinities with No. 198.

The subject of the Bard was treated by several English artists of the late eighteenth and early nineteenth centuries. The earliest illustrations are drawings by Richard Bentley (collection of Wilmarth S. Lewis, Farmington, Connecticut), and there are well-known paintings of the subject by Thomas Jones (National Museum of Wales, Cardiff), William Blake (Tate Gallery, London), and John Martin (Laing Art Gallery, Newcastle, and Yale Center for British Art, New Haven). Engravings based on drawings by Philip James de Loutherbourg, Richard Corbould, Henry Fuseli, and Richard Westall were published in 1784, 1796, 1801, and 1808.[4] With the possible exception of the illustration by Westall, which is discussed below, none of these works seem to have much relation to either of West's treatments of the subject.

West painted No. 198 too late for it to be included in the lists of his works published in Public Characters and subsequently, but the smaller version, dated 1778 (No. 199), upon which he evidently based No. 198 does

The Bard, drawing by West or Raphael West. Private collection

appear in the lists. The lists also include a drawing of the subject,[5] which may be a large and elaborate drawing now in a private collection in Illinois (p. 266).[6] It shows an entirely different composition, with Edward and his soldiers dominating the scene, and is slightly reminiscent of one of the illustrations by Richard Bentley. A drawing which shows essentially the same composition as No. 198 went through the market in 1966,[7] and three further related drawings are in the Pierpont Morgan Library.[8]

A large painting of the *Bard* now in the San Antonio Museum of Art, which was sold at Christie's in 1968, and again in 1969 and 1970, as by West,[9] is either by or after Richard Westall, who exhibited a painting of *The Bard, from Gray* at the Royal Academy in 1801. The San Antonio painting corresponds to a detail of Westall's frontispiece for Thomas Park's edition of *The Poetical Works of Thomas Gray* published in 1808.[10] It is possible that this small engraving, which shows distinct similarities in composition with Nos. 198 and 199, inspired West to undertake his large painting of the subject (No. 198) in the following year.

[1] A letter dated 16 January 1815 from William Bromley, the father of John Charles, to West states that the plate of the *Bard* "engraved by my son . . . has not yet been printed" (Historical Society of Pennsylvania, quoted in Kraemer 1975, p. 51.).
[2] H. W. Starr and J. R. Hendrickson, eds., *The Complete Poems of Thomas Gray*, Oxford, 1966, p. 209.
[3] Sir Joshua Reynolds, *Discourses on Art*, Robert Wark, ed., New Haven, 1966, p. 238. This reference was pointed out by Edward Morris in his entry for No. 198 in Liverpool 1976.
[4] See F. I. McCarthy, "The Bard of Thomas Gray: Its Composition and its Use by Painters," *National Library of Wales Journal*, XIV, 1965, pp. 105–13, and Arthur S. Marks, "The Source of John Martin's 'The Bard,'" *Apollo*, LXXXIV, Aug. 1966, "The Paul Mellon Foundation for British Art: Notes on British Art 6," pp. 1–2.
[5] *PC*, p. 569 ("The Drawing of the Bard from Gay [*sic*]," West, Gallery); *UM*, p. 532 (. . . from Gray . . .); *BA*, p. 19; Galt, p. 234; Dillenberger, p. 186 (478).
[6] Pen, etc., 19 × 36¼ in., on several sheets joined together. It should be pointed out, however, that this drawing looks more like the work of Raphael West than of Benjamin. It does have a West family provenance, but that would be consistent with works by Raphael as well as with those by his father.
[7] Pen, sepia ink, and wash, 8⅜ × 4⅜ in.; sold Sotheby's, London, 23 Nov. 1966, lot 249.
[8] Black chalk on red-ruled paper, 5⅛ × 3½ in.; black chalk on blue paper, 10¾ × 17⅝ in.; and pen and brown ink, 5⅜ × 4 in.; Kraemer 1975, pp. 50–51 (88–90) and pls. 58 and 59.
[9] Christie's, London, 22 Nov. 1968, lot 5; 20 June 1969, lot 1; and 19 Nov. 1970, lot 3.
[10] This connection was pointed out by Nancy Heiner.

199 The Bard 1778

TATE GALLERY LONDON

Oil on panel: 11⁹⁄₁₆ × 9 in. (29.4 × 22.8 cm.)

Signed lower right: *B. West 1778*

PROV: Acquired by Mortimer Brandt, New York in 1969; Sabin Galleries, London, from whom purchased by the Tate Gallery in 1974

LISTED: *PC*, p. 567 ("The Sketch of the Bard—from Gray," West, Gallery); *UM*, p. 531; *BA*, p. 18; Galt, p. 231; Dillenberger, p. 179 (408)

LIT: *The Tate Gallery 1974–6: Illustrated Catalogue of Acquisitions*, London, 1978, pp. 41–42

Although No. 199 evidently served as a sketch for No. 198, there is an interval of over thirty years between the dates on the two works. There are numerous differences in detail, most notably in the Bard's dress and in the addition of ravens and eagles

199

(from the third stanza of the poem) in the lower left of No. 198, but, apart from the manner in which the Bard holds his lyre, the pose and placement of the figure in both paintings are similar. As discussed in the entry for No. 198, the Bard in No. 199 may have had his origin as a figure of Moses.

A slight drawing of a bearded figure on a cliff in a pose similar but not identical to that in No. 199 belonged at one time to a descendant of the artist. This drawing does seem to show Moses carrying the tables of the law rather than a bard holding a lyre.

200 The Stolen Kiss (?)1769

GOVERNOR'S MANSION, ATLANTA, GEORGIA

Oil on canvas: 55¾ × 37½ in. (141.5 × 95 cm.)

Signed lower right: *B. West 17[?]69*

PROV: (?) Painted for General Lawrence (? Stringer Lawrence, 1697–1775); (?) Park or Pauch Esq., by 1804 (? Sir Robert Palk, 1717–1798); Milch Galleries, New York; Hirschl & Adler Galleries, New York, from whom acquired for the Governor's Mansion in Atlanta in 1967

EXH: *The Painter and the New World*, Museum of Fine Arts, Montreal, 1967 (208a) as "The Preparation of Psyche"; *American Paintings for Public and Private Collections*, Hirschl & Adler Galleries, New York, 1967–68 (11) as "Preparation of Psyche"

(?) LISTED: *PC*, p. 564 ("The stolen kiss" painted for General Lawrence and in the possession of Park, Esq.); *UM*, p. 529; Barlow, p. 433; *BA*, p. 16 (. . . Pauch, Esq.); Galt, p. 224; Dillenberger, p. 162 (237)

The early lists of West's works record two paintings of the *Stolen Kiss*. No. 200 is presumably one of them. A painting of the subject in the Museum of Fine Arts, Boston (No. 202) is signed and dated *1819* and hence would seem to have been painted too late to be on the lists, but, nonetheless, may be identical with the other (No. 201).

The subject of the stolen kiss comes from the pastoral drama *Il Pastor Fido* (or *The Faithful Shepherd*) by Giovanni Battista Guarini (1527–1612), which had a great and long-lived popularity in England. It was first translated in 1602, and between that year and 1736

there were no less than seven English editions.[1] West's two known paintings (Nos. 200 and 202) are both based on the first scene of the second act. This scene consists of a dialogue between the shepherd Mirtillo and his friend Ergasto, in which Mirtillo describes his encounter of a year earlier with Amarillis. Dressed as a girl in his sister's garments, Mirtillo observes the maidens of Arcadia having a kissing contest, with Amarillis, who has the fairest mouth, acting as judge. Mirtillo sneaks into the game, and his kiss not only wins the contest but also causes him to fall in love with Amarillis.

The date on this painting is extremely difficult to read. It is recorded as *1763* in the catalogues of two exhibitions in which No. 200 appeared in 1967, but that year is impossibly early. On stylistic grounds, it is likely that West painted No. 200 around 1770. For that reason we have tentatively associated it with the painting of the subject which West painted for General Lawrence, whose patronage of West seems to have occurred at about that time (see No. 251). West may have painted No. 200 as a companion to a lost *Angelica and Medoro* (No. 190), which was in the same collection.

The erotic content, which is inherent and explicit in the literary source, probably explains why West did not exhibit any of his paintings of the *Stolen Kiss* prior to the year before his death. Although he did exhibit paintings of *Angelica and Medoro* (No. 188) in 1764, *Rinaldo and Armida* (No. 228) in 1776, and *Cymon and Iphigenia* (Nos. 195, 196) in 1764 and 1766, as well as subjects from classical mythology with erotic content during the 1760s and 1770s, the dalliance depicted in Nos. 200 and 202 recalls too blatantly what was already being thought of as the dubious morality of French Rococo painting.[2] *Il Pastor Fido* itself suffered a sharp decline in English estimation during the second half of the eighteenth century for similar reasons.[3]

[1] See Nicholas J. Perella, *The Critical Fortune of Battista Guarini's "Il Pastor Fido,"* Florence, 1973, pp. 64–79.
[2] West's first biographer contrasts his early historical subjects, *Agrippina Landing at Brundisium* (No. 33) and *Regulus* (No. 10) with the debased state of the painting he had seen in France in 1763: "there it was humiliated to cherish and stimulate the lascivious passions, and the gaieties of frivolity and shew." (*Public Characters* 1805, p. 535).
[3] Perella, op cit., pp. 128–35.

201 The Stolen Kiss

LOCATION UNKNOWN

PROV: John Hobart, second Earl of Buckinghamshire (1723–1793)

LISTED: *PC*, p. 564 ("The stolen Kiss"—the late Lord Buckinghamshire); *UM*, p. 529; *BA*, p. 16; Galt, p. 225 ("The drawing of the Stolen Kiss"); Dillenberger, p. 163 (244)

Galt lists No. 201 as a drawing, and in *Public Characters* and the other early lists, this work and three others in the Buckinghamshire collection are listed with dittoes immediately following a work which is identified as a drawing. However, since three of the four Buckinghamshire pictures are currently known (Nos. 228, 243, and 535) and all three are oil paintings, the implicit identification of these works as drawings is clearly wrong. No. 201 appears as the first entry on a page in Galt's catalogue, and it is apparent that Galt translated the misleading "ditto" from *Public Characters* into the word "drawing" in keeping with his editorial practice of not beginning any page with a "ditto." Galt recorded the picture as still in the collection of a man who had died twenty-seven years previously, so it seems obvious that he did not insert the word "drawing" on the basis of familiarity with the actual work.

In the lists No. 201 appears between "Rebecca Receiving the Bracelets at the Well", (No. 243), which

200

202

is signed and dated *1775*, and "Rinaldo and Armida" (No. 228), which is signed and dated *1773*. These two paintings both measure 49 × 63 in.; if, as seems likely, No. 201 formed part of a group with them, then it presumably would have been of the same size (which is also the size of No. 202), and would have had a similar date. For a discussion of the possibility that Nos. 201 and 202 may be the same work, see the following entry.

202 The Stolen Kiss (?)1819

MUSEUM OF FINE ARTS, BOSTON

Oil on canvas: 48¾ × 62¾ in. (123.8 × 159.4 cm.)

Signed lower left: *Benjamin West 1819*

PROV: Offered by West's sons to the United States in 1826 (24) and sold by them, Robins, London, 22–25 May 1829, lot 155 ("The Stolen Kiss," 4 ft. 2 in. × 5 ft. 2 in.), bt. by G. Walker for £81.18.0.; George R. White, Boston; his sister, Mrs. Frederick J. Bradbury, Boston, by whom bequeathed to the Museum of Fine Arts in 1930

EXH: RA 1819 (157) "The stolen Kiss Vide Guarini's Pastor Fido, act ii, scene 1"; BI 1820 (214), . . ., 5 ft. 6 in. × 6 ft. 9 in. (including frame); West's Gallery 1822–28 (127)

LIT: Farington Diary, 3 April 1819 (Farington 1978—, xv, p. 5346); Boston 1969, I, pp. 283–84 (1020), II, fig. 99

The Boston catalogue cites an old label on the back of No. 202 describing it as West's last work. This claim is not strictly accurate (see No. 124); nonetheless, West was recorded as working on No. 202 within a year of his death and at a time when his health was failing. On 3 April 1819, Joseph Farington described in his diary a visit from Sir John Hayes, West's physician:

Hayes called and spoke of Mr. West as being in a poor state of health and of injuring himself by professional application. He has for a fortnight past been daily employed in preparing a picture for the Exhibition "*The Lover's Kiss*" from *Pastor Fido*. He is in his painting room at 8 o'clock in the morning and remains there till 6 in the evening, and is much exhausted by His over application. When Hayes observed on the injury he did himself, He said, "He must complete what He was engaged upon though it should cause his death."

West did complete the painting in time to send it, along with three other works, to the Royal Academy exhibition of 1819, his last appearance there. Two of the other three paintings (Nos. 7 and 26), and possibly the third as well (see No. 365), were works that West had painted at a much earlier date.

West also probably began No. 202 before 1819, although Farington's diary establishes that he was

working on it in that year. It is even possible that No. 202 is identical with No. 201, which the lists of his works establish had been painted definitely prior to 1793 and probably earlier still. One other work known to have been in the same collection as No. 201 was painted before 1770 (No. 535) and the other two are dated 1773 and 1775 (Nos. 228 and 243). Features of No. 202, particularly Mirtillo's hair and the pose of one of the heads on the right, recall paintings such as *Fidelia and Speranza* of 1776 (No. 222) and suggest that No. 202 had its origins in the 1770s as well, but the severe profile of Amarillis, which is a conspicuous and discordant element of the composition, is more reminiscent of paintings from after 1800, such as the *Cupid and Psyche* of 1808 (No. 152). Thus it is probable that West began No. 202 long before it was completed in its present form. Whether or not it could be a picture that he had previously sold must remain a question. He certainly did reacquire some of his earlier paintings (including Nos. 7 and 26, which he exhibited with No. 202 in 1819) and he did repaint previously completed works, much to the distress of Farington and Lawrence.[1] The size of No. 202 is also approximately the same as the probable size of No. 201, further encouraging the suspicion that they might be the same work, but there seems to be no documentary evidence to confirm it.

[1]Farington Diary, 3 Sept. 1819 (Farington 1978—, xv, p. 5403).

203 Milton's Messiah

LOCATION UNKNOWN

EXH: RA 1809 (68) "Milton's Messiah, from the sixth book of Paradise Lost":

> Full soon among them he arriv'd, in his right hand
> Grasping ten thousand thunders, which he sent
> Before him, such as in their souls infix'd
> Plagues: they, astonish'd, all resistance lost,
> All courage; down their idle weapons dropt;
> O'er shields and helms and helmed heads he rode
> On throne and mighty seraphims prostrate,
> That wish'd the mountains now might be again
> Thrown on them, as a shelter from his ire!

Nothing is known about this painting apart from its inclusion in the catalogue of the Royal Academy exhibition of 1809. Suggestions have been made that a painting of the *Messiah* dated *1814* (No. 399) may be the same work as No. 203, which West repainted after exhibiting it in 1809, but the former painting is based on a passage from Revelation and does not have much evident relation to the lines from *Paradise Lost* quoted by West in 1809. A work whose imagery is closer to that of the quoted lines is the *Destruction of the Beast and False Prophet* of 1804 (No. 410). Enemies, who drop their weapons, and a Messiah with thunders in his right hand, who rides "O'er shields and helms and helmed heads," are both present in No. 410. However, Milton's immediately preceding lines (VI, 827 ff.) describe the Messiah riding in a chariot rather than on horseback; furthermore, West exhibited No. 410 at the Royal Academy in 1804 accompanied by a quotation from the nineteenth chapter of Revelation, which it illustrates more closely than Milton; so it seems that No. 203 cannot be identified with No. 410 either.

West also did several drawings showing what appears to be Miltonic imagery. The most elaborate of these is in the British Museum,[1] and related drawings are at Swarthmore[2] and in a private collection.[3] These three show a standing figure of Christ accompanied by an armed St. Michael triumphing over a seated or fallen satanic figure. In the privately owned drawing Christ does stand upon a chariot, but none of the three tallies sufficiently with the lines quoted by West in 1809 to suggest that they reflect the appearance of the missing painting.

[1] Pen and wash, 9¾ × 13¾ in.
[2] Pen and wash, 11⅛ × 10⅛ in.
[3] Pen and wash, 10½ × 12½ in.; exhibited New York 1962 (21).

204 The Grecian Daughter Defending Her Father 1794

NEWARK MUSEUM, NEWARK, NEW JERSEY

Oil on panel: 19 × 23 in. (48.5 × 58.5 cm.)

Signed upper right: *B. West/1794*

PROV: Painted for George Bowles, Wanstead (died 1817); Childs Gallery, Boston, from whom purchased by the Newark Museum in 1956

EXH: RA 1794 (23) "The Grecian daughter defending her father"; Allentown 1962 (22)

LISTED: *BA*, p. 19 ("The Grecian Daughter defending her father from the Tyrant—Its companion, the Couch scene of King Lear and his Daughter", painted for Mr. Bowles of Wanstead); Dillenberger, p. 188 (496)

The painting illustrates the final scene (act v, scene 3) of *The Grecian Daughter*, a tragedy by Arthur Murphy (1727–1805) first performed at the Drury Lane Theater in 1772. The daughter in the play's title is Euphrasia, whose father Evander, the rightful King of Syracuse,

204

has had his throne usurped by the tyrant Dionysius. In the moment shown, Dionysius intends to murder Evander, but Euphrasia throws herself between them, telling Dionysius to kill her rather than her aged father. The scene and play close with Euphrasia killing Dionysius, whereupon Evander returns to his throne. This is the climax of the play, but the most famous incident occurs in the second act, when Euphrasia suckles her starving father, who has been imprisoned by Dionysius, the idea for which Murphy was said to have derived from paintings of *Roman Charity*.[1]

Prior to West, William Hamilton, John Hoppner, and Robert Edge Pine had all made drawings or paintings of the subject.[2] West, in painting the *Grecian Daughter*, probably was inspired by performances of the play, since Murphy's tragedy was currently popular, but comparison of No. 204 with Hamilton's and Pine's more conventionally theatrical works demonstrates how far West departed from the details of costume, etc., as they would have appeared in an actual eighteenth-century production. He exhibited No. 204 together with a small version of *Lear and Cordelia* (No. 215) at the Royal Academy in 1794 and the two pictures are listed as companions in *La Belle Assemblée*. The Shakespearean painting, which is signed and dated *1793*, repeats a composition West had originally painted in the early 1780s (see No. 212). Hence, No. 204, which is dated *1794*, seems certainly to have been later in conception, and the fact that it was destined to be a companion to No. 215 must have dictated its appearance as much or more than current performances in the theater.

Nos. 204 and 215 appear only in the list of West's works published in *La Belle Assemblée* in 1808, and there they are at the very end among a small group of works which had evidently been overlooked when the earlier

lists were prepared. The Mr. Bowles for whom they are recorded as painted was George Bowles, of The Grove, Wanstead, who is best known as Angelica Kauffmann's greatest patron.[3]

A drawing of the subject was included in the group of West's drawings sold by Benjamin West, Jr. in 1839.[4]

[1] W. Oxberry, ed., *The Grecian Daughter: A Tragedy by Mr. Arthur Murphy*, London, 1821, pp. iii–iv.
[2] A painting by Hamilton, signed and dated *1780* and exhibited at the Royal Academy in that year, was sold, Sotheby's, London, 23 March 1977, lot 77. A print after this composition by James Caldwall, was published in 1789, and two impressions of it were sold by West's sons, Christie's, London, 1 July 1820, lot 76. A *Grecian Daughter* by Hoppner was exhibited at the Polygraphic Rooms in the Strand *c.* 1788 (no. 16). A print after Pine's *Grecian Daughter* by Caroline Watson was published in 1784.
[3] Lady Victoria Manners and G. C. Williamson, *Angelica Kauffmann, R.A.*, London, 1924, p. 58, and Cummings 1968, p. 120.
[4] S. Leigh Sotheby, London, 1 June 1839, lot 74.

205 Moonlight

LOCATION UNKNOWN

(18½ × 14 in.) (47 × 35.5 cm.)

PROV: Offered by West's sons to the United States in 1829 (137, "Moonlight—the Beckoning Ghost," 1 ft. 6½ in. × 1 ft. 2 in.)

EXH: RA 1804 (130) "Moonlight":

> What beck'ning ghost along the moonlight shade,
> Invites my steps, and points to yonder glade?
> "Tis she!"   *Vide Pope's Elegy*

LISTED: *PC*, p. 565 ("The small picture of Moonlight and the 'Beckoning Ghost' from Pope's Elegy," West, Painting-room); *UM*, p. 530; Barlow, p. 434; *BA*, p. 17; Galt, p. 228; Dillenberger, p. 171 (325)

The lines that accompanied No. 205 in the Royal Academy catalogue of 1804 are the opening lines of Alexander Pope's *Elegy to the Memory of an Unfortunate Lady*, first published in 1717.

206 Moonlight

LOCATION UNKNOWN

LISTED: *PC*, p. 567 ("The picture of Moonlight (small)," West, Gallery); *UM*, p. 531; *BA*, p. 18; Galt, p. 232; Dillenberger, p. 181 (423)

No. 206 may have been a second version of No. 205, but since both works have disappeared, and we do not know the appearance of either, their relationship is a matter of speculation.

207 Hamlet: Act IV, Scene V (Ophelia before the King and Queen) 1792

CINCINNATI ART MUSEUM, CINCINNATI, OHIO

Oil on canvas: 109 × 152½ in. (277 × 387 cm.)

Signed: *Benj West/1792*

PROV: Commissioned by John and Josiah Boydell for £525 to be part of Boydell's Shakespeare Gallery; sold, Christie's, London, 17–20 May 1805, second day, lot 56 ("Ophelia appearing before the King and Queen"), bt. by Robert Fulton (1765–1815) for £131.5.0.; placed on loan by Fulton in the Pennsylvania Academy of the Fine Arts, Philadelphia, until 1816; by descent to Fulton's widow and heirs, Mrs. Dale and Mrs. Roosevelt, and lent by them to the American Academy of Fine Arts, New York, 1816–28; purchased by Nicholas Longworth, Cincinnati (? for $430.00),[1] *c.* 1828; presented by his son, Joseph Longworth, to the Cincinnati Art Museum in 1882

EXH: The Shakespeare Gallery, Pall Mall, *c.* 1792–1805; PAFA 1807–16 (in published catalogues 1811–16, as "Ophelia" in 1811, and as "Hamlet (Act 4th, scene 5)" in 1812–16); AAFA 1816–28 ("Ophelia's Madness. Hamlet IV: 5," lent by Mrs. Fulton 1816–20, by Mrs. Dale 1821–27, and by Mrs. Roosevelt in 1828)

ENGR: Engraving (17¼ × 23¼ in.) by Francis Legat, pub. by J. and J. Boydell, 1 Dec. 1802, titled "Shakespeare/Hamlet/Act IV Scene V/Elsinore—King, Queen, Laertes, Ophelia, etc.," and accompanied by a quotation of lines 161–83 of this scene; outline engraving (3³⁄₁₆ × 4⁵⁄₁₆ in.) by A. Roumique, pub. in Hamilton 1831 (56) as "Scene from Hamlet"

LISTED: *UM*, p. 529 ("Ophelia and her brother before the King and Queen," Shakespeare Gallery); Barlow, p. 434 ("Ophelia distracted, before the king and queen," in the collection of Robert Fulton); *BA*, p. 19 ("Ophelia before the King and Queen, companion to the large picture of King Lear in the storm" [No. 210]; painted for the Shakespeare Gallery, but now in the Academy at Philadelphia); Dillenberger, pp. 165 (262) and 187 (487)

LIT: Farington Diary, 26 May 1804 and 5 May 1807 (Farington 1978—, VI, p. 2331 and VIII, p. 3038); V and A Cuttings, III, p. 814 (26 May 1805); Hamilton 1831 (56); Tuckerman 1867, p. 101; T. S. R. Boase, "Illustration of Shakespeare's Plays in the Seventeenth and Eighteenth Centuries," *Journal of the War-burg and Courtauld Institutes*, X, 1947, p. 102; Tinkcom 1951, p. 390 (Sir Augustus Foster); Theodore Sizer, "The American Academy of the Fine Arts," in Mary Bartlett Cowdrey, *American Academy of Fine Arts and American Art Union*, New York, 1953, pp. 18 and 47; W. Moelwyn Merchant, *Shakespeare and the Artist*, London, 1959, p. 72 and pl. 21a (Legat engraving); Winifred H. Friedman, *Boydell's Shakespeare Gallery*, New York and London, 1976, pp. 152, 239, and fig. 50 (Legat engraving); Alberts 1978, p. 342

As the various titles under which No. 207 was exhibited and engraved indicate, the painting shows the moment from the fourth scene of the fifth act of *Hamlet* when Laertes, already incensed at the death of Polonius, first observes Ophelia's madness. She is depicted scattering herbs and flowers, in accordance with the lines beginning, "There's rosemary, that's for remembrance . . .," which appear as part of the quotation printed on the Legat engraving.

No. 207 was West's second large painting for the Boydell Shakespeare Gallery. The earlier scene from *King Lear*, completed in time for the gallery's opening in 1789, is No. 210 below. An account from West to Boydell, dated 25 September 1792, "for the history of Ophelia with her brother before the King and Queen and *c.* from Hamlet—£525.0.0" is in the Historical Society of Philadelphia. Both paintings were engraved as part of a series of 100 large plates taken from the larger pictures in the Boydell gallery.[2] On 26 May 1804, West told Farington that he had looked over the Shakespeare prints and was sorry to see their poor quality; he approved of the print from his *Lear* by William Sharp, but mentioned "the print from *His Ophelia* as being a very inadequate performance."

Following the demise of the gallery, Robert Fulton purchased Nos. 207 and 210, and a painting of *Orlando and Oliver* from *As You Like It* by Raphael West.[3] The press announced at the time that Fulton had acquired them to be "the first ornament of a Gallery which is to be established" in Philadelphia, and Fulton did deposit them in the newly instituted Pennsylvania Academy of the Fine Arts, where they remained from 1807 until the year after Fulton's death in 1815. The three paintings were then transferred by Mrs. Fulton to the American Academy of Fine Arts in New York, which included them in its opening exhibition in 1816, and they remained together there until 1828, when they were dispersed. Before the paintings went to America in 1807, West retouched them. The noticeable difference between Laertes's hair in the Legat engraving of 1802 and its appearance in No. 207 is probably a result of this retouching.

In Philadelphia Nos. 207 and 210 were seen some time before 1812 by the British diplomat Sir Augustus Foster, who subsequently described them in his memoirs. After admiring No. 210, he continued:

A Picture that is hung opposite to this and of which the subject was taken from Hamlet, was extravagant and disgusting. The King and Queen appear as if they each had a Crick in the Neck. They told me it was also by West, but I could not believe it.

Two small versions of the subject are recorded (Nos. 208 and 209).

[1] This figure is given by Theodore Sizer in Mary Bartlett Cowdrey, *American Academy of Fine Arts and American Art Union*, New York, 1953, p. 47, and is evidently taken from the American Academy of Fine Arts Minutes for 7 November 1828. The Minutes, as cited by Sizer, do not record Longworth as the purchaser.

[2] Reproduced in *The Boydell Shakespeare Prints*, introduction by A. E. Santaniello, New York (Arno Press), 1979. Boydell also published 100 smaller plates as illustrations to a complete edition of Shakespeare's plays, which are also included in the Arno volume of 1979.

[3] *Orlando and Oliver* by Raphael West was lot 16 on the third day of the Shakespeare Gallery sale, Christie's, London, 20 May 1805, where it was catalogued as by Benjamin West. It fetched £25.4.0., as opposed to the price of £131.5.0. for No. 207 and £210.5.0. for No. 210. The engraving after it by William Charles Wilson, made as part of the Boydell series, is reproduced in Kraemer 1975, p. 89, fig. 53.

207

208 Hamlet: Act IV, Scene V (Ophelia before the King and Queen)

LOCATION UNKNOWN

(21 × 27 in.) (53.5 × 68.5 cm.)

PROV: Offered by West's sons to the United States in 1826 (103) and sold by them Robins, London, 22–25 May 1829, lot 99 ("Ophelia Before the King—Hamlet," 1 ft. 9 in. × 2 ft. 3 in., "Study for the large Picture of the same subject.—[Lot 163]"), bt. by Smith for £57.5.0.; (?) L. Dulacher, by 1833

EXH: West's Gallery 1822–28 (97) "Ophelia before the King—Hamlet"; (?) SA 1833 (306) "Hamlet, King, Laertes, Ophelia, etc.—Hamlet, Act IV, Scene 5," lent by L. Dulacher, Esq.

LISTED: PC, p. 565 ("The small picture of Ophelia before the King and Queen, with her Brother Laertis," West, Painting-room); UM, p. 530; Barlow, p. 434; BA, p. 17; Galt, p. 227; Dillenberger, p. 170 (313)

See No. 209.

209 Hamlet: Act IV, Scene V (Ophelia before the King and Queen)

LOCATION UNKNOWN

(21 × 27 in.) (53.5 × 68.5 cm.)

PROV: Sold by West's sons, Robins, London, 22–25 May 1829, lot 163 ("Ophelia Before the King.—Hamlet," 1 ft. 9 in. × 2 ft. 3 in.) bt. by Smith for £52.10.0.

Two small versions of No. 207 are listed in the sale of paintings from West's estate on 22–25 May 1829. The first of those, lot 99 (No. 208) was described as a "Study for the large Picture of the same subject.—(Lot 163)." Lot 163 (No. 209), however, was not the large picture, which had gone to America in 1807. Both lot 99 and lot 163 were listed with the same measurements. Hence, it is possible that the two lots were the same work, erroneously included twice, but the cross reference in the entry for lot 99 suggests that there were indeed two works. Both seem to have been bought by the same purchaser, who was probably an agent buying on behalf of the West family, but for slightly different prices.

Neither of the two small versions is now known. One of them is fairly fully recorded in early lists, etc., of West's works; that documentation is given under No. 208, although it is impossible to say to which of the two pictures sold in 1829 it in fact applies.

210 King Lear: Act III, Scene IV (King Lear in the Storm) 1788

See color illustration, p. 100

MUSEUM OF FINE ARTS, BOSTON

Oil on canvas: 107 × 144 in. (271.8 × 365.7 cm.)

Signed lower left: *B. West 1788/retouched 1806*

PROV: Commissioned by John and Josiah Boydell for £525 to be part of Boydell's Shakespeare Gallery; sold Christie's, London, 17–20 May 1805, third day, lot 55 ("King Lear in the Storm"), bt. by Robert Fulton for £210.5.0.; placed on loan by Fulton in the Pennsylvania Academy of the Fine Arts, Philadelphia, until 1816; by descent to Fulton's widow and heirs, Mrs. Dale and Mrs. Roosevelt, and lent by them to the American Academy of Fine Arts, New York 1816–28; bought by the Boston

Athenaeum in 1828 for $600.00; deposited by the Athenaeum in the Museum of Fine Arts, Boston, in 1876, and bought by the museum in 1979 (Henry H. and Zoe Oliver Sherman Fund)

EXH: The Shakespeare Gallery, Pall Mall, 1789–1805; PAFA 1807–16 (in published catalogues 1811–16); AAFA 1816–28 (lent by Mrs. Fulton 1816–20, by Mrs. Dale 1821–27, and by Mrs. Roosevelt in 1828)

ENGR: Engraving (17⅜ × 23⁵⁄₁₆ in.) by William Sharp, pub. by John and Josiah Boydell, 26 March 1793, titled "Shakspeare/King Lear/Act III. Scene IV/'Off, off, you lendings:/Come: unbutton here'—[Tearing off his clothes]"; outline engraving (3¼ × 4¹⁄₁₆ in.) by Normand *fils*, pub. in Hamilton 1831 (45) as "Lear in the Storm"

LISTED: UM, p. 529 ("King Lear in the Hovel," Shakespeare Gallery); Barlow, p. 434 ("King Lear in the storm," in the collection of Robert Fulton); BA, p. 19 ("The large picture of King Lear in the storm at the hovel on the heath; painted for the Shakespear Gallery, but now in the Academy at Philadelphia"); Dillenberger, pp. 165 (263) and 186 (486)

LIT: V and A Cuttings, II, p. 405 (Nov. 1788) and III, p. 814 (26 May 1805); [Richard Cumberland], *The Observer*, IV, no. 99, London, 1788, pp. 58–60; Henry Fuseli, "A Catalogue of Pictures in the Shakespeare Gallery," *Analytical Review*, May 1789, p. 112; *The Diary or Woodfall's Register*, 16 May 1789; *Public Advertiser*, 5 June 1789; Farington Diary, 26 May 1804 and 5 May 1807 (Farington 1978—, VI, p. 2331 and VIII, p. 3038); Hamilton 1831 (45); Charles Robert Leslie, *Autobiographical Recollections*, 1860, I, p. 28; Tuckerman 1867, pp. 101 and 627; T. S. R. Boase, "Illustration of Shakespeare's Plays in the Seventeenth and Eighteenth Centuries," *Journal of the Warburg and Courtauld Institutes*, X, 1947, p. 107; Tinkcom 1951, p. 390 (Sir Augustus Foster); Theodore Sizer, "The American Academy of the Fine Arts," in Mary Bartlett Cowdry, *American Academy of Fine Arts and American Art Union*, New York, 1953, pp. 18 and 47; Helmut von Erffa, "King Lear by Benjamin West," *Bulletin of the Rhode Island School of Design*, XLIII, Dec. 1956, pp. 6–8; W. Moelwyn Merchant, *Shakespeare and the Artist*, London 1959, p. 72; Evans 1959, pp. 76–77 and pl. 57; Cummings 1968, p. 101; Boston 1969, I, p. 283 (1019) and II, fig. 100; Winifred H. Friedman, *Boydell's Shakespeare Gallery*, New York and London, 1976, pp. 149–52, 239, and fig. 46; Wainwright 1978, p. 109; Alberts 1978, p. 342; Judy Sund, "Benjamin West: A Scene from King Lear," *Bulletin of the Detroit Institute of Arts*, LVIII, 1980, pp. 127–36.

No. 210 was the first of two paintings done by West for the Boydell Shakespeare Gallery; the second is No. 207 above. This gallery, which was certainly the most ambitious venture in patronage in eighteenth-century England, opened to the public on 4 May 1789 with an exhibition of thirty-four paintings and eventually contained some 167 works before its demise in 1805.[1] The project was undertaken by the printsellers Alderman John Boydell and his nephew Josiah Boydell and led to two series of engravings: 100 large plates, which were sold by subscription, and a like number of smaller engravings, which appeared as illustrations in a nine-volume complete edition of Shakespeare's plays. Although in a few cases the larger and smaller plates were based on the same painting, more frequently the different sizes of the engravings reflected the different sizes of two distinct sets of paintings, with the larger paintings being conceived on a public and monumental scale, rather than one determined by the needs of the engraver. The two paintings by West are both very

large, and both were engraved as large plates, that after No. 210 by William Sharp having been generally acknowledged as one of the most successful prints in the series.[2]

No. 210, which shows Lear and his companions on the heath, as described in the fourth scene of the third act of *King Lear*, is one of three major paintings from *King Lear* in the Boydell series. In narrative sequence it fits between *Lear Cursing Cordelia*, from the opening scene of the play, painted by Henry Fuseli (Art Gallery of Ontario, Toronto) and *Lear Weeping over the Dead Body of Cordelia*, from the final scene, painted by James Barry (Tate Gallery, London). These three paintings are all approximately the same size, and all three were commissioned and completed in time to appear together in the opening exhibition of the Boydell gallery in 1789.[3] However, to what extent either the Boydells or the artists may have conceived of the three as a sequence of related works is not known. The same scene from *Lear* as that depicted in this painting was also painted by Robert Smirke and engraved by Lewis Schiavonetti as one of the smaller plates in the Boydell's illustrated editions of Shakespeare's plays.

Between 1700 and 1830 the heath scene from *Lear* was the most frequently depicted of all Shakespearean subjects,[4] and it would seem to have been one of the plum commissions of the Boydell undertaking. West received £525 for No. 210, as opposed to Barry's £315 and Fuseli's £262.10.0., for their *Lear* paintings, and William Sharp was paid £840 to engrave it, a figure far surpassing that recorded for any other engraving in the series.[5] Whether West chose the subjects of his Boydell paintings, or whether they were chosen for him, is not recorded. The Boydells had made more money from the sale of engravings after his paintings, in particular the *Death of General Wolfe* (No. 93), than from the work of any other artist, and West himself was present at the dinner at which the gallery was conceived. George Romney, who was also present at the same dinner, is generally credited with first suggesting the project, but West was never reticent about looking after his own interests. Certainly, the fact that his son Raphael received a commission for a large painting from *As You Like It* for the series is a testimonial to West's influence.

The main figures in No. 210 are, from left to right, Gloucester, the Fool, Lear, Kent, and Edgar. The line quoted on the Sharp engraving immediately precedes the entrance of Gloucester carrying a torch. Two small figures visible in the distance in the lower left represent Cordelia and her maid Arante who, according to Shakespeare's text, do not belong in this scene. Their inclusion reflects eighteenth-century performances of *Lear*, all of which followed the adaptation by Nahum Tate, first performed in 1681. Tate introduced into the play a romance between Edgar and Cordelia, and the latter in the third act, instead of being in France, where Shakespeare has sent her, wanders onto the heath, where she is attacked by two ruffians and saved by Edgar. On the other hand, West's main figures do not accord with Tate's version, which eliminates the Fool. He was thought to lower the tone of the play and, hence, was never seen on the eighteenth-century stage.

West completed No. 210 by November of 1788, when according to an unidentified clipping in the Victoria and Albert Museum, it was already in the hands of the engraver. An oil sketch, which West exhibited at the Royal Academy in 1789 simultaneously with the appearance of No. 210 in the opening exhibition of the Boydell gallery, is No. 211 below. West retouched Nos. 207 and 210 in his studio between 1805 and 1807, but what he may have done to No. 210 at that time is difficult to determine. Copies of No. 210 are in the Museum of the Rhode Island School of Design[6] and in a private collection,[7] and a copy in watercolor of a detail of the figure of Edgar from the lower right of

James Gillray, *Shakespeare Sacrificed*. Etching, 1789

No. 210 was in the collection of the late Winifred Friedman.[8] Joseph Farington mentioned in his diary that he called on West on 5 May 1807, and found Ward coloring a print from No. 210 prior to the painting's being sent to America along with No. 207 in the following week.[9] A copy by Rembrandt Peale is also recorded.[10]

In James Gillray's attack on the Boydell gallery published on 20 June 1789, *Shakespeare Sacrificed;—or— The Offering to Avarice*, which contains caricatures of figures from several of the paintings in the gallery's opening exhibition, West's Fool is shown working a bellows while a bonfire consumes a pile of Shakespeare's plays (*above*).[11] A somewhat friendlier burlesque of the undertaking appeared in Richard Cumberland's *Observer* in the form of a mock-Greek manuscript which discusses a group of pictures commissioned by a rich citizen named Philoteuchus to illustrate the tragedies of Aeschylus. In this, West's Lear is Oedipus, and West himself is the artist Parrhasius who "though born in the colony of Miletus on the coast of Asia, was an adopted citizen of Athens and in great credit there for his celebrated picture on the death of Epaminondas." Other critical response to No. 210 seems to have been generally favorable. The treatment of Lear as a powerful figure, rather than the feeble old man portrayed by David Garrick and other eighteenth-century actors, was, however, described in the *Public Advertiser* as "an outrage upon nature." Fuseli described No. 210 as "a striking commentary on the advantages and disadvantages of a settled method . . . the progress of his pencil is as inexorable as the storm." West himself told two American visitors in 1807 that it was "his best piece done in his greatest stile." In America from 1807 on, it was a central attraction in the exhibitions of the new academies in Philadelphia and New York successively, and it is the one major painting ("one of the finest of West's pictures") which Charles Robert Leslie recalled in his *Autobiographical Recollections* that he had seen in America before his departure for England in 1811. At about the same time, Sir Augustus Foster, who was horrified by No. 207, admired No. 210, although his opinion of the vigorous "Old Monarch" echoed that of the *Public Advertiser*.

For discussion of precedents, analysis of the work's style, and consideration of sources and affinities, see the articles by von Erffa and Sund, published in 1956 and 1980, and the catalogue entry by Frederick Cummings from 1968.

See also pp. 152 and 157 (note 139) above.

[1] An account of the gallery is given by Winifred H. Friedman, op. cit.; see also *The Boydell Shakespeare Prints*, with an introduction by A. E. Santaniello, New York, 1979.
[2] Friedman, pp. 85 and 91–92. West himself described Sharp's engraving as one of the few acceptable prints in the series (Farington Diary, 26 May 1804, Farington 1978–, VI, p. 2331).
[3] The two paintings by Barry and Fuseli were both bought by John Green in 1805, and in his sale in 1830, they were bought by Henry Bone on behalf of Joseph Neeld, MP of Grittleton House, Wilts. In the previous year Bone buying for Neeld had been a major purchaser at the West sale; consequently for the next 130 years the Barry and Fuseli hung together with a major group of Wests. They were sold by the Neeld descendants on 16 November 1962 in a sale that included ten Wests, including six major pictures from the Revealed Religion series.
[4] Sund, p. 130 and note 17, citing the unpublished dissertation by Esther Gordon Dotson, *Shakespeare Illustrated, 1779–1820* (New York University, 1972).
[5] These figures are from Friedman, pp. 220–45. According to her lists, the £525 received by West for each of his two paintings was surpassed only by the £1,000 paid to Reynolds for a large scene from *Macbeth* (Petworth) and equalled the fees of £525 paid to Reynolds for the *Death of Cardinal Beaufort* and *Henry VI, Part II* (also at Petworth), to Romney for a scene from *The Tempest* (destroyed), and to Gavin Hamilton for one from *Coriolanus* (location unknown).
[6] Oil on panel or (?) possibly paper mounted on panel, $17\frac{1}{2} \times 25\frac{1}{2}$ in. See also the entry for No. 211.
[7] Oil on canvas, 28×36. We are indebted to David Moore-Gwyn of Sotheby's for information about this painting.
[8] Ill. in Friedman op. cit., fig. 48.
[9] Farington does not give Ward's first name. He was most probably the painter James Ward (1769–1859), whose address in 1807 was 6 Newman Street, a few doors away from West at 14 Newman Street.
[10] Charles Coleman Sellers, *Charles Willson Peale*, 1947, II, p. 247.
[11] Friedman, pp. 76–78 and fig 11, and Draper Hill, *Mr. Gillray: The Caricaturist*, London, 1965, p. 35 and pl. 31.

211 King Lear: Act III, Scene IV (King Lear in the Storm) *c.* 1788
See color illustrations, pp. 101, 106

DETROIT INSTITUTE OF ARTS

Oil on canvas: $20\frac{1}{2} \times 27\frac{1}{2}$ in. (52×70 cm.)

Signed lower left: *B. West* (this signature does not appear to be in West's hand)

PROV: Evidently still in West's possession 1804–8; William Beckford, Bath, by 1838; Beckford's daughter, Euphemia, wife of the tenth Duke of Hamilton; by descent to the twelfth Duke of Hamilton, by whom sold, Christie's, London, 17 June–20 July 1882, 10th day, lot 1068, bt. by H. Graves and Co. for £31.10.0.; Thomas B. Walker, Minneapolis, by 1909; Harry W. Peterson, 1937; Frank Gunter, Champaign, Illinois, from whom purchased by the Detroit Institute of Arts (Gibbs–Williams Fund) in 1977

EXH: RA 1789 (88) "King Lear, a finished sketch for the Gallery of Shakespear"; BI 1862 (183) lent by the Duke of Hamilton; Minneapolis Public Library, 1909 (91) lent by Thomas B. Walker; Walker Art Galleries, Minneapolis, 1927; *Cinco siglos de obras maestras*, Museo de Jade, San Jose, Costa Rica, 1978 (2)

LISTED: PC, p. 566 ("King Lear in the Storm at the

Hovel," West Gallery); *UM*, p. 530; *BA*, p. 17; Galt, p. 229; Dillenberger, p. 174 (352)

LIT: V and A Cuttings, II, pp. 467 and 478 (both 1789); *Public Advertiser*, 5 June 1789; Lansdown 1893, p. 13; R. H. Adams, *The Walker Art Galleries, Minneapolis*, Minneapolis, 1927, p. 170 (317); Winifred H. Friedman, *Boydell's Shakespeare Gallery*, New York and London, 1976, p. 150; Judy Sund, "Benjamin West: A Scene from *King Lear*," *Bulletin of the Detroit Institute of Arts*, LVIII, 1980, pp. 127–36

No. 211 differs from No. 210 in a number of details, most notably in the position of Edgar and in the head of Kent. It can thus be identified as the "finished sketch" for No. 210 which West exhibited at the Royal Academy in 1789, since a review of the Boydell gallery, which appeared in the *Public Advertiser* on 5 June compared the sketch and the finished picture and noted that in the latter, "the figure of Edgar and some other parts of the picture are varied from the sketch and they are improved." Prior to the discovery of No. 211 and its acquisition by Detroit in 1977, a small version of No. 210 in the Rhode Island School of Design had been thought to be the exhibited sketch;[1] however, that painting does not differ from No. 210 in any significant detail, so could not have been the sketch referred to in the *Public Advertiser*. The Rhode Island painting is the same size as the engraving after No. 210 by William Sharp, and is evidently either a copy made after No. 210 for the sake of the engraver or possibly the proof of the engraving which Joseph Farington saw being colored by Ward in West's studio in 1807.[2] For a fuller discussion see the article by Judy Sund published in 1980.

Although No. 211 was acquired by William Beckford, who was a major patron of West in the years 1796–99, it appears that Beckford did not buy No. 211 at that time, since in lists of West's works published in the first decade of the nineteenth century it is described as hanging in West's gallery. No. 211 is not mentioned in any descriptions of Fonthill Abbey and does not appear in the catalogues of the Fonthill sales in 1822 and 1823, so Beckford probably acquired it only after he left Fonthill in 1822 but, since it equally does not appear in the catalogues of the sales of works from West's estate in 1829, West or his heirs must have sold it by then. It is first recorded in Beckford's possession in 1838 when an unidentified visitor saw it in Beckford's dining-room at Lansdown Crescent in Bath and described it in a letter to his daughter as "West's original sketch for his great picture of King Lear for Boydell's Shakespeare Gallery." The letter continues:

A most wonderful performance. The expression of the face of the poor mad king is astonishing; the colouring rich and mellow—nothing of West's usually hard outline. The whole picture is full of energy and fire, and seems to have been struck off with the greatest ease and rapidity. "Do observe the face of Edgar," said Mr. Beckford. "Under his assumed madness you trace a sentiment of respect and anxiety for the monarch; he could not forget that it was his sovereign."

The visitor then tells Beckford that he has seen most of West's great pictures, "but there is more genius in that sketch than in anything I ever saw of his."

See also pp. 101–2 above.

[1] See, for example, Cummings 1968, p. 101.
[2] Farington Diary, 5 May 1807 (Farington 1978–, VIII, p. 3038). See also the entry for No. 210.

212 Lear and Cordelia *c.* 1784

LOCATION UNKNOWN

Oil on canvas: ($42 \times 56\frac{1}{2}$ in.) (106.5×143.5 cm.)

PROV: Peter, Duke of Courland, Mitau and Berlin (died 1800); his daughter, Pauline, Princess of Hohenzollern-Hechingen; sold in Munich, c. 1886.

(?) ENGR: Engraving by Daniel Berger, c. 1786 (see also under No. 214)

LISTED: *PC*, p. 563 ("King Lear and his Daughters"—Duke of Courland); *UM*, p. 529; Barlow, p. 434; *BA*, p. 16; Galt, p. 224 ("a small picture of King Lear and his Daughters," for the Duke of Courland); Dillenberger, p. 161 (226)

LIT: *Public Characters* 1805, pp. 546–47; Dunlap 1834, p. 67 (Dunlap 1918, I, pp. 71–72); *Verzeichniss der Gemäldesammlung Seiner Hoheit des Fürsten zu Hohenzollern-Hechingen*, Löwenberg, n.d. (359); Otto Clemen, "Kunstgeschichtliches aus Mitau," *Repertorium für Kunstwissenschaft*, XLI, 1919, p. 241, n. 10

Although No. 212 has evidently disappeared, it presumably showed the same moment from *King Lear* as Nos. 213 and 215, the two known paintings of the subject, and as a mezzotint, which is discussed under No. 214. These works are loosely based on the seventh scene of the fourth act of *King Lear*, set in the French camp where Lear has been brought after his ravings on the heath. The mezzotint, which incorrectly identifies the subject as Act V, Scene 1, is inscribed:

> Cor.—*Speak to me sir, who am I?*
> Lear— *You are a soul in bliss ; but I am bound*
> *Upon a wheel of fire, that my own tears*
> *Do scald like molten lead*

The words spoken by Lear are lines 46–48 of act IV, scene 7; those of Cordelia are either a fabrication or reflect some seventeenth- or eighteenth-century alteration of Shakespeare's text. The figure on the right in all the known versions could be either Kent or the Doctor, who plays the more active role during Cordelia's interview with her father. The title used for the subject in the early lists of West's works, "King Lear and His Daughters," establishes that the two female figures standing behind Cordelia are Goneril and Regan (and they could hardly be anybody else), but Goneril and Regan should not appear in this scene. Since contemporaries of West such as Robert Smirke managed to paint the scene more or less in accordance with Shakespeare's text,[1] it would seem either that West was extremely careless, or that he deliberately sought to create a generalized sense of the play rather than exact delineation of a specific passage from it.

At least four versions of the subject are recorded, and their histories are somewhat opaque. The first to leave West's possession, and perhaps the first to have been painted, was acquired by the Duke of Courland along with a scene from *Romeo and Juliet* (No. 217), dated *1778*. The Duke's minister, Heinrich von Offenberg, was in London in 1778 and 1779, and he may have commissioned the painting from *Lear* then, when he certainly did buy the *Romeo and Juliet*, but his published letters from London to the Duke mention only the latter work. The biography of West published in *Public Characters of 1805* states that in 1781 the Duke of Courland complimented West with a gold medal and rewarded the artist with great liberality for the two pictures he commissioned. Although this passage suggests that both pictures were completed by 1781, it does not say so explicitly, and the suggestion seems to be contradicted by William Dunlap's statement that when Dunlap first arrived in London in June 1784 he found West working on a picture of *Lear and Cordelia* for the Empress Catherine of Russia. The Empress Catherine was, of course, not the Duke of Courland, but her predecessor the Empress Anne had been the Duchess of Courland, and the Duchy of Courland, in Latvia, was closely tied to the Russian court (West's patron's father had been

Anne's lover and grand chamberlain when she assumed the Russian throne; she created him Duke of Courland in 1737, and he was re-established in the Duchy by Catherine in 1763). Since a version of the subject is not otherwise recorded as having gone to Russia, it seems likely that Courland and Russia became scrambled somewhere between West's explanation of the destination of his picture and Dunlap's recollection of that explanation when writing his history many years later. Thus, his testimony indicates that, although the Duke may have complimented and rewarded West in 1781, at that time he had probably received only the painting from *Romeo and Juliet*, and that the companion picture from *King Lear* followed in or after 1784. It is recorded in the Duke's possession in August 1786, when Daniel Berger made a drawing after it in preparation for an engraving.[2] The Courland *Lear* passed by family descent into the Hohenzollern-Hechingen collection, which was dispersed in 1886. A catalogue of the Hohenzollern-Hechingen collection lists its dimensions as $42 \times 56\frac{1}{2}$ in.,[3] which correspond reasonably closely to those of the scene from *Romeo and Juliet* (No. 217), as one would expect of companion pictures. A version of the subject in the Huntington Library in San Marino, California (No. 213) also has similar dimensions; that picture, however, does not appear to be entirely by West's hand and seems to have been in an English collection in the nineteenth century.

In addition to Nos. 212, 213, and two other known or recorded versions (Nos. 214 and 215), a *Lear and Cordelia* and a companion design from Shakespeare (presumably a version of No. 217), both painted on cast-iron panels, were sold by West's sons in 1829;[4] they were not listed in the sales catalogue as by West, and it seems likely that they were copies, possibly made in his studio, but by another hand.

West's son Benjamin sold a drawing of "King Lear and Cordelia" in 1839,[5] and there are drawings of the subject in the British Museum[6] and the Toledo Museum of Art.[7] Both of these show the composition in reverse of that in the known versions of the painting, as well as a number of significant differences in details. The Toledo drawing does not include Goneril and Regan, but does show both Kent and the Doctor, while in the British Museum drawing the two sisters replace the second male figure. Both of these drawings echo the composition of three drawings in the Pierpont Morgan Library catalogued by Ruth Kraemer as showing "Esau Selling His Birthright for a Dish of Pottage," in which the aged Jacob is in the position of Lear and Esau in that of Cordelia.[8] There is no firm evidence to establish which drawings came first, but since West evidently never painted the Esau subject, it seems likely that he probably made the Old Testament drawings initially, and adapted the composition to the Shakespearean subject after abandoning his plans to carry out the other. The *Lear* drawing in the British Museum is signed and dated *1783*, which is in line with Dunlap's testimony that West was working on a painting of the subject in June of 1784.

[1] The engraving after Smirke's painting for Boydell is reproduced in *The Boydell Shakespeare Prints*, New York, 1979.
[2] Mentioned in a letter from Offenberg to the Duke, 25 August 1786, cited by Clemen. No engraving of the subject by Berger is known to the compilers of the present catalogue.
[3] The recorded measurements of this version contradict the "small" in Galt's list, but, as in other cases, Galt's adjective can be dismissed as a misreading of the earlier lists of West's works. We are indebted to Dr. Walter Kaufhold, Director of the Fürstlich Hohenzollernsches Museum, in Sigmaringen, for information about the Hohenzollern-Hechingen collection (letter to Helmut von Erffa, 6 June 1968).
[4] Robins, London, 20–22 June 1829, lot 174.
[5] S. Leigh Sotheby, London, 1 June 1839, lot 68 (reed pen and bistre, washed).
[6] Sepia wash, $4\frac{3}{4} \times 7$ in., signed lower left: *B. West 1783* (1871-6-10-763).
[7] Sepia wash, $7\frac{3}{4} \times 10\frac{1}{8}$ in., signed lower left: *BW*.
[8] Kraemer 1975, pp. 23–24 (33–35) and pl. 22.

213 Lear and Cordelia

HENRY E. HUNTINGTON LIBRARY AND ART GALLERY, SAN MARINO, CALIFORNIA

Oil on canvas: $42\frac{1}{2} \times 57$ in. (108 × 145 cm.)

PROV: (?) Sold by West's sons, Robins, London, 20–22 June 1829, lot 152 ("Una and the Lion, and Lear and Cordelia, unfinished," by the late B. West); (?) Gage family, Hengrave Hall, Suffolk; sold anonymously, Christie's, London, 27 November 1909, lot 104, bt. by Neiss; T. J. Blakeslee, New York; acquired by the Huntington Library in 1912

(?) LISTED: *PC*, p. 565 ("A Sketch of King Lear and his Daughter," West, Painting-room); *UM*, p. 530; *BA*, p. 17; Galt, p. 228; Dillenberger, p. 172 (329)

LIT: C. H. Collins Baker, *Catalogue of British Paintings in the Henry E. Huntington Library and Art Gallery*, San Marino, 1936, pp. 98–99; [Robert R. Wark], *The Huntington Art Collection*, San Marino, 1970, p. 48 (66); Kraemer 1975, p. 23

No. 213 does not appear to be entirely by West's hand; most notably, the head of Cordelia is uncharacteristic both in modelling and in physical type; there are also very evident signs of repainting around it. It thus seems likely that No. 213 was the unfinished version of the subject sold by West's heirs on 20–22 June 1829, and that it was subsequently completed by another artist. If that is correct, it cannot be equated with the painting sold by West to the Duke of Courland before 1786 (No. 212), although the sizes correspond closely.

214 Lear and Cordelia

LOCATION UNKNOWN

$(18\frac{1}{2} \times 23\frac{1}{2}$ in.) (47 × 59.5 cm.)

PROV: Offered by West's sons to the United States in 1826 (60), and sold by them, Robins, London, 22–25 May 1829, lot 92 ("King Lear and Cordelia," $18\frac{1}{2} \times 23\frac{1}{2}$ in.), bt. by Smith for £57.15.0.

EXH: West's Gallery 1821 (8), 1822–28 (10)

(?) ENGR: Mezzotint ($18 \times 22\frac{15}{16}$ in.) by Richard Earlom, pub. 1 January 1799 by B. B. Evans, as "Shakespeare. King Lear. Act v. Scene 1":

> Cor.—*Speak to me sir, who am I?*
> Lear— *You are a soul in bliss : but I am bound*
> *Upon a wheel of fire, that my own tears*
> *Do scald like molten lead*

LISTED: *PC*, p. 565 ("The small picture of King Lear and his Daughter," West, Painting-room); *UM*, p. 530; Barlow, p. 434; *BA*, p. 16; Galt, p. 226; Dillenberger, p. 167 (287)

The measurements of the version of "King Lear and Cordelia" sold by West's sons in May 1829 were the same as those of the version now in the Folger Shakespeare Library (No. 215), but since No. 215 has an old label on the verso indicating that it was once in the Bowles collection, it must be the version listed in the early catalogues as painted for Mr. Bowles, rather than one that remained in the artist's possession until sold by his sons in 1829.

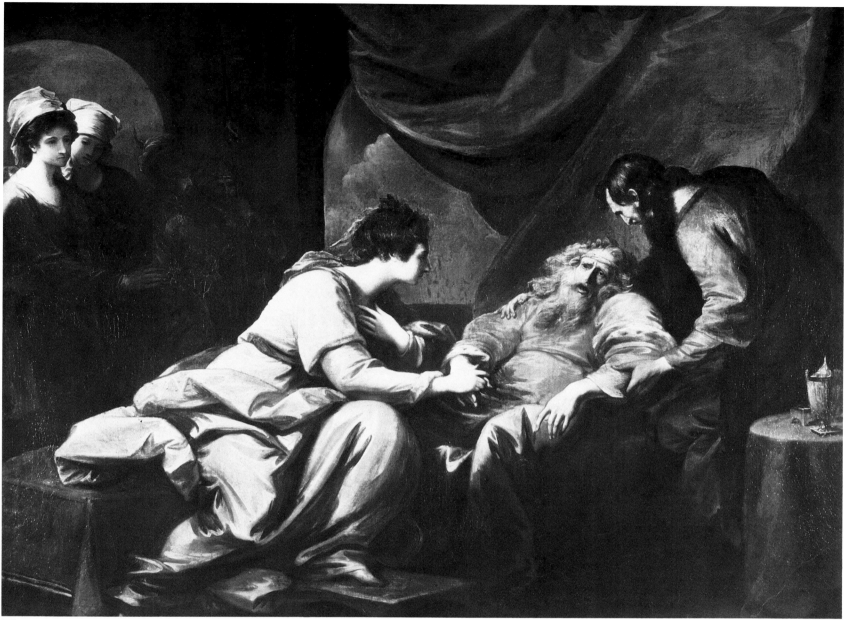

213

No. 214 was presumably the model for the mezzotint of the subject by Richard Earlom (*right*) published in 1799; its recorded dimensions are approximately the same as those of the print, and it is quite possible that it was made for the engraver's use. The print, which differs in some details from both known versions of the painting (Nos. 213 and 215), may also reflect the appearance of the lost first version (No. 212), but that version had gone to eastern Europe at least thirteen years before the print appeared. An elaborately and boldly painted-over proof of the mezzotint, in which the painting gives every appearance of having been done by West himself, is in the Royal Shakespeare Gallery in Stratford-upon-Avon. This proof has a signature and date of *1792* in the lower left corner. The signature does not appear to be in West's hand, but if the date is not simply a fabrication, it indicates that the mezzotint was engraved well before its publication date, although perhaps still after No. 212 had been sent to Courland. Since No. 215 is signed and dated *1793*, the painted-over proof may have served West as a preliminary sketch for that slightly altered version of the composition.

Lear and Cordelia, mezzotint by Richard Earlom, (?) after No. 214

215

215 Lear and Cordelia 1793

FOLGER SHAKESPEARE LIBRARY, WASHINGTON, D.C.

Oil on canvas: 19 × 23⅝ in. (48.5 × 60 cm.)

Signed lower left: *B. West 1793*

PROV: Painted for George Bowles, Wanstead (died
1817); Col. W. P. Kennedy; bought by H. C. Folger
from McGirr, 20 September 1929

EXH: RA 1794 (17) "Cordelia making herself known
to her father, King Lear"

LISTED: *BA*, p. 19 ("The Grecian Daughter defending
her father from the tyrant—Its companion, the
Couch scene of King Lear and his Daughter", painted for Mr. Bowles of Wanstead); Dillenberger,
p. 188 (497)

As indicated by the entry in *La Belle Assemblée*, West
painted No. 215 and a companion picture of the *Grecian
Daughter* (No. 204) for Mr. Bowles in Wanstead.[1] The
two paintings appeared together at the Royal Academy
in 1794, the year after the date on No. 215 (No. 204
is dated *1794*).

This picture shows essentially the same composition
as West's other known treatments of the subject (see
Nos. 213 and 214), but does not include two soldiers
in the background and differs in a number of lesser
details.

[1] The Bowles provenance is confirmed by an old label on the
back of No. 215, as is also the subsequent ownership of Col.
W. P. Kennedy (letter from Giles E. Dawson, Curator of
Books and Manuscripts, The Folger Shakespeare Library,
to Helmut von Erffa, 26 May 1955).

216 Macbeth and the Witches *c.* 1793

LOCATION UNKNOWN

PROV: Sold by West's sons, Robins, London, 20–22
June 1829, lot 60 ("Macbeth and the Weird Sisters")

EXH: RA 1793 (546) "Macbeth and the witches; a
sketch"

LISTED: *PC*, p. 564 ("The Sketch of Macbeth and the
Witches," West, Painting-room); *UM*, p. 530;
Barlow, p. 434; *BA*, p. 16; Galt, p. 225; Dil-
lenberger, p. 167 (280)

LIT: Kraemer 1975, p. 91

No. 216 has been lost since 1829. A drawing of this subject in the Pierpont Morgan Library,[1] which is ascribed
by Ruth Kraemer to Raphael West, appears to be
derived from John Martin's *Macbeth* exhibited at the
British Institution in 1820.[2] Hence, it presumably does
not reflect the appearance of West's sketch exhibited
in 1793.

[1] Pen and graphite on oatmeal paper, 10 9/16 × 14 11/16 in.,
Kraemer 1975, p. 91 (221), and pl. 115.
[2] Location unknown; a version is in the National Gallery of
Scotland. See William Feaver, *The Art of John Martin*,
Oxford, 1975, p. 48, pl. 30.

217 Romeo and Juliet (?)1775–78

NEW ORLEANS MUSEUM OF ART

Oil on canvas: 44½ × 59 in. (113 × 150 cm.)

Signed lower right: *B. West. London/1778*

PROV: Purchased from West for 60 guineas in 1779 by
Heinrich von Offenberg on behalf of Peter, Duke of
Courland, Mitau and Berlin (died 1800); Count
Karl Lanckoronski, Vienna; Count Antoine Lanck-
oronski, Geneva (died 1965); Newhouse Galleries,
New York, from whom acquired by the New Orleans
Museum of Art in 1973

ENGR: Stipple engraving printed in colors (oval,
11⅝ × 9⅝ in., reversed), by G. Scorodomow, showing
a bust-length detail of the two main figures, pub. 26
June 1775 by V. M. Picot, London; line engraving,
(5 1/16 × 6½ in., reversed) by William Sharp, pub. 24
June 1783 by John Boydell; (?) engraving by Daniel
Berger, *c.* 1786

LISTED: *PC*, p. 563 ("Romeo and Juliet"—Duke of
Courland); *UM*, p. 529; Barlow, p. 434; *BA*, p. 16;
Galt, p. 223 ("A small picture of Romeo and Juliet,"
for the Duke of Courland);[1] Dillenberger, p. 161
(225)

LIT: *Public Characters* 1805, pp. 546–47; Otto Clemen,
"Kunstgeschichtliches aus Mitau," *Repertorium für
Kunstwissenschaft*, XLI, 1919, pp. 240–42

No. 217 shows the moment in the Balcony scene (act
III, scene 5) of *Romeo and Juliet*, when, as dawn breaks,
Romeo is about to make his departure in response to
the warning from Juliet's nurse of the imminent arrival
of Lady Capulet.

Although the date on the painting is *1778*, the date
of *1775* on the engraving by Scorodomow, showing a
detail from No. 217, indicates that West had at least
begun that part of the composition by then.

In 1778 Heinrich von Offenberg, the *Kammerjunker*
(chamberlain) of the Duke of Courland, arrived in
London and sent to his employer an engraving of
No. 217 (possibly either the Scorodomow print or the
Sharp engraving, which, although not published until
1783, may have already existed in proof). The Duke
thereupon had Offenberg purchase the painting itself.
Offenberg and a companion, Herr von Kleist, called
on West on 1 May 1779 to inquire about the painting,
and Offenberg reported that the picture was ready and
that West had corrected Juliet's elongated neck in a
masterly fashion.[2] West also had ordered a very beautiful frame made for the painting. On 3 May, Offenberg
paid West sixty guineas for the painting and an additional £9.0.6. for the frame. West subsequently presented Offenberg with a sketch of the *Death of General Wolfe*
(No. 93). The Duke also acquired a painting of *Lear
and Cordelia* (No. 212) from West, and in 1781 presented
the artist a gold medal, although, as discussed in the
entry for No. 212, West had at that date probably only
painted No. 217. In 1786 both paintings were in the
Duke's residence, Schloss Friedrichsfelde, near Berlin,
where the artist Daniel Berger copied them in order
to make engravings.

A copy or version of No. 217 belonged in 1979 to
Mrs. Benjamin G. Lockerd in Fort Smith, Arkansas.

[1] See No. 212, note 3, regarding Galt's "small" picture.
[2] "Das Bild war fertig und der nicht uns allein, sondern auch
West selbst zu langgestreckte Hals von Julien meisterhaft
geändert" (Clemen, p. 241).

217

218

218 Una and the Lion (Mary Hall in the Character of Una) 1771

WADSWORTH ATHENEUM, HARTFORD, CONNECTICUT

Oil on canvas: $65\frac{3}{4} \times 86\frac{1}{4}$ in. (167×219 cm.)

Signed lower right: *B. West 1771*

PROV: Sold anonymously, Christie's, London, 9 May 1940, lot 90; Arnold Seligman, Rey and Company, New York, from whom purchased by the Wadsworth Atheneum in 1941

EXH: RA 1772 (274) "Una. From Spenser's Fairy Queen, Book I, Canto 3, Verses 4 and 5."

ENGR: Mezzotint ($17\frac{5}{8} \times 22\frac{7}{8}$ in.) by Richard Earlom, pub. 10 Aug. 1772 by John Boydell

LIT: *Middlesex Journal*, no. 480, 25–28 April 1772; John Chaloner Smith, *British Mezzotinto Portraits*, London, 1878–83, I, pp. 249–50; Evans 1959, pp. 45, 53, and pl. 30; Laurel Bradley, "Eighteenth-Century Paintings and Illustrations of Spenser's *Faerie Queene*: A Study in Taste," *Marsyas*, XX, 1979–80, pp. 41–42 and fig. 15

No. 218 is the first of three Spenserian subjects painted and exhibited by West in the 1770s; the other two are Nos. 220 and 222 below. It also appears to have been one of the first paintings of a subject from Spenser to have been done by an eighteenth–century artist.[1] When it was exhibited, a critic in the *Middlesex Journal* found the subject sufficiently unfamiliar that he provided his readers with a full quotation of the relevant lines from *The Faerie Queene*: "This is founded upon a passage in Spencer, which, as that author is but little read at present, I shall take the liberty of giving you at length":

IV One day, nigh wearie of the yrkesome way,
From her unhastie beast she did alight;
And on the grasse her dainty limbs did lay
In the secrete shadow, far from all mens sight:
From her fayre head her fillet she undight,
And layd her stole aside. Her angels face,
As the great eye of heaven, shyned bright,
And made a sunshine in the shady place;
Did ever mortal eye behold such heavenly grace.

V It fortuned, out of the thickest wood
A ramping Lyon rushed suddeinly,
Hunting full greedy after salvage blood.
Soone as the royall virgin he did spy,
With gaping mouth at her ran greedily,
To have at once devourd her tender corse;
But to the pray when as he drew more ny,
His bloody rage aswaged with remorse,
And, with the sight amazd, forgat his furious forse.

VI In stead thereof he kist her wearie feet,
And lickt her lilly hands with fawning tong.[2]

This quotation is a slightly edited rendering of the lines cited but not quoted by West in the catalogue of the Royal Academy exhibition.

According to J. C. Smith's catalogue entry for the mezzotint by Richard Earlom, No. 218 is a portrait of a Miss Hall. The information Smith gives about her is:

Born in Jamaica; daughter of Thomas Hall of Kirkpatrick and Worcester; married Richard James Laurence, of Fairfield, Jamaica, Esq. Died at Montague-place, Montague-square, Jan. 20, 1815, aged 66, buried in the chapel of St. John's Wood, Marylebone.

If this information is correct, the sitter would have been twenty-two years old when West painted the picture. No. 218 would have been the first of West's allegorical portraits, preceding his portrait of Alderman Sawbridge as a Roman tribune (No. 694), which appeared at the Academy in 1773, and various portraits or presumed portraits of ladies as Rachel (No. 247), Rebecca (No. 243), and Armida (No. 228), which the artist painted later in the decade. In this departure, West was certainly following the lead of Reynolds, who had exhibited no less than four portraits of sitters in mythological or allegorical guises at the first Royal Academy exhibition in 1769 but, in depicting his subject as Una, West preceded Reynolds, whose portrait of Mary Beauclerk as Una appeared at the Royal Academy in 1780 (Fogg Museum of Art, Cambridge, Massachusetts). George Stubbs also exhibited a *Portrait of a Young Lady in the Character of Una* at the Academy in 1782 (Fitzwilliam Museum, Cambridge, England).[3] Like the majority of West's portraits (including allegorical portraits such as Nos. 247 and 694), this painting does not appear in any of the early lists of West's works.

West evidently left unfinished a second version of the subject (No. 219). A drawing of Una was with the Bernard Black Gallery in 1972,[4] and another is at Swarthmore,[5] as is also a drawing for her donkey (illus. p. 437).[6] A drawing of a lion at Swarthmore does not appear to be related to No. 218 and may have been made as a study for the lion in *Death on the Pale Horse* (see No. 402).

[1] For a useful survey of eighteenth-century paintings based on *The Faerie Queene* see the article by Laurel Bradley cited above.

[2] We are indebted to Brian Allen for transcribing this review and bringing it to our attention.

[3] The portraits by Reynolds and Stubbs are reproduced by Bradley, figs. 19 and 20.

[4] Pen and ink, $10\frac{1}{4} \times 12\frac{1}{2}$ in.

[5] Black chalk, $7\frac{1}{8} \times 9$ in.

[6] Black and white chalk, $10\frac{5}{8} \times 8\frac{1}{2}$ in.

219 Una and the Lion

LOCATION UNKNOWN

PROV: Sold by West's sons, Robins, London, 20–22 June 1829, lot 152 ("Una and the Lion, and Lear and Cordelia, unfinished")

220 The Cave of Despair 1772

See color illustration, p. 82

YALE CENTER FOR BRITISH ART, NEW HAVEN, PAUL MELLON COLLECTION

Oil on canvas: 24 × 30 in. (61 × 76 cm.)

Signed right side: *B. West/Painted 1772*

PROV: (?) Offered by West's sons to the United States in 1826 (122) and sold by them, Robins, London, 22–25 May 1829, lot 77 (24 × 30 in.) bt. by Hicks for £42; Sabin Galleries, London, from whom purchased by Paul Mellon prior to 1968

EXH: (?) RA 1773 (309) "The Cave of Despair, From Spencer's Fairy Queen"; West's Gallery 1821 (89) "Cave of Despair":

The Cave of Despair, outline engraving by Henry Moses after No. 220

That darkesome cave they enter, where they find
That cursed man low sitting on the ground,
Musing full sadly in his sullen mind;
His griesly lockes long growen and unbound,
Disordred hong about his shoulders round.
And hid his face, through which his hollow eyne
Lookt deadly dull, and stared as astound;
His raw-bone cheekes, through penurie and pine,
Were shronke into his jawes, as he did never dine.

His garment, nought but many ragged clouts,
With thornes together pind and patched was,
The which his naked sides he wrapt about;
And him beside there lay upon the gras
A dreary corse, whose life away did pas,
All wallowed in his own yet luke-warme blood,
That from his wound yet welled, fresh, alas!
In which a rusty knife fast fixed stood.
And made an open passage for the gushing flood.

Which piteous spectacle approving trew,
The woful tale that Trevisan had told,
Whenas the gentle Red-crosse knight did vew,
With firie zeale he burnt in courage bold
Him to avenge, before his blood were cold;
And to the villein sayd.

Faery Queen, Book i. canto 9

West's Gallery, 1822–28 (138), with same quotation, less the last six lines; *American Art in Alumni Collections*, Yale University Art Gallery, New Haven, 1968 (10), lent by Mr. and Mrs. Paul Mellon; *Painters and Engraving: The Reproductive Print from Hogarth to Wilkie*, Yale Center for British Art, New Haven, 1980 (54); Washington and Philadelphia, 1980

ENGR: Mezzotint ($16\frac{13}{16} \times 20\frac{11}{16}$ in.) by Valentine Green, pub. 1 June 1775 by John Boydell; outline engraving ($7 \times 8\frac{1}{4}$ in.), drawn by Henry Corbould, engraved by Henry Moses, pub. 2 Dec. 1811 by Moses as pl. x in Moses 1811; outline engraving of a detail of the figure of Despair, signed: *R. R. Dec. 21. 1821.*

LISTED: *PC*, p. 567 ("The Cave of Despair—from Spenser," West, Gallery); *UM*, p. 531; Barlow, p. 435; *BA*, p. 18; Galt, p. 231; Dillenberger, p. 180 (418)

LIT: Moses 1811 (x); Dafforne 1863,: 11 p. 219; Graves 1906, VIII, p. 213 (Horace Walpole, 1773); Rosenblum 1960, p. 78; John Gage, "Turner's Academic Friendships: C. L. Eastlake," *Burlington Magazine*, cx, 1968, pp. 680–81, fig. 49; Kraemer 1975, pp. 83–84; Laurel Bradley, "Eighteenth-Century Paintings and Illustrations of Spenser's *Faerie Queene*: A Study in Taste," *Marsyas*, xx, 1979–80, pp. 37–38, fig. 8

No. 220 shows the climactic moment of canto 9 of *The Faerie Queene*. The entire episode of the Cave of Despayre (or Despaire) is described by Spenser in stanzas 21–54; the lines quoted in the catalogues of the exhibitions in West's gallery in the 1820s, from stanzas 35–37, are less immediately relevant to the moment shown by West than are stanzas 51–52. In these, the Red Cross Knight, goaded by Despaire, raises his arm to kill himself, only to be stopped by Una, who seizes the knife from his hand. Despaire is described in stanzas 35 and 36. He sits with "swords, ropes, poison, fire" (stanza 50), which he has offered as suicidal weapons, on one side of him, and with what appears to be a "table plaine" painted with fiends and tormenting ghosts (stanza 49), on the other. The painting on the table, the dismaying sight of which drives the Knight to his attempt to kill himself, is not discernible in No. 220, but the fiendish figures can be seen in the outline engraving by Henry Moses after the painting and somewhat less clearly in No. 221 and in the Green mezzotint. The "drearie corse" of Sir Terwin (stanzas 27–30 and 36) is in the lower right corner, and Sir Trevisan, with "curld uncombed heares upstaring stiffe, dismayd with uncouth dread" (stanza 22), stands behind the Red Cross Knight, whom he has brought to the cave. The "ghastly Owle, shrieking his balefull note," and "wandring ghosts" (stanza 33) are in the upper right corner.

Two versions of the composition are known (Nos. 220 and 221). Both are of high quality and appear to be by West's hand. No. 220 is signed and dated in the place and manner shown in the Moses engraving (*left*), whereas No. 221 evidently is not, and we have, therefore, assumed that No. 220 was West's prime version of the subject, while No. 221 would be the "copy painted upon by West" sold by the artist's sons in June 1829; however, neither painting has a complete provenance and it is possible that some parts of their histories are confused. Apart from the figures on Despaire's "table," which are visible in No. 221 but not in No. 220, there are few appreciable differences in composition or detail between the two works.

Drawings for the composition differing considerably from the final paintings are in a private collection,[1] at Swarthmore,[2] and in the Museum of Fine Arts in Montreal.[3] Additionally, the drawing for Una's donkey (illus. p. 437), mentioned under No. 218, may have been re-used for this painting, where the beast reappears in a similar position. A drawing of the final composition, which appears to be a copy, not by West's hand, was with the Bernard Black Gallery in 1968,[4] and a second, similar drawing on tracing paper is in the Pierpont Morgan Library.[5] It has been suggested about both these drawings that they were made by or for an engraver; however, their sizes do not correspond with those of either of the two known prints after the picture.

As noted in 1960 by Robert Rosenblum and in 1980 by Dorinda Evans in the catalogue of *Benjamin West and His American Students*, No. 220, dated 1772 and exhibited in 1773, marks a radical change in West's subjects, and constitutes his first notable effort to evoke the terrible sublime as it had been defined by Edmund Burke in *A Philosophical Enquiry into the Origin of our Ideas of the Sublime and Beautiful* (1756–57). In contrast to West's dependence upon classicizing artists such as Raphael and Poussin in his earlier subject pictures, the imagery in No. 220 draws upon Salvator Rosa, the bones, etc., recalling particularly those in Salvator's *Democritus in Meditation* (Royal Museum of Fine Arts, Copenhagen, but in an English collection in the eighteenth century).[6] This departure presumably provoked Horace Walpole's one-word comment about No. 220: "Outré." Among other important early examples of the sublime, Reynolds's *Count Ugolino and His Children* (Knole House, Kent) appeared at the same Royal

Academy exhibition in 1773, and the *Old Man and Death* by Joseph Wright of Derby (Wadsworth Atheneum, Hartford, Connecticut) was exhibited the following year at the Society of Artists. Wright's *Hermit Studying Anatomy* (Derby Museum and Art Gallery), which is closer in imagery to the West, as well as being overtly derived from the *Democritus* by Salvator, dates from the same period, *c.* 1771–73.

An obscure artist named William Dawes (exhibited 1760–74) exhibited a *Red Cross Knight in the Cave of Despair* (location unknown) at the Society of Artists in 1764, and a drawing by Fuseli from *c.* 1769 is in the Art Institute of Chicago. John Hamilton Mortimer and Edward Edwards may have also painted the same subject before West.[7] Subsequently, as Spenser's popularity grew, the Cave of Despair became a fairly common theme. It was the subject set for the painting prize at the Royal Academy in 1818, and the winning picture by Joseph Severn was evidently derived from West's composition.[8] On 11 August 1829, J. M. W. Turner wrote to Charles Eastlake, who was then in Rome: "I should have liked to have bought West's *Cave of Despair* and lament I did not." Turner's lost opportunity had come in the auctions of West's paintings in May and June of 1829, when both Nos. 220 and 221 were sold. His interest had probably been aroused because of visiting Eastlake in Rome in the winter of 1828–29, while Eastlake was painting a picture of the same subject commissioned by Sir John Soane, and the mention of West's picture in his letter follows a report about Soane's concern over Eastlake's progress.[9]

See also pp. 77–83 above.

[1] Pencil and ink, $11\frac{1}{2} \times 11$ in.; exhibited New York 1962 (25) as "Study for 'Despair in a Cave.'"
[2] Two drawings in black chalk, on both sides of one sheet, $10\frac{1}{8} \times 11\frac{1}{4}$ in.
[3] Pen and black chalk, $10\frac{1}{2} \times 8\frac{1}{8}$ in.
[4] Pencil, $11 \times 14\frac{3}{4}$ in.; exhibited, New York 1968 (17).
[5] $13\frac{3}{4} \times 16$ in. (Kraemer 1975, pp. 83–84, no. 206).
[6] See Benedict Nicolson, *Joseph Wright of Derby*, London and New York, 1968, 1, pp. 52–53.
[7] See Nancy L. Pressly, *The Fuseli Circle in Rome: Early Romantic Art of the 1770s* (exhibition catalogue), Yale Center for British Art, New Haven, 1979, pp. 28–29.
[8] The painting, which was exhibited at the RA in 1820, was sold Christie's, London, 28 June 1963, lot 163; see Gage, p. 680.
[9] Gage, p. 681.

221 The Cave of Despair

DUXBURY ART COMPLEX, DUXBURY, MASSACHUSETTS

Oil on canvas: 25×30 in. (63.5 × 76 cm.)

PROV: (?) Sold by West's sons, Robins, London, 20–22 June 1829, lot 62 ("The Cave of Despair, from Spencer; copy painted upon by the late B. West" . . .); (?) Robert Hamilton, Bloomfield House, Norwood, Surrey, by whom sold, Foster, London, 17 March 1832, lot 236 (West, "Pair, The Cave of Despair and Companion"); Vose Galleries, Boston, 1969

For reasons discussed under No. 220, we have equated No. 221 with the copy "painted upon" by West sold in June 1829, although No. 221 is not appreciably inferior to No. 220. The entry in the sale catalogue implies that the copy was fundamentally by another hand, but neither painting shows palpable evidence of having been worked on by two artists. Nonetheless, since the two pictures are so similar to one another in almost every detail, it seems perhaps more likely that one of them is the work of a skilled and conscientious copyist, rather than that West himself would have repeated his own work in such a painstaking fashion without some variations.

If the two pictures are properly identified here, it seems marginally more likely that No. 221 was the painting sold with an unidentified companion by Robert Hamilton in 1832, since No. 220 had been bought three years before by another purchaser, a Mr. Hick or Hicks, none of whose other purchases at the same time could conceivably be described as a companion.[1] It is impossible to say what the companion picture in 1832 may have been.

[1] In the marked catalogue transcribed by Graves for the sale of pictures by West, Robins, London, 22–25 May 1829, lots 55 "Christ Healing the Infirm" (No. 334), 75 "Cupid and Psyche" (No. 152), 77 "The Cave of Despair" (No. 220), 122 "Genius Calling Forth the Fine Arts" (No. 435), and 123 "The Four Quarters of the Globe Bringing Treasures to Britannia" (No. 438) are listed as bought by "Hicks." A partly marked catalogue in the New-York Historical Society lists the purchaser of lot 55 as "Mr. Hick of Bolton" and of lot 123 as "Mr. Hick."

222 Fidelia and Speranza 1776

PUTNAM FOUNDATION, TIMKEN ART GALLERY, SAN DIEGO, CALIFORNIA

Oil on canvas: $54\frac{3}{4} \times 42\frac{1}{2}$ in. (139 × 108 cm.)

Signed lower left: *B. West/1776*

PROV: Vose Galleries, Boston, from whom acquired by the Putnam Foundation in 1969

EXH: RA 1777 (364) "Fidelia and Spiranza; from Spencer's Fairy Queen"

ENGR: Mezzotint ($23\frac{1}{2} \times 17\frac{1}{16}$ in.) by Valentine Green, pub. 9 Nov. 1778 by John Boydell

LIT: John Chaloner Smith, *British Mezzotinto Portraits*, London, 1878–83, II, p. 598 (160); *Grenville L. Winthrop: Retrospective for a Collector* (exhibition catalogue), Fogg Museum of Art, Cambridge, Mass., 1969, p. 132; Martin E. Petersen, *American Paintings in the Collection of the Putnam Foundation*, San Diego, Calif., 1977, p. 14

The painting shows two daughters of Caelia (heavenly), residents with their sister Charissa in the House of Holiness, to which Una brings the Red Cross Knight in canto 10 of *The Faerie Queene*:

Thus as they gan of sundry things devise,
    Loe two most goodly virgins came in place,
    Ylinked arme in arme in lovely wise,
    With countenance demure, and modest grace,
    They numbred even steps and equall pace:
    Of which the eldest, that *Fidelia* hight,
    Like sunny beames threw from her Christall face,
    That could have dazd the rash beholders sight,
And round about her head did shine like heavens
        light.

She was araied all in lilly white,
    And in her right hand bore a cup of gold,
    With wine and water fild up to the hight,
    In which a Serpent did himselfe enfold,
    That horrour made to all, that did behold;
    But she no whit did chaunge her constant mood:
    And in her other hand she fast did hold
    A booke, that was both signd and seald with
        blood,
Wherein darke things were writ, hard to be
        understood.

Her younger sister, that *Speranza* hight,
    Was clad in blew, that her beseemed well;

221

222

Not all so chearefull seemed she of sight,
As was her sister; whether dread did dwell,
Or anguish in her hart, is hard to tell;
Upon her arme a silver anchor lay,
Whereon she leaned ever, as befell:
And ever up to heaven, as she did pray,
Her steadfast eyes were bent, ne swarved other way.

Una, on her donkey,[1] and her companion approach in the lower left corner.

A preparatory drawing showing a similar composition but with many differences in detail was formerly in the collection of Mrs. F. Howard.[2] A larger and more highly finished drawing of the subject, which follows this painting closely in all details except facial features and hair styles, and which is signed and dated *1784* (that is, eight years later than the painting), is in the Grenville L. Winthrop Collection in the Fogg Museum.[3]

Although there seems to be no contemporary documentation to substantiate the hypothesis, it is possible that West painted No. 222 as an allegorical portrait of, presumably, two sisters. This idea was put forth in connection with the Green mezzotint by J. C. Smith, who proposed that Fidelia might be the same Miss Hall depicted by West as Una in No. 218. Like that painting, No. 222 does not appear on any of the early lists of West's works, which may indicate that the artist thought of it as a portrait, as well as the fact that it probably left his possession long before the lists were drawn up, as a commissioned portrait would have. A painting by Copley of the *Red Cross Knight, Fidelia and Speranza* shown at the Royal Academy in 1793 (National Gallery, Washington) is a group portrait of three Copley children.[4]

[1] Which, once again, appears to be based upon the drawing mentioned under No. 218 and ill. p. 437.
[2] Pen and brown ink, 9½ × 7¾ in., sold Sotheby's, London, 22 March 1979, lot 6 (as "Faith and Hope"), ill. in cat.
[3] Brown ink and watercolor, 20 × 15 in.; discussed and ill. in the Fogg catalogue cited above.
[4] See Prown 1966, II, pp. 342, 445, and fig. 592. Prown suggests that Copley may have chosen this atypical subject in an effort to compete with West.

223 The Dead Ass, from Sterne *c.* 1800

MUSEUM OF FINE ARTS, HOUSTON, TEXAS

Oil on canvas: 19⅞ × 14¾ in. (50.5 × 37.5 cm.)

Signed lower right: *B. West*

PROV: Offered by West's sons to the United States in 1826 (52), and sold by them, Robins, London, 22–25 May 1829, lot 25 (19½ × 14½ in.), bt. by W. Ward for £23.2.0., evidently on behalf of Benjamin West, Jr.; sold by Mrs. Albert F. West, Christie's, London, 19 March 1898, lot 131 ("A Peasant, seated on a bench," 12½ × 16 in.), bt. by Parsons; purchased by Joseph S. Cullinan, Houston, in New York in the 1920s, and given by his family to the Houston Museum in 1953

EXH: West's Gallery 1822–28 (2); BI 1833 (27) lent by B. West; *The Hand and the Spirit: Religious Art in America, 1700–1900*, University Art Museum, Berkeley, California, etc., 1972–73

LISTED: *PC*, p. 567 ("The Traveller laying his Piece of Bread on the Bridle of the dead Ass—from Sterne," West, Gallery); *UM*, p. 531; Barlow, p. 435; *BA*, p. 18; Galt, p. 230; Dillenberger, p. 177 (389)

LIT: Dillenberger 1977, p. 25, pl. 19

West painted two small companion pictures (Nos. 223 and 224) illustrating passages from *A Sentimental Journey* by Laurence Sterne. The former is based on the chapter entitled "Nampont. The Dead Ass." The dead ass is visible on the road in the background, and its owner, who had been returning to his home in Franconia from a pilgrimage to Spain, sits dejectedly in the foreground, gazing at the ass's bridle, on which he has placed the portion of their joint crust of bread that would have been its share were it still alive. The old man's hat, decorated with a pilgrim's shell and a saddle lie to the left of the bridle.

No. 223 is signed but not dated. Jane Dillenberger has argued that it was probably painted between 1772 and 1780,[1] and there is circumstantial evidence, which is discussed under No. 224, to suggest that both paintings may have been begun in the 1770s. However, although No. 224 is lost, the outline engraving after it by Henry Moses bears within the image West's signature and the date *1800*, and that later year seems more consistent with West's handling in No. 223, than does a date in the 1770s. For the model for the pilgrim, see the discussion under No. 224.

[1] In correspondence with Helmut von Erffa; see also the entry in *The Hand and the Spirit* exhibition catalogue.

224 The Captive, from Sterne *c.* 1800

LOCATION UNKNOWN

(19½ × 14½ in.) (49.5 × 36.8 cm.)

(Signed lower right: *B. West/1800*)

PROV: Offered by West's sons to the United States in 1826 (51), and sold by them, Robins, London, 22–25 May 1829, lot 24 (19½ × 14½ in.), bt. by W. Ward for £16.16.0., evidently on behalf of Benjamin West,

Jr.; sold by Mrs. Albert F. West, Christie's, London, 19 March 1898, lot 132 ("A Prisoner in a Cell," 19 × 14 in.), bt. by Cohen

EXH: West's Gallery 1822–28 (1); BI 1833 (29) lent by B. West

ENGR: Outline engraving ($7\frac{7}{16} \times 5\frac{11}{16}$) drawn by Henry Corbould, engraved by Henry Moses, pub. 1 May 1811 by Moses as pl. IV in Moses 1811

LISTED: *PC*, p. 567 ("The Captive—from Sterne," West, Gallery); *UM*, p. 531; Barlow, p. 435; *BA*, p. 18; Galt, p. 230; Dillenberger, p. 177 (390)

LIT: Moses 1811 (IV)

In the chapter of *A Sentimental Journey* entitled "The Captive, Paris," Yorick tries to imagine the miseries of confinement by visualizing a captive in his dungeon cell. Sterne describes Yorick looking through a grated door, whereas in No. 224 Yorick peers through a window on the left, but apart from that West follows Sterne's text, which describes the captive sitting upon the ground upon a little straw, his legs chained, his sole activity scratching notches into sticks with a rusty nail to record the days. Sterne does not mention *graffiti* on the walls, and the inscriptions *1740, CA 1754, VI,* and *Paris 1760* seem to be West's addition, without reference to the narrative.

According to the Robins sale catalogue of 22–25 May

The Captive, from Sterne, outline engraving by Henry Moses after No. 224

1829, the features of Yorick in No. 224 are those of Sterne: "The painter has completed the personification, by introducing the portrait of his esteemed friend, the sentimental Sterne, in the character of Yorick—thus contemplating with emotion the phantom of his own creative imagination." West's Yorick does appear to be Sterne, but the likeness does not seem to be copied from any one known portrait.[1] The statement from the Robins catalogue claims that West had been a friend of Sterne, and the fact that West painted or drew a portrait of Sterne's daughter (No. 657) also indicates a personal connection between the two men. See also No. 646.

No. 224 has disappeared, but its appearance is known from the outline engraving by Henry Moses (*above*), which bears a facsimile of West's signature and the date *1800* within the image, on the end of the block of stone upon which the captive reclines. The companion picture, the *Dead Ass, from Sterne* (No. 223), which is known, is not dated, but the handling of paint in it seems characteristic of West's manner of painting around 1800.

When No. 224 was sold in 1829, the catalogue entry described the model for the prisoner as a poor Yorkshire laborer, whom Reynolds had employed as the model for the chief figure in his *Ugolino* (Knole House, Kent). That painting appeared at the Royal Academy in 1773; the model was "Old George" White, whose features, according to Horace Walpole, were recognizable in no less than six different pictures in the Royal Academy exhibition of 1772.[2] White was apparently also the model for the pilgrim in No. 223, and the Robins catalogue of May 1829 claimed additionally that White ("Sir Joshua's famed old labourer"), then in his hundredth year, served as model for yet another picture by West, *Tobias Curing His Father's Blindness* (No. 293), which is signed and dated *1803*. The chief figure in No. 293 does appear to be taken from the same model as the figures in Nos. 223 and 224, and, hence, the date of *1803* on No. 293 corroborates the *1800* on the engraving after No. 224. The question of whether the model for Reynolds's aged Ugolino could have posed for these works painted some thirty years later is stilled by his reported longevity. If White had indeed reached the

223

age of one hundred in 1803, he would have been seventy years old when Reynolds painted him.

Nevertheless, despite the evidence for accepting the *1800* on Moses's print after this painting, there are reasons to think that Nos. 223 and 224 had their origins in some fashion considerably earlier, probably in the 1770s. Sterne died in 1768. West must have been in touch with his daughter between 1768 and 1775 when an engraving after No. 657 served as a frontispiece to her book, and he may initially have made the designs of Nos. 223 and 224 at that time, possibly to serve as illustrations in a planned but unrealized life of Sterne.[3] Sterne had considerable vogue among artists in the 1770s, subjects such as that of No. 224 appealing to an early taste for the sublime, which is also reflected in Reynold's *Ugolino* and in such works by West as the *Cave of Despair* (No. 220). John Hamilton Mortimer exhibited a drawing of the *Captive* (location unknown) at the Society of Artists in 1774,[4] and Joseph Wright of Derby painted a *Captive* in the same year (location unknown; copy in the Derby Art Gallery), exhibiting either it or a second version at the Royal Academy in 1778. Wright also painted or began paintings of two

further subjects from Sterne, one of which, *An Old Man and His Ass* (location unknown), is the same subject as West's companion to his *Captive*.[5]

A second *Captive*, described in 1829 as a study, is No. 225 below. A drawing, which shows the prisoner in a similar position as in No. 224, scratching on a stick and a similarly located window in the upper left, but which is otherwise quite different in effect, is in the Historical Society of Pennsylvania.[6]

[1] See Kerslake 1977, I, pp. 260–69, II, pls. 763–70. Additionally, see the drawing in the Ford Collection, New York Public Library, reproduced as the frontispiece to Gardner D. Stout's edition of *A Sentimental Journey*, Berkeley and Los Angeles, 1967.
[2] Whitley 1928a, II, pp. 265–66.
[3] See Lewis Perry Curtis, ed., *Letters of Laurence Sterne*, Oxford, 1935, pp. 448–52.
[4] An etching after Mortimer's drawing is illustrated in *John Hamilton Mortimer ARA 1740–1779* (exhibition catalogue), Towner Art Gallery, Eastbourne, and Iveagh Bequest, Kenwood, 1968, p. 43 (82).
[5] Benedict Nicolson, *Joseph Wright of Derby*, London and New York, 1968, I, pp. 60–61, 150–51, 241–42, 246–47, and II, pls. 162, 184, and 220. Wright left *An Old Man and His Ass*

unfinished, and Nicolson does not assign it a date. The third subject, *Maria and Her Dog Sylvio*, exists in two versions, of which the first (private collection) is signed and dated *1777*.
[6] Charcoal and wash, inscribed *Barabas* on the mount.

225 The Captive, from Sterne

LOCATION UNKNOWN

PROV: Sold by West's sons, Robins, London, 20–22 June 1829, lot 153 ("The Captive from Sterne, a study, by the late B. West . . .—beginning of Telemachus in the Island of Calypso, by ditto— View from Greenwich Hill, by ditto")

226 Rinaldo and Armida 1766–90

RUTGERS UNIVERSITY ART GALLERY, NEW BRUNSWICK, NEW JERSEY

Oil on canvas: 26 × 32 in. (66 × 81.5 cm.)

Signed bottom center: *B. West 1766, Retouched 1790*

226

PROV: Peter Delmé (1748–1789); his sale, Christie's, London, 13 Feb. 1790, lot 25; John Rushout, second Lord Northwick (1770–1859); his sale, Phillips, Thirlestone House, Cheltenham, 26 July–30 Aug. 1859, lot 67 (as "Renaldo and Amida"), bt. by J. E. Dixon, America, for £27.6.0.; the Revd. George Warrington Eccles, Flushing, New York, 1898; Willet L. Eccles, by whom given to Rutgers University in 1952

EXH: Philadelphia 1938 (12) as "Angelica and Medoro"

LIT: Evans 1959, p. 20, pl. 16

No. 226 depicts the well-known and frequently painted scene described in the sixteenth book of *Gerusalemme Liberata* by Torquato Tasso (1544–1595) in which Rinaldo holds a mirror, so that Armida can see her love reflected, while he sees his reflected in her eyes. In the background are two knights, Ubaldo and Guelfo, who have come in search of Rinaldo. Robert Rosenblum pointed out in 1960 that this work shows an obvious dependence upon the painting of the same subject by Domenichino now in the Louvre.[1] West himself owned

a small *Rinaldo and Armida* by or ascribed to Domenichino,[2] but it seems unlikely that it would have been in his possession as early as 1766.

An oil sketch is No. 227 below. West painted this same scene again, in a different composition, in Nos. 229 and 230, and he exhibited yet another picture (No. 228) as "Rinaldo and Armida" at the Royal Academy in 1776, although that painting is not based on the same passage from Tasso. Only two of these pictures appear on the early lists of West's works: No. 228 and one other, listed in *La Belle Assemblée* as "for Caleb Whiteford, Esq." There is no way of proving which version Whiteford owned, but for reasons discussed under No. 229, it seems somewhat more likely to have been that picture than No. 226 or No. 230.

West was given the opportunity to retouch this painting when it was sold in 1790 following the death of Peter Delmé. The painting does show very evident retouching, presumably done at that time, but comparison with the oil sketch (No. 227) establishes that he did not substantially alter the composition.

In subject, and to some extent in style, No. 226 follows two other scenes of amatory dalliance based on

similar literary sources: *Angelica and Medoro*, which appeared at the Society of Artists in 1764 (see No. 188) and *Cymon and Iphigenia*, of which West exhibited versions in 1764 and 1766 (Nos. 195 and 196).

[1]Rosenblum 1960, p. 78.
[2]Sold, Christie's, London, 23–24 June 1820, 2nd day, lot 41, Domenichino, "Rinaldo and Armida, in a garden scene," panel, 6 × 6½ in.

227 Rinaldo and Armida *c.* 1766

NICOLAS M. EUSTATHIOU

Oil on paper mounted on board: 15½ × 19 in. (39.5 × 48.5 cm.)

PROV: By descent in the family of Raphael West to Aubyn Raphael Margary, by whom sold, Sotheby's, London, 2 March 1983, lot 67

No. 227 is a sketch in grisaille for No. 226. It shows no major compositional differences from the finished painting, but there are numerous slight alterations of details. The garland of flowers which hangs across

227

Rinaldo's chest in No. 227 has been moved down to his arm in the painting; another garland embellishes his sword in No. 226, but not in the sketch; the cherubs in the lower right corner, who are nude in No. 227, have been supplied with some draperies in No. 226, etc.

It was West's practice throughout his career to make monochrome sketches in oil on paper for his more ambitious paintings. No. 227 would seem to be the earliest such sketch to have come to light. An analogous sketch (No. 36), of approximately the same size, is for *Agrippina Landing at Brundisium with the Ashes of Germanicus* (No. 33), of 1768.

228 Rinaldo and Armida 1773

See color illustration p. 78

LOS ANGELES COUNTY MUSEUM OF ART

Oil on canvas: 49 × 63 in. (124.5 × 160 cm.)

Signed lower left: *B. West/1773*

PROV: John Hobart, second Earl of Buckinghamshire (1723–1793); his daughter Amelia Anne, wife of the second Marquess of Londonderry; by family descent to Lady Mairi Bury (daughter of the seventh Marquess of Londonderry), Mount Stewart, Newtownards, County Down, Northern Ireland, until 1977; Thos. Agnew and Sons, London; Coe Kerr Gallery, New York, from whom purchased by the Los Angeles County Museum in 1982

EXH: RA 1776 (320) "Rinaldo and Armida"

LISTED: *PC*, p. 564 ("Rinaldo and Armida"—late Lord Buckinghamshire); *UM*, p. 529; *BA*, p. 16; Galt, p. 225; Dillenberger, p. 163 (245)

No. 228 does not show the same scene from *Gerusalemme Liberata* as Nos. 226, 229, and 230, and it is even questionable that it is based on Tasso at all. When it appeared on the market in 1977 it was called "Cymon and Iphigenia," and it does seem closer to West's earlier treatment of that subject (No. 196) than it does to any of his other paintings of Rinaldo and Armida. Nevertheless, if the male figure on the left of No. 228 distinctly recalls the figure of Cymon in No. 196, the central female figure makes a somewhat inappropriate Iphigenia, who is traditionally depicted as bare-breasted and asleep.

The reason for cataloguing No. 228 as a painting of *Rinaldo and Armida* here is that it has a remarkably complete provenance, which establishes it as the picture bearing that title in the early lists of West's works and exhibited as "Rinaldo and Armida" at the Royal Academy in 1776. No. 228 appeared together at the Academy with *Isaac's Servant Tying the Bracelet on Rebecca's Arm* (No. 243), and the two paintings shared the same history until 1978.

In the entry for No. 243 we propose that both pictures may be allegorical portraits of the second wife of Lord Buckinghamshire, their first owner. If this hypothesis is correct, and portraiture rather than accurate illustration of a text was West's first purpose, it may partly explain why he took such liberties with the ostensible subjects of both paintings.

229 Rinaldo and Armida 1780–96

LOCATION UNKNOWN

(52 × 64 in.) (132 × 162.5 cm.)

Signed lower right: *B. West/1780/Retouched/1796*

PROV: (?) Caleb Whitefoord; (?) F. B. Greenstreet, London, by whom sold, Christie's, London, 17 Dec. 1926, lot 49 (as "Venus and Adonis with cupids, Mars in the background"), bt. by Turner; (?) sold anonymously, Christie's, London, 28–29 July 1927, lot 320 (as "Rinaldo and Armida"); Albert Rosenthal, New Hope, Pennsylvania; his estate sale, Samuel T. Freeman and Co., New Hope, 13–16 Sept. 1939, lot 1258

(?) LISTED: *PC*, p. 564 ("Rinaldo and Armida"— Caleb Whitford, Esq.); *UM*, p. 529; Barlow, p. 433; *BA*, p. 16 (for Caleb Whitefoord, Esq.); Galt, p. 224; Dillenberger, p. 162 (235)

Nos. 229 and 230, which is a reduced replica with significant differences only in the background, illustrate the same lines from *Gerusalemme Liberata* as No. 226. They differ considerably in composition from the earlier work, and they show Armida, aided by a *putto*, holding the mirror, rather than Rinaldo.

No. 229 is or was the largest of West's paintings of the subject, and hence seems the most likely among Nos. 226, 229, and 230 to have been the version included in the early lists of his works. Three of those lists indicate that a *Rinaldo and Armida* belonged to "Caleb Whitford"; the fourth, in *La Belle Assemblée*, that it was painted "for Caleb Whitefoord," thus implying that it was a commissioned work. Since the only list with a correct spelling of Whitefoord's name is that of *La Belle Assemblée*, and since it is in general the most reliable of the lists, its "for" is credible. Caleb Whitefoord (1734–1810), a sometime journalist, famous wit, and friend and neighbor of Benjamin Franklin in London, was certainly in touch with West around or shortly after 1780. He sat to Gilbert Stuart, who was then working in West's studio, for a portrait which Stuart exhibited at the Royal Academy in 1782, and in 1783 or 1784 he lent West a portrait of Franklin to use in the *Signing of the Preliminary Treaty of Peace* (No. 105), in which Whitefoord was himself supposed to be represented as secretary of the British delegation to the conference. Hence the date of *1780* on No. 229 seems consistent with the little we know about Whitefoord's contacts with the artist. West, however, must either have failed to deliver the painting for some sixteen years, or had it back in his studio by 1796, when he retouched it.

No. 229 had been lost since 1939, and from a photograph it is impossible to tell the nature or extent of West's retouching.

230 Rinaldo and Armida 1797

GEORGE E. DOTY

Oil on panel: 13 × 16 in. (33 × 40.5 cm.)

Inscribed verso: *Rinaldo & Armida/B. West/1797*

PROV: (?) Mrs. Galbraith, Ontario; sold anonymously, Sotheby Parke Bernet, New York, 21 Nov. 1979, lot 53, where bt. by the present owner

No. 230 is a small version of No. 229, differing from it most notably in the arrangement of curtains and foliage in the background, some variations in Armida's dress, and the addition of drapery partly covering the *putto* in the upper right. The date of *1797* on the back of the picture suggests that West probably began it while retouching No. 229 in 1796 or shortly thereafter.

An old photograph of what appears to be this version of the composition shows an identical signature *B. West/1780/Retouched/1796* in the same spot as that on No. 229. That signature was evidently forged, and no trace of it can now be seen on No. 230. Nor does it appear on another old photograph of No. 230 in the Witt Library, which lists the owner as Mrs. Galbraith.

230

231

231 Musidora and Her Two Companions
1795–1806

PRIVATE COLLECTION

Oil on canvas: $20\frac{1}{2} \times 28\frac{1}{2}$ in. (52 × 72.5 cm.)

Signed upper right: *B. West 1795/Retouched 1806*

PROV: Offered by West's sons to the United States in 1826 (127, "Musidora," 1 ft. $8\frac{1}{2}$ in. × 2 ft. 4 in.), and sold by them, Robins, London, 20–22 June 1829, lot 66 ("Damon and Musidora, from Thompson's Seasons . . . considered one of the very finest specimens of the Master; colouring in the gusto of the Venetian school"); probably acquired *c.* 1829 by James Morrison (1789–1857) of Balham Hill and later Basildon Park; Captain Archibald Morrison, Basildon Park, Berkshire, 1914; sold anonymously, Christie's, London, 21 Nov. 1975, lot 79 (as "Nymphs Surprised by a Young Man"), bt. by Weitzner; M. Knoedler and Co., New York

EXH: (?) RA 1796 (175+) "Nymphs Bathing"; *Third National Loan Exhibition: Pictures from the Basildon Park and Fonthill Collections*, Grosvenor Gallery, London, 1914–15, (53) as "Nymphs Surprised while Bathing" from Basildon Park

LISTED: *PC*, p. 565 ("The small picture from Thomson's Seasons, of Miranda and her two Companions," West, Painting-room); *UM*, p. 530; *BA*, p. 17; Galt, p. 227; Dillenberger, p. 170 (315)

Although No. 231 has consistently been assigned a variety of incorrect titles throughout its history, it illustrates a variant version of one of the best-known passages in James Thomson's *Seasons*. The story of Damon and Musidora, in which Damon inadvertently spies Musidora bathing in a stream, comes from lines 1289–1370 of "Summer," one of the four books of *The Seasons*, published between 1726 and 1730. In all editions after 1744 Musidora bathes alone, but in the first published versions of "Summer" she has two companions, Sacharissa and Amoret, who bathe with her. There is no analogous scene with a "Miranda" in *The Seasons*, and that name in *Public Characters* and other early lists of West's works is clearly a mistake for Musidora. Damon wearing a red coat is visible in the left background of No. 231.

An analogous story of voyeurism is that of Arethusa from Ovid, in which the river god Alpheus observes the nymph Arethusa bathe. West exhibited an *Arethusa* at the Royal Academy in 1802, and copies of that painting were subsequently exhibited in the United States under the title "Musidora" (see No. 119). West's own *Musidora* and *Arethusa* paintings are clearly distinguished on the list of works offered by West's sons to the United States in 1826 by different measurements; furthermore Ovid's Arethusa does not have any companions, nor should she wear a stylish eighteenth-century bonnet.

West evidently exhibited the painting at the Royal Academy in 1796, the year after he painted it, but, for some reason, without its being listed in the exhibition catalogue. Algernon Graves's dictionary of Royal Academy contributors lists for 1796 a "175+ Nymphs bathing" in addition to "175 Moses and Aaron before Pharaoh" (No. 252). Since only the latter entry appears in copies of Academy catalogues known to the compilers of this catalogue, we surmise that Graves took his "175+" from a marginal notation made by a visitor to the Royal Academy, who supplied his own title for an exhibited but uncatalogued picture. As a work titled or identifiable as "Nymphs Bathing" is not otherwise recorded in any source from West's lifetime, the exhibited picture was probably this one, whose proper subject again eluded detection both when it was exhibited in 1914 and when it was sold in 1975.

SUBJECTS FROM THE OLD TESTAMENT AND APOCRYPHA

232 The Expulsion of Adam and Eve from Paradise 1791

LOCATION UNKNOWN

(72 × 108 in.) (183 × 274 cm.)

PROV: Painted for George III (1797 account: "The Expulsion of Adam and Eve from Paradise," 1791, £525; 1801 account, p. 209: for the Windsor Chapel, Antediluvian Dispensation, 1, . . .); never delivered and ownership returned to West's sons by George IV in 1828; sold by them, Robins, London, 22–25 May 1829, lot 154 (6 ft. × 9), bt. by Smith for £441, apparently on behalf of Raphael West; sold by Raphael West, Robins, London, 16 July 1831, lot 40

EXH: RA 1791 (147) "The Expulsion of Adam and Eve from Paradise, for His Majesty's chapel, Windsor Castle"; West's Gallery 1821 (47), 1822–28 (98)

LISTED: *PC*, p. 560 ("The Expulsion of Adam and Eve from Paradise," George III, for his Majesty's Chapel, Windsor, Patriarchal Dispensation); *UM*, p. 527; *AA*, p. 66 (Antediluvian and Patriarchal Dispensation . . . 9 ft. × 6); Barlow, p. 431; *BA*, p. 14 (Antediluvian Dispensation); Galt, p. 218; Dillenberger, p. 143 (63)

LIT: Meyer 1975, p. 264; Dillenberger 1977, pp. 58–63 passim

In narrative sequence, No. 232 is or was the first of West's series of paintings devoted to the History of Revealed Religion and intended for the Royal Chapel in Windsor Castle. For a consideration of that undertaking as a whole and the works painted for it, see Appendix I. The list of West's paintings published in Joel Barlow's *Columbiad* includes an "Adam and Eve Created" for the chapel before No. 232, but that subject is recorded in no other source, and it seems certain that it was never painted. Neither No. 232 nor any other pre-Mosaic subject appears on the architectural drawings for the chapel dating from *c.* 1779–80 (ill. pp. 577–9), and it may be that West did not initially plan to include any subjects from what he later termed the Antediluvian and Patriarchal Dispensation(s). He did eventually paint or commence five pre-Mosaic subjects for the chapel (Nos. 232, 234, 236, 240, and 245), but none of them prior to 1790 (the date on a sketch for No. 234). On the diagrams dated 1801 in the Friends Historical Library at Swarthmore College for a revised arrangement of the chapel paintings (ill. p. 580) Nos. 234, 236, 240, and 245 and a fifth subject, "12 Tribes in Egypt," are shown on a wall devoted to Old Testament subjects. The *Expulsion* does not appear there with them, but a subject listed simply as "Adam" is included on what seems to be an end wall of the rearranged chapel as part of a triptychal arrangement of smaller pictures, with a "Last Supper" (see No. 344) at the center, situated beneath a much larger "Crucifixion" (see No. 356).

Although No. 232 has disappeared, we have some idea of what it looked like from a finished oil sketch (No. 233). The early lists of West's works include one drawing of the subject.[1] Ruth Kraemer has tentatively associated a drawing in the Pierpont Morgan Library with the chapel *Expulsion*,[2] but the figures in that drawing do not correspond very closely with those in No. 233.

[1] *PC*, p. 568 ("The Drawing of the Expulsion of Adam and Eve," West, Gallery); *UM*, p. 531; Galt, p. 232; Dillenberger, p. 182 (441)
[2] Black chalk, 7⅞ × 4⅞ in. (Kraemer 1975, p. 32, no. 50 and pl. 29).

233 The Expulsion of Adam and Eve from Paradise *c.* 1790–1805

ART INSTITUTE OF CHICAGO

Oil on canvas: 19½ × 28½ in. (49.5 × 72.5 cm.)

PROV: Offered by West's sons to the United States in 1826 (104), and sold by them, Robins, London, 22–25 May 1829, lot 88 (1 ft. 7 in. × 2 ft. 4½ in.), bt. by Hayes for £45.3.0.; (?) Graves and Son, London; Samuel Putnam Avery, New York, by whom sold to Thomas Clarke, New York, by 1891; sold by Clarke, American Art Galleries, New York, 14–18 Feb. 1899, lot 355, bt. by Harry W. Watrous for $200; George F. Harding, Chicago (deceased 1939); George F. Harding Museum, Chicago, until 1982 when transferred to the Art Institute of Chicago

EXH: RA 1805 (86) "The Expulsion of Adam and Eve from Paradise, Genesis, chap. iii":

> Ver. 21. Unto Adam also, and to his wife, did the Lord God make coats of skins, and clothed them.
>
> Ver. 22. And the Lord God said, Behold, the man is become as one of us, to know good and evil. And now, lest he put forth his hand and take also of the tree of life, and eat and live for ever.
>
> Ver. 23. Therefore the Lord God sent him forth from the garden of Eden to till the earth, whence he was taken.

West's Gallery 1821 (73); *The Thomas B. Clarke Collection of American Pictures*, Pennsylvania Academy, Philadelphia 1891 (192); *Retrospective Exhibition of American Paintings*, World's Columbian Exposition, Chicago, 1893 (2861b); Brooklyn 1922 (23) lent by Harry W. Watrous.

LISTED: *PC*, p. 566 ("The Expulsion of Adam and Eve from Paradise," West, Gallery); *UM*, p. 530; Barlow, p. 435; *BA*, p. 17; Galt, p. 229; Dillenberger, pp. 174 (353) and 214

LIT: Meyer 1975, p. 264; Dillenberger 1977, p. 62, pl. 36

No. 233 can be identified with reasonable certainty as the oil sketch painted *c.* 1790 for the large picture of the *Expulsion* for the Royal Chapel at Windsor (No. 232), which West exhibited at the Royal Academy in 1791. In the same year West also exhibited a second chapel painting, the "Abating of the Waters after the Deluge" (No. 234). That painting is lost, but a small version (No. 235), which is known and is exactly the same size as No. 233, is signed and dated *B. West 1790/Retouched 1803*. The two small versions (Nos. 233 and 235) appeared together at the Royal Academy in 1805.

234 The Deluge 1791

LOCATION UNKNOWN

(72 × 108 in.) (183 × 274 cm.)

PROV: Painted for George III (1797 account: "The picture of the Deluge" for the Chapel, 1791, £525; 1801 account, p. 209: for the Windsor Chapel, Antediluvian Dispensation, 2, . . .); never delivered and ownership returned to West's sons by George IV in 1828; (?) offered by West to the Pennsylvania Academy in 1809 (the "Deluge," 9 ft. 6 in. × 6 ft., £200); sold by West's sons, Robins, London, 22–25 May 1829, lot 166 ("The Waters Subsiding After the

233

Deluge," 6 ft. × 9), bt. by Sandby for £472.10.0., apparently on behalf of Raphael West; sold by Raphael West, Robins, London, 16 July 1831, lot 41

EXH: RA 1791 (169) "The Abating of the Waters after the Deluge, for his Majesty's chapel, Windsor-castle"; West's Gallery 1821 (50), not in subsequent catalogue, but added by hand in that for 1828 replacing no. 131 the *Death of Nelson* (No. 108)

LISTED: *PC*, p. 560 ("The Deluge," George III, for his Majesty's Chapel, Windsor, Patriarchal Dispensation); *UM*, p. 527; *AA*, p. 66 (Antediluvian and Patriarchal Dispensation, . . . 9 ft. × 6); Barlow, p. 431; *BA*, p. 14 (Antediluvian Dispensation); Galt, p. 218; Dillenberger, p. 144 (64)

LIT: Meyer 1975, pp. 258–60, 264; Dillenberger 1977, pp. 58–63

The *Expulsion* and the *Deluge* (Nos. 232 and 234) are listed together under 1791 in West's account of 1797 recording the works he had done since 1780 for George III. Both appeared in the same Royal Academy exhibition in 1791, and oil sketches for them (Nos. 233 and 235) were exhibited together in 1805, so it would seem that West thought of the pictures as a pair. In 1829 the two larger pictures were apparently bought in by Raphael West, and when they were resold in 1831, along with a *Crucifixion* (No. 356), the catalogue suggested that the three paintings might become part of a chapel arrangement, "the centre to admit of the upright picture of the Crucifixion, that to the right, the Expulsion, and that to the left, the Deluge." The subjects do not appear in any of the drawings from *c.* 1780 for the chapel at Windsor. In the diagrams of 1801, the *Deluge* appears on the far left of the lower range of subjects on a wall devoted to Old Testament subjects, while the *Expulsion* appears to be on the end wall, as "Adam," under the *Crucifixion* (ill. p. 000).

A "Deluge" was among the works that West offered to sell to the Pennsylvania Academy of the Fine Arts in 1809. We have included that offer in the provenance above for No. 234, but strictly speaking West could not have sold No. 234 to the Pennsylvanians, since it already belonged to the King. He probably intended to paint a replica for Philadelphia but, since his offer was not taken up by the Academy, the replica almost certainly was never painted.

Like No. 232, No. 234 is lost, but its appearance is probably reflected in No. 235. The early catalogues of West's *oeuvre* list one drawing of the subject.[1] A drawing of "The Waters subsiding after the Deluge" was exhibited by West's sons in 1823 and sold by Benjamin West, Jr. in 1839.[2] A drawing now in Boston appears to be a copy after the composition, rather than a study for it.[3] Many elements of the composition also appear in a large drawing of *Noah Sacrificing* in the collection of Mr. and Mrs. Erving Wolf. A drawing of the *Deluge* in the Pierpont Morgan Library has no compositional resemblance to No. 235. It does have a West-Margary family provenance and is ascribed by Ruth Kraemer to Raphael West.[5]

[1] *PC*, p. 568 ("The Drawing of the Deluge," West, Gallery); *UM*, p. 531; Galt, p. 232; Dillenberger, p. 182 (442).
[2] West's Gallery 1823 (Room of Drawings, no. 52) and S. Leigh Sotheby, London, 1 June 1839, lot 116.
[3] Watercolor and body-color, 9 × 12 11/16 in.; ill. in Meyer 1975, p. 260, fig. 19, and in Dillenberger 1977, p. 62, pl. 37; exhibited, San Antonio 1983, no. 10.
[4] Pen and ink on blue prepared paper, 22 × 32 in. (San Antonio 1983, no. 8).
[5] Pen and black ink, and grey wash, arched top, 6 3/16 × 16 13/16 in. (Kraemer 1975, pp. 93–94, no. 226 as "Shipwreck Scene," and pl. 118).

235 The Deluge 1790–1803
See illustration, p. 122

DR. ROBERT ERWIN JONES

Oil on canvas: 19½ × 29 in. (49.5 × 73.5 cm.)

Signed lower left: *B. West 1790/Retouched 1803*, and inscribed verso on the stretcher in different hands: *B. West* and *bought of Benj. West Esq./July 1805*

PROV: Sold by West to N. W. Ridley Colborne (1779–1854), July 1805; anonymous sale, Christie's, London, 26–27 April 1973, lot 300, bt. by Pearson; Sabin Galleries, London

EXH: RA 1805 (77) "The deluge, Genesis, chap. viii":

Ver. 6. So after forty days, Noah opened the window of the ark which he had made;

Ver. 7. And sent forth a raven, which went out, going forth and returning, until the waters were dried up upon the earth.

Ver. 8. Again, he sent a dove from him, that he might see if the waters were diminished from off the earth;

Ver. 9. But the dove found no rest for the sole of her foot; therefore she returned unto him into the ark (for the waters were upon the whole earth), and he put forth his hand and received her, and took her to him into the ark.

Ver. 10. And he abode yet other seven days, and again he sent forth the dove out of the ark;

Ver. 11. And the dove came to him in the evening, and lo in her mouth was an olive leaf that she had plucked; whereby Noah knew that the waters were abated from the earth.

San Antonio 1983 (9)

LISTED: *PC*, p. 566 ("The Deluge," West, Gallery); *UM*, p. 530; Barlow, p. 435; *BA*, p. 18; Galt, p. 229; Dillenberger, p. 192 (442)

In addition to the inscriptions on the stretcher of No. 235 recorded above, there is also glued to the stretcher a letter from West to Ridley Colborne dated 15 July 1805, about West's readiness to part with the picture of the *Deluge* that Colborne had admired. Colborne's opportunity to admire it had been provided by that year's Royal Academy exhibition. The date of *1790* on No. 235 suggests that West began the painting as an oil sketch for the lost No. 234, which he exhibited in 1791. The retouching of 1803 presumably turned the preparatory sketch into an exhibitable picture. No. 233, which is the same size as this painting, and No. 232 seem to have had parallel early histories.

In the catalogue of the exhibition of West's paintings of religious subjects that took place in San Antonio in 1983, Nancy Pressly has proposed that West exhibited the sketches (Nos. 233 and 235) at the Royal Academy in 1791, and that the lost large paintings (Nos. 232 and 234) were painted and exhibited in 1805. This reversal of the sequence presented here is contradicted by the facts that West specified in the Academy catalogue that the pictures he exhibited in 1791 were "for his Majesty's chapel," and that West himself assigned the date of 1791 to Nos. 232 and 234 in his account for George III prepared in 1797. Mrs. Pressly's catalogue also includes an essay devoted to Nos. 235 and 236, discussing possible sources, related works, and the intellectual context in which they were painted.

236 Noah Sacrificing *c.* 1801
See color illustration, p. 98

SAN ANTONIO MUSEUM OF ART, SAN ANTONIO, TEXAS

Oil on canvas: 72 × 138 in. (182.9 × 350.5 cm.)

PROV: Painted for George III (1801 account, p. 210: for the Windsor Chapel, Antediluvian Dispensation, 3, "Noah and his Family sacrificing," £525); never delivered and ownership returned to West's sons by George IV in 1828; sold by them, Robins, London, 22–25 May 1829, lot 53 (11 ft. 6 in. × 6 ft., "Painted by command of His Late Majesty, for his intended Chapel in Windsor Castle,/Genesis, chap. 8./Verse 20. And Noah builded an altar unto the Lord; and took of every clean beast and of every clean fowl, and offered burnt offerings on the altar."), bt. by H. P. Bone for £26.5.0. on behalf of Joseph Neeld, MP, Grittleton House, Wilts.; by descent to Captain L. W. Neeld, Grittleton House (died *c.* 1962); sold by John Bourne, Christie's, London, 3 July 1964, lot 84, bt. by Dent; Central Picture Galleries, New York, 1964; Spencer A. Samuels, New York, from whom purchased by the San Antonio Museum of Art

EXH: West's Gallery 1821 (85), 1822–28 (126); San Antonio 1983 (11)

LISTED: *PC*, p. 560 ("Noah Sacrificing," George III, for his Majesty's Chapel, Windsor, Patriarchal Dispensation); *UM*, p. 527; *AA*, p. 66 (Antediluvian and Patriarchal Dispensation . . . 9 ft. × 6); Barlow, p. 431; *BA*, p. 14; Galt, p. 218; Dillenberger, pp. 144 (66) and 214

LIT: Kraemer 1975, pp. 31–32; Meyer 1975, p. 264; Dillenberger 1977, p. 63, pl. 38

For an extended consideration of No. 236 from a variety of perspectives, see the catalogue of the exhibition *Revealed Religion* (San Antonio 1983), which Nancy Pressly organized around this work. Identification of No. 236 with West's painting for the Royal Chapel at Windsor is substantiated by the correspondence of its measurements with those given in the Robins catalogue of May 1829. The measurements in the sale catalogue are for a picture eleven and a half feet high, rather than wide, but that appears to have been a careless transposition. No. 236 appears in West's account for George III of 1801, but not that of 1797, which indicates that it was painted between those years. It is the only work for the chapel listed in the account of 1801 with a price by it (supposedly indicating that it had been painted), as well as the only work sold in 1829 as a chapel painting, that had not been exhibited at the Royal Academy. The reason was that it had not, in fact, been completed; it received a relatively low price in 1829, evidently because of its unfinished state.

The subject does not appear on the architectural schemes for the chapel from *c.* 1780. In the diagrams of 1801 at Swarthmore, "Sacrifice Noah" appears second from the left, between the "Deluge" and "Abraham Sacrificing," in the bottom row of a wall devoted to Old Testament subjects (ill. p. 580). No. 236 is approximately 30 in. wider than the other horizontal compositions intended for the chapel. That may have been because West initially intended it to go below *Moses Receiving the Laws* (No. 258), which is the largest work he actually painted for the chapel and is some 30 in. wider than the paintings placed on either side of it in the scheme recorded in the diagrams of 1801. However, in those diagrams *Abraham and His Son Isaac Going to Sacrifice* (No. 240), rather than No. 236, is under No. 258.

A drawing of the subject which incorporates additional imagery that appears in West's *Deluge* is in the collection of Mr. and Mrs. Erving Wolf (see No. 235). Ruth Kraemer has also associated two drawings in the Morgan Library and a further drawing now in the Bayou Bend Collection in Houston, with the chapel painting.[1] The latter drawing shows no obvious connection with the composition of No. 236.

In Lawrence's full-length portrait of West, painted between 1818 and 1821 (Frontispiece), the larger of two pictures in the background may have been intended by Lawrence to represent No. 236. In 1819 West described the portrait as showing him delivering a discourse "on the immutability of colors on the Rainbow system and their proper stations in a good organized picture."[2] This had been the subject of his discourse to the students at the Royal Academy in December 1817, which Lawrence attended.[3] The picture within Lawrence's picture appears to be approximately the same size as No. 236, and the rainbow is in roughly the same position on the canvas. Somewhat ironically, in light of West's "immutability," the colors of Lawrence's rainbow are reversed, and the doves and other details from the right side of No. 236 are not discernible. For the smaller painting in the background of the portrait see No. 513.

[1] Kraemer 1975, p. 31, no. 48 (black chalk, $3\frac{1}{4} \times 3\frac{1}{8}$ in.) and p. 32, no. 49 (pen and brown ink, $3\frac{7}{8} \times 3\frac{1}{8}$ in.). The Houston drawing is in pen and wash, $4\frac{1}{4} \times 8\frac{1}{2}$ in.
[2] Letter to John Trumbull, 21 May 1819, quoted by Charles C. Cunningham, letter to the editor, *Art in America*, XXXIX, April 1951, p. 95.
[3] Farington Diary, 12 Dec. 1817 (Farington 1978—, XIV, p. 5120).

237 Abraham Entertaining the Angels

LOCATION UNKNOWN

Oil on panel: $7 \times 8\frac{1}{2}$ in. (18×21.5 cm.)

PROV: Sold by Mrs. Albert F. West, Christie's, London, 18–19 March 1898, lot 137, bt. by Sir C. Robinson for £2.15.0.

There is no record of any painting of this subject by West apart from the sale catalogue of 1898, which establishes a family provenance, but does not guarantee correct identification of the subject, or that the work was certainly by West.

238 Lot and His Daughters Conducted by Two Angels 1810

See color illustrations, pp. 110, 123

DETROIT INSTITUTE OF ARTS

Oil on panel: $47\frac{1}{4} \times 78$ in. (120×198 cm.)

Signed lower right: *B. West/1810*

PROV: Purchased from John Wilson of the European Museum in 1819 by Sir John Fleming Leicester, Bt. (later the first Lord de Tabley, died 1827); his sale, Christie's, London, 7 July 1827, lot 45, bt. by Jackson for £105; given by Mrs. Newton Jackson in memory of her son Leyton Thomas, who died in 1906, to Radley College, Oxfordshire; sold Phillip, Son, & Neale, London, 6 April 1970, lot P90, bt. by Leger Galleries, by whom sold to the Detroit Institute of Art in the same year

EXH: RA 1811 (188) "Lot and his daughters conducted by two Angels":

> And when the morning arose, then the angels hastened Lot, saying, "arise, take thy wife and thy two daughters, which are here, lest thou be consumed in the iniquity of the city."
>
> And while he lingered, the men laid hold upon his hand, and upon the hand of his wife, and upon the hand of his two daughters; the Lord being merciful unto him; and they brought him forth, and set him without the city.
>
> And it came to pass, when they had brought them forth abroad, that he said, "escape for thy life; look not behind thee, neither stay thou in all the plain; escape to the mountain, lest thou be consumed."

> The sun was risen upon the earth when Lot entered into Zoar.
>
> Then the Lord rained upon Sodom, and upon Gomorrah, brimstone and fire from the Lord out of heaven.
>
> And he overthrew those cities, and all the plain, and all inhabitants of the cities, and that which grew upon the ground.
>
> But his wife looked back from behind him, and she became a pillar of salt.
>
> *Genesis, chap. xix, ver. 15, 16, 17, 23, 24, 25, and 26*

BI 1814 (146) "Lot and his family conducted by two angels from the burning city destroyed by fire from heaven," with a quotation from Genesis, xix, 16 and 23, and measurements as 5 ft. 6 in. × 7 ft. 10 in. (including frame); Sir John Leicester's Gallery, 1819 (26)

ENGR: Etching ($4\frac{1}{4} \times 6\frac{7}{16}$ in.) by John Young, pub. as no. 30, opp. p. 14, in his *Catalogue of Pictures by British Artists in the Possession of Sir John Fleming Leicester, Bart.*, 1821

LISTED: Dillenberger, p. 214

LIT: Farington Diary, 15 March 1811 (Farington 1978—, XI, p. 3894); V and A Cuttings, III, pp. 890 and 891 (reviews of BI 1814); Hazlitt 1930–34, XVIII, pp. 13–14; William Carey, *A Descriptive Catalogue of a Collection of Paintings by British Artists in the Possession of Sir John Fleming Leicester, Bart.*, London, 1819, pp. 77–80 (26); John Young, *A Catalogue of Pictures by British Artists, in the possession of Sir John Fleming Leicester, Bart.*, London, 1821, p. 14 (30); Hall 1962, pp. 102 and 122 (111); Dillenberger 1977, p. 121, pl. 82

Sir John Fleming Leicester purchased No. 238 in January 1819 by exchanging the *Destruction of the Beast and False Prophet* (No. 410), which he had purchased from West in 1818, and paying an additional 100 guineas. John Wilson of the European Museum probably had the painting on consignment from West rather than owning it himself, as No. 410 subsequently returned to West's (or his sons') possession. No. 238 hung in the Leicester house in London and is recognizable in the engraved frontispiece to William Carey's catalogue of the collection published in 1819.

The combination of a scene of Old Testament disaster and extensive landscape may have been partly inspired by the depictions of similar subjects painted and exhibited by Turner in the first years of the nineteenth century. Turner painted a *Destruction of Sodom*, c. 1805 (Tate Gallery), but No. 238 has greater compositional affinities with somewhat earlier paintings such as the *Tenth Plague of Egypt* of 1802 (Tate Gallery). In the collection of Sir John Fleming Leicester it hung amidst a distinguished group of paintings by Turner.

Joseph Farington first saw No. 238 on 15 March 1811, and was "much struck" with it. The painting seems to have attracted little attention when exhibited at the Royal Academy that year, but it drew several notices when West re-exhibited it at the British Institution in 1814. The most quotable and least sympathetic was that of William Hazlitt, who described No. 238 as "one of those highly finished specimens of *metallurgy* which too often proceed from the President's hardware manufactory." The entries in the catalogues of the Leicester collection by Carey and Young both praised the picture (the former at length) and emphasized the fact that West painted it when in his seventy-second year.

A drawing for the figures, with a much less extensive landscape, is in the Vassar College Art Gallery.[1]

See also p. 123 above.

[1] Black and white chalk on blue paper, $9 \times 16\frac{5}{16}$ in. (*Vassar College Art Gallery: Selection from the Permanent Collection*, Poughkeepsie, New York, 1967, p. 31).

239 Hagar and Ishmael 1776–1803

See color illustration, p. 137

METROPOLITAN MUSEUM OF ART, NEW YORK

Oil on canvas: $76 \times 54\frac{1}{2}$ in. (193×138.5 cm.)

Signed lower right: *B. West/1776* and lower left: *B. West 1803*

PROV: Thomas Dawson, first Lord Cremorne; (?) unidentified "nobleman in Ireland"; in West's possession again by October 1802, offered by him to the Pennsylvania Academy in 1809 ("The picture, life [-sized], of Hagar and Ishmael," 6 ft. × 4 ft. 2 in., £150); offered by his sons to the United States in 1826 (21), and sold by them, Robins, London, 22–25 May 1829, lot 135 (6 ft. 3 in. × 4 ft. 6 in.), bt. by Armstrong for £52.10.0; Arthur E. S. Seguin (1809–1852) by 1851; by descent to Mrs. E. S. R. Seguin; on deposit in the Pennsylvania Academy from c. 1851 to c. 1864 and at the Metropolitan Museum from 1881 to 1923, when purchased by the museum from Mrs. Seguin

EXH: RA 1776 (318) "Hagar and Ishmael"; RA 1804 (211) "Hagar and Ishmael":

> And God heard the voice of the lad: and the angel of God called to Hagar out of heaven, and said unto her, What aileth thee Hagar? Fear not; for God hath heard the voice of the lad where he is.
>
> Arise, lift up the lad, and hold him in thine hand; for I will make of him a great nation.
>
> *Genesis, chap. xxi. ver. 17, 18*

BI 1806 (North Room, 94); PAFA 1851 (16) lent by S. Seguin, and again in most subsequent years through 1859; *Retrospective Exhibition of American Paintings*, Metropolitan Museum of Art, New York, 1895–96

ENGR: Mezzotint ($26\frac{5}{16} \times 20\frac{7}{8}$ in.) by Valentine Green, pub. 30 April 1805 by Green, dedicated to the Countess of Chesterfield

LISTED: *UM*, p. 531 ("The Angel appearing to Hagar and her sick Son," West, Gallery); not listed by Barlow, but probably identical with the "Abraham sending away Hagar with her child" mentioned on p. 436 among the works painted since the list had been drawn up; *BA*, p. 19 ("Hagar and Ishmael, figures as large as life; painted for Lord Cremorne, but now in the possession of a nobleman in Ireland"); Dillenberger, pp. 187 (490) and 211

LIT: Farington Diary, 14–28 April, 8 August, and 13 Nov. 1803, 29 March, 3 and 12 April, and 6 July 1804 (Farington 1978—, VI, pp. 2011–20, 2100–2, 2163–64, 2282–85, 2289, 2296–97, and 2372); *Morning Post*, 14 April 1803; Whitley 1928b, pp. 54–56; Evans 1959, pp. 52–53, pl. 38; Gardner and Feld 1965, pp. 28–29; Kraemer 1975, pp. 8–9; Dillenberger 1977, pp. 24–25, pl. 16; Alberts 1978, pp. 280–84, 289, 302

Although in *La Belle Assemblée* No. 239 is described as having been painted for Lord Cremorne, W. T. Whitley, who does not indicate his source, states that Lord Cremorne purchased the picture following the Royal Academy exhibition of 1776 because the figure of Ishmael chanced to bear a strong resemblance to his son, and that Lord Cremorne sold it following the latter's death. Lord Cremorne had two sons: the elder, from his first marriage, died at Cambridge in 1778; the younger, Thomas, who would have been five years old in 1776, died in 1787. Lord Cremorne's second wife, whom he married in 1770, was a granddaughter of William Penn and had been born in Philadelphia.

After re-acquiring the picture, West substantially repainted it and submitted it to the Royal Academy in 1803. Since it had been exhibited previously, in 1776, it was ineligible for exhibition, and in the midst of considerable debate, much of it carried on in the public press, it was withdrawn, although West succeeded in having it included in the following year's exhibition. In 1803 he defended his action of sending the work to the Academy a second time on two counts: he had not remembered that it had been exhibited before, and, more significantly, he had repainted it so extensively that it was effectively a new picture:

In Octr. last I began to prepare the pictures which I intented for the ensuing Exhibition among that number was that of Hagar & Ishmael which I sent to the Royal Academy on the [illegible]—the others not being in readiness on account of my ill state of health: the picture of Hagar I first painted in the year 1776 & whether exhibited, or not, in that year, I have not the least recollection . . . The picture has been reconsidered & intirely repainted by me, the Angel has been erased & a new one substituted. Hagar & Ishmael have undergone alterations, & new Draperies have been introduced, the back ground intirely changed, so that in every respect it is a *new picture* as much as that picture which is in the Chapel at the Foundling Hospital [No. 325] differs from that which I painted for Macklin's Gallery some years ago; on that picture as on the Hagar there are two dates shewing the time when painted and that when they underwent alterations; different dates may be seen on many of my other works which have ever been viewed as new pictures & it will prove to posterity how anxious I have been to leave the few works I have done as perfect as was in my power to make them.[1]

A drawing in the Victoria and Albert Museum (*right*), which is signed and dated *1776*,[2] may record the appearance of No. 239 before West repainted it. In the drawing, the angel does have a different pose, and there are also significant differences in the figures of Hagar and Ishmael and in other details, as claimed by the artist. The Victoria and Albert drawing also suggests that the original figure of Hagar was based on Mrs. West, and that of Ishmael on Raphael West, who would have been ten years old in 1776. Hagar in the drawing is also similar in appearance and dress to the mother in the *Golden Age* of 1776 (No. 419), who has traditionally been identified as Mrs. West; that picture may also at one time have been intended to represent Hagar and Ishmael.

A large finished drawing of the subject with a somewhat different composition, which is signed and dated *1788*, is in the Addison Gallery of American Art at Andover.[3] A sketchier drawing showing yet another composition was formerly in the collection of Mrs. Claire Francis,[4] and another is in the Pierpont Morgan Library.[5] Two drawings of the subject were exhibited in West's gallery in 1823 (Room of Drawings, nos. 10 and 48).

[1] Draft of a letter from West to the Council of the Royal Academy, dated 16 April 1803, now in Historical Society of Pennsylvania. A draft of a letter on the subject from West to George III, dated 20 November 1803, is in the same collection.
[2] Black and white chalk and some color on grey paper, 12⅛ × 8⅞ in.
[3] Pen and brown ink and blue wash, 17½ × 20¼ in.
[4] Black chalk, 6¾ × 8¼ in., sold, Christie's, London, 14 March 1967, lot 48, subsequently with Bernard Black Gallery, New York.
[5] Kraemer 1975, p. 8 (9) and pl. 4; see also pp. 60 (110), 65 (129), and 68 (145) for additional drawings which Kraemer more tentatively associates with the subject.

240 Abraham and His Son Isaac Going to Sacrifice *c.* 1799

NEATH BOROUGH COUNCIL, NEATH, GLAMORGANSHIRE

Oil on canvas: 72 × 113 in. (183 × 287 cm.)

PROV: Painted for George III (1801 account, p. 210: for the Windsor Chapel, Patriarchal Dispensation, 4, "The Call of Abraham going to sacrifice his son Isaac," £600); never delivered and ownership returned to West's sons by George IV in 1828; sold by them, Robins, London, 22–25 May 1829, lot 164 (6 ft. × 9 ft. 8 in.), bt. for £47.5.0. by Morgan (Charles Morgan, Caeforgan, Llanrhidian, Glamorganshire); by descent in the Morgan family until *c.* 1907, when sold in Swansea; J. C. Romback, Melyncryhan, Neath, by whom presented to the Borough of Neath in 1909[1]

EXH: (?) RA 1799 (298 or 837) "Abraham and his son Isaac going to Sacrifice":

Behold the fire and the wood, but where is the lamb for a burnt offering? and Abraham said, my son, God will provide himself a lamb for a burnt offering.

West's Gallery 1821 (41), 1822–28 (141)

Hagar and Ishmael, drawing by West for No. 239. Victoria and Albert Museum, London

240 (detail)

LISTED : *PC*, p. 560 ("Abraham and his Son Isaac going to Sacrifice," George III, for his Majesty's Chapel, Windsor, Patriarchal Dispensation); *UM*, p. 527; *AA*, p. 66 (Antediluvian and Patriarchal Dispensation . . . 9 ft. × 6); Barlow, p. 431; *BA*, p. 14; Galt, p. 218; Dillenberger, pp. 144 (68) and 214

LIT : Meyer 1975, p. 264; Dillenberger 1977, pp. 55, 63, pl. 39

No. 240 is one of the four pictures painted by West for the Royal Chapel at Windsor between 1797 and 1801 which appear in his account of the latter year but not that of the former. In the Swarthmore diagrams of 1801 (p. 580) the subject appears in the center of the bottom row, under "The Law" (see No. 258), on the side wall devoted to the Old Testament.

We have no firm evidence to indicate which versions of the subject West exhibited in 1799 and 1801. It seems most probable that No. 240 appeared at the Royal Academy in 1799, but it was not stated to be for the chapel in the catalogue, unlike most other completed chapel pictures. In catalogues of the 1799 exhibition, the subject appears twice (under nos. 298 and 837). This may have been due to clerical error and does not constitute certain evidence that two versions of the picture were exhibited in the same year;[2] nevertheless, No. 240 and a small version of the composition dated *1799* (No. 241) are sufficiently dissimilar in numerous details that West could have sent them both to the same exhibition. A version of the subject which appeared at

the Royal Academy two years later can probably be identified as that bought by William Beckford (No. 242), and one exhibited in 1817 was probably No. 241, possibly for the second time.[3]

In an engraving by John Le Keux after a drawing by George Cattermole (ill. p. 150), which shows the Great Room in West's gallery in 1821, No. 240 is visible to the right of the door leading to the Inner Room, under *St. Peter's First Sermon* (No. 385).

A drawing for the figure of Isaac is in the Morgan Library.[4] Two additional drawings which have been associated with the subject were formerly in the collection of Mrs. F. Howard.[5]

[1]Information about the painting's history after 1829 was kindly supplied to Helmut von Erffa by Merlin Thomas of Neath in 1963 and 1964. We are also indebted to Mr. I. H. K. Thorne of the Neath Borough Council for further information and assistance.
[2]The title is listed twice in all catalogues that we have been able to consult, but Algernon Graves lists "Jacob's Covenant with Laban" as 298 (see No. 249).
[3]To exhibit the same work at the Royal Academy twice was contrary to that institution's rules (see No. 239), but by 1817, if the infringement was not simply overlooked, West's age and position were sufficient to discourage potential critics from making a fuss. West also evidently exhibited both Nos. 246 and 295 for a second time in 1817.
[4]Kraemer 1975, p. 51 (91) and pl. 60, black chalk heightened with white on brown prepared paper, 11¼ × 7¼ in.
[5]Sold Sotheby's, London, 22 March 1979, lot 5.

241 Abraham and His Son Isaac Going to Sacrifice 1799

WICHITA ART MUSEUM, WICHITA, KANSAS

Oil on canvas: 20¼ × 29¼ in. (51.5 × 74.5 cm.)

Signed lower right: *B. West 1799*

PROV : Offered by West's sons to the United States in 1826 (124), and sold by them, Robins, London, 22–25 May 1829, lot 162 (1 ft. 8½ in. × 2 ft. 4 in.), bt. by Smith for £43; (?) Caunter, Esq., 1833; Berry-Hill Galleries, New York, 1975, by whom sold to the present owner

EXH : (?) RA 1799 (298 or 837) (see No. 240); RA 1817 (143) "Abraham and his son Isaac going to sacrifice":

> And Abraham rose up early in the morning, and saddled his ass, and took two of his young men with him, and Isaac his son; and clave the wood for the burnt offering, and rose up, and went unto the place of which God had told him.
>
> And Abraham said unto his young men, Abide ye here with the ass; and I and the lad will go yonder and worship, and come again to you.
>
> And Isaac spake unto Abraham his father, and said, My father: and he said, Here am I, my son. And he said, Behold the fire and the wood; but where is the lamb for a burnt offering?

And Abraham said, My son, God will provide himself a lamb for a burnt offering; so they went both of them together.

Genesis, chap. xxii, ver. 3, 5, 7, 8

West's Gallery 1821 (41); (?) SBA 1833 (165) lent by Caunter, Esq.; San Antonio 1983 (14)

LISTED : *PC*, p. 567 ("Abraham and Isaac—'Here is the wood and fire, but where is the lamb to sacrifice,'" West, Gallery); *UM*, p. 531; Barlow, p. 435; *BA.*, p. 18; Galt, p. 231; Dillenberger, p. 179 (407)

LIT : V and A Cuttings, III, p. 858, and IV, pp. 1109 and 1133 (1817, exhibition reviews); *Connoisseur*, CLXXXVIII, Feb. 1975, adv. p. 42

No. 241 is a smaller version of the previous entry, but it differs from that work in numerous details, most notably in the position of Isaac, but also very conspicuously in the dress of Abraham. It is not a monochromatic sketch, like several of West's studies for paintings for the Royal Chapel, but a strongly colored and completely finished picture in its own right. Since correspondence in size seems to establish that No. 241 remained in West's sons' possession until sold by them in 1829, it follows that No. 241 was the picture of this subject that West exhibited at the Royal Academy in 1817, when he was seventy-eight years old, along with two other sketches for, or versions of, pictures originally painted for the chapel at Windsor and exhibited between 1798 and 1800, the *Naming of John* (Nos. 294 and 295) and the *Birth of Esau and Jacob* (Nos. 245 and 246). Contemporary press notices described the latter two as originally designed for the chapel, and described No. 241 as painted "some years past." Another painting of *Abraham and Isaac* by West (No. 242) was put up for sale by William Beckford in May 1817 during the first two weeks of that year's Royal Academy exhibition. That coincidence may explain not only the somewhat fulsome praise given to No. 241 by the press but also the avoidance of any indication of the existence of yet another version (No. 240), which might have adversely affected the price of No. 242.

The history of No. 241 between 1829 and 1975 is not known, and it is impossible to say whether it or No. 242

was the picture exhibited at the Society of British Artists in 1833.

242 Abraham and His Son Isaac Going to Sacrifice *c.* 1801

LOCATION UNKNOWN

72 × 120 in. (183 × 305 cm.)

PROV : Acquired by William Beckford, Fonthill Abbey, Wilts., *c.* 1801; put up for sale by him, 6 Harley St., London (Christie's), 9–12 May 1817, lot 99, bt. in for 115 guineas; in the Fonthill catalogue (Christie's), 17–22 Sept. 1822, lot 97; sold, Fonthill Abbey (Phillips), 10–15 October 1823, lot 199 (. . . "a noble gallery picture") for £189; (?) Caunter, Esq., 1833 (cf. No. 241)

EXH : (?) RA 1801 (134) "Abraham and Isaac going to sacrifice":

> Genesis, chap. xxii.
> Ver. 7. And Isaac spake unto Abraham his father, and said, my father: and he said, here am I, my son: and he said, behold the fire and the wood: but where is the lamb for a burnt-offering?
> Ver. 8. And Abraham said, my son, God will provide himself a lamb for a burnt-offering———

(?) SBA 1833 (165), lent by Caunter, Esq.

LISTED : *PC*, p. 561 ("Abraham and Isaac going to Sacrifice," painted for, and in the possession of Wm. Beckford, Esq., of Fonthill); *UM*, p. 528; Barlow, p. 432; *BA.*, p. 14 (6 ft. × 10 ft.); Galt, p. 220; Dillenberger, p. 151 (132)

LIT : Rutter 1823, p. 31; Alexander 1957, pp. 20, 196, and 207

Although the evidence is only circumstantial, it seems likely that William Beckford commissioned No. 242 from West after seeing No. 240 exhibited in the Royal Academy in 1799. The latter constituted an integral part of the iconographical program for Windsor, whereas No. 242 seems to have had no such place in any of Beckford's schemes for Fonthill, unlike many of the other pictures he acquired from West, and it may be that he was attracted to the subject because of the semi-nude youth in the foreground of No. 240. If the size of 6 × 10 ft., given in *La Belle Assemblée*, is correct, then No. 242 was approximately the same size as No. 240. The description of it in the catalogue of the Fonthill sale of 1823 as "a noble gallery picture" gives further indication both that it was a good-sized painting and that it had not been intended for a specific architectural context.

On 22 December 1801 West wrote to Beckford, who was then in Paris, "Your favorite picture of Abraham and his son Isaac going to sacrifice, I gave according to your order into the hands of Mr. Foxhall."[1] Mr. Foxhall was Edward Foxhall of the firm of upholsterers Foxhall & Fryer, who regularly bought and sold pictures on Beckford's behalf.[2] In May 1817 Beckford tried unsuccessfully to sell the picture by auction. In a letter written a few days later, possibly in response to a subsequent offer, he declared:

> I do not wish to let the West go for a penny under £200 . . . My reason for not sacrificing the West for £100 is its grandeur and feeling of movement (?) . . . Every grand historical picture of any merit is important, and some merit the *Abraham* certainly has: there is something grandiose in its landscape, and the whole is pervaded with a certain solemnity and harmony. £200, yes, but anything less would be a shame.[3]

He finally sold it along with the abbey itself in 1822; in the following year, according to John Rutter, it hung in the Grand Drawing-Room in the Eastern Transept.

[1] Benjamin West to William Beckford, 22 December 1801, formerly in the collection of the Duke of Hamilton, sold Sotheby's, London, 5–6 July 1977, lot 272.
[2] See Alexander 1957, p. 47, n. 1, et passim.
[3] William Beckford to Gregorio Franchi, 16 May 1817, trans. by Boyd Alexander, in Alexander 1957, p. 207. The question mark is Alexander's, according to whom Beckford began to alter the last phrase but did not complete the alteration.

241

243 Isaac's Servant Tying the Bracelet on Rebecca's Arm 1775
See color illustrations, pp. 79, 80

YALE CENTER FOR BRITISH ART, NEW HAVEN

Oil on canvas: 49 × 63 in. (125 × 160 cm.)

Signed lower right: *B. West/1775*

PROV : John Hobart, second Earl of Buckinghamshire (1723–1793); his daughter Amelia Anne, wife of the second Marquess of Londonderry; by family descent to Lady Mairi Bury (daughter of the seventh Marquess of Londonderry), Mount Stewart, Newtownards, County Down, Northern Ireland, until 1977; Thos. Agnew and Sons, London, from whom acquired by the Yale Center in 1978

EXH : RA 1776 (319) "Isaac's servant tying the bracelet on Rebecca's arm"

LISTED : *PC*, p. 564 ("Rebecca Receiving the Bracelets at the Well," late Lord Buckinghamshire); *UM*, p. 529; Barlow, p. 434; *BA*, p. 16; Galt, p. 224; Dillenberger, p. 163 (243)

The title under which No. 243 is here listed is that which appeared in the Royal Academy catalogue in 1776. In the biblical account, in Genesis 24, Rebecca's encounter is with Abraham's servant rather than Isaac's.

No. 243 was apparently painted as a companion to No. 228, showing either *Cymon and Iphigenia* or *Rinaldo and Armida*, together with which it appeared at the Royal Academy in 1776 and with which it shared the same history until 1978. In both West seems to have employed the same model for the principal figure; and in both she is the object of the rapturous or respectful attention of a subordinate male figure. Lord Buckinghamshire had remarried in 1770, following the death of his first wife, and it is not unlikely that he may have commissioned the two paintings as allegorical representations of his new wife. This would explain why the two paintings passed to Lord Buckinghamshire's youngest daughter, the only child of the second marriage. No. 247, showing Mrs. Henry Thompson as Rachel at the well, is an analogous example of the combination of portraiture and biblical subject matter painted in the same year as No. 243.

Although No. 243 and three other pictures in the Buckinghamshire collection are all listed with dittoes following a work identified as a drawing in *Public Characters* and other lists, implicit description of these works as drawings is clearly erroneous, since three of them (Nos. 228, 243, and 535) can be identified as known paintings.

A drawing for the composition, with some differences in details is in the Museum of Fine Arts, Boston.[1] There is also a drawing of "Rebecca at the Well," unrelated compositionally to No. 243, in the Morgan Library. That drawing does not appear to be in West's hand, but it does have a West family provenance and it is inscribed *One of the first attempts at historical composition by Benjn West. while in Philadelphia 1757*.[2]

[1]Black chalk, $10\frac{1}{4} \times 14\frac{1}{8}$ in. This is probably the drawing of the subject sold S. Leigh, Sotheby, London, 1 June 1839, lot 11.
[2]Kraemer 1975, pp. 3–4, no. 1, and pl. 1, chalk and wash, $13\frac{5}{16} \times 20\frac{5}{8}$ in.

244 [?] Rebecca Coming to David

LOCATION UNKNOWN

PROV: Sir Jacob Ashley, *c.* 1804

LISTED: *PC*, p. 564 ("Rebecca coming to David," Sir Jacob Ashley); *UM*, p. 529; Barlow, p. 434 ("Rebecca coming to Jacob"); *BA*, p. 16; Galt, p. 224; Dillenberger, p. 163 (241)

Nothing is known of this work apart from the information provided in the lists. The title of "Rebecca Coming to David" describes an event that does not take place in the Bible, and is perhaps a mistake for "Rebecca Coming to Isaac," or either "Abigail" or "Bathsheba Coming to David."

245 The Birth of Jacob and Esau *c.* 1800

BOB JONES UNIVERSITY, GREENVILLE, SOUTH CAROLINA

Oil on canvas: 72×101 in. (183×257 cm.)

PROV: Painted for George III (1801 account, p. 210: for the Windsor Chapel, Patriarchal Dispensation, 5, "The Birth of Jacob and Esau," £525); never delivered and ownership returned to West's sons by George IV in 1928; sold by them, Robins, London, 22–25 May 1829, lot 160 (6 ft. × 9), bt. by Armstrong for £47.5.0.; sold anonymously, Christie's, London, 25 July 1958, lot 166, bt. by Frost & Reed, Ltd., Bristol; gift of Harry and Oscar Dwoskin to Bob Jones University, 1963

EXH: RA 1800 (144) "Isaac, when he first saw his twin sons, Esau and Jacob, painted for His Majesty's Chapel, Windsor Castle"; West's Gallery 1821 (29), 1822–28 (19)

LISTED: *PC*, p. 560 ("The Birth of Jacob and Esau," George III, for his Majesty's Chapel, Windsor, Patriarchal Dispensation); *UM*, p. 527; *AA*, p. 66 (Antediluvian and Patriarchal Dispensation, . . . 9 ft. × 6); Barlow, p. 432; *BA*, p. 14; Galt, p. 218; Dillenberger, pp. 144 (69) and 213

LIT: Jones 1963; Jones 1968, p. 65 (344), ill. p. 185; Meyer 1975, p. 264; Dillenberger 1977, pp. 63 and 64, pl. 40

This subject does not appear in the architectural schemes for the Windsor chapel from *c.* 1780. In the Swarthmore diagrams of 1801 it appears second from the right, between "Abraham Sacrificing" and the "12 Tribes in Egypt," and below the "Brazen Serpent," in the bottom range of the wall devoted to Old Testament subjects (ill. p. 580).

West exhibited a sketch for the picture (No. 246) four years before the finished work, and he had conceived the composition long before then. A drawing now in the same collection as No. 245, which shows basically the same scene, is signed and dated *1783*.[1] This drawing is probably the drawing of the subject recorded in the early lists of West's works.[2] A slighter drawing of the composition, less close in detail and without Isaac, is in one of West's sketchbooks in the Historical Society of Pennsylvania.

[1]Pen and wash, $12\frac{1}{8} \times 16\frac{3}{4}$ in.
[2]*PC*, p. 568 ("The Drawing of the Birth of Jacob and Esau," West, Gallery); *UM*, p. 531; *BA*, p. 19; Galt, p. 232; Dillenberger, p. 182 (434). See also No. 249, note 4.

246 The Birth of Jacob and Esau *c.* 1796

LOCATION UNKNOWN

($15\frac{1}{2} \times 21$ in.) (39.5×53.5 cm.)

PROV: Offered by West's sons to the United States in 1826 (63), and sold by them, Robins, London, 22–25 May 1829, lot 5 ($15\frac{1}{2} \times 21$ in.), bt. by H. P. Bone for £22.10.0.

EXH: RA 1796 (243) "The birth of Jacob and Esau; a sketch, for His Majesty's Chapel, Windsor"; (?) RA 1817 (129) "The birth of Esau and Jacob. Vide Genesis, chap. xxv."

LISTED: *PC*, p. 556 ("The Birth of Jacob and Esau," West, Gallery); *UM*, p. 531; Barlow, p. 435; *BA*, p. 18; Galt, p. 230; Dillenberger, p. 176 (375)

LIT: V and A Cuttings, III, p. 858 (May 1817)

The *Birth of Jacob and Esau* that West exhibited at the Royal Academy in 1796 (No. 246) was identified in the catalogue as a sketch for the chapel at Windsor, and the "Birth of Esau and Jacob" exhibited in 1817 was identified in a press notice as "originally designed" for the chapel. Since apart from the large picture for the chapel, which West had exhibited in 1800 (No. 245), no other version of the subject is recorded, it seems that the venerable President violated the Academy's rules by exhibiting either No. 245 or No. 246 for the second time. The re-exhibited work was more probably the latter, since its earlier exhibition was the more likely to have been forgotten, and West may have worked it up from a sketch into a finished work in the intervening years. The two other paintings that he sent to the Academy in 1817 (Nos. 241 and 295) were probably making their second appearance there as well.

H. P. Bone, who bought both Nos. 246 and 295 in 1829, bought extensively for Joseph Neeld MP. Neither of these two pictures appeared in the Neeld sales of 1945 and 1962, and we have found no evidence to confirm that the two were indeed in the Neeld collection.

245

247 Jacob and Rachel (Mary, wife of Henry Thompson, as Rachel) 1775

CHRYSLER MUSEUM, NORFOLK, VIRGINIA

Oil on canvas: 50 × 39¼ in. (127 × 99.5 cm.)

Signed lower right: *B. West/1775*

PROV: Sold anonymously (property of a lady), Sotheby's, London, 22 Nov. 1961, lot 87 ("Mary, wife of Henry Thompson, Kirby Hall, as Rachel, Jacob & Laban's wife at the Well"), bt. by Graham; Graham Galleries, New York, from whom acquired by Walter P. Chrysler, Jr. in 1967; given by him to the Chrysler Museum in 1971

EXH: New York 1962 (12)

LIT: *Gazette des Beaux-Arts*, LXXI, 1968, p. 68 (258)

There is considerable confusion in the documentation of West's versions of the story of Jacob and Rachel (Nos. 247 and 248). He did not exhibit any pictures of this subject, but he may have exhibited the related "Jacob's Covenant with Laban" at the Royal Academy in 1799 (see No. 249). A *Jacob and Rachel* was sold by the dealer Noel Desenfans in 1786, but that picture was not large enough to be identified as No. 247. *Public Characters* and the other early lists of West's works include a painting of "Jacob drawing water at the well for Rachel and her flock," but since Jacob is not shown in the act of drawing water in this painting, that identification seems unlikely for it as well. Various other subjects on the lists of West's works, such as "Rebecca Coming to Jacob" (see No. 244) and the "Woman of Samaria at the Well with Christ" (see No. 318), of which no paintings are now known, could be confused references to No. 247, but such identification is entirely speculative. If, as indicated by the title under which the work appeared at Sotheby's in 1961, No. 247 was painted as a commissioned portrait, its non-appearance on the early lists would have been consistent with the exclusion from them of most portraits. Nonetheless, a painting of the similar subject of Rebecca at the well (No. 243), painted in the same year as No. 247, which also may have been intended as a quasi-portrait, does appear in the lists under its biblical title. The title under which No. 247 was sold in 1961 presumably reflects a traditional identification. Mrs. Thompson was born Mary Spence; she married Henry Thompson of Kirby Hall near York in 1769. By 1775, the date on No. 247, she had been married six years and had borne at least one child, so the scene of biblical courtship shown in the picture would not seem to reflect her situation at the time. The other figures may also be portraits, but, if so, their identifications have been lost. The youthful Jacob on the left appears too young to represent Henry Thompson, who would have been thirty-two years old in 1775.[1]

Paintings of the meeting of Jacob and Rachel traditionally show the couple embracing (but cf. No. 248). The departure from tradition in No. 247 can probably be explained by the demands of portraiture. The presence of sheep in the lower left corner, rather than camels as in scenes of Rebecca at the well, such as No. 243, confirms that the subject is Jacob and Rachel.

For drawings of the subject see under No. 248.

[1] For details see *Burke's Landed Gentry*, 5th ed., 1871, II, p. 1373.

248 Jacob and Rachel (?)c. 1765–70

LOCATION UNKNOWN

(Oil on canvas: 39 × 33 in. [? including frame]) (99 × 84 cm.)

PROV: Noël Desenfans, London, by whom sold, 125 Pall Mall, London, 8 April 1786, lot 310 ("Jacob and

247

Rachel at the well," on canvas, 3 ft. 3 in. × 2 ft. 9 in.) for £52.10.0.; Polygraphic Society, London, by *c.* 1788; (?) Mrs. Evans, by 1804

EXH: Polygraphic Society, London, *c.* 1788, (12) "Jacob and Rachel," 33½ × 28½ in.

ENGR: (?) Stipple engraving printed in colors (19¼ × 14⅞ in.) by William Nutter, pub. by Rudolph Ackermann, Jan. 1825

LISTED: (?) *PC*, p. 562 ("Jacob drawing water at the well for Rachel and her Flock," in the possession of Mrs. Evans); *UM*, p. 528; *BA*, p. 15; *Galt*, p. 222; Dillenberger, p. 157 (190)

See the discussion under No. 247. The painting of *Jacob and Rachel* sold by Noël Desenfans in 1786 was much smaller than No. 247 and, hence, cannot be that work. It almost certainly was the painting of the subject owned and exhibited by the Polygraphic Society *c.* 1788, since the Society's catalogue states that its painting had cost fifty guineas, which is the amount Desenfans's painting had realized two years previously.[1] The sizes listed in the two catalogues do not correspond exactly with one another, but the measurement listed in the Polygraphic Society's catalogue included frames, and those in the Desenfans catalogue evidently did as well (see No. 312). The differences then between the two sets of dimensions may have been the result of a new frame. The identification of No. 248 with the painting of the subject listed in the early catalogues of West's works as belonging to Mrs. Evans is conjectural.

Jacob and Rachel, stipple engraving by William Nutter, possibly after No. 248

The composition may be recorded in a color engraving by William Nutter (1754–1802), which Rudolph Ackermann published twenty-three years after Nutter's death. The print (*above*) shows Jacob drawing water at the well, and thus, unlike No. 247, shows an image that fits the title used in the early lists of West's works for the painting belonging to Mrs. Evans. The painting shown in this print would probably have dated from fairly early in the artist's career, possibly from the late 1760s. Two drawings, which evidently show the same subject but have no relation to either No. 247 or the composition shown in the Nutter engraving, were formerly in the collection of Mrs. F. Howard. In one, Jacob stands to the left of the well, while Rachel approaches from the right with a vase on her head.[2] In the other, which is larger and more highly finished, she sits to the left holding a vase, while he leans over a trough or well, from which sheep are drinking, on the right.[3] This drawing is signed and dated *1783*.

For the Polygraphic Society see No. 139. Although the Society owned, exhibited, and reproduced No. 248, no polygraphic reproduction is known to the compilers of this catalogue.

[1] The Polygraphic Society in the same catalogue included two paintings by de Loutherbourg, no. 2 *Winter* and no. 15 *Summer*, which it described as having cost £150 at "Mons. Des Enfans's" sale.

[2] Chalk, 19 × 16 in., sold Sotheby's, London, 22 March 1979, lot 5.

[3] Pen, ink, and some watercolor, $15\frac{3}{4} \times 22\frac{1}{8}$ in., signed lower right: *B. West 1783*; sold Sotheby's, London, 22 March 1979, lot 16 as "Rebecca at the Well," and ill. in the catalogue.

249 Jacob and Laban 1798

GEORGE E. DOTY

Oil on canvas: $14\frac{1}{4} \times 19\frac{1}{4}$ in. (36 × 49 cm.)

Signed lower left: *B. West 1798*

PROV: Offered by West's sons to the United States in 1826 (67), and sold by them, Robins, London, 22–25 May 1829, lot 7 ("Jacob and Laban," $14 \times 19\frac{1}{2}$ in.), bt. by John Nash for £31.10.0.; his sale, Christie's, London, 11 July 1835, lot 73 ("Jacob and Laban"; a well coloured picture); John Allnutt (1773–1863); his sale, Christie's, London, 20 June 1863, lot 405 ("Jacob, Laban, and Rachel, with sheep and goats in a landscape"); Renaissance Galleries, Philadelphia, by *c.* 1936; Hirschl & Adler Galleries, New York, *c.* 1967; given by Abraham Adler and Norman Hirschl to the Morgan State College Gallery of Art in 1968; Ira Spanierman, Inc., New York, 1980; purchased by the present owner in 1983

EXH: (?) RA 1799 (298) "Jacob's covenant with Laban for Rachel" (see below); West's Gallery 1822–28 (21); Philadelphia 1936; Philadelphia 1938 (48)

ENGR: Colored aquatint ($6\frac{1}{2} \times 8\frac{3}{4}$ in.), not inscribed and never published, but signed *B. West/1783* within the image

LISTED: *PC*, p. 567 ("Jacob, and Laban with his two Daughters," West, Gallery); *UM*, p. 531; Barlow, p. 435; *BA*, p. 18; Galt, p. 231; Dillenberger, pp. 178 (397) and 213

The story of Jacob and Laban is from Genesis 29–31. In the painting, Laban stands on the left and Jacob is the younger man next to him. The seated female figure on the right probably represents Rachel, while in the center of the painting, behind Jacob, an oddly masculine Leah holds her hands to her head and looks out over her shoulder. Rachel's position suggests that the painting shows the moment when she hides Laban's idols by sitting on them, but her seat in No. 249 is concealed by a sheep, whereas a scrupulous rendering of the biblical story would show her on the camel's furniture in which she had placed the idols. None of the early titles recorded above indicate precisely what moment No. 249 is supposed to show, but the commentary in the Robins sale catalogue of May 1829 does describe the subject as the parting of Jacob and Laban.

The dimensions listed above are those of the painted surface, and they correspond with the measurements recorded in the sale catalogue of 1829. At some time after 1829 the painting was relined and mounted on a larger stretcher, measuring $16\frac{1}{2} \times 21$ in. This larger size is recorded in the catalogue of the West exhibition in Philadelphia in 1938, and a photograph of No. 249 made when it belonged to Morgan State College shows the picture with the added area painted over to extend the composition. The additional paint has since been removed.

Although No. 249 is signed and dated *1798*, its origins stem from much earlier. An aquatint of the subject is signed and dated *1783*, and it seems to be based on a related pair of drawings at Swarthmore, which are not dated but appear earlier yet.[1] Despite changes in dress and pose, the positions of the three main participants remain essentially the same through the progression. The most conspicuous alterations are in the figure below and behind Jacob in No. 249 (? Leah), who is shown in a less twisted pose in the print of 1783 and is standing in the Swarthmore drawings. This figure is clearly female in the earlier works but less obviously so in No. 249. The shadowy male figure behind the cattle on the right side of the painting is not included in the earlier treatments of the subject, and there are numerous additional differences, but the basic composition was established by 1783. West was then at work on the project for George III's chapel in Windsor Castle, as he was still in 1798, but he does not seem to have intended at either time to include a painting of this subject in that scheme.

Algernon Graves lists "Jacob's covenant with Laban for Rachel" as no. 298 in the Royal Academy exhibition of 1799,[2] but in actual catalogues of that year's exhibition, it is not included, while *Abraham and His Son Isaac Going to Sacrifice* appears twice, as nos. 298 and 837. This may have been a clerical error, and it is plausible that West would have exhibited No. 249, which had been painted the year before, rather than two versions of No. 240, each with the same quotation, but we have been unable to find confirmation of Graves's indication that he did so.

The early catalogues list one drawing of "Jacob and Laban,"[3] which may have been a large and highly finished drawing now in the Wichita Art Museum. Although evidently a work of the 1780s, this drawing is not related compositionally to No. 249, and appears to show an earlier moment in the Old Testament narrative.[4]

[1] Black chalk, $7\frac{3}{4} \times 12\frac{1}{4}$ in., and $6\frac{5}{8} \times 10\frac{5}{8}$ in.

[2] Graves 1906, VIII, p. 216.

[3] *PC*, p. 568 ("The Drawing of Jacob and Laban," West, Gallery); *UM*, p. 532; *BA*, p. 19; Galt, p. 233; Dillenberger, p. 184 (457).

[4] Pen and wash, $13\frac{1}{2} \times 19$ in., exhibited, New York 1968 (8) as "An Allegory of Man," ill. on cover of the catalogue. This drawing has also been called "Arrival of the Hunter" (Christie's, London, 18 Oct. 1966, lot 33) and "Esau Selling His Birthright" (by the present owner). Another drawing which does show Esau selling his birthright appeared on the market in 1984 (pen and wash, $10\frac{3}{4} \times 14\frac{3}{4}$ in., signed lower right: *B. West/1783*; exhibited *British Drawings*, Anthony Reed, London, and Davis & Langdale, New York, 1984, no. 6). This drawing is inscribed *Jacob and Esau/Benjn West* on the verso and was probably the "Jacob and Esau" sold by Benjamin West, Jr., S. Leigh Sotheby, London, 1 June 1839, lot 105.

250 Jacob Blesseth Joseph's Two Sons (?)1766

See color illustration, p. 77

ALLEN MEMORIAL ART MUSEUM, OBERLIN COLLEGE, OBERLIN, OHIO

Oil on canvas: $40\frac{1}{16} \times 51$ in. (101.8 × 129.5 cm.)

(?)Signed lower left: *B. [West 17]66*

PROV: Richard, Lord Grosvenor (later the first Earl Grosvenor) by 1778; by family descent to the second Duke of Westminster (died 1953); sold by his estate, Sotheby's, London, 15 July 1959, lot 128, bt. by Nicholson; John Nicholson Gallery, New York; purchased by the Allen Memorial Art Museum in 1961

EXH: SA 1768 (177) "Jacob Blesseth Joseph's Two Sons Ephraim and Manasseh"; New York 1962 (16)

ENGR: Mezzotint ($15\frac{11}{16} \times 20\frac{1}{2}$ in.) by Valentine Green, pub. 1 Jan. 1778 by John Boydell, *From the Original Picture in the Collection of the Right Honourable Lord Grosvenor*; mezzotint ($15\frac{11}{16} \times 20\frac{3}{8}$ in.) by William Wilson; engraving by J. Rogers as a vertical composition

LISTED: *PC*, p. 561 ("Jacob blessing Joseph's Sons," Earl Grosvenor); *UM*, p. 528; Barlow, p. 432; *BA*, p. 14; Galt, p. 220; Dillenberger, pp. 151 (139) and 211

LIT: Buckler 1826, p. 4; Gatty 1938–39, p. 81 (Horace Walpole, 1768); Wolfgang Stechow, *Catalogue of European and American Paintings in the Allen Memorial Art Museum, Oberlin College*, Oberlin, 1967, pp. 160–61 and fig. 151; Kraemer 1975, p. 5; Dillenberger 1977, pp. 20–21, pl. 9

The traces of signature on No. 250 are barely legible and the reading of the digits *66* is open to question.[1] A drawing of the composition, which shows numerous differences in detail and hence would seem to be a study for No. 250 rather than after it, is signed and dated *1768*.[2] That is the year when No. 250 appeared at the Society of Artists, and there is no obvious explanation of why West would have waited two years to exhibit the picture if it had indeed been painted in 1766. Among reliably dated works by West the painting's closest stylistic affinities are with *Leonidas and Cleombrutus* (No. 13), which is signed and dated *1768* and was also exhibited in that year. There is, nevertheless, some evidence to support an argument that No. 250 may have been begun before 1768. It was apparently painted as a companion to *Elisha Raising the Shunamite's Son* (No. 279), which is the same size and entered the same collections as No. 250. Prints of the two by Valentine Green were exhibited together in 1768 and published as a pair ten years later. Either No. 279 or another treatment of the subject was exhibited a year earlier than No. 250. No. 279 also bears or bore a dubiously legible signature and date of *1766*, and a version of that composition (No. 280) is inscribed *Begun 1765/and finished 1814, Oct. 10th/B. West.* However, since that inscription was evidently written only in 1814 it cannot be considered absolutely reliable either, and in any case it provides only tangential evidence for the date of No. 250.

Nos. 250 and 279 are the only two pictures of biblical subjects West exhibited during the 1760s. Children figure prominently in both, as they do in several other pictures exhibited by the artist in 1767, and 1768 (such

as Nos. 8, 13, 33, and 163), following the birth of his first child, Raphael Lamar West, in April 1766. In No. 250, which shows Joseph, who had made good in Egypt, with his father, who had come to him from their native land, there are unmistakable parallels with West, who had successfully established himself in England, and his father, who had come over from Pennsylvania in 1764.

The subject of this painting is from Genesis 48. West appears to have planned two or three pictures of related subjects for the Royal Chapel at Windsor. In his account for George III of 1801, "Joseph and his brothers in Egypt" and the "Death of Jacob surrounded by his sons in Egypt" are both described as "composed, not painted."[3] The latter subject also appears on the early published lists of his works;[4] the former does not. Additionally, Joel Barlow lists a "Bondage of the Israelites in Egypt."[5] A rough drawing of "Joseph and His Brethren" at Swarthmore appears to date, on stylistic grounds, from the same approximate period as No. 250 and thus to provide a tenuous link between West's biblical subjects of the 1760s and his later work for George III.[6] The Swarthmore drawing may be identical with a drawing of "Joseph making himself known to his Brethren" recorded on the early lists of West's works.[7] A drawing of the "Death of

Jacob" is one of a group of three large outline drawings of subjects intended for the chapel formerly in the collection of Mrs. F. Howard.[8]

[1]Letter from Chloe Hamilton to Helmut von Erffa, 9 August 1962. Old photographs of No. 250 and *Elisha Restores to Life the Widow's Son* (No. 279), which was sold with it in 1959, both show complete signatures *B. West 1766*, neither of which is still legible.

[2]Pen, ink, and body-color, 12⅝ × 16⅜ in., Pennsylvania Academy of the Fine Arts, Philadelphia; ill. in Kraemer 1975, p. 6, fig. 3. In the Oberlin catalogue, Wolfgang Stechow, who accepts the validity of the *66* on No. 250, suggests that the date on the drawing was added later.

[3]1801 account, nos. 6 and 7 (Galt 1820, p. 210), both under Patriarchal Dispensation.

[4]*PC*, p. 560; *UM*, p. 527; Barlow, p. 432; *BA*, p. 14; Galt, p. 218; Dillenberger, p. 144 (70).

[5]Barlow, p. 432 (Patriarchal Dispensation).

[6]Black chalk, 13 × 18½ in. A drawing in the Morgan Library showing a different composition may also be related to this subject; see Kraemer 1975, p. 24 (36).

[7]*PC*, p. 568 (West, Gallery); *UM*, p. 19; Galt, p. 234; Dillenberger, p. 185 (473).

[8]Pen and black ink on blue prepared paper, each 22 × 32 in., sold Sotheby's, London, 22 March 1979, lot 26. For the other two, see Nos. 236 and 254.

249

251

190, 200, and 318). Although the entry for No. 251 in *Public Characters* suggests that the picture listed as belonging to Park was a second version; the entries for the subsequent two pictures (Nos. 190 and 200) indicate the opposite: that the works painted for Lawrence subsequently belonged to Park. The entry for No. 251 in *La Belle Assemblée* states that it was originally painted for Lawrence as well, although "Park" has now become "Pauch." If we are right in identifying General Lawrence as Stringer Lawrence, the "father of the Indian army," then the "Park" in *Public Characters* and "Pauch" in *La Belle Assemblée* are confused references to the former governor of Madras and Lawrence's lifelong friend, Robert Palk, to whom Lawrence bequeathed all his effects.[3] Stringer Lawrence was also an associate of Clive of India, who granted him an annuity of £500 following his return from India in 1759, and it seems likely, therefore, that his patronage of West around 1771 was connected in some fashion with that of Clive, which commenced at about the same time (see No. 101), and with that of Giles Stibbert, a younger officer in the Indian army, who also bought works by West around 1771 (see Nos. 7 and 26).

A drawing of the subject was sold by West's descendants in 1898.[4] A drawing now in the Morgan Library is on paper watermarked 1801 and is unrelated in composition to No. 251.[5]

[1] A letter from Robert Frank to Helmut von Erffa, 4 March 1953, gives the Houghton-Crewe-Frank provenance.
[2] Drawing in the Huntington Library and Art Gallery, San Marino, California, engraved in mezzotint by Richard Earlom (ill. in Sidney Hutchison, *The History of the Royal Academy 1768–1968*, London, 1968, pl. 4).
[3] See the *Dictionary of National Biography* entries for Lawrence and Palk, also Kerslake 1977, I, pp. 164–65.
[4] Christie's, London, 18–19 March 1898, as part of lot 100.
[5] Kraemer 1975, p. 42 (68).

252 Moses and Aaron before Pharaoh 1796

BOB JONES UNIVERSITY, GREENVILLE, SOUTH CAROLINA

Oil on canvas: 148 × 115 in. (376 × 292 cm.)

Signed lower right: *B. West 1796*

PROV: Painted for George III (1797 account: "Moses and Aaron before Pharo," 1797, £1,050; 1801 account, p. 210: for the Windsor Chapel, Mosaical Dispensation, 9, "Moses and his brother Aaron before Pharaoh, their Rods turned into Serpents," £1,050; never delivered and ownership returned to West's sons by George IV in 1828; sold by them, Robins, London, 22–25 May 1829, lot 48 (12 ft. 6 in. × 10 ft.), bt. by H. P. Bone for £42 on behalf of Joseph Neeld, MP, Grittleton House, Wilts.; by descent in the Neeld family until sold by Miss C. K. M. Neeld, Christie's, London, 16 Nov. 1962, lot 92 (as "Moses Pleading with Pharaoh for the Children of Israel"), bt. by Weitzner; purchased by Bob Jones University in 1963

EXH: RA 1796 (175) "Moses and Aaron before Pharaoh, for His Majesty's Chapel, Windsor"; West's Gallery 1821 (55), 1822–28 (82)

LISTED: *PC*, p. 560 ("Moses and Aaron before Pharaoh; their Rods turned into Serpents," George III, for his Majesty's Chapel, Windsor, Mosaical Dispensation); *UM*, p. 527; *AA*, p. 66 (9 ft. × 14); Barlow, p. 432 (15 ft. × 14); *BA*, p. 14 (10 ft. × 14); Galt, p. 218; Dillenberger, pp. 145 (75) and 213

LIT: V and A Cuttings, III, pp. 726, 761, 767–69 (all 1796); Jones 1963, frontispiece; Jones 1968, p. 65 (345), ill. p. 186; Meyer 1975, p. 264; Dillenberger 1977, p. 65, ill. p. 66, pl. 41

251 The Compassion of Pharaoh's Daughter for the Infant Moses *c.* 1771

UNIVERSITY OF NOTRE DAME ART GALLERY, NOTRE DAME, INDIANA

Oil on canvas: 59 × 45½ in. (150 × 115.5 cm.)

PROV: Painted for General Lawrence (? Stringer Lawrence, 1697–1775); Park or Pauch Esq. by 1804 (? Sir Robert Palk, 1717–1798); Lord Houghton;[1] the first Marquess of Crewe (died 1945); Robert Frank, London, 1953; E. and A. Silberman Galleries, New York, by whom sold, Parke-Bernet, New York, 27 Nov. 1968, lot 178; gift of Walter and William Klauer to the University of Notre Dame in 1970

EXH: RA 1771 (211) "The Compassion of Pharaoh's daughter for the infant Moses"; New York 1962 (8)

LISTED: *PC*, p. 564 ("Pharaoh's Daughter with the Child Moses—Park Esq. The original painted for General Lawrence"); *UM*, p. 529; Barlow, p. 433; *BA*, p. 16 (". . . Pauch, Esq., originally painted for General Lawrence"); Galt, p. 224; Dillenberger, p. 162 (236)

No. 251 is apparently neither signed nor dated, but its identification as the picture West exhibited in 1771 is appropriate on stylistic grounds. It is more or less recognizable hanging above Reynolds's *Venus Chastising Cupid* in Charles Brandoin's view of that year's Academy exhibition.[2]

The early catalogues of West's works list four pictures painted by West for General Lawrence (Nos. 251,

252

In the architectural drawings for the chapel at Windsor dating from *c.* 1780, the subject of *Moses and Aaron before Pharaoh* is on the extreme left in the upper row on a side wall, above the New Testament subject of the *Baptism* (ill. p. 577). Although clearly recognizable there, it is shown as a horizontal composition without much similarity to West's final realization of the subject in No. 252. In the Swarthmore diagrams, from 1801 it appears as a vertical composition on the extreme left of the center range of the side wall devoted to Old Testament subjects (ill. p. 580).

In West's account of 1801 of his pictures painted for George III, No. 252 is preceded by the "Calling of Moses, his Rod turned into a Serpent before the Burning Bush, composed but not painted." Barlow also lists a "Moses Called." There is no evidence to suggest that West ever painted either subject.

Because of its large size, No. 252 attracted considerable critical attention when exhibited in 1796, but the response was generally lukewarm with several critics expressing preference for West's smaller paintings.

An oil sketch is No. 253 below.

253 Moses and Aaron before Pharaoh *c.* 1796

LOCATION UNKNOWN

(37 × 30 in.) (94 × 76 cm.)

PROV: Offered by West's sons to the United States in 1826 (34), and sold by them, Robins, London, 22–25 May 1829, lot 90 (3 ft. 1 in. × 2 ft. 6 in.), bt. by Smith for £63

EXH: RA 1813 (76) "Moses and Aaron before Pharaoh, King of Egypt":

> And Moses stretched forth his hand toward heaven and there was a thick darkness in all the land of Egypt three days. *Exodus, chap. x, ver. 22*

BI 1820 (259) "Moses and Aaron before Pharaoh":

> 10. And Moses and Aaron went in unto Pharaoh, and they did so as the Lord had commanded: and Aaron cast down his rod before Pharaoh, and before his servants, and it became a serpent. *Exodus, chap. vii, ver. 10*
>
> 11. Then Pharaoh also called the wise men, and the sorcerers; now the magicians of Egypt, they also did in like manner with their enchantments: And Moses stretched forth his hand toward heaven; and there was a thick darkness in all the land of Egypt three days.
> *Exodus, chap. x, ver. 22*

4 ft. 3 in. × 3 ft. 7 in. (including frame); West's Gallery 1821 (60), 1822–28 (88)

LISTED: *PC*, p. 566 ("Moses and Aaron before Pharaoh," West, Gallery); *UM*, p. 530; Barlow, p. 434; *BA*, p. 17; Galt, p. 228; Dillenberger, p. 173 (346)

LIT: Courtauld Cuttings, II, p. 47 (review, 1813) and p. 148 (review, 1820); V and A Cuttings, III, p. 868 (review, 1813)

Despite the quotation printed in the Royal Academy catalogue of 1813, it is probable that the "Moses and Aaron before Pharaoh" which West exhibited in that year was a sketch for No. 252 and that it was identical with the version of the subject that appeared at the British Institution in 1820 accompanied also in that catalogue by the same lines about the plague of darkness. These, however, were preceded by another quotation which is appropriate to the subject shown in No. 252. The painting exhibited in 1820 remained in

West's sons' possession and, when sold by them in 1829, was described in the catalogue as "A beautiful, and highly wrought study for the great and impressive picture of the same subject, painted for the projected Chapel at Windsor." There is no record otherwise of West's ever having undertaken a painting of Moses invoking the plague of darkness, nor is there any evidence to suggest that he painted a third version of *Moses and Aaron before Pharaoh* in any form. Furthermore, the title and the accompanying quotation in the catalogue of 1813 contradict each other, as in the biblical narrative Moses and Aaron are not before Pharaoh when Moses calls darkness down upon Egypt. According to contemporary reviews the exhibited picture of 1813 was small and showed "the expression of awful denunciation in the Prophets, and of surprise and terror in the Egyptian priests and King," all of which accords with what one would expect of a sketch for No. 252.

254 Pharaoh and His Host Lost in the Red Sea *c.* 1792

LOCATION UNKNOWN

(150 × 120 in.) (381 × 305 cm.)

PROV: Painted for George III (1797 account: "The destruction of Pharo and his Host," 1792, £1,050; 1801 account, p. 210: for the Windsor Chapel, Mosaical Dispensation, 10, "Moses destroying Pharaoh and his host in the Red Sea," £1,050); never delivered and ownership returned to West's sons by George IV in 1828; sold by them, Robins, London, 22–25 May 1829, lot 150 (12 ft. 6 in. × 10 ft.), bt. by Bone for £115.10.0., possibly on behalf of Joseph Neeld, MP, Grittleton House, Wilts.

EXH: RA 1792 (124) "The Triumph of Moses over Pharaoh and his host, Exod., chap. 14, ver. 27, painted for His Majesty's chapel, Windsor Castle"; West's Gallery 1821 (49), 1822–28 (75)

LISTED: *PC*, p. 560 ("Pharaoh and his Host lost in the Red Sea, while Moses stretches his Rod over them," George III, for his Majesty's Chapel, Windsor, Mosaical Dispensation); *UM*, p. 527; *AA*, p. 66 ("The Israelites having passed the Red Sea, Moses stretcheth his Rod over Pharaoh and his Host, who are overwhelmed by the water," 9 ft. × 14); Barlow, p. 432 ("Pharaoh's Army lost in the sea"); *BA*, p. 14 (10 ft. × 14); Galt, p. 218; Dillenberger, p. 145 (76)

LIT: Helmut von Erffa, "A Lost Painting," *Worcester Art Museum News Bulletin and Calendar*, XXVI, 4, Jan. 1961; Kraemer 1975, pp. 32–33; Meyer 1975, p. 264; Dillenberger 1977, p. 65.

A horizontal drawing of this subject appears in the architectural schemes for the Windsor chapel from *c.* 1780; it is second from the left in the upper row of subjects on a side wall, adjacent to *Moses and Aaron before Pharaoh* and above *Christ Healing the Sick* (ill. p. 577). In the Swarthmore diagrams of 1801, "Red Sea/ Pharo," is a vertical composition second from the left in the center row of the side wall devoted to Old Testament subjects (ill. p. 580).

A related oil sketch is No. 255 below. Drawings of the subject were sold by West's heirs in 1839[1] and 1898;[2] one of these probably was the drawing of the "Destruction of Pharaoh" exhibited in West's gallery in 1823.[3] There are drawings in the Museum of Fine Arts, Boston[4] and the Morgan Library, New York.[5] An outline drawing formerly in the collection of Mrs. F. Howard and sold under the title "Moses Striking the Rock" is compositionally closer to the first idea

appearing in the architectural schemes for the chapel, though in reverse, than it is to the Worcester sketch (No. 255) and the drawings in Boston and New York, and hence appears to be an earlier visualization of the subject.[6]

[1] S. Leigh Sotheby, London, 1 June 1839, lots 24 (pen and bistre, washed) and 91 (sepia, outline).
[2] Christie's, London, 18 March 1898, lot 93 (six drawings), bt. by Parsons for 2 shillings.
[3] Room of Drawings, no. 16.
[4] Pen and wash, 12¾ × 9⅞ in., ill. Kraemer 1975, p. 33, fig. 23.
[5] Pen and brown ink over black chalk, 14⅛ × 12¼ in., Kraemer, p. 32 (51), pl. 30.
[6] Pen and black ink, on blue prepared paper, 22 × 32 in.; sold, Sotheby's, London, 22 March 1979, lot 26, together with companion drawings cited under entries Nos. 236 and 250.

255 Pharaoh and His Host Lost in the Red Sea *c.* 1792

See color illustration, p. 99

WORCESTER ART MUSEUM, WORCESTER, MASSACHUSETTS

Oil on canvas: 37½ × 29¼ in. (95 × 74.5 cm.)

PROV: Offered by West's sons to the United States in 1826 (35), and sold by them, Robins, London, 22–25 May 1829, lot 168 (37 × 30 in.), bt. by Blamise (or Blamire) for £63; purchased from P. & D. Colnaghi, London, by the Worcester Art Museum in 1960

EXH: West's Gallery 1821 (63), 1822–28 (94); San Antonio 1983 (16)

LISTED: *PC*, p. 566 ("Pharaoh and His Host drowned in the Red Sea," West, Gallery); *UM*, p. 531; Barlow, p. 435; *BA*, p. 18; Galt, p. 229; Dillenberger, pp. 175 (367) and 212

LIT: Helmut von Erffa, "A Lost Painting," *Worcester Art Museum News Bulletin and Calendar*, XXVI, 4, Jan. 1961; Kraemer 1975, pp. 32–33; Meyer 1975, p. 260 and fig. 21; Dillenberger 1977, p. 66, pl. 42

The Robins sale catalogue of May 1829 praised lot 150, West's large painting of *Pharaoh and His Host* (No. 254) for the "angel, clad in white raiment, stretching his protecting hands over the Israelites," and it praised lot 168 (No. 255) for "the Angel stretching his arms over the protected of Heaven." Although the latter was not identified as a sketch for the former in the catalogue, the evident similarity in this detail is indicative of their connection. No. 255 is sketchier and less finished than many other sketches for, or small versions of, chapel pictures (such as Nos. 233, 235, and 241), and unlike those examples it was not exhibited during the artist's lifetime. The greater detail in the upper right corner suggests, however, that West started to work No. 255 up into a finished and exhibitable picture, but never completed it.

256 Moses Striking the Rock 1783–1803

ROYAL ACADEMY OF ARTS, LONDON

Pen and brown ink and wash, heightened with white: 23 × 44 in. (58.5 × 112 cm.)

Signed lower left: *B. West/1783/Retouched 1803*

PROV: In the possession of West's heirs in 1823

EXH: RA 1784 (435) "Moses striking the rock, a design for His Majesty's chapel in Windsor Castle"; West's Gallery 1823 (Room of Drawings, 56); London 1963 (77); Washington and Philadelphia 1980; San Antonio 1983 (17)

256

LISTED: *PC*, p. 568 ("The large sketch, in oil, on paper, of the Water gushing from the Rock when struck by Moses," West, Gallery); *UM*, p. 532; *BA*, p. 19; Galt, p. 233; Dillenberger, 1977, pp. 184 (460) and 212

LIT: Carl Goldstein, "Towards a Definition of Academic Art," *Art Bulletin*, LVII, 1975, pp. 102–9

No. 256 is one of a group of three drawings which West exhibited at the Royal Academy in 1784. The other two were the "Triumph of Death" (see No. 402) and the *Last Supper* (No. 345). All three were identified in the catalogue as designs for the chapel at Windsor. The drawing of the "Triumph of Death" is in the same collection as No. 256 and is usually known by the title which West employed for later treatments of the subject: "Death on the Pale Horse" (Nos. 401 and 403). Neither of these drawings became a completed picture for the chapel, although West did identify an oil version of *Death on the Pale Horse* as a sketch for the chapel in the Royal Academy catalogue of 1796 (No. 403), and at the end of his life he painted a large version of the subject (No. 401). The subject of Moses striking the rock does not appear on any list or diagram of chapel subjects and hence seems to have been dropped from the program some time after 1784.

No. 256, like No. 402, is on several pieces of paper joined together. Both drawings are dated *1783* and bear the further inscription *retouched 1803*. A third drawing of a subject related to the chapel, the *Death of Aaron* (No. 265), is dated *1790, retouched 1803* and is also on several sheets of paper pieced together. Nevertheless, despite this common feature, the piecing together of different sheets was probably done when the drawings were originally made. What these drawings also have in common is extremely heavy use of body-color, and this probably was a product of the retouching in 1803. On 18 November of that year Joseph Farington called on West and recorded in his diary:

West shewed me several drawings begun at different periods,—now retouching them.—said He knew as much of *Composition* when he was 26 years old as now, but his judgement in heightening, & of effect is better.[1]

Although Nos. 256, 265, and 402 are described in the early catalogues as oil on paper, there is no reason to believe that those listings are for other works; the white which is used extensively in all three (and in a number of other drawings) looks very much like oil paint. The last digit of the date *1783* on No. 256 is bisected by the edge of what appears to be a stain and is consequently difficult to read. Although it was recorded as *1788* in 1963, to the compilers of this catalogue a reading of *1783* has seemed more convincing.

A drawing formerly in the collection of Mrs. F. Howard, which was incorrectly identified as "Moses Striking the Rock," when sold in 1979, shows *Pharaoh and His Host Lost in the Red Sea* (see No. 254).

[1]Farington 1978—, VI, p. 2166.

257 Moses Receiving the Laws 1773

LOCATION UNKNOWN

EXH: RA 1774 (312) "Moses receiving the tables, a design for a picture, intended to have been painted for St. Paul's Cathedral"

LIT: V and A Cuttings, I, p. 106 (1774); Galt 1820, pp. 14–15; Carey 1820, pp. 695–96; C. R. Leslie and Tom Taylor, *The Life and Times of Sir Joshua Reynolds*, London, 1865, II, p. 38; Whitley 1928a, I, p. 293; Croft-Murray 1970, pp. 67–68; Meyer 1975, p. 247

In 1773, a plan was put forward by several members of the recently founded Royal Academy to provide their services gratuitously to decorate St. Paul's Cathedral with paintings. The artists were Sir Joshua Reynolds, James Barry, Giovanni Battista Cipriani, Nathaniel Dance, Angelica Kauffmann, and West. Because of the opposition of Dr. Richard Terrick, the Bishop of London (see No. 705), the plan was dropped by October of 1773. West's use of the past tense in the entry for No. 257 which appeared in the Royal Academy catalogue in 1774 reflects the fact that the project was by then dead. The word "design" is probably indicative that the work was a drawing.

Although the design has disappeared and West never executed the actual painting for St. Paul's, he painted a large picture of the subject a decade later for the chapel in Windsor Castle (No. 258). It is possible that that work reflects the earlier composition. A small sketch of a single figure of Moses receiving the laws in a pose similar to that in No. 258 may also and more directly reflect the earlier composition (No. 261). A drawing showing a different visualization of Moses either receiving or breaking the tables of the law is known,[1] but in that drawing the violent Moses with head lowered and wild hair appears more akin to West's *Bard* of 1809 (No. 198) than to any figure West was likely to have drawn as early as 1774.

[1]Formerly in the collection of H. H. Margary, crayon, $10\frac{3}{4} \times 7$ in.

258 Moses Receiving the Laws 1784

PALACE OF WESTMINSTER, LONDON

Oil on canvas: 216×147 in. (549×373 cm.)

Signed: *B. West, 1784*

PROV: Painted for George III (1797 account: "Moses receiving the Law on Mount Sinia [*sic*], 18 ft. × 12 ft. 2 in., 1784, £1,260; 1801 account, p. 210: for the

Moses Receiving the Laws, drawing by West for No. 258. Yale Center for British Art, New Haven

Windsor Chapel, Mosaical Dispensation, 11, . . .); never delivered and ownership returned to West's sons by George IV in 1828; sold by them, Robins, London, 22–25 May 1829, lot 85 (18 ft. 2 in. × 12 ft. 3½ in.), bt. by Ward for £545; presented to the Royal Courts of Justice through the National Art Collection fund by the Earl of Crawford and Balcarres in 1946; installed in the Palace of Westminster, in St. Stephen's Entrance, c. 1959

EXH: RA 1784 (126) "Moses receiving the law on Mount Sinai, painted for His Majesty's chapel in Windsor-castle"; West's Gallery 1821 (79), 1822–28 (120)

ENGR: Mezzotint (34½ × 23¾ in.) by Richard Earlom, pub. 4 June 1814 by Boydell & Co.; unlettered lithograph (13¾ × 17 in.) by an unidentified artist reproducing five heads from the composition

LISTED: *PC*, p. 560 ("Moses receiving the Law on Mount Sinai," George III, for his Majesty's Chapel, Windsor, Mosaical Dispensation); *UM*, p. 527; *AA*, p. 66 (12 ft. × 18); Barlow, p. 432 (18 ft. × 12); *BA*, p. 14 (10 ft. × 14); Galt, p. 218; Dillenberger, pp. 145 (77) and 212

LIT: *Public Characters* 1805, p. 552; Dunlap 1834, I, p. 67 (Dunlap 1918, I, p. 72); von Erffa 1956, pp. 4–5; R. J. B. Walker, "A Mosaic Law Painting in Parliament," *Country Life,* CXXIV, 18 Sept. 1958, pp. 605–6; R. J. B. Walker, "A Catalogue of Paintings, Drawings, Sculpture and Engravings in the Palace of Westminster," unpublished [London, Ministry of Works, 1959]; Mount 1964, pp. 86 and 93; Kraemer 1975, p. 63, fig. 41; Meyer 1975, p. 264 et passim; Dillenberger 1977, pp. 53–57, 65, 67, pl. 43 et passim; Pressly 1983, p. 44

No. 258, which repeats the subject that West had planned to paint for the abortive program of decorating St. Paul's Cathedral (see No. 257), was a central work in West's plan for George III's chapel in Windsor Castle. A drawing at Windsor shows it as the main picture on an end wall where it is situated over the altar and over a smaller picture of the *Last Supper* (No. 344) and flanked on either side by empty niches (ill. p. 579). In one of West's sketchbooks in the Yale Center for British Art, a small and faint drawing shows what appears to be a similar arrangement, but in place of the empty niches on either side there are two tall narrow pictures, with empty rectangular panels above them.[1] The paintings in this sketch are not sufficiently defined for their subjects to be discernible, but they must represent No. 258 with the *Call of the Prophet Isaiah* and the *Call of the Prophet Jeremiah* (Nos. 283 and 286) on either side of it, a scheme which West evidently devised before 1782 (the date on a sketch for No. 283). By 1801 that plan was abandoned, and in one of the Swarthmore diagrams a painting of "The Laws" is the central vertical composition on the side wall devoted to Old Testament subjects (ill. p. 580). In that diagram, "The Laws" is larger than the pictures on either side, as No. 258 was and is in fact, being approximately 6 ft. taller and 2 ft. wider than the four pictures intended to flank it. The price of 1,200 guineas that West charged George III for No. 258 was 200 guineas more than that for any other chapel picture, including the *Ascension* (No. 380), which is almost the same size and in the Swarthmore diagrams is shown in the analogous position at the center of the opposite wall devoted to New Testament subjects.

Samuel Shoemaker mentioned in his diary seeing the large, finished picture in West's studio in Newman Street on 5 March 1784 (Historical Society of Pennsylvania), and William Dunlap described seeing it there when he arrived in London in June of the same year. Dunlap, however, must have been mistaken in his recollection of either the time or the place, as in June 1784 No. 258 was on view at the Royal Academy, and

he must have first seen it there, as well as in West's studio after its return.

In a watercolor view of the Royal Academy exhibition of 1784 by Johann Heinrich Ramberg (British Museum), No. 258 appears as the central picture of a triptych, with the *Call of the Prophet Isaiah* (No. 283) on its left and the *Call of the Prophet Jeremiah* (No. 286) on its right,[2] reflecting thus the arrangement sketched in the drawing at Yale which is cited above. These paintings also hung on either side of No. 258 in the posthumous exhibitions in West's gallery in the 1820s. In the sale of his pictures in May 1829 they appeared as the next two lots following No. 258 and were described in the catalogue as "side components of the great picture." No. 258, but not the flanking pictures, is visible through a doorway in the Inner Room, in the Cattermole/Le Keux engraving of West's gallery in 1821 and less distinctly in a painting of the gallery by John Pasmore in Hartford (ill. pp. 150 and 151).

Charles Merrill Mount has pointed out the features of John Trumbull in a head on the left side of the painting, and those of Gilbert Stuart in the profile head on the lower right.[3] Both of these artists, who were in West's studio at the time, may have assisted in the execution of the large painting. Additionally, Stuart seems to have painted a picture of Moses related to West's figure in No. 258 (see No. 260), and the figure of Moses from No. 258 appears in the background of the portrait of West by Stuart in the National Portrait Gallery in London.

In addition to the related works cited in the entries for Nos. 257 and 259–61, what appears to be a copy of No. 258 is in a private collection in France.[4] This picture has the same measurements as the Earlom mezzotint after No. 258. A drawing of the composition is in the same sketchbook at Yale that includes the sketch for the wall, mentioned above, on the facing page.

[1] Pencil, double page size 6 5/16 × 8 in. (B1977.14.4079, p. 9 recto).
[2] Meyer 1975, p. 252.
[3] See Mount 1964, p. 93. For likenesses of Trumbull, see Jaffe 1975, pp. 14, 53, and 229; for Stuart, see Mount 1964, following p. 128.
[4] Oil on paper mounted on panel, 34½ × 23½ in.

259 Moses Receiving the Laws *c.* 1784

PRIVATE COLLECTION

Oil on paper mounted on panel: 45¾ × 28½ in. (116 × 72.5 cm.)

PROV: Offered by West's sons to the United States in 1826 (140), and sold by them, Robins, London, 22–25 May 1829, lot 125 (2 ft. 11 in. × 4 ft. 2 in.), bt. by Bone for £78.15.0.; sold by the estate of Pierre G. Jeannerat, Sotheby's, London, 14 March 1984, lot 105; P. & D. Colnaghi, Ltd.

EXH: 125 Pall Mall 1814 (9); 125 Pall Mall 1818 (10)

LISTED: *PC*, p. 568 ("The large Sketch, in oil, [on paper] of Moses receiving the Laws on Mount Sinai," West, Gallery); *UM*, p. 531; *BA*, p. 19; Galt, p. 232; Dillenberger, p. 182 (436)

No. 259 was listed in 1826 among the "Original Designs in Chiaro Scuro for the large Pictures which were painted for his late Majesty's Chapel in Windsor Castle" and described when sold in 1829 as "a splendid study, intended for the centre division of the projected Altar-piece" of the chapel. Despite some discrepancy between the dimensions of the present work and those recorded in 1826 and 1829, No. 259 is a

258

259

monochromatic sketch, similar to other sketches that
West utilized for his large paintings intended for the
Royal Chapel at Windsor. The composition repeats
that shown in the drawing of *c.* 1780 for the altar wall
of the chapel (ill. p. 579). In the final version (No. 258),
West substantially re-arranged the group of spectators
in the lower half of the canvas. The relation of this
sketch to the sketch of the same subject that West
intended for St. Paul's Cathedral (No. 257) can only
be a matter of conjecture. He probably painted (or
composed) Nos. 260 and 261 before he painted No. 259,
and they may more closely reflect the appearance of
the earlier sketch.

The Bone who bought No. 259 in 1829 was presumably the enamel painter Henry Pierce Bone, who
bought extensively for Joseph Neeld at the West sale.
The painting did not appear in the Neeld sales of 1945
and 1962 and, as with Nos. 246 and 295, two other
chapel sketches which were also bought by Bone, there
is no evidence that No. 259 was in fact in the Neeld
collection.

260 Moses Receiving the Laws *c.* 1777

ST. PANCRAS PARISH CHURCH, LONDON

Oil on canvas: $77\frac{1}{2} \times 29$ in. (197×73.5 cm.)

PROV: Fitzroy Chapel, Fitzroy Square, London, until
World War II (the chapel was destroyed in 1945);
since then in the church hall of St. Pancras Parish
Church

LIT: Mason 1879, p. 277; London County Council,
*Survey of London, XXI: Tottenham Court Road and
Neighbourhood: The Parish of St. Pancras, Part III,*
London, 1949, p. 48; Dillenberger 1977, p. 86

260

Neither No. 260 nor a companion painting of *Christ Blessing* (No. 332) appears on the early lists of West's *oeuvre*. The earliest reference to them known to the authors of this catalogue is in George Mason's biography of Gilbert Stuart published in 1879: "There are two pictures in Fitzroy Chapel, Fitzroy Square, London. One represents Moses Kneeling and receiving the Commandments; the other is a whole length of our Savior, designed by West, and painted by Stuart." Although Mason's phrasing is ambiguous, the "designed by West, and painted by Stuart" evidently refers to both works. There is nothing distinctive in the handling in either painting to suggest that they were actually executed by West, and it seems unlikely that Mason, whose book was based largely on material from Stuart's daughter, would have made such a statement without reason for it. On the other hand, if the execution is Stuart's, the design is certainly West's, as stated by Mason. The close similarity of the Moses in No. 260 to the Moses in No. 258 is evident, although there are conspicuous differences in the draperies and the placing of one of the tables of the law.

Traditionally the two paintings from the Fitzroy Chapel seem to have been thought of as by West; according to the *Survey of London* he painted them for the chapel, and it is quite likely that he donated them. The Fitzroy Chapel, which was located not far from West's home in Newman Street, was the church West attended. Its founder, the Reverend Robert Anthony Bromley, was a friend of West and an art critic or art historian, who shamelessly puffed West in his writings and was generally believed to have helped West prepare his presidential Academy discourses.[1]

Nos. 260 and 332 may have had their origins in designs for stained glass. Both show single hieratic figures, of a type that West rarely painted otherwise, set against neutral gold backgrounds in narrow vertical compositions. The present frames are not original. Both canvases have additions of approximately 4 in. along the bottom, and marks of an arched frame are evident at the top of No. 260. Two smaller versions (Nos. 261 and 333) have trefoil Gothic arches at the tops, which make the purpose as designs for glass seem still more likely. The actual glass may have been that mentioned by the American loyalist refugee Samuel Curwen in a diary entry for 15 May 1776: "Visited Pinchbeck's to view stained glass; most elegant figures, finest tints in the new revived art, by a Mr. Jervais; among which were two full lengths of Christ and Moses, bought at seventy guineas by a clergyman, and presented to Westminster Abbey."[2] Curwen does not mention West in connection with these windows, and the pairing of Christ and Moses was so common that the glass may have been by another artist entirely. Nevertheless, West and Thomas Jervais, the glassmaker to whom Curwen certainly was referring, did work together in the 1780s at Windsor; and on 26 June 1777, a year after Curwen's visit, Jervais initially recommended to the Warden of New College, Oxford, that West, rather than Reynolds, provide the designs for windows that Jervais was to execute for New College.[3] That suggests not only that Jervais was aware of West, but that he may have previously worked from designs by West. The full-lengths of Christ and Moses in glass, which Curwen saw at Pinchbeck's, seem to have disappeared: removed, destroyed, or possibly never installed in Westminster Abbey. Two additional paintings of Moses and Christ, which appear to have been copies of either Nos. 260 and 332 or the smaller versions, 261 and 333, were until recently in St. Margaret's, Westminster, and it may be that their presence there was in some way connected with the glass which Curwen believed destined for the abbey next door.[4] Therefore, it seems more probable than not that the glass Curwen saw in May of 1776 was based on West's designs, but if we accept also Mason's statement that Stuart executed Nos. 260 and

332, it follows that these two works could not have served as the cartoons, as Stuart did not meet West until the latter part of 1776. They were probably painted after 1777, while Stuart was living with West in Newman Street. Bromley took the lease of the land for the Fitzroy Chapel in 1777 and West may have then set his new pupil and assistant to painting the two pictures for the chapel on the basis of sketches such as Nos. 261 and 333, which West had made earlier as designs for glass. The design for the painting of Moses would not then have been based on the Moses in the large painting for Windsor (No. 258), which West painted only in 1784 but it may well have derived from the earlier design for St. Paul's, which West had exhibited in 1774 (No. 257).

[1] For the Fitzroy Chapel, see the volume of the *Survey of London* cited above. For Bromley, see especially Mitchell 1967, pp. 270–72 and Dillenberger 1977, pp. 3–5. West painted portraits of Bromley and his wife (Nos. 598 and 599).
[2] Curwen 1842, p. 56.
[3] Christopher Woodforde, *The Stained Glass of New College, Oxford*, London, 1951, pp. 39–40; see also Meyer 1979, p. 55.
[4] These paintings were on canvas, 38 × 15 in. each. According to a letter from Howard M. Nixon to Barbara Coffey dated 11 Oct. 1979, they were found to be in such hopelessly deteriorated condition in the early 1960s that they were thrown away. Photographs taken in 1962 confirm their bad condition and also suggest that they were works of very dubious quality.

261 Moses Receiving the Laws *c.* 1774–76

LOCATION UNKNOWN

Oil on panel: 20¼ × 7⅛ in. (51.5 × 18 cm.)

PROV: Mrs. E. K. Rule, London

Mrs. Rule, the last recorded owner of this painting and of a companion picture of *Christ Blessing* (No. 333), was a descendant of the artist. It is possible that these two works were painted by West before 1776 as designs for stained glass and that they were subsequently utilized by Gilbert Stuart as the modellos for Nos. 260 and 332. The figure of Moses in No. 261 may have derived from the Moses in No. 257, which West exhibited in 1774 as a design for St. Paul's Cathedral.

262 Moses and Aaron Sacrificing *c.* 1795

LOCATION UNKNOWN

150 × 120 in. (381 × 305 cm.)

PROV: Painted for George III (1797 account: "Moses consecrates Aaron and his sons," 1795, £1,050; 1801 account, p. 210: for the Windsor Chapel, Mosaical Dispensation, 12 . . .); never delivered and ownership returned to West's sons by George IV in 1828; sold by them, Robins, London, 22–25 May 1829, lot 51 (12 ft. 6 in. × 10 ft.), bt. by Dolman for £68.5.0.

EXH: RA 1795 (144) "Moses consecrateth Aaron and his sons, their sin offering"; West's Gallery 1821 (46), 1822–28 (68) "Moses and Aaron Sacrificing, Exodus, chap. 29":

> Verse 4. And Aaron and his sons thou shalt bring unto the door of the tabernacle of the congregation, and shalt wash them with water.

> Verse 5. And thou shalt take the garments, and put upon Aaron the coat, and the robe of the ephod, and the ephod, and the breast-plate, and gird him with the curious girdle of the ephod.

> Verse 6. And thou shalt put the mitre upon his head, and put the holy crown upon the mitre.

> Verse 7. Then shalt thou take the anointing oil, and pour it upon his head, and anoint him.

> Verse 8. And thou shalt bring his sons, and put coats upon them.

> Verse 9. And thou shalt gird them with girdles, (Aaron and his sons), and put the bonnets on them: and the priest's office shall be theirs for a perpetual statute: and thou shall consecrate Aaron and his sons.

> Verse 10. And thou shalt cause a bullock to be brought before the tabernacle of the congregation: and Aaron and his sons shall put their hands upon the head of the bullock.

LISTED: *PC*, p. 560 ("Moses consecrateth Aaron and his Sons to the Priesthood," George III, for his Majesty's Chapel, Windsor, Mosaical Dispensation); *UM*, p. 527; *AA*, p. 66 (9 ft. × 14); Barlow, p. 432 (15 ft. × 10); *BA*, p. 14 (10 ft. × 14); Galt, p. 218; Dillenberger, p. 145 (78)

LIT: Farington Diary, 28 and 29 April 1795 (Farington 1978—, II, pp. 331–32); V and A Cuttings, III, pp. 716, 738, 744, 747 (1795); Meyer 1975, p. 264; Dillenberger 1977, p. 65

This subject does not seem to appear on the architectural schemes for the Windsor chapel from *c.* 1780.[1] On the Swarthmore diagrams of 1801 it appears as "The Priests Instituted" on the extreme right in the center row on the side wall devoted to Old Testament subjects (ill. p. 580). In left-to-right sequence, it follows the *Brazen Serpent*, although in biblical sequence it should precede.

No. 262 is recognizable on the right-hand wall, adjacent to *Death on the Pale Horse* (No. 401), in a view of the posthumous exhibition in West's gallery painted by John Pasmore (ill. p. 151).[2] An oil sketch is No. 263 below.

[1] It should be noted that the two horizontal drawings in the upper right on the main side wall in the architectural schemes both contain motifs that can be connected with this subject: two children who could be Aaron's sons in one and a sacrificial bullock and a scene of anointment in the other (see ill. p. 577). However, neither scene fits very well with the biblical text, and it seems more likely as suggested by Meyer (1975, p. 249, n. 6), that they represent the "Twelve Tribes Drawing Lots" and "David Anointed King," neither of which was to become a completed painting.
[2] The painting is behind a supporting column in the engraved view of the gallery by Cattermole and Le Keux.

263 Moses and Aaron Sacrificing *c.* 1795

BOB JONES UNIVERSITY, GREENVILLE, SOUTH CAROLINA

Oil on canvas: 37½ × 28⅞ in. (95.5 × 73.5 cm.)

Signed lower left: (?) *B. West 1795*

PROV: Offered by West's sons to the United States in 1826 (36), and sold by them, Robins, London, 22–25 May 1829, lot 133 (2 ft. 4 in. × 3 ft.), bt. by Bone for £105 on behalf of Joseph Neeld, MP, Grittleton House, Wilts.; by descent in the Neeld family until sold, Christie's, London, 13 July 1945, lot 166 (as "The Sacrifice"); W. Katz, London, by 1960; Central Picture Galleries, New York, 1969

EXH: West's Gallery 1821 (74) "Aaron Sacrificing (a sketch)"; San Antonio 1983 (19)

LISTED: *PC*, p. 566 ("Moses consecrating Aaron and his Sons to the Priesthood," West, Gallery); *UM*, p. 531; Barlow, p. 435; *BA*, p. 18; Galt, p. 229; Dillenberger, pp. 176 (370) and 213

263

Aaron Stopping the Plague, outline engraving by Henry Moses after No. 264

LIT: Meyer 1975, p. 264; Dillenberger 1977, p. 67, pl. 44

This oil sketch for No. 262 is unfinished and appears to have been worked on in some areas by another hand. The signature is barely discernible.

264 Aaron Stopping the Plague *c.* 1792

LOCATION UNKNOWN

(28 × 37 in.) (71 × 94 cm.)

PROV: Offered by West's sons to the United States in 1826 (80), and sold by them, Robins, London, 22–25 May 1829, lot 149 (2 ft. 4 in. × 3 ft. 1 in.), bt. by Powell for £16.16.0.

EXH: RA 1792 (319) "Aaron stopping the plague; a sketch"; West's Gallery 1822–28 (47)

ENGR: Outline engraving ($7\frac{7}{16} \times 5\frac{5}{8}$ in.) by H. Moses, pub. 1 May 1811 by H. Moses as pl. v in Moses 1811

LISTED: *PC*, p. 569 ("The Sketch, in oil, of Aaron standing between the Dead and Living to stop the Plague," West, Gallery); *UM*, p. 532; *BA*, p. 19; Galt, p. 234; Dillenberger, p. 186 (480)

LIT: Moses 1811 (v); Kraemer 1975, p. 33

The subject of No. 264 is from Numbers 16:42–48. Although it appears on none of the lists of works intended for the chapel at Windsor, it is so closely related in subject to works West was painting for the chapel at precisely the time he exhibited No. 264 that it seems probable that it was initially intended for that project, and later, like No. 256, dropped from the scheme before any of the lists were drawn up. In all accounts it is described as a sketch rather than a finished painting. The measurements of the sketch in West's sons' list of 1826 and the sale catalogue of 1829 indicate that it was a horizontal composition, which would have been appropriate for a subject intended for a subordinate position in the chapel. However, the outline engraving by Henry Moses (*above*) shows a vertical composition. Moses may have reproduced only part of No. 264, but it is perhaps more likely that the measurements of the sketch were mistakenly transposed in 1826 and 1829,[1] and that West originally intended the subject for one of the larger vertical spaces in the chapel. The re-transposed dimensions of 37 × 28 in. are close to those of Nos. 253, 255, 263, and 267, the sketches for the four large Old Testament paintings that West did complete for the chapel between 1790 and 1796. See also No. 265.

A rapid drawing of the subject, related to the Moses engraving but significantly different in detail, is in the Pierpont Morgan Library.[2]

[1] In 1826 numerous measurements were transposed including those of a group of sketches related to chapel pictures; see Nos. 259, 284, 287, 317, 335, 381, 386, and 396; those of the three Old Testament subjects remained transposed in 1829.

[2] Kraemer 1975, p. 33 (52) and pl. 31, pen and brown ink, $4\frac{15}{16} \times 4\frac{15}{16}$ in., signed.

265

265 The Death of Aaron 1790–1803

BALTIMORE MUSEUM OF ART

Pen and ink and wash heightened with white:
28⅝ × 19 in. (72.5 × 48.5 cm.)

Signed lower left: *B. West 1790/retouched 1803*

PROV: Drawn as a study for a painting intended for
George III (1801 account, p. 211: for the Windsor
Chapel, Mosaical Dispensation, 14, "The Death of
Aaron on Mount Hor, composed, but not painted");
by descent in the West family to H. H. Margary,
Bagshot, Surrey; Thos. Agnew and Sons, London;
Bernard Black Gallery, New York, 1963; purchased
by the Baltimore Museum of Art in 1964

EXH: RA 1804 (554) "The death of Aaron"; West's
Gallery 1823 (Room of Drawings, 54)

LISTED: *PC*, p. 568 ("The Sketch, in oil, of the Death
of Aaron, on paper," West, Gallery); *UM*, p. 531;
BA, p. 19; Galt, p. 233; Dillenberger, pp. 145 (80),
183 (446) and 212

LIT: *Art Quarterly*, XXVI, 1963, p. 117 (adv., as "The
raising of Saul"); Meyer 1975, p. 264

No. 265 is one of a group of drawings related to the
Royal Chapel in Windsor Castle which West retouched
in 1803. Others include *Moses Striking the Rock*
(No. 256), and *Death on the Pale Horse* (No. 402). All
these works were described as sketches in oil on paper
in *Public Characters* and the other early lists of West's
oeuvre, apparently because of West's extensive use of
body-color. No. 265, like Nos. 256 and 402, is on
several sheets of paper joined together. The two latter
drawings are both dated *1783*, and they appeared
together at the Royal Academy in 1784. No. 265, which
is smaller than those two drawings, bears the date *1790*
and was first exhibited in 1804, following its
retouching.

Although the subject appears on only one list of
chapel subjects and on none of the drawings and
diagrams showing purported arrangements of pictures
in the chapel, there is no reason to doubt that West
composed No. 265 for the chapel as indicated in his
account of 1801. Like No. 256, which was identified as
a design for the chapel when exhibited in 1784 but
appears on none of the lists, the subject of this work
appears to have been part of the chapel scheme only
briefly. In conception and in subsequent disappearance
from the chapel plans, it may have been linked with
the related subject of *Aaron Stopping the Plague* (No. 264),
which was exhibited as a sketch in 1792 but does not
appear on any of the lists of chapel subjects.

**266 Moses Showing the Brazen Serpent to the
Israelites** *c.* 1790

BOB JONES UNIVERSITY, GREENVILLE, SOUTH
CAROLINA

Oil on canvas: 148 × 115 in. (376 × 292 cm.)

PROV: Painted for George III (1797 account: "Moses
Shewing the Brazen serpent to the Israelites," for the
Chapel in Windsor Castle, 1790, £1,050; 1801
account, p. 210: for the Windsor Chapel, Mosaical
Dispensation, 13 . . .); never delivered and ownership returned to West's sons by George IV in 1828;
sold by them, Robins, London, 22–25 May 1829, lot
76 (12 ft. 6 in. × 10 ft.), bt. by Bone for £68.5.0. on
behalf of Joseph Neeld, MP, Grittleton House, Wilts.;
by descent in the Neeld family until sold by Miss
C. K. M. Neeld, Christie's, London, 16 Nov. 1962,
lot 93, bt. by Weitzner; purchased by the present
owner in 1963

EXH: RA 1790 (36) "Moses showing the brazen serpent to the Israelites, painted for His Majesty's chapel, Windsor Castle"; West's Gallery 1821 (22), 1822–28 (33)

LISTED: *PC*, p. 560 ("Moses sheweth the Brazen Serpent to the People to be healed," George III, for his Majesty's Chapel, Windsor, Mosaical Dispensation); *UM*, p. 527; *AA*, p. 66 (9 ft. × 14); Barlow, p. 432 (15 ft. × 10); *BA*, p. 14 (10 ft. × 14); Galt, p. 218; Dillenberger, pp. 145 (79) and 212

LIT: V and A Cuttings, II, pp. 561, 565, and 566 (reviews, 1790); Passavant 1836, I, pp. 55, 187; Jones 1963; Jones 1968, p. 65 (346), ill. p. 187; Meyer 1975, pp. 260–61, 264, and fig. 22; Dillenberger 1977, pp. 65, 68, pl. 45; Pressly 1983, pp. 21–22, fig. 10

This subject does not appear in the architectural schemes from *c.* 1780 for the Windsor chapel. In the Swarthmore diagrams from 1801 it is second from the right in the center range of the side wall devoted to Old Testament subjects, between "The Laws" (No. 258) and the "Priests Instituted" (No. 262) (ill. p. 580). In proper biblical order, the subject of No. 266 (from Numbers 21:6–9) should follow that of No. 262 (from Exodus 29:4–10), rather than precede it as it does in the general left-to-right sequence of the Swarthmore diagram.

In addition to the sketch at Andover listed below (No. 267), there is also a drawing in the same collection which is slightly less close in composition to this painting.[1] Another slighter and sketchier drawing of the subject was formerly in the collection of H. H. Margary.[2]

[1] Sepia, 13½ × 11½ in.
[2] Pen and ink, 5⅝ × 5¼ in., sold Sotheby's, London, 25 Oct. 1961, lot 23.

267 Moses Showing the Brazen Serpent to the Israelites 1790

ADDISON GALLERY OF AMERICAN ART, PHILLIPS ACADEMY, ANDOVER, MASSACHUSETTS

Oil on canvas: 38 × 29 in. (96.5 × 73.5 cm.)

Signed bottom center: *B. West 1790*

PROV: Renaissance Galleries, Philadelphia, 1938

EXH: Philadelphia 1936; Philadelphia 1938 (39); Allentown 1962 (19)

LISTED: Dillenberger, p. 212

LIT: Meyer 1975, p. 264

This sketch for No. 266 corresponds with the large painting in all significant details. There are slight differences in the serpent around the neck of the boy at Moses' feet, and in the figure behind the boy, who is clothed in No. 266 and nude in No. 267.

Unlike most of the other sketches for chapel pictures, No. 267 does not appear on any of the early lists of West's works and it seems to have gone completely unrecorded until the 1930s. In size and medium it is consistent with several of the chapel sketches such as Nos. 255 and 263, but it stands apart from them in remaining like a drawing in effect rather than having been worked up into a completed picture.

268 Moses Showing the Brazen Serpent (?)*c.* 1786

LOCATION UNKNOWN

(96 × 60 in.) (244 × 152.5 cm.)

PROV: (?) Christ Church, Barbados

ENGR: Engraving (12³⁄₁₆ × 9¾ in.) by John Hall, pub. 30 Aug. 1793 by Thomas Macklin, and utilized as the frontispiece to vol. I of Macklin's *Bible*, London, 1800

(?) LISTED: *PC*, p. 562 ("Moses with the Law, and John the Baptist [see No. 297], in the Church of Barbadoes, as large as life") and p. 563 ("Moses shewing the Brazen Serpent"); *UM*, p. 528 (listed twice on the same page); *AA*, p. 69 ("Moses with the Tables of the Laws," 8 ft. × 5, in Christ Church in the Island of Barbados); Barlow, p. 433 ("Moses shewing the Brazen Serpent," under "In Different Churches"); *BA*, p. 15 (as in *PC*, p. 562); Galt, pp. 221 and 222; Dillenberger, pp. 154 (161), 155 (165), and 158 (196)

No. 268 is one of four compositions by West which appeared as engravings in Thomas Macklin's great illustrated *Bible* (*see over page*), published in 1800. The others are *Saul and the Witch of Endor*, *St. John the Baptist*, and *Christ Showing a Little Child as the Emblem of Heaven* (Nos. 275, 297, and 325). Paintings by West of two of the four subjects (Nos. 297 and 325) were in Macklin's sale in 1800, where they were identified as "original Pictures" painted for Macklin's *Bible*. No. 268 was not in the sale, but paintings of *Moses* and *St. John*, both described as "after West," were sold together in one lot among a group of works catalogued as "Copies."[1] These copies were presumably made for Macklin's engravers to work from. The available evidence does not suggest that Macklin ever owned Nos. 268 and 275.

The list of West's works in *Public Characters of 1805* (repeated in the *Universal Magazine* and by Galt) includes two paintings of *Moses* described either explicitly or implicitly as in a church in Barbados, in each instance listed together with paintings of the *Resur-*

267

Moses Showing the Brazen Serpent, engraving by John Hall after No. 268

269 Moses Shown the Promised Land 1801
See color illustration, p. 104

METROPOLITAN MUSEUM OF ART, NEW YORK

Oil on panel: $19\frac{3}{4} \times 28\frac{3}{4}$ in. (50×73 cm.)

Signed bottom center: *B. West 1801*

PROV: Study for a painting intended for George III (1801 account, p. 211: for the Windsor Chapel, Mosaical Dispensation, 16 "Moses sees the Promised Lane from the top of Mount Abarim, and Death, a sketch in oil colours"); offered by West's sons to the United States in 1826 (56), and sold by them, Robins, London, 22–25 May 1829, lot 29 (1 ft. $8\frac{1}{2}$ in. $\times$ 2 ft. 5 in.), bt. by Albert for £25.4.0.; sold anonymously, Sotheby's, London, 7 July 1965, lot 132 (as "Let there be Light"), bt. by Weitzner;[1] M. Knoedler & Co., New York; given to the Metropolitan Museum of Art by Mr. and Mrs. James Fosburgh in 1969

EXH: RA 1801 (243) "Moses, from the top of Mount Pisgah, is shown the promised land, Deuteronomy, chap. xxxiv. ver. 1":

> And Moses went up from the plains of Moab unto the mountain of Nebo, to the top of Pisgah, that is over against Jericho, and the Lord shewed him all the land of Gilead, unto Dan.

West's Gallery 1821 (75), 1822–28 (4); *American Painting 1750–1950*, M. Knoedler & Co., New York, 1969 (6)

ENGR: Outline engraving ($6\frac{13}{16} \times 9\frac{11}{16}$ in.) by Henry Moses, pub. 1817 by H. Moses and incorporated in later editions of Moses 1811

LISTED: *PC*, p. 567 ("Moses shewn the promised Land," West, Gallery); *UM*, p. 531; Barlow, p. 435; *BA*, p. 18; Galt, p. 230; Dillenberger, pp. 177 (383) and 213

LIT: Moses 1811 (only in later editions); Meyer 1975, pp. 261, 264, and fig. 23; Dillenberger 1977, pp. 65 and 69, pl. 46

No. 269 is one of two works listed in West's account of 1801 of his works painted for George III as a "sketch in oil colours" of a subject intended for the chapel at Windsor. The other is *Joshua Passing the River Jordan* (No. 270). He exhibited both at the Royal Academy in 1801 without indication in the catalogue of their connection with the chapel scheme. Both subjects also appear on subsequent lists as full-sized pictures for the chapel,[2] but, as in the case of many other titles on those lists, there is no evidence to suggest that the large versions were ever painted. The subject of No. 269 does not appear on the architectural drawings from *c.* 1780 for the chapel. On the Swarthmore diagrams of 1801 it appears as the "Death of Moses" on the extreme left of the top row of the side wall devoted to Old Testament subjects (ill. p. 580). Although Moses is clearly alive in No. 269, chapter 34 of Deuteronomy, from which West quoted the first verse in the Royal Academy catalogue, describes the death of Moses following his view of the Promised Land from Mount Pisgah. The name Mount Abarim, which West used in the 1801 account, is from Deuteronomy 32:49.

Jerry Meyer has pointed out the similarity of West's imagery in No. 269 with that of Philip James de Loutherbourg's frontispiece for Macklin's *Bible*, published in 1800. Although the de Loutherbourg purportedly shows the Creation, it contains many elements which make it also appear to be a representation of Moses.[3]

---

rection and *John the Baptist* similarly identified as in Barbados. The double appearance of these subjects in these catalogues seems obviously erroneous, and in *Academic Annals*, Joel Barlow's *Columbiad*, and *La Belle Assemblée*, there are only single entries for each subject. Unfortunately, the two entries in *Public Characters*, the *Universal Magazine* and Galt, for the painting of *Moses* describe the figure in one case as "with the Law" and in the other as "shewing the Brazen Serpent," and these two differing titles are repeated separately in *Academic Annals* and in the *Columbiad*, for what is or was presumably one work. The *Resurrection* (No. 362) is now in St. George's Parish Church in Barbados, but the paintings of *St. John* and *Moses* are not presently known, nor is there any record of them in Barbados,[2] and it is conceivable that they never reached the island. Because of the coincidence of the subjects of the missing pictures with those of two of the illustrations in Macklin's *Bible*, for which the original paintings are also missing and which are otherwise unrecorded in the early lists of

West's works, we have catalogued them as the same works (Nos. 268 and 297). The sizes recorded for the *Moses* and the *St. John* in *Academic Annals* (each as 8×5 ft) are almost certainly too large, since those listed for the *Resurrection* are 9×6 ft. (or 108×72 in.), whereas the actual painting is 84×60 in., but it is possible that the recorded dimensions included the frames. The relative sizes of the three suggest that the two smaller works were intended to flank the *Resurrection* as wings of a triptych. The *Resurrection* is signed and dated *1786*. West may have painted Nos. 268 and 297 somewhat later, but before they were engraved in 1793 and 1796 respectively.

---

[1]Peter Coxe, Burrell, and Foster, London, 5 May 1800 and following days, lot 41.

[2]Letter from E. M. Shilstone (Hon. Secretary of Barbados Museum and Historical Society) to Helmut von Erffa, 4 Aug. 1956.

---

[1]The painting also appears and is reproduced in Christie's catalogue for 16 July 1965, lot 118 (withdrawn).

[2]For *Moses Shown the Promised Land*, the references are: *PC*, p. 560 (Mosaical Dispensation); *UM*, p. 527; *AA*, p. 66

(9 ft. × 6); Barlow, p. 432; *BA*, p. 14 (6 ft. × 10); Galt, p. 218; Dillenberger, p. 145 (82).

[3] See the discussion by Rüdiger Joppien in *Philippe Jacques de Loutherbourg 1740–1812*, the Iveagh Bequest, Kenwood, 1973, no. 70, where the oil version, signed and dated *1800*, is reproduced.

270 Joshua Passing the River Jordan with the Ark of the Covenant 1800

See color illustration, p. 104

ART GALLERY OF NEW SOUTH WALES, SYDNEY, AUSTRALIA

Oil on panel: 21 × 30 in. (53.3 × 76.2 cm.)

Signed bottom center: *B. West 1800*

PROV: Study for a painting intended for George III (1801 account, p. 211: for the Windsor Chapel, Mosaical Dispensation, 17 "Joshua Commanding the Ark and Congregation to pass the river into the Promised Land, a sketch in oil colour"); offered by West's sons to the United States in 1826 (113), and sold by them, Robins, London, 22–25 May 1829, lot 46 (1 ft. 8½ in. × 2 ft. 5 in.), bt. by Albert for £42; purchased by the Art Gallery of New South Wales in 1971

EXH: RA 1801 (295) "Joshua passing the river Jordan, with the Ark of the Covenant, Joshua, chap. iii. ver. ii":

Behold, the ark of the covenant of the Lord of all the earth, passeth over before you into Jordan.

West's Gallery 1821 (83), 1822–28 (110)

LISTED: *PC*, p. 567 ("Joshua crossing the River Jordan with the Ark," West, Gallery); *UM*, p. 531; Barlow, p. 435; *BA*, p. 18; Galt, p. 230; Dillenberger, pp. 177 (384) and 213

LIT: *Art Gallery of New South Wales: Picturebook*, Sydney, 1972; Meyer 1975, p. 264; Dillenberger 1977, pp. 65 and 70, pl. 47

No. 270 has the identical early history to that of No. 269, up to and including the West sale of 1829, when both pictures were acquired by the same purchaser. Both appear in West's account of 1801 as sketches in oil colours. The subjects are also included on the later published lists of West's works as full-sized pictures for the Windsor chapel,[1] but it is unlikely that large versions were ever painted. The subject of No. 270 does not appear on the architectural drawings for the chapel dating from *c*. 1780. On the Swarthmore diagrams of 1801, "12 Tribes/Joshua" is second from the left on the top row of the side wall devoted to the Old Testament, following the "Death of Moses" (ill. p. 580). "12 Tribes/Joshua" may refer to the subject of No. 270, but West also projected the "Twelve Tribes drawing Lots for the Lands of their Inheritance,"[2] which he apparently never painted at all, as another subject for the chapel, and it is possible that he intended the space for it. The available evidence suggests that in 1801 West was not certain which post-Mosaic Old Testament subjects he intended to paint for the chapel or exactly where they would go. In addition to the "12 Tribes/Joshua" on the top row, he also included "12 Tribes in Egypt," a title that appears on none of the accounts or lists, at the extreme right of the bottom row of subjects in the same diagram, following the *Birth of Jacob and Esau* (cf. No. 245), and, to complicate things further, the space to the right of center in the top row, which follows immediately after that with "12 Tribes/ Joshua" in the normal sequence of subjects in this diagram, is blank.[3] The following and last remaining space on this wall, on the extreme right of the uppermost row, contains "David Anointed King," another subject which West evidently never painted, although

like the "12 Tribes Drawing Lots," it appears among the chapel subjects on all the early published lists of his works.[4] One other related subject, "Moses presenting Joshua to Eleazer the priest, and Congregation, as commanded," is included on West's account of 1801 with the notation "composed, but not painted," but appears on no other early lists.[5] The two remaining Old Testament subjects that can be associated with the chapel, the *Call of Isaiah* and the *Call of Jeremiah* (Nos. 283 and 286), which West painted and exhibited in 1784 as companions to *Moses Receiving the Laws* (No. 258), do not appear on the Swarthmore diagrams at all.

A drawing at Swarthmore appears to show the subject of the priests bearing the Ark of the Covenant over the Jordan but has little resemblance compositionally to No. 270.[6]

[1] For *Joshua Passing the Jordan*: *PC*, p. 560 (Mosaical Dispensation); *UM*, p. 527; *AA*, p. 66 (9 ft. by 6); Barlow, p. 432; *BA*, p. 14 (6 feet by 10); Galt, p. 218; Dillenberger, p. 146 (83).
[2] *PC*, p. 561 (Mosaical Dispensation, 6 feet × 10); *UM*, p. 527; *AA*, p. 67 (9 ft. × 6); Barlow, p. 432 (9 ft. × 6); *BA*, p. 14; Galt, p. 218; Dillenberger, p. 146 (84).
[3] Dillenberger supplies a title in his schematic reproduction of the diagram (Dillenberger 1977, pl. 32), but there is none in the space on the actual sheet (see p. 580).
[4] 1801 account, no. 20 ("The prophet Samuel anointing David the son of Jesse, a sketch"); *PC*, p. 561 (Mosaical Dispensation, 6 ft. × 10); *UM*, p. 527; *AA*, p. 67 (9 ft. × 6); Barlow, p. 432 (9 ft. × 6); *BA*, p. 14; Galt, p. 218; Dillenberger, p. 146 (87).
[5] 1801 account, no. 15; Dillenberger, p. 145 (81).
[6] Black chalk, 10¾ × 7 in.

271 Hannah Presenting Samuel to Eli *c.* 1778–80

HIS GRACE THE DUKE OF RUTLAND

Oil on canvas: 20 × 26 in. (51 × 66 cm.)

PROV: (?) Painted for the fourth Duke of Rutland (1754–1787)

LISTED: *UM*, p. 528 ("Samuel presented to the Altar by his Mother," in the possession of the Duke of Rutland); (?) *BA*, p. 19 (as "Christ Blessing Little Children"; see discussion below)

LIT: The Revd. Irvin Eller, *The History of Belvoir Castle*, London, 1846, pp. 204–5

No. 271 and *Christ among the Doctors* (No. 314), which are the same size, must have been painted as companion works. The two were recorded as belonging to the Duke of Rutland in the *Universal Magazine* in 1805. They are not included as a pair in any of the other early lists, but *La Belle Assemblée* records a "Christ Blessing Little Children" and "Christ among the Doctors" as "both painted for the late Duke of Rutland, and at Belvoir Castle," and as there is no record otherwise of a version of the former subject in the Rutland collection, the work referred to under that title may have been No. 271, whose presence in the possession of the fifth Duke at Belvoir Castle was confirmed by Irvin Eller in 1846. Since the fifth Duke held the title from 1787 to 1857, the "late Duke" in *La Belle Assemblée* was the fourth Duke, who succeeded in 1779 and died in 1787. The one other picture known to have been painted by West for a Duke of Rutland, (No. 47), appeared at the Royal Academy in 1778. Nos. 271 and 314 were probably painted at approximately the same time. West may have undertaken them as preliminary sketches for works proposed but never carried out for the chapel in Windsor Castle, a project begun in 1779. The subject of No. 314 appears in various documents related to the chapel; that of No. 271 does not.

Eller quoted prices of £40 for Nos. 271 and 314. Two

Hannah Presenting Samuel to Eli, (?) studio replica of No. 271. George E. Doty

272

paintings of the same subjects in the collection of George E. Doty are approximately the same size and are reportedly identical in composition to the two Rutland paintings.[1] They are not signed and seem to have no recorded histories prior to 1968. Nonetheless, it seems likely that they are contemporary replicas, possibly painted by one of West's studio assistants.[2]

[1] The version of No. 271 is in oil on canvas, $19 \times 25\frac{1}{2}$ in., sold by Sir John Dilke, Bt., Parke-Bernet, New York, 25 Sept. 1968, lot 15; and sold anonymously, Christie's, New York, 9 June 1978, lot 4.
[2] We have not been able to see Nos. 271 and 314, nor to obtain photographs, and are grateful to Barbara Dayer Gallati for reporting that they are still at Belvoir Castle (letter of 17 June 1985).

272 Hannah Presenting Samuel to Eli 1800

MR. AND MRS. RICHARD MANNEY

Oil on canvas: $13\frac{1}{4} \times 17\frac{1}{4}$ in. (33.5 × 44 cm.)

Signed lower right: *B. West/1800*

PROV: Offered by West's sons to the United States in 1826 (65), and sold by them, Robins, London, 22–25 May 1829, lot 6 ("Samuel, when a child, presented to Eli," $12\frac{1}{2} \times 17$ in.), bt. by Albert for £17.17.0.; (?) Robert Hamilton, Bloomfield House, Norwood, Surrey; sold, Foster, London, 16 March 1832, lot 205 (as "The Prophet Eli"); Charles Meigh; Renaissance Galleries, Philadelphia, 1938; sold anonymously, Parke-Bernet, New York, 17 Dec. 1969, lot 90

EXH: RA 1801 (688) "Hannah presenting Samuel to Eli, First Book of Samuel, chap. i":

> Ver. 26. And she said, O my Lord, as thy soul liveth, my Lord, I am the woman that stood by thee here, praying unto the Lord.
>
> Ver. 27. For this child I prayed: and the Lord hath given me my petition which I asked of him.
>
> Ver. 28. Therefore I also lend him to the Lord, as long as he liveth, he shall be lent to the Lord.

West's Gallery 1822–28 (18); Philadelphia 1936; Philadelphia 1938 (51)

ENGR: Engraving ($12\frac{7}{16} \times 17\frac{7}{16}$ in.) by S. Bennett, pub. by S. Bennett (undated)

LISTED: *PC*, p. 567 ("Samuel when a Boy presented to Eli," West, Gallery); *UM*, p. 531; Barlow, p. 435; *BA*, p. 18; Galt, p. 230; Dillenberger, pp. 176 (378) and 213

No. 272, which is signed and dated *1800*, shows the same subject as the previous entry. In 1800 West also painted a second treatment (No. 315) of the companion subject of No. 271, *Christ among the Doctors* (No. 314). The two later pictures are both smaller than Nos. 271 and 314, and they are both new compositions rather than repetitions of the earlier works. Nevertheless, apart from similar twisted columns in the backgrounds, Nos. 272 and 315 do not have much in common with one another; they are not the same size, and they do not seem to have been thought of as companion pieces.

A slight drawing is at Swarthmore.[1]

The early catalogues also list a "Naming of Samuel" in West's possession, but with the subtitle "and the prophesy of Zacharias,"[2] which suggests that this title is probably a mistake for the small version of the *Naming of John* (No. 295).

[1] Black chalk, $5\frac{3}{4} \times 7\frac{1}{4}$ in.
[2] *PC*, p. 366; *UM*, p. 531; Barlow, p. 435; *BA*, p. 18; Galt, p. 230; Dillenberger, p. 176 (373).

273 The Messenger Announcing to Samuel the Loss of the Battle

LOCATION UNKNOWN

LISTED: *PC*, p. 569 ("The Sketch, in oil, on paper, of the Messenger announcing to Samuel the Loss of the Battle," West, Gallery); *UM*, p. 532; *BA*, p. 19; Galt, p. 234; Dillenberger, p. 186 (481)

Nothing is known about this work apart from its appearance on the early lists, and no such incident occurs in the Bible. Helmut von Erffa has suggested that the title under which the sketch was listed may have been an error and that it could have been an illustration of I Samuel, 4:12–18, in which a messenger tells Eli of the loss of a battle against the Philistines. That subject is possibly represented in a rather slight and sketchy drawing at Swarthmore (*right*) showing a soldier wearing a helmet and leading a horse approaching a bearded elderly man who is accompanied by three other less well-defined figures.[1] On the other hand, the title might also be a mistake for "Saul and the Witch of Endor" (cf. No. 275), in which Samuel himself is the messenger who announces to Saul the forthcoming loss of a battle.

[1] Black chalk, $6\frac{1}{4} \times 9\frac{1}{8}$ in.

The Messenger Announcing to Samuel the Loss of the Battle, (?) drawing by West for No. 273. Swarthmore College, Pennsylvania

274 Historical Landscape: Saul before Samuel and the Prophets 1812

See color illustrations, pp. 124, 125

HENRY E. HUNTINGTON LIBRARY AND ART GALLERY, SAN MARINO, CALIFORNIA, GIFT OF THE VIRGINIA STEELE SCOTT FOUNDATION

Oil on canvas: 64×101 in. (162.5 × 257 cm.)

Signed left: *B. West/1812*

PROV: Offered by West's sons to the United States in 1826 (6), and sold by them, Robins, London, 22–25 May 1829, lot 96 ("Saul Prophecying," 5 ft. 7 in. × 8 ft. 7 in.), bt. by Shaddon for £63; Torre Abbey sale, Christie's, London, 26 Feb. 1859, lot 73, bt. by Burgley (? or Bayley) for £23.2.0.; T. J. Blakeslee sale, American Art Assoc., New York, 21 April 1915, lot 162 (as "Conversion of St. Paul"); Vose Galleries, Boston; St. Paul's Church, Richmond, Va., 1943–73; Kennedy Galleries, New York, from whom acquired by the Virginia Steele Scott Foundation

EXH: RA 1812 (162) "Historical landscape: Saul before Samuel and the Prophets":

And Saul went thither to Naioth in Ramah, and the spirit of God was upon him also; and he went on and prophesied, until he came to Naioth in Ramah.

And he stripped off his clothes also, and prophesied before Samuel in like manner, and lay down naked all that day and all that night. Wherefore they say, Is Saul also amongst the prophets? *Samuel, Book I, Chap. xix. Ver. 23, 24*

BI 1813 (150) same title, but with quotation of verse 24 only, 7 ft. 3 in. × 10 ft. 2 in. (including frame); 125 Pall Mall, 1816 and 1818 (2) "Saul Prophecying, Samuel, I, chap. x, vers. 8, 9, 10, 11"; West's Gallery 1821 (23), 1822–28 (34) "Saul Prophesying, I Samuel, chap. 10":

Verse 9. And it was so, that when he had turned his back to go from Samuel, God gave him another heart: and all those signs came to pass that day.

Verse 10. And when they came thither to the hill, behold, a company of prophets met him, and the spirit of God came upon him, and he prophesied among them.

Brooklyn 1922 (29) as "The Conversion of St. Paul," lent by Vose and Company, Boston

LISTED: Dillenberger, p. 214

LIT: Farington Diary, 31 Jan. 1812 (Farington 1978—, XI, p. 4072); V and A Cuttings, III, p. 854 (1812); Courtauld Cuttings, II, pp. 5 (1812) and 59 (1813); Evans 1959, pp. 88 and 95, pl. 63 (as "The Conversion of St. Paul"); Constable 1962–68, II, p. 66 (letter, 6 May 1812); Rothenberg 1967, p. 280, note 150; Dillenberger 1977, p. 122, pl. 83

Although quotations or citations from the Bible describing separate incidents when Saul prophesied accompanied No. 274 in different exhibitions during West's lifetime, the description of Saul stripping off his clothes and laying down naked occurs only in the passage from chapter 19 of I Samuel quoted in 1812 and 1813.

On 31 January 1812, Farington described No. 274 as "a large Historical Landscape lately begun," and it is noteworthy that at both the Royal Academy and the British Institution West headed his title with the words "Historical Landscape". The Robins sale catalogue of 1829 implies that West was emulating Poussin in this painting, but West's concern with historical landscape was probably more immediately inspired by the pictures Turner had been exhibiting at the Royal Academy since 1800. No. 274, which first appeared in the same Royal Academy exhibition as Turner's *Snowstorm: Hannibal and His Army Crossing the Alps* (Tate Gallery), was generally well received, and was described by one reviewer as the only historical picture in the exhibition "which lays claim to any great degree of praise."[1] John Constable praised No. 274 to his fiancée as "truly an heroic landscape," whereas he found Turner's *Hannibal* "scarcely intelligible."

Jacob Rothenberg has noted a resemblance between Saul in No. 274 and the so-called Theseus of the Elgin Marbles, which West had copied in 1808 (see Nos. 498 and 501).

A drawing for the landscape background was formerly in the collection of H. H. Margary.[2] See also p. 125 above.

[1] Courtauld Cuttings, from an unidentified source.
[2] Pen and ink, $5\frac{1}{2} \times 9$ in., sold, Sotheby's, London, 25 Oct. 1961, lot 21.

275 Saul and the Witch of Endor 1777

See color illustration, p. 83

WADSWORTH ATHENEUM, HARTFORD, CONNECTICUT

Oil on canvas: $20\frac{1}{2} \times 27$ in. (52 × 68.5 cm.)

Signed bottom right: *B. West 1777*

PROV: Daniel Daulby, Liverpool (purchased 1779);[1] Renaissance Galleries, Philadelphia, by 1935; Mrs. Frederic S. Gould, Santa Barbara, California, by whom given to the Wadsworth Atheneum in 1948

EXH: Philadelphia 1936; Philadelphia 1938 (31) lent by Renaissance Galleries; *Romantic Painting in America*, Museum of Modern Art, New York, 1943 (206) lent by Mrs. Gould; *From Colony to Nation*, Art Institute of Chicago, 1949 (129); Allentown (1962) (11); *Art of the United States 1670–1966*, Whitney Museum, New York, 1966 (290); *La Peinture romantique anglaise et les préraphaélites*, Petit Palais, Paris, 1972 (324)

ENGR: Engraving ($16\frac{7}{8} \times 23\frac{1}{4}$ in.) by William Sharp, pub. by J. & J. Boydell,[2] *From an Original Picture in the Collection of Daniel Daulby, Esqr of Liverpool*, and dedicated to Daulby by Thos. Macklin [*sic*], as "The Witch of En-Dor," accompanied by the following lines:

And he said unto her, what form is he of? And she said, an old man cometh up, and he is covered with a mantle.

And Saul perceived that it was Samuel, and he stooped with his face to the ground, and bowed himself.

Vide the 1ˢᵗ Book of Samuel. 28ᵗʰ Chapter & 14ᵗʰ Verse

engraving (12 × 10 in.) by F. Shipster, pub. 4 July 1797 by Thos. Macklin, and included in vol. II of Macklin's *Bible*, 1800; steel engraving by Winkles, Karlsruhe

LISTED: *UM*, p. 529 ("The Ghost of Samuel appearing to Saul, at Liverpool"); Dillenberger, p. 211

LIT: Evans 1959, p. 68; Irwin 1966, pp. 51 and 138, pl. 44; Rosenblum 1967, pl. 12, n. 28; Kraemer 1975, pl. 54; David Bindman, *Blake as an Artist*, Oxford and New York, 1977, p. 30, and pl. 18; Dillenberger 1977, pp. 30, pl. 21; Pressly 1983, p. 13 and fig. 1

Saul's visit to the Witch of Endor and the appearance of the ghost of Samuel, who predicts Saul's forthcoming defeat and death, are described in I Samuel 28:3–20. The incident is the subject of a painting by Salvator Rosa now in the Louvre (ill. p. 83), which, via the engraving by A. Laurentius, undoubtedly provided West's main inspiration.[3] The subject was also treated by John Hamilton Mortimer[4] and Henry Fuseli, at approximately the same time as West, and by William Blake in 1783.[5]

West did not exhibit No. 275, which was therefore overlooked by the compilers of all but one of the early lists of his work, but it was engraved three times. A copy, which appears to be after the engraving by William Sharp, is in the Victoria and Albert Museum.[6] Another copy bearing a mistaken attribution to Fuseli was at one time in the Oscar Rheinhart Collection in Winterthur, Switzerland.[7] A picture of *Saul and the Witch of Endor* painted by Charles Robert Leslie soon after his arrival in England, which Leslie painted under West's direction and sold with West's help in 1814 to Sir John Fleming Leicester, appears to have been an independent composition, rather than a copy.[8]

A drawing of the subject was sold by Benjamin West, Jr. in 1839,[9] and a drawing of the prostrate Saul was sold by Mrs. F. Howard in 1979.[10] A drawing in the Morgan Library showing a distinctly different treatment of the subject and on paper watermarked 1812,[11] may be related to Leslie's painting and is possibly by Leslie rather than West.

See also pp. 77–84 above.

[1] A copy of a letter dated 15 Oct. 1779 from West to Daulby about the possible sale of the picture for 30 guineas is in the files of the Wadsworth Atheneum (partly quoted in Pressly 1983, pp. 15 and 24, n. 4).
[2] The proof in the British Museum is undated, but according to W. S. Baker, *William Sharp Engraver, with a descriptive catalogue of his works*, Philadelphia, 1875, p. 42, the second state is dated 1788.
[3] See Luigi Salerno, *Salvator Rosa*, Milan, 1963, p. 113 and pl. XXIV.
[4] See John Sunderland, "John Hamilton Mortimer and Salvator Rosa," *Burlington Magazine*, CXII, 1970, pp. 524–25, no. 32. Another painting by Mortimer of similar imagery inspired by the Rosa *Saul and the Witch of Endor* and quite possibly an influence on West was *Sextus Pompeius Consulting Erictho before the Battle of Pharsalia*, exhibited in 1771 and engraved by Robert Dunkarton in 1776.
[5] Drawings by Fuseli are in the Victoria and Albert Museum (dated 1777) and the Kunsthaus, Zurich. A watercolor by Blake is in the New York Public Library.
[6] Oil on canvas, 16¼ × 23¼ in.
[7] Letter from Bruno Bischofberger, Zurich, to Helmut von Erffa, 11 Nov. 1968. Yet another copy was sold Christie's, London, 1 October 1976, lot 147 (35½ × 48 in.).
[8] Exhibited RA 1814 (206). See Leslie 1860, I, p. 40, II, p. 319; and Hall 1962, pp. 100–101 and 116.
[9] S. Leigh Sotheby, London, 1 June 1839, lot 75 (black and white chalk on blue paper).
[10] Black and white chalk on blue paper, 9¾ × 11¾ in., sold Sotheby's, London, 22 March 1979, lot 5.
[11] Kraemer 1975, pp. 53–54 (94) and pl. 62, pen and ink and wash, 7⅞ × 12½ in.

Nathan and David, mezzotint by Valentine Green after No. 276

276 Nathan and David *c.* 1775

LOCATION UNKNOWN

(84 × 108 in.) (213.5 × 274 cm.)

PROV: Offered by West to the Pennsylvania Academy in 1809 ("The picture, life[-sized], of Nathan and David," 8 ft. × 7 ft., £200); offered by his sons to the United States in 1826 (4) and sold by them, Robins, London, 22–25 May 1829, lot 137 ("Nathan and David," 7 ft. × 9, "II Samuel, chap. xii. verse 7. And Nathan said unto David, Thou art the man"); bt. by G. Wigg for £33.12.0.

EXH: RA 1775 (336) "Nathan and David. 'Thou art the man.'"; West's Gallery 1821 (90), 1822–28 (135)

ENGR: Mezzotint (21 × 26 in.) by Valentine Green, pub. by V. Green & Son, 10 August 1784; engraving (3¼ × 4 in.) by S. Sangster, pub. 1831

LISTED: *PC*, p. 565 ("Nathan and David—'Thou art the Man'—as large as Life," West, Painting-room); *UM*, p. 530; Barlow, p. 434; *BA*, p. 16; Galt, p. 226; Dillenberger, p. 167 (289)

LIT: V and A Cuttings, I, p. 117 (*Public Advertiser*, May 1775)

The subject of No. 276 is taken from the twelfth chapter of the second Book of Samuel. The prophet Nathan tells David the story of a rich man who feeds a traveller by taking a poor man's only lamb rather than one of his own. When David expresses his outrage at the rich man's cruelty and greed, Nathan reveals ("Thou art the man") that the tale really refers to David himself, who had taken Uriah's wife, Bathsheba, when he already had many wives of his own, and had then sent Uriah off to die in battle.

Although there was a nine-year time lag between the exhibition of No. 276 at the Royal Academy and the publication of the mezzotint by Valentine Green

(*above*), the print bears the words "Painted by B. West . . ." and, hence, presumably reproduces No. 276, which is the only recorded painting of the subject by West.

A drawing of "Nathan and David" also appears on the lists of West's work.[1] A drawing dated 1783 went through the market in 1944,[2] and a drawing dated 1784 was in the possession of P. & D. Colnaghi in 1979. The dates on both of these drawings are well after 1775 when No. 276 was exhibited, and it is possible that they were made in connection with the Green print; there are, however, a number of differences between the Colnaghi drawing and the print (most conspicuously Nathan wears a hood in the former and is bare-headed in the latter), and exactly what purpose they served is not entirely evident.

A drawing identified as "King David Rising after the Death of His Child," a subject from the same chapter of II Samuel as No. 276, was sold by Benjamin West, Jr. in 1839.[3]

[1] *PC*, p. 568 (West, Gallery); *UM*, p. 532; *BA*, p. 19; Galt, p. 234; Dillenberger, p. 185 (472).
[2] Christie's, London, 4 Aug. 1944, lot 85, pen and ink and wash, 11¼ × 15½ in.
[3] S. Leigh Sotheby, 1 June 1839, lot 115, pen and ink, washed with sepia.

277 The Plague Stayed by the Repentance of David 1798

AMHERST COLLEGE, AMHERST, MASSACHUSETTS

Oil on paper mounted on panel: 31 × 22 in. (78.5 × 56 cm.)

Signed lower left: *B. West/1798*

PROV: Sold by West's sons, Robins, London, 20–22 June 1829, lot 53 ("The Angel sheathing the Flaming Sword, . . . I Book Chron. chap. 21"); Frank G. Logan, Chicago; his sale, Kende Galleries, New

York, 1–3 Feb. 1945, lot 172 (as "Elias convincing the False Prophets of Baal"), bt. by Renaissance Galleries, Philadelphia; Victor Spark, New York, from whom acquired by Amherst College in 1950

EXH: RA 1800 (335) "A drawing in oil colours—King David prostrate at the altar he built at the threshing place of Arunah";

And when the Angel stretched out his hand upon Jerusalem to destroy it, the Lord repented him of the evil, and said to the Angel that destroyed the people (by three days pestilence), stay now thy hand. And the Angel of the Lord was by the threshing place of Arunah the Jesubite.

2d Samuel, chap. xxiv. ver. 16

277

Amherst 1950 (as "Elijah Convincing the False Prophets of Baal")

ENGR: Stipple engraving ($25\frac{1}{4} \times 18\frac{1}{16}$ in.) by Thomas Cheesman, pub. by Jˢ Minasi, 1 March 1813, as "The Plague Stayed by the Repentance of David":

And David built there an altar unto the Lord, and offered burnt offerings and peace offerings, and called upon the Lord, and he answered him from Heaven by fire upon the altar of burnt offerings. And the Lord commanded the Angel, and he put up his sword again unto the sheaf thereof.

1ˢᵗ Book of Chron. Chap. 21, v. 26 & 27

LISTED: *PC*, p. 568 ("The Sketch, in oil, on paper, of David prostrate, whilst the destroying Angel sheathes the Sword," West, Gallery); *UM*, p. 531; *BA*, p. 19; Galt, p. 233; Dillenberger, pp. 183 (448) and 213

LIT: Morgan and Toole 1950, pp. 212–13 and ill. opp. p. 212 (as "Elijah Convincing the False Prophets of Baal"); Evans 1959, pl. 62 (as "Elijah" . . .); Helmut von Erffa, *Art Journal*, xx, 1960–61, pp. 124 and 195

Although West exhibited No. 277 with a quotation from the second book of Samuel, the subject is more precisely described in the quotation from I Chronicles printed with the Cheesman engraving. Both passages, which are quoted above, describe the same event.

The angel in No. 277 is based on the angel in the *Destruction of the Assyrian Camp by the Destroying Angel* (No. 282), which West had exhibited in 1791. The latter is a drawing; No. 277 is a sketch and was identified as such when exhibited in 1798. West may have undertaken them as sketches of possible subjects to be part of the series of biblical subjects he was painting for George III for Windsor Castle, but neither subject appears on any of the lists of works intended for the Windsor chapel. No. 277 is also close in date, approximately the same size, in the same medium, and similar in its visionary violence to two of the sketches of Apocalyptic subjects for Fonthill Abbey which West exhibited in 1798 (Nos. 404 and 409), but whereas those sketches became the property of William Beckford, No. 277 remained in West's possession, and no documentation is known that connects it with Beckford's commissions.

278 Elijah Raising the Widow's Son 1774–1819

PHILADELPHIA MUSEUM OF ART

Oil on canvas: $63\frac{5}{8} \times 81\frac{3}{4}$ in.) (161.5 × 207.5 cm.)

Signed right: *Benj West 1774/Retouched 1819*

PROV: Offered by West to the Pennsylvania Academy in 1809 ("The picture, life[-sized], of Elijah raising the Widow's son," 7 ft. × 5 ft., £150); offered by his sons to the United States in 1826 (5, as "Raising the Shunamite's Son," 6 ft. × 6 ft. 6 in.), and sold by them, Robins, London, 22–25 May 1829, lot 167 (as "Raising the Shunamite's Son," 6 ft. × 6 ft. 6 in.), bt. by Erskine for £33.12.0.; Bloomfield Moore; given by Mrs. Moore to the Philadelphia (then Pennsylvania) Museum in 1899

EXH: RA 1775 (334) "The Prophet Elijah restoring to life the widow's son"; (?) BI 1820 (111) "Elijah raising the Widow's Son," 4 ft. 9 in. × 5 ft. 9 in. (including frame); West's Gallery 1821 (27), 1822–28 (129); Philadelphia 1938 (25) as "The Schunamite's Son Restored to Life by Elisha"

ENGR: Steel engraving ($4\frac{9}{16} \times 6\frac{1}{4}$ in.) by W. Holl, pub. by Fisher, Son & Co., London

LISTED: *PC*, p. 565 ("Elijah raising the Widow's Son to Life," West, Painting-room); *UM*, p. 530; Barlow, p. 434; *BA*, p. 16; Galt, p. 226; Dillenberger, pp. 167 (290) and 211

LIT: V and A Cuttings, I, p. 117 (1775); Courtauld Cuttings, II, p. 148 (1820); Dillenberger 1977, pp. 24, 26–27, and pl. 13

No. 278, which illustrates I Kings 17:17–24, and Nos. 279–81, which show the similar subject of "Elisha Raising the Shunamite's son," from II Kings 4:18–37, have been consistently confused. Because of the conjunction of dates there can be little doubt that No. 278 was the "Prophet Elijah restoring to life the widow's son" exhibited by West in 1775, and it seems to have been the picture of similar title and dimensions offered

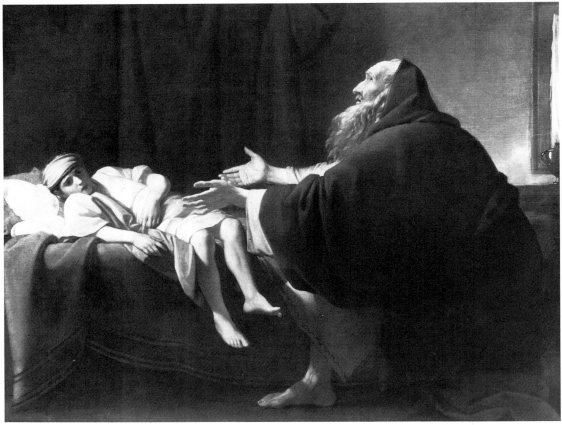

278

by West to the Pennsylvania Academy in 1809–10. In 1820, pictures of both *Elijah* and *Elisha* appeared at the British Institution where they were described by a contemporary reviewer as having been painted by West "at an early period of his profession," and the conjunction of that date with West's retouching of No. 278 in 1819 suggests that one of these pictures was probably No. 278 again, although listed with incorrect measurements. The measurements recorded for the "Raising of the Shunamite's Son" offered by West's sons to the United States in 1826, and sold by them in 1829 are also slightly at odds with the present dimensions of No. 278 but, since no other comparably large versions of either the *Elijah* or *Elisha* subjects are otherwise recorded, that picture must have been No. 278 as well.

A drawing for the figure of Elijah is at Swarthmore. The model seems to have posed for several works painted by West between 1771 and 1774 (Nos. 159, 292, 312, 321, etc.).

¹Black and white chalk on brown paper, 10⅜ × 9⅜ in.

279 Elisha Raising the Shunamite's Son (?)1766

J. B. SPEED ART MUSEUM, LOUISVILLE, KENTUCKY

Oil on canvas: 40 × 50 in. (101.5 × 127 cm.)

Signed bottom left: *B. West* [?] 1766

PROV: Richard, first Earl Grosvenor; by family descent to the second Duke of Westminster (died 1953); sold by his estate, Sotheby's, London, 15 July 1959, lot 127 (as "Elijah Raising the Widow's Son"), bt. by Nicholson; John Nicholson Gallery, New York; purchased by the J. B. Speed Museum in 1964

(?) EXH: SA 1767 (175) "Elisha restores to life the Shunamite's Son"; SA 1768 (special exhibition in honor of the King of Denmark) (121)

ENGR: Mezzotint (15¹¹⁄₁₆ × 20½ in.) by Valentine Green,

pub. 1 Jan. 1778 by John Boydell;¹ line engraving by Isaac Taylor, pub. 1809, by R. Philips; outline engraving (6³⁄₁₆ × 8⅛ in.) by H. Moses, pub. 1 Nov. 1814, by the Society for Promoting Christian Knowledge; engraving by J. B. Longacre; steel engraving (4½ × 6⁹⁄₁₆ in.) by W. Radclyffe, pub. by Fisher, Son and Co., London.²

LISTED: *PC*, p. 561 ("The Shunamite's Son Raised to Life by the Prophet Elisha," in the possession of the Earl of Grosvenor); *UM*, p. 528; Barlow, p. 432; *BA*, p. 14; Galt, p. 220; Dillenberger, pp. 151 (138) and 211

LIT: V and A Cuttings, I, p. 75 (*Public Advertiser*, May 1767); Graves 1907, VIII, p. 275 (Horace Walpole, 1767); Buckler 1926, p. 4; Gatty 1938–39, p. 81 (Walpole 1767); Addison Franklin Page, "A Biblical Story: Benjamin West," *J. B. Speed Art Museum Bulletin*, XXIV, June 1964, pp. 5–7; Rosenblum 1967, pp. 53–54, fig. 49; von Erffa 1973, p. 12; Dillenberger 1977, pp. 24, 26–27 and pl. 15

The story of Elisha raising the Shunamite's son comes from the second book of Kings 4:18–37. For the similar subject of Elijah and the widow's son, from the first Book of Kings, see the preceding entry (No. 278).

The early lists of West's works indicate that he painted three versions of *Elisha Raising the Shunamite's Son* (Nos. 279–81), and, of these, No. 279 seems most likely to have been the painting of the subject which West exhibited at the Society of Artists in 1767. Some copies of that year's catalogue included indication of an anonymous owner, "the Reverend Mr. . . . (Enquire of Mr. Newton, Mortimer Street)," so it appears that Lord Grosvenor, whose son owned No. 279 in 1804, was not the painting's first owner. "Mr. Newton, Mortimer Street" was not Thomas Newton, Bishop of Bristol, who did own a version of the subject (No. 281), but the painter Francis Milner Newton (1720–1794), who was Secretary of the Society of Artists.

Jacob Blesseth Joseph's Two Sons (No. 250), which is

the same size and which appeared at the Society of Artists in 1768, is a companion to No. 279. Valentine Green exhibited engravings after the two subjects in 1768, although he did not publish them until 1778. The British Museum proof of the Green print after No. 279 is unlettered; that of No. 250 is identified as after the picture belonging to Lord Grosvenor, and it would seem likely that Lord Grosvenor acquired the two paintings as a pair. They hung together in the Drawing-Room at Eaton Hall in 1826 (when Elisha was already wrongly identified as Elijah; cf. No. 278 above), and remained together in the Westminster collection until 1961.

The date on No. 279 is now barely legible,³ but in a photograph made at the time of the Westminster sale in 1959 is appears to be *1766*, which is consistent with its appearance at the Society of Artists in the following year.

Benjamin West, Jr. sold a drawing of the subject in 1839, identifying it as "a study for the picture."⁴ Additionally No. 281, which in 1804 was described as "a small sketch" of the subject, may have been a preparatory study for this painting, and if the dates in the inscription on No. 280 are reliable, West also probably began that version before No. 279 but completed it much later.

Charles Willson Peale painted a copy in watercolor after No. 279 in West's studio in 1767 (estate of the late Charles Coleman Sellers). A copy by John Trumbull is in the Wadsworth Atheneum in Hartford, Connecticut,⁵ and the kneeling mother in the lower left served as a model for a similar kneeling figure in Trumbull's *Brutus and His Friends at the Death of Lucretia* (Yale University Art Gallery, New Haven).⁶ Trumbull painted both works in America in 1777, basing them on the Green mezzotint after No. 279. In 1829 West's sons also sold a work identified as a copy of the subject after West.⁷

The different publications of Horace Walpole's marginal comments in his catalogues of the exhibition of the Society of Artists for 1767 record different opinions of No. 279. The painting was listed last in the catalogue of the five works West exhibited that year, and the remark quoted by Gatty was, "best of the five, but heavy." The notation quoted by Graves was "Not so fine," in contrast to the previous two entries (Nos. 8 and 163), both of which (as recorded by Graves), Walpole deemed "very fine."

¹Although the proof in the British Museum bears the publication date of 1778, Green exhibited a proof of the print at the Society of Artists in 1768 (245) as a companion to a proof after No. 250 (246).
²We have not been able to ascertain whether the later prints are after No. 279 or one of the two other versions of the picture.
³Letter from Addison Franklin Page to Helmut von Erffa, 21 May 1964.
⁴S. Leigh Sotheby, 1 June 1839, lot 102 (black chalk).
⁵Jaffe 1975, p. 326 and fig. 23.
⁶Ibid., p. 315 and fig. 21.
⁷Robins, London, 20–22 June 1829, lot 61, under paintings.

280 Elisha Raising the Shunamite's Son (?)1765–1814

GEORGE WALTER VINCENT SMITH ART MUSEUM, SPRINGFIELD, MASSACHUSETTS

Oil on canvas: 40 × 54 in. (101.5 × 137 cm.)

Signed lower left: *Begun 1765/and finished, 1814 Oct. 10th/B. West*

PROV: (?) Offered by West's sons to the United States in 1826 (28 "Elijah Raising the Widow's Son," 3 ft. 5 in. × 4 ft. 6 in.); and sold by them, Robins,

279

281 Elisha Raising the Shunamite's Son
c. 1765–66

LOCATION UNKNOWN

PROV: Painted for Dr. Newton, Bishop of Bristol; the Revd. Hand

LISTED: *PC*, p. 563 ("A small sketch of the Shunamite's Son restored, &c."—Rev.—Hard); *UM*, p. 529; *BA*, p. 15 (. . . Rev.—Hand, painted for Dr. Newton, Bishop of Bristol); Galt, p. 223; Dillenberger, p. 160 (219)

See No. 279. All we know about this version of the subject comes from the early lists of West's works. As a "small sketch," painted for Dr. Newton, No. 281 was probably painted in the 1760s and utilized as a study for No. 279. Dr. Newton was an important early patron for whom West painted at least two other pictures in the 1760s, including the *Fright of Astyanax* (No. 163) that appeared at the Society of Artists in 1767 at the same time as No. 279 (see also No. 675). The Revd. "Hard," or "Hand," as corrected in *La Belle Assemblée*, was Newton's stepson (the son of his second wife by her previous marriage), who is mentioned in Newton's autobiography as taking as much delight in Newton's pictures as Newton himself did.[1]

[1] *The Lives of Dr. Edward Pocock, The Celebrated Orientalist, by Dr. Twells; of Dr. Zachary Pearce, Bishop of Rochester . . . and of Dr. Thomas Newton, Bishop of Bristol, by Themselves; and of the Rev. Philip Skelton, by Mr. Burdy*, London, 1816, p. 190.

London, 22–25 May 1829, lot 58 ("Elisha Raising the Widow's Son," 4 ft. 5 in. × 3 ft. 6 in.) bt. by Capt. Murray, for £53.11.0; Art Collector's Association, London, from whom purchased in 1922 by George Walter Vincent Smith (1832–1923)

EXH: BI 1820 (223) "The Shunamite's Son restored to life by the Prophet Elisha," 4 ft. 8 in. × 5 ft. 8 in. (including frame); West's Gallery 1821 (56), 1822–28 (103)

LISTED: *PC*, p. 564 ("The Prophet Elisha raising the Shunamite's Son," West's house at Windsor); *UM*, p. 529; Barlow, p. 433; *BA*, p. 16; Galt, p. 225; Dillenberger, pp. 165 (266) and 214

LIT: Courtauld Cuttings, II, p. 148; *George Walter Vincent Smith Art Gallery Bulletin*, IV, Feb. 1938 (ill.)

No. 280, which must have been in West's possession in 1814 in order for him to finish and inscribe it on 10 October (his birthday) of that year, can accordingly be identified as the version of the subject listed in the early catalogues of his works as in his house at Windsor (which he gave up in 1809) and as the version that he exhibited at the British Institution in the year of his death. Approximate correspondence in measurements and lack of an alternative candidate also suggest that it was the "Elijah Raising the Widow's Son" offered by his sons to the United States in 1826, and the "Elisha Raising the Widow's Son" sold by them in May 1829.

There is an addition to the original canvas of approximately 3 in. or 4 in. along the right edge, showing more of the table and candelabra than are visible in No. 279. There are also traces of red drapery under the window on the left and projecting above the sill, which seem to be later additions, and much of the handling of paint throughout appears to date from 1814, when West "finished" the picture, rather than from 1765. It is also possible that West continued to work on No. 280 before exhibiting it. When exhibited in 1820, it was described as "comparatively feeble."

280

282

282 The Destruction of the Assyrians by the Destroying Angel c. 1791

ROYAL ACADEMY OF ARTS, LONDON

Wash, heightened with white on pink paper: 25 × 18 in. (63.5 × 45.5 cm.)

PROV: Sold by West's sons, Robins, London, 20–22 June 1829, lot 149 ("The Destroying Angel, a magnificent sketch . . . damaged")

EXH: RA 1791 (504) "The destruction of the Assyrians by the destroying Angel"; London 1963 (54)

LISTED: PC, p. 568 ("The large drawing of the Destruction of the Assyrian Camp by the destroying Angel," West, Gallery); UM, p. 532; BA, p. 19; Galt, p. 233; Dillenberger, pp. 184 (458) and 214

LIT: Dillenberger 1977, p. 109

The subject is from II Kings 19:35. West subsequently painted a similar angel, probably based on No. 282, in No. 277, which he exhibited in 1800.

Although this work was not described as a drawing in the catalogue of the Royal Academy exhibition of 1791, it hung in the Exhibition Room of Sculpture and Drawings. The exhibited work can hence be equated with the "large drawing" that appears on the early lists of West's works and with the "magnificent" but damaged sketch sold in 1829. The damage consists of a tear (now repaired, but readily discernible) across the angel's wing in the upper right corner.

John Dillenberger asserts that the drawing was done for Fonthill Abbey, but that is incorrect. Fonthill was not begun until 1796, and there is no documentary evidence to connect No. 282 with Beckford patronage.

A related drawing was in the collection of Professor and Mrs. Charles H. Morgan, Amherst, Massachusetts, in 1962.[1]

[1] Pen and wash on brown paper, 7¾ × 3⅞ in.; exhibited Allentown 1962 (20). This drawing is possibly the "Destroying Angel" sold by Mrs. Albert F. West, Christie's, London, 18–19 March 1898, lot 118.

283 The Call of the Prophet Isaiah c. 1784

BOB JONES UNIVERSITY, GREENVILLE, SOUTH CAROLINA

Oil on canvas: 150 × 61 in. (381 × 155 cm.)

PROV: Painted for George III (1797 account: "The Inspiration of the Prophet Isaiah," 1784, as a companion to No. 286 with a price of £525 for the pair; 1801 account, p. 211: for the Windsor Chapel, The Prophets, 18, "The Prophets Isaiah and Jeremiah," £525); never delivered and ownership returned to West's sons by George IV in 1828; sold by them, Robins, London, 22–25 May 1829, lot 87 ("The Prophet Isaiah," 12 ft. 6 in. × 5 ft.), bt. by Bone for £31.10.0. on behalf of Joseph Neeld, MP, Grittleton House, Wilts.; by descent in the Neeld family until sold by Miss C. K. M. Neeld, Christie's, London, 16 Nov. 1962, lot 99; purchased by Bob Jones University in 1963

EXH: RA 1784 (121) "The call of the Prophet Isaiah, for his Majesty's chapel in Windsor"; West's Gallery 1821 (80), 1822–28 (121)

ENGR: See No. 284

LISTED: PC, p. 561 ("The Call of Isaiah and Jeremiah," each 5 ft. × 14, George III, for his Majesty's Chapel, Windsor, Mosaical Dispensation); UM, p. 527; AA, p. 67; BA, p. 14; Galt, p. 218; Dillenberger, pp. 146 (86) and 212 (as "Isaiah's Lips Anointed with Fire")

LIT: von Erffa 1956; Jones 1963; Jones 1968, p. 65 (347) and ill. p. 188; Meyer 1975, pp. 252 and 264; Dillenberger 1977, pp. 54, 56, and 65; Evans 1980, p. 95, fig. 68; Pressly 1983, p. 46, fig. 22a

No. 283 forms a pair with the Call of the Prophet Jeremiah (No. 286); West painted them to form part of a triptych flanking No. 258, the large Moses Receiving the Laws. Neither appears on either the architectural drawings of c. 1780 for the chapel at Windsor or the Swarthmore diagrams of 1801, but they are on West's accounts for George III of 1797 and 1801, and on all the early lists of his works, except Barlow's, always as a pair. At the

283

Royal Academy in 1784 they hung on either side of No. 258. West's sons hung the three paintings together in similar fashion in the exhibitions of their father's works after his death, and in the sale catalogue of 1829 No. 286 was described as "Designed for one of the side compartments of the great picture of Moses receiving the laws." In one of the drawings for the chapel from *c.* 1780 (ill. p. 579), *Moses Receiving the Laws* (No. 258) is shown above a painting of the *Last Supper* (No. 344), but with empty niches on either side of it, so it would seem that the idea of painting the two flanking pictures was conceived by West after that drawing was made but before 1782, which is the date on a preparatory study for No. 283 (No. 284). An arrangement of the end wall incorporating Nos. 283 and 286 is shown in a rough drawing in one of his sketch books at Yale, facing a drawing for No. 258 (ill. p. 300). In his reorganized scheme of 1801 West abandoned the triptych, locating No. 258 in the middle of a series of Old Testament subjects on a side wall of the chapel and leaving out Nos. 283 and 286 entirely.

The subject of No. 283 is from Isaiah 6:5–7:

> Then said I, Woe is Me! for I am undone: because I *am* a man of unclean lips, and I dwell in the midst of a people of unclean lips: for mine eyes have seen the King, the Lord of hosts.
>
> Then flew one of the seraphims unto me, having a live coal in his hand, which he had taken with the tongs from the altar:
>
> And he laid it upon my mouth, and said, Lo, this hath touched thy lips; and thine iniquity is taken away, and thy sin purged.

Related oil sketches are Nos. 284 and 285 below. There are drawings in the sketchbook in the Yale Center for British Art mentioned above,[1] in the Addison Gallery of American Art, Phillips Academy, Andover,[2] and in the Witt Collection, Courtauld Institute of Art.[3] No. 284 shows essentially the same composition as No. 283, but No. 285 and all three drawings display considerable differences in the positions of both Isaiah and the angel.

[1] Black chalk, approx. 3 × 2 in.
[2] Pencil, $17\frac{3}{8} \times 8\frac{5}{8}$ in. (San Antonio 1983, no. 20, ill. in the catalogue, also ill. in von Erffa 1956, p. 2).
[3] Black and white chalk on blue paper, $12\frac{11}{16} \times 10\frac{5}{16}$ in.; sold by Benjamin West, Jr., S. Leigh Sotheby, London, 1 June 1839, lot 108 ("Studies for the Figure of the angel in the picture of the Prophet Isaiah." Black chalk, on blue paper, heightened with white); ill. von Erffa 1956, p. 3.

284 The Call of the Prophet Isaiah 1782

MUSÉE DES BEAUX-ARTS, BORDEAUX

Oil on canvas: $36\frac{5}{8} \times 14\frac{1}{8}$ in. (93 × 36 cm.)

Signed lower left: *B. West 1782*

PROV: Offered by West's sons to the United States in 1826 (141, included among "Original Designs in Chiaro Scuro for the large Pictures which were painted for his late Majesty's Chapel in Windsor Castle"), and sold by them, Robins, London, 22–25 May 1829, lot 126 ("The Prophet Isaiah," 1 ft. 2 in. × 3 ft.), purchaser not listed, but evidently the same as the purchaser of No. 287 since the two pictures have identical later histories; sold anonymously, Christie's, London, 8 July 1927, lot 96 (as a pair with No. 287), bt. by the Comtesse de la Béraudière; B. Chesnais, Paris, from whom purchased by the city of Bordeaux in 1967

EXH: West's Gallery 1822–28 (not numbered, exhibited with No. 287 on either side of 26 "The Nativity of our Saviour" (No. 298); Bregenz 1968

284

[1]The two etchings are reproduced in von Erffa 1956, p. 6. Proofs of both are in the Library of Congress.

285 The Call of the Prophet Isaiah

SPENCER MUSEUM OF ART, UNIVERSITY OF KANSAS, LAWRENCE, KANSAS

Oil on canvas: $33\frac{1}{2} \times 13\frac{3}{4}$ in. (85 × 35 cm.)

PROV: (?) The Earl of Huntingdon; Kleinberger and Co., New York; gift of Mr. and Mrs. Howard Hurwitz to the University of Kansas Museum in 1955

LISTED: Dillenberger, p. 212 (as "The Calling of Jeremiah")

LIT: von Erffa 1956; Meyer 1975, p. 264

This oil sketch, like No. 284, is in monochrome. Although it clearly shows the same subject, it differs considerably in composition from Nos. 283 and 284 and may represent an earlier stage in West's conception of the subject. The pose of the figure of Isaiah is essentially the same as that in a small sketch on the sheet in the Witt collection cited in the entry for No. 283.

285

(477) as "Jakob und der Engel"; *Peintures du dix-huitième siècle au Musée des Beaux-Arts de Bordeaux*, Galerie Cailleux, Paris, and Musée des Beaux-Arts, Bordeaux, 1969–70 (46); *La peinture britannique de Gainsborough à Bacon*, Galerie des Beaux-Arts, Bordeaux, 1977 (60)

ENGR: Uninscribed etching ($13\frac{1}{8} \times 6$ in.)

LISTED: Dillenberger, p. 212

LIT: Meyer 1975, pp. 252–53, 264, and fig. 9; Dillenberger 1977, p. 57, pl. 34

Nos. 284 and 287 are a pair of monochrome oil sketches for Nos. 283 and 286. The composition of No. 283 follows that of No. 284 closely, but there are a number of slight changes in detail, for example in Isaiah's right hand, in the relation of the angel's foot to Isaiah's draperies, and in the position of the draperies above the angel's head.

An etching of the subject corresponds in detail to No. 284 rather than to No. 283. Whether West himself made this etching and a companion etching after No. 287 has not been established.[1]

286 The Call of the Prophet Jeremiah *c.* 1784

See color illustration, p. 91

ST. MARTIN'S CHURCH, LAUGHARNE, DYFED, WALES

Oil on canvas: *c.* 150 × 57 in. (381 × 145 cm.)

PROV: Painted for George III (1797 account: "The Inspiration of the Prophet Isaiah," 1784, as a companion to No. 283 with a price of £525 for the pair; 1801 account, p. 211: for the Windsor Chapel, The Prophets, 18, "The prophets Isaiah and Jeremiah," £525); never delivered and ownership returned to West's sons by George IV in 1828; sold by them, Robins, London, 22–25 May 1829, lot 86 ("The Prophet Jeremiah," 12 ft. 6 in. × 5 ft., "Designed for one of the side compartments of the great picture of Moses receiving the laws"), bt. for £29.8.0. by Charles Morgan, Llanrhidian, Glamorganshire; Herbert Eccles, Laugharne; presented to the church by a Mr. Bolton, *c.* 1937

EXH: RA 1784 (121) "The call of the prophet Jeremiah, for his Majesty's chapel in Windsor Castle"; West's Gallery 1821 (77), 1822–28 (118)

ENGR: See No. 287

LISTED: *PC*, p. 561 ("The Call of Isaiah and Jeremiah," each 5 ft. × 14, George III, for his Majesty's Chapel, Windsor, Mosaical Dispensation); *UM*, p. 527; *AA*, p. 67; *BA*, p. 14; Galt, p. 218; Dillenberger, p. 146 (86)

LIT: von Erffa 1956; Meyer 1975, pp. 252 and 264; Dillenberger 1977, pp. 54, 56, and 65

No. 286 is one of the pair of pictures West painted to flank *Moses Receiving the Laws* (No. 258) on the end wall of George III's chapel in Windsor Castle. The other is the *Call of the Prophet Isaiah* (No. 283), together with which this painting was always exhibited and listed until the two paintings were bought by different purchasers in 1829. For a discussion of the place of the two in the schemes for the chapel see the entry for No. 283. The history of No. 286 after 1829 is obscure. When given to the parish church in Laugharne it was in a deteriorated state and was not known to be by West. It has since been properly identified and has recently undergone conservation.[1]

The subject is from chapter 1 of the Book of Jeremiah. The almond branch held by the angel is mentioned in verse 11.

An oil sketch is No. 287 below. A drawing for the angel and group of cherubs in the upper right corner is in the British Museum.[2]

The leg under the cherub furthest to the right, which has no visible connection to his body, evidently should be concealed by a cloud, which has become transparent over the years. In the oil sketch (No. 287), there are only two cherubs, rather than three as in this painting, and the partly concealed leg in No. 286 is a vestige of this earlier grouping. The drawing in the British Museum shows three cherubs in positions corresponding to those in No. 286 and with cloud completely filling the area of the vestigial leg. There are also *pentimenti* around the fingers of the prophet's left hand, and illegible traces of what seems to have been a signature are discernible above and to the left of his right foot.

[1]We are indebted to the Revd. J. Iorworth Thomas, the former vicar at Laugharne, for information about the history of No. 286 and for much additional assistance.
[2]Pen and sepia ink, 16 × $11\frac{1}{4}$ in. (1920–6–15–3).

287 The Call of the Prophet Jeremiah *c.* 1782

MUSÉE DES BEAUX-ARTS, BORDEAUX

Oil on canvas: $36\frac{5}{8} \times 14\frac{1}{8}$ in. (93 × 36 cm.)

PROV: Offered by West's sons to the United States in 1826 (142, included among "Original Designs in Chiaro Scuro for the large Pictures which were painted for his late Majesty's Chapel in Windsor Castle"), and sold by them, Robins, London, 22–25 May 1829, lot 124 ("The Prophet Jeremiah," 1 ft. 2 in. × 3 ft.), bt. by Renton for £13.13.0.; sold anonymously, Christie's, London, 8 July 1927, lot 96 (as a pair with No. 284), bt. by the Comtesse de la Béraudière; B. Chesnais, Paris, from whom purchased by the city of Bordeaux in 1967

EXH: West's Gallery 1822–28 (see No. 284); Bregenz 1968 (478) as "Szene aus dem Leben Aarons"; *Peintures du dix-huitième siècle au Musée des Beaux-Arts de Bordeaux*, Galerie Cailleux, Paris, and Musée des Beaux-Arts, Bordeaux, 1969–70 (47) as "Scène de la vie d'Aaron"; *La peinture britannique de Gainsborough à Bacon*, Galerie des Beaux-Arts, Bordeaux, 1977 (61)

ENGR: Uninscribed etching ($13\frac{13}{16} \times 6$ in.)

LISTED: Dillenberger, p. 214

LIT: Meyer 1975, pp. 252–53, 264, and fig. 10; Dillenberger 1977, p. 57, pl. 35

See No. 284, with which this work has always been a companion. No. 287 stands in the same relation to No. 286 as No. 284 to No. 283, and the etching, listed above, is after No. 287 rather than No. 286, corresponding to the companion etching after No. 284. The chief compositional differences between No. 286 and this painting are in the cherubs in the upper right corner, as discussed in the preceding entry.

288 Daniel Interpreting to Belshazzar the Writing on the Wall 1775

See color illustration, p. 84

BERKSHIRE MUSEUM, PITTSFIELD, MASSACHUSETTS

Oil on canvas: $50\frac{3}{4} \times 73\frac{1}{2}$ in. (129 × 186.5 cm.)

Signed bottom center, on scroll at Daniel's feet: *B. West 1775*

PROV: Offered by West to the Pennsylvania Academy in 1809 ("The picture of Daniel interpreting the hand writing," 6 ft. × 4 ft. 2 in., £150); offered by his sons to the United States in 1826 (16), and sold by them, Robins, London, 22–25 May 1829, lot 145 (4 ft. 2 in. × 6 ft.), bt. by Sir M. W. Ridley, Bt., for £136.10.0.; (?) General Bulwer, Heydon Hall, Norfolk; sold anonymously ("property of a nobleman"), Christie's, London, 27 Feb. 1909, lot 109, bt. by T. Permain for £23.2.0.; gift of Zenas Crane to the Berkshire Museum in 1909

EXH: RA 1776 (317) "Daniel interpreting to Belshazzar the writing on the wall"; BI 1820 (3) 5 ft. 2 in. × 7 ft. (including frame); West's Gallery 1821 (78), 1822–28 (119); BI 1833 (25) lent by Sir M. White Ridley, Bt., MP

ENGR: Mezzotint ($18\frac{3}{8} \times 26$ in.) by Valentine Green, pub. 19 May 1777 by John Boydell; stipple engraving ($10\frac{3}{8} \times 14\frac{3}{8}$ in.) by Geo. Graham, pub. 24 June 1793 by J. and J. Boydell; engraving by Tomlinson, pub. 1809 by Philips; outline engraving ($6\frac{7}{16} \times 8\frac{13}{16}$ in) by Henry Moses, pub. 1 March 1815 by the Society for Promoting Christian Knowledge; engraving ($4\frac{7}{8} \times 6\frac{15}{16}$ in.) by J. Taylor, pub. by Keymer & Co., Yarmouth

287

LISTED: *PC*, p. 565 ("Daniel interpreting the Handwriting on the Wall," West, Painting-room); *UM*, p. 530; Barlow, p. 434; *BA*, p. 16; Galt, p. 226; Dillenberger, p. 168 (243)

LIT: Courtauld Cuttings, II, p. 148 (1820); Landis 1926, p. 250; Dillenberger 1977, pp. 25, 30 (with a reproduction of the Green mezzotint, pl. 20); William H. Gerdts, "The Paintings of Washington Allston," in William H. Gerdts and Theodore E. Stebbins, Jr., "*A Man of Genius": The Art of Washington Allston*, Boston, 1979, pp. 106–8 and fig. 43

The subject is from the fifth chapter of the Book of Daniel.

There are a number of retouched areas on No. 288, which account for some slight discrepancies between it and the Green mezzotint. According to Gerald Hoepfner of the Williamstown Conservation Laboratory, who examined the painting in January 1980, the retouchings were probably done by West,[1] which seems entirely possible, since the painting remained in the artist's possession, and we know from Farington that West did retouch earlier paintings during the last years of his life. It should be noted that there are even greater discrepancies between No. 288 and the Moses engraving of 1815 (*below*), which shows additional figures and a Veronese-like colonnade in the background.

Dillenberger and Gerdts both state that No. 288 was re-exhibited as a result of the success of John Martin's *Belshazzar's Feast* at the British Institution in 1821. In fact, however, West's picture had been re-exhibited at the British Institution in the previous year, and its being shown again in West's gallery in Newman Street in 1821, along with ninety-three other works by West, can hardly be described as a response to Martin's success. West's precocity in treating the subject in 1775, and the relationship of paintings of the subject by West, Martin, and Washington Allston are discussed by Gerdts.

A drawing for the three standing figures on the left side of the painting is at Swarthmore.[2]

[1] Kindly communicated by Christine Bauer Podmaniczky in letters of 13, 18, and 27 January 1980.
[2] Black and white chalk, 18 × 12 in.

Daniel Interpreting to Belshazzar the Writing on the Wall, outline engraving by Henry Moses after No. 288

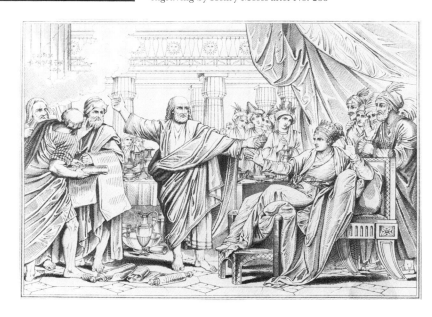

Daniel in the Lion's Den, stipple engraving by R. Hunt after No. 289

289 A Head, Representing Daniel in the Lion's Den *c.* 1799

LOCATION UNKNOWN

PROV: (?) Sold by West's sons, Robins, London, 20–22 June 1829, lot 98 ("Daniel in the Lion's Den, an early picture")

EXH: RA 1799 (571) "A head, representing Daniel in the lion's den"

ENGR: Stipple engraving ($8\frac{15}{16} \times 6\frac{3}{16}$ in) by R. Hunt

This subject does not appear on any of the early lists of West's paintings, and no painting of the subject is now known. It is possible that the work exhibited in 1799 and the "early picture" sold in 1829 were separate paintings. A *Daniel* about which nothing else is known also went through Christie's in 1802.[1]

A drawing dated *1798* was in the collection of the late Iolo A. Williams.[2]

[1]The United Cabinet of Sir Simon Clarke, Bart. and George Hibbert, Esq., Christie's, London, 14–15 May 1802, lot 18, B. West *Daniel*, "In the best manner of this intelligent artist," bt. by Coxe for £110.5.0.
[2]Pen and wash, $8\frac{7}{8} \times 7\frac{1}{4}$ in.

290 The Trial of Susannah *c.* 1756–59

LOCATION UNKNOWN (PROBABLY DESTROYED)

PROV: Painted for a Mr. Cox of Philadelphia

LIT: Galt 1816, pp. 72–74; Carey 1820, p. 515; Dunlap 1834, I, p. 44 (Dunlap 1918, I, p. 44); Mathew Pilkington, *A General Dictionary of Painters*, new ed., revised, etc., by Allan Cunningham, London, 1840, p. 646

In 1816 Galt wrote that it was not known what had become of this picture, but in 1834 Dunlap stated that he knew it. In 1840 Allan Cunningham indicated that it had been destroyed in a fire.

No. 290 was West's second historical picture, following the *Death of Socrates* (No. 4). Galt states that West's

patron, an otherwise unidentified Mr. Cox, commissioned a historical subject from West, allowing the young artist to choose the subject, and that West in reading the Bible to his mother some time before had been led to think that the trial of Susannah was a fine subject. In fact, the story of Susannah does not come from the Bible proper but from the Apocrypha. According to Galt, the canvas was about the size of a half-length portrait and contained more than forty figures; West drew the principal figures from living models and believed that in composition the picture was superior to the *Death of Socrates*. However, Dunlap, who claimed to have seen the picture, wrote that West apparently "made ample use of a print on the subject, which had fallen in his way."

291 Tobias Curing His Father's Blindness 1771

PRIVATE COLLECTION

Oil on panel: $10\frac{3}{4} \times 11$ in. (27.5 × 28 cm.)

Signed lower left: *B. West/1771*

PROV: Offered by West's sons to the United States in 1826 (85), and sold by them, Robins, London, 22–25 May 1829, lot 15 ("Tobit's Return," 11 × 12 in.), bt. by W. Ward on behalf of West's sons; by descent in the West family to Mrs. F. Howard, by whom sold, Sotheby's, London, 22 March 1979, lot 10, bt. by Thos. Agnew & Son on behalf of the present owner.

EXH: RA 1771 (216) "Tobias curing his father's blindness," as a companion to no. 215 "The prodigal son received by his father" (No. 320); West's Gallery 1821 (21) "Tobit," 1822–28 (55) "Tobit's Return"

LISTED: *PC*, p. 564 ("The small picture of the Return of Tobias," West, Painting-room); *UM*, p. 530; Barlow, p. 434; *BA*, p. 16; Galt, p. 225; Dillenberger, p. 167 (281)

The story of Tobias, the subject of Nos. 291, 292, and 293, is from the Apocryphal Book of Tobit. The figure on the left is the Archangel Raphael; the dog leaping up before him also figures in the story. The fish, with the gall of which Tobias cures the blindness of his father Tobit, is not visible in Nos. 291 or 292, but is in a later treatment of the subject, No. 293.

Although No. 291 is the smaller of the two earlier versions of the subject, which show the same composition, it was evidently the picture which West exhibited in 1771 as a companion to the small version of the *Return of the Prodigal Son* (No. 321). The background in the upper left corner of No. 291 appears unfinished, but, since the painting is signed and seems to have been exhibited in the year it was painted, the condition of this area may be due instead to a later uncompleted retouching by the artist, who retained No. 291 in his own possession until his death.

A drawing related to Nos. 291 and 292 is in a private collection in New York. Another drawing of the subject in the Victoria and Albert Museum, which shows a different composition from any of the three paintings, although traditionally ascribed to West does not appear to be in his hand. A pair of paintings, one a sketch for the other, which were exhibited as by West in 1968–69, are also not by him.[1]

[1]$50 \times 39\frac{3}{4}$ in. and 23×18 in., exhibited Bregenz 1968 (475 and 476 and ills. 163 and 164).

292 Tobias Curing His Father's Blindness 1772

ST. VINCENT HEALTH CENTER, ERIE, PENNSYLVANIA

Oil on canvas: 47 × 52 in. (119.5 × 132 cm.)

Signed lower left: *B. West pinxt./1772*

PROV: Baruch Feldman, Philadelphia; the Sisters of St. Joseph's, Erie, Pennsylvania

291

This virtually unknown painting is signed and dated a year later than No. 291. It seems likely that West sold this work before he had a chance to exhibit it and, since it is not recorded on the lists of his works, that its existence was forgotten.

No. 292 follows No. 291 closely in composition. There are differences in the backgrounds, in the placement of the left hand of Tobit's wife Anna, in several lesser details, and in the colors, which are generally more subdued. Tobias has red hair in No. 291 and dark hair in No. 292, and Raphael's garment, which is red in the former work, is brown in the latter.

The model for Tobit seems also to have posed for the father in No. 321 and for figures of old men in several other works painted by West at approximately the same time (Nos. 159, 160, 278, and 312). West's later Tobit in No. 293 of 1803 does not appear to have been painted from the same model, although, ironically, the model for that picture was said to have been "Old George" White, who was at the peak of his activity as a widely recognized model at precisely the time West painted No. 292.

293 Tobias Curing His Father's Blindness 1803

DELAWARE ART MUSEUM, WILMINGTON, DELAWARE

Oil on canvas: $45\frac{3}{4} \times 62\frac{1}{4}$ in. (116×158 cm.)

Signed lower left: *B. West/1803*

PROV: Offered by West to the Pennsylvania Academy in 1809 ("The picture, life[-sized], of Tobias bringing the Fish to his Father," 5 ft. × 4 ft. 2 in., £200); offered by his sons to the United States in 1826 (17, "Tobit and the Angel," 3 ft. 10 in. × 5 ft. 2 in.), and sold by them, Robins, London, 22–25 May 1829, lot 106 ("Tobit and the Angel," 3 ft. 10 in. × 5 ft. 2 in.), bt. by Holloway for £42; Newman F. McGirr, Philadelphia, 1920; Robert H. Richards, Wilmington; given by his widow to the Wilmington Society of Fine Arts in 1960

EXH: RA 1804 (91) "Tobias received by his blind father, whose sight was restored by the gall of a fish"; BI 1806 (North Room, 64) "The return of Tobias to his blind father," 5 ft. 2 in. × 6 ft. 6 in. (including frame); West's Gallery 1821 (81), 1822–28 (105) as "Tobit and the Angel"

ENGR: Mezzotint ($14\frac{7}{8} \times 20\frac{13}{16}$ in.) by Valentine Green, pub. by Green, 25 Sept. 1805

LISTED: *UM*, p. 531 ("Tobias returned to his blind father," West, Gallery); not listed by Barlow, but "Tobet and Tobias with the fish" is mentioned by him on p. 436 among the works painted since the list had been drawn up; Dillenberger, p. 213

LIT: Elizabeth H. Hawkes, *American Painting and Sculpture: Delaware Art Museum*, Wilmington, 1975, p. 16 (2), ill. pl. 17

This picture, which West painted over thirty years after Nos. 291 and 292, shows a slightly earlier moment in the story of Tobias and Tobit. Tobias carries the fish with the gall of which he will restore his blind father's sight, as shown in Nos. 291 and 292. The Archangel Raphael and the dog are again present, but Anna, Tobit's wife, is not.

According to the entry in the Robins sale catalogue of May 1829 for No. 293, Tobit (referred to as "The father of Tobit") was based on a study "supplied by Sir Joshua's famed old labourer," then in his hundredth year. This is a reference to "Old George" White, who posed frequently for Reynolds and other artists in the early 1770s. See also *The Captive, from Sterne* (No. 224), for which, according to the same source, White also served as model.

292

293

SUBJECTS FROM THE NEW TESTAMENT

294 The Naming of John the Baptist *c.* 1798

LOCATION UNKNOWN

(72 × 108 in.) (183 × 274 cm.)

PROV: Painted for George III (1801 account, p. 211:
for the Windsor Chapel, The Prophets, 20, "The prophesying of Zacharias at the birth of John his son,"
£525); never delivered and ownership returned to
West's sons by George IV in 1828; sold by them,
Robins, London, 22–25 May 1829, lot 148 ("The
Naming of John," 6 ft. × 9), bt. by Armstrong for
£36.15.0.

EXH: RA 1798 (87) "The prophecy of Zacharias at the
naming of John the Baptist, for His Majesty's Chapel
at Windsor"; West's Gallery 1821 (32), 1822–28 (15)
"The Naming of John"

LISTED: *PC*, p. 561 ("The naming of John; or the
Prophecies of Zacharias," George III, for his
Majesty's Chapel, Windsor, Gospel Dispensation,
6 ft. × 10); *UM*, p. 527; *AA*, p. 67 (9 ft. × 6); Barlow,
p. 432 ("John Baptist called and named," 9 ft. × 6);
BA, p. 14 (6 ft. × 12); Galt, p. 219; Dillenberger,
p. 146 (91)

LIT: Meyer 1975, p. 264; Dillenberger 1977, p. 71

This subject does not appear on the architectural drawings of *c.* 1780 for the Windsor chapel. In the Swarthmore diagrams of 1801 it is on the extreme left of the
bottom row of the side wall devoted to the New Testament (ill. p. 580). Of the five horizontal compositions
in this row, none of which appears on the drawings of
c. 1780, it is the only one to bear the notation
"finished"; the other four are all described only as
"designed," and none of them seems ever to have been
painted.[1]

A preparatory study is No. 295 below. Since that
work is lost as well, and no drawings for the composition
have been identified, No. 294 is the only painting for
the Windsor chapel which we know that West completed of which we do not have a reasonable idea of
the appearance.

[1]The other four subjects are the "Birth of our Saviour"; the
"Wise Men Offering"; "Christ in Egypt" (with "among
the doctors" scratched out); and "Christ among the Doc^{tr}."
The title "Christ in Egypt" appears only in this diagram.
For versions of the other subjects, see the entries for
Nos. 298, 309, and 314.

295 The Naming of John the Baptist *c.* 1795

LOCATION UNKNOWN

(15½ × 21 in.) (39.5 × 53.5 cm.)

PROV: Offered by West's sons to the United States in
1826 (62), and sold by them, Robins, London, 22–25
May 1829, lot 4 ("Naming of John," 15½ × 21 in.,
"The first study for the large Picture"), bt. by H. P.
Bone for £63

EXH: RA 1795 (77) "The naming of John the Baptist";
(?) RA 1817 (142) "The naming of John":

The Infant St. John, mezzotint by Valentine Green after No. 296

And it came to pass, that on the eighth day they
came to circumcise the child; and they called
him Zacharias, after the name of his father.

And his mother answered and said, Not so; but
he shall be called John.

St. Luke, chap. i, ver. 59, 60

LISTED: *PC*, p. 566 (as "The Naming of Samuel and
the prophesying of Zacharias," West, Gallery); *UM*,
p. 531; Barlow, p. 435; *BA*, p. 18; Galt, p. 230; Dillenberger, p. 176 (373). All the later lists repeat the
title as the "Naming of Samuel"

LIT: V and A Cuttings, III, p. 858 (May 1817)

The listing of a "Naming of Samuel" belonging to West
in the early catalogues of his works is clearly erroneous
and must refer to No. 295, which remained in West's
possession until his death. Although the picture was not
identified as a sketch for the chapel picture (No. 294)
when exhibited in 1795, the proximity of date, and the
identification in the Robins catalogue of May 1829
make clear that it was. See also the entry for No. 246,

the sketch for the *Birth of Jacob and Esau*, exhibited in
1796, which West probably re-exhibited together with
this picture in 1817. The two works were recorded as
being the same size, and they seem to have been
thought of as companions. They were lots 4 and 5 in
the Robins sale of 22–25 May 1829, and were there
bought by the same purchaser.

296 The Infant St. John *c.* 1781

LOCATION UNKNOWN

(17½ × 13 in.) (44.5 × 33 cm.)

PROV: Offered by West's sons to the United States in
1826 (99, "St. John," 1 ft. 5½ in. × 1 ft. 1 in.), and
sold by them, Robins, London, 22–25 May 1829, lot
22 ("The Infant St. John," 1 ft. 5½ in. × 1 ft. 1 in.),
bt. by Dunlop for £40.19.0.

EXH: West's Gallery 1821 (71), 1822–28 (85) "The
Infant St. John"

ENGR: Mezzotint ($9\frac{1}{8} \times 7\frac{1}{2}$ in.) by Valentine Green, pub. 21 Dec. 1781 by Green; mezzotint by J. Sartain, as "Innocence"; engraving by C. Muss; steel engraving by G. H. Phillips

LISTED: Dillenberger, p. 211 (the Green engraving)

LIT: Kraemer 1975, p. 7

It may be that West painted No. 296 for the sake of the mezzotint by Valentine Green (*opposite*). The painting was not exhibited during West's lifetime, nor does it appear on any of the early lists of his works, but the number of prints of it by different engravers indicates that the image must have had considerable popular appeal. There is a companion print by Green, published on the same day, after *Virtue and Innocence* (No. 425).

A drawing is in the Morgan Library.[1]

[1] Kraemer 1975, p. 7 (6), and pl. 3: graphite on brown paper, $15\frac{13}{16} \times 11\frac{3}{4}$ in., squared for transfer.

297 St. John the Baptist (?)c. 1786

LOCATION UNKNOWN

(96 × 60 in.) (244 × 152.5 cm.)

PROV: (?) Christ Church, Barbados; Thomas Macklin, London; his sale, Peter Coxe, Burrell, and Foster, London, 5 May 1800 and following days, lot 52; the European Museum, London, 1812–13

EXH: The European Museum, London, 1812 (310), 1813 (51)

ENGR: Engraving ($12\frac{1}{16} \times 10\frac{1}{16}$ in.) by John Landseer, pub. 28 May 1796 by Thomas Macklin and included as an illustration to vol. v of Macklin's *Bible*, with a line indentifying the source as Luke, ch. 3, v. 4

(?) LISTED: *PC*, p. 562 ("Moses with the Law, and John the Baptist, in the Church of Barbadoes, as large as life") and p. 563 ("John shewing the Lamb of God, in a Church at Barbadoes"); *UM*, p. 528 (listed twice on the same page); *AA*, p. 69 ("John the Baptist," 8 ft. × 5, in Christ Church in the Island of Barbadoes); Barlow, p. 433 ("John Seeing the Lamb of God," under "In different Churches"); *BA*, p. 15 (as in *PC*, p. 562); Galt, pp. 221 and 222; Dillenberger, pp. 154 (162), 155 (166), and 158 (197)

See No. 268, the painting of *Moses* that, like No. 297, served as the basis of an engraved illustration in Macklin's *Bible*. We have tentatively equated these two paintings, both of which have disappeared, with paintings of the subjects recorded in the early lists of West's works as in Barbados. If No. 297 was in fact painted for Barbados, it may never have gone, or may have gone there for only a brief period, as it was sold by Thomas Macklin in London in 1800 and was probably the *St. John* exhibited and offered for sale at the European Museum in London in 1812 and 1813. The entry in the European Museum's catalogue for 1812 described the exhibited work as "St. John divinely inspired, exclaiming 'The voice of one crying in the wilderness, prepare ye the way of the Lord, make his paths straight.'" This quotation is from chapter 3, verse 4, of Luke, and the same verse is cited in the caption to the plate after No. 297 in Macklin's *Bible* (*right*). Some of the titles listed in the early catalogues for the Barbados *St. John* describe John as "shewing the Lamb of God," which does not seem to fit his action in No. 297. However, the duplications and contradictions in these titles (cf. No. 268) make their accuracy suspect, and in any case the banner tied to John's cross in No. 297 bears the words *Ecce Agnus Dei*. For other images of John see also Nos. 296 and 316.

A "St. John, after West," presumably a copy after No. 297, was lot 41 in the same sale in 1800 of Macklin's collection in which No. 297 was lot 52.

298 The Nativity c. 1792–94

H.M. TREASURY AND THE NATIONAL TRUST,
PETWORTH HOUSE, SUSSEX

Oil on paper: 196 × 101 in. (498 × 256.5 cm.)

PROV: Cartoon for a window commissioned by George III for St. George's Chapel, Windsor (1797 account: "The Nativity of our Saviour, a cartoon," 1792, £525; 1801 account, p. 211; listed with paintings for the King's Chapel in Windsor Castle, 22, "The Birth of our Saviour, a cartoon for a painted-glass window, by Mr. Forrest," £525); sold by West's sons, Robins, London, 22–25 May 1829, lot 36 ("The Nativity of our Saviour," 15 ft. 6 in. × 8 ft. 6 in., "A Cartoon, from which the painted glass Window in St. George's Chapel, Windsor, was executed"), bt. by the third Earl of Egremont for £189; by family descent to the third Lord Leconfield (died 1952); accepted by the Treasury in part payment of death duties in 1957

EXH: RA 1799 (168) "The nativity of Our Saviour, a cartoon designed for a painted window in the Collegiate Church, Windsor"; West's Gallery 1821 (20), 1822–28 (26)

LISTED: *PC*, p. 560 ("The Cartoon of the Nativity of our Saviour," for the Collegiate Church, Windsor); *UM*, p. 527; Barlow, p. 431; *BA*, p. 13; Galt, p. 217; Dillenberger, pp. 141 (41), 147 (94), and 213

LIT: Collins Baker 1920, p. 133 (591); Meyer 1979, pp. 59 and 61, fig. 7

For a thoroughgoing discussion of West's designs for windows in St. George's Chapel, Windsor, see the article by Jerry D. Meyer, published in 1979. The *Nativity* window was executed by a glassmaker named Forrest and installed as the west window of the south aisle in 1794.[1] It formed one of a group of three windows in the aisles of the chapel devoted to Christ's birth, the other two showing the *Angels Appearing to the Shepherds* (cf. No. 306) and the *Wise Men's Offering* (No. 309). The windows in the aisles were replaced in the 1840s and 1850s by windows designed by Thomas Willement.[2] See also Nos. 356 and 360.

St. John the Baptist, engraving by John Landseer after No. 297

298

The listing of the designs and cartoons for the windows, and of the windows themselves in the early catalogues of West's works is confusing. In West's account for George III of 1801, studies and cartoons for the windows are identified as such but listed together with the subjects intended for the Royal Chapel in Windsor Castle,[3] while the actual windows are not included. In *Public Characters* and the other early catalogues of West's *oeuvre*, the designs and cartoons are listed without a separate heading immediately after the series of paintings from the life of Edward III (Nos. 56–76) painted by West for the Audience Chamber at Windsor, though it seems highly unlikely that the cartoons were actually situated there. The windows themselves appear separately with works "In different Churches,"[4] and several of the subjects, including that of No. 298, reappear again with the works intended for the Royal Chapel in the castle.[5] None of the subjects West had designed for windows for St. George's Chapel was in fact carried out as a painting for the Royal Chapel. How seriously West intended to paint any of them is open to question. Three of the subjects also appear on the Swarthmore diagrams of 1801, including a "Birth of Our Saviour" second from the left on the bottom row of the side wall devoted to New Testament subjects, but since these diagrams were made after West had been told to stop work on the chapel, the evidence they provide is not compelling.

Although the window was completed and installed in 1794, West did not exhibit the cartoon (No. 298) until 1799. He had previously exhibited a design for the window at the Royal Academy in 1793 (No. 299). A nativity group repeating the lower half of No. 298 can probably be identified as the "Birth of Our Saviour" which West exhibited in 1796 (No. 300). A drawing by Mather Brown after the angel in No. 298 is in the Huntington Library and Art Gallery.[6]

Drawings of the Nativity which are not closely related to any known painting are in the Philadelphia Museum of Art[7] and in the collection of Julius Held.[8] A painting at Swarthmore, which was included in the West exhibition at Brooklyn in 1922, does not appear to be by him.[9]

[1] *Windsor Guide*, 1807, p. 79.
[2] Hope 1913, II, pp. 416 and 421.
[3] cf. Galt 1820, pp. 211–13.
[4] References for the *Nativity* are: *PC*, p. 562 ("The Birth of our Saviour," in the Collegiate Church of Windsor, 9 × 16 ft.); *UM*, p. 528; *AA*, p. 68 (18 × 9 ft.); *BA*, p. 15; Galt, p. 221; Dillenberger, p. 154 (157).
[5] *PC*, p. 561 ("Christ's Birth," 6 × 10 ft., Gospel Dispensation); *UM*, p. 527; *AA*, p. 67 (9 ft. × 6); Barlow, p. 432 (9 ft. × 6); *BA*, p. 14 (6 ft. × 12); Galt, p. 219; Meyer, p. 264; Dillenberger, p. 146 (90).
[6] Ill. in Evans 1982, p. 40, fig. 18.
[7] Pen and ink, 3 × 3 in., signed. See No. 301 below.
[8] Sepia wash, $8\frac{7}{8} \times 12\frac{7}{8}$ in., signed and dated *1801*.
[9] Oil on canvas, $19 \times 23\frac{3}{4}$ in., Brooklyn 1922 (6) lent by Albert Rosenthal.

299 The Nativity *c.* 1793

LOCATION UNKNOWN

PROV: (?) Mr. Tomkins, Doctors Commons, by *c.* 1804

EXH: RA 1793 (47) "The nativity of our Saviour, the design for a window in the collegiate church, Windsor"

(?) LISTED: *PC*, p. 564 ("The drawing representing Christ's Nativity," Mr. Tomkins, Doctors Commons); *UM*, p. 529; *BA*, p. 16; Galt, p. 224; Dillenberger, p. 163 (242)

300 The Nativity *c.* 1796

LOCATION UNKNOWN

Oil on canvas: (27 × 20 in.) (63.5 × 51 cm.)

PROV: Offered by West's sons to the United States in 1826 (82) and sold by them, Robins, London, 22–25 May 1829, lot 56 ("The Nativity of Our Saviour," 2 ft. 4 in. × 1 ft. 8. in., "The first study for the lower compartment of the same design, for the stained-glass Window of St. George's Chapel"), bt. by Dolman for £54.12.0.; Arthur Wilkin, Cousley Wood, Woodhurst, Sussex; Mortimer Brandt, New York, 1967

EXH: (?) RA 1796 (420) "Birth of our Saviour"; (?) West's Gallery 1821 (76) "The Nativity (a sketch)", 1822–28 (51) "The Nativity of Our Saviour"

LISTED: PC, p. 567 ("Christ's Nativity," West, Gallery); UM, p. 531; Barlow, p. 435; BA, p. 18; Galt, p. 230; Dillenberger, p. 177 (385)

The figures in No. 300 are virtually identical with those in the lower part of No. 298, and there can be little doubt that it was the work sold in 1829 as the first study for the lower compartment of the design. However, despite the words of the sale catalogue, No. 300 is more likely a replica than a first study. See also No. 311, which shows a freer but comparable reworking of the lower portion of the composition of another of the windows for St. George's Chapel.

301 The Nativity 1818

ST. MARYLEBONE PARISH CHURCH, LONDON

Oil on canvas: 60 × 48 in., arched top (152.5 × 122 cm.)

Inscribed lower right corner:

> Christ's Nativity announced by the Angel of the Lord to Shepherds. And the Angel said unto them, fear not for behold, I bring you good tidings of great joy, which shall be to all people. For unto you is born this day in the city of David, a Saviour, which is Christ the Lord. And this shall be a sign unto you and they came with haste, and found Mary and Joseph, and the Babe wrapped in swaddling clothes lying in a manger. Luke Chap 2nd This picture by Benjamin West Esq. President of the Academy of Arts in London, and Historical Painter to His Majesty, is presented by him as a gratuitous offering to the communion of the Parish of St. Mary le bone—in which Parish he has lived as a housekeeper forty-five years when he painted this picture in 1818

PROV: Presented by West in 1818 to St. Marylebone Parish Church, where it was originally situated above the altar (see No. 308); from 1883 until 1949 in Old St. Marylebone Church; now over a side altar of the parish church

EXH: RA 1818 (36) "The nativity of our Saviour," with the biblical quotation from Luke 2: 10–12 which is inscribed on the painting and quoted above

LISTED: Dillenberger, p. 214

LIT: V and A Cuttings, III, pp. 832 and 838 (1818); Art Journal, 1859, p. 195; T. Harris, A Brief Account of the Parish of St. Marylebone, London, 1885, pp. 13–15; Croft-Murray 1970, p. 291; Dillenberger 1977, pp. 113–14; Gerald L. Carr, "Benjamin West's Altar Paintings for St. Marylebone Church," Art Bulletin, LXII, 1980, pp. 293–303

In 1816–17 West painted a transparency of the "Annunciation to the Shepherds" to be situated at the center of the organ and above the altar of St. Marylebone Parish Church (No. 308). For this large work he charged the church 800 guineas, which price evidently was taken amiss by some members of the church's vestry; according to Farington they had expected West to give the transparency.[1] West sub-

301

sequently painted No. 301 and present it gratuitously to the church, where it was installed below the transparency and immediately above the altar. The article by Gerald Carr includes extensive documentation from the parish records about both works. The composition of the two together, with angel above and a scene of the Nativity below, echoes that of West's Nativity window for St. George's Chapel (see No. 298), but the grouping of the figures in this picture is distinct from that in any earlier painting. A small drawing in the Philadelphia Museum, though quite different in composition, does have certain features in common with No. 301 (notably the position of Joseph behind the Virgin and a conspicuous burst of light) and may represent an early idea for the composition.[2]

No. 301 was vandalized in 1859 by an assailant who made two large cuts across the center of the picture.

These have been restored, but the painting remains in a very deteriorated condition.

[1] Farington Diary, 18 March 1818 (Farington 1978–, xv, p. 5175).
[2] Pen and ink, 3 × 3 in.

302 Madonna and Child c. 1765

LOCATION UNKNOWN

(11 × 8½ in.) (28 × 21.5 cm.)

PROV: Offered by West's sons to the United States in 1826 (97, . . . , 11 × 8 in.), and sold by them, Robins, London, 22–25 May 1829, lot 41 ("Madonna and Child," 11 × 8½ in.), bt. for £23.12.0. by R. Boston

EXH: West's Gallery 1821 (19), 1822–28 (74)

The description of this lost work in the Robins sale catalogue of May 1829 is:

Painted in 1765, subsequently to West's return from Italy. Highly wrought, and composed and coloured in the feeling of the Italian school. The artist's passionate admiration of the Correggiesque style is identified with this elegant cabinet picture.

It is noteworthy that West associated the name of Correggio with a picture of a similar subject which he exhibited in 1773 (No. 303). He much later told Joseph Farington that in 1765 "his mind was full of Correggio" (see No. 128). West had copied the *Madonna with St. Jerome* by Correggio in Parma in 1762 and 1763 (see No. 505). See also No. 676 and several portraits of Mrs. West and Raphael (Nos. 535–39), which have similar imagery.

303 The Holy Family *c.* 1773

LOCATION UNKNOWN

EXH: RA 1773 (311) "A Holy Family, in imitation of Correggio's manner"

Nothing is known about this work apart from its appearance at the Royal Academy in 1773. The wording of the entry in the Academy catalogue suggests that it was an independent picture in the manner of Correggio, rather than a copy, and the mention of Correggio anticipates that reference to that master accompanying No. 302 in the Robins catalogue of 1829.

West did paint a large copy of a *Holy Family* by Mengs while he was in Italy (No. 511). Ann C. Van Devanter has argued that a *Holy Family* in Old St. Joseph's Church in Philadelphia, based on an engraving of a *Hagar and Ishmael* by Federico Barocci, was painted by West in Italy,[1] but the style seems remote from that of works painted by West in Italy whose provenances give much surer guarantees of their authenticity (see Nos. 506, 510, 511 and 516). A *Holy Family* in the parish church in Tetbury, Gloucestershire, which has been ascribed to West, is also not by him.

[1] Ann C. Van Devanter, "A *Holy Family* attributed to Benjamin West," *Antiques*, XCVIII, 1970, pp. 773–75.

304 The Angels Appearing to the Shepherds 1774

LOCATION UNKNOWN

Oil on canvas: 88 × 56 in. (223.5 × 142 cm.)

Signed: *B. West 1774*

PROV: Commissioned by Joseph Wilcocks in 1772 to be presented anonymously by him to Rochester Cathedral; lent to St. Mary's, Chatham, in 1826, the loan made into a gift in 1886, and still there in 1907; Vose Galleries, Boston, 1922; sold "to close an estate," American Art Association, New York, 20–21 February 1924, lot 214 (... 88 × 56 in.), bt. by Ehrich Galleries, New York

EXH: RA 1774 (310) "The angels appearing to the shepherds; for the altar of a cathedral"; Brooklyn 1922 (15) lent by Vose and Company, Boston

ENGR: Engraving (5⅜ × 3 in.) by William Sharp, pub. as the frontispiece to vol. I of *Discourses on Various Subjects* by Jacob Duché, MA, London, 1779

LISTED: *PC*, p. 562 ("the Angels announcing the Birth of our Saviour, in the Cathedral Church of Rochester," 10 ft. × 6); *UM*, p. 528; *AA*, p. 68 (12 ft. × 8); Barlow, p. 433; *BA*, p. 15; Galt, p. 220; Dillenberger, pp. 153 (149) and 211

LIT: V and A Cuttings, I, p. 106 (*Public Advertiser*, 30 April 1774); Joseph Wilcocks, *Roman Conversations; or, A Short Description of the Antiquities of Rome: interspersed with Characters of Eminent Romans; and Reflections,*

304

Religious and Moral, on Roman History, 2nd. ed., London, 1797, pp. xxxix–xli; Carey 1820, p. 696; G. H. Palmer, *The Cathedral Church of Rochester*, London, 1899, pp. 94–95; Dillenberger 1977, pp. 41–42

Joseph Wilcocks, who commissioned No. 304, was the son of a former Bishop of Rochester. West had been introduced to him in Rome by Thomas Robinson (see Nos. 689 and 714). According to Carey, Wilcocks commissioned No. 304 following the collapse in October 1773 of the scheme of the recently founded Royal Academy to decorate St. Paul's Cathedral with paintings (see No. 257). That assertion is contradicted by the date of 6 January 1773 on a letter from Wilcocks to West in the Historical Society of Pennsylvania, in which there is reference to earlier correspondence about the commission in the December of the previous year. This makes No. 304 the earliest of West's major religious commissions. West exhibited the completed painting at the Royal Academy in 1774 along with designs for an altarpiece for St. Stephen Walbrook (see Nos. 388 and 389) and for the never-realized picture for St. Paul's (No. 257).

According to a guide to Rochester Cathedral published in 1899, No. 304 was installed over the altar only in 1788, and according to the same source, it was sent to the church of St. Mary's in Chatham in 1826, where it still remained when the guide was published. No. 304 is not now at Chatham, and inquiries at both Chatham and Rochester have failed to uncover any information about what subsequently happened to it. It probably can be identified as a picture sold in New York in 1924, which according to the auction catalogue was signed and dated *1774*, and which seems to accord with descriptions of the Rochester painting when it was exhibited in that year. There are significant discrepancies between the measurements appearing in the American Art Association sales catalogue and those listed in *Public Characters* and the other early catalogues of West's works for the Rochester painting, but since the measurements in *Public Characters*, published in 1804, and *Academic Annals*, published in 1805, signifi-

cantly contradict each other, and since the lists date from thirty years after the picture was painted, they cannot be taken as trustworthy evidence of the work's actual size. A hypothesis that the painting may have been cut down at some time prior to 1924 is not tenable, since an engraving published in 1779 in a collection of sermons by Jacob Duché shows the same composition as the work sold in 1924, without any additional area that might subsequently have been removed. Duché's preface describes that engraving and a companion one (based on No. 351) as taken from two of West's "most capital paintings."[1]

Joseph Wilcocks's letter to West of 6 January 1773, is of such exceptional interest in revealing the attitudes of an eighteenth-century patron and the relations between patron and artist, as well as in accounting for some of the differences between the painting and two earlier sketches discussed below, that it should be quoted at length. The Bishop of Chester and former Dean of Rochester mentioned by Wilcocks was Dr. William Markham, whose portrait West painted at about this time (No. 655).

I ought to return you many thanks for your kind letter, written last Christmas day which I found here on my arrival from bath.—In relation to it suffer me to trouble you with the few following lines.

My father was for 25 years Bishop of *Rochester*: during all which have I partook of the benefits of his station. In memory of those benefits I ought to wish to do some act of gratitude to *that* place.—A picture by your hand, on the subject I mentioned to you, would be surely a proper ornament for the Altar Piece of the very ancient & (...) *Cathedral* of Rochester.

But it must *not on any account* be known that I have any concern in the gift.—I hope the Bishop of Ches-

The Angels Appearing to the Shepherds, engraving by William Sharp after No. 304

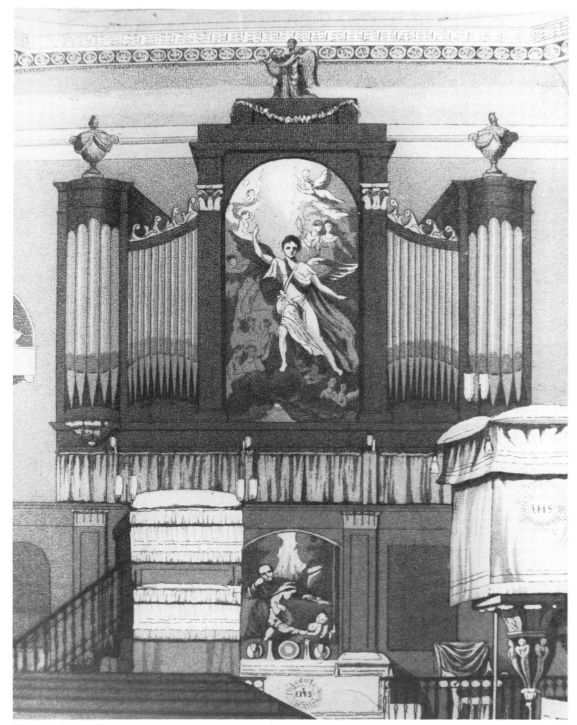

St. Marylebone Church, detail from an engraving made between 1818 and 1826 showing Nos. 301 and 308 in situ

above the wings of the organ are recorded in a nineteenth-century print showing the interior of the church.[4] Although Adams was evidently wrong in stating that No. 308 was to be copied on glass, it was described in most accounts as a transparent picture and was situated before a window. No. 301 is below, and the relation of the two echoes the *Nativity* window in St. George's Chapel (see No. 298), as was noted by contemporary reviewers quoted by Carr. The angel also is reminiscent of the main angel in No. 307, a sketch for the window showing the *Angels Appearing to the Shepherds* at Windsor.

[1] Historical Society of Pennsylvania.
[2] Quoted by Taylor, pp. 146–47.
[3] Ibid.
[4] For the full print see Dillenberger 1977, p. 113, pl. 78. Our illustration is a detail showing the arrangement of the altar.

309 The Wise Men's Offering *c.* 1794–96

LOCATION UNKNOWN

(192 × 108 in.) (488 × 274 cm.)

PROV: Cartoon for a window commissioned by George III for St. George's Chapel, Windsor (1797 account: "The Wise Man's Offering to Christ, a cartoon", 1794, £525; 1801 account, p. 211: listed with paintings for the King's Chapel in Windsor Castle, 23, "The Wise Man's Offering, a cartoon for a painted-glass window, by Mr. Forrest," £525

EXH: (?) RA 1797 (251) "The Wise Men's offering, executed on glass in the Collegiate Church, Windsor"

LISTED: See p. 324; *PC*, p. 560 ("The Cartoon of the Kings presenting Gifts to our Saviour," for the Col-

legiate Church, Windsor); *UM*, p. 527; Barlow, p. 431; *BA*, p. 13 (9 ft. × 16); Galt, p. 217; Dillenberger, pp. 141 (42) and 147 (95)

The window for which No. 309 was a cartoon was installed at the west end of the north aisle of St. George's Chapel in 1796. According to the *Windsor Guide* of 1807, it showed:

> the infant Jesus, in a reclining posture in the lap of the Virgin Mary, behind whom is Joseph, and in the front are the wise men of the east presenting offerings, whose various countenances and habits, bespeak them of different and distant countries. Over these is a luminous star, and the angel of the Lord . . .[1]

The window was replaced in the mid-nineteenth century. What became of the cartoon (No. 309) is not known. The wording of the entry in the Royal Academy catalogue for 1797 does not indicate whether the cartoon itself or a smaller study for the window such as No. 310 was exhibited.

For cartoons for other windows at Windsor see Nos. 298, 306, 357, and 361. "The Wise Men's Offering," like most of the other subjects executed as windows in the St. George's Chapel, appears also on early lists of West's works among the subjects planned for the Royal Chapel in Windsor Castle;[2] it is also on the Swarthmore diagram dated 16 August 1801 devoted to New Testament subjects, at the center of the bottom row with the notation "Designed" (p. 580). However, no actual picture of the subject is known to have been painted for the Royal Chapel.

An oil sketch of the design is No. 310, below. A drawing of the subject, which is evidently different in composition from Nos. 309 and 310, was owned by the Bernard Black Gallery in 1968.[3]

[1] *Windsor Guide* 1807, p. 80. The window is listed in *PC*, p. 562 (9 ft. × 16); *UM*, p. 528; *AA*, p. 68 (18 ft. × 9); *BA*, p. 15; Galt, p. 221; Dillenberger, p. 154 (158).
[2] *PC*, p. 561 ("The Kings Bringing Presents to Christ," 6 ft. × 12, Gospel Dispensation); *UM*, p. 527; *AA*, p. 67; Barlow, p. 432 (9 ft. × 6); *BA*, p. 14; Galt, p. 219; Dillenberger, p. 147 (96).
[3] Pen and ink, 4 × 7⅜ in.; see New York 1968 (29).

310 The Wise Men's Offering 1794

MR. AND MRS. RICHARD MANNEY

Oil on canvas: 50¾ × 23 in. (129 × 58.5 cm.)

Signed lower right: *B. West/1794*

PROV: Offered by West's sons to the United States in 1826 (41), and sold by them, Robins, London, 22–25 May 1829, lot 68 ("The Wise Men's Offering," 4 ft. × 1 ft. 11 in.), bt. by H. P. Bone for £47.5.0. on behalf of Joseph Neeld, MP, Grittleton House, Wilts.; by descent in the Neeld family until sold, Christie's, London, 13 July 1945, lot 164, bt. by the Revd. W. R. Corbould, Carshalton, Surrey; sold, Sotheby's, London, 16 April 1958, lot 71, bt. by J. Mitchell; Childs Gallery, Boston, 1958; Robert S. Draper, South Miami, Florida; French and Company, New York; gift of Mr. and Mrs. James W. Fosburgh to the Metropolitan Museum of Art, New York, 1964; sold by the museum and acquired by the present owners by 1970

EXH: (?) RA 1797 (see No. 309); (?) 125 Pall Mall 1816 (11); (?) 125 Pall Mall 1818 (7); West's Gallery 1821 (26 or 44), 1822–28 (42 or 66); BI 1833 (41) lent by Joseph Neeld

LISTED: *PC*, p. 565 ("The Large Sketch of the Window at Windsor of the King's Presenting Gifts to the Infant Christ," West, Painting-room); *UM*, p. 530; *BA*, p. 17; Galt, p. 227; Dillenberger, pp. 170 (310) and 213

312

went through the market in 1778, 1786, and 1795, is confirmed by the approximate correspondence of its measurements with those listed in the Kerry catalogue in 1778. The larger dimensions in the Desenfans catalogue presumably included the frame.

Drawings identified as showing "Simeon and the Child" were sold by descendants of the artist in 1839 and 1979.[1]

[1]S. Leigh Sotheby, London, 1 June 1839, lot 18 (pen and bistre, washed); and Sotheby's, London, 22 March 1979, lot 17 (pencil, brown, grey and white washes, $5\frac{1}{4} \times 6\frac{3}{4}$ in.).

313 Simeon with the Child Jesus in His Arms
c. 1796

LOCATION UNKNOWN

($20\frac{1}{2} \times 26$ in.) (52×66 cm.)

PROV: (?) William Beckford; in West's possession in 1816; offered by West's sons to the United States in 1826 (57, "Simeon and the Child," 1 ft. $8\frac{1}{2}$ in. × 2 ft. 2 in.), and sold by them, Robins, London, 22–25 May 1829, lot 3 ("Simeon," $20\frac{1}{2} \times 26$ in.), bt. by Pickering for £21

EXH: RA 1796 (171) "Simeon with the Infant Saviour;" 125 Pall Mall 1816 (14) "Simeon"; 125 Pall Mall 1818 (11); West's Gallery 1821 (72), 1822–28 (5)

LISTED: *PC*, p. 561 ("Simeon with the Child in his Arms," painted for and in the possession of Wm. Beckford, Esq. of Fonthill); *UM*, p. 528; Barlow, p. 432; *BA*, p. 14; Galt, p. 219; Dillenberger, p. 151 (130)

If the measurements given for No. 313 in 1826 and 1829 are correct, it was, unlike No. 312, a horizontal composition. Although in several exhibitions and in the Robins sale of May 1829 this version was simply titled "Simeon," the description in the Robins catalogue establishes that the picture included a child: "An interesting group, to which the colouring is judiciously distributed. The flesh tones of old age and infancy are harmoniously relieved on the russet-coloured drapery; and the subject is wrought with becoming breadth."

The early lists of West's works include a picture of the subject painted for William Beckford, but there is no confirming evidence from any of the Beckford sales or otherwise that Beckford ever owned such a picture, whereas there is ample evidence that No. 313 was in the possession of West and his heirs, at least from 1816 to 1829. It may be that Beckford did acquire No. 313 and subsequently returned it to West, possibly in exchange for another work.

314 Christ among the Doctors *c.* 1778–80

HIS GRACE THE DUKE OF RUTLAND

Oil on canvas: 20 × 26 in. (51 × 66 cm.)

PROV: Painted for the fourth Duke of Rutland (1754–1787)

LISTED: *UM*, p. 528 ("Christ among the Doctors," in the possession of the Duke of Rutland); *BA*, p. 19 (painted for the late Duke of Rutland, and at Belvoir Castle); Dillenberger, p. 188 (494)

LIT: The Revd. Irvin Eller, *The History of Belvoir Castle*, London, 1846, p. 204

This painting is a companion to *Hannah Presenting Samuel to Eli* (No. 271). Versions of both compositions

The subject is from Luke 2:22–39. West exhibited pictures of Simeon at the Royal Academy in 1772 and 1796. No. 312 is not dated, but it must have been the earlier of the two. The model for Simeon seems to have posed frequently for West between 1771 and 1774 (see No. 159).

Eton College has no record of when or how it acquired the painting, but it must have arrived there between 1795 and 1804, when the catalogue of West's works in *Public Characters* appeared. The identification of No. 312 with the "Presentation in the Temple" and the "Simeon Offering Christ in the Temple" which are in the collection of George E. Doty.[1] See No. 271 for further discussion.

A later treatment of the subject differing in composition is No. 315 below. Additionally, the subject appears among the works intended for George III's chapel in Windsor Castle on several of the early published lists of West's works,[2] and on the Swarthmore diagrams of 1801 with the notation "designed" (ill. p. 580). It is not on the drawings of *c.* 1780 or on West's accounts of 1797 and 1801, and there is no evidence to indicate that West ever painted the subject on a large scale. Nonetheless, the two works do not seem radically unlike sketches for pictures that West did paint for the chapel.

The distinctive features of the standing man furthest to the right appear to have been based on those of Gilbert Stuart, who was in West's studio from 1777 to 1782 (cf. No. 258).

[1] The version of No. 314 (*right*) is in oil on canvas, $19\frac{3}{4} \times 25\frac{3}{8}$ in.
[2] *PC*, p. 561 ("Christ among the Doctors," George III, for his Majesty's Chapel, Windsor, Gospel Dispensation, 6 ft. × 10); *UM*, p. 527; *AA*, p. 67 (6 ft. × 9); Barlow, p. 432 (9 ft. × 6); *BA*, p. 14; Galt, p. 219; Dillenberger, p. 147 (97).

315 Christ among the Doctors 1800

LOCATION UNKNOWN

($11 \times 15\frac{1}{2}$ in.) (28 × 39.5 cm.)

Signed lower right: *B. West 1800* (from Moses engraving)

PROV: Offered by West's sons to the United States in 1826 (88), and sold by them, Robins, London, 22–25 May 1829, lot 10 ($11 \times 15\frac{1}{2}$ in.), bt. by Pickering for £14.14.0.

EXH: West's Gallery 1822–28 (62)

ENGR: Outline engraving ($6\frac{15}{16} \times 9\frac{1}{4}$ in.) by Henry Moses, pub. 1 April 1813 by Moses and included in later editions of Moses 1811 (*below*)

LISTED: *PC*, p. 567 ("Christ among the Doctors in the Temple," West, Gallery); *UM*, p. 531; Barlow, p. 435; *BA*, p. 18; Galt, p. 230; Dillenberger, p. 177 (382)

LIT: Moses 1811 (only in later editions); Dillenberger 1977, p. 73, pl. 49 (Moses engraving)

See Nos. 314 and 272.

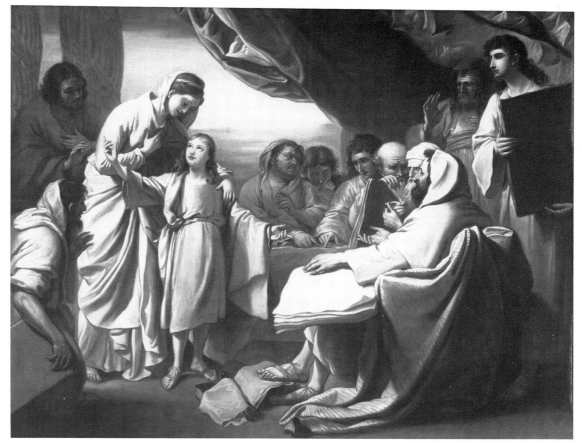

Christ among the Doctors, (?) studio replica of No. 314. George E. Doty

Christ among the Doctors, outline engraving by Henry Moses after No. 315

316 The Baptism *c.* 1794

BOB JONES UNIVERSITY, GREENVILLE, SOUTH CAROLINA

Oil on canvas: 148 × 115 in. (376 × 292 cm.)

PROV: Painted for George III (1797 account: "The descent of the Holy Ghost on our Saviour at the River Jordan," 1794, £1,050; 1801 account, p. 212: for the Windsor Chapel, The Prophets, 24, "John the Baptist baptizing our Saviour, on whom the Holy Ghost descends"); never delivered and ownership returned to West's sons by George IV in 1828; sold by them, Robins, London, 22–25 May 1829, lot 72 ("Baptism of Our Saviour," 12 ft. 6 in. × 10 ft.), bt. by Bone for £52.10.0., on behalf of Joseph Neeld, MP, Grittleton House, Wilts.; by descent in the Neeld family until sold by Miss C. K. M. Neeld, Christie's, London, 16 Nov. 1962, lot 94, bt. by Weitzner; purchased by the present owner in 1963

EXH: RA 1794 (132) "The Holy Spirit descending upon Christ after his Baptism at the River Jordan, for his Majesty's Chapel in Windsor Castle": West's Gallery 1821 (28), 1822–28 (40) (both with quotation from Matthew 3:13–16)

ENGR: Stipple engraving ($27\frac{3}{16} \times 19\frac{3}{8}$ in.) of a detail of a mother and child, by M. A. Bourlier, pub. by Bourlier, 2 August 1813; stipple engraving ($18\frac{1}{2} \times 13\frac{1}{4}$ in.) of detail of John, by Edward Scriven; lithograph ($12\frac{7}{8} \times 8\frac{1}{16}$ in., reversed) of detail of Christ, inscribed within the image *B. West/1802* and in the lower margin *This is my beloved son &c*; lithograph ($12\frac{5}{16} \times 8\frac{7}{8}$ in., reversed) of detail of John, altered in several details, inscribed within the image *B. West 1801* and in the lower margin *John the Baptist*

LISTED: *PC*, p. 561 ("The Descent of the Holy Ghost on Our Saviour at the River Jordan," George III, for his Majesty's Chapel, Windsor, Gospel Dispensa-

tion, 10 ft. × 14); *UM*, p. 527; *AA*, p. 67 (9 ft. × 14); Barlow, p. 432 (15 ft. × 10); *BA*, p. 14; Galt, p. 219; Dillenberger, pp. 147 (98) and 212

LIT: V and A Cuttings, III, p. 709 (1795); Jones 1963; Jones 1968, p. 65 (348), ill. p. 189; Kraemer 1975, pp. 54–55; Meyer 1975, pp. 256–57, 264–65 and fig. 14; Dillenberger 1977, pp. 71, 81, and pl. 50

The *Baptism* appears first in the sequence of New Testament subjects in the architectural drawings of *c.* 1780 for the Royal Chapel in Windsor Castle (ill. p. 577) as a large vertical composition on the extreme left on a side wall. It reappears, as do the four companion compositions, in the same position in one of the Swarthmore diagrams of 1801 (p. 580). In West's account of 1801 for George III two further New Testament subjects, "Christ's Temptation and Victory in the Wilderness" and "Christ beginneth to preach at Nazareth, his native place," each described as "a sketch," follow No. 316 and precede, "Christ Healeth the Sick and Blind, &c in the Temple" (No. 334), which is next to No. 316 on both the drawings of *c.* 1780 and the diagram of 1801; however, there is no evidence that either the "Temptation" or the "Nazareth" subject was ever carried beyond an initial sketch.[1]

Although an interval of approximately fourteen years separates No. 316 from the sketches in the earlier architectural schemes, its composition is recognizably based on the one appearing there. As Meyer has pointed out, several changes occur, most notably in the elimination of a semi-nude male figure who reclines in the lower right corner in the drawings and in the position of John the Baptist.

The dependence of John the Baptist upon the *Apollo Belvedere* was first discussed by Katharine Shepard writing about West's lithograph after this figure;[2] Meyer has also suggested that his pose is reminiscent of the Adam in Dürer's *Adam and Eve* engraving of 1504.

319

319 The Good Samaritan (?)*c*. 1763–66

LOCATION UNKNOWN

(27 × 36 in.) (68.5 × 91.5 cm.)

PROV: Offered by West's sons to the United States in
1826 (116), and sold by them, Robins, London, 22–
25 May 1829, lot 136 (2 ft. 3 in. × 3 ft.), bt. by Sir
M. W. Ridley for £31.10.0.; (?) sold anonymously,
Christie's, London, 13 Feb. 1925, lot 96 (28 × 35 in.),
bt. by Mason; sold again, Christie's, London, 8 Feb.
1926, lot 38 (28 × 35 in.), bt. by Napier

LISTED: *PC*, p. 566 ("The Good Samaritan," West,
Painting-room); *UM*, p. 530; Barlow, p. 434; *BA*,
p. 17; Galt, p. 228; Dillenberger, p. 172 (338)

The text accompanying No. 319 in the Robins sale
catalogue of May 1829 consisted of one sentence: "A
composition interesting to the collector, principally
from the circumstance of its being one of the very early
efforts of the master's ingenious pencil." This comment
seems markedly temperate in comparison to the fulsome praise bestowed on virtually every other work in
the sale, and suggests not only that the painting did

not arouse the enthusiasm of the catalogue's compiler,
but also that it must have been fairly uncharacteristic
of the master's style. In the light of that and of the description of the work as "very early," it is perhaps
reasonable to accept the painting of the subject which
went through Christie's in 1925 and 1926 as No. 319.
Although it has little in common with any of West's
mature works, there are some similarities in the treatment of the foliage with that in the early *Angelica and
Medoro* and *Choice of Hercules* (Nos. 188 and 143). The
clumsy details in conjunction with a sophisticated effect
of light and a spacious Claudian landscape strongly
suggest that the painting is a copy after an unidentified
seventeenth-century work.

A large and fairly complete drawing of the composition in a private collection in Philadelphia has a West
family provenance and the initials *RL* in the lower left
corner.[1] It does not appear to be by Benjamin West,
but it is plausible as a copy made after either this painting or the work upon which it is based. The initials may
refer to Richard Livesay, who was a student and
assistant of West.

[1]Black chalk, 15½ × 20¼ in., formerly in the collection of Mrs.
Claire Francis, a descendant of the artist.

320 The Return of the Prodigal Son *c*. 1765–67

LOCATION UNKNOWN

PROV: Painted for James Johnson (1705–1774), Bishop
of Worcester

LIT: Galt 1820, p. 9; Dillenberger 1977, p. 21

West seems to have painted three pictures of the *Prodigal Son*, only one of which is now known (No. 322). Our
information about the earliest of them comes from two
sentences in Galt:

Dr. Markham in 1765 introduced Mr. West to Dr.
Newton, Bishop of Bristol, Dr. Johnson, Bishop of
Worcester, and Dr. Drummond, Archbishop of
York. Dr. Newton engaged him to paint the Parting
of Hector and Andromache, and afterwards sat to
him for his portrait, in the back ground of which a
sketch of the picture was introduced: and for the
Bishop of Worcester he painted the Return of the
Prodigal Son.

The Earlom engraving of West's portrait of Newton
(No. 675) showing the *Fright of Astyanax* (No. 163) in
the background was published on 1 December 1767,
giving a date by which Nos. 675 and 163, the two works

cited in the same sentence with No. 320, must have been painted. Archbishop Drummond, the third patron introduced to West by Dr. Markham in 1765 had also started to patronize the artist by 1767. Hence, the context in which Galt mentioned No. 320 implies a similar date for it as well. Such an early date suggests that it was probably not either of the versions of the subject exhibited by West in 1771 and 1773 (Nos. 321 and 322). The version painted for the Bishop of Worcester is not recorded as such on any of the lists of West's works and may simply have been forgotten at the time the first lists were drawn up almost forty years after No. 320 was painted.

Although West may have been introduced to the Bishop of Worcester by Dr. Markham (for whom see No. 655), as stated by Galt, by the summer or autumn of 1766 he had a further connection with Dr. Johnson via his Philadelphia contemporary Francis Hopkinson, whose mother, née Mary Johnson (see No. 641), was a cousin of the Bishop. Francis Hopkinson visited England in 1766 and stayed alternately with West in London and with his distinguished kinsman at Hartlebury Castle near Worcester. A long poem entitled "Genius" written by Hopkinson in England apostrophizes West and the Bishop jointly, referring to the latter as "Patron of Genius."[1]

[1]George Everett Hastings, *The Life and Works of Francis Hopkinson*, Chicago, 1926, pp. 150–51.

321 The Return of the Prodigal Son c. 1771

LOCATION UNKNOWN

(11 × 12 in.) (28 × 30.5 cm.)

PROV: Offered by West's sons to the United States in 1826 (83), and sold by them, Robins, London, 22–25 May 1829, lot 16 (11 × 12 in.), bt. by Pickering for £16.16.0.

EXH: RA 1771 (215) "The Prodigal Son Received by His Father," as a companion to no. 216 "Tobias curing his father's blindness" (No. 291); Polygraphic Society, London, 1788 (6) "Prodigal Son, a Picture painted by and in the Possession of Mr. West", 16 × 16 in. (including frame)

ENGR: Mezzotint (18 × 20¾ in.) by John Young, pub. 21 Oct. 1789 by Young

LISTED: *PC*, p. 564 ("the small picture of the Return of the Prodigal Son," West, Painting-room); *UM*, p. 530; Barlow, p. 434; *BA*, p. 16; Galt, p. 226; Dillenberger, p. 167 (282)

LIT: Gardner and Feld 1965, pp. 26–27; Kraemer 1975, pp. 6–7

The *Prodigal Son* which West sent to the Royal Academy in 1771 had as a companion a painting of *Tobias Curing His Father's Blindness*. We have equated that work with No. 291, which is signed and dated 1771. Both pictures remained in West's possession and were always listed together until they were bought by different purchasers in the sale of his estate of May 1829.

No. 321 was one of three works by West which were reproduced by the polygraphic process, and which were exhibited together with the reproductions in the rooms of the Polygraphic Society in the Strand in 1788 (for the others see Nos. 139 and 248). The price of a reproduction of No. 321 was £1.11.6. One such copy subsequently belonged to Thomas Jefferson, having been sent to him by John Trumbull in 1788.[1]

A painting of the subject in the Metropolitan Museum of Art, long ascribed to West and associated by Gardner and Feld with the painting exhibited in 1771, is not by him. Another painting of the *Prodigal Son* which evidently went through auction in New York in 1935 appears from a reproduction to have nothing to do with West.[2] A drawing in the Pierpont Morgan Library may represent the subject but has no evident connection with Nos. 321 and 322.[3]

[1]Marie Kimball, "Jefferson's Works of Art at Monticello", *Antiques*, LIX, April 1951, pp. 298 and 308.
[2]Plaza, New York, 16 June 1935 (reference from the Witt Library; we have been unable to find a catalogue of this sale). This seems to be the same picture previously sold Sotheby's, London, 4 July 1928, lot 131 (45 × 60 in.).
[3]Kraemer 1975, pp. 6–7 (5), red chalk on grey paper, 6⅜ × 6⅜ in.

322 The Return of the Prodigal Son 1772

PRIVATE COLLECTION

Oil on canvas: 50 × 40 in. (127 × 102 cm.)

Signed and dated: 1772

PROV: Sir James Earle, c. 1804; by descent to the present owner

EXH: RA 1773 (307) "The prodigal son received by his father."

LISTED: *PC*, p. 563 ("The Return of the Prodigal Son," Sir James Earle); *UM*, p. 529; Barlow, p. 433 (Greenwich Hospital); *BA*, p. 15 (for Sir James Earle); Galt, p. 223; Dillenberger, pp. 157 (191) and 159 (213)

This painting, which had been lost to sight since the early nineteenth century, was brought to our attention as this catalogue was going to press.[1] It shows a similar conception of the subject as the mezzotint by John Young after No. 321, but with full-length figures and numerous differences in details.

Although Barlow gives Greenwich Hospital as the location of a version of the subject, that is not repeated in any other source and appears to be an error.

[1]We are indebted to James Miller for telling us about the painting and for providing further information in letters of 25 and 26 April and 15 June 1984.

323 Christ Showing a Little Child as the Emblem of Heaven (?) 1776

LA SALLE COLLEGE, PHILADELPHIA

Oil on canvas: 49¼ × 39¼ in. (125 × 99.5 cm.)

Signed on left side, below Christ's elbow: *B. West/London/[?]1776*

PROV: Given by West in 1777 to Johann Caspar Lavater (1741–1801), Zurich; the Markgraf Carl-Friedrich von Baden, Karlsruhe, (died 1829); by family descent to Colonel-Commandant U. Wille, Zurich (died 1959);[1] sold by his daughter, Elizabeth Albers-Schoenberg, Sotheby's, London, 17 June 1970, lot 38, bt. by Leger Galleries, London; Central Picture Galleries, New York, 1972; purchased by La Salle College in 1973

ENGR: Engraving (10⅛ × 8½ in.) by Johann Heinrich Lips, pub. as "Solcher ist das Reich Gottes!" in the *Physiognomische Fragmente* by Johann Caspar Lavater, Leipzig and Winterthur, 1775–78, vol. IV, opp. p. 450; engraving (7⅞ × 6½ in.) of a detail of the head of the child, by Lips, dated 1779 and titled "Horum est Regnum Coeloeum," pub. in the first French edition of the *Physiognomische Fragmente* (1781–86), III, pl. v, opp. p. 135; mezzotint (14 × 12 9/16 in.) of the same detail within a *trompe l'oeil* frame by F. Haid, dated 1787; engraving (7⅞ × 6⅝ in.) of the same detail by T. Holloway, pub. by H. Murray, T. Holloway, and

The Return of the Prodigal Son, mezzotint by John Young after no. 321

325

& Foster, London 29 May 1801, lot 14; presented by John Wilmot, Thomas Everett, Thomas Bernard, and John Puget to the Foundling Hospital in 1801 to be placed over the altar of the chapel

EXH: (?) Macklin's Gallery, Pall Mall; (?) RA 1800 (134)

> And Jesus called a little child unto him, and set him in the midst of them;
> And said, verily, I say unto you, except ye be converted, and become as little children, ye shall not enter into the kingdom of Heaven.
>
> *Matthew, chap. xviii. ver. 2 and 3*

ENGR: Engraving ($12 \times 9\frac{7}{8}$ in.) by John Hall, pub. by Thomas Macklin, 29 Aug. 1795, and included in Macklin's *Bible*, pub. 1800, vol. v, as "Of Such is the Kingdom of Heaven, vide Mark. Ch. 9 v. 36.37"; mezzotint ($26\frac{3}{4} \times 21$ in.) by Valentine Green, pub. by Green, 21 June 1807, inscribed with a quotation from Matthew 18: 2, 3, 5, and a dedication to the governors and guardians of the Foundling Hospital; outline engraving ($7\frac{7}{16} \times 5\frac{11}{16}$ in.) drawn by Henry Corbould, engraved by Henry Moses, and pub. by Moses, 1 May 1811, as pl. IV in Moses 1811; line engraving ($7\frac{7}{16} \times 5\frac{11}{16}$ in.) by G. Cooke, pub. by the Society for Promoting Christian Knowledge, 1 May 1822; engraving by J. Taylor, pub. by Keymer, Yarmouth; engraving by J. W. Cook

LISTED: *UM*, p. 528 ("The picture over the Communion Table, Foundling Hospital, Christ shewing a little child as the Emblem of Heaven"); *AA*, p. 68 (12 ft. × 8); Dillenberger, pp. 155 (164) and 212

LIT: Edwards 1808, p. 23; Moses 1811 (VI); R. H. Nichols and F. A. Wray, *The History of the Foundling Hospital*, London, 1935, ill. opp. p. 214; Boase 1963, pp. 166 and 177; Benedict Nicolson, *Treasures of the Foundling Hospital*, Oxford, 1972, pp. 79–80 (81); Kraemer 1975, pp. 30–31; Dillenberger 1977, pp. 98–100, pl. 67

No signature or date is presently visible on No. 325, but West stated in 1803 that the painting bore two dates, showing the time when it was painted and the time when it underwent alteration.[1]

The earlier date was probably between 1790, the date on an oil sketch of the composition (No. 326), and 1795, when the picture was engraved for Macklin's *Bible*. The second date must have been 1801. When the painting was acquired by the Foundling Hospital following the death of Thomas Macklin, it was found to have been injured by an improper varnish; so between 29 July and 15 September 1801, West restored and retouched the painting. He did this work without charge, and in return was elected a governor of the hospital. In 1816, while the chapel of the hospital was being renovated, the picture was returned to him again for further repair.[2]

In 1803 West claimed that No. 325, like *Hagar and Ishmael* (No. 239), was "in every respect a new picture" due to his additional work, hence the two dates on the canvas. The original appearance of the work is recorded in the engraving by John Hall in the Macklin *Bible* and in a related oil sketch (No. 327). As in the case of No. 239 West did not modify the composition significantly in repainting the picture; the most marked changes being in the features of several figures, including most conspicuously those of Christ, and in the draperies. No. 325 is presently very dark and appears to be in a deteriorated condition due to the extensive use of bitumen, which may have been applied as part of this repainting (and which may also have been what necessitated West's subsequent work in 1816).

West exhibited versions of this subject at the Royal Academy in 1792 (a finished sketch), 1800, and 1810, and at the British Institution in 1806. No. 328 below,

which is signed and dated *1810*, can be identified as the picture exhibited in that year, and No. 326 was probably the sketch exhibited in 1792, but which version was exhibited in 1800 is a matter for speculation. If it was No. 325, its appearance at the Academy coincided with an attempt of Macklin's estate to sell it.

A copy of the picture was sold by West's heirs in June 1829;[3] this may be the unfinished version of the composition, now in a private collection, which does not appear to be entirely in West's hand.[4]

[1] Draft of a letter from West to the Council of the Royal Academy, dated 16 April 1803, now in the Historical Society of Pennsylvania. The relevant passages are quoted under No. 239.
[2] See Nicolson for extensive documentation from the records of the Foundling Hospital about the picture's acquisition and its subsequent history.
[3] Robins, London, 20–22 June 1829, lot 181 ("Copy of the Altar Piece at the Foundling Hospital").
[4] Oil on canvas, 22 × 16 in.

326 Christ Showing a Little Child as the Emblem of Heaven 1790

DOUGLAS TURNER

Oil on canvas mounted on panel: $27\frac{3}{8} \times 19\frac{7}{8}$ in. (69.5 × 50.5 cm.)

Signed bottom right: *B. West 1790*

PROV: Offered by West's sons to the United States in 1826 (94), and sold by them, Robins, London, 22–25 May 1829, lot 12 ("Christ Showing a Little Child as the Emblem of Heaven," 2 ft. 3 in. × 1 ft. 9 in., "the first study for the admired picture presented to the Governors of the Foundling Hospital, as an Altar-Piece for the Chapel"), bt. by H. P. Bone for £31.10.0., on behalf of Joseph Neeld, MP, Grittleton House, Wilts.; by descent in the Neeld family until sold, Christie's, London, 13 July 1945, lot 171 ("The Emblem of Heaven," panel, 27 × 20 in., signed and dated *1790*)

EXH: (?) RA 1792 (421) "Christ shewing a little child, 'of such is the kingdom of Heaven,'—A finished sketch"; (?) BI 1806 (50) "Christ shewing a little child as the emblem of Heaven"; West's Gallery 1821 (43) "Christ comparing the Kingdom of Heaven to Little Children"; West's Gallery 1822–28 (65) "Christ shewing a Little Child as the Emblem of Heaven"

LISTED: *PC*, p. 566 ("Christ shewing a little child as the Emblem of Heaven," West, Gallery); *UM*, p. 530; Barlow, p. 435; *BA*, p. 18; Galt, p. 229; Dillenberger, p. 174 (359)

Although a second apparently autograph small version in oil of this composition is known (No. 327), because of discrepancies in measurements it cannot be equated with the "first study" in the Robins sale of 22–25 May 1829. No. 326, which is signed and dated *1790*, seems, therefore, to have been the "finished sketch" of the subject exhibited by West in 1792, and, since we know that it remained in his possession, to have been the version of the subject which he exhibited at the British Institution in 1806. No. 327, which belonged to Thomas Macklin, was evidently painted in 1794 to serve as the model for John Hall's engraving published in 1795, the large size of No. 325 necessitating a reduced version for that purpose.

No. 326 is in deteriorated condition, with extensive losses of areas of original paint. It appears to have been painted originally in monochrome and subsequently to have been painted over in colors, probably by West himself.

327

327 Christ Showing a Little Child as the Emblem of Heaven 1794

DR. ROBERT ERWIN JONES

Oil on canvas: 22 × 18 in. (56 × 45.5 cm.)

Signed lower right: *B. West/1794*

PROV: Thomas Macklin; sold anonymously, Peter Coxe, Burrell & Foster, London, 12–13 May 1803, second day, lot 30 ("The children presented to the Saviour in the Temple," a sketch from which the plate for Macklin's *Bible* was engraved); sold anonymously, Christie's, London, 6 April 1973, lot 130

ENGR: Engraving ($12 \times 9\frac{7}{8}$ in.) by J. Hall, as under No. 325

See No. 326.

328 Christ Showing a Little Child as the Emblem of Heaven 1810

TRAFALGAR GALLERIES, LONDON

Oil on canvas: $89\frac{1}{2} \times 70\frac{1}{2}$ in. (227.5 × 179 cm.)

Signed lower left: *B. West/1810*

PROV: Purchased by Richard Hart Davis, MP, Bristol, in June 1810 for 1,000 guineas; Philip John Miles, Leigh Court, near Bristol; John Wanamaker; Bishop Hoban, Cleveland; Schweitzer Gallery, New York; sold, Christie's, New York, 11 Jan 1979, lot 64

EXH: RA 1810 (92) "Christ teacheth to be humble":

> And Jesus called a little child unto him, and set him by him, and said, verily I say unto you, except ye be converted, and become as little children, ye shall not enter into the kingdom of Heaven. Whosoever therefore shall humble himself as this little child, the same is the greatest in the kingdom of Heaven. And whoso shall receive one such little child in my name, receiveth me.
>
> *Matthew, chap. xviii, verses 2, 3, 4, and 5*

ENGR: Uninscribed line engraving ($11\frac{13}{16} \times 16$ in.); etching ($5\frac{9}{16} \times 4\frac{1}{2}$ in.) by John Young, pub. in *A Catalogue of the Pictures at Leigh Court, near Bristol; the seat of Philip John Miles, Esq., MP*, London, 1822

LIT: Farington Diary, 3, 6, and 7 April and 26 and 27 June 1810 (Farington 1978–, x, pp. 3625–28 and

3675–76); John Young, *A Catalogue of the Pictures at Leigh Court, near Bristol; the seat of Philip John Miles, Esq., MP, with etchings from the whole collection*, London, 1822, p. 23 (50).

There are several references in Farington's diary to No. 328, West's third and last major composition devoted to the subject of Christ showing a small child. On 3 April 1810, Thomas Lawrence told Farington that West had begun it since 15 March and that, although the figures were larger than life, it was already completed and was one of the best pictures West had ever executed. Three days later, on 6 April, Farington and Richard Westall called on West and saw the work, "this day finished." They agreed it was West's best picture, and Farington recorded West's explanation of the speed with which he executed it:

> He said He had begun and completed it in 20 days, but His design was before settled and drawn in upon another canvas which took him 4 or 5 days, so that upon this picture He had only to endeavour to paint it as well as He could.

On 7 April, Farington added that West had sent to Sir George Beaumont and Mr. Knight[1] to see the picture. Neither had been much struck with it, but in June, after No. 328 had appeared at the Royal Academy, West told Farington that Hart Davis from Bristol, who was forming a collection of pictures by the best modern artists, had called on him and offered him 1,000 guineas for the picture. "West was struck with His generosity, & accepted His offer, expressing that it was a sum above any price He should have mentioned." Farington had evidently never heard of West's new patron, as on the next day he added the further information that he had learned that Davis had been "a very fortunate Commercial speculator." West, on the other hand, had had previous contact with Davis in May 1809, when he sold him a painting ascribed to Titian from his own collection (see No. 521).

The sum of 1,000 guineas, which West told Farington and which is recorded also in the catalogue of the Miles collection, was indeed a remarkably high price for a work that is not particularly large. In 1804 West testified that he had received 800 guineas for the much larger and more complex *Alexander III of Scotland Saved from the Fury of a Stag* and had thought himself very handsomely paid (see No. 54). For pictures such as No. 245 for the chapel at Windsor measuring approximately 72 × 100 in. (i.e., larger than No. 328) West had charged George III 500 guineas, and he had asked 1,000 guineas for works that are much larger yet, such as Nos. 252 or 316, measuring 148 × 115 in. However, the price for No. 328 was soon to be surpassed by the 3,000 guineas which West received the following year from the directors of the British Institution for the large *Christ Healing the Sick* (No. 336).

The preliminary canvas mentioned by West to Farington was probably No. 329 below. A squared drawing of the composition, with some slight differences in details, is in the Historical Society of Pennsylvania.[2] A somewhat sketchier drawing showing Christ in a position similar to that in the earlier No. 323, but with a girl holding the child on the right was at one time in the collection of Herbert Margary.[3]

[1] Probably Richard Payne Knight, although another Knight, John Knight of Portland Place, collected works by West.
[2] Pen and ink, $7\frac{11}{16} \times 6\frac{1}{8}$ in., signed *B. West/1810*.
[3] Present location unknown. Although most of the works formerly owned by Herbert Margary were sold by Mrs. Howard, Sotheby's, London, 22 March 1979, this drawing does not seem to have been among them.

329 Christ Showing a Little Child as the Emblem of Heaven *c.* 1810

LOCATION UNKNOWN

328

Oil on canvas: *c.* $89\frac{1}{2} \times 70\frac{1}{2}$ in. (227.5 × 179 cm.)

PROV: Sold by West's sons, Robins, London, 20–22 June 1829, lot 85 ("Christ shewing a little child as the Emblem of Heaven, a sketch on canvas, . . . same size as the picture painted for Hart Davis, Esq.")

LIT: Farington Diary, 6 April 1810 (Farington, 1978—, x, pp. 3626–27)

See No. 328.

330 Christ Blessing Little Children 1781

ROYAL ACADEMY OF ARTS, LONDON

Oil on canvas: $44\frac{1}{2} \times 83\frac{1}{4}$ in. (113 × 211.5 cm.)

PROV: In the possession of the Royal Academy by 1782

EXH: Included in the catalogues of Royal Academy exhibitions, beginning in 1811, along with diploma pictures in the Council Room (as "Christ blessing little children, Matthew chap 22, v. 21"); BI 1844 (135); BI 1854 (161); Manchester 1857 (103); *International Exhibition*, Philadelphia, 1876 (185); London 1963 (10)

ENGR: Mezzotint ($24\frac{13}{16} \times 32\frac{1}{8}$ in.) by Valentine Green, pub. 1 May 1782 by Green, inscribed *Painted by B. West . . . 1781 . . . engraved from the original Picture in the Possession of the Royal Academy*, and dedicated to the Queen

LISTED: Dillenberger, p. 211

LIT: Dillenberger 1977, pp. 20–21, pl. 10

Although No. 330 shows a subject related to the theme of Christ showing a little child, of which West painted several versions (Nos. 323–29), it is in fact a different subject, showing Christ holding one child on his lap and laying His hand on the head of another, rather than pointing to Heaven as in No. 323, etc. No. 330

330

has always been known as *Christ Blessing Little Children*. In the Royal Academy catalogues from 1811 on, the entries included a reference to Matthew 22:21, but that verse, although memorable ("Render therefore unto Caesar . . ."), clearly has little to do with what is shown in No. 330. Descriptions of children being brought to Christ may be found in Matthew 19:13–15, Mark 10:13–16, and Luke 18:15–17. The words "of such is the kingdom of Heaven," from Matthew 19:14 were used by West as the title for the sketch of *Christ Showing a Little Child* exhibited in 1792 (see No. 326) but that sketch and the other works related to it more directly illustrate Matthew 18:2–6, which West quoted in the Academy catalogues of 1800 and 1810.

The catalogue of the *Treasures of the Royal Academy* exhibition of 1963 states that it is not clear how this painting came to the Academy. It has been claimed that it was a diploma picture, which new members of the Academy are required to present to the Institution, but that is not the case. Founding members of the Academy such as West were not required to present diploma pictures. The inscriptions on the Green mezzotint, indicating that West painted the picture in 1781 and that it belonged to the Academy by the following May, when the print was published, suggest that West painted No. 330 to present to the Academy following its move to new quarters in Somerset House in 1780. It appears over the fireplace of the Assembly Room (or Council Room) in the *Royal Academicians in General Assembly* of 1795 by Henry Singleton (ill. p. 113), which includes at least one other work, Reynolds's *Self-Portrait*, presented by a founding member to the Academy on the occasion of the move.[1]

A drawing for the composition of No. 330 was with the Leger Galleries, London, in 1976.[2] What may have been a sketch or second version is No. 331 below. A "Christ blessing little children" listed in *La Belle Assemblée* as painted for the Duke of Rutland is probably

a mistake for the *Hannah Presenting Samuel to Eli* painted by West for the Duke of Rutland (see No. 271).

[1]See Sidney C. Hutchison, *The History of the Royal Academy 1768–1968*, London, 1968, pp. 65–66.
[2]Pencil and chalk on blue paper, $5\frac{3}{8} \times 8\frac{7}{8}$ in.

331 **Christ Blessing Little Children**

LOCATION UNKNOWN

PROV: Sold by West's sons, Robins, London, 20–22 June 1829, lot 58 ("The Parting of Hector and Christ Blessing Little Children")

332 **Christ Blessing** *c.* 1777

ST. PANCRAS PARISH CHURCH, LONDON

Oil on canvas: $77\frac{1}{2} \times 29$ in. (197 × 73.5 cm.)

PROV: Fitzroy Chapel, Fitzroy Square, London, until World War II (the chapel was destroyed in 1945); since then in the church hall of St. Pancras Parish Church

LIT: Mason 1879, p. 277; London County Council, *Survey of London, XXI: Tottenham Court Road and Neighbourhood: The Parish of St. Pancras Part III*, London, 1949, p. 48; Dillenberger 1977, p. 86

See the entry for *Moses Receiving the Laws* (No. 260), a companion picture which was also formerly in Fitzroy Chapel. Both pictures were evidently painted by Gilbert Stuart on the basis of designs by West.

A smaller version is No. 333. A related drawing is at Swarthmore.[1] Additional versions in oil of Nos. 260 and 332, which may have been copies, were formerly in St. Margaret's, Westminster.[2]

[1]Black crayon, $17\frac{1}{2} \times 6$ in.
[2]Oil on canvas, each 38 × 15 in. See the entry for No. 260.

332

333 Christ Blessing *c.* 1774–76

LOCATION UNKNOWN

Oil on panel: 20¼ × 7⅛ in. (51.5 × 18 cm.)

PROV: Mrs. E. K. Rule, London

See No. 261.

334 Christ Healing the Sick *c.* 1780–81

LOCATION UNKNOWN (POSSIBLY DESTROYED)

(150 × 120 in.) (381 × 305 cm.)

PROV: Painted for George III (1797 account: "The picture of our saviour receiving the sick and lame, etc., to be healed," for his Majesty's Chapel in Windsor Castle, 12 ft. 7 in. × 9 ft. 2 in., 1780, £1,050; 1801 account, p. 212: for the Windsor Chapel, The Prophets, 27, "Christ healeth the Sick and Blind, &c. in the Temple," £1,050; never delivered and ownership returned to West's sons by George IV in 1828; sold by them, Robins, London, 22–25 May 1829, lot 55 ("Christ Healing the Infirm in the Temple," 12 ft. 6 in. × 10 ft.), bt. by Hicks (or Hick) for £110.5.0.; (?) the church of St. Etheldreda, Fulham, where it was badly damaged during World War II and subsequently destroyed

EXH: RA 1781 (80) "An Historical picture, representing the sick, possessed, &c., brought to our Saviour to be healed, painted for his Majesty's chapel in Windsor—castle"; West's Gallery 1821 (31), 1822–28 (45), in both as "Christ Healing the Infirm in the Temple"

> St. Matthew, chap. 4, Verse 23. And Jesus went about all Galilee, teaching in their synagogues, and preaching the gospel of the kingdom, and healing all manner of sickness, and all manner of disease among the people.
> Verse 24. And his fame went throughout all Syria: and they brought unto him all sick people that were taken with divers diseases, and torments, and those which were possessed with devils, and those which were lunatic, and those which had the palsy; and he healed them.

ENGR: Stipple engraving (22 7⁄16 × 17⅛ in.) by Benjamin Smith, pub. 1 July 1813, by Boydell & Co

LISTED: *PC*, p. 561 ("Christ healing the Sick in the Temple," George III, for his Majesty's Chapel, Windsor, Gospel Dispensation, 10 ft. × 14); *UM*, p. 527; *AA*, p. 67 (9 ft. × 14); Barlow, p. 432 (15 ft. × 10); *BA*, p. 14; Galt, p. 219; Dillenberger, p. 147 (101)

LIT: V and A Cuttings, I, p. 202 (*Morning Herald*, 1781); Meyer 1975, p. 265; Dillenberger 1977, pp. 71 and 74; Goodison 1977, pp. 278–79

No. 334 was the first picture West painted for the Royal Chapel in Windsor Castle and the first to be exhibited. In the architectural drawings of *c.* 1780 (ill. p. 577), the subject appears second from the left in the main sequence of New Testament subjects, following the *Baptism* (No. 316) and preceding the *Ascension* (No. 380). It is in the equivalent position in the Swarthmore diagrams of 1801 (p. 580) and it is perhaps worth noting that it is the only subject from Christ's ministry between the Baptism and the Last Supper (see No. 344) which West painted for the Windsor chapel. Two further subjects, "Christ's Temptation and Victory in the Wilderness" and "Christ beginneth to preach at Nazareth," each described as a sketch, are included in his account of his work on the chapel submitted to George III in 1801, but he did not complete paintings of either subject.[1]

A letter in the Tate Gallery files indicates that a large painting of the subject, which two representatives of the National Gallery identified as West's painting for Windsor, was given to the church of St. Etheldreda in Fulham before the Second World War. Having been hopelessly damaged during the war, it was subsequently destroyed.[2] The composition is known from the engraving by Benjamin Smith and from the oil sketch (*below*). No. 334 itself is recognizable, hanging next to *Christ Rejected* (No. 353), in the Cattermole/Le Keux engraving of West's gallery in Newman Street in 1821 (ill. p. 150).

A drawing either for or after the foreground group of a kneeling mother with two children was sold in New York in 1928.[3] This may be the "Study of a Group in the picture Christ healing the Sick, which was painted by command of His Majesty George the Third, for his intended Chapel in Windsor Castle," which was sold in 1839.[4] See also the drawings discussed in the entry for *Christ Raising the Widow's Son* (No. 343).

Paintings of *Christ Healing the Sick* and *Christ Expelling the Money Lenders* formerly in the collectin of the Earl of Darnley,[5] and acquired by the City Art Museum of St. Louis in 1957 as works by West, are not by him; they are now ascribed by the museum to a French artist, Nicolas Colombel. A picture of the related subject of *Christ Healing the Blind Man* in the parish church of St. Mary Magdalene, Sternfield, Suffolk, which has traditionally been thought to be by West, and which was purportedly given to the church by Charles Long (Lord Farnborough), appears to be the work of a younger, nineteenth-century artist.[6] For West's later treatments of the subject, see Nos. 336–38 below.

[1] See No. 316.
[2] Letter from Judith G. Scott, Acting Secretary of the Central

Christ Healing the Sick, stipple engraving by Benjamin Smith after No. 334

Council for the Care of Churches, to the Director of the Tate Gallery, 19 Dec. 1956.

3 A. C. Goodyear Collection, Anderson Galleries, New York, 16 Feb. 1928, lot 131 ($6\frac{1}{2} \times 9\frac{1}{2}$ in.).

4 S. Leigh Sotheby, 1 June 1839, lot 12 ("... Sketch in pen and oil colour").

5 Christie's, London, 1 May 1925, lots 90 and 91.

6 Nikolaus Pevsner, *The Buildings of England: Suffolk*, London and Beccles, 1961, p. 437, and W. Fayle-Parr, *The Parish Church of St. Mary Magdalene, Sternfield*, 1961.

335 **Christ Healing the Sick** *c.* 1780–81

FITZWILLIAM MUSEUM, CAMBRIDGE, ENGLAND

Oil on canvas: $35\frac{3}{8} \times 27\frac{1}{2}$ in. (90 × 70 cm.)

PROV: Offered by West's sons to the United States in 1826 (147, 2 ft. 4 in. × 3 ft., included among "Original Designs in Chiaro Scuro for the large Pictures which were painted for his late Majesty's Chapel in Windsor Castle"), and sold by them, Robins, London, 22–25 May 1829, lot 128 (3 ft. × 2 ft. 4 in.), bt. by Wood for £49.7.0; given by Charles Fairfax Murray to the Fitzwilliam Museum in 1908

EXH: 125 Pall Mall 1814, either (2) "Christ Healing the Infirm" or (8) "Christ Receiving the Lame and Blind to Heal Them"; (?) Pall Mall 1816 (10) "Christ Healing in the Temple, St. Matthew chap. iv., verses 23–24"

LISTED: (?) PC, p. 566 ("Christ healing the Sick, Lame, and Blind in the Temple," West, Gallery); (?) *UM*, p. 530; (?) Barlow, p. 434; (?) *BA*, p. 17; (?) Galt, p. 228; Dillenberger, pp. 173 (341) (?) and 211

LIT: Meyer 1975, p. 265; Dillenberger 1977, p. 74, pl. 51; Goodison 1977, pp. 278–79

335

No. 335, which is a study for No. 334, is one of several monochromatic oil sketches for the Windsor chapel which were sold together as a group in 1829. Since West composed two major but distinct compositions devoted to the subject of Christ healing the sick (Nos. 334 and 336) and retained oil sketches of both until his death, it is not possible to differentiate the references to the sketches in early lists and catalogues of his works, where measurements or further descriptions are not given.

336 **Christ Healing the Sick** 1811

TATE GALLERY, LONDON

Oil on canvas: 108 × 168 in. (274 × 427 cm.)

PROV: Painted by West to present to the Pennsylvania Hospital, in Philadelphia, but purchased by the directors of the British Institution in 1811 for 3,000 guineas; presented by the British Institution to the National Gallery in 1826; badly damaged in the Tate Gallery flood of 1928

EXH: BI 1811 (special exhibition of No. 336); BI 1812 (214) "Our Saviour healing the sick in the Temple," 11 ft. 6 in. × 16 ft. 3 in. (including frame),

> And the blind and the lame came to him in the Temple, and he healed them.
> And when the Chief Priests and Scribes saw the wonderful things that he did, and the children crying in the Temple, and saying, Hosanna to the son of David; they were sore displeased.
> *St. Matthew, chap. xxi, verse 14–15*

BI 1821 (115); BI 1824 (171)

ENGR: Engraving ($18\frac{7}{16} \times 28\frac{3}{8}$ in.) by Charles Heath, pub. 15 May 1822 by G. & W. Nicol; outline engraving ($4\frac{3}{16} \times 5$ in.) by Normand *fils*, pub. in Hamilton 1831 (226)

LISTED: (See discussion below.) PC, p. 563 ("Christ receiving the Sick and Lame in the Temple, in the Pennsylvania Hospital, Philadelphia," 11 ft. × 18); *UM*, p. 529; Barlow, p. 433; *BA*, p. 15; Galt, p. 222; Dillenberger, p. 159 (206) and 214

LIT: Farington Diary, 15, 18, 23, and 29 March, 8 April, 23 May, 15 July, and 21 Nov. 1811, 8 July 1812, 6 July 1813, and 1 July 1816 (Farington 1978—, XI, pp. 3893, 3895, 3898, 3902, 3908, 3936, 3970, 4035, XII, pp. 4156, 4387, and XIV, p. 4864); Z. [Ange Denis Macquin], *Description of the Picture, Christ Healing the Sick in the Temple, painted by Benjamin West, Esq. . . . and now in the British Gallery, Pall Mall. From the Phoenix Sunday and Monday Newspaper . . .*, London, 1811; M. Heurtault, *Description du tableau de Mr. W. representant Jésus guérisant l'aveugle et le boiteux dans le temple. Fragment d'un discours sur l'état présent des beaux-arts en Angleterre*, London, 1811, with text printed in French and English; V and A Cuttings, III, pp. 835, 839–40 (1811), 864 (1821), and 865 (1813); [William Richard Hamilton], *Memorandum on the Subject of the Earl of Elgin's Pursuits in Greece*, 2nd. ed., London, 1815, p. 53; *Report from the Select Committee of the House of Commons on the Earl of Elgin's Collection of Sculptured Marbles, etc.*, London, 1816, p. 152; Galt 1820, pp. 185–87; Carey 1820, p. 697; John Thomas Smith, *Nollekens and His Times*, 2nd. ed., London, 1829, II, pp. 395–97; Hamilton 1831 (226); Dunlap 1834, II, p. 124 (Dunlap 1918, II, p. 262); Tom Taylor, ed., *Life of Benjamin Robert Haydon, Historical Painter*, London, 1853, I, pp. 170 and 185; Morton and Woodbury 1895, pp. 305–9; Hart 1908, pp. 17, 26–27; "Famous Early-19th Century Painting Restored," *Pennsylvania Hospital Bulletin*, VIII, no. 4, Winter 1950–51; Evans 1959, pp. 5, 87, 93–94; Haydon 1960–63, I, pp. 230, 419,

Christ Healing the Sick, engraving by Charles Heath after No. 336

463, II, p. 519; Constable 1962–68, I, pp. 62–63; Irwin 1968, pp. 74–75; Kraemer 1975, p. 52; Dillenberger 1977, pp. 115–16; Alberts 1979, pp. 348, 352–53; Evans 1980, p. 151

On 1 September 1800, the president and secretary of the Pennsylvania Hospital in Philadelphia wrote to West describing the purpose of their hospital and soliciting the gift of a painting for its nearly finished building. West replied on 8 July 1801 with the promise of a painting 10 × 16 ft., including frame, which would illustrate Matthew 21:14–15 and for which he had already made a design.[1] Prior to writing in July, West had in May 1801 exhibited a drawing in oil color of the subject at the Royal Academy, which he described in the catalogue as "for a large picture to be painted after, for the Pennsylvania hospital . . .," and it appears from the inscription on No. 337, which is presumably the work exhibited in 1801, that he had begun it as early as 1794, long before being approached by the hospital. He did not complete the promised picture for a decade, and although it is described as "in the Pennsylvania Hospital," in the early published lists of West's works, which began to appear in 1804, it never reached the hospital. Instead, as soon as it was completed it was purchased by the British Institution, and West promised the hospital that he would paint a second improved version of the subject for it. That second version, which he completed in 1815, is No. 338 below.

When the young American painter Thomas Sully arrived in London in July 1809 he found West at work on No. 336. However, in a letter dated 5 September 1810 West indicated that the painting would not be ready to be shipped to America before the following spring.[2] On 4 March 1811, James Rush, the son of Benjamin Rush, reported to his father from London that it was finished: "I myself saw the last touch of the brush upon it, a few days ago."[3] At that time West had evidently already been approached by the British Institution, for which Rush believed West would paint a copy of No. 336 before sending the original off to Philadelphia. West did the opposite, selling No. 336 to the British Institution, and painting the copy for Philadelphia. On 15 March Joseph Farington called on West to see the recently finished work:

> I found Sir Thos. Bernard there who has been very active in forwarding the subscription set on foot by Patrons of the British Institution to raise £3000 by subscription of £50 from each Subscriber for the purpose of giving that sum to Mr. West for this picture to be considered as a commencement of a national gallery.

On 18 March Farington recorded that Bernard had told Robert Smirke two days before that it had been purchased. West retained No. 336 in his studio for a short time to make an outline copy, which was to be the basis of No. 338, and it was placed on exhibition at the British Institution on 15 April 1811. West subsequently presented each of the subscribers with a medal which bore on the obverse a profile portrait of himself, based on a bust by Sir Francis Chantrey, and on the reverse the names of forty subscribers headed by that of the Prince Regent. The medals were dated 1815 and were in bronze except for that of the Prince which was in gold.[4]

The price of 3,000 guineas which West received for No. 336 was by far the highest price he received for any single work, and it was generally believed to be the highest price ever paid to a modern artist.[5] Since West had been one of the chief movers in the foundation of the British Institution in 1805 and one of its strongest supporters, and since he also had close personal ties with several of the Institution's directors, the purchase seems (and seemed to some at the time) possibly to have been made for reasons other than the quality of the picture itself,[6] but the Institution fulfilled the intention recorded by Farington, by presenting No. 336 to the newly created National Gallery in 1826, and, on other grounds as well, the purchase seems to have been a success. Because of the special circumstances under which No. 336 was acquired and exhibited, particularly the much publicized price, it received a considerable amount of attention. Four years later, Benjamin Robert Haydon wrote that its reputation had been such, "for the time that the usual address about the weather was forgotten, and 'have you seen the picture?' became its substitute." On 15 July 1811, three months after the exhibition of No. 336 had opened, West told Farington attendance at the British Institution had been so heavy that the Institution, after paying him his 3,000 guineas and all other expenses, would still make a £2,000 profit on the picture, which "happily proved that he had not overcharged the *King*" by asking "only £1500" for the design for the never-realized *Crucifixion* window for St.

George's Chapel (see No. 356).[7] A year later, on 8 July 1812, Farington recorded that the British Institution had received a total of over £9,300 from subscriptions toward paying for No. 336, from money received at the door of the exhibition room, and from subscriptions for the print to be made after the picture.

The published critical response seems to have been uniformly laudatory. On 23 May 1811, Farington reported after dining with a group of artists at Sir Thomas Lawrence's that "the exaggerated praise of it which is so much kept up in the newspapers was thought disgusting." Lawrence defended the picture, while Fuseli declared "he would not have been the painter of it for double the three thousand guineas given for it." Among the other recorded opinions of the picture are those of John Constable's mother, who went to see it on 28 April 1811 and decided that she saw no reason that her own son, "should not in due time, with diligence & attention, be the performer of a picture worth £3000." Haydon described it in his diary as "hard, red & mean, well-composed in some [parts]. Nothing can be more despicable than the forms. How the people have been duped. Upon the whole it is one of his best." But Haydon, who had decidedly mixed feelings about West, wrote to the *Examiner* to defend the British Institution's purchase of the picture, and indeed the purchase was probably a major factor behind Haydon's commencing to paint analogous large-scale religious pictures in the following year.[8]

West and Haydon had both drawn or painted from the Elgin Marbles in 1808 (see Nos. 498–503). West subsequently wrote two letters of appreciation to the Earl of Elgin, which were published in 1811 in William Richard Hamilton's *Memorandum on the Subject of the Earl of Elgin's Pursuits in Greece*. In the second of the two letters, dated 20 March 1811, he invited Lord Elgin to come and see No. 336: "This picture I am the more desirous of showing to your Lordship, as I have conducted it on those dignified principles of refined art, which I found so superior in the Athenian sculpture, with which you have enriched your country." In 1816, in testimony submitted to the Select Committee appointed by the House of Commons to consider the purchase of the Marbles for the British Museum, West reiterated his assertion of their importance for No. 336 (or, more precisely, for No. 338, which was then on exhibition), as well as for the more recently painted *Christ Rejected* (No. 353). In what way these works were affected by the Parthenon sculptures is not very obvious, but in 1811, when writing about No. 336, West claimed, "it has been my ambition (though at a very advanced period of life) to introduce those refinements in art, which are so distinguished in your Collection," and he continued that if he had seen the Marbles earlier, "more character, and expression, and life, would have pervaded all my humble attempts in Historical Painting." Thus it appears that for West the Parthenon sculptures provided examples of a more naturalistic art than he had previously practiced. To Haydon, who had studied the Marbles before West and certainly knew them much more thoroughly, such claims were ludicrous. Although in his *Autobiography* he gave West credit for a "grandeur of soul" in recognizing the majesty of the Parthenon sculptures, he also asserted the priority of his own *Dentatus* over *Christ Healing the Sick* in embodying their principles,[9] and in marginal notes to his copy of Hamilton's *Memorandum*, next to West's assertions about conducting No. 336 on principles learnt from the Marbles, Haydon wrote: "Where? Shew us a hand, a head, a foot, a back, or a limb executed on those sublime dignified principles. Not only would it puzzle Mr. West himself to do it, but I suspect it would puzzle the Greek artists more than any of us, those who of course were the best acquainted with their own principles."[10]

The paralytic woman on the right side of Nos. 336

and 338 has been said to be a likeness of Mrs. West, who by 1811 was in declining health;[11] she died in 1814. A Philadelphia newspaper in 1821 declared that all the principal figures in the painting were portraits and identified the sick man in front as the blind brother of the artist James Barry.[12]

Although No. 336 does not repeat any details from West's earlier picture of *Christ Healing the Sick* for George III (see Nos. 334 and 335), it does show the same subject. It is in fact closer in composition than No. 335 to the sketch of the subject in the architectural drawings of *c*. 1780 for the chapel at Windsor, and is a development of that earlier composition, whereas in the Windsor composition West put distinctly different figures in the foreground at Christ's feet.[13] An intervening oil sketch is No. 337 below. A drawing for two women carrying baskets on their heads in the background is in the Pierpont Morgan Library.[14]

A copy, which corresponds closely in all details to the Heath engraving of No. 336, is in the William Penn Memorial Museum in Harrisburg, Pennsylvania.[15] A copy of the group of figures supporting a sick man, from the foreground of No. 336, is in the Victoria and Albert Museum in London.[16]

No. 336 is visible in the background of Thomas Lawrence's portrait of West exhibited at the Royal Academy in 1811 and now in the Yale Center for British Art. Figures from either No. 336 or No. 338 also are in the background of a portrait of West by George Watson (1767–1837) in the National Gallery of Scotland. This picture, which appeared at the Royal Academy in 1816, was probably painted in 1815, when Watson visited London,[17] so No. 338, which West completed in 1815, evidently served as the model.

See also pp. 142–7 above.

[1] This correspondence from the archives of the Pennsylvania Hospital is published in the hospital's *Bulletin* for 1950–51.
[2] To Robert Barclay, pub. in Hart 1908, pp. 26–27.
[3] Library Company of Philadelphia. We are indebted to Bruce Laverty of the Historical Society of Pennsylvania for a transcript of this letter.
[4] Details about the medal including the names on the reverse are provided by J. T. Smith.
[5] See Smith, ibid. According to Gerald Reitlinger (*The Economics of Taste: The Rise and Fall of Picture Prices 1760–1960*, London, 1961, p. 70) the price was only surpassed by the 100,000 francs (approximate £4,000) paid by Napoleon to Jacques-Louis David for the *Coronation of Napoleon* now in the Louvre.
[6] Benjamin Robert Haydon recorded an aspersion supposedly made by envious members of the Royal Academy: "Mr. West was an old man, and it was *merely* a reward for his life," *Examiner*, 2 Feb. 1812, p. 76.
[7] According to rather confused entries in West's account of 1801 prepared for George III, he had asked the King for 1,000 guineas for the design and another 1,000 for the cartoon, for a total of 2,000 guineas, rather than £1,500. The highest price he charged George III for any single painting was £1,365 (or 1,300 guineas), which he asked for each of the three largest paintings for the Audience Chamber in Windsor Castle (Nos. 58, 67, and 74).
[8] For Haydon's letter to the *Examiner* see note 6 above. His own works in a similar vein are the *Judgment of Solomon* (130 × 154 in.), begun in 1812, and *Christ's Entry into Jerusalem* (192 × 228 in.) begun in 1814. Both are reproduced in Eric George, *The Life and Death of Benjamin Robert Haydon*, 2nd ed., Oxford, 1967, pls. 17 and 6.
[9] *Autobiography* (2nd ed.), I, pp. 94 and 170.
[10] Haydon 1960–63, III, p. 519, with more of the same.
[11] Hart 1908, p. 17.
[12] *Relf's Philadelphia Gazette and Daily Advertiser*, 1 Aug. 1821, p. 2. On the other hand, John Robinson in the pamphlet about No. 338 published in 1818 denied that there were any direct portraits in the pictures. Barry's brother was named Redmond Barry. He did not go blind until *c*. 1814 after West painted No. 336. A lithographic likeness reproduced on a broadside soliciting charitable donations on his behalf after he was blinded shows remarkable similarities to the figure in No. 336 and suggests that he was indeed the model

for this figure. We are indebted to William Pressly for a copy of the broadside and for much further information about Redmond.
[13] This was pointed out by Mrs. Dorothy Kemper in correspondence with Helmut von Erffa in 1974 about No. 337.
[14] Black chalk on grey-brown paper: 6⅝ × 9⅝ in. (Kraemer 1975, p. 52, no. 92).
[15] Oil on canvas: 36 × 56 in.; acquired by the museum in 1970.
[16] Oil on canvas: 9½ × 11½ in., Forster Bequest. Although catalogued by the museum as a sketch by West, the close correspondence in detail with the Heath engraving after No. 336 and the absence of West's usually recognizable handling suggest that it is a copy.
[17] *National Gallery of Scotland: Catalogue of Paintings and Sculpture*, Edinburgh, 1957, p. 290.

337 Christ Healing the Sick (?)1794–1801

M. H. DE YOUNG MEMORIAL MUSEUM, SAN FRANCISCO

Oil on paper mounted on canvas: 29¼ × 46 5/16 in. (74.5 × 117.5 cm.)

Inscribed lower left, on the step below Christ's feet: *B. West [?] 1794. Retouched 1795 & 1801*

PROV: Offered by West's sons to the United States in 1826 (38), and sold by them, Robins, London, 22–25 May 1829, lot 44 (2 ft. 5 in. × 3 ft. 10 in., and identified as the original design for No. 336), bt. by H. P. Bone, on behalf of Joseph Neeld, MP, Grittleton House, Wilts.; by descent in the Neeld family until sold, Christie's, London, 13 July 1945, lot 165; Appleby Brothers, London, 1957; given by David Pleydell-Bouverie to the De Young Museum in 1960

EXH: RA 1801 (307) "Christ healing the sick, a drawing in oil colour for a large-picture to be painted after, for the Pennsylvania hospital, in the city of Philadelphia" (with quotation from Matthew 21:14 and 15); 125 Pall Mall 1814, either (2) "Christ Healing the Infirm" or (8) "Christ Receiving the Lame and Blind to Heal Them" (see No. 335); (?)125 Pall Mall 1816 (10) "Christ Healing in the Temple, St. Matthew chap. iv., verses 23–24"; West's Gallery 1821 (45) "Christ healing the Sick and the Lame in the Temple a sketch of the large Picture in the possession of the Directors of the British Institution"; West's Gallery 1822–28 (90); BI 1833 (20) lent by Joseph Neeld; *The Hand and the Spirit; Religious Art in America 1700–1900*, University Art Museum, Berkeley, California, etc., 1972–73

ENGR: Outline engraving (4¾ × 7¼ in.) by Edwards, pub. 1 Aug. 1807 by John Bell.

LISTED: See No. 335

No. 337 is an early study for No. 336, though differing from it in numerous details. The backgrounds are different, and there are many additional figures in the larger work, but the position of Christ, the main figure groups on either side of him, and the paralytic woman on the right side of the composition are essentially the same. The composition is derived from that in the sketch of the subject in the architectural drawings of *c*. 1780 for the chapel at Windsor (ill. p. 577), transformed into a horizontal composition by the addition of the group around the paralytic woman on the right.

The inscription on No. 337 is faint and extremely difficult to read. In the catalogue of the Neeld sale in 1945, the painting was described as signed and dated *1796*, but to both authors of the present catalogue, a reading of *1794. Retouched 1795 & 1801* has seemed more convincing. In either case, the inscription indicates that West began No. 337 long before the Pennsylvania Hospital approached him in 1800 with the invitation that led to his painting Nos. 336 and 338, but the date of *1801* for the second retouching of No. 337 accords with the date of West's acceptance of the invitation and his exhibition of a sketch of the subject at the Royal Academy. The fact that West repainted No. 337 at least twice accounts for the conspicuous *pentimenti* and other signs of repainting.

An outline engraving of this composition published by John Bell in 1807 is comparable in technique and size to engravings after the *Death of General Wolfe* and *Death on the Pale Horse* (Nos. 93 and 403), both of which were published by Bell in *La Belle Assemblée* in 1808; so the print after No. 337 may have been intended for that publication as well.

338 Christ Healing the Sick 1815
See color illustration, p. 144

PENNSYLVANIA HOSPITAL, PHILADELPHIA

Oil on canvas: 120 × 180 in. (305 × 457 cm.)

Signed bottom center: *Benj. West/1815*

PROV: Presented by West to the Pennsylvania Hospital in 1817; on loan to the Pennsylvania Academy 1847–53, and 1982–83

EXH: 125 Pall Mall 1815 and 1816; PAFA 1847–53; *Centennial Exhibition*, Memorial Hall, Philadelphia, 1876

ENGR: Outline keys pub. in the pamphlets by Macquin and Robinson listed below

LISTED: Galt, p. 234 ("The second picture of Christ healing the Sick"); Dillenberger, pp. 189 (513) and 214.

LIT: Farington Diary, 23 March 1811 and 23 July 1814

(Farington 1978–, XI, p. 3898 and XIII, p. 4564); V and A Cuttings, IV, pp. 904 (1815) and 1034 (1816); [Ange Denis Macquin], *Description of the Picture Christ Healing the Sick in the Temple Painted by Benjamin West, Esq., . . . and Presented by the Author to the Pennsylvania Hospital*, Philadelphia, 1817; John Robinson, *A Description of and Critical Remarks on The Picture of Christ Healing the Sick in the Temple: Painted by Benjamin West, Esq. . . . And Presented by Him to the Pennsylvania Hospital*, Philadelphia, 1818 (and later editions); Galt 1820, pp. 186–87; Morton and Woodbury, 1895, II, pp. 305–21; Sartain 1899, pp. 176–77; Hart 1908, pp. 17, 29–33; Edward Biddle and Mantle Fielding, *The Life and Works of Thomas Sully*, Philadelphia, 1921, p. 347, nos. 2199 and 2200; "Famous Early-19th Century Painting Restored," *Pennsylvania Hospital Bulletin*, VIII, no. 4, Winter 1950–51; Evans 1959, pl. 4; Dillenberger 1977, pp. 115–17; Alberts 1979, pp. 348, 352, 378

See No. 336, which West painted with the intention of presenting to the Pennsylvania Hospital. When that picture was completed in 1811, ten years after West had promised it to the hospital, West sold it to the British Institution instead and promised a second, improved, version for the hospital in its place. The first inkling that something was afoot appears in a letter dated 4 March 1811, written by the son of Dr. Benjamin Rush, who states that the painting's arrival in America would be delayed until the fall of 1811, while West made a copy for the British Institution.[1] Either the younger Rush was misinformed or West changed his plans during the following two weeks, as entries in Farington's

diary from 15 and 18 March 1811 indicate that by then West had sold the original version (No. 336) to the British Institution. On 23 March Farington recorded that West told him "on Wednesday the 27*th* inst. He shd. shut himself up in order to make an outline from it for a Picture which he shd. present to the Hospital at Philadelphia." After the exhibition of No. 336 opened in April 1811 at the British Institution, West wrote to Samuel Coates, the secretary of the hospital, to tell him that he had sold the promised picture, "but with a reserve on my part to make another for the Hospital, which I have commenced on a more improved plan of composition, and in the course of the ensuing summer shall complete it. I hope with equal, or more power, as it is my wish to do so."[2]

West did not finish No. 338 in the summer of 1811, and apparently did not start seriously to work on it for three more years. On 17 March 1814, he wrote to Joseph Wharton in Philadelphia that, having now finished the large *Christ Rejected* (No. 353), "I shall next finish my picture for the Hospital—that it may be ready for going to Philadelphia by the first conveyance which offers for that city."[3] Farington saw the painting in West's painting-room on 23 July 1814, but West did not complete it for almost another year. An announcement appeared in the press on 30 June 1815 stating that it was now finished and would be placed together with *Christ Rejected* on exhibition at 125 Pall Mall. The two pictures remained on exhibition there into (and probably through) the following year, and it was only in the summer of 1817 that No. 338 was dispatched to America. On 2 March 1817, West wrote to the president of the hospital that he would detain No. 338

337

"for as short a Time as possible," while he completed two other pictures that he intended to present with it, in order to put them "into that perfect Union of Colour and Effect which ought to prevail." He evidently never completed these paintings, and No. 338 eventually went without them. On 5 August 1817, West wrote to the daughter of Joseph Wharton (who had died in the meantime) that the picture was about to be sent on the ship *Electra*: "what a real joy would this occurrence have afforded your venerable Father."[4] By 11 August the *Electra* had sailed, and West wrote to the Lords of the Treasury to thank them for allowing the painting to leave the country duty free.[5] According to John Sartain, the painter Joshua Shaw (1777–1860) escorted the picture on its voyage.

Following West's initial promise of a picture in 1801 the officials of the hospital consulted Gilbert Stuart and Charles Willson Peale about where to install it.[6] West, writing to Joseph Wharton in 1814, urged that a special room be erected for No. 338 and sent a plan of what he had in mind. A Philadelphian named Caleb Cresson, who called on West in February 1816, warned the hospital that West would not send the picture until a proper place was prepared for it, and West wrote in the following month,

> When the Room is so much advanced as to ascertain the Time of the Completion, and in a dry state to receive the Picture, I will have it ship'd for Philadelphia with its Frame in a safe and proper Manner—I wish it to be placed opposite the Entrance into the intended Room, midway of which on either side, there should be a low Fire place for warming the Room in Winter, and over which Fireplaces I will compliment each with a Picture.[7]

The pictures to be hung over the fireplaces were a portrait of the artist (No. 531) and a portrait of Benjamin Franklin (see No. 618). West had previously mentioned them to a group of visitors from Philadelphia who called on him in January 1816,[8] but, as we have seen, they did not accompany No. 338 to America. However, the hospital was soon given a pair of juvenile landscape and seascape paintings by West (Nos. 480 and 481), and these hung with the large picture instead. The hospital erected a special building for the painting and raised $1,710 from voluntary contributions to pay for it.[9] In writing to the president of the hospital on 2 March 1817, West reported receiving a letter from Thomas Sully "stating his opinion of how very appropriate the Room is." Once No. 338 was installed, the hospital made a substantial profit from the admissions charge paid by visitors coming to see the work, as West had predicted that it would. The painting remained in its original site until 1847, when it was placed on loan in the Pennsylvania Academy; the building was demolished in 1893. Two descriptive pamphlets about the picture were published for the hospital. The first, which appeared anonymously in 1817, was a slightly modified reprint of the pamphlet by Macquin which initially accompanied No. 336 at the British Institution in 1811. The second, dated 23 February 1818, was by a Philadelphia painter named John Robinson. Both pamphlets contained engraved keys to the painting; that in the second one was based on an outline sketch by Thomas Sully.

West began No. 338 by copying No. 336 and, although there are numerous changes in details, it follows the composition of the earlier painting closely, with only one significant departure. That departure is the addition of a group of four figures slightly to the right of the painting's center. These four figures, a man carrying a raving boy and, immediately to their left, the boy's two sisters, one of whom points to him while the other wrings her hands, replace a single figure of a man with a cloak flying out behind him in No. 336, who points to the palsied or paralytic woman on the right side of the composition. A man carrying a boy

appears in West's earlier treatment of the subject for the chapel at Windsor (see No. 334). By introducing this group into No. 338, West told the Philadelphians, he had made their picture a better picture than the one they should have received in the first place: "I think my exertions are more complete in appropriate character, as I have introduced a demoniac with his attendant relations, by which circumstance is introduced most of the maladies which were healed by Our Saviour."[10]

A drawing for the raving boy was sold by West's son in 1839,[11] and three drawings, all of which are dated *1815*, and all of which are inscribed or otherwise traditionally have been identified as for the boy, are known.[12] These three drawings differ considerably from one another, and none of them is very close to the figure as he appears in the finished picture.

No. 338 was cleaned and restored by Hannah Mee Horner in 1950 and by Joseph Amarotico in 1981–82.

[1] See No. 336.
[2] This letter and West's other letters to the Pennsylvania Hospital are in the hospital's archives and are quoted in the history of the hospital by Morton and Woodbury and in an issue of the hospital's *Bulletin* devoted to No. 338 published in 1950–51.
[3] Hart 1908, pp. 29–30.
[4] Ibid., pp. 31–32. A note from the shipping agents dated 6 Aug. 1817, is published by Morton and Woodbury, p. 311.
[5] Ibid., p. 33.
[6] Incomplete letter dated 5 Dec. 1801 (Historical Society of Pennsylvania).
[7] 10 March 1816 (Morton and Woodbury, pp. 309–10).
[8] See No. 524.
[9] James J. Levick, MD, "Benjamin Hornor Coates, MD," *Pennsylvania Magazine of History and Biography*, VI, 1882, p. 23.
[10] 10 Sept. 1815 (Morton and Woodbury, p. 315).
[11] S. Leigh Sotheby, London, 1 June 1839, lot 97 ("The Demoniac Boy, a study for an additional group introduced into the picture of Christ healing the Sick, which was presented by Mr. West to the Hospital at Philadelphia," Pen and ink, washed with bistre).
[12] In the Toledo Museum of Art (pen, 6¾ × 10 in.); the Delaware Art Museum (pen, 5½ × 3¾ in.); and Historical Society of Pennsylvania.

339 The Raising of Lazarus 1780

WADSWORTH ATHENEUM, HARTFORD, CONNECTICUT

Oil on canvas: 101 × 130 in. (257 × 330 cm.)

Signed bottom center: *B. West 1780*

PROV: Commissioned as the altarpiece for Winchester Cathedral, where it remained until 1900; gift of J. Pierpont Morgan to the Wadsworth Atheneum in 1900

EXH: RA 1780 (123) "The raising of Lazarus; an altarpiece for the Cathedral of Winchester"

ENGR: Mezzotint (25 × 32⅜ in.) by Valentine Green, pub. 1 May 1780 by V. Green & Son

LISTED: *PC*, p. 562 ("The Raising of Lazarus, in the Cathedral of Winchester," 10 ft. × 14); *UM*, p. 528; *AA*, p. 68 (13 ft. × 9); Barlow, p. 433; *BA*, p. 15; Galt, p. 220; Dillenberger, pp. 153 (151) and 211

LIT: *Gentleman's Magazine*, L, 1780, p. 317, and LXVIII, 1798, pp. 1033–34; V and A Cuttings, I, p. 188 (1780); the Revd. William Gilpin, *Observations on the Western Parts of England, related Chiefly to Picturesque Beauty*, London, 1808, pp. 49–50; the Revd. John Milner, *The History Civil and Ecclesiastical and Survey of the Antiquities of Winchester*, London, 1809, II, pp. 39–40; Carey 1820, p. 696; Evans 1959, pl. 8; Dillenberger 1977, p. 44, pl. 26

William Carey states that the success of West's altarpiece for St. Stephen, Walbrook (No. 388) at the Royal Academy in 1776 procured him commissions for

this work for Winchester and *St. Michael* (No. 406) for Trinity College, Cambridge. In 1777 West exhibited the Trinity College altarpiece, but only a sketch (No. 340) for No. 339, and it took him three more years to complete and exhibit the large painting.

In addition to the sketch, related works include a drawing sold in 1839,[1] and possibly a drawing sold in 1964.[2] Other drawings by West which have been identified as showing the raising of Lazarus seem more probably related either to a later and different composition (No. 341) or to different subjects such as the lost *Christ Raising the Widow's Son* (No. 343) or the *Raising of Jairus's Daughter*.[3]

[1] S. Leigh Sotheby, London, 1 June 1839, lot 98, "The Raising of Lazarus, the finished drawing for the large picture in the Cathedral at Winchester. In colors."
[2] Sotheby's, London, 8 Jan. 1964, lot 6, black chalk on buff paper, 10⅞ × 16⅝ in.
[3] No painting of the "Raising of Jairus's Daughter" by West is known or recorded, but a group of rather slight drawings in the Pierpont Morgan Library, which have been catalogued by Ruth Kraemer as depicting the raising of Lazarus, shows a scene set in an interior and more likely are sketches of this subject. See Kraemer 1975, pp. 11–12 (13v, 14, and 15), pl. 7.

340 The Raising of Lazarus 1776–1814

SWARTHMORE COLLEGE, SWARTHMORE, PENNSYLVANIA

Oil on canvas: 30¼ × 35¼ in. (77 × 89.5 cm.)

(?) Signed left: *B. West 1776*, and lower right: *Retouched 1814*

PROV: Offered by West's sons to the United States in 1826 (148) and sold by them, Robins, London, 22–25 May 1829, lot 118 (2 ft. 6 in. × 3 ft., "painted in chiaro scuro. The original study for the great Altarpiece in Winchester Cathedral"), bt. by Morgan (? Charles Morgan, Caeforgan, Llanrhydian, Glamorganshire) for £31.10.0; Ehrich Galleries, New York, 1922; Frederic Newlin Price, by whom presented to the Benjamin West Society at Swarthmore College before 1933

EXH: RA 1777 (366) "Lazarus; a study for a large picture to be painted for the cathedral church of Winchester, 'Jesus saith unto them, Loose him, and let him go'"; (?) 125 Pall Mall 1814 (5) and (?) 1816 (6), both with a citation of John 11 : 43, 44; Philadelphia, 1921 (9); Brooklyn 1922 (9); Philadelphia 1938 (29); Allentown 1962 (10)

LISTED: (?) *PC*, p. 568 ("The sketch, in oil, of the Raising of Lazarus," West, Gallery); (?) *UM*, p. 532; (?) *BA*, p. 19; (?) Galt, p. 234; Dillenberger, pp. 185 (468) and 211

LIT: V and A Cuttings, I, p. 147 (1777); *Catalogue of the Works of Art belonging to the Benjamin West Society and to Swarthmore College*, Swarthmore, Pennsylvania, 1933; Evans 1959, pl. 7

This monochrome sketch for No. 339 corresponds with the large picture in composition and all major details. The most conspicuous difference is in the position of the head of the sister who kneels between Lazarus and Christ.

Some details in the early histories of Nos. 340 and 341, another sketch of the same subject which also remained in the possession of West and his heirs until 1829, may be confused.

The painting was damaged in a fire in August 1982. A strip of canvas approximately 4 in. wide running vertically through the center of the picture was badly charred and all detail there seems to have been totally obliterated. Signatures, which were recorded on No. 340 in 1938 and in 1962, are also no longer visible.

339

340

341 The Raising of Lazarus 1788

GLASGOW ART GALLERY AND MUSEUM

Oil on paper on canvas: $29\frac{3}{8} \times 46\frac{1}{4}$ in.
(74.5 × 117.5 cm.)

Signed lower center to the right of Lazarus's legs: *B. West/1788*

PROV: Offered by West's sons to the United States in 1826 (39), and sold by them, Robins, London, 22–25 May 1829, lot 134 (2 ft. 5 in. × 3 ft. 10 in.), bt. by Ward; bequest of Archibald McLellan to the city of Glasgow in 1854

EXH: RA 1791 (135) "The resurrection of Lazarus, a finished sketch"; (?) 125 Pall Mall 1814 (5) and (?) 1816 (6); BI 1833 (38) lent by W. J. Ward

(?) LISTED: *PC*, p. 564 ("The Raising of Lazarus," West's House at Windsor); *UM*, p. 529; Barlow, p. 434; *BA*, p. 16; Galt, p. 225; Dillenberger, pp. 165 (267) and 215

LIT: *Summary Catalogue of British Oil Paintings*, Art Gal-

341

lery and Museum, Glasgow, 1971, p. 90 (258); Kraemer 1975, p. 12

The date on No. 341 contradicts a description of it in the Robins catalogue of May 1829 as earlier than the Winchester altarpiece (No. 339).

A drawing for the figure of Lazarus in this composition is at Swarthmore,[1] and a compositional drawing, which repeats foreground figures from the lower left and right corners of No. 341 but otherwise differs in most details, is at Nottingham.[2]

[1]Crayon and white on grey paper: 14 × 10 in., ill. in Dillenberger 1977, pl. 27.

[2]Sepia ink and wash on grey paper: 6 × 8 in.

342 The Raising of Lazarus

LOCATION UNKNOWN

PROV: Sold by West's sons, Robins, London, 20–22 June 1829, lot 78 ("The Raising of Lazarus, . . ., not quite finished")

See No. 343 below.

343 Christ Raising the Widow's Son

LOCATION UNKNOWN

Oil on paper: $44 \times 21\frac{1}{2}$ in. (112 × 54.5 cm.)

PROV: Offered by West's sons to the United States in 1826 (150, "Christ Raising the Widow's Son," 3 ft. 8 in. × 1 ft. $9\frac{1}{2}$ in.)

EXH: 125 Pall Mall 1816 (7) "Widow's Son Restored, St. Luke, chap. xxii, verses 19, 20"

LISTED: *PC*, p. 568 ("The large Sketch, in oil, on paper, of Christ raising the Widow's Son," West, Gallery); *UM*, p. 532; *BA*, p. 19; Galt, p. 233; Dillenberger, p. 184 (459)

The citation which accompanied No. 343 in the Pall Mall catalogue of 1816 refers to a description of the Last Supper and is obviously incorrect. The correct citation should be Luke 7:11–17.

No. 343 is one of the small number of works that appear on the list of pictures offered by West's sons to the United States in 1826 but do not reappear in the main Robins sale catalogue of 22–25 May 1829. It is conceivable that it is identical with the not-quite-finished *Raising of Lazarus* sold on 20–22 June 1829, a work for which there is otherwise no documentation (see No. 342 above).

Two drawings of the subject were exhibited in West's gallery in 1823,[1] and two drawings were included in the sale of West's drawings on 1 June 1839.[2] Three drawings of Christ raising a male figure, which show a city gate in the background, as described in Luke 7:12, rather than a cave as in the *Raising of Lazarus*, and which hence probably show this subject, are currently known.[3] But they differ considerably from one another in composition, and it is impossible to say which, if any of them, reflects the composition of No. 343.

[1]West's Gallery 1823, Room of Drawings (14 and 29).

[2]S. Leigh Sotheby, London, 1 June 1839, lots 30 ("Christ raising the Widow's Son," pen and ink, washed with bistre) and 67 ("Raising the Widow's Son," pen and ink, washed with bistre).

[3]British Museum (1920-6-15-8); with Hirschl & Adler Galleries, New York, 1979; and formerly in the collection of Mrs. F. Howard (sold Sotheby's, London, 17 March 1979, lot 17, as "The Raising of Lazarus," signed and dated *1789 Windsor*).

344 The Last Supper 1784

TATE GALLERY, LONDON

Oil on canvas: $72\frac{1}{4} \times 109$ in. (183.5 × 277 cm.)

PROV: Painted for George III (1797 account: "The picture of the Last Supper," 1784, £735; 1801 account, p. 212: for the Windsor Chapel. The Prophets, 29, "A Last Supper, painted for the King's Chapel," £735; given by George IV to the National Gallery in 1828; transferred to the Tate Gallery in 1921

EXH: RA 1785 (219) "The Lord's Supper, painted for His Majesty's chapel in Windsor Castle"; West's Gallery 1821 (38), 1822–28 (14)

ENGR: Mezzotint ($20\frac{9}{16} \times 30\frac{1}{4}$ in.) by Richard Earlom (unlettered proof printed in color in the British Museum); stipple engraving ($16\frac{7}{8} \times 23\frac{1}{8}$ in.) by Thomas Ryder, pub. 2 Jan. 1797, by John & Josiah Boydell, *from the original picture in the Chapel Royal at Windsor*; outline engraving ($3\frac{3}{16} \times 4\frac{1}{2}$ in.) by Normand *fils*, pub. in Hamilton 1831 (127)

LISTED: *PC*, p. 561 ("Christ's last Supper," George III, for his Majesty's Chapel, Windsor, Gospel Dispensation, 6 ft. × 10); *UM*, p. 527; *AA*, p. 67; Barlow, p. 432 (15 ft. × 10); *BA*, p. 14; Galt, p. 219; Dillenberger, pp. 148 (103) and 212

LIT: V and A Cuttings, I, pp. 253, 255 (1785); Hamilton 1831 (127); Shoemaker 1878, p. 408 (1784); Meyer 1975, pp. 249–53, 256, 265, and fig. 7; Kraemer 1975, p. 28; Dillenberger 1977, pp. 54, 58, 71, and 74, pl. 52; Pressly 1983, p. 47, fig. 23a

West painted two large paintings of the *Last Supper* (Nos. 344 and 346) for George III at approximately the same time, both of them to serve as altarpieces for chapels at Windsor Castle. No. 344, which is slightly the earlier of the two, was for the Royal Chapel, while No. 346 was for St. George's Chapel.

In the architectural drawings for the Royal Chapel from around 1780, a *Last Supper* is on the end of the wall over the altar and under the large *Moses Receiving the Laws* (ill. p. 579), and in the Swarthmore diagrams of 1801 the subject is located in the analogous position on an end wall, this time under the *Crucifixion* (ill. p. 580) and with pictures—or spaces for pictures—on either side.

We know from the diary of Samuel Shoemaker, who saw No. 344 in West's room in Windsor Castle, that it was "just finished" on 10 October 1784. It appeared at the Royal Academy the following spring. It is noteworthy that Shoemaker saw No. 344 at Windsor, rather than in West's London studio, and, if we can trust the inscription on the Ryder print after it published in 1797, No. 344 was the one picture painted by West for the chapel at Windsor which was in fact utilized in the castle.[1] No. 344 is also unique in that it is the one completed picture for the chapel that did not appear in the Robins sale of West's estate on 22–25 May 1829. When George IV returned ownership of the other pictures to West's sons, he retained No. 344 and presented it to the recently founded National Gallery instead.[2] Nonetheless, No. 344 was, like all the other pictures for the chapel, physically in the possession of West's sons following their father's death and was exhibited by them along with his other works in his former house and studio in Newman Street. It is recognizable hanging on the end wall next to the door into the inner room in the Cattermole-Le Keux engraving of the Great Room as it was installed in 1821 (ill. p. 150).

A sketch of the composition is No. 345 below. A much slighter drawing is in one of West's sketchbooks in the Yale Center for British Art. Another drawing of the composition, which has been squared for transfer is in the collection of Mr. and Mrs. Erving Wolf,[3] and a drawing of the figure of Christ is in the Pierpont Morgan Library.[4] A monochrome copy is in the Beeston St. Lawrence parish church, in Norfolk.[5]

[1]We have not been able to confirm this. Hamilton 1831 repeats the information given in the inscription on the Ryder print; that should be reliable, but it is conceivable that already in 1797 the two *Last Suppers* (Nos. 344 and 346) were being confused. The latter was definitely installed in St. George's Chapel at Windsor.

[2]A letter from Raphael West to the Marquis of Lansdowne, dated 7 January 1828, refers to George IV's intention of retaining one picture from the group he was returning to West's sons (A. Aspinall, *The Letters of King George IV 1812–1830*, Cambridge, 1938, III, p. 379).

[3]Pencil, $16 \times 24\frac{1}{2}$ in. (San Antonio 1983, no. 21).

[4]Kraemer 1975, p. 28 (40) and pl. 26: black chalk, $4\frac{1}{4} \times 5\frac{5}{8}$ in.

[5]Oil on canvas, $38\frac{1}{2} \times 51$ in.

344

345

345 The Last Supper *c.* 1784

RICHARD N. TETLIE

Pen and ink and wash, heightened with white: $22\frac{1}{2} \times 31\frac{3}{4}$ in. $(57 \times 80.5$ cm.)

PROV: (?) Sold by Mrs. Albert F. West, Christie's, London, 19 March 1898, lot 138 (under "Pictures," sepia, unframed, 22×31 in.), bt. by Obach together with lot 139 (No. 99) for £5.15.0.; John Levy, New York, 1952

EXH: RA 1784 (437) "The last supper, a design for a picture for his Majesty's chapel in Windsor-castle"

LISTED: *PC*, p. 567 ("The Sketch on Paper of Christ's Last Supper," West, Gallery); *UM*, p. 531; *BA*, p. 18; Galt, p. 231; Dillenberger, p. 180 (412)

This drawing, which shows the same composition as the large painting of the *Last Supper* exhibited by West at the Royal Academy in 1785 (No. 344) can be equated with the "design" of the subject which he had exhibited the year before. That design was one of three works which he exhibited in 1784 as designs for pictures for His Majesty's chapel in Windsor Castle. The other two were, *Moses Striking the Rock* (No. 256) and *Death on the Pale Horse* (No. 402), which was exhibited as "The Triumph of Death." Although No. 345 is somewhat smaller than the other two works, all three have approximately the same height, are in comparable media, and are on several sheets of paper joined together. Nos. 256 and 402 both bear inscriptions indi-

346

cating that they were drawn in 1783 and retouched in 1803. No legible signature is visible on this work.

West painted two large *Last Suppers* (Nos. 344 and 346) for which three sketches are known or recorded. Some exhibition or sales catalogues explicitly associate a sketch with the altarpiece in St. George's Chapel (No. 346), but the early lists and the catalogues of the exhibitions in Pall Mall between 1814 and 1818, make no connection. Only two sketches of the *Last Supper* are recorded in the lists, and it is impossible to say with absolute certainty which these are, but since No. 345 is on paper, we have equated it with the "Sketch on Paper" included in the lists. On the other hand, it seems somewhat more likely that West would have shown a painting on canvas (i.e., No. 347) rather than No. 345 in his exhibitions in Pall Mall.

346 The Last Supper 1786

DETROIT INSTITUTE OF ARTS

Oil on canvas: 98 × 140½ in. (248.9 × 356.9 cm.)

Signed lower left: *B. West 1786*

PROV: Painted for George III (1797 account: "The picture of the Last Supper which His Majesty made a present of to the Collegiate Church Windsor", 1786, £735; 1801 account, p. 212: for St. George's

Chapel, Windsor, 28 . . .); removed from its original situation in 1863; sold by the Dean and Canons of Windsor, Sotheby's, London, 23 June 1978, lot 132, bt. by Somerville; Somerville and Simpson and P. & D. Colnaghi, London, from whom bought by the Detroit Institute of Arts in 1980

EXH: Washington and Philadelphia 1980 (11)

LISTED: *PC*, p. 562 ("The Supper, over the Communion-table in the Collegiate Church of Windsor," 8 ft. × 13); *UM*, p. 528; *AA*, p. 68 (12 ft. × 9); Barlow, p. 433; *BA*, p. 15; Galt, p. 220; Dillenberger, pp. 147 (102), 153 (153), and 212

LIT: *Windsor Guide*, 1792, p. 63; Farington Diary, 17 Sept. 1804 (Farington 1978—, VI, p. 2412); Pyne 1819, I, p. 182; John Thomas Smith, *A Book for a Rainy Day*, London, 1845, p. 77; Papendiek 1887, II, p. 278; Hope 1913, II, pp. 388–89, 426–27; W. S. Lewis, ed., *Horace Walpole's Correspondence*, XI, New Haven, 1944, p. 363 (letter of 9 Oct. 1791); von Erffa 1969, pp. 22 and 29; Kraemer 1975, pp. 28–29; Dillenberger 1977, pp. 96–97; Meyer 1979, pp. 56, 58, fig. 5

No. 346, the second *Last Supper* painted by West for George III in a span of two years, was commissioned by the King as part of an ambitious scheme of rede-

corating the east end of St. George's Chapel. It was, until removed in 1863, situated under the huge *Resurrection* window (see No. 360) which had been commissioned in 1782 and installed in 1786. A drawing of the choir of the chapel by the architectural draughtsman John Carter showing West's altarpiece below the intended window appeared at the Royal Academy in 1785.[1] No. 346 is signed and dated *1786*, and it was put in place, in a neo-Gothic reredos designed by Thomas Sandby and carved by Henry Emlyn, in December 1786.[2] Several contemporary or early nineteenth-century views of the interior of the chapel show it in situ (ill. p. 90).[3] After its removal in 1863 it hung for a period in the ambulatory behind the altar.

No. 346 is somewhat larger than No. 344, which was intended for an analogous position in George III's chapel in the castle. The compositions of the two paintings are not dissimilar, but the point of view in No. 346 is lower, and the figural scale is larger. The positions of John and Peter on either side of Christ have been reversed, and Judas has been moved from the right background of No. 341 to pace melodramatically before the table in No. 346.

John Thomas Smith (1766–1833) claimed to have sat for the apostle John in No. 346, but Mrs. Papendiek wrote that the model for John was Raphael West (who was exactly the same age as Smith). West, of course, may have used both as models for the same figure.

Sketches for No. 346 are Nos. 347 and 348 below. A drawing which appears to be a first idea for this composition, with Judas before the table, is in the Pierpont Morgan Library.[4] Another drawing was sold by Benjamin West, Jr. in 1839.[5]

In 1791 Horace Walpole sent to Mary Berry a report of the recent additions to St. George's Chapel, in which he mentioned No. 346 following a remark (quoted under No. 360) about the window above: "and there is a Judas below so gigantic, that he seems more likely to burst by his bulk than through guilt." Similar criticisms were acknowledged and dismissed in the account of No. 346 that appeared in the *Windsor Guide*: "those who only affect to be critics pretend that the figure of Judas is too predominant, 'though real judges esteem the whole a masterly composition."

[1] (452) *View of the choir of St. George's chapel, Windsor, in which is introduced the intended painted window and altarpiece, as designed by Mr. West.* A drawing by West and Carter of the window had appeared at the Academy two years before in 1783 (see No. 360).
[2] The most important documentation for this work is provided in "An Account of all the great works which have been executed in St. George's Chapel Windsor from the year 1782 to ye end of 1792," published in Hope 1913, II, pp. 388–91; Emlyn's accounts are published ibid., pp. 391–94. A letter dated 29 December 1786, and published in the *Gentleman's Magazine*, Jan. 1787, p. 82, describes West's painting as installed and much admired.
[3] See also No. 360, note 1.
[4] Black chalk, $5\frac{13}{16} \times 8\frac{1}{2}$ in. (Kraemer 1975, pp. 28–29, no. 42, and pl. 27).
[5] S. Leigh Sotheby, London, 1 June 1839, lot 88 ("Design for the Altar Piece, in St. George's Chapel Windsor." Black chalk, washed with bistre).

347 The Last Supper 1787

UNIVERSITY OF VIRGINA MUSEUM OF ART,
CHARLOTTESVILLE, VIRGINIA

Oil on canvas: $19\frac{1}{2} \times 27\frac{1}{2}$ in. (49.5 × 69.8 cm.)

Signed lower left: *B. West 1787*

347

PROV: Sold anonymously, Christie's, London, 20 June 1975, lot 59; Central Picture Galleries, New York, from whom purchased by the University of Virginia Art Museum in 1976 (gift of Mr. and Mrs. Frederick Palmer Weber)

(?) EXH: RA 1804 (28) "The Last Supper, the original sketch for the great picture over the communion table in the Collegiate Church, Windsor"; BI 1806 (North Room, 90) "Sketch for the picture of the Last Supper, the altar-piece of St. George's Chapel, Windsor"; 125 Pall Mall 1814 (6) "The Lord's Supper, St. Luke, chap. xxii, verses 19, 20"; 125 Pall Mall 1816 (8), 1818 (9)

(?) LISTED: *PC*, p. 567 ("Christ's Last Supper [in brown colour]," West, Gallery); *UM*, p. 531; *BA*, p. 18; Galt, p. 230; Dillenberger, p. 176 (379)

No. 347 is a sketch in grisaille for the previous painting. Although showing basically the same composition, it differs from No. 346 in several significant details such as the positions of the apostles' heads on both the right and left sides of the picture, and the arrangement of the arches in the background. These differences would seem to establish that West painted No. 347 as a study for No. 346 rather than as a copy or replica after it; nonetheless, No. 347 is signed and dated *1787*, whereas No. 346 is dated *1786*. Thus, he evidently completed it only after completing the larger picture.

We have tentatively equated No. 347 with the "Last Supper—in brown colour" on the early lists of West's works; with the *Last Supper* exhibited at the Royal Academy in 1804, where it was identified as the original sketch for No. 346; and with the sketches or paintings of the subject that West exhibited on several subsequent occasions during his lifetime. Because of a substantial discrepancy in measurements we cannot identify it as the study for No. 346 which West's sons sold in 1829 (see No. 348), and since West seems to have painted two sketches for No. 346, as well as one for the slightly earlier No. 344, it is not possible to be certain of which is which in all the early records of his works.

348 The Last Supper *c.* 1786

LOCATION UNKNOWN

($10\frac{1}{2} \times 14$ in.) (26.5 × 35.5 cm.)

PROV: Offered by West's sons to the United States in 1826 (64), and sold by them, Robins, London, 22–25 May 1829, lot 21 ("The study for the admired picture, placed over the table of the Altar of the choir of St. George's chapel, Windsor," $10\frac{1}{2} \times 14$ in.), bt. by Nash for £57.15.0.; sold by Sir William W. Knighton, Bt., Christie's, London, 23 May 1885, lot 451 ($10\frac{1}{2} \times 15\frac{1}{2}$ in.).

349

349 Christ in the Hall of Caiaphas *c.* 1814

MUSEUM OF FINE ARTS, BOSTON

Oil and gouache on paper: $12\frac{1}{2} \times 18\frac{1}{4}$ in. (31.5 × 46.5 cm.)

PROV: Sold by Benjamin West, Jr., S. Leigh Sotheby, London, 1 June 1839, lot 86 ("Christ in the Hall of Caiaphas, the finished drawing from which Mr. West intended to paint a picture, the size of his Christ Rejected," pen and bistre, worked up with oil); John Hubbard Sturgis, Boston (1834–88); given by his daughter to the Museum of Fine Arts in 1942

LIT: *Bulletin of the Museum of Fine Arts, Boston*, XLI, June 1943, p. 35; Kraemer 1975, pp. 54–55, fig. 37

No. 349 illustrates the scene in which Christ is taken to the house of the high priest Caiaphas, immediately following his arrest in the Garden of Gethsemane. It shows Christ in the center, Caiaphas to the left, and Peter denying Christ on the right. Behind are the soldiers who had arrested Christ, and in the arches above is the crowing cock. West painted two paintings of the subject of *St. Peter Denying Christ* (Nos. 350 and 351), but No. 349 seems to have been a sketch for a much vaster work that he never carried out.

In the sale of drawings by West in 1839, there were two lots similarly identified as designs for a picture of *Christ in the Hall of Caiaphas* which was to have been the size of *Christ Rejected* (No. 353). No. 349 was presumably the second of two, (lot 86), which was described as worked up in oil.[1] The implication of the wording of the entries in the sale catalogue is that West undertook the subject after *Christ Rejected*, which he completed in 1814. As such, the picture would have been one of his last major undertakings. This is confirmed by an inscription (probably written by Benjamin West, Jr.) on a related drawing in the Pierpont Morgan Library: *The last design by Benj West-/1819.*[2]

A drawing for the composition showing significant differences but also fundamental similarities in the architecture and the position of Christ and Caiaphas is in the Georgia Museum of Art, University of Georgia,[3] and in addition to the dated drawing mentioned above, there are three further related drawings in the Pierpont Morgan Library.[4] Many of these draw-

350

ings, like No. 349, are on several sheets of paper joined together.

[1] The other was lot 27, "Christ in the Hall of Caiphas, a design for a picture which Mr. West intended to paint the size of Christ Rejected." Pen and ink washed.
[2] Kraemer 1975, p. 59 (107) pl. 68 (pen, ink, and wash, approx. 24 × 22⅝ in.). Although Kraemer catalogues this drawing as "Peter's Denial of Christ," she points out that it is closely related to No. 349.
[3] Ink, 11½ × 18½ in. formerly in the collection of Mrs. E. K. Rule, a descendant of the artist.
[4] Kraemer 1975, p. 54 (96) pl. 67 (ink and wash, 6 × 2½ in.); ibid., p. 55 (97) pl. 63 (black chalk, 5 × 4⅛ in.); and ibid., p. 55, (98) (black chalk, 6⅝₁₆ × 7¹³₁₆ in.).

350 St. Peter Denying Christ 1778–79

ST. JOHN'S CHURCH, PERLETHORPE, NOTTINGHAMSHIRE

Oil on canvas: 60 × 58 in. (152.5 × 147.5 cm.)

PROV: Painted for Charles Pierrepont Medows, later Viscount Newark, and first Earl Manvers

EXH: RA 1779 (342) "St. Peter, accused by the damsel, denies our Saviour"

LISTED: *PC*, p. 562 ("Peter denying our Saviour, in the Chapel of Ld. Newark"); *UM*, p. 528; Barlow, p. 433; *BA*, p. 15; Galt, p. 221; Dillenberger, p. 154 (159)

LIT: Carey 1820, p. 696

A second smaller version of this composition is in the Royal Collection (No. 351). It has been described as the version exhibited in 1779, but William Carey stated in 1820, "In 1778 and 9, he painted and exhibited 'Christ denying St. Peter,' [*sic*] for the chapel of Lord Newark." The Lord Newark referred to by Carey was Charles Pierrepont Medows (1737–1816), a friend of West's of long standing (see No. 658), who was created Viscount Newark in 1796 and was known by that title in 1804 when the first of the published lists of West's works appeared. In 1806 he became Earl Manvers. In 1788 he inherited Thoresby in Nottinghamshire, which has remained in the possession of the Manvers family

Copy by Raphael West after the figure of Christ in No. 350

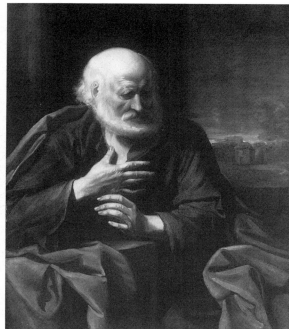

Copy ascribed to John Singleton Copley after the figure of Peter in No. 350

John Singleton Copley, *Samuel and Eli*, 1780. Oil on canvas, $77\frac{1}{2} \times 59\frac{7}{8}$ in. Wadsworth Atheneum, Hartford, Connecticut

to the present time. No. 350 has been in its present location since the church was built in the 1850s, and is recorded in the church's inventories as having come from the previous church at Thoresby.

In addition to the second version of the composition in the Royal Collection (No. 351) and a third version sold by West's sons in 1829 (No. 352), separate paintings of details of the figures of Christ (which went through Sotheby's in 1980)[1] and of St. Peter (in a private collection, London)[2] are also known. The former (*above*) is inscribed on the verso: *To the Lord Bishop of Bristol, from Raphael West. Painted when he was twelve years and nine months old. 1779*. Raphael was born on 8 April 1766, and accordingly would have reached the specified age in January 1779. The Lord Bishop of Bristol at the time was West's old patron Thomas Newton (see No. 675). The painting itself, although undoubtedly a remarkable achievement for a twelve-year-old child, does have all the hallmarks of a copy by a less assured artist, and there seems to be no reason to question the veracity of the inscription. In 1779 the precocious Raphael exhibited *An old man's head* at the Royal Academy (no. 374), and it is possible that that work was a copy from the St. Peter in No. 350. It is unlikely, however, that the head of an old man by Raphael could be the copy of the head of Peter mentioned above, which is altogether bolder and freer in handling than the copy of the head of Christ. The *St. Peter*, which has a landscape background in the right distance, appears to have been painted by John Singleton Copley (*above*),[3] and it would seem that Copley used this figure as a model for the Eli in his *Samuel and Eli* of 1780 (*above*). For discussion of the possibility that Copley also painted part of No. 351 see the following entry.

[1] Oil on canvas, 36 × 28 in., sold Sotheby's, London, 5 Nov. 1980, lot 194.
[2] Oil on canvas, 41 × 34 in.
[3] We are indebted to Professor Jules Prown for his opinion of this painting (letter of 25 June 1980).

351 St. Peter Denying Christ *c.* 1778–79

HER MAJESTY THE QUEEN

Oil on canvas: $48\frac{3}{4} \times 49$ in. (124 × 124.5 cm.)

PROV: Presented by West to George III (1801 account,

351

p. 215: "A picture of Peter denying our Saviour, of which His Majesty honoured me by accepting, two half-length figures, the size of life")

ENGR: Engraving ($5\frac{3}{8} \times 3$ in., reversed and with full-length figures), by William Sharp, pub. as the frontispiece of vol. II of *Discourses on Various Subjects* by Jacob Duché, London, 1779; mezzotint (21×20 in.) by Valentine Green, pub. [?] 1 May 1780; steel engraving by William Holl, pub. by Fisher Son & Co

LISTED: *PC*, p. 559 ("The Damsel accusing Peter," George III, Queen's House); *UM*, p. 527; Barlow, p. 418; *BA*, p. 13; Galt, p. 216; Dillenberger, pp. 137 (10) and 211

LIT: Evans 1959, pl. 36; Mount 1964, p. 57; Millar 1969, p. 130 (1150) and pl. 117; Meyer 1975, p. 247

The composition of No. 351 is essentially that of No. 350. The former is smaller than the latter, and several auxiliary details which appear in No. 350, such as the lamp above Peter's head and the moon in the sky above Christ's have been omitted. Also the spear held by the soldier on the right edge of the composition is behind his head, rather than before it as in No. 350.

In 1964 Charles Merrill Mount claimed that John Singleton Copley executed the figure of Peter in No. 351, basing it on the head of Eli in his *Samuel and Eli* now in the Wadsworth Atheneum, and that Gilbert Stuart painted the other two main figures. Mount was evidently unaware of the earlier No. 350, and his assignment of chronological precedence to Copley's *Samuel and Eli*, which is signed and dated *1780*, is undermined by the fact that West exhibited No. 350 in May of 1779 (an engraving after No. 351 appeared in 1779 as well), but his ascription of the Peter in No. 351 to Copley, evidently on purely visual grounds, is given enhanced credibility by the subsequent appearance of a separate painting of Peter, discussed under No. 350, which also seems to be the work of Copley. There are visible differences in the handling of the paint between the two Peters in Nos. 350 and 351, and the freer handling in No. 351, particularly discernible in the hands, is close to that in the single figure of Peter ascribed to Copley. There are also much more marked differences between the Peter in No. 351 and the other two main figures in the painting than between the corresponding figures in No. 350, supporting Mount's claim that Peter's companions in No. 351 are by a different hand. Christ and the maid in No. 351 are less linear, more conventionally lit and modelled, somewhat different in physiognomy, and generally less characteristic of West than their counterparts in No. 350. Hence, it is not improbable that they were painted by an assistant, and there are sufficient similarities between the Christ in No. 351 and the *Christ Blessing* from the Fitzroy Chapel (No. 332), for which there is documentary evidence to suggest that it was painted by Stuart, to make Mount's attribution persuasive. The question is complicated by the fact that Raphael West also painted a copy of the Christ in No. 350, but Raphael's copy and the corresponding figure of Christ in No. 351 do not appear to be by the same hand.

The circumstances under which Copley and Stuart would have painted a joint copy after West (if this painting is indeed that) can only be guessed at. Copley and West seem to have been close in the years 1778–79, and their overlapping interest in painting the *Death of Chatham* (see No. 104) dates from precisely this time. It should be noted also that West gave No. 351 away, and he may have chosen to do so, rather than to sell it, because it was not a work by his own hand. The related *Christ Blessing* (No. 332) and a companion *Moses* (No. 260), which we believe to have been painted by Gilbert Stuart from West's designs, are also works

which West probably gave away at approximately the same time.

If West had scruples about selling No. 351, he had none about claiming it for himself otherwise, and it appears on all the early lists of his works. Three engravings of the composition are known or recorded, and all of them seem to have been based on No. 351, rather than No. 350, as they follow No. 351 in showing the soldier's spear behind rather than before his head. The engraving by Sharp, which reproduces the composition in reverse and extended vertically to allow full-length figures, appeared as a book illustration in 1779,[1] and Valentine Green's mezzotint was listed in a catalogue published on 1 January 1780, described as "from the Original Picture in his Majesty's Collection."[2] Hence, West must have presented No. 351 to the King before the end of 1779. As Meyer has suggested the gift may have helped prime the pump for the commission for the great series of religious paintings for the Royal Chapel at Windsor, upon which West was engaged by October of that year. Ironically, although George III was to pay the artist over £20,000 for religious paintings over the following twenty-two years, No. 351, a gift, is the only biblical painting by West to remain in the Royal Collection.

[1] See No. 304.
[2] No proof of the Green mezzotint is known to the compilers of this catalogue. Information about it comes from Millar and from Alfred Whitman, *Valentine Green*, London, 1902, p. 149 (221).

352 St. Peter Denying Christ

LOCATION UNKNOWN

PROV: Sold by West's sons, Robins, London, 20–22 June 1829, lot 187 ("Peter Denying Christ")

353 Christ Rejected 1814
See illustration, p. 145

PENNSYLVANIA ACADEMY OF THE FINE ARTS, PHILADELPHIA

Oil on canvas: 200×260 in. (508×660 cm.)

Signed lower left: *Benj West/1814*

PROV: Offered by West's sons to the United States in 1826 (1, . . ., 16 ft. 10 in. × 22 ft.), and sold by them, Robins, London, 22–25 May 1829, lot 104 (16 ft. 9 in. × 22 ft.), bt. by Smith for £3,150, on behalf of Benjamin West, Jr.; Joseph Harrison, Jr., Philadelphia, by 1862; given by his widow to the Pennsylvania Academy in 1878

EXH: 125 Pall Mall 1814; 125 Pall Mall 1816; West's Gallery 1821 (30), 1822–28 (43); Niblo's, New York, 1829; Independence Hall, Philadelphia, 1830; New York, 1831; Glasgow, 1832; PAFA 1843 (lent by Benjamin West, [Jr.], London); PAFA 1864 (514) lent by Joseph Harrison, Jr., (and re-exhibited there on numerous occasions subsequently)

ENGR: Five stipple engravings (each 15×20 in.) of details from the painting (*I The Centurion and his Family*, *II The Enraged Multitude, with Joseph of Arimathea and James the Less*, *III St. Peter, with Part of the Enraged Multitude*, *IV Barabbas, with the Condemned Thieves*, *V Mary, the Wife of Cleophas, with Pious Women from Galilee*), drawn by Henry Corbould and engraved by Edward Scriven, pub. 1 July 1814 by T. Clay as *Select Groups from the Grand Picture of Christ Rejected . . .*; six stipple engravings of details of heads (*Mary the Mother of Christ*, *Mary Magdalene*, *The Wife of Pontius Pilate*, *One of the Pious Women from Galilee*, *He who casts the Robe of Decision upon Christ*, *The Scoffer*),

drawn by Corbould and engraved by Scriven, pub. 18 April 1820 by R. Ackermann and E. Scriven, as *Elements of the Human Figure*; steel engraving (25×36 in.) by John Sartain, 1862, commissioned by Joseph Harrison

LISTED: Galt, p. 234; Dillenberger, pp. 189 (511) and 214

LIT: Farington Diary, 21 Nov. 1811, 31 Jan. and 8 and 22 July 1812, 18 Jan. and 25 Aug. 1813, 27 May, 27 June, 26 Aug., and 10 Oct. 1814, 18 July 1817 (Farington 1978–, XI, pp. 4035, 4072, XII, pp. 4156, 4161–62, 4284, 4414; XIII, pp. 4525, 4537, 4575, 4593; XIV, p. 5057); Courtauld Cuttings, II, pp. 26 (1812) and 68 (1813); V and A Cuttings, III, pp. 823, 892 (1814), IV, p. 937; *Christ Rejected: Catalogue of the Picture, representing the above subject; together with sketches of other Scriptural subjects; painted by Benjamin West, Esq., now exhibiting at No. 125 Pall Mall*, London, 1814 (and reprinted with different accompanying material in 1816, 1821, 1822, etc.); C. Langford, *A Description of the Picture, Christ Receiving the Sentence of Death; with Reflections on Each Principal Character: Painted by Benjamin West, Esq. President of the Royal Academy and now Exhibiting in a Commodious Room Adjoining Carlton House*, London, 1814; A. D. MacQuin, *A description of the picture, Christ rejected by the Jews . . .*, London, 1814 (reprinted Philadelphia, 1830); *Select groups (in five plates) from the grand picture of Christ Rejected Painted by Benjamin West, Esq. . . . . Drawn from the Original Picture by Henry Corbould, Esq. Engraved by Edward Scriven*, with explanatory text in English signed R. H. (Robert Hunt) and text in French signed A. D. M. (Ange Denis Macquin), London, 1814; *Poulson's Advertiser* (? Philadelphia), 13 Feb. 1830; *Literary Rambler* (Glasgow), Sept. 1832; Dunlap 1834, I, pp. 305, 308 (Dunlap 1918, I, pp. 361–62, 366); E. Strahan, *Art Treasures of America*, New York, 1879, II, p. 104, and III, p. 37; Sartain 1899, pp. 168–69, 231–33; Hart 1908, pp. 29–30; Whitley 1928b, pp. 231–32; Hazlitt 1934, XVIII, pp. 28–34; Evans 1959, pp. 92–99, and pl. 70; Haydon 1960–63, pp. 362–63; Constable 1962–68, I, p. 94, and IV, p. 23; Kraemer 1975, pp. 55–56; Dillenberger 1977, pp. 117–19, 121; Alberts 1978, pp. 367–68; Evans 1980, p. 21, fig. 6

The subject of No. 353, in the words of the catalogue published to accompany it when first exhibited in 1814, is "Christ rejected by the Jewish High Priest, the Elders, and the People when brought to them by Pilate from the Judgment Hall." The event is variously described in all four Gospels, and the catalogue contains quotations from Matthew 27, Mark 15, Luke 23, and John 19, preceded by lines from Isaiah 53 which foretell Christ's Passion. According to the description in the catalogue, the architectural setting denotes "the Roman magnificence wherever they had established imperial sway." On the left are Roman soldiers with a standard bearing a portrait of the Emperor Tiberius. At the center of the composition are Pilate, who offers to release either Christ or Barabbas, and the chief priests and elders, who demand that Christ be crucified. Slightly to the right of center, before the gesticulating priests and elders, are Joseph of Arimathea, James the Less, and Peter, who turns away and weeps in remorse for having denied Christ; and further to the right are Barabbas and the two condemned thieves. In the lower right corner are the Virgin Mary supported by St. John, Mary Magdalene kneeling on the Cross, and the third Mary accompanied by pious women from Galilee. To their left, below Christ, is the executioner showing two boys the instruments of the Crucifixion. In the gallery in the background above Pilate are Herod and Pilate's wife.

Following the description of the painting, the catalogue also included a paragraph headed "Object of the Artist":

It has been Mr. West's object, in the delineation of this subject, to excite feelings in the spectator similar to those produced by a perusal of the Sacred Texts, which so pathetically describe these awful events. As part of the means for accomplishing this end, several incidents, which were in connection with the main circumstance, have been introduced to contrast with the meekness and sufferings of the "Man of Sorrows", and to shew the simplicity and purity of the Gospel Dispensation, in opposition to the gaudy and earthly objects of the Heathen and Jewish systems. The delineation of nearly the whole scale of human passions, from the basest to those which partake most of the divine nature, has thus been necessarily attempted.

Elsewhere, the catalogue states, "For such a subject an Epic composition was demanded; for it seemed every way proper that the principal characters, as well as the Divine Christ himself, should be brought together on the canvas, . . ." This echoes West's earlier ideas about "Epic representation" in the treatment of historical subjects, which are quoted in the entry for the *Death of Nelson* (No. 108).

West seems to have undertaken the painting as a sequel to *Christ Healing the Sick* (No. 336), which he sold for an unprecedented price in March of 1811 and which had extraordinary popular success when exhibited at the British Institution. He evidently painted an oil sketch of the subject as early as July 1811 (see No. 354), and on 21 November 1811, he told Joseph Farington that he was beginning a painting 16 ft. high and 22 ft. wide. At that time the canvas was being prepared; West intended to start painting on it in the following January and expected to finish it in six months. Farington saw the large canvas on 31 January 1812, but West did not complete the large painting within six months, and several entries in Farington's diary from 1812 and 1813 contain reports of his progress on the work. Accounts of the state of completion of the picture and descriptions of it also began to appear in the press as early as December 1812, and it was seen and discussed by numerous visitors to West's studio before it was finally completed (for example, Constable's uncle, David Pike Watts, went to see it in December 1813). On 17 March 1814, West wrote to Joseph Wharton in Philadelphia that it was now completed.[1]

While at work on No. 353, West told Farington on 18 January 1813, that he had been offered 8,000 guineas for the picture. An undated and unidentified press cutting (in the Courtauld Institute files), which describes the picture as nearly finished, states that he had been offered 10,000 guineas and "five hundred guineas beyond any sum that may be offered higher than ten thousand guineas." John Constable's mother wrote to her son on 8 March 1813, a year before No. 353 was completed, that she had heard West had been offered £12,000, or £6,000 and the full profits from one year's exhibition, and other similarly high figures were mentioned in the press.[2] West accepted none of these offers, retaining the picture and exhibiting it himself, and it may be that they were all more or less fictitious, the rumors of such sums serving, of course, to generate public interest in the exhibition of the work. Fifteen years after its completion, although bought in at the Robins sale of 1829, No. 353 was bought in for a price of 3,000 guineas, which was by far the highest price achieved by any work in the posthumous sales of West's works and the same amount as the much-publicized price which West had received for *Christ Healing the Sick* (No. 336) in 1811.

The exhibition of No. 353 took place in premises in Pall Mall, which had served from 1769 to 1779 as the first home of the Royal Academy. This was Crown property adjacent to Carlton House, and according to

a paragraph that appeared in the press prior to the exhibition's opening, it was appropriated to West's use at the command of the Prince Regent. A drawing in the Pierpont Morgan Library, dated 21 December 1813, showing No. 353 in an interior hung with heavy draperies, evidently reflects West's plans for the installation.[3] Farington visited the exhibition room on 27 May 1814, when workmen were still there preparing it. Private views of the exhibition began on 1 June, and it opened to the public on Thursday, 9 June. A notice in the press dated 22 October 1814, announced that due to continuing interest the exhibition would stay open until further notice, every day except Sunday, from ten a.m. until the evening. In 1815 and 1816 the painting was joined by No. 338, the second version of *Christ Healing the Sick*, on exhibition in London before being sent to Philadelphia, and a design of the *Crucifixion* presumably related to West's unrealized west window for St. George's Chapel (see No. 356). Then in November 1817, they were replaced by the large, final version of *Death on the Pale Horse* (No. 401). At all times, the main works were accompanied by from ten to fifteen small pictures or sketches of religious works. According to the entry in the Robins sale catalogue, 240,000 people saw No. 353 during the public exhibition. An account book recording daily receipts for the first two months of the exhibition in 1814 shows an average daily attendance of close to 400 people and a daily income of from £20 to £25, based on the sale of admission tickets at one shilling apiece and catalogues at sixpence.[4] Against this income West had weekly expenses of £7.17.0. for the wages of a secretary, two attendants, and a porter, and £5.3.0. for advertising, leaving him an average net profit of well over £100 per week.

In addition to the catalogue published in 1814, which itself contained a description of the picture and the brief statement of the "Object of the Artist" quoted above, further descriptive and critical pamphlets were published by Ange Denis Macquin, who had previously written one for *Christ Healing the Sick* in 1811, and by C. Langford. The critical response appears to have been less extensive and less wholeheartedly laudatory than that to *Christ Healing the Sick* three years before, the most memorable being a six-page extremely hostile diatribe by William Hazlitt.[5]

Following West's death, the painting hung opposite the large *Death on the Pale Horse* (No. 401) in the Great Room in West's gallery in Newman Street; it is visible in both the Cattermole/Le Keux engraving and the Pasmore painting of the gallery (ill. pp. 150 and 151). Bought in in 1829, it was taken the same year by Benjamin West, Jr., to America, where it was exhibited in New York, Philadelphia, and, according to William Dunlap, throughout the Union. It was back in Britain and exhibited in Glasgow in September 1832.[6] The subsequent history of the picture is somewhat obscure. According to John Sartain, a picture restorer from Philadelphia named Richardson learned that the painting was rolled up and in storage in a shop in Rathbone Place in London. Richardson subsequently told Joseph Harrison of Philadelphia (1811–1874) about it, and Harrison arranged to buy it and bring it to Philadelphia. Sartain does not indicate when Harrison bought it. *Christ Rejected* was exhibited at the Pennsylvania Academy in 1843, and, although catalogued as lent by Benjamin West, London, it seems unlikely that a work of such large dimensions would have been sent across the Atlantic again to be part of single exhibition. So it may have been there because of Harrison; otherwise the first sure year that it is recorded in Harrison's possession is 1862, when Sartain made an engraving after it. After Harrison's death it was given by his widow to the Pennsylvania Academy, there rejoining *Death on the Pale Horse*, which hangs opposite.

West's oil sketch of 1811 is No. 354 below. In addi-

tion to the drawing catalogued here as No. 355, two rather slight compositional drawings on the same sheet, differing considerably from No. 353 and with Christ at the center in both, were formerly in the collection of H. H. Margary.[7] A larger detailed drawing of the hat and robe worn by the chief priest, containing notes of the colors and the jewels on the breast-plate was formerly in the collection of Mrs. E. K. Rule.[8]

A large sepia drawing of "Christ before Pilate," after West, by "Corbold" (*sic*) was sold by West's descendants in 1898.[9] This was presumably a copy of No. 353 made by Henry Corbould to be the basis of an engraving and may be identical with No. 355 below. A "print on the largest dimensions ever engraved" after No. 353 was announced, and the exhibition in Pall Mall was closed for a short time to allow an "eminent draughtsman," who must have been Corbould, to make a drawing after the picture the same size as the proposed plate. This plate, if it had been the size of the Corbould drawing ($31\frac{1}{2} \times 41\frac{1}{2}$ in.), would indeed have been huge, larger than any other engraving after West, but it never appeared, and in its stead two series of stipple engravings by Edward Scriven after drawings by Corbould of details of the painting were published in 1814 and 1820. Several highly detailed paintings in sepia monochrome in oil on paper (usually mounted on board) which correspond to the Scriven prints are known, and would appear to be copies by Corbould after No. 353.

In 1821 William Dunlap painted a large picture of *Christ Rejected*, based on the Scriven prints of details of No. 353 and upon printed descriptions of the picture, which he had never seen. This picture he exhibited successfully in Philadelphia, Boston, New York, and elsewhere, accompanying the exhibition with a pamphlet acknowledging his debts to West. When Dunlap finally saw No. 353 in New York in 1829, he discovered that his groupings "were as different as if he had never read a description of his picture." Dunlap then repainted his picture removing the borrowed figures and replacing them with others of his own invention.[10]

Statements in the literature on Thomas Sully, that Sully made a copy of No. 353 to serve as the basis of a key,[11] probably confuse the latter with No. 338, of which there is a key based on a drawing by Sully. No key to No. 353 is known, and Sully, like Dunlap, could not have seen the picture until it came to America in 1829.

The figures of Pilate and the chief priest next to him appear on an otherwise bare canvas of much smaller dimensions than No. 353 in the lower right corner of George Henry Harlow's portrait of West exhibited at the Royal Academy in 1815.[12]

See also pp. 142–152 above.

---

[1] Quoted in Hart 1908, pp. 29–30.

[2] A price of 10,000 guineas, or 7,000 and the profits from the first year's exhibition is quoted in Whitley 1928b, p. 232.

[3] Kraemer 1975, pp. 55–56 (99) and pl. 64. Another drawing intended for the same purpose is referred to by Kraemer.

[4] Historical Society of Pennsylvania, Philadelphia, extra-illustrated Galt, II, pp. 106–12. On 26 August 1814, West told Farington that the average attendance had been 472 persons per day.

[5] Farington's diary entry for 27 June 1814, which was ultimately prompted by the appearance of Hazlitt's criticism, cites the negative attitudes of several patrons.

[6] We are indebted to Hamish Miles for pointing out an announcement in the *Literary Rambler*, Glasgow, Sept. 1832, in which the picture is described as "having just returned from a voyage across the Atlantic" (letter to Helmut von Erffa, 20 Feb. 1960).

[7] Crayon on white paper, sheet size 6 × 11 in.

[8] Pen and ink, $12\frac{5}{8} \times 7\frac{1}{2}$ in.

[9] Christie's, London, 18 and 19 March 1898, lot 147.

[10] See Dunlap 1918, I, pp. 335–62, passim. Dunlap also exhibited a *Barabbas and the Thieves*, described as "Sketch

354

from West," at the National Academy of Design, New York, 1826 (81).
[11] Edward Biddle and Mantle Fielding, *The Life and Works of Thomas Sully*, Philadelphia, 1921, p. 347 (2201).
[12] Versions (both approximately 20 × 16 in.) in the collection of Simon Houfe and formerly with Victor Spark, New York.

354 Christ Rejected 1811

MEMORIAL ART GALLERY OF THE UNIVERSITY OF ROCHESTER, ROCHESTER, NEW YORK

Oil on paper, mounted on panel: $30\frac{1}{4} \times 42\frac{1}{4}$ in. (77 × 107.5 cm.)

Signed lower center (on step): *B. West July 15th 1811*

PROV: John Bligh (1767–1831), fourth Earl of Darnley, by 1824; by descent to the eighth Earl, by whom sold, Christie's, London, 1 May 1925, lot 90; Appleby Brothers, London, 1957; John Nicholson Gallery, New York, 1961; acquired by Rochester in 1964 (Marion Gould Fund)

EXH: RA 1815 (110) "The original sketch for the great picture of Christ rejected, 'He is brought as a lamb to the slaughter, and as a sheep before her shearers is dumb, so he openeth not his mouth.' Isaiah, chap. liii, part of ver. 7"; BI 1824 (161) lent by the Earl of Darnley; Washington and Philadelphia 1980

LISTED: Galt, p. 234 ("The sketch of Christ Rejected"); Dillenberger, pp. 189 (510) and 214

LIT: Farington Diary, 21 Nov. 1811, 22 July 1812, and 5 June 1815 (Farington 1978—, XI, p. 4035, XII, p. 4161, and XIII, p. 4638); V and A Cuttings, IV, pp. 924, 939, and 949; *Burlington Magazine*, XCIX, Dec. 1957, p. iv (adv.); *Art Quarterly*, XXIV, Winter 1961 (adv.); Dillenberger 1977, p. 118, pl. 80

On 21 November 1811, West told Joseph Farington that he intended to paint a large picture of "Pilate Shewing Christ to the Jews" (i.e., *Christ Rejected*, No. 353) and showed him a small painted study for it. Farington noted a date on the study indicating that it had been painted the previous July. That is consistent with the date of 15 July 1811 on No. 354, and it seems evident, therefore, that the latter was the painted study Farington saw. On 22 July 1812, West showed Farington the large painting of *Christ Rejected*, upon which he was laying in the first color, and pointed out several alterations differing from the small study: "He found that it was necessary to introduce more objects in order to fill up & give interest. Upon a small scale there did not seem to be a want of them, but upon a large scale it was necessary."

Although in general No. 353 follows No. 354 closely, without conspicuous alterations in composition, there are many more objects and figures in the large picture,

confirming what Farington recorded. In No. 353 there are five women standing behind the Virgin in the lower right corner of the composition, whereas in No. 354 there are four. St. John, who supports the Virgin's outstretched arm in No. 353 is an addition, and there is one more pious woman from Galilee behind Mary Magdalene. The two thieves behind Barabbas in No. 353 and a group of soldiers between Barabbas and the Virgin are not included in No. 354. On the left side of No. 353 a bald man in the lower left corner, several other figures, and a Roman standard have been added. There are also additional figures in the galleries in the background and numerous lesser changes in details and expression.

The scale of the figures in relation to the overall size of the composition is somewhat larger in No. 353 than in No. 354 and the horizontal spaces have been reduced. Thus Christ appears somewhat closer to the left edge of the composition in the large painting; the high priest is closer to Pilate; Joseph of Arimathea is closer to the priest, and so on across the painting.

Like most of West's sketches on paper, No. 354 is on several sheets joined together. The arched top, which is separated from the rest of the composition by a seam running across the picture, is not typical of West and may be a later addition.

When the work appeared at the Royal Academy in 1815, the year following the opening of the exhibition of No. 353 in Pall Mall, it seems to have been universally praised, one critic declaring it "decidedly superior to the picture itself." Sir George Beaumont told Farington that it was the one work in the exhibition to have "the true quality of art, ... that comprehensiveness and completeness which is found in the work of the great masters ... Since the time of LeBrun there has been no artist to be compared with West."

355 Christc Rejected (?)1814

LOCATION UNKNOWN

(Drawing, sepia, 31½ × 41½ in.) (80 × 105.5 cm.)

PROV: (?) sold by Mrs. Albert F. West, Christie's, London, 19 March 1898, lot 147 ("Christ before Pilate," after West by Corbould, sepia drawing, 31½ × 41½ in.), bt. by Misell for £1.12.0.

EXH: 125 Pall Mall 1818 (12) "Drawing of Christ Rejected"

When a drawing of this subject was exhibited in 1818 as one of the group of pictures and sketches accompanying *Death on the Pale Horse* in Pall Mall, the entry in the catalogue was accompanied by a note: "Proposals for publishing by subscription, a Print from this Picture, to be had of Mr. Smart the Secretary; and of whom may be had a Description of the Painting of the same subject." Hence, it seems likely that the exhibited drawing may have been a drawing made after the painting in connection with the announced print (which never appeared) rather than an otherwise unrecorded study for the painting. If so, although not identified as such in the catalogue, it was probably not drawn by West himself but by Henry Corbould, as we know that West's descendants sold a large drawing of the subject by Corbould in 1898. For a fuller discussion see the entry for No. 353. Corbould made drawings, which served as the basis of engravings, after several of West's works and was almost certainly the "eminent draughtsman" who, according to an announcement in the press, was making a drawing the size of the intended plate, "on the largest dimensions ever engraved," after the painting.[1]

[1] V and A Cuttings, IV, p. 937.

356 The Crucifixion 1796

LOCATION UNKNOWN

(90 × 72 in.) (228.5 × 183 cm.)

PROV: Design for a window commissioned by George III for St. George's Chapel, Windsor (1797 account: "The Crucifying of our Saviour [an oil picture], and the cartoon from that picture [. . .] for the great west window, Collegiate Church," 1797, £2,100; 1801 account, p. 212: listed with paintings for the King's Chapel in Windsor Castle, no. 30, "The Crucifixion, a study in oil colour, for the glass painting by Messrs. Jervis and Forrest to colour from, and the cartoon the size of the window," £1,050; sold by West's sons, Robins, London, 22–25 May 1829, lot 47 ("The Crucifixion of Our Saviour," 7 ft. 6 in. × 6 ft.," Painted by command of His late Majesty. From this design a painted glass was to be executed for the large west window in St. George's Chapel, at Windsor"), bt. by W. Ward for £388.10.0. on behalf of Raphael West; sold by Raphael West, Robins, London, 16 July 1831, lot 39

EXH: RA 1797 (21) "The crucifixion"; BI 1807 (19) "Crucifixion of Our Saviour," 9 ft. 3 in. × 7 ft. 6 in. (including frame); (?) 125 Pall Mall 1816; (?) 125 Pall Mall 1818 (1); West's Gallery 1821 (91), 1822–28 (139)

LISTED: See p. 324; *PC*, p. 560 ("The design of our Saviour's Crucifixion, painted in colours"); *UM*, p. 527; Barlow, p. 431; *BA*, p. 13; Galt, p. 217; Dillenberger, pp. 140 (38) and 148 (104)

LIT: Farington Diary, 16 Dec. 1796, 11, 14, 17, and 31 Jan., 22 Feb. and 6 Nov. 1797, 17 Sept. and 11 Dec. 1804, and 15 July 1811 (Farington 1978—, III, pp. 720–21, 743–44, 747, 749–51, 760, 777, 915–17, VI, pp. 2412–13, 2468, and XI, p. 3970); V and A Cuttings, III, pp. 780 and 787; *Windsor Guide* 1807, pp. 73–74; Thomas Willement, *An Account of the Restoration of the Collegiate Chapel of St. George, Windsor*, London, 1844, p. 10; Hope 1913, pp. 471–72, note 100; Kraemer 1975, pp. 15–16, and 58; Dillenberger 1977, pp. 58 and 96; Alberts 1978, p. 226; Meyer 1979, pp. 62–65

No. 356, the design for a window intended for St. George's Chapel, Windsor, and No. 357, the cartoon based on it, have both disappeared. The window itself was destroyed in 1864, but a partial record of its appearance is provided by a drawing at Windsor, which is discussed below.

The painter Richard Westall, who saw No. 356 in West's studio in December 1796, told Joseph Farington that it was

the strangest thing He ever saw. All sorts of shapes are introduced, & every incident which is described in Scriptures is introduced in it, forming altogether a most absurd jumble.—West seemed delighted with the performance and said He had formed his composition on the Greek model, and that a Groupe of Virgins in one corner serves as the Chorus.

Although Westall saw the "painted design" in 1796 and described it then as "intended for the West window of Windsor Chapel," West himself in the account prepared in 1797 of his works for George III gave 1797 as the date of Nos. 356 and 357, and it may be that he did not receive the actual commission until the latter year. According to the *Windsor Guide* of 1807, West

exhibited a cartoon of the *Crucifixion* to His Majesty in 1797, and, that being approved, Mr. Forest (or Forrest) was engaged to paint it on glass.[1]

The glass-painter Forrest had previously executed three windows in the side aisles of St. George's Chapel after designs by West (see Nos. 298, 306, and 309), completing the third of them, showing the *Wise Men's Offering*, in 1796. The commission for a *Crucifixion* for the large west window of the nave was the last commission given to West by George III for St. George's Chapel, and it was the most important. The size of the window, whose dimensions were determined by the existing architecture, was to be 36 ft. high by 28 ft. across, making it the largest single composition ever undertaken by the artist (and according to the *Windsor Guide* making the cartoon the largest picture in the world). The similar space of the east window of the nave, which also had glass based on designs by West, (see Nos. 360, 367, and 369), had been divided into three compositions, a central *Resurrection* flanked by separate scenes on either side, whereas West treated the west window as one undivided design.

For the west window West charged the King 2,000 guineas (the same total as for the east window), dividing the price into 1,000 guineas each for the design (No. 356) and for the cartoon (No. 357). These prices were the highest West received from George III, indeed the highest he received for any work until the British Institution paid him 3,000 guineas for *Christ Healing the Sick* (No. 336) in 1811, and they seem to have attracted criticism. In conversation with Farington in December 1804, West defended himself against what had been said about the price, implying that 2,000 guineas was a low price for a picture of such size, "containing near 70 figures, many of them Colossal in size," and in 1811, when the British Institution was about to make a profit on *Christ Healing the Sick* after paying 3,000 guineas for it, West told Farington, "that it had happily proved that He had not overcharged the King" for the *Crucifixion* window.[2]

The Crucifixion. Drawing showing the unfinished window based on Nos. 356 and 357 (St. George's Chapel, Windsor)

The first reference to the *Crucifixion* window in Farington's diary occurs on 16 December 1796, recording Richard Westall's description quoted above. This painted design was evidently the *Crucifixion* that in January 1797 West told Farington he had completed by the previous October and presumably the same *Crucifixion* that West exhibited at the Royal Academy in May 1797, although he exhibited it without indication that it was for St. George's Chapel. On 17 September 1804, Farington and several companions called on Forrest, the glass-maker, in Windsor and saw part of the window, upon which, according to Farington, Forrest had been working for five years and had completed less than half. In 1807, the *Windsor Guide* reported that Forrest had been working on the window for ten years and had completed about 500 of the window's 1,000 square feet, with considerably more glass painted and ready for burning. But the *Guide* also mentioned rumors that the window would never be finished and cited as one reason Forrest's "ill state of health, which he seems to have injured by close application." The rumors proved accurate. Forrest died that same year.[3] His widow attempted to carry on the work, but the window was never completed or installed. The unfinished glass remained in storage until 1846, when it was sent to Calcutta, and installed there as the east window of St. Paul's Cathedral. This window was destroyed in a cyclone in 1864, and its appearance is known only from an engraving showing the interior of the cathedral at the time of its consecration in 1847.[4] As this engraving shows a window twice as high as wide and hence with proportions considerably different from those recorded for West's cartoon (and those of the actual west window of St. George's Chapel), and as all evidence indicates that the glass was never completed, the composition of the window shown as installed in Calcutta was modified substantially from what West and Forrest had originally intended.

A squared drawing in watercolors in the Windsor Chapter Library, which is inscribed on the mount, *Sketch of an unfinished Window painted on Glass by Mr. Forrest from a cartoon by Benj. West Esq. intended for the great West Window of St. George's Chapel, Windsor*, although incomplete and crude, provides the best evidence of what the window originally was supposed to look like (ill. p. 361). The most plausible explanation of this drawing is that it was made after Forrest's death to record what he and Mrs. Forrest had done before the unfinished glass was put into storage. The lower right hand corner is blank, and several individual squares throughout the composition are blank as well, doubtlessly indicating areas of glass that had not been completed at the time that the drawing was made. The drawing shows a composition wider than it is high, and bears the notation: "Width of the Window 28 ft. 7 in. Height of ditto 23 ft. 8 in."[5] Although the width recorded here corresponds to the dimension listed in West's account of 1801 and repeated on several other occasions, the height clearly does not. These measurements as well as the drawing itself would seem to indicate that Forrest had not completed the bottom third of the composition. The measurements of the actual west window of St. George's Chapel are remarkably close to West's 36 × 28 ft., and a window of that size would comprise an area of approximately 1,000 square feet as reported in the *Windsor Guide* of 1807, so there seems little reason to believe that West ever intended the window to be of the reduced size and different proportions recorded in the drawing at Windsor.

West painted No. 356 at the time he was experimenting with the so-called Venetian Secret (for which see also Nos. 22, 133, and 543), but to what extent he used the Secret in No. 356 is not clear. West told Farington in January 1797 that Thomas Provis had first approached him about the discovery in December 1795 and that he had subsequently made an experiment

under the direction of Provis's daughter. Following this experiment, which was a failure, West told Farington tht he did not see the Provises again until 31 October 1796, "after he had completed his picture of the Crucifixion. At that time West declared that he had been quite ignorant of the Secrets of the process, though he had made the experiment mentioned." After 31 October he resumed experiments with the process and Miss Provis communicated all the Secret to him. Nevertheless, both Provis and his daughter separately told Farington on several occasions that West had attempted to imitate their process in the *Crucifixion*. According to the father, West put off seeing them "during which time West painted his Crucifixion in which he attempted to make use of the discovery but at last found himself defficient in information. He then applied to Provis with excuses for the delay."[6] When No. 356 appeared at the Royal Academy in 1797, it was described by at least two reviewers as painted in a new process or manner, and was criticized by one for "an odd mixture of the raw and the gaudy" and by the other for "a dark and purpurine hue."

In addition to the *Crucifixion* intended for St. George's Chapel, a "Crucifixion" destined for George III's chapel in Windsor Castle is included in the early published lists of West's works.[7] There is no evidence that he ever painted this second picture, and as in the case with other subjects he designed for St. George's Chapel, the reappearance of the title may simply reflect a confusing together of the works intended for the two chapels at Windsor.[8] The subject does appear on the Swarthmore diagram of 1801 (ill. p. 580), but as noted elsewhere, these diagrams, made after West had been told to stop work on the chapel, contain several subjects from St. George's Chapel which do not appear to have been thought of earlier in conjunction with the Royal Chapel. In the Robins sale of May 1829, No. 356 was explicitly described as a design for the west window of St. George's Chapel. A *Crucifixion* sold by Raphael West in 1831 together with two works intended for the Royal Chapel in Windsor Castle (Nos. 232 and 234) was most probably No. 356 again, after it had been bought in in 1829, not a second otherwise unrecorded "Crucifixion" painted for George III's chapel.

Related drawings are in the Pierpont Morgan Library[9] and in the collection of Julius Held.[10] Several other drawings were at one time in the collection of H. H. Margary.[11]

[1] The window itself is listed in *PC*, p. 562 ("The Crucifixion, in the window of the Collegiate Church of Windsor," [28 × 36]); *UM*, p. 528; *AA*, p. 68 (36 ft. × 28); *BA*, p. 15; Galt, p. 221; Dillenberger, p. 154 (155). The wording in the lists misleadingly implies that the window had been installed in St. George's Chapel. See Meyer 1979, passim, for a thorough discussion of the windows for St. George's Chapel and for a summation of the available information about Forrest. Although West listed both Jervis and Forrest in his account of 1801, it appears that Jervis (Thomas Jervais), who had been responsible for the earlier *Resurrection* window at the east end of the chapel, did not work on the west window.

[2] In December 1804 the price West defended was 2,000 guineas, which is in accord with all other documentation. In 1811 he told Farington that he had asked £1,500, which seems to be a mistake.

[3] A letter from West to Mrs. Forrest dated 8 October 1807, which refers to "the late Mr. Forrest," is in the Historical Society of Pennsylvania. See also Meyer 1979, p. 62, n. 35.

[4] Reproduced in *A Short History of St. Paul's Cathedral Calcutta*, Calcutta, 1956, p. 5; a detail is reproduced in Meyer 1979, p. 64, fig. 10.

[5] It also bears the notation: "Each frame 11 inches Square."

[6] Farington Diary, 11 Jan. 1797. Other entries repeating the Provises' assertions about the *Crucifixion* are 31 Jan. and 27 Feb. 1797. West's explanation is in the entry for 17 Jan. 1797.

[7] *PC*, p. 561 (Gospel Dispensation, 16 × 28 ft.); *UM*, p. 527; *AA*, p. 67 (28 ft. × 36); Barlow, p. 432 (36 ft. × 28); *BA*,

p. 14 (28 ft. × 36); Galt, p. 219; Meyer 1975, p. 265; Dillenberger, p. 148 (106).

[8] None of the measurements given in note 7 has any similarity to those of any of the pictures actually painted by West for George III's chapel, while those listed by Barlow and in the *Academic Annals*, and *La Belle Assemblée* are identical (though transposed in two cases) with those of No. 357, the cartoon based on No. 356.

[9] Black chalk on blue paper, 12⅜ × 9⅜ in. (Kraemer 1975, pp. 15–16, no. 21 and pl. 11). For other Crucifixion drawings in the same collection, see No. 358.

[10] Pen, ink and colored chalks, 11 7/16 × 9½ in.; ill. in Meyer 1979, fig. 9.

[11] The most important of these is a small drawing of the composition in black and white chalks on blue paper, 6 5/16 × 4¾ in.

357 The Crucifixion *c.* 1797

LOCATION UNKNOWN

(432 × 336 in.) (1097 × 853 cm.)

PROV: Cartoon for the window discussed in the preceding entry (1797 account: listed together with No. 356; 1801 account, p. 212: listed together with No. 356 under no. 30, . . . "the cartoon the size of the window," and also under no. 31, "The west end window of St. George's Chapel, 28 feet wide by 36 high, for them to draw the figures from on the glass," £1,050)

LISTED: See No. 298; *PC*, p. 560 ("The Cartoon from the above design [No. 356], for the west window in the Collegiate Church, painting on glass, 36 feet high by 28"); *UM*, p. 527; Barlow, p. 431; *BA*, p. 13; Galt, p. 217; Dillenberger, pp. 140 (39) and 148 (105)

LIT: See No. 356

No. 357 is (or was) the cartoon based on No. 356. It may be identical with the *Crucifixion* mentioned in Farington's diary in 1817 and discussed in the following entry.

358 The Crucifixion (?)1817

LOCATION UNKNOWN

(432 × 336 in.) (1097 × 853 cm.)

LIT: Farington Diary, 22 May 1817 (Farington 1978–, XIV, p. 5023); Kraemer 1975, pp. 58–59; Dillenberger 1977, pp. 212, 123

All that is known about this work is an entry in Joseph Farington's diary dated 22 May 1817 recording conversation at a dinner at Sir George Beaumont's:

Mr. West now almost 79 years old, told us that beside the great picture of *Death on the Pale Horse*, which He now has in hand, He has upon a Canvass 36 feet high by 28 feet deep, a picture drawn in, the subject, *The Crucifixion*.

Neither Farington nor any one else mentions ever seeing the actual work in West's studio. At this advanced stage of West's life, it seems more likely that such an ambitious undertaking would have been the reworking of an earlier composition, as was the *Death on the Pale Horse* (No. 401), which he mentioned to Farington along with the large *Crucifixion*, rather than a completely new design. Thus No. 358, which presumably the artist never completed, was probably closely related to Nos. 356 and 357. Indeed the dimensions cited by Farington are the same as those recorded for No. 358, the cartoon for the west window of St. George's Chapel, and it may be that the work West referred to in 1817 was the cartoon itself, returned to him when the project of making a window based on it was abandoned following the death of Forrest, the glass-maker.

Ruth Kraemer has associated three drawings in the Pierpont Morgan Library with this late *Crucifixion*.[1] However, the attribution of these three drawings to West is open to question (Kraemer ascribes the puzzling draughtsmanship to West's old age), and there is no real evidence to connect them with the picture mentioned by Farington.

[1] Kraemer 1975, pp. 58–59, nos. 104, 105, 106, and plates 66 and 67.

359

359 The Madre-dolorosa 1798

LOCATION UNKNOWN

Oil on canvas: $25\frac{3}{4} \times 18\frac{1}{2}$ in. (65.5 × 47 cm.)

Signed lower left: *B. West 1798*

PROV: William Beckford, Fonthill Abbey, Wilts., by *c.* 1804; in the Fonthill catalogue (Christie's), 17 Sept. 1822, lot 21, and sold, Fonthill Abbey (Phillips) 10–15 Oct. 1823, lot 38 for £19.19.0. (in both catalogues as "The Virgin and Dead Christ" and with "St. Anthony of Padua" [No. 417] as a companion); Arthur E. S. Seguin (1809–1852) by 1851; by descent to Mrs. E. S. R. Seguin; on deposit in the Pennsylvania Academy from *c.* 1851 to *c.* 1864 and at the Metropolitan Museum from 1881 to 1923, when purchased by the museum from Mrs. Seguin; sold by the Metropolitan Museum, Parke-Bernet, New York, 27 March 1956, lot 36, bt. by the Archie Shore Galleries

EXH: PAFA 1851 (274) "The Virgin and the Dead Christ," lent by S. Seguin, 1864 (519) lent by Mrs. Seguin

LISTED: *PC*, p. 561 ("The Madra Dolo Roso," painted for, and in the possession of Wm. Beckford, Esq. of Fonthill); *UM*, p. 528; Barlow, p. 432 ("The Madre Dolorosa"), *BA*, p. 14 ("The Madre-dolorosa"); Galt, p. 219; Dillenberger, p. 150 (129)

LIT: Storer 1812, p. 20; Bryson Burroughs, *Catalogue of Paintings: The Metropolitan Museum of Art*, New York, 1920, p. 328 and fig. 57; Kraemer 1975, pp. 92–93

Helmut von Erffa questioned the attribution of No. 359 to West. Photographs made before it was sold by the Metropolitan Museum show that it was in deteriorated condition, and that parts of it seemed to have been clumsily repainted. Nonetheless, it appears to be by West. A signature and date of *1798* are visible in photographs, and that date fits with No. 359's Beckford provenance. West exhibited works painted for William Beckford and intended for Fonthill Abbey at the Royal Academy in 1797, 1798, and 1799. At the Academy in 1799 West exhibited "The Vision of St. Anthony of Padua (a sketch for a picture to be painted for the Abbey at Fonthill)." This sketch was probably No. 418, which remained in West's possession, and the picture for Fonthill was No. 417, which the Fonthill sale catalogues of 1822 and 1823 identified as the companion of No. 359. In 1812 Nos. 359 and 417 hung opposite each other in a dressing room at Fonthill. The subjects of both works, which hardly reflect conventional English Protestant tastes, must have been dictated by Beckford.

A drawing showing the Virgin and dead Christ in positions similar to those in No. 359, but in a horizontal composition with additional figures, is in the collection of the University of Glasgow.[1] A drawing by Raphael West of the Virgin and the dead Christ, which Ruth Kraemer has associated with No. 359, is in the Pierpont Morgan Library.[2]

[1] Pen and ink, $5\frac{3}{4} \times 8$ in., signed lower right: *B. West 1799*.
[2] Kraemer 1975, pp. 92–93 (224) and pl. 116.

360 The Resurrection c. 1782
See color illustration, p. 91

MUSEO DE ARTE DE PONCE, PUERTO RICO

Oil on canvas: 118×52 in. (arched top) (300 × 132 cm.)

PROV: Painted together with Nos. 367 and 369 as a design for a window commissioned by George III for St. George's Chapel, Windsor (1797 account: "The design in colours on canvas of our Saviour's Resurrection and the Cartoons from those designs—thirty feet in height by thirty in breadth for [. . .] the Collegiate Church of Windsor," 1782, £2,200; 1801 account, p. 212: listed with paintings for the King's chapel in Windsor Castle, 32, "The Ressurection, a study in oil colour, for glass painting by Messrs. Jervis and Forrest to colour from," £525); sold by West's sons, Robins, London, 22–25 May 1829, lot 141 ("The Resurrection of Our Saviour," 10 ft. × 4 ft. 6 in., "designed for the centre compartment of the Great Window"), bt. by Bone for £157.10.0., on behalf of Joseph Neeld, MP, Grittleton House, Wilts.; by descent in the Neeld family until sold by Miss C. K. M. Neeld, Christie's, London, 16 Nov. 1962, lot 97, bt. by Weitzner; acquired by the Ponce Museum (Fundación Luis A. Ferré) in the same year

EXH: RA 1783 (16) "Design for the east window of St. George's chapel, Windsor: in the centre, the resurrection; on the right hand, St. Peter and St. John; on the left, the three Marys" [see also Nos. 367 and 369]; West's Gallery 1821 (62), (?) 1822–28 (28)

LISTED: See p 324; *PC*, p. 560 ("The design of our Saviour's Resurrection, painted in colours, with the Women going to the Sepulchre; also Peter and John"); *UM*, p. 527; *BA*, p. 13 (12 ft. × 10 [with the two side panels]); Galt, p. 217; Dillenberger, pp. 140 (36), 148 (32), and 215

LIT: V and A Cuttings, I, p. 232 (1783); *Windsor Guide* 1792, pp. 51–55; *Windsor Guide* 1807, pp. 74–76; Thomas Willement, *An Account of the Restorations of*

the Collegiate Chapel of St. George, Windsor, London, 1844, pp. 6–8; Papendiek 1887, I, pp. 277–78, II, pp. 38–39, 97; Charlotte Barrett, ed., *Diary and Letters of Madame d'Arblay (1778–1840)*, London, 1905, III, pp. 84, 152, 154–55; Hope 1913, II, pp. 388–92, 426–27, 429; W. S. Lewis, ed., *Horace Walpole's Correspondence*, XI, New Haven, 1944, p. 363 (letter of 9 Oct. 1781); Julius S. Held, *Museo de Arte de Ponce, Fundación Luis A. Ferré: Catalogue I: Paintings of the European and American Schools*, Ponce, Puerto Rico, 1965, p. 194 and pl. 159; Kraemer 1975, pp. 19–23, fig. 16; Dillenberger 1977, pp. 51, 96, and pl. 29; Meyer 1979, pp. 55–58, fig. 2; Wynne 1982, p. 60; Pressly 1983, p. 54, fig. 27a

No. 360 is the design for the central compartment of the tripartite east window of St. George's Chapel, Windsor. The companion designs for the two flanking compositions are Nos. 367 and 369 below. The actual window was removed (and evidently destroyed) in 1863, but its appearance is recorded in a number of early nineteenth-century views of the interior of the chapel (ill. p. 90).[1]

This window was the first of a series of windows designed by West for St. George's Chapel between 1782 and 1797.[2] According to contemporary guides to Windsor, the idea for installing a new east window in the chapel was first proposed by George III, at whose request in the beginning of 1782, Dr. Lockman, Canon of the chapel, prepared a plan for a subscription to pay for the window. In his account of 1797 of his work for the King, West gives the date of 1782 as the date of both the designs (Nos. 360, 367, and 369) and the cartoon (see No. 361), so it would seem that he was given the commission in that year. The designs appeared at the Royal Academy in the following year, 1783, along with a drawing of the proposed window, in which the figures were drawn by West and the architectural setting by the antiquarian draughtsman John Carter.[3] A second drawing by Carter showing the window appeared at the Academy in 1785.[4] The latter drawing, according to its title, showed not only West's intended window but also the intended altarpiece of the *Last Supper* (No. 346) which West painted in 1786 to go under it. The actual window was executed in glass by Thomas Jervais and his assistant, a Mr. Forrest (who was to receive the commission to carry out West's subsequent designs for windows for St. George's Chapel instead of Jervais) and evidently installed before 1 January 1787, when Fanny Burney (later Mme. d'Arblay) recorded in her diary seeing the glass in place for the first time.

Fanny Burney's evidence of when the window was put in place is sustained by records, published by Hope, of payments to carpenters, masons, and glaziers for work on the window, which run from 7 August 1785 to 18 March 1787.[5] On the other hand, Mrs. Papendiek describes a temporary installation of the central *Resurrection* panel of the window during George III's illness in the autumn of 1788. According to her account, when the central panel was installed, everyone decided that it was too narrow, whereupon West was commissioned to prepare additional cartoons for the two side compartments. Mrs. Papendiek further states that the window was finally put up permanently after the King's recovery, that is in the spring of 1789. Although Mrs. Papendiek, like Fanny Burney, was a member of the court at Windsor in the 1780s, this account seems wrong. It is not only contradicted by what we know from other sources about the date of the installation, but also by the fact that West had exhibited a design for the window including two side panels as early as 1783. The cartoon for the *Resurrection* (No. 361) was exhibited in the chapel in October 1786, presumably in the place where the completed glass would go, and it may be this event, which is described by Fanny Burney, that was subsequently remembered in a confused fashion as the later temporary installation of the glass itself by Mrs. Papendiek in her memoirs.

A "Resurrection" which appears among the pictures intended for George III's chapel in Windsor Castle on some of the published lists of West's works seems to be no more than the window for St. George's Chapel reappearing in the wrong place.[6] There is no evidence apart from those lists to suggest that West ever painted or intended to paint a Resurrection for the Royal Chapel.

A design for the window in pen and ink and washed in colors was sold by Benjamin West, Jr. in 1839.[7] Five early sketches for the composition are in a sketchbook now in the Yale Center for British Art,[8] and what appear to be further early compositional sketches, varying considerably in detail from No. 360, are at Swarthmore[9] and in the Pierpont Morgan Library.[10] A sheet of studies for the figure of Christ in a number of slightly different positions and of the angel next to him is in the Royal Collection.[11] A separate drawing of Christ and the angel in positions essentially the same as those shown in No. 360 passed through the market in 1977.[12] A large, squared, and highly finished drawing (*right*), which corresponds closely to No. 360 in most major details, but with a much more muscular figure of Christ, is in the Delaware Art Museum.[13] Fanny Burney criticized the figure of Christ in the cartoon (No. 361) as "somewhat too earthly; He seems athletic as an Hercules, and rather as if He derived His superiority from strength of body than from influence of divinity." This criticism, which seems appropriate for the Christ in the Delaware drawing but not for the slim figure in No. 360, suggests that West altered the figure in the cartoon, and that his alteration is reflected in the Delaware drawing. Hence this drawing was probably made after No. 360 was painted, and is possibly a copy after No. 361. Ruth Kraemer also associates a drawing of the Risen Christ and two other slighter studies in the Morgan Library with No. 360.[14] A drawing of a head of Christ, which is signed and dated *1783* and is closer to the head in No. 360 than to that in the Delaware drawing, is in the Historical Society of Pennsylvania.[15] A drawing of an angel removing the stone of the sepulcher, which is also signed and dated *1783* (private collection),[16] appears to be related to the angels in the earlier compositional drawings mentioned above, but there is no angel in a corresponding position in No. 360. Another drawing of an angel with a stone was at one time in the possession of descendants of the artist.[17]

According to the *Windsor Guide*, the window based on No. 360 included among the cherubim and seraphim at the top of the composition a portrait of Prince Octavius, who died in 1783.[18] It is not possible to identify Octavius in No. 360, and since his death occurred on 3 May 1783, after the design was already completed and on exhibition at the Royal Academy, it is unlikely that he would be there, unless West added him later. He does, however, seem to be recognizable in a figure at the top and center of the group in the Delaware drawing discussed above; the pose and features of this figure differ considerably from those of the cherub in the comparable position in No. 360.

In a letter to Mary Berry dated 9 October 1791, Horace Walpole commented on the east window:

> Jarvis's window over the altar after West is rather too sombre for the Resurrection, though it accords with the tone of the choir; and the Christ is a poor figure scrambling to heaven in a fright, as if in dread of being again buried alive; and not ascending calmly in serene dignity.

[1] In addition to the drawing reproduced on p. 90, a watercolor drawing (Royal Collection) by Charles Wild from *c.* 1818 was the basis of an engraving published in Pyne 1819, I, opp. p. 182 and reproduced in Dillenberger 1977, pl. 66. Other views are reproduced in von Erffa 1969, p. 32, and Carr 1980, p. 295, fig. 5.

The Resurrection, drawing for or after No. 361. Delaware Art Museum, Wilmington, Delaware

[2]For the others see Nos. 298, 306, 309, and 356. The series of windows and their place in West's *oeuvre* are discussed at length in the article devoted to them published by Jerry D. Meyer in 1979.

[3]RA 1783 (441) "Drawing of the window in St. George's chapel, Windsor. The figures by Mr. West, the architecture by Mr. Carter."

[4]RA 1785 (452) John Carter, "View of the choir of St. George's chapel, Windsor, in which is introduced the intended painted window and altarpiece, as designed by Mr. West."

[5]The relevant accounts are in Hope 1913, II, pp. 391–92; other accounts published by Hope for subsequent work on the chapel (pp. 392–94) do not include reference to the east window. The *Windsor Guide* of 1802 lists the slightly more inclusive dates of 1785–88 for the execution of the window (p. 75).

[6]*AA*, p. 67 (28 ft. × 32); Barlow, p. 432 ("Christ's Resurrection. Peter, John and the women at the Sepulchre," 36 ft. × 28); Meyer, p. 265; Dillenberger, p. 148 (107).

[7]S. Leigh Sotheby, London, 1 June 1839, lot 82, "The Resurrection of Our Saviour. A design for the large East Window in St. George's Chapel, Windsor." Pen and ink, washed in colors.

[8]Pencil and black chalk, each $6\frac{3}{8} \times 4\frac{1}{8}$ in. (page size).

[9]Black chalk, $12\frac{1}{2} \times 6\frac{5}{8}$ in.

[10]Black chalk, $12\frac{13}{16} \times 7\frac{1}{2}$ in. (Kraemer 1975, pp. 19–21, no. 26, and pl. 17).

[11]Pencil, pen and brown ink, and wash, $7\frac{7}{8} \times 12\frac{1}{8}$ in. (San Antonio 1983, no. 29).

[12]Pencil, pen and brown ink, and wash, $8\frac{3}{4} \times 12$ in., signed lower left, *B. West* (Sotheby's, London, 24 Nov. 1977, lot 2).

[13]Pencil, $23\frac{3}{8} \times 14\frac{1}{4}$ in.

[14]Kraemer 1975, pp. 21–22, nos. 27, 28, 29, and pl. 18.

[15]This is possibly the "Study of the Head of Christ, in the Cartoon of the Resurrection, painted on glass by Jervis, for St. George's Chapel, Windsor." Outline, in pen and bistre. Sold by Benjamin West, Jr., S. Leigh Sotheby, London, 1 June 1839, lot 15.

[16]Pen, 20 × $12\frac{3}{4}$ in.

[17]Black chalk, $11\frac{1}{2} \times 6\frac{5}{8}$ in.

[18]See Nos. 574 and 575.

361 The Resurrection *c.* 1782

LOCATION UNKNOWN

PROV: Cartoon for the window discussed in the preceding entry (1797 account: listed together with No. 360; 1801 account, p. 213: listed with pictures for the Royal Chapel in Windsor Castle, 33, "And the cartoon the size of the window at the east end of St. George's Chapel, 28 feet wide by 36 high, to draw from on the glass," £1,050 . . .)

EXH: St. George's Chapel, Windsor, Oct. 1786 (see No. 360)

LISTED: See No. 298, *PC*, p. 560 ("The Cartoon from the above design [No. 360], for the east window, painted in the Collegiate Church of Windsor, on glass, 36 feet high by 28 wide"); *UM*, p. 527; Barlow, p. 419; *BA*, p. 13; Galt, p. 217; Dillenberger, pp. 140 (37), 148 (109)

LIT: See No. 360

This cartoon, like all but one of the other cartoons for the windows in St. George's Chapel, has disappeared. Its appearance, in so far as that differed from the design (No. 360), may be reflected in a drawing in the Delaware Art Museum, which is discussed in the preceding entry.

West's accounts of 1797 and 1801 give different dimensions for the cartoon, with a discrepancy of 6 ft. between them for the vertical measurement. The published lists of West's works all follow the measurements in the 1801 account of 36 × 28 ft. (the horizontal measurement incorporating the two side compartments as well as the central *Resurrection*), but they also include a separate listing for the actual window and there give its measurements as 32 × 28 ft.[1] Whatever the actual height, in width the central *Resurrection* panel was, of course, much narrower than the window as a whole. In views of the window in situ (ill. p. 90), it appears to be approximately twice as high as wide.

[1]*PC*, p. 562; *UM*, p. 528; *AA*, p. 68; *BA*, p. 15; Galt, p. 221; Dillenberger, p. 153 (154).

362 The Resurrection 1786

ST. GEORGE'S PARISH CHURCH, BARBADOS

Oil on canvas: 84 × 60 in. (213.5 × 152.5 cm.)

Signed lower right: *B. West 1786*

PROV: Commissioned by Henry Frere, Lower Estate Plantation, Barbados, for St. George's Church, but not put in place in the church until *c.* 1820

EXH: RA 1786 (20) "The Resurrection of Our Saviour"

LISTED: *PC*, p. 562 ("The Resurrection of our Saviour, in the Church of Barbadoes," 10 ft. × 6) and p. 563 ("The Resurrection of our Saviour, in a Church at Barbadoes"); *UM*, p. 528 (listed twice on the same page); *AA*, p. 69 ("The Picture in Christ Church in the Island of Barbadoes representing our Saviour's Resurrection," 9 ft. × 6); Barlow, p. 433; *BA*, p. 15; Galt, p. 221; Dillenberger, pp. 154 (160), 158 (195) and 215

362

LIT: V and A Cuttings, I, pp. 279 and 285 (1786); Neville Connell, "St. George's Parish Church, Barbados," *Journal of the Barbados Museum and Historical Society*, XX, May 1953, pp. 133–36; "The Resurrection in St. George's Church," *Barbados Advocate-News*, Sunday, 15 March 1970; Dillenberger 1977, p. 51

The tradition in Barbados that No. 362 was commissioned from the artist is confirmed by a contemporary review of the Royal Academy exhibition of 1786, which describes the picture as "painted for a foreign altar." Henry Frere, who commissioned No. 362 during a trip to London, was President of the Barbados Legislative Council. Because of a disagreement between Frere and the rector of the church for which No. 362 was intended, after the painting arrived on the island it was not installed in the church but stored in an outbuilding on Frere's estate, and there had the eyes of the centurion in the lower left corner punched out by a local workman. In 1974 the painting fell from its frame and suffered some further damage.

The published lists of West's works include additional pictures of Moses and St. John (see Nos. 268 and 297) as situated along with No. 362 in the same location in Barbados. Although it is possible that West and his patron may at one time have intended a triptych with No. 362 at the center, West exhibited this painting without companion pictures in 1786, and there is no documentary evidence to indicate that the two additional pictures were painted at the same time. Nor is there any to indicate that they ever reached Barbados. Whereas No. 362 is the most celebrated art treasure on the island, there is no record or memory there of the other works.[1]

West painted No. 362 four years after No. 360, his design for the *Resurrection* window in St. George's Chapel, Windsor, and while the actual window was being executed. It is possible that the commission for the church of the same name in Barbados was inspired by Frere's seeing or knowing about the *Resurrection* for Windsor. The figures of Christ and the angel in No. 362 are loosely based on the central figures in No. 360, and it is noteworthy that when No. 362 appeared at the Royal Academy in May 1786 a criticism of the Christ as too "Herculean" anticipated Fanny Burney's comment that West's resurrected Christ seemed "athletic as an Hercules" when she saw the cartoon of the Windsor window (No. 361) in October of the same year.

Closely related paintings of the subject are Nos. 363 and 364 below. A drawing of the composition is in the Historical Society of Pennsylvania.[2]

[1] Letter from E. M. Shilstone, Hon. Secretary of the Barbados Museum and Historical Society, to Helmut von Erffa, 4 Aug. 1956.
[2] Black chalk, $6\frac{3}{4} \times 5\frac{3}{8}$ in.

363 The Resurrection 1794

SWARTHMORE COLLEGE, SWARTHMORE, PENNSYLVANIA

Oil on canvas, mounted on panel: $22\frac{5}{8} \times 17\frac{7}{8}$ in. (57.5×45.5 cm.)

Signed lower center: *B. West 1794*

PROV: Offered by West's sons to the United States in 1826 (66), and sold by them, Robins, London, 22–25 May 1829, lot 8 ("Resurrection of Our Saviour," 2 ft. × 1 ft. 6 in.), bt. by John Nash for £31.10.0.; his sale, Christie's, London, 11 July 1835, lot 86; acquired by Swarthmore between 1933 and 1938

363

EXH: RA 1795 (140) "The Resurrection of our Saviour"; (?) West's Gallery 1821 (25) "The Resurrection of Our Saviour (a sketch)"; Philadelphia 1938 (43)

ENGR: Engraving ($3\frac{3}{16} \times 2\frac{3}{4}$ in.) by Freeman, pub. by S. Leigh

LISTED: *PC*, p. 567 ("Christ's Resurrection," West, Gallery); *UM*, p. 531; *BA*, p. 18; Galt, p. 232; Dillenberger, pp. 180 (419) and 213

Nos. 363 and 364 both repeat with modifications the composition of No. 362. In this version there are significant differences in the angel, in Christ's dress, and in the position of his head and hands. There is a large stone in the lower right corner, more of the steps are visible, and there is more space around both figures.

The histories of Nos. 360 and 362, which West exhibited at the Royal Academy in 1783 and 1786 respectively, are clear cut. No. 363, which is signed and dated *1794*, can also be identified as the *Resurrection* that West exhibited at the Academy in the following year. But he exhibited further paintings of the subject in 1808 and 1819, and three or probably four (see No. 366) *Resurrections* in addition to No. 360 appeared in the two main sales of his estate in 1829. Three further paintings of the subject (Nos. 363, 364, and 365) are currently known, along with Nos. 360 and 362, but their histories are far from complete, and the attempts in this catalogue to equate these works with works listed in various earlier records, are necessarily somewhat speculative.

The dimensions of No. 363 correspond loosely with two works in the Robins sale of 22–25 May 1829: lots 8 and 114. Since No. 363 was probably exhibited in 1795 as "The Resurrection of Our Saviour," it is perhaps reasonable to think that it retained that title and that in 1829 it was lot 8, which bore the same title, although the title of lot 114, "Christ and the Angel," also fits No. 363 (see No. 366). Both lot 8 and another *Resurrection*, in the sale of 22–25 May 1829, lot 52 (see No. 365), were bought by the architect John Nash, and hence it is possible that some of the succeeding histories of these two works have been confused.

364 The Resurrection

STANFORD UNIVERSITY MUSEUM OF ART, STANFORD, CALIFORNIA

Oil on canvas: 87×62 in. (221×157.5 cm.)

PROV: (?) Sold by West's sons, Robins, London, 20–22 June 1829, lot 87 ("The Resurrection, very finely coloured and suited for an altarpiece"); given by Thomas Welton Stanford (the brother of the founder of Stanford University) to the Stanford Museum *c*. 1900

LISTED: Dillenberger, p. 215

LIT: Dillenberger 1977, pp. 50–51, and pl. 28

This large unsigned painting has no certain recorded history prior to the beginning of this century. It cannot be equated with any picture of the Resurrection in the main sale of pictures from West's estate on 22–25 May 1829; its size, however, suggests that it may have been the "Resurrection" described as "suited for an altarpiece" in the sale of sketches, unfinished pictures, and lesser works on 20–22 June 1829. The late date at which it was presumably painted would have prevented it from appearing on the early published lists of West's works, and it does not appear to have been exhibited. West did exhibit a *Resurrection* at the Royal Academy as late as 1819, but that work was described in the catalogue as a sketch, as was also the *Resurrection* which he exhibited in 1808, and it seems unlikely that he would have described a work as large as No. 364 as a sketch.

No. 364 is, like No. 363, essentially a replica of the *Resurrection* of 1786 in Barbados (No. 362). In the dress and pose of the angel, and in the position of Christ's right hand, it follows No. 363 rather than No. 362. In Christ's head, and in the treatment of his draperies, it is closer to the earlier work. The painting of the flesh in the figure of Christ in No. 364 is notably flaccid, with little articulation of muscle and bone. To both authors of this catalogue, the handling has suggested that it was painted, or at least completed, considerably later than Nos. 362 and 363. The treatment of the angel, which is visibly superior to that of the figure of Christ, supports a hypothesis that the picture was worked on at two (or more) different periods, and the relatively weak handling of the main figure suggests that No. 364 may have been one of the paintings upon which West worked at the very end of his life. It is also possible that the picture was completed by another hand.

365 The Resurrection

PHILADELPHIA MUSEUM OF ART

Oil on paper mounted on board: $15\frac{3}{4} \times 12$ in. (40×30.5 cm.)

PROV: Offered by West's sons to the United States in 1826 (72) and sold by them, Robins, London, 22–25 May 1829, lot 52 ("The Resurrection of Our Saviour," 16×13 in.), bt. by John Nash for £52.10.0.; his sale, Christie's, London, 11 July 1835, lot 78 ("The Resurrection; a coloured sketch"); (?) Thomas Francis Robins (to whom No. 365 was given as a Christmas gift in 1872); Renaissance Galleries, Philadelphia; Hammer Galleries, New York; given to the Philadelphia Museum of Art by Mr. and Mrs. D. Clifford Ruth, Bryn Mawr, Pennsylvania, in 1967

EXH: (?) RA 1808 (117) "The Resurrection of our Saviour; a sketch"; (?) RA 1819 (111) "The Resurrection of our Saviour; a sketch"; West's Gallery 1821 (36) "The Resurrection of Our Saviour (a sketch)", (?) 1822–28 (20) "The Resurrection of our Saviour" angel show evident signs of retouching as well.[3]

Such signs of very late work make No. 365 the most likely candidate for identification as the sketch of the *Resurrection* which West exhibited at the Royal Academy in 1819. It could easily also have been the sketch of the subject which West exhibited at the Academy in 1808, the subsequent repainting and additions of new figures legitimitizing the sketch's reappearance eleven years later. The sketch that West exhibited in 1808 appeared, described as "a small picture," at the end of the *Belle Assemblée* list of West's works, which was published in that year, along with several other works that West had exhibited in 1808 (see Nos. 46 and 458–61). None of these pictures appears in any of the other early lists of West's works.

If No. 365 is correctly identified as the *Resurrection* described as a sketch in either 1808 or 1819, it seems likely that it was one of the two sketches of the subject exhibited in West's gallery in the 1820s. Because of its dimensions, it appears to have been lot 52 in the Robins sale of 22–25 May 1829, which was purchased by John Nash and subsequently included in the sale following Nash's death in 1835. That history, if correct, would seem to invalidate part of a provenance recorded in an inscription on the back of the picture,[4] which we accordingly have not included above. "A Resurrection; a Sketch" lent by Robert Vernon to the British Institution in 1833 was probably, in fact, an "Ascension" (see No. 384).

[1] Black chalk on grey paper: $12\frac{11}{16} \times 8$ in. (Kraemer 1975, pp. 22–23, no. 31, and pl. 20).
[2] See Farington Diary entries 27 Aug. 1818 and 3 Sept. 1819 (Farington 1978—, xv, pp. 5254–55 and 5403).
[3] Retouchings by the artist are recorded in a "Record of Conservation, October 13—November 6, 1967" by Theodor Siegl in the curatorial files of the Philadelphia Museum.
[4] The inscription reads: *Thomas Francis Robins* [?] *Esquire/ Memento of grateful regard from/Christmas Eve 1872/Painted by Sir Benjamin West Originally in the Collection of the Hon. Col. Stuart/twin brother of Francis 9th Earl of Moray.* Although the ninth Earl of Moray had a brother, James, who was a colonel, it was the tenth Earl who had a twin brother, Archibald Stuart, as mentioned in the inscription. James, the brother of the ninth Earl, died in 1808; Archibald, the twin brother of the tenth Earl, died in 1832.

365

364

LISTED: (?) *BA*, p. 20 ("a small picture of the Resurrection of our Saviour"; in the possession of Mr. West); (?) Dillenberger, p. 189 (503)

LIT: Kraemer 1975, pp. 22–23, fig. 17

No. 365 is on several sheets of paper joined together, a vertical joint running from top to bottom along the right side being particularly noticeable. West frequently extended his compositions in similar fashion, and in most cases the additions do not necessarily seem to have been made at a later date than the main part of the painting or drawing. However, in No. 365 the group of soldiers in the lower right corner, whose limbs and bodies extend on to the added strip does look like

a later addition. A preparatory drawing in the Pierpont Morgan Library shows the figures of Christ and the angel with no hint of the group of figures in the lower right,[1] and the crude but expressive handling displayed in this group is not only distinct from the linear treatment visible in the underlying outlines of Christ and the angel, but also distinct from the handling in almost any other work which we can accept as by the artist's hand. Although such an observation might suggest that these figures were added by another hand, it is perhaps more likely that they were added at the very end of West's life when his hand was beginning to falter but when, as we know from Farington, he continued to retouch earlier works.[2] The figures of Christ and the

366 The Resurrection (Christ and the Angel)

LOCATION UNKNOWN

(24 × 18 in.) (61 × 45.5. cm.)

PROV: Offered by West's sons to the United States in
1826 (98, "Christ and the Angel," 1 ft. 6 in. × 2 ft.),
and sold by them, Robins, London, 22–25 May 1829,
lot 114 ("Christ and the Angel," 2 ft. × 1 ft. 6 in.),
bt. by Halliwell for £31.10.0.

EXH: West's Gallery 1821 (51), 1822–28 (77)

LIT: Kraemer 1975, pp. 22–23

No painting with the title "Christ and the Angel" was
exhibited or otherwise recorded during West's lifetime.
The title appears for the first time in the catalogues of
the posthumous exhibitions in West's gallery, and may
have been applied by West's sons to a work which had
previously been exhibited or recorded under another
title. Whether or not this was the case, the picture
which was exhibited from 1821 to 1828 and sold in 1829
as "Christ and the Angel" was probably a representation of the Resurrection. Although the words "Christ
and the Angel" do not necessarily indicate the Resurrection, the comment which accompanied lot 114 in
the Robins sale of 22–25 May 1829 ("*A chaste and most
pleasing cabinet picture*. The Saviour, to speak in the professional phrase, is a pure specimen of the colouring of
the naked; and the action of the figure is admirably
expressed") indicates that the picture showed a nude,
or more likely, semi-nude, figure of Christ in some form
of action, and thus makes it sound very much like
West's pictures of the Resurrection. Ruth Kraemer has
associated a drawing in the Morgan Library with this
lot in the Robins sale, but, as she has pointed out, that
drawing has a basic similarity with the oil sketch of the
Resurrection in the Philadelphia Museum (No. 365),
whose measurements do not correspond with those of
the "Christ and the Angel" sold in 1829. Although the
title could perhaps fit all the known versions of the
Resurrection by West except No. 360, the suggestion of
action on the part of Christ implies that this picture
may have been yet another variant of the Barbados
composition of 1786 (No. 362), in which Christ strides
vigorously from the tomb.

Both lot 114 and lot 8 in the sale of 22–25 May 1829
had measurements of 24 × 18 in., and they sold for identical prices. In this catalogue we have equated lot 8
with No. 363 above, but if both works showed essentially the same subject, it is impossible to be certain that
the identification is correct.

367 The Three Marys Going to the Sepulchre
c. 1782

NATIONAL TRUST, TATTON PARK, CHESHIRE

Oil on canvas: 64 × 34¼ in. (162.5 × 87 cm.)

PROV: Painted together with Nos. 360 and 369 as a
design for a window commissioned by George III for
St. George's Chapel, Windsor (the subject is not
listed by name in West's accounts of 1797 and 1801,
but the existence of Nos. 367 and 369, and of the corresponding cartoons, Nos. 368 and 370, is implied by
West's use of the plural "Cartoons from those
designs" in 1797 [cited under No. 360], and either
the designs or the cartoons are listed in the 1801
account, p. 213: no. 33, "And two side pictures,"
£525, following the entry for No. 361, the cartoon
for the central compartment of the east window);
sold by West's sons, Robins, London, 22–25 May
1829, lot 142 ("The Three Maries Going to the Sepulchre," 5 ft. 3 in. × 2 ft. 10 in., "Designed for the
third compartment of the Great Window" . . .), bt.
by Egerton (presumably Wilbraham Egerton, 1781–

367

1856, of Tatton Park) for £54.12.0.; by family descent to Maurice Egerton, fourth Lord Egerton of Tatton (1874–1958), by whom bequeathed to the National Trust

EXH: RA 1783 (16) as for No. 360; West's Gallery 1821 (64) "The Maries going to the Tomb of Jesus, St. Luke, chap. 24 Verse 1. Now upon the first day of the week, very early in the morning, they came unto the sepulchre, bringing the spices which they had prepared."

ENGR: Mezzotint ($17\frac{3}{8} \times 9\frac{7}{16}$ in.) by Valentine Green, pub. 4 June 1784 by Green

LISTED: See p. 324; *PC*, p. 560 ("The design of our Saviour's Resurrection, painted in colours, with the Women going to the Sepulchre; also Peter and John"); *UM*, p. 527; Barlow, p. 431 ("Peter, John and women at the Sepulchre"); *BA*, p. 13; Galt, p. 217; Dillenberger, pp. 140 (36) and 215

LIT: Kraemer 1975, p. 21; Meyer 1979, pp. 56–58 and fig. 4

No. 367 is the design for the right-hand compartment of the great east window in St. George's Chapel, Windsor, which is discussed in the entry for No. 360.

The cartoon for the compartment is No. 368 below. A drawing of the composition, which conforms closely in detail to No. 367, is in the Yale Center for British Art.[1] A much slighter pencil sketch is in the Philadelphia Museum of Art.[2]

[1]Pen and ink, with sepia and blue wash, $16\frac{1}{4} \times 8\frac{1}{4}$ in. (San Antonio 1983, no. 30).
[2]The correct identification of this drawing is pointed out in Meyer 1979, pp. 57–58, n. 19.

368 The Three Marys Going to the Sepulchre
c. 1782

LOCATION UNKNOWN

PROV: See No. 367

No. 368 is or was the cartoon based on No. 367 for the window discussed under No. 360. Like all the cartoons for the Windsor windows except No. 298, it has disappeared without a trace and may have been destroyed soon after the window was made.

369 Sts. Peter and John Running towards the Sepulchre *c.* 1782

LOCATION UNKNOWN

(63×34 in.) (160×86.5 cm.)

PROV: See No. 367; sold by West's sons, Robins, London, 22–25 May 1829, lot 140 ("Peter and John Going From the Sepulchre," 5 ft. 3 in. × 2 ft. 10 in., "The original design for one of the side compartments of the magnificent stained glass Window, executed by the command of His late Majesty, and set up at the east end of St. George's Chapel, at Windsor"), bt. by Kershaw for £47.5.0.

EXH: RA 1783 (16) as for No. 360; West's Gallery 1821 (61) "St. Peter and St. John running towards the Sepulchre. St. John, chap. 21. Verse 4. So they ran both together; and the other disciple did outrun Peter, and came first to the sepulchre."

ENGR: Mezzotint ($17\frac{5}{16} \times 9\frac{7}{16}$ in.) by Valentine Green, pub. 4 June 1784 by Green (*right*)

LISTED: As for No. 367

LIT: Kraemer 1975, p. 21; Meyer 1979, pp. 56–57 and fig. 3

No. 369 is the design for the left-hand compartment of

Sts. Peter and John Running towards the Sepulchre, mezzotint by Valentine Green after No. 369

369

the east window in St. George's Chapel, Windsor, which is discussed in the entry for No. 360.

Kershaw, who bought No. 369 in 1829, also bought the large *Death on the Pale Horse* (No. 401), but whereas *Death on the Pale Horse* soon reappeared in the possession of Raphael West, thus suggesting that Kershaw acted as Raphael's agent, No. 369 has not been heard of since.

A drawing of the composition corresponding in size to a similar drawing of the pendant composition (No. 367) is in the Museum of Fine Arts, Boston.[1]

[1] Pen and ink, with sepia and blue wash, $16\frac{1}{2} \times 8\frac{1}{2}$ in., signed lower center *B. West/1783* (San Antonio 1983, no. 31).

370 Sts. Peter and John Running towards the Sepulchre *c.* 1782

LOCATION UNKNOWN

PROV: See No. 367

No. 370 is (or was) the cartoon based upon No. 369 for the window discussed under No. 360.

371 The Women at the Sepulchre (The Angel at the Tomb of Christ) (?) 1768

LOCATION UNKNOWN

PROV: Sold by William Smith, MP, Christie's, London, 28 May 1824, lot 29 ("The Maries at the Sepulchre," painted for Mr. Chas Price in 1768), bt. in at £16.10.0.

(?) ENGR: Engraving ($4\frac{7}{8} \times 3\frac{7}{8}$ in.) by T. Pollock (*below*); engraving by T. Smith

LISTED: *PC*, p. 563 ("The Marys at the Sepulchre, for General Stibert"); *UM*, p. 529; Barlow, p. 433 ("The two Marys at the Sepulchre," under "Various Collections"); *BA*, p. 15 ("The Marys at the Sepulchre, W. Smith Esq., first painted for W. Locke, Esq."); Galt, p. 233; Dillenberger, p. 159 (210)

West exhibited pictures with the title "The Women at the Sepulchre," or some slight variant, at the Royal Academy in 1792, 1800, 1805, and 1818. Of these only one (No. 375) can be identified with reasonable certainty. In addition, we know that he painted one and perhaps two versions of the subject well before 1792 (Nos. 371 and 372). A number of other pictures, which

The Women at the Sepulchre, engraving by T. Pollock, (?) after No. 371

evidently were not exhibited during West's lifetime, are recorded in early lists and sales under variants of the title "The Angel at the Tomb," and show essentially the same subject. There is considerable confusion in sorting out the documentation for virtually all these works.

The earliest date recorded for any of them is the statement in the sale catalogue of 1824, cited above, that No. 371 was painted in 1768. Either this or another painting of the subject was sold at auction in 1774 (see No. 372 below) and what clearly is or was an early painting of the subject by West is reproduced in the two engravings listed above.

The information from the 1824 sale catalogue is contradicted by most of the early lists of West's works, but partly confirmed by the list in *La Belle Assemblée*. According to *Public Characters*, the *Universal Magazine*, and Galt, West painted a version of the subject for General Stibert (Giles Stibbert) along with *Alexander's Confidence in His Physician Philip* and *Caesar Reading the History of Alexander's Exploits* (Nos. 7 and 26), which follow immediately after it in the lists with their owners indicated by dittoes. That No. 7 belonged to Stibbert can be confirmed by the inscription on an engraving published in 1772. No such confirmation exists for No. 371, and it seems probable that the Stibbert listing in *Public Characters*, although repeated in two other lists, was an error that is corrected in *La Belle Assemblée*. There the corresponding "Marys at the Sepulchre" has a ditto beside it, indicating that it had the same ownership as the preceding work on the list ("'Leonidas ordering Cleombrotus into Banishment' [see No. 13]: W. Smith, Esq., first painted for W. Locke, Esq.,") while the "for General Stibert" has slipped down to accompany "Alexander and his Physician," following No. 371. This is much more plausible, since Smith's ownership of No. 371 is confirmed by the 1824 catalogue mentioned above, but whether the ditto in *La Belle Assemblée* is supposed to indicate only that No. 371 belonged to Smith, or that the painting shared the complete history of No. 13, is not clear. W. Locke was presumably William Lock or Locke of Norbury (1732–1810), and we know that at least one other work which he had acquired in the 1760s, *Celadon and Amelia* by Richard Wilson, belonged to Smith before 1800.[1] Furthermore, according to the catalogue of 1824, No. 371 was painted in 1768, the date on No. 13, with which it supposedly shared the Locke provenance. On the other hand, the catalogue of 1824 says nothing about Locke, but states that No. 371 was painted for a Chas Price (? Chase Price, MP, 1731–1777) prior to being owned by Smith, and there is no satisfactory way to reconcile the two sources.

A drawing of the composition reproduced in the Pollock and Smith engravings is at Swarthmore.[2] There is also a drawing of the subject in gouache with a vertical composition in the Butler Institute of American Art in Youngstown, Ohio.[3] This drawing is signed and dated *1782* and shows a fundamentally different composition from that in the two engravings and the Swarthmore drawing.

[1] W. G. Constable, *Richard Wilson*, London, 1953, p. 165 (24b), and Farington 1978–, III, p. 840 (17 May 1797).
[2] Pen and wash: $6\frac{7}{8} \times 5\frac{3}{8}$ in.
[3] Gouache: 19×14 in., signed lower left *B. West/1782*. This may be the drawing recorded in the early lists: *PC*, p. 568 ("The Drawing of the Women looking into the Sepulchre," West, Gallery); *UM*, p. 531; *BA*, p. 19; Galt, p. 231; Dillenberger, p. 183 (449).

372 The Women at the Sepulchre (The Angel at the Tomb of Christ)

LOCATION UNKNOWN

PROV: Sold by Samuel Dickenson, Esq., of East Smithfield, Christie's, London, 11–12 March 1774, lot 69

Nothing is known about this work apart from its appearing at auction at the remarkably early date of 1774. It was quite probably connected in some way with the work discussed in the preceding entry, and it is conceivable that Nos. 371 and 372 are the same work, although Samuel Dickenson is not among the various owners recorded for No. 371.

A "Maries at the Sepulchre" sold from the collection of W. H. Trant of 10 Berkeley Square in 1832[1] could be any one of several works, including Nos. 371, 372, and 373.

[1] Foster, London, 9, 11, 12 June 1832, lot 124.

373 The Women at the Sepulchre (The Angel at the Tomb of Christ) *c.* 1792

PRIVATE COLLECTION

Oil on canvas: $16\frac{1}{8} \times 21\frac{1}{4}$ in. (41 × 54 cm.)

EXH: RA 1792 (401) "The three women at the sepulchre"

ENGR: Engraving ($16 \times 21\frac{1}{4}$ in.) by James Stow, pub. by Stow, 1 May 1792

LISTED: (?) *PC*, p. 565 (either "The Angel Sitting on the Stone of the Sepulchre," or the following entry, "Second picture of the same, but differing in composition," both in West's Painting-room); *UM*, p. 530; Barlow, p. 434; *BA*, p. 17; Galt, p. 228; Dillenberger, p. 172 (326 or 327)

No. 373 is reproduced in an engraving by James Stow (*opposite*) published on 1 May 1792, a date coinciding with the opening of that year's Royal Academy exhibition. Therefore, we have equated it with "The three women at the sepulchre" exhibited by West at the Academy in 1792. The engraving by Stow is the same size as No. 373, and it is possible that West painted the picture for the sake of the engraver. In its present state No. 373 appears too unfinished to have been displayed publicly, but its condition may be due to West's subsequent reworking of a previously finished painting. It may perhaps be one of the pictures of the "Angel Sitting on the Stone of the Sepulchre" recorded in West's gallery on the early lists of his works, but it does not seem to have appeared in any of the posthumous exhibitions or sales of pictures from his estate.

Paintings showing the same composition are in a private collection in Philadelphia[1] and in the cathedral of St. John the Divine in New York.[2] Neither appears to be by West's hand, and both evidently are copies made either after No. 373 or after the engraving; the Philadelphia picture has approximately the same dimensions as No. 373 and as the print.

A large drawing of an angel in a pose similar to that of the angel in No. 373 is signed and dated *B. West 1788 Windsor . . . retouched by B. West in Nov. 1812* (National Museum of Wales, Cardiff).[3] A slighter drawing dated *1812* shows a generally similar composition, in which the angel appears to be based on the Cardiff drawing, and in which there is also a group of soldiers on the right, balancing the women on the left (Museum of Fine Arts, Boston).[4]

[1] Oil on panel: $16\frac{1}{2} \times 24\frac{1}{2}$ in.
[2] Oil on canvas: $58\frac{1}{2} \times 76\frac{1}{2}$ in.
[3] Pen and gouache: $29\frac{1}{8} \times 23\frac{7}{8}$ in. (ill., *Burlington Magazine*, CXV, 1973, p. 252, fig. 102).
[4] Sepia wash: $7 \times 9\frac{5}{8}$ in.

374 The Women at the Sepulchre (Angels at the Tomb of Christ) *c.* 1800

LOCATION UNKNOWN

PROV: Offered by West's sons to the United States in 1826 (54), and sold by them, Robins, London, 22–25

373

May 1829, lot 27 ("Angels at the Tomb of Our Saviour," 14½ × 11 in.), bt. by Archbutt for £27.6.0.; sold by Archbutt, Stanley, London, 9 July 1830, lot 157 ("The Maries at the Sepulchre") for £18.18.0.; M. Colnaghi, by 1834

EXH: RA 1800 (74) "The Women at the Sepulchre of Jesus Christ":

> And they entered in, and found not the body of the Lord Jesus; and behold two men stood by them in shining garments, and said unto them, why seek ye the living among the dead? he is not here, but is risen.   *St. Luke, chap. xxiv. vers. from 3 to 6*

West's Gallery 1821 (7), 1822–28 (7) "Angels at the Tomb of Our Saviour;" SBA 1834 (398) "Angels at the Tomb," lent by M. Colnaghi

ENGR: Engraving (10⅝ × 8¼ in.) by J. Porter, pub. by Colnaghi, 1834 (*over page*)

LISTED: *PC*, p. 567 ("The Women Looking into the Sepulchre, and beholding two Angels where the Lord lay," West, Gallery); *UM*, p. 531; Barlow, p. 435; *BA*, p. 18; Galt, p. 231; Dillenberger, p. 178 (398)

The Women at the Sepulchre, engraving by James Stow after No. 373

The Women at the Sepulchre, engraving by J. Porter after No. 374

LIT: Kraemer 1975, p. 39

The painting of the *Women at the Sepulchre* which West exhibited at the Royal Academy in 1800 was accompanied by a passage from the twenty-fourth chapter of Luke, which describes two angels standing in the sepulchre. On all other occasions when West appended scriptural quotations to versions of the subject he employed lines from the twenty-eighth chapter of Matthew, in which a single angel rolls back the stone from the door, then sits upon it. Although several paintings showing a single angel are now known, no painting by West showing two angels in the tomb can currently be identified. It seems reasonable, however, to equate the painting exhibited in 1800 with the one work included in the early lists of West's works that is described as showing the women beholding two angels, and to equate this work in turn with a picture that appeared in the posthumous exhibition of West's works and in the sales of 1829 bearing a somewhat different title but one which described "Angels" (rather than "Angel") "at the Tomb." The picture exhibited in 1800 is presumably also the work reproduced in an engraving published by Colnaghi in 1834, and hence the picture of the subject which Martin Colnaghi lent to an exhibition in the same year.

A slight sketch of the composition is in the Pierpont Morgan Library.[1]

[1] Kraemer 1975, p. 39 (65), and pl. 15; sepia, $4\frac{1}{8} \times 3\frac{1}{4}$ in.

375 The Women at the Sepulchre (The Angel at the Tomb of Christ) 1805

BROOKLYN MUSEUM, NEW YORK

Oil on panel: $34\frac{1}{8} \times 32\frac{1}{2}$ in. (86.5 × 82.5 cm.)

Signed lower left: *B. West 1805*

PROV: Offered by West's sons to the United States in 1826 (81), and sold by them, Robins, London, 22–25 May 1829, lot 17 ("The Maries at the Sepulchre," 2 ft. 10 in. × 2 ft. 10 in.), bt. by Vernon for £52.10.0.; owned by Robert Vernon in 1833; Harlow C. Curtiss, Buffalo (by whom acquired in Toronto, probably in the early 1890s); by family descent to Mrs. John S. Curtiss, from whom purchased by the Brooklyn Museum in 1948

EXH: RA 1805 (83) "Mary Magdalen and the other Mary at the Sepulchre, St. Matthew, chap. xxviii":

> Ver. 1. Now on the end of the Sabbath, when the first day of the week began to dawn, Mary Magdalen and the other Mary came to see the sepulchre;
> Ver. 2. And behold there was a great earthquake, for the angel of the Lord descended from heaven, and came and rolled back the stone from the door, and sat upon it;
> Ver. 3. And his countenance was like lightning, and his raiment white as snow;
> Ver. 4. And for fear of him the keepers were astonished, and became as dead men.
> Ver. 5. But the angel answered and said unto the women, Fear ye not, for I know that ye seek Jesus that was crucified;
> Ver. 6. He is not here, for he is risen as he said; come, see the place where the Lord lay.

125 Pall Mall 1818 (6) "The Women at the Sepulchre," with a citation of Matthew 28:1–7; West's Gallery 1821 (34) "Maries at the Sepulchre," with a quotation from Matthew 28:1–4, 1822–28 (48) "Maries at the Sepulchre," without quotation; BI 1833 (14) "The Maries at the Sepulchre," lent by Robert Vernon

LISTED: Dillenberger, p. 213

LIT: Evans 1959, p. 5 and pl. 3; Kraemer 1975, pp. 91–92

The date of *1805* on No. 375 makes it probable that this painting was the "Mary Magdalen and the other Mary at the Sepulchre" which West exhibited at the Royal Academy in that year, even though the painting shows three women while the title in the catalogue mentioned only two.[1] No. 375 was evidently painted too late to be in the early lists of West's works, but it can be equated with a picture of "The Women at the Sepulchre" or "The Maries at the Sepulchre" that appeared in exhibitions of the artist's work from 1818 to 1828 and that was sold in 1829.[2]

Unlike No. 373, this painting includes soldiers (the astonished keepers mentioned in Matthew 28:4) as well as the three women and the angel. The pose of the angel is closely related to that in two smaller oil paintings or sketches discussed below (Nos. 377 and 378), several drawings,[3] and a lithograph of 1801 inscribed *He is not here: for he is risen* (ill. p. 63),[4] but it repeats none of them exactly.

Extensive *pentimenti* are visible throughout No. 375. Ghostly figures are visible above and next to the head of the central Mary, and there is considerable confusion in the area adjacent to the angel's left foot. There are also painted-over architectural elements in the background, and the upper left side of the painting has been left unfinished.

[1] No known version of the subject (or variant of the subject) by West shows only two women at the sepulchre.
[2] The Cattermole/Le Keux engraving of West's gallery in 1821 (ill. p. 150) confirms that no. 34 in that exhibition had approximately the size of No. 375. No. 34 is on the far end of the left wall, the center work in a vertical tier of three paintings.
[3] These are: (a) Delaware Art Museum: pen, wash, and gouache: 18 × 23 in. (b) Historical Society of Pennsylvania: pen and wash: $16\frac{3}{4} \times 19\frac{3}{4}$ in. (c) Princeton University Art Museum: sepia: $10\frac{11}{16} \times 7\frac{13}{16}$ in. (d) Pierpont Morgan Library, New York: pen: $6\frac{3}{8} \times 10\frac{3}{8}$ in. (Kraemer 1975, pp. 91–92, no. 223, where ascribed to Raphael West). See also the drawings mentioned in the entries for Nos. 373 and 377.
[4] Lithograph: $12\frac{7}{16} \times 9$ in. inscribed lower right *B. West. 1801* and below margin *He is not here: for he is risen*; published in P. André, ed., *Specimens of Polyautography: Consisting of Impressions taken from Original Drawings made on stone purposely for this work*, London, 1803.

376 The Women at the Sepulchre (The Angel at the Tomb of Christ)

LOCATION UNKNOWN

EXH: RA 1818 (114) "The Women at the Sepulchre," with a quotation from Matthew 28:1–6, as under No. 375, but omitting verse 4

It is impossible to identify the picture West exhibited at the Academy in 1818. At that late date, it was possibly an earlier work rather than one recently painted. The omission in the catalogue entry of verse 4 from Matthew 28, which refers to the keepers, suggests that these figures may not have been included in the exhibited work, and, hence, that the work may have been No. 373, making a second appearance at the Academy, or a second version of that composition. See also No. 377 below.

377

377 The Angel at the Tomb of Christ (The Women at the Sepulchre) (?)1812–13

JOSEPH F. McCRINDLE

Oil on panel: $15\frac{3}{4} \times 11\frac{1}{4}$ in. (40 × 28.5 cm.)

Signed lower right (near the angel's left foot): *B. West/ [?] 1812*, and lower center (on the rocks below the angel's foot): *B. West/1813*

PROV: Offered by West's sons to the United States in 1826 (76), and sold by them, Robins, London, 22–25 May 1829, lot 30 ("Angel at the Tomb of Christ," 1 ft. 3 in. × 11 in.), bt. by J. Morrison (James Morrison, MP, of Balham Hill and Basildon Park, 1789–1857); by descent to Walter Morrison; sold, Sotheby's, London, 22 March 1972, lot 111 (as "Angel of the Resurrection"), bt. by B. Sewall

EXH: West's Gallery 1821 (42) "The Angel at the Tomb of Christ, St. Matthew, chap. 23. Verse 3. His countenance was like lightning, and his raiment white as snow"; West's Gallery 1822–28 (32) without quotation; *Third National Loan Exhibition: Pictures from the Basildon Park and Fonthill Collections*, Grosvenor Gallery, London, 1914–15 (70)

375

(?) LISTED: *PC*, p. 565 (either "The Angel Sitting on the Stone at the Sepulchre" or the following entry, "Second picture of the same, but differing in composition," both in West's Painting-room); *UM*, p. 530; Barlow, p. 434; *BA*, p. 17; Galt, p. 228; Dillenberger, p. 172 (326 or 327)

The Morrison provenance and the dimensions of No. 377 identify it as lot 30 in the Robins sale of 22–25 May 1829, which can in turn be equated with no. 76 on West's sons' list of works offered to the United States in 1826. It also seems highly probable that it was the one picture with the same title included in the posthumous exhibitions in West's gallery from 1821 to 1828. The small size of that work is confirmed by the Cattermole/Le Keux engraving of the gallery published in 1821 (ill. p. 150).[1]

The line from Matthew 28 which accompanied No. 377 in the catalogue of West's gallery in 1821 also appears in the quotation with which West accompanied paintings of the *Women at the Sepulchre* in catalogues in 1805 and 1818 (see Nos. 375 and 376). The subjects are essentially the same in all these works, although in No. 377 the women are relegated to a cor-

ner of the composition as they are also in No. 378 below. The angel in No. 377 is closely related to those in Nos. 373, 375 and West's lithograph of 1801 (ill. p. 63). A drawing of an angel in the same pose as that in No. 377 belongs to the Central Picture Galleries, New York.[2] The women and soldiers squeezed into the lower corner below a dominant frontally posed central figure make the composition reminiscent of that of the *Messiah* (No. 399) which is signed and dated *1814*. There are also distinct similarities between the angels in No. 377 and 399, which appear to have been painted from the same model, and, more generally, in the tonality and

The Angel at the Tomb of Christ, stipple engraving by John Ogborne after No. 378

378

handling in the two paintings. A third work sharing many of the same qualities is No. 365, the small sketch of the *Resurrection,* which hung as a pendant to No. 377 in West's gallery in 1821 and which seems very evidently to have been repainted by the artist near the end of his career.[3]

[1] "The Angel at the Tomb of Christ," no. 42 in the exhibition of 1821, is the small work on the extreme right side of the far wall. The similarly small work hanging pendant to it on the left is no. 36 "The Resurrection of our Saviour (a sketch)" (see No. 365 above).
[2] Pen and ink: $4\frac{9}{16} \times 3\frac{3}{4}$ in.
[3] The late date of No. 377 raises the question of its having been the *Women at the Sepulchre* which West exhibited at the Royal Academy in 1818 (see No. 376), but it seems unlikely that he would have employed that title for a work in which the women play such a subordinate role.

378 The Angel at the Tomb of Christ (The Women at the Sepulchre) (?)*c.* 1797

SALANDER–O'REILLY GALLERIES, NEW YORK

Oil on paper laid down on board: $6\frac{1}{2} \times 8\frac{1}{4}$ in. (16.5 × 21 cm.)

PROV: Sold, Sotheby's, London, 12 Nov. 1980, lot 64; sold, Christie's, London, 19 Nov. 1982, lot 69

EXH: *British Drawings,* Anthony Reed, London, and Davis & Langdale, New York, 1984 (7)

ENGR: Stipple engraving $(6\frac{3}{4} \times 5\frac{5}{16}$ in.) by John Ogborne, pub. 1 Sept. 1797 by T. Simpson, and Darling & Thompson

(?) LISTED: *PC,* p. 565 ("A small Sketch of ditto," West, Painting-room [following "Angel sitting on the Stone at the Sepulchre" and "Second picture of the same, but differing in composition" see Nos. 373 and 377]); *UM,* p. 530; *BA,* p. 17; Galt, p. 228; Dillenberger, p. 172 (328)

This small sketch appeared on the market in 1980. Its composition is the same as that of a print published in 1797, and the size of the sketch and the print are virtually identical. Although No. 378 appears to have been clumsily repainted in places, notably in two of the faces in the lower left corner, the handling otherwise appears to be West's. Hence, it appears probable that the sketch served as the basis for the print, rather than having been copied after or painted over an impression of the engraving.

379 The Angel at the Tomb of Christ (The Women at the Sepulchre)

LOCATION UNKNOWN

(Oil on canvas)

PROV: Sold by West's sons, Robins, London, 20–22 June 1829, lot 193 ("The Angel at the Tomb, large sketch on canvas, and study for Achilles" [see No. 172])

380 The Ascension *c.* 1781–82

BOB JONES UNIVERSITY, GREENVILLE, SOUTH CAROLINA

Oil on canvas: 211 × 114 in. (536 × 290 cm.)

PROV: Painted for George III (1797 account: "The Assension of our [Saviour]," 1781, £1,050; 1801 account, p. 213: for the Windsor Chapel, The Prophets, 34, "The Assumption of our Saviour," for the King's Chapel," . . .); never delivered and ownership returned to West's sons by George IV in 1828; sold by them, Robins, London, 22–25 May 1829, lot 169 ("The Ascension," 17 ft. 7 in. × 9 ft. 6 in.), bt. by Bone for £73.10.0. on behalf of Joseph Neeld, MP, Grittleton House, Wilts.; presented by Neeld to Harrow School c. 1839 to serve as altarpiece of the school chapel; returned to Neeld c. 1854; by descent in the Neeld family until sold by Miss C. K. M. Neeld, Christie's, London, 16 Nov. 1962, lot 98, bt. by Weitzner; purchased by the present owner in 1963

EXH: RA 1782 (144) "The ascension of Our Saviour, painted for his Majesty's chapel at Windsor"; West's Gallery 1821 (69) "The Ascension of our Saviour, Acts, chap. 1":

> Verse 9. And when he had spoken these things, while they beheld, he was taken up and a cloud received him out of their sight.
> Verse 10. And while they looked steadfastly towards heaven as he went up, behold two men stood by them in white apparel;
> Verse 11. Which also said, Ye men of Galilee, why stand ye gazing up into heaven, shall so come in like manner as ye have seen him go into heaven.
> Verse 12. Then returned they unto Jerusalem from the Mount, called Olivet

ENGR: Stipple engraving ($30\frac{3}{8} \times 17\frac{7}{16}$ in.) by G. S. and J. G. Facius, pub. 2 Jan. 1797 by John and Josiah Boydell

LISTED: *PC*, p. 561 ("Christ's Ascension," George III, for his Majesty's Chapel, Windsor, Gospel Dispensation, 12 ft. × 18); *UM*, p. 527; *AA*, p. 67; Barlow, p. 432; *BA*, p. 14; Galt, p. 219; Dillenberger, pp. 149 (110) and 212

LIT: V and A Cuttings, I, p. 227 (*Morning Herald*, 1782); Jones 1963; Jones 1968, p. 65 (349), ill. p. 190; Meyer 1975, p. 256, fig. 11, and p. 265; Kraemer 1975, pp. 17–18; Dillenberger 1977, pp. 51–56, 71, and pl. 54; Evans 1982, p. 20 and fig. 6; Pressly 1983, p. 22 and fig. 11

No. 380 was the second painting for the Royal Chapel in Windsor Castle to be exhibited by West at the Royal Academy, in 1782. It is a considerably larger work than No. 334, which the artist had shown in the previous year, and was destined for a more important position in the scheme. In the architectural drawings of c. 1780, it is the center work of a wall devoted to New Testament subjects, and it fills the space between the base and the entablature, whereas its four companions on either side (Nos. 316, 334, 385, and 394) have smaller horizontal compositions above them (ill. p. 577). The subject reappears in the same position in one of the Swarthmore diagrams of 1801, but with the notation "Designed and canvas now preparing" (p. 580). Since No. 380 had been completed and exhibited almost twenty years before 1801, this notation suggests that West intended to replace it in the Windsor program, most probably with a large version of the composition shown in No. 383 below.

No. 380 and *Moses Receiving the Laws* (No. 258), are both approximately the same in height, but No. 380 is 33 in. narrower than No. 258. This discrepancy would not have mattered as long as No. 258 was to hang on the end wall of the chapel above the altar, as initially planned, but in the Swarthmore diagrams of 1801 the *Laws* is situated on a long wall in a position analogous to that of the *Ascension* and presumably opposite to it. Thus the difference in sizes may have been one of the factors that led West to intend to replace No. 380 with a new version of the subject based on No. 383, which is proportionately wider than No. 380. It is also worth nothing that while the painting is considerably larger than the pictures that were to hang on either side of it, West charged George III the same price of 1,000

380

guineas for each of these works, but for No. 258 he asked for a further 200 guineas.

The American-born painter Mather Brown, who had arrived in London in April 1781, and Raphael West, who was sixteen years old in 1782, posed for the angels in No. 380. Brown is the more scantily clad angel on the right. These two figures seem to have dominated critical response to the picture. According to the *Morning Herald*:

The Angels from their attributes certainly remind the spectator of academical figures, and rather approach the form of Antinous or Mercury; They are however delicately pencilled, and seem of a celestial nature, without the vulgar symbol of wings, which are so often made use of to express etherial purity.

The *Morning Chronicle*, on the other hand, found them indecent.[1]

In the posthumous exhibition of West's works in 1821 in his former home and studio in Newman Street, No. 380 hung at the center of one of the side walls of the Inner Room (No. 258 was at the center of the wall facing the door, and No. 54 was opposite No. 380), but it seems to have been replaced by a smaller painting of the subject (probably No. 381) in subsequent years.[2] In the sale of 22–25 May 1829, it was accompanied by a note in the catalogue: "For this large picture no space could be afforded in the gallery: it will not therefore be exhibited until the opening of the third day of the sale." It also went for a fraction of the price fetched by No. 258. Joseph Neeld, who acquired it, later presented it to Harrow School, where it was placed over the altar of the chapel designed by C. R. Cockerell and consecrated in 1839. When that chapel was replaced in 1854 by a new Gothic structure designed by Gilbert Scott, the painting was returned to Neeld.[3]

An oil sketch is No. 381 below. A squared drawing of the composition, which is probably a copy after No. 380 made in conjunction with the Facius engraving, was with Bernard Black Gallery, New York, in 1968.[4] It does not appear to be by West himself. Three slighter compositional sketches are in the Royal Library at Windsor.[5] Another rather sketchy compositional drawing, which seems to show the subject of the Ascension but is not very similar to any known painting of the subject by West, was formerly in the collection of Mrs. F. Howard.[6] A study for the figure of Christ was on the market in London in 1959,[7] and other studies of details are in the Pierpont Morgan Library[8] and at Swarthmore College.[9]

[1] Cited in Evans 1982, p. 20.
[2] This assertion is based on the sequence of catalogue numbers which, if correctly interpreted, indicate that the exhibited picture would have been in a corner and in a space too small for No. 380. No. 54 was also withdrawn after 1821.
[3] We are indebted to A. D. K. Hawkyard, Archivist of Harrow School, for this information (letter of 15 June 1983).
[4] Black chalk, $31\frac{3}{4} \times 17\frac{1}{2}$ in., illustrated in *A Benjamin West Portfolio*, Bernard Black Gallery, New York, 1968.
[5] All three in pencil, each approximately $5\frac{1}{2} \times 3$ in. These three drawings were originally mounted together on a sheet along with several other slight compositional sketches and a design for the chapel wall devoted to New Testament subjects. The compositional sketches include studies for Nos. 316, 385, and 394, as well as for No. 380; they evidently were made not as first studies for the picture themselves, but for the compositions shown in the architectural drawings for the chapel made c. 1780 such as that ill. on p. 577.
[6] Pencil, $10 \times 7\frac{1}{2}$ in., sold Sotheby's, London, 22 March 1979, lot 33.
[7] Crayon on blue paper, $13\frac{3}{4} \times 9\frac{7}{8}$ in.
[8] Two drawings, both in black chalk, heightened with white, on blue paper, $15\frac{5}{8} \times 14$ in., and $14 \times 12\frac{1}{4}$ in. (Kraemer 1975, pp. 17–18, nos. 23 and 24, and pls. 12 and 13).
[9] Black chalk, heightened with white, on blue paper, $12\frac{5}{8} \times 10$ in., ill. in Kraemer 1975, p. 16, fig. 10 (recto) and fig. 11 (verso).

381

381 The Ascension c. 1781–82

TATE GALLERY, LONDON

Oil on canvas: $49\frac{3}{4} \times 28$ in. (126.5 × 71 cm.)

PROV: Offered by West's sons to the United States in 1826 (143, . . . 2 ft. 4 in. × 4 ft. 2 in., listed among the "Original Designs in Chiaro Scuro for the large Pictures which were painted for his late Majesty's Chapel in Windsor Castle"), and sold by them, Robins, London, 22–25 May 1829, lot 129 (3 ft. × 2 ft. 4 in.), bt. by Bone for £52.10.0. on behalf of Joseph Neeld, MP, Grittleton House, Wilts.; by descent in the Neeld family until sold, Christie's, London, 13 July 1945, lot 163; presented to the Tate Gallery by the National Art Collections Fund in 1945

EXH: (?) West's Gallery, 1822–28 (89); *American Painting*, Tate Gallery, London 1946 (224)

LISTED: Dillenberger, p. 212

LIT: Evans 1959, p. 53 and pl. 39; Meyer 1975, p. 265; Kraemer 1975, pp. 17–18, fig. 12

No. 381 is a monochrome sketch for No. 380, and the compositions of the two works are virtually identical. There are differences in the hair and features of several figures (most notably Christ and the angel on the left), in details of drapery, and in the positions of some hands.

The documentation for Nos. 381 and 383 may be confused. Both remained in the possession of West and his heirs until 1829. In 1801 West exhibited a version of the subject with the title "Sketch for a large picture for His Majesty's chapel at Windsor, representing the

Ascension," which certainly fits No. 381, but the exhibited work was probably not No. 381. The Swarthmore diagrams of 1801 indicate that by that year West intended to replace No. 380 in the chapel scheme with a new version of the subject, which was "Designed and canvas now preparing" (see p. 580). Hence, it seems more likely that West would have exhibited the sketch of the composition that was currently engaging him, rather than a sketch painted almost twenty years before and showing a composition with which he was evidently not satisfied. For fuller discussion see under No. 383.

That No. 381 was lot 129 in the Robins sale of 22–25 May 1829, despite a discrepancy in the measurements, is confirmed by its position in the sale among a group of eight works which were described in the entry for lot 124 (No. 287) as painted in "Chiaro Scuro." All of them were designs for large paintings in the same sale that had originally been painted for the chapel at Windsor. The identification is also confirmed by the Neeld provenance of No. 381, since Bone, who purchased lot 129, bought at least twenty-four pictures for Joseph Neeld at the sale.

382 The Ascension 1798

WASHINGTON COUNTY MUSEUM OF FINE ARTS, HAGERSTOWN, MARYLAND

Oil on canvas: $20\frac{1}{2} \times 16\frac{1}{2}$ in. (52×42 cm.)

Signed lower center: *B. West 1798*

PROV: (?) Sold by West's sons, Robins, London, 20–22 June 1829, lot 50 ("The Ascension, A sketch by the late B. West, P.R.A. one of the most admired compositions of the master"); (?) J. H. Mann, 1865; sold, Christie's, London, 4 July 1947, lot 172; E. and A. Silberman Galleries, New York, 1951; purchased by the Washington County Museum in 1953

EXH: (?) BI 1865 (132) "The Ascension a sketch," lent by J. H. Mann; Allentown 1962 (26)

LISTED: Dillenberger, p. 213

LIT: Kraemer 1975, p. 18; Dillenberger 1977, p. 76, pl. 55 (detail)

No. 382 is signed and dated, and, hence, would seem to have been thought of by the artist as a completed work, but in appearance it is more like a drawing than an oil painting or even an oil sketch. X-ray photographs made by the Washington County Museum in 1953 revealed that it is painted over another composition.

There are some similarities in detail between Nos. 382, 383, and 384, and the date of *1798*, on No. 382 suggests that it may have been undertaken by West as a sketch for a new *Ascension* to replace No. 380 in the Revealed Religion series, but then abandoned and replaced in turn by No. 383.

A drawing for the two angels at the center of No. 382 was at one time in the collection of Paul F. Grigaut.

383 The Ascension *c.* 1801

See color illustration, p. 105

P. & D. COLNAGHI, LTD., LONDON AND NEW YORK

Oil on canvas: $49\frac{1}{2} \times 34$ in. (125.5×86.5 cm.)

Signed lower left: *B. West 18 . . .* (the last two digits are illegible; there are also faint traces of an illegible second signature slightly above.)

PROV: Offered by West's sons to the United States in 1826 (32), and sold by them, Robins, London, 22–25 May 1829, lot 80 (4 ft. 2 in. × 2 ft. $10\frac{1}{2}$ in.), bt. by the third Earl of Egremont for £210; by family

descent to John Wyndham, seventh Baron Leconfield and second Baron Egremont, by whom sold, Sotheby's, London, 19 July 1978, lot 19; P. & D. Colnaghi, Ltd., London and New York

EXH: (?) RA 1801 (167) "A sketch for a large picture for His Majesty's chapel at Windsor, representing the Ascension of our Saviour, Acts of the Apostles, chap. i":

> Ver. 10. And while the apostles looked stedfastly toward heaven, as our Saviour went up, behold, two men stood by him in white apparel;
> Ver. 11. Which also said, ye men of Galilee, why stand ye gazing up into heaven? This same Jesus which is taken up from you into heaven, shall so come in like manner as ye have seen him go up into heaven.

BI 1807 (28) . . ., 5 ft. 8 in. × 4 ft. 3 in. (including frame); (?) 125 Pall Mall 1818 (8), with citation of St. Luke, chap. xxiv, verse 51; (?) West's Gallery 1821 (53) ". . . St. Luke, chap. 24, Verse 51. And it came to pass, while he blessed them, he was parted from them, and carried up into heaven."; (?) West's Gallery 1822–28 (59) without quotation; Washington and Philadelphia 1980

LISTED: (?) PC, p. 566 ("The Ascension of our Saviour," West, Gallery); UM, p. 531; Barlow, p. 435; BA, p. 18; Galt, p. 230; Dillenberger, pp. 176 (374) and 213

LIT: Collins Baker 1920, p. 133 (77); Kraemer 1975, p. 18

Although West painted and exhibited in 1782 a large painting of the *Ascension* for the Royal Chapel at Windsor (No. 380), the Swarthmore diagrams of 1801 bear the words "Designed and canvas preparing" in the space where the *Ascension* appears (see p. 580). These words suggest that West was in the process of replacing

382

the completed large picture with a new version of the subject. A second large painting of the Ascension is not known, and probably it was never painted, since precisely at the time West described the canvas as "now preparing" he was instructed to stop work on the paintings for the chapel.[1] Three smaller works (Nos. 382, 383, and 384) do, however, show the subject in a fashion radically different from No. 380 and appear to have been painted as studies for the new composition. No. 382, which is signed and dated *1798*, was evidently done before the other two, and was itself replaced by the composition shown in No. 383, with the small No. 384 being intermediary between the two. No. 383 is the largest and most highly finished of these three works and, hence, would seem most likely to have been the version of the subject shown at the Royal Academy in 1801, where it was identified as a sketch for a large picture for the Windsor chapel. Because of correspondence in measurements, No. 383 can be identified with certainty as the version of the subject exhibited by West at the British Institution in 1807.[2] In addition, because it was the largest and most highly finished treatment of the subject remaining in the artist's possession, it is the most likely candidate for identification as the version exhibited in 1818, and as one of the versions included in the posthumous exhibitions of West's art in the 1820s. For similar reasons, we have tentatively equated the work with the painting of the subject which *Public Characters* and the other early lists of West's works describe as being in the artist's possession.

According to the diagrams of 1801, West intended the *Ascension* and *Moses Receiving the Laws* (No. 258) to hang in corresponding positions on opposite walls in the reorganized chapel, and, as noted in the entry for No. 380, discrepancy in proportion between No. 380 and 258 may have been one of the reasons West intended to replace the completed picture with a new treatment of the subject. In contrast to No. 380, this version has virtually the same proportions, on a smaller scale, as No. 258, and whereas No. 380 has an arched top, No. 383, like No. 258, and in accordance with the shape of the space shown for the subject in the Swarthmore diagrams, has a rectangular one. Additionally, by 1801 West may simply have wanted a more dynamic composition than the one he had painted two decades earlier in his second picture for the chapel.

A rather slight compositional sketch, which shares features with both Nos. 383 and 384, went through the market in 1973.[3]

[1]See the letter dated 26 Sept. 1801 (printed in Galt 1820, pp. 193–98), in which West states that he had been instructed by James Wyatt to suspend work on the paintings for the chapel on "the fifteenth of last month," viz. on 15 August 1801. The exact date on the Swarthmore diagram which includes the *Ascension* is difficult to read; it is transcribed as "Aug. 25, 1801" in Dillenberger 1977, pl. 33. Helmut von Erffa read it as "Aug. 26, 1801"; Allen Staley and Nancy Pressly (in Pressly 1983, p. 18) as "Aug. 16, 1801." There is no question about the *Aug.* and the *1801*. See also Appendix I.
[2]Subtraction of the measurements of No. 383 from those given in the British Institution catalogue, gives differences of $18\frac{1}{4}$ in. in the vertical dimension and 17 in. in the horizontal, which are accounted for by the frame.
[3]Sotheby's, London, 29 Nov. 1973, lot 55 (pencil, grey ink, and black and white chalk, $6\frac{3}{4} \times 4\frac{3}{4}$ in.).

384 The Ascension *c.* 1798–1801

NEWARK MUSEUM, NEWARK, NEW JERSEY

Oil on paper: 11×8 in. (28×20.5 cm.)

Signed lower left: *B. W.*

PROV: Offered by West's sons to the United States in 1826 (87), and sold by them, Robins, London, 22–25

May 1829, lot 49 ($11 \times 7\frac{1}{2}$ in.), bt. by Vernon for £47.5.0.; Argosy Gallery, New York; gift of A. Edward Masters to the Newark Museum in 1959

EXH: (?) BI 1833 (22) as "the Resurrection; a Sketch," lent by Robert Vernon; Allentown 1962 (27)

LISTED: (?) *PC*, p. 567 ("The small sketch of Christ's Ascension," West, Gallery); *UM*, p. 531; *BA*, p. 18; Galt, p. 231; Dillenberger, pp. 179 (403) and 213

LIT: Kraemer 1975, p. 18

As noted in the entry for No. 383, this version shows a composition intermediary between those of Nos. 382 and 383. Certain details, such as the apostles standing on the right, echo No. 382, while in the positions of Christ and the angels it points to No. 383.

Because of the correspondence in measurements, No. 384 can be equated with the small *Ascension* bought by Robert Vernon in 1829, and it would seem to be the work erroneously (but understandably) identified as a sketch of the "Resurrection" that Vernon lent to the British Institution in 1833, which is otherwise unrecorded among the works by West that Vernon is known to have owned.

385 St. Peter's First Sermon 1785

BOB JONES UNIVERSITY, GREENVILLE, SOUTH CAROLINA

Oil on canvas: 148×116 in. (376×295 cm.)

Signed bottom right: *B. West/1785*

PROV: Painted for George III (1797 account: "The Picture of St. Peter's first Sermon," 1785, £1,050; 1801 account, p. 213: for the Windsor Chapel, The Prophets, 35, "Peter's first Sermon, or the Apostles receiving the Cloven Tongues," ...); never delivered and ownership returned to West's sons by George IV in 1828; sold by them, Robins, London, 22–25 May 1829, lot 82 (12 ft. 6 in. × 10 ft.), bt. by Bone for £105 on behalf of Joseph Neeld, MP, Grittleton House, Wilts.; by descent in the Neeld family

384

until sold by Miss C. K. M. Neeld, Christie's, London, 16 Nov. 1962, lot 95, bt. by Weitzner; purchased by the present owner in 1963

EXH: RA 1785 (153) "St. Peter's first sermon after being filled with the Holy Ghost, painted for His Majesty's chapel, Windsor Castle"; West's Gallery 1821 (40) ... "Acts, chap. 2":

Verse 1. And when the day of Pentecost was fully come, they were all with one accord in one place.

Verse 2. And suddenly there came a sound from heaven as of a rushing mighty wind, and it filled all the house where they were sitting.

Verse 3. And there appeared unto them cloven tongues like as of fire, and it sat upon each of them.

Verse 4. And they were all filled with the Holy Ghost, and began to speak with other tongues, as the Spirit gave them utterance.

Verse 14. But Peter standing up with the eleven, lifted up his voice and said unto them, Ye men of Judea, and all ye that dwell at Jerusalem, be this known unto you, and hearken to my words.

West's Gallery 1822–28 (58), with same quotation

ENGR: Stipple engraving ($22\frac{9}{16} \times 17\frac{1}{4}$ in.) by Benjamin Smith, pub. by Boydell & Co., 19 May 1814; engraving ($6\frac{3}{8} \times 4\frac{1}{2}$ in.) by W. Holl, pub. by Fisher & Son, in the *Royal Family Bible*

LISTED: *PC*, p. 561 ("The Inspiration of St. Peter," George III, for his Majesty's Chapel, Windsor, Gospel Dispensation, 10 ft. × 14); *UM*, p. 527; *AA*, p. 67 (9 ft. × 14); Barlow, p. 432 ("Peter's first sermon, Descent of the Holy Spirit," 15 ft. × 10); *BA*, p. 14; Galt, p. 219; Dillenberger, pp. 149 (111) and 212

LIT: V and A Cuttings, 1, p. 255 (1785); Jones 1963; Jones 1968, p. 65 (350), ill. p. 191; Meyer 1975, p. 256, fig. 12, and p. 265; Dillenberger 1977, p. 71 and pl. 56; Pressly 1983, p. 21, fig. 8

In the drawings made *c.* 1780 showing architectural schemes for the Royal Chapel in Windsor Castle, this composition appears second from the right among the vertical compositions devoted to New Testament subjects on what was evidently supposed to represent a side wall of the chapel (ill. p. 577). The subject reappears in the same position in one of the Swarthmore diagrams of 1801 (p. 580).

The composition appears to have been based upon that of the huge *St. Denis Preaching the Faith in France* exhibited by Joseph-Marie Vien in the Salon of 1767 (Church of Saint-Roch, Paris). There are also similarities with Vien's earlier *Marcus Aurelius Distributing Food and Medicine*, which had been commissioned in 1764 for the Château de Choisy (now Musée de Picardie, Amiens).

An oil sketch of the composition is No. 386 below. Three slight drawings are in the print room at Windsor,[1] and a drawing showing what appears to be the same subject, but with a completely different composition, is at Swarthmore.[2] A drawing for the infant near Peter's feet went through Sotheby's in 1982.[3] An unfinished copy of the painting was sold by West's sons in 1829.[4]

[1]Pencil, $3\frac{7}{8} \times 3\frac{1}{8}$ in.; pencil, $3\frac{7}{8} \times 3\frac{1}{4}$ in.; pencil, $3\frac{3}{4} \times 3\frac{1}{8}$ in. See No. 380, note 5.
[2]Black chalk, $6\frac{1}{4} \times 9\frac{1}{8}$ in.
[3]Black, red, and white chalk on blue paper, $11\frac{3}{4} \times 9\frac{1}{4}$ in., signed lower left: *B. West 1785*, sold Sotheby's, London, 11 Nov. 1982, lot 78.
[4]Robins, London, 20–22 June 1829, lot 166 ("St. Peter's First Sermon, copied from the large picture, companion to the preceding [copy of the *Baptism*, see No. 316],——not finished").

385

386

386 St. Peter's First Sermon *c.* 1785

LOCATION UNKNOWN

Oil on canvas: 36 × 28 in. (91.5 × 71 cm.)

PROV: Offered by West's sons to the United States in 1826 (144, . . ., 2 ft. 4 in. × 3 ft., included among "Original Designs in Chiaro Scuro for the large Pictures which were painted for his late Majesty's Chapel in Windsor Castle"), and sold by them, Robins, London, 22–25 May 1829, lot 127 (3 ft. 6 in. × 2 ft. 4 in.), bt. by Hayes for £50.8.0.; E. and A. Silberman Galleries, New York (*c.* 1949–62)

EXH: 125 Pall Mall 1814 (3) "Peter's Sermon, Acts, chap ii, verse 7"; 125 Pall Mall 1818 (5) "St. Peter's First Sermon, Acts, chap. ii, verses 1, 2, 3, 4, 14"; West's Gallery 1821 (57) "St. Peter's First Sermon (a sketch)"; New York 1962 (14)

LIT: Meyer 1975, p. 265

387 The Apostles Imprisoned (Peter Delivered from Prison) 1800

MUSEUM OF FINE ARTS, BOSTON

Oil on paper, mounted on panel: 14¼ × 10¾ in. (36.2 × 27.3 cm.)

Signed lower left: *B. West/[?]Windsor/1800*

PROV: Offered by West's sons to the United States in 1826 (55), and sold by them, Robins, 22–25 May 1829, lot 26 ("Angels Delivering St. Peter," 14½ × 11 in.), bt. by H. P. Bone for £47.5.0., on behalf of Joseph Neeld, MP, Grittleton House, Wilts.; by descent in the Neeld family until sold, Christie's, London, 13 July 1945, lot 176; Mrs. C. B. E. Franklin; Christie's, London, 23 July 1954, lot 139; Frost & Reed, Ltd., London; Sotheby's, London, 15 May 1957, lot 122; Mrs. Robert Frank, London, from whom purchased by the Museum of Fine Arts (Ellen Kelleran Gardner Fund) in 1958

EXH: RA 1800 (63) "The Apostles imprisoned":

But the Angel of the Lord by night opened the prison doors, and brought them forth, and said,

go, stand and speak in the temple to the people, all the words of this life
Acts of the Apostles, chap. v. ver. 19 and 20

West's Gallery 1821 (6) "The Angel delivering St. Peter;" West's Gallery 1822–28 (3) "Angels delivering St. Peter;" BI 1833 (36) "The Angel delivering St. Peter; a Sketch," lent by Joseph Neeld

LISTED: *PC*, p. 567 ("The Angel loosening the Chains of St. Peter in Prison," West, Gallery); *UM*, p. 531 ("The Angels" . . .); Barlow, p. 435 ("The Angel unchaining Peter in Prison"), *BA*, p. 18; Galt, p. 231; Dillenberger, pp. 178 (399) and 213

LIT: Boston 1969, pp. 281–82 (1017), fig. 96

Although West exhibited No. 387 in 1800 as "The Apostles imprisoned," accompanying it with a quotation from the fifth chapter of Acts, the painting shows the release of St. Peter from prison as described in Acts 12:1–11. All early references to the picture except the Royal Academy catalogue describe it as showing St. Peter being unchained or delivered from prison. Details such as the sleeping soldiers, which are conspicuous in No. 387, are mentioned only in the later passage.

In 1783 West had made a drawing of the subject of "St. Peter Delivered from Prison," which is inscribed *a sketch from memory of the picture painted by Salvator Rosa in the possession of the Earl of Chesterfield*,[1] and in 1788 he made a second drawing of the subject to serve as model for one of the reliefs on the pulpit in the chapel in Greenwich Hospital.[2] No. 387 does not repeat the composition of either of these earlier drawings.

[1] 15¾ × 11⅝ in., sold by Mrs. Claire Francis, Christie's, London, 14 March 1967, lot 40, ill. in the cat.
[2] 14½ × 14½ in., signed: *B. West 1788/Windsor* (National Maritime Museum, Greenwich). For the Greenwich pulpit see No. 397, note 2.

388 Devout Men Taking the Body of St. Stephen 1776

ST. STEPHEN WALBROOK, LONDON

Oil on canvas: 216 × 120 in. (549 × 305 cm.)

Signed lower left: *B. West 1776*

PROV: Presented to St. Stephen Walbrook in 1776 by the Rector, Dr. Thomas Wilson (1703–1784)

EXH: RA 1776 (96) "Devout men taking the body of St. Stephen; an altarpiece"

ENGR: Mezzotint (34 13/16 × 22½ in.) by Valentine Green, pub. by J. Boydell, 16 Oct. 1776; this plate was reworked by Robert Dunkarton and republished by Boydell, 1 Jan. 1801; outline engraving (5 × 2⅛ in.) by Normand *fils*, pub. in Hamilton 1831, no. 170

LISTED: *PC*, p. 562 ("The Death of St. Stephen, in the Church of St. Stephen, Walbrook," 10 ft. × 18); *UM*, p. 528; *AA*, p. 68 (18 ft. × 12); Barlow, p. 433 ("St. Stephen stoned to death"); *BA*, p. 15; Galt, p. 220; Dillenberger, pp. 153 (150) and 211

LIT: V and A Cuttings, I, p. 56; Farington Diary, 22 Feb. 1804 (Farington 1978–, VI, p. 2251); Carey 1820, p. 696; Galt 1820, p. 15; Hamilton 1831: Curwen 1842, p. 52; Croft-Murray 1970, p. 291 (6); T. W. Matthews, *St. Stephen Walbrook: A Short History*, p. 9; Jerry D. Meyer, "Benjamin West's 'St. Stephen Altarpiece': a Study in late eighteenth-century Protestant Church Patronage and English History Painting," *Burlington Magazine*, CXVIII, 1976, pp. 634–43; Dillenberger 1977, p. 42 and pl. 23

The title used by West at the Royal Academy in 1776 indicates that No. 388 shows the aftermath of the first Christian martyrdom, as described in the Acts of the Apostles 8:12. It does not depict the "Stoning of St.

387

Stephen" or the "Death of St. Stephen," although variants of both titles appears in the early lists of West's works.

A press cutting in the Victoria and Albert Museum, which appears to be from 1773, provides the following information:

> We hear that the ingenious Mr. Benjamin West, of Panton-Square, having signified his inclination to paint the Martyrdom of St. Stephen to be placed in the East window of St. Stephen's, Walbrook, the Rev. Dr. Wilson, the Rector, eagerly embraced the opportunity of engaging so celebrated a Painter, and desired Mr. West to accept 150 guineas from him to shew the high esteem he has for the ornamenting of churches in general, and particularly a church where he had been so long Rector. Mr. West has been pleased to accept this as a present, not at all adequate to so noble a design.

This curious definition of the payment as a present perhaps explains the description of No. 388 as a "gratuitous picture" by William Carey in 1820. West was recorded by Samuel Curwen as having said in April 1776 that he was to receive 600 guineas, "which Mr. West esteems so small a price that he considers it a gift to the church." It seems likely that Curwen got the figures confused, and 600 guineas, an amount considerably higher than anything the artist is known to have been paid prior to that date, may have been the amount that West felt he should have received. In 1804 West told Farington that he had received £150 (not even guineas) for the picture. But if West was paid so little for No. 388 that he thought of it as a gift, the work brought him further returns, since, according to Carey, the success of No. 388 at the Royal Academy in 1776 procured the artist commissions for altarpieces for Trinity College, Cambridge (No. 406) and Winchester Cathedral (No. 339). No. 388 had been preceded by West's altarpiece for Rochester (No. 304) and by the aborted scheme of decoration for St. Paul's Cathedral (see No. 257).[1]

The shape of the canvas was dictated by the shape of the east window of the church, where No. 388 was originally installed.[2] In 1852 it was removed to its present situation on the north wall.[3]

West's missing sketch, which appeared at the Royal Academy two years before the large painting, is No. 389 below.

[1] See the article published by Jerry Meyer in 1976 for a fuller discussion of the circumstances under which No. 388 was painted, the stylistic sources, and a consideration of the picture in relation to other treatments of St. Stephen, and analogous subjects.

[2] A view by Thomas Malton of the interior of the church c. 1792 with No. 388 in its original location is reproduced by Meyer, fig. 18.

[3] Photographs of the east window in its present form, with modern stained glass, and of No. 388 in its present location are reproduced in the guide to the church by T. W. Matthews.

389 Devout Men Taking the Body of St. Stephen

c. 1773–74

LOCATION UNKNOWN

Oil on paper

PROV: In West's sons' possession in 1821

EXH: RA 1774 (311) "Devout men taking the body of St. Stephen; a design for a picture to be painted for the altar of the church of St. Stephen Walbrook"; 125 Pall Mall 1814 (10) "St. Stephen, Acts, chap. vii, verses 57, 58, 59, 60"; 125 Pall Mall 1816 (5) with same citation; West's Gallery 1821 (52) "St. Stephen, a sketch of the large Picture in St. Stephen's Church, Walbrook"

388

390

LISTED: *PC*, p. 568 ("The large Sketch, in oil, of the Death of St. Stephen, on paper," West, Gallery); *UM*, p. 531; Galt, p. 232; Dillenberger, p. 182 (438)

LIT: V and A Cuttings, I, p. 106 (*Public Advertiser*, 30 April 1774); Carey 1820, p. 696

390 St. Paul Persecuting the Christians 1786

SMITH COLLEGE MUSEUM OF ART, NORTHAMPTON, MASSACHUSETTS

Oil on canvas: $35\frac{1}{2} \times 9$ in. (90 × 23 cm.)

This painting is framed together with Nos. 392 and 393. See the entry for No. 392 for all three works.

391 The Conversion of St. Paul *c.* 1786

PROV: Sold by West's sons, Robins, London, 20–22 June 1829, lot 132 ("Two narrow pictures, the Conversion of St. Paul and Companion")

EXH: (?) RA 1791 (426) "The conversion of St. Paul; a finished sketch, a design for the painted window in St. Paul's church Birmingham"

See No. 392.

392 The Conversion of St. Paul 1786
See color illustration, p. 92

SMITH COLLEGE MUSEUM OF ART, NORTHAMPTON, MASSACHUSETTS

Oil on canvas: $50\frac{1}{2} \times 23\frac{1}{2}$ in. (128.5 × 59.5 cm.)

Signed lower left: *B. West 1786*

PROV: (?) In the collection of Henry Hope (1736–1811) by 1802; (?) his sale, Christie's, London, 27–29 June 1816, lot 90 ("The Conversion of St. Paul") for £106.1.0.; Lederer, London; sold anonymously, Christie's, London, 1 Dec. 1950, lot 149 (as "The Conversion of Saul," $51 \times 23\frac{1}{2}$ in.), bt. by Frost and Reed; Charles D. Childs, Boston, from whom purchased by the Smith College Museum of Art in 1951 (gift of the Misses Wing)

EXH: (?) RA 1801 (80) "A sketch for a painted window in St. Paul's church, Birmingham, representing Saul's miraculous conversion, Acts of the Apostles, chap. ix":

> Ver. 1. And Saul yet breathing out threatenings and slaughter against the disciples of the Lord, went unto the high priest,
> Ver. 2. And desired of him letters to Damascus to the synagogues, that if he found any of this way, whether they were men or women, he might bring them bound unto Jerusalem.
> Ver. 3. And as he journeyed, he came near Damascus; and suddenly there shined round about him a light from heaven.
> Ver. 4. And he fell to the earth, and heard a voice saying unto him, Saul, Saul, why persecutest thou me?
> Ver. 6. And he trembling and astonished said, Lord, what wilt thou have me to do? And the Lord said unto him, arise, and go into the city, and it shall be told thee what thou must do.
> Ver. 11. And the Lord said unto Ananias, arise, and go into the street which is called Straight, and inquire in the house of Judas, for one called Saul of Tarsus: for behold he prayeth.

> Ver. 17. And Ananias went his way, and entered into the house, and putting his hands on him, said, brother Saul, the Lord, even Jesus, that appeared unto thee in the way as thou camest, hath sent me, that thou mightest receive thy sight, and be filled with the Holy Ghost

(?) LISTED: *PC*, p. 562 ("St. Paul's Conversion; his Persecution of the Christians; and the Restoration of his Sight under the hands of Ananias, in one frame, divided in three parts," Henry Hope); *UM*, p. 528; Barlow, p. 433 ("St. Paul's Conversion," with "St. Paul persecuting the Christians and His restoration to Sight by Ananias" listed after it as separate works, all three in the collection of Mr. Hope); Galt, p. 221; Dillenberger, pp. 155–56 (173–75) and 212

LIT: H. R. Hitchcock, "An 'Altarpiece' by Benjamin West, P.R.A.," *Smith College Museum of Art Bulletin*, nos. 29–32, June 1951, pp. 12–18, and figs. 5–8; Evans 1959, pp. 66–67, pls. 48 and 49; Dillenberger 1977, p. 105 and pl. 72

No. 392 is framed together with *St. Paul Persecuting the Christians* and the *Restoration of St. Paul's Sight, under the Hand of Ananias* (Nos. 390 and 393). The three form a triptych, with two smaller canvases showing cherubs, which do not appear to be by West's hand, above the side compartments.[1] The three larger paintings were described as "in one frame, divided in three parts" in *Public Characters* in 1804. Neither the catalogue of the Hope sale in 1816 nor the Christie's sale catalogue of 1 December 1950, describes more than a single picture of the *Conversion of St. Paul*, but as the two side compartments are so definitely subordinate to the central scene of the *Conversion* and are so closely related to it in subject, the omissions should probably not be interpreted as indicating that Nos. 390 and 393 were separated from No. 392.

West exhibited sketches of the *Conversion of St. Paul* at the Royal Academy in 1791 and 1801, describing both of them in the catalogue as for a painted window in St. Paul's Church, Birmingham.[2] Henry Hope probably owned the second of the two. Although there is no proof that Hope bought his pictures at the time of the Royal Academy exhibition, he only settled in England in 1794, and it is reasonable to think that he would have been attracted to works that he saw exhibited, rather than other versions of the same subjects remaining in the artist's studio. Henry Hope's one well-documented act of patronage of West occurred in 1802 (see No. 640). The sketch of the *Conversion of St. Paul* exhibited in 1791 may have been the version of the subject sold by West's sons on 20–22 June 1829 (see No. 391 and note 4 below).

The painted window in St. Paul's Church, Birmingham, referred to in both Royal Academy catalogues, was executed by Francis Eginton of Soho in 1789 and installed in 1791.[3] It is still intact and consists of three lights reproducing the compositions of Nos. 390, 392, and 393 (ill. p. 92). The central light has a semicircular arched top and shows Christ with his right hand raised and looking downward at Paul, in both these respects differing from No. 392, to which otherwise it corresponds closely. However, *pentimenti* indicate that No. 392 has been altered and that its appearance was previously considerably closer to that of the window. Traces of an arched top and of the outlines of the former position of the figure of Christ are still discernible in the painting.[4]

[1] Oil on canvas, each $12\frac{3}{4} \times 9\frac{7}{8}$ in.
[2] Both catalogue entries refer only to the *Conversion*, without indicating if West exhibited a triptych, or only the central scene, but the passage accompanying the picture exhibited in 1801, which is quoted above, includes verses describing events that are depicted in the two side compartments.

393

[3] The window is inscribed *DESIGNED BY B. WEST, ESQ. & EXECUTED BY F. EGINTON, MDCCLXXXIX*. Eginton is said to have rented the paintings from West for 80 guineas to use as his models. For the window, see also Robert K. Dent, *The Making of Birmingham*, London, 1894, p. 163; L. R. Ettlinger and R. G. Holloway, *Architectural Review*, CI, 1947, pp. 226–28; Marcus Whiffen, *Stuart and Georgian Churches: The Architecture of the Church of England Outside London, 1603–1837*, London, 1948, p. 104.

[4] In September 1985 Simon Dickinson of Christie's kindly brought to our attention three further paintings of the same subjects identical in most details with Nos. 390, 392, and 393, and it is possible that those three works rather than No. 392 and its companions had the early history listed above. They were purchased from Robert Frank by Ray L. Murphy in 1948 and have no recorded earlier history. The three are in oil on canvas; the central painting is $49\frac{1}{2} \times 23$ in.; the two side compartments are each $35\frac{1}{4} \times 9\frac{1}{4}$ in. The central *Conversion of St. Paul* has an arched top, and the position of Christ in it corresponds to that of the figure in the window rather than to the one in No. 392. There are also significant differences in the angels around Christ in the two paintings. The two sets of paintings now known presumably account for the two sketches shown by West in 1791 and 1801.

393 The Restoration of St. Paul's Sight, under the Hands of Ananias 1786

SMITH COLLEGE MUSEUM OF ART, NORTHAMPTON, MASSACHUSETTS

Oil on canvas: $35\frac{1}{2} \times 9$ in. (90 × 23 cm.)

This painting is framed together with Nos. 390 and 392. See the entry for No. 392 for all three works. A drawing for this composition is at Swarthmore.[1]

[1] Pen, $17 \times 5\frac{5}{8}$ in.

394 Paul and Barnabas Rejecting the Jews and Receiving the Gentiles *c.* 1793
Illustrated over page

PENNSYLVANIA ACADEMY OF THE FINE ARTS, PHILADELPHIA

Oil on canvas: 147 × 115 in. (373 × 292 cm.)

PROV: Painted for George III (1797 account: "Paul and Barnabas rejecting the Jews and receiving the Gentiles," 1793, £1,050; 1801 account, p. 213: for the Windsor Chapel, The Prophets, 36, . . .); never delivered and ownership returned to West's sons by George IV in 1828; sold by them, Robins, London, 22–25 May 1829, lot 39 ("Paul and Barnabas," 12 ft. 6 in. × 10 ft., "Painted by command of His late Majesty for his intended Chapel in Windsor Castle"), bt. by L. Girarde for £378; bequeathed (? by Girarde) to the city of Philadelphia before 1843; transferred to the Pennsylvania Academy in 1848 in exchange for a portrait of the Marquis de Lafayette by Thomas Sully

EXH: RA 1793 (140) "St. Paul and Barnabas rejecting the Jews and receiving the Gentiles, for His Majesty's chapel in Windsor Castle"; West's Gallery 1821 (37), 1822–28 (50), in both as "Paul and Barnabas, Acts, chap. 13":

> Verse 45. But when the Jews saw the multitudes, they were filled with envy, and spake against those things which were spoken by Paul, contradicting and blaspheming.
> Verse 46. Then Paul and Barnabas waxed bold, and said, it was necessary that the word of God should first have been spoken to you; but seeing ye put it from you, and judge yourselves unworthy of everlasting life, lo, we turn to the Gentiles.

Artist's Fund Society, Philadelphia, 1843 (19) "Paul and Barnabas at Lystra," lent by the City of Philadelphia; PAFA 1847 and frequently thereafter

LISTED: *PC*, p. 561 ("Paul and Barnabas rejecting the Jews, and receiving the Gentiles," George III, for his Majesty's Chapel, Windsor, Gospel Dispensation, 10 ft. × 14); *UM*, p. 527; *AA*, p. 67 (9 ft. × 14); Barlow, p. 432; *BA*, p. 14; Galt, p. 219; Dillenberger, p. 149 (113)

LIT: Henderson 1911, pp. 320–21; Meyer 1975, p. 256, 265, and fig. 13; Dillenberger 1977, p. 71 and pl. 57

The subject of Paul and Barnabas, shown in essentially the same composition as No. 394, appears on the extreme right, in the sequence of New Testament compositions in the drawings of *c.* 1780 for the chapel at Windsor (ill. p. 577). It reappears, with the notation "Finished," in the same position in the Swarthmore diagrams of 1801 (p. 580). It is the final subject in biblical sequence among the pictures actually painted by West for the chapel. Barlow includes one further title, "The Apostles preaching and working miracles," between *Peter's First Sermon* (see No. 385) and *Paul and Barnabas*, but that subject appears on no other list and West seems never to have painted it.

No. 394 is conspicuously visible on the far wall, hanging pendant to *St. Peter's First Sermon* (No. 385), in the engraved view by Cattermole and Le Keux and in the painting by John Pasmore showing posthumous exhibitions in West's gallery (ill. pp. 150 and 151).

Oil sketches or versions are Nos. 395 and 396 below. A small drawing of the composition is in the print room at Windsor Castle.[1]

[1] Pencil, $3\frac{3}{4} \times 4$ in. This is one of the group of drawings discussed in entry No. 380, note 5.

395 Paul and Barnabas Rejecting the Jews and Receiving the Gentiles *c.* 1793

PRIVATE COLLECTION

Oil on canvas: 36 × 28 in. (91.5 × 71 cm.)

PROV: Offered by West's sons to the United States in 1826 (37, . . . 3 ft. × 2 ft. 4 in.), and sold by them, Robins, London, 22–25 May 1829, lot 132 ("Paul and Barnabas Preaching," 2 ft. 4 in. × 3 ft., "The original design for the Large Picture"), bt. by Ward for £120.15.0.

EXH: RA 1807 (175) "Paul and Barnabas rejecting the Jews and receiving the Gentiles, the finished study, from which the large picture was painted for His Majesty's chapel at Windsor", with a quotation from Acts 13:46 (cf. No. 394 above); (?) 125 Pall Mall 1814 (4); (?) West's Gallery 1821 (33), 1822–28 (82), in both described as a sketch

LISTED: (?) *PC*, p. 566 ("St. Paul and Barnabas rejecting the Jews and turning to the Gentiles," West, Gallery); *UM*, p. 530; Barlow, p. 435; *BA*, p. 17; Galt, p. 228; Dillenberger, p. 173 (348)

Two small versions of *Paul and Barnabas* appeared in the West sons' offer of works to the United States in 1826 and in the Robins sale of 22–25 May 1829. The one that received the far higher price in 1829 (No. 395) was described in the catalogue as a colored study, made as a prototype for the large picture. The other (No. 396) was listed in 1826 and in 1829 among a group of studies in "Chiaro Scuro." Hence, the version of the subject which West exhibited in 1807 as a "finished study" would seem to have been No. 395, which is a finished picture in colors rather than a monochromatic sketch. The question of which version appeared in various subsequent exhibitions can only be guessed at, but it seems reasonable to assume that West and his sons would have given preference to No. 395.

394

396 Paul and Barnabas Rejecting the Jews and Receiving the Gentiles *c.* 1793

LOCATION UNKNOWN

(36 × 28 in.) (91.5 × 71 cm.)

PROV: Offered by West's sons to the United States in 1826 (145, . . ., 2 ft. 4 in. × 3 ft., included among "Original Designs in Chiaro Scuro for the large Pictures which were painted for his late Majesty's Chapel in Windsor Castle"), and sold by them, Robins, London, 22–25 May 1829, lot 131 ("Paul and Barnabas Preaching," 3 ft. × 2 ft. 4 in.), bt. by Pickering for £31.10.0.

397 St. Paul Shaking the Viper from His Hand after the Shipwreck 1789
See color detail, p. 88

CHAPEL OF ST. PETER AND ST. PAUL, THE ROYAL NAVAL COLLEGE, GREENWICH

Oil on canvas: 300 × 168 in. (762 × 427 cm.)

Signed lower left: *B. West/1789*

PROV: Commissioned from the artist *c.* 1782; completed and installed in its present situation in 1789

ENGR: Engraving (25½ × 14 9/16 in.) by F. Bartolozzi, pub. with a dedication to the Commissioners and Governors of the Royal Hospital for Seamen at Greenwich, on 1 Jan. 1791, by B. West and J. Barney; engraving (6 1/16 × 4 5/16 in.) by W. J. White, showing the central area of the composition, pub. by Keymer & Co., Yarmouth, 1813

LISTED: *PC*, p. 562 ("St. Paul shaking the Viper off his Finger," 27 ft. × 15, in the Chapel at Greenwich); *UM*, p. 528; *AA*, p. 68 (27 ft. × 16); Barlow, p. 433; *BA*, p. 15; Galt, p. 220; Dillenberger, pp. 153 (152) and 212

LIT: V and A Cuttings, II, pp. 340 and 445; Farington Diary, 1 Jan. 1795, 22 Feb. and 3 March 1804 (Farington 1978–, II, p. 285, and VI, pp. 2251 and 2259); [John Cooke and John Maule], *An Historical Account of the Royal Hospital for Seamen at Greenwich*, London, 1789, pp. 100–107; *Public Characters*, 1805, p. 553; Whitley 1928a, p. 48; "The Royal Naval College: Greenwich Chapel Restored," *The Times* (London) 13 June 1955; Helmut von Erffa, letter to the editor, *The Times* (London) 16 June 1955; The Revd. Basil Watson, *A Short Guide to the Chapel of St. Peter and St. Paul*, Greenwich, n.d. (*c.* 1955), pp. 2, 6–7, and 23–24; von Erffa 1969, pp. 24–25; Croft-Murray 1970, p. 291; Esther Sparks, "'St. Paul Shaking off the Viper,' an Early Romantic Series by Benjamin West," *Museum Studies* (Art Institute of Chicago), VI, 1971, pp. 59–65; Dillenberger 1877, pp. 101–5, pls. 68 and 69; Alberts 1978, p. 185

The chapel of the Royal Naval Hospital (now College) at Greenwich, originally built by Christopher Wren and Thomas Ripley, was gutted by fire in January 1779 and subsequently rebuilt by James Stuart and William Newton (ill. p. 88). For the new chapel, West not only painted the huge picture over the altar (No. 397), but also provided designs for numerous further paintings executed by Biagio Rebecca,[1] for relief sculptures on the reader's desk and pulpit,[2] and for free-standing statues in the vestibule.[3] In 1795 he told Joseph Farington that he received 1300 guineas for the large picture and 5 guineas each for twenty-five drawings (these presumably were the designs from which Rebecca and the sculptors worked).[4] By 1804, however, when Farington recorded West's testimony against Copley on behalf of Sir Edward Knatchbull, the stated price had dropped to £1,200, with which West "thought himself well paid."[5]

According to contemporary newspaper accounts, the commission for the chapel was originally given to Copley, but transferred to West due to the intervention of George III.[6] A letter from James Stuart to his Clerk of the Works, Robert Mylne, which is cited by Lesley Lewis with the suggestion that it was written in August 1782, evidently requested the return of Stuart's designs for the chapel from Mylne to allow West to show them to "His Majesty with the sketch of his picture inserted in its place."[7] This letter appears to be the first recorded mention of West in connection with the chapel. Whether at this time he had been given the commission, or whether his showing a sketch to the King was part of his campaign to take the commission away from Copley, is not clear. He exhibited a finished sketch for the yet unpainted large picture at the Royal Academy in 1787 (No. 398). In 1789 he exhibited only one relatively modest work at the Academy (No. 211, the sketch for one of his pictures for Boydell's Shakespeare Gallery), and one newspaper commented that the reason was West's "attention to his large picture for Greenwich, which is not in that state of forwardness that may be expected." A letter from J. Ibbetson to West dated 17 April 1789, announces on behalf of the directors that, the chapel being very nearly completed, the picture is "much wanted," and expresses the hope that "you will not fail to finish it, and have it put up, within two months at least from the date hereof, agreeable to your Engagement when you last attended them; as any failure therein will be productive of great inconvenience" (Historical Society of Pennsylvania). The picture was not finished within two months, and a letter from West to Ibbetson in the Public Records Office, which is dated 26 August 1789, promises that it will be completed within twelve or fifteen days. By then, however, the painting may already have been in place, as another letter in the same collection requests a scaffolding so that West can put the final touches on it.[8]

No. 397 is the only major oil painting by West to remain in the situation for which it was painted. Apart from cartoons for stained glass it was by far the largest picture painted by the artist prior to the last decade of his life. In his testimony against Copley in 1804, West described the painting as containing about fifty figures, the largest of which were eight feet high. The subject is from the Acts of the Apostles 28:1–6 and shows St. Paul on the island of Malta, following the wreck of the ship that was taking him prisoner to Rome. According to a guide to the Greenwich Hospital published in 1789:

The picture consists of three groups. The lower part represents Marines and Prisoners bringing ashore various articles which have been preserved from the wreck. Near these is an elegant figure supposed to be a Roman lady of distinction, clasping with affection an urn containing the ashes of her deceased husband who had fallen in the wars of Judea. Before her is an aged, infirm man who, being unable to assist himself is carried in the arms of two robust young men.

In the middle part of the piece is the principal group, consisting of St. Paul shaking into the fire the viper that had fastened on his hand, the Brethren who accompanied him, his friend the Centurion, and a band of Roman soldiers with their proper insignia.

The figures above these, on the summit of the rocks, form the third group; and consist of the hospitable inslanders lowering down fuel and other necessaries for the relief of the sufferers.

The sea and wrecked ship appear in the background, and combine to exhibit a scene that cannot fail of having a proper effect on the minds of seafaring men, and of impressing them with a due sense of their past preservation and their present comfortable situation and support in this glorious asylum for naval misfortune and naval worth.[9]

No. 397 has undergone several cleanings. In 1954 and 1955 the entire chapel underwent extensive restoration, and, according to an anonymous article in *The Times*, consideration was given to removing the West, but "The amount of work involved and the expense were, however, eventually decisive against doing so."

Apart from the oil sketch (No. 398), there are compositional drawings, all of which differ considerably from the finished painting, in the Art Insitute of Chicago,[10] the Historical Society of Pennsylvania,[11] and the Museum of Fine Arts, Boston.[12] A large drawing of the composition, which is close to the finished painting and is probably after it, rather than a preparatory study, is in the National Maritime Museum, Greenwich.[13] A drawing for the figure of Paul was lent to the Graham Gallery, New York, in 1962 by Mr. and Mrs. Daniel Fraad, Jr.,[14] and another drawing with a draft of a letter about the commission was with the Bernard Black Gallery, New York, in 1968.[15]

[1]The chief paintings by Rebecca for which West provided designs are fourteen figures in grisaille of the Apostles and Evangelists in simulated niches between the clerestory windows. Drawings for these figures are in the National Maritime Museum, Greenwich, and the subjects along with those of West's other designs for the chapel (cf. notes 2 and 3 below) are included in the early lists of West's works: *PC*, p. 562 (In the Council-chamber, Greenwich Hospital); *UM*, p. 528; Barlow, p. 433; *BA*, p. 15 (erroneously as in the collection of Henry Hope); Galt, pp. 221–22; Dillenberger, pp. 156–57 (177–87) and 215. In addition, not on the lists, but evidently designed by West and executed by Rebecca as well is a grisaille *Ascension* in the low arch between the cornice and ceiling above No. 397. A drawing

397

for this composition (brown ink and wash, $5\frac{1}{8} \times 12\frac{1}{8}$ in.) is at Swarthmore and is reproduced in Brooks 1925, fig. 7. The painting is described as designed by West and executed by Rebecca in the guide by Cooke and Maule published in 1789 (p. 105).

[2] The reader's desk, which has been separated from the pulpit and relegated to storage in the dome of the chapel has four reliefs of the prophets *Daniel, Micah, Zacariah,* and *Malachi.* The pulpit has six reliefs in Coade stone showing scenes from the Acts of the Apostles: the *Conversion of St. Paul, Cornelius and the Angel, Peter delivered from Prison, Elymas Struck Blind, Paul Preaching at Athens,* and *Paul before Felix.* Drawings for both series are in the National Maritime Museum, and the subjects are listed in the early catalogues of West's works (see note 1). One of the pulpit reliefs, *Paul Preaching at Athens,* is reproduced in Dillenberger 1977, p. 104, pl. 71.

[3] *Faith, Hope, Charity,* and *Meekness* in Coade stone (for which see also No. 110). Drawings, which do not appear to be entirely in West's hand, are in the National Maritime Museum, and the subjects are included in the early catalogues of West's works (see note 1). The lists include *Innocence,* but the corresponding drawing is inscribed *Meekness.* According to Watson (p. 18) the captions which were originally on the pedestals of the statues have been removed, as Meekness "was hardly a desirable or inspiring virtue to be inculcated in Naval Officers." Margaret Whinney ascribes these four figures to John Bacon (*Sculpture in Britain 1530–1830,* Harmondsworth, 1964, p. 166). Rupert Gunnis (*Dictionary of British Sculptors, 1660–1851,* rev. ed., London, n.d., p. 106, under Coade) lists them as designed by West.

[4] The works enumerated in notes 1–3 total twenty-nine. The most likely explanation for the discrepancy is that West may not have been paid for the four drawings for the vestibule statues (cited in note 3) which do not appear to be entirely in his hand (two are signed) and which would have been only of minimal use in the execution of large free-standing sculptures.

[5] For this controversy see No. 54 Prown 1966, II, pp. 360–71, and Farington Diary, 1 and 3 March 1804 (Farington 1978—, VI, pp. 2257–60).

[6] A variant account in the *Morning Herald,* cited by Whitley, ascribed the intervention to Lord North. See also Prown 1966, II, p. 319.

[7] Lesley Lewis, "The Architecture of the Chapel at Greenwich Hospital," *Art Bulletin,* XXIX, 1947, p. 262.

[8] Both letters cited in von Erffa 1969, p. 25.

[9] Cooke and Maule, p. 105. This description, which was probably provided by West, is reprinted in later guides to the hospital.

[10] Pen and wash, $12 \times 14\frac{3}{4}$ in.; ill. by Sparks, fig. 2.

[11] Pen and wash; Sparks, fig. 3.

[12] Two drawings, pen and wash, $19\frac{3}{8} \times 13\frac{7}{16}$ in. and $16\frac{3}{8} \times 10\frac{1}{8}$ in.; Sparks, figs. 4 and 5.

[13] Pen and wash, $26 \times 14\frac{3}{4}$ in., signed lower right: *B. West/1789.*

[14] Pencil; exhib., New York 1962 (18).

[15] Black crayon, $5 \times 6\frac{3}{4}$ in.; exhib. New York 1968 (11).

398 St. Paul Shaking the Viper from His Hand after the Shipwreck 1786

TATE GALLERY, LONDON

Oil on canvas: $51 \times 28\frac{1}{2}$ in. (129.5 × 72.5 cm.)

Signed lower right: *B. West 1786*

PROV: Offered by West's sons to the United States in 1826 (40, "The Shipwreck of St. Paul," 4 ft. × 2 ft. 4 in.), and sold by them, Robins, London, 22–25 May, 1829, lot 37 ("St. Paul Shaking the Viper from his Finger," 4 ft. × 2 ft. 4 in., and with a long description of the subject), bt. by H. P. Bone for £126 on behalf of Joseph Neeld, MP, Grittleton House, Wilts.; by descent in the Neeld family until sold, Christie's, London, 13 July 1945, lot 162; presented to the Tate Gallery by the National Art Collections Fund, 1945

EXH: RA 1787 (88) "St. Paul shaking the viper from his hand after the shipwreck. A finished sketch to paint a picture from, for the New Chapel in Greenwich Hospital"; 125 Pall Mall 1816 (9) "St.

398

386

Paul's Shipwreck. Acts, chap. xxviii, verses 1, 2, 3, 4, 5, 6, 7, 8"; 125 Pall Mall 1818 (4); West's Gallery 1822–28 (44); BI 1833 (45) lent by Joseph Neeld; *American Painting*, Tate Gallery, London, 1946 (225)

LISTED: *PC*, p. 566 ("St. Paul Shaking the Viper from his Finger," West, Gallery); *UM*, p. 531; Barlow, p. 435; *BA*, p. 18; Galt, p. 229; Dillenberger, pp. 175 (363) and 212

LIT: V and A Cuttings, II, p. 340; Farington Diary, 3 March 1804 (Farington 1978–, VI, p. 2259); Passavant 1836, I, p. 187; Evans 1959, p. 80 and pl. 61; Sparks 1971 (see No. 397), pp. 64–65, fig. 6; Dillenberger 1977, p. 102, pl. 70

The composition of No. 398 corresponds closely to that of No. 397, but there are many small differences in details, for example, in the position of St. Paul's head.

In testimony given in 1804 and recorded by Farington, West estimated that it had taken him ten days to paint No. 398.[1]

[1] See No. 397, note 5.

399 The Messiah 1814
See color illustration, p. 141

MR. AND MRS. P. D. THOMSON

Oil on panel: $51 \times 39\frac{1}{2}$ in. (130×100 cm.)

Signed bottom center: *B. West 1814*

PROV: Offered by West's sons to the United States in 1826 (31), and sold by them, Robins, London, 22–25 May 1829, lot 57 ("The Messiah," 4 ft. 1 in. × 3 ft. 3 in.), bt. by Dolman for £47.5.0.; Arthur Wilkin, Cousley Wood, Woodhurst, Sussex; David David, Inc., Philadelphia, 1970; Sloan and Schatzberg, Inc., New York; Trafalgar Galleries, London, 1977, by whom sold to the present owner

EXH: 125 Pall Mall 1816 (4) "Messiah, Revelations, chap. i, verse 7"; 125 Pall Mall 1818 (3); West's Gallery 1821 (86); 1822–28 (136)

LIT: "Notable Works of Art now on the Market," *Burlington Magazine*, CXXIX, Dec. 1977, pl. XLII; Dillenberger 1977, p. 124, pl. 85

The seventh verse of the first chapter of Revelation, which West cited but did not quote in his catalogues of 1816 and 1818, is as follows:
Behold he cometh with clouds; and every eye shall see him, and they *also* which pierced him; and all kindreds of the earth shall wail because of him. Even so, amen.
West had previously exhibited a picture entitled "Milton's Messiah, from the sixth book of Paradise Lost" at the Royal Academy in 1809 (No. 203), but the quotation with which he accompanied it in the catalogue does not fit No. 399 at all, whereas the verse quoted above does. To the soldiers that "pierced him" on the bottom of the picture, the eyes which "shall see him" on the left, and the clouds, West has added the four beasts described in chapter four of Revelation.

Although some of the imagery is related to that in a small oil sketch in Philadelphia of the *Resurrection* (No. 365), No. 399 does not appear to be the reworking or repetition of any known earlier work, and, hence, it is one of the last independent compositions of any importance to have been begun and carried through by the artist.

400 John Called to Write the Revelation 1797

THE SARAH CAMPBELL BLAFFER FOUNDATION, HOUSTON, TEXAS

Oil on paper on panel: $56\frac{3}{4} \times 25\frac{1}{2}$ in. (144×65 cm.)

Signed lower left: *B. West/1797*

400

PROV: Painted for William Beckford, Fonthill Abbey, Wilts.; possibly one of the two pictures identified as "Scene from the Revelations" in the Fonthill sale catalogue of 17–22 Sept. 1822 (Christie's), lots 26 and 27, and probably one of the four subjects from Revelations, in the Fonthill sale catalogue of 10–15 Oct. 1823 (Phillips), lots 152, 153, 349 and 350; given to the church of St. Andrew, Totteridge, in 1918 by the children of Sir Samuel Bagster Boulton, Bart.; sold by the church, Sotheby's, London, 9 July 1980, lot 73; Noortman & Brod, Ltd., New York; Hirschl & Adler Galleries, New York

EXH: RA 1798 (219) "The Son of Man, in the midst of the Seven Golden Candlesticks, appearing to John the Evangelist, and commanding him to write.— Rev. i, v. 13, for the New Abbey at Fonthill"; *Inaugural Exhibition*, Noortman & Brod, New York, 1981 (25a); San Antonio 1983 (35)

LISTED: *PC*, p. 561 ("John Called to write the Revelation," painted for and in the possession of Wm. Beckford Esq., of Fonthill); *UM*, p. 528; Barlow, p. 432; *BA*, p. 14; Galt, p. 219; Dillenberger, pp. 150 (125) and 213

LIT: Dillenberger 1977, p. 77, pl. 58

Nos. 400 and 405 are companion works whose recorded histories are identical. Together with Nos. 404 and 409, they seem to have been painted as sketches for paintings or windows for a planned but never-realized Revelation Chamber for Fonthill Abbey.

William Beckford began the planning and building of Fonthill Abbey in Wiltshire in 1796. On 22 December of that year, Joseph Farington recorded in his diary: "Mr. Beckford of Fonthill talks of encouraging the English arts.—West is to paint a picture for him"[1] In the following May, Farington was told by Robert Smirke that Beckford had ordered four pictures from Smirke, and that Beckford's agent Edward Foxhall "told Smirke, Beckford has ordered pictures from West of value of £3,000 and has paid in advance £1,000."[2] In 1797 West identified one work which he exhibited at the Royal Academy as for a window of the new abbey (see No. 408 below). No. 400 and the three companions all appeared at the Academy in 1798 and were identified in the catalogue as for the new abbey at Fonthill, but not as designs for windows. The earliest reference to a Revelation Chamber is in Farington's diary entry dated 22 December 1798, repeating what James Wyatt, the architect of Fonthill, had told him:

The Revelation Chamber is to have walls 5 feet thick in which are to be recesses to admit coffins. Beckford's Coffin is to be placed opposite to the door. The room is not to be entered by strangers, to be viewed through wire gratings. The floor is to be Jasper. . . . West is to paint all the pictures for this room, and is now limited to £1,000 a year while He is proceeding with the pictures.[3]

By the following September plans had been changed, as Farington recorded on 15 September 1799, "West not to paint the pictures for the Revelation Chamber, only to finish what he has begun."[4] A draft of an account prepared by West for Nicholas Williams, Beckford's agent, and dated 30 September 1799 also states that there had been an alteration in the commission; West had commenced and now had orders to finish four pictures from the Revelation, two of them at 300 guineas each and two at 400 guineas.[5] On 14 January 1800, West denied a rumor that he had lost his commission from Beckford, telling Farington that Williams had been with him "to know if he was getting on with the Revelation Chamber pictures,"[6] but it would seem that the project must have been stopped soon after. There are no further references to the chamber in Farington's diary, or in other sources; a Revelation Chamber does not appear in descriptions or plans of Fonthill Abbey

as it was built; and no later finished pictures by West that can be associated with this commission seem to exist.

The four pictures that, according to the account of September 1799, West had commenced, must have been of the four subjects from Revelation which he had exhibited in 1798. It is noteworthy that those pictures had been exhibited prior to Farington's first mention of the chamber, in which, as in subsequent references, implication is given that the actual pictures had not yet been painted. Since two (and probably three) of the four paintings of these subjects that can be identified, including No. 400, are signed and dated *1797*, it is plausible to identify them as the works exhibited in 1798 and, since no other versions of these four subjects are known, as the four subjects from Revelation in the Fonthill sale of 1823 as well. The later identification is complicated by the fact that the lists of West's works include two additional Revelation subjects at Fonthill. One of these, *St. Michael* (No. 408), was sold under its own title in 1823 and hence presents no problems, but the other, the *Angel in the Sun* (No. 411), was not, and, as the picture cannot presently be identified, its relation to the four pictures exhibited in 1798 remains somewhat uncertain. What does seem clear is that the pictures dated *1797* and exhibited in 1798 must have been distinct from the versions of the subjects mentioned in the document of September 1799 and upon which West was supposedly working in January 1800. The lack of record of any larger or more finished versions of these compositions suggests that they were never painted, and it would seem that Beckford took the four initial sketches and hung them at Fonthill instead.

Nos. 400 and 405 are both sketches, rather than finished works that would command the high prices (300 or 400 guineas each) quoted by West in the account of 30 September 1799. Both are in oil on several sheets of paper pieced together and mounted on panel. No. 400 is nearly monochromatic. The apostle and his eagle in No. 400 are contained within a central rectangular sheet, and the composition has been extended by four additional sheets. As these sheets contain the figures of Christ and the candlesticks mentioned in the title under which the work was exhibited in 1798, as well as West's signature and the date *1797*, they do not appear to be later additions. The shapes of Nos. 400 and 405 suggest that they may have been intended as designs for stained glass windows. West did designs or cartoons for at least three windows for Fonthill (see Nos. 408, 414, and 416) but he usually identified designs for glass as such when he exhibited them, and no such identification accompanied either No. 400 or No. 405 in the Royal Academy catalogue in 1798. Farington's description of the Revelation Chamber quoted above states that West was to paint pictures for the room, not that he was to design windows, but, on the other hand, in 1823, John Rutter wrote that the Revelation Chamber was so called "from the subjects proposed for the painted windows; several of the designs for which, from the Apocalypse, were prepared by the late President of the Royal Academy."[7] It is, of course, perfectly possible that in Beckford's changing plans for the chamber paintings were envisioned at one time and stained glass windows at another.

The subject of John before the figure of Christ and the seven golden candlesticks appears as the first of the Apocalyptic subjects in one of West's drawings of *c.* 1780 for a wall of the Royal Chapel at Windsor (p. 578) and on the Swarthmore diagrams of 1801 (p. 580). It is also among the subjects for the Windsor chapel in *Public Characters* and the other early lists of West's works.[8] West never painted the subject for George III, and there is not much similarity between the composition of No. 400 and that of the small sketch in the earlier wall design, but since he had been planning to paint the subject for some seventeen years before he in fact

did so in No. 400, it seems likely that the composition is a development of what he intended to do for George III's chapel. None of the other Apocalyptic subjects that West painted for Beckford repeat subjects that appear on any of the lists of subjects for Windsor. Nevertheless, the appearance at the Royal Academy in 1796 of a version of *Death on the Pale Horse* that had been painted as a sketch for the chapel (No. 403) probably prompted Beckford's patronage of West, and, in general terms, the series of subjects from Revelation planned but never realized as part of the Windsor scheme constituted a conspicuous precedent for the series of subjects from Revelation planned, but never completely realized as planned, for Fonthill.

[1] Farington 1978—, III, p. 726.
[2] 15 or 16 May 1797 (ibid., III, p. 840).
[3] Ibid., III, p. 1117. See also p. 1106 (8 December 1798).
[4] Ibid., IV, p. 1278.
[5] Historical Society of Pennsylvania, Philadelphia, extra-illustrated Galt, III, p. 69.
[6] Farington 1978—, IV, p. 1349.
[7] Rutter 1823, pp. 111–12.
[8] *PC*, p. 561; *UM*, p. 528; *AA*, p. 67; Barlow, p. 432; *BA*, p. 14; Galt, p. 219; Dillenberger, p. 149 (115).

401 Death on the Pale Horse 1817
See illustration, p. 148

PENNSYLVANIA ACADEMY OF THE FINE ARTS, PHILADELPHIA

Oil on canvas: 176 × 301 in. (447 × 765 cm.)

Signed lower right: *Benj West/ Oct.r 10/1817*

PROV: Offered by West's sons to the Pennsylvania Academy in 1823 and 1824,[1] and to the United States Government in 1826 (2, "Death on the Pale Horse," 12 ft. 6 in. × 25 ft. 6 in.); sold by them, Robins, London, 22–25 May 1829, lot 98 ("Death on the Pale Horse: or the Opening of the Five Seals," 15 ft. × 25 ft. 3 in.), bt. by Kershaw for £2,100, apparently as agent for Raphael West; purchased from Raphael West by the Pennsylvania Academy in December 1835 for £1,200

EXH: 125 Pall Mall 1818 [1817] "Death on the Pale Horse or the Opening of the First Five Seals"; West's Gallery 1821 (48), 1822–28 (72); AAFA, New York, 11 April–July 1836; Independence Hall, Philadelphia, 5 Aug.–31 Oct. 1836; David Wright's Diorama, Boston, 26 May–15 July 1837; Providence, Rhode Island, 20 July–10 Aug. 1837; Pennsylvania Museum (Memorial Hall), Philadelphia, 1893

ENGR: Lithograph (8 × 7½ in.) of a detail of the central horse's head, inscribed *B. West/Oct 10, 1816* and *From the Lithographic Press of Henry Bankes 148 New Bond Street*

LIT: Farington Diary, 29 Oct. 1815, 16 July and 6 Nov. 1816, 17 Feb., 22 May, 18 July, 24 and 25 Nov. 1817 (Farington 1978—, XIII, p. 4725; XIV, pp. 4874, 4920, 4974, 5023, 5056, 5111, 5113); V and A Cuttings, IV, pp. 956, 1093, 1129–30, and 1136 (reviews, 1817); J. G. [John Galt] *A Description of Mr. West's Picture of Death on the Pale Horse; or the Opening of the First Five Seals; exhibiting under the immediate Patronage of His Royal Highness the Prince Regent at no. 125 Pall Mall, near Carlton House*, London, 1817 (and frequently reprinted under different titles to accompany exhibitions of the painting); Carey 1817 (reprinted Philadelphia 1836); Dunlap 1834, II, pp. 147–48 (Dunlap 1918, II, pp. 290–91); Adams 1874, III, pp. 433 and 548; Jared B. Flagg, *The Life and Letters of Washington Allston*, New York, 1892, p. 122; Sartain 1899, pp. 166–69; Hazlitt 1930–34, XVIII, pp. 135–40 (1817); Kimball 1932; "Famous Early-19th Century Painting Restored," *Pennsylvania Hospital Bulletin*, VIII, no. 4, Winter 1950–51, p. 9 (Caleb Cresson, Jr., 1816); Charles Coleman Sellers, "Pale Horse on the Road," *Antiques*, LXV, 1954, pp. 384–87; Cunningham 1956, pp. 210–11; Evans 1959, pp. 61–65, 74–76, pl. 45; Hall 1962, pp. 103–4; Gardner 1966, fig. 1; Rothenberg 1967, p. 280; Norman D. Ziff, "Mortimer's 'Death on a Pale Horse,'" *Burlington Magazine*, CXII, 1970, p. 532; Keyes 1973; Kraemer 1975, p. 27; Dillenberger 1977, pp. 89–93, 118, 121, and pl. 81; Alberts 1978, pp. 378 and 379; Staley 1980

No. 401 is the third of the three vast religious compositions which West painted and exhibited in the last decade of his life, its exhibition in a special gallery at 125 Pall Mall in 1817 following those of *Christ Healing the Sick* (No. 336) at the British Institution in 1811 and of *Christ Rejected* (No. 353) in Pall Mall in 1814. It is also West's largest and last treatment of a subject that had occupied him since 1783 and of which he had exhibited earlier versions in 1784 and 1796 (Nos. 402 and 403). Those two earlier works were both identified when exhibited as preparatory studies for a large picture for George III's chapel at Windsor, but by the time West painted No. 401, the chapel project had been long dead, and the painting was undertaken as an independent picture on a scale exceeding that of any of the works painted for the chapel.

The first two versions of the subject appeared at the Royal Academy under the titles "The triumph of Death, from the Revelation" and "The opening of the four seals (vide Revelation)" respectively. West subsequently exhibited No. 403 in Paris in 1802 as "la Mort sur le cheval pâle" and at the British Institution in 1806 as "Death on the Pale Horse," the title he used for No. 401 in 1817. A pamphlet published to accompany the exhibition in 1817 gives the picture the subtitle "The Opening of the First Five Seals" and opens with a quotation of the first eleven verses of the sixth chapter of the Book of Revelation:

And I saw when the Lamb opened one of the seals, and I heard, as it were the noise of thunder, one of the four beasts saying, Come and see.

And I saw, and behold a white horse: and he that sat on him had a bow; and a crown was given unto him: and he went forth conquering, and to conquer.

And when he had opened the second seal, I heard the second beast say, Come and see.

And there went out another horse that was red: and power was given to him that sat thereon to take peace from the earth, and that they should kill one another: and there was given unto him a great sword.

And when he had opened the third seal, I heard the third beast say, Come and see. And I beheld, and lo a black horse; and he that sat on him had a pair of balances in his hand.

And I heard a voice in the midst of the four beasts say, a measure of wheat for a penny, and three measures of barley for a penny; and *see* thou hurt not the oil and wine.

And when he had opened the fourth seal, I heard the voice of the fourth beast say, Come and see.

And I looked, and behold a pale horse: and his name that sat on him was Death, and Hell followed with him. And power was given unto them over the fourth part of the earth, to kill with sword, and with hunger, and with death, and with beasts of the earth.

And when he had opened the fifth seal, I saw under the altar the souls of them that were slain for the word of God, and for the testimony which they held:

And they cried with a loud voice, saying How long, O Lord, holy and true, dost thou not judge and avenge our blood on them that dwell on the earth?

And white robes were given unto every one of them; and it was said unto them, that they should rest yet for a little season until their fellow servants also and their brethren, that should be killed as they were, should be fulfilled.

The central figure in No. 401 is Death, riding the pale horse, who appears upon the opening of the fourth seal as described in the eighth verse quoted above. The monsters of Hell are behind him, while manifestations of killing by the sword, by famine, by pestilence,[2] and by wild beasts are in the foreground and to the left. To the right are the riders on the white, red and black horses, who are seen following the opening of the first three seals, and further to the right, in the sky, are the white-robed souls who are revealed by the opening of the fifth seal. These souls do not appear in West's earlier versions of the subject, and their inclusion in No. 401 explains the apparent inconsistency of its subtitle in 1817, indicating that the picture shows the opening of five seals, in contrast to the title "The opening of the four seals" which West employed for No. 403 in 1796. The same subject when treated by other artists, as for example Dürer in the well-known woodcut published in 1498, is frequently known as the "Four Horsemen of the Apocalypse," but neither West nor any of his contemporaries ever seems to have used such a title.

Joseph Farington recorded on 29 October 1815, that West had resolved to paint a large "Death upon the Pale Horse" from his painted sketch. According to Charles Robert Leslie (quoted by Dunlap) Raphael West drew the whole of the outline on the large canvas from the small sketch. On 13 February 1816, Leslie called on West with a Philadelphian named Caleb Cresson, Jr., who described No. 401 as "chalk'd out, tho' no appearance of a Pencil on it." By 24 August 1816, when John Quincy Adams called on West, the head of Death was completed, or "settled," and the head of the horse was nearly finished. On 6 November Farington reported that West was painting on it with his left hand, "his right hand being wrapped up with gout." It was nearly finished and much improved when Adams called again on 30 June 1817, and on 18 July Farington was told that West expected to complete it about the beginning of September. He did complete it in October, and the painting is signed and dated *October 10, 1817*, West's seventy-ninth birthday.

West intended the exhibition to open that day, but on 17 October,[3] an announcement appeared in the press that an "unexpected occurrence" had forced the postponement of the exhibition. That occurrence was the necessity of repairing the roof of the gallery at 125 Pall Mall where No. 401 was to be exhibited. The painting was taken to the Royal Academy in Somerset House, where West continued to work on it, and it was finally seen by the public on the twenty-sixth of the following month, following a private view two days earlier.[4] It remained on view there at least until September 1818, when in a letter dated 28 September West described it as "now before the public in exhibition."[5] Following West's death, No. 401 and *Christ Rejected* (No. 353) hung opposite each other in the Great Room in the gallery which West's sons opened to the public on the site of his former home and studio in Newman Street (see ills. pp. 150 and 151). The two now hang opposite each other in the Pennsylvania Academy, but they were acquired separately and came to America at different times. The later exhibition

history of No. 401 is discussed at length in the article by Sellers published in 1954.

When No. 401 appeared on exhibition in 1817 it was accompanied by a short explanatory pamphlet signed *J.G.* Those initials belonged to the writer John Galt, who in the previous year had published the first of his two volumes of biography of the artist. Galt's pamphlet was soon followed by a more substantial publication, 172 pages long, written by William Carey. The contents of Galt's text, which contains passages such as "Mr. West was of the opinion," were clearly dictated by the artist. Carey, on the other hand, seems to have taken on his as an independent venture, which he published himself. West was accused of puffing his own work via Carey, but the latter in the preface to his pamphlet stated that it was not based on West's interpretation, and subsequently both West and Carey made statements denying any collaboration or consultation.[6] The two publications do not significantly contradict each other, but Carey's much fuller discussion includes several references to an eighteenth-century interpretation of the Book of Revelation by Moses Lowman.[7] This work is not mentioned by Galt, and, except for one detail in No. 401, there is little evidence to indicate to what extent West himself was influenced by Lowman. The part of Lowman's thesis cited by Carey in relation to No. 401 is an interpretation of the sixth chapter of Revelation as a prophetic description of the Church under the Romans, with each seal or rider corresponding to a specific period. Thus, according to Lowman, the period represented by the second seal and the rider on the red horse was from the reign of Trajan to that of Commodus, and characterized by wars between the Romans and the Jews. In No. 401 between the legs of the red horse are visible numerous figures, a Jewish candelabrum, and a red banner inscribed *SPQR*.[8] Both Galt and Carey identify this part of the painting as representing the destruction of Jerusalem by Titus in A.D. 70, which though not precisely within the period of the second seal as defined by Lowman, certainly is close enough to suggest that West was aware of such equations. This part of the composition is substantially different in Nos. 402 and 403, which both show scenes of warfare but without the specific Roman–Jewish details of No. 401, thus suggesting that West may have only become aware of Lowman when he began to work on the large painting in 1815. Carey cites Lowman's historical analogies for the other riders as well, although there are no corresponding details in No. 401 to link them with specific historical periods. In the more remote distance between and beyond the legs of the red horse and above the heads of the Roman army is a further scene of conflict on a seashore, which Carey and Galt both describe as the conflict between the Saracens and the Crusaders, a historical reference not dependent upon this part of Lowman though briefly mentioned by him elsewhere as prophesied in the sixteenth chapter of Revelation.

Stylistic sources for No. 401 have been proposed by Grose Evans and Norman Ziff. Carey, but not Galt, drew comparisons between No. 401 and earlier treatments of related subjects by Dürer and John Hamilton Mortimer. The figures in the center foreground of No. 403, who appear with only slight changes in No. 401, reminded a French critic in 1802[9] of an analogous family group in the foreground of Poussin's *Plague of Asdod* (Musée du Louvre), and in the same year Farington recorded Jacques-Louis David's comment that West was a caricature of Rubens. The dependence of No. 401 on hunting scenes by Rubens is suggested by the strong similarity of the pale horse and the most conspicuous horse in *Alexander III of Scotland Saved from a Stag by Colin Fitzgerald* (No. 54), which is also analogous in subject matter to pictures by Rubens. There is an even more marked similarity between the horse in No. 402, West's first version of the composition, and that in No. 54, and it is noteworthy that No. 402 and an earlier version of No. 54 (No. 55) appeared together at the Royal Academy in 1784. Grose Evans has pointed out that Leigh Hunt mentions an engraving after Rubens's *Lion Hunt* as one of the few works by artists other than West himself which Hunt remembered on the walls of West's home in Newman Street. This was evidently "The Lion Hunt, a print colored and touched upon in oil by Rubens, for the engraver to work from; very splendid and fine," sold by West's heirs in 1824,[10] which should probably be identified as the Bolswert engraving of the well-known *Lion Hunt* in Munich, but we should also note that the horses in Nos. 54 and 401 suggest that West may have looked at the horseman on the left side of Rubens's *Wolf and Fox Hunt* (ill. p. 191), which had also been engraved. As pointed out by William Hazlitt, the infant falling from his dying mother's breast in the center foreground seems to be borrowed from the child falling from his drunken mother's lap in Hogarth's print *Gin-Lane*. The head of the pale horse, which differs somewhat from the corresponding horses in Nos. 402 and 403, may, as proposed by Jacob Rothenberg, reflect West's study of the Horse of Selene from the pedimental sculptures of the Parthenon, which he saw for the first time only in 1807 or 1808 (see Nos. 498–503).

The chief preparatory studies connected with No. 401, though not undertaken with it specifically in mind, are Nos. 402 and 403. Since No. 401 is painted over an outline drawn by Raphael West on the basis of No. 403, the composition follows the main lines of the earlier sketch closely. In some places where West made changes, such as the sword of the horseman on the left, the bow of the rider on the white horse, or the serpents in the upper right, Raphael's outlines following the earlier composition are still visible. In proportion No. 401 is slightly more vertical and less horizontal than No. 403, and consequently the lateral spacing of

the figures has been contracted throughout. For example, the fallen figure in the foreground with his back to us is to the left of the pale horse in No. 403, but under it in No. 401. In addition to alterations already cited, one other significant change in No. 401 is the conversion of the rider on the white horse from a fierce warrior leaning forward to shoot his bow to a figure of Christ, still carrying a bow, but gazing beatifically upward at the white-robed souls of the fifth seal, who, as previously noted, do not appear in Nos. 402 and 403. In the upper left an eagle attacks a heron; this detail does not appear in No. 403,[11] but in the upper left of No. 402 of 1783–84 there are two eagles and a heron. The standing man with a spear on the left is clean shaven and with a full head of hair in No. 401, bearded and balding in No. 403, and there are numerous other lesser variations of detail between the two works. Changes between Nos. 402 and 403 are discussed in the entry for the latter.

A painting of *Death on the Pale Horse* on the scale of No. 401 but corresponding in detail to No. 403 rather than No. 401, appeared in the background of a portrait of West by James Green (1771–1834), which may have been either of two portraits of West exhibited by Green at the Royal Academy in 1817 and 1820. The full-length portrait was purchased by the Metropolitan Museum of Art in New York in 1923, evidently in damaged condition.[12] It was cut down the following year, and a three-quarter-length likeness of West and a separate detail of the central pale horse were preserved as independent pictures. Both of them were lent to the West exhibition at the Graham Gallery in New York in 1962 as works by West himself, the latter under the title "Death on A Pale Horse" (no. 9).

[1] Correspondence between Raphael West and Joseph Hopkinson, 17 Jan. and 7 April 1824 (Pennsylvania Academy of Fine Arts), cited in Sellers, p. 385.
[2] Although the biblical passage does not use the word

"pestilence," both early descriptions of the painting by Galt and Carey do, equating it with the phrase "to kill . . . with death" in verse 8.
[3] Letter from West to a Mr. Anderdon, Historical Society of Pennsylvania, Philadelphia (extra-illustrated Galt, III, p. 100).
[4] For details of the postponement, see William Carey, *To the President and Members of the Artist's Fund Society of Philadelphia*, 2nd ed., Philadelphia, 1838, postscript pp. 34–35, and an undated manuscript letter by West in the Historical Society of Pennsylvania, Philadelphia (extra-illustrated Galt, II, p. 70).
[5] Letter from West to Jane Porter, 28 Sept. 1818 in the British Museum (Department of Prints and Drawings, extra-illustrated Royal Academy Catalogues, Anderdon Collection, VIII, 151).
[6] As cited in note 4 above.
[7] Moses Lowman, *A Paraphrase and Notes on the Revelation of St. John*, London, 1737.
[8] The initials are not visible in a photograph, but are clearly legibly on the banner immediately to the right of the candelabrum on the painting itself.
[9] Quoted in *Public Characters of 1805*, pp. 556–57.
[10] Christie's, London, 28 May 1824, lot 22.
[11] Two eagles and a heron appear in an outline engraving after No. 403; see the discussion in the entry for that work.
[12] The portrait by Green was one of a group of works by or ascribed to West which the Metropolitan Museum purchased from the Seguin family in 1923 (see No. 422). It was exhibited at the Pennsylvania Academy between 1851 and 1862 as a self-portrait by West without reference to Green. Green's other exhibited portrait of West may be a bust-length painting (29 × 24½ in.) now in the Delaware Art Museum.

402 **Death on the Pale Horse** 1783–1803

ROYAL ACADEMY OF ARTS, LONDON

Pen and brown ink and wash, heightened with white: 22½ × 44 in. (57 × 112 cm.)

402

Signed bottom right of center: *B. West 1783, retouched 1803*; also signed to the left of center, below the legs of the pale horse: *B. West/1783*

PROV: In the possession of West's heirs in 1823

EXH: RA 1784 (442) "The triumph of Death, from the Revelations, a design for a picture for his Majesty's chapel in Windsor-castle"; West's Gallery 1823 (Room of Drawings, 50); London 1963 (67)

LISTED: *PC*, p. 568 ("The large Sketch, in oil, on paper, of Death on the pale horse," West, Gallery); *UM*, p. 532; *BA*, p. 19; Galt, p. 233; Dillenberger, pp. 183 (454) and 212

LIT: Carey 1817, pp. 47–48, 96, 115; Kimball 1932; Evans 1959, pp. 64–65, pl. 42; Norman D. Ziff, "Mortimer's 'Death on the Pale Horse,'" *Burlington Magazine*, CXII, 1970, p. 532; Keyes 1973; Kraemer 1975, pp. 26–27, fig. 20; Meyer 1975, pp. 257–58, 265 and fig. 15; Dillenberger 1977, p. 78, pl. 59, and pp. 89–93; Staley 1980

West exhibited this work at the Royal Academy in 1784 in the Exhibition-Room of Sculptures and Drawings, along with three other drawings or studies for works he intended to paint. One of them was probably the oil sketch (No. 55) for *Alexander III of Scotland Saved from a Stag by Colin Fitzgerald* (No. 54), which has significant stylistic similarities with No. 402, as discussed in the preceding entry. The other two, *Moses Striking the Rock* (No. 256) and the *Last Supper* (No. 345), were identified in the catalogue as designs for pictures for George III's chapel at Windsor, as was also No. 402. Nos. 256 and 402 are both in the collection of the Royal Academy at Burlington House. The subject of the former was apparently dropped from the scheme for the chapel, and no later version is known. The latter was the basis for a moderately sized painting, which West exhibited at the Academy in 1796 as a sketch for the chapel (No. 403), and for the huge painting, which West completed and exhibited in 1817, well after all plans for the chapel had been abandoned (No. 401). For a consideration of the place of the subject within schemes for the chapel see under No. 403.

No. 402, like No. 256, is on several pieces of paper joined together. Both are dated *1783* with the further inscription *retouched 1803*. As discussed in the entry for the latter, West's retouchings in 1803 seem to have consisted of heightening these drawings with white. The joining together of the papers must have occurred when the drawings were first made, and West did not modify the composition of No. 402 in 1803 to bring it into conformity with the painting of 1796 (No. 403) that he had based on it. The differences between the two are discussed in the following entry. The description of No. 402 as oil on paper in the lists of West's works echoes that of No. 256 and several other drawings by West in which he used body-color so heavily that it does look like oil paint.

A drawing in black chalk and india ink and identified as a "Study for Death on the Pale Horse" was sold by Benjamin West, Jr. in 1839.[1] Ruth Kraemer has associated a drawing of an Apocalyptic horseman in the Morgan Library with No. 402, but there is virtually no similarity in compositions.[2] Several other drawings of analogous subjects, which do not appear to be by Benjamin West but may be by his son Raphael, are also known.[3] A drawing of a lion, which is possibly a study for the lion in the lower left corner in Nos. 401, 402 and 403 is at Swarthmore,[4] and a drawing of a bat's head, used for one of the demons behind the figure of Death, is in the British Museum.[5] A drawing for the four horses in No. 54, which West may also have used for No. 402, is cited in the entry for No. 54.

[1] S. Leigh Sotheby, London, 1 June 1839, lot 66.
[2] Kraemer 1975, p. 27 (39), and pl. 24 (pen and brown ink

over black chalk, 14 × 18¾ in.).
[3] Discussed ibid.
[4] Black chalk, 6¾ × 9¾ in.
[5] Black chalk, 7¾ × 6¼ in. (1920-6-15-14). What appears to be another drawing for the same creature is in an English private collection.

403 Death on the Pale Horse 1796
See color illustrations, pp. 86, 146, 149

DETROIT INSTITUTE OF ARTS

Oil on canvas: 23½ × 50½ in. (59.5 × 128.5 cm.)

Signed lower right: *B. West 1796*

PROV: (?) Henry Thomson, RA; in the collection of the third Earl of Egremont, Petworth House, Sussex, by 1820; by descent to John Wyndham, seventh Baron Leconfield and second Baron Egremont, by whom sold, Sotheby's, London, 19 July 1978, lot 18 (as "Triumph of Death"); P. & D. Colnaghi, Ltd., London, from whom acquired by the Detroit Institute in 1979

EXH: RA 1796 (247) "The opening of the four seals (vide Revelation), a sketch, for His Majesty's Chapel, Windsor"; Salon du Musée central des Arts, Paris, 1802 (second supplement, no. 756) "Esquisse représentant la Mort sur le cheval pâle, ou l'ouverture des sceaux, 6ᵉ c. des Révél, v. 7 et 8" (with quotation); (?) BI 1806 (North Room, No. 18) "Death on the pale horse"; (?) 125 Pall Mall 1814 (7) "Death on the Pale Horse"; BI 1833 (13) as "The Triumph of Death," lent by the Earl of Egremont; RA 1871 winter (39); Washington and Philadelphia 1980

ENGR: Outline engraving (3 9/16 × 7½ in.) pub. by J. Bell, 30 May 1807 and reissued 1 March 1808 opp. p. 55 of vol. IV of *La Belle Assemblée*; outline engraving (3 × 6½ in.) by Normand *fils*, pub. in Hamilton 1831 (211)

LISTED: *PC*, p. 566 ("Death on the pale Horse; or the Opening of the Seals," West, Gallery); *UM*, p. 530; Barlow, p. 434; *BA*, p. 17; Galt, p. 228; Dillenberger, pp. 173 (343) and 213

LIT: Farington Diary, 23 April 1796, I, 2, 12, and 24 Sept., and 19 Nov. 1802 (Farington 1978—, II, p. 528; V, pp. 1820, 1823, 1851, 1875, and 1935); V and A Cuttings, III, pp. 726, 757, 761, 768 and 769 (exhibition reviews, 1796); *Journal des Arts* (Paris) 1802; *Public Characters* 1805, pp. 555–57; *La Belle Assemblée* 1808, p. 55; Carey 1817, pp. 47–48, 96, 102–3, 115; Carey 1820, pp. 696–97; Hamilton 1831 (211); Jared B. Flagg, *The Life and Letters of Washington Allston*, New York, 1892, pp. 43–44; Lansdown 1893, p. 13; Collins Baker 1920, p. 133 (219); Kimball 1932, fig. 1 et passim; Keyes 1973; Kraemer 1975, p. 27; Meyer 1975, p. 265; Dillenberger 1977, pp. 90–93, pl. 64; Alberts 1978, pp. 261–63, 270; Staley 1980; Pressly 1983, pp. 19, 58, 61–64, fig. 34

West identified No. 403 as a sketch for the Windsor chapel when he exhibited it in 1796, and it is clearly a development of No. 402, which he identified as a design for the chapel when he exhibited it twelve years before. A group of pictures from Revelation appear to have been part of the chapel project from its commencement, and one of the architectural drawings from c. 1780 shows a sequence of five Revelation subjects in the smaller spaces above a series of empty arches possibly representing windows (ill. p. 578). The second from the left of these shows the four horsemen of the Apocalypse, but, like the other sketchy designs in the smaller spaces in these early drawings, it shows little similarity to West's later treatment of the subject on

a larger scale. In the Swarthmore diagrams of 1801, four Revelation subjects, including *Death on the Pale Horse* (second from the left), make up the uppermost row of the side wall devoted to the New Testament (p. 580). These four titles all bear the notation "Designed."[1] The lists of West's pictures published in 1804 and subsequent years contain groups of six or seven subjects from Revelation among the works painted for the chapel at Windsor,[2] but it seems certain that he never completed any of them on the scale of the finished chapel pictures. None of them appears on West's account of 1797, which included only completed works and, rather surprisingly, none appears on the 1801 account either, although that list did include subjects that West intended to paint as well as ones that he actually had painted. Nos. 402 and 403 were the only exhibited Revelation subjects which West identified as for the chapel, but one other, the *Destruction of the Beast and False Prophet* (No. 410), which West exhibited in 1804, was originally composed for the chapel as well.

The anomalous position that these subjects seem to have held in the chapel project may have been a result of George III's dislike of them. That dislike was stated explicitly in a remark quoted at second-hand by Farington in 1804: "The King told Lysons that the pictures which West had painted for the Chapel at Windsor should not be put up, except the Altar piece, & *that* should not be a Bedlamite scene from the Revelations."[3] It is possible that prior expression of distaste for such subjects by George III kept West from completing *Death on the Pale Horse* for the chapel, although he had designed it as early as 1783, and also from including any subjects from Revelation on his account of 1801 of work for the King, which was intended for the King's eyes. As far as we know, the only examples of a "Bedlamite scene from the Revelations" intended by West for the chapel which George III could have seen before 1801 to provoke such hostility were Nos. 402 and 403.

West's own high opinion of No. 403 is reflected in the fact that it was the one example of his work which he took to Paris and exhibited in the Salon during the Peace of Amiens of 1802. Though conceived as a sketch for a larger work, it was one of two works engraved to illustrate the account of his life published in *La Belle Assemblée* in 1808, the other engraving being after his most famous picture, the *Death of General Wolfe* (No. 93). William Beckford told a visitor in 1838 that West considered it his best work and had refused to sell it to the Prince Regent, and, according to William Carey, West refused to sell it to Bonaparte. Although the picture remained in the artist's possession until c. 1819, it was exhibited on several occasions and must also have been fairly conspicuous in his studio. The young Washington Allston, who arrived in London in 1801 and who could only have seen it in Newman Street, cited it in a letter home written on 25 August of that year as *the* highest example of contemporary painting.

Exactly when West sold No. 403 is not recorded. The *Recollections of the Late William Beckford* state that after West refused the Prince Regent's offer of £100, "being distressed for money, he parted with it, I believe, to Mr. Thompson, the artist, for £50." "Mr. Thompson" was presumably Henry Thomson (1773–1843), who was West's next-door neighbor in Newman Street and had frequent contact with West during the last few years of his life. Hence, that he might have been the purchaser of the picture seems plausible. By June 1820 No. 403 was in the possession of the Earl of Egremont, who may have acquired it from Thomson, but we know from Farington that in the summer of 1819 Egremont visited West's studio, and that he solicited prices for several works through the agency of another artist, the portrait painter Thomas Phillips (1770–1845). So it is also possible that Egremont acquired No. 403 at this time, and that the "Mr. Thompson, the artist" qualified by "I believe" in the reminiscence quoted above was in fact a mistaken reference to Phillips acting on behalf of Lord Egremont.

No. 403 is clearly based on No. 402, but with numerous and significant changes. Most obvious are the replacement of the kneeling figure with arms outstretched in the lower left corner by a man holding a spear and the joining of this figure and the standing man behind into a compact group with the fallen horseman to their right. The small figures to their left at the edge of the painting, who appear to represent a fleeing family in No. 402, have been changed to a group around a youth being struck by lightning in No. 403. Similarly, the figures fleeing before the horsemen on the extreme right of No. 402 are replaced by a distant scene of battle and a body of water in the painting. The nude figure scratching the ground to the right of center has been given an empty cup, and the figure behind, whose head is lowered in No. 402, has been substantially changed as well. Figures representing the Demons of Discord and Envy[4] have been added in the sky in the upper right, and a group of two eagles attacking a heron, which appears in the upper left part of the sky in No. 402, has disappeared in No. 403. Rather curiously, these birds are present in the outline engraving published in 1807, which in all other respects follows No. 403 closely. In No. 401, the final version of the subject, West re-incorporated two birds. Otherwise, No. 403, rather than No. 402, served as the model for the large picture, although West again made significant changes, which are discussed in the entry for No. 401.

Two copies of this painting, both of which have been frequently exhibited and reproduced as works by West, are in the Philadelphia Museum of Art. Neither appears to be by West's hand. In articles published in 1931 and 1932 Fiske Kimball, the then director of the Philadelphia Museum, argued that the larger of the two was the version of the subject which West exhibited in Paris in 1802, but there is no documentary evidence to support this claim, and it flatly contradicts Carey's statement made in 1820 that the "sublime production, which is at once the glory of Lord Egremont's collection, and the triumph of modern art" was the picture shown in Paris. A copy after the central horse and rider from No. 403 in the background of a portrait of West by James Green is discussed under No. 401. In 1825 William Dunlap painted a *Death on the Pale Horse* based on the "etched outline" (i.e., the outline engraving of 1807 after No. 403) and "the printed descriptions" (probably of No. 401). This painting on a 10 × 20 ft. canvas he exhibited privately and successfully at the American Academy of Fine Arts in New York, in Norfolk, Virginia, and in Albany and several other cities in upstate New York.[5]

[1] The other three subjects were "Son of Man Seen by John," which West had already painted for William Beckford (cf. No. 400); "Destruction of Old Beast and False Prophet," which he subsequently painted and exhibited in 1804 (cf. No. 410); and "Day of Judgement," which he may have originally designed for the ceiling of the chapel (drawing formerly in the collection of Mrs. F. Howard, ill. p. 579). There is also a sketch for a *Last Judgment* in the Morgan Library (Kraemer 1975, p. 43, no. 72, and pl. 43).

[2] *PC*, p. 561; *UM*, p. 528; *AA*, p. 67; Barlow, p. 432; *BA*, p. 14; Galt, p. 219; Meyer, p. 265; and Dillenberger, pp. 149–50 (115–21). The additional titles are "Saints Prostrating Themselves before the Throne of God"; "General Resurrection, the end of Death" (included only by Barlow); "Christ's second coming" (included only by Barlow); and "The New Jerusalem." For a drawing possibly related to the first of these subjects see Kraemer 1975, p. 43 (71), pl. 42.

[3] Farington Diary, 1 Dec. 1804 (Farington 1978–, VI, p. 2461). "Lysons" was Samuel Lysons (1763–1819), an

404

antiquarian, who was both a favorite of the Royal Family and a close friend of Farington's.

[4] Cf. Carey 1817, p. 17.

[5] Dunlap 1918, I, pp. 350–54.

404 A Mighty Angel Standeth upon the Land and upon the Sea (?)1797

LOCATION UNKNOWN

Oil on paper, mounted on panel: 31 × 21 in. (78.5 × 53.5 cm.)

Signed lower right: *B. West/*[?]*1797*

PROV: Painted for William Beckford, Fonthill Abbey, Wilts.; possibly one of the two pictures identified as "Scene from the Revelation" in the Fonthill catalogue of 17–22 Sept. 1822 (Christie's) lots 26 and 27, and one of the four subjects from Revelation in the

Fonthill sale of 10–15 Oct. 1823 (Phillips), lots 152, 153, 349 and 350; probably the "fine sketch of angel" bought by Sir John Fleming Leicester (Lord de Tabley) from William Carey in 1825 for 80 guineas, and sold in the de Tabley sale, Christie's, London, 7 July 1827, lot 18 ("The angel, from the Revelations, standing on earth and sea," study on carton, of cabinet size), bt. by Jackson for £42; sold anonymously, Christie's, London, 13 July 1931, lot 51 (as "The Archangel Gabriel"), bt. by Feldman; Hannah Mee Horner, Upper Darby, Pennsylvania, 1938; Mrs. Linden T. Harris, Drexel Hill, Pennsylvania, 1959

EXH: RA 1798 (76) "A mighty Angel standeth upon the Land and upon the sea.—Rev., Chap. 10, for the new abbey at Fonthill"; Philadephia 1938 (41, as "The Archangel Gabriel")

LISTED: *PC*, p. 561 ("The mighty Angel, one Foot upon Sea, and the other on Earth," painted for, and in the possession of W. Beckford, Esq. of Fonthill); *UM*, p. 528; Barlow, p. 432; *BA*, p. 14; Galt, p. 219; Dillenberger, pp. 150 (127), 212 (as "Archangel Gabriel") and 213 (as "The Mighty Angel, one Foot upon Sea, the Other on Earth")

LIT: Evans 1959, pp. 60–61 and pl. 41 (as "The Archangel Gabriel," 1798); Hall 1962, pp. 102, 106, and 122 (112); Kraemer 1975, p. 37; Dillenberger 1977, p. 109

No. 404 is one of four paintings exhibited by West in 1798 which were evidently done as studies for pictures for the never-realized Revelation Chamber at Fonthill Abbey (for which see No. 400). It seems to have been painted as a pair with No. 409, which is the same size, and which is signed and dated *1797*, as is also No. 400. In the Philadelphia catalogue of 1938, the date on No. 404 was given as "1792," but that date is highly improbable, and it seems likely that the compiler misread the final digit as a "2" rather than a "7."[1]

Although there is a possibility that the histories of Nos. 404 and 411 are confused, it seems probable that the latter was the subject from Revelation that remained in Beckford's possession until his death, while the four subjects originally exhibited in 1798 (including No. 404) were sold together in 1823. In 1828 Beckford commissioned a painting of the identical subject from Francis Danby (collection of Robert Rosenblum, New York),[2] which he perhaps would not have done if he had still owned No. 404, whereas the reappearance of this painting at auction in the de Tabley sale in 1827 may have rekindled his enthusiasm for such subjects.

A drawing for No. 404 is in the collection of Mr. and Mrs. Erving Wolf.[3]

[1] The signature and date are too faint in a photograph to allow confirmation of either reading.
[2] See *The Bristol School of Artists: Francis Danby and Painting in Bristol 1810–1840*, City Art Gallery, Bristol, 1973, pp. 37–38 and 65. The painting is illustrated in Eric Adams, *Francis Danby: Varieties of Poetic Landscape*, New Haven and London, 1973, fig. 53.
[3] Black and white chalk on grey paper, 15 × 9¼ in. (San Antonio 1983 (36). See also No. 411.

405 The Woman Clothed with the Sun *c.* 1797

HIRSCHL & ADLER GALLERIES NEW YORK

Oil on paper on panel: 56¾ × 25½ in. (144 × 65 cm.)

PROV: As for No. 400

EXH: RA 1798 (232) "The woman cloathed with the sun fleeth from the persecution of the dragon, for the new abbey at Fonthill"; *Inaugural Exhibition*, Noortman & Brod, New York, 1981 (25b); San Antonio 1983 (37)

405

406

LISTED: *PC*, p. 561 ("The Woman clothed in the Sun," painted for, and in the possession of Wm. Beckford, Esq. of Fonthill); *UM*, p. 528; Barlow, p. 432; *BA*, p. 14; Galt, p. 219; Dillenberger, pp. 150 (124) and 213

LIT: Dillenberger 1977, p. 109 and pl. 76

No. 405 is a companion to No. 400, and, as far as is known, the two works had always been together until they parted company in 1985. For questions pertinent to both see the entry for No. 400. The subject of this painting is from the twelfth chapter of Revelation.

A drawing for the central figure in No. 405 belongs to Mr. and Mrs. Erving Wolf.[1] A sheet of sketches of a winged figure holding a child, probably also related to No. 405, is in the Morgan Library.[2]

[1] Black and white chalk on blue paper, $11\frac{1}{4} \times 8$ in. (San Antonio 1983, no. 38).
[2] Black chalk, $9\frac{1}{8} \times 7\frac{5}{8}$ in. (Kraemer 1975, pp. 37–38, no. 60, and pl. 39).

406 St. Michael 1777

TRINITY COLLEGE, CAMBRIDGE

Oil on canvas: 172×80 in. (437×203 cm.)

Signed lower left: *B. West 1777*

PROV: Presented to Trinity College by Dr. John Hinchliffe (Master of the College from 1768 to 1789) to be the altarpiece in Trinity College Chapel

EXH: RA 1777 (365) "St. Michael the Archangel; an altar piece for Trinity Chapel, Cambridge"

LISTED: *PC*, p. 562 ("St. Michael chaining the Dragon, in Trinity College, Cambridge," 15 ft. × 8); *UM*, p. 528; *AA*, p. 69 ("St. Michael casting the Old Beast into the Bottomless pit, in Trinity Chapel Cambridge," 18 ft. by 10); Barlow, p. 433; *BA*, p. 15; Galt, p. 220; Dillenberger, pp. 153 (148) and 211

LIT: V and A Cuttings, I, p. 147 (*General Advertiser*, April 1777); Farington Diary, 13 Sept. 1805 (Farington 1978–, VII, p. 2616); Carey 1820, p. 696; Robert Willis and John Willis Clark, *The Architectural History of the University of Cambridge and the Colleges of Cambridge and Eton*, Cambridge, 1886, II, pp. 584–85 and fig. 38 (showing No. 406 in its original location); Rogers 1966, pp. 424–25, fig. 5; Kraemer 1975, pp. 10–11, fig. 6; Dillenberger 1977, p. 42

No. 406 illustrates verses 1–3 of chapter 20 of Revelation:

And I saw an angel come down from heaven, having the key of the bottomless pit and a great chain in his hand.

And he laid hold on the dragon, that old serpent, which is the Devil, and Satan, and bound him a thousand years,

And cast him into the bottomless pit, and shut him up, and set a seal upon him, that he should deceive the nations no more, till the thousand years should be fulfilled: and after that he must be loosed a little season.

Although this passage does not identify the angel as St. Michael, it is the source for the chains in the angel's left hand and for the main image of an angel overcoming a single satanic foe. In verses 7–9 of chapter 12 of Revelation, Michael and his angels fight against Satan (the great red dragon) and his angels, casting them out of heaven, a passage which West subsequently illustrated in No. 408 below.

According to Carey, the success at the Royal Academy in 1776 of No. 388, West's altarpiece for St.

See also No. 516.
[3] See Pressly 1981, pp. 43–45 and pls. 33 and 34.
[4] Both in black chalk, heightened with white on blue paper, $15\frac{1}{4} \times 9\frac{1}{2}$ in. (ill. Kraemer 1975, p. 11, fig. 7) and $6\frac{3}{4} \times 5\frac{1}{8}$ in.
[5] Black chalk, $5\frac{11}{16} \times 3$ in. (Kraemer 1975, p. 10, no. 13 and pl. 6).
[6] Raphael's *St. Michael* may be identical with a painting of the subject which in 1982 was stolen from Anthony Dallas & Sons, Ltd., London (*left*).

(?)Raphael West, *The Battle between Michael and Satan*, exhibited 1782. Oil on canvas, 50 × 40 in.

407 St. Michael 1776

See color illustration, p. 85

JAMES RICAU

Oil on paper mounted on canvas: $46\frac{1}{2} \times 29\frac{1}{2}$ in. (118×75 cm.)

Signed lower right: *B. West/1776*

PROV: Sold anonymously, Christie's, London, 14 Dec. 1949, lot 107, bt. by Potter; M. Knoedler and Co., New York, by 1957; currently on extended loan to the Brooklyn Museum

EXH: New York 1962 (13) lent by James Ricau

LISTED: Dillenberger, p. 211

LIT: Rogers 1966, p. 424, fig. 4; Kraemer 1975, p. 10; Dillenberger 1977, pp. 34 and 42, and pl. 25

No. 407, which is signed and dated *1776*, a year earlier than No. 406, clearly served as a sketch for that work. The most important change between the two is that in No. 407 St. Michael holds a thunderbolt in his right hand, whereas in No. 406 he holds a spear. Barry's St. Michael in the drawing and print mentioned under No. 406 also holds a thunderbolt.

West did not exhibit No. 407; it was not in any of the posthumous sales; and, since it does not appear on any of the early lists of his works, it probably left his possession long before they were drawn up.

408 St. Michael 1797

TOLEDO MUSEUM OF ART, TOLEDO, OHIO

Oil on canvas: $50\frac{1}{2} \times 23\frac{9}{16}$ in. (128.3×59.9 cm.)

PROV: Painted for William Beckford, Fonthill Abbey, Wilts.; in the Fonthill sale catalogue of 17–22 Sept. 1822 (Christie's), lot 89 ("St. Michael and the Falling Angels: a grand design," with lot 90, "St. Thomas à Becket," described as the companion picture [see No. 415]), and sold, 10–15 October 1823 (Phillips), lot 250 (as above, with an accompanying note that the two lots "were painted by the artist for Mr. Beckford as a design for stained windows"), for £22.11.6.; Charles Mitchell, London, by *c.* 1941, and sold by him to the Toledo Museum in 1959

EXH: RA 1797 (242) "Michael casteth out the Dragon and his Angels, for a window at the new abbey, Font Hill"; Allentown 1962 (25); Washington and Philadelphia 1980; San Antonio 1983 (39)

LISTED: PC, p. 561 ("St. Michael and his Angels fighting and casting out the Red Dragon and his Angels," painted for and in the possession of Wm. Beckford, Esq. of Fonthill); UM, p. 528; Barlow, p. 432; BA, p. 14; Galt, p. 219; Dillenberger, pp. 150 (123) and 213

LIT: Farington Diary, 28 April 1791 (Farington 1978–, III, p. 828); Storer 1812, p. 19; Rogers 1966 passim; Kraemer 1975, pp. 10–11; Dillenberger 1977, p. 109 and pl. 75

Stephen, Walbrook, procured him the commissions for No. 406 for Trinity College and for No. 339 for Winchester Cathedral. Dr. Hinchliffe, the Master of Trinity College, and (according to Willis and Clark) the donor of the picture, had previously been Assistant Master at Westminster School under Dr. Markham (see No. 655), and, hence, seems to have been at least peripherally associated with the circle of Anglican divines who provided significant early patronage for West. The subject of St. Michael may have been intended to commemorate Michaelhouse, one of the two early Cambridge colleges which were refounded as Trinity.[1] Additionally, it is worth noting that Dr. Hinchliffe, who was also Bishop of Peterborough, had taken a conspicuous stand in the House of Lords in 1775 in favor of coercion against the American colonies, and, although he subsequently modified his views, it was perhaps not until after he had commissioned this monumental depiction of biblical coercion.

No. 406 and a preparatory oil sketch (No. 407) which is signed and dated *1776*, were West's first paintings of Apocalyptic subjects. Millard Rogers has pointed out their dependence upon the *St. Michael* by Guido Reni in S. Maria della Concezione in Rome, of which West evidently owned a copy or version.[2] Nos. 406 and 407 may also have been partly inspired by James Barry's drawing of *St. Michael* from the early 1770s done for the aborted scheme of decorating St. Paul's Cathedral (for which see No. 257). Barry also published a print of the subject in 1777.[3]

There are two related drawings at Swarthmore[4] and one in the Pierpont Morgan Library.[5]

West's son Raphael exhibited a painting of the *Battle between Michael and Satan. From Milton* at the Royal Academy in 1782 (when he was sixteen years old).[6]

[1] Kindly suggested by Dr. Philip Gaskell, Librarian of Trinity College.
[2] Sold by West's sons, Christie's, London, 6 July 1820, lot 99.

408

In No. 408 St. Michael does not hold a chain, as he does in Nos. 406 and 407, and this picture, as indicated by the title in the early lists of West's works, illustrates the twelfth chapter of Revelation, in which Michael and his angels cast out the great red dragon and his angels, and not the twentieth chapter, in which an angel binds Satan and casts him into the bottomless pit.

No. 408 was the first Apocalyptic subject painted by West for William Beckford. Although it and the *St. Thomas à Becket* (No. 415) are of an identical size and were identified as companion pictures in the Fonthill sales of 1822 and 1823, they were not originally exhibited as a pair. No. 408 was shown at the Royal Academy in 1797 and described as for a window at the new abbey, while No. 415 was exhibited the following year and identified as for Fonthill but not for a window. No window is known to have been produced after No. 408, while No. 415 was the basis for a cartoon exhibited in 1799 (No. 416) and for the only recorded window actually made for Fonthill after West's designs. Whether or not either No. 408 itself or the window that was to have been based on it was ever destined for the unrealized Revelation Chamber at Fonthill Abbey (discussed under No. 400) is not known. The south wing of the abbey as built did contain "St. Michael's Gallery," which was decorated with stained glass windows,[1] but in 1812, both Nos. 408 and 415 were described by James Storer as hanging in the state bedchamber, in the north wing of the abbey.

Beckford's birthday was 29 September, the feast day of St. Michael.

[1] Rutter 1823, pp. 52–53 and pl. LXXVI; and Alexander 1957, pp. 17–18.

409 The Beast Riseth Out of the Sea 1797
See color illustration, p. 109

PROFESSOR AND MRS. THOMAS J. MCCORMICK

Oil on panel: $31\frac{1}{2} \times 21\frac{1}{2}$ in. (80 × 54.5 cm.)

Signed lower right: *B. West 1797*

PROV: Painted for William Beckford, Fonthill Abbey, Wilts.; possibly one of the two pictures identified as "Scene from the Revelation" in the Fonthill catalogue of 17–22 Sept. 1822 (Christie's), lots 26 and 27, and one of the four subjects from Revelation in the Fonthill sale of 10–15 Oct. 1823 (Phillips), lots 152, 153, 349 and 350; Childs Gallery, Boston, from whom acquired by the present owner in 1958

EXH: RA 1798 (95) "The beast riseth out of the sea.— Rev. Chap. 13, for the New Abbey at Fonthill"; *A Rationale for Modern Art*, American Federation of Arts, 1959 (17); San Antonio 1983 (40)

LISTED: *PC*, p. 561 ("The Beast rising out of the Sea," painted for, and in the possession of Wm. Beckford, Esq. of Fonthill); *UM*, p. 528; Barlow, p. 432; *BA*, p. 14; Galt, p. 219; Dillenberger, pp. 150 (126) and 214

LIT: Farington Diary, 12 Feb. 1798 (Farington 1978–, III, p. 982); Dillenberger 1977, p. 109 and pl. 77

No. 409 is one of the four Apocalyptic subjects which West exhibited in 1798 and which were evidently painted as studies for pictures intended for the Revelation Chamber at Fonthill Abbey (for which see No. 400). It is approximately the same size as No. 404 and was presumably sold as a pair with it in 1823. It was also, presumably, the "Beast from Revelations" seen in February 1798 by Ozias Humphry, who told Joseph Farington that it was the "finest conception ever come from mind of man." Nancy Pressly in the catalogue of

410

the exhibition in San Antonio in 1983 cites further, less enthusiastic, comment about the painting; she also suggests that the prominent head of a lion in No. 409 can be seen as a slightly veiled reference to Britain and, hence, that it is difficult not to see radical political commentary underlying the religious imagery.[1]

See also p. 108 above.

[1] Mrs. Pressly develops this argument, with reference to contemporary Millenarian ideas, in an essay devoted to West's Apocalyptic imagery (Pressly 1983, pp. 57–66).

410 The Destruction of the Beast and False Prophet 1804

MINNEAPOLIS INSTITUTE OF ARTS

Oil on panel: 39 × 56½ in. (99 × 143.5 cm.)

Signed bottom center: *B. West 1804*

PROV: Purchased by Sir John Fleming Leicester in May 1818 for £300; exchanged by him in January 1819 with John Wilson of the European Museum in part payment for *Lot and His Daughters* (No. 238) and returned to the artist;[1] offered by West's sons to the United States in 1826 (27), and sold by them, Robins, London, 22–25 May 1829, lot 38 ("The Overthrow of the Old Beast and False Prophet," 3 ft. 4 in. × 4 ft. 8 in.), bt. by W. Ward for £199.10.0., apparently on behalf of West's heirs; sold by Mrs. Albert F. West, Christie's, London, 18–19 March 1898, lot 142 ("Death on the Pale Horse," 39 × 55 in.) bt. by McLean for £1.10.0.; Blakeslee Galleries, New York, by whom sold, American Art Association, Plaza Hotel, New York, 21–23 April 1915, lot 208 (as "Death on the Pale Horse"), where bt. by the Minneapolis Institute of Arts (Dunwoody Fund)

EXH: RA 1804 (30) "The destruction of the beast and false prophet, from Revelations, chap. xix. ver. 11 and 20":

> And I saw heaven opened, and behold a white horse: and he that sat upon him was called Faithful and True; and in righteousness he doth judge and make war.
> And the beast was taken, and with him the false prophet that wrought miracles before him, with which he deceived them that had received the mark of the beast and them that worshipped his image. These both were cast alive into a lake of fire burning with brimstone.

European Museum, London, 1819 (602) "The Messiah on a White Horse"; (?) BI 1820 (200) "The White Horse and his Legions, who overthrow the Old Beast and false Prophet. Vide Revelations XIX, verses 11–14," 4 ft. 3 in. × 4 ft. 9 in. (including frame); West's Gallery 1822–28 (49); BI 1833 (5) lent by B. West; *Horse Show*, M. H. de Young Memorial Museum, San Francisco, 1932 (38); *Dog, Cat and Horse Show*, Toledo Museum of Art, 1934; Philadelphia 1938 (55)

LISTED: *PC*, p. 566 ("The Destruction of the old Beast and false Prophet—Revelations," West, Gallery); *UM*, p. 530; Barlow, p. 434; *BA*, p. 17; Galt, p. 228; Dillenberger, pp. 173 (340) and 213

LIT: Farington Diary, 17 April 1804 (Farington 1978–, VI, p. 2299); *St. James Chronicle* 5–8 May 1804 (exhibition review); *Public Characters* 1805, pp. 555–56; Courtauld Cuttings, II, p. 148 (exhibition review by R. H., 17 July 1820); *Bulletin of the Minneapolis Institute of Arts*, V, 1916, pp. 12–14; Kimball 1932, pp. 409–10, fig. 4; Evans 1959, p. 79, pl. 56; Hall 1962, pp. 101–2, 121 (110); Kraemer 1975, p. 42; Meyer 1975, p. 458, fig. 18 and p. 265; Dillenberger 1977, pp. 71 and 78, fig. 60; Pressly 1983, p. 48, fig. 24

Although No. 410 was not identified as a study for the Royal Chapel at Windsor when exhibited at the Royal Academy in 1804, West connected it with that under-

397

taking in a letter to Sir John Fleming Leicester in 1818: "This composition is one of the subjects in Revelation, which I composed to paint a large Picture after for that great work of Revealed Religion—of which that Picture of Death on the Pale Horse was another."[2] The subject is not among the Apocalyptic subjects shown in the architectural drawings for the chapel from *c.* 1780, but it does appear on the Swarthmore diagrams of 1801, second from the right in the uppermost row of the wall devoted to New Testament subjects, where it is described as "Designed" (ill. p. 580). It is also included as part of the Revelation Dispensation in the published lists of West's works.[3] For a consideration of the place of the subjects from Revelation in the chapel scheme see No. 403. Whether West painted No. 410 itself as a study from which he expected to paint a larger picture for the chapel is open to question. He completed no pictures for the chapel after 1801, and a suspicion that by 1804 he was no longer thinking of the chapel project as a viable scheme is encouraged by his failure to have included reference to the chapel in the entry for No. 410 in the Academy catalogue, contrary to his usual practice in previous years. In writing to Sir John Fleming Leicester he referred to the composition of No. 410, rather than the picture itself, as composed for the great work of Revealed Religion, and we know from the inscription on the Swarthmore diagram that the subject indeed had been composed for the chapel several years before 1804, when the Windsor project was still alive. In November 1803, at a time when he might well have been working on the painting, West told Farington that he was going ahead with the chapel pictures at his own expense, but the success of the sketch of *Death on the Pale Horse* (No. 403) in Paris in 1802, rather than hope of completing the chapel, may have provided the more immediate inspiration for him to work up another Apocalyptic design into a comparable exhibitable picture. In this regard, it is noteworthy that the account of West's career published in *Public Characters of 1805* in October 1804 paired these two pictures together without describing them as sketches or connecting them with the chapel.

The measurements of 4 ft. 3 in. × 4 ft. 9 in. (51 × 57 in.), given in the catalogue of the British Institution for "The White Horse and His Legions" exhibited there in 1820, do not correspond very well with those of No. 410, but a long description of the exhibited picture in a contemporary review describes No. 410 accurately. Since No. 410 had returned to West's possession in the previous year and hence was conspicuously available for exhibition, it seems more likely that the measurements given in the British Institution catalogue were wrong than that West exhibited another, otherwise unrecorded version of the picture. It should also be noted that Sir John Fleming Leicester in 1818 and 1819 referred to No. 410 as "The Messiah," and subsequently it was listed as "The Messiah on a White Horse" in the European Museum's catalogue of 1819. If the use of this title stemmed from West himself, there is a possibility that one or more of the pictures exhibited and otherwise recorded as the "Messiah" might either be identified with or related to No. 410 (see Nos. 399 and 203).

No. 410 was sold in 1898 as "Death on the Pale Horse" and was generally known as such until 1932, when Fiske Kimball pointed out its proper identification. Although it shows a different subject based on a different passage in the book of Revelation than West's paintings of *Death on the Pale Horse*, there are nonetheless significant similarities in the imagery, and not only the anonymous article in *Public Characters*, which was published in the year No. 410 was painted, but West himself writing to Sir John Fleming Leicester in 1818, linked the two subjects together.

A drawing is in the Pierpont Morgan Library.[4]

[1]For the exchange, see Hall 1962, pp. 102 and 121–22. Wilson's copy of the catalogue of the European Museum for 1819 bears a note indicating that the painting was returned to West (collection of R. J. Lloyd, to whom we are indebted for communicating this information).
[2]Hall 1962, p. 101.
[3]*PC*, p. 561 (Revelation Dispensation); *UM*, p. 529; *AA*, p. 67 (6 ft. by 9); Barlow, p. 432; *BA*, p. 14 (6 ft. × 10); Galt, p. 219; Meyer, p. 265; Dillenberger, p. 149 (118).
[4]Black chalk with white on blue-grey paper, 9¼ × 7 in. (Kraemer 1975, p. 42, no. 70 and pl. 41).

411 The Angel in the Sun *c.* 1801

LOCATION UNKNOWN

(31 × 20 in.) (78.5 × 51 cm.)

PROV: Painted for William Beckford, Fonthill Abbey, Wilts. (died 1844); (?) sold, Messrs. English and Son, Bath, 25 Nov. 1845, lot 327 (as "The Opening of the Seventh Seal," canvas, 31 × 20 in.) for £22.1.0, bt. in

LISTED: *PC*, p. 561 ("The Angel in the Sun assembling the Birds of the Air, before the Destruction of the Old Beast," painted for, and in the possession of Wm. Beckford, Esq. of Fonthill); *UM*, p. 528; Barlow, p. 432; *BA*, p. 14; Galt, p. 220; Dillenberger, p. 151 (134)

LIT: *Bath and Cheltenham Gazette*, 26 Nov. 1845; Kraemer 1975, pp. 36–37; Dillenberger 1977, pp. 108–9

In a letter dated 22 December 1801, West wrote to William Beckford, who was then in Paris, that he had delivered a picture of Abraham and Isaac (No. 242) to Beckford's agent, "and the one representing the Angel in the sun from Revelation (not finished when you left London) it is my intention to exhibit in the Royal Academy next May."[1] He did not exhibit the picture in 1802, or in any other year, and no painting of the subject is now known. That the picture was painted and belonged to Beckford is confirmed by its appearance in the lists of West's works, and by the fact that in addition to the Revelation subjects by West which appeared in the Fonthill sale of 1823, all of which can be equated with previously exhibited works, one further such subject was included in an inventory made immediately after Beckford's death in 1844,[2] and sold by his estate in 1845. In the inventory the picture was listed as "The Opening of the Sixth Seal" and in the sale it was "The Opening of the Seventh Seal," neither of which is appropriate for the angel in the sun, who is described in verses 17 and 18 of chapter 19 of Revelation. The angel with one foot on the earth, a subject which West also painted for Beckford (No. 404), on the other hand, is one of several angels who appear in chapters eight, nine and ten of Revelation following the opening of the seventh seal. Hence it might seem that No. 404 rather than this painting was the picture that remained in Beckford's collection. However, No. 404 appears to have been the "Angel, from the Revelations, standing on earth and sea" in the de Tabley sale in 1827, so, unless Beckford subsequently bought it back, the more probable explanation of the titles used in 1844 and 1845 is that the compiler of the inventory and the provincial auctioneer, who did not agree with one another about the subject, did not recognize what specific passage from Revelation the picture illustrated.

Although the painting is lost, a drawing in the Toledo Museum of Art (*right*) shows the angel in the sun and may reflect the composition of the oil paintings.[3] The angel in that drawing is similar to the one in No. 404, and it is possible that No. 411 was based on the earlier work. Its relation otherwise to the four

Apocalyptic subjects exhibited in 1798 and intended for the Revelation Chamber at Fonthill is not clear.

In addition to the drawing at Toledo, Ruth Kraemer has associated a drawing in the Morgan Library with this subject.[4] A sketch was sold by West's heirs in 1829, and two ambiguously titled drawings, which may have been related to No. 404 or No. 411, were sold by Mrs. Albert F. West in 1898.[5]

[1]Beckford papers, formerly collection of the Duke of Hamilton, sold, Sotheby's, London, 6 July 1977, lot 272.
[2]Letter from Boyd Alexander to Helmut von Erffa, 28 April 1956.
[3]Pen and wash, 13½ × 11 in. (San Antonio 1983, no. 41).
[4]Graphite, 9¼ × 9⅜ in. (Kraemer 1975, pp. 36–37, no. 59, and pl. 38).
[5]Robins, London, 20–22 June 1829, lot 55, and Christie's, London, 18–19 March 1898, lots 118 ("The Destroying Angel") and 127 ("The Angel of death," 30 × 22 in.).

The Angel in the Sun, (?) drawing for or after No. 411. Toledo Museum of Art, Toledo, Ohio

SAINTS

412 St. George Destroying the Dragon 1787

Oil on canvas: 77 × 86 in. (195.6 × 218.4 in.)

Signed lower left: *B. West/1787*

PROV: Painted for George III (1797 account: "St. George destroying the Dragon," 1787, £630; 1801 account, p. 213: for His Majesty's State Rooms in Windsor Castle, 4, . . .)

EXH: BI 1833 (16) lent by William IV

LISTED: *PC*, p. 560 ("St. George destroying the Dragon," King's Audience-room, Windsor Castle); *UM*, p. 527; Barlow, p. 431; *BA*, p. 13 (8 ft. × 6); Galt, p. 217; Dillenberger, pp. 140 (35) and 212

LIT: Brayley and Britton 1801, pp. 238–41; *Windsor Guide* 1807, p. 49; Millar 1969, pp. xix and 130 (1151)

See No. 56 for a discussion of the Audience Chamber at Windsor, for which this picture was painted. It is visible over the mantel in the watercolor view of the Audience Room by Charles Wild (ill. p. 94). No. 412 and the *Institution of the Order of the Garter* (No. 67) were the first two pictures painted for the chamber. The significance of St. George for the Order of the Garter, for Windsor, and for George III explains why this subject was assigned the central place in the Audience Chamber, although it does not belong to the sequence of historical events from the reign of Edward III to which all the other pictures in the series were devoted.

An oil sketch is No. 413 below. Two drawings of the same subject by Raphael West, one of which is signed and dated *1783*, have significant elements in common with No. 412 and would seem to have been of some significance for the painting.[1] But it should be noted that Raphael West was only seventeen years old in 1783, and it seems likely that his drawings reflect other sketches by his father, which have since disappeared. There is also a general similarity between Raphael's drawings, No. 412, and two other compositions upon which Benjamin West was working at approximately the same time, *Alexander III of Scotland Saved from a Stag by Colin Fitzgerald* and *Death on the Pale Horse* (Nos. 54 and 401). West exhibited designs for both of these works at the Royal Academy in 1784 (Nos. 55 and 402).

[1] The dated drawing (reproduced here) is in ink and wash: $26\frac{1}{2} \times 19\frac{7}{8}$ in. (exhibited *Old Master and English Drawings*, Kate de Rothschild and Morton Morris and Company, London, 30 June–11 July 1980, no. 27). This drawing may have been the "St. George and the Dragon; a drawing," which Raphael exhibited at the Royal Academy in 1784. The second drawing, which is much sketchier, is signed with initials *RW* but not dated (location unknown).

413 St. George Destroying the Dragon 1786

Oil on canvas: $15\frac{1}{8} \times 11\frac{1}{8}$ in. (38.5 × 28.5 cm.)

Signed lower left: *B. West 1786*

PROV: Offered by West's sons to the United States in 1826 (70), and sold by them, Robins, London, 22–25 May 1829, lot 111 ("St. George and the Dragon,"

412

Raphael West, *St. George Destroying the Dragon*, drawing (cf. No. 412). Private collection

413

14 × 11 in.), bt. by Ward for £38.17.0.; J. A. Ward in 1833; Vose Galleries, Boston; Mr. and Mrs. John F. Braun, Merion, Pennsylvania, 1938; Victor Spark, New York, 1951; purchased by the Reading Public Museum and Art Gallery (Edith H. Seyfert Fund) in 1951

EXH: West's Gallery 1822–28 (25); BI 1833 (50) lent by J. A. Ward; Philadelphia 1938 (36) lent by Mr. and Mrs. John F. Braun

LISTED: *PC*, p. 567 ("The Sketch of St. George and the Dragon," West, Gallery); *UM*, p. 531; *BA*, p. 18; Galt, p. 231; Dillenberger, p. 179 (410)

The date of *1786* on No. 413 is the earliest date that can be associated with any of the sketches or pictures for the Audience Chamber at Windsor. The shape, which is vertical rather than horizontal as in No. 412, suggests that the destination of the final version had not yet been decided when West painted this sketch.

414 St. Margaret of Scotland 1799

THE LORD BISHOP OF LONDON

Oil on paper mounted on canvas: $108 \times 39\frac{5}{8}$ in. (274.5×100.5 cm.)

Signed bottom center: *B. West 1799*

PROV: Cartoon for a stained glass window intended for Fonthill Abbey; offered by West's sons to the United States in 1826 (19), and sold by them, Robins, London, 22–25 May 1829, lot 173 ("Saint Margaret of Scotland," 10 ft. × 3 ft. 4 in., "a cartoon, the study for a stained glass window, intended to be executed by Jervis and Pearson, for Fonthill Abbey, in Wiltshire"), bt. by Thompson for £15.15.0; in Fulham Palace, London, 1974

EXH: RA 1799 (136) "St. Margaret, Queen of Scotland, a cartoon designed for a painted window in the new abbey at Fonthill"; West's Gallery 1822–28 (96)

LISTED: Dillenberger, p. 213 (as "Margaret of Anjou")

LIT: Kraemer 1975, pp. 37–38; Dillenberger 1977, p. 109; Hamilton-Phillips 1981, pp. 167–70, fig. 13

See No. 416, the cartoon of *St. Thomas à Becket*, with which this work was exhibited in 1799. The two cartoons have evidently been together ever since. Unlike the former, however, No. 414 did not serve as the basis of an actual window executed for Fonthill, nor does it appear in any of the early lists of West's works.

No smaller version in oil, analogous to No. 415 of *St. Thomas*, is known or recorded for the *St. Margaret*. Two related drawings, neither of which is very close to the final cartoon, are at Swarthmore.[1] Ruth Kraemer has associated a rough sketch of a female saint, which is on a sheet of disparate studies in the Pierpont Morgan Library, with this subject as well.[2]

[1] Brown chalk, $10\frac{1}{2} \times 3\frac{1}{2}$ in.; and black chalk heightened with white on blue paper, 12×9 in. (sheet size) (Hamilton-Phillips 1981, figs. 15 and 14). The latter drawing also contains two smaller studies for Nos. 415 and 416.
[2] Black chalk, $9\frac{1}{8} \times 7\frac{5}{8}$ in. (sheet size) (Kraemer 1975, pp. 37–38, no. 60, verso).

415 St. Thomas à Becket 1797
See color illustration, p. 103

TOLEDO MUSEUM OF ART, TOLEDO, OHIO

Oil on canvas: $50\frac{1}{2} \times 23\frac{3}{8}$ in. (128.3×59.4 cm.)

Signed lower left: *B. West 1797* and inscribed upon the plinth upon which the Saint stands *St THOs BECKET*

PROV: Painted for William Beckford, Fonthill Abbey, Wilts.; in the Fonthill sale catalogue of 17–22 Sept. 1822 (Christie's), lot 90 ("St. Thomas à Becket," companion picture to lot 89, "St. Michael and the Falling Angels" [see No. 408]), and sold, 10–15 October 1823 (Phillips), lot 251 (as above, with an accompanying note: "the two preceding lots were painted by the artist for Mr. Beckford as a design for stained glass windows; a copy of the latter [No. 415] now forms a window in the angle of the north east or 'Becket passage'"), for £21.10.6.; Charles Mitchell, London, by c. 1941, and sold by him to the Toledo Museum in 1959

EXH: RA 1798 (267) "St. Thomas à Becket, for the new abbey at Fonthill"; Allentown 1962 (24); San Antonio 1983 (42)

LISTED: *PC*, p. 561 ("A whole length figure of Thomas of Becket, larger than Life," painted for, and in the possession of Wm. Beckford, Esq. of Fonthill); *UM*, p. 528; Barlow, p. 432; *BA*, p. 14; Galt, p. 220; Dillenberger, pp. 151 (133) and 213

414

When the *St. Michael* (No. 408) appeared at the Royal Academy in 1797, the catalogue identified it as for a window for Fonthill Abbey. In the following year, No. 415 was described simply as "for the new abbey at Fonthill," but in 1799 the larger version (No. 416) appeared along with *St. Margaret of Scotland* (No. 414), a companion work the same size, each accompanied by the words, "a cartoon designed for a painted window in the new abbey at Fonthill." There is no record of windows having been executed after either No. 408 or No. 414 but Nos. 415 and 416 did provide the basis for a window which was installed in the "Becket passage" of the east transept of Fonthill, and which is now in the church of St. Mark's, or Lord Mayor's Chapel, in Bristol.[1] Although both Nos. 415 and 416 are in color, the window is in grisaille with only a few areas of reddish color for some details of the robes. It was described by Rutter in 1823 as "a lofty painted glass window, in chiaro-scuro by Pearson of the celebrated Archbishop, after a design by the late President West." In showing Becket beardless and in other details the window follows No. 416, the cartoon, rather than No. 415.

The Pearson mentioned by Rutter was James Pearson, who had previously executed windows for Brasenose College, Oxford, and for Salisbury Cathedral. The reason that only one design by West was carried out by Pearson for Fonthill is given by Joseph Farington in his diary entry for 1 November 1797. James Wyatt, the architect of Fonthill, told Farington that Beckford was furious at Pearson's proposed charges:

> Pearson had said to Wyatt He shd. charge for each figure in painted glass to be copied from Wests *Paintings of Saints* for the purpose, 100 or 120 or 150 gs. Pearson had been mentioned by West to Beckford, but rather as a *stranger* than as an *acquaintance*. Beckford called at Wests to see one of the figures finished; Pearson, *accidentally on purpose*, came in—Beckford told Wyatt He soon *saw through him*, but left it to Wyatt to settle—Pearson also demanded a sum of money *in advance*.—Wyatt privately desired His nephew Jefferey Wyatt to write as from himself to Eggington, who resides near Birmingham to know his terms for such work. Eggington replied *50 guineas a figure*, 7 Feet ½ high & 3 Feet ½ wide—and to finish 8 figures in two years. This difference appeared to make Pearsons charge monstrous.—Beckford, however, offers Pearson a figure to execute at 100 gs. if He chooses.[2]

The "Eggington" who underbid Pearson was Francis Eginton, who had previously executed a window of the *Conversion of St. Paul* for St. Paul's in Birmingham after designs by West (Nos. 390, 392, and 393). With his son William Raphael Eginton he subsequently produced a large amount of glass for Fonthill, but after designs by William Hamilton rather than by West.[3]

Two slight sketches are on the same sheet with a sketch for No. 414 at Swarthmore.[4] A larger more highly finished drawing is in the Nelson-Atkins Museum in Kansas City;[5] a drawing for the saint's upraised left arm went through Sotheby's in 1964;[6] and Ruth Kraemer associates a sketch of a bishop on a sheet in the Morgan Library with this subject.[7]

[6]Sotheby's, London, 22 Jan. 1964, lot 8, black and white chalk, 15½ × 10½ in.
[7]Black chalk, 9⅝ × 7⅝ in. (sheet size) (Kraemer 1975, pp. 37–38, no. 60, verso).

416 St. Thomas à Becket *c.* 1799

THE LORD BISHOP OF LONDON

Oil on paper mounted on canvas: 108½ × 40 in. (276 × 101.5 cm.)

PROV: Cartoon for a stained glass window for Fonthill Abbey; offered by West's sons to the United States in 1826 (18), and sold by them, Robins, London, 22–25 May 1829, lot 174 ("Saint Thomas a-Becket," 10 ft. × 3 ft. 4 in., "The companion cartoon to the preceeding [No. 414], intended as the prototype for a window executed in stained glass at Fonthill Abbey"), bt. by Thompson for £15.15.0; in Fulham Palace, London, 1974

EXH: RA 1799 (170) "St. Thomas à Becket, a cartoon designed for a painted window in the new abbey at Fonthill"; West's Gallery, 1822–28 (106)

LISTED: PC, p. 568 ("The small whole length of Thomas à Becket, in oil, on canvas," West, Gallery); UM, p. 532; BA, p. 19; Galt, p. 234; Dillenberger, pp. 185 (469) and 213

LIT: Dillenberger 1977, p. 109

416 (detail)

LIT: Storer 1812, p. 19; Rutter 1823, p. 31; Rogers 1966, passim; Kraemer 1975, p. 38; Dillenberger 1977, p. 109 and pl. 74

Although *Public Characters* and other early catalogues of West's works list a larger-than-life *Thomas à Becket* in the collection of William Beckford and a small whole length version in the possession of the artist, it is clear that they have the information reversed. The larger version (No. 416) remained in West's possession and was sold by his sons in 1829, while No. 415, which is less than life-sized, and its companion piece, *St. Michael* (No. 408), hung as pendants in the state bedroom at Fonthill Abbey in 1812 and remained at Fonthill until sold in 1823.

[1]Reproduced in Wynne 1982, p. 64, pl. 48.
[2]Farington Diary, 1 Nov. 1797 (Farington 1978—, III, p. 912). For Pearson, see Wynne 1982, pp. 60–65.
[3]William Hamilton exhibited designs for glass for Fonthill Abbey at the Royal Academy in 1799 (392) and 1800 (120 and 140), indicating in the catalogue in the former year that the glass was executed by "F. Egerton of Birmingham."
[4]Black chalk heightened with white on blue paper, 12 × 9 in. (sheet size).
[5]Black chalk heightened with white on blue paper, 17½ × 11⅞ in.

The Vision of St. Anthony of Padua, (?) drawing for Nos. 417 and 418. Swarthmore College, Swarthmore, Pennsylvania

25 May 1829, No. 418 showed the "ecstacy of the saint on beholding the infant Saviour;" a further comment about the grave coloring, "compatible with the retired sentiment associated with the habits of a monkish cell," suggests that the scene was set in the interior of a monastic cell. The apparent discrepancy between Storer's description of St. Anthony receiving the Christ Child into his arms and the Robins catalogue's description of him seeing the Child seems to be explained by a drawing at Swarthmore (*left*), which is evidently a study for this subject.[1] That drawing shows a figure in Franciscan robes kneeling before an altar and gazing upwards into a glory of clouds and light, in the midst of which a small figure of the Christ Child is seemingly poised to leap into the Saint's arms.

St. Anthony of Padua was William Beckford's patron saint, to whom Beckford expressed sincere, if somewhat eccentric, devotion throughout his mature life. A statue of St. Anthony with the infant Christ in his arms by John Charles Rossi stood above the altar in the Oratory at Fonthill Abbey.

[1]Black and white chalk on brown paper, $6\frac{3}{4} \times 5\frac{1}{4}$ in.

418 The Vision of St. Anthony of Padua *c.* 1799

LOCATION UNKNOWN

$(26 \times 18\frac{1}{2}$ in.$)$ $(66 \times 47$ cm.$)$

PROV: Offered by West's sons to the United States in 1826 (61), and sold by them, Robins, London, 22–25 May 1829, lot 23 ("St. Anthony of Padua," 2 ft. 2 in. × 1 ft. $6\frac{1}{2}$ in.), bt. by Pike for £21

EXH: (?) RA 1799 (546) "The vision of St. Anthony of Padua, a sketch for a picture to be painted for the abbey at Fonthill"; West's Gallery 1822–28 (16)

LISTED: *PC*, p. 567 ("St. Anthony of Padua and the Child," West, Gallery); *UM*, p. 531; Barlow, p. 435; *BA*, p. 18; Galt, p. 231; Dillenberger, p. 178 (396)

Although Nos. 418 and 417, both of which have disappeared, can reasonably be identified respectively as the sketch exhibited by West at the Royal Academy in 1799 and the picture for Fonthill Abbey referred to in the Academy catalogue, it should be noted that in other instances (see No. 400), the exhibited sketch itself became Beckford's property, and the painting that would have been based on it was never carried out. Nos. 417 and 418 seem to have been the identical size. Comments about No. 418 from the Robins catalogue of May 1829 are quoted in the entry for No. 417.

417 The Vision of St. Anthony of Padua *c.* 1799

LOCATION UNKNOWN

$(25\frac{3}{4} \times 18\frac{1}{2}$ in.$)$ $(65.5 \times 47$ cm.$)$

PROV: Painted for William Beckford, Fonthill Abbey, Wilts.; in the Fonthill sale catalogue of 17–22 Sept. 1822 (Christie's), lot 22, and sold, Fonthill Abbey, 10–15 Oct. 1823 (Phillips), lot 39 (in both catalogues as "St. Anthony of Padua" with "The Virgin and Dead Christ" [No. 359] as a companion)

LISTED: *PC*, p. 561 ("St. Anthony of Padua," painted for and in the possession of Wm. Beckford, Esq. of Fonthill); *UM*, p. 528; Barlow, p. 432; *BA*, p. 14; Galt, p. 219; Dillenberger, p. 150 (128)

LIT: Storer 1812, p. 20; Hamilton-Phillips 1981, pp. 170–71

The *Description of Fonthill Abbey* published by James Storer in 1812 mentions a painting in the West Dressing Room showing "the Vision of St. Anthony of Padua, receiving into his arms the infant Christ." Storer does not name the artist, but as the painting hung opposite the *Madre-dolorosa* by West (No. 359), it seems likely that the picture was No. 417, which was described as a companion to No. 359 in the Fonthill catalogues of 1822 and 1823. The *Madre-dolorosa* measured $25\frac{3}{4} \times 18\frac{1}{2}$ in., and presumably its companion piece would have had the same dimensions.

The catalogues of the Fonthill sales and the early lists of West's works describe the subject of No. 417 simply as "St. Anthony of Padua," but the title under which West exhibited a sketch for the picture in 1796 (presumably No. 418) confirms that it showed the vision of St. Anthony. According to the Robins sale catalogue of 22–

ALLEGORICAL SUBJECTS

419 The Golden Age 1776

See color illustration, p. 81

TATE GALLERY, LONDON

Oil on canvas: oval, $25\frac{3}{4} \times 30\frac{1}{8}$ in. (65.5×76.5 cm.)

Signed right side, slightly below center: *B. West/1776*

PROV: Richard, first Earl Grosvenor (1731–1802); sold anonymously (The Property of a Nobleman), Peter Coxe, London, 2 July 1812, lot 53; presumably bought back by West; owned by his sons in 1821; offered by them to the United States in 1826 (125), and sold by them, Robins, London, 22–25 May 1829, lot 153 ("The Golden Age," 2 ft. 2 in. × 2 ft. 6 in.), bt. by Bone for £136.10.0. on behalf of Joseph Neeld, MP, Grittleton House, Wilts.; by descent in the Neeld family until sold, Christie's, London, 13 July 1945, lot 170; Leger Galleries, London; James Green; Samuel Eckman, Jr., by whom sold, Sotheby's, London, 11 Oct. 1967, lot 46, bt. by Leger; purchased by the Tate Gallery in 1967

EXH: (?) RA 1776 (321) "A domestic scene"; West's Gallery 1821 (94) 1822–28 (142) "The Golden Age"; BI 1833 (37) lent by Joseph Neeld; RA 1878 winter (78) "The Golden Age; Portrait of Mrs. West," lent by Sir John Neeld, Bt.

ENGR: Mezzotint ($18\frac{7}{16} \times 22$ in.) by Valentine Green, pub. 4 June 1777 by John Boydell; stipple engraving ($11\frac{5}{8} \times 9\frac{15}{16}$ in.) by Facius, pub. 1 Jan. 1778 by Boydell

LISTED: PC, p. 562 ("The Golden Age," in the possession of the Earl of Grosvenor); UM, p. 528; Barlow, p. 432; BA, p. 14; Galt, p. 220; Dillenberger, p. 152 (146)

LIT: Leslie 1860, 1, pl. 61; *The Tate Gallery 1967–68*, London, 1968, p. 52; Kraemer 1975, p. 66

West probably exhibited No. 419 at the Royal Academy in 1776 under the title "A domestic scene," but it has always been known since as "The Golden Age", the title on the print by Valentine Green published in 1777. The Robins sale catalogue of 1829 described it as depicting the three periods of life—infancy, puberty, and old age—while, "In the characteristics of the happy drama, all affects that dignified simplicity of the pastoral habits of society, coeval with the patriarchal days of Abraham." Although West never used a more explicit title in connection with No. 419, it is possible that he painted the picture as an illustration of a specific Old Testament subject, showing Hagar (whose ragged skirt indicates her lowly status) and Ishmael in the foreground, and Abraham and Sarah in the background. West also painted and exhibited the *Hagar and Ishmael* (No. 239) now in the Metropolitan Museum in 1776, but he substantially repainted it in 1803, altering the details of Hagar's dress. A drawing for No. 239 (ill. p. 289), which is signed and dated *1776*, does show Hagar dressed virtually identically to the mother in No. 419. There is no evident allusion in the imagery to the Ovidian Golden Age.

When No. 419 was exhibited in 1878, it bore the subtitle "Portrait of Mrs. West." It is quite likely that the artist's wife was the model for the mother in No. 419;

she also was probably the model for Hagar in No. 239. It seems less likely that her appearance in No. 419 directly corresponds to her actual role as a mother in 1776, since her youngest child, born in August 1772, would have been too old to have served as the model for the baby. There is also no particular resemblance between the seated patriarch in the background of No. 419 and West's father, who was beardless. West's mother had been dead since 1756. The painting is therefore in no way a West family portrait; nonetheless the mother in No. 419 so closely resembles Mrs. West in a family portrait (No. 546), which West probably began before No. 419 but exhibited later, that there must have been some connection between the two works in the artist's mind. Charles Robert Leslie wrote that West thought of the family portrait as an "Ages of Man" and that he repeated it, "with great variations, substituting loose draperies for the modern dresses." No. 419 probably was that so-called repetition, which in Leslie's opinion "immediately became commonplace" and served as a warning to artists "of the danger of endeavoring to improve on incidents taken from real life."

In the early lists of West's works, the *Golden Age* is described as belonging to the Earl Grosvenor. In 1812 it was sold anonymously, as "The Property of a Nobleman," but described in the catalogue entry as "Painted by the President of the Royal Academy for the late Earl Grosvenor." West must have bought it back in or after 1812 as it was in his sons' possession in 1821 and was sold by them in 1829.

A large drawing in the National Gallery of Canada, which shows the composition of No. 419 but as a rectangle, is probably identical with the drawing of "The Golden Age" described in the lists of West's works as belonging to him.[1] This drawing is signed but not dated and was probably done after No. 419 rather than as a study for it. The style of draughtsmanship suggests that West may not have drawn it until the 1780s; in this it would be comparable to the rather similar drawing in the Fogg Museum dated *1784* after *Fidelia and Speranza* of 1776 (No. 222). A drawing in pencil repeating No. 419, with greater accuracy and as an oval, appears to be a copy not by West's hand.[2] A smaller drawing sold in 1969 as "The Three Ages of Man," which is signed and dated *1783* shows the same subject but with a different composition.[3]

An oval copy of No. 419 was acquired by the University of Nebraska Art Galleries in 1961 and stolen in 1962.[4] There is also a copy of No. 419 framed as a rectangular painting in the Princeton University Art Museum.[5] No. 419 was also copied in miniature on a vase made in Berlin around 1805.[6]

[1] Pen and wash: $12\frac{5}{8} \times 16\frac{1}{8}$ in., signed lower right *B. West*; PC, p. 568; UM, pp. 531–32; BA, p. 19; Galt, p. 233; Dillenberger, p. 183 (451); probably sold S. Leigh Sotheby, London, 1 June 1839, lot 110 ("The Golden Age, the design for the picture," pen and bistre, washed).
[2] Pencil, $12\frac{3}{4} \times 20\frac{3}{16}$ in., Yale Center for British Art, New Haven.
[3] Pen, ink and watercolor, $3\frac{1}{2} \times 4\frac{7}{8}$ in., signed lower left *B. West/1783*; sold Christie's, London, 14 Oct. 1969, lot 34. Another drawing sold in the same sale as lot 35, *The Golden Age*, has no relation with No. 419 in subject or composition.
[4] Oil on canvas, $24\frac{3}{4} \times 29\frac{7}{8}$ in.
[5] Oil on canvas, $24\frac{3}{4} \times 30\frac{1}{8}$ in., bequeathed to Princeton by C. O. von Kienbusch; exhibited Brooklyn 1922 (8, as "Portrait of Mrs. West and Child," lent by Ehrich Galleries).
[6] See *Porzellankunst: Berliner Porzellane von Rokoko bis zum Empire*, Schloss Charlottenburg, Berlin, 1969, p. 36 (No. 418) and pl. 83.; kindly pointed out to us by Dr. Rüdiger Joppien.

420 The Harmony of Affection 1808

LOCATION UNKNOWN

(50×54 in., or possibly vice versa) (127×137 cm.)

PROV: Offered by West to the Pennsylvania Academy in 1809 ("The Harmony of Affection," 4 ft. 6 in. × 4 ft. 2 in., £250)

EXH: RA 1808 (174) "The harmony of Affection"; BI 1809 (197) . . . 69 × 72 in. (including frame)

LIT: Hall 1962, p. 100 (letter from West to Sir John Fleming Leicester, 25 March 1808)

On 25 March 1808, West wrote to Sir John Fleming Leicester, who was in the process of buying *A Bacchante* (No. 123) from the artist, in an attempt to interest him in another work:

I am at present painting a picture expressive of the harmony of love over creation—the figures are the size of the Cupid in the picture I parted with to Mr. Agar [No. 127]—it is intended for the approaching exhibition at the Royal Academy—it will be done by the beginning of the next month: I shall be happy to shew it to you when compleat—and at which time you may have your choice of either that or the *Baccanti*.

Leicester bought the *Bacchante* for 150 guineas, rather than the new picture, for which West asked twice as much. The *Harmony of Affection* was completed in time to appear at the Royal Academy in 1808, and West also exhibited it at the British Institution in 1809, but it seems to have disappeared completely after 1809. In subject and possibly in appearance it may have had some similarity to *Omnia Vincit Amor* (No. 422) of 1809, in which the main figure of Amor corresponds not only in size but also in action to the figure of Cupid in No. 127, mentioned by West in his letter. Discrepancies in sizes and in dates, as well as the rules of the Royal Academy forbidding the exhibition of the same work there twice, preclude the possibility of identifying the *Harmony of Affection* and *Omnia Vincit Amor* as the same picture.

421 A Lady Leading Three Children along the Path of Virtue to the Temple

LOCATION KNOWN

LISTED: PC, p. 563 ("A Lady leading Three Children along the Path of Virtue to the Temple"); UM, p. 529; Barlow, p. 433 ("A mother leading her children to the Temple of Virtue," listed under "In Different Churches"); BA, p. 15 ("A Lady leading three Children of Virtue to the Temple"); Galt, p. 222; Dillenberger, pp. 155 (167) and 158 (202)

This lost work, which is known only from the early lists of West's paintings, appears in all of them except that in *The Columbiad* in conjunction with several group portraits (Nos. 602, 607, 610, and 651), and it is probable that No. 421 was a group portrait of a mother and her children, although there is no explicit indication in any of the variations of the title that it was. There are temples with the word *VIRTUTIS* inscribed upon them in the backgrounds of two of West's group portraits of the children of Archbishop Drummond (Nos. 608 and 611), and it is possible that No. 421 is identical with No. 611, which otherwise does not appear on the lists.

Barlow's indication that No. 421 was in a church is not repeated in any other list and is clearly an error.

422 Omnia Vincit Amor 1809

See color illustrations, pp. 138, 139

METROPOLITAN MUSEUM OF ART, NEW YORK

Oil on canvas: $70\frac{3}{8} \times 80\frac{1}{2}$ in. (179×204.5 cm.)

Signed lower right: *B. West 1809*

PROV: Offered by West's sons to the United States in 1826 (9, "The Triumph of Love over Animated

Nature," 6 ft. × 7), and sold by them, Robins, London, 22–25 May 1829, lot 143 ("Omnia Vincit Amor," 6 ft. × 7), bt. by Bone for £63; Henry Pierce Bone (1779–1855); sold by him, Christie's, London, 12 March 1847, lot 124, bt. by Smith; Arthur E. S. Seguin (1809–52) by 1851; by descent to Mrs. E. S. R. Seguin; on deposit in the Pennsylvania Academy, Philadelphia, from c. 1851 to c. 1864, and at the Metropolitan Museum from 1881 to 1923, when purchased by the museum from Mrs. Seguin

EXH: RA 1811 (63) "Omnia Vincit Amor, or the Power of Love in the Three Elements," or, in some editions of the catalogue, "The omnivincent Amour guiding the three elements"; West's Gallery 1821 (58), 1822–28 (86) "Omnia Vincit Amor"; PAFA 1851 (241), and almost every year thereafter through 1864, as "The Triumph of Love" lent by S. Seguin; *Retrospective Exhibition of American Paintings*, Metropolitan Museum of Art, New York, 1896 (208) as "The Triumph of Love"

LIT: Dunlap Diary, 23 June 1833 (Dunlap 1930, III, p. 701); Dunlap 1834, II, p. 124 (Dunlap 1918, II, p. 262); Evans 1959, pp. 77, 79–80, pl. 60; Gardner and Feld 1965, pp. 35–36; Kraemer 1975, pp. 51–52, 68–69

The title "Omnia Vincit Amor" comes from the tenth *Eclogue* of Virgil (line 69), but the imagery of No. 422 has nothing to do with the Virgilian narrative. It has been suggested,[1] however, that it may have been inspired by John Dryden's translation of the tenth *Eclogue*, which includes the lines:

In hell, and earth, and seas and heaven above,
Love conquers all; and we must yield to Love.

No. 422 shows the conquering figure of Cupid or Love grasping three reins leading to a lion, a web-footed horse or hippocampus, and an eagle, representatives of earth, seas, and heaven. These constitute the "Three Elements" of West's title. The fourth element, fire, which is also present in the torch held by Cupid in his right hand, is not subject to the same form of control. Some, presumably early, issues of the Royal Academy catalogue for 1811 give the title of No. 422 as "The omnivincent Amour guiding the three elements." This was soon replaced by the more correctly Latin and Virgilian "Omnia Vincit Amor," but the word "guiding" accompanying the bastard Latin–French of the first title fits the action of the picture. Also appropriate to the imagery is the title used by West's sons in 1826, "The Triumph of Love over Animated Nature," which they may have felt would be more comprehensible to an American public.

West had previously shown Cupid holding reins leading to two doves as a subsidiary detail in the background of *Venus Relating to Adonis the Story of Hippomenes and Atalanta* (No. 112) of 1767, and as the main motif in No. 127, which he exhibited as "Cupid" in 1798 and retouched in 1803 and 1808. No. 422, which a recent cleaning has revealed to be signed and dated *1809*, appears to be an extension of the idea of No. 127, but intervening between the two came the lost *Harmony of Affection* (No. 420), which West exhibited at the Royal Academy in 1808, and which seems to have had a great deal in common with both works. The pose and headdress of Venus on the left are borrowed with little change from the Thetis in *Thetis Bringing the Armor to Achilles*, which West painted in several versions between 1804 and 1808 (Nos. 170–75).

Grose Evans, who is repeated by Gardner and Feld, states that the pose of Cupid is based on the Laocoon. A more likely and appropriate source, however, would have been the *Dioscuri* or *Horse Tamers* on the Quirinal Hill in Rome. There are also echoes of the Parthenon frieze, which West first saw in 1807 or 1808 (see

Nos. 498–503). The head of West's sea-horse appears to be based on the head of the horse of Selene from the east pediment of the Parthenon, but may not be, since a similar horse's head appears in Nos. 110 and 111, which were completed by May 1807.

Thomas Sully, who arrived in London in July 1809, told William Dunlap in 1833 that he had watched West at work on No. 422, and that West had the wing of a macaw in his studio to use as a model for the wing of one of the *genii* (the word quoted by Sully from West) in the picture: "I never paint without having the object before me, if it is to be had." Sully also told Dunlap that West was working on No. 422 in Raphael West's small room, while *Christ Healing the Sick* (No. 336) was in his large studio.

Ruth Kraemer has identified a drawing of doves in the Pierpont Morgan Library as a study for those held by Venus in No. 422.[2] A drawing of a nude youth in the same collection, tentatively proposed by Kraemer as a first study for Cupid in the painting, is not, but is a study for Isaac in No. 240 instead. A drawing for the lion is in Wilmington.[3]

No. 422 is one of the works bought in the West sales of 1829 either by the enamelist Henry Bone (1755–1834) or his son Henry Pierce Bone (1779–1855) which were not purchased on behalf of Joseph Neeld. It is the most important of a group of paintings, either by West or formerly attributed to him, which the Metropolitan Museum of Art acquired from the descendants of the opera singers Arthur and Anne Seguin. Former Metropolitan Museum catalogues, presumably on the basis of information given the museum by the Seguin heirs, state that the Seguins had acquired these paintings as collateral for a loan and brought them to the United States with them in 1839. That is palpably untrue, for No. 422 and at least one other work in the

Metropolitan Museum (No. 194), since they appeared in a sale of works owned by Henry Pierce Bone in 1847. They were in America and did belong to a member of the Seguin family by 1851, when they were placed on extended loan in the Pennsylvania Academy of Fine Arts in Philadelphia.

Charles Robert Leslie painted a copy of No. 422 some time before 1816, when it was lent to the American Academy of Fine Arts in New York by Major General Scott (present location unknown).[4]

[1] For this suggestion and for much of the content of this entry we are indebted to Jennifer Licht who presented a seminar report on No. 422 at Columbia University in 1978.
[2] Black chalk on blue paper, 12⅛ × 5¹³⁄₁₆ in. (Kraemer 1975, pp. 68–69, no. 148 verso and pl. 81).
[3] Black and white chalk, 12¼ × 16½ in. (see also No. 110).
[4] William Dunlap (1918, II, p. 262, note) mentions Leslie's copy "brought to this country by one of our travelling connoisseurs."

423 Time Bringing Truth to Light

LOCATION UNKNOWN

PROV: Sold by West's sons, Robins, London, 20–22 June 1829, lot 79

This work was sold among the paintings in the sale of sketches, unfinished pictures, and lesser works from West's estate in June 1829. Otherwise, it seems to have gone completely unrecorded. A sheet of six sketches in the British Museum (*below*) showing varying treatments of the subject is probably related, but it is impossible to determine which, if any, of the sketched compositions was utilized by West in the painting.[1] The pose of the naked figure of Truth in the upper left sketch is very similar to that of Venus in *Venus Lamenting Adonis* of 1803 (No. 118).

Time Bringing Truth to Light,
(?) sheet of drawings for No. 423.
British Museum, London

A drawing copied after Poussin's painting of the subject in the Louvre is in the Victoria and Albert Museum, where it is ascribed to West, but it does not appear to be by him. A painting on the market in 1975 and published as "Truth discovered by Time" by West is also not by him.[2]

[1] Black chalk, 9 × 6½ in. (1920–6–15–15)
[2] "Notable Works of Art Now on the Market," *Burlington Magazine*, CXVII, Dec. 1975, pl. XXX.

Allegorical Figure Celebrating the Battle of Waterloo, (?) drawing for No. 424

424 The Figure of Victory, Designed for a Monument to Perpetuate the Memorable Battle of Waterloo *c.* 1815

LOCATION UNKNOWN

PROV: Sold by West's sons, Robins, London, 20–22 June 1829, lot 112

Like No. 423, No. 424 was sold with the paintings in the sale of lesser works from West's estate in June 1829. Described as a design for a monument in the catalogue, it may have been a painted design analogous to the sketch for a monument to the memory of Lord Nelson of 1807 (No. 110).

The Battle of Waterloo took place on 18 June 1815. On 31 August Sir George Beaumont wrote to West on behalf of the Lords Commissioners of His Majesty's Treasury soliciting designs for a commemorative monument. West replied in a long letter dated 20 September 1815, which is printed in Galt, proposing an elaborate building embellished by "the pen, the pencil, and the chisel."[1] His letter does not include any mention of an allegorical figure of Victory; nonetheless, the wording in the sale catalogue suggests that West painted No. 424 in connection with this never-realized monument.

Two drawings of a winged figure holding a palm frond, an olive branch, and a banner inscribed *WATERLOO* probably reflect the appearance of No. 424.[2] Three further drawings related to this composition are in the Pierpont Morgan Library.[3] One of

them is circular, and Ruth Kraemer has proposed that it was intended as a design for a commemorative medal, rather than the monument. A drawing formerly in the collection of a descendant of the artist showing the figure of Victory accompanying a lion and another figure carrying a spear and a shield (? Britannia) also appears to be related to these undertakings.[4]

The figure in the two larger drawings mentioned above echoes the angels from the Book of Revelation painted or drawn by West in Nos. 404 and 411, and he is also prefigured by an angel or allegorical figure accompanied by two eagles in a drawing made by West in Paris in 1802.[5]

[1] Galt 1820, pp. 235–39, where the letter is dated 30 Sept. 1815. The actual letter, dated 20 Sept. 1815, is in the Historical Society of Pennsylvania, Philadelphia.
[2] Pen and watercolor, 8⅜ × 5⅞ in. (Art Gallery of Ontario, Toronto, ill. in Kraemer 1975, p. 57, fig. 38) and (ill. *left*) pen, brown ink, and wash, 10½ × 6⅝ in., signed lower left: *B. West 1816* (sold, Christie's, London, 21 Nov. 1978, lot 68).
[3] All three in pen and brown ink, 6 3/16 × 6⅞ in., 4⅛ × 2 3/16 in.,

and 5⅞ × 4⅛ in. (Kraemer 1975, pp. 56–58, nos. 101–3, and pl. 65).
[4] Pen and brown ink, 4 × 2¾ in.
[5] Pen, black ink, and grey wash on mauve prepared paper, 12⅛ × 8⅝ in., signed lower right: *Paris/B. West Sepr 5th 1802* (sold, Sotheby's, London, 21 Nov. 1978, lot 67).

425 Virtue and Innocence *c.* 1781

LOCATION UNKNOWN

EXH: (?) PAFA 1819 (41) "Innocence (with the Lamb)"

ENGR: Mezzotint (9⅛ × 7½ in.) by Valentine Green, pub. 21 Dec. 1781 by Green

No. 425 is known only through the mezzotint by Valentine Green (*below*), which was published as a companion print to a mezzotint after the *Infant St. John* (No. 296). The legends on both prints explicitly state *Painted by B. West*, but the paintings by West may have been made primarily for the sake of the prints.

Virtue and Innocence, mezzotint by Valentine Green after No. 425

DECORATIVE PROGRAMS

1 London, Royal Academy
Nos. 426–431

426 The Graces Unveiling Nature *c.* 1780

ROYAL ACADEMY OF ARTS, LONDON

Oil on canvas: circular, 60 in. (152.3 cm.) in diameter

PROV: Painted with four companion pictures for £125 for the ceiling of the Council Chamber of the Royal Academy in Somerset House; removed in 1836 to the Academy's new premises in Trafalgar Square (part of the present National Gallery); removed again in 1868 to Burlington House, and installed in the present situation in the ceiling of the vestibule of Burlington House in 1899

LIT: Joseph Baretti, *A Guide through the Royal Academy,* London, n.d. [1781], pp. 25–26; Raymond Needham and Alexander Webster, *Somerset House Past and Present,* London, 1905, p. 224; Evans 1959, p. 45; Charles Merrill Mount, "An American Artist in London: Gilbert Stuart—I," *Country Life,* CXXXV, 20 Feb. 1964, p. 379; Mount 1964, pp. 57–58; Sidney C. Hutchison, *The History of the Royal Academy,* London, 1968, pp. 66, 84, 153, 194 and pl. 40; Edward Croft-Murray, "Decorative Paintings for Lord Burlington and the Royal Academy," *Apollo,* LXXXIX, 1969, pp. 16–19 and figs. 14–18; Croft-Murray 1970, pp. 68, 291, and pl. 128

The ceiling of the Council Chamber (or Assembly Room) of the second home of the Royal Academy in Somerset House was embellished with decorative paintings provided by West, Angelica Kauffmann and Biagio Rebecca. Sir William Chambers, Treasurer of the Royal Academy, was the architect of Somerset House and must have been responsible for the overall scheme. The paintings are no longer in Somerset House, but during the restoration of the Royal Academy's former premises there in the 1970s photographic reproductions were installed in their original places. West's five paintings were at the center of the ceiling, with Nos. 428–31 placed radially around No. 426. Around them, four roundels by Angelica Kauffmann represented *Design, Painting, Composition,* and *Genius;* and twelve monochrome medallions by Rebecca showed great artists of the past. The paintings by West and Angelica Kauffmann have been installed in the entrance hall of the present Royal Academy in Burlington House since 1899; those by Rebecca have disappeared.

In 1781 Joseph (or Giuseppe) Baretti, the Secretary for Foreign Correspondence of the Royal Academy, published a guide to the Academy's new premises in which he described the subjects of West's panels as follows:

The center Picture in this ceiling represents the *Graces unveiling Nature,* exhibited under the figure of the Ephesian Diana, meaning probably, that nothing but what is graceful in the stores of Nature, should be a subject for the Artist's pencil. The other four explain themselves sufficiently. They represent the four Elements (from which the imitative Arts collect the objects of their imitation) under the forms of female Figures attended by Genii with fire, water, earth, and air, exhibited in different forms and modifications.

Although later writers have followed Baretti in calling No. 426 the *Graces Unveiling Nature,* the activity is essentially the same as that in a painting by Rubens usually known as *Nature Adorned by the Graces* (Glasgow Art Gallery). The Rubens also shows a multi-breasted Nature based on the Diana of Ephesus and probably was the source of inspiration for the imagery in No. 426, although compositionally the works are completely dissimilar.

West's receipt made out to Chambers for £125, which he was paid for the five paintings, is dated 9 June 1780,[1] and thus gives an approximate indication of when the works were completed and installed. The Academy's first exhibition in Somerset House took place in 1780.

The original appearances of Nos. 426 and 428–31 may have been substantially affected by various restorations the paintings have undergone, the most recent having been in 1962–63. Nonetheless, although West was paid for the pictures, it is difficult to accept the actual execution as by him. In 1964 Charles Merrill Mount asserted that the panels "bear the inimitable mark" of Gilbert Stuart's brush. Both authors of the present catalogue agree. Stuart was in West's employ from 1777 to 1782, and he certainly seems to have pain-

Detail of the ceiling of the entrance hall of the Royal Academy, Burlington House, showing Nos. 426, 428, 429, 430 and 431

ted some works for which West took credit (see Nos. 260 and 332) as well as assisting with the drapery, etc., in others. Stuart exhibited three works under his own name at the Royal Academy in 1779 and two in 1781, but had nothing there in 1780, possibly because the pressure of completing the ceiling panels for the new premises allowed him no time to prepare anything of his own. West, on the other hand, exhibited nine works at the Academy in 1780 and was in the midst of the busiest period of his career, so his entrusting to an assistant the execution of a decorative commission that he probably did not consider entirely worthy of himself is understandable. The other two groups of decorative works discussed below (Nos. 432–34 and 435–39), as well as the decorative paintings in the chapel at Greenwich Hospital (see No. 397) were carried out either partly or completely by other hands.

An oil sketch for No. 426 is No. 427 below. A drawing formerly in the collection of Mrs. F. Howard contains a rough design for the placement of Nos. 428–31 around No. 426 and a sketch of what appears to be an alternative design for the center roundel (i.e., instead of that shown in No. 426).[2] Drawings in pen, ink, and gouache of all five compositions, which do not appear to be by West's hand, are in the Museum of Fine Arts, Boston. The one after (or for) No. 426 has the name *Cipriani* inscribed on the mount.

427

426

428

[1] In the Somerset House Accounts, now belonging to the Royal Institute of British Architects; published by Croft-Murray, *Apollo*, LXXXIX, 1969, pp. 18–19.

[2] Pencil and body-color, $20\frac{3}{4} \times 13$ in., on the reverse of a design probably intended for the ceiling of the Royal Chapel in Windsor Castle (sold Sotheby's, London, 22 March 1979, lot 29).

427 The Graces Unveiling Nature *c.* 1780

PRIVATE COLLECTION

Oil on canvas: circular, $10\frac{3}{4}$ in. (27.3 cm.) in diameter

Signed bottom center: *B—West*

PROV: Julius Weitzner, New York, by whom sold to the Nelson Gallery of Art, Kansas City in 1932; acquired by the present owner from the Nelson Gallery

Unlike No. 426, this small sketch is signed and does appear to have been painted by West. In the finished picture there are notable differences in the treatment of the figure of Nature and in the positions of the heads of one of the Graces and of one of the *putti* in the lower right.

It would seem reasonable to expect West to have painted similar sketches as the basis of the four other ceiling panels (Nos. 428–31), especially if he intended them to be carried out by another hand, but no such sketches have come to light.

428 Air *c.* 1780

ROYAL ACADEMY OF ARTS, LONDON

Oil on canvas: irregularly shaped, 43×73 in. (109×185.5 cm.)

PROV: As for No. 426

LIT: As for No. 426; in addition: Gerdts 1974, pp. 30–31, ill. 2–1

429

430

431

429 Earth *c.* 1780

ROYAL ACADEMY OF ARTS, LONDON

Oil on canvas: irregularly shaped, 43 × 73 in. (109 × 185.5 cm.)

PROV: As for No. 426

LIT: As for No. 426

430 Fire *c.* 1780

ROYAL ACADEMY OF ARTS, LONDON

Oil on canvas: irregularly shaped, 43 × 73 in. (109 × 185.5 cm.)

PROV: As for No. 426

LIT: As for No. 426

431 Water *c.* 1780

ROYAL ACADEMY OF ARTS, LONDON

Oil on canvas: irregularly shaped, 43 × 73 in. (109 × 185.5 cm.)

PROV: As for No. 426

LIT: As for No. 426

II Windsor Castle,
Marble Gallery: Nos. 432–34

432 Hymen Leading and Dancing with the Hours before Peace and Plenty 1789

LOCATION UNKNOWN; PROBABLY DESTROYED

(Watercolor: 96 × 120 in.) (244 × 305 cm.)

PROV: Painted, together with Nos. 433, 434, and a transparency, for £250 by West, one of his sons, and Biagio Rebecca in 1789 as decorations for the Marble Gallery in Windsor Castle (1797 account: 1789, "Myself and Son Aiding [?] and Assisting [?] Mr. Rebecca in painting the Transparency and water colour pictures for the Marble Gallery in Windsor Castle"—£250; 1801 account, p. 214: "Myself and son, with Mr. Rebecca, for painting transparent and water coloured pictures to adorn the marble gallery at a great evening entertainment in the Castle given by their Majesties to the nobility"—£250)

LISTED: *PC*, p. 560 ("The picture, in water colours, representing Hymen leading and dancing with the Hours before Peace and Plenty," . . . for the Marble Gallery in Windsor Castle, in his Majesty's possession at Windsor); *UM*, p. 527; Barlow, p. 431; *BA*, p. 13 (. . ., 3 ft. × 10); Galt, p. 217; Dillenberger, p. 141 (44)

LIT: *Gentleman's Magazine*, LIX, 1789, p. 564; von Erffa 1969, p. 21; Croft-Murray 1970, p. 292

Nos. 432, 433, and 434 were painted as adornments for festivities at Windsor in April and May 1789 celebrating George III's return to health following his attack of apparent insanity the previous autumn. A brief mention of the decorations in the *Gentleman's Magazine* appears in a description of a gala given by the Princess Royal on 1 May 1789, but without stating that they were done specifically for that entertainment, and it is possible that they were initially commissioned for some earlier event such as a concert described by Lady Duncannon in her diary on 5 April, which A. P. Oppé cited in relation to the details that West incorporated in preparatory drawing at Windsor for the *Recovery of His Majesty in the Year 1789* (No. 107).[1] What Nos. 432–34 may have looked like is a mystery apart from what we are told by their titles, and even that information is questionable. The name "Hymen," which appears in the title of No. 432 on all the early lists of West's works, may have been a slip for "Hygiea," the goddess of health and a more appropriate deity for the occasion. The dimensions listed for the three works in *La Belle Assemblée*, if reliable, indicate that they were so large that they would have presented storage problems once they were no longer wanted as decorations. Hence, they probably have long since been destroyed.

There is no space called the Marble Gallery in the present-day Windsor Castle, and no Marble Gallery appears in the extensive index in W. St. John Hope's *Windsor Castle: an Architectural History*. However, the *Gentleman's Magazine* situated West's and Rebecca's works in the Stone rather than Marble Gallery, and Hope does state that the Stone Gallery was the old name for what is now a wide vestibule on the ground floor on the north side of the former brick court.[2]

West's account of 1797 indicates that Biagio Rebecca rather than West himself had the main responsibility in a shared enterprise. Nevertheless, there may have

been a clearer division of labor, as the *Gentleman's Magazine* describes "paintings" by West on one side of the gallery, and "transparencies" by Rebecca on another, and the early lists of West's works, while listing three pictures in watercolor, mention no transparencies. Rebecca (1735–1808), who worked together with West on several occasions (see Nos. 397 and 426), went to Windsor at about this time to paint decorative borders in the state apartments.[3] Fanny Burney described a transparency done by Rebecca at Kew Palace on 10 March 1789, to celebrate George III's recovery: "The King—Providency—Health—and Britannia, were displayed with elegant devices."[4] West's son involved in the project was presumably Raphael West (1766–1850).

[1] Oppé 1950, p. 99 (641).
[2] Hope 1913, II, p. 557.
[3] Papendiek 1887, p. 233.
[4] Austin Dobson, ed., *Diary and Letters of Madame D'Arblay (1778–1840)*, London, 1905, IV, p. 269, cited in Croft-Murray 1970, p. 260 (16) with further references. West displayed a transparency before his house in Windsor to celebrate the King's return there on 14 March 1789.

433 Boys with the Insignia of Riches 1789

LOCATION UNKNOWN; PROBABLY DESTROYED

(Watercolor: 96 × 120 in.) (244 × 305 cm.)

PROV: As for No. 432

LISTED: *PC*, p. 560 ("The picture, in water colours, of Boys with the Insignia of Riches," . . . for the Marble Gallery in Windsor Castle, in his Majesty's possession at Windsor); *UM*, p. 527; Barlow, p. 431; *BA*, p. 13 (. . . 8 ft. × 10); Galt, p. 217; Dillenberger, p. 141 (45)

434 Boys and the Insignia of the Fine Arts 1789

LOCATION UNKNOWN; PROBABLY DESTROYED

(Watercolor: 96 × 120 in.) (244 × 305 cm.)

PROV: As for No. 432

LISTED: *PC*, p. 560 ("The Companion [of No. 433] with Boys, and the Insignia of the Fine Arts"); *UM*, p. 527; Barlow, p. 431; *BA*, p. 13 (. . . 8 ft. × 10); Galt, p. 217; Dillenberger, p. 141 (46)

III Windsor Castle,
Queen's Lodge: Nos. 435–39

435 Genius Calling Forth Arts and Sciences 1789
See color illustration, p. 93

M. H. DE YOUNG MEMORIAL MUSEUM, SAN FRANCISCO

Oil on canvas: oval, $19\frac{1}{2}$ × $24\frac{3}{4}$ in. (49.5 × 63 cm.)

Signed lower left: *B. West/1789*

PROV: Painted with four companion pictures (Nos. 436–39) and several drawings as designs for a ceiling in the Queen's Lodge in Windsor (1797 account: "1788, Nine designs for the Ceiling of the Queen's Lodge Windsor—for Mr. Haas to work from" £525; 1801 account, p. 214: "By His Majesty's commands I made nine designs for the ceiling in the Queen's Lodge, Windsor, for Mr. Haas to work the ceilings from. Viz. 1. Genius inspiring the fine arts to adorn the useful arts and sciences. 2. Agriculture. 3. Manufactures. 4. Commerce. 5. Botany. 6. Chemistry. 7. Celestial Science. 8. Terrestrial Science. and 9. To adorn Empire." £525); offered by West's sons to the United States in 1826 (132) and sold by them, Robins, London, 22–25 May 1829, lot 122 ("Genius Calling Forth the Fine Arts," 1 ft. $7\frac{1}{2}$ in. × 2 ft.), bt. by Hicks (? or Hick) for £29.8.0.; (?) John Hick, Mytton Hall, Whalley, Lancashire; sold by Frank Bulkeley Smith, American Art Association, New York, 22–23 April 1920, lot 44 ("Allegorical," $19\frac{1}{2}$ × $23\frac{3}{4}$ in., ill. in cat.); Scott and Fowles, New York, by 1921; Alfred Ramage; his niece, Mrs. Robert E. McConnell, Jr., Middleburg, Va.; sold Parke-Bernet, New York, 6 Dec. 1973, lot 131, bt. in; Vose Galleries, Boston, 1976; Hirschl & Adler Galleries, New York; given by Mr. and Mrs. John D. Rockefeller, Jr., to the De Young Museum in 1979

EXH: RA 1790 (110) "A sketch: Genius calling forth Arts and Sciences; part of a design in the Queen's Lodge, Windsor, intended to show the utility they are of to this, as a commercial nation"; Philadelphia 1921 (14) as "Apollo and the Muses," lent by Scott and Fowles; Brooklyn 1922 (14) "Apollo and the Muses," lent by Scott and Fowles

ENGR: Engraving (oval, $19\frac{3}{4}$ × $24\frac{5}{8}$ in.) by Francesco Bartolozzi, pub. by West, 1 Oct. 1789

LISTED: *PC*, p. 560 ("Designs, from which the Ceiling in the Queen's Lodge was done: Genius calling forth the Fine Arts to adorn Manufactures and Commerce, and recording the Names of eminent Men in those pursuits" . . .); *UM*, p. 527; *BA*, p. 13 (. . . 3 ft. × 4); Galt, p. 217; Dillenberger, p. 412 (48)

LIT: *Windsor Guide* 1792, pp. 98–99; Brayley and Britton 1801, p. 260; Farington Diary, 27 Nov. 1802 (Farington 1978–, VI, p. 2173); Robert Huish, *The Public and Private Life of George the Third*, London, 1821, pp. 539–40 (G. Hardinge, 1789); Papendiek 1887, pp. 235–36; C. E. Vulliamy, *Royal George*, New York, 1937, p. 252; von Erffa 1969, pp. 20–21, 33; Croft-Murray 1970, p. 292

The most complete account and description of the decorations in the Queen's Lodge at Windsor, for which Nos. 435–39 are the preparatory designs, appeared in a late eighteenth-century guide to Windsor:[1]

> In the beginning of the year 1789, a ceiling was affixed up in the Drawing-Room of the Queen's Lodge, by an artist of the name of Haas, of a peculiar and novel art, to which no name has yet been applied; but the figures are in imitation of, and have all the force and effect of the best oil painting; with this great advantage, that the various groups of figures may be distinctly seen at any point of view. Only one simple article is used by the artist, which is *stained marble dust*; this is strewed with a piece of card, either on board or canvas. The composition of, as well as the manner of using the cement, is known only to the artist himself, which, upon trial, has been proved to resist the various changes of the weather.
>
> The ceiling consists of several subjects. In the centre, in an oval, is genius reviving the arts; in the four corners, are agriculture, manufactory, commerce, and riches, depicted by emblematical figures in the different vocations, with the symbols of the several sciences. The intermediate compartments are in imitation of bas relief, and are representations of astronomy, navigation, electricity, geography, fortification, gunnery, chemistry, and botany. The whole is beautifully ornamented with festoons of oak leaves, interspersed with roses, lilies, and thistles; the arms of the royal family, etc. This is the first production of the artist, except some few portraits, in which he has been tolerably successful. The subjects of the ceiling, are from the designs of Benjamin West, Esq.

The memoirs of Mrs. Papendiek, an assistant keeper of Queen Charlotte's wardrobe, also include a discussion of the ceiling. She gives the date as 1790, places the ceiling in the card room rather than the drawing-room, gives the name of the artist as Hawes rather than Haas, and describes the subject as "the four quarters of the globe, with their different inhabitants and productions, with Britannia in the centre, calling them forth, as it were." This subject sounds like a somewhat confused conflation of the images in Nos. 435, 438, and 439, and Mrs. Papendiek's memoirs, which she wrote in the 1830s, are certainly less reliable than the contemporary or near-contemporary *Guide*, which purported to describe what was there at the time.

West evidently painted sketches in oil only for five of the compartments of the ceiling: the central oval one and those in the four corners as described in the *Windsor Guide*. He exhibited two of them (Nos. 435 and 436) at the Royal Academy in 1790, two more in 1791 (Nos. 437 and 438), and all five were included in the sale of pictures from his estate on 22–25 May 1829. The catalogue of the sale describes No. 439 rather than No. 435 as the design for the central compartment, but since that catalogue was written forty years after the ceiling was painted, nine years after West died, and six years after the Queen's Lodge was demolished, it also seems like a less authoritative source than the *Windsor Guide*. A description of the Queen's Lodge published in Brayley and Britton's *Beauties of England and Wales* in 1801 also situates No. 435 in the center of the ceiling, and No. 435 does appear first on all the early lists of West's designs for the ceiling.

The eight subjects in imitation of bas-relief in the intermediate compartments evidently all fit into four frieze-like horizontal compositions, for which West only provided drawings. One such drawing, signed and dated *Windsor 1788*, in the Victoria and Albert Museum shows *Astronomy* and *Navigation*,[2] and another drawing, also dated *1788 Windsor*, which is in a similar style, depicts *Botany* and probably constitutes part of the panel that *Botany* would have shared with *Chemistry*.[3] Together the five paintings and the four intermediate compartments make up the "nine designs" cited by West in his two accounts of his works for George III.[4] Additionally, four further drawings, made probably to fit around the curves of the oval central compartment, are known. These are all signed and dated *1788*, are inscribed *Queen's Lodge, Windsor*, and also bear inscriptions identifying their subjects as *Sculpture*, *Painting*, *Architecture*, and *Music*.[5] They presumably correspond to the festoons of oak leaves, etc., mentioned in the *Windsor Guide*, but they do not show the arms of the royal family.

Haas, who executed the ceiling panels, was one of a group of Germans working at Windsor in the late eighteenth century whose primary responsibility was to provide elaborate table decorations.[6] From the eighteenth-century practice of making patterns in colored sands for the center of tables, they developed techniques of fixing their designs, thus allowing them to be used as decorations for walls or ceilings. Although the *Windsor Guide* states that no name had yet been applied to the art, it did become known as "*marmortinto*." Mrs. Papendiek calls Haas a confectioner, and his technique, as she describes it, of pouring colored sands through small funnels, sounds like that a confectioner would use in decorating a cake. Unfortunately, the fruits of his labors have disappeared, since the Queen's Lodge, which was built between 1778 and 1782 by Sir William Chambers, was pulled down by George IV in 1823. The ceiling by West and Haas was the only feature of the building that the *Windsor Guide* deemed worth mentioning.

West gives the date of 1788 for his designs for the ceiling in his account of 1797 of his work for George III, and his drawings for the ceiling are dated *1787* and *1788*. Nonetheless, there must have been a time lag between West's preparation of the designs, and the installation of Haas's completed panels on the ceiling. The date of 1789 given in the *Windsor Guide* is confirmed by a Welsh visitor to Windsor in the spring of 1789 who reported seeing the ceiling and having the allegorical figures explained to him by the Princess Royal. This visit took place after the King returned to Windsor on 14 March, following his illness.

In 1803 Joseph Farington recorded a long narration by West describing Queen Charlotte's hostility toward him. It included the following account of what must have been the Queen's Lodge ceiling:

> During the King's illness a ceiling which the King had ordered was put up, and the Queen was informed of it. This had been done under West's direction. She ordered it to be taken down. The King on his recovery was removed to Windsor . . . Soon afterwards He required West to go through certain apartments with [him] & among them that for which He had ordered the Ceiling. Though taken down by the Queen's order it had been put up again in consequence of the King having spoken about it after His recovery. On looking at it now, He observed a *crack* in it, & asked How that came. The person who put it up said that it was in consequence of it having been taken down. The King asked who ordered it to be taken down. The Man paused: no answer was made.—The King asked if the Queen had ordered it to be taken down: Silence implied the affirmation: The King said no more.—West has continued to feel coldness on the part of Her Majesty.

Two of West's known paintings for the ceiling (Nos. 435 and 436) are signed and dated *1789*, while No. 437 is dated *1791*, suggesting that he continued to work on them in preparation for exhibiting them at the Royal Academy after Haas had made his copies.

The measurements of 3 × 4 ft. (or 36 × 48 in.) listed for the designs in *La Belle Assemblée* clearly do not fit Nos. 435–38, but may correspond to the sizes of the actual decorations by Haas.

The title which West employed for No. 435 in the Royal Academy catalogue of 1790, "Genius calling forth Arts and Sciences, part of a design in the Queen's Lodge, Windsor, intended to show the utility they are of to this, as a commercial nation," was probably intended in part to explain the program of the ceiling as a whole. The commercial orientation of the allegorical message echoes aspects of James Barry's series of monumental paintings done between 1777 and 1783 for the Society of Arts, Manufactures, and Commerce,[7] and the position of Genius at the center of West's cycle of paintings parallels that of Orpheus, the artist and giver of civilization, as the single most prominent figure in Barry's. The title for No. 435 in the early lists of West's works, "Genius calling forth the Fine Arts to adorn Manufactures and Commerce, and recording the Names of eminent Men in those pursuits," seems somewhat misleading since no active recording of names is visible in No. 435, but it also suggests some inspiration from Barry's great work, in which the celebration of eminent men constitutes an important feature.

Apart from the presiding Genius, the most prominent figures in No. 435 are three female figures in the lower right representing Painting, Architecture, and Sculpture. The figure of Sculpture leans on a relief bust of George III. Three smaller figures making music are visible through the opening above Painting and below Genius's left arm. A globe, a sextant, and (?) a compass in the left background evoke Navigation and perhaps Geography, while the large telescope and the sphere held by a female figure in the right background belong to Astronomy. Much of this imagery also appears in the drawing of *Astronomy* and *Navigation* mentioned above. The telescope in No. 435 is aimed at a device in the sky in the upper left consisting of an H with a disk attached to it. This is the traditional symbol for the planet Uranus, which had been discovered by Sir William Herschel (1738–1822) in 1781.[8] Two smaller spheres or disks accompanying it may represent the satellites that Herschel had discovered for the planet. The same device also appears in slightly different form and accompanied by seven smaller spheres in a drawing signed and dated *Windsor 1788* in which the main motif is a rearing horse.[9] That drawing has no further relation to No. 435 and may have been intended for a work commemorating Herschel's observations, which were generously and enthusiastically supported by George III. The names of Herschel and Newton are inscribed on the drawing of *Astronomy* and *Navigation* intended for one of the side compartments of the ceiling.

A drawing showing the composition of No. 435 in somewhat simpler form is signed and dated *1787*.[10] It includes the four main figures and the personification of Music at the center, but excludes most of the background details. On the right, a male figure looks through a telescope by holding it up to his eye.

1 *Windsor Guide*, Windsor, 1792, pp. 98–99 (and reprinted in numerous later editions). We are indebted to Annette Blaugrund, who wrote a report on the Queen's Lodge ceiling at Columbia University in 1980, for bringing the relevant passage to our attention and for much additional assistance with entries 435–39.

2 Sepia ink and blue wash, $5\frac{7}{8} \times 31\frac{1}{4}$ in., signed lower left: *B. West/Windsor 1788*.

3 Pen and wash, $14 \times 18\frac{1}{2}$ in., signed lower right: *B. West 1788/Windsor* (Courtauld Institute Galleries, London). This is probably the drawing of "Botany" sold by Mrs. Albert F. West, Christie's, London, 18 March 1898, lot 108, bt. by Fairfax Murray.

4 The actual list of subjects in West's account of 1801 (see above under PROV.) does not agree entirely with the description from the *Windsor Guide*, and the other early lists of his works provide yet another set of titles, which do not agree with the others. In addition to the titles recorded in the entries for Nos. 435–39, the early lists include the following: "Peace and Riches cherishing the Fine Arts"; "Printing aided by the Fine Arts"; "Astronomy making new Discoveries in the Heavens"; and "Civil and Military Architecture defending and adorning Empire" (*PC*, p. 560; *UM*, p. 527; *BA*, pp. 13–14; Galt, p. 218; Dillenberger, pp. 142–43 [50–56]). Since these lists and the accounts for George III were drawn up long after the works were done,

they seem less likely to be reliable than the description in the *Windsor Guide*, although they may have been provided by West himself.

[5] All in pen and ink, approx. $12\frac{1}{4} \times 15\frac{3}{4}$ in. *Sculpture* and *Painting* were sold by Mrs. F. Howard, Sotheby's, London, 22 March 1979, lot 30; *Architecture* and *Music* are in the Delaware Art Museum, Wilmington. *Music* is illustrated in von Erffa 1969, p. 33.

[6] Sylvia Groves, "The Art of Sand Painting," *Country Life*, CIX, 9 March 1951, pp. 696–97.

[7] For which, see Pressly 1981, pp. 86–122.

[8] Information kindly supplied by Professor Owen Gingerich, Smithsonian Astrophysical Observatory, in letters to Helmut von Erffa, 14 Aug. and 1 Sept. 1973.

[9] Pencil, pen and brown ink, blue and brown washes, $10\frac{1}{2} \times 8\frac{3}{4}$ in. Sold by Mrs. F. Howard, Sotheby's, London, 22 March 1979, lot 31.

[10] Black chalk and wash, $13\frac{3}{4} \times 18\frac{1}{2}$ in. (Cincinnati Art Museum), possibly the "Genius calling forth the Fine Arts," outline in pen and ink, and washed a peculiar brown, sold by West's son, S. Leigh Sotheby, London, 1 June 1839, lot 41.

436 Agriculture (Husbandry Aided by Arts and Commerce) 1789

MINT MUSEUM OF ART, CHARLOTTE, NORTH CAROLINA

Oil on paper, mounted on panel: oval, 20×24 in. (51×61 cm.)

Signed bottom center: *B. West 1789*

PROV: As for No. 435 until 1829; offered by West's sons to the United States in 1826 (134) and sold by them, Robins, London, 22–25 May 1829, lot 121 ("Husbandry Aided by Arts and Commerce," 1 ft. $7\frac{1}{2}$ in. × 2 ft.), bt. by Bone for £27.6.0. on behalf of Joseph Neeld, MP, Grittleton House, Wilts.; by descent in the Neeld family until sold, Christie's, London, 13 July 1945, lot 173; Spink and Son, London; sold by Colin Cooper, Sotheby's, London, 17 March 1971, lot 17; purchased by the Mint Museum in 1972

EXH: RA 1790 (117) "A sketch. agriculture, part of a design in the Queen's Lodge, Windsor"

ENGR: Engraving (oval, $19\frac{5}{8} \times 24\frac{5}{8}$ in.) by Francesco Bartolozzi, pub. by West, 11 May 1790

LISTED: *PC*, p. 560 ("Designs, from which the Ceiling in the Queen's Lodge was done . . . Husbandry aided by Arts and Commerce"); *UM*, p. 527; *BA*, p. 13; Galt, p. 217; Dillenberger, p. 142 (49)

LIT: As for No. 435; in addition, "New Acquisition," *Mint Museum of Art Newsletter*, VII, no. 1, Jan 1973

As noted in the Robins sale catalogue of May 1829, No. 436 not only shows a genre subject as part of the allegorical program of the Queen's Lodge ceiling, but also depicts the Ages of Man.

A drawing dated *1787*, which shows essentially the same composition, but which is round rather than oval and with many differences in detail, is at Hampton Court.[1]

[1] Black chalk, $16\frac{3}{4}$ in. in diameter; signed lower left: *B. West 1787*.

437 British Manufactory (Manufactory Giving Support to Industry) (Etruria) *c.* 1789–91

CLEVELAND MUSEUM OF ART

Oil on paper, mounted on panel: oval, $20\frac{1}{8} \times 25\frac{1}{2}$ in. (51×65 cm.)

Signed bottom center: *B. West 1791*

PROV: As for No. 435 until 1829; offered by West's sons

436

437

British Commerce, drawing for No. 438. Museum Nacional de Arte Antigua, Lisbon

to the United States in 1826 (133) and sold by them, Robins, London, 22–25 May 1829, lot 120 ("Manufactory Giving Support to Industry," 1 ft. 7½ in. × 2 ft.), bt. by E. Armstrong for £15.15.0.; Mrs. S. J. Tuttle, Boston, in 1878; William MacBeth, New York, from whom purchased in July 1919 for the John Huntington Collection, Cleveland Museum

EXH: RA 1791 (167) "British manufactory; a sketch"; Allentown 1962 (97 as "Etruria"); *Neo-Classicism: Style and Motif*, Cleveland Museum of Art, 1964 (77 as "Etruria"); *The Age of Neo-Classicism*, Council of Europe and Arts Council of Great Britain, Royal Academy, London, 1972 (272 as "Etruria")

LISTED: *PC*, p. 560 ("Designs, from which the Ceiling in the Queen's Lodge was done . . . Manufactory giving Support to Industry in Boys and Girls"); *UM*, p. 527; *BA*, p. 14; Galt, p. 218; Dillenberger, p. 142 (51)

LIT: As for No. 435; in addition: Gardner Teall, "Benjamin West's *Etruria*," *International Studio* LXXXIX, Jan. 1928, pp. 45–46; Jean Gorely, "Josiah Wedgwood and the Museum in the 18th-century World," *American Collector*, XVII, June 1948, p. 15, fig. 8

This painting has been frequently exhibited and published under the title "Etruria"; nevertheless, the description of lot 120 in the Robins sale catalogue of 22–25 May 1829 establishes that it was sold there under the title "Manufactory Giving Support to Industry." Hence it can be identified as the "Manufactory" of the *Windsor Guide*, the "Manufactures" listed among the designs for the Queen's Lodge in West's account of 1801 for George III (see No. 435 under PROV.), and the "British manufactory; a sketch," which West exhibited at the Royal Academy in 1791. The manufactures displayed include spinning in the left background, a loom in the right, and vase painting in the foreground.

The title "Etruria" was evidently applied to No. 437 at some time because the foreground scene recalls and probably was inspired by the manufacturing activity of Josiah Wedgwood at Etruria in Staffordshire. One

of the boys seated in the immediate foreground holds a vase which appears to be the celebrated *Portland Vase* in the British Museum, but more likely represents one of Wedgwood's copies in black jasper-ware. The *Portland Vase* had been brought to England and sold to the Dowager Duchess of Portland by Sir William Hamilton in 1784. Her son, the third Duke of Portland, lent it in 1786 to Josiah Wedgwood, who after extended effort produced a satisfactory copy only in October 1789; he first exhibited it in his London showrooms in the following year. That is later than the installation of West's and Haas's ceiling in the Queen's Lodge, but since No. 437 is dated 1791 West evidently continued to work on it prior to exhibiting it in that year, and he could easily have added or altered the details of the vase. The sources (if any) of the details on the vase standing in the foreground and that on which the woman is painting are yet to be identified. Similar dancing figures appear in the background of *A Bacchante* (No. 123) of 1797.

438 British Commerce (The Four Quarters of the Globe Bringing Treasures to Britannia) *c.* 1787–91

LOCATION UNKNOWN

(19½ × 24 in.) (49.5 × 61 cm.)

PROV: As for No. 435 until 1829; offered by West's sons to the United States in 1826 (135) and sold by them, Robins, London, 22–25 May 1829, lot 123 ("The Four Quarters of the Globe Bringing Treasures to Britannia," 1 ft. 7½ in. × 2 ft.), bt. by Hicks (? or Hick) for £22.11.0.; (?) John Hick, Mytton Hall, Whalley, Lancashire

EXH: RA 1791 (189) "British Commerce; a sketch."

LISTED: *PC*, p. 560 ("Designs, from which the Ceiling in the Queen's Lodge was done . . . The Four Quarters of the World bringing Treasures to the Lap of Britannia"); *UM*, p. 527; *BA*, p. 14; Galt, p. 218; Dillenberger, p. 142 (55)

LIT: As for No. 435

Although the actual appearance of No. 438 is unknown, the Robins sale catalogue of 22–25 May 1829 described it as showing personifications of the four quarters of the globe. A drawing in Lisbon (*left*), dated *1787*, which shows personifications of the four continents before Britannia probably represents an early stage of the composition.[1] Unlike preparatory drawings for Nos. 436 and 439, which are round, and unlike the paintings themselves, which are oval, the drawing in Lisbon is rectangular, suggesting that West probably drew it before the program for the Queen's Lodge ceiling was very far advanced. It shows Europe leading Asia, Africa, and, at a little distance, America on the left; an enthroned Britannia with crown and sceptre and accompanied by her lion on the right; and between them, Mercury, the god of merchants, in a pose reminiscent of the well-known statue by Jean-Baptiste Pigalle (Musée du Louvre). Below Mercury, *putti* pour out a cornucopia of the world's treasures. The title "The Four Quarters of the Globe Bringing Treasures to Britannia" does not appear in the *Windsor Guide*'s description of the Queen's Lodge ceiling, but the central figure of Mercury in the drawing suggests that No. 438 should be identified as the design for the compartment described by the *Guide* as depicting "Commerce," a title which also appears in West's account of 1801 for George III (see No. 435). No. 438 would also then be the "British Commerce," which West exhibited at the Royal Academy in 1791.

[1] Pen and sepia and blue washes, 6⅞ × 9½ in., signed lower left: *B. West 1787* (Museu Nacional de Arte Antigua, Lisbon); see Edgar Breitenbach, "Two Drawings by Benjamin West," *Master Drawings*, XV, 1977, pp. 401–3, pl. 48.

439 Riches (Marine and Inland Navigation Enriching Britannia) *c.* 1788–89

WELLESLEY COLLEGE MUSEUM, WELLESLEY, MASSACHUSETTS

Oil on paper mounted on panel: 19 × 21¼ in. (48.5 × 54 cm.)

PROV: As for No. 435 until 1829; offered by West's sons to the United States in 1826 (136) and sold by them, Robins, London, 22–25 May 1829, lot 119 ("Marine and Inland Navigation Enriching Britannia," 1 ft. 7½ in. × 2 ft.); Robert Frank, London, 1952; Hirschl & Adler Galleries, New York, 1962

EXH: *Selections from the Collection II*, Hirschl & Adler Galleries, New York, (?) 1960 (29)

LISTED: *PC*, p. 560 ("Designs, from which the Ceiling in the Queen's Lodge was done . . . Marine and Inland Navigation enriching Britannia"); *UM*, p. 527; *BA*, p. 14; Galt, p. 218; Dillenberger, p. 142 (52)

LIT: As for No. 435

No. 439 bears an inscription on the back: *Sir Benjamin West, P.R.A. "Marine and Inland Navigation Sketch for Command Picture of one of Royal Palaces,"* and it clearly seems to be the "Marine and Inland Navigation" included in the early lists of West's works and sold by his sons in 1829. By process of elimination, it can also be equated with the design for "Riches," described in the *Windsor Guide* as the subject of one of the four corner compartments of the Queen's Lodge ceiling. For Nos. 435–38 the subjects mentioned in the *Windsor Guide* are either the same or correspond directly with titles used by West in 1801 for his account of the works he had painted for George III, but that is not the case with "Riches," for which there is no equivalent title in the account (see No. 435 under PROV.). No. 439 was the only one of the five painted designs for the ceiling which West did not exhibit at the Royal Academy in 1790 or 1791, and it is possible that by 1801 he had forgotten about it.

No. 439 is unfinished and was described as such in the Robins catalogue of May 1829. Its dimensions are slightly different from those of the other known designs (Nos. 435–37) and from the dimensions listed for it in the Robins catalogue. A hypothetical explanation for

the difference from the other designs is that West may have intended No. 439 to serve as the design for the central compartment of the ceiling, as the Robins catalogue states that he did. Although, according to the *Windsor Guide*, No. 435 rather than No. 439 provided the design that was actually used at the center of the ceiling, the enthroned central figure of Britannia flanked by symmetrically balanced figures and the rounder shape of the design do suggest that thematically and compositionally No. 439 would have pro-

vided a more imposing central focus for the ceiling as a whole. West himself, however, must not have been entirely satisfied with the painting since he neither completed nor exhibited it.

A drawing of the composition dated *1788* is round, like that for No. 436 discussed above, but unlike that drawing, it does not show any significant differences in detail from the painting.[1]

[1]Pen; signed lower right *B. West 1788/Windsor* (collection of H. H. Margary).

439

GENRE SUBJECTS

440 An Assembly (La Belle Assemblée) 1806

D. B. ROBB

Oil on canvas: 16 × 12 in. (40.5 × 30.5 cm.)

Signed lower left: *B. West 1806*

PROV: (?) Painted for John Bell (1745–1831); George Henry Boughton, RA (1833–1905); then by descent to the present owner

No. 440 has a torn but partly legible letter affixed to the back:

Newman Street Octr 8th 1806

Dear Sir,

I felt myself much mortified when you and Mr Bell did me the favour of a call on Sunday last, that it was not in my power to see you at that time—as I wished to have shown you my design for La Belle Assemblee. This composition has given me more trouble to prepare than [. . .] Regulus, Wolfe and Nelson did—for I [. . .] to [. . .] out of nothing, that is, to give to the fash[. . .]ble and [. . .] part of community something (?) to do—[. . .] to the [. . .] which it is to be of it [. . .] effected at last, and if Mr. Bell, and [. . .] with a call on Sunday next, you [. . .] to judge [. . .] truth.

My respects to Mr. Bell [. . .] assured that I am with friendship

Yours with [. . .]
[. . .] njⁿ West

The tone of this letter suggests that the unidentified recipient was the secretary or agent of Mr. Bell, and that West prepared the "design for La Belle Assemblee" for the latter. Although No. 440 is an oil painting, rather than a drawing, it is presumably either the design referred to in the letter or is based upon it. It does show the fashionable part of the community, presided over by a statue of the three Graces, and, on the left by a painting of Diana, goddess of chastity, and her attendants.

Mr. Bell was John Bell, the proprietor of *La Belle Assemblée or Bell's Court and Fashionable Magazine*, a periodical which he had started in February of 1806. The June issue of *La Belle Assemblée* contained the following announcement:

In the Supplemental Number, to be published with the Sixth Number, on the first of August next, will be given a Frontispiece, characteristic of the Work, and a suitable appendage to the Volume—The most Eminent Artist of the modern age, the man to whom the British School is chiefly indebted for the present renown and lustre of its character, has presented the Proprietors of this Work with a Design for the Frontispiece, which will be engraven in a stile of excellence correspondent with its merits.

West almost certainly was the "most Eminent Artist" referred to in the announcement, and No. 440 most probably was the design for the frontispiece. However, no supplement appeared accompanying the sixth number of *La Belle Assemblée*, or indeed until the following January, and no engraving after No. 440 ever appeared. The reason was presumably West's failure to produce his design on time. Despite the promise in the June issue, accompanied by the statement that a design had been presented, the letter attached to the back of No. 440 indicates that West only had something ready to show to Bell long after the announced date

440

of publication. Engravings after the *Death of General Wolfe* and the oil sketch of *Death on the Pale Horse* (Nos. 93 and 403) did appear in *La Belle Assemblée* in 1808, as did also a biography of the artist and a catalogue of his works.[1]

[1] The biography of West appeared in five parts, running from January to May 1808, in vol. IV, and the catalogue was published in a supplemental number accompanying the June issue. An engraving published by Bell, on 1 August 1807, after No. 337, West's sketch for the large *Christ Healing the Sick*, is approximately the same size as the two that appeared in *La Belle Assemblée* and may have been intended for the magazine as well.

441 Beggar Woman and Child

ANTHONY BURTON CAPEL PHILIPS

Oil on canvas: 18 × 13¼ in. (45.5 × 33.5 cm.)

PROV: Sold by West's sons, Robins, London, 22–25 May 1829, lot 14 ("Beggar Woman and Child," 1 ft. 6 in. × 1 ft. 2½ in.) bt by Phillips (? Philips) for £13.13.0.; by family descent to the present owner

EXH: West's Gallery, 1822–28 (70) "Beggar Woman and Child"; Liverpool 1976 (72)

(?) LISTED: *PC*, p. 566 ("Sketch of a Mother and her

Child on her lap," West, Gallery); *UM*, p. 531; *BA*, p. 18; Galt, p. 230; Dillenberger, p. 178 (394)

The discussion of No. 441 in the Robins sale catalogue of May 1829 begins with the words, "Studies painted from the life," and implies that No. 441 is one of several such studies made by the artist for his own pleasure. However, No. 441 is virtually the only work of its kind by West now known, although a few others such as No. 442, which evidently showed comparable subjects, are recorded.

442 Children Eating Cherries *c*. 1801

LOCATION UNKNOWN

(7 × 9 in.) (18 × 23 cm.)

441

PROV: Offered by West's sons to the United States in 1826 (89) and sold by them, Robins, London, 22–25 May 1829, lot 50 ("Children Eating Cherries," 7 × 9 in.), bt. by E. (or C.) Morgan for £45.3.0.

EXH: RA 1801 (136) "Children eating cherries"; West's Gallery 1822–28 (60)

LISTED: *PC*, p. 567 ("Children eating Cherries"); *UM*, p. 531; Barlow, p. 435; *BA*, p. 18; Galt, p. 230; Dillenberger, p. 178 (393)

The Robins catalogue of 22–25 May 1829, described this tiny work as showing a simple group of cottage children. A copy after No. 442, evidently by another hand, appeared among the "Coloured Drawings" as lot 11 in the secondary sale of works from West's estate on 20–22 June 1829.

The initial of the purchaser of No. 442 in 1829 is given as "C" in one marked catalogue and "E" in another. If the former is correct, he was probably the Charles Morgan of Caeforgan, Glamorganshire, who purchased several other works by West at the same sale (i.e., Nos. 104 and 107).

443 A Drayman Drinking 1796

See color illustration, p. 114

DR. AND MRS. HENRY C. LANDON III

Oil on canvas: 15½ × 21 in. (39.5 × 53.5 cm.)

Signed lower left: *B. West/1796*

PROV: Offered by West's sons to the United States in 1826 (102) and sold by them, Robins, London, 22–25 May 1829, lot 83 ("Characters in the Streets of London," 1 ft. 3 in. × 1 ft. 8½ in.), bt. by Ward for £52.10.0.; William James Ward (1800–1840) in 1833; Hirschl & Adler Galleries, New York, 1971; Mann Galleries, Miami, 1973; Craig and Tarlton, Raleigh, North Carolina, from whom purchased by the present owner in 1973

EXH: RA 1797 (98) "A drayman drinking"; West's Gallery 1822–28 (93) "Characters in the Streets of London"; BI 1833 (1) "Labourers resting: a Scene in the neighborhood of London," lent by W. J. Ward

LISTED: *PC*, p. 566 ("The Brewer's Porter and Hod-carrier," West, Gallery); *UM*, p. 531; Barlow, p. 435; *BA*, p. 18 ("The Brewer's Porter and Hod carrier drinking porter at the door of an Ale-house"); Galt, p. 230; Dillenberger, p. 176 (376)

LIT: Farington Diary, 21 May 1797 (Farington 1978—, III, p. 842); *True Briton*, 25 May 1797; Herman Warner Williams, Jr., *Mirror to the American Past: A Survey of American Genre Painting: 1750–1900*, Greenwich, Conn., 1973, pp. 28–29, fig. 9 and color pl. I (as "The Old George Inn")

No. 443 includes a view of the dome of St. Paul's in the background, as does also West's portrait of Kosciuszko of 1797 (No. 650), but it is questionable that the painting depicts a specific site. The *George III* inscribed on a sign in the upper right is presumably the name of the ale house to which it is attached, rather than of a street. The owner or licensee of the establishment, whose name appears over the door is J. Thorogood. The other signs consist of an advertisement for Whitbread's Entire[1] and recruiting posters for the army and navy.

On 21 May 1797, West told Joseph Farington that he could have sold No. 443, "his little picture of the Dray Horse," which was then on view at the Royal Academy, but that he would not sell any of his small pictures. Instead, he intended to make a collection of such works to sell together, "to make an independence for others." No. 443 was evidently not the first work in this proposed collection, but followed several other small genre paintings (Nos. 444, 447, 451, and 453) which West had exhibited in the previous few years. He retained virtually all of them until his death.

The title "Characters in the Streets of London," under which West's sons sold the painting in 1829, is also inscribed on the back of a drawing dated *1799* showing a group of figures outside a pub (Yale Center for British Art). This drawing, although showing a similar subject, has no compositional resemblance to No. 443, and the inscription on the back was not written by West himself but probably by his son Benjamin West, Jr., when he sold the drawing in 1839.[2] A much sketchier drawing in the British Museum, showing a horseman on the right and, on the left, a man wearing

The Flower Girls, stipple engraving by R. Hunt after No. 444

an apron and holding a tankard, in a pose similar to that of the hod-carrier in No. 443, may represent an early idea for the painting, but is also quite different from the finished work.[3]

A review of the Royal Academy exhibition of 1797 in the *True Briton* questioned whether the subject of No. 443 was suitable to the pencil of the Academy's President, decided the picture was not unworthy of his hand, suggested that West's representation of life did have some moral purpose in view, and concluded that he indulged himself "in a familiar incident" as a form of relaxation. Although this criticism may fairly represent public response to works such as No. 443, as a descent from West's usual high-minded subjects to

indulge in a type of low-life scene normally associated with an artist such as George Morland, nevertheless the painting does embody a moral message, which is distinctly reminiscent of and probably inspired by Hogarth's engraving of *Beer Street*. In the words of the sale catalogue of 1829, the beer drinking in "this truly English scene" (painted at a time when England was at war with France) is being done by "specimens of a class of beings, useful, honest, hardy, and happy, regaling at an ale-house door; looking independent, saucy, and free from care, as the venerated monarch, who patronised the philosophic painter, delighted to boast his 'honest common people.'" In addition to the idealization of the subject, the conspicuous use of signs,

the scaffolding on the left, and the woman with a basket on her head on the right also recall Hogarth's print.

See also p. 113 above.

[1]"Entire" was the name of a new dark brew introduced in 1722 which became so popular with London porters that it became known as "Porter." The firm of Whitbread, founded in 1742, was the largest English brewer in the 1790s. See H. A. Monckton, *A History of the English Public House*, London, 1969, and Peter Mathias, *The Brewing Industry in England 1700–1830*, Cambridge, 1959.
[2]Pen and wash, 9 × 13 in. signed lower left *B. West 1799*. Sold by Benjamin West, Jr., S. Leigh Sotheby, London, 1 June 1839, lot 29, "Characters in the Streets of London," pen and bistre, washed with the same.
[3]Black ink, $6\frac{1}{2} \times 5\frac{1}{2}$ in. (1920–6–15–27)

444 A Flower Girl and Child *c.* 1793

LOCATION UNKNOWN

(15 × 11 in.) (38 × 28 cm.)

PROV: Sold by West's sons, Robins, London, 22–25 May 1829, lot 179 ("A Flower Girl and Child," 15 × 11 in.), bt. by Penny for £21; (?) sold by John Allnut (1773–1863), Christie's, London, 20 June 1863, lot 432 ("A Woman and child-small")

EXH: (?) RA 1793 (138) "A woman selling rosemary"

ENGR: Stipple engraving ($16\frac{1}{2} \times 11\frac{1}{2}$ in.) by R. Hunt as "The Flower Girls" (*left*)

This lost work, if correctly identified as the "Woman Selling Rosemary" exhibited by West in 1793, was evidently the earliest of the group of small pictures which West discussed with Joseph Farington in 1797 (see No. 443). The first six of Francis Wheatley's paintings of the *Cries of London* had appeared at the Royal Academy in 1792 and may well have inspired West to try his hand at this type of subject.[1]

No. 444 appeared in the main sale of paintings from West's estate, 22–25 May 1829. A copy followed in the lesser sale a month later,[2] and a drawing of the subject was sold by the artist's younger son in 1839.[3]

[1]Wheatley exhibited six more *Cries* in 1793 and a final two in 1795. The Royal Academy catalogues did not identify the specific subjects, but a flower seller was the subject of the first engraving to be published in the series of prints of *The Cries of London*, on 2 July 1793, and, hence, the painting on which it was based presumably part of the group exhibited in 1792. See Mary Webster, *Francis Wheatley*, London, 1970, pp. 81–85 and 173–74.
[2]Robins, London, 20–22 June 1829, lot 59 ("Flower Girl and Child," after West).
[3]S. Leigh Sotheby, London, 1 June 1839, lot 60 ("A Flower Girl and Child," outline, in bistre, washed with the same).

445 Fly Fishing, Evening 1809

LOCATION UNKNOWN

PROV: Sold by West's sons, Robins, London, 20–22 June 1829, lot 72 ("Fly fishing, Evening, in which are introduced portraits of the artist and Sir Anthony Carlisle")

LIT: Farington Diary, 2 Aug. 1809 (Farington 1978—, x, p. 3520); Alberts 1978, p. 344

No. 445 is one of the three recorded paintings of fishing subjects by West. The others are Nos. 446 below and 468, a landscape which incorporates a group of anglers in the foreground. A drawing in the Huntington Library, which has been ascribed to West, also shows a fishing scene.[1]

West evidently painted No. 445 in 1809, and may never have carried it beyond a sketch. Sir Thomas Lawrence described it to Joseph Farington on 2 August 1809:

He told me West has been on a fishing party with Carlisle & others, in the neighborhood of Carshalton.—While there [he said] He shd. make a sketch of the party thus amusing themselves. He did so, but Carlisle sd. in it He made Himself the principal figure, & only introduced them as looking towards Him.

Carshalton is in Surrey, just south of London, approximately ten miles from Charing Cross. Sir Anthony Carlisle (1768–1840) was an eminent surgeon and Professor of Anatomy at the Royal Academy from 1808 until 1824.

 Pen and brown ink, with wash, $13\frac{5}{16} \times 10\frac{15}{16}$ in.; see Kraemer 1975, p. 80 (197).

446 Gentlemen Fishing 1794

LOCATION UNKNOWN

Oil on slate: $11\frac{3}{8} \times 16\frac{1}{4}$ in. (29 × 41.5 cm.)
Signed lower left: *B. West/1794*

PROV: Offered by West's sons to the United States in 1826 (115, "A Fishing Party," 1 ft. × 1 ft. 4 in.), and sold by them, Robins, London, 22–25 May 1829, lot 175 ("Fishing Party," 1 ft. 6 in. × 2 ft. 1 in.), bt. by Smith for £31.10.0.; sold by Arthur N. Gilbey,

Christie's, London, 25 April 1940, lot 136 ("Gentlemen Fishing from a Punt," slate, $11\frac{3}{8} \times 16\frac{1}{4}$ in.), bt. by Nicolson

EXH: RA 1795 (69) "Gentlemen Fishing"; West's Gallery 1828 (114) "Sir Hugh Palliser Fishing" (not in printed catalogue, but added by hand in place of "Mr. West's Garden" [No. 465])

LISTED: PC, p. 566 ("Gentlemen Fishing in the Water at Dagenham Breach," West, Gallery); UM, p. 531; BA, p. 18; Galt, p. 229; Dillenberger, p. 175 (369)

LIT: V and A Cuttings, III, p. 716 (1795)

This painting on slate, which was photographed at the time of its sale in 1940, but which has since disappeared, corresponds in size with the "Fishing Party" offered by West's sons to the United States in 1826. Since it is signed and dated *1794* there can be little doubt that it is also identical with the *Gentlemen Fishing* exhibited by West at the Royal Academy in 1795, which was described by a contemporary reviewer as showing more talent in a few square inches "than is to be found in as many acres of his painted statues!" What is puzzling is the discrepancy in the measurements given in the sale catalogue of 1829. Since the works offered by West's sons to the United States in 1826 invariably reappeared in the main estate sale three years later, the larger size in the later publication should probably be explained as an error on the part of the cataloguer rather than

as an indication that another and otherwise unknown work was sold under the same title.

The entry in the catalogue of 1829 includes the following description:

This scene represents a still water near Daggenham Reach, a famed site for the rod, with a party collected for a day's sport, by the late Sir Hugh Palliser, Governor of Greenwich Hospital. The artist, who was an intimate friend of the Admiral, and like himself, skilled in the rod, used to recreate in the summer season at his apartments, and meet some of the renowned anglers of the last century. On one of those visits the sketch for this picture was made, in which is introduced the portrait of the governor and the painter, with others whose identity now elude research.

Sir Hugh Palliser (1723–1796) was appointed governor of Greenwich Hospital in 1780. West may have known him because of his work in the chapel of Greenwich Hospital in the 1780s (see No. 397). Their fishing site, Dagenham Breach (as in *Public Characters*, not "Reach" as in the Robins catalogue), was a lake formed in 1707 by a breach in the river-wall on the north side of the Thames, fifteen miles downstream from London Bridge and some eight or nine from Greenwich. The shipping visible in the background of No. 446 would have been on the Thames proper.

For other pictures painted on slate see Nos. 453 and 470.

446

448

447 Harvest Home c. 1795

LOCATION UNKNOWN

EXH: RA 1795 (80) "Harvest home"

LISTED: *PC*, p. 566 ("Harvest Home," West, Gallery); *UM*, p. 530; Barlow, p. 435; *BA*, p. 18; Galt, p. 229; Dillenberger, p. 175 (360)

LIT: von Erffa 1952, pp. 163–64; Kraemer 1975, p. 35

See No. 453.

448 The Milk-woman in St. James's Park c. 1801

SIMON HOUFE

Oil on panel: 39 × 56½ in. (99 × 143.5 cm.)

PROV: Sold by West's sons, Robins, London, 20–22 June 1829, lot 86 ("St. James Park with a view of Westminster Abbey, scene, morning; a highly interesting topographical picture represented with great local fidelity ... not quite finished"); sold anonymously, Christie's, London, 20 Jan. 1928, lot 158 (as "St. James's Park," 1815); Albert E. Richardson, PRA, Ampthill, by whom bequeathed to the present owner

LISTED: *PC*, p. 566 ("The Milk-woman in St. James's

Park," West, Gallery); *UM*, p. 530; Barlow, p. 435; *BA*, p. 17 ("The Milk-woman in St. James's Park, with Children receiving milk from the cow"); Galt, p. 229; Dillenberger, p. 174 (351)

LIT: Leigh Hunt, *The Town: Its Memorable Characters and Events*, London 1848, II, p. 298; Grant 1958, III, p. 222, and fig. 214

Milk-maids kept cows and sold milk in St. James's Park from the late seventeenth century until 1905.[1] In the eighteenth century the wealthy and fashionable visited the park in the morning to drink sillabub, a mixture of wine with milk straight from the cow. Cattle also appear in other eighteenth-century paintings of St. James's Park, the best-known being Gainsborough's *Mall in St. James's Park* of 1783 in the Frick Collection. West's painting shows the east end of the park near Whitehall, where milk was traditionally sold, looking south toward Westminster Abbey. According to West's grand-nephew, Leigh Hunt: "Mr. West ... was so pleased with this pastoral group of cows and milk-drinkers in the park, that he went out of the line of his art to make a picture of it."

Although No. 448 was hanging in the gallery of West's house by the time the list of his works in *Public Characters of 1805* was drawn up, it is not quite finished, and was described as such when sold in 1829. The fact that it is not finished probably explains why it was not

signed and why it was relegated to the secondary sale of works from his estate in June 1829. The most obviously incomplete area is that of the group of milk-maids and their customers in the right middle distance, but several faces and other details here and there throughout are only roughly drawn in. The painting is the same size as *Paddington Passage-boats Returning from Uxbridge in the Evening* (No. 466), which is also on panel, and it seems probable that West intended the two works as companion pieces. No. 466 is signed and dated *1801* and was exhibited at the Royal Academy in 1802.

[1] See Guy Williams, *The Royal Parks of London*, London, 1978, pp. 32–36, and the Hon. Mrs. Evelyn Cecil, *London Parks and Gardens*, New York, 1907, pp. 61–68.

449 A Mother Inviting Her Little Boy to Come to Her through a Small Stream of Water

LOCATION UNKNOWN

(16 × 21 in.) (40.5 × 53.5 cm.)

PROV: Offered by West's sons to the United States in 1826 (59, "A Child fearful of crossing a Brook," 16 × 21 in.) and sold by them, Robins, London, 22–25 May 1829, lot 28 ("Child Afraid of Crossing the Water," 16 × 21 in.) bt. by E. Moseley for £44.2.0.

EXH: West's Gallery 1821 (15) "Child crossing the Water"; 1822–28 (6) "Child afraid of crossing the Water"

LISTED: *PC*, p. 566 ("A mother inviting her little Boy to come to her through a small Stream of Water," West, Gallery); *UM*, p. 531; Barlow, p. 435; *BA*, p. 18; Galt, p. 230; Dillenberger, p. 176 (373)

450 Mothers with Their Children Dabbling in a Brook 1798

PRIVATE COLLECTION

Oil on canvas: 19 × 26 in. (48.5 × 66 cm.)

Signed lower right: *B. West/1798*

PROV: Offered by West's sons to the United States in 1826 (68, "Mothers with their Children at a Brook," 1 ft. 6½ in. × 2 ft. 2 in.), and sold by them, Robins, London, 22–25 May 1829, lot 93 ("Mothers with their Children Dabbling in a Brook," 18½ × 26 in.), bt. by Satterby for £31.10.0.; Albert Francis Joseph Horatio Nelson (1890–1957), sixth Earl Nelson, by whom sold *c*. 1950; M. Kleinberger, New York; Vose Galleries, Boston, by whom sold to the present owner in 1952

EXH: RA 1798 (551 or 622) "A landscape with women and children" (both entries had the same title); West's Gallery, 1822–28 (22) "Mothers with their Children dabbling in a Brook"

LISTED: *PC*, p. 567 ("Mothers with their Children, in water," West, Gallery); *UM*, p. 531; Barlow, p. 435; *BA*, p. 18; Galt, p. 230; Dillenberger, p. 177 (386)

No. 450 must be the *Mothers with their Children Dabbling in a Brook* sold by West's sons in 1829 and the "Mothers with their Children, in water" recorded in *Public Characters* and the other early lists of West's works. Since it is signed and dated *1798* it can also be identified as a work exhibited by West at the Royal Academy that year under a title which appears twice in the Academy catalogue: "A landscape with women and children" (see also No. 487). Although the figures dominate the landscape setting in No. 450, the background vista is sufficiently extensive to have allowed West to describe the painting as a landscape with figures.

451 Reapers with a View near Windsor 1795

LOCATION UNKNOWN

(19½ × 27 in.) (49.5 × 68.5 cm.)

Signed lower right: *B. West/1795/Windsor*

PROV: Offered by West's sons to the United States in 1826 (53, "Landscape-Harvest," 1 ft. 7½ in. × 2 ft. 3 in.) and sold by them, Robins, London, 22–25 May 1829, lot 64 ("Reapers, with a View near Windsor," 19½ × 27 in.) bt. by Dolman for £23.2.0.; Frost and Reed, Bristol, 1956; M. Bernard, London

EXH: RA 1796 (157) "A harvest scene"; West's Gallery 1822–28 (17) "Reapers, with a View near Windsor"

LISTED: *PC*, p. 567 ("The Reaping of Harvest, with Windsor in the back-ground," West, Gallery); *UM*, p. 531; Barlow, p. 435 ("Reaping scene"); *BA*, p. 18; Galt, p. 230; Dillenberger, p. 177 (380)

LIT: V and A Cuttings, III, p. 768 (1796); von Erffa 1962, pp. 631–32, fig. 6; Kraemer 1975, pp. 35–36

The entry in the Robins sale catalogue of 22–25 May 1829, describes the setting of No. 451 as a corn field on the borders of Windsor Great Park, and identifies four of the onlookers in the right background as Mrs. West, Mrs. Brounker, Sir Francis Bourgeois, RA, and John Trumbull. Since there are five figures in the group of onlookers, the remaining male figure may represent West himself. Trumbull was in England in 1795 as secretary to a diplomatic mission led by John Jay. Bourgeois (1756–1811) had been appointed landscape

450

451

painter to George III in 1794. Mrs. Brounker was a friend or companion to Mrs. West; a drawing by West dated *1781* shows the two ladies sewing together in the parlor of the Wests' home in Newman Street.[1]

A sheet of sketches, which includes two figures in poses close to those of the two central reapers in No. 451 and a view of Windsor Castle corresponding to that in the background, is in the Pierpont Morgan Library.[2]

For other views of Windsor Castle, see Nos. 473–75. No. 451 appeared in the same Royal Academy exhibition as No. 474, showing wood cutters in Windsor Great Park, but the sizes of the two works are sufficiently different to negate any question of their having been painted as companion pieces.

[1] Ink and wash, $4\frac{3}{4} \times 7$ in., signed lower left: *B. West 1781*; and inscribed on mount: *Mrs. West and her Friend Mrs. Brounker/in the Parlour of her House in Newman Street/Benj.ⁿ West* (see *English Watercolors*, Davis & Langdale, New York, 1982, no. 46, ill.).

[2] Black chalk, $7\frac{7}{16} \times 6$ in. (Kraemer 1975, pp. 35–36, no. 56, pl. 34).

452 Savage Warrior Taking Leave of His Family
c. 1760

ROYAL COLLEGE OF SURGEONS OF ENGLAND, LONDON

Oil on canvas: $23\frac{9}{16} \times 19$ in. (60×48 cm.)

PROV: Painted for John Murray (*c.* 1715–1775), Venice; Dr. John Hunter (1728–1793), London; the Hunterian Museum, London; transferred to the Royal College of Surgeons in 1800

EXH: *The European Vision of America*, Cleveland Museum of Art, etc., 1975–77 (186)

ENGR: Engraving ($5\frac{13}{16} \times 3\frac{11}{16}$ in., reversed), by Francesco Bartolozzi, pub. Venice, 1763, as the frontispiece to *Storia degli stabilimenti europei in America* (an anonymous Italian translation of Edmund Burke, *An Account of the European settlement in America*, London, 1757)

LISTED: Barlow, p. 433 ("Savage Warrior taking leave of his family," under "Various Collections"); Dillenberger, p. 164 (254)

LIT: [Edmund Burke], *Storia degli stabilimenti europei in America*, Venice, 1763, I, pp. i–viii; Barlow 1807, p. 430; William Le Fanu, *A Catalogue of the Portraits and Other Paintings, Drawings, and Sculpture in the Royal College of Surgeons in England*, Edinburgh and London, 1960, p. 83 (247); von Erffa 1973, p. 5; Alberts 1978, pp. 39–40, 50; Hugh Honour, "Benjamin West's 'Indian family,'" *Burlington Magazine*, CXXV, 1983, pp. 726–33

West painted No. 452 in response to a request from John Murray, the British Resident in Venice (see No. 673), which had been passed on to him by Colonel Joseph Shippen, one of the artist's travelling companions on the voyage from Philadelphia to Italy in 1760. While West went to Rome in June 1760 after they had arrived at Leghorn, Shippen and John Allen, the third member of the group, travelled first to Venice and reached Rome only in September, after West had been forced by ill health to return to Leghorn. Shippen included the request for No. 452 in a letter written from Rome on 17 September. Murray had commissioned an unidentified artist to paint representations of the four quarters of the globe, but the artist had been unable to complete the commission "for want of knowing the particular Dress of our Indians to distinguish America." Hence, Shippen asked West for a painting of an Indian warrior and his squaw, which Robert Rutherford of the shipping firm of Rutherford and Jackson in Leghorn could send to Murray. Shippen specifically instructed: "It would be best that each figure be at least 18 inches high that the particularities of the dress may be plainly distinguished. The Warriour's face should be painted and Feather in his head. He ought to have his gun Tomahawk and spear, but no Dog with him as he is supposed going out to war."[1]

If West's composition was utilized in a series of paintings of the four continents done by a Venetian artist in the early 1760s, those works are not known to the compilers of this catalogue. It did serve as the basis of

an engraving by Francesco Bartolozzi (ill. p. 57) published in Venice in 1763 as the frontispiece to an Italian translation of Edmund Burke's *Account of the European Settlements in America*.[2] This print was accompanied by a long explanatory note stating that it was based on a painting done the year before in Livorno by a talented young man, who was a native of Pennsylvania. The note continues that the artist himself had provided a written description in order that the work would be better understood. The rest of the note (for which see Appendix II), therefore, would seem to have been written by West himself.[3] In addition to its explanation of Indian costume, etc., it contains two points of interest relating to No. 452 as a composition, rather than as an ethnographic document. First, it mentions the dog that Shippen had told West to exclude:

> In the entrance of the hut is a little Indian child who is straining to hold the dog so that he does not follow his master, in order to demonstrate that the man is going to war and not leaving for a hunt; since in that case the dog would be his inseparable companion.

Second, it explains the gesture of the departing warrior as pointing to his crop of corn or maize, which is represented by one or two plants on the edge of the composition. According to West's explanation, a warrior would never leave his home until the crop was sufficiently advanced to provide for his family during his absence, and in No. 452 his gesture says to his wife that since the corn is in flower he can go with a calm heart.

West submitted a painting rather than a drawing to Murray because it was to be used as the basis for another painting, and for that color would have been important, whereas if the composition had been intended only for Bartolozzi's print, a drawing in black and white would have sufficed. Additionally, at this early stage of his career West was more comfortable with paint than in drawing.[4] The Indian warrior shows a remarkable advance over the artist's only known earlier depiction of a nude or semi-nude figure, in the *Death of Socrates* of *c.* 1756 (No. 4). The transformation was the result of West's exposure to classical sculpture in Rome. His reported exclamation, "My God, how like it is to a young Mohawk warrior!,"[5] made before the *Apollo Belvedere*, may be apocryphal, but there can be little doubt that in No. 452 he tried to make his Indian warrior like the *Apollo Belvedere*.

Francesco Bartolozzi (1728–1815), a native of Florence, began his career as an engraver in Venice and continued to work in Venice and elsewhere in Italy until 1764. His subsequent life followed a course parallel to that of West. The royal librarian Richard Dalton, who was travelling in Italy on behalf of George III, and whom West met in Venice in 1762, was at least partly responsible for West's going to England in 1763.[6] Dalton also induced Bartolozzi to travel to England the following year to take an appointment as engraver to the King. Bartolozzi remained in England until 1802; in 1768 he, like West, was a founding member of the Royal Academy; and he was responsible for numerous subsequent engravings after works by West as part of his vast output of prints in England.

The engraving by Bartolozzi has long been known and properly identified,[7] but No. 452 itself was catalogued and exhibited as the work of an unknown artist until its proper identification was pointed out by Hugh Honour in 1983. Although the painting must have been in John Hunter's collection by 1793, the artist responsible for it was not recorded in early manuscript catalogues of the Hunterian Museum.[8] Nevertheless, No. 452 is the one work painted by West prior to the *Death of General Wolfe* (No. 93) of 1770–71 that is specifically mentioned by Joel Barlow in his brief biography preceding the list of the artist's works published in *The Columbiad* in 1807. According to Barlow, No. 452 "staggered the connoisseurs in Italy" and "excited great admiration at Venice." Barlow mentions the fact that it was engraved by Bartolozzi before either he or West went to England, and his following remark, "The artists were surprised to find that the expression of the passions of men did not depend on the robes they wore," suggests that he saw it as a significant precursor of the modern dress in the *Death of General Wolfe*, which he discusses in the following sentence. No other early biographer of West mentions the painting, and it appears only on Barlow's list of his works.

No. 452 is West's only recorded painting of a purely Indian subject, although American Indians do appear conspicuously in a number of other paintings (Nos. 85, 92, 93, and 647). An engraving entitled *The American*, showing a single Indian in a mountainous landscape, appeared as an illustration in a publication that we have not identified.[9] Two illustrations based on drawings by West showing confrontations between colonial troops and Indians appeared in the second edition,

published in 1766, of *An Historical Account of the Expedition against the Ohio Indians, in the year MDCCLXIV, Under the Command of Henry Bouquet, Esq.*, by West's former mentor Dr. William Smith (see No. 699).[10] A further illustration, engraved by Bartolozzi, showing a Cuban Indian chief addressing Columbus, first published in 1794, was included in 1801 in the third edition of *The History, Civil and Commercial, of the British Colonies in the West Indies* by Bryan Edwards.[11]

[1] Pennsylvania Academy of the Fine Arts, Philadelphia, partly quoted by Alberts, pp. 39–40, and in full by Honour, p. 729.
[2] The *Account* was published anonymously in 1757 and had numerous later editions; the Italian translation was from the second edition.
[3] West presumably wrote his explanation in English, although it was published in Italian. The transcription and translation into English in Appendix II are by Lewis Andrews.
[4] See No. 689 and Galt 1816, p. 119.
[5] Galt 1816, p. 105. See also above, p. 155, note 5.
[6] Letter from Robert Rutherford to Joseph Shippen, 22 April

1763 (American Philosophical Society, Philadelphia), partly quoted in Alberts 1978, p. 52. See also No. 195.
[7] See A. de Vesme, *Francesco Bartolozzi: Catalogue des Estampes*, Milan, 1928, p. 403 (1598).
[8] Manuscript catalogues compiled by William Clift in 1816 and 1820 are cited by Le Fanu.
[9] Engraved by E. Martin, with the inscription *Vol. 2, Page 229* printed above the image. An impression detached from its original source is mounted in a scrapbook on American Indians in the American History Room of the New York Public Library.
[10] *The Indians giving a Talk to Colonel Bouquet in a Conference at a Council Fire near his Camp on the Banks of Muskingum in America, in Oct. 1764*, engraved by Charles Grignion, and *The Indians delivering up the English Captives to Colonel Bouquet near his Camp at the Forks of Muskingum in North America in Novr. 1764*, engraved by Peter Canot, both ill. in Abrams 1982, figs. 6 and 7. Drawings of the two compositions are in the Yale Center for British Art.
[11] *An Indian Cacique of the Island of Cuba, addressing Columbus concerning a future state*, pub. 18 Nov. 1794 by L. Stockdale.

452

453 Sheep Washing 1795

RUTGERS UNIVERSITY ART GALLERY, NEW BRUNSWICK, NEW JERSEY

Oil on slate: $12\frac{1}{4} \times 17$ in. (31 × 43 cm.)

Signed lower right: *B. West 1795*

PROV: Offered by West's sons to the United States in 1826 (114) and sold by them, Robins, London, 22–25 May 1829, lot 144 ("Sheep Washing," $12 \times 16\frac{1}{2}$ in.), bt. by Sir M. W. Ridley, for £73.10.0.; (?) Robert Vernon in 1833; sold anonymously, Christie's, London, 16 June 1938, lot 140; sold by Arnold Seligmann, Rey, & Co., Inc., Parke-Bernet, New York, 23–25 Jan. 1947, lot 289; John Levy Galleries, New York, from whom acquired by Rutgers University as a gift of Dr. Ralph G. Wright in 1952

EXH: RA 1796 (197) "Washing of Sheep"; West's Gallery 1821 (2), 1822–28 (113) "Sheep Washing"; (?) BI 1833 (12) "Sheep Shearing," lent by Robert Vernon

LISTED: *PC*, p. 566 ("Washing of Sheep," West, Gallery); *UM*, p. 530; Barlow, p. 435; *BA*, p. 18; Galt, p. 229; Dillenberger, p. 175 (362)

LIT: von Erffa 1952, pp. 160–65, fig. 1; Kraemer 1975, pp. 35–36

The chief activity shown in No. 453 is the washing of sheep, but to the right of the pool there is also a man shearing a sheep. Hence, it seems likely that No. 453 was the "Sheep Shearing" lent by Robert Vernon to the British Institution in 1833, since that title is otherwise unrecorded in the documentation of West's art.

When West's sons sold No. 453 in 1829, the catalogue entry included the comment, "This subject has afforded a delightful theme for many poets . . ." In 1952 Helmut von Erffa pointed out the similarity of West's imagery to the following lines from "Summer," one of the four long poems which make up *The Seasons* by James Thomson:

Urged to the giddy brink, much is the toil,
The clamour much, of men, and boys, and dogs,
Ere the soft fearful people to the flood
Commit their woolly sides; and oft the swain,
On some impatient seizing, hurls them in.
Emboldened then, nor hesitating more,
Fast, fast they plunge amid the flashing wave,
And panting labour to the farthest shore.
Repeated this, till deep the well-washed fleece
Has drunk the flood, and from his lively haunt
The trout is banished by the sordid stream,
Heavy and dripping to the breezy brow
Slow move the harmless race; . . .   *lines 376–88*

453

In the same article, von Erffa also suggested a connection between the lost *Harvest Home* (No. 447) and Thomson's "Autumn." Ruth Kraemer more recently has described both works as illustrations of *The Seasons* and has also proposed that a third painting, *Reapers* (No. 451) may also have had a basis in Thomson's poetry. It should be noted, however, that neither West himself nor his sons ever directly associated Thomson with any of the three paintings, and, hence, it seems unlikely that the artist intended them to be seen as illustrations. That, of course, in no way lessens the affinities between these works and the relevant poetry, and, without a doubt, West's treatment of pastoral life in these works does reflect literary conventions, although possibly unconsciously on the part of the artist.

Nos. 453 and 451 are both dated *1795* and both appeared at the same Royal Academy exhibition in 1796, but they are different sizes and hence should not be thought of as companions. Both belong to the group of small pictures which West told Joseph Farington in 1797 that he intended to keep together and sell as a group (see No. 443), and both remained in his possession until his death. *Harvest Home* (No. 447) may have belonged to this group as well, but we do not know its size, as it did not appear in a posthumous sale of works from West's estate, and it would seem that the artist sold it apart from the others before his death.

No. 453 is one of three known works painted by West on slate; the others are *Gentlemen Fishing*, dated *1794* (No. 446), and a landscape dated *1799* or possibly *1794* (No. 470). Presumably his use of this unusual support in these three works, which are all approximately the same size, was a technical experiment, reflecting that same interest in techniques which was to involve him in the imbroglio of the "Venetian Secret" in 1796–97 (see No. 543, etc.).

A drawing signed and dated *1783*, was evidently the basis for No. 453.[1] It shows essentially the same composition, although with numerous differences in details, as one might expect in light of the interval of twelve years between the two works. The drawing, like many

of West's drawings from the 1780s, appears to have been made as a finished work in its own right, rather than as a study for a picture, and it would seem that when West conceived his plan of painting a collection of small genre pictures in the 1790s, he turned back to this earlier composition as the starting point for one of them.

[1] Pen and wash, $11 \times 19\frac{3}{4}$ in., signed lower right: *B. West 1783* (Victoria and Albert Museum, London), ill. in von Erffa 1962, fig. 2. West's heirs sold drawings of "Sheep-Washing" in 1839 (S. Leigh Sotheby, London, 1 June 1839, lot 114, sepia washed with colors) and in 1898 (Christie's, London, 18 March 1898, lot 107).

454 The Student (Man Reading by Candlelight) *c.* 1758–59

LOCATION UNKNOWN

PROV: Bought by a Mr. Myers, *c.* 1758–59

LIT: Galt 1816, pp. 82–83; Sawitzky 1938, p. 461 (5)

According to Galt, West painted No. 454 in New York during his visit to the city in 1758 or 1759.

> He happened, during his residence there, to see a beautiful Flemish picture of a hermit praying before a lamp, and he was resolved to paint a companion to it, of a man reading by candle light. But before he discovered a method of producing, in daylight, an effect on his model similar to what he wished to imitate, he was frequently baffled in his attempts. At length, he hit on the expedient of persuading his landlord to sit with an open book before a candle in a dark closet; and he found that, by looking in upon him from his study, the appearance was exactly what he wished for.

Galt states that a Mr. Myers bought No. 454 and a copy by West after an engraving of Salvator Rosa's *Belisarius* (No. 517), and that West subsequently lost sight of both works. The only information Galt gives about this patron is that he remained loyal to England during the American Revolution.

455 Three Girls Shelling Peas *1783*

LOCATION UNKNOWN

Pen and wash: 14×11 in. (35.5×28 cm.)

Signed lower right: *Benj. West/1783*, and inscribed bottom center: *The Three Sisters*

PROV: Given by West to John Barnard, Berkeley Square, London, 23 May 1784; his sale, Greenwood, London, 16 Feb. 1787 ff., eighth night, lot 35 ("Girls shelling Peas"), bt. for £33.1.6. by John Bertels; his sale, Christie's, London, 6 Feb. 1793, lot 57 ("The Three Sisters . . . from Mr. Barnard's collection"); Blumka Gallery, New York, 1954; Graham Gallery, New York, 1962

EXH: New York, 1962 (17)

LIT: V and A Cuttings, II, p. 340

This drawing exists in at least four versions. One, which is virtually identical with No. 455 in all details, is in the Nelson-Atkins Museum in Kansas City.[1] Another, with an arched top and somewhat looser drawing of details, went through the market in 1969;[2] and another, which is slighter and sketchier yet, is in the National Gallery of Scotland in Edinburgh.[3] All four drawings bear signatures, and all except the one in Edinburgh also bear the date *1783* and inscriptions identifying the subject as "The Three Sisters." The version in Kansas City was sold in 1929 as "The Northwick Sisters,"[4] but that identification does not seem very probable. The three daughters of John Rushout, who was created first Lord Northwick in 1797, were celebrated beauties, sometimes known as "The Three Graces," but as the recorded dates of the marriages of two of them are 1797 and 1808 (the third sister never married), it seems unlikely that they would have been old enough in 1783 to pose for the girls shown in No. 455. Contemporary sales catalogues and other mentions of No. 455 do not specify the sitters.

The drawing, bearing the initials *J.B.* on the mount, is also inscribed on the verso: "Given to me by Himself the 23d May 1784. J. B." Since a drawing of "Girls shelling Peas" appeared in the sale of the collector John Barnard in 1787 it seems reasonable to equate No. 455 with the drawing in his sale. It would then be the subject of an anecdote recorded in a press clipping of which we have been unable to determine the source:

> A drawing of Mr. West's was sold at Mr. Barnard's late sale for 35 guineas:—and a curious anecdote belongs to it.—Mr. West finding it was to be brought to auction, desired Mr. Greenwood would let him have it to retouch;—the subject was pretty, and consisted of a *group of girls shelling peas*,—It was embellished in his best manner;—and upon its being consigned again to Mr. Greenwood, Mr. West desired Mr. Flaxman to bid for it up to 32 or 33 guineas:—at the same time he commissioned Mr. Bertels to buy it at any rate, as he had a friend who wished to have it.—By this manouvering the drawing was knocked down at the above price, and the artist is thereby enabled to say, that his drawings and Raphael's studies are equally invaluable.

Although West may have commissioned Mr. Bertels to buy the drawing on behalf of an unidentified friend, Bertels retained his expensive acquisition, and it was sold again following his death six years later with its Barnard provenance cited in the catalogue. Some or all of the other versions may date from when No. 455 was back in West's hands to be retouched before the Barnard sale.

[1] Pen and wash, $14\frac{3}{16} \times 11$ in.
[2] Pen, 13×11 in.; sold Sotheby's, London, 6 Nov. 1969, lot 123.
[3] Pen and wash, 16×10 in.
[4] Christie's, London, 17 June 1929, lot 24.

456 **Three Ladies Making Music** 1798

LOUISE CRANE

Oil on canvas: 13 × 18 in. (33 × 45.5 cm.)

Signed at middle of left side: *B. West 1798*

PROV: Sold anonymously, Christie's, London, 6 July 1925, lot 100 (as "Duet"); Victor Spark, New York; Mrs. W. Murray Crane, New York

A drawing showing the three figures in the same positions as in No. 456, but with some differences in costume (most notably the lady at the keyboard does not wear a hat) and without any background detail, was with Thos. Agnew and Sons in 1982.[1]

[1] Pencil, 3⅝ × 6⅛ in., signed lower left: *B. West/98*. Formerly in the collection of H. H. Margary, a descendant of the artist.

457 **Two Young Ladies at Play** *c.* 1766

EXH: SA 1766 (183)

Nothing is known about this early work apart from its having been exhibited at the Society of Artists in 1766. Although not identified as such in the exhibition catalogue, it may have been a double portrait rather than a painting of a genre subject.

455

456

LANDSCAPES

458 A View of the City of Bath, as Seen from the High Grounds Eastward of Prior Park House 1807

LOCATION UNKNOWN

(Chalk and crayon on colored paper: 24 × 38 in.) (61 × 96.5 cm.)

(Signed and dated: *1807*)

PROV: Sold by Mrs. Albert F. West, Christie's, London, 19 March 1898, lot 128 ("A View of Bath," drawing, 24 × 38 in., signed and dated *1807*), bt. by Robinson for 10 shillings

EXH: RA 1808 (416) "A View of the City of Bath, as seen from the high grounds eastward of Prior Park House"; (?) West's Gallery 1823 (Room of Drawings, no. 30 or 44) both as "View near Bath"

LISTED: *BA*, p. 20 ("A view of Bath from the high ground eastward of Prior-Park House," drawing, in the possession of Mr. West); Dillenberger, p. 189 (505)

LIT: Farington Diary, 10 and 19 Nov. and 4 Dec. 1807 (Farington 1978—, VIII, pp. 3138–39, 3144, and 3157)

West visited Bath from the middle of July until early November 1807 for the sake of his wife's health. What we know about this trip comes almost entirely from Joseph Farington's diary. In July West told Farington that he intended to stay in Bath for only a fortnight, leaving his wife there with a companion, the widow of the sculptor Thomas Banks, the Wests' next-door neighbor in Newman Street, but he seems to have remained for the entire period. On 10 November, three days after his return, he called on Farington and described the place and what he did there at some length:

He spoke of Bath & its vicinity with rapture as abounding with picturesque scenery. Take Bath & 20 miles round it He sd. & there is not in the world anything superior to it. Rocks of the finest forms for a painter that He had ever seen, large, square forms. *Quarry's* worked out, now most picturesque & romantic ... Take *Tivoli* away & Rome & its vicinity of 20 miles not to be compared with Bath & its neighbourhood. ...

West had the carriage at Bath in which He & Mrs. West & Mrs. Banks went from London, & He used it in all His excursions, hiring 2 or 4 Horses as the distance might require. He employed his mornings in making sketches, & made a design of "the discovery of the good qualities of the Bath water."

On 19 November Farington called on West and found him working on the design of "the discovery of the virtues of Bath waters," *Prince Bladud Contemplating the Medicinal Virtues of the Bath Waters by Observing their Effect on Swine* (No. 46): "He shewed me also several studies He had made in & near Bath with Chalk & Crayon upon coloured paper, very good, His power seeming in no respect to have diminished." Two weeks later, on Friday, 4 December, Farington recorded the dinner conversation at Sir George Beaumont's: "Sir George spoke in the highest manner of the excellent Landscape sketches made by West while at Bath saying they were of as high a character as the designs of Nicolo Poussin, 'the true Heroic Landscape.'"

West exhibited No. 46 and four further drawings of views made near Bath (Nos. 458–61) at the Royal Academy in 1808, and the five works appear together as the final five entries in the list of his works published in *La Belle Assemblée* that same year. No. 46 now belongs to the Royal Academy, but the four landscapes have all disappeared.

Prior Park House, mentioned in West's title for No. 458, is the Palladian mansion some two miles south of Bath built *c.* 1735–50 by John Wood the Elder.

459 A View within Prior Park, near the City of Bath 1807

LOCATION UNKNOWN

(Chalk and crayon on colored paper)

EXH: RA 1808 (441) "A View within Prior Park, near the city of Bath"; (?) West's Gallery 1823 (Room of Drawings, no. 30 or 44) both as "View near Bath."

LISTED: *BA*, p. 20 ("A view in Prior Park, near Bath," drawing, in the possession of Mr. West); Dillenberger, p. 189 (507)

LIT: As for No. 458

See No. 458.

460 A View on the River Avon above the City of Bath 1807

LOCATION UNKNOWN

(Chalk and crayon on colored paper)

EXH: RA 1808 (459) "A View on the river Avon above the city of Bath"; (?) West's Gallery 1823 (Room of Drawings, no. 30 or 44) both as "View near Bath"

LISTED: *BA*, p. 20 ("A view on the river Avon, at Bath," drawing, in the possession of Mr. West); Dillenberger, p. 189 (508)

LIT: As for No. 458

See No. 458.

461 A View of the Rocks at Bristol Wells 1807

LOCATION UNKNOWN

(Chalk and crayon on colored paper)

EXH: RA 1808 (389) "A View of the Rocks at Bristol Wells, with the ceremony of conducting down the river Avon the Man of War presented by the City of Bristol to Government"; West's Gallery 1823 (Room of Drawings, no. 36) "St. Vincent's Rocks"

LISTED: *BA*, p. 20 ("A view of the Rocks at Bristol Wells," drawing, in the possession of Mr. West); Dillenberger, p. 189 (506)

LIT: As for No. 458

See No. 458. Bristol and Bath, where West stayed in 1807, are only some ten miles apart. The "Rocks" of West's title in 1808 were St. Vincent's Rocks at the suburb of Clifton on the western side of Bristol, and the "Wells" a warm spring usually called the Hotwells, which flows from the Rocks. There was a hotel at the Hotwells in the early nineteenth century (pulled down in 1822), and the dramatic scenery of the Avon Gorge in its vicinity provided a favorite subject for local landscape painters.[1]

[1]See *The Bristol School of Artists: Francis Danby and Painting in Bristol 1810–1840*, Bristol City Art Gallery, 1973, passim.

462 Chepstow Castle 1799

LOCATION UNKNOWN

LIT: Farington Diary, 25 Oct. 1799 (Farington 1978—, IV, p. 1291)

West visited Chepstow in September 1799 on a trip down the River Wye organized by the Duke of Norfolk. On 25 October 1799, Joseph Farington called on West and recorded in his diary: "West shewed me 3 pictures, views of Inside of Tintern Abbey—the Outside etc.—and Chepstow Castle etc. which he has drawn in." One picture of *Tintern Abbey* appeared on the early lists of West's works and in the sale on 22–25 May 1829, of works from his estate (No. 471). The other two pictures are unknown and unrecorded, apart from Farington's one brief mention of them; hence, it is possible that they were not carried beyond being drawn in.

Four years later Farington travelled down the Wye and, following his return to London, when discussing the trip with West, the latter described Chepstow as, "a place for a Poussin to pass His life in, to notice all the variations produced by changes in the Atmosphere on objects so picturesque."[1]

[1]Farington Diary, 2 Oct. 1803 (Farington 1978—, VI, p. 2137; Farington's account of his trip is ibid., pp. 2125–34).

463 Cranford Bridge 1791–1801

LOCATION UNKNOWN

Oil on canvas: 28 × 36 in. (71 × 91.5 cm.)

Signed right center: *B. West 1791/retouched 1801*

PROV: Offered by West's sons to the United States in 1826 (119) and sold by them, Robins, London, 22–25 May 1829, lot 147 ("View of Cranford Bridge," 2 ft. 3 in. × 3 ft.), bt. by Ward for £89.5.0.; J. A. Ward in 1833; sold anonymously, Christie's, London, 5 May 1916, lot 95 ("River scene with bridge; figures and sheep in the foreground," 27½ × 36 in.); Mrs. Charles F. Williams, Philadelphia, by 1923; Miss Mary A. Williams; Abram T. Eastwick, Norristown, Pennsylvania, 1938

EXH: RA 1805 (194) "Cranford Bridge"; (?) BI 1806 (South Room, no. 5) "A shepherd driving sheep through a ford"; West's Gallery 1822–28 (123) "View of Cranford Bridge"; BI 1833 (49) "View of Cranford Bridge," lent by J. A. Ward; Philadelphia 1921 (16) "Landscape with Bridge," lent anonymously; Philadelphia 1938 (40) "Landscape with Bridge," lent by Abram T. Eastwick

LISTED: *PC*, p. 567 ("Cranford Bridge," West, Gallery); *UM*, p. 531; *BA*, p. 18; Galt, p. 230; Dillenberger, p. 177 (387)

LIT: A. E. B. [Arthur Edwin Bye], "Landscape with Coaching Party by Benjamin West," *Pennsylvania Museum Bulletin*, XVIII, May 1923, pp. 8–10, ill. p. 10

Cranford is a village in Middlesex on the eastern edge of the present Heathrow airport. It takes its name from the small river Crane, and in the eighteenth century was the site of a bridge on the main road from London to Windsor. In the words of the Robins catalogue of May 1829, "This very masterly painting will perpetuate the memory of a spot, over which the honoured King George the Third had passed a thousand times, in his way to and fro from the seat of government, and his quiet retreat at Windsor."

The *Landscape: Driving of Sheep and Cows to Water* (No. 484), must have shown a subject similar to the scene in the foreground of No. 463, and it is possible that the former rather than the latter was the

463

"Shepherd driving sheep through a ford" exhibited by West at the British Institution in 1806. However, it should be noted that the foreground of No. 463 shows a shepherd driving his sheep through a ford, not simply to it, and it includes no cattle. The size of No. 463 confirms its identification as the *Cranford Bridge* sold by West's sons in 1829 rather than the considerably smaller *Driving of Sheep and Cows to Water*.

464 View from Greenwich Hill *c.* 1810

LOCATION UNKNOWN

PROV: Sold by West's sons, Robins, London, 20–22 June 1829, lot 153 ("The Captive from Sterne, a study, by the late B. West . . .—beginning of Telemachus in the Island of Calypso, by ditto—View from Greenwich Hill, by ditto")

LIT: Farington Diary, 30 June 1810 (Farington 1978–, X, pp. 3679–80); Grant 1958, III, pp. 221–22

The circumstances under which No. 464 was sold in 1829, in a minor sale as part of a lot of three works, one a sketch and one only a beginning, suggest that it also was probably unfinished, although the catalogue gives no explicit information about its condition. It was presumably the painting West was planning to paint when he visited Greenwich with Joseph Farington and Henry Edridge on 30 June 1810:

> At one o'Clock went with Mr. West & Edridge to Greenwich Park, where we remained a considerable time, contemplating the view of London from Flamstead House, which West had formed a design to paint as being the finest of its kind in Europe. He said He had had this in His mind from the time of his first coming to England, when on His way from Dover He left the carriage with a Gentleman who had spoken of this situation, and when He came to this point and saw the scene before Him He was struck with the magnificence of it. . . . West proposed to make Greenwich Hospital with the colonnade of the building in the Park His Center, having the advantage of this long line, & to include London on the left & Black wall on the right of His picture. Edridge held a Handkerchief while West measured the proportion of the Canvass which wd. be required, & determined it to be in the proportion of three wide to two deep. . . .
> West said that in painting this view from near Flamstead House, viz: at the top of the Hill looking down upon the Hospital, He should omit many of

the trees which stood in the way & interrupted some principal circumstances. He considered that His object shd. be to give the true character of the scene with all its magnificence, & not to allow it to be broken by these interruptions.

Flamstead (or Flamsteed) House in Greenwich Park is the site of the Royal Observatory. The view from Greenwich Hill is one of the most frequently painted in England, and, as we learn from Farington, West claimed to have intended to paint it ever since he came to England. Nevertheless, the immediate impetus may have been provided by Turner's view of London from Greenwich, which had been exhibited the year before (Tate Gallery, London).

465

A drawing of the view from the hill, showing the Queen's House, Greenwich Hospital, and a distant prospect beyond, which West may have made in preparation for No. 464, is in the Yale Center for British Art.[1]

[1] Black chalk, $5\frac{3}{8} \times 12\frac{5}{8}$ in., formerly in the collection of H. H. Margary.

465 Mr. West's Garden, Gallery, and Painting-room *c.* (?) 1808–9

NATIONAL PORTRAIT GALLERY, WASHINGTON, D.C.

Oil on canvas: 13×16 in. (33×40.5 cm.)

Signed lower left: *B. West* and illegibly dated

PROV: In the possession of West's sons in 1820s; Sabin Galleries, London, from whom purchased by the National Portrait Gallery in 1977

EXH: West's Gallery, 1821 (68) "Mr. West's Garden, upon which the present large Room is erected", and 1822–28 (114) "Mr. West's Garden, upon which the present large Room was erected" (in copies of the 1828 edition of this catalogue, this entry is scratched out and replaced by "Sir Hugh Palliser fishing," [see No. 446]); Washington and Philadelphia 1980

(?) LISTED: *PC*, p. 567 ("Mr. West's Garden, Gallery, and Painting Room," West, Gallery); *UM*, p. 531; Barlow, p. 435; *BA*, p. 18; Galt, p. 231; Dillenberger, p. 180 (417)

No. 465 shows the garden behind West's home at 14 Newman Street in London, off Oxford Street, where he lived from 1774 until his death. From the main house, just visible on the left, a long passageway or gallery leads to his large painting room at the end of the garden. A description of the garden by Leigh Hunt calls it "very small but elegant, with a grass plot in the middle and busts upon stands under an arcade."[1] This garden disappeared in 1821, when West's sons built a large gallery or "Great Room" (as it is referred to in the catalogues of 1821–28) in its place in order to exhibit their father's pictures. West's sons sold the premises in 1829, as the last item of the Robins sale of 22–25 May, and the buildings no longer exist. The site is presently a parking lot belonging to the post office.

The figures appear to be the artist and his wife, their two sons, Raphael and Benjamin, with their wives, and West's two grandchildren, Maria and Benjamin, the children of Raphael and Benjamin, Jr. respectively. The youngest Benjamin was born in 1804 (see No. 544), so, if the boy seated on the bench in No. 465 in fact represents him, his evident age of four or five suggests that West painted No. 465 in 1808 or 1809. Such a late date is not incompatible with the style of the painting, but it would seem to be contradicted by the inclusion of a work whose title fits No. 465 on the lists of West's works, one of which was drawn up as early as 1802. It is not very likely that West would have shown a family other than his own in his own garden, so it seems either that No. 465 is a second treatment of the subject, painted too late to be included on the lists of West's works, or, perhaps more probably, that West added the

figures of the family group around 1808 to a view of the garden which he had initially painted much earlier. The latter alternative is in keeping with West's practice in his later years of retouching and revising earlier works.

A drawing of the garden, with much larger figures in the foreground, and seen from a different angle, but with the painting room still in the background, is in the Toledo Museum of Art.[2] In style this drawing appears to date from the early 1780s, and the figures in it almost certainly represent the artist himself under a parasol, his wife, and their two sons, whose different ages (Raphael would have been fourteen years old in 1780, Benjamin eight) are reflected in their different sizes. Cats and dogs figure prominently both in the drawing and in No. 465.

The passageway or gallery shown in No. 465 is the "Gallery," where according to the lists of West's works the artist hung drawings, sketches, and smaller pictures (such as No. 465), and the larger structure beyond is the "Painting-room" of the lists, where he not only worked, but also hung more pictures, including all the larger ones.

[1] Leigh Hunt, *The Autobiography of Leigh Hunt*, London, 1850, 1, pp. 147–48.
[2] Ink, 7¼ × 9⅛ in., signed lower right: *B. W.*, and bearing an old inscription on the mount: *Mr. West's Family in the Garden of their Residence in Newman St. London.*

466 The Paddington Passage-boats Returning from Uxbridge in the Evening 1801

DETROIT INSTITUTE OF ARTS

Oil on panel: 39½ × 56⅝ in. (100.5 × 144 cm.)

Signed lower center (on the side of the bridge): *B. West 1801*

PROV: Offered by West's sons to the United States in 1826 (29, "Landscape—Paddington Canal and Pleasure Boats," 3 ft. 4 in. × 4 ft. 8 in.) and sold by them, Robins, London, 22–25 May 1829, lot 59 ("Paddington Canal," 3 ft. 4 in. × 4 ft. 8 in.), bt. by Henry Pierce Bone (1779–1855) for £63; Daniel H. Farr, New York, by 1921; Victor Spark, New York, by 1954; Hirschl & Adler Galleries, New York, from whom acquired by the Detroit Institute of Arts in 1957 (gift of Dexter M. Ferry, Jr.)

EXH: RA 1802 (191) "The Paddington passage-boats returning from Uxbridge in the evening"; BI 1806 (South Room, no. 17) "The Paddington boats returning from Uxbridge"; West's Gallery 1822–28 (134) "The Paddington Canal Boats"; Philadelphia 1921 (17) "The Paddington," lent by Daniel H. Farr, Esq.

LISTED: *PC*, p. 566 ("Uxbridge Passage-boat on the Canal," West, Gallery); *UM*, p. 530; Barlow, p. 435

466

("Passage boat on the Canal"); *BA*, p. 17 ("Uxbridge Passage-boats on the Canal, returning in the evening"); Galt, p. 228; Dillenberger, p. 173 (347)

LIT: John Thomas Smith, *Nollekens and His Times*, London, 1828, I, pp. 383–84; Nancy J. Rivard, "American Paintings at the Detroit Institute of Arts," *Antiques*, CXIV, 1978, p. 1046, pl. II; Alberts 1978, ill. between pp. 270 and 271

The canal between Uxbridge in Middlesex, a rural market town fifteen miles west of London, and Paddington in London, to the north of Hyde Park, opened on 10 July 1801. It was later linked up with the Grand Union Canal (the chief canal from the Midlands to London) and extended through the Regent's Park to Limehouse and the Thames. Passage-boats plying the canal provided an inexpensive and pleasant way for Londoners to visit the countryside. Among those who made the trip was the sculptor Joseph Nollekens (1737–1823), whose excursion was found sufficiently memorable by his biographer, John Thomas Smith, to call for the following account:

> I ought to have noticed in a former page, that when it was customary for so much company to visit Uxbridge by the barges drawn by horses gaily decked out with ribands, Mr. and Mrs. Nollekens, with all the gaiety of youthful extravagance, embarked on board, and actually dined out on that gala-day at their own expense. The sights they saw on this memorable aquatic excursion afforded them mutual conversation for several weeks; and Mrs. Nollekens actually tired her friends with letters upon their canal adventures from Paddington to Uxbridge, and from Uxbridge to Paddington. In these epistles, she most poetically expatiated upon the clearness of the water, the fragrance of the flowers, the nut-brown tints of the wavy corn, and the ruddy and healthful complexions of the cottager's children, who waited anxiously to see the vessel approach their native shores.

To this passage Smith added a footnote mentioning No. 466:

> The pleasures of a similar excursion induced the late venerable President West to paint a picture of the barge he went by, on the crowded deck of which he has introduced his own portrait, and also those of several of his friends who were that day on board. This pleasing and singular picture adorns the splendid Gallery of West's works, daily exhibiting at his late house in Newman-Street.

This was written in 1828, when No. 466 was on view in West's gallery. The author, who was Keeper of Prints at the British Museum, and the subject of his book were both friends of Mr. and Mrs. West. In the following year, the catalogue of the Robins sale of 22–25 May 1829, also mentioned that the artist and his wife "and several of their old and esteemed friends" are depicted on the deck of the barge. West is presumably the man with a walking stick standing toward the front of the closer of the two barges.

The horses pulling the first barge are on the extreme left of the composition, and lines connecting them to the barge are faintly visible. A second barge seen in the distance is similarly drawn by a pair of horses. In the foreground a man turns a bridge to allow the barges to pass.

Since No. 466 is signed and dated *1801* and was completed in time to be sent to exhibition in the following April, West must have made his excursion and commenced his picture soon after the canal's opening in July 1801. He probably intended the *Milk-woman in St. James's Park* (No. 448), which is the same size and also on panel, as a companion.

467 The Bathing Place at Ramsgate *c.* 1780–88

YALE CENTER FOR BRITISH ART, NEW HAVEN, PAUL MELLON COLLECTION

Oil on canvas: 14 × 17½ in. (35.5 × 44.5 cm.)

PROV: In West's possession in 1791; T. Laughton, Royal Hotel, Scarborough; sold, Sotheby's, London, 18 March 1964, lot 81; Mr. and Mrs. Paul Mellon

EXH: *Presences of Nature: British Landscape 1780–1830*, Yale Center for British Art, 1982 (II.3)

ENGR: Stipple engraving (4 1/16 × 5 in.) by William Birch, pub. by Birch, 1 Dec. 1788, and included in 1791 as an illustration in Birch's *Délices de la Grande Bretagne*

LIT: William Birch, *Délices de la Grande Bretagne*, Hampstead-Heath, 1791; Grant 1958, III, p. 221; Alberts 1978, ill. between pp. 270 and 271

Ramsgate is a seaside town in south-eastern England, on a peninsula at the eastern-most tip of Kent. Apart from the sea itself, its most prominent topographical features are its chalk cliffs, one of which fills the right side of No. 467. Although Ramsgate and the neighboring communities of Margate and Broadstairs, in the area known as the Isle of Thanet, started to become popular as sites for bathing in the sea in the second half of the eighteenth century, Ramsgate's chief development as a resort came after 1800. A well-known Victorian painting, *Life at the Seaside* or *Ramsgate Sands* (Royal Collection) by William Powell Frith (1819–1909), seems to show the same location as No. 467, with the cliff similarly on the right, but all the structures shown by West in his background had evidently been pulled down by Frith's time, and not one building in Frith's extensive background existed when West painted No. 467.[1]

Bathing machines, which figure prominently in the painting and are also visible in Frith's background, are said to have been invented in 1753 by a resident of Margate named Benjamin Beale. These huts, constructed on wheels so that they could be taken into the sea, permitted the swimmer to undress and enter the water privately at a time when the bathing suit was still unknown. The machine in the water in the background of No. 467 has its "modesty hood" extended so that its undressed occupant can maintain his or her privacy until submerged in the waves.

Since the work was engraved in 1788, it must have been painted before then, but probably not long before. A pencil drawing ascribed to West in the Yale Center for British Art showing a bathing machine is inscribed *Margate 1767*,[2] but it has no direct relation to No. 467, and West's handling in the painting appears to belong to a later date. There is also a drawing in the Metropolitan Museum of Art showing the site much as it appears in No. 467, but with bathers and machines in different positions.[3] Similar scenery is in the background of *General Monk Receiving Charles II on the Beach at Dover* (No. 84) of 1781.

[1] Nikolaus Pevsner, in "Frith and the Irregular," *Architectural Review*, CXX, Sept. 1956, p. 191, identifies the structures in Frith's painting.
[2] Black chalk, 14 × 21½ in.
[3] Pen and ink, with some body-color on blue paper, 4½ × 7 in., signed lower left: *B W*.

468 View on the Susquehanna River 1767

HENRY FRANCIS DU PONT WINTERTHUR MUSEUM, WINTERTHUR, DELAWARE

Oil on canvas: 14 × 17⅞ in. (35.5 × 45.5 cm.)

Signed lower left: *B. West 1767*

467

PROV: Offered by West's sons to the United States in 1826 (71) and sold by them, Robins, London, 22–25 May 1829, lot 170 ("View on the Susquehannah," 13½ × 17½ in.), bt. by Ward for £23.2.0.; J. A. Ward in 1833; M. Bernard, London, by 1956; Mr. and Mrs. Daniel Fraad, Jr., New York, 1962; given by them to the Winterthur Museum in 1963.

EXH: West's Gallery 1821 (3), 1822–28 (27) "View on the Susquehannah"; (?) BI 1833 (51) "A Fishing Party" lent by J. A. Ward; New York 1962 (11) lent by Mr. and Mrs. Daniel Fraad, Jr.

LISTED: *PC*, p. 564 ("A View on the Banks of the River Susquehannah, in America," Mr. West's House at Windsor); *UM*, p. 529; Barlow, p. 434 ("View on the Susquehanna"); *BA*, p. 16; Galt, p. 225; Dillenberger, p. 166 (273)

LIT: Colonel M. H. Grant, "Some 'Unexpected' Landscapes," *Connoisseur*, CXXIX, 1952, p. 78, fig. ii; Grant 1958, III, p. 222, fig. 215

No. 468 appears to have been subjected to repainting or overpainting on one or more occasions in the past. Since the painting remained in West's possession until his death fifty-three years after the date on the canvas, at least some retouching may have been done by the artist himself. Photographs taken at different times since 1950 show significant differences in the appearance of areas of foliage, presumably reflecting the removal within the last thirty years of earlier overpainting.

The date of *1767* indicates that West painted No. 468 in England, even though it shows an American subject. The Susquehanna flows southward through east-central Pennsylvania into the Chesapeake Bay. Lancaster, Pennsylvania, lies approximately ten miles east of the river, and it seems reasonably likely that West may have seen the Susquehanna during his stay in Lancaster, which occurred probably in 1755–56. That visit, however, was over a decade before 1767, and, no matter how vivid the artist's memories may have been, the view in No. 468 must be largely a product of the imagination.

In the foreground of No. 468 are one hunter, shooting at a flock of ducks or geese, and a group of three fishermen slightly further into the picture. According to the Robins catalogue of 22–25 May 1829, "The principal figure in the diminutive group, is a *whole length portrait* of an esteemed friend of the painter, THE LATE DR. BRAGGE, placed on this congenial site, in playful compliment to his celebrity, as one of the *cognos* of the old Cottonian school of fly-fishing." Dr. Bragge was Richard Bragge (died *c.* 1778), an art dealer who collected pictures on the Continent and brought them to England to sell. There is no record of his ever having

468

visited America, so the nature of the playfulness of West's compliment is evident.[1] He must be the heavy-set man standing in the center of the group of fishermen. A sketch by West dated *1769* showing him holding a fishing rod but in a pose unrelated to any of the figures in No. 468 is at Swarthmore.[2] The old Cottonian school of fly-fishing takes its name from Charles Cotton (1630–1687), who contributed a treatise on fly-fishing to the fifth edition of Izaak Walton's *Compleat Angler*.

[1] See Frank Simpson, "Dutch Paintings in England before 1760," *Burlington Magazine*, xcv, 1953, p. 40. Bragge's estate sale took place on 5–7 February 1778.
[2] Black chalk on brown paper, $6\frac{3}{8} \times 4\frac{5}{8}$ in., inscribed lower right *Doc^r Bragg 1769*.

469 A View on the River Thames at Hammersmith

LOCATION UNKNOWN

$(14 \times 17\frac{1}{2}$ in.$)$ $(35.5 \times 44.5$ cm.$)$

PROV: Sold by West's sons, Robins, London, 22–25 May 1829, lot 176 ("View near Hammersmith," 1 ft. 2 in. × 1 ft. $5\frac{1}{2}$ in.), bt. by Ward for £45.4.0.; (?) J. A. Ward in 1833; (?) Serjeant Ralph Thomas, London, from whom bought by John Linnell (1792–1882) in 1845

EXH: West's Gallery 1821 (5), "View near Hammersmith," and 1822–28 (31) "A View on the River Thames at Hammersmith" (in the catalogue of 1828 the title of no. 31 has been scratched out, with "Arion" [see No. 122] inserted in its place, while "View at Hammersmith" has been added by hand in place of "Mr. West and Family" [see No. 546] for no. 117); (?) BI 1833 (47) "View on the River; an Evening Scene," lent by J. A. Ward

LISTED: *PC*, p. 564 ("A View on the River Thames at Hammersmith," Mr. West's House at Windsor); *UM*, p. 529; Barlow, p. 434 ("View on the River

Thames"); *BA*, p. 16; Galt, p. 225; Dillenberger, p. 166 (272)

LIT: A. T. Story, *The Life of John Linnell*, London 1892, I, p. 23; Grant 1958, III, p. 221; Katharine Crouan, *John Linnell: A Centennial Exhibition*, Fitzwilliam Museum, Cambridge, England, 1982, p. 1

Hammersmith is on the north bank of the Thames in the western suburbs of London, between Fulham and Chiswick. West evidently acquired a country house on Hammersmith Terrace overlooking the river in 1769.[1] How long he kept it is not known; he must have given it up by the time he took a house in Windsor in the early 1780s. The Hammersmith house later belonged to the painter John Linnell (1792–1882), who for a brief period around 1804–5 had been one of West's pupils. According to Linnell's biographer, one of the artist's recollections from his visits to West was of seeing a small painting of boats on the river near Hammersmith, and he later acquired it as well as the house.

The Robins catalogue of 22–25 May 1829, described West's "View near Hammersmith" as showing, "The sentiment of the stillness of a fine summer evening, reposing on the tranquil bosom of the 'silver Thames.'" John Linnell described it as, "a sweet Claude-like view of the effect of sun and water with barges and boats and trees mingled. Painted with a firm delicate hand with great love of nature and of that particular spot."

[1] See Alberts 1978, p. 102.

470 The Sun Setting Behind a Group of Trees on the Banks of the Thames at Twickenham (Landscape—Evening) (?) 1799
See color illustrations, pp. 115, 116

DEERFIELD ACADEMY, DEERFIELD, MASSACHUSETTS

Oil on slate: 12 × 17 in. (30.5 × 43 cm.)

Signed lower right: *B. West* [?] *1799*

PROV: (?) Offered by West's sons to the United States in 1826 (130 "A Landscape—Evening," 1 ft. 6 in. × 2 ft.), and sold by them, Robins, London, 22–25 May 1829, lot 60 ("Landscape—Evening," $11\frac{1}{2} \times 16\frac{1}{2}$ in.), bt. by Dunlop for £23.2.0.; Vose Galleries, Boston, from whom purchased by Mrs. L. D. Potter, Greenfield, Mass.; presented by Mrs. Potter and Miss Lucia Russell to Deerfield Academy in memory of their father Charles P. Russell

(?) EXH: West's Gallery 1822–28 (24) "Landscape, Evening"

(?) LISTED: *PC*, p. 566 ("The Sun Setting behind a group of Trees on the Banks of the Thames at Twickenham," West, Gallery); *UM*, p. 531; Barlow, p. 435 ("Sun setting at Twickenham on Thames"); *BA*, p. 18; Galt, p. 229; Dillenberger, p. 175 (364)

No. 470 must be the "Landscape—Evening," lot 60 in the Robins sale of 22–25 May 1829, described as "*A twilight effect, the scene on the banks of the Thames, above Windsor, and wrought in the style and feeling of Rembrandt.*" The entry also mentions that the picture included a barge at anchor, with no one on the deck.

Although Twickenham is not above Windsor, but a few miles to the west of London across the river from Richmond Park, it seems likely that the work is also identical with "The Sun Setting behind a group of trees on the banks of the Thames at Twickenham," from the early lists of West's works. The painting does not show sufficient topographical detail to have allowed a cataloguer to distinguish one river bank from another with any certainty. It was presumably the "Landscape—Evening" included in the posthumous exhibitions in West's gallery, and the "Landscape—Evening" offered by West's sons to the United States in 1826 was probably the same work, since, despite the discrepancy in measurements from those in the sale catalogue of three years later, the latter repeated the title. No. 469 also showed an evening scene on the river, but that work was identified in the exhibitions of the 1820s and in the sale of 1829 as a view at or near Hammersmith.

A copy of No. 470 in watercolors went through the market in 1974.[1] This work, although bearing a signature, does not appear to be by West's hand.

For other works on slate, see Nos. 446 and 453. Those paintings, which are both approximately the same size as No. 470, bear dates of *1794* and *1795* respectively. Although the date accompanying West's signature on No. 470 appears to be *1799*, it is not impossible that we have misread the final digit, and that it is "4" rather than "9," since we might expect the artist to have made all his experiments using this unusual support at roughly the same time.

[1] $7\frac{1}{4} \times 10\frac{1}{2}$ in.; sold, Sotheby's, London, 18 July 1974, lot 150.

471 The Ruins of Tintern Abbey, on the Banks of the River Wye 1799

LOCATION UNKNOWN

Oil on canvas: 36 × 28 in. (91.5 × 71 cm.)

Signed lower left: *B. West/Decm 31 1799*

PROV: Offered by West's sons to the United States in 1826 (45) and sold by them, Robins, London, 22–25 May 1829, lot 65 ("View of Tintern Abbey," 3 ft. × 2 ft. 4 in.), bt. by William Pitt Amherst, first Earl Amherst (1773–1857) for £69.6.0.; by descent to the fifth Earl Amherst, by whom sold Robinson & Fisher, London, 29 July 1937, lot 45; McClees Galleries, Philadelphia, 1938; sold anonymously, Sotheby Parke Bernet, New York, 20 May 1971, lot 97

EXH: RA 1800 (672) "The ruins of Tintern Abbey, on the banks of the river Wye"; West's Gallery 1822–28 (11) "View of Tintern Abbey"; *British Country Life through the Centuries*, 39 Grosvenor Square, London, 1937 (363A) lent by the Earl Amherst; Philadelphia 1938 (49) lent by McClees Galleries

LISTED: *PC*, p. 566 ("Fintern [*sic*] Abbey," West, Gallery); *UM*, p. 530; *BA*, p. 17 ("Tintern Abbey"); Galt, p. 228; Dillenberger, p. 173 (342)

LIT: Farington Diary, 25 Oct. 1799 and 2 Oct. 1803 (Farington 1978–, IV, p. 1291, and VI, p. 2137); Kraemer 1975, p. 78

The ruins of Tintern Abbey stand on the west bank of the River Wye in Monmouthshire, five miles above Chepstow. The structure was a Cistercian monastery, founded in 1131, but largely rebuilt as a Gothic building in the thirteenth century. West visited Tintern in September 1799 on a trip down the Wye organized by

471

the Duke of Norfolk, and he subsequently began three pictures based on the trip, which he showed to Joseph Farington in October: "views of Inside of Tintern Abbey—the Outside etc.—and Chepstow Castle etc. which he has drawn in." No. 471 is the only one of these pictures now known and it may be the only one that West completed (for the other two see Nos. 462 and 472). West exhibited it at the Royal Academy the following year, and he discussed it with Farington in the autumn of 1803, after the latter had visited the Wye valley:

> Of Tintern Abbey He spoke with great delight. He had in his picture of it endeavored to give some idea of the effect produced on first entering it, but He had not time to go into *the detail of the building*.

The small figures in No. 471 represent the party with which West visited the abbey. The Robins catalogue of 22–25 May 1829 states that the picture shows the Duke of Norfolk and his friends, but names only West

among the members of the group. The catalogue of the *Country Life* exhibition of 1937 names five figures: West; Charles, eleventh Duke of Norfolk (1746–1815); Other Archer, sixth Earl of Plymouth (1789–1833); his mother, the Countess of Plymouth and widow of the fifth Earl; and her sister, the Hon. Mrs. Clive. The Earl of Plymouth, who had inherited his title three months before the Wye excursion, was ten years old at the time and is readily identifiable as the child standing in the group of figures at the center of the picture. In the following year his mother remarried, and her second husband, the first Earl Amherst, was the purchaser of No. 471 in 1829. The identification of the figures in No. 471 in 1937 probably stemmed from her, as her descendants still owned the picture at the time.[1]

The view in No. 471 is from the west end of the nave looking toward the presbytery and the large east window. The extant tracery of the east window is more complete than shown by West, the discrepancy being explained by the artist's lack of time "to go into the detail of the building." The trees and vines growing in and over the structure, which also figure prominently in other eighteenth- and nineteenth-century views of the abbey, have since been stripped away.

[1] West in describing his trip to Joseph Farington on 16 October 1799 (Farington 1978–, IV, p. 1287) mentioned as members of the group that made the trip down the Wye: "the Duke of Norfolk, and Countess of Plymouth & Her Sister Mrs. Clive with Her Husband, also Captn. Morris."

472 The Ruins of Tintern Abbey, on the Banks of the River Wye 1799

LOCATION UNKNOWN

LIT: Farington Diary, 25 Oct. 1799 (Farington 1978–, IV, p. 1291)

See the previous entry. In contrast to that work, which shows the inside of Tintern Abbey, No. 472, which Joseph Farington saw drawn in in West's studio, showed the outside. West may never have completed it.

473 Landscape Representing the Country near Windsor *c.* 1785

HER MAJESTY THE QUEEN

Oil on canvas: 60 × 84¾ in. (152.4 × 215.3 cm.)

Signed: *B. West*

PROV: Offered by West's sons to the United States in 1826 (10 "Landscape view of Windsor Castle, with the Royal Hunt," 5 ft. × 7) and sold by them, Robins, London, 22–25 May 1829, lot 67 ("A Large Landscape, with His Late Majesty Hunting and Windsor Castle in the Distance," 5 ft. × 7), bt. by H. P. Bone for £73.10.0.; bought by King Edward VII from Colonel Tatham in 1904

EXH: RA 1785 (31) "Landscape representing the country near Windsor"; West's Gallery 1822–28 (41) "A Large Landscape, with his late Majesty hunting, and Windsor Castle in the distance"

LISTED: *PC*, p. 565 ("The large Landscape from Windsor Forest," West, Painting-room); *UM*, p. 530; Barlow, p. 434; *BA*, p. 17; Galt, p. 227; Dillenberger, p. 169 (307)

LIT: V and A Cuttings, I, pp. 255 and 261, II, pp. 444 (all 1785), 448 (n.d.) and 481 (January 1789); *Morning Post*, 13 Jan. 1789; Dunlap 1834, I, pp. 258–59 (Dunlap 1918, I, pp. 305–6); John Thomas Smith, *A Book for a Rainy Day: or Recollections of the Events of the Years 1766–1833*, ed. by Wilfred Whitten, London, 1905, p. 129; Whitley 1928, II, p. 73; Millar

473

1969, I, pp. 135–36 (1168), II, pl. 118; Alberts 1978, p. 188

No. 473 is the earliest of seven landscapes (Nos. 473–79), which West painted showing views at or near Windsor, where he rented a house in Park Street from the early 1780s until 1809.[1] The view includes Windsor Castle in the far distance seen from the south-west. Sir William Chambers's Queen's Lodge, built between 1778 and 1782 (see No. 435) is visible before it. The vantage point is from Windsor Great Park to the west of the Long Walk. John Thomas Smith identified the gnarled tree on the left side of No. 473 as a venerable beech tree standing near Sandpit Gate. Smith himself exhibited a painting of the tree at the Royal Academy in 1787, two years after West exhibited No. 473. On a hill beyond the tree on the left edge of the painting is a large house, which Sir Oliver Millar has tentatively identified as Cranbourne Lodge, a structure built in the seventeenth century and pulled down in 1830. In West's time it was occupied by the Duke of Gloucester.

In the middle distance are several mounted horsemen accompanied by hounds, which early sources identify as George III and the Royal Hunt. Their quarry, a stag, is visible through the trees on the right. In the foreground, framed by a sow with a litter of piglets on the left and cattle on the right, a peasant carrying a bundle of faggots returns to his family and their ramshackle hut. This little group echoes and

almost certainly was inspired by depictions of similar scenes by Thomas Gainsborough in works such as the *Woodcutter's Return*, shown at the Royal Academy in 1782.[2] The entry for No. 473 in the Robins catalogue of 22–25 May 1829, describes the foreground scene as "no poetic fiction, but a veritable pastoral of the happy cot," and it calls the entire painting a "graphic allegory" in which the King and his friends joined in rural sport link the "peaceful home" of the woodman with the castle, "so long the residence of royalty, and that domestic peace, the example of which dispensed moral good to every grade of the subjects of this virtuous king and queen of England."

While West was at work on No. 473, he gave William Dunlap a lesson in the disposition of light and shadow, using the masses of foliage on the oak tree on the right as an example. Dunlap wrote that this happened probably in the summer of 1785, but it must have been somewhat earlier, as West completed No. 473 in time to send it to the Royal Academy in the spring of that year. At the Academy critics recognized the landscape as a new departure in West's art, but did not receive it with much enthusiasm. The fullest comment is from an unidentified clipping in the Victoria and Albert Museum:

This performance consists of a view near Windsor. Cottages are introduced in one part of the scene—in another a sow and pigs, with cattle. The trunk of the withered tree in the front ground is by no means

a natural representation; nor indeed have we opportunity to compliment the Artist on any part of his performance. The foliage of the trees, and the verdure of the earth, possess neither force nor spirit. The pigs in *pageantry* are unpleasing objects, and the cattle appear out of nature.—Labour and practice have made Mr. *West* a painter; Genius has assisted but sparingly.

Another briefer comment was: "Mr. West, in his preposterous landscape, has disposed his sow and litter in a direction toward Windsor Castle. We infer, of course, that the artist knows how to drive his pigs to a good market."

No. 473 was mentioned again in the press four years later, in January 1789:

Mr. West's landscape with Windsor Castle in the distance has this anecdote related of it, that while it was in hand, his Majesty came to Mr. West, and desired him to introduce a lion in it;—Mr. West complied, and it was some time before his Majesty was convinced that the King of the Forest appeared out of his place in an English landscape!—This instance occurred a full three years since![3]

A variant of this story, which must refer to the same painting, appeared in the *Morning Post* on 13 January 1789. According to this account, the incident happened not three years before, but in the autumn of 1788; West himself introduced the lion into the picture to amuse Prince Adolphus; when the King saw the lion, he declared it looked like a dog, and "then deliberately took up a pencil and drew it through the figure, and then drawing a fantastic sketch showed it to the painter as a proper drawing of the animal." Of the two stories, the former sounds the more convincing. In January 1789 George III was suffering from apparent insanity (see No. 107), and the anecdotes were reported in the press as early manifestations of his condition. "Three years since" was three years before the King's first attack in October 1788, and the incident, whether having any actual relation to his illness or not, would have seemed highly relevant at the time. West must have been the source of the stories, but perhaps only indirectly, and the discrepancies between the two probably reflect variations that crept in before they reached the newspapers.

No. 488 below may have been painted as a reduced replica of No. 473. West painted further views of the castle from the Great Park in Nos. 474, 475, and 451, and he included additional views of it from the south, with the Queen's Lodge standing before it, in the backgrounds of his full-length portraits of Queen Charlotte (Nos. 556 and 558) and in the *Apotheosis of Prince Alfred and Prince Octavius* (No. 575). A large number of drawings either by or attributed to West also show the castle and its vicinity. Of these, two slight sketches on one sheet, which show distant views of the castle, seem loosely related to No. 473.[4] West also did several drawings of the ancient trees in Windsor Great Park, but none corresponding to those shown in this work.[5] West's son Raphael exhibited a drawing of "An old tree in Windsor forest" at the Royal Academy in 1791 (no. 583), and numerous drawings and prints of trees and forest scenery ascribed variously to Raphael and to Benjamin West, Jr., are known.[6]

[1] West probably took the house in Windsor around 1780, at the time he began his series of paintings for the Royal Chapel in Windsor Castle. He was certainly there by 10 November 1784, when Samuel Shoemaker visited him (*Pennsylvania Magazine of History and Biography*, II, 1878, pp. 35–40). He gave it up in November 1809 (Alberts 1978, p. 437).

[2] Collection of the Duke of Rutland, Belvoir Castle; see Ellis K. Waterhouse, *Gainsborough*, London, 1958, p. 119 (960) and pl. 227. Another painting by Gainsborough with similar imagery is the *Cottage Door with Children Playing* in the Cincinnati Art Museum, possibly exhibited at the Royal Academy in 1778; ibid., p. 117 (940) and pl. 192. It is worth noting that the entry for No. 473 in the Robins catalogue of May 1829 mentions Gainsborough, not, however, as a source of inspiration for West's figures, but rather as an admirer of West's treatment of forest trees.

[3] V and A Cuttings, II, p. 481, which gives the date of January 1789. The source is unknown. The clipping continues with a second anecdote:

Another incident recurred to is, his Majesty having sent to Mr. West, and commanded him to paint the large Ox, which Mr. Bakewell had conveyed to Windsor for Royal inspection,—the orders were to paint the animal as large as life. If the artist, however, had suspicions of calamitous symptoms, he brooded over them in silence!

Confirming that there is at least some truth in this story, there is a drawing by West of an ox in the Historical Society of Pennsylvania; it is inscribed *The Ox brought from Lord Warwick's Park, and shewn to His Majesty at Windsor Jan 1st 1787* and has the dimensions of 6 ft. by 10 ft., the height and length of the animal, noted upon it.

[4] Pen and ink, $4\frac{5}{16} \times 7\frac{3}{16}$ (sheet size), on the reverse of a drawing of Prometheus (Philadelphia Museum of Art). The Philadelphia drawing is not dated, but a closely related drawing of Prometheus in the Fogg Art Museum is signed and dated *1783*.

[5] See Kraemer 1975, pp. 75–76 (174–78), fig. 44, and pls. 96 and 97. The most famous of the old trees at Windsor was Herne's Oak, which stood in the Home Park and which No. 473 does not show. In 1839 the artist's younger son sold a drawing by West of Herne's Oak (S. Leigh Sotheby, London, 1 June 1839, lot 53), and that drawing is probably identical with one now in Boston, which bears an inscription on the mount in Benjamin West, Jr.'s hand identifying it

as Herne's Oak (ill. in Kraemer, pl. 76, fig. 44).
[6] See Kraemer 1975, pp. 98–101. Several further such drawings have passed through the market in recent years.

474 Landscape: Wood Cutters in Windsor Great Park 1795

INDIANAPOLIS MUSEUM OF ART, INDIANAPOLIS, INDIANA

Oil on canvas: 28 × 36 in. (71 × 91.5 cm.)

Signed lower right: *B. West, 1795*

PROV: Offered by West's sons to the United States in 1826 (46, "Landscape—Wood Cutters in Windsor Great Park," 1 ft. 4 in. × 3 ft.) and sold by them, Robins, London, 22–25 May 1829, lot 152 ("Landscape—Falling of Trees in Windsor Great Park," 2 ft. 4 in. × 3 ft.), bt. by Egerton (? Wilbraham Egerton, 1781–1865, of Tatton Park, Cheshire); Mr. and Mrs. Nicholas H. Noyes, Indianapolis, by whom given to the Herron (now Indianapolis) Museum of Art in 1950

EXH: RA 1796 (189) "Landscape with wood cutters"; West's Gallery 1822–28 (38) "Landscape, Falling of Trees in Windsor Great Park"; New York 1962 (7); *The Painter and the New World*, Montreal Museum of Fine Arts, 1967 (196)

LISTED: PC, p. 566 ("Falling of Trees in the great Park at Windsor," West, Gallery); UM, p. 530; BA, p. 17; Galt, p. 229; Dillenberger, p. 173 (349)

LIT: V and A Cuttings, III, pp. 768, 769, and 783 (all 1796); Wilbur D. Peat, "A Landscape by Benjamin West," *Bulletin of the Art Association of Indianapolis*, XXXVIII, April 1951, pp. 3–6; Evans 1959, p. 73, pl. 54

No. 474 includes a distant view of Windsor Castle in

the background. The view is similar to that in No. 473, of a decade earlier, but from a vantage point further to the east.

The painting received generally favorable attention when it was exhibited in 1796, but with reservations on the part of one writer about the background ("very much too blue") and about the figures on the part of another ("rather too much of the enamelling hue").

See also *Reapers with a View near Windsor* (No. 451), which is also dated 1795 and appeared together with No. 474 in the Royal Academy exhibition of 1796.

475 A View of Windsor from Snow Hill, Windsor Great Park 1799–1803

TATE GALLERY, LONDON

Oil on paper mounted on canvas: 24 × $33\frac{1}{2}$ in. (61 × 85 cm.)

Inscribed bottom center: *retouched 1803*

PROV: Offered by West's sons to the United States in 1826 (47, "Landscape—View in Windsor Forest," 2 ft. × 2 ft. 9 in.) and sold by them, Robins, London, 22–25 May 1829, lot 159 ("View of Windsor Castle from the Great Park," 2 ft. × 2 ft. 9 in.), bt. by Bone for £105 on behalf of Joseph Neeld, MP, Grittleton House, Wilt.; by descent in the Neeld family until sold, Christie's, London, 13 July 1945, lot 169; purchased by the Tate Gallery in 1945

EXH: RA 1799 (391) "A View of Windsor from Snow Hill, Windsor Park"; West's Gallery 1822–28 (133) "View of Windsor Castle from the Great Park"; BI 1833 (46) "View of Windsor Castle, from the Great Park," lent by Joseph Neeld; *American Painting*, Tate Gallery, London, 1946 (227a)

474

475

ENGR: Engraving ($4\frac{1}{16} \times 6\frac{1}{16}$ in.) by B. Comte, pub. 1 July 1801 opp. p. 198 of vol. 1 of *The Beauties of England and Wales*, by Edward Wedlake Brayley and John Britton

LISTED: *PC*, p. 566 ("View of Windsor Castle from Snow-hill, in the Great Park," West, Gallery); *UM*, p. 531; *BA*, p. 18; Galt, p. 230; Dillenberger, p. 176 (371)

LIT: Farington Diary, 1 Jan. 1799 and 14 May 1803 (Farington 1978—, IV, p. 1123 and VI, p. 2030)

The view of Windsor Castle in No. 475 appears to be from a vantage point somewhere between those utilized by the artist for Nos. 473 and 474. Snow Hill is at the end of the Long Walk, approximately three miles from the castle. A companion view of Snow Hill is No. 476 below. In both Nos. 475 and 476 West avoided the formal view straight down the Long Walk, and, although he must have painted No. 475 from a point not far from the Walk, the painting gives no hint of its existence.

Joseph Farington called on West on New Year's Day 1799 and found him "washing up in oil colours 2 landscape sketches on paper—made in Windsor Park.—He

recommended to me to do the same." Since Nos. 475 and 476 are on paper, and since West completed them in the winter or spring of 1799 in time to exhibit them at that year's Royal Academy exhibition, they must be the two sketches seen by Farington. No. 475 is inscribed *retouched 1803* and hence is presumably also the work mentioned by Farington after a visit to West on 14 May 1803: "He was painting with spectacles on and was retouching one of his studies made in Windsor Park." No. 476, which West evidently did not retouch in 1803 bears a signature and date of *1799*; if No. 475 was similarly signed, the signature has disappeared. Both works are on several pieces of paper joined together. Both show pencil outlines under the paint, confirming the information from Farington that West worked up the pictures from sketches made in the park. No. 475 is now rather dark and has a prevailing golden color, which is probably due in part to varnish and to the discoloration of the paper; however, it was described in the Robins sale catalogue of 1829 as being an autumn scene: "a rich and glowing landscape, represented under that deep-toned mysterious effect of atmosphere which is so inspiring to the picturesque genius of poetry and painting, and so peculiar to the climate."

476 A View of Snow Hill, Windsor Great Park
1799

See color detail p. 118

VICTORIA AND ALBERT MUSEUM, LONDON

Oil on paper mounted on canvas: $23\frac{1}{2} \times 33$ in. (51.5×84 cm.)

Signed lower left: *B. West 1799*

PROV: Offered by West's sons to the United States in 1826 (48, "Landscape," 2 ft. × 2 ft. 9 in.) and sold by them, Robins, London, 22–25 May 1829, lot 156 ("View in Windsor Great Park," 2 ft. × 2 ft. 9 in.), bt. by Smith for £68.5.0.; acquired by the Victoria and Albert Museum in 1885

EXH: RA 1799 (657) "A view of Snow Hill, Windsor Great Park"; West's Gallery 1822–28 (128) "View in Windsor Great Park"

LISTED: *PC*, p. 566 ("Cattle drinking at a Watering-place in the Great Park, Windsor, with Mr. West drawing," West, Gallery); *UM*, p. 531; Barlow, p. 435; *BA*, p. 18; Galt, p. 229; Dillenberger, p. 175 (366)

476

LIT: Farington Diary, 1 Jan. 1799 (Farington 1978—, IV, p. 1123); Whitley 1928b, p. 312; William T. Whitley, *Gilbert Stuart*, Cambridge, Mass., 1932, pp. 21–22; Grant 1958, III, p. 221, fig. 213; Devanter 1973, p. 767, fig. 3 and pl. IV; Kraemer 1975, p. 72

See No. 475, which appeared together with No. 476 at the Royal Academy in 1799. Whereas the former shows the view from Snow Hill in Windsor Great Park, the latter depicts the hill itself. It does not show Windsor Castle, or any other marked topographical features. The equestrian statue of George III, the so-called "Copper Horse," which now stands atop of Snow Hill at the end of the Long Walk, was only erected between 1829 and 1831.

The early lists of West's works and the Robins sale catalogue of May 1829, both indicate that No. 476 includes a self-portrait of the artist sketching. Additionally, the Robins catalogue identifies his companion as James Dyer, a former soldier in the Horse Guards and life model at the Royal Academy schools, who was West's servant for fifty years. According to the same source, the two horses are also portraits of West's own saddle horses.

Ruth Kraemer has loosely associated two small drawings in the Pierpont Morgan Library with No. 476; one shows a man wearing a broad-rimmed hat similar to that worn by West in the painting, while in the other the subject, who leans against a horse, wears a long coat and crosses his legs, as does West as he leans against a tree in No. 476.[1]

[1]Black chalk, $1\frac{3}{4} \times 1\frac{1}{2}$ in., and brown and black chalk, $3\frac{15}{16} \times 3\frac{13}{16}$ in. (Kraemer 1975, p. 72, nos. 159 and 160).

477 View from the East Terrace of Windsor Castle Looking over Datchet (?)1792

See color illustration p. 116

TATE GALLERY, LONDON

Oil on canvas: $11\frac{1}{8} \times 14\frac{5}{8}$ in. (28.5 × 37 cm.)

Signed lower left: *B. West/Windsor/[?]1792*

PROV: Sold by West's sons, Robins, London, 22–25 May 1829, lot 146 ("Landscape View from the Terrace at Windsor Looking over Datchet," 1 ft. × 1 ft. 3 in.), bt. by Ward for £33.12.0.; William James Ward (1800–1840) in 1833; bought by the Tate Gallery in 1941

EXH: West's Gallery 1822–28 (80) "A Landscape, View from the Terrace at Windsor looking over Datchet"; BI 1833 (11) lent by W. J. Ward

LISTED: *PC*, p. 566 ("View from the East-end of Windsor Castle looking over Datchet," West, Gallery); *UM*, p. 530; *BA*, p. 18; Galt, p. 229; Dillenberger, p. 175 (361)

LIT: Evans 1959, p. 73, pl. 55

Nos. 477 and 478 are views from Windsor Castle, rather than of it, looking to the east and to the north respectively. Datchet, which is shown in the former, is a village on the opposite bank of the Thames beyond the Home Park. The wall running across the foreground is that of the East Terrace, built by King Charles II.

The signature and date on No. 477 are very faint, and the reading of the date is questionable. The Tate Gallery catalogues record it as *1791*.

In 1967, Mrs. Claire Francis, a descendant of the artist, sold a drawing showing the same view from a slightly different vantage point.[1]

[1]Pen and wash, $4\frac{7}{8} \times 7\frac{1}{8}$ in.; sold Christie's, London, 14 March 1967, lot 29.

478

478 View from the North Terrace of Windsor Castle Looking over Eton 1798

MUSEUM OF FINE ARTS, BOSTON

Oil on paper: 11 × 17½ in. (28 × 44.5 cm.)

Signed lower left: *B. West, 1798, Windsor*

PROV: Sold by Benjamin West, Jr., S. Leigh Sotheby, London, 1 June 1839, lot 64 ("View of Eton College, taken from the Terrace at Windsor," in oil colour); John Hubbard Sturgis (1834–1888); given by his daughters to the Museum of Fine Arts in 1942

No. 478 shows the view looking northward from Windsor Castle. Eton College Chapel, to the left of center, is the most prominent feature in the landscape. As in No. 477, the foreground consists of a low terrace wall and a view over part of the Home Park. Nevertheless, despite the similarities in composition and concept, the two are not companion works. No. 478 is larger than No. 477; it is on a different support; and whereas the latter appeared in the main sale of paintings by West in 1829, No. 478 was sold in a sale of drawings ten years later. Also, if the date of *1792* on No. 477 is correctly read, an interval of six years separates the two works.

479 A View of Tangier Mill, near Windsor

LOCATION UNKNOWN

(29 × 21 IN.) (73.5 × 53.5 CM.)

PROV: Offered by West's sons to the United States in 1826 (100) and sold by them, Robins, London, 22–25 May 1829, lot 139 ("A View of Tangier Mill, near Windsor," 2 ft. 5 in. × 1 ft. 9 in.), bt. by Ward for £73.10.0.; (?) William James Ward (1800–1840) in 1833

EXH: West's Gallery 1822–28 (81) "A View of Tangier Mill, near Windsor"; (?) BI 1833 (35) "Landscape, with Figures," lent by W. J. Ward

LISTED: *PC*, p. 564 ("The picture of Tangere-mill, at Eton," Mr. West's House at Windsor); *UM*, p. 529; Barlow, p. 434; *BA*, p. 16; Galt, p. 225; Dillenberger, p. 166 (274)

No. 479 evidently depicted the ancient Tangier flour mill in Eton, in a view that also incorporated part of Windsor Castle. The wooden mill, which is no longer standing, was situated on the edge of the Thames a short distance to the south-east of Eton College and

approximately a third of a mile north of Windsor Castle, with a largely unimpeded prospect of the castle over the river. According to the Robins catalogue of May 1829, "From hence, along the wooded banks of the lock, and the park wall, which form a vista, is seen one of Windsor's oldest towers." The same entry also mentions the mastery of West's treatment of the figures in No. 479, suggesting that they were sufficiently prominent to allow our tentative equation of this work with the "Landscape, with Figures" lent by W. J. Ward to the British Institution in 1833.

The dimensions listed for No. 479 in 1826 and 1829 indicate that it was a vertical composition rather than the more usual horizontal of West's other landscapes, and it is perhaps worth noting that in *Public Characters*, and in the other early lists of his works, the wording of the entry is "picture of" the mill, rather than "view of," which appears in the preceding two entries (for Nos. 468 and 469).

480 Storm at Sea (?)c. 1752–53

PENNSYLVANIA HOSPITAL, PHILADELPHIA

Oil on panel: 13¼ × 43 in. (33.5 × 109 cm.)

PROV: Presented to the Pennsylvania Hospital by Thomas Rogers in 1818 or 1819

EXH: Philadelphia 1938 (1); *Seascape and the American Imagination*, Whitney Museum of American Art, New York, 1975

LIT: Dunlap Diary, 22 June 1833 (Dunlap 1930, III, p. 697); Dunlap 1834, I, p. 40 (Dunlap 1918, I, p. 39); John F. Watson, *Annals of Philadelphia and Pennsylvania in Ye Olden Times*, Philadelphia, 1845, I, p. 575; Sawitzky 1938, p. 445 (1), ill. no. 1; Flexner 1952, pp. 15–16

According to John F. Watson's *Annals of Philadelphia*, first published in 1830, the young West painted No. 480 and a second picture now also belonging to the Pennsylvania Hospital (No. 481) as over-mantels in a house in which he boarded while living in Philadelphia. They remained in the house, in Strawberry Alley, until a later owner, a merchant named Thomas Rogers, had the cedar panels upon which they were painted removed from the walls and cleaned.[1] Rogers's attention to the two works was evidently due to West himself, as Watson recorded that another Philadelphian, Samuel R. Wood, had told him that West had asked Wood "to seek out and preserve those early efforts of his mind." Rogers presented the two works to the Penn-

480

sylvania Hospital, where they hung with West's large *Christ Healing the Sick* (No. 338), presumably as overmantels in the places which the artist had intended to fill with portraits of himself and Benjamin Franklin (Nos. 531 and 618). An entry, evidently for 8 August 1818, in the minutes of the Pennsylvania Hospital acknowledges Thomas Rogers's gift of two paintings "executed by B. West in the fifteenth year of his life" and authorized the President to give Rogers "a certificate for life admission to the picture room" in return.[2] The same entry instructs Zaccheus Collins "to superintend the cleaning of the paintings and the fixing of them in such situations as he may deem proper." The two were hanging with *Christ Healing the Sick* on 22 June 1833, when William Dunlap recorded in his diary that he had seen them.

If West painted Nos. 480 and 481 in the "fifteenth year of his life," they date from 1752–53 and, hence, are among the earliest works now known by the artist. Sawitzky considered No. 480 West's earliest preserved work and assigned it an earlier date: *c.* 1749–52, and Flexner has argued for the yet earlier date of *c.* 1748–49. Dunlap both in his diary and in his *History of the Rise and Progress of the Arts of Design* described No. 480 as copied from a print, "with a perfect lack of skill, as might be expected" (in the words of the *History*). Although the print which West copied has not been identified, Roger Stein in the catalogue of the exhibition *Seascape and the American Imagination* suggests that No. 480 is close in format to works by Claes Claesz. Wou (*c.* 1592–1665). As far as we know, at the age of fifteen West had not yet seen the sea, but, according to Galt, he had been profoundly impressed by the sight of ships in Philadelphia.[3]

[1] Watson states that Rogers had the paintings taken down in 1825, but this date is contradicted by the earlier date of the Pennsylvania Hospital's acknowledgment of his gift. It is also worth asking why the Pennsylvania Hospital needed to have the pictures cleaned in 1818 or 1819, if Rogers had them cleaned when they were removed from the walls, as Watson states he did.
[2] Archives of American Art: Microfilm, roll P: 87, frame 92, p. 314 of the *Minutes of the Pennsylvania Hospital: Excerpts relating to art, artists and their productions*. In the microfilm, it is not clear whether the date of 14 August 1818 belongs to the entry about Rogers's gift or the preceding entry. The following entry excerpted from the minutes is dated 26 July 1819.
[3] Galt 1816, p. 26.

481 Landscape with Cow (?) *c.* 1752–53
See illustration, p. 12

PENNSYLVANIA HOSPITAL, PHILADELPHIA

Oil on panel: $26\frac{3}{4} \times 50\frac{1}{4}$ in. (68 × 127.5 cm.)

PROV: As for No. 480

EXH: Philadelphia 1938 (2)

LIT: As for No. 480; in Sawitzky 1938, pp. 445–46 (2), ill. no. 2

The documentation of the early history of this work is the same as that for No. 480. In 1814 William Dunlap described it as West's "own composition," rather than a copy: "a white cow, who is the hero of the piece, and sundry trees, houses, men, and ships, combined in a manner perfectly childish."

See also No. 482. Both No. 481 and the lost No. 482 probably depended upon the example of William Williams (1727–1791), one of whose landscapes West is said to have copied at the outset of his career (see No. 523). Flexner has suggested that West may have partly based No. 481 on drawings made with a *camera obscura*.

[1] Carey 1820, p. 514.

482 Landscape Composition *c.* 1746

LOCATION UNKNOWN

PROV: Painted by West for Edward Penington (1726–1796)

LIT: Galt 1816, p. 26; Sawitzky 1938, p. 446 (3) and cf. ill. no. 3; Flexner 1952, p. 10; Dickason 1970, p. 130 (letter from West to Thomas Eagles, 10 Oct. 1810); Alberts 1978, p. 12

John Galt in his account of the young West's beginnings as an artist states that a relative, a Mr. Pennington (or Penington) presented the eight-year-old boy his first box of paints and canvases. After West had painted one picture (see No. 509), Penington took him for a stay of several days in Philadelphia. There, West painted a picture for Penington: "a picturesque view of a river, with vessels on the water, and cattle pasturing on the banks." This was evidently the same picture that West described in a letter written in 1810 as "a landscape—in which were ships, cattle, & other things which I had been accustomed to see."[1] According both to this letter and to Galt, West was still working on the picture when he met the artist William Williams (1727–1791), who lent him books by du Fresnoy and Jonathan Richardson and otherwise encouraged the aspiring artist. Our other chief source for West's early career, William Carey, does not tell the same story, but states that West saw and copied a landscape by Williams before he met the artist himself (see No. 523).

A painting of a river with boats and cattle sounds not unlike No. 481, but the circumstances recorded by Galt suggest that it was another work painted several years previously. A landscape (*below*) now in the Abby Aldrich Rockefeller Folk Art Center in Williamsburg, Virginia, which was lent by the Rosenbach Galleries to the West exhibitions in Philadelphia and Brooklyn in 1921 and 1922, was described in the catalogues of both exhibitions as "supposed to be the second painting done by Benjamin West."[2] William Sawitzky on the basis of those claims included it in his fundamental study of West's American works published in 1938, equating it with the picture painted for Penington. However, there seems little reason to accept the Wil-

liamsburg painting as that work. Unlike No. 481, which was at the Pennsylvania Hospital before West's death, and was accepted as an early work by West by Dunlap in 1833, its history prior to 1921 is a blank. Not only does it not have much resemblance to No. 481, but it shows considerably more advanced technical facility in the control of perspective on the part of the artist. Galt's and West's accounts are the only reasons we have for considering the painting a work by West at all, and those accounts lead us to expect a less accomplished work. In 1952 Flexner rejected the attribution to West, and it is no longer ascribed to West by the authorities in Williamsburg.[3]

[1] West's letter to Thomas Eagles is an account of what he knew about the life of William Williams, and it provides an abbreviated description of his own early life as appropriate background. In it he states that Mr. Penington gave him his first paints in Philadelphia and that No. 482 was his "first attempt" in painting. This seems to telescope separate incidents described in Galt's more ample narrative. They are also separated, although with somewhat different details, by William Carey (Carey 1820, p. 514).
[2] Philadelphia 1921 (23) and Brooklyn 1922 (18).
[3] We are indebted to Graham Hood, Chief Curator, Colonial Williamsburg, for helpful correspondence about this work.

483 Landscape (?)1756

LOCATION UNKNOWN

PROV: William Henry (1729–1786), Lancaster, Pennsylvania; his son

LIT: Tinkcom 1951, p. 382 (Sir Augustus Foster)

The British diplomat Sir Augustus Foster visited a son of West's early patron William Henry (see No. 637) at some date between 1804 and 1812 and saw in his home several works by West. Among them was "a Landscape that appeared to be a Copy from some Italian Painting and represented a confused tumble of an Italian Town and Mountain with Dutch or German Figures, Chinese Rocks and English Ships." After listing the other pictures, Foster went on, "The colouring and drawing in all is very bad and hard, tho the Two

Unknown artist, *Imaginary Landscape*. Oil on canvas, 23 × 36 in. Abby Aldrich Rockefeller Folk Art Collection

Cows which are in the Landscape have something natural about them that is pleasing." This painting may have been signed and dated *1756* (see No. 637). The description sounds similar to accounts of No. 482, and ships, cows, towns, and rocks are to be seen in No. 481, but No. 483 was presumably a separate work painted for Henry at a later date than those two paintings.

484 A Landscape: Driving of Sheep and Cows to Water (?)*c.* 1794

LOCATION UNKNOWN

(11½ × 15½ in.) (29 × 39.5 cm.)

PROV: Offered by West's sons to the United States in 1826 (73 "Landscape and Cattle," 11½ × 1 ft. 3½ in.) and sold by them, Robins, London, 22–25 May 1829, lot 34 ("A Landscape, Driving of Sheep and Cows to Water," 11½ × 15½ in.), bt. by Pickering for £22.1.0.

EXH: (?) RA 1794 (265) "A Landscape" or (270) "A Landscape"; West's Gallery 1822–28 (29) "A Landscape, driving of Sheep and Cows to Water."

LISTED: *PC*, p. 566 ("Driving of Sheep and Cows to Water," West, Gallery); *UM*, p. 531; Barlow, p. 435; *BA*, p. 18; Galt, p. 229; Dillenberger, p. 175 (365)

West exhibited two pictures at the Royal Academy in 1794 with the same uninformative title of "A Landscape." We have tentatively equated them with Nos. 484 and 486, two missing works, both of which were sold by West's sons in 1829 with titles describing them as landscapes, but not identifying them as views of specific locations. Needless to say, the cryptic titles allow latitude for guessing about what works went with them, but there are surprisingly few recorded works by West which we can consider as possible candidates. Apart from Nos. 484 and 486, the most likely are Nos. 469 and 470, but both of those paintings are works for which he probably would have used more specific titles identifying the sites depicted and possibly the times of day as well.

Since West's sons sold No. 484 in 1829, it presumably was not the "Landscape, with cattle" sold by Mrs. Albert F. West in 1898 (No. 485). That work's dimensions, as recorded in 1898, also do not correspond with

those listed for No. 484 in 1826 and 1829. The painting of "A shepherd driving sheep through a ford," which West exhibited at the British Institution in 1806, can probably be identified as *Cranford Bridge* (No. 463), which West exhibited at the Royal Academy in the previous year, rather than as No. 484.

485 A Landscape, with Cattle

LOCATION UNKNOWN

(7 × 9 in.) (18 × 23 cm.)

PROV: Sold by Mrs. Albert F. West, Christie's, London, 19 March 1898, lot 135 ("A Landscape, with cattle," 7 × 9 in.), bt. by Cohen for 5 shillings

EXH: (?) *Spring Exhibition*, Whitechapel Art Gallery, 1906 (87) "Figures and Cattle at a Stream," lent by M. H. Colnaghi

LIT: David Howard Dickason, *William Williams: Novelist and Painter of Colonial America 1727–1791*, Bloomington, Indiana, 1970, p. 25

David Dickason, on the basis of no visible evidence, equates No. 485 with West's first painting (see No. 509).

486 A Landscape (?)*c.* 1794

LOCATION UNKNOWN

(15 × 21 in.) (38 × 53.5 cm.)

PROV: Offered by West's sons to the United States in 1826 (109) and sold by them, Robins, London, 22–25 May 1829, lot 165 ("A Landscape," 1 ft. 3 in. × 1 ft. 9 in.), bt. by Armstrong for £31.10.0.

EXH: (?) RA 1794 (265) "A Landscape" or (270) "A Landscape"; West's Gallery 1822–28 (107) "A Landscape"

See No. 484. The entry in the Robins sale catalogue of 22–25 May 1829 described No. 486 as "Characteristic of the scenery of Cumberland, with one of the beck's, or small cascades, which abound in the well watered regions of that romantic country."

487 A Landscape with Women and Children
c. 1798

LOCATION UNKNOWN

EXH: (?) RA 1798 (551 or 622) "A Landscape with women and children" (both entries had the same title)

See *Mothers with their Children Dabbling in a Brook* (No. 450), which was certainly one of the two works which West seems to have exhibited at the Royal Academy in 1798 under the title "A Landscape with Women and Children." It is possible that the inclusion of the same title twice in the same catalogue was an error. If not, and if West did exhibit two works in one year that the title could fit, then the second painting has disappeared without a trace.

488 A Landscape, with a Hunt on the Second Ground *c.* 1798

LOCATION UNKNOWN

PROV: William Beckford (1759–1844), Fonthill Abbey, Wilts.; in the Fonthill sale catalogue of 17–22 Sept. 1822 (Christie's), lot 20, and sold, Fonthill Abbey, 10–15 Oct. 1823 (Phillips) lot 20 (in both catalogues as "A small landscape with figures, stag hunt")

EXH: RA 1798 (632) "A Landscape, with a hunt on the second ground"

LISTED: *PC*, p. 561 ("A small Landscape, with a Hunt passing in the back-ground," painted for and in the possession of Wm. Beckford, Esq. of Fonthill); *UM*, p. 528; Barlow, p. 432; *BA*, p. 14; Galt, p. 220; Dillenberger, p. 151 (131)

See *Landscape Representing the Country near Windsor* (No. 473), which shows a scene of stag hunting in the background. It is possible that West painted No. 488 as a reduced replica of that painting, but the mention of a hunt in all variations of the title of No. 488 suggests that this detail may have constituted a more conspicuous feature of the painting than do the tiny figures in the middle distance in No. 473. West painted stag hunts in the foreground in Nos. 54 and 55.

ANIMALS

489 Cats and Dogs 1793

LOCATION UNKNOWN

(Oil on panel: $8\frac{1}{2} \times 11\frac{1}{4}$ in.) (21.5×28.5 cm.)

(Signed and dated: *1793*)

PROV: Sold by Mrs. Albert F. West, Christie's, London, 18–19 March 1898, lot 134, bt. by McLean for £3

490 A Bull's Head before 1760

LOCATION UNKNOWN

LIT: Whitley 1928a, p. 195 (*Literary Gazette*, 1832); Wainwright 1978, p. 111 (Nicholas Biddle, diary, 24 June 1807)

In 1807 Nicholas Biddle (1786–1844), who was serving in London as the secretary to the American envoy, James Monroe, asked West about a signboard showing a bull's head in one of the streets of Philadelphia. West did not remember it, but by the time he talked to Biddle, he had been gone from Philadelphia for forty-seven years, and his failure of memory probably should be interpreted as such, rather than as a denial of the work. Another reference to a sign showing a bull's head appeared in the *Literary Gazette* in 1832: "we observe in a New York journal that a Bull's Head, one of the earliest productions of West, which has hung there for more than sixty years, has been purchased by an English gentleman."

491 A Drove of Oxen *c.* 1755–56

LOCATION UNKNOWN

LIT: Wainwright 1978, p. 111 (Nicholas Biddle, diary, 24 June 1807)

See No. 490. In the same diary entry in which Nicholas Biddle recorded that West did not remember a sign of a bull's head in Philadelphia, Biddle wrote that West had painted "a sign still at Lancaster of a drove of oxen." West told Biddle that he painted it at about the same time as he painted his early *Death of Socrates* (No. 4), when he was about thirteen or fourteen years old. It seems likely, however, that West made his trip to Lancaster, where he painted the *Death of Socrates*, at a slightly later date, in 1755–56, when he would have been sixteen or seventeen years old.

492 Fish

LOCATION UNKNOWN

PROV: Sold by West's sons, Robins, London, 20–22 June 1829, lot 71 ("Fish, Very Fine")

A large drawing of a fish is in the Pierpont Morgan Library.[1]

[1]Black chalk, $33\frac{1}{2} \times 10\frac{5}{8}$ in. (Kraemer 1975, p. 80, no. 197).

A Donkey, drawing for Nos. 218 and 220. Swarthmore College, Swarthmore, Pennsylvania

MISCELLANEOUS STUDIES

493 A Child

PRIVATE COLLECTION

Oil on canvas: $9\frac{7}{8} \times 7\frac{3}{4}$ in. (25 × 19.5 cm.)

This detail of a child holding a ball and a doll appears to have been cut from a larger unfinished picture.

494 Three Heads

LOCATION UNKNOWN

(20 × 26 in.) (50.8 × 86 cm.)

PROV: Offered by West's sons to the United States in 1826 (129, "Three Heads," 1 ft. 7 in.×2 ft. 1 in.), and sold by them, Robins, London, 22–25 May 1829, lot 117 ("Three Heads," 1 ft. 8 in.×2 ft. 2 in.), bt. by Morgan for £13.13.0.

The entry in the Robins sale catalogue contained the following discussion of No. 494:

> These studies were the result of an experiment by the masterly hand of West, to ascertain the capacities of a menstruum, brought to this country by an ingenious Italian. It is to be regretted that it rested here, for its properties were such, as to induce the belief that the same menstruum had been used by the great masters of the old Italian school, and that much of the recondite character which is so admired in the *chiaro scuro* of their works, was effected through its medium. The proprietor of this secret disappeared, to the great regret of the Artist, and perhaps to the disparagement of the art, which might have derived considerable aid from a discovery that promised new means to the professor, for rendering his thoughts with superior facility, richness, and effect.

The most celebrated or notorious technical secret supposedly brought to England from Italy with which West experimented was that of the "Venetian Secret," for which see No. 543, etc. It is possible that No. 494 was one of West's experiments in that technique. However, none of Joseph Farington's many references to West's experiments with the Venetian Secret mentions a study of three heads, and the details quoted above are sufficiently at odds with the recorded history of the Secret to suggest that No. 494 was the product of another, presumably unrelated, experiment.

495 Academical Study from Wilson the Black

LOCATION UNKNOWN

PROV: Sold by West's sons, Robins, London, 20–22 June 1829, lot 82 ("Academical Study on canvas, from Wilson the Black")

496 Two Prismatic Spheres (?)c. 1797

LOCATION UNKNOWN

PROV: Sold by West's sons, Robins, London, 20–22 June 1829, lot 99 ("The two Prismatic Spheres, Illustrative of the system of colouring and referred to by the Professor of Painting to the Royal Academy")

493

The entry in the sale catalogue quoted above indicates that No. 496 did not illustrate one of West's own lectures but was referred to by the Professor of Painting of the Royal Academy. During West's tenure of office as President, the Academy had four Professors of Painting: James Barry, Henry Fuseli, John Opie, and Henry Tresham. Nevertheless, West did discuss a system of coloring by the example of distributing prismatic colors over a ball in his lecture to the Royal Academy students in 1797,[1] and it seems much more likely that he would have painted No. 496 to illustrate his own lectures than those by one of his colleagues. A drawing in the British Museum of a globe or sphere, although monochromatic, may also have been done in connection with this lecture.[2] Before discussing the prismatic coloration of the ball, West discussed its illumination in light and dark. See also No. 522.

[1]Galt 1820, p. 113.
[2]Black and white chalks on grey paper: $8\frac{5}{8} \times 10\frac{3}{4}$ in. (50–10–21–1).

497 Design for a Pediment

LOCATION UNKNOWN

PROV: Sold by West's sons, Robins, London, 20–22 June 1829, lot 57 ("Design for a Pediment")

The most important pediment designed by West (indeed, the only one known to the authors of this catalogue) is that of the King William Block of Greenwich Hospital (see No. 110). A large drawing for it is in the National Maritime Museum at Greenwich. Whether No. 497 was related to this project is not known, since the only information we have about No. 497 is the brief title from the Robins catalogue of June 1829. If it was for the Greenwich pediment, it seems strange that the fact was not mentioned in the catalogue. West did make designs for further pediments destined for Greenwich but never executed.[1]

[1]See No. 110, note 3.

COPIES

I Paintings based on the Elgin Marbles: Nos. 498–503

498 Battle of the Centaurs 1808

LOCATION UNKNOWN

(Oil on canvas: 66 × 120 in.) (167.5 × 308 cm.)

LIT: Farington Diary, 30 March and 21 May 1808 and 2 and 22 March 1809 (Farington 1978–, IX, pp. 3249–50, 3282, 3413, and 3424–25); [William Richard Hamilton], *Memorandum on the Subject of the Earl of Elgin's Pursuits in Greece*, 2nd ed., London, 1815, pp. 47–55, 150, 152; Tom Taylor, ed., *Life of Benjamin Robert Haydon, Historical Painter*, 2nd ed., London, 1853, I, pp. 96, 117–18, and 170; A. H. Smith, "Lord Elgin and His Collection," *Journal of Hellenic Studies*, XXXVI, 1916, pp. 297, 303–4; Haydon 1960–63, I, pp. 89–92, 212–13, and II, pp. 517–19; Rothenberg 1967, pp. 228–30, 242–45, 274–81, 321–26, 414–18; Kraemer 1975, pp. 63–64; Alberts 1978, pp. 348–52.

The Elgin Marbles, sculptures chiefly from the Parthenon in Athens, were brought by Thomas Bruce, seventh Earl of Elgin, from Athens to London between 1801 and 1811. In 1807 those that were then in England were installed in a shed built by Lord Elgin in the grounds of a house he had leased at the corner of Park Lane and Piccadilly. They remained there until 1811. Following an interlude when they were kept at Burlington House, in 1816 they entered the British Museum, where they remain.

West evidently first saw the sculptures in the winter of 1807–8. On 30 March 1808, he told Farington,

that they were sublime specimens of the purest sculpture & that when the summer arrives He means to devote much time to study from them. He sd. that this He wd. do though in His 70th year & had on this acct. a wish to be again only 20 years of age that He might labour to profit by them.

On 21 May he told Farington that he would begin his studies in July and August. A letter from Lord Elgin inviting West to work in his "Musaeum" is dated 1 September 1808, but, as the letter indicates, it followed an earlier oral invitation:

I am extremely mortified to find that the letter which was to have been written to you in consequence of our last conversation has by accident, not reached its destination. But, I hope this circumstance has not prevented your proceeding as agreed on. The more so as I had on that very day an opportunity of communicating with Mr. Hamilton on the subject.[1]

At Park Lane West found Benjamin Robert Haydon, who had been given permission to draw from the Marbles in May, already at work. According to Haydon's memoirs:

While I was drawing there, West came in and seeing me said with surprise, "Hah, hah, Mr. Haydon, *you* are admitted, are you? I hope you and I can keep a secret." The very day after he came down with large canvasses, and without at all entering into the principles of these divine things hastily made compositions from Greek history, putting in the Theseus, the Illysus, and restoring defective parts;—that is, he did that which he could do easily and which he did not require to learn how to do, and avoided doing that which he could only do with difficulty and which he was in great need of learning how to do.

In another passage in his memoirs, Haydon states that when West came, he did not draw the Marbles: "He merely made a set of rattling compositions, taking the attitudes as models for his own inventions." West, on the other hand, told Farington on 22 March 1809 that "during the last Autumn He had made drawings from the statues & Basso relevios in that Collection & with the figures & groupes had made compositions of fabulous subjects." He had been employed for about three weeks and proposed to complete during the next summer what he had begun. West also wrote a letter on 6 February 1809, to Lord Elgin, thanking him for allowing him to study the Marbles. There he states,

I must premise to your Lordship, that I considered loose and detached sketches from these reliques, of little use to me, or value to the arts in general. To improve myself, therefore, and to contribute to the improvement of others, I have deemed it more important to select and combine whatever was most excellent from them into subject and composition.

The letter then describes six canvases which West had painted (Nos. 498–503). Three of them (Nos. 499 or 500, 501, and 502) appeared in the secondary sale of pictures from his estate on 20–22 June 1829, but there is no later trace or record of any of them. We do, nonetheless, have some idea of what they showed from West's descriptions; in this catalogue we have quoted these descriptions in the appropriate entry for each work, while the sequence of entries follows that of West's letter.

The paragraph devoted to the first composition (No. 498) is:

From the Centaurs in *alto relievo*, I have taken the figures of most distinguished eminence, and formed into groupes for painting; from which selection, by adding female figures of my own, I have composed the Battle of the Centaurs. I have drawn the figures the size of the originals, on a canvass five feet six inches high, by ten feet long.

This composition clearly derived from the Parthenon metopes, which are in high relief, and of which all those collected by Lord Elgin, from the south side of the Parthenon, show struggles between Lapiths and centaurs. A drawing by West in the Pierpont Morgan Library shows figures from Metopes VII, IX, XXVII, and XXVIII.[2] This drawing and one other in the same collection based on the Theseus or Heracles (see No. 501) confirm Farington's statement that West did make drawings from the Marbles. They are, however, the only such drawings now known, and they are relatively slight productions. So it seems probable that West did paint Nos. 498–503 directly on his canvases before the sculptures, as Haydon states he did, rather than base the compositions on his drawings, as what he told Farington implies. In both drawings he took great liberties with the originals, adding heads and other missing parts, which, according to Haydon, he did in the paintings as well.

West evidently chose his seemingly bizarre manner of working from the sculptures in response to a request from Lord Elgin, who wrote on 1 September 1808:

My request to you is that you would have the goodness of making any sketches from the subjects in my Musaeum in the view of pointing out how far, either individually or in groupes they may be worthy of being imitated in painting. For this purpose the Musaeum will be open to you at all times.

West in his letter of the following February to Lord Elgin stated:

In order to render the subjects which I selected, with perspecuity, and the effect, which arises from combined parts and the order of arrangements, comprehensive, I have ventured to unite figures of my own invention with those of Phidias; but as I have endeavoured to preserve, with the best force of my abilities, the style of Phidias, I flatter myself, the union will not be deemed incongruous or presumptuous. Your Lordship may perhaps be inclined to think with me, that a point, and, if I may so express it, a kind of climax, is thus given to those works, by the union of those detached figures, with the incorporation of the parts of individual grandeur, and abstracted excellence of Phidias. For what I have done, my Lord, I had the example of Raphael, and most of the Italian masters of the greatest celebrity. Is it not, moreover, this combination of parts which comes the nearest to perfection in refined and ideal art? For, thus combining what is excellent in art with what possesses character in nature, the most distinguished works have been produced, in painting, poetry, and sculpture.

In following this system of combination, I had the singular good fortune, by your Lordship's liberality, to select from the first productions of sculpture which ever adorned the world in that department in art; which neither Raphael, nor any of the distinguished masters, had the advantage to see, much less to study, since the revival of art. I may therefore, declare with truth, my Lord, that I am the first in modern times who have enjoyed the much coveted opportunity, and availed myself of the rare advantage of forming compositions from them, by adapting their excellencies to poetic fictions and historical facts. . . .

To your Lordship I have to return my sincere thanks, for the means you have afforded me of adding my name to that of Phidias, by arranging his figures in my own compositions, and adapting them to subjects, by which my sketches may be rendered more acceptable, as well as more improving to myself in the higher point of my profession.

West wrote this letter not simply to express his gratitude but to serve as a public document. He offered it to Prince Hoare to publish in the *Academic Annals*,[3] but according to Farington, "This letter had too much of *self* in it to be proper for publication in the Academic Annals & was also too incorrect." It was, however, printed in the *Memorandum on the Subject of the Earl of Elgin's Pursuits in Greece* published in the following year by Lord Elgin's secretary, William Richard Hamilton. In a second edition of the *Memorandum*, published in 1811, it was joined by a second letter written by West on 20 March 1811. That letter says nothing about Nos. 498–503 but does assert the importance of West's studies of the Elgin Marbles for his recently completed *Christ Healing the Sick* (No. 336). West also praised the sculptures in a discourse to the Royal Academy students on 10 December 1811.[5] His health kept him from testifying in 1816 before the Select Committee of the House of Commons, which was considering the purchase of the Marbles, but the Committee sent him thirty questions to which he provided written responses that were published in the *Minutes of Evidence*.[6] In these he stated that he had *drawn* the most distinguished of the Marbles, suggested that his study had been of importance for both No. 336 and *Christ Rejected* (No. 353), which he had completed in 1814, and, more generally, testified to the pre-eminent quality of the sculptures. In all of this activity, West was the most prominent advocate of the Elgin Marbles, the only British artist of an older generation to value them so highly, and his enthusiasm was certainly a crucial factor affecting the Committee's decision to acquire them for the British Museum.[7] Appropriately, a painting of 1819 by Archibald Archer showing the Marbles installed in their new premises in the British Museum includes West prominently seated in the foreground together with the museum's Chief Librarian, Sir Joseph Planta (ill. p. 132).

In September 1809 Benjamin Robert Haydon called on West to see the sketches he had made from the Marbles. Haydon immediately concluded that West had learned nothing from the sculptures, in contrast to his own mastery of their principles:

I saw instantly his figures were sketched in, in the Westian manner,—His figures were sitting on Horses to be sure, but with no more of the refined characteristics of sitting in various forms than that their legs were astride, and a Horse was between them—

He studied here as he has studied everywhere else—all his life; he came down with immense canvasses, sketched all the figures in an hour, put them into a composition, surveyed them, with the same superficial glance as he had surveyed nature, and all these hidden, deep seated exquisite beauties passed unheeded by—I have heard him talk of them in raptures, when I have been with him, and wondered why he never talked to me scientifically about them or pointed out any particular beauties.

Haydon also filled the margins of his copy of the *Memorandum on the Subject of the Earl of Elgin's Pursuits in Greece* with invective against West, most of it in the same vein, and he repeated it again in passages in his *Autobiography*, two of which are quoted above. He was legitimately offended by West's claim in the letter to Lord Elgin of 6 February 1809, to have been "the first in modern times" to study the sculptures and to form compositions from them, and both the marginal notes and the *Autobiography* contain his counter claims of having drawn from the Marbles long before West and of having utilized their principles in his *Assassination of Dentatus*, which he completed and exhibited in 1809. Although West's compositions based on the Marbles are known to us only from written accounts, there can also be little doubt that Haydon's criticisms of them had some legitimacy. Certainly Haydon's own magnificent drawings from the Marbles reveal a scrupulous and searching observation of a kind that West never devoted to anything. But as A. H. Smith first observed, Haydon was not entirely fair to West. In making compositions from the Marbles, rather than detailed studies, West was doing what Lord Elgin had asked him to do. Additionally, in 1808, West was seventy years old, while Haydon was twenty-two, and the latter's criticism reflects not only the antagonism of an ambitious young man toward an established older one, but also a basic conflict between the naturalistic bias of a nineteenth-century artist and the more idealizing orientation of the preceding century. Elsewhere in his *Autobiography* Haydon was more generous, contrasting the tepid response to the Marbles of Fuseli, his teacher, with that of West:

He [Fuseli] did not behave with the same grandeur of soul that West did. He [West], too, was in the decline of life; he, too, used to talk of art since nature, and of the beau-ideal; but he nobly acknowledged that he knew nothing until he saw the marbles, and bowed his venerable head before them as if in reverence of their majesty.

Peace and honour to his memory! There was more true feeling in his submission to their principles than in all Fuseli's boastful sneers.

Finally, we should note that the aging West's admiration for the Marbles evoked what remains not only the cruellest but also the most memorable attack of the many that the artist drew throughout his long life. Lord Elgin's removal of the sculptures from Athens was not universally approved; among his detractors, Lord Byron devoted five stanzas of *Childe Harold's Pilgrimage* to Lord Elgin's plunder and subsequently published a satirical poem "The Curse of Minerva," on the same subject. In the latter, Byron introduces West, following a reference to Lord Elgin's efforts to sell the Marbles to the state:

Meanwhile, the flattering, feeble dotard West,
Europe's worst dauber, and poor Britain's best,
With palsied hand shall turn each model o'er,
And own himself an infant of fourscore.[9]

Ironically, before West saw the Marbles and became their most visible champion, he had expressed an opinion of their removal to England not unlike Byron's. In 1807 Nicholas Biddle recorded a conversation in which West "Agreed with me about Elgin, a sad barbarian who collected merely to sell & whose boxes are now lying in some corner of London."[10]

See also pp. 130–4 above.

[1]The letter (in the British Museum) is quoted by Smith, p. 303, and by Rothenberg, pp. 244–45. Mr. Hamilton was William Richard Hamilton, Lord Elgin's private secretary.
[2]Black chalk, $3\frac{3}{16} \times 4\frac{3}{8}$ in. (Kraemer 1975, p. 63, no. 119 and pl. 76).
[3]For the *Academic Annals*, see Dillenberger 1977, p. 49, note 14.
[4]There is also a third edition, which we have used, published in 1815 and described on the title-page as the second edition. In this edition, West's two letters comprise Appendix A, pp. 47–56.
[5]Galt 1820, pp. 150–52.
[6]*Report from the Select Committee of the House of Commons on the Earl of Elgin's Collection of Sculptured Marbles, Etc.*, London, 1816, pp. 148–54. West's testimony is dated 18 March 1816.
[7]Rothenberg 1967, pp. 420–21.
[8]See Rothenberg 1967, pp. 245–51, pls. 66–71, and Frederick Cummings, "Phidias in Bloomsbury; B. R. Haydon's Drawings of the Elgin Marbles," *Burlington Magazine*, CVI, 1964, pp. 323–28.
[9]Lines 175–78. For a full discussion of Byron and the Earl of Elgin, see William St. Clair, *Lord Elgin and the Marbles*, London, 1967, pp. 187–202.
[10]Wainwright 1978, p. 114.

499 Theseus and Hercules in Triumph over the Amazons 1808

LOCATION UNKNOWN

(Oil on canvas: 66 × 120 in.) (167.5 × 305 cm.)

PROV: (?) Sold by West's sons, Robins, London, 20–22 June 1829, lot 150 ("Three Sketches, large canvas— the Theseus and Neptune, and the Triumphal Possession [*sic*], from the Elgin Marbles")

LIT: As for No. 498

See No. 498. West's letter to Lord Elgin describes Nos. 499 and 500 together in one paragraph:

From the equestrian figures in *relievo*, I have formed the composition of Theseus and Hercules in triumph over the Amazons, having made their Queen Hippolita a prisoner. In continuation, and as a companion to this subject, I have formed a composition, in which Hercules bestows Hippolita in marriage upon Theseus. Those two are on the same size with the Centaurs.

The "equestrian figures in *relievo*" are the horsemen of the Panathenaic procession from the Parthenon frieze, which is in low relief. Hence, the sketch of the "Triumphal Possession" sold by the artist's sons in 1829 was probably either No. 499 or No. 500, which West evidently also based on the frieze.

500 Hercules Bestows Hippolita in Marriage upon Theseus 1808

LOCATION UNKNOWN

(Oil on canvas: 66 × 120 in.) (167.5 × 305 cm.)

PROV: See No. 499

LIT: As for No. 498

See Nos. 498 and 499. West described Nos. 499 and 500 together in one paragraph, which is quoted in the entry for No. 499.

501 Theseus and the Minotaur 1808

LOCATION UNKNOWN

(Oil on canvas: 72 × 108 in.) (183 × 274 cm.)

PROV: As for No. 499

LIT: As for No. 498

See No. 498. The description of No. 501 is:

From the large figure of Theseus, I have drawn a figure of that hero, of the same size with the sculpture. Before him, on the ground, I have laid the dead body of the Minotaur which he slew. As, by this enterprise, he was extricated from the Labyrinth by the aid of Ariadne, I have represented that Princess sitting by his side, gazing on him with affection. In the back-ground, are the Athenian youths, whom he delivered from bondage; and near them, the ship "with black sails," (in the poetic fancy of Pindar,) which brought him to Crete. The size of this canvass is six feet high, by nine feet long.

The "large figure of Theseus," now generally identified as either Heracles or Dionysus, from the East Pediment, is the most complete of the extant Parthenon pedimental sculptures. A drawing of a seated male nude figure, which appears to be loosely based upon it, is in the Pierpont Morgan Library.[1] Jacob Rothenberg has suggested that the figure of Saul in *Saul before Samuel and the Prophets* (No. 274) of 1812 derives from the Theseus.

[1]Black chalk, heightened with white on blue-grey paper: $7\frac{9}{16} \times 11\frac{7}{8}$ in. (Kraemer 1975, pp. 63–64, no. 120, and pl. 77).

502 Neptune and Amphitrite 1808

LOCATION UNKNOWN

(Oil on canvas: 72 × 108 in.) (183 × 274 cm.)

PROV: As for No. 499

LIT: As for No. 498

See No. 498 and No. 501, to which No. 502 was a companion piece:

From the figure of Neptune, I have formed a companion to the Theseus. In this composition, I have shown Neptune reclining, with his left arm upon the knees of Amphitrite, while with his right he strikes the earth with his trident, and creates the horse. Around him, is Triton, with his train of marine gods; in the back ground, are equestrian exhibitions; and in the distance, ships at anchor.

Although the Elgin Marbles include a fragment of the torso of the figure of Neptune, or Poseidon, which stood together with Athena at the center of the west pediment of the Parthenon, West's "figure of Neptune," whom he represented reclining, was probably based on the reclining figure from the north angle of the same pediment. This figure is usually identified as a river god, either the Cephisus or the Ilissus, but was also called Neptune at the time the sculptures came to England.[1] Although headless, it is otherwise the best preserved of the pedimental sculptures, and it was and is probably the most admired of any of the figures from the Parthenon.[2]

[1]The index to *The Report from the Select Committee of the House of Commons on the Earl of Elgin's Collection of Sculptured Marbles, Etc.*, London, 1816, begins with the warning that the titles "Ilissus" or "River God" are both used for a statue, "which was sometimes called Neptune."
[2]In West's written testimony (ibid., pp. 150–53), he refers at several points to the Theseus and the Ilissus as standing supreme, not only among the Parthenon sculptures, but among all works of art. In 1816, he did refer to the figure of Ilissus by that name, and he does separately mention (on p. 150) the breast and shoulders of the Neptune. In 1808 and 1809, however, he would have known much less about the proposed identifications of the various figures.

503 Alexander and Bucephalus 1808

LOCATION UNKNOWN

(Oil on canvas)

LIT: As for No. 498

See No. 498. West's final paragraph describing his compositions is:

> From the casts in plaster of Paris, taken from the moulds which your Lordship had made at Athens, I selected such figures as I was enabled to form into a composition; the subject of which is, Alexander, and his horse Bucephalus: it is on a canvass smaller than those before mentioned.

Strictly speaking, West did not base this work on the Marbles from the Parthenon. Along with the actual sculptures from the Acropolis, Lord Elgin also brought back eighteen casts from the frieze of the Parthenon, twenty-four casts from the frieze and metopes of the Temple of Theseus, twelve casts from the Choragic Monument of Lysicrates, and one cast from a sarcophagus at Agrigento. Since West's composition included a horse, it seems likely that he did base it on casts from the Parthenon. The entire west frieze is devoted to horsemen preparing, and, while only two slabs from this part of the actual frieze came to England, Lord Elgin's workers had taken molds of all of it.[1]

In his discourse of December 1811, West drew the Academy students' attention to the equestrian groups as examples of the mental power displayed in the Elgin Marbles.[2] His studies of them were particularly criticized by Benjamin Robert Haydon (quoted under No. 498).

[1]D. E. L. Haynes, *An Historical Guide to the Sculptures of the Parthenon*, London, 1971, pp. 12, 23–24, and fig. 10, which reproduces a photograph of a detail of the cast that might well have served as the basis for No. 503.
[2]Galt 1820, pp. 150–51.

II Copies after Earlier Paintings: Nos. 504–23

504 Copy after Venus Lamenting over the Dead Body of Adonis by a Follower of Annibale Carracci 1762

LOCATION UNKNOWN

PROV: Painted in the summer of 1762 for William Allen (1704–1780) and James Hamilton (c. 1710–1783), Philadelphia; Allen's daughter, Anne Penn (1746–1830, wife of John Penn, 1729–1795); her nephew, Thomas Dawson Allen (1813–1882)

LIT: Copley-Pelham 1914, p. 163 (letter from John Singleton Copley to Henry Pelham, 29 Sept. 1771); Richardson 1978, p. 22 (letter from West to Joseph Shippen, 1 Sept. 1763)

During his visit to Italy from 1760 to 1763 West painted copies after "a number of the best pictures in Italy"[1] for Chief Justice William Allen (for whom see No. 581) and Lieutenant-Governor James Hamilton (see No. 633) in partial return for their support of his travels. West painted six copies for them (Nos. 504, 506, 510, 511, 516, and 520), all of which are documented in his and other contemporary correspondence.

In September 1771 John Singleton Copley visited Philadelphia and saw the six copies in the home of Chief Justice Allen. In a letter to his half-brother Henry Pelham describing what he saw, Copley does not mention West but he does describe the six pictures, mistak-

ing the original artist of one (No. 511) and being somewhat uncertain of the subject of another (No. 510). Pelham in turn visited Philadelphia in the winter of 1774–75 and wrote to Copley on 16 February 1775, that he had seen and admired "the several Copies of which you gave me a very just discription."[2] They were then in the home of Governor John Penn, the husband of Anne Allen, the daughter of Chief Justice Allen (see No. 584). They remained in her possession until her death in 1830, and all six are mentioned by name in her will.[3] Five of them, including No. 504, she left to her nephew Thomas Dawson Allen. Four of those five are now known, but the fifth picture, No. 504, has disappeared.

West was hospitalized in Florence in the winter and spring of 1762. On 11 May of that year, he wrote to Joseph Shippen that he was cured, but not yet sufficiently strong to paint.[4] In another letter, written on 1 September 1763, after his journey to London, West reported to Shippen that as soon as he was able, he painted or began to paint three copies in Florence for his Philadelphia patrons: No. 511 after Mengs, No. 520

after Titian, and No. 504 after "a celebrated picture of Hannibal Caracci, in the Prince Corsini's palace, of Venus lamenting over the dead body of Adonis. In a reasonable time I got this picture done." This activity was in the summer of 1762 before West set off from Florence on a trip to Venice and Lombardy. No. 504 may have been the first of these three copies that West completed, as on 22 April 1763, Robert Rutherford wrote to Joseph Shippen that it was then in his apartment in Leghorn, but he was still waiting for the other two to arrive. All three had arrived by 21 June 1763, when Rutherford wrote to Shippen that he was sending them on the schooner *Cato* sailing for Salem, and that the ship's captain, Jonathan Gardiner, had promised to forward them to Judge Allen in Philadelphia.[5]

The painting West copied in No. 504 is still in the Corsini Gallery in Florence (*below*), but is no longer generally accepted as a work by Annibale Carracci. According to a suggestion by the late Rudolf Wittkower it may be by the Bolognese painter Alessandro Tiarini (1577–1668).[6] There are distinct echoes of the painting in West's first treatment of the same subject after his

(?)Alessandro Tiarini, *Venus Lamenting Adonis*. Oil on canvas, Galleria Corsini, Florence

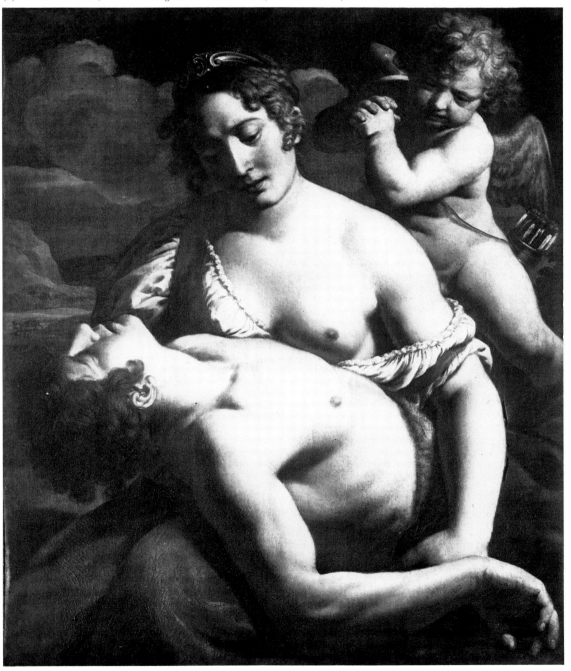

arrival in London (No. 117), although he replaced the half-length figures with full-length ones in a horizontal composition and a more spacious landscape setting.

[1] William Allen to Messrs. David Barclay & Sons, London, 10 Oct. 1762; quoted in Richardson 1978, p. 20.
[2] Copley-Pelham 1914, p. 293.
[3] Information about Anne Penn's will kindly supplied by Anthony A. Barnes in a letter to Helmut von Erffa, dated 30 Nov. 1967.
[4] Richardson, 1978, p. 18.
[5] Both letters from Rutherford to Shippen are in the American Philosophical Society, Philadelphia.
[6] Annotation on a photograph in the Photograph Collection of the Department of Art History and Archaeology, Columbia University.

505 Copy after the Madonna and Child with St. Jerome by Correggio 1762–63

LOCATION UNKNOWN

PROV: Sold by West's sons, Robins, London, 20–22 June 1829, lot 76 ("St. Gerolimo, a fine copy from the celebrated picture by Correggio")

LISTED: *PC*, p. 565 ("Copy from Correggio's celebrated picture at Parma, viz. the St. Gerolemo, now in the National Gallery," West, Painting-room); *UM*, p. 530; *BA*, p. 17; Galt, p. 227; Dillenberger, p. 169 (306)

LIT: Farington Diary, 13 Sept. 1802 (Farington 1978—, v, p. 1852); *Public Characters* 1805, p. 529; Galt 1816, pp. 144–45; Carey 1820, p. 517; Trumbull 1953, pp. 62–63, 70; Jaffe 1975, pp. 51, 326; Alberts 1978, pp. 49–50, 55; Evans 1980, pp. 24–25, 71–72

West began No. 505 on a visit to Parma in the autumn of 1762. He left it unfinished, evidently because of illness,[1] when he went on to Venice, but he stopped at Parma in June 1763, when he was travelling from Rome to London, and finished it then. It remained in his studio until his death, and two of his students, Matthew Pratt and John Trumbull, painted copies of it (National Gallery of Art, Washington, and Yale University Art Gallery, New Haven, respectively).[2] Trumbull completed his copy in the winter of 1780–81

Matthew Pratt, Copy after No. 505. Oil on canvas, 30⅝ × 23⅝ in. National Gallery of Art, Washington D.C.

in Tothill Field Prison, where he had been sent after being arrested as a spy in November 1780, and where West brought or sent No. 505 for him to work from. Trumbull described No. 505 as a small copy, which "approaches much nearer to the exquisite delicacy of expression and harmony of clair-obscure of the original, than any other I have seen."

The *Madonna and Child with St. Jerome*, or *St. Gerolamo*, by Correggio (Galleria Nazionale, Parma) was an immensely celebrated painting in the eighteenth century; Trumbull described it as "universally regarded as one of the three most perfect works of art in existence." It was one of the works brought by the French to Paris after 1796, to be included in the Musée Napoléon, so West had an opportunity to see it again when he visited Paris in 1802. According to Joseph Farington's diary, on 13 September 1802:

He got upon a Stool and examined closely the famous picture of St. Jerom, by Correggio. West said no part of the picture was injured but the small piece of Drapery under the foot of Christ, and a little under the Chin of the Magdalen. He said He was well acquainted with the picture, having copied it at Parma, and formed himself upon it.

This assessment contradicted that of other contemporary witnesses who were distressed by what they believed had been done to the picture in Paris. Trumbull saw it in the Louvre in 1797, when, according to his autobiography, written much later, it was "under the hands of some mender of pictures, who deserves to be flayed alive for the butchery he was inflicting upon this exquisite work." West soon altered his favorable opinion, and on 3 October 1802, he read to Farington a declaration about the state of the paintings and statues in Paris, in which he described the *St. Jerome* as "in a worse state than when He saw it in Italy; but . . . He has been assured by an Artist who copied it that the injury which it has received was done some time ago in that Country."[3] In 1788 West advised his student Johann Heinrich Ramberg, who was about to set off on a trip to Italy, to make a copy of the *St. Jerome* the size of the original, and in his letter of instruction to Ramberg he included a lengthy analysis of Correggio's use of color in the painting.[4] West's statement that he "formed himself" upon the original of No. 505 is sustained by the evidence of many of his paintings, as well as by what he said about them (see, in addition to his advice to Ramberg, his comments to Farington quoted in the entry for *Venus and Cupid* [No. 128] of 1765). In 1773 he exhibited at the Royal Academy a painting under the title "A Holy Family, in imitation of Correggio's manner" (No. 303).

In 1771 John Singleton Copley wrote to Henry Pelham that he had seen a copy of a *Holy Family* by Correggio at Justice Allen's home in Philadelphia,[5] but the picture he saw must have been No. 511 the *Holy Family* copied by West from a painting by Mengs rather than Correggio.

[1] All West's early biographers mention the copy. The anonymous biography in *Public Characters of 1805* states that illness had caused him to leave it incomplete on his first visit to Parma.
[2] The Pratt copy (*left*), made in 1764–66, is oil on canvas, 30⅝ × 23⅝ in. The Trumbull, painted in 1780–81, is oil on canvas, 31½ × 23⅝ in. (ill. in Jaffe 1975, fig. 33).
[3] Farington 1978—, v, p. 1899. According to Farington the declaration was addressed to the administration of the museum (the Musée Napoléon) and was translated into French by J.-M. Langlois and signed by West. A copy of it, in French, signed by West, and dated *Londres le 8 Nov. 1802* is in the Historical Society of Pennsylvania. On 15 October 1802, West sent a similar declaration, in English, to George III (see A. Aspinall, ed., *The Later Letters of George III*, Cambridge, 1968, IV, pp. 54–56).
[4] Forster-Hahn 1967, pp. 378–79, 381–82.
[5] Copley-Pelham 1914, pp. 163–64.

506 Copy after the Cumaean Sibyl by Domenichino *c.* 1761

FERENS ART GALLERY, KINGSTON-UPON-HULL, HUMBERSIDE

Oil on canvas: $45\frac{1}{2} \times 36$ in. (115.5 × 91.5 cm.)

PROV: Painted before 1762 for William Allen (1704–1780) and James Hamilton (*c.* 1710–1783), Philadelphia; Allen's daughter, Anne Penn (1746–1830, the wife of John Penn, 1729–1795); her nephew Thomas Dawson Allen (1813–1882); by family descent to the Hon. Margaret Hammond, by whom bequeathed to the Ferens Art Gallery in 1941

LIT: Copley-Pelham 1914, p. 163; Richardson 1978, pp. 17 and 25 (letters from West to Joseph Shippen 11 May 1762 and 1 Sept. 1763)

No. 506 must be the painting referred to in a letter from West to Joseph Shippen dated 11 May 1762 as a copy of the *St. Cecilia*. By that date, not only had the painting and a companion (No. 510) been completed and sent to America, but West had learned of their safe arrival and installation in the home of his patron, Lieutenant-Governor James Hamilton (see Nos. 504 and 633). As West had been hospitalized in Leghorn and Florence since the summer of 1761, he probably painted the two copies before then, in the first seven or eight months of 1761 before he was forced to retire to Leghorn.

Although West called No. 506 a copy of the *St. Cecilia*, and it could easily be taken as a picture of that patron saint of music, it is a copy of the well-known *Cumaean Sibyl* by Domenichino in the Galleria Borghese in Rome. West used the same painting, but much more freely and in reverse, as the basis of his posthumous portrait of the first Lady Griffin (No. 629), painted *c.* 1772.

507 Copy after the Portrait of Cardinal Bentivoglio by Van Dyck *c.* 1762

LOCATION UNKNOWN

PROV: (?) Sold by West's sons, Robins, London, 20–22 June 1829, lot 35 ("Studies from Van Dyck, by the late B. West . . . painted in Italy")

LISTED: *PC*, p. 565 ("Mr. West's small copy from Vandyke's picture of Cardinal Bentivoglio, now in the National Gallery at Paris," West, Painting-room); *UM*, p. 530; *BA*, p. 17; Galt, p. 227; Dillenberger, p. 169 (305)

The portrait of Cardinal Guido Bentivoglio, by Anthony Van Dyck is in the Pitti Palace in Florence. West presumably copied it there either in 1762, at the same time that he painted Nos. 504, 511, and 520, or during a brief stay in Florence in June 1763 as he was leaving Italy. Neither West nor Robert Rutherford mentions the picture in their letters to Joseph Shippen, and the only explicit documentation we have for it comes from the early lists of West's works. However, since they establish that it remained in West's possession at least until 1804 (the date of the list in *Public Characters*), and since West must have painted it in Italy, No. 507 probably should be identified as the "Studies from Van Dyck . . . painted in Italy," which West's sons sold in 1829, although the reason for the plural title is not known. The "now in the National Gallery at Paris" in the early lists of West's works refers to the original's having been taken there to be part of the Musée Napoléon.

Samuel F. B. Morse in 1811–12 painted "a copy from Mr. West's copy from Vandyke,"[1] but it could have been after either No. 507 or No. 508, both of which would have been available to him in West's studio.

[1] From a letter from Morse to his parents, 30 January 1812, quoted in Evans, p. 161.

506

508 Copy after the Portrait of Cornelis van der Geest by Van Dyck 1806

LOCATION UNKNOWN

PROV: Sold by West's sons, Robins, London, 20–22 June 1829, lot 154 ("Copy from Vandyke's Govartius, and Portrait of a Lady"); Joseph Harrison, Philadelphia, 1853

EXH: PAFA 1853 (50) lent by Joseph Harrison

LIT: Farington Diary, 17, 18 and 20 Nov. 1806 (Farington 1978–, VIII, pp. 2909 and 2912); Whitley 1928b, p. 111

Van Dyck's portrait of Cornelis van der Geest (or *Govartius*), now in the National Gallery in London, belonged prior to 1825 to John Julius Angerstein, who in 1806 lent it to the newly founded British Institution. West copied it there, and showed his copy, along with a copy of Rembrandt's *Mill* (No. 515), to Joseph Farington, when Farington called at the British Institution on 18 November 1806. West told Farington that he observed the same process in both copies: "viz; by laying on the *high lights* with *pure white* & giving tone to it by *thin colours only* which preserved the clearness." Two days later Farington had dinner with the painter Richard Westall who "spoke of the copy made by West of the picture of *Govartius* by Vandyke and said it was far superior to any other copy made at the British Institution."

According to W. T. Whitley, who does not indicate his source, West's copy of the *Govartius* was begun for him by a Miss Hay, and West added to it two hands holding a book (the original painting by Van Dyck consists only of a head and ruff). Miss Hay was a protégée of West's who is mentioned several times in Farington's diary during 1806 because of a *contretemps* between West and Lady Beaumont over which of them should possess a copy by Miss Hay of a *Head of Christ* by Guido Reni belonging to West.[1] Farington reports that Miss Hay was the daughter of a shoemaker living in Chandos Street. She could have been either a Miss J. Hay, whose name appears in Royal Academy exhibition catalogues from 1797 to 1812, or, perhaps more probably, Miss M. Hay, who is only in the catalogues from 1807 to 1809; both were listed with addresses in Chandos Street.

[1] Farington Diary, 25, 26 and 30 April, 1 May and 14 Nov. 1806 (Farington 1978—, VII, pp. 2734, 2736, 2740, 2746, and VIII, p. 2905). West's *Head of Christ* by Guido Reni is now in the National Gallery, London, catalogued as an imitation of Reni (Michael Levey, *National Gallery Catalogues: The Seventeenth and Eighteenth Century Italian Schools*, London, 1971, pp. 193–94, no. 271).

509 Copy or Imitation after Grevling (The First Attempt in Painting by Mr. West, when a Boy, in America)

LOCATION UNKNOWN

(Oil on canvas: [?] 11 × 15 in.) (28 × 38 cm.)

PROV: Offered by West's sons to the United States in 1826 (138, "The first attempt in Painting by Mr. West, when a boy, in America," 1 ft. 1 in. × 1 ft. 5 in.) and sold by them, Robins, London, 22–25 May 1829, lot 180 ("The First Picture Painted by the Venerable Founder of this Gallery when in His Childhood," 11 × 15 in.) bt. by Ward for £26.5.0.; (?) Eli Bowen, Pottsville, Pennsylvania, by whom offered for sale for $200.00 to the Pennsylvania Academy of Fine Arts, Philadelphia, in 1847[1]

EXH: West's Gallery 1821 (66), "The Picture first painted by Mr. West, when a child"; West's Gallery 1822–28 (124) "The first Picture painted by the late Mr. West, when a child"

LIT: Galt 1816, pp. 21–24; Carey 1820, p. 514; Flexner 1952, p. 9; Evans 1959, pp. 11 and 110–11, n. 5; Kraemer 1975, p. 3; Alberts 1978, p. 11

William Carey's obituary of West, published in 1820, states that a Mr. Pendleton, West's cousin, gave the young artist his first materials for painting, and with these aids West "made some copies." In Galt's account of West's early life, published four years previously, the relative is Mr. Pennington, rather than Pendleton (he, in fact, seems to have been Edward Penington, 1726–1796), and the present included not only the materials for painting, but also "six engravings by Grevling." Galt claims that while West "immediately began to imitate the figures in the engravings," his first work was not "a mere copy, but a composition from two of the engravings." Galt also says that West's mother admired the work and would not let him finish it, "lest he should spoil what was already in her opinion perfect, even with half the canvas bare." This description of its unfinished state was based on first-hand knowledge, as Galt states that he saw the picture in the same room, presumably West's studio, with *Christ Rejected* (No. 353), which West painted between 1811 and 1814. West's sons exhibited No. 509 in the posthumous exhibitions of their father's works and sold it in 1829. It seems to have resurfaced in 1847 in Pottsville, Pennsylvania, but has since disappeared entirely. Apart from being small and unfinished,[2] what it looked like is a mystery. None of our various sources indicate its subject, which suggests that it did not have a recognizable subject.

510

James Thomas Flexner proposed, or assumed, that Galt's "Grevling" was Hubert-François Gravelot (1699–1773), the prolific French draughtsman, who lived and worked in England from 1733 to 1746. This identification has been accepted by Ruth Kraemer, but was questioned by Grose Evans, who proposed on phonetic grounds that Grevling was more probably Simon Gribelin (1661–1733). Since we know neither the subject nor the appearance of the work, further speculation about its source does not seem very fruitful; nonetheless, we should observe that West's earliest known historical composition, the *Death of Socrates* (No. 4), painted *c.* 1756, is largely a copy from an engraving after Gravelot. Since that painting has a provenance precluding its identification as the picture belonging to and sold by West's sons in the 1820s, the two must be separate works, but it is possible that Galt confused what the elderly West had told him about them in an account of what had taken place over sixty years before.

For an entirely different description of West's first painting see the letter from the artist to Thomas Eagles, dated 10 October 1810, which is quoted and discussed in the entry for No. 482.

[1] Bowen's letter dated 25 October 1847 and a reply dated 9 November from John L. Lewis, the Secretary of the Academy, rejecting the offer, are in the archives in the Pennsylvania Academy.
[2] West's list of works offered to the United States in 1826 and the Robins sale catalogue of 1829 give differing measurements; they are, however, within 2 in. of each other, and in either case indicate that the painting was small.

510 Copy after a Sibyl by Mengs *c.* 1761

Oil on canvas: $45\frac{1}{2} \times 36$ in. (115.5 × 91.5 cm.)

PROV: As for No. 506

LIT: As for No. 506

No. 510 is one of the copies West painted in Rome for Chief Justice Allen and Lieutenant-Governor Hamilton of Pennsylvania. Its history and documentation are the same as those of No. 506, copied by West from a well-known painting by Domenichino in the Villa Borghese. West must have painted Nos. 506 and 510 at approximately the same time, probably in the first part of 1761, and he probably thought of them as companion works. Nevertheless, unlike No. 506, the latter is not a copy of a famous picture by a much-admired earlier artist, but after a contemporary or near-contemporary work by Anton Raphael Mengs (1728–1779) now or recently in London.[1] That work, like West's copy, is in the vein of seventeenth-century paintings of similar subjects, recalling in particular Guercino's *Persian Sibyl* in the Pinacoteca Capitolina, a work which West himself later was to emulate directly in his portrait of the second Lady Griffin (No. 630).

While in Italy West subsequently painted a second copy from Mengs for his American patrons (No. 511). The two chief accounts of West's stay in Italy both make abundantly clear Mengs's impact and importance for West when he arrived in Italy,[2] and, of course, the fact that he chose to copy paintings by Mengs gives further evidence to corroborate what they say. Mengs was the only living artist whom West is known to have copied after leaving America, and had the largest influence of any single artist on the development of West's art.

In 1771 Copley described No. 510 as "I think a Niobe, I cannot be certain."

[1] With Chaucer and Van Dam Galleries, London in 1977; ill. *Burlington Magazine*, CXIX, Nov. 1977, p. cxviii (adv.). See also Dieter Honisch, *Anton Raphael Mengs und die Bildform des Frühklassizismus*, Recklinghausen 1965, pp. 117 (214) and 124 (250). The late Howard Hibbard first pointed out that No. 510 appears to be derived from an eighteenth-century source, rather than from a seventeenth-century one, as hitherto had been assumed.

[2] See Galt 1816, pp. 118–23 and Carey 1820, pp. 515–17.

Anton Raphael Mengs, *Holy Family*, engraving by Manuel Salvador Carmona, 1781

511 Copy after a Holy Family by Mengs 1762

Oil on canvas: 81 × 58 in. (205.5 × 147.5 cm.)

PROV: As for No. 506

LIT: Copley-Pelham 1914, pp. 163–64; Richardson 1978, pp. 21–25 (letter from West to Joseph Shippen, 1 Sept. 1763)

511

West painted No. 511 in Florence in 1762 along with Nos. 504 and 520. It seems to have been his first undertaking after recovering from illness and the operation on his ankle that had taken place in Florence at the beginning of that year.[1] In his letter to Joseph Shippen of 1 September 1763, after describing his difficulty in working again after his long confinement, he continues:

My first application was to serve my worthy and honored patrons in the copies they desired, as far as lay in my power; and as, just at that time, Lord

Fordwich had ordered up from Leghorn to Florence the picture that Mr. Mings had painted for him, of a Holy Family, and was so obliging as to give me leave to copy it. I thought myself happy in having such an opportunity of studying upon my favorite master, since he was gone from Rome, and the season of the year was not proper for me to go thither to seek for other studies. I concluded also that nothing could be more agreeable to you and my other friends than the copy of so capital a piece. . . . I got through the copy in about two months . . . nothing but such a study after Mings could have made me go through with so large a copy, and in so short a time, and I thought it a happy instance of my cure, that after so much labor I was not again laid up with a fresh fit of my usual violent pains.

West then goes on to discuss Nos. 504 and 520, but despite the implication in his letter that he completed No. 511 before those two works, No. 504 preceded it to Leghorn, from where they were to be shipped to America. On 22 April 1763, the Leghorn merchant Robert Rutherford wrote to Joseph Shippen that he had received No. 504 but was still waiting for Nos. 511 and 520. They were all there by 21 June 1763 when Rutherford wrote again, announcing that he was sending them.

We have been unable to locate the *Holy Family* by Mengs, which West copied.[2] However, confirmation that No. 511 is indeed after Mengs is provided by a Spanish engraving of a *Holy Family* by Mengs (ill. p. 445), which shows an identical grouping of the Virgin and the two infants in the foreground. The owner of the painting in 1762, Lord Fordwich, became the third Earl Cowper two years later. Mengs left Rome for Spain in August 1761, hence the mention of his being away. West's assertion that the season was not proper for him to go to Rome, reflects his belief that the summer heat there had brought on his illness, and thus indicates the time of year when he painted Nos. 504, 511, and 520. That approximate date is consistent with his description of his activities otherwise in his two letters to Shippen.

On 29 September 1771, after visiting Chief Justice Allen, John Singleton Copley described among the works he had seen a "Holy Family at whole length as large as life from Coregio." Despite Copley's misattribution of the source, this picture must have been No. 511. Copley went on to describe it at some length and he also made a slight sketch to give Henry Pelham a better idea of the painting.

[1]See Alberts 1978, pp. 46–47, and Adrian W. Zorgniotti, MD, "Benjamin West's Osteomyelitis: a Translation," *Bulletin of the New York Academy of Medicine*, XXXIX, 1973, pp. 702–7.
[2]It may have been the lost *Holy Family*, measuring 7 × 5 ft., recorded in Dieter Honisch, *Anton Raphael Mengs und die Bild-form des Frühklassizismus*, Recklinghausen, 1965, p. 125 (254), as intended for England.

512 Copy after a Painting of St. Ignatius Loyola, Ascribed to the School of Murillo *c.* 1756–58

LOCATION UNKNOWN

LIT: Galt 1816, p. 71; Carey 1820, p. 515

Both William Carey and John Galt mention No. 512 in their accounts of West's early career in America in the 1750s. Carey describes it as a "copy of a Saint Ignatius, taken on board a Spanish prize." Galt discusses it more fully:

Governor Hamilton, who, at that period presided with so much popularity over the affairs of the province, possessed a few pictures, consisting, however, chiefly of family portraits. Among them was a St. Ignatius, which was found in the course of the preceding war on board a Spanish prize, and which Mr. Pennington obtained leave for West to copy. The

Artist had made choice of it himself, without being aware of its merits as a work of art, for it was not until several years after that he discovered it to be a fine piece of the Murillo school, and in the best style of the master.

For Governor Hamilton, see No. 633. Mr. Pennington was West's relative, who gave him his first set of paints (see No. 509). Both No. 512 and the painting West copied it from have disappeared. No painting of St. Ignatius by Murillo is known, or recorded apart from this reference in the West literature,[1] and Galt's words constitute a pretty vague attribution.

According to Galt, No. 512 was greatly admired by all who saw it, and William Smith, Provost of the College of Philadelphia, induced West to paint his portrait (No. 699) "in the style and attitude of the St. Ignatius."

[1]Diego Angulo Iñiguez, *Murillo*, Madrid, 1981, II, pp. 495–96 (2.023).

513 Copy after the Death of Ananias by Raphael 1785

LOCATION UNKNOWN

(Signed and dated: *1785*)

PROV: Sold by West's sons, Christie's, London, 23–24 June 1820, second day, lot 31 ("A Set of the Seven Cartoons, in colours. These were formerly in the possession of Sir James Thornhill, who coloured five of the set; a sixth was painted upon in oils by Mr. West, but not finished; and the seventh, the Death of Ananias, is painted upon and carefully finished by Mr. West, who has inscribed his name upon it with the date 1785"); evidently bought in, and sold again, Robins, London, 20–22 June 1829, lot 51 ("Complete set of Raphael's Cartoons; copied from the originals at Hampton Court, upon the off-tracts made by Dorigny for his series of engravings. Two of the set Ananias and Christ's Charge to Peter, finished by the late B. West PRA. N.B. These are the same as the paintings, the engravings being reversed.")

Despite the slight differences in the description in the two sales catalogues, the sets of copies after the Raphael tapestry cartoons offered for sale by West's sons in 1820 and 1829 must have been the same. Both catalogues indicate that West himself painted on only two of them (Nos. 513 and 514). The sale in 1820 was of West's collection, rather than works by the artist himself, and these two copies were the only works by him, or partly by him, included in it.

Sir James Thornhill (1676–1734), who is mentioned in the catalogue of 1820, made three different sets of drawings from the tapestry cartoons between 1729 and 1731.[1] Sir Nicholas Dorigny (1657–1746), who is mentioned in the 1829 catalogue, was a French engraver who produced a set of engravings after the cartoons between 1712 and 1719. The cartoons, which are now in the Victoria and Albert Museum, were in the eighteenth century at Hampton Court. According to Galt, West's first excursion from London, after arriving in England in August 1763, was to Hampton Court to see them.[2] He later had the cartoons under his care as Surveyor of the King's Pictures.

In Sir Thomas Lawrence's full-length portrait of West, painted between 1818 and 1821 (Frontispiece), the artist stands next to an easel upon which there is a copy of the *Death of Ananias*, presumably No. 513. The portrait supposedly shows West presenting one of his discourses to the Royal Academy students. We know from Farington's diary that West intended to discuss the *Death of Ananias* on 17 December 1816, when the cartoon itself had been brought from Hampton Court to the Royal Academy for the students to copy. Ill health evidently kept him from presenting that dis-

course, but he was able to address the students the following year and may have discussed the Raphael then, using his own copy in place of the original cartoon. Farington's brief summary of the discourse of 1817 does not mention Raphael, but it is a secondhand account derived from Lawrence, who had been present and whose picture seems to have been inspired by what he had seen.[3]

The tapestry cartoons show subjects chiefly from the Acts of the Apostles. West himself did a series of six drawings showing scenes from the Acts (National Maritime Museum, Greenwich), which served as the models for reliefs in Coade stone on the pulpit of the chapel at Greenwich (see No. 397). The series does not include the *Death of Ananias* or *Christ's Charge to Peter* (see No. 514) but does repeat other subjects from the cartoons.

On 11 May 1762, West wrote to Joseph Shippen from Florence that the Duke of Grafton wanted him to paint a copy of the *Madonna della Sedia* by Raphael in the Pitti Palace, but in his following letter to the same recipient, dated 1 September 1763, he wrote that illness had forced him to make his excuses to the Duke of Grafton for not serving him.[4] A copy of the *Madonna della Sedia* did hang in West's London studio where both John Trumbull[5] and Thomas Sully[6] copied it, but it was evidently a copy painted by West's former student John Downman (1750–1824) on a trip to Italy in 1773–75.[7] In 1788 West also advised another former student, Johann Heinrich Ramberg (1763–1840) to copy the "Madona Dela Saggala" by Raphael when he visited Florence.[8]

A drawing ascribed to West in the Pierpont Morgan Library shows a water-bearer copied from Raphael's fresco of the *Fire in the Borgo* in the Stanza dell'Incendio of the Vatican.[9]

[1]Edgar de N. Mayhew, *Sketches by Thornhill*, London, 1967, p. 10.
[2]Galt 1820, p. 5.
[3]Farington Diary, 10, 13, and 14 Dec. 1816, and 12 Dec. 1817 (Farington 1978–, XIV, pp. 4940, 4942–44, and 5120.) See also No. 236. West also discussed the *Death of Ananias* in another discourse on 10 Dec. 1811 (Galt 1820, p. 163).
[4]Richardson, 1978, pp. 18 and 22.
[5]Trumbull 1953, pp. 61–62, and Jaffe 1975, p. 46.
[6]Edward Biddle and Mantle Fielding, *The Life and Works of Thomas Sully*, Philadelphia, 1921, pp. 19 and 360 (2325).
[7]Sold by West's sons, Christie's, London, 23 June 1820, lot 1.
[8]Forster-Hahn 1967, p. 383.
[9]Black chalk, $22\frac{3}{4} \times 16\frac{9}{16}$ in. (Kraemer 1975, p. 81, no. 202, and pl. 106).

514 Copy after Christ's Charge to Peter by Raphael *c.* 1785

LOCATION UNKNOWN

PROV: As for No. 513

See No. 513. Although the Robins sale catalogue of 20–22 June 1829 states that West finished No. 514, the earlier Christie's catalogue of 23 June 1820, states that it was painted upon by West, but not finished.

515 Copy after The Mill by Rembrandt 1806

LOCATION UNKNOWN

LIT: Farington Diary, 17 and 18 Nov. 1806 (Farington 1978–, VIII, p. 2909); Whitley 1928b, p. 111

See No. 508, West's copy after the portrait of Cornelis van der Geest by Van Dyck. West copied the *Mill* at the British Institution at the same time, and according to W. T. Whitley, both copies were begun by his protégée Miss Hay. West had tea with Joseph Farington on

17 November 1806 and told him that he was making a copy of Rembrandt's *Mill*; the following day Farington visited the British Institution and saw West at work on the copy. While Farington's diary records the process used by West in both Nos. 508 and 515 (quoted under No. 508), it makes no mention of Miss Hay in relation to either.

The *Mill* came to England as part of the Orleans collection in 1792, and was lent to the British Institution in 1806 by William Smith, MP (1756–1835). It is now in the National Gallery in Washington. Although it was an immensely admired painting in the nineteenth century, its ascription to Rembrandt is no longer universally accepted.

516 Copy after the Herodias by Guido Reni 1763

FERENS ART GALLERY, KINGSTON-UPON-HULL, HUMBERSIDE

Oil on canvas: 49 × 36 in. (124.5 × 91.5 cm.)

PROV: As for No. 506

LIT: Copley-Pelham 1914, p. 163; Richardson 1978, pp. 23, 24 (letter from West to Joseph Shippen, 1 Sept. 1763)

West painted No. 516 in Rome in the winter or spring of 1763. It was the last of the copies he made for Governor Hamilton and Chief Justice Allen, his patrons in Philadelphia, and it reached Leghorn too late to accompany the other copies that Robert Rutherford sent to America in June 1763 (Nos. 504, 511, and 520).[1]

West described No. 516 in his letter to Joseph Shippen of 1 September 1763, as "a copy of Guido's finest, Herodias in Cardinal Corsini's palace." The original remains in the Corsini Palace. Although referred to by West as a painting of Herodias and usually catalogued as such, it has also been called a painting of Salome, the daughter of Herodias. In the biblical account of the decapitation of John the Baptist (Mark 6:14–28), Salome presents John's head on a charger to Herodias. In 1788 the *Herodias* by Guido was one of the works West recommended copying to his former pupil Johann Heinrich Ramberg during Ramberg's forthcoming tour of Italy.[2]

Prior to painting No. 516, West had made some sort of copy of the *Apostles Peter and Paul* by Guido Reni now in the Brera in Milan, but then in the Palazzo Zampieri in Bologna, where he visited in the autumn of 1762. This copy is mentioned in the travel diary of Dr. John Morgan (1735–1789), who saw the original two years later. Apparently making copies of the picture was forbidden, but, according to Morgan, "Mr West by coming in frequently & then retiring to a neighbouring street & taking it down by parts, returning often to correct & compare it, took a copy of it."[3] A copy made under such circumstances in a neighbouring street was perhaps more likely to have been a drawing than a painting. There is no further record of it, but in 1788 West recommended the *Apostles Peter and Paul* to Ramberg as a painting he might copy.[4]

West also wrote to Joseph Shippen about how long it would take to paint a copy of the *St. Michael* by Guido in the church of Sta. Maria della Concezione in Rome, which had figures half-again life-size.[5] There is no evidence to indicate that he ever did paint a copy of the *St. Michael*, but he did later own a version or copy of it,[6] and it had an evident impact on his own paintings of the same subject (Nos. 406–8).

[1]Letter from Robert Rutherford to Joseph Shippen, 21 June 1763 (American Philosophical Society, Philadelphia), and also mentioned by West in his letter to Shippen of 1 September.

[2]Forster-Hahn 1967, p. 383.

516

[3]*The Journal of Dr. John Morgan of Philadelphia: From the City of Rome to the City of London 1764*, Philadelphia, 1907, pp. 76–77 (entry for 16 July 1764).

[4]Forster-Hahn 1967, p. 383.

[5]Richardson 1978, p. 19 (letter of 11 May 1762).

[6]Sold by West's sons, Christie's, London, 6 July 1820, lot 99.

517 Copy after the Belisarius by Salvator Rosa
c. 1758–59

LOCATION UNKNOWN

PROV: Bought by a Mr. Myers, New York

LIT: Galt 1816, p. 83; Kraemer 1975, p. 41

John Galt described No. 517 as one of two works painted by West during his visit to New York in 1758 or 1759 that were bought by a Mr. Myers. The other was a genre picture (No. 454), which was inspired by West's sight of a Flemish painting of a hermit praying before a lamp, but which evidently was not a copy. Both paintings had disappeared by the time Galt wrote his first volume. Galt stated that West based No. 517 on the engraving by Robert Strange (1721–1792) after Salvator Rosa's painting of *Belisarius*, but that is not possible. Ruth Kraemer has pointed out that the Strange

447

engraving was not published until 1764, and she suggests that West copied an earlier engraving by Cristoforo dell'Acqua of 1709.

During West's lifetime, the original *Belisarius* by Salvator Rosa hung as the focal point of a Belisarius Chamber in Raynham Hall in Norfolk and was a seminally influential image, either directly or via engravings, for later eighteenth-century painting. According to Galt, West saw the painting itself long after he had painted No. 517 and "was gratified to observe that he had instinctively coloured his copy almost as faithfully as if it had been painted from the picture instead of the engraving." West also painted several independent pictures of Belisarius (see Nos. 42–45). His future pupil, John Trumbull, while still in America also painted a copy after an engraving of the Salvator Rosa (Wadsworth Atheneum, Hartford).[1]

In addition to painting No. 517 and one other recorded copy or imitation (No. 518) after Salvator, West also drew an *Angel Releasing St. Peter from Prison*, which is inscribed: *A Sketch from Memory of the Picture painted by Salvator Rosa in the possession of the Earl of Chesterfield*, and dated *1783*.[2]

[1] Jaffe 1975, pp. 33 (fig. 24) and 315–16.
[2] Pen and brown ink, 15¾ × 11⅜ in., sold by Mrs. Claire Francis, Christie's, London, 14 March 1967, lot 40, ill. in the catalogue.

518 Jason and the Dragon, in Imitation of Salvator Rosa

LOCATION UNKNOWN

PROV: (?) Sold by West's sons, Robins, London, 20–22 June 1829, lot 160 ("Copy from Salvator Rosa")

LISTED: *PC*, p. 566 ("Jason and the Dragon—in imitation of Salvator Rosa," West, Gallery); *UM*, p. 530; Barlow, p. 434; *BA*, p. 17; Galt, p. 228; Dillenberger, p. 173 (344)

Raphael West, Copy after *Jason and the Dragon* by Salvator Rosa. Pen, 17½ × 11½ in.

The meaning of the word "imitation," used in the lists of West's works for No. 518, rather than "copy," is not clear. It seems likely that No. 518 was thought of after West's death as a copy from Salvator Rosa, since there is no other recorded candidate for identification as the copy sold by his sons in 1829. West presumably based No. 518 either upon the *Jason and the Dragon* by Salvator now in the Montreal Museum of Fine Arts, which was in England in the eighteenth century, or upon the etching by Salvator showing a slightly different composition.

It is possible that West painted No. 518 to serve as a model for his son Raphael West (1766–1850). Raphael did draw a copy of Salvator's etching of *Jason and the Dragon* (below),[1] and several drawings by him of the similar subject of Cadmus slaying the dragon are very much in the manner of Salvator.[2] Raphael probably made these drawings before 1785, the date on a related etching of *Hercules Slaying the Hydra*.[3]

[1] Pen and brown ink, 17½ × 11½ in.; sold by Mrs. F. Howard, Sotheby's, London, 22 March 1979, lot 4 (as by Benjamin West).
[2] See Kraemer 1975, pp. 87–88, fig. 51 and pl. 109. Another drawing of "Cadmus Slaying the Dragon" was sold by Mrs. Howard, Sotheby's, London, 22 March 1979, lot 38, ill. in the catalogue.
[3] Kraemer 1975, p. 87 and fig. 50.

519 A Group of Legendary Saints in Imitation of Rubens

LOCATION UNKNOWN

LISTED: *PC*, p. 567 ("The Sketch of a Group of Legendary Saints, in imitation of Rubens," West, Gallery); *UM*, p. 531; *BA*, p. 18; Galt, p. 231; Dillenberger, p. 179 (404)

As in the preceding entry, the meaning of the word "imitation" is open to question. Nothing is known about this "imitation" apart from the title cited in the lists of West's works, and that is too imprecise to allow us to identify its source or sources.

West must have painted No. 519 by 1804 for it to have been included in the list of his works in *Public Characters of 1805*. Hence it seems unlikely that a drawing of a group of saints carrying palm fronds in the British Museum, which is signed and dated *1817*, has any relation to it.[1] That drawing does not appear to be based on Rubens.

[1] Bistre and blue wash, 7⅞ × 8³⁄₁₆ in., signed lower left: *B. W./m.* [?] *1817* (1920–6–15–11).

520 Copy after the Venus of Urbino by Titian
1762

LOCATION UNKNOWN

PROV: Painted for William Allen (1704–1780) and James Hamilton (c. 1710–1783), Philadelphia; Allen's daughter, Anne Penn (1746–1830, the wife of John Penn, 1729–1795); her nephew Andrew Allen

LIT: Copley-Pelham 1914, pp. 163–64, 307 and 333 (letters from John Singleton Copley to Henry Pelham, 29 Sept. 1771, and 14 March and 25 June 1775); Richardson 1978, pp. 22–25 (letter from West to Joseph Shippen, 1 Sept. 1763); Alberts 1978, p. 48

No. 520 is one of the copies West painted in Italy for his Philadelphia patrons, Chief Justice William Allen and Lieutenant-Governor James Hamilton. The circumstances under which he painted it are detailed in his long letter of 1 September 1763 to his former travelling companion Joseph Shippen. Following his operation and convalescence in Florence at the beginning of

1762, the first copy West made was after a *Holy Family* by Mengs (see No. 511). Upon completing that, West began two further copies, No. 504 after a *Venus Lamenting Adonis* believed by him to have been painted by Annibale Carracci, and No. 520 after the *Venus of Urbino* by Titian in the Uffizi. Although in his letter to Shippen he initially mentioned No. 520 before No. 504, he evidently painted the latter first:

> In a reasonable time I got this picture done, and set about the Titian, when just as it was dead colored in, the fire broke out in the gallery, and put everything there in confusion, and stopped the work of copying there, upon that picture, for some time.

The fire mentioned by West occurred in the west wing of the Uffizi on 12 August 1762.[1] West took advantage of the forced interruption of his labor and set off on a trip to Bologna, Parma, and Venice. Upon his return from Venice to Florence, probably in the late autumn of 1762, he finished the copy of the Titian. In the following spring, on 22 April 1763, Robert Rutherford wrote to Joseph Shippen from Leghorn mentioning that No. 504 was there, but that he was still waiting for Nos. 511 and 520. Rutherford wrote again on 21 June stating that the further two pictures had arrived and that he was sending the three copies to America. He then singled out No. 520 for special praise: "*The Copy of the Venus* is I think by far the most beautifull, most exact, & best I ever saw, of a great many I have seen at different times of this famous Picture."[2]

In Philadelphia the painting was one of the pictures which John Singleton Copley saw in the home of Chief Justice Allen in 1771 and which Copley's half-brother Henry Pelham saw at the home of Governor Penn in 1774–75. Copley writing to Pelham in 1771 included a long discussion of No. 520, and when he was in Italy in 1775 and saw actual works by Titian he mentioned it twice in letters to Pelham as giving an idea of the original paintings. On the first occasion, in a letter from Rome on 14 March, he qualified the reference with, "yet I beleave was you to see them together you would think the coppy less broken and varigated in the tints of Flesh than the original."[3] Writing from Florence in June, Copley gave Pelham a fuller description of the *Venus of Urbino*, this time describing West's copy as having "more of an Inamil'd look than the original."

[1] Luciano Berti, *The Uffizi*, Florence, 1971, p. 13.
[2] Both letters in the American Philosophical Society, Philadelphia.
[3] In the preceding sentence Copley mentioned both the *Venus* and the *Danaë* by Titian, and Jules Prown has interpreted this passage to refer to a copy by West of the *Danaë* (Prown 1966, II, p. 252). No copy of Titian's *Danaë* by West is otherwise recorded.

521 Copy after a Venus and Adonis by or after Titian *c.* 1798–1809

LOCATION UNKNOWN

PROV: Sold by West's sons, Robins, London, 20–22 June 1829, lot 95 ("Venus and Adonis, a splendid copy from the celebrated picture of Titian in the Collection of Mr. Miles")

The version of the *Venus and Adonis* by Titian which in 1829 was in the collection of Mr. Miles (Philip John Miles, MP, of Leigh Court, near Bristol) had belonged previously to West. According to Harold Wethey, it had come to England in the 1790s as part of the Orleans collection and was given to West rather than included in the exhibition and sale of the Orleans pictures in 1798–99. West sold it to Richard Hart Davis of Bristol (for whom see No. 328) in 1809, and the Davis collection passed *en masse* to Miles.[1] Wethey records the Titian as last heard of in the sale of the collection of

Baron von Heyl in Munich in 1930 and catalogues it as a workshop replica of Titian's *Venus and Adonis* in the Prado.

The painting by Titian shows Adonis departing from Venus to go hunting, rather than Venus grieving over the dead Adonis as shown in the painting ascribed to Annibale Carracci which West copied in Florence in 1762 (see No. 504). West had painted pictures based on both moments from the story of Venus and Adonis long before the painting from which he copied No. 521 came into his possession (see Nos. 112, 116, and 117), but he also painted a further group of paintings of the same subject around 1800 (Nos. 113, 114, 115, and 118), and it seems likely that these were at least partly inspired by his new acquisition. The Adonis in No. 114 in particular seems to echo his counterpart in the paintings by Titian.

[1] Harold E. Wethey, *The Paintings of Titian*, London, 1975, III, p. 191 and pl. 191. See also John Young, *A Catalogue of the Pictures at Leigh Court, near Bristol; the seat of Philip John Miles, Esq., MP, with etchings from the whole collection*, London, 1822, p. 4 (4).

522 A Crystal Vase, from Titian

LOCATION UNKNOWN

PROV: Sold by West's sons, Robins, London, 20–22 June 1829, lot 92 ("A Crystal Vase, from Titian")

There are several crystal vases in pictures by Titian. The one that West most likely copied is in the center of the great *Diana and Actaeon* in the Sutherland collection (on extended loan to the National Gallery of Scotland). West could have copied the vase either from the original painting, which came to London as part of the Orleans collection and was on quasi-public view in the Stafford Gallery in the early nineteenth century, or from what may have been a version or copy in his own possession.[1]

It is possible that West painted No. 522 to use in a discourse to the Royal Academy students. In his discourse for 1797, although not referring to a vase or to No. 522, he did discuss a theory of prismatic colors with the example of light falling on a ball, and he urged his students to acquire practical knowledge of the system by copying pieces by Titian and other artists.[2] See also No. 496.

[1] Sold by West's sons, Christie's, London, 28 May 1824, lot 78 "The Bath of Diana, a noble study for the very large picture of the same subject in the Stafford Gallery." Harold Wethey (*The Paintings of Titian*, London, 1975, III, p. 142) identifies this picture as a copy of the *Diana and Callisto* in the Sutherland collection, but the title "Bath of Diana" is more appropriate to the companion *Diana and Actaeon*, in which the goddess is shown being bathed by her attendants. West's "Bath of Diana" should not be confused with yet another putative Titian in his collection, which his sons put up for sale twice under the title "The Death of Actaeon" (Christie's, London, 23 June 1820, lot 85, and 28 May 1824, lot 80). Descriptions in the catalogues preclude identifying it as a version of either of the Sutherland paintings or of the *Death of Actaeon* by Titian in the National Gallery in London. It was finally sold by the family, Christie's, 19 March 1898, lot 157 as "A Grand Stag Hunt" (see also Whitley 1928a, pp. 31–34).
[2] Galt 1820, pp. 111–15.

523 Copy after a Landscape by William Williams (?)c. 1747

LOCATION UNKNOWN

LIT: Carey 1820, p. 514

William Carey in his obituary of West states that after the aspiring artist had been given his first set of paints and had painted some copies in his native Springfield, Pennsylvania (see No. 509), he visited Philadelphia: "He there resided with his brother-in-law, and accidentally saw and copied one of Williams's landscapes." This copy is not mentioned in John Galt's account of West's early career, nor in any other early source, but since Carey's story of West's life, like Galt's, was based on interviews with the old artist, it deserves equal respect. Indeed Carey probably deserves more, since it seems likely that West would have begun to paint by painting copies, whereas Galt's repeated descriptions of West's earliest works as original compositions manifesting his innate genius hardly ring true.

William Williams (1727–1797), West's earliest mentor, had himself only recently begun to paint when West first met him at the end of the 1740s (in 1810 West wrote that he met Williams in 1747).[1] No known painting by Williams can be reliably dated earlier than 1766, and the one landscape that is generally accepted as by him (Newark Museum, Newark, New Jersey) bears a signature and date of 1772.[2] Hence we have no credible evidence of what the landscape that West supposedly copied over twenty years earlier may have looked like, apart from that provided by West's own early landscapes, which are discussed in entries for Nos. 480–83.

[1] Letter from West to Thomas Eagles, 10 Oct. 1810, quoted in Dickason 1970, p. 130.
[2] David Howard Dickason, *William Williams: Novelist and Painter of Colonial America*, Bloomington, Indiana, 1970, pp. 166–69, ill. p. 167.

PORTRAITS OF WEST AND FAMILY

524 Self-Portrait *c.* 1758–59
See color illustration, p. 2

YALE UNIVERSITY ART GALLERY, NEW HAVEN

Watercolor on ivory (miniature): oval, $2\frac{1}{2} \times 1\frac{13}{16}$ in. (6.3 × 4.6 cm.)

PROV: Presented by the artist to Elizabeth Steele (later Mrs. Wallace), Philadelphia; her daughter, Mrs. John Cook; lent by C . . . Esq (John Cook, died *c.* 1845) to the Pennsylvania Academy in 1817; his son, William Wallace Cook (died *c.* 1846); sold by D. Thomas, Philadelphia, in 1847 to Joseph West (a nephew of Benjamin) for $147; given by Joseph West to his son Clement L. West prior to 1857, when the latter advertised it for sale; his daughter, Mrs. Edward Wilcox, by 1875, and then by descent to Colonel Cornelius de W. Wilcox, West Point, N.Y.; Ehrich Galleries, New York, 1922; Mrs. John Hill Morgan, Farmington, Conn., by 1924; given to the Yale University Art Gallery in 1940 (the Lelia A. and John Hill Morgan Collection, 1940.529)

EXH: PAFA 1817 (87) "Miniature of Mr. West, painted by himself, in the 18th year of his age":

This picture, the property of C . . . Esq. of Philadelphia was shown to Mr. West in January 1816. The dialogue between himself and his visitors on the occasion is characteristic of the painter, and of sufficient interest to deserve insertion.

Mr. C. opened the object of our visit by saying that some years ago he had waited on Mr. W. with the picture of a Great Man [George Washington] an American, and had now the pleasure of showing him the picture of another great man, also an American; at the same time presenting the miniature. He looked at it earnestly. "This is a curiosity. Where did this picture come from, sir?" I replied, from Philadelphia. "This is indeed, a very great curiosity! This, sir, was done for me, and by me. Who does it belong to?" I said, "To yourself; you gave it, sir, to a Miss Steele, who married a Mr. W., and was the mother of my wife."

"Yes, sir, and well I remember it; 'tis now sixty years ago; and there is something more about it that, may be, you don't know. We were very much in love with one another, sir, and the old lady, her mother, whose memory I honor, didn't like my intended profession, and she knew, too, there was such a place as Swedes Church, where people sometimes got married. There again," looking earnestly at the picture, "this I did, and gave her previous to my going to New York, whither I was sent for to paint some portraits. Now this is not a bad picture for one who had never seen a miniature!"

He continued some time musing on the picture, frequently exclaiming, "This is, indeed, a very great curiosity!" Altering its position to different shades of light, at length, "Walk with me into my picture gallery," said he, "I will send for my son and daughter; I should like to show them this picture, it will gratify them." We followed him; he still kept his eyes fixed on the miniature. Mr. C.,

adverting to it, observed there was no collar to the coat, and said something about the dress of a Quaker. "Sir, said Mr. W., "I was once a Quaker, and have never left the principle. I was once present by the king's desire when seven bishops waited on him. The Quakers were mentioned. The king said, '*I was born to fill the station, and am head both of Church and State. I remain in the line of my duty. But had I been left to my own free choice, I should have been a Quaker myself.*'"

We returned to the parlor, where were Mr W 's son and daughter and a lad about thirteen, as we supposed, his grandson. He showed them the miniature, and recounted its history. His son, after listening to him and looking at it closely, exclaimed: "Is this picture to go back, sir?" "It is the property of this gentleman," said Mr. W. He remarked that he could see the likeness of the lad in it, and continued at intervals, while we stayed with him, to look at it with undiminished attention.

Speaking of Mr Leslie, he said: "That young man will be a great painter; he astonishes us all at the Academy! How is it that there is more intellect in Americans than there is in our people? I perceive it in most of those who come to me."

He gave us a history of his "Christ Healing the Sick." Said he had painted a better picture than that for the Pennsylvania Hospital; that he had given instructions for a room to be built there for its exhibition; that one person had offered him £7,000 for it, and the profits of the first year's exhibition; another had offered £10,000 for it; that if the managers could build such a room, he could present them with two other pictures. "I do not say what those pictures shall be; but, sir, I authorize you on this condition to promise them two more pictures."

He pressed us to visit his painting of "Christ Rejected," having presented me with a ticket for myself and friends, returned the miniature, particularly requesting that I would have engraved on the back of it that it was painted in 1756, by himself.

Brooklyn 1922 (32d) lent by Ehrich Galleries; *Miniatures Painted in America 1720–1850*, Metropolitan Museum of Art, New York, 1927 (56); *Five Centuries of Miniature Painting*, Brooklyn Museum, 1936 (257); *American Art: 1750–1800 Towards Independence*, Yale University Art Gallery, New Haven, and the Victoria and Albert Museum, London, 1976 (7)

LIT: Thompson Westcott, "Queries: West's Auto-Miniature," *Pennsylvania Magazine of History and Biography*, VI, 1882, pp. 495–96; J. T. Stern, ed., *Our Kindred. The McFarland and Stern Families of Chester County, Pa and New Castle, Delaware*, West Chester, 1885, p. 167, ill. p. 17; Hart 1908, pp. 4–6; Harry B. Wehle, *American Miniatures, 1730–1850*, New York, 1927, p. 16; Brinton 1936; Sawitzky 1938, pp. 436, 452–53 (14); Devanter 1973, p. 764, fig. 1

The main source of information about No. 524 is the interview with West recorded in the Pennsylvania Academy catalogue of 1817, quoted above.[1] The miniature is set in a silver locket, which is engraved on the reverse: *Benjn. West/Aged 18/Painted by himself/in the year 1756/& presented to Miss Steele/of Philadelphia*. This locket would seem to confirm the reliability of the account of the miniature's early history, and the inscription fulfills the request made by West to his visitors in 1816. Nevertheless, it should be pointed out that West made his statement some sixty years after he painted the miniature, when his memory was certainly not infallible. West's remark, "this I did and gave her previous to my going to New York, whither I was sent for to paint some portraits," suggests a date later than

1756, since his one known visit to New York probably did not take place until 1758 or 1759, shortly before his departure for Italy in the spring of 1760 (see No. 648). The style and assurance of handling in No. 524 also seem more compatible with a date closer to 1759 than to 1756.

West's collarless coat in No. 524, which his visitors commented upon, is similar to the coats worn by his father and brother in the *West Family* of *c.* 1772–73 (No. 546), where they contrast with the more elegant and worldly dress of the now successful painter. However, West's reply to his visitors—"I was once a Quaker, and have never left the principle"—was, to say the least, misleading, since, as Charles Henry Hart established in 1908, West was not a Quaker either by birth or by adoption.[2] The son and daughter to whom West showed the miniature were Benjamin West, Jr. and his wife, who with their son had come to live with West in 1815.[3] The comment about Quakers, which George III is said to have made when West and seven bishops waited upon him, must have been made during the deliberations sought by George III to assess the propriety of West's proposed paintings for the chapel in Windsor Castle. Galt cites a similar comment made by the King in response to the bishops' judgment that "even a Quaker" might contemplate the works with edification.[4]

No. 524 is the only known miniature which can be ascribed with reasonable certainty to West's hand. A related drawing showing what appears to be the same subject with his hat tucked under his arm as in No. 524 and with the same oval shape is in a sketchbook that West evidently used during the later 1750s in Philadelphia (Historical Society of Pennsylvania).[5] A companion drawing on the same page showing a young lady may represent Miss Steele, and would seem to indicate that West drew her or intended to draw her in miniature as well. Additional similarly composed drawings, probably also done for miniatures, are on other pages of the book.

[1]The entry in the Pennsylvania Academy catalogue was evidently based on a slightly longer description of the interview in John Cook's journals. A copy made in 1848 by Preston C. F. West (a son of the Joseph West who bought No. 524 in 1847) of a transcription of the relevant portion of John Cook's journal made by *his* son, William Wallace Cook, was formerly in the files of A. Duveen and Company. This description gives the exact date of the visit (25 January 1816) and names John Cook's companions (Mr. William Vaughan and Mr. John Osely or Oseley) but gives no further information about No. 524. Also in the former Duveen files was a letter about the work from Joseph West to a Mrs. Sanguinetti, dated 6 December 1875, which corroborates some details of the miniature's later history.
[2]Hart 1908, pp. 1–3.
[3]Farington Diary, 11 July 1815, Farington 1978–, XIII, p. 4667.
[4]Galt 1820, pp. 55–56.
[5]Reproduced by Sawitzky, as are several other drawings from the sketchbook. The sketchbook consists of thirty sheets, each $6\frac{1}{2} \times 3\frac{7}{8}$ in., and contains some seventy portrait sketches in pencil; see Sawitzky, pp. 438–39.

525 Self-Portrait 1760

LOCATION UNKNOWN

PROV: Said to have been given by West to William Henry (1729–1786) in 1760 and to have belonged to Henry's son in the early nineteenth century

LIT: Tinkcom 1951, p. 382 (Sir Augustus Foster)

Sir Augustus Foster, a British diplomat who visited Lancaster, Pennsylvania, some time between 1804 and 1812, was taken to see the pictures belonging to a son of West's early patron William Henry (for whom see No. 637). No. 525 was the first work he mentioned following a somewhat garbled account of West's early life:

527

He painted a Portrait of himself and gave it, on his leaving America as a memento to Mr. Henry, observing that he felt as if he should one day become a distinguished artist and requested the Picture might be carefully preserved. It had, however, become totally ruined by the damp, the Colouring being completely peeled off.

We know from Galt that West did see William Henry in Philadelphia while waiting to sail to Italy in April 1760.[1]

[1]Galt 1816, p. 85.

526 Self-Portrait c. 1776
See color illustration, p. vi

BALTIMORE MUSEUM OF ART

Oil on canvas: $30\frac{1}{4} \times 25\frac{1}{8}$ in. (76.8 × 63.8 cm.), painted oval

PROV: (?) Possibly sold by West's sons, Robins, London, 20–22 June 1829, lot 100, 142, or 161 (all three lots were self-portraits); (?) Sir Robert Peel (1788–1850), second Baronet; sold by Sir Robert Peel (1867–1925), fourth Baronet, Willis's Rooms, London, 29–30 November 1917, lot 83; Daniel H.

Farr, Philadelphia; William G. Warden, Philadelphia, by 1921; Mr. and Mrs. Jacob Blaustein, Baltimore, 1942; given in their memory to the Baltimore Museum in 1981 by their children

EXH: Philadelphia 1921 (2); Brooklyn 1922 (2); *Eighteenth Century English, American and French Paintings*, Daniel H. Farr, Philadelphia, 1927 (30); Philadelphia 1938 (21); *From Colony to Nation*, Art Institute of Chicago, 1949 (128); *Rendezvous for Taste*, Peale Museum, Baltimore, 1956 (140); Allentown 1962 (8); *From El Greco to Pollock: Early and Late Works*, Baltimore Museum of Art, 1968 (47); *Maryland Heritage*, Baltimore Museum of Art, 1976 (20); Boston 1976 (21)

LIT: Harvey M. Watts, "The Benjamin West Exhibition at the Art Alliance, Philadelphia," *Art and Archaeology*, Jan. 1922, ill. p. 20; Devanter 1973, pp. 765–66, pl 1; Sona K. Johnston, *American Paintings 1750–1900 from the Collection of the Baltimore Museum of Art*, Baltimore, 1983, pp. 179–80 (158), and frontispiece

No. 526 shows the artist holding a board or small easel upon which can be seen what appears to be a drawing

in monochrome greys of the two standing figures from the right side of the *Death of General Wolfe* (No. 93). This reference to the painting which more than any other established West's reputation suggests that he did not paint No. 526 until after the *Death of General Wolfe* made its first public appearance at the Royal Academy exhibition of 1771, and probably not until after William Woollett's engraving of the picture, published in January 1776, began to achieve an unprecedented popular and commercial success. The vigorous touch in No. 526 is more consistent with West's handling in portraits such as No. 590 of 1777 than with that in portraits from around 1770–71 such as No. 662.[1] Gilbert Stuart's portrait of Woollett (ill. p. 213) shows one of the same two standing figures from the painting of the *Death of General Wolfe* in its background, and it may be that what West is holding in his hand in No. 526 is meant to represent not a drawing, but a marked proof of the Woollet engraving.

The large round beaver hat and the angle from which West views himself in No. 526 suggest his conscious emulation of the well-known self-portrait by Rubens in the English Royal Collection, which by 1776 he certainly would have known firsthand. As Dorinda Evans has pointed out, the young Gilbert Stuart, who arrived in West's studio in 1777 echoed both pictures in a *Self-Portrait* which he painted in 1778 (Redwood Library and Athenaeum, Newport, Rhode Island).[2]

A copy, which has traditionally been accepted as by West, is in the National Gallery in Washington.[3] Although the Washington picture is a work of considerable quality, the brushwork is consistently less free than that in No. 526, while at the same time the detail is less precise, suggesting that it is not by West's hand but quite possibly a contemporary copy made by one of the younger artists working in West's studio, of whom the most likely is, of course, Stuart. The National Gallery painting lacks the painted oval of No. 526, the fall of drapery in the background, and the figures from the *Death of General Wolfe* on the sheet which the artist holds.[4] Several other copies, of varying degrees of incompetence, also exist.

[1] Jules Prown has suggested that West's brushwork in No. 590 reflects the impact of Copley's arrival in England (Prown 1966, II, p. 274, note 25). The suggestion seems equally germane to No. 526.
[2] Evans 1980, p. 52; the self-portraits by Stuart and by Rubens are reproduced ibid., pp. 54 and 55, figs. 33 and 34.
[3] Oil on canvas: $30\frac{1}{4} \times 25\frac{3}{8}$ in. Reproduced in color as the frontispiece of Evans 1959, on the cover of Alberts 1978, etc., and frequently exhibited as a work by West.
[4] X-ray photographs made during an examination of the Washington portrait in the conservation department of the National Gallery on 27 September 1983, reveal that the painting did at one time have a painted oval and background draperies corresponding to those in No. 526, which have been painted over. We are grateful to Linda Ayres and Anne Hoenigswald, of the National Gallery, and to Sona Johnston and Margaret Ash, of the Baltimore Museum, for making it possible to study the two paintings side by side and for their helpful discussions of the two works.

527 Self-Portrait (?) 1792
Illustrated p. 451

ROYAL ACADEMY OF ARTS, LONDON

Oil on panel: 40×52 in. (101.5×132 cm.)

Signed, bottom left: *B. West/[?]1792*

PROV: Sold by West's sons, Robins, London, 20–22 June 1829, lot 88 ("Portrait of the late Benjamin West, Esq. in the President's Chair, with Somerset House in the background, painted by himself"); presented to the Royal Academy in April 1830 by Joseph Neeld, MP

EXH: (?) RA 1804 (37) "Portrait of himself"; *Exhibition of the Royal House of Guelph*, New Gallery, London, 1891 (262); *British Art*, Royal Academy, London, 1934 (250); *British Self-Portraits*, Arts Council of Great Britain, 1962 (39); London 1963 (25); *Bicentenary Exhibition*, Royal Academy, London, 1968–69 (54)

ENGR: Engraving ($3\frac{7}{8} \times 3\frac{3}{16}$ in.) of a detail of West's head only, without any background, by Christian Josi, pub. in the *European Magazine*, XXVI, Sept. 1794, opp. p. 163; engraving ($4\frac{1}{8} \times 3$ in.) also of the head only by F. Bolt, dated *1796*, and inscribed in German; engraving ($8\frac{5}{8} \times 7\frac{7}{16}$ in.) of a bust-length detail with a contracted version of Somerset House in the background, by Thomas Holloway, pub. by Holloway, 25 April 1798, as an ill. to the first English edition of the *Physiognomische Fragmente* by Johann Caspar Lavater (1789–98), III, pl. 171, between pp. 150–51

(?) LISTED: *PC*, p. 566 ("Mr. West's Portrait, half length," West, Painting-room); *UM*, p. 530; *BA*, p. 17; Galt, p. 228; Dillenberger, p. 172 (332)

LIT: J. E. Hodgson and Fred A. Eaton, *The Royal Academy and its Members, 1768–1830*, London, 1905, p. 377;

Constable 1962–68, III, p. 28 (letter of April 1830); Devanter 1973, p. 770, fig. 5

The date accompanying West's signature on No. 527 is difficult to read and has been recorded as *1793* in various exhibition catalogues published by the Royal Academy. Whether West painted No. 527 in 1792 or 1793, the painting commemorates his election to the presidency of the Royal Academy on 17 March 1792. Somerset House, the Academy's home, is visible in the background, and the chair upon which West sits is the same chair in which he is shown presiding over the assembled Academicians in the group portrait of 1795 by Henry Singleton (ill. p. 113). The hat in the lower right corner is presumably the hat that he wears in Singleton's picture and that he wore on all formal occasions at the Academy, "to do honour to the office."[1] The piece of sculpture on the right side of the painting is a cast of the *Belvedere Torso* and may represent the cast which had been brought from Rome and presented to the Academy by Joseph Nollekens. From the sixteenth through the eighteenth centuries, the *Torso* commanded almost universal respect as a font of artistic wisdom, largely because of the admiration Michelangelo was said to have expressed for it; in 1780, in Sir Joshua Reynolds's tenth Discourse, West's predecessor as president of the Royal Academy singled it out as the embodiment of the perfection of the "science of abstract form."[2] On a table before the *Torso* is a stack of four books, two of which are labelled *HISTORY OF ENGLAND* and *HISTORY OF GREECE*, emblematic not only of West's sources, but also of the role of the Academy as a learned body and its traditional commitment, repeatedly expressed in Reynolds's *Discourses*, to history painting as the highest form of artistic endeavor. Also on the table are a portfolio, a magnifying glass, some paper, and a quill pen, the latter perhaps intended to suggest the intellectual and quasi-literary responsibilities West inherited as Reynolds's successor.

No. 527 is the largest and most ambitious of West's known self-portraits. A second, smaller but similarly emblematic self-portrait, which bears the date *1793*, is No. 529 below. Although there is a possibility of confusion between the two, it seems somewhat more likely that No. 527 was the self-portrait exhibited by West at the Royal Academy in 1804, and it was probably the half-length self-portrait described in the early lists of West's works as being in his painting-room. In 1829, No. 527 was the only one of the four self-portraits in the Robins sale of 20–22 June to be accompanied by a description in the catalogue, allowing it to be identified. It was evidently purchased some months after the sale by Joseph Neeld who, through the agency of Henry Pierce Bone, had been a major buyer at the earlier West sale of 22–25 May 1829. A letter of April 1830 from John Constable to Charles Robert Leslie, written while Constable was serving as a member of the Hanging Committee at the Royal Academy, reports that the portrait "is bought by a Mr. Neal, who has presented it very properly to the R.A."

A second version, which was in America by 1802, is No. 528 below. An unfinished copy of a detail of West's head and shoulders, in which the artist holds a scroll of paper before him in his right hand, is in a private collection.[3] Another copy is recorded as having been in a private collection in New York in 1934.[4]

[1] Whitley 1928a, II, p. 161.
[2] Sir Joshua Reynolds, *Discourses on Art*, Robert R. Wark, ed., New Haven and London, 1975, p. 177. See also Haskell and Penny 1981, pp. 311–14. James Barry included the *Belvedere Torso* in the background of his self-portrait of 1767 (National Portrait Gallery, London). The *Torso*, on a monumental scale, is also visible on the left side of the Singleton's group portrait of the Academicians (p. 113).
[3] Oil on canvas: $27\frac{1}{2} \times 24\frac{3}{8}$ in.
[4] Photograph in the Frick Art Reference Library.

528 Self-Portrait (?) c. 1792

THE BROOK CLUB, NEW YORK

Oil on canvas: $40\frac{1}{4} \times 50\frac{1}{2}$ in. (102×128.5 cm.)

PROV: Edward Savage (1761–1817), New York, by 1802; Moses Kimbalt, Boston, by 1892; Ehrich Galleries, New York; purchased by the Brook Club in 1907

EXH: Columbian Gallery, New York, 1802; *Exhibition of Paintings, Portraits painted in Europe by early American Artists*, Union League Club, New York, 1922 (7)

LIT: Ehrich 1918, p. 157; Diego Suarez, *The Collection of Portraits of American Celebrities and other Paintings belonging to the Brook*, New York, 1962, pp. 14–15, ill. p. 14; Rita Susswein Gottesman, *The Arts and Crafts in New York 1800–1804*, New York, 1965, pp. 32–33; Devanter 1973, p. 770

No. 528 is a replica of the previous entry. Since it was in America by 1802 and indeed was exhibited before No. 527 was first seen publicly, it may have been painted more or less contemporaneously. Edward Savage (1761–1817), the proprietor of the Columbian Gallery, where No. 528 was exhibited in 1802, had been in London between 1791 and 1794.[1]

[1] See Dunlap 1918, I, p. 381, note 1.

529 Self-Portrait 1793
See color illustration, p. 3

SOCIETY OF DILETTANTI, LONDON

Oil on panel: $36 \times 27\frac{1}{2}$ in. (91.5×70 cm.)

Inscribed lower left (on sheet of paper under the artist's left hand): *Benjamin West Esqr/painted this pictu[re]/in 1793*

PROV: Presented by the artist to the Society of Dilettanti in 1818

EXH: London 1868 (945)

ENGR: Stipple engraving (oval, $3\frac{1}{8} \times 2\frac{1}{2}$ in.) of a detail of West's head and shoulders, by James Hopwood, pub. 1 Jan. 1805 by H. D. Symonds as the frontispiece to the *Universal Magazine*, XVIII, no. 3, May 1805 (accompanying an article about West); stipple engraving ($5\frac{1}{4} \times 4\frac{1}{16}$ in.) by W. T. Fry, pub. 12 July 1820 by T. Cadell, as the frontispiece to Galt 1820

LIT: Lionel Cust, *History of the Society of Dilettanti*, London, 1898, pp. 230–31; Cecil Harcourt-Smith, *The Society of Dilettanti: Its Regalia and Pictures*, London, 1932, pp. 78–80 (32), pl. XXVIII; Millar 1969, I, p. XIX and fig. IX; Devanter 1973, pp. 768–70 and pl. V

The inscription on No. 529 quoted above differs considerably from West's usual manner of signing his works. This departure from the artist's normal practice may be explained by the painting's special destination as a presentation piece, in which case it seems probable that the inscription was added at the time West presented No. 529 to the Society of Dilettanti. West was elected to membership of the Society in 1792, but he only presented the portrait some twenty-six years later, in April 1818. In a letter to Sir Henry Englefield, the Society's secretary, dated 25 April 1818, West offered the painting to the Society, promised to provide a proper frame for it, and also asked to be allowed to retain it through the following summer in order to make copies to be sent to Rome and Florence.[1] Nonetheless, No. 529 certainly records West's appearance in the 1790s (he was fifty-five years old in 1793), rather than two years before his death, and he may have added the wordy inscription to emphasize the fact.

Whether or not West initially intended No. 529 for

the Society of Dilettanti is open to question. He was elected to the presidency of the Royal Academy and to membership of the Society in the same year, the latter election being a consequence of the former, and No. 529, like No. 527, which is dated *1792* or *1793*, commemorates his role in the Academy, rather than in the Society. The chair in which West sits in No. 529 is similar to that in No. 527, although less of it shows, and in his right hand he holds a paper inscribed: *By Command./Decem.ʳ 10th 1768. Royal Aacademy [sic] of/arts London.* 10 December 1768 was the day on which George III had signed the Instrument of Foundation, creating the Royal Academy, an action which West had played a major role in bringing about.[2] Above the paper is a bust of the King, the patron of the Academy and of West, and before the bust lie two books, inscribed *BIBLE* and *HISTORY OF ENGLAND*. These volumes correspond to those shown by West in No. 527 but with the significant difference that the Bible has replaced a history of Greece.

The bust of George III in the background shows the monarch in Roman guise wearing a wreath of laurel around his head. Although what appears to be the molding of a frame running along the left edge of the picture suggests that West may have at one time intended to include a painting in the background, the monochromatic grey and the projection of one shoulder in front of the adjacent curtain establish that the bust is sculpted rather than painted. The features do not appear to be derived from any of West's portraits of the King (Nos. 547–52). It is possible that West modelled the likeness on an actual piece of sculpture, but if so, we have not succeeded in identifying his source.

No. 529 is smaller than No. 527, but it was evidently the image of himself by which West preferred to be remembered. Apart from presenting it to the Society of Dilettanti, where it joined a much-admired self-portrait by Reynolds,[3] he proposed sending copies of it abroad, and in engraved versions it provided the first likeness to accompany a published account of West's life,[4] as well as the frontispiece to Galt's life.

Although West wrote to Sir Henry Englefield in 1818 that he intended to make two copies of No. 529 in response to requests from the capital at Rome and the gallery at Florence (i.e., the Museo Capitolino and the Uffizi), no self-portrait by West seems to have reached either city.[5] Three copies of No. 529 are currently known, and it is possible that they include the two intended for Rome and Florence (Fogg Art Museum, Harvard University, and in private collections in England and in the United States). At least one of these copies appears to have been included in the sales of pictures from West's estate in 1829, and it is possible that all three were.[6] None of them, however, shows much sign of having been painted by West's hand, and it seems unlikely that, at the age of eighty, he would have undertaken the routine task of making the copies himself, rather than entrust them to one of his sons. All three copies are approximately the same size as No. 529. The version in the Fogg Museum corresponds closely with it in all details, but lacks the inscription under the artist's left hand. The two versions in private collections are somewhat less finished (the books and the paper West holds in his right hand are uninscribed) and show some minor changes in detail, most notable in the replacement of the curtains, which hang behind West in No. 529 and the Fogg painting, by what appears to be the framing of a window and a diamond-patterned wallpaper.

A copy in miniature in enamel after No. 529 by Henry Bone is in the National Gallery of Ireland, and a squared drawing by Bone, which is signed and dated 1804 and which was made presumably for the enamel, is in the National Portrait Gallery in London. Bone exhibited a portrait of West at the Royal Academy in 1804.

530

[1] Quoted by Cust; a draft of the letter is in the Historical Society of Pennsylvania.
[2] See Galt 1820, pp. 34–44, and Sidney C. Hutchison, *The History of the Royal Academy: 1768–1968*, London, 1968, pp. 42–45 and 209–13, where the Instrument of Foundation is transcribed. The words on the paper in No. 529 do not correspond exactly to the wording of the Instrument.
[3] Reproduced as the frontispiece to Cust.
[4] It should be noted, however, that an engraving after No. 527 accompanied a very brief article about West in the *European Magazine* in 1794.
[5] Letter from Wolfram Prinz to Helmut von Erffa, 13 Feb. 1967.
[6] Four self-portraits by West were sold, Robins, London, 20–22 June 1829, lots 88, 100, 142, and 161. Lot 88 was described in the sale catalogue as showing Somerset House in the background, and it can therefore be equated with the painting fitting that description that Joseph Neeld presented to the Royal Academy in the following year (No. 527). The other three were not accompanied by any distinguish-

ing descriptions and cannot be identified. However, the copy of No. 529 now in an American private collection has a Neeld provenance (sold Christie's, London, 13 July 1945, lot 167); like all the other pictures by West in the Neeld collection, it probably was sold by West's sons in 1829, and since there were no self-portraits in the main Robins sale of 22–25 May 1829, from which most of the Neeld pictures were acquired, it must, like No. 527, have been in the subsequent sale on 20–22 June 1829.

530 Self-Portrait 1806

PENNSYLVANIA ACADEMY OF THE FINE ARTS, PHILADELPHIA

Oil on canvas: 36 × 28 in. (91.5 × 71 cm.)

Signed upper right: *B. West 1806*

PROV: Given by West to Robert Fulton, who brought

the painting to the United States in 1806; Ehrich Galleries, New York, by 1918; Albert Rosenthal; Henry R. Hallowell, Philadelphia; given to the Pennsylvania Academy by Mr. and Mrs. Hallowell in 1964

EXH: (?) PAFA 1807; AAFA 1816 (22) lent by Mrs. Fulton; Philadelphia 1921 (1); Brooklyn 1922 (1) lent to both by Ehrich Galleries; *Early American Portraits*, Minneapolis Institute of Arts, 1924 (6); *Early American Portraits*, Carnegie Institute, Pittsburgh, 1925 (45) lent by Ehrich Galleries; *Colonial Portraits*, Robert C. Vose Galleries, Boston, 1930 (21); Philadelphia 1938 (59) lent by Henry R. Hallowell, Philadelphia; *In this Academy: the Pennsylvania Academy of the Fine Arts, 1805–1976*, PAFA 1976 (89)

LISTED: *BA*, p. 19 ("Mr. West painting the portrait of Mrs. West, in one picture half figures, large as life; in the Academy at Philadelphia"); Dillenberger, p. 187 (488)

LIT: *Delaplaine's Repository of the Lives and Portraits of Distinguished Americans*, Philadelphia, 1817, pp. 203–4; Cadwallader D. Colden, *The Life of Robert Fulton*, New York, 1817, p. 10; Dunlap 1834, I, p. 231 (1918, I, p. 273); Ehrich 1918, p. 153; Brinton 1936 (9); Devanter 1973, pp. 770–71, pl. VI; Alberts 1978, p. 342, ill.

No. 530, which shows West, palette and maulstick in hand, painting a portrait of Mrs. West, was one of two portraits given by West to Robert Fulton in 1806, on the occasion of the latter's return from England to America. The other was a portrait of Fulton (No. 620). Both works were described in *La Belle Assemblée* in 1808 as being in the Academy in Philadelphia, but it seems unlikely that either portrait was there for more than a brief period at the time of the Academy's opening; see No. 620 for a fuller discussion.

The brief biography of Robert Fulton published in *Delaplaine's Repository* in 1817 contained the statement, "Before they separated, the portrait of each of the friends was painted by the other, and these pictures were carefully cherished as remembrances of their attachment." The implication that Fulton rather than West painted No. 530 is contradicted in the more substantial and authoritative biography of Fulton by Cadwallader D. Colden, published in the same year, which explicitly states that No. 530 was painted by West himself, and it was contradicted earlier by the inclusion of the painting in the list of West's works published in *La Belle Assemblée* in 1808. The handling of the paint in No. 530 also is characteristic of West. Nonetheless, it is not impossible that No. 530 was begun by Fulton and completed by West. The direction of West's gaze in the painting is unusual for a self-portrait, which normally reflects the necessity of the painter's looking directly into a mirror in order to be able to record his own features. The frozen action and the resultant and somewhat disturbing stiffness of No. 530 are also not consistent with the majority of West's portraits, but are at least superficially reminiscent of the engravings by James Ward after Fulton's portraits of Mary, Queen of Scots, and Lady Jane Grey, and there is a distinct resemblance between No. 530 and Fulton's equally stiff portrait of the third Earl Stanhope holding a printer's plate, his one English painting now known (collection of Henry H. Livingston).[1]

A copy of No. 530 in watercolors is in the Philadelphia Museum of Art. For the portrait of Mrs. West on the easel in No. 530, see No. 534 below.

[1] See Evans 1980, pp. 116–19, figs. 93, 95 and 96.

531 Self-Portrait *c.* 1816–17

LOCATION UNKNOWN

(Oil on panel)

PROV: Commenced as an intended gift of the artist to the Pennsylvania Hospital, Philadelphia, but never completed; sold by West's sons, Robins, London, 20–22 June 1829, lot 161* ("Whole length portrait of the late B. West . . . by Leslie")[1]

LISTED: (?) Galt, p. 234 ("Portrait of Himself, left unfinished"); Dillenberger, p. 190 (516)

LIT: Farington Diary, 3 Sept. 1816 (Farington 1978–, XIV, p. 4896); Dunlap 1834, I, p. 86 (Dunlap 1918, I, p. 95); Morton and Woodbury, 1895, II, pp. 309–11; Evans 1980, pp. 168–69

In January 1816 West told a group of visitors from Philadelphia that if the managers of the Pennsylvania Hospital would build an appropriate room, he would present them not only the large *Christ Healing the Sick*, which he recently had completed (No. 338), but also two additional pictures: "I do not say what those pictures shall be; but, sir, I authorize you on this condition to promise them two more pictures."[2] On 10 March of the same year he wrote to the hospital making a similar promise and specifying that he intended the two pictures to "compliment" a pair of low fireplaces on each side of the room. On 2 March 1817, in response to news from the hospital that the room was ready, he wrote again to say that he was preparing two pictures to accompany the large one and that he would detain No. 338 for a short time: "otherwise I shall be deprived of the opportunity of putting the other two into that perfect union of Colour and Effert which ought to prevail.—When that is accomplished I will consign the three Pictures to America . . ." Despite this promise, the several letters quoted by Morton and Woodbury about the shipping of No. 338 and its reception in Philadelphia contain no further mention of the two companion pictures, and it is evident that they were not sent.

West never specified what the subjects of the two pictures would be. They are, however, described in a letter written by Charles Robert Leslie in 1833 or 1834 to William Dunlap. After discussing West's gift of No. 338 to the Pennsylvania Hospital, Leslie continues:

He had begun his own portrait to present to the hospital. It was a whole length on a mahogany panel; he employed me to dead color it for him. He had also made a small sketch of a picture of Dr. Franklin, to present with it. The doctor was seated on the clouds, surrounded by naked boys, and the experiment of proving lightning and electricity to be the same was alluded to.

The sketch of a picture of Dr. Franklin must certainly be the sketch now in the Philadelphia Museum (No. 618). The whole-length portrait of West, dead-colored by Leslie, seems, equally certainly, to have been the whole-length portrait sold by West's sons in 1829 as a work by Leslie. No whole-length self-portrait by West is otherwise known, nor does the literature on Leslie contain any mention of an independent portrait by him of West.[3] Leslie's use of the word "begun" implies that the painting was never finished, and, hence, No. 531 may have been the unfinished self-portrait included as the last entry in Galt's list of West's works published in 1820. Galt's list is mainly copied from the much earlier list published in *Public Characters*, but at the very end it includes seven large and important late works that do not appear on the other lists. As the only recorded full-length self-portrait of the artist, which must have been fairly elaborate in composition and imagery if the sketch for its intended companion (No. 618) is in any way a guide, as well as a work which the available documentation suggests was

only undertaken in 1816 or 1817, No. 531 is the strongest candidate for identification as the self-portrait listed by Galt.[4]

No. 531 must also be the picture about which Farington recorded West's speaking to Lawrence on 3 September 1816:

He told Sir Thos. that he had been requested to send His Portrait, a whole Length to Philadelphia, and He desired the consent of Sir Thos. to copy the Portrait of Himself painted by Sir Thos. as being an approved likeness, and to the *Head only copied* He wd. add the figure. To this Sir Thomas gave his consent readily.

The portrait by Lawrence to which West referred had been painted and exhibited in 1811 and is now in the Yale Center for British Art.[5]

[1] This lot was the second of two lots numbered 161 in the sale. The other, preceding one, was a *Self-Portrait*.
[2] See the account of the visit published in the catalogue of the Pennsylvania Academy exhibition of 1817, quoted under No. 524.
[3] See Tom Taylor, ed., *Autobiographical Recollections by the Late Charles Robert Leslie, R.A.*, 2 vols., London, 1860. Vol. 2 contains a list of Leslie's principal pictures (pp. 319–25). In 1898, Mrs. Albert F. West sold a "Portrait of Benjamin West, in profile, seated," as by "Leslie (of America)" (Christie's, London, 18–19 March 1898, lot 150, 35½ × 28 in.). Kenneth Garlick also records a copy by Leslie in the Boston Athenaeum of Thomas Lawrence's half-length seated portrait of West now in the Yale Center for British Art (see note 5 below).
[4] A full-length portrait of West by Lawrence (RA 1821, no. 193) is in the Wadsworth Atheneum, Hartford (Frontispiece). A full-length portrait by James Green was formerly in the Metropolitan Museum (see No. 401). That painting was exhibited PAFA 1851–62 as a self-portrait of the artist.
[5] Oil on panel, 60 × 47½ in. (Kenneth Garlick, "A catalogue of the paintings, drawings and pastels of Sir Thomas Lawrence," *Walpole Society*, XXXIX, 1962–64, p. 195).

532 Self-Portrait (?) 1819

NATIONAL MUSEUM OF AMERICAN ART, WASHINGTON, D.C.

Oil on board: $32\frac{3}{8} \times 25\frac{5}{8}$ in. (82.2 × 65.1 cm.)

Signed lower left: (?) *B. West/Oct. 1819* and also inscribed on the charcoal box in the lower right corner: [illegible]/*Oct. 1819*

PROV: H. N. Barlow, Washington, by whom sold, Latimer and Cleary, Washington, 8 January 1876, lot 124, bt. for $500 by the Joint Committee of Congress for the Library of Congress; transferred to the National Collection of Fine Arts (the present National Museum of American Art) in 1917

EXH: *The Painter and the New World*, Montreal Museum of Fine Arts, 1967 (138); Washington and Philadelphia 1980

LIT: Theodore Bolton, "A Portrait of Benjamin West Painted by Himself," *Art in America*, VIII, 1920, pp. 298–301, ill. p. 299; Devanter 1973, p. 771 and pl. III; Alberts 1978, p. 384, ill. opp. p. 271

The signature or signatures on No. 532 are not readily visible to the naked eye and are not discernible in a photograph. That in the lower left has been variously described as *BW/1818*,[1] *B. West PRA./Oct. 1819*,[2] and *B. West/Oct. 1819*.[3] If the signature is indeed by West, and if the date of *Oct. 1819* is correctly read, No. 532 is one of two known works signed and dated by the artist in the same month, when he was entering his eighty-second year, and only five months before his death. The other painting, *Boys and Grapes* (No. 124), which bears the specific date of *October 10th 1819* (West's birthday), was described on the list of works offered by West's sons

532

Sir Francis Chantrey, *Benjamin West*.
Marble, 1818. Royal
Academy of Arts, London.

to the United States in 1826 as the artist's last picture. The two paintings do not show much similarity in handling, and it is difficult to accept them as works from the same time by the same artist. Whereas the flaccid modelling in No. 124 seems reasonably consistent with a number of other late works by the artist (such as No. 364), the relatively firm yet subtle modelling of No. 532, is not only at variance with what we might assume West capable of at a time when his health was rapidly failing, but also unlike his modelling of flesh at any earlier stage of his career. The treatment of the still-life details in the two works is also radically unlike. Thus, although we should be cautious about forming rigid presuppositions of how the artist's very last works should look, it would seem that No. 532 is probably not entirely and perhaps not even partly a work by West's own hand.

The identification of the subject of No. 532 as West is not open to serious question. His appearance, although quite unlike that in earlier self-portraits showing him at a younger age, is comparable to that in the portraits from later years by Lawrence (Frontispiece) and Chantrey (dated 1818, exhibited at the Royal Academy in the same year, and now belonging to the Academy as Chantrey's diploma work). Indeed the similarities in the down-turned mouths and the lines around the nose between No. 532 and the bust by Chantrey, raise the possibility that the bust rather than West himself may have served as the model for the picture. Since the Chantrey bust was in the Royal Academy from 1818 on and, therefore, available to students in the Academy's schools, those similarities also suggest the possibility that No. 532 might have been painted by someone who had no personal contact with the subject.

[1] Letter from Thomas N. Beggs, Director, National Collection of Fine Arts, to Helmut von Erffa, 4 April 1952.
[2] Letter from Robert Hunter, Research Assistant, National

533

Collection of Fine Arts, to Helmut von Erffa, 4 Nov. 1968. This report was based on examination of No. 532 under a microscope.

[3] Letter from Joshua C. Taylor, Director, National Collection of Fine Arts, to Helmut von Erffa, 25 September 1972. In this letter, which followed re-examination of No. 532 in the Conservation Laboratory, Mr. Taylor specifically denied that the letters *P.R.A.* (which had been recorded by Mr. Hunter four years earlier) were legible in either inscription.

533 Self-Portrait with Raphael West 1773

YALE CENTER FOR BRITISH ART, NEW HAVEN, PAUL MELLON COLLECTION

Oil on canvas: circular, $26\frac{1}{2}$ in. (67.25 cm.) in diameter

PROV: Bequeathed to Sir Henry Fitzherbert, third Baronet (1783–1858), Tissington Hall, Derbyshire, by his uncle Phelp Perrin;[1] then by family descent to Sir William Fitzherbert, seventh Baronet (1874–1963); Hirschl & Adler Galleries, New York; acquired by Paul Mellon in 1971

EXH: *Treasures from Midland Houses*, City Art Gallery, Birmingham, 1938 (135) lent by Sir William Fitzherbert

ENGR: Mezzotint ($13\frac{3}{4} \times 10\frac{13}{16}$ in.) with the image in a *trompe-l'oeil* frame ($9\frac{3}{8}$ in. in diameter) by Valentine Green, inscribed *B. West pinxit 1773*, and pub. by Green, 13 Feb. 1775

According to the inscription on the Green mezzotint,

West painted No. 533 in 1773, when he was thirty-five years old. Raphael Lamar West (1766–1850), the older of his two sons, who looks over his shoulder, would have been seven years old at the time. Raphael at an earlier age also appears with his mother in a companion composition known in several versions, one of which (No. 536) shares the same provenance and is now in the same collection as No. 533.

[1] Letter from W. C. C. Weetman to Helmut von Erffa, 17 July 1962, transcribing an excerpt from a catalogue of paintings at Tissington Hall compiled by Lady Nora Fitzherbert, the wife of the seventh Baronet. Phelp Perrin was the son of William Perrin of Jamaica (died 1795) and the brother of the wife of Sir William Fitzherbert, first Baronet (1748–1791; married in 1777).

534 Mrs. Benjamin West (Elizabeth Shewell West) *c.* 1806

LOCATION UNKNOWN

Elizabeth Shewell (1741–1814) was, like Benjamin West, a native of Pennsylvania. The two evidently were acquainted as early as 1755 and became engaged to be married before West sailed for Italy in April 1760. When West decided to remain in England in 1764, she joined him there, having been accompanied on the voyage by West's father and by the painter Matthew Pratt (1734–1805), her cousin.[1] Her marriage to West took place on 2 September 1764.

No. 534 is known only through its appearance in No. 530 as a picture within a picture. Although it is conceivable that the portrait never existed independently, it seems improbable that West would have depicted himself painting a picture that he never painted and, if Robert Fulton began No. 530 (as discussed in the entry for that picture), it seems even more improbable that he would have taken such a liberty. In 1806, the date on No. 530, Mrs. West would have been sixty-five years old.

Despite the fact that West and his wife lived harmoniously together for fifty years, no independent portrait of her by him is now known, and none appears in any of the early lists of his works. He did, however, paint her with their son Raphael West (see Nos. 535–39) and in family groups (Nos. 465 and 546), and there can be little doubt that she served frequently as his model during the 1760s and 1770s, her features being recognizable in many of West's works. He also made drawings of her on several occasions. In 1803 Joseph Farington mentioned in his diary seeing a drawing done in America around 1755,[2] and until recent years a large and handsome profile drawing inscribed *Mrs. West 1775* remained in the possession of the artist's and his model's descendants.[3]

An oil painting in the Addison Gallery of American Art in Andover, Massachusetts, which was exhibited in Philadelphia in 1938 and Allentown in 1962 as a portrait of Mrs. West by West, appears neither to be by West, nor to show his wife.[4]

[1] A portrait of her by Matthew Pratt is in the Pennsylvania Academy of the Fine Arts (ill. in Evans 1980, p. 30, fig. 12).
[2] Farington Diary, 9 May 1803 (Farington 1978–, VI, p. 2027).
[3] Pencil: $19\frac{7}{8} \times 15$ in.
[4] Sold anonymously, Christie's, London, 18 March 1924, lot 80 (as "Mrs. Elizabeth West"); exhibited Philadelphia 1938 (60) and Allentown 1962 (31).

535 Mrs. West with Raphael West before 1770

THE MARQUESS OF LOTHIAN

Oil on canvas: 30×25 in. (76.2×63.5 cm.) with the image in a circular painted frame, approximately 26 in. in diameter

PROV: In the possession of John Hobart, second Earl of Buckinghamshire (1723–1793), by 1770; his daughter, Henrietta, wife of the sixth Marquess of Lothian (1763–1824)

EXH: RA 1885, winter (199), lent by the Marquess of Lothian; *Fair Women*, Grafton Gallery, London, 1894 (101)

ENGR: Mezzotint ($14\frac{1}{4} \times 11$ in.) by Valentine Green, pub. by Robert Sayer, 10 July 1770

LISTED: *PC*, p. 564 ("a Mother and Child—the late Lord Buckinghamshire"); *UM*, p. 529; Barlow, p. 434; *BA*, p. 16; Galt, p. 225; Dillenberger, p. 163 (246)

LIT: Graves 1906, VIII, p. 212 (Walpole, 1770)

No. 535 is one of a series of closely related paintings showing the artist's wife holding their eldest son (Nos. 535–39). One of these, possibly No. 538, which appeared at the Royal Academy in 1770 under the title "A portrait of a mother and child," was identified by Horace Walpole in marginal notes in his copy of the Academy catalogue as a portrait of West's own wife and child. To this identification Walpole added the comment, "the Earl of Buckingham has one of these." Since there was no Earl of Buckingham in 1770, we can interpret that comment as a reference to the second Earl of Buckinghamshire, who was credited in the early lists of West's works as owning a "Mother and Child" by the artist, and to whom we can trace the provenance of No. 535. If Walpole's comment was written at the time of the Royal Academy exhibition of 1770, as we might normally assume, it establishes the fact that West must have completed and sold No. 535 prior to that year's exhibition. In No. 535 and other versions of the

535

composition, the apparent age of Raphael West, who was born in April 1766, also suggests a date earlier than 1770. Further confirmation that West must have painted a version or versions considerably before the spring of 1770 is provided by the fact that Valentine Green exhibited a mezzotint after the composition at the Society of Artists in that year, since Green would have required a picture to work from, as well as sufficient time to engrave his plate. It should be pointed out, however, that no version of the subject known to the compilers of this catalogue bears a date. Hence, it is impossible to establish with certainty the date of any one of the pictures or the sequence in which West painted them.

In addition to the versions and related pictures discussed in separate entries below, there are good contemporary copies at Blickling Hall, Norfolk,[1] in the Cleveland Museum of Art,[2] and in a private collection in Germany.[3] And still more copies are known.

The composition depends upon the *Madonna della Sedia* by Raphael (ill. p. 19), with which West was acquainted from his stay in Florence in 1761–62.[4] A copy of the *Madonna della Sedia* was in West's studio by 1780, when John Trumbull copied it,[5] but the copy copied by Trumbull had most probably been painted by John Downman during his visit to Italy in 1773–75, after West had painted No. 535. It was sold by West's sons in 1820.[6]

[1] Oil on canvas, 30 × 25 in. This painting may also have belonged to the second Earl of Buckinghamshire, who owned Blickling Hall. Blickling passed, via his second daughter, to her great nephew, the eighth Marquess of Lothian, and was bequeathed to the National Trust by the eleventh Marquess of Lothian. Because of its apparent Buckinghamshire provenance, this picture has also been identified as the work referred to by Horace Walpole in 1770 (as quoted above), and in 1960 it was exhibited with the implicit claim that it was West's original (*Portrait Groups from National Trust Collections*, Arts Council of Great Britain, 1960, no. 2). The compilers of this catalogue have not been able to study the Blickling painting and No. 535 side by side and have not seen No. 535 at first hand, but the available photographic evidence suggests that No. 535 is the superior work, and that the painting at Blickling is a copy. We are indebted to David Moore-Gwyn, to the Marquess of Lothian, and to St. John Gore for helpful correspondence about the two works.

[2] Oil on canvas, 26¼ × 26 in.; reproduced in *Connoisseur*, XXIII, 1909, p. 80, as in the collection of Castle Smith, Esq., 27 Netherhall Gardens, London. According to a note on pp. 115–16 of the same issue, Smith acquired the picture from the widow of the grandson of Benjamin West, Jr. (i.e., of West's great-grandson). Smith also owned a portrait of West by Lawrence (now in the Yale Center for British Art), for which Kenneth Garlick lists a similar provenance: "West's son and grandson whose widow bequeathed it to her daughter-in-law from whom it passed to the family solicitor, Castle Smith" (*Walpole Society*, XXXIX, 1962–64, p. 195). Christie's records confirm that Castle Smith was the solicitor for Mrs. Albert F. West, who sold several family pictures in 1898 (see No. 544).

[3] Oil on canvas, 26 × 26 in.

[4] See Richardson 1978, p. 18 (letter from West to Joseph Shippen, 11 May 1762).

[5] Jaffe 1975, p. 46. Thomas Sully also made a copy of the *Madonna della Sedia* in West's studio in 1809.

[6] Christie's, London, 23 June 1820, lot 1.

536 Mrs. West with Raphael West (?)*c.* 1773

YALE CENTER FOR BRITISH ART, NEW HAVEN, PAUL MELLON COLLECTION

Oil on canvas: circular, 26½ in. (67.25 cm.) in diameter

PROV: As for No. 533

EXH: *Treasures from Midland Houses*, City Art Gallery, Birmingham, 1938 (141)

No. 536 is a replica of the previous entry and a companion to No. 533, West's portrait of himself with Raphael. Nos. 533 and 536 share identical histories, and it seems likely that West painted the two works at the same time to form a pair. If that is so, he painted No. 536, which shows Raphael at a considerably younger age than he is in No. 533, several years after he painted No. 535. Nos. 533 and 536 are framed as round pictures and hence do not display painted frames as part of their compositions corresponding to the frame in No. 535, but otherwise No. 536 is virtually indistinguishable from No. 535 in all details.

537 Mrs. West with Raphael West

LOCATION UNKNOWN

PROV: Catherine II of Russia

ENGR: Stipple engraving (oval, 9⅝ × 7⅞ in.) by Senodomof, not dated but inscribed *From the Original Picture in the Possession of the Empress of Russia*

This painting is known to the compilers only through the engraving by Senodomof (*below*), which shows the same composition as in Nos. 535 and 536, but reversed.[1] The print identifies the painting's owner as the Empress of Russia (i.e., Catherine the Great). The second Earl of Buckinghamshire, who owned No. 535, had served as ambassador to St. Petersburg from 1762 to 1765, and it may be that he commissioned No. 537 as a replica of his picture to present to the Empress.

[1] A proof is in the British Museum. Although the inscription is in English, the lack of the publication data required of English prints and the name of the engraver, which we have been unable to find in standard dictionaries, suggest a continental, possibly Russian, origin.

538 Mrs. West with Raphael West (?)*c.* 1770
See color illustration, p. 19

UTAH MUSEUM OF FINE ARTS, SALT LAKE CITY

Oil on canvas: circular, 36 in. (91.5 cm.) in diameter

Signed lower right: *B. West*

PROV: Purchased in the 1920s by Hugh A. Green, London; sold by his widow *c.* 1960 to Eunice Chambers, Hartsville, South Carolina; Hirschl & Adler Galleries, New York, by 1965; Reynolda House, Winston-Salem, North Carolina, 1967–76; Hirschl & Adler Galleries, New York, 1982; gift of the Marriner S. Eccles Foundation to the Utah Museum of Fine Arts, 1982

EXH: (?) RA 1770 (198) "A portrait of a mother and child"; *American Art From the Colonial and Federal*

Mrs West with Raphael West, stipple engraving by Senodomof after No. 537

Periods, Hirschl & Adler Galleries, New York, 1982 (22); *Raphael and America*, National Gallery of Art, Washington 1983 (4)

LIT: Barbara B. Lassiter, "American Paintings in the Reynolda House Collection," *Antiques*, XCVIII, 1970, pp. 758–65, pl. II

No. 538 shows essentially the same composition as Nos. 535–37 but with a somewhat expanded format in a painting of larger dimensions. In the added space are the arm and back of a chair in the lower right, a ledge or table top in the lower left, and a drapery or curtain in the upper part of the canvas. Additionally, Mrs. West's right hand is visible encircling her son's waist, Raphael's right shoulder is bare rather than covered as in Nos. 535–37, and there are a few other changes in lesser details.

No. 538 is here tentatively equated with the "portrait of a mother and child" which West exhibited at the Royal Academy in 1770. All we know about that painting comes from Horace Walpole's marginal comment in his Academy catalogue: "His own wife and child, the woman fine, the child poor, and its hand wretched. The Earl of Buckingham has one of these." As discussed in the entry for No. 535, this comment establishes that No. 535 was not the exhibited picture. It also indicates that the exhibited picture included a noticeably "wretched" hand, something that does not seem to be true of Nos. 535–37. "Wretched," however, does seem to be an appropriate adjective for the prominently visible hands in No. 538. A still more conspicuous display of hands, of both mother and child, can be seen in No. 539 below, but, at least as transcribed in the Picot engraving, none of them appears

so emphatically bad as in No. 538. It should also be said that the exhibited picture must have been sufficiently similar to No. 535 for Walpole to refer to the latter as "one of these," and that No. 538 is the largest and most ambitious known painting in this sequence of works, and hence, the one that West probably would have chosen to exhibit.

539 Mrs. West with Raphael West (?)*c.* 1771

LOCATION UNKNOWN

(?) EXH: RA 1771 (217) "A mother and child"

ENGR: Engraving printed in colors (oval, $7\frac{5}{8} \times 6\frac{1}{8}$ in.) by Victor Marie Picot, pub. by Picot, 26 Aug. 1781, and inscribed *From an Original Picture of B. West's*

No. 539 is not a replica of Nos. 535–38, but a separate composition in which the child (presumably Raphael West again) kneels on his mother's lap and waves toward the spectator. It is known only through the Picot engraving (*left*), which shows the mother facing to the right, rather than to the left as in Nos. 535, 536, and 538; Picot, however, may have reversed the composition in the engraving process, as Senodomof presumably did in the print after No. 537.

West exhibited pictures of mothers and children at the Royal Academy in 1770 and 1771. That exhibited in 1770 is here tentatively identified as No. 538; that in 1771 even more tentatively as No. 539 for the reason that there is no other obvious candidate. If the identification of No. 538 as the picture exhibited in 1770 is correct, it seems unlikely that West would have returned to the Academy in the following year with Nos. 535, 536, or 537, all of which show the same composition on a reduced scale; whereas No. 539, although still related, does show a significant development or re-thinking of the subject.

Mrs. West with Raphael West, engraving by Victor Marie Picot after No. 539

540 Raphael West *c.* 1796

LOCATION UNKNOWN

LIT: Farington Diary, 12 and 17 Jan. 1797 (Farington 1978–, III, pp. 745 and 750)

Raphael Lamar West (1766–1850) was the elder of the artist's two sons. He appears in double portraits with his father (No. 533), with his mother (Nos. 535–39), and with his brother (Nos. 541–43), but No. 540 is the only recorded independent picture of him. All that we know about it comes from Joseph Farington, who wrote in his diary that West had painted a head of Raphael some time before 31 October 1796, and that shortly after that date he copied that head onto a new canvas and to it added a head of his second son, Benjamin. The new canvas (No. 543) was undertaken as an experiment in the "Venetian Secret." Whether or not West had previously used or attempted to use the technique in No. 540 is not clear from Farington's account. However, on 12 January 1797, Thomas Provis (for whom see No. 543), in a meeting with several members of the Royal Academy, accused West of lying about when he had painted No. 540 in an evident attempt to establish that he had not employed the Secret in painting it, when in fact (or according to Provis) he had.

541 Raphael West and Benjamin West, Jr. 1775

LOCATION UNKNOWN

$(41 \times 31\frac{1}{2}$ in.) $(104 \times 80$ cm.)

(Signed and dated: *1775*)

Raphael West and Benjamin West Jr, (?) drawing for No. 541

PROV: Sold by Mrs. Albert F. West, Christie's, London, 19 March 1898, lot 143 ("Portraits of Raphael West and Benjamin West, sons of Benjamin West P.R.A., when young with a dog," unframed, 41 × 31½ in., signed and dated *1775*), bt. by Obach for £10.10.0.

(?) EXH: RA 1775 (338) "Portraits of two young gentlemen"

LISTED: *PC*, p. 566 ("Sketch of his two sons, when Children," West, Painting-room); *UM*, p. 350; *BA*, p. 17; Galt, p. 228; Dillenberger, p. 172 (333)

No. 541 is the first of three recorded double portraits of Raphael (1766–1850) and Benjamin (1772–1848), the two sons of the artist. Of the three, only one (No. 543) is currently known.

A drawing of two children (*above*) dated *1774*, sold in 1967 by Mrs. Claire Francis, a descendant of the artist, was identified as a portrait of the two boys when it was sold;[1] it may have been related to No. 541, which is recorded as having been dated *1775*.

[1] Pen and brown ink, 7 × 7½ in., Christie's, London, 14 March 1967, lot 36.

542 Raphael West and Benjamin West, Jr.

LOCATION UNKNOWN

LISTED: *PC*, p. 566 ("Sketch of his two Sons, when Boys," West, Painting-room); *UM*, p. 530; *BA*, p. 17; Galt, p. 228; Dillenberger, p. 172 (334)

543 Raphael West and Benjamin West, Jr. 1796
See color illustration, p. 134

NELSON-ATKINS MUSEUM OF ART, KANSAS CITY, MISSOURI

Oil on canvas: 35¼ × 28¼ in. (89.5 × 71.7 cm.)

PROV: Sold by Mrs. Albert F. West, Christie's, London, 19 March 1898, lot 144 ("Portraits of the Same [i.e., the same subjects as in lot 143 as recorded under No. 541 above], when older, the one in brown coat, the other with yellow vest, standing together," unframed, 36 × 29 in.), bt. by Obach for £1.10.0.; William Rockhill Nelson, Kansas City (died 1915); his daughter, Laura Nelson Kirkwood; presented to the museum by the Laura Nelson Kirkwood Residuary Trust in 1944

EXH: RA 1797 (189) "Portraits of two brothers"; Washington and Philadelphia 1980

544

LISTED: *PC*, p. 566 ("Sketch of his two Sons, when young Men," West, Painting-room); *UM*, p. 530; *BA*, p. 17; Galt, p. 228; Dillenberger, p. 172 (335)

LIT: Faringdon Diary, 19 Dec. 1796, and 6, 12, 17, and 18 Jan. 1797 (Faringdon 1978—, III, pp. 722, 739, 743–44, 749–51); John Gage, "Magilphs and Mysteries," *Apollo*, LXXX, 1964, p. 39, fig. 1; Alberts 1978, p. 226

According to Faringdon's diary, West began No. 543 shortly after 31 October 1796, and he must have substantially completed it by 19 December of the same year when John Opie described it to Faringdon following a visit to West's studio. Raphael West was thirty years old in 1796, and his brother twenty-four.

No. 543 is the most thoroughly documented of West's experiments in the so-called Venetian Secret. On 17 January 1797 West told Faringdon that the originators of the Secret, Thomas Provis and his daughter, Ann Jemima, first approached him about their method in December 1795. West had then made an experiment by sketching a head under the direction of Miss Provis, but that experiment had proven unsatisfactory because the canvas used was "of a bad color." West, still according to what he told Faringdon, did not see the Provises again until 31 October 1796, when they agreed to resume the experiments. He then sketched a subject (which is identified elsewhere by Faringdon as a version of *Cupid Stung by a Bee*, see No. 133). "At this time He had a head of His son Raphael painted some months before, this by way of *continuing his experiments* He copied on a Canvass prepared agreeable to Provis's process and added to it a Head of His son Benjamin." The head of Raphael is catalogued as No. 540 above.

Faringdon saw the two pictures on 18 January 1797, and felt that by using the technique West had made a manifest advance over his previous work. When No. 543 appeared at the Royal Academy in the following May, it was overshadowed in the eyes of the critics by two more ambitious works, a *Crucifixion* (No. 356) and *Cicero Discovering the Tomb of Archimedes* (No. 22), in which West also used or was believed to have used the new technique, but some of the comments attracted by those pictures—"remarkable for a dark and purpurine hue" (No. 356)—were described as applicable to all West's pictures "in this new manner." By 6 June 1797, while the Royal Academy exhibition was still open, West seems to have become disillusioned with the technique, telling Farington that "Provis's grounds are too *cold* & purple." The chief ingredients of the Secret, which not surprisingly led to this result, are conveniently summarized by John Gage: pure linseed oil, dark absorbent grounds, and a "Titian Shade" used as a universal shadow color and consisting of equal quantities of lake, indigo, and Prussian or Antwerp blue, combined with a larger amount of ivory black.

544 [?] Mrs. Benjamin West, Jr. with Benjamin West III 1805

DULWICH COLLEGE PICTURE GALLERY, LONDON

Oil on canvas: $36\frac{1}{8} \times 28$ in. (92 × 71 cm.)

Signed lower right: *B. West. 1805*

PROV: Sold by Mrs. Albert F. West, Christie's, London, 19 March 1898, lot 146 ("Portrait of a lady, in brown dress, holding a child on her lap, in white frock and cap," unframed), bt. by Murray for £13.13.0.; given by Fairfax Murray to Dulwich College in 1911

LIT: Edward Cook, *Catalogue of the Dulwich Collection*, London, 1914, p. 301 (586); Alberts 1978, p. 470 (note)

Although the subjects of this painting were not identified when it was sold in 1898, it was sold by a member of the West family as part of a group of works which included other family portraits (Nos. 541 and 543), and it was catalogued by Sir Edward Cook in 1914 as a portrait of West's daughter-in-law. That daughter-in-law appears to have been the wife of West's younger son, Benjamin, rather than the wife of Raphael.[1] In November 1803 West told Joseph Farington that his younger son had married a beautiful young lady, and on 24 March 1804 he reported that Benjamin had brought his wife to town and "that she was a very fine young woman,—and in a state likely to add to the family." That addition, in the form of a boy also named Benjamin, would have occurred some time later in 1804, a date that seems in keeping with the evident age of the child shown in No. 544, which is dated *1805*.

According to Robert Alberts, Benjamin West, Jr.'s wife was the daughter of Edward Dickinson of Perthall.[2] In 1815 when she and her husband came to live with West following the death of his wife, Farington described their son as an only child.[3] Charles Henry Hart stated in 1908 that Benjamin West III died after West but did not live to attain his majority or to leave issue.[4] This assertion is contradicted by various sources. When the family pictures including No. 544 appeared at auction in 1898, the Christie's sale catalogue stated that the works "formed part of the Collection of Benjamin West, P.R.A., and have remained in the possession of the family since the Artist's death," and according to Christie's files the seller was a Mrs. Albert F. West. She seems to have died in the same month as the sale, and she was identified by H. W. O. Margary (a descendant of Raphael West) in a letter to Charles Henry Hart as the wife of the great-grandson of the artist, i.e., the daughter-in-law of the child (West's grandson) shown in No. 544.

[1]Raphael married in 1798 and had one child, a daughter, who in 1829 married Thomas George Margary.
[2]Alberts 1978, p. 307.

[3]Farington Diary, 11 July 1815 (Farington 1978–, XIII, p. 4667).
[4]Hart 1908, p. 10.
[5]See also No. 535, note 2, for another provenance purportedly in the family of Benjamin West, Jr.

545 John West *c.* 1764–70

LIBRARY OF THE SOCIETY OF FRIENDS, LONDON

Oil on canvas, mounted on panel: $26\frac{3}{4} \times 22$ in. (68 × 56 cm.)

Inscribed lower right: *Geo Fox/first Quaker*

PROV: Bought by the library in 1923

No. 545 was offered to the library of the Society of Friends in 1923 as a portrait of George Fox (1624–1691), the founder of the Society. The library acquired the painting after determining that it was not a portrait of Fox, but of John West, the father of Benjamin. This identification is confirmed by the likenesses of John West in Nos. 546 and 85.

John West (1690–1776) was born at Long Crendon in Buckinghamshire and emigrated to Pennsylvania in 1715 or 1716, leaving in England a pregnant wife, who was to die while giving birth to West's older half-brother. John West married his second wife, the mother of Benjamin and several other children, in America in 1720. In 1738, when Benjamin West was born, he was an innkeeper in Springfield, Pennsylvania, although he may have had other occupations at other times.[1] His second wife died in 1756, and in the summer of 1764 he returned to England accompanying Elizabeth Shewell, who became the wife of Benjamin West in September of the same year. Subsequently, until his death in 1776, he seems to have lived chiefly with his eldest son, Thomas, Benjamin West's half-brother, in Reading in Berkshire.

As Charles Henry Hart pointed out in 1908, John West was not a Quaker either at the time he settled in Pennsylvania or when Benjamin was born.[2] He did become a member of the Society of Friends later in his life, in 1759, and the hat and the collarless coat which he is shown wearing in No. 545 were both characteristic

545

of Quaker attire in the eighteenth century. John and Thomas West appear similarly clad as part of the group around William Penn in *Penn's Treaty with the Indians* (No. 85) of 1771 and in a group portrait with Benjamin West's family painted by West shortly after the birth of his second son in 1772 (No. 546). In the present painting John West appears somewhat younger than he does in either of those works. That, along with the rather dry handling of the paint, suggests a date somewhere between 1764 and 1770.

A slightly larger portrait of John West, which appears to be a copy of No. 545, is in the Friends Historical Library at Swarthmore College.[3]

[1]Alberts 1978, p. 8 and passim.
[2]Hart 1908, pp. 2–3.
[3]Oil on canvas: $29\frac{1}{2} \times 24\frac{1}{2}$ in. This may have been the portrait of John West with the same dimensions lent to the winter exhibition of the Royal Academy in 1873 by T. S. Norton.

546 The West Family *c.* 1772

YALE CENTER FOR BRITISH ART, NEW HAVEN, PAUL MELLON COLLECTION

Oil on canvas: $20\frac{1}{2} \times 26\frac{1}{4}$ in. (52 × 66.5 cm.)

Signed lower left: *B. West/177[?]*

PROV: By descent in the family of Raphael West to Aubyn Margary, Leek, Staffordshire; Thos. Agnew and Sons, London, from whom acquired by Paul Mellon in 1964

EXH: RA 1777 (367) "A small picture of a family"; West's Gallery 1821 (67) "Mrs. West's Family. The property of Mr. R. L. West"; West's Gallery 1822–28 (117) "Mr. West and Family"; BI 1833 (28) lent by Raphael West; *Painting in England 1700–1850, from the Collection of Mr. and Mrs. Paul Mellon*, Royal Academy, London, 1964–65 (146) and Yale University Art Gallery, New Haven, 1965 (216); *American Art from Alumni Collections*, Yale University Art Gallery, 1968 (8); *Bicentenary Exhibition*, Royal Academy, London, 1968–69 (50); *American Self-Portraits 1670–1973*, National Gallery, Washington, 1974 (5); New Haven and London, 1976 (21); *The Conversation Piece: Arthur Devis and His Contemporaries*, Yale Center for British Art, 1980 (60); New Haven 1983 (3)

ENGR: Stipple engraving ($19\frac{7}{8} \times 25\frac{5}{16}$ in.) by G. S. and I. G. Facius, pub. 26 July 1779 by John Boydell, with a dedication to *Her Imperial Majesty of all the Russia's*, stipple engraving ($6\frac{9}{16} \times 8\frac{5}{8}$ in.) by Pariset, pub. 1781 by Mr Breton, Paris, also with a dedication to the Empress of Russia; stipple engraving printed in colors ($9\frac{15}{16} \times 12\frac{1}{4}$ in.) by Grant and Bonnefoy, undated, pub. by Smith in Oxford Street

LISTED: *PC*, p. 565 ("Mr. West's small picture of his Family," West, Painting-room); *UM*, p. 530; Barlow, p. 434; *BA*, p. 17; Galt, p. 226; Dillenberger, pp. 164 (258) and 169 (303)

LIT: V and A Cuttings, I, p. 147 (*General Advertiser*, April 1777); Dunlap 1834, pp. 137–38 (Dunlap 1918, II, pp. 277–78); Charles Robert Leslie, *A Handbook for Young Painters*, London, 1855, pp. 292–93; Leslie 1860, I, pp. 60–61; Graves, 1906, VIII, p. 213 (Horace Walpole, 1777); Hart 1908, p. 7; Devanter 1973, p. 766, pl. II; Dillenberger 1977, p. 5, pl. I; Alberts 1978, ill. between pp. 78 and 79

The subjects of No. 546 are, from left to right, West's eldest son, Raphael; Mrs. West holding her recently born second son, Benjamin, on her lap; the artist's half-brother Thomas West (1716–1792); his father John

West (1690–1776); and the artist himself, palette in hand, on the extreme right. Although the date on the painting is not entirely legible, the birth date of the artist's younger son in August 1772 provides approximate indication of when West must have commenced it. The painting is described by Charles Robert Leslie as recording the first visit of West's father and half-brother to see the newest addition to the family. Raphael West would have been six years old in August 1772.

West did not exhibit No. 546 until 1777, the year following the death of his father (for whom see No. 545), and he may not have completed it until then. Although he exhibited it without identifying the subjects, they were, of course, instantly recognized, and at least one critic, writing in the *General Advertiser*, questioned West's taste in exhibiting publicly a painting of such a personal subject. It was engraved two years later, and via the print, which is almost the same size as the paint-ing itself, it became one of West's best-known pictures. In his *Autobiographical Recollections* Charles Robert Leslie described seeing the engraving in the window of a print shop in Philadelphia and the great impression that the natural and simple treatment of the subject had then made on him. Subsequently a proof of the engraving hung in Leslie's drawing-room in London. Leslie des-cribed the picture as West's most original work and dis-cussed it at length in his lectures given at the Royal Academy (published as *A Handbook for Young Painters*) as well as in his autobiography. He also claimed that David Wilkie greatly admired the composition.

Several commentators have noted the contrast between the artist's curled wig and elegant dressing-gown, and the straight hair and simple Quaker dress of his father and half-brother. Leslie described the painting as showing the two Quakers sitting "for a few minutes in silent meditation, which will soon be ended by the old man's taking off his hat and offering up a prayer for the mother and infant." Leslie also stated that West himself thought of the picture as a treatment of "The Ages of Man," and that West repeated it "with great variations, substituting loose draperies for the modern dresses." This reference may be to the *Golden Age* (No. 419), which West painted at approximately the same time as No. 546 and which has been inter-preted as a family portrait in the guise of "The Ages of Man." The *Golden Age*, however, in no way repeats the composition of No. 546.

Copies of the entire composition of No. 546 and of the left half are known,[1] and a drawing of the composi-tion is in the Princeton University Art Museum.[2] None of these works is by West.

[1] Oil on panel, 20 × 22 in., private collection, Kentucky (as of 1961), and oil on panel, 15 × 13 in., sold anonymously, Christie's, London, 23 Nov. 1973, lot 19.
[2] $20\frac{1}{16} \times 26\frac{3}{8}$ in.

546

PORTRAITS OF THE ROYAL FAMILY

547 George III *c.* 1776

THE EARL OF ELGIN AND KINCARDINE

Oil on canvas: 36 × 28 in. (91.5 × 71 cm.)

PROV: Painted for George III (1801 account, p. 208, no. 9, "The Portrait of His Majesty, the same size, companion" [i.e., companion to No. 553, which is listed immediately above No. 547 and described as "Kit-cat size"], £84 [for the two portraits]); given by George III to Martha, Countess of Elgin (widow of the fifth Earl of Elgin), *c.* 1806

EXH: *Royal Gifts*, Christie's, London, 1961–62 (160)

ENGR: Mezzotint (15¼ × 11⅞ in.) by Edward Fisher, pub. by Fisher, 28 Feb. 1778

LISTED: Dillenberger, p. 138 (24)

LIT: Millar 1969, I, p. 128 (under no. 1138)

No. 547 appears to be the first of several portraits painted by West of George III. In it, as in most of the subsequent portraits, the King is shown wearing the ribbon and star of the Order of the Garter. A companion portrait of Queen Charlotte is No. 553 below. There is evidence (discussed in the entry for No. 553) to suggest that West painted that picture in 1776, and it would seem likely that he painted No. 547 at the same time. It must have been completed before February 1778, the date of the publication of Edward Fisher's mezzotint engraving.

George III's patronage of West began in 1768 with the commission for the *Departure of Regulus from Rome* (No. 10). His initial interest in West was as a painter of historical subjects, and between 1768 and 1773 West painted seven historical pictures for the King, all of which were placed in the Warm Room at Buckingham House. Later, beginning in 1779, West received major commissions from George III for paintings of religious subjects for the Royal Chapel in Windsor Castle, for designs for stained glass for St. George's Chapel at Windsor, and for paintings of subjects from the reign of Edward III for the Audience Chamber in Windsor Castle. In the intervening years, however, West's royal commissions consisted entirely of portraiture. Eleven portraits of members of the royal family bearing dates between 1776 and 1783 remain in the Royal Collection, and several others, which either were at one time in the Royal Collection (such as Nos. 547 and 553) or were painted independently of royal commission (? No. 551), date from the same period.

Nos. 547 and 553 seem almost certainly to have been the Kit-cat portraits of George III and Queen Charlotte included in West's account prepared in 1801 of his pictures painted for the King. They were subsequently presented to the Countess of Elgin in appreciation of her service as governess of Princess Charlotte, the daughter of George IV.

A small version of No. 547 is No. 548 below. West copied the pose in a small double portrait of the King and Queen (No. 559), which appear to have been painted as a study for a never-realized larger picture, and he repeated the head, with little or no change, in Nos. 551 and 552.

547

In addition to the portraits of George III listed here (Nos. 547–52 and 559–61), West also portrayed him allegorically resuming power after his first attack of apparent insanity (No. 107), included his bust in a self-portrait (No. 529), and included him as a tiny distant figure in the hunting field in a landscape view of Windsor (No. 473).

Several portrait drawings of George III by West are recorded,[1] but the only one of them known to the compilers of this catalogue is an oval profile in the Royal Collection, which bears no evident relationship to any of West's paintings of the King.[2]

[1]Black chalk on blue paper, sold by Benjamin West, Jr., S. Leigh Sotheby, London, 1 June 1839, lot 61; and a drawing about which no information is given, sold by Mrs. Albert F. West, Christie's, London, 18 March 1898, lot 94.
[2]Black and white chalk on blue paper, oval, 7⅞ × 6¾ in. (see Oppé 1950, p. 99 [no. 639], and pl. 2).

548 George III *c.* 1776
Illustrated over page

NICOLAS M. EUSTATHIOU

Oil on copper: 10¹³⁄₁₆ × 8⅞ in. (27.5 × 22.5 cm.)

PROV: By descent in the family of Raphael West to Aubyn Raphael Margary, by whom sold, Sotheby's, London, 2 March 1983, lot 44

No. 548 is a smaller version of the previous entry, to which it corresponds closely in all significant details, but with an addition of an area of sky on the right side of the composition. West probably painted it as a reduced replica of the commissioned portrait to keep for himself. Since it remained in his own possession, it presumably served as his model for later likenesses of the King such as Nos. 551 and 552.

548

549 George III 1779

HER MAJESTY THE QUEEN

Oil on canvas: $100\frac{1}{2} \times 72$ in. (255.3×182.9 cm.)

Signed slightly below the center of the right side:
B. West/1779

PROV: Painted for George III (1801 account, p. 208,
no. 14, "A whole-length portrait of His majesty—
Lord Amherst and the Marquis of Lothian in the
background," £262.10.0)

EXH: RA 1780 (116) "Portrait of His Majesty, two
general officers on horseback and the royal navy in
the background"; *1776: The British Story of the American Revolution*, National Maritime Museum,
Greenwich, 1976 (122)

LISTED: *PC*, p. 559 ("The whole length portrait of his
Majesty, in regimentals, with Lord Amherst and the
Marquis of Lothian on horseback in the back
ground," George III, now at Hampton Court); *UM*,
p. 527; *BA*, p. 13; Galt, p. 216; Dillenberger, p. 138
(18)

LIT: V and A Cuttings, I, p. 188 (*London Courant*, 4 May
1780); Millar 1969, I, p. 128 (1138), II, pl. 108

No. 549 is the most ambitious of West's portraits of
George III. It shows the King in military uniform,
wearing the star and sash of the Order of the Garter,
and holding a partly unrolled scroll of paper which is
inscribed: *Plans of the Camps of Cox Heath, Warley, St.
Eden [Port]smouth and Plymouth/with a General Return of
your Majesty's Forces in Great Britain/Aug*± *18 1779*. On
a table behind the King are the crown, orb, and scepter,
and an ermine cloak spills down to the floor. A three-
cornered hat is on a chair in the lower right. Through
an arch on the right side of the painting are visible two
mounted officers, a groom in royal livery, and three
soldiers. Further in the distance are the tents of a military camp and several ships, the most prominent of
which fires a salute and is inscribed *ROYAL GEORGE*
on the stern.

West's account prepared in 1801 of pictures painted
for George III identifies the two mounted officers in
the background of No. 549 as Lord Amherst and the

Marquis of Lothian. The former, who had served as
commander of the victorious British forces in North
America during the Seven Years' War, was commander of the land forces in Great Britain in 1779. The latter was Colonel of the first Horse Guards. The words
on the scroll which the King holds refer to military and
naval installations, and the painting commemorates
the preparation made in the summer of 1779 in
response to a threat of invasion by the French, who had
formed an alliance with the rebellious Americans in the
previous year.[1]

A smaller version is No. 550 below, and a companion
portrait of the Queen, which West exhibited along with
No. 549 at the Royal Academy in 1780, is No. 556. In
1783 West exhibited a second portrait of George III,
here tentatively identified as No. 551.

[1]See Millar 1969 for a fuller discussion; this entry is derived
almost entirely from that very thorough treatment.

550 George III *c.* 1779

HISTORICAL SOCIETY OF PENNSYLVANIA,
PHILADELPHIA

Oil on canvas: $17\frac{1}{4} \times 12\frac{3}{8}$ in. (44×31.5 cm.)

(?) Signed at left: *B. West/1778*

PROV: Purchased by the Society, 2 August 1910

EXH: Philadelphia 1938 (27)

LIT: Sawitzky 1942, p. 45; Millar 1969, I, p. 128 (under
no. 1138); Wainwright 1974, p. 81

This painting is a small version of No. 549. It shows
several differences in detail and, hence, appears to have
been painted as a study for the larger work rather than
as a reduced replica. There is no arch in the upper right,
and the draperies, which partially mask the arch in
No. 549, have a simpler fall. The King is dressed

550

549

551

Duke of York, the second son of George III. The proper identification was pointed out by Oliver Millar. The likeness of the King is obviously based on that in Nos. 547 and 548.

George III wears armor in this version, rather than contemporary dress as in No. 549, but both works show him in a military guise. A crown is on a table behind the King on the left in both pictures, and there are similar views of naval vessels in the distance on the right. The most prominent ship in No. 551, however, does not appear to be the *Royal George*, shown in No. 549, which sank dramatically and disastrously (with the loss of 900 lives) in August 1782.

No. 551 has no recorded history prior to the twentieth century, and there is no known evidence to indicate that it was a royal commission. It is here tentatively equated with the portrait of George III that West exhibited at the Royal Academy in 1783. The latter work drew the criticism in the *Morning Herald* that it appeared "as if it had been painted from a lay figure, on account of the awkward disposition of the arms and drapery; and by reason of the scarlet tinge on the complexion, one would conceive it had been viewed through the medium of stained glass." This comment is not very specific, but in referring to the disposition of the drapery on the figure, it does seem more appropriate to No. 551 than to any other known portrait of George III by West. The King does look younger in No. 551 than he does in No. 549, which West had exhibited at the Academy three years earlier, but since West copied the features from a portrait painted some seven years before, that evident anomaly would not preclude his having painted No. 551 as late as 1783. The handling, which is freer than that in Nos. 547–50, appears consistent with a date of 1782–83.

552 George III 1813

BISHOPTHORPE PALACE, YORK

Oil on panel: 62 × 57 in. (157.5 × 144.8 cm.)

Signed lower left: *Painted by B. West 1813/From the likeness he painted/of His Majesty in 1776*

PROV: Commissioned by Edward Venables Vernon (later Harcourt) (1757–1847), Archbishop of York from 1807 to 1847, and presented by him to Bishopthorpe Palace (the seat of the Archbishops of York) in 1813

LIT: John Ingamells, *Catalogue of Portraits at Bishopthorpe Palace*, York, 1972, pp. 19–20, pl. 14

This ambitious late portrait of George III is, as the inscription states, based on an earlier likeness, either No. 547 or No. 548. In 1813, when West painted the work, he would have had no alternative to using an earlier portrait, as the King's insanity prevented the possibility of any fresh sittings.

The painting was evidently commissioned by the then Archbishop of York, Edward Venables Vernon, who later assumed the name of Harcourt when he inherited the estates of the Earls Harcourt. A letter from West to the Archbishop, dated 26 July 1813, is in the Bishopthorpe Archive and published by John Ingamells in his catalogue of the portraits at Bishopthorpe:

... the Portrait of His Majesty into which picture I have introduced the late Earl of Harcourt Bearing the Cap of Maintenance—was sent by Decons Waggon to Bishopthorpe on the 24th Inst . . . the Dowager Lady Harcourt—and those that her Ladyship wished to see the picture, have so highly approved of it—as have also some of my friends, and a few of our distinguished artists concurring in sentiments with them, have added to my professional pleasure.

This picture containing the Portrait of my King,

similarly in both works, but he wears his hat in No. 550, whereas it lies on a chair before him in No. 549.

The catalogue of the West exhibition of 1938 states that No. 550 is signed and dated *1775*. Sawitzky in 1942, repeated by Wainright in 1974, recorded the date as *1778*. Neither a signature nor a date is visible in a photograph, and neither was discernible in an examination of the painting itself in 1981. Since the military imagery in Nos. 549 and 550 evidently reflects British preparations to repel an anticipated French invasion in the summer of 1779 (in No. 549 the King holds a report dated 18 August 1779), dates of either *1775* or *1778* seem improbably early for any version of the composition. A corresponding small portrait of the Queen (No. 557) does bear a signature accompanied by the date of *1775*, but they do not appear to be in West's hand.

551 George III (?)*c.* 1783

CLEVELAND MUSEUM OF ART

Oil on canvas: 49⅞ × 39¾ in. (126.5 × 101 cm.)

Signed lower right: *B. West*

PROV: Dr. T. Fisher, Sidcup, Kent (in 1910); Elsa Woolworth Miller, Cleveland; her sale, Kende Galleries, New York, 14 October 1944, lot 75 (as a portrait of "Frederick, Duke of York"); given to the Cleveland Museum of Art in 1952 by Mr. and Mrs. Lawrence S. Robbins

EXH: (?) RA 1783 (73) "Portrait of His Majesty"

LIT: (?) V and A Cuttings, I, p. 232 (*Morning Herald*, 1783); Millar 1969, I, p. 128 (under no. 1138); *Cleveland Museum Bulletin*, LX, Jan. 1973, p. 35

This portrait was sold in 1944 and acquired by the Cleveland Museum in 1952 as a portrait of Frederick,

552

553

as well as that He was the Protector of my Pencil for the last seven and forty year—and as the Earl of Harcourt was my friend for nearly fifty: could I have rendered such a subject more worthy of art as a picture, to record their likeness, and their virtues to posterity, it would have been done; but such as it is, I can assure your Grace, my humble professional abilities have been exerted—and I have to lament that they were not more adequate to the high sense of feeling I had on the occasion of painting the picture for your Grace, as a deposit at Bishopthorpe. A letter dated 5 August 1813 from the Archbishop to West acknowledging the arrival of the painting is now in the Pierpont Morgan Library and is also quoted by Ingamells.

The late Earl Harcourt, mentioned by West in his letter, was George Simon Harcourt (1736–1809), the second Earl Harcourt and first cousin of the Archbishop. If West's memory was trustworthy when he claimed that they had been friends for nearly fifty years, they must have met very close to the time West came to England. In No. 552 the Earl stands on the right side. Since the Earl had been dead for four years in 1813 and furthermore is shown as a relatively young man, his portrait, like that of the King, must have been based on an earlier likeness.[1] The beefeater on the left side of the painting is evidently not a specific portrait.

The opening words on the scroll which George III holds are *I have called you together*. The crown is on a table to the left, as it is also in Nos. 549–51, but No. 552 is the only portrait by West in which the King is shown enthroned and wearing robes of state. In keeping with the formal dress, he wears the collar of the Order of the Garter rather than the star, as in Nos. 547–51.

---

[1] See Ellis K. Waterhouse, *Reynolds*, London, 1941, pls. 18 and 217 for two earlier portraits of the second Earl. The second of the two, painted *c*. 1780–81, shows him as recognizably the same man and at approximately the same age as the figure in No. 552. No record of an independent portrait of the Earl by West is known to the compilers of this catalogue.

553 **Queen Charlotte** *c*. 1776

THE EARL OF ELGIN AND KINCARDINE

Oil on canvas: 36 × 28 in. (91.5 × 71 cm.)

Signed middle of right side: *B. West Pinxt.*/*1766*/*Kew*/*Palace*

PROV: As for No. 547 (1801 account, p. 208, no. 8, "The portrait of Her Majesty, the Kit-cat size," £84 [the price is for both Nos. 553 and 547, which immediately follows in the list and is described as a companion])

EXH: *Royal Gifts*, Christie's, London, 1961–62 (161)

ENGR: Mezzotint (14½ × 11 in.) by Valentine Green, pub. by J. Brydon, Feb. 1790

LISTED: Dillenberger, p. 138 (23)

LIT: Millar 1969, 1, p. 129 (under no. 1142)

No. 553 is a companion to No. 547 and shares the same history.

No small version of No. 553 corresponding to No. 548 is currently known. However, a portrait of the Queen, described as "painted from life," which cannot now be identified, was sold by West's heirs in 1829 (see No. 554). A second version is No. 555 below, and the Queen reappears in the same dress and pose in a small sketch of a double portrait with George III (No. 559) and, with very slight modification of pose, in a finished double portrait with the Princess Royal (No. 562). West also painted the Queen in two full-length portraits (Nos. 556 and 557), in profile with the King (Nos. 560–61), and in the sketch of the *Recovery of His Majesty in the year 1789* (No. 107).[1]

No. 553 bears a signature, but the date of *1766* accompanying West's name is impossibly early. The artist's first contact with the royal family came only in 1768, and Kew Palace, which is mentioned in the inscription became the King's country residence only in 1772.[2] No. 562, to which No. 553 is closely related, bears the date of *1776*, and that would seem to be the probable date of No. 553 as well. Although it is possible that West painted No. 553 after he painted No. 562, the words *Kew Palace* on the former painting suggest that the Queen posed for the picture at Kew. Hence, it appears to have been the original from which West copied the likeness of Queen Charlotte into Nos. 559 and 562, rather than a replica of part of the double portrait. A related drawing of Queen Charlotte in the Royal Collection is discussed under No. 562 below.

[1] For portraits of Queen Charlotte by other artists see Michael Levey, *A Royal Subject: Portraits of Queen Charlotte*, London, 1977.
[2] John Brooke, *King George III*, London, 1972, p. 283.

554 **Queen Charlotte**

LOCATION UNKNOWN

PROV: Sold by West's sons, Robins, London, 20–22 June 1829, lot 114 ("Portrait of the late Majesty Queen Charlotte, painted from life . . . considered a very faithful resemblance")

Nothing is known about this painting apart from its appearance in the sale of works from West's estate on 20–22 June 1829. The wording of the entry in the sale catalogue suggests that No. 554 was not the small version of West's full-length *Queen Charlotte* now in the Historical Society of Pennsylvania (No. 557), which is palpably not a "faithful resemblance." On the other hand, it could well have been a version of No. 553, corresponding to No. 548, which is a small version of the companion to No. 553.

555 Queen Charlotte 1777

YALE CENTER FOR BRITISH ART, NEW HAVEN, PAUL
MELLON COLLECTION

Oil on canvas: $36\frac{1}{8} \times 28$ in. (91.7 × 71.1 cm.)

Signed middle of left side: *B. West/1777*

PROV: Presumably acquired by the fifth Duke of Leeds
(for whom see No. 600); then by family descent until
sold by the trustees of the tenth Duke of Leeds Will
Trust, Christie's, London, 23 Nov. 1973, lot 70;
Sabin Galleries, London; Mr. and Mrs. Paul Mellon

EXH: *International Confederation of Dealers in Works of Art*,
Metropolitan Museum of Art, New York, 1974–75
(1); New Haven 1983 (2)

No. 555 is a replica of No. 553. It differs from that painting in details of the drapery in the background, the floral decoration on the upholstery of the chair upon which the Queen sits, and the conspicuous inclusion of a crown on the left side.

The future fifth Duke of Leeds (who succeeded to the dukedom in 1789) served as Lord Chamberlain of the Queen's household from 1777 to 1780, and during that period he probably either commissioned or was given No. 555, which is dated *1777*.

556 Queen Charlotte 1779

HER MAJESTY THE QUEEN

Oil on canvas: $101 \times 71\frac{1}{2}$ in. (256.5 × 181.6 cm.)

Signed lower left: *Benj. West/1779*

PROV: Painted for George III (1801 account, p. 208,
no. 15, "A whole-length portrait of Her Majesty,
with all the Royal Children in the back-ground,"
£262.10.0.

EXH: RA 1780 (130) "Portrait of Her Majesty, and the
royal family in the background"; *The King's Pictures*,
Royal Academy, London, 1946–47 (111)

LISTED: *PC*, p. 559 ("The whole length portrait of her
Majesty with the 14 Royal Children," George III,
Windsor Castle); *UM*, p. 527; *BA*, p. 13 (where this
picture is evidently listed twice: as a companion to
No. 549 at Hampton Court, and again at Windsor
Castle); Galt, p. 216; Dillenberger, p. 138 (19 and
21)

LIT: V and A Cuttings, I, p. 188 (*London Courant*, 4 May
1780); Millar 1969, I, p. 128 (1139), II, pl. 109;
Michael Levey, *A Royal Subject: Portraits of Queen
Charlotte*, London, 1977, p. 13 and pl. 8

No. 556 is a companion to No. 549, which shows King
George III. The two paintings appeared together at
the Royal Academy in 1780. The Queen's crown on
the right side of No. 556 balances the King's on the left

555

side of No. 549, and there are views into background vistas on the left of No. 556 and on the right of No. 549. However, while the embellishments and background details of the latter are military, those of No. 556 are domestic. A spaniel lies at the Queen's feet. In the background are Windsor Castle and the Queen's Lodge, with thirteen of the royal children arrayed in the middle distance.

The early lists of West's works describe No. 556 as showing fourteen children in the background. That number is incorrect, but West's replica of the picture (No. 558), which is dated *1782* does show fourteen children, the fourteenth, Prince Alfred, having been born after West completed No. 556. West's own account of

the pictures he had painted for George III simply describes the painting as showing *all* the royal children, and it does include all the children born by the time he painted it. The youngest of them, Prince Octavius, who was born on 23 February 1779, is at the center of the group, wearing baby clothes and riding in a little carriage. The eldest two, the Prince of Wales (the future George IV) and Prince Frederick, stand on the left. Prince William and Prince Edward stand on the right. Prince Ernest pulls the baby's carriage, and Prince Adolphus pushes it. Prince Augustus lies on the ground before them, while Charlotte, the Princess Royal, and four of her sisters, the Princesses Augusta, Elizabeth, Mary, and Sophia, stand in a group behind the car-

556

riage. For other portraits of all these children see Nos. 562–75.

A small version, evidently painted as a sketch for No. 556 is No. 557 below, and a reversed replica is No. 558.

557 **Queen Charlotte** *c.*1779

HISTORICAL SOCIETY OF PENNSYLVANIA, PHILADELPHIA

Oil on canvas: $17\frac{1}{4} \times 12\frac{1}{4}$ in. (44 × 31 cm.)

(?) Signed lower left: *B. West 1775*

PROV: Purchased by the Society, 2 August 1910

EXH: Philadelphia 1938 (28)

LIT: Sawitzky 1942, pp. 25–26; Wainwright 1974, pp. 48–49

No. 557 is a small version of the previous entry; it corresponds to No. 550, which is in the same collection and is a small version of No. 549. Both small pictures appear to have been painted as preparatory sketches for the full length portraits, and both show significant differences in detail from the finished pictures. There are differences in the details and arrangements of the Queen's dress between Nos. 557 and 556, and the backgrounds of the two works are radically different. Instead of showing a view at Windsor, No. 557 includes what appears to be Westminster Abbey, and it shows none of the royal children. The back of a chair to the left of the Queen blocks part of the view, and there are no draperies in the upper left, as there are in No. 556. There are draperies in the upper right of No. 557, whereas the base of a column fills the corresponding area in No. 556.

The signature and the date of *1775* on No. 557 do not appear to be in West's hand, and it seems unlikely that he would have painted the sketch at such an early date, four years before the large painting for which it is a study. The facial features in No. 557 show very little resemblance to those of the Queen as she appears in Nos. 553–56 and in portraits by other artists, suggesting that West undertook the sketch as a compositional study and did not paint it directly from his royal subject.

557

558

558 **Queen Charlotte** 1782

HER MAJESTY THE QUEEN

Oil on canvas: $89 \times 55\frac{1}{4}$ in. (226.1 × 140.3 cm.)

Signed lower right: *B. West 1782*

PROV: Painted for George III (1797 account: "The whole length portrait of her Majesty, with the Royal Children introduced in to the background, and placed in Windsor Castle," 1780, £262.10.0.; 1801 account, p. 215: "A second whole length of Her Majesty, with all the Royal children in the background, which was placed in Windsor Castle, but at present in the Queen's Palace, London," £262.10.0.)

LISTED: *PC*, p. 559 ("The same [i.e., No. 556] repeated," in Windsor Castle); *UM*, p. 527; *BA*, p. 13; Galt, p. 216; Dillenberger, p. 138 (22)

LIT: Millar 1969, I, p. 128 (1140)

No. 558 is a replica with modifications of No. 556. It is slightly smaller than the original and shows the composition in reverse. Although it is dated *1782*, West may have begun it in 1780, the date given in his account of 1797 (that account lists only works painted by West for George III after 1780, when the King started to pay West an annual stipend of £1,000; No. 558 is the first work listed there).

The subject includes fourteen children, rather than the thirteen shown in No. 556. The additional child is Prince Alfred, born on 22 September 1780, who has usurped not only the carriage from Prince Octavius but also his dress and his pose, forcing the latter to take a seat between the front wheels of the carriage. By including Alfred, West depicted in the painting all but one of the fifteen children of George III and Queen Charlotte. He never painted Princess Amelia, who was born only in 1783.

Other changes from No. 556 are in the dogs at the Queen's feet, the carpets, elimination of detail along the left edge of No. 558, and a different arrangement of columns and draperies in the upper left corner. The Queen's Lodge, which has moved from the left back-

559

560

ground of No. 556 to right background of the present painting is seen from a direction more to the west, but is not reversed, and the towers of the castle behind it appear to have grown taller.

559 George III and Queen Charlotte *c.* 1776

PRIVATE COLLECTION

Oil on copper: $15\frac{3}{16} \times 21\frac{3}{4}$ in. (38.5 × 55 cm.)

PROV: By descent in the West family to the present owner

No. 559 combines West's Kit-cat portraits of George III (No. 547) and Queen Charlotte (No. 553) into a single composition. It is of small size and is on copper, a support which West used on at least one other occasion for a small version of a royal portrait (No. 548), but which he seems to have used rarely otherwise. No larger version of the composition is known or recorded. West repeated the figure of Queen Charlotte in another double portrait, showing her with the Princess Royal (No. 562), which is dated *1776*, and once that painting was underway, it seems unlikely that West's patrons would have wanted a large version of No. 559 as well.

560 George III and Queen Charlotte 1789

HER MAJESTY THE QUEEN

Oil on panel: oval, $22\frac{3}{8} \times 31\frac{1}{2}$ in. (56.8 × 80 cm.)

Signed lower left: *B. West/1789*

PROV: No. 560 is not recorded in either of West's accounts of works painted for George III, but it was, nonetheless, almost certainly a royal commission. It was installed in the Audience Chamber in Windsor Castle by 1791

LIT: Brayley and Britton 1801, p. 223; Pyne 1819, I, p. 166; W. S. Lewis, ed., *Horace Walpole's Correspondence*, XI, New Haven, 1944, p. 363 (letter of 9 Oct. 1791); Millar 1969, I, pp. 128–29 (1141)

Oliver Millar has demonstrated that this double portrait, showing the King and Queen in profile, was originally installed as part of the canopy over the throne in the Audience Chamber in Windsor Castle. The date of *1789* corresponds with the dates of West's other paintings for the same chamber (Nos. 56–76 and 412), which bear dates from 1787 to 1789. In a letter of 1791 Horace Walpole described the "gaudy, clumsy throne, with a medallion at top of the King's and Queen's heads, over their own—an odd kind of tautology, whenever they sit there!" Walpole's letter does not give much information about the medallion, but a description of the room published in 1801 describes the medallion as showing profiles of their Majesties and mentions West as the artist.

The painting has little obvious relationship to West's earlier portraits of the King and Queen, but the profile head of the King and the elaborate hat of the Queen are echoed in the roughly contemporary *Recovery of His Majesty in 1789* (No. 107). Another double profile portrait, which may have been painted as a study for No. 560, is No. 561 below.

561 George III and Queen Charlotte

LOCATION UNKNOWN

PROV: Sold by West's sons, Robins, London, 20–22 June 1829, lot 119 ("Profiles of their late Majesties, designed for a Medal")

Although this work was described in 1829 as designed for a medal, no such medal is known to the compilers of this catalogue. It seems more likely that it was painted as a study for or version of the medallion portrait listed above (No. 560).

562 Queen Charlotte with Charlotte, Princess Royal 1776

HER MAJESTY THE QUEEN

Oil on canvas: $66\frac{1}{4} \times 81$ in. (168.3 × 205.7 cm.)

Signed center left (on a portfolio protruding from behind the bust of Athena): *Benj. West/1776*

PROV: Painted for George III (1801 account, p. 208: no. 11, "Her Majesty and Princess Royal, in one picture," £157

EXH: RA 1777 (362) "Her Majesty with the Princess Royal"

ENGR: Mezzotint ($18\frac{9}{16} \times 22\frac{5}{8}$ in.) by Valentine Green, pub. 25 March 1778 by John Boydell

LISTED: *PC*, p. 559 ("The Queen with the Princess Royal, in one picture, whole lengths," George III, in the King's Closet at St. James's); *UM*, p. 527; *BA*, p. 13; Galt, p. 216; Dillenberger, p. 137 (12)

LIT: Graves 1906, VIII, p. 213 (Horace Walpole, 1777); Millar 1969, I, p. 129 (1142), II, pl. 114; Alberts 1978, p. 131

No. 562 shows the Queen together with her oldest daughter, Charlotte (1766–1828), who in 1776 bore the title of Princess Royal and in 1797 was to become Queen of Württemberg. Mother and daughter are engaged in needlework. A bust of Athena is on a table to the left and the towers of Westminster Abbey are visible in the distance beyond. Among the papers and portfolios scattered on the table around the bust, bars of music are discernible on the sheet nearest to the foreground. A rolled sheet behind it bears the inscription [*dise*]*gnio da Raffae*[*llo*].

A separate painting of the Princess Royal, which may have been related to this work, is No. 563 below. The figure of the Queen is almost identical with West's treatment of her in Nos. 553 and 555, the only significant difference being in the position of her right arm. A drawing of the Queen in the Royal Collection at Windsor shows her in the same pose as in No. 562.[1]

Nos. 562 and 570 were the first of West's royal portraits to appear at the Royal Academy. Horace Walpole's comment about the former, when he saw it in 1777, was "Bad and too old for the Queen."

[1] Black and white chalk on blue paper, $10\frac{7}{8} \times 8\frac{1}{4}$ in. Oppé 1950, p. 99 (640) and pl. 3.

563 Charlotte, Princess Royal

LOCATION UNKNOWN

PROV: Sold by West's sons, Robins, London, 20–22 June 1829, lot 117 ("Portrait of her late Royal Highness the Princess Royal")

No. 563 and the two preceding lots in the Robins sale of 20–22 June 1829 (Nos. 566 and 567) were described together as, "painted with great fidelity from the Life." All three have disappeared.

562

564 George, Prince of Wales, with Prince Frederick 1777

HER MAJESTY THE QUEEN

Oil on canvas: $95\frac{1}{2} \times 65\frac{1}{2}$ in. (242.6×166.4 cm.)

Signed: *B. West/1777*

PROV: Painted for George III (1801 account, p. 208: no. 12, "His R.H. the Prince of Wales and Prince Frederic (Duke of York), in one picture whole length," £210

EXH: RA 1778 (330) "Portraits of their Royal Highnesses the Prince of Wales and Prince Frederick"

ENGR: Mezzotint ($23\frac{5}{8} \times 16\frac{3}{16}$ in.) by Valentine Green, pub. 4 Nov. 1779 by John Boydell

LISTED: *PC*, p. 559 ("The Prince of Wales and Duke of York, in one picture, whole lengths," George III, in the King's Closet at St. James's); *UM*, p. 527; *BA*, p. 13; Dillenberger, p. 137 (13)

565

568

LIT: V and A Cuttings, I, pp. 169 (*General Advertiser*, May 1778) and 171 (review dated 2 April 1778 from an unidentified source); Millar 1969, I, p. 129 (1143), II, pl. 110

No. 564 shows the two eldest children of George III: George, Prince of Wales (1762–1830), who was subsequently to become King George IV; and Frederick (1763–1827), the future Duke of York, Bishop of Osnabrück, and Commander-in-Chief of the British Army. The Prince of Wales wears the collar of the Garter over state robes, while his brother wears both the collar of the Garter and that of the Bath. On a table to the left are the Prince of Wales's crown and the plumed hat of the Order of the Garter.

A replica is No. 565 below. Separate paintings of the two brothers, which may have been painted as studies for this work are Nos. 566 and 567. Both, along with No. 563, showing the Princess Royal, were described in 1829 as "painted with great fidelity from the Life."

565 Prince George and Prince Frederick 1778

HERMITAGE, LENINGRAD

Oil on canvas: $94\frac{1}{2} \times 65\frac{3}{8}$ in. (240 × 166 cm.)

Signed right side: *Painted by B. West/Historical Painter to His Majesty/London 1778*

PROV: Presented by George III to Catherine II of Russia (1801 account, p. 208: no. 13 "A second picture of Ditto" [i.e., No. 564], for the Empress of Russia, sent by His Majesty, £210

LISTED: Dillenberger, p. 139 (25)

LIT: [Alexandra Kroll], *The State Hermitage: English Paintings: Catalogue* (in Russian), Leningrad, [1969], p. 115, ill.; Larissa Dukelskaya, *The Hermitage: English Art Sixteenth to Nineteenth Century*, Leningrad, 1979, p. 129, pl. 130

According to West's account of his works for George III submitted to the King in 1801, No. 565 was painted for George III and given by the King to Catherine II. The catalogues of English pictures in the Hermitage give a slightly different provenance, indicating that Catherine II herself commissioned the painting for the Chesmensky Palace, which had been built between 1774 and 1777.

566 George, Prince of Wales

LOCATION UNKNOWN

PROV: Sold by West's sons, Robins, London, 20–22 June 1829, lot 115 ("Portrait of his Present Majesty when a Youth")

567 Prince Frederick

LOCATION UNKNOWN

PROV: Sold by West's sons, Robins, London, 20–22 June 1829, lot 116 ("Portrait of HRH the late Duke of York")

568 Prince William and Prince Edward 1778

HER MAJESTY THE QUEEN

Oil on canvas: $96 \times 65\frac{1}{2}$ in. (243.8 × 166.4 cm.)

Signed lower right: *Benj. West, 1778*

PROV: Painted for George III (1801 account, p. 208: no. 16, "Whole-length portraits of Prince William (Duke of Clarence) and Prince Edward (Duke of Kent), in one picture," £262.10.0)

EXH: RA 1780 (7) "Portraits of their Royal Highnesses Prince William Henry and Prince Edward"

ENGR: Mezzotint ($12\frac{3}{4} \times 10\frac{3}{4}$ in.) by Valentine Green

Prince William, engraving and aquatint by Francesco Bartolozzi and Paul Sandby after No. 569

A drawing of Prince Edward for No. 568 was with the Leger Galleries in 1976.[1] A painting of Prince William sold by West's sons in 1829 (No. 569) was not a study for No. 568, but a separate composition.

[1] Black and white chalk on blue paper, $8\frac{1}{2} \times 4\frac{3}{4}$ in. (*Exhibition of English Watercolours*, Leger Galleries, London, 1976, no. 67 and pl. xiv).

569 Prince William 1781

LOCATION UNKNOWN

PROV: Sold by West's sons, Robins, London, 20–22 June 1829, lot 69 ("Whole-length portrait of HRH the Duke of Clarence, represented in the naval uniform of a midshipman on the deck of a ship of war")

ENGR: Engraving and aquatint $(20\frac{13}{16} \times 16\frac{15}{16}$ in.) by Francesco Bartolozzi and Paul Sandby, pub. 15 Jan. 1782 by Anthony Poggi and John Boydell under the title, "His Royal Highness Prince William Henry Serving as Midshipman on board His Majesty's Ship Prince George, dedicated to the Navy of Great Britain"; lithograph $(10\frac{1}{2} \times 8\frac{7}{16}$ in.) by W. Day, pub. Jan. 1832 by Rudolf Ackermann under the title, "His Majesty William IV When Midshipman in the Year 1781"

Although echoing the naval imagery of No. 568, No. 569 does not repeat the composition, but shows the Prince actually in service, standing on the deck of the *Prince George*. West may have painted the picture for the sake of the engraving by Bartolozzi and Sandby (*left*). The date of publication of that plate, and the date given in the title of a later lithograph indicate that it was painted some three years after No. 568.

570 Six Children of George III 1776

See color illustration p. 89

HER MAJESTY THE QUEEN

Oil on canvas: $66\frac{1}{4} \times 71$ in. (168.3 × 180.3 cm.)

Signed lower left: *B. West/1776*

PROV: Painted for George III (1801 account, p. 208: no. 10, "Six of the Royal Children in one picture, size of life," £315)

EXH: RA 1777 (363) "Portraits of six of the Royal Children"

ENGR: Mezzotint $(18\frac{9}{16} \times 22\frac{9}{16}$ in.) by Valentine Green, pub. 29 Sept. 1778 by John Boydell, under the title "Their Royal Highnesses" and with accompanying inscriptions identifying each child

LISTED: PC, p. 559 ("Princes Ernest and Augustus; Princesses Augusta, Elizabeth, and Mary, in one picture, whole lengths," George III, in the King's Closet at St. James's); UM, p. 527; B, p. 13 ("Dukes of Cumberland and Sussex; Princesses Augusta, Elizabeth, and Mary, in one picture)"; Galt, p. 216; Dillenberger, p. 137 (14)

LIT: V and A Cuttings, I, p. 147 (*General Advertiser*, April 1777); Graves 1906, VIII, p. 213 (Horace Walpole, 1777); Millar 1969, I, p. 129 (1145), II, pl. 115

The six children shown in No. 570 are, from left to right: Prince Ernest (1771–1851), the future Duke of Cumberland and King of Hanover; Prince Augustus (1773–1843), the future Duke of Sussex; Princess Elizabeth (1770–1840); Princess Mary (1776–1857);

of a detail showing a half-length portrait of Prince William, pub. 1 Feb. 1780 by Green, under the title "His Royal Highness Prince William Henry Knight of the Most Ancient Order of the Thistle, now serving aboard his Majesty's Ship the Prince George Commanded by the Hon[ble] Rob[t] Digby, Rear Admiral of the Blue"; lithograph of a detail showing a vignetted bust-length portrait of Prince William, pub. after 26 June 1830 by J. Lambert under the title, "His present Majesty William IVth at 14 Years of Age"

LISTED: PC, p. 559 ("Prince William and Prince Edward, in one picture, whole lengths," George III, in the King's Closet at St. James's); UM, p. 527; BA, p. 13; Galt, p. 216; Dillenberger, p. 137 (15)

LIT: Millar 1969, I, p. 129 (1144), II, pl. 111

Prince William (1765–1837) and Prince Edward (1767–1820) were the third and fifth children of George III, their sister the Princess Royal having been born between them, in 1766. Prince William was created Duke of Clarence in 1789 and succeeded to the throne as William IV in 1830. Prince Edward, who became Duke of Kent in 1799, was to be the father of Queen Victoria.

Prince William wears the ribbon, star, and mantle of the Order of the Thistle and points on a large globe to the English Channel. His brother points to a ship's model, which bears the name *PRINCE GEORGE* on its stern and sits on a base embellished with a relief of Britannia. A banner with a rearing horse of Hanover partly conceals the relief. The ship and globe commemorate William's entry into the navy as a midshipman aboard the *Prince George*.

Prince Adolphus (1774–1850), the future Duke of Cambridge; and Princess Augusta (1768–1840). Prince Ernest is holding a string attached to a small wagon on which Adolphus and Mary ride. Adolphus and Mary, the two youngest children depicted in No. 570, also reappear in No. 573.

An elaborate drawing in the Victoria and Albert Museum shows essentially the same composition, but with five rather than six children.[1] Oliver Millar has suggested that it may be for a different family group, but the similarities with No. 570 are so great that it must have been sketched as an early idea for this picture, which the birth of Princess Mary on 25 April 1776, forced West to modify.[2] In the drawing, Prince Adolphus sits alone on the wagon. There are also significant changes in the dress of the children, particularly noticeable in that of the Princes Ernest and Augustus, who wear dresses in the drawing. A drawing of Prince Augustus dressed as he is in this work and in the same pose (dictated by his action of throwing a ball to the small spaniel in the lower left corner of the picture) was with the Leger Galleries in 1976.[3] He reappears in a similar pose and also playing with a dog in the backgrounds of West's full-length portraits of Queen Charlotte (Nos. 556 and 558).

Horace Walpole described No. 570 in 1777 as "Bad and without grace."

[1] Black and white chalk on blue paper, $9\frac{7}{8} \times 13\frac{1}{4}$ in. (Millar 1969, 1, fig. 37): this drawing was probably sold by Benjamin West, Jr., S. Leigh Sotheby, London, 1 June 1839, lot 63 ("Portraits of the Dukes of Cumberland and Sussex, the Princess Augusta, Elizabeth and Mary, in one drawing," black chalk on blue paper).

[2] The lists of West's works give the names of only five Royal children, but as the omitted name is that of Prince Adolphus, rather than Princess Mary, this discrepancy with the finished picture appears to be the result of error rather than to record the initial pre-Mary commission.

[3] Black and white chalk on blue paper, $6 \times 7\frac{3}{4}$ in., inscribed lower right, *Prince Augustus* (*Exhibition of English Watercolours*, Leger Galleries, London, 1976, no. 69, pl. xiv).

571 Prince Augustus 1780

HER MAJESTY THE QUEEN

Oil on canvas: $36 \times 27\frac{3}{4}$ in. (91.4 × 70.5 cm.)

Signed lower right: *B. West 1780*

PROV: Painted for Queen Charlotte (1801 account, p. 215: "A portrait of Prince Augustus, half length, for the Queen"); by descent to the second Duke of Cambridge (1819–1904, the nephew of the sitter); his sale, Christie's, London, 11 June 1904, lot 117; Sir Augustus C. FitzGeorge, by whom sold, Willis's Rooms, London, 15 March 1934, lot 25, bt. by Lady Cynthia Colville, evidently on behalf of Queen Mary

EXH: (?) RA 1782 (97) "His Royal Highness Prince Augustus Frederick"

LISTED: Dillenberger, p. 143 (59)

LIT: V and A Cuttings, 1, p. 227 (*Morning Herald*, 1782); Millar 1969, 1, p. 130 (1146)

A second version of this portrait, which is virtually identical in all details, is No. 572 below. It is possible that parts of the histories of the two works, both of which have provenances tracing back to members of the royal family, are confused.

The Round Tower at Windsor Castle is in the background. Prince Augustus (1773–1843), who was created Duke of Sussex in 1801, also appears in No. 570 of 1776.

West initially painted the shirt collar as opened less widely; *pentimenti* showing its former position are visible on Augustus's neck and chest.

572 Prince Augustus

HER MAJESTY THE QUEEN

Oil on canvas: $36\frac{1}{2} \times 27\frac{3}{4}$ in. (91.7 × 70.5 cm.)

PROV: Princess Sophia (1777–1848, the sitter's sister); bequeathed by her to Queen Victoria

LIT: Millar 1969, 1, p. 136 (1169)

As noted in the previous entry, the histories of Nos. 571 and 572 may be partly confused. No. 572 is not signed, whereas No. 571 is, and Oliver Millar catalogues it as a work after West rather than by him. Nonetheless, the handling is consistent with West's work, and it seems reasonable to the compilers of the present catalogue to accept both paintings as by his hand.

573 Prince Adolphus, Princess Mary, and Princess Sophia 1778

HER MAJESTY THE QUEEN

Oil on canvas: $95\frac{1}{2} \times 59$ in. (242.6 × 149.9 cm.)

Signed lower left: *B. West/1778*

PROV: Painted for George III (1801 account, p. 208: no. 17, "Whole-length portraits of Prince Adolphus and his sisters, in one picture," £262.10.0.)

EXH: RA 1780 (17) "Portraits of their Royal Highnesses Prince Adolphus, Princess Mary, and Princess Sophia"; *British Portraits*, Royal Academy, London, 1956–57 (311)

LISTED: Dillenberger, p. 139 (26)

571

573

LIT: Millar 1969, I, p. 130 (1147), II, pl. 112

The two older children shown in No. 573, Prince Adolphus (1774–1850) and Princess Mary (1776–1857) also appear in No. 570 of 1776, as the two youngest children shown there. In this work, dated *1778*, they are shown with their sister Princess Sophia, born on 3 November 1777 (died 1848). The setting is Kew, and the pagoda designed by Sir William Chambers, which still stands in Kew Gardens, is visible in the background.

A drawing of Princess Mary and Princess Sophia was with the Leger Galleries in 1976.[1]

[1] Black and white chalk on blue paper, $6 \times 7\frac{3}{4}$ in., inscribed lower left: *Princesses* (*Exhibition of English Watercolours*, Leger Galleries, London, 1976, no. 68, ill. on cover of catalogue).

574 Prince Octavius *c.* 1782

HER MAJESTY THE QUEEN

Oil on canvas: $50\frac{1}{2} \times 40$ in. (128.3×101.6 cm.)

Signed lower left: *B. West 178*[?]

PROV: Painted for George III (1797 account: "The whole length portrait of Prince Octavius," 1781, £73.10.0.; 1801 account, p. 214: "Painted for His Majesty a whole-length portrait of Prince Octavius holding the King's sword," £73.10.0.)

EXH: RA 1782 (93) "His Royal Highness Prince Octavius"; London 1868 (949)

ENGR: Stipple engraving ($14\frac{1}{4} \times 10\frac{7}{8}$ in.) by George Sigmund Facius and John Gotlieb Facius, pub. 1 March 1785 by John Boydell

LISTED: *PC*, p. 559 ("Prince Octavius, whole length," George III, in the King's Closet at St. James's); *UM*, p. 527; *BA*, p. 13 ("Prince Octavius [dead])"; Galt, p. 216; Dillenberger, pp. 137 (16) and 143 (58)

LIT: V and A Cuttings, I, p. 227 (*Morning Herald*, 1782); Millar 1969, I, p. 130 (1148), II, pl. 113

Prince Octavius, as his name implies, was the eighth son of George III and Queen Charlotte. He was born on 23 February 1779, too late to be included in either of West's major group portraits of the younger royal children painted in 1776 and 1778 (Nos. 570 and 573), but he does appear in the group of royal children in the background of West's two full-length portraits of Queen Charlotte of 1779 and 1782 (Nos. 556 and 558). His death in 1783 is commemorated in No. 575. In this painting he is playing with a sword from the Royal Collection, which has been identified and is now at Windsor.[1] The painting was presumably painted at Buckingham House (now Palace); visible in the distance on the left are the Horse Guards, seen across St. James's Park, and the dome of St. Paul's further away.

The last digit of the date accompanying West's signature on the painting is difficult to read. Oliver Millar has recorded the date as *1783*, but that seems unlikely since West exhibited the picture in the previous year. West himself in 1797 recorded the date as *1781*, when Octavius would have been two years old.

A very slight drawing of a child playing with a sword, which West may have sketched as a first idea for No. 574, is in the possession of one of the artist's descendants.[2] A large and carefully finished watercolor drawing dated *1783*, which shows Octavius in profile but dressed as in No. 574 (illus. p. 480), was sold by Mrs. Albert F. West in 1898.[3] This drawing, done in the year of Octavius's death and possibly as long as two years after West painted No. 574, may have been made in conjunction with No. 575.

Although Nos. 574 and 571 (or 572) showing Prince Augustus appeared at the same Royal Academy exhibition in 1782, where they must have hung close to one another (nos. 93 and 97 in the catalogue), the paintings are of different sizes and are not companion pieces.

[1] Millar, loc. cit.
[2] Black chalk on white paper, $5\frac{1}{2} \times 7$ in.
[3] Christie's, London, 18 March 1898, lot 117 ("Prince Octavius, in buff dress with blue sash," water-colour drawing), bt. by Murray. This drawing (black chalk and gouache, $23\frac{1}{4} \times 16\frac{1}{4}$ in., ill.), has subsequently been catalogued, incorrectly, as "Jack Plowden as a child" (i.e., Philadelphia 1938, p. 57, no. 29).

575 The Apotheosis of Prince Alfred and Prince Octavius 1783

HER MAJESTY THE QUEEN

Oil on canvas: 94¼ × 60⅜ in. (239.4 × 153.4 cm.)

Signed lower right: *B. West 1783*

PROV: Painted for George III (1797 account: "The picture of the Apotheosis of Prince Octavius and Prince Alfred," 1783, £315; 1801 account, p. 215: "Painted for His Majesty the apotheosis of Prince Octavius and Prince Alfred, in one picture, the size of life," £315)

EXH: RA 1784 (81) "The apotheosis of Prince Alfred and Prince Octavius"

ENGR: Engraving (21⅝ × 15¹¹⁄₁₆ in.) by Robert Strange, pub. 1786 by Strange under the title "Ah! si qua Fata aspera!" and dedicated to the Queen

LISTED: *PC*, p. 559 ("The apotheosis of Prince Alfred and Octavius," George III, Queen's House); *UM*, p. 527; Barlow, p. 431 ("Apotheosis of the two young princes"); *BA*, p. 13; Galt, p. 216; Dillenberger, p. 137 (9)

LIT: V and A Cuttings, II, p. 308; Farington Diary, 22 Dec. 1799 (Farington 1978—, IV, pp. 1329–30); James Dennistoun, *Memoirs of Sir Robert Strange, Knt., and of His Brother-in-Law Andrew Lumisden*, London, 1855, II, pp. 193–207, passim; Whitley 1928a, I, pp. 309–10; Waterhouse 1953, p. 192, pl. 169; Millar 1969, I, p. 130 (1149), II, pl. 116; Alberts 1978, p. 179

Prince Alfred (1780–1782) and Prince Octavius (1779–1783), the thirteenth and fourteenth children of George III and Queen Charlotte, died within nine months of one another, on 20 August 1782, and 3 May 1783. The death of the latter seems to have particularly affected the King ("there will be no Heaven for me, if Octavius is not there"). In addition to showing Octavius here being received into heaven by the younger brother who had predeceased him, West also included him among the heavenly host in the stained glass window of the *Resurrection* for St. George's Chapel (see Nos. 360 and 361), upon which he was working at the time of Octavius's death.

The view in the lower left corner of No. 575 is of the Queen's Lodge at Windsor and Windsor Castle seen from the south. A less extensive view of these structures

from the same direction also appears in the backgrounds of Nos. 556 and 558, the two full-length portraits of Queen Charlotte in the Royal Collection. The background of the former includes Octavius, as the youngest member of the family, at the center of his brothers and sisters grouped together before the more distant buildings. No. 558, which is dated *1782*, also includes Prince Alfred, and is the only one of West's royal portraits, apart from No. 575, to show him.

Prince Octavius's likeness in No. 575 is similar to that in the profile drawing dated *1783* discussed under No. 574 (*below left*). It is not certain, however, whether that drawing was made before or after Octavius's death on 3 May 1783. Although it could have served as the basis for the portrait in No. 575, it could equally have been made subsequent to No. 575 as a modified repetition of a detail of the painting. Whatever the circumstances under which it was made, it is a finished work in its own right, showing the Prince in different dress, and it seems unlikely that West made it to serve as a study for the painting.

A squared drawing for the three principal figures in No. 575, which includes the view of Windsor in the lower left, is in the Witt Collection, Courtauld Institute of Art, London,[1] and a sheet of separate studies for the three figures is in the Museum of Fine Arts, Boston.[2]

The engraving after No. 575 by Robert Strange (1721–1792) was described by James Dennistoun as the only plate made by Strange after a work by a living artist. Strange made the engraving while residing in Paris and was evidently permitted by George III to take No. 575 to France in order to do so. He presented the completed plate, as well as a large number of impressions to the King and Queen, and in return, at West's suggestion, he received a knighthood. An undated, but contemporary newspaper notice about the Strange engraving describes the idea of West's picture as "evidently from Peter's [*sic*] Lady and Child." This comment presumably alludes to *An Angel Carrying the Spirit of a Child to Paradise* (*below*) exhibited by the Reverend Matthew William Peters at the Royal Academy in 1782.

[1] Pen and wash: 7½ × 8¾ in. (Millar 1969, I, fig. 38).
[2] Pen and wash: 17⁷⁄₁₆ × 11¹⁵⁄₁₆ in. (Millar 1969, I, fig. 39).

Prince Octavius, drawing by West of the subject of Nos. 574 and 575. Pennsylvania Academy of the Fine Arts, Philadelphia

Matthew William Peters, *An Angel Carrying the Spirit of a Child to Paradise*, stipple engraving by William Dickinson, *c.* 1782

575 503

576 The Royal Family (?)c. 1791

LOCATION UNKNOWN

PROV: Sold by West's sons, Robins, London, 20–22 June 1829, lot 102 ("Study of their late Majesties and the Royal Children")

Nothing is known about this study apart from its appearance in the sale of 20–22 June 1829, and no finished group portrait by West showing the King and Queen together with some or all of the royal children is now known. However, in 1838 a group portrait of the royal family went through Christie's and was described in the sale catalogue as by West and Richard Livesay, a pupil and studio assistant of West.[1] That listing suggests that the painting (below), which is now at Upton House, was primarily, if not entirely, by Livesay,[2] but it could have been based on a study by West. The painting is not dated, but it represents the introduction of the Duchess of York to the royal family, and, therefore, must have been painted reasonably close to 29 September 1791, when the Duke and Duchess of York were married. That date is consistent with the little that is known about Livesay's activities as a portraitist. In 1791 his address listed in the Royal Academy catalogue was Windsor (according to Samuel Redgrave he moved there in order to assist West on his royal commissions),[3] and he had no less than nineteen entries listed in the Academy catalogue, all of them for portraits. On the other hand, West's activity as court portraitist was concentrated in the late 1770s and early 1780s, and it seems unlikely that he would have been commissioned to paint an elaborate group portrait as late as 1791, or that he would have undertaken one on his own.

[1] Christie's, London, 23 June 1838, lot 119 (sold anonymously), West and Livesay, "The Royal Family. This picture was painted expressly for George III, and represents the introduction of the Duchess of York to the Royal Family. King George III, Queen Charlotte, and George IV, occupy with the Duchess of York, the centre; immediately behind George III are the Princesses Royal, Augusta, Elizabeth, Mary, Sophia, and Amelia, the youngest in front; the late King is in conversation with the Duke of York, who occupies the extreme right of the spectator."

[2] It has subsequently been catalogued as by Livesay without mention of West (Christie's, London, 14 July 1922, lot 127, and the second Viscount Bearsted, Catalogue of Pictures and Porcelains at Upton House, Banbury, London, c. 1952, pp. 15–16).

[3] Samuel Redgrave, A Dictionary of Artists of the English School, London, 1874, p. 262.

577 Princess Amelia

LOCATION UNKNOWN

PROV: Sold by West's sons, Robins, London, 20–22 June 1829, lot 118 ("her RH the Princess Amelia, daughter of George II")

In the Robins sale of 20–22 June 1829, No. 577 was sold in sequence following three portraits of children of George III, No. 566 (lot 115), No. 567 (lot 116), and No. 563 (lot 117), but No. 577 was described in the catalogue as showing the Princess Amelia (1711–1786), the aunt of George III, rather than his daughter (1783–1810) of the same name. Nothing is known about the picture apart from its appearance in the 1829 sale.

Richard Livesay, *The Royal Family*, c. 1791. Oil on canvas, $37\frac{3}{4} \times 49\frac{1}{2}$ in. National Trust, Upton House, Oxfordshire

578

578 Prince William and Princess Sophia of Gloucester 1779

SIR VICTOR FITZGEORGE-BALFOUR

Oil on canvas: 60 × 84 in. (152.5 × 213.5 cm.)

Signed lower left: *B. West—1779*

PROV: By descent in the family of the sitters' first cousin, Adolphus (1774–1850), first Duke of Cambridge

EXH: RA 1779 (343) "Prince William and Princess Sophia, children of their Royal Highnesses the Duke and Duchess of Gloucester"

Prince William (1776–1834), who in 1805 succeeded his father as second Duke of Gloucester, and Princess Sophia (1773–1844) were the niece and nephew of George III. In 1779 they would have been three and six years old respectively.

West painted this work shortly after painting four group portraits of the children of George III (Nos. 564, 568, 570, and 573), which bear dates from 1776 to 1778, and in scale and imagery it is a comparable work. The crown and Garter robes on the bench to the right would have belonged to the children's father, the King's brother, since the young Prince depicted in the picture was to be elected to the Order of the Garter only fifteen years after West painted No. 578. In other details, No. 578 seems to celebrate the reconciliation between George III and the Duke of Gloucester which had come about in 1777–78 following their estrangement caused by the King's displeasure over the Duke's marriage. The most visible feature of that reconciliation was the provision made by Parliament for allowances for the Duke's children in the event of his death.[1] Since the Duke of Gloucester was in poor health and had been close to death in 1777, the protection of his children was a genuine concern. Thus, the young children stand between a relief of the British lion, who appears to stride protectively toward them, and a statue of the Roman wolf suckling Romulus and Remus, who sets an example of the appropriate care of orphans. While Princess Sophia points to the lion, Prince William holds a purse, in explicit reference to the Parliamentary provision.

The towers in the background are analogous to those in the portrait of the Queen and Princess Charlotte (No. 562), and would seem to represent Westminster Abbey. The spread-legged seated pose of the wolf is evidently based on that of the once-celebrated "*Dog of Alcibiades*" at Duncombe Park.[2]

A double portrait of the two sitters painted by Angelica Kauffmann in Rome in 1787 belongs to the Earl Waldegrave.[3]

[1] John Brooke, *King George III*, London, 1972, pp. 277–81.
[2] See Gervase Jackson-Stops, "King of Restorers: Bartolomeo Cavaceppi (1719–99)," *Country Life*, CLXXIV, 1983, pp. 1758–59.
[3] Exhibited Bregenz 1968 (32 and ill. no. 18).

PORTRAITS OF OTHER IDENTIFIED SUBJECTS

579 William Abercromby, Esq., of Glassaugh, Banffshire *c.* 1773–78

LOCATION UNKNOWN

Oil on canvas: 30 × 25 in. (76 × 63.5 cm.)

PROV: By descent in the family of the sitter to R. W. Duff, Fetteresso Castle, Stonehaven, Scotland, by whom sold, Christie's, London, 12 June 1931, lot 67 (as by Gilbert Stuart), bt. by Col. Sir George Abercromby, Bt. (1886–1964)

LIT: William T. Whitley, *Gilbert Stuart*, Cambridge, Mass., 1932, p. 39 (as by Stuart)

Although No. 579 and its companion, No. 580, were sold in 1931 as by Gilbert Stuart and were accepted by Whitley as works by Stuart painted in 1783 or 1784, they appear to be works by West from the mid-1770s.

According to the Christie's catalogue of 1931, William Abercromby of Glassaugh was the eldest son of General James Abercromby (1706–1781), who commanded at the Battle of Ticonderoga.

580 Mrs. William Abercromby *c.* 1773–78

PRIVATE COLLECTION

Oil on canvas: 30 × 25 in. (76 × 63.5 cm.)

Inscribed verso: *Mrs. William Abercromby of Glassaugh*

PROV: By descent in the family of the sitter to R. W. Duff, Fetteresso Castle, Stonehaven, Scotland, by whom sold, Christie's, London, 12 June 1931, lot 66 (as by Gilbert Stuart), bt. by Wyatt; sold by Mr. and Mrs. Marvin Frankel, Christie's, London, 23 March 1979, lot 140 (as by West); Hirschl & Adler Galleries, New York

EXH: *American Art from the Gallery's Collection*, Hirschl & Adler Galleries, New York, 1980 (3); *American Art from the Colonial and Federal Periods*, Hirschl & Adler Galleries, 1982 (21)

LIT: As for No. 579

See the entry for No. 579, to which this painting is the companion. According to the Christie's catalogue of 1931, the subject of No. 580 is Mary, the daughter of Sir Robert Abercromby, third Baronet, of Birkenbog, who married her cousin, William Abercromby of Glassaugh.

581 William Allen *c.* 1763

See color illustration, p. 21

PRIVATE COLLECTION

Oil on canvas: 50 × 40 in. (127 × 101.5 cm.)

PROV: By descent in the family of the sitter to the present owner

LIT: Walker 1897, frontispiece (etching after No. 581 by Albert Rosenthal); Lehigh 1960, p. 15

579

William Allen (1704–1780) served as Mayor of Philadelphia and from 1750 to 1774 as Chief Justice of Pennsylvania. He was one of the wealthiest men in eighteenth-century Pennsylvania (the present city of Allentown is on a tract of land he owned), and, along with his brother-in-law, Governor James Hamilton (No. 633), he provided substantial financial support for West during his stay in Italy by commissioning copies from the young artist (see Nos. 504, 506, 510, 511, 516, and 520).[1] West travelled to Italy with one of William Allen's sons, John, whose portrait he painted while in Italy (No. 582), and he subsequently painted additional portraits of other members of the family (see Nos. 583, 584, and 726).

William Allen was in England in August 1763, when West arrived in London, and he remained until the following summer. According to Galt, West spent about a month with Allen in Bath in the autumn of 1763. He probably painted No. 581 then, when his sitter was fifty-nine years old. William Allen next returned to London in 1776 as a loyalist fleeing the American Revolution. In Bath West must have had exposure to Thomas Gainsborough, who had settled there in 1759, and the visible break in No. 581 from the Mengs-Batoni style of West's earlier portraits (such as No. 582), should probably be ascribed to the artist's knowledge of one or more of Gainsborough's half-length portraits from the early 1760s of "oldish men of strong character," which No. 581 distinctly resembles.[3]

A portrait of William Allen in Independence National Historical Park in Philadelphia, which has traditionally been thought to be an American work by West,[4] does not appear to be by him and is now ascribed by the National Park Service to Robert Feke. See also p. 30 above.

---

[1] For a biography of William Allen see the *Dictionary of American Biography*. For his patronage of West see pp. 21–5 above and Richardson 1978.

[2] Galt 1820, p. 5.

[3] Ellis Waterhouse, *Gainsborough*, London, 1958, p. 20 and pls. 57–60.

[4] Allentown 1962 (1).

582 John Allen *c.* 1760
See color illustration, p. 16

PRIVATE COLLECTION

Oil on canvas: 49⅛ × 39⅛ in. (125 × 99.5 cm.)

PROV: By descent in the family of the sitter to the present owner

EXH: Allentown 1962 (4)

LIT: Lehigh 1960, p. 13, ill. p. 21; von Erffa 1973, p. 5

John Allen (1739–1778) was the eldest son of West's early patron Chief Justice William Allen (see No. 581). West travelled to Italy together with John Allen and Joseph Shippen. According to Galt they parted company shortly after their arrival at Leghorn in June 1760, West immediately going to Rome, Allen and Shippen remaining in Leghorn to tend to mercantile matters, then travelling to Venice.[1] They evidently intended to meet in Rome at the end of the summer, but when Allen and Shippen arrived there on 28 August, they found that West had returned to Leghorn.[2] On 3 September Shippen wrote to Robert Rutherford, the agent in Leghorn, saying that he and Allen planned to remain in Rome for about a month. Their subsequent movements are not recorded, but John Allen must have passed through Leghorn again while travelling northwards during the following autumn or winter. He seems to have been in London by March 1761,[3] and he was back in Philadelphia after a long stay in Bristol by October 1762.[4] At some stage in his travels he advanced West sixty pounds, and in acknowledging and approving that act in a letter dated 19 August 1761, Chief Justice Allen asked that John send West £100.[5] In return for this largesse West painted copies for Chief Justice Allen and Governor Hamilton, his brother-in-law (see No. 504, etc.), but it is possible that the advance from John Allen also paid for No. 582.

The most likely opportunity that John Allen might have had to pose for West would have been after rejoining him in Leghorn in the autumn of 1760. West by that time had painted at least one portrait in Rome in emulation of Anton Raphael Mengs (No. 689), and the influence of Mengs is evident in No. 582. Van Dyck dress, such as that in No. 582, started to appear in portraits of English sitters painted in Rome by Pompeo Batoni in the early 1750s.[6] West himself wears similar costume in a portrait drawing made by Angelica Kauffmann in 1763,[7] and he utilized it in at least one other portrait dating probably from 1760 or 1761 (No. 730). For a third male portrait from this period, see also No. 658.

See also p. 17 above.

[1] Galt 1816, pp. 90–91.
[2] Letter from Joseph Shippen to Robert Rutherford, 3 Sept. 1760 (American Philosophical Society, Philadelphia).
[3] Walker 1897, p. 44.
[4] Ibid., p. 51 and Richardson 1978, pp. 19–20.
[5] Walker 1897, p. 47 and Richardson 1978, p. 16.
[6] See *Pompeo Batoni (1708–87) and his British Patrons*, the Iveagh Bequest, Kenwood, 1982 (exhibition catalogue by Edgar Peters Bowron), pp. 37–42 (nos. 11, 12, and 14).
[7] Peter Walch, "An Early Neoclassical Sketchbook by Angelica Kauffmann," *Burlington Magazine*, CXIX, 1977, p. 102 and fig. 51. (ill. above p. 17).

583 Andrew Allen *c.* 1763–64

PRIVATE COLLECTION

Oil on canvas: 42 × 36 in. (106.5 × 91.5 cm.)

PROV: By descent in the family of the sitter to the present owner

LIT: Lehigh 1960, p. 13, ill. p. 23

Andrew Allen (1740–1825) was the second son of West's early patron Chief Justice William Allen (see No. 581). He was in England, studying law at the Middle Temple, London, from 1761 to 1764. He also appears in West's group portrait *The Cricketers* (Nos. 726 and 727). If the traditional identification of the sitters in *The Cricketers* is correct, one version of that picture must date from between West's arrival in England in August 1763 and Arthur Middleton's departure for America in December of the same year. No. 583 presumably was painted at approximately the same time, certainly by the summer of 1764 when Andrew returned to Philadelphia.

584 Anne Allen (Mrs. John Penn) *c.* 1763

MRS. HOPE G. INGERSOLL

Oil on canvas: 50½ × 40 in. (128 × 101.5 cm.)

PROV: Mrs. Frederick Tudor, Boston, 1916; by descent to the present owner

EXH: Museum of Fine Arts, Boston, 1916, and on extended loan there 1923–1942

Anne Allen (1746–1830) was the daughter of Chief Justice William Allen (see No. 581) and the younger sister of the brothers depicted by West in Nos. 582, 583, 726, and 727. In 1766 she became the wife of John Penn (1729–1795), the grandson of William Penn, who in 1763 became Lieutenant-Governor of Pennsylvania.

Although this painting has been separated from Nos. 581–83, all of which remain together in the possession of the descendants of Andrew Allen, confirmation of the identification of the sitter is provided by a portrait of Anne Allen painted in 1773 by Richard Brompton and now in the same collection as Nos. 581–

583

584

83. There is no recorded documentation of contact between West and Anne Allen. On stylistic grounds, it seems highly improbable that he painted No. 584 before leaving America in 1760, and it seems equally improbable that he painted it while in Italy. Nevertheless, the works by West to which is has closest affinities are the portrait of the Countess of Northampton and her daughter, painted in Venice in 1762 (No. 676), and the *Angelica and Medoro*, possibly begun in Rome in 1763 and completed in time to be exhibited in London in the spring of 1764 (No. 188). It seems likely, therefore, that West painted No. 584 shortly after his arrival in England in August 1763, possibly as a commission from Chief Justice Allen, with whom he spent a month in Bath, and whose portrait (No. 581) he also painted, probably at that time. Anne Allen was not then in England, or is not known to have been. Hence West would not have painted the portrait from life, but on the basis of a miniature or some other likeness provided by the subject's father. Like No. 581, No. 584 suggests awareness of works by Gainsborough that West may have seen in Bath, an awareness reflected in the ambitious landscape background, the inclusion of a dog, and, particularly, the averted gaze of the subject.[1] Apart from the portrait of the Reverend William Smith (No. 699), which West modelled on a painting of St. Ignatius, Nos. 581 and 584 are his earliest known portraits in which the subjects do not look directly at the viewer.

[1] For relevant works by Gainsborough from the late 1750s and early 1760s, see Ellis Waterhouse, *Gainsborough*, London, 1958, pls. 61–69.

585 Sir Edward Astley, Bt. 1773

THE LORD HASTINGS

Oil on canvas: 49 × 39½ in. (124.5 × 100.5 cm.)

Signed upper left: *Painted by B. West/1773*

PROV: In the possession of the Order of Gregorians, Norwich, by 1771; presented by the Order to the family of the sitter in the last decade of the eighteenth century; by family descent to the present owner

ENGR: Mezzotint (17¾ × 13⅞ in.) by Richard Earlom (*right*), inscribed *Sir Edward Astley, Bart., Representative*

in Parliament for the County of Norfolk, and Grand of the most ancient & honorable Order of Gregorians in Norwich, 1771. Taken from an original Painting in the Possession of that Society

LIT: Duleep Singh 1927, II, pp. 5–6 (19)

Sir Edward Astley, fourth Baronet (1729–1802), of Melton Constable Park in Norfolk was a Member of Parliament for Norfolk from 1768 to 1790. In this painting, which was evidently executed for the Order of Gregorians, an eighteenth-century society similar to the Freemasons, he is seen wearing the badge of a Grand (or officer) of the Order and with a gold sword of the Gregorians on the table at his side.

The portrait became the property of the Astley family when the society ceased to exist at the end of the eighteenth century.[1]

[1] Letter from the twenty-first Baron Hastings to Francis Hawcroft, 20 July 1955, and kindly forwarded by him to Helmut von Erffa.

586 Sir Joseph Banks *c.* 1771–1773
See illustration, p. 29

PRIVATE COLLECTION

Oil on canvas: 92 × 63 in. (234 × 160 cm.)

PROV: W. Milnes, 1862; sold anonymously, Christie's, London, 14 April 1866, lot 186, bt. by Horsley for 100 guineas

EXH: RA 1773 (310) "A whole length of a gentleman with a New Zealand mantle around him"; *International Exhibition*, South Kensington, 1862 (79) lent by W. Milnes (as by Joseph Wright of Derby)

ENGR: Mezzotint (22⅜ × 14⅞ in.) by J. R. Smith, pub. by S. Hooper and J. R. Smith in 1773, as "Mr. Banks"; republished by Molteno Colnaghi & Co., 1 May 1788, with the title altered to "Sir Joseph Banks, Bt."

LIT: Graves 1906, VIII, p. 213 (Horace Walpole, 1773)

Sir Joseph Banks (1743–1820), the great naturalist who was President of the Royal Society from 1778 to 1820, travelled to the South Pacific on the *Endeavour* with

Sir Edward Astley, Bt., mezzotint by Richard Earlom after No. 585

Captain Cook on Cook's first voyage, which lasted from August 1768 to June 1771. West must have painted No. 586 sometime between the summer of 1771 and the spring of 1773, when it appeared at the Royal Academy. Although Banks was not named in the catalogue, he is identified (and the painting described as "good") in Horace Walpole's marginal notations. The catalogue's description of the subject as "a gentleman with a New Zealand mantle around him" makes the identification secure, since John Raphael Smith's engraving after the picture is inscribed with Banks's name, and both painting and engraving show the subject surrounded by objects from New Zealand and Polynesia, which Banks collected during the voyage.[1]

Banks had no children. When No. 586 was sold at Christie's in 1866, Charles Horsley, its purchaser, was told by the auctioneer that the vendor (presumably the W. Milnes who had lent it to the *International Exhibition* four years before) was a grand-nephew of Banks. It had been requested for the *International Exhibition* under the belief that it was by Reynolds, and it was re-attributed there to Joseph Wright of Derby by Richard Redgrave, who was responsible for the British paintings in the exhibition. In 1866, Horsley was told that there should never have been any confusion over the attribution, since "it was well known that it was painted by West for the family of Sir Joseph."[2]

See also No. 647, which was sold in 1927 as a portrait of Banks, but does not show him. No. 586 itself, although known via the mezzotint by Smith, has not been seen publicly since 1866 and was brought to our attention only since this catalogue went to press.[3]

[1] See J. C. Beaglehole, ed., *The Endeavour Journal of Joseph Banks 1768–1771*, 2 vols., Sydney, 1962, I, pp. 62–64. The objects collected by Banks are now in the British Museum (Natural History).

[2] From letters written by Redgrave on 26 May 1862 and by Horsley on 16 April 1866, belonging to the picture's present owner.

[3] We are indebted to David Moore-Gwyn for telling us about No. 586 and for copies of the correspondence cited above.

587 Sir Francis Baring, Bt. 1804
See color illustration, p. 112

BARING BROTHERS & CO. LTD., LONDON

Oil on canvas: 50 × 40 in. (127 × 101.5 cm.)

Signed lower center: *B. West 1804*

PROV: By family descent to the first Earl of Northbrook (1826–1904)

EXH: London 1868 (47), lent by Lord Northbrook

LISTED: PC, p. 563 ("Sir Francis Baring and Part of his Family, containing six Figures as large as Life," Sir Francis Baring); *UM*, p. 529; Barlow, p. 434; *BA*, p. 16; Galt, p. 224; Dillenberger, p. 161 (228)

LIT: Farington Diary, 2 Sept. 1804, 13 Sept. and 3 Nov. 1806 (Farington 1978–, VI, p. 2403, and VII, pp. 2851 and 2895)

Sir Francis Baring, Bt. (1740–1810) was the founder of the financial house of Baring Brothers. On 2 September 1804, Joseph Farington noted, "West has lately been finishing a family picture of Portraits of Sir Francis Baring & His relatives." That picture was the picture of "Sir Francis Baring and Part of his Family, containing six Figures as large as Life" which is on all the early lists of West's works, including (in slightly abbreviated form) the list published by Joel Barlow in *The Columbiad*. Since Barlow stated that his list had been given him by West in 1802, the picture's inclusion there suggests that it had been commissioned by that year. Baring acquired a painting by West of *Belisarius and the Boy*

(No. 42) at approximately the same time. In 1802 West had completed a group portrait of another merchant-banking family, that of Henry Hope (No. 640), and it seems likely that Baring's commission to West was inspired by that work. Baring already owned a group portrait by Sir Joshua Reynolds of Lord Lansdowne, Lord Ashburton, and Colonel Isaac Barré, and in 1806 he commissioned a further group portrait of himself and two of his partners from Thomas Lawrence.[1] According to Farington, Baring thought of these three works as related: "Sir Francis will then He says have three pictures,—one of his Political friends,—by Sir Joshua,—one of his domestic connexions by West, and this of his Brother and commercial friend by Lawrence." But that relationship did not work to West's advantage: on 3 November 1806, when Lawrence had completed the three heads in his picture, Farington recorded that Lawrence's portraits

> have given great satisfaction, & the more so from being compared with those painted by West.—Sir Francis asked Lawrence whether West ever took the opinion of any Artists upon his works? adding that while West was painting for Him, He made a few observations but West paid no regard to them.

The group portraits by Reynolds and Lawrence are still in the possession of the descendants of Sir Francis Baring. West's group portrait was cut down at some time, perhaps as a result of Sir Francis's evident dislike, and part of it is preserved in the single figure of Sir Francis seated (No. 587). *Pentimenti* of a woman's bodice and crossed arms, discernible under the landscape in the upper right corner of No. 587, establish that Sir Francis was not originally depicted alone. His remarkably informal pose makes the painting appear entirely uncharacteristic of West's portrait style at any stage of his career, but the pose becomes understandable if we imagine Sir Francis seated on the left of his family in a position analogous to that of Henry Hope on the left of his family portrait (No. 640). The alteration also explains, on the one hand, why there is no contemporary record of the single portrait of Baring although there is documentation for the group portrait, and, on the other, how the group portrait, which would have had considerable family interest, could disappear without a trace from a family collection that has remained largely intact. The dismemberment must have taken place before 1868 when No. 587 was lent in its present form to the National Portrait Exhibition which took place in that year.

[1] Ill. in *Sir Joshua Reynolds: Loan Exhibition at 45 Park Lane*, London, 1937, pl. 87 and in Kenneth Garlick, *Sir Thomas Lawrence*, London, 1954, pl. 60.

588 Lady Diana Mary Barker of Speen House, Berkshire 1766

MINNEAPOLIS INSTITUTE OF ARTS

Oil on canvas: 37 × 33 in. (94 × 83.8 cm.)

Signed lower right: *B. West 1766*

PROV: Presented to the Minneapolis Institute of Arts in 1931 by James F. and Louise H. Bell, in memory of James S. and Sallie W. Bell

EXH: Philadelphia 1938 (11); Washington and Philadelphia 1980

589 Mrs. Shute Barrington 1808

CUMMER GALLERY OF ART, JACKSONVILLE, FLORIDA

Oil on canvas: 50 × 40 in. (127 × 101.5 cm.)

Signed lower left: *B. West 1808*

PROV: The Hon. Shute Barrington, Bishop of Durham (1734–1826); his great-nephew, Uvedale Price (1805–1830), Mongewell Park, Oxon.; by family descent to Thomas Price; his sale, Christie's, London, 6 May 1893, lot 62, bt. by Vokins; A. Tooth and Sons, London; Barbizon House, London; Macbeth Galleries, New York; R. L. Skofield, sale Parke-Bernet, New York, 1 Feb. 1940, lot 67; Newhouse Galleries, New York; John C. Meyers, Ashland, Ohio; purchased by the Cummer Gallery in 1960

EXH: Brooklyn 1922 (30) lent by Tooth

LIT: W. Roberts, "The Honorable Mrs. Shute Barrington by Benjamin West, PRA, 1738–1820. Painted for the Bishop Shute Barrington, and hung at their estate, Mongewell Park, Oxon.," unpublished typescript, 1920, Frick Art Reference Library; *Catalogue of Paintings and Other Art Objects, Cummer Gallery of Art*, Jacksonville, [n.d., *c.* 1961], p. 27; Robert W. Schlageter, "Cummer Gallery of Art," *Antiques*, CXII, 1977, p. 954

The sitter, the daughter of Sir John Guise, Bt., married in 1770 the Hon. Shute Barrington, then Bishop of Llandaff and subsequently Bishop of Salisbury from 1782 to 1791 and Bishop of Durham from 1791 to 1826. She died in 1807. No. 589 is signed and dated *1808* but has traditionally been thought to have been painted at a much earlier date. Since the sitter wears no rings, William Roberts proposed that the picture was painted before her marriage in 1770. According to this theory, the background showing the towers of Durham Cathedral (where Shute Barrington assumed the bishopric only in 1791) was added following her death, and West signed and dated the painting at that time. Stylistically, however, No. 589 does not appear to be as early as the 1760s (or the 1770s); rather the handling appears not unlike that in West's portrait of Robert Fulton, which is signed and dated *1806* (No. 620). Hence, it seems reasonable to accept the date of *1808* on the canvas as indication of when the picture was painted. If that is correct, No. 589 is a posthumous portrait based, presumably, on earlier works by other artists. According to Roberts, No. 589 hung together with a portrait of Bishop Barrington at Mongewell Park in Oxfordshire, which Mrs. Barrington had inherited from her brother and which remained the property of her husband following her death. It seems likely that the Bishop commissioned No. 589 as a companion to a portrait of himself, possibly the one exhibited by Lawrence at the Royal Academy in 1796, which has a background of church architecture, and which is the same size (Merton College, Oxford).

588

589

590

591

590 Sir Thomas Beauchamp-Proctor, Bt., of Langley Park, Norfolk 1777

TATE GALLERY, LONDON

Oil on canvas: $49\frac{3}{4} \times 39\frac{1}{2}$ in. (126.5 × 100.5 cm.)

Signed lower left: *B. West 1777*

PROV: By descent in the family of the sitter's son, George Edward Beauchamp, to Major General George Edward Henry Beauchamp (1834–1894); presented by his daughters to the Tate Gallery in 1941 through the National Art Collections Fund, following the death of his widow in the previous year

LIT: Prown, 1966, II, p. 274, n. 2

This portrait of Sir Thomas Beauchamp-Proctor, second Baronet (1756–1827), appears to be the earliest of several related pictures by West, which include a portrait of Sir Thomas's wife (No. 591) and a double portrait of his sister and her husband, John Custance (No. 607).

Jules Prown has noted the similarity in handling in No. 590 and Copley's earliest English portraits (such as his portrait of West in the Fogg Museum) and has suggested that West may have been influenced by the example of his compatriot.

Later portraits of Sir Thomas Beauchamp-Proctor by Romney, Opie, and Henry William Pickersgill were still at Langley Park at the beginning of the century.[1]

[1]Duleep Singh 1927, I, pp. 376–77.

591 Lady Beauchamp-Proctor 1778

TATE GALLERY, LONDON

Oil on canvas: $49\frac{3}{4} \times 39\frac{1}{2}$ in. (126.5 × 100.5 cm.)

Signed lower left: *B. West/1778*

PROV: As for No. 590

EXH: (?) RA 1778 (332) "Portrait of a Lady; half-length"

ENGR: Mezzotint ($13\frac{7}{16} \times 11$ in.) by James Watson, pub. 25 March 1779 by John Boydell

Mary, daughter of Robert Palmer of Holme Park, Sonning, Berkshire, married Sir Thomas Beauchamp-Proctor (see No. 590) on 5 March 1778. The painting, which shows her adorning a term of Hymen with flowers, obviously commemorates that event. The same altar and a very similar *putto* also appear in No. 607, which was painted by West in the same year in commemoration of the marriage of Sir Thomas Beauchamp-Proctor's sister.

A full-length portrait of the sitter painted by Romney in 1782–83 is in the Huntington Library in San Marino and several other portraits of her are recorded.[1]

A small version of No. 591, which was sold anonymously in 1932, appears to be a copy of the Watson mezzotint.[2]

[1]See C. H. Collins Baker, *Catalogue of British Paintings in the Henry E. Huntington Library Art Gallery*, San Marino, 1936,

pp. 84–85 and pl. xxxix; and Duleep Singh 1927, I, pp. 375–76.
[2]Oil on panel, $11 \times 9\frac{1}{2}$ in., sold Puttick & Simpson, London, 31 May 1932, lot 25 (photograph in the Witt Library).

592 Peter Beckford 1797

METROPOLITAN MUSEUM OF ART, NEW YORK

Oil on canvas: $57 \times 45\frac{1}{2}$ in. (145 × 115.5 cm.)

Signed lower right: *B. West 1797*

PROV: William Beckford, Fonthill Abbey, Wilts.; by family descent to the twelfth Duke of Hamilton (died 1895) and sold by his estate, Christie's, London, 6–7 Nov. 1919, lot 75, bt. by Tooth; John R. Morron, by whom bequeathed to the Metropolitan Museum in 1950

LISTED: *PC*, p. 561 ("Four Half Lengths," painted for and in the possession of Wm. Beckford, Esq. of Fonthill); *UM*, p. 528; *BA*, p. 14; Galt, p. 220; Dillenberger, p. 151 (135)

LIT: Albert Ten Eyck Gardner, "Beckford's Gothic Wests," *Metropolitan Museum of Art Bulletin*, XIII, Oct. 1954, pp. 41–49; Gardner and Feld 1965, pp. 34–35; Kraemer 1975, p. 71; Hamilton-Phillips 1981, pp. 158–64, fig. 2

592

The "Four Half Lengths" included in *Public Characters* among the works painted by West for William Beckford can be identified as the four portraits by West in the Hamilton Palace sale of 1919, of which two, Nos. 592 and 593, are now in the Metropolitan Museum of Art and two, Nos. 594 and 615, are in the National Gallery of Art in Washington. These four paintings remained in Beckford's possession until his death in 1844 and they appear in an inventory of works in his possession made at that time.[1] From Beckford they passed to his younger daughter, Susan Euphemia, the wife of the tenth Duke of Hamilton. The article by Martha Hamilton-Phillips published in 1981 provides a thorough discussion of the four.

No. 592 is described in the inventory of 1844 as "Portrait of Peter Beckford, Esq. with a map in his Hand." In the painting itself that map can be seen to be of Jamaica. The subject could be either William Beckford's great-grandfather, who served as Lieutenant-Governor of Jamaica and died in 1710, or Beckford's grandfather, who became Speaker of the Jamaican Assembly and died in 1735; both of them were named Peter. It has been assumed that Nos. 592 and 593 show William Beckford's grandfather and grandmother, the Speaker and his wife, but the seventeenth-century garb in No. 592 suggests that it may represent the elder Peter, William's great-grandfather. In either case, the picture and its companion were painted long after the subjects' deaths.

Although not painted from life, Nos. 592 and 593 should not be confused with the imaginary portraits of recipients of the Order of the Garter, adorning King Edward's Gallery in the north wing of Fonthill Abbey, none of which seem to have been painted by West.[2] The four half-length portraits may have been among the family portraits hung in the Oak Parlour in the south transept of the abbey, where Beckford normally dined.[3] A reference in a letter written by Beckford in 1822, when the abbey was open to the public before being sold, refers to visitors "regretting not yet being able to *retire* beyond West's great dauberies," which Boyd Alexander has interpreted as indicating that West's portraits hung above wainscoting concealing water-closets.[4]

A preparatory drawing for No. 592 showing slight differences in pose and details (i.e., there is no map of Jamaica) is at Swarthmore.[5] Similar drawings for the other three portraits are also known. Portraits of the subjects of all four pictures by Andrea Casali and William Hoare are known to have been at Fonthill House (the predecessor of Fonthill Abbey)[6] and West probably based the features in his pictures upon them. As this group of pictures included portraits of both Beckford's grandfather and his great-grandfather, it does not help to identify the subject of No. 592.

[1] We are indebted to the late Boyd Alexander for sending Helmut von Erffa a list of works by West from the manuscript inventory in the Beckford Papers, which until 1977 were in the collection of the Dukes of Hamilton.

[2] The inventory of 1844 includes, in addition to the four family portraits and three other pictures by West (Nos. 71, 211, and 411), six historical portraits listed as "the High Constable of France," "Alfonso, King of Spain," "John of Brittany," "Edward the 4th," and two of "Henry the 7th." These had hung in King Edward's Gallery, but we have been unable to find any further documentation to confirm that they were painted by West. They are described in two early accounts of Fonthill Abbey (Storer 1812, p. 22, and Rutter 1823, p. 38) but neither mentions the artist, which they probably would have done, if the painter had been West. The second "Henry the 7th" on the inventory was probably a mistake for a painting of John of Gaunt, which is included by both Storer and Rutter.

[3] See Alexander 1957, pp. 16 and 18, and Lees-Milne 1976, pp. 60 and 65. It should be noted, however, that these portraits are not mentioned in Rutter's and Storer's descriptions of the room.

593

[4] Alexander 1957, p. 336.

[5] Black and white chalk on blue paper, $11\frac{1}{16} \times 9\frac{1}{4}$ in. (Hamilton-Phillips 1981, fig. 6).

[6] They are mentioned in a letter written in 1768 or 1769 by Robert Drysdale, Beckford's first tutor (information provided by Boyd Alexander in a letter to Helmut von Erffa, 7 July 1959).

593 Mrs. Peter Beckford 1797

METROPOLITAN MUSEUM OF ART, NEW YORK

Oil on canvas: $57 \times 45\frac{1}{2}$ in. (145 × 115.5 cm.)

Signed lower right: *B. West/1797* and inscribed verso on a lining canvas: *Busbua Beckford/wife of Peter Beckford Esqr. and/Daughter & Heir of Colonel Justives Hering*

PROV: As for No. 592 (lot 76 in the Hamilton sale, 6–7 Nov. 1919, as "Busbua, wife of Peter Beckford")

LISTED: As for No. 592

LIT: As for No. 592 (fig. 3 in Hamilton-Phillips 1981)

See No. 592. Although No. 593 bears an inscription and was sold in 1919 as a portrait of "Busbua Beckford," it was listed in the inventory of 1844 only as "Portrait of Mrs. Beckford seated at a table with a book. Wife of the above Peter Beckford, Esq." Busbua is a mis-spelling of "Bathshua," the name of William Beckford's grandmother, the wife of the Speaker Peter Beckford, but the conspicuous error in spelling brings into question the reliability of the identification, and it seems possible, therefore, that the subject could be either the grandmother or the great-grandmother of West's patron. Whoever she is, she is not the same Mrs. Peter Beckford (who was married to William Beckford's first cousin, the author of *Thoughts on Hunting*) painted by Sir Joshua Reynolds in the full-length portrait now in the Lady Lever Art Gallery in Port Sunlight.

A drawing for the composition of No. 593 is at Swarthmore,[1] and a study for the sitter's right hand

594

by Alderman Beckford after 1755 and pulled down by William Beckford in 1807. A visitor to Beckford in Bath in 1838 saw No. 594 and its companion, No. 615, showing Beckford's aunt, and mentioned the view of Fonthill in the background of the former. He also contrasted No. 594 unfavorably with Reynolds's portrait of Mrs. Peter Beckford, the wife of William Beckford's cousin, which Beckford also had at Bath (now in the Lady Lever Art Gallery, Port Sunlight): "West certainly knew nothing of portrait painting. The tout ensemble of the portrait in question is as dry and hard as if painted by a Chinese novice."[1]

In the inventory made at the time of William Beckford's death (see No. 592), the painting is listed as "Portrait of Mrs. Beckford, mother of the late William Beckford Esq., seated at a table."

Guy Chapman supplied dates of 1790 and 1793 for No. 594, but neither seems to have been based on any firm evidence. A charge of £84, for "painting the Portrait of Mr. Beckford's Mother," appears on an account sent by West to Nicholas Williams, Beckford's agent, on 30 September 1799. This would seem to indicate that West painted No. 594 after Nos. 592 and 593, which are both signed and dated 1797, and after the death of the sitter in 1798. Thus the commission may have been inspired by Mrs. Beckford's death, and her features in No. 594 may have been based upon an earlier portrait by Andrea Casali.

A preparatory drawing, with a slighter sketch for the same composition on the verso, is in the Pierpont Morgan Library.[2] In the sketch on the verso, the flowers, which are on the left in the painting, are on the right, and the sitter has one arm raised, as if in the act of arranging them. In No. 594 itself, numerous *pentimenti* are discernible around the sitter's head.

[1]Quoted from Lansdown 1893, p. 9.
[2]Black and white chalk on grey paper, $10\frac{9}{16} \times 8\frac{1}{2}$ in. (Kraemer 1975, pp. 71–72, no. 158, pls. 86 and 87).

595 Captain Christopher Codrington Bethell (?)1769

LOCATION UNKNOWN

Oil on canvas: 29×24 in. (73.6×60.9 cm.)

PROV: By descent to Bethel Walrond, Dulford House, Devon; sold anonymously, Christie's, London, 30 June 1888, lot 129, bt. by B. Smith for £6.10.0.; sold

595

lying upon an open book is in the Pierpont Morgan Library.[2]

[1]Black chalk, heightened with white, on blue paper, $10\frac{5}{8} \times 8\frac{7}{8}$ in. (Hamilton-Phillips 1981, fig. 7).
[2]Black chalk, heightened with white, on blue-grey paper, $5\frac{15}{16} \times 8\frac{9}{16}$ in. (Kraemer 1975, p. 71, no. 156 and pl. 88).

594 Mrs. William Beckford c. 1799

NATIONAL GALLERY OF ART, WASHINGTON, D.C.

Oil on canvas: $57\frac{1}{2} \times 45\frac{3}{8}$ in. (146×115.5 cm.)

PROV: William Beckford, Fonthill Abbey, Wilts.; by family descent to the twelfth Duke of Hamilton (died 1895) and sold by his estate, Christie's, London, 6–7 Nov. 1919, lot 74 (as "Lady Elizabeth Gordon, mother of William Beckford, Esq."), bt. by Tooth; Thomas B. Clarke, New York (died 1931); Andrew Mellon, by whom presented to the National Gallery in 1947

EXH: Brooklyn 1922 (24) as "Elizabeth Gordon, Countess of Sutherland," lent anonymously; *Portraits by Early American Artists of the 17th, 18th & 19th Centuries Collected by Thomas B. Clarke*, Philadelphia Museum of Art, 1928

LISTED: As for No. 592

LIT: Lansdown 1893, p. 9; Guy Chapman, *Beckford*, London, 1937, pp. 9 and 93, ill. opp. p. 40; Kraemer 1975, pp. 71–72; Lees-Milne 1976, pp. 12–13; Hamilton-Phillips 1981, pp. 158–67, fig. 5

See No. 592. Although the identity of the sitter was confused in the catalogue of the Hamilton sale of 1919 and remained confused in subsequent years, there can be no doubt that No. 594 represents William Beckford's mother, née Maria Hamilton, who married Alderman Beckford, William's father, in 1756 and died in 1798. She is shown seated before the portico and one of the wings of Fonthill House (or Fonthill Splendens), built

596

597

anonymously, Christie's, London, 22 June 1979, lot 134; 11 April 1980, lot 143; and again, Christie's, New York, 24 April 1981, lot 2

Captain Christopher Codrington Bethell (1728–1797) was the third son of Sir William Codrington, first Baronet, of Dodington in Gloucestershire. The surname of Bethell, which he assumed, was that of his maternal grandfather. An inscription on the back of No. 595 includes the date of *1769*, when the subject would have been somewhat over forty years old.

596 Dr. Samuel Boudé *c*. 1755–56

NATIONAL GALLERY OF ART, WASHINGTON, D.C.

Oil on canvas: 35⅝ × 30⅛ in. (90.5 × 76.5 cm.)

PROV: By descent in the family of the sitter to Mrs. Henry S. Heistand, Marietta, Pennsylvania (as of 1934); Knoedler Gallery, New York, 1948; Edgar William and Bernice Chrysler Garbisch, by whom presented to the National Gallery of Art in 1964

EXH: *Loan Exhibition of Historical and Contemporary Portraits*, Lancaster, Pa., 1912 (24); *American Painting of the 18th and Early 19th Century*, Knoedler Gallery, New York, 1948 (3); *American Primitive Paintings from the Collection of Edgar William and Bernice Chrysler Garbisch: Part II*, National Gallery of Art, Washington, 1957; Boston 1976 (2)

LIT: Sawitzky 1938, pp. 437 and 451 (11), ill.; Flexner 1952, pp. 24–25

Samuel Boudé was a physician and apothecary in Lancaster, Pennsylvania, where West spent several months, most probably in 1755–56. According to Flexner, Mrs. Boudé (No. 597) was a distant family connection of the artist, her sister being married to Matthew Clarkson, whose brother was married to West's sister Rachel.

Nos. 596 and 597 have both been heavily restored. Sawitzky, who saw the paintings in 1934, described them as being in very deteriorated condition, and that description is confirmed by the illustrations accompanying his article.

597 Mrs. Samuel Boudé *c*. 1755–56

NATIONAL GALLERY OF ART, WASHINGTON, D.C.

Oil on canvas: 35⅝ × 30⅛ in. (90.5 × 76.5 cm.)

PROV: As for No. 596

EXH: As for No. 596 (no. 25 in the Lancaster exhibition of 1912, no. 4 in New York 1948, and no. 3 in Boston 1976)

LIT: As for No. 596 (no. 12 in Sawitzky)

See No. 596. An almost identical pose can also be seen in No. 690, the portrait of Sarah Ursula Rose, which West also painted while in Lancaster in 1755–56.

598 The Reverend Robert Anthony Bromley

LOCATION UNKNOWN

PROV: Sold by West's sons, Robins, London, 20–22 June 1829, lot 94 ("Small whole length Portraits of the Rev. Bromley and his Wife")

Nothing is known about Nos. 598 and 599 apart from the entry in the sale catalogue cited above. The wording of the catalogue suggests that two separate pictures were sold as one lot, rather than a single double portrait. It is not known if West painted additional versions which belonged to the sitters.

The Reverend Robert Anthony Bromley (1736–1800) was the founder and minister of the Fitzroy Chapel, which West attended and to which he donated two pictures (Nos. 260 and 332). Bromley was the author of *A Philosophical and Critical History of the Fine Arts* published in two volumes in 1793 and 1795, and it was believed that he helped West prepare his presidential Academy discourses.[1] The first volume of his book, which praised the *Death of General Wolfe* as the one great modern example of history painting, while insulting Fuseli and ignoring Copley, provoked a considerable rumpus in the Royal Academy as a consequence of Copley's motion to have it removed from the Academy's library. That motion did not succeed but the Academicians did vote not to purchase the second volume, with almost the entire membership of the Academy apart from West seeming to disapprove of the book.[2]

[1] Mitchell 1967, p. 270.
[2] See Farington Diary, 10 Dec. 1793–19 April 1794, passim (Farington 1978–, I, pp. 111–81); Alberts 1978, pp. 205–9; and Mitchell 1967, pp. 270–72.

599 Mrs. Bromley

LOCATION UNKNOWN

PROV: As for No. 598

600 Francis Godolphin Osborne, Marquess of Carmarthen (later Fifth Duke of Leeds)
(?) 1769

LOCATION UNKNOWN

Oil on canvas: 29 × 24 in. (73.5 × 61 cm.)

(?) Signed and dated: *1769*

PROV: Henry Sherwood, Crawford House, Dorset; sold anonymously, Sotheby's, London, 17 June 1970, lot 47; Douglas Wing, Old Hall Gallery, Rye, Sussex; sold anonymously, Sotheby's, London, 17 Nov. 1971, lot 77, bt. by G. Henley

When sold in 1970, No. 600 was described as indistinctly signed and dated. A subsequent owner reported that the date could be read as *1769*.[1] Francis Godolphin

Osborne (1751–1799), who was to succeed to the dukedom of Leeds in 1789, bore in 1769 the courtesy title of Marquess of Carmarthen. In that year he became an Oxford M.A., hence the academic robes. Another very similar portrait of the sitter, presumably painted at approximately the same time, is in the National Portrait Gallery in London.[2] Reynolds painted portraits of him in 1764[3] and as one of the members of the Society of Dilettanti in 1778–79 (Society of Dilet-

600

601

tanti, London). A later portrait by Lawrence shows him in Garter robes (private collection).

The fourth Duke of Leeds, the father of the subject of this painting, was a first cousin of Archbishop Drummond, West's patron, and in the 1730s the two had taken the Grand Tour together. In 1767, two years before painting No. 600, West had painted a portrait of Archbishop Drummond's two eldest sons, also wearing academic robes (No. 608).

[1] Letter from D. C. Cooke, Old Hall Gallery, Iden, Rye, dated 15 July 1970, to Richard Ormond, in the files of the National Portrait Gallery, London.
[2] This portrait is attributed to West in the Gallery's current catalogue (1981, p. 339, no. 801); it had previously been ascribed to George Knapton. Despite its similarities to No. 600, in the opinion of the compilers of the present catalogue, it is probably not by West.
[3] See *Realism through Informality*, Leger Galleries, London, 1983 (exhibition catalogue), no. 5.

601 Stephen Carmick *c.* 1755–56

SANTA BARBARA MUSEUM OF ART, PRESTON MORTON COLLECTION

Oil on canvas: $47\frac{1}{2} \times 37\frac{1}{4}$ in. (120.5 × 94.5 cm.)

PROV: By descent in the family of the sitter to Louis G. Carmick, Washington, D.C. (in 1938); Hirschl & Adler Galleries, New York, 1959
EXH: *International Exhibition*, Philadelphia, 1876 (1164)

lent by Louis Carmick; *250 Years of Art in Pennsylvania*, Westmoreland County Museum of Art, Greensburg, Pennsylvania, 1959 (131)

LIT: Alan Burroughs, *Limners and Likenesses: Three Centuries of American Painting*, Cambridge, Mass., 1936, pp. 72–73; Sawitzky 1938, p. 452 (13)

Stephen Carmick (1719–1774) was born near Camden, New Jersey, and became a merchant in Philadelphia. Alan Burroughs recorded a rather shaky belief held by the family of the sitter that the picture originally had West's signature on the back and the date 1759. Sawitzky questioned the reliability of this information, and suggested that the style of the work puts it close to West's Lancaster paintings of 1755–56, such as No. 596.

602 The Cartwright Children 1768

PRIVATE COLLECTION

Oil on canvas: 58 × 76 in. (147.5 × 193 cm.)

Signed lower left: *B. West/1768*

PROV: By descent in the Cartwright family to the present owner

LISTED: *PC*, p. 563 ("The family picture, half lengths, of Mrs. Cartwright's Children"); *UM*, pp. 528–29; *BA*, p. 15; Galt, p. 222; Dillenberger, p. 158 (199)

LIT: Charles Merrill Mount, "A Hidden Treasure in Britain," *Art Quarterly*, XX, 1959, p. 221, fig. 3; *Aynhoe Park: An Illustrated Survey of the Northamptonshire Home of the Cartwright Family*, English Life Publications, Derby [1953], p. 29

No. 602 shows the children of William Cartwright (*c.* 1705–1768) of Aynhoe Park, Northamptonshire, by his second wife, Elizabeth Cottrell Dormer. According to a label on the frame, the children, from left to right, are William (1754–1829), Clement (1761–1828), Bridget (1752–1794), Mary (1756–1793), and

Elizabeth (1749–1838). Clement and Bridget hold a volume of drawings in red chalk, evidently the work of Elizabeth, who has a porte-crayon in her right hand. The globe on the table to the left is turned to show the coast of North America and the words "The Western Atlantic."

The children's mother was the daughter of Sir Clement Cottrell Dormer (died 1758) of Rousham House in Oxfordshire, which is only a few miles away from Aynhoe Park. Between 1765 and 1771 West also painted portraits of her brother, Sir Charles Cottrell Dormer, and of Sir Charles's wife and son (Nos. 603, 604, and 605). The William Cartwright depicted by West in No. 602 subsequently became a general, and Clement a Fellow of All Souls. None of the children ever married, and No. 602 descended in the family of their older half-brother Thomas Cartwright (1736–1772).

A drawing for the composition is in the British Museum.[1]

[1]Black and white chalk on grey paper: 9 × 11⅞ in. (1920–6–15–2).

602

603

604

603 Sir Charles Cottrell Dormer 1772

C. COTTRELL-DORMER

Oil on canvas: 50 × 40 in. (127 × 101.5 cm.)

Signed lower left: *Benj West/1772* and inscribed by another hand: *Sir Charles/Cottrell Dormer K[t].*

PROV: By descent in the family of the sitter to the present owner

No. 603 is the third of three portraits painted by West of Sir Charles Cottrell Dormer (1719–1779) of Rousham House in Oxfordshire and of his family. The other two are Nos. 604 and 605 below. In addition West also painted the family of Sir Charles's sister, Mrs. William Cartwright (No. 602). In this painting, Sir Charles is shown wearing the chain and badge of the office of Master of the Ceremonies, a court position, which he was the fourth member of his family in succession to hold, and which was subsequently inherited by his son Clement, depicted in No. 605. His right hand rests on a book entitled *Memorandums of Ceremony*, and the sheet of paper behind is inscribed *Lettre de Cr[éance]* (i.e., the credentials of a foreign ambassador, whose

presentation at court would have been supervised by the Master of the Ceremonies). Earlier portraits in the same collection depicting Sir Charles's predecessors in the office include similar details.

604 Lady Cottrell Dormer 1765

C. COTTRELL-DORMER

Oil on canvas: 92 × 47 in. (233.5 × 119.5 cm.)

Inscribed lower right: *Lady Cottrell Dormer 1765*; and lower left: *Jane, Eldest Daughter of Chas Caesar Adelmare Esqre and Grand Daughter of Chas Caesar Adelmare Esqre MP of Pennington Place Herts.—Sister of Harriot Wife of Robert Chester Esqre—Born 1732 died 1802. Married 1st Sir Chas Cottrell Dormer of Rousham, K[t]. M.C. 2[d] Gen[l] the Honble George Lane Parker 2[d] son of George 2[d] Earl of Macclesfield.* Neither inscription is in West's hand

PROV: As for No. 603

LIT: *Rousham Park*, n.d., Oxford Publishing Co., Oxford (ill. in situ)

No. 604 is installed as one of a series of portraits, most of which date from the seventeenth century, in elaborate plaster-work frames in the Great Parlour of Rousham House. This room, which was originally designed by William Kent *c.* 1738, was remodelled in 1764 by Thomas Roberts of Oxford, who provided the frames. The date of *1765* on No. 604 suggests that it may have been commissioned in order to be incorporated into this scheme of decoration. The other two Wests at Rousham (Nos. 603 and 605), both of which are later and smaller, hang separately in the Dining Room.

A portrait of the sitter by Reynolds, signed and dated *1764*, is also at Rousham.

605 Clement Cottrell Dormer 1771

C. COTTRELL-DORMER

Oil on canvas: oval, 31 × 26½ in. (78.5 × 67.5 cm.)

Signed lower left: *B. West 1771*, and inscribed upper left, by another hand: *Clement Cottrell Dormer*

PROV: As for No. 603

Clement
Cottrell Dormer

605

and the view from an interior space over enclosed parkland on the left distinctly recalls Zoffany's portrait of *Queen Charlotte with Her Two Eldest Sons* of *c.* 1765 in the Royal Collection, which is also close in size.[3] West, who had been painting historical pictures for George III since 1768, certainly must have been familiar with the King's Zoffanys. Zoffany was away from England from the summer of 1772 until 1779, and No. 606 may represent a deliberate venture by West into his territory during his absence. In one respect, West was successful in this, since he replaced Zoffany during the 1770s as George III's favorite artist, painting not only historical subjects, but also a major series of royal portraits. The first securely dated one of these, No. 562 of 1776, showing Queen Charlotte and the Princess Royal, is a double portrait, like No. 606, with a view from indoors to the out of doors in the left background, but it is on a much larger scale than No. 606 or the paintings by Zoffany cited above. Other group portraits by West on a reduced scale include one of his own family (No. 546), probably painted or begun shortly before No. 606, and The *Cricketers* (Nos. 726 and 727) from 1763–64.

[1]This manuscript belongs to the owner of No. 606. It is on business paper headed *Philadelphia Offices, No. 6 Strawberry Street* and bears no address, heading, signature or date.
[2]A letter from Richard Wells dated 1760 contains the instruction, "My direction is under the care of Crafton and Colson, London" (Smith, p. 176). The firm was situated at 166 Fenchurch Street in 1772 and at 9 Great St. Helens in 1774. We are indebted to Lewis Andrews for this and other information pertinent to No. 606.
[3]See Millar 1969, I, pp. 149–51 (1199, 1201, and 1207), and II, pls. 26–28, 30, and 32.

607 Mr. and Mrs. John Custance 1778
See color illustrations, pp. 30, 31

NELSON-ATKINS MUSEUM OF ART, KANSAS CITY, MISSOURI

Oil on canvas: 59 × 83 in. (150 × 211 cm.)

Signed lower right: *B. West 1778*

PROV: By descent in the family of the sitters to Lady Alfred Douglas (daughter and heiress of Col. Frederic Hambledon Custance) and still in her possession at Weston House, the Custance family seat, in January 1927; sold anonymously, Christie's, London, 20 May 1927, lot 110, bt. by Madame Herz; Jacques Seligmann & Co.; purchased by the Nelson Gallery in 1934

EXH: RA 1779 (344) "A gentleman and lady in commemoration of their marriage"; *Inaugural Exhibition*, Springfield Museum of Fine Arts, Springfield, Mass., 1933 (6); *A Survey of American Painting*, Baltimore Museum of Art, 1934 (6); Philadelphia 1938 (32)

(?) LISTED: *PC*, p. 563 ("The family picture of Sir Edmund Baker, Nephew, and Niece, half lengths"); *UM*, p. 529; *BA*, p. 15 ("The family picture of Sir Edmund Bacon's Nephew and Niece, half lengths"); Galt, p. 222 (as in *PC*); Dillenberger, p. 158 (200)

LIT: John Beresford, ed., *Diary of a Country Parson, the Reverend Woodforde*, 5 vols., 1924–31 (frontispiece to vol. II, 1926); Duleep Singh 1927, II, p. 389, ill. opp. p. 392

John Custance (1749–1822) of Weston House, near Norwich, was part of a closely-knit group of Norfolk families that included also Sir Thomas and Lady Beauchamp-Proctor, of Langley Park (see Nos. 590 and 591), and Sir Edmund Bacon of Raveningham Hall, the premier Baronet of England. No. 607 commemorates the marriage of John Custance to Frances Beauchamp-Proctor, the sister of Sir Thomas

Clement Cottrell Dormer (1757–1808) was knighted and succeeded his father as Master of the Ceremonies in 1779. He resigned the office in 1796. In 1771, he would have been fourteen years old.

606 Mr. and Mrs. Robert Crafton 1773
See color illustration, p. 32

PRIVATE COLLECTION

Oil on canvas: 40⅛ × 50⅜ in. (102 × 128 cm.)

Signed lower right: *Painted by B. West/in London 1773*

PROV: By descent in the family of Richard Wells (died 1801), the son of Mrs. Crafton by her first marriage; sold anonymously, Christie's, New York, 3 June 1982, lot 7

LIT: John Jay Smith, ed., *Letters of Doctor Richard Hill and His Children*, privately printed, Philadelphia, 1854, p. xviii, note

The chief source of information about this painting is the volume of Hill family letters cited above. A manuscript letter or copy of a portion of a letter, dating evidently from the nineteenth century and offering to sell the painting, gives essentially the same information.[1] Mrs. Crafton was the daughter of Richard Partridge, agent in London for the provinces of Pennsylvania, New Jersey, Rhode Island, and Connecticut. She is shown with her second husband, Robert Crafton, who seems either to have been a partner in a firm of hosiers in London, Crafton & Colson, or related to the Crafton of that firm.[2] Mrs. Crafton's first husband had been Dr. Gideon Wells. Her son by that marriage, Richard Wells, settled in Philadelphia in 1750. There he is said to have met West and to have given West letters of introduction to his mother and stepfather. The nineteenth-century sources state that West and the Craftons became intimate friends and that West presented No. 606 to the sitters.

No. 606 is a virtually unique example by West of a conversation piece in the scale and manner of Johann Zoffany (1733–1810). In size it corresponds to two paintings by Zoffany in the Royal Collection, one of which was exhibited at the Royal Academy in 1773,

Beauchamp-Proctor, and the sister-in-law of Sir Edmund Bacon. Bacon married her sister, Anne, on 29 January 1778. The exact date of the Custances' marriage is not known but it evidently took place in 1778, the date on this painting, which clearly celebrates the event; their first child was born in February 1779. The marriage of Sir Thomas and Lady Beauchamp-Proctor took place in the same year as well, on 5 March 1778, and West's portrait of the latter (No. 591) contains an altar and a bust of Hymen, which equally clearly refer to that event. The same altar appears in both Nos. 591 and 607; the cherub above Mrs. Custance's head echoes the one accompanying Lady Beauchamp-Proctor; and there are similar garlands of flowers in both works. No. 607 is, however, a much more ambitious painting than No. 591 and, indeed, the prominence of the figure of Hymen, who is as large as, and as alive as, either member of the couple being portrayed, makes the picture considerably more than just a portrait. The use of allegory and many of the specific details echo paintings by Reynolds such as the portrait of Lady Elizabeth Keppel exhibited at the Society of Artists in 1762 (Woburn Abbey) and *Three Graces Adorning a Term of Hymen* exhibited at the Royal Academy in 1774 (Tate Gallery).[1]

The equation of No. 607 with the painting listed in *Public Characters* as "Edmund Baker, Nephew and Niece" and in *La Belle Assemblée* as "Sir Edmund Bacon's Nephew and Niece" is speculative. The substitution of Bacon for Baker in *La Belle Assemblée* appears to be the correction of an error in *Public Characters* and hence to be the more reliable identification of what is certainly the same work. The Custances' children would have been nieces and nephews of Sir Edmund, as would also have been the children of Sir Thomas Beauchamp-Proctor. No portrait by West that can be properly identified as showing a niece and nephew of Sir Edmund is now known, and none is mentioned by Duleep Singh who described the family collections at Weston House, Langley Park, and Raveningham Hall when they were all still relatively intact. On the other hand, the painting is one of West's most ambitious portraits, one that he exhibited at the Royal Academy and, hence, one that he would have been likely to remember and record when making up the lists of his works. It seems probable, therefore, that No. 607 is the work referred to in the lists, the actual kinship of the sitters to Sir Edmund Bacon (brother-in-law and sister-in-law), becoming confused in the same manner that Bacon became Baker in *Public Characters*. The twenty-five years between 1779, when West presumably saw No. 607 for the last time, and 1804, when the first list was published, probably account for the confusion.

The Custance family figures conspicuously in the diaries of Parson James Woodforde (1740–1803), who from 1776 held a living at Weston, where John Custance was the local squire.

[1] See Ellis K. Waterhouse, *Reynolds*, London, 1955, pls. 76 and 152.

608 The Drummond Brothers 1767

See illustration, p. 47

ADDISON GALLERY OF AMERICAN ART, PHILLIPS ACADEMY, ANDOVER, MASSACHUSETTS

Oil on canvas: $94\frac{1}{2} \times 58\frac{3}{8}$ in. (240 × 148.5 cm.)

Signed lower center: *B West 1767*

PROV: Probably painted for Robert Hay Drummond (1711–1776), Archbishop of York and father of the sitters; thence by descent in the family of the elder brother, who in 1787 became tenth Earl of Kinnoull; Scott and Fowles, New York by 1921–22; William Macbeth, Inc., New York; acquired by the Addison Gallery in 1932

EXH: SA 1768 (176) "Portraits of two gentlemen, whole length"; Philadelphia 1921 (3) lent by Scott and Fowles; Brooklyn 1922 (3); Philadelphia 1938 (14)

ENGR: Mezzotint ($24\frac{1}{4} \times 15\frac{1}{4}$ in.) by Valentine Green, inscribed *B. West, pinxit, 1768*, and *Mr. Robert Drummond & Mr. Thomas Drummond, Sons of Robert Archbishop of York*; this print was exhibited SA 1769 (272) as "A mezzotinto proof of two gentlemen; whole length. After Mr. West," but was evidently never published

LISTED: *PC*, p. 562 ("Two whole lengths of the late Archbishop of York's two eldest Sons"); *UM*, p. 528; *BA*, p. 15; Galt, p. 222; Dillenberger, p. 157 (188)

LIT: Gatty 1938–39, p. 81 (Horace Walpole, 1768); Comstock 1932, p. 351, fig. 1

The subjects are Robert Auriol Drummond (or Hay-Drummond), the future tenth Earl of Kinnoull (1751–1804) and his brother Thomas (1752–1773). The two boys, who in 1767 were sixteen and fifteen years old respectively, were the eldest sons of West's early patron Robert Drummond, Archbishop of York and younger brother of the ninth Earl of Kinnoull. This painting appeared at the Society of Artists in 1768 along with *Agrippina Landing at Brundisium with the Ashes of Germanicus* (No. 33), which West also painted for the Archbishop. The date of *1767* on No. 608 indicates that it was completed before No. 33, which is signed and dated *1768*. According to Galt's account of the genesis of the latter painting, Archbishop Drummond frequently invited West to dine and then "seemed to turn the conversation on the celebrity which the patronage of the arts had in all ages reflected on the most illustrious persons and families, addressing himself with particular emphasis to his sons." When he commissioned No. 33, one of the sons fetched the volume of Tacitus from which the Archbishop, or a son, read the appropriate passage.[1] The prominence given to the sons and to the Archbishop's concern with them in this account, which must stem from what West told Galt some fifty years later, suggests the central importance that their education played in the prelate's life at this time. According to the *Dictionary of National Biography*, he instructed his children himself:

> History, of which he had an extensive and accurate knowledge, was his favorite subject, and his son gratefully records "the perspicacious and engaging manner" in which he imparted his instruction, and the lucidity with which he traced the continuity and connection of all history, sacred and profane, "with the zeal and fervour of honest conviction."[2]

This devotion to education is reflected in the academic gowns worn by both boys in No. 608, the books and globe on the floor, and the statue of Athena in the upper right corner. The older brother holds in one hand a scroll, upon which the name *Regulus* is discernible, and with the other points upward to a temple in the background, upon which are inscribed the words *VIRTUTI/S* over the entrance and *HONORI/S* on the drum.[3] This imagery was probably dictated to the artist by the Archbishop, who may have been inspired by a similar double portrait of the third Earl of Shaftesbury and his brother painted by John Closterman *c.* 1702 (National Portrait Gallery, London).[4]

Robert and Thomas and much of the same imagery reappear in No. 611 of 1781 along with a third figure traditionally identified as their sister Abigail. Another Drummond family portrait painted by West in 1776 (No. 610) includes two other brothers traditionally identified as Peter (1754–1799) and George (1761–1807), and a female figure who may have been the wife of Peter. There were still two more brothers, John (1756–1780) and Edward (1758–1829), of whom no portraits by West are presently known.

Nos. 608, 610, and 611 appear to have remained in

the possession of the Earls of Kinnoull, the descendants of the elder of the brothers in No. 608, until early in the twentieth century. The three were lent to exhibitions in 1921 and 1922 in Philadelphia and Brooklyn by New York dealers. In the Brooklyn catalogue, No. 608, which was lent by Scott and Fowles, was listed without indication of provenance, but Nos. 610 and 611, both of which were lent by Knoedler, were each described as coming "direct from the Kinnoull family."

A second version of No. 608, which evidently remained in the artist's possession, is No. 609 below. A preparatory drawing for the composition is in the British Museum.[5]

[1] Galt 1820, pp. 12, 26.
[2] E. V. [the Revd. Canon Venables] in *DNB*, xvi, pp. 38–40. The son quoted was probably not one of the sitters in No. 608, but a younger brother, the Revd. George Hay Drummond (see No. 610), who wrote a memoir of his father as the preface to a collection of his sermons, published in 1803.
[3] These inscriptions can no longer be read on No. 608, but they are visible in the engraving by Valentine Green and can also be made out in the replica (No. 609).
[4] See *John Closterman: Master of the English Baroque 1660–1711*, National Portrait Gallery, London, 1981, pp. 17–18 (17).
[5] Black chalk on grey paper: $15 \times 10\frac{1}{8}$ in. (1920-6-15-4).

609 The Drummond Brothers

LOCATION UNKNOWN

Oil on canvas: $64 \times 39\frac{1}{2}$ in. (162.5 × 100.5 cm.)

PROV: Sold by West's sons, Robins, London, 20–22 June 1829, lot 148 ("Sons of Dr. Drummond, late Archbishop of York"); sold anonymously, Christie's, London, 27 Oct. 1961, lot 157, bt. by Derrick; sold, Sotheby's, London, 18 June 1969, lot 124, bt. by Blady

The picture of the sons of Archbishop Drummond sold by West's sons in 1829 cannot be equated with No. 608 which belonged to the family of the sitters, but it can reasonably be identified with a second, smaller version of the picture which appeared on the market in 1961 and 1969. That picture is an exact replica of No. 608 in all significant details. The temple in the upper left background, which is somewhat abraded in No. 608, is more clearly visible in this painting.

610 Three Members of the Drummond Family
1776

MINNEAPOLIS INSTITUTE OF ARTS

Oil on canvas: 60 × 72 in. (152.5 × 183 cm.)

Signed left: *B. West/1776*

PROV: The Revd. Dr. Drummond (? George Hay Drummond, 1761–1807); subsequently as for No. 608 until *c.* 1920; M. Knoedler and Co., New York, by 1921; acquired by the Minneapolis Institute of Arts in 1931

EXH: Philadelphia 1921 (4); Brooklyn 1922 (4); Philadelphia 1938 (30)

LISTED: *PC*, p. 563 ("Three of the Children of the late Archbishop of York, with the Portrait of the Archbishop, half lengths," in the possession of the Revd. Dr. Drummond); *UM*, p. 528; *BA*, p. 15; Galt, p. 222; Dillenberger, p. 158 (198)

LIT: "The Drummond Family by Benjamin West," *Bulletin of the Minneapolis Institute of Arts*, xx, 1931, pp. 166–68; Comstock 1932, p. 351; Prown 1966, II, p. 274

610

The catalogue of the West exhibition at Brooklyn in 1922 identifies the man in uniform on the right of No. 610 as Peter Auriol Hay Drummond (1754–1799), an officer in the West Yorkshire Militia and the third son of Archbishop Robert Drummond. The woman next to him is, according to the same source, his wife, whom he had married in 1775, and the figure in student dress holding a picture is his youngest brother George Hay Drummond (1761–1807). The painting George Hay Drummond holds shows West's patron Archbishop Drummond wearing Garter robes and is copied from a portrait of the Archbishop painted by Reynolds in 1764–65 (versions in the St. Louis City Art Museum and the Scottish National Portrait Gallery). Archbishop Drummond died in the year that West painted No. 610, but not until 10 December, and since the other three subjects of the painting do not display any indica-

tion of mourning, it seems probable that the painting was undertaken before his death, and not as a memorial tribute to the deceased. Nonetheless, it is possible that the portrait of the Archbishop was introduced after his death and after the rest of the picture had been painted.

The identification provided in 1922 for the three main sitters in this painting presumably depended on family tradition which may or may not have been reliable. Archbishop Drummond does not seem to have had any daughter living in 1776, so, despite the fact that the early lists of West's works describe the sitters as three of the children of the Archbishop, identification of the female figure, who conspicuously displays a wedding ring, as the recently married wife of one of his sons is plausible. Peter Auriol and George Hay Drummond would have been twenty-two and fifteen years old respectively in 1776.

611 Three Members of the Drummond Family
1781

Oil on canvas: 60 × 51 in. (152.5 × 129.5 cm.)

Signed lower right: *B. West 1781*

PROV: Evidently painted for Robert Auriol Drummond (1751–1804), who in 1787 became tenth Earl of Kinnoull, then by family descent until *c.* 1920; M. Knoedler and Co., New York, by 1921; Percy R. Pyne II, Roslyn, New York, by 1932; sold Parke-Bernet, New York, 12 January 1940, lot 236

EXH: *Early American Pictures*, M. Knoedler and Co., New York, 1921; Brooklyn 1922 (32); Philadelphia

501

611

which is faintly legible on the scroll held by Robert in No. 608, is also repeated as the one legible word printed in the book held by the seated female figure in No. 611. On the pages of this book there are several ghostly traces of portraits, which West evidently had initially included then covered over with lines simulating lines of printed text. These paintings, which must have been intended as family portraits, recall the inclusion of a painted portrait of Archbishop Drummond in No. 610, another Drummond family group.

Nos. 608 and 610 both are on the early lists of West's works, with titles recorded in a manner that leaves no doubt about their identification. No. 611 does not appear to be on the lists, but if the female figure was intended to represent Robert's and Thomas's mother, then it is possible that it should be equated with *A Lady Leading Three Children along the Path of Virtue to the Temple* (No. 421), which probably was a group portrait, although not explicitly identified as such in the lists.

612 Mrs. Dundas and Her Daughter 1777

PRIVATE COLLECTION

Oil on canvas: $62\frac{1}{2} \times 49\frac{1}{8}$ in. (158.5 × 125 cm.)

Signed lower left, on front edge of steps: *B. West 1777* and inscribed upper right, by another hand: *Jean. 2nd wife of 2nd Pres^t Dundas / and her daughter Grizzel*

PROV: By descent in the Dundas family

The President Dundas mentioned in the inscription on No. 612 was Robert Dundas, of Arniston, who in 1760 became Lord President of the Court of Session in Edinburgh. This position had previously been held by his father, hence the *2nd Pres^t* of the inscription. His second wife, whom he married in 1756, and who is depicted in No. 612 together with their daughter, was a daughter of William Grant, Lord Prestongrange, a judge in the Court of Session. A portrait of Mrs. Dundas painted by Andrea Soldi in 1757 is at Arniston House, and a portrait of Grizzel as Hebe is No. 613 below. See also No. 624, a portrait of the fourth wife of Mrs. Dundas's uncle, Sir Archibald Grant (the brother of Lord Prestongrange). Lady Grant, the subject of No. 624, was the widow of Andrew Millar of London, while Mrs. Dundas's mother was the daughter of a Revd. Mr. Millar, so there may have been yet further familial connections between these two ladies to explain why West painted them both at approximately the same time. One other picture by West dated *1777* and showing a member of the Edinburgh legal community is No. 616 below.

In No. 612, mother and daughter are sacrificing at an altar to Diana, the virgin goddess, whose statue is on a pedestal to the left. Similar altars, dedicated to Hymen and decorated with *putti* rather than animal heads, appear in West's portraits of Lady Beauchamp-Proctor (No. 591) and Mr. and Mrs. Custance (No. 607), both dated *1778*. In No. 612, however, unlike these works, the classically draped figures are shown full-length and at a scale considerably smaller than that of life. The use of classical dress and accoutrements had been prefigured among West's portraits most notably in the portrait of Alderman Sawbridge (No. 694) painted *c.* 1772. There are also marked similarities between No. 612 and *Fidelia and Speranza* (No. 222), including not only the arches in the backgrounds, but also the arrangement of the hair of the principal figures, and it is possible that the exhibition of *Fidelia and Speranza* at the Royal Academy in 1777 inspired the commission for No. 612.

1938 (33); *The Arts in America in the Eighteenth Century*, Allen Memorial Art Museum, Oberlin College, Oberlin, Ohio, 1946 (17); *American Painting 1700–1950*, Honolulu Academy of Art, Honolulu, Hawaii, 1950; Washington and Philadelphia 1980

(?) LISTED: See No. 421

LIT: Comstock 1932, p. 351 and fig. IV

The entry for No. 611 in the catalogue of the West exhibition in Brooklyn in 1922 identifies the three sitters as Robert Auriol Drummond (1751–1804), Thomas Drummond (1752–1773), and their sister Abigail Drummond (1750–1766), the latter two being depicted posthumously. The two male portraits do appear to show Robert and Thomas Drummond, whom West had previously depicted in 1767 in No. 608, the older brother having graduated from academic garb in the fourteen-year interval. The deceased younger brother,

Thomas, is shown still in his scholar's robes and in a pose almost identical to that in No. 608. If the third figure is Abigail Drummond, the likeness must have been based on a portrait of her made before her death at the age of sixteen, but it does not seem to show such a young girl. Alternatively, the figure might represent Robert's first wife, who had died on 29 March 1780, or his second wife, whom he married on 3 June 1781, or possibly even his mother, who had died in 1773.

Archbishop Drummond died in 1776, so No. 611 most probably was commissioned by Robert, his eldest son, who at thirty years of age in 1781 was not only his father's heir but also in line to inherit his uncle's earldom, to which he succeeded six years later. No. 611 is an explicit sequel to No. 608. The temple in the background, to which Robert points, echoes that in No. 608, and the words *VIRTUTIS* and *HONORIS* reappear over the entrance and on the drum. The word *Regulus*,

Jean. 2⁵ Wife of 2ⁿᵈ Presᵗ Dundas and her daughter Grizzel.

613 Grizzel Dundas as Hebe *c.* 1777

PRIVATE COLLECTION

Oil on canvas: 29 × 23⅞ in. (73.5 × 60.5 cm.)

Inscribed: *Grizzel, Daughter of the 2nd President Dundas*

PROV: By descent in the Dundas family

No. 613 has been ascribed to the Scottish painter David Martin (1737–1797), but it appears much more characteristic of West. Other pictures by West showing female subjects as Hebe are Nos. 721 and 733.

See also No. 612. No. 613 must have been painted at approximately the same time. Grizzel, who took her name from her maternal grandmother, the wife of William Grant, Lord Prestongrange, subsequently became Mrs. Robert Colt.

614 Dr. Enoch Edwards 1795

AMHERST COLLEGE, AMHERST, MASSACHUSETTS

Oil on canvas: 36 × 27¾ in. (91.5 × 70.5 cm.)

Signed upper left: *B. West/1795*, and inscribed on the papers held by the sitter: *London, Dec^m 5, 1795 B. West*

PROV: Traditionally said to have been given by West to the wife of the sitter; Major Evan Edwards (brother of the sitter) and thence by family descent to a Mrs. Cabanis of South Carolina, from whom purchased in 1912 by Herbert Lee Pratt, Glen Cove, Long Island; presented by him to Amherst College in 1938

EXH: (?) RA 1796 (153) "Portrait of a Gentleman"; PAFA 1843 ("Portrait of a Gentleman," lent by Mrs. Edwards); *Early American Paintings*, Brooklyn Museum, 1917 (132); Brooklyn 1922 (31); *Early American Portraits*, Carnegie Institute, Pittsburgh, 1925 (46); Philadelphia 1938 (45); Amherst 1950 (9); *The Art of Philadelphia Medicine*, Philadelphia Museum of Art, 1965 (31)

LIT: Charles Henry Hart, *Works of American Artists in the Collection of Herbert L. Pratt*, New York, 1917, pp. 22–24; Morgan and Toole, 1950, pp. 211–12, ill.

Enoch Edwards (1751–1802) was a native of Philadelphia. Trained as a physician, he was Associate Justice of the Court of Common Pleas in Pennsylvania at the time West painted him. His wife, the half-sister of the painter Henry Benbridge, was a distant relative, by marriage, of Mrs. West.

Edwards visited London at least twice in the 1790s. Two letters from West to his brother William West in Upper Darby, Pennsylvania, dated 27 July 1794, and 18 September 1796, were both written on the occasion of Edwards's imminent returns to his native land.[1] The earlier of the two is a letter of introduction for Edwards, to whom West had given a commission to purchase lands in Pennsylvania. Edwards carried out that commission in conjunction with William West, and West's second letter contains an expression of his approval of the lands so procured: "I have had much conversation with the Dr. on the subject, and the more I know of such purchases the better I am satisfied." Edwards must have been back in London by December of 1795, the date on No. 614, and, if the tradition that the picture was painted by West as a gift for Edwards's wife is true, West's generosity can probably be explained as a form of compensation to Edwards for acting as his agent in the transaction. See also No. 698.

Edwards appears at a much earlier age as part of a group portrait by Henry Benbridge now in the Philadelphia Museum of Art.[2]

[1] Hart 1908, pp. 23–26.
[2] See *Henry Benbridge (1743–1812): American Portrait Painter*, National Portrait Gallery, Washington, 1971 (catalogue by Robert G. Stewart), p. 60 (65).

615 Elizabeth, Countess of Effingham *c.* 1797–99

NATIONAL GALLERY OF ART, WASHINGTON, D.C.

Oil on canvas: 57¾ × 45½ in. (146.5 × 115.5 cm.)

Signed lower right: *B. West*

PROV: As for No. 594 (lot 77 in the Hamilton sale, Christie's, London, 6–7 Nov. 1919)

EXH: *Portraits by Early American Artists of the 17th, 18th, & 19th Centuries Collected by Thomas B. Clarke*, Philadelphia Museum of Art, 1928 (158)

LIT: Lansdown 1893, p. 9; Hamilton-Phillips 1981, pp. 158–67, fig. 5

See Nos. 592 and 594. No. 615 shows Elizabeth (1725–1791), a daughter of Peter Beckford, the Speaker of the House of Assembly in Jamaica. She was the sister of Alderman Beckford and aunt of William Beckford, the builder of Fonthill Abbey and West's patron. Her first husband was Thomas Howard, second Earl of Effingham (1714–1763). Following his death, she married his kinsman Field-Marshal Sir George Howard (died 1796).

Like Nos. 592, 593 and 594, this painting is a posthumous portrait, which West probably based on an earlier portrait of the sitter by Andrea Casali at Fonthill House. It is included in the inventory of Beckford's property made after his death and was mentioned along with No. 594 among the pictures seen by a visitor to Beckford in Bath in 1838.

613

Grizzel, Daughter of the 2ⁿᵈ President Dundas.

614

615

616

A preparatory drawing is in the British Museum.[1]
That drawing does not include the coronet which is so
conspicuously displayed in No. 615 and has drapery in
the upper left corner. *Pentimenti* in the sky of the painting indicate that it originally had drapery in the upper
left corner and possibly across the entire background.

[1]Black and white chalk on blue paper, $17\frac{3}{8} \times 11\frac{1}{2}$ in.
(Hamilton-Phillips 1981, fig. 10).

616 James Veitch, Lord Eliock 1777

FACULTY OF ADVOCATES, EDINBURGH

Oil on canvas: $29\frac{1}{4} \times 24\frac{3}{4}$ in. (74.3×62.9 cm.)

Signed upper left: *B. West/1777*

PROV: By descent in the family of the sitter to David
Somerwell, Gilminscroft, Ayrshire, by whom presented to the Faculty of Advocates in 1975

James Veitch (1712–1793) of Edinburgh, took the title
of Lord Eliock when appointed a judge in 1761. In
No. 616 he is shown wearing the robes of a senator of
the College of Justice.

617

617 Harry Fetherstonhaugh c. 1772

THE PROVOST AND FELLOWS OF ETON COLLEGE

Oil on canvas: 30 × 25 in. (76 × 63.5 cm.)

PROV: Presented to the Headmaster of Eton by the
sitter

EXH: *Eton Leaving Portraits*, Tate Gallery, London, 1951
(25)

LIT: Cust 1910, p. 18 (21), pl. VIII

Harry Fetherstonhaugh (1754–1846) of Uppark in Sussex was the son of Sir Matthew Fetherstonhaugh, Bt.,
whose baronetcy he inherited in 1774. He is perhaps
best known as the protector in 1780–81 of Emma Hart,
the future Lady Hamilton. He was at Eton from 1766
to 1772, and No. 617 is a so-called Eton leaving
portrait, presented by students to the Headmaster on
the occasion of their leaving the school. Two other leaving portraits by West are Nos. 656 and 724.

A copy of No. 617 is at Uppark,[1] where there are
also portraits of Sir Harry by Nathaniel Dance and
Pompeo Batoni.[2] A second version at Uppark of
another picture by West apparently depicts Joshua
Iremonger, a relative (see Nos. 644 and 645).

[1] Oil on canvas: 29½ × 24½ in.
[2] The latter, dated *1776*, is reproduced as the frontispiece of
Uppark and its People, by Margaret Meade-Fetherstonhaugh
and Oliver Warner, London, 1964, which contains an
account of Sir Harry's life.

618 Benjamin Franklin c. 1816–17
See color illustration, p. 140

PHILADELPHIA MUSEUM OF ART

Oil on paper on canvas: 13¼ × 10 in. (33.5 × 25.5 cm.)

PROV: Sold by Mrs. Albert F. West, Christie's,

London, 19 March 1898, lot 140 ("Benjamin
Franklin Discovering Electricity; attended by
Cupids," 13¼ × 10 in.), bt. by Obach for £19.19.0.;
Godefroy Mayer, Paris, by 20 April 1898, and still
in his possession in 1910; Kennedy and Co., New
York; Mr. and Mrs. Wharton Sinkler, Philadelphia,
by whom given to the Philadelphia Museum of Art
in 1958

EXH: Philadelphia 1938 (56); *Life in America*,
Metropolitan Museum of Art, New York, 1939 (34);
Life in Philadelphia, Philadelphia Museum of Art,
1940 (66); *Franklin Portraits*, Philadelphia Museum
of Art, 1948; *From Colony to Nation*, Art Institute
of Chicago, 1949 (131); *Benjamin Franklin: Exhibition of
Portraits Marking the 250th Anniversary of the Birth of the
Society's Founder*, American Philosophical Society,
Philadelphia, 1956 (35)

LIT: Dunlap 1834, I, p. 86 (Dunlap 1918, I, p. 95);
Tuckerman 1867, p. 101; Lilian M. C. Randall, ed.,
*The Diary of George A. Lucas: An American Art Agent
in Paris, 1857–1909*, Princeton, 1979, II, p. 861 (entry
for 20 April 1898); Godefroy Mayer, *No. 30: Old
Paintings, Drawings, Miniatures* (dealer's catalogue),
Paris, 1910, p. 15 (83); John Clyde Oswald, *Benjamin
Franklin in Oil and Bronze*, New York, 1926, pp. 26–
27; Sellers 1962, pp. 401–2, pl. 35; H. L. W.
[Hobart Lyle Williams], "Benjamin Franklin Draw-
ing Electricity from the Sky," *Philadelphia Museum of
Art Bulletin*, LX, 1964–65, pp. 36–37

No. 618 is a sketch for a never-realized painting that
West intended to paint and present to the Pennsylvania
Hospital as a companion to *Christ Healing the Sick* (see
Nos. 336 and 338), and it is referred to in a letter from
Charles Robert Leslie about West's gift to the hospital
(quoted by Dunlap):

I can bear witness of his great satisfaction, when he
heard that the exhibition of it [No. 338] had so much
benefitted the institution. He had begun his own
portrait to present to the hospital. It was a whole
length on a mahogany panel; he employed me to
dead color it for him. He had also made a small
sketch of a picture of Dr. Franklin, to present with
it. The doctor was seated on the clouds, surrounded
by naked boys, and the experiment of proving lightning and electricity to be the same was alluded to.

The two portraits were evidently the two pictures envisioned by West in a letter of March 1816 as hanging
over two fireplaces in the room housing *Christ Healing
the Sick*.[1] For the self-portrait, see No. 531.

The experiment of proving the identity of lightning
and electricity, referred to by Leslie, took place in June
1752. Instructions about how to conduct such an
experiment were published by Franklin in the *Pennsylvania Gazette*, on 19 October 1752, and a description
of the actual experiment, based on what Franklin had
told him, was published by Joseph Priestley in 1767.[2]
The main incident shown in No. 618, the spark of electricity passing from a key attached to a kite string to
Franklin's raised knuckle is mentioned in both sources.
Franklin's features in No. 618 are, according to Sellers,
based on an engraving or copy after a miniature
portrait by Jean-Baptiste Weyler painted c. 1782.[3]
Needless to say, the *putti* and Franklin's situation on
a cloud are West's invention. The actual experiment
took place under the protection of a shed in a field near
Philadelphia, and Franklin was assisted in it by his son
William Franklin, who was then in his twenties.

West evidently had some contact with Franklin in
Philadelphia (see No. 619) prior to Franklin's
departure for England in 1757. Both men were living
in London between 1765 and 1775, and Franklin was
godfather to West's second son born in 1772. West,
however, never seems to have painted him from life,
and the only other portrait of Franklin by West, in the
Signing of the Preliminary Treaty of Peace in 1782 (No. 105),

is based on a portrait by Joseph Siffred Duplessis. A portrait of Franklin lent to the British Institution in 1846 and 1859 by the Earl of Yarborough and identified on both occasions as by West, is a copy of the portrait by David Martin (1737–1798) now in the White House. West's authorship of the copy is accepted by Sellers on the basis of a misinterpretation of a statement by the engraver Edward Savage, who published a mezzotint after the Martin portrait, but there is no real evidence or reason to believe that either the former Yarborough copy (which subsequently belonged to John D. Rockefeller, Jr.) or another copy in the collection of the Earl Stanhope was executed by West.[4] Other portraits at one time ascribed to West are discussed by Sellers.[5]

[1] See No. 338.
[2] Leonard W. Labaree and Whitfield J. Bell, Jr., eds., *The Papers of Benjamin Franklin*, IV, New Haven, 1961, pp. 366–69.
[3] Sellers 1962, pp. 404–8.
[4] Ibid., pp. 336–39.
[5] Ibid., pp. 402–4.

619 Sarah Franklin (Mrs. Richard Bache)
1756–57

LOCATION UNKNOWN

LIT: Sellers 1962, pp. 47, 52; Leonard W. Labaree and Whitfield J. Bell, Jr., eds., *The Papers of Benjamin Franklin*, VII, New Haven and London, 1963, p. 278, n. 4, and ibid., VIII, 1965, pp. 91–92; Marks, 1974, pp. 26–27

Sarah Franklin (1744–1808), later Mrs. Richard Bache, was the daughter of Benjamin Franklin, generally referred to by her father as Sally. Franklin's household accounts, which are quoted by Sellers, show entries, dated 1756 or 1757 by Sellers, for payments to West: one for £2.10.0. to "B. West for drawing Sally's Picture" and a second for the same amount. Franklin left Philadelphia to become agent for the province of Pennsylvania in London in the spring of 1757, and the likeness commissioned from West was evidently intended to be a reminder of his daughter which he could take with him. This may have been the portrait referred to by Franklin in a letter to his wife written from London on 10 June 1758: "I fancy I see more likeness in her Picture than I did at first, and look at it often with Pleasure, as at least it reminds me of her." The less than whole-hearted enthusiasm on the part of Franklin for the portrait, which is evident from this letter, has been taken by Sellers as an explanation of why there is no portrait painted from life by West of his distinguished compatriot. It also explains why as early as the autumn of 1757 Franklin had commissioned a second portrait of Sally by John Hesselius, which was to be sent to him in London.[1] Hesselius's portrait, like West's, has disappeared.

[1] This portrait is referred to in letters of 22 Nov. 1757 and 10 June 1758, published in Labaree and Bell, VII, p. 278, and VIII, pp. 91–92.

620 Robert Fulton 1806
See color illustration, p. 153

NEW YORK STATE HISTORICAL ASSOCIATION, COOPERSTOWN, NEW YORK

Oil on canvas: $35\frac{1}{2} \times 27\frac{1}{2}$ in. (90 × 70 cm.)

Signed lower right: *B. West/1806* and less distinctly on the balustrade to the left of the sitter

PROV: Given by West to the sitter, who brought the picture to the United States in 1806; by descent in the family of Mrs. William Cutting (sister of the wife of the sitter) to Robert Fulton Cutting; Macbeth Gallery, New York; acquired by the New York State Historical Association in 1947

EXH: (?) PAFA 1807; AAFA 1816 (46) lent by Mrs. Fulton; AAFA 1821 (51), 1825 (20), 1826 (56); *From Colony to Nation*, Art Institute of Chicago, 1949 (132); Amherst 1950; *An Albany Microcosm*, Albany Institute of History and Art, Albany, New York, 1957; New York 1962 (3); Washington and Philadelphia 1980

ENGR: Engraving ($4\frac{7}{8} \times 3\frac{7}{8}$ in.) by W. S. Leney, pub. by Joseph Delaplaine, Philadelphia, 1815, and included in *Delaplaine's Repository of the Lives and Portraits of Distinguished Americans*, I, part II, Philadelphia, 1817, opp. p. 201

LISTED: *BA*, p. 19 ("The half length portrait of R. Fulton, Esq., in the Academy at Philadelphia"); Dillenberger, p. 187 (489)

LIT: Cadwallader D. Colden, *The Life of Robert Fulton*, New York, 1817, p. 10; *Delaplaine's Repository of the Lives and Portraits of Distinguished Americans*, Philadelphia, 1817, pp. 203–4; Dunlap 1834, I, p. 231 (Dunlap 1918, I, p. 273); H. W. Dickinson, *Robert Fulton: Engineer and Artist: His Life and Works*, London and New York, 1913, p. 278; Thomas Addis Emmet, "Note XVIII: History of the Portraits of Robert Fulton Painted by Miss Elizabeth Emmet while his Pupil, and Since Falsely Credited to Benjamin West," in *Memoir of Thomas Addis and Robert Emmet*, New York, 1915, II, pp. 523–27; R. W. G. Vail, "The Robert Fulton Portrait," *Proceedings of the American Antiquarian Society*, XLV, 1935, pp. 183–92; *American Collector*, XVI, 1947, frontispiece and p. 4; Morgan and Toole, 1950, p. 214

Robert Fulton (1765–1815), a native of Pennsylvania, lived in England from 1786 to 1797 and again from 1804 to 1806. He came originally as an artist and, during his first stay in London, became both a student and close friend of West. Around 1793 or 1794 he gave up painting to devote himself to his scientific interests, and when he returned to London from France, where he had lived from 1797 to 1804, he came as the inventor of a torpedo, which he hoped to sell to the British government. No. 620, which shows a ship being blown up in the left background, records a successful demonstration of the effectiveness of Fulton's torpedoes, which took place at Walmer Roads, near Deal on 15 October 1805.[1]

According to the biography of Fulton by Cadwallader D. Colden published in 1817, No. 620 and a second picture showing West painting a portrait of Mrs. West (see No. 530) were given to Fulton by West and brought to America when Fulton returned to his native land in October 1806. In May 1805 Fulton had purchased two large and important pictures by Benjamin West (Nos. 207 and 210) and one by Raphael West, all painted originally for the Boydell Shakespeare Gallery, and it was announced at the time that they had been bought "for the Museum at Philadelphia." West retouched the pictures for Fulton in September 1806[2] and probably painted No. 620 at the same time, when the two men must have had frequent and close contact. Upon his return Fulton did place Nos. 207 and 210 on loan in the Pennsylvania Academy of the Fine Arts in Philadelphia, where they remained until after his death.[3] They are listed as there in *La Belle Assemblée*, published in 1808. No. 620 and the self-portrait given by West to Fulton (No. 530) immediately follow Nos. 207 and 210 in the *Belle Assemblée* list and are both described as "in ditto." However, these pictures, unlike Nos. 207 and 210, do not appear in exhibition cata-

logues published annually by the Pennsylvania Academy from 1811 onwards; thus it seems that if Fulton lent the portraits to the Academy after his return to America in 1806, he soon took them back into his own possession. The loan or promised loan of the two large paintings led to West's being elected the first honorary member of the Pennsylvania Academy, which had been founded in 1805, and to Fulton being elected the second. Subsequently, Fulton continued to exert himself for West, proposing in 1807 and again in 1810 that the Academy should form or acquire collections of West's works, in the latter year even devising an elaborate scheme of fund-raising to pay for the undertaking.[4] Hence, while Colden states that Nos. 620 and 530 "were offerings of friendship, and were made and received as tokens of the attachment formed between the family of that great painter and his young friend at an early day ...," it can be seen that Fulton generously reciprocated by his activities on West's behalf.

A second version (No. 621), whose later history may be confused with that of No. 620,[5] was sold by West's heirs in 1829. Several copies of the composition, often with slight changes in detail, are known. A miniature, purportedly painted by Fulton himself, is in the New-York Historical Society in New York City. An engraving inscribed *Miss Emmett Pinxit* and *W. S. Leney Sculpsit*, which shows a different type of vessel and no explosion in the left background, served as frontispiece to Colden's life of Fulton published in 1817. This would appear to have been made after a painting now in the American Antiquarian Society in Worcester, Massachusetts. "Miss Emmett" was Elizabeth Emmet, an amateur artist and daughter of one of Fulton's lawyers, Thomas Addis Emmet. In 1915 her nephew, also named Thomas Addis Emmet, argued with considerable passion that Miss Emmet painted her portrait of Fulton from life in 1814 and that No. 620 and all other versions of the composition were based on it. Although accepted by R. W. G. Vail, this argument is untenable; the existence of West's portrait prior to 1814 is documented, and Miss Emmet almost certainly copied her picture from No. 620 while it was in Fulton's possession. The same W. S. Leney was responsible both for the engraving after No. 620 which appeared in *Delaplaine's Repository* in 1817 and for that after Miss Emmet's copy in Colden's biography published in the same year. The two engravings are almost identical in size, and, apart from the different backgrounds, they are so similar in appearance that Thomas Addis Emmet argued that they were from the same plate. Close examination of the two, however, reveals slight differences in almost every line and establishes that the two prints must have been made from different plates. Miss Emmet's copy, which initially belonged to Colden, was later ascribed to John Wesley Jarvis until identified by Vail in 1935. It served as the model for a statue of Fulton erected before the Fulton Ferry House in Brooklyn in 1873.[6]

[1] See Colden, pp. 58–60 and Dickinson, pp. 192–94.
[2] A letter from Fulton to Joel Barlow in September 1806, mentions that "Mr. West has been retouching my pictures," quoted by Dickinson, pp. 199–200.
[3] Rutledge 1955, p. 249.
[4] Thomas B. Brumbaugh, "The Pennsylvania Academy's Early Days: A Letter of George Clymer to Robert Fulton," *Pennsylvania Magazine of History and Biography*, XCII, 1968, pp. 384–86.
[5] The provenances of both pictures given here are those published by R. W. G. Vail in 1935 on the basis of correspondence with Mrs. Alice Crary Sutcliffe, a great-granddaughter of Robert Fulton.
[6] Reproduced in Alice Crary Sutcliffe, "Fulton's Invention of the Steamboat," *Century Magazine*, LXXVIII, Oct. 1909, p. 825. In this sculpture, by M. J. Seelig & Co., Fulton is standing, rather than seated, and leaning on a model of the *Nassau*, his first steam ferry-boat.

623

Jane Galloway was certainly "very young" in February 1758, but it is questionable if she would have been referred to as a "lady" at the age of twelve or thirteen, and if she would have been thought of as belonging to the same age group as West and her future husband, who were seven and thirteen years older respectively. Furthermore, the quasi-erotic imagery of parts of the poem ("And from such lips nectareous sweets must flow") is so dubiously appropriate for a subject of such tender years, that it seems unlikely that this painting did in fact inspire the poem. For another, more likely, possibility see No. 701 below.

[1] See Theodore Hornberger, "Mr. Hicks of Philadelphia," *Pennsylvania Magazine of History and Biography*, LIII, 1929, pp. 343–51. The attribution to Shippen goes back to 1842, but is questioned by Hornberger, who cites evidence that the author was a Mr. Hicks. Other possible authors that have been suggested are Francis Hopkinson and Thomas Godfrey. See Alberts 1978, p. 23.

623 Sir Sampson Gideon, Bt. (later Lord Eardley) 1764

LOCATION UNKNOWN

Oil on canvas: 49 × 39 in. (124.5 × 99 cm.)

Signed lower left: *B. West 1764*

PROV: By descent in the family of the sitter to Sir Francis Fremantle, Bedwell Park, Hertfordshire (1872–1943); sold, Christie's, London, 14 Dec. 1945, lot 35; sold anonymously, Christie's, London, 26 March 1952, lot 102; the Old Print Shop, New York, in 1957

LIT: Waagen 1857, p. 281

Sampson Gideon (1745–1824), the subject of No. 623, was the son of Sampson Gideon (1699–1762), a wealthy Jewish financier who provided significant service to the British government in the 1740s and 1750s. The elder Sampson Gideon's wish to be made a baronet was frustrated because of his religion, but in compensation his son, who was brought up as a Christian, received a baronetcy in 1759 at the age of thirteen. Sir Sampson married in 1766 the daughter of Sir John Eardley Wilmot, Chief Justice of the Common Pleas (she was the sister of the subject of No. 718); in July 1789 he took the surname of Eardley; and in September 1789 he was created Baron Eardley of Spalding.

Sir Sampson, who wears student dress and rests his left hand upon a book in No. 623, was nineteen years old and a student at Lincoln's Inn at the time the picture was painted. The painting appears to have been the first of several portraits of students in academic robes painted by West in the 1760s (others are Nos. 600 and 608). West painted No. 623 at approximately the same time as his portrait of Andrew Allen (No. 583) and the group portrait of *The Cricketers* (Nos. 726 and 727). Andrew Allen and his younger brother James were students at the Middle Temple at the same time Sir Sampson was at Lincoln's Inn, and it may have been via the Allens, with whom West had a longstanding connection from Philadelphia, that he received the commission for No. 623.

No. 623 was seen and described by Gustav Waagen in 1857 as part of the rich collection of paintings, chiefly acquired by the elder Sampson Gideon, at Belvedere, near Erith in Kent.

624 Jane, Lady Grant (?)1777

PRIVATE COLLECTION

Oil on canvas: 49 × 40 in. (124.5 × 102 cm.)

(?) Signed and dated: *1772*

PROV: By family descent

621 Robert Fulton *c.* 1806

LOCATION UNKNOWN

PROV: Sold by West's sons, Robins, London, 20–22 June 1829, lot 143 ("Portrait of the late Mr. Fulton, the celebrated Engineer"), bt. by Charles Blight (son-in-law of Robert Fulton); by family descent to Robert Fulton Ludlow

622 Jane Galloway (Mrs. Joseph Shippen) *c.* 1757

See color illustration, p. 7

HISTORICAL SOCIETY OF PENNSYLVANIA, PHILADELPHIA

Oil on canvas: 49¾ × 39¼ in. (126.5 × 99.5 cm.)

PROV: By descent in the Shippen family to Elizabeth Swift Shippen, by whom presented to the Historical Society of Pennsylvania in 1914

EXH: PAFA 1824 (4), and 1825 (5); Allentown 1962 (3); *Three Centuries of American Art*, Philadelphia Museum of Art, 1976 (56)

LIT: Thomas Balch, *Letters and Papers Relating Chiefly to the Provincial History of Pennsylvania*, Philadelphia, 1855, pp. xxv–xxvi; Sawitzky 1938, pp. 442, 445 (17) ill.; Sawitzky 1942, p. 43; ill. p. 225; Charles Coleman Sellers, *Charles Willson Peale*, Philadelphia, 1947, II, pp. 362–65; Wainwright 1974, p. 80, ill. opp. p. 20; Richardson 1978, p. 6, note 5; Alberts 1978, p. 24

Jane Galloway (1745–1801) became in 1768 the wife of Joseph Shippen (1732–1810), with whom West travelled to Italy in 1760.

Sawitzky dates No. 622 *c.* 1757, when the sitter would have been approximately twelve years old. It has been suggested that the painting was the "Portrait of Miss **—** by Mr. West," apostrophized in verse in the *American Magazine* in February 1758 by an anonymous writer signing himself "Lovelace," who supposedly was Joseph Shippen.[1] This poem was prefaced by a note stating "The lady who sat, the painter who guided the pencil, and the poet who so well described the whole are all natives of this place and very young."

624

EXH: *Artist and Patron in the North East 1700–1860*, Aberdeen Art Gallery, 1975 (13)

The sitter was the widow of Andrew Millar of London. In 1770 she became the fourth wife of Sir Archibald Grant, second Baronet, of Monymusk, Aberdeenshire (1696–1778). She died in October 1788. A label on the reverse of No. 624 notes that she was "rich but noted for the infirmity of her temper."

Although No. 624 has been recorded as signed and dated *1772*, a somewhat later date seems more likely. A label on the frame gives the date as 1777, in which year West also painted No. 612, a double portrait of Sir Archibald Grant's niece, Mrs. Dundas, with her daughter Grizzel.

625 George Harry Grey, Lord Grey (later the Fifth Earl of Stamford) 1765

PRIVATE COLLECTION

Oil on canvas: 49¼ × 39⅜ in. (125 × 100 cm.)

Signed lower right: *B. West 1765*

625

626

627

PROV: By descent in the Grey family to Sir John Foley Grey, Bt., Enville Hall, Staffordshire, by whom sold, Christie's, London, 15 June 1928, lot 120, bt. by Martin; sold by Daniel H. Farr, Plaza Galleries, New York, 23 March 1935, lot 76; sold anonymously, Christie's, London, 31 May 1935, lot 106, bt. by Meatyard; Mrs. E. Lovette West, Bronxville, New York

LIT: St. John Gore, "Portraits and the Grand Tour," *Apollo*, CVIII, July 1978, p. 29

George Harry Grey (1737–1819), who bore the title Lord Grey when West painted him, succeeded his father as fifth Earl of Stamford in 1768. He was in Rome in 1760 and he may have been acquainted with West from that time. A double portrait of the sitter and his travelling companion Sir Henry Mainwaring painted by Nathaniel Dance in Rome in 1760 was sold by Sir John Foley Grey in 1928 at the same time as No. 625.[1] His wife, whom he married in 1763, was a Cavendish-Bentinck, the daughter of the second Duke of Portland and sister of the third Duke whose portrait West also was to paint (see Nos. 683 and 684). Hence it is also possible that the commission for No. 625 was a consequence of West's ice-skating virtuosity, since Galt mentions "some of the Cavendishes" among the audience whose admiration for his exploits on the ice in Kensington Gardens led to his encouragement as a portrait-painter.

Two other portraits by West which were also sold in 1928, and which are here tentatively identified as portraits of the fifth Earl's younger brothers, are Nos. 626 and 627 below. A portrait of the fifth Earl's wife, which has been traditionally ascribed to West, is at Dunham Massey, the home of the Grey family. That painting is approximately the same size as a portrait of the subject of No. 625 by or attributed to Mengs, in the same collection (ill. p. 17), and was evidently painted as a companion piece.[2] It is less precise in handling than No. 625 and does not appear to be by West.

[1] See *Nathaniel Dance 1735–1811*, the Iveagh Bequest, Kenwood, London, 1977, no. 4.
[2] Galt 1820, pp. 26–31.
[3] Illustrated *Apollo*, CVIII, 1978, p. 29, fig. 9. The portrait of the Countess of Stamford has dimensions of 37½ × 28 in. Those of Mengs's portrait are 38 × 29 in. Dunham Massey now belongs to the National Trust.

626 [?] **Booth Grey** *c.* 1765–66

SWARTHMORE COLLEGE, SWARTHMORE, PENNSYLVANIA

Oil on canvas: 29½ × 24½ in. (75 × 62 cm.)

PROV: By descent in the Grey family to Sir John Foley Grey, Bt., Enville Hall, Staffordshire, by whom sold, Christie's, London, 15 June 1928, lot 122 (as "Portrait of an Officer"), bt. by Leger; Howard Young Galleries, New York; Mrs. E. Lovette West, Bronxville, New York, by whom given to Swarthmore College in 1944

No. 626 is one of three paintings by West sold by John Foley Grey in 1928. One was identified in the sale catalogue as a portrait of George Harry Grey, the fifth Earl of Stamford (No. 625). The other two (Nos. 626 and

627) were not identified at the time of the sale, but the former has since been described as a portrait of Booth Grey (1740–1802), a younger brother of the fifth Earl. If this identification is valid, No. 627 probably represents a third brother, John Grey (1743–1802). No signature or date is visible on No. 626, but No. 627 is recorded as having been signed and dated *1766*, a year later than the date on No. 625, West's portrait of the Earl. Whereas No. 625 measures approximately 50 × 40 in., Nos. 626 and 627 share a smaller size and would appear to have been painted as companion pictures. Although we have not been able to ascertain exactly when or why No. 626 was first identified as Booth Grey after being sold as an unidentified portrait, the identification seems plausible both on the grounds of the picture's provenance and because of the similarities in the features of the sitter with those of his putative elder brother in No. 625.

627 [?] **John Grey** (?)1766

LOCATION UNKNOWN

Oil on canvas: 29 × 24½ in. (73.5 × 62 cm.)

(?) Signed and dated: *1766*

PROV: By descent in the Grey family to Sir John Foley Grey, Bt., Enville Hall, Staffordshire, by whom sold, Christie's, London, 15 June 1928, lot 121 (as "A Gentleman"), bt. by Martin

See No. 626. Although No. 627 was described as signed and dated *1766* when sold in 1928, no signature or date is discernible on a photograph made at that time.

628

628 Sir John Griffin Griffin *c.* 1772

DEPARTMENT OF THE ENVIRONMENT, AUDLEY END, ESSEX

Oil on canvas: 67 × 51 in. (170 × 129.5 cm.)

PROV: By descent in the family of the sitter's third cousin and heir, Richard Neville, second Lord Braybrooke (1750–1825); purchased by the Department of the Environment in 1971

LIT: Richard, Lord Braybrooke, *The History of Audley End*, London, 1836, p. 118; Department of the Environment, *Audley End, Essex*, London, 1958, p. 26; R. J. B. Walker, *Audley End: Catalogue of the Pictures in the State Rooms*, London, 1973, p. 21 (1)

Sir John Griffin Griffin (1719–1797) was born John Griffin Whitwell and changed his surname to Griffin in 1749, when he became heir to the Griffin properties, including the estate of Audley End. In 1784 he successfully claimed the dormant barony of Howard de Walden, becoming fourth Lord Howard de Walden, and in 1788 he was also created first Baron Braybrooke. He was a distinguished soldier, who served in the War of the Austrian Succession and in the Seven Years' War. At the time West painted him, he was a lieutenant-general. In 1796, the year before his death, he became a field marshal. No. 628 shows him in his tent in general's uniform and wearing the star of the Order of the Bath, which he had received in 1761. A full-length portrait of the sitter wearing the robes of the

Order of the Bath by Biagio Rebecca (1735–1808) is also at Audley End.

Portraits by West of Sir John Griffin Griffin's two wives are Nos. 629 and 630 below. The artist's receipt, dated 26 March 1772, and for 140 guineas, is in the Braybrooke archives: "Received of Sir John Griffin for painting a whole-length portrait of himself, a kitkat of his Lady and ditto of his late Lady."[1] A manuscript inventory dated August 1797, cited by Walker, describes the three portraits as in the ground-floor library designed by Robert Adam at the eastern end of the south wing of Audley End, with No. 628 over the fireplace and Nos. 629 and 630 over the doors. Since *c.* 1830 the three paintings have been over the fireplace and the two doors of the South Library on the first floor of the same house.

[1] Quoted from the Walker catalogue. The Braybrooke archives are deposited in the Essex Record Office, Chelmsford.

629 Anna Maria, Lady Griffin *c.* 1772

DEPARTMENT OF THE ENVIRONMENT, AUDLEY END, ESSEX

Oil on canvas: 35 × 42 in. (89 × 106.5 cm.)

PROV: As for No. 628

LIT: As for No. 628 (Walker, p. 21, no. 2)

See No. 628. No. 629 is a posthumous portrait of the first wife of Sir John Griffin Griffin. They were married *c.* 1749, and she died in 1764 at the age of forty-two. She was the daughter of a Colonel John Schutz and granddaughter of Baron von Schutz who had come to England with George I.

In West's receipt of 1772 for the three portraits at Audley End (quoted under No. 628), Nos. 629 and 630 are listed only as kitkats of Sir John's first and second wives. They are described in the third Lord Braybrooke's *History of Audley End*, published in 1836, as in the costumes of the sibyls of Domenichino and Guercino. No. 629 appears to be based loosely, and in reverse, upon the painting by Domenichino of the *Cumaean Sibyl* in the Galleria Borghese in Rome. West had painted a copy (No. 506) after the Domenichino *Sibyl* while in Rome in 1761, but since that copy went straight from Italy to America, it would not have served him as a model while painting No. 629 a decade later.

630 Catherine, Lady Griffin *c.* 1772

DEPARTMENT OF THE ENVIRONMENT, AUDLEY END, ESSEX

Oil on canvas: 35 × 42 in. (89 × 106.5 cm.)

PROV: As for No. 628

LIT: As for No. 628 (Walker, p. 22, no. 7)

See Nos. 628 and 629. No. 630 shows the second wife of Sir John Griffin Griffin, whom he married in 1765. She was born in 1747, the daughter of William Clayton of Harleyford, Buckinghamshire, and she died in 1809. In 1784 she became Lady Howard de Walden, when her husband succeeded to that title.

West based No. 630 upon the painting by Guercino of the *Persian Sibyl* in the Capitoline Museum in Rome (*opposite*). Unlike No. 629, which has only a loose similarity to its compositional source, No. 630 is virtually a copy after the Guercino, with no significant departures in composition or detail apart from the features of the sitter and the change in proportion of the canvas from vertical to horizontal.

631 Richard, Lord Grosvenor, later first Earl Grosvenor *c.*1771

COUNCIL OF THE CITY OF CHESTER, ENGLAND

Oil on canvas: 96 × 57 in. (244 × 145 cm.)

PROV: Presented by the sitter to the corporation of Chester

ENGR: Mezzotint (21¾ × 14⅞ in.) by W. Dickinson, inscribed *The Right Honourable Lord Grosvenor, Mayor of the City of Chester, 1760, and Mayor of the Royal Cheshire Militia*

LISTED: *PC*, p. 562 ("A whole length portrait of the late Lord Grosvenor"); *UM*, p. 528; *BA*, p. 15; Galt, p. 222; Dillenberger, p. 157 (189)

LIT: Joseph Hemingway, *History of the City of Chester*, Chester, 1831, II, p. 187

Richard Grosvenor (1731–1802) succeeded to his father's baronetcy in 1755, became Baron Grosvenor of Eaton in 1761, and Earl Grosvenor and Viscount Belgrave in 1784. He was one of West's most important patrons, owning at least ten works by the artist in addition to No. 631 and its companion No. 632.

The sitter was Mayor of Chester in 1759–60 and Member of Parliament for the city from 1754 to 1761, when he was raised to the peerage. His younger brother Thomas Grosvenor, whom West depicted in No. 632, succeeded him as Mayor and was M.P. for Chester from 1755 to 1795. The minutes of the Chester City Assembly for 23 October 1760 record that the two brothers were to be asked to present their portraits to the corporation to hang in the Court Room of the Exchange.[1] According to Joseph Hemingway's history of Chester, published in 1831, the pictures were painted in 1771,

629

Guercino, *The Persian Sibyl*. Oil on canvas, Museo Capitolino, Rome

630

631

632 (detail)

a date for which there seems to be no confirming evidence, but which is plausible on stylistic grounds. Since West did not arrive in England until 1763, he obviously could not have undertaken the pictures at the time they were initially requested by the Assembly. In 1831 the two portraits hung in the council room in the Exchange, accompanying a portrait of George III presented to the corporation by the second Earl Grosvenor. The Exchange was destroyed by fire in 1862, and the two paintings now hang in the Assembly Room of the present Chester Town Hall together with additional portraits of descendants of the first Earl.

The two pictures show the brothers in full dress robes as mayors of Chester, displaying the emblematic trappings of office. In No. 631 Lord Grosvenor stands before a bust inscribed with the name of Hugh Lupus, the first Norman Earl of Chester and ancestor of the Grosvenor family. In the background is part of Chester Castle, which was traditionally believed to have been erected by William the Conqueror in 1069 and to have been Hugh Lupus's seat.

A preparatory drawing, which shows numerous differences in detail but is basically similar in pose and composition, was sold by Mrs. F. Howard in 1979.[2]

[1]Chester City Record Office, Ref. AB/4 f. 186. We are indebted to Miss Annette M. Kensett, the Chester City Archivist, for this and other information about the two paintings (letter of 29 April 1981).
[2]Pencil, pen and brown ink, 13¼ × 9 in., sold, Sotheby's, London, 22 March 1979, lot 2.

632 Thomas Grosvenor of Swell Court c. 1771

COUNCIL OF THE CITY OF CHESTER, ENGLAND

Oil on canvas: 96 × 57 in. (244 × 145 cm.)

PROV: Presented by the sitter to the City of Chester

LIT: As for No. 631

No. 632 is a companion picture to No. 631. The subject is the younger brother of Richard, first Earl Grosvenor, the subject of No. 631. He served as Mayor of Chester in 1760–61 and as M.P. for Chester from 1755 to 1795.

633 Governor James Hamilton 1767

INDEPENDENCE NATIONAL HISTORICAL PARK, PHILADELPHIA

Oil on canvas: 95 × 61 in. (241 × 155 cm.)

Signed lower left: *B. West pinxit London/1767*

PROV: By collateral descent to the son-in-law of Mrs. James Lyle (see No. 634), Henry Beckett, Bordentown, New Jersey, by whom bequeathed in 1871 to the Spring Garden Institute, Philadelphia; presented by the Institute to the city of Philadelphia, and transferred to Independence Hall in 1892

EXH: Washington and Philadelphia 1980

LIT: Dunlap 1834, I, p. 101 (Dunlap 1918, I, p. 114); Tuckerman 1867, p. 101; Charles Henry Hart, letters to the Philadelphia *Times*, 6 Nov. 1892 and 3 Oct. 1894; Henderson 1911, pp. 326–29; Sellers 1939, p. 77; William Sawitzky, *Matthew Pratt 1734–1805*, New York, 1942, p. 82; Alberts 1978, pp. 75–76

James Hamilton (c. 1710–1783) served as Lieutenant-Governor of Pennsylvania from 1748 to 1754 and from 1759 to 1763. He was the brother-in-law of Chief Justice William Allen (see No. 581) and joined Judge Allen in commissioning copies from West in Italy, thus providing important financial support for the young

633

artist. West had earlier copied a painting in Hamilton's collection (see No. 512). Galt states that Hamilton was in England when West arrived in 1763, but that seems to be wrong.[1] He travelled to England in November 1765 to seek medical attention for a disorder on his nose that his physician feared might become cancerous, and he returned to Philadelphia in November 1767 in perfect health.[2]

No. 633 was on the easel in West's studio on 13 February 1767, when Charles Willson Peale arrived in London and called on West. Peale is said to have posed for the Governor's hand on the table in the painting.

In a letter quoted by William Dunlap, Thomas Sully mistook No. 633 for a work by Matthew Pratt, although it was, nonetheless, "a very worthy picture, and worthy to pass for one of West's." In 1867 Henry Tuckerman listed it among West's works, but Charles

Henry Hart reattributed it to Pratt in a letter to the Philadelphia *Times* in 1892. Hart subsequently corrected the mistake in a second letter in 1894, after cleaning had revealed West's signature. At the time No. 633 arrived at Independence Hall in 1892 it was evidently in extremely deteriorated condition. It underwent conservation in 1894 and again in 1918.

A half-length copy, which Sawitzky tentatively ascribed to Matthew Pratt, belonged in 1942 to Mrs. William D. Disston of Philadelphia. A half-length copy by William Cogswell and a bust-length copy by J. Augustus Beck are in the Historical Society of Pennsylvania.[3]

[1]Galt 1820, pp. 3–4.
[2]Walker 1897, pp. 62–63 and 71.
[3]Sawitzky 1942, pp. 54–55, and Wainwright 1974, pp. 89–90.

634

634 William Hamilton and His Niece Anna Hamilton 1785–1813

Oil on canvas: $92\frac{3}{4} \times 72$ in. (235.5 × 183 cm.)

Inscribed lower right: *This picture was begun/in 1785 and completed in/[?]1813/London Benjn West*

PROV: By descent in the family of Anna Hamilton (Mrs. James Lyle) to Charles Kuhn, by whom deposited with the Society in 1873

LIT: Hart 1908, pp. 26–27; Henderson 1911, pp. 345–46, ill. opp. p. 344; Sawitzky 1942, pp. 55–56; Wainwright 1974, pp. 90–91

William Hamilton (1745–1813) of the "Woodlands," in West Philadelphia is said by Sawitzky to have been a grandson of Governor James Hamilton (see No. 633), but since the latter never married this assertion is unlikely. He seems to have been a nephew of Governor Hamilton. His niece, born Anna Hamilton in 1769, married James Lyle in 1792 and died in 1798. William Hamilton never married.

The inscription on No. 634 is not entirely legible. Sawitzky read the date of completion as *1812* rather than *1813*. Apart from the inscription, our chief source of information for No. 634 is a letter dated 5 September 1810, from West to Robert Barclay, Hamilton's agent and banker in London.[1] The letter acknowledges that West had received Hamilton's instructions to complete the picture and indicates West's intention to repaint it all, except the faces, but not to charge Hamilton more than his prices had been when the picture was begun: sixty guineas for each of the two whole-length figures. West proposed sending the completed picture to America together with the first version of *Christ Healing the Sick* (No. 336), which he was painting for the Pennsylvania Hospital. Since that picture never went to America, and the replica (No. 338) was only sent in 1817, No. 634 probably went separately upon its completion in 1812 or 1813.

William Hamilton and his niece must have been in London in 1785, when West began No. 634. At that time Anna Hamilton would have been sixteen years old and still unmarried. When West took up the painting again in 1810 she had been dead for over a decade. West's letter to Robert Barclay indicates that he received no further sittings from William Hamilton in order to complete the picture and that the faces of both sitters remain as he had originally painted them. The Empire chair in the lower left corner and other details confirm that he did repaint the rest of the work as promised.

A drawing for the composition in the British Museum, which shows numerous differences in detail from the finished picture, must date from around 1785.[2]

[1]Hart 1908, pp. 26–27. The letter belongs to the Historical Society of Pennsylvania. Sawitzky and Wainwright record its date as 5 September 1811.
[2]Black and white chalk on beige paper: $10\frac{1}{4} \times 7\frac{1}{4}$ in. (1920-6-15–23).

635 Mrs. Richard Hare (Martha Harford Hare) 1775

Oil on canvas: $34\frac{1}{2} \times 27$ in. (87.5 × 68.5 cm.)

Signed lower left: *B. West, London, 1775*

PROV: By descent in the family of the sitter

EXH: Philadelphia 1936; Philadelphia 1938 (26) lent by Horace Binney Hare, Berwyn, Pennsylvania

635

LIT: Tuckerman 1867, p. 101

Martha Harford was born in Bath in 1720, became the second wife of Richard Hare in 1745, and died in 1786. In No. 635 she holds a letter inscribed *Philadelphia 1775*, which, according to family tradition, represents the letter sent to her by her son Robert Hare (1752–1811), who had travelled to Philadelphia in 1773, telling her that he intended to remain and make his home in America. According to that same tradition, No. 635 was painted for him and sent to him in Philadelphia.[1]

[1] Most of the information in this entry comes from the catalogue of the West exhibition in Philadelphia in 1938, where no source is given. It must, however, have come from the Hare family, in whose possession the picture has always remained.

636 Edward Hase 1768

PRIVATE COLLECTION

Oil on canvas: 29⅜ × 24⅜ in. (74.5 × 62 cm.)

636

Signed: *B. West pinxit. 1768*

PROV: By descent in the family of the sitter to the present owner

LIT: Duleep Singh 1927, II, p. 347

Edward Hase (1733–1804), of Salle in Norfolk, was the younger brother and heir of John Hase, who assumed the name of Lombe upon inheriting the estates of a maternal uncle and subsequently became Sir John Lombe, first Baronet. His daughter's son, in whose descendants' possession No. 636 remains, took the name Evans-Lombe.

637 William Henry (?) 1756

HISTORICAL SOCIETY OF PENNSYLVANIA, PHILADELPHIA

Oil on canvas: 36¾ × 30½ in. (93.5 × 77.5 cm.)

PROV: By descent in the family of the sitter to Elizabeth Henry Jordan (Mrs. John Jordan); presented by the Jordan family to the Historical Society of Pennsylvania in 1902

EXH: PAFA 1847 (274) lent by John Jordan, Jr.; Philadelphia 1938 (5)

LIT: Galt 1816, pp. 35–36; Francis Jordan, Jr., *The Life of William Henry*, Lancaster, 1910, pp. 27–28, ill. frontispiece; Henderson 1911, pp. 342–43; Landis 1925, pp. 57–58; Sawitzky 1938, pp. 437 and 448 (6); Sawitzky 1942, p. 61; Tinkcom 1951, p. 382 (Sir Augustus Foster); Flexner 1952, pp. 23–26; ill. opp. p. 24; Wainwright 1974, p. 111, ill. p. 38; Alberts 1978, p. 18

William Henry (1729–1786) was a gunsmith in Lancaster, Pennsylvania, at the time West painted him. He was also an inventor and was to become an important figure in the American revolutionary war. He commissioned the early *Death of Socrates* (No. 4) from West, and he named his youngest son, who was born in 1777, Benjamin West Henry. West told Nicholas Biddle in 1807 that Henry "might have made a great man,"[1] and, according to Galt, towards Henry West "always cherished the most grateful affection."[2]

West painted No. 637 and a companion portrait of Mrs. Henry (No. 638) during a visit to Lancaster, which probably took place in 1755–56. The Henrys were married on 8 March 1756, and it seems likely that West would have painted them after rather than before that event.[3] Although Galt's account of Henry's patronage of West is somewhat confusing, it seems to suggest that West's performance in Nos. 637 and 638 so impressed Henry that the latter told the young artist not to waste his time on portraits but to devote himself to history painting, thereupon proposing the subject of the *Death of Socrates*. Henry also acquired several further works by West. Sir Augustus Foster, a British diplomat who was taken to visit William Henry's son sometime between 1804 and 1812, reported seeing not only Nos. 637, 638, and 4, but also a portrait of an unidentified lady (see No. 690), a landscape (No. 483), and a self-portrait (No. 525). Foster also wrote that West's name was "annexed to all that I saw and the year 1756 faintly traced along side of it."

The rifle Henry holds is presumably one of his own manufactures. The castellated structure on the edge of a lake in the background has not been identified.

[1] Wainwright 1978, p. 111.
[2] Galt 1816, pp. 85–86.
[3] See Flexner 1952, p. 23; Jordan, repeated by Sawitzky, gives the date of the marriage as January 1755.

638 Mrs. William Henry (?) 1756

HISTORICAL SOCIETY OF PENNSYLVANIA, PHILADELPHIA

Oil on canvas: 36½ × 30½ in. (92.5 × 77.5 cm.)

PROV: As for No. 637

EXH: PAFA 1847 (275) lent by John Jordan, Jr.; Philadelphia 1938 (6)

LIT: Francis Jordan, Jr., *The Life of William Henry*, Lancaster, 1910, p. 28, ill. opp. p. 29; Henderson 1911, pp. 342–43; Landis 1925, pp. 57–58; Sawitzky 1938, pp. 437 and 448–49 (7); Sawitzky 1942, pp. 61–62; Tinkcom 1951, p. 382; Flexner 1952, pp. 23–26; Wainwright 1974, p. 111; Alberts 1978, p. 18

Ann Wood (1732 or 1734–1799) married William Henry (see No. 637) in 1756. West presumably painted Nos. 637 and 638 at the same time, not long after the couple were married. Sarah Ursula Rose, whom West also painted (No. 690), was Mrs. Henry's younger half-sister.

637

638

Lord Hood, engraving by William Angus after No. 639

639 Lord Hood *c.* 1760–63

LOCATION UNKNOWN

PROV: Sir John Dick, Bt. (1720–1804), in 1782

ENGR: Engraving ($5\frac{3}{4} \times 3\frac{1}{2}$ in.) by W. Angus, inscribed *Rt. Hon. LORD HOOD/From a Painting by West in the Possession of S^r. In^o. Dick*, pub. 1 July 1782 by I. Fielding, I. Sewell, and I. Debrett, in the *European Magazine*, I, for June 1782; line engraving by Birrell, pub. 1785 by I. Fielding

Samuel Hood (1724–1816), the distinguished naval commander, was raised to the peerage as Lord Hood following his brilliant victory and the surrender of the French Admiral de Grasse in the Battle of the Saints in the Caribbean in April 1782. In 1796 he became the first Viscount Hood.

No. 639 is known only through an engraving, which accompanied a biographical article about Hood that appeared in the *European Magazine* the month after the news of Hood's great victory reached England. Since Hood himself did not return to England during this period, the engraving must have been based on a portrait made before the Battle of the Saints made him a national hero. The inscription on the engraving provides the only documentary evidence connecting West to this portrait. Sir John Dick was the British Consul in Leghorn when West arrived in Italy in 1760, and as Hood was stationed in the Mediterranean from April 1760 to April 1763, it is likely that West painted

No. 639 at that time. The engraving is at least superficially reminiscent of West's portrait of Captain Charles Pierrepont Medows (No. 658), which bears an inscription stating that West painted it at Leghorn for Sir John Dick in 1761.

A portrait of Hood, which was lent to exhibitions in 1867 and 1891 by the fourth Viscount Hood as a work by West,[1] remains together with a companion portrait of Lady Hood in the possession of the present Lord Hood, but the two paintings are not, in our opinion, by West.

[1] *National Portrait Exhibition*, London, 1867 (727); *Guelph Exhibition*, New Gallery, London, 1891 (128). The two paintings are illustrated in Dorothy Hood, *The Admirals Hood*, London, 1942, opp. pp. 24 and 81.

640 The Hope Family 1802

MUSEUM OF FINE ARTS, BOSTON

Oil on canvas: $70 \times 100\frac{3}{4}$ in. (177.8 × 255.9 cm.)

Signed lower left: *B. West/1802*

PROV: Painted for Henry Hope (1736–1811), London; Blakeslee Galleries, New York; purchased by the Museum of Fine Arts in 1906 (Abbott Lawrence Fund, 06. 2362)

EXH: Philadelphia 1938 (54); *Survey of American Painting*, Carnegie Institute, Pittsburgh, 1940 (81); Boston 1976 (17)

LISTED: *PC*, p. 562 ("Mr. Hope's Family, containing nine figures as large as life," in the collection of

640

Henry Hope, Esq.); *UM*, p. 528; Barlow, p. 433; Galt, p. 221; Dillenberger, p. 156 (176)

LIT: Farington Diary, 7 March 1802 and 3 March 1804 (Farington 1978–, v, pp. 1755–56 and VI, p. 2260); "Painting by West," *Museum of Fine Arts Bulletin*, VI, 1906, p. 21; W. J. J. C. Bijleveld, "De Hope-groep in Boston," *Historie in Woord en Beeld*, Assen, 1939, pp. 19–33; David Watkin, "'The Hope Family' by Benjamin West," *Burlington Magazine*, CVI, 1964, pp. 571–72, fig. 28; David Watkin, *Thomas Hope 1769–1831 and the Neo-Classical Idea*, London, 1968, pp. 2–4, and pl. 1; Boston 1969, I, pp. 282–83 (1018), and II, fig. 98

From 1906, when No. 640 was acquired by the Museum of Fine Arts in Boston, to 1964, when it was the subject of a fundamental article by David Watkin, the figures in this painting were identified as the family of Adrian Hope. That identification was presumably inspired by the inscription *ADRIAN HOPE/ESQ* on the framed portrait of a man leaning on the table in the lower left, and undoubtedly, the man depicted in that picture is Adrian Hope (1709–1781), one of the founders of the banking firm of Hope and Co., in Amsterdam. The man seated on the left is Henry Hope (1736–1811), Adrian's nephew. The elderly woman seated to the right of the painting's center is Henry

Hope's widowed sister, Harriet Hope Goddard, and on the extreme right is her daughter Ann, who in 1782 had married John Williams, the man standing immediately behind her. Williams (1757–1813), the son of a Cornish clergyman, started work as a clerk for Hope and Co., rose to be a partner, and, after his marriage to Henry Hope's niece, adopted the surname of Hope. The five children in the painting are evidently children of John Williams Hope and his wife. According to the Boston catalogue of 1968 they are, from left to right: Henry (born 1785), Adrian (born 1788), Elizabeth (1794–1860), Henrietta Dorothea Maria (1790–1830), and Francis (1798–after 1864). Another son, William (1802–1855), who was to become a famous and eccentric *bon-vivant* and collector of diamonds, was evidently born too late to be included in the picture.[1]

On a chest in the upper left corner of No. 640 is a model of a building which Watkin identifies as the mansion at Weglegen near Haarlem in Holland that Henry Hope had built for himself between 1785 and 1788.[2] The red-figured *lekythos* on the pedestal before the model was presumably in the collection of Henry Hope; it subsequently belonged to Sir Henry Englefield.[3] The seascape in the center background appears to be copied from a Dutch picture, by or similar to paintings by Willem van de Velde (1633–1707).[4]

On 7 March 1802, West dined with Joseph Faring-

ton, who recorded in his diary: "West is painting large family pictures for Mr. Hope of Cavendish Square. The portraits are half lengths. West's price is 70 guineas for a half length, the whole wd. come to 470 guineas.—Mr. Hope said He could give him 500 guineas." Despite Farington's use of the plural "pictures," he was referring to No. 640, as a second reference to the picture in the diary two years later, on 3 March 1804, makes clear. On this occasion West was testifying in the dispute between Copley and Sir Edmund Knatchbull over Copley's charges for a group portrait of the Knatchbull family:[5]

He was then asked the size and price of a family picture of portraits which He had painted for Mr. Henry Hope. He sd. it was 9 feet wide by 6 feet high,—that there were 9 portraits in it, some nearly whole lengths & several as wd. be considered as Half lengths; That he had on receiving the Commission made an estimate of the price which He reckoned at £470 but Mr. Hope sent him 500 guineas which He acknowledged to be a very liberal act.

There seems to be no way to reconcile the price of seventy guineas for a half-length, which Farington recorded in 1802, and the total of either 470 pounds or guineas, which West calculated as the appropriate charge.

Henry Hope, "the most eminent merchant of his

time," had managed the firm of Hope and Co. in Amsterdam from 1780 to 1794. When Holland was invaded by the French in the latter year, he retired from business, and moved to London. In England, he was an important patron of West, owning at least five pictures by him in addition to No. 640 (Nos. 22, 180, 189, 193, and 392).[6] He never married, and John Williams Hope was his chief heir in 1811. John Williams Hope had remained in Amsterdam in 1794, running the family business there until 1808. The Peace of Amiens between France and England, which lasted from March 1802 to April 1803, evidently allowed him to visit England and provided the opportunity for the family to pose together for West in the spring of 1802. In that year Henry Hope made over the house at Weglegen to John Williams Hope, and that transaction undoubtedly explains why a model of the house figures so prominently in West's painting. The scene of shipping in the picture in the background may have been chosen also as a reference to the voyage that made the family gathering possible.

A rather sketchy drawing of a family group around a table in the Museum of Fine Arts, Boston, may represent an early idea for the composition of No. 640.[7] It is, however, substantially different in almost every detail and shows only six figures rather than the nine in No. 640.

Copies of No. 640 are in the collection of Charles J. Duveen, New Hope, Pennsylvania,[8] and in a private collection in New York.[9]

[1] We have been unable to confirm the identification given in the Boston catalogue, and some of the information provided there is contradicted by other sources. The obituary for Henry Hope in the *Gentleman's Magazine* (LXXXI, March 1811, pp. 292–93) indicates that at that time John Williams Hope had only three surviving children, and the account of the life of John Williams Hope in the *Dictionary of National Biography* states that when he died in 1813 he had only two surviving children, Henrietta Dorothea Maria and William Williams Hope.

[2] The building itself is illustrated in Jakob Rosenberg, Seymour Slive, and E. H. Ter Kuile, *Dutch Art and Architecture 1600 to 1800*, Harmondsworth and Baltimore, 1966, pl. 203 (B). It now serves as the seat of the Provincial Government of North Holland.

[3] Illustrated in Henry Moses, *Vases from the Collection of Sir Henry Englefield Bart.*, London, 1848, pl. 35, and in J. D. Beazley, *Attic Red-Figure Vase Painters*, Oxford, 1942, p. 473, no. 92.

[4] Although it is tempting to think that the seascape records a painting in Henry Hope's collection, it does not seem to represent any work included in the sales of his estate in 1816. Two paintings by Willem van de Velde did appear in the sale of 27 June 1816 (lots 23 and 24), but one was a large *Battle-Piece* and the other its companion.

[5] See Prown 1966, II, pp. 360–71.

[6] It should be noted that Henry Hope's second cousin, Thomas Hope of Deepdene (1769–1831) also bought paintings by West (see Nos. 146, 170, and 176).

[7] Black chalk and white, $10\frac{1}{8} \times 14\frac{3}{4}$ in. (66.14).

[8] Watercolor and tempera on ivory, $9\frac{1}{2} \times 12\frac{1}{4}$ in. Differences in detail between this copy and No. 640 are discussed in the Boston catalogue.

[9] Oil on canvas, 24 × 31 in.

641 Mrs. Thomas Hopkinson 1767

HISTORICAL SOCIETY OF PENNSYLVANIA, PHILADELPHIA

Oil on canvas: 30 × 25 in. (76 × 63.5 cm.)

Signed lower left: *B. West pinxit London/1767*

PROV: Placed on permanent deposit in the Historical Society of Pennsylvania by Oliver Hopkinson, 1891

EXH: *Historical Portraits*, Pennsylvania Academy of the Fine Arts, Philadelphia, 1887–88 (199); Philadelphia 1938 (15)

LIT: Sawitzky 1942, pp. 68–69; Wainwright 1974, p. 117

The subject of No. 641 was born in 1718 and died in 1804. Her maiden name was Mary Johnson. She was the wife of Thomas Hopkinson (1709–1751) of Philadelphia and the mother of Francis Hopkinson (1737–1791).

Francis Hopkinson was in London in 1766 and 1767, and he resided with West for part of that time. His mother did not accompany him, and West could not have painted No. 641 directly from life in 1767. Francis Hopkinson, however, did have with him a portrait of Mrs. Hopkinson, which he showed to the Bishop of Worcester on 10 August 1766, and West may have based No. 641 upon it.[1] That portrait could conceivably have been a miniature showing the same sitter, which now also belongs to the Historical Society of Pennsylvania. The miniature has been catalogued by Sawitzky and Wainwright as a copy, with some changes, after No. 641. In 1927 it was attributed to Matthew Pratt by Harry Wehle; that attribution is accepted by Wainwright but was rejected by Sawitzky in his earlier catalogue of the Historical Society's collection and in his monograph on Pratt.[2]

A portrait of the sitter's daughter, Mary Hopkinson, in the National Museum of American Art in Washington, has traditionally been ascribed to West as well. It also could not have been posed for by the subject and has been said to have been painted from a miniature supplied by her fiancé, Dr. John Morgan, in 1764.[3] The painting shows very little sign of having been done by West. It might, however, have been painted by Matthew Pratt, who came from Philadelphia to London to work in West's studio in July 1764. Since John Morgan, for whom the picture was supposedly painted, only arrived in London after an extended continental trip some months later, Pratt would have had as much opportunity as West to paint the portrait in London, and, unlike West, he could also have painted the sitter from life after his own return to Philadelphia in 1768.[4]

[1] George Everett Hastings, *The Life and Works of Francis Hopkinson*, Chicago, 1926, p. 134.

641

642

[2]William Sawitzky, *Matthew Pratt: 1734–1805*, New York, 1942, pp. 86–87.

[3]See Arthur S. Marks, "Angelica Kauffmann and Some Americans on the Grand Tour," *American Art Journal*, XII, Spring 1980, p. 12 and fig. 4.

[4]For comparable works by Pratt see the monograph by Sawitzky; Evans 1980, pp. 24–31; and Virginius Cornick Hall, Jr., *Portraits in the Collection of the Virginia Historical Society*, Charlottesville, 1981, p. 20 and pls. 3 and 4.

642 **Ann Inglis** *c.* 1757

DELAWARE ART MUSEUM, WILMINGTON, DELAWARE

Oil on canvas: 30 × 25 in. (76 × 63.5 cm.), painted oval

PROV: Mrs. Charles G. Rupert, Wilmington (in 1938); sold Samuel T. Freeman & Co., Philadelphia, 28–30 April 1947, lot 392, bought by A. Sussell, Philadelphia; presented by Mr. and Mrs. Daniel Moore

Bates and other donors to the Delaware Art Museum in 1948

EXH: *Portraits in Delaware 1700–1850*, Delaware Art Museum, 1958 (58); *American Portraits*, Community Gallery, Lancaster, Pa., 1971 (24)

LIT: Theodore Bolton and Harry Lorin Binsse, "Wollaston, an early American Portrait Manufacturer," *Antiquarian*, June 1931, p. 50 (as by Wollaston); Sawitzky 1938, pp. 443–44, 453–54 (15); Elizabeth H. Hawkes, *American Painting and Sculpture: Delaware Art Museum*, Wilmington, 1975, p. 14 (1)

The attributions of Nos. 642 and 643 to West and the identifications of the sitters as Ann and Mary Inglis are due to Sawitzky. Prior to 1938 both paintings had been described as portraits of Mrs. John Inglis (*c.* 1717–1750) of Philadelphia, who was the mother of Ann and Mary, and No. 642 had been ascribed to John Wollaston. Ann Inglis married Gilbert Barkly in 1761. Both paintings were presumably executed a few years earlier, shortly before West left Philadelphia in 1760. Sawitzky dates them *c.* 1757.

643 **Mary Inglis** *c.* 1757

PRIVATE COLLECTION

Oil on canvas: 30 × 25 in. (76 × 63.5 cm.)

PROV: By descent in the family of the daughter of the sitter, Mary Helen Hering, who in 1794 married Henry Middleton (1770–1846), to Dr. and Mrs. Henry Middleton Fisher, Philadelphia (in 1938); Mrs. Charles Morris Young, Radnor, Pennsylvania

LIT: John Alexander Inglis, *The Family of Inglis of Auchindinny and Redhall*, Edinburgh, 1914, ill. opp. p. 64 (as "Mrs. John Inglis"); Sawitzky 1938, pp. 454–55 (16)

Mary Inglis was the younger sister of Ann Inglis (see No. 642). On 10 April 1761, she married Julines Hering (1732–1797), a wealthy Jamaican planter and distant relative of William Beckford. She died in Bath in 1818. Henry Middleton (1770–1846), the child shown in West's *Middleton Family* of 1770–71 (No. 661), married her daughter, Mary Helen Hering, in 1794.

Prior to the publication of Sawitzky's article in 1938, No. 643 was identified, like No. 642, as a portrait of Mrs. John Inglis, but without attribution to any artist. No. 643 must have been painted at approximately the same time as No. 642, shortly before West's departure from Pennsylvania.

644 **Joshua Iremonger** *c.* 1765–70

PRIVATE COLLECTION

Oil on canvas: 29½ × 24½ in. (75 × 62 cm.)

PROV: Sold anonymously, Christie's, London, 24 July 1936, lot 78 (as "Josiah Iremonger," from the collection of George Marsham, Esq.); McClees Galleries, Philadelphia, 1936; Hammer Galleries, New York; Henry W. Rustin, New York

EXH: Philadelphia 1936

LIT: C. H. Bonte, "Benjamin West and Other Early American Painters," *Philadelphia Inquirer*, Sunday, 15 Nov. 1936, p. 18, ill.

Although the label on this painting identifies the sitter as Josiah Iremonger, the subject must be either Joshua Iremonger (died 1804) of Wherwell Priory, Hampshire, or, more probably, his son of the same name (*c.* 1744–1817). The elder of the two was the older half-brother of Sarah, Lady Fetherstonhaugh, the wife of Sir Matthew Fetherstonhaugh of Uppark in Sussex and mother of Sir Harry Fetherstonhaugh, who was painted by West in an Eton leaving picture of *c.* 1772 (No. 617). There is a copy of the Eton portrait of Sir Harry at Uppark, where there is also a second version of No. 644, which is listed in the guidebook to the house as "Reputedly a Member of the Iremonger Family" by an unknown artist (No. 645). An earlier portrait of the elder Joshua Iremonger by Arthur Devis, dated 1748, is at Uppark as well.

Although Nos. 644 and 645 evidently show the same sitter, they vary considerably in details, and the former shows him at a younger age. It seems likely that it was painted for the sitter, or his immediate family, probably during the latter 1760s, and that No. 645 was painted at a later date for his relatives at Uppark.

645 **Joshua Iremonger** *c.* 1772–75

NATIONAL TRUST, UPPARK, SUSSEX

Oil on canvas: 29½ × 24¾ in. (75 × 63 cm.)

644

645

PROV: Presumably at Uppark since the eighteenth century

LIT: *Uppark: Sussex*, the National Trust, 1962, p. 37 (listed as "English, 18th Century, 'Reputedly a Member of the Iremonger Family'")

No. 645 appears to show the same subject as the previous entry but in different dress, with a fuller face, and at a somewhat more advanced age. As No. 645 is the same size as the version at Uppark of West's portrait of Sir Harry Fetherstonhaugh (see No. 617) and shows the sitter in similar dress, the two paintings may have been commissioned at the same time. No. 645 is listed in the guidebook to Uppark only as a painting by an unknown eighteenth-century English artist. Nevertheless, it certainly depends upon No. 644, while the numerous changes make it more than simply a copy, thus differentiating it from the version of No. 617 at Uppark. The handling seems characteristic of West's painting in the mid-1770s.

646 Mrs. William James c. 1768

LOCATION UNKNOWN

LIT: Lewis Perry Curtis, ed., *Letters of Laurence Sterne*, Oxford, 1935, pp. 412–14

Mrs. William James (died 1798) and her husband (? 1721–1783) were close friends of Laurence Sterne during the last year of Sterne's life.[1] A portrait of her by West is known only through references in two of Sterne's letters. The first, dated by Lewis Perry Curtis "? 17 February 1768," is to a "L. S. Esq.," who Curtis suggests may have been either Luke Scrafton or Laurence Sullivan. It discusses a dinner engagement at the James home for the following Sunday:

> do not be late, for we will go half an hour before dinner, to see a picture executed by West, most admirably—he has caught the character of our friend—such goodness is painted in that face, that when one looks at it, let the soul be ever so much un-harmonized, it is impossible it should remain so.

In the second letter, written a day later to Mr. and Mrs. James, Sterne postpones the engagement for a week:

> The Sunday following I will assuredly wait upon you—and will come a quarter before four, that I may have both a little time, and a little day light, to see Mrs. J[ames]'s picture.

Curtis suggests that Archbishop Drummond (see Nos. 608–10) introduced West to Sterne, and that Sterne introduced the artist to Mr. and Mrs. James. West also painted a portrait of Sterne's daughter (No. 657) and two small pictures illustrating subjects from *A Sentimental Journey* (Nos. 223 and 224).

[1] For biographical details see Curtis, pp. 302–3, notes 5 and 7.

647 [?] Sir William Johnson, Bt. c. 1767–70
See color illustration, p. 59

NATIONAL GALLERY OF ART, WASHINGTON, D.C.

Oil on canvas: $79\frac{3}{4} \times 54\frac{1}{2}$ in. (203×138.5 cm.)

PROV: Sold anonymously, Sotheby's, London, 7 Dec. 1927, lot 54 (as "Portrait of Sir Joseph Banks, P.R.S.," 85×58 in.), bt. by F. Sabin; Miss E. Dina Brown, Henfield, Sussex; M. Knoedler and Co., New York; Andrew W. Mellon, by whom presented to the National Gallery in 1940

EXH: *Masterpieces of American Historical Portraiture*, M. Knoedler and Co., New York, 1936 (not in catalogue); *Painting and Sculpture from the Mellon Collection*, National Gallery, Washington, 1949 (496); *The Painter and the New World*, Montreal Museum of Fine Arts, 1967 (85); *The European Vision of America*, Cleveland Museum of Art, etc., 1975–77 (177)

LIT: *National Gallery of Art: Preliminary Catalog of Paintings and Sculpture*, Washington, 1941, p. 213 (496); Milton W. Hamilton, "Joseph Brant—'The Most Painted Indian,'" *New York History*, XXXIX, 1958, pp. 122–23; Evans 1959, pp. 46 and 119, note 53, pl. 33; Milton W. Hamilton, "The Johnson Portraits," in *The Papers of Sir William Johnson*, XIII, Albany, New York, 1962, p. xi; Ellwood Parry, *The Image of the Indian and the Black Man in American Art 1590–1900*, New York, 1974, pp. 31–34; Dillenberger 1977, pp. 23–24, pl 13; James Thomas Flexner, *Lord of the Mohawks: A Biography of Sir William Johnson*, 2nd ed., Boston and Toronto, 1979, p. 346, ill. opp. p. 351

This impressive and well-known picture of a seated man, who wears a combination of European and American Indian dress, and an Indian, who holds a peace pipe and points to a scene of an Indian family by a waterfall in the background, is neither signed nor dated and has no recorded history prior to 1927, when it was sold as a portrait of Sir Joseph Banks. West did paint a portrait of Banks, which appeared at the Royal Academy in 1773, but that work is known (No. 586). It has no connection with No. 647, the features of whose subject do not much resemble those of Banks in No. 586 and other portraits of him. Banks visited Newfoundland in the summer of 1766 to collect plants, but his trip to North America, although cited in the 1927 sale catalogue, is hardly sufficient to explain the emphasis on American Indians in No. 647.

Since the picture entered the National Gallery it has always been known as a portrait of Colonel Guy Johnson (c. 1740–1788), the nephew and son-in-law of Sir William Johnson, who was depicted by West in No. 92. Guy Johnson succeeded Sir William in 1774 as Superintendent of Indian Affairs in upstate New York. The National Gallery catalogue of 1941 dates the picture c. 1779 and identifies the seated man's companion as Joseph Brant (also known as Thayendanega), an educated Mohawk who served as Guy Johnson's secretary and visited England together with Johnson in the winter of 1775–76. Later National Gallery catalogues move the date of No. 647 from c. 1779 to 1775–76, thus making it coincide with the joint visit. There is, however, no compelling evidence to substantiate the identification of either sitter. Brant, who became something of a celebrity in London, was painted by George Romney in March and April 1776 in a portrait (National Gallery of Canada) that shows very little similarity with the Indian in No. 647, and Milton W. Hamilton, in the article about portraits of Brant cited above, dismisses the identification in No. 647 as "highly unlikely."[1] Hamilton also describes the likeness of Guy Johnson in No. 647 as "highly idealized," because of the contrast with written descriptions and with another supposed portrait of Guy Johnson, by an unknown artist in the New York State Historical Association in Cooperstown, New York.[2] The probable date of No. 647, discussed below, raises additional questions about the possibility of Guy Johnson and Joseph Brant having posed for the picture.

If the identification of the main sitter as Joseph Banks is untenable, and as Guy Johnson uncertain at best, the most likely alternative seems to be that No. 647 shows Sir William Johnson, Bt. (1715–1774), Guy's uncle, father-in-law, and predecessor as Superintendent of Indian Affairs. There is no documentary evidence to substantiate this identification either, and as comparison with known portraits of Sir William neither confirms nor contradicts it, it can only be put forward as a tentative suggestion.[3]

The question of the identification of the subject of No. 647 is of course connected with the question of the painting's date. Although it is not possible to assign it a precise date on stylistic grounds, the carefully drawn detail and relatively dry handling make a date as late as 1775 or 1776, when Guy Johnson visited London, unlikely. The painting seems closer to West's full-length portraits of the later 1760s, such as the *Governor James Hamilton* (No. 633) and the *Drummond Brothers* (No. 608), both dated 1767, than to West's portraits of a decade later, such as No. 610 of 1776, No. 590 of 1777, or the numerous royal portraits that occupied him from 1775 to 1779. The cross-legged pose of the Indian echoes that of Thomas Drummond in No. 608. The use of pointing fingers and the relation of foreground to background are also reminiscent of that painting and of several other portraits (notably Nos. 631 and 632) that can be dated either certainly or probably to the following few years.

Iconography provides less certain evidence for dating the picture, since West would presumably have responded to the requirements of the sitter, but the prominent American Indians in No. 647 link it to a series of works, commencing with *General Johnson Saving*

a *Wounded French Officer from the Tomahawk of a North American Indian* (No. 92), which is undated but must have been begun in the 1760s, and culminating in the *Death of General Wolfe* (No. 93) of 1770 and *William Penn's Treaty with the Indians* (No. 85) of 1771. The shaven-headed and semi-naked Indian in the foreground is similar to Indians in all three of those works. The pose of one of the Indians in the background is almost identical with that of the Indian in the *Death of Wolfe*, and the squaw nursing a papoose recalls a similar detail in the lower right corner of *Penn's Treaty*. The dress of the seated man is reminiscent of that of the officer in a green coat immediately behind the Indian in the *Death of Wolfe*. His mixture of Indian and European attire and many of the smaller details of hats, moccasins, beaded knee bands and shoulder straps, although not identical, are distinctly similar, and while the coat is green in No. 93, the coat worn by the corresponding figure in West's sketch for the *Death of General Wolfe* (No. 99) is red.

Unfortunately, the identity of that officer in the *Death of Wolfe* is not certain. His dress, including the green coat, has been described as an accurate depiction of the uniform of Rogers' Rangers, the best known of the American rangers serving in the British Army, some of whom were with Wolfe at Quebec.[4] Robert Rogers, the commander of the unit bearing his name, was not there. As noted in the entry for No. 93, the words *Sr. Wm. Johnson/MOHAWK RIVER* appear on the powder horn carried by the figure in this uniform, suggesting that he may have been intended to represent Johnson, although Johnson was not at Quebec either, nor was he a ranger. Whether or not that identification is tenable, the inscription in No. 93 seems to be the strongest clue provided by West to help us identify the figure similarly clad and similarly accompanied by an Indian in No. 647. If he is indeed Sir William Johnson, the waterfall in the background would be Niagara, the scene of a great victory by Johnson over the French in 1759. His Indian companion may have been intended to represent Hendrick, a Mohawk chief who was killed while commanding the Indians during Johnson's victory at Lake George in 1755 (the battle in which the incident shown by West in No. 92 took place), or he may less specifically represent the people whom Sir William commanded in several campaigns during the Seven Years' War and with whom he lived in close association and remarkable harmony.

Sir William Johnson never visited England after emigrating to America in 1738, but his son, Sir John Johnson (1742–1830), was in London from 1765 to 1767 and may have commissioned the picture from the artist at that time. The likeness would then have been based on a miniature or other material provided by Sir William's son.[5] The Johnson family had social aspirations; Sir William hoped and expected to be raised to the peerage, and his son was knighted in 1765;[6] so the desire to have a full-length portrait by a well-known artist in the tradition of those of the English aristocracy does not seem out of character. John Johnson had studied in Philadelphia from 1757 to 1759 under West's teacher, Provost Smith (see No. 699), and must have been acquainted with West from there. Additionally, one of the letters of introduction he carried in 1765 was to General Robert Monckton,[7] whose portrait West had painted in 1764 (No. 665), and who later was to be represented in the *Death of General Wolfe*. It is not impossible that sight of No. 665, West's first full-length portrait, which shows a British officer in the exotic setting of a Caribbean island, inspired John to commission No. 647, another full-length portrait, which shows an officer in the exotic setting of the North American wilderness.

It should be acknowledged that, if Sir John Johnson commissioned No. 647 while in England, there is a surprising lack of any allusion to the deed in the surviving

Johnson correspondence. On the other hand, two letters, written by agents in New York City and Schenectady to Sir William Johnson shortly after John's return in September 1767, mention a picture or pictures being shipped to Sir William.[8] One refers to "Your Brother's Picture," which would seem not to be No. 647, and there is no proof that the shipment had any direct connection with John's travels. But it seems more likely than not that it did, and the fact that the picture or pictures did not accompany him suggests that they were too large to be included in his personal luggage.

The possibility that the subject of No. 647 is Sir John Johnson, rather than his father or cousin, should also be considered. Unlike Sir William, Sir John could have posed for the picture. In 1765, when he arrived in London, he was twenty-three years old and had served as a captain of militia in the campaign against Pontiac two years before.[9] Other less likely candidates are Robert Rogers, the ranger, (1727–1795), and Sir William (later Viscount) Howe (1729–1814). Rogers visited London in 1765, when he published two books and was considerably lionized, and he was there again in 1769–70. Several details of dress in No. 647, such as the moccasins and the hat, correspond to the uniform of Roger's Rangers as shown in the *Death of Wolfe*, but the red coat seems to conflict with all descriptions of Rogers's uniform. Howe served in America in the Seven Years' War. He was supposedly a friend of West,[10] and has been traditionally identified as the officer in ranger uniform in the *Death of Wolfe*. However, the figure in that painting almost certainly does not represent Howe, who was not a ranger, and it is questionable that he would have chosen to be portrayed in such guise in a full-length portrait. Neither Rogers nor Howe had the strong personal connections with American Indians of Sir William Johnson and his family, and for that reason alone, neither man seems as likely to be the subject of No. 647 as any one of the Johnsons.[11]

[1] A painting of an American Indian in the Yale University Art Gallery (30 × 25 in.) has been called a portrait of Brant by West. It is not by West, but is a copy of a painting of a Cherokee or Creek Indian by William Hodges belonging to the Royal College of Surgeons in London (see *The European Vision of America*, no. 185). Another portrait supposedly of Brant by Gilbert Stuart belongs to the New York Historical Association in Cooperstown, New York (ill. in Flexner, *Lord of the Mohawks*, opp. p. 292).

[2] See *The Papers of Sir William Johnson*, XIII, p. 636. No certain portraits of Guy are known. An engraving ascribed to Francesco Bartolozzi (ibid., II, p. 256) has been described at various times as a likeness of Guy, of Sir William Johnson, and of Sir John Johnson, Sir William's son.

[3] See Milton W. Hamilton, "The Johnson Portraits" (as cited above). The chief relevant likenesses are: a portrait by John Wollaston of c. 1751 in the Albany Institute of History and Art, Albany, New York (*The Papers of Sir William Johnson*, II, frontispiece); a miniature in the Public Archives of Canada, Ottawa, which may have been based on the Wollaston portrait (ibid., VII, frontispiece); a mezzotint by J. (or more probably Charles) Spooner published in London in 1756 after a lost drawing by T. Adams (ibid., II, p. 160); a painting in the New-York Historical Society, New York, identified by William Sawitzky as a copy made in 1838 by Edward L. Mooney after a lost portrait painted by Thomas McIlworth in 1763 (Flexner, *Lord of the Mohawks*, opp. p. 293); and a portrait in an English private collection traditionally ascribed to Sir Joshua Reynolds (*1776: The British Story of the American Revolution*, Greenwich, 1976, no. 326).

[4] Burt Garfield Loescher, *The History of Rogers Rangers*, San Francisco, 1946, p. 283.

[5] West's model conceivably could have been the miniature mentioned in note 3. The putative likenesses ascribed to Bartolozzi and Reynolds, mentioned in notes 2 and 3, if they show Sir William, must also have been based on a similar, or possibly the same, source.

[6] Milton W. Hamilton, "An American Knight in Britain: Sir John Johnson's Tour 1765–1771," *New York History*, XLII, 1961, p. 123.

[7] Ibid., p. 121.

[8] Letters written by Daniel Campbell, Schenectady, 15 Nov. 1767, and by Hugh Wallace, New York, 8 Dec. 1767 (*The Papers of Sir William Johnson*, v, pp. 794–95 and 853).

[9] The chief likenesses of, or supposedly of, John Johnson are: an oil painting by John Mare at Johnson Hall near Johnstown, New York, which has also been called a portrait of Sir William Johnson (ibid., II, p. xii, and IV, p. xi); a portrait in pastels also at Johnson Hall (ibid., VII, p. 900); and an engraving published in 1793 and showing him at a more advanced age (ibid., XI, frontispiece).

[10] See Galt 1820, pp. 26–31, and Alberts 1978, pp. 22–23, 60–61, and 421. West was said by Archibald Robertson to have painted the head of Howe in the *Death of General Warren at the Battle of Bunker's Hill* by John Trumbull, for whom Howe refused to sit (Dunlap 1930, III, p. 733).

[11] We are indebted to Richard Brender for assistance with this entry, and to Deborah Chotner and Nicolai Cikovsky, Jr., of the National Gallery, for comments made in 1983 and 1984 in response to an earlier draft, which neither of them found convincing.

648 William Kelly *c.* 1759

LOCATION UNKNOWN

LIT: Galt 1816, pp. 84–85; Carey 1820, p. 515; Dunlap 1834, I, p. 46 (Dunlap 1918, I, p. 46); Sawitzky 1938, pp. 439 and 462; Wayne Craven, "Painting in New York City 1750–1775," in Ian M. G. Quimby, ed., *American Painting to 1776: A Reappraisal*, Winterthur, Del., and Charlottesville, Va., 1971, pp. 274–76

Early accounts of West's life mention a visit to New York *c.* 1759, immediately prior to his voyage to Italy in the spring of 1760. According to Dunlap, this visit lasted eleven months. No works painted by West in New York are now known.

The portrait of Mr. Kelly is mentioned specifically in the early accounts because West heard of Chief Justice Allen's plan to send a ship to Italy while Kelly was sitting to him. West charged Kelly ten guineas, the price to which he had raised his charge for a half-length portrait while in New York, and Kelly when paying him also gave him a letter to deliver to his agent in Philadelphia. When opened this letter proved to contain instructions to the agent to pay West an additional fifty guineas as a present from Kelly to help the young artist in his projected voyage. Hence, Kelly, who is described by Galt only as a merchant, was one of West's early major benefactors. The portrait was presumably one of the last painted by West prior to his departure from America.

649 Mrs. Thomas Keyes and Her Daughter *c.* 1806

PRIVATE COLLECTION

Oil on canvas: 33 × 23¼ in. (84 × 59 cm.)

PROV: Childs Gallery, Boston, 1957; Alexander Gallery, New York

The subjects of this portrait were described by Charles D. Childs in 1957 as the wife and daughter of Dr. Thomas Keyes of Baltimore, painted in London *c.* 1806. The sources for the identification and the date are not known. No signature or date is presently visible on the painting, but the style seems consistent with a date near 1806. If West painted No. 649 as early as 1802 it might be identical with the otherwise unidentified "Portraits of a Mother and Her Daughter" (No. 739) exhibited by him in that year.

650 General Tadeusz Kosciuszko 1797

See color illustration, p. 133

ALLEN MEMORIAL ART MUSEUM, OBERLIN COLLEGE, OBERLIN, OHIO

649

Oil on panel: 12 5/16 × 17 5/16 in. (31.5 × 44 cm.)

Signed lower left: *B. West/1797* and inscribed on a sheet of paper on the table, center left: *Genl Co . . . osko/ London* (the rest of the inscription is concealed by an inkwell)

PROV: Offered by West's sons to the United States in 1826 (no. 90) and sold by them, Robins, London, 22–25 May 1829, lot 138 ("General Kosciusko," 12 × 16½ in.), bt. by Bone for £42 on behalf of Joseph Neeld, MP, Grittleton House, Wilts.; by descent in the Neeld family until sold, Christie's, London, 13 July 1945, lot 175; M. Knoedler and Co., New York, from whom purchased by the Allen Memorial Art Museum in 1946

EXH: RA 1798 (618) "Portrait of General Kosciusko"; West's Gallery 1822–28 (63); *The Arts in America in the Eighteenth Century*, Allen Memorial Art Museum, 1946 (18); *From Colony to Nation*, Art Institute of Chicago, 1949 (130); *They Gave Us Freedom*, Colonial Williamsburg, Va., 1951 (48); *The French in America*, Detroit Institute of Arts, 1951 (244); *Paintings and Drawings from Five Centuries*, Knoedler, New York, 1954 (54); *The Century of Mozart*, Nelson Gallery–Atkins Museum, Kansas City, 1956 (106); *Masterpieces from American University Museums*, Malmö, Sweden, etc., 1956–57; *Art Across America*, Munson-Williams-Proctor Institute, Utica, New York, 1960 (109); New York 1962 (4); *Style, Truth and the Portrait*, Cleveland Museum of Art, 1963 (47); *Treasures from the Allen Memorial Art Museum*, Minneapolis Institute of Arts, 1966; *Romantic Art in Britain*, Detroit Institute of Arts and Philadelphia Museum of Art, 1968 (53)

LISTED: *PC*, p. 567 ("Kosciusco on a Couch, as he appeared in London 1797," West, Gallery); *UM*, p. 531; Barlow, p. 435; *BA*, p. 18; Galt, p. 231; Dillenberger, p. 179 (405)

LIT: Farington Diary, 8 June 1797 (Farington 1978–, III, p. 852); Chloe Hamilton, "A Portrait of General Kosciusko by Benjamin West," *Allen Memorial Art Museum Bulletin*, IX, 1952, pp. 81–91; Wolfgang Stechow, *Catalogue of European and American Paintings and Sculpture in the Allen Memorial Art Museum*, Oberlin, 1967, pp. 161–63; Alberts 1978, pp. 221–22

The circumstances under which West painted No. 650 are described in the diary of Joseph Farington, who called on West on 8 June 1797:

West saw General Kosciosceau yesterday. He went with Dr. Bancroft & Trumbull.—The Genl. was laid on a Couch—had a black silk band round his head—& was drawing Landscapes, which is his principal amusement.—He speaks English, appears to be abt. 45 yrs. of age; and abt. 5 feet 8 Inches high. One side of him is paralytic—the effect of a cannon shot passing over him—He had two stabbs in his back—one cut in his head. He asked abt. the mutiny at the Nore—is agitated by the thoughts of revolutions and wishes to proceed to America, where he expects to find peace. He proposes going to Bristol and from thence to America (Philadelphia). The Emperor of Russia behaved kindly to him—gave him an estate & then allowed him to sell it, which He did for abt. 10,000.—He lodges at the Hotel in Leicester Fields formerly the house of Hogarth. West shewed me a small picture which He yesterday began to paint from memory of Koscioscow on a Couch.

For a full discussion of No. 650, see the article by Chloe Hamilton published in 1952. Tadeusz Kosciuszko (1746–1817), the Polish general and patriot, had been badly wounded and taken prisoner by the Russians in the Battle of Maciejowice in October 1794. Following his release from imprisonment in 1796 upon the advent of Paul I as czar (cf. the reference to the kind behavior of the Emperor of Russia in the quotation above), he travelled via Sweden and England to asylum in America, where he had previously served with distinction in the American revolutionary war. He reached London on 30 May 1797, and a contemporary newspaper report of his arrival, quoted by Hamilton,[1] describes his wounds, his activity of drawing landscapes, and his gratitude to the present Emperor of Russia, anticipating or echoing what West was to tell Farington following his visit on 7 June.

John Trumbull, who accompanied West on the visit, had, like Kosciuszko, been a colonel in the Northern Army under General Horatio Gates during the American Revolution, and the two men may have been previously acquainted.[2] If not, they must have been aware of one another and may have been given letters of introduction by Gates or some other mutual acquaintance. In 1797 Trumbull was serving as an American diplomat in London and living at 29 Berners Street, around the corner from West in Newman Street. Dr. Bancroft was presumably the American-born inventor and physician Edward Bancroft (1744–1821), who lived in London and spied on behalf of both the Americans and English during the revolutionary war.

No. 650 is one of a group of closely related portraits of Kosciuszko. A likeness modelled in wax by Catherine Andras was the basis of an engraving by William Sharp published in 1800, and a portrait drawing by Richard Cosway was engraved by Antonei Cardon and published on 1 January 1798.[3] Both prints show Kosciuszko reclining on a couch before a window, although in

neither is the view through the window recognizably that of St. Paul's Cathedral, as it is in No. 650. The Cardon engraving after Cosway also includes a Polish officer's cap and a sword, similar to those on the low table in the foreground of No. 650. The sword in the Cardon engraving is accompanied by a scroll with the words "From the Whig Club of England to Gen'l Kosciuszko 1797." The presentation of this sword is recorded elsewhere in biographies of Kosciuszko,[4] and presumably West intended to represent the same sword, although as Hamilton points out, his differs slightly from that shown in the Cosway/Cardon print. Kosciuszko was evidently reluctant to pose for artists; according to some accounts, Cosway sketched him through a keyhole, and as we learn from Farington, West did not sketch or paint Kosciuszko from life but began No. 650 from memory following his visit.

On 10 June 1797, three days after the visit recorded by Farington, West presented Kosciuszko a drawing of *Hector and Andromache* (No. 165, ill. p. 133), which Kosciuszko in turn presented to Thomas Jefferson before his departure from America in the following year.

[1] From the *Gentleman's Magazine*, LXVII, pt. 2, July 1797, p. 609.
[2] According to Jaffe 1975, p. 27, Trumbull worked together with Kosciuszko in fortifying Ticonderoga. This, however, seems unlikely; Trumbull was at Ticonderoga in the summer and autumn of 1776; Kosciuszko, according to the *Dictionary of American Biography*, did not arrive there until the following year. Trumbull does not mention Kosciuszko in his autobiography, although he does describe his own military career in considerable detail.
[3] Both are reproduced by Hamilton, figs. 2 and 3.
[4] Monica M. Gardner, *Kosciuszko*, London, 1942, p. 121.

651 [?] The Lane Children

LOCATION UNKNOWN

LISTED: *PC*, p. 563 ("The Family picture of Lunes, Esq.'s children, half lengths"); *UM*, p. 529; *BA*, p. 15 (… "Lane, Esq.'s Children" …); Galt, p. 222 (… "Lunis, Esq.'s Children); Dillenberger, p. 158 (201)

Nothing is known about this work apart from its appearance in *Public Characters* and the other early lists of West's paintings, where it immediately follows three other group portraits (Nos. 610, 602, and 607). In four lists, the name is spelled in three different ways, and there is no way to ascertain which is correct. "Lane" seems most probable.

652 George, First Lord Lyttelton c. 1773

LOCATION UNKNOWN

PROV: Painted c. 1773 for Thomas Newton, Bishop of Bristol (1704–1782)

ENGR: Mezzotint (oval, 13 × 11 in.) by Robert Dunkarton, pub. 14 Feb. 1774 by R. Dunkarton, J. Boydell, and H. Parker, inscribed *from the Original Picture in the Collection of Dr. Newton, Lord Bishop of Bristol*; engraving (oval, 5½ × 4 in.), by Joseph Collyer, undated but with a line identifying it as from the painting in the possession of the Bishop of Bristol and, hence, presumably from before Newton's death in 1782; No. 652 was also the basis of several smaller prints by Collyer and other engravers published between 1779 and 1806 as illustrations to editions of Lyttelton's poems

LIT: *The Works of the Right Reverend Thomas Newton, D. D., Late Lord Bishop of Bristol, and Dean of St. Paul's, London, with some account of his Life, and anecdotes of several of his Friends, written by Himself*, London, 1782, I, pp. 97–98; Rose Mary Davis, *The Good Lord Lyt-*

George, First Lord Lyttelton, mezzotint by Robert Dunkarton after No. 652

telton: A Study in Eighteenth Century Politics and Culture, Bethlehem, Pa., 1939, pp. 400–01; Kerslake 1977, I, pp. 173–75

West produced three versions of his portrait of the patron of literature, improver of landscape, politician, poet, and scholar George Lyttelton (1709–1773), who was created Baron Lyttelton in 1756. Of these, two (Nos. 653 and 654) are now known, but the unlocated No. 652 was the first, from which the others were copied. According to the edition of Bishop Newton's *Works* published in the year of Newton's death, Lord Lyttelton

did the Bishop the honour of sitting for his picture for him to Mr. West, and he himself and his family all agreed, that it was the truest resemblance and the best portrait of him that ever was drawn. After his death, Mr. West copied it for Lord Hardwick and for Governor Lyttelton, now Lord Westcote; the prints of Lord Lyttelton are also taken from this picture.

The reliability of this account is confirmed by Rose Mary Davis, who cites further manuscript sources, and by the inscriptions on the Dunkarton and Collyer prints after No. 652. Bishop Newton had been an important early patron of West (see Nos. 163 and 281) and was himself portrayed by the artist in No. 675.

The engravings by Dunkarton (*above*) and Collyer reproduce No. 652 as an oval. Otherwise, Nos. 653, 654, and the engravings after No. 652 show no significant differences in composition or detail. Lord Lyttelton wears a peer's parliamentary robe in all three. No. 653 bears an inscription identifying the subject as sixty-four years old in 1773, and the sources quoted by Davis indicate that Lord Hardwicke commissioned No. 654 in June 1773. Lord Lyttelton died on 22 August of the same year.

Charles Coleman Sellers has suggested that the American sculptress Patience Wright may have taken advantage of Lyttelton's posing for West to have modelled a bust of him in wax at the same time. Her bust was mentioned by Horace Walpole in a letter dated 11 February 1773,[1] so, if Sellers is right, Lord Lyttelton must have posed for No. 652 before then.

[1] Charles Coleman Sellers, *Patience Wright: American Artist and Spy in George III's London*, Middletown, Conn., 1976, pp. 57 and 231–32.

653

653 George, First Lord Lyttelton 1773

VISCOUNT COBHAM

Oil on canvas: 29 × 24½ in. (73.5 × 62 cm.)

Inscribed upper right: *George Ld Lyttelton/aetatis sua 64. anno Dom.ⁿⁱ/1773*

PROV: Painted for William Henry Lyttelton, Baron Westcote and later Baron Lyttelton, brother of the sitter (1724–1808); by family descent to the present owner

EXH: *Guelph Exhibition*, New Gallery, London, 1891 (146) lent by Lord Cobham

LIT: As for No. 652; illustrated in Kerslake 1977, II, pl. 494

654 George, First Lord Lyttelton *c*. 1773

PRIVATE COLLECTION

Oil on canvas: 29¾ × 24¾ in. (75.5 × 63 cm.)

PROV: Commissioned in 1773 by Philip Yorke, second Earl of Hardwicke, Wimpole Hall, Cambridgeshire (1720–1796); H. V. Yorke; Sabin Galleries, London, 1970; National Bank of Commerce of Seattle, London; sold anonymously, Sotheby's, London, 17 March 1982, lot 36

EXH: *English Portraits 1500–1830*, Sabin Galleries, London, 1970 (36)

LIT: As for No. 652

A copy of No. 652 for Lord Hardwicke is mentioned in the passage from Bishop Newton's *Works* and in the manuscript material used by Rose Mary Davis, both cited in the entry for No. 652. According to the latter source, in June 1773 the Earl of Hardwicke made a request to Lord Lyttelton for a portrait to place in his collection at Wimpole, to which Lyttelton replied "that he believed he could have no better likeness than a copy from the portrait drawn by Benjamin West." Lord Hardwicke had earlier in the same year also requested a portrait from the aging fourth Earl of Chesterfield.[1] Kerslake cites references by Musgrave in 1798 and George Scharf in 1879 recording No. 654's presence at Wimpole.[2]

[1]Kerslake 1977, I, p. 51.

[2]Ibid., p. 174. The identification of No. 654 as the Hardwicke picture and the provenance given above come from the Sabin catalogue of 1970.

655 William Markham, Archbishop of York

c. 1771–77

NATIONAL PORTRAIT GALLERY, LONDON

Oil on canvas: 30 × 25 in. (76 × 63.5 cm.)

PROV: By descent in the family of the sitter to Peter G. Markham, Waikato, New Zealand; P. & D. Colnaghi, London, from whom purchased by the National Portrait Gallery in 1966

EXH: *National Exhibition of Works of Art*, Leeds, 1868 (3241)

LIT: *Burlington Magazine*, CIX, 1967, p. 259, ill.

William Markham (1719–1807) became Master of Westminster School in 1753; Dean of Rochester in 1765; Dean of Christ Church, Oxford, in 1767; Bishop

of Chester in 1771; and Archbishop of York in 1777. An old label on the back of No. 655 states that the painting shows him when Bishop of Chester, and in style the painting appears consistent with West's works of the early 1770s.

According to Galt, Dr. Markham, who was then Master of Westminster School, called on West soon after the artist arrived in London and subsequently was responsible for introducing West both to some of the leading figures of intellectual life in London, including Samuel Johnson and Edmund Burke, and to three Anglican divines who were to become major patrons of the artist: Thomas Newton, Bishop of Bristol; James Johnson, Bishop of Worcester; and Robert Hay Drummond, Archbishop of York.[1] Markham himself does not seem to have acquired any works by West apart from No. 655.

Portraits of Markham painted by Reynolds in *c*. 1759–61 and *c*. 1778 are at Christ Church, Oxford, and a later portrait by Hoppner is in the Royal Collection.[2]

[1]Galt 1820, pp. 6–7 and 9.

[2]Ellis Waterhouse, *Reynolds*, London and Boston, 1941, pls. 66 and 203; and Millar 1969, II, pl. 177.

655

656

have been based on a portrait painted some time earlier, or the likeness may have been painted (or drawn) specifically for the sake of being reproduced in the *Letters*. The latter alternative seems perhaps more likely, but it should be observed that Lydia Sterne's connection with West was probably due to her father's association with West's patron Robert Hay Drummond, Archbishop of York. In the months following Sterne's death on 18 March 1768, Lydia corresponded with the Archbishop and had at least one meeting with him when he subscribed ten guineas to an appeal to help Sterne's widow and daughter.[1] In that same year West completed and exhibited the most ambitous and important of his pictures painted for Archbishop Drummond, *Agrippina Landing at Brundisium with the Ashes of Germanicus* (No. 33), which depicts the devotion of a wife to a deceased husband. No. 657, which shows Lydia with a bust of Sterne, depicts the similar devotion of a daughter to a dead father, and, although the painting is (or was) on the more modest and intimate scale of portraiture, the laurel wreath and pseudo-Roman appearance of the bust make explicit classical allusions. Lydia Sterne was in London in May and June 1769 and West could have painted her picture at that time, possibly with the intention of its being used as an illustration to a life of Sterne which Lydia was attempting to induce John Wilkes and John Hall Stevenson to write.[2] By 22 July 1769, she was at Angoulême in France, and she evidently did not return to England again until June of 1775.[3] See also Nos. 223 and 224. The latter contains a portrait of Sterne.

[1] Lewis Perry Curtis, ed., *Letters of Laurence Sterne*, Oxford, 1935, pp. 433–39. Curtis (p. 413, note 6) points out that Sterne-Drummond-West relationship in connection with West's portrait of Mrs. William James (No. 646).
[2] Ibid., pp. 448–52.
[3] Ibid., p. 449 et passim. The dedication of Lydia's edition of Sterne's letters is dated "London, June, 1775." Advertisements for the edition, including the announcement that it would be "Embellished with an elegant engraving of Mrs. Médalle, from a picture by Mr. West," appeared in the *London Chronicle* on 6–8 July 1775 and subsequently in other periodicals (see Wilbur L. Cross, ed., *The Letters of Laurence Sterne to His Most Intimate Friends*, New York, 1904, I, pp. xv–xvi and 60).

Lydia Sterne de Médelle, engraving by James Caldwall after No. 657

656 Charles Maynard *c.* 1771

THE PROVOST AND FELLOWS OF ETON COLLEGE

Oil on canvas: 36 × 30 in. (91.5 × 76 cm.)

PROV: Presented to the Headmaster of Eton by the sitter

LIT: Cust 1910, p. 17 (17), pl. VIII

Charles Maynard (1751–1824) was the eldest son of Sir William Maynard, fourth Baronet. He succeeded his father as fifth Baronet in 1772, and his cousin as the second Viscount Maynard in 1775.

No. 656, like Nos. 617 and 724, is an Eton leaving portrait, painted, according to Cust, in 1771. Charles Maynard entered Eton in 1764 and was in the sixth form (or final year) in 1769.

657 Lydia Sterne de Médalle (?)*c.* 1769

LOCATION UNKNOWN

ENGR: Engraving (4½ × 3 in.) by James Caldwall (*right*), pub. by T. Becket, 10 Aug. 1775, and utilized as the frontispiece to *Letters of the late Rev. Mr. Laurence Sterne, to his most intimate Friends*, edited by Lydia Sterne de Médalle, 25 Oct. 1775; engraving (6⅛ × 4¼ in.) by P. Rothwell, pub. by J. Bumpus, 30 May 1818

Lydia Sterne, the daughter of Laurence Sterne, was born in 1747 and in 1772 married Jean-Baptiste-Alexandre-Anne Médalle. No. 657 is known only through engravings, the earliest of which was made to serve as the frontispiece of the edition of Sterne's letters published by his daughter in 1775. The engraving may

658 Captain Charles Pierrepont Medows (later Viscount Newark and first Earl Manvers) 1761

Oil on canvas: 33 × 27 in. (84 × 69 cm.)

Inscribed, *verso*: *Captain Medows now Lord Newark—painted by Benj. West at Leghorn for the english consul Sir John Dick 1761*

PROV: Painted for Sir John Dick, Bt. (1720–1804); then by descent in the family of the sitter

Charles Pierrepont Medows (1737–1816) was the nephew and heir of Evelyn Pierrepont (1711–1773), the second Duke of Kingston. In 1796 he succeeded to the titles of Baron Pierrepont and Viscount Newark, and in 1806 he became the first Earl Manvers. Before acquiring his titles and inheriting the estate of Thoresby, where No. 658 remains, Medows had been an officer in the Royal Navy, serving as captain of the frigate *Shannon* at the capture of Louisbourg in 1758 and again as part of the British fleet off Gibraltar the following year.[1] In 1760 the *Shannon* was still at Gibraltar when the *Betty Sally* bringing West and his companions from Philadelphia to Italy arrived there. Since England was at war with France (the Seven Years' War), the *Betty Sally* joined a convoy conducted by two English men-of-war to sail through the Mediterranean from Gibraltar to Leghorn. One of the naval vessels was the *Shannon*, and, according to all the early biographies of West, during the voyage commenced a friendship between Captain Medows and the artist which continued for the rest of their lives.[2] No. 658 is not mentioned in the biographies, nor does it appear on the early lists of West's works, but another painting which West painted for Medows does (No. 350).

The inscription on the back of No. 658, which must date from between 1796 and 1806 when the subject was known as Lord Newark, indicates that West painted Medows in the year following their first meeting. The artist spent some four months in Leghorn in 1761 in the home of Robert Rutherford, and there, according to Galt, "Mr. (afterwards Sir John) Dick, then the British Consul at Leghorn, and his lady also treated him with great partiality, and procured for him the use of the Imperial baths."[3] The apparent age of the sitter in No. 658 accords with that of Medows, who was twenty-four years old in 1761 (a year older than West), as does the uniform with Medows's professional calling. Stylistically, No. 658 is not dissimilar to other portraits which we believe to have been painted by West shortly after his arrival in Italy, such as No. 582, of his travelling companion John Allen, and No. 730. Although none of these paintings is securely documented in the way that much of West's later *oeuvre* is, they are consistent with one another and with what we might expect of the young artist at this time.

[1] Wm. Laird Clowes, *The Royal Navy*, London, 1897–1903, III, pp. 183 and 212.
[2] *Public Characters* 1805, pp. 525–26; Galt 1816, p. 90; Carey 1820, p. 515.
[3] Galt 1816, p. 124; see also Richardson 1978, p. 17 (letter from West to Joseph Shippen, 11 May 1762).

658

659 [?] William Middleton *c.* 1770

Oil on canvas: 49¼ × 39 in. (125 × 99 cm.)

PROV: By descent in the family of the sitter to the sixth Baron de Saumarez, Shrubland Park, Suffolk; included in sale catalogue, Sotheby's, London, 23 June 1971, lot 96 (as "Portrait of the Hon. Henry Middleton, President of the Continental Congress") but withdrawn; currently on extended loan to the Middleton Place Foundation, Charleston, South Carolina

No. 659 is one of four closely related portraits of members of the Middleton family of South Carolina (Nos. 659–62). Although there has been some confusion over the identity of the sitter in No. 659, the picture most probably represents William Middleton (1710–1785) of Crowfield, South Carolina, and Crowfield Hall, Suffolk. William Middleton inherited estates in both England and America. He was born in South Carolina but moved to England in 1754 and resided in Suffolk for the rest of his life.

No. 659 was catalogued by Sotheby's in 1971 as a portrait of William Middleton's younger brother Henry Middleton (1717–1784), who remained in America and served briefly as President of the Continental Congress. That identification was evidently based on a framed photograph of No. 659 in the Charleston Library Society, which is inscribed thus on the mat, but the reliability of the inscription of the photograph is undermined by the accompanying ascription of the picture to Copley. Henry Middleton is not known to have visited England after his early school days, and, hence, it appears that he never would have had the opportunity to sit to West for his portrait.

No. 659 was described as a portrait by West of William Middleton by the Reverend Edmund Farrer in 1907[1] and in an inventory made by Lady de Saumarez shortly after the Second World War.[2] According to the latter, quoting Sir William Fowle Fowle Middleton, Bt., Nos. 659 and 660, showing William Middleton's son, were the first two portraits painted by West after his arrival in England in 1763; however, a date closer

659

dleton, by the Reverend Edmund Farrer in 1907, Lady de Saumarez subsequently confused the sitter with an earlier Thomas Middleton (1719–1766), the brother of William Middleton.[1] That identification is out of the question because of the youthful appearance of the sitter in West's picture. In 1971 the painting was catalogued at Sotheby's as a portrait of Arthur Middleton (1742–1817), the first cousin of Thomas Middleton of Crowfield. The reason for this identification appears to have been the similarity in features of the subject of No. 660 to those of Arthur Middleton in No. 661. However, that similarity can be explained as family resemblance, and certainly it does not constitute proof of the subject's identity. There is an equally strong resemblance in appearance with the subject of a painting by an unidentified artist at Drayton Hall near Charleston, of a slightly older man holding a child, which until 1980 belonged to descendants of Thomas Middleton of Crowfield, and which, according to family tradition, has always been described as a portrait of him with his daughter Mary, born in 1775.[2] It seems most likely, therefore, that No. 660 does represent Thomas Middleton of Crowfield, as stated by Farrer in the earliest recorded reference to the picture.

The sitter is shown in Van Dyck costume, as are his cousins in Nos. 661 and 662. The latter work is signed and dated 1770; the former was painted either in that year or early in the following; and it seems likely that West painted No. 660 at approximately the same time, when the subject would have been seventeen years old.

[1] See No. 659, notes 1 and 2. Elsewhere in her inventory Lady de Saumarez cites Sir William Fowle Fowle Middleton's reference to No. 660 as a portrait of his uncle Thomas, which would make it a portrait of William Middleton's son (i.e., Thomas Middleton of Crowfield), rather than his brother.

[2] Letter from Letitia Galbraith, Administrator of Drayton Hall, 30 September 1980.

661 Arthur Middleton, His Wife Mary Izard, and Their Son Henry Middleton c. 1770–71

DR. HENRY MIDDLETON DRINKER

Oil on canvas: $44\frac{3}{4} \times 66$ in. (113.5×167.5 cm.)

Signed lower left: *Benj. West*

PROV: By family descent to the present owner; currently on extended loan to the Middleton Place Foundation, Charleston, South Carolina

EXH: *Loan Exhibition of Historical Portraits*, Pennsylvania Academy of the Fine Arts, Philadelphia, 1887–88 (285); *Gallery of National Portraiture and Historical Scenes*, Pennsylvania Academy of the Fine Arts, Philadelphia, 1926 (24); Philadelphia 1938 (19)

ENGR: Detail of the head of Arthur Middleton ($5\frac{1}{8} \times 4\frac{1}{8}$ in.) by J. B. Longacre, after a drawing by T. Middleton after No. 661

LIT: Tuckerman 1867, p. 101; Anna Wells Rutledge, "Artists in the Life of Charleston," *Transactions of the American Philosophical Society*, XXXIX, part 2, 1949, p. 116 and fig. 7; Helen G. McCormack, "Expatriate Portraits: Charlestonians in Museums outside Charleston," *Antiques*, XCVIII, 1970, pp. 788–90; Ann C. Van Devanter, "The Signers' Wives," *Antiques*, CVIII, 1975, p. 120; Sarah Lytle, "Middleton Place," *Antiques*, CXV, 1979, p. 780

Arthur Middleton (1742–1787) was the eldest son of Henry Middleton (1717–1784) of Middleton Place in South Carolina, and the nephew of William Middleton (see No. 659). In 1754 he was sent to England with his uncle, and he remained there until 1763. Before his departure from England in December 1763, he was probably one of the five young men depicted by West in *The Cricketers* (Nos. 726 and 727, ill. p. 24).

to 1770, when West painted two further Middleton portraits (Nos. 661 and 662), seems more likely for both works. The further statement in Lady de Saumarez's inventory that West repainted No. 659 later in his life does seem confirmed by the free handling in the waistcoat and other details of the clothing.

[1] Typescript for *Portraits in Suffolk Houses (East)*, in the Ipswich, Suffolk, Public Library.

[2] Typescript at Shrubland, Suffolk. Copies of the relevant portions of this typescript and the Farrer typescript were kindly sent to Helmut von Erffa by Janet Green of Sotheby's in July 1971. The Sir William Fowle Fowle Middleton, Bt. (1784–1860), quoted by Lady de Saumarez, was the grandson of William Middleton.

660 [?] **Thomas Middleton of Crowfield** c. 1770

THE LORD DE SAUMAREZ

Oil on canvas: 49×39 in. (124.5×99 cm.)

PROV: Probably painted for William Middleton (1710–1785) of Crowfield, Suffolk, the sitter's father; thence by descent in the family of Sir William Fowle Middleton, Bt. (1749–1830), the sitter's elder brother, to the Hon. Mrs. Llewellen Palmer, daughter of the fifth Baron de Saumarez; included in sale catalogue, Sotheby's, London, 23 June 1971, lot 99 (as "Portrait of the Hon. Arthur Middleton"), but withdrawn; currently on extended loan to the Middleton Place Foundation, Charleston, South Carolina

Thomas Middleton of Crowfield (1753–1779) was the second son of William Middleton (see No. 659). Born in South Carolina, he was raised in England, where the family moved in 1754. In 1774, accompanied by his first cousin of the same name (see No. 662), he returned to South Carolina to reside at the family estate of Crowfield, and he died there in 1779.

Although the subject of No. 660 was identified as a portrait of Thomas Middleton, the son of William Mid-

661

In August 1764 he married Mary Izard of Charleston, whose cousin, Ralph Izard, is also depicted in *The Cricketers*. Arthur Middleton and his wife spent three years, from 1768 to 1771, travelling in England and on the continent of Europe, and their first child, Henry, was born in London on 28 September 1770. Arthur Middleton succeeded his father in 1776 as a member of the Continental Congress, and he was one of the signers of the Declaration of Independence. His son, Henry Middleton (1770–1846), was to be at various times a member of the United States Congress, Governor of South Carolina, and American Ambassador to Russia. In 1794 Henry Middleton married Mary Helen Hering of Bath, the daughter of Mary Inglis, depicted by West in No. 643.

West must have painted No. 661 some time after the birth of Henry Middleton on 28 September 1770, and before the departure of the Middleton family for America in August 1771. He also painted Arthur Middleton's younger brother Thomas at approximately the same time (No. 662). See the entry for No. 660 for the question of Arthur Middleton being the subject of that work as well. The pose of Thomas Middleton of Crowfield in the portrait at Drayton Hall showing him with his daughter, which is mentioned in the entry for No. 660, is clearly derived from that of Arthur Middleton in No. 661.

662 Thomas Middleton of The Oaks 1770

GIBBES ART GALLERY, CHARLESTON, SOUTH CAROLINA

Oil on canvas: $49\frac{1}{2} \times 39$ in. (125.5 × 99 cm.)

Signed lower left: *B. West 1770*

PROV: By family descent to Alicia H. Middleton, Bristol, Rhode Island, by whom given to the Gibbes Art Gallery in 1937

EXH: *Art in South Carolina*, Gibbes Art Gallery, 1970 (35); *Art in the Lives of South Carolinians*, Gibbes Art Gallery, 1979 (36)

LIT: Langdon Cheves, "Middleton of South Carolina," *South Carolina Historical and Genealogical Magazine*, I, 1900, p. 252, note 2; Alicia Middleton, Nathaniel Russell Middleton, Jr., and Nathaniel Middleton, *Life in Carolina and New England During the Nineteenth Century*, Bristol, Rhode Island, 1929, pp. 68–70, ill. opp. p. 74; Francis W. Bilodeau, "American Art at the Gibbes Art Gallery in Charleston," *Antiques*, XCVIII, 1970, p. 782

Thomas Middleton (1753–1797) of The Oaks was the youngest son of Henry Middleton (1717–1784) of Middleton Place and the younger brother of the Arthur Middleton (1742–1787) depicted by West in No. 661.

The Oaks, which he inherited, was an estate in Berkley County, South Carolina, that had been in the Middleton family since 1678. He was sent to England to be educated and returned to South Carolina in 1774, travelling together with his first cousin Thomas Middleton of Crowfield, who was painted by West in No. 660. West's portraits of the two cousins are the same size, and both show the subjects wearing Van Dyck dress. It seems likely that they were painted at approximately the same time,[1] as companion pictures, although they ended up belonging to different branches of the Middleton family on opposite sides of the Atlantic.

A copy of No. 662 belongs to a descendant of the sitter.

[1] No. 660 is not dated. The date on No. 662 is recorded as *1773* in the Gibbes Art Gallery catalogue, but Martha R. Severens, Curator of the Gibbes Art Gallery, has written (17 Jan. 1979) that recent cleaning reveals it to be *1770*.

663 Thomas Mifflin *c.* 1758–59
See color illustration, p. 8

HISTORICAL SOCIETY OF PENNSYLVANIA, PHILADELPHIA

Oil on canvas: $51\frac{1}{2} \times 38\frac{1}{2}$ in. (131 × 98 cm.)

662

contains reference to their friendship of many years before, is in the Rutgers University Library.

[1] Dunlap 1918, opp. p. 48. The picture is not mentioned in Dunlap's text.

664 Elizabeth Milward *c.* 1770–75

PHILBROOK ART CENTER, TULSA, OKLAHOMA

Oil on canvas: 30 × 25 in. (76 × 63.5 cm.)

PROV: Ainslie Galleries, New York; Laura A. Clubb

According to the files of the Philbrook Art Center, the sitter was from Eaton Dovedale, in Derbyshire.

665 General Robert Monckton *c.* 1764
See color illustration, p. 25

TRUSTEES OF LADY GALWAY'S CHATTELS SETTLEMENT

Oil on canvas: $94\frac{1}{2} \times 68\frac{3}{8}$ in. (240 × 173.5 cm.)

Inscribed lower right: *General Hon.*ble *Robert Monckton*

PROV: Painted for the sitter; thence by descent in the family of his brother, William Monckton, second Viscount Galway; currently on extended loan to the National Army Museum, London

EXH: SA 1764 (133) "A Gentleman, whole length"; *National Portrait Exhibition*, London, 1867 (407); *National Exhibition of Works of Art*, Leeds, 1868 (3152)

ENGR: Mezzotint ($19\frac{1}{2} \times 14$ in.) by James Watson, pub. by W. Austin

LIT: *Public Characters* 1805, p. 532; Carey 1820, p. 518; Galt 1820, p. 6; von Erffa 1973, p. 6, fig. 2; Alberts 1978, pp. 60 and 63

General Robert Monckton (1726–1782) was the second son of the first Viscount Galway. In 1759 he served as second-in-command under Wolfe at Quebec, where he was wounded, and he is shown by West with his arm in a sling in the *Death of General Wolfe* (No. 93). He subsequently served in Philadelphia in 1760 and was appointed Governor of New York in the following year. In 1762 he led a successful British expedition against Martinique, and in the summer of 1763 he returned to England. In 1765 he became Governor of Berwick-on-Tweed. In No. 665 he holds a roll of paper in his right hand inscribed *Plan of Martinique*, and the details of soldiers and a burning fortress in the background, as well as the cannon and tent in the foreground, all evidently commemorate his Caribbean victory.

Although West exhibited No. 665 only as a portrait of "A Gentleman" at the Society of Artists in 1764, all the early sources identify it as the exhibited picture. Hence, it was one of the first three works to be exhibited by the artist following his arrival in England in August 1763. The fullest account of the circumstances under which West painted and exhibited No. 665 is given by William Carey, who states that General Monckton heard reports of the young American Quaker who had arrived in London after studying painting in Italy:

> This brave officer had only recently returned from America, and he had, there, either seen or heard of Mr. West's brother, who had acted as captain in the Pennsylvania militia, under General Wayne, in 1757. These circumstances induced him to visit Mr. West and his pictures: and he was so struck with their merit that he sat to him for his own whole-length portrait. His friends being pleased with the likeness and military spirit of the picture, they pressed the artist to remain in England, and recommended him earnestly in his own circle. The portrait by an

664

PROV: Bequeathed by William Mifflin to the Historical Society of Pennsylvania in 1910

EXH: Philadelphia 1938 (9); *Life in America*, Metropolitan Museum of Art, New York, 1939 (14); *Life in Philadelphia*, Philadelphia Museum of Art, 1940 (67); *Centennial Exhibition*, Pennsylvania State University, State College, Pennsylvania, 1955 (4); *Faces of America*, Brooklyn Museum, Brooklyn, New York, 1967–68 (14); *Philadelphia Painting and Printing to 1776*, Pennsylvania Academy, Philadelphia, 1971 (33); *American Art 1750–1800: Towards Independence*, Yale University Art Gallery, New Haven, and Victoria and Albert Museum, London, 1976 (8)

LIT: Henderson 1911, p. 348; Theodore Bolton and Harry L. Binsse, "Wollaston, An Early Portrait Manufacturer," *Antiquarian*, XVI, 1931, pp. 50–52; Sawitzky 1938, pp. 443 and 457–58 (21); Sawitzky 1942, pp. 106–7; Wainwright 1974, pp. 174–75, ill. p. 37

Thomas Mifflin (1744–1800) graduated from the College of Philadelphia in 1760. He was subsequently a member of the first Continental Congress, a general in the revolutionary war, and Governor of Pennsylvania. Together with his wife, he is the subject of a well-known double portrait painted by Copley in 1773, which also belongs to the Historical Society of Pennsylvania.

No. 663 itself was referred to as a work by Copley by Helen Henderson the year after it entered the collection of the Historical Society of Pennsylvania, and Bolton and Binsse ascribed it to John Wollaston in 1931. It was, however, reproduced as a painting by West in the 1918 edition of William Dunlap's *History of the Rise and Progress of the Arts of Design in the United States*,[1] and it was included in the West exhibition in Philadelphia in 1938 and in William Sawitzky's seminal article on West's American work published in the same year. Sawitzky dates the painting *c.* 1758–59, when the sitter was fourteen or fifteen years old. A letter from West to Mifflin, dated 10 November 1795, which

American Quaker made a great noise; he got some sitters; and artists and amateurs flocked to his apartments to inspect the works of a painter from the New World. Romney, who had only settled in London the year before, Gainsborough, Wright of Derby, and Wilson were among his visitors. General Monckton took him to Reynolds at his house in Leicester-fields, and Reynolds paid him the compliment to call at the general's house and view the portrait. The Exhibition for 1764 was just then about to open in Spring Gardens; and at the express request of Reynolds and Wilson, he exhibited the whole-length of General Monckton, with his picture of *Cymon and Iphigenia* [No. 195], and that of *Angelica and Medoro* [No. 188].

The public success of these pictures, Carey continues, was one of the factors that induced West to abandon his plan to return to America.

Carey's statement that General Monckton introduced West to Reynolds is of particular interest in relation to No. 665.[1] West's imagery and use of subordinate details in the picture make it distinctly reminiscent of several of Reynolds's portraits of military and naval officers painted in the previous decade; the pose recalling the *Apollo Belvedere* recalls even more strongly that of Reynolds's *Commodore Keppel* of 1753–54 (National Maritime Museum, Greenwich); and it seems reasonable to think that West's patron encouraged the young artist, who had not previously undertaken a portrait of comparable scale or ambition to model his work on Reynolds's examples.[2] No portrait of Monckton by Reynolds is recorded. A portrait by Hudson, which demonstrates by contrast how dependent upon Reynolds West was, is in the same collection.[3]

West repeated the elaborate contemporary detail of No. 665 in a few other portraits (most notably in Nos. 628 and 647), but like Reynolds he soon turned to more generalized imagery in his portraits, frequently embellishing them with classicizing rather than contemporary detail. Unlike Reynolds, however, West also soon transposed the specificity and contemporaneity of portraits such as No. 665 into history painting: in *General Johnson Saving a Wounded French Officer from the Tomahawk of an American Indian* (No. 92) and in the *Death of General Wolfe* (No. 93), in which General Monckton, wearing the same uniform as in No. 665, plays a prominent role.

See also p. 31 above.

[1] Carey is contradicted by Galt, who states that the Mr. Patoune with whom West had travelled from Italy, introduced West to Reynolds (Galt 1820, p. 5).
[2] For the *Commodore Keppel*, see Ellis K. Waterhouse, *Reynolds*, London, 1939, pl. 27. For other military portraits see ibid., pls. 37, 60, 61, 78 and 86, and p. 25 above.
[3] *Thomas Hudson 1701–1779*, the Iveagh Bequest, Kenwood, 1979 (62).

666 **Samuel More** 1796

ROYAL SOCIETY OF ARTS, LONDON

Oil on canvas: $49\frac{1}{2} \times 39\frac{1}{2}$ in. (125.5 × 100.5 cm.)

Signed lower left: *B. West 1796*

PROV: Commissioned by the Society in 1796 for £66.8.0.

ENGR: Engraving ($16\frac{3}{4} \times 13\frac{5}{8}$ in.) by William Sharp, pub. 30 Nov. 1798 by Samuel More

LIT: Farington Diary, 11 July 1796 (Farington 1978–, II, p. 602); Henry Trueman Wood, *A History of the Royal Society of Arts*, London, 1913, pp. 327 and 518, ill. opp. p. 326

Samuel More served as Secretary to the Society of Arts in London from 1769 to 1799. In No. 666 the medal

he holds in his left hand is one of the premiums awarded annually by the Society. More himself was presented a gold medal by the Society in 1794, and in No. 666 he wears it attached to a button hole. Additional medals lie on the table before him. The design by James Stuart showing Britannia receiving awards from Minerva and Mercury can be seen clearly on the medal More wears. The volume in his right hand contains an inscription, which is only partly legible, referring to the Society's awards. That inscription is more completely legible on the engraving by Sharp: *Premiums offered in 1796 by the Society for the Encouragement of Arts Manufactures and Commerce*. One of the books on the desk in the foreground is entitled in the Sharp print, *Transact[ions] of the Society*. The chair behind him is the so-called President's Chair designed by William Chambers, which is still in use in the Society's Great Room.

Joseph Farington called on West on 11 July 1796, while he was at work on No. 666.

666

667 **Robert Morris** *c.* 1752

CHESTER COUNTY HISTORICAL SOCIETY, WEST CHESTER, PENNSYLVANIA

Oil on canvas: $18\frac{1}{2} \times 18$ in. (47 × 45.5 cm.)

PROV: Painted for John and Elizabeth Morris of Marple Township, Pennsylvania, the parents of the sitter; by family descent to Mrs. John E. Cornwell, West Chester, Pennsylvania, by whom presented to the Chester County Historical Society in 1984

EXH: *Pennsylvania at the Jamestown Exposition*, Hampton Roads, Virginia, 1907 (208); Philadelphia 1938 (3)

LIT: George Smith, *History of Delaware County, Pennsylvania*, Philadelphia, 1862, p. 513; Hart 1908, pp. 6–7; Brinton 1936; Sawitzky 1938, pp. 436–37 and 446–48 (5); Flexner 1952, pp. 16–17

No. 667 and its companion No. 668 are referred to in

a manuscript which in 1938 belonged to Mrs. John Cornwell, the owner of the two portraits, and which was quoted in the entry for the pictures in the catalogue of the West exhibition in Philadelphia in that year:

John and Elizabeth (Taylor) Morris had five children, Mary, Robert, Jane, Phebe and Hannah. There are two very curious portraits of Robert and Jane Morris, which are among the earliest paintings of Benjamin West. John Morris owned a store and took Benjamin West, when a small boy, to assist him in waiting on customers; finding that he had great talent for drawing, Mr. Morris bought and gave to the child a box of colours, with which he took the likenesses of the two Morris children about the year 1752.

The origins of the account are not known to the present writer. Galt describes a Dr. Jonathan Morris as a neighbor of the West family in Chester County, Pennsylvania, who gave the young Benjamin West "a present of a few dollars to buy materials to paint with."[1] This Dr. Morris was almost certainly Jonathan Morris (1729–1819) of Newtown Square, Pennsylvania, with whom West corresponded after settling in England, and the two stories of gifts to West of a box of colors and of money to buy materials may be recollections of the same act of generosity by a member of the Morris family. William Dunlap mentioned finding in Germantown, Pennsylvania, "a portrait painted in West's youth of a gentleman of the Morris family."[2] Nothing further is known about this picture; if correctly identified by Dunlap, it indicates further Morris patronage of the young West.

In 1862 George Smith described Nos. 667 and 668 as the only early works by West that he had been able to locate. At that time they belonged to a daughter of a sister of the two children. William Sawitzky examined the paintings in 1934 when they were in deteriorated condition, as the illustrations accompanying his article confirm. They were restored and partly repainted before being exhibited in Philadelphia in 1938.

The early date claimed for these pictures in the manuscript account cited above seems to be confirmed by the stiff (and charming) naïveté displayed in both of them. In 1752 West would have been fourteen years old. Along with the early landscape and seascape in the Pennsylvania Hospital (Nos. 480 and 481), Nos. 667 and 668 are the earliest paintings now known that we can reasonably accept as works by the artist.

[1]Galt 1816, p. 32.
[2]Dunlap 1834, p. 45 (Dunlap 1918, I, p. 45), and Sawitzky 1938, p. 462 (14).

667

668 Jane Morris c. 1752
See color illustration, p. 4

CHESTER COUNTY HISTORICAL SOCIETY, WEST CHESTER, PENNSYLVANIA

Oil on canvas: 18½ × 18 in. (47 × 45.5 cm.)

PROV: As for No. 667

EXH: As for No. 667, except no. 209 at Hampton Roads, 1907; and no. 4, Philadelphia, 1938

LIT: As for No. 667 (in Sawitzky 1938, pp. 446–47, no. 4)

669 John Sawrey Morritt 1765
See color illustration, p. 26

PRIVATE COLLECTION

Oil on canvas: 50 × 40 in. (127 × 101.5 cm.)

Signed lower right: *B. West/1765*

PROV: By descent in the family of the sitter

EXH: (?) SA 1765 (154) "Portrait of a gentleman in Vandyke dress, three quarters"

LIT: Bea Howe, "Pioneer of the Woolwork Picture," *Country Life*, CXI, 7 March 1952, pp. 656–58

John Sawrey Morritt (1738–1791), the son of Bacon Morritt of Cawood in Lancashire, purchased Rokeby Park, at the junction of the Rivers Greta and Tees near Barnard Castle, in 1769, four years after the date on No. 669. Since it is a three-quarter-length portrait of a man wearing Van Dyck costume, it probably can be safely identified as the "Portrait of a gentleman in Vandyke dress, three quarters" exhibited by West in 1765.

Portraits by West of the subject's wife and his sister are Nos. 670 and 671. A notebook dated 1805, which is quoted by Bea Howe in an article about the subject of No. 671, mentions three portraits by West at Rokeby of three members of the family, including one of "Mr. Morritt." In the same collection, there is also a bust-length portrait of John Sawrey Morritt wearing black Van Dyck dress, rather than red as in No. 669, but which, nonetheless, appears to have been copied from No. 669.[1] It is inscribed on the back: *J. S. Morritt Esq./ Anne Morritt.* The Anne Morritt of the inscription was presumably the subject's older sister (see No. 671), who was an artist in her own right.

No. 669 is in the manner of the male portraits that West had painted in Italy, such as Nos. 582 and 730, recalling the portrait styles of Batoni and Mengs. Both paintings show their subjects in Van Dyck costume.

[1]Oil on canvas, 30 × 25 in. We are indebted to William Hood, Conservator of Paintings at the Bowes Museum, for information about this work (letter of 25 February 1985).

670 Mrs. John Sawrey Morritt c. 1765
See color illustration, p. 27

PRIVATE COLLECTION

Oil on canvas: 50 × 39½ in. (127 × 100.5 cm.)

Signed lower right: *B. West/17[ ]*

PROV: As for No. 669

EXH: (?) SA 1765 (153) "Portrait of a lady in masquerade dress, half length"

LIT: As for No. 669

No. 670 is a companion to No. 669 and shows the wife of John Sawrey Morritt, Anne (died 1809), the daughter of Henry Peirse of Bedale. The last two digits of the date on No. 670 are illegible, but West probably painted it in 1765, the same year as No. 669, and it may have been the "Portrait of a lady in masquerade dress" which he exhibited in that year. However, the identification is made slightly problematic by the fact that the "gentleman in Vandyke dress" which West exhibited in 1765 was described as "three quarters," whereas the "lady in masquerade dress" was "half length." Although the terms themselves are loose enough to be virtually interchangeable, it is questionable that West would have described companion pictures, which are identical in size, differently in successive entries in the same exhibition catalogue.

The notebook from 1805 cited by Bea Howe (see No. 669) described the portraits by West at Rokeby as showing "Mr. Peirse, Mr. Morritt and Mrs. Anne Morritt—the latter of whom has graced the house with some extraordinary efforts of her needle." Mr. Morritt is the subject of No. 669, but there seems to be no portrait of Mr. Peirse now at Rokeby, and although the subject of No. 670 is Mrs. Anne Morritt, the lady who graced Rokeby with the efforts of her needle was her sister-in-law, Miss (rather than Mrs.) Anne Morritt, the subject of No. 671.

671 Anne Elizabeth Morritt *c.* 1773–78

PRIVATE COLLECTION

Oil on canvas: 48½ × 38½ in. (123 × 98 cm.)

PROV: As for No. 669

LIT: As for No. 669

Anne Elizabeth Morritt (1726–1797) was the elder sister of John Sawrey Morritt, the subject of No. 669. She was a skilled artist in needlework, specializing in making copies in woolen yarns after actual paintings. Many of her works, including the one depicted in No. 671, are still at Rokeby, and several are reproduced in the article about her work by Bea Howe in *Country Life* (for which see also No. 670).

On stylistic grounds, No. 671 would seem to be somewhat later than Nos. 669 and 670, dating perhaps from the mid-1770s, when the sitter would have been around fifty years old.

672 Moses the Jew before 1760

LOCATION UNKNOWN

(Miniature)

PROV: Sarah Hill Dillwyn, Philadelphia; Thomas Chalkley James, Philadelphia (1766–1835)

LIT: John Jay Smith, ed., *The Letters of Doctor Richard Hill and His Children*, privately printed, Philadelphia, 1854, p. 251

This work is known only from a brief mention in a letter written by a Philadelphian, Sarah Hill Dillwyn (1738/39–1826), during a trip to England with her husband in July 1784: "I gave little Tommy James a miniature of Moses the Jew; B. West wishes he had it, as being one of his early production; if thou can procure it without mentioning my name, I should be glad." The recipient of this letter was Margaret Hill Morris (1737–1816), the writer's sister. Little Tommy James is identified by John Jay Smith as Thomas Chalkley James (1766–1835), who was to become an eminent obstetrician and a professor of medicine at the University of Pennsylvania.

There are two further references to West in letters written by Sarah Dillwyn to her sister during the same trip and also published by Smith: "Did I tell thee that Benny West came to see us?"; and "The last time I spent a day in town, Benny West, his wife, and two

671

sons came to see me."[1] The two sisters were almost exact contemporaries of the artist, and the informal "Benny" suggests a close friendship, dating possibly from childhood, certainly from before West's departure from Philadelphia in 1760.

[1] Smith, pp. 249 and 253. We are indebted to Mr. William J. Little of Baltimore for bringing this correspondence to our attention (letter of 9 October 1980).

673 John Murray 1762

LOCATION UNKNOWN

LIT: Alberts 1978, p. 50

John Murray (*c.* 1715–1775) was the British Resident in Venice from 1754 to 1766 and, hence, was there when West visited the city in the autumn of 1762. West's travelling companions of 1760, John Allen and Joseph Shippen, had earlier visited Venice in the summer of 1760, shortly after their arrival from America,

while West had gone directly to Rome. They met Murray, and on his behalf Shippen solicited from West the painting of the *Savage Chief Taking Leave of His Family* (No. 452). When West arrived in Venice two years later Murray seems to have been extremely solicitous of him. According to a letter to Joseph Shippen written by West on 1 September 1763, after he had arrived in London, but recounting his activities since May of 1762, "The particular kindness of Mr. Murray, at Venice, made my stay there much longer than I ever imagined, for which I am in great measure obliged to you, good sir, and Mr. Allen, by your speaking so advantageously of me, when you were there."[1]

Our only information about No. 673 comes from a letter written by Robert Rutherford, of the Leghorn firm of Jackson and Rutherford, on 22 April 1763, also to Joseph Shippen, in which there is a reference to West's painting a half-length portrait of Murray for forty "zeccheenis" and a portrait of Lady Northampton and her daughter (No. 676) for fifty.[2] Rutherford may have had this information directly from West,

537

674

or it may have come from West's companion on the visit to Venice, Henry Matthews, who had formerly been the manager of the firm of Jackson and Rutherford.

[1] Richardson 1978, p. 23.
[2] American Philosophical Society, Philadelphia; cited in Alberts 1978, pp. 50 and 427 (note).

674 Richard Newcome, Bishop of St. Asaph 1767

QUEEN'S COLLEGE, CAMBRIDGE, ENGLAND

Oil on canvas: 56 × 44¾ in. (142.3 × 113.8 cm.)

Inscribed lower left: *Richd Newcome L^d B^p of/St Asaph/ B. West PINXIT/1767*

EXH: *Cambridge Portraits: From Lely to Hockney*, Fitzwilliam Museum, Cambridge, 1978 (10, ill. in cat.)

Richard Newcome (1700/1–1769) was admitted to Queen's College as a pensioner in 1718 and held a fellowship there from 1723 to 1734. He served as Bishop of Llandaff from 1755 to 1761, and as Bishop of St. Asaph from 1761 to his death. It is not known when and how No. 674 was acquired by his old college.

Newcome's name is not recorded by Galt et al. among those of the prelates who gave West substantial early support. The date of 1767 on No. 674, nevertheless, does suggest that the commission must have been somehow connected with the patronage that West was contemporaneously receiving from the Archbishop of York and the Bishops of Worcester and Bristol.

675 Thomas Newton, Bishop of Bristol *c.* 1767

TRINITY COLLEGE, CAMBRIDGE, ENGLAND

Oil on canvas: 50 × 40 in. (127 × 101 cm.)

Signed lower right: *B. West Pinxit*, and also inscribed with the name of the sitter

ENGR: Mezzotint (17 11/16 × 14 in.) by Richard Earlom, pub. 1 Dec. 1767 by J. Boydell; engraving (5½ × 4½ in.) by Samuel Freeman, pub. by B. Blake

LIT: Galt 1820, p. 9; von Erffa 1973, pp. 7 and 9; Alberts 1978, p. 73

Thomas Newton (1704–1782) served as Bishop of Bristol from 1761 until 1782. In 1768 he also became Dean of St. Paul's Cathedral in London.

Galt lists Newton as one of the three bishops to whom Dr. Markham, the Master of Westminster School, introduced West in 1765. The other two were Robert Drummond, the Archbishop of York, and James Johnson, Bishop of Worcester. All three commissioned or purchased paintings from West in the following years. Newton acquired at least two early paintings by West in addition to No. 675: the *Parting of Hector and Andromache* (No. 163) and *Elisha Restores to Life the Shunamite's Son* (No. 281).[1] A painting of the former subject appears in the background of No. 675,[2] and this detail is mentioned by Galt. In 1773, Newton, as Dean, encouraged the abortive scheme of several members of the Royal Academy, including West, to decorate St. Paul's Cathedral with paintings (see No. 257).

In addition to the painting in the background, No. 675 also includes volumes inscribed *Holy BIBLE* and *Newton/MILTON* on a desk next to which the Bishop is seated. The latter volume leans on a bust of Milton and was certainly intended to represent the edition of Milton's works published by Newton beginning in 1749. Further evidence of the Bishop's activity as a writer is provided by the sheet of paper lying under his right hand, upon which the word *Dissertations* is written. This alludes to Bishop Newton's main theological work, *Dissertations on the prophecies, which have remarkably been fulfilled, and at this time are fulfilling in the world,* commenced in 1754, a work which, it has been claimed, was of major importance for West's great series of paintings devoted to the History of Revealed Religion painted for George III.[3]

[1] The lists of West's works in *Public Characters* (p. 562) and the *Universal Magazine* (p. 528) precede the group of six paintings in the collection of Henry Hope (see No. 640) with the notation "First painted for the late Bishop of Bristol." The list in *La Belle Assemblée* contains the same claim for Hope's pictures but the actual titles are left out so that it appears to be made for West's designs for Greenwich Hospital. It is possible that Newton did own one or more of the paintings that subsequently belonged to Hope (Nos. 180, 189, and 193), but the other three works in the group (Nos. 22, 392, and 640) were only painted after his death.
[2] The painting in the background appears in the mezzotint by Richard Earlom (ill. p. 249), but not in the smaller print by Samuel Freeman.
[3] See Dillenberger 1977, pp. 60–61 et passim.

676 Anne, Countess of Northampton, and Her Daughter, Lady Elizabeth Compton 1762
See color illustration, p. 18

BASS MUSEUM OF ART, MIAMI BEACH, FLORIDA

Oil on canvas: 52 × 42 in. (132 × 106.5 cm.)

Signed lower right: *B. West/Venice/1762*

PROV: Sold anonymously, Christie's, London, 7 April 1933, lot 135, bt. by Marshall; sold again, Christie's, London, 26 May 1933, lot 18, bt. by Edwards; sold

675

anonymously, Anderson Galleries, New York, 17–18 May 1934, lot 137; given by Chester Dale to the Minneapolis Institute of Arts in 1945; sold by the museum in 1958 to Julius Weitzner, New York and London; presented by Mr. and Mrs. John Bass to the Bass Museum (opened in 1964)

LIT: "A West Portrait of the Italian Period," *Bulletin of the Minneapolis Institute of Arts*, XXXIV, 1945, pp. 96–101; von Erffa 1973, p. 5; Alberts 1978, p. 50

Lady Anne Somerset (1740/41–1763), the daughter of the fourth Duke of Beaufort, married Charles Compton, the seventh Earl of Northampton (1737–1763) in 1759. Their only child, Lady Elizabeth Compton, was born in June 1760. In 1782 she married George Augustus Henry Cavendish, who was subsequently created Earl of Burlington, and she died in 1835.

The seventh Earl of Northampton was appointed Ambassador Extraordinary and Plenipotentiary to Venice in August 1762, and he arrived there on 17 October.[1] The exact dates of when West was in Venice are not known, but a letter from the Earl dated 13 November 1762, referring to the expected arrival in Venice of George III's librarian, Richard Dalton, whom West met in Venice, establishes that at least part of his stay must have been after that date.[2] West's activity as a painter while in Venice is described in a letter from Robert Rutherford in Leghorn to Joseph Shippen dated 22 April 1763, which reports that he painted two portraits while there, "being both, I believe, half lengths," and the second being "Lady Northampton's, the Ambassador's Lady in the Character of a Madonna, with her Child in her Arms, which gained great applause; 50 zeccheenis are given him for it."[3] The other portrait painted by West during the visit is No. 673 above, for which, according to the same source, he received forty *zecchini*.

As the birth and death dates given above indicate, Lady Elizabeth Compton, who was slightly over two years old when West painted No. 676, was orphaned within a year, her mother dying in Italy on 18 May 1763, and her father in France in the following October. Twenty years later she was to be the subject of a memorable full-length portrait by Reynolds, now in the National Gallery of Art in Washington.[4]

The "Character of a Madonna, with her Child in her Arms," which Rutherford noted in No. 676, was obviously inspired by Renaissance paintings that West had seen since his arrival in Italy. The composition of No. 676 seems to be an amalgam of those of the *Madonna della Granduca* and the *Madonna della Sedia* (ill. p. 19) by Raphael (Pitti Palace, Florence), and the relation of foreground figures to background space echoes that of the *Madonna and Child with St. Jerome* by Correggio in Parma, of which West had started a copy in the autumn of 1762, before going on to Venice (No. 505). West painted several later paintings of mothers and children which also show strong debts to Renaissance Madonnas, most notably Nos. 535–39. A drawing of a mother and child, or Madonna and Child in a sketchbook that West used both in Italy and after settling in England (Royal Academy, London) may be a preliminary sketch for No. 676 although it differs from the painting in numerous details.

[1] D. B. Horn, *British Diplomatic Representatives 1689–1789*, London, 1932, p. 85.
[2] Michael Levey, *Later Italian Pictures in the Collection of Her Majesty the Queen*, London, 1964, p. 30.
[3] American Philosophical Society, Philadelphia; cited in Alberts 1978, pp. 50 and 427 (note).
[4] Ellis K. Waterhouse, *Reynolds*, London, 1941, pl. 230.

677 Spencer Compton, Eighth Earl of Northampton, with His Wife and Children
c. 1764–65

678

THE MARQUESS OF NORTHAMPTON, CASTLE ASHBY, NORTHAMPTON

Oil on canvas: 100 × 76 in. (254 × 193 cm.)

Inscribed lower left: *Spencer/8th Earl of North^ton & Jane his Wife./His Son, Aft^wds 1st Marquis/& Lady Frances Compton/(by West.)* (not by West's hand)

PROV: By descent at Castle Ashby

As the inscription on No. 677 indicates, the picture shows the eighth Earl of Northampton (1738–1796) together with his first wife, Jane, their daughter, Lady Frances Compton, and their son, Charles (1760–1828), who succeeded to his father's titles and in 1812 was created first Marquess of Northampton. Castle Ashby, seen from the south-east is in the background.

No. 677 has traditionally been described as painted in 1764 or 1765, and this approximate date is sustained by the apparent age of the future first Marquess in the painting. The eighth Earl's first wife died in November

1767, and he had no children by his second marriage. West had painted the wife and daughter of the seventh Earl while in Venice in 1762 (No. 676). The eighth Earl was the brother of the seventh Earl and succeeded to the title upon the death of the latter in October 1763.

678 Captain John Neale Pleydell Nott *c.* 1768–72

NATIONAL TRUST, LYDIARD PARK, LYDIARD TREGOZE, WILTSHIRE

Oil on canvas: 37½ × 32¾ in. (95.2 × 83.2 cm.)

PROV: By descent in the family of the sitter to Colonel Richard Ffolliott Willis, by whom bequeathed to the National Trust in 1956; lent by the Trust to the Corporation of Swindon to hang at Lydiard Park at Colonel Willis's request

679

680

LIT: Ellis Waterhouse, "The Willis Family at Lydiard Park," in *National Trust Studies*, 1980, p. 53, fig. 7

John Neale Pleydell Nott (1732–1781) was a captain in the Royal Navy. He was killed in action against the French while commanding the *Centaur* in the Caribbean in April 1781. No. 678 is neither signed nor dated, but the apparent age of the sitter and the style of the painting suggest that it was executed in the late 1760s or early 1770s.

679 Admiral Ommanney 1773

NATIONAL GALLERY OF IRELAND, DUBLIN

Oil on canvas: 30 × 25 in. (76 × 63.5 cm.)

Signed center right: *B. West/1773*

PROV: Purchased by the Gallery from Langdon Douglas in 1922

LIT: National Gallery of Ireland, *Catalogue of Oil Pictures in the General Collection*, Dublin, 1932, p. 136 (838)

The identification of the subject of this painting comes from an old label on the verso of the frame. Although there have been several officers of the name of Ommanney in the Royal Navy, the earliest one for whom the compilers of this catalogue have been able to find any record was Rear-Admiral Cornthwaite Ommanney, who died in 1801 at the age of sixty-five. He would have been approximately thirty-seven years old in 1773, the date on No. 679, an age that would seem to be considerably less than that of the subject shown in the picture.

The sitter rests his right hand upon an astronomical globe, showing signs of the zodiac.

680 Charles Willson Peale *c.* 1769

THE NEW-YORK HISTORICAL SOCIETY, NEW YORK

Oil on canvas: 28¼ × 23 in. (72 × 58.5 cm.)

PROV: It is generally assumed that West gave No. 680 to the sitter; purchased by Thomas J. Bryan from the Peale Museum in Philadelphia, when the museum closed in 1854, and given by Bryan to the New-York Historical Society in 1867

EXH: Washington and Philadelphia 1980

LIT: Charles Coleman Sellers, *Charles Willson Peale*, New York, 1969, p. 61, fig. 13; *Catalogue of American Portraits in the New-York Historical Society*, New Haven and London, 1974, II, p. 608 (1574); Alberts 1978, pp. 77–78

The American painter Charles Willson Peale (1741–1827) studied in London under West from February 1767 to March 1769. Since Peale and West never met again, No. 680, which is not signed or dated, must have been painted during this period, and it was presumably given by the artist to the sitter. When Peale left London, West also gave him an adjustable sitter's chair.[1] In America in 1771, Peale reciprocated by painting a portrait of one of West's brothers, identified by Sellers as John West, Jr., of Fairfax County, Virginia, as a present for West.[2] The two men remained in contact via correspondence until after 1800.

[1] See Sellers 1969, p. 74.
[2] Referred to in a letter from Peale to John Beale Bordley, 20 Nov. 1771 (quoted and discussed in Charles Coleman Sellers, *Portraits and Miniatures by Charles Willson Peale*, Philadelphia, 1952, p. 245, no. 966).

681 Elizabeth Peel *c.* 1757–58

PENNSYLVANIA ACADEMY OF THE FINE ARTS, PHILADELPHIA

Oil on canvas: 47¼ × 34⅛ in. (120 × 86.5 cm.)

PROV: Ehrich Galleries, New York; John Frederick Lewis, Philadelphia, by whom bequeathed to the Pennsylvania Academy in 1923

EXH: *In This Academy*, PAFA 1976 (88)

LIT: Sawitzky 1938, pp. 443–44, 455–56 (18)

The sitter is said to have been the daughter of Oswald Peel of Philadelphia, and to have married a Mr. Harris. Sawitzky, who dates the picture *c.* 1757–58, points out the strong influence of John Wollaston, describing it as "an almost literal copy" of the *Portrait of Margaret Oswald* by Wollaston (ill. p. 6).

682 Lady Juliana Penn *c.* 1773

LOCATION UNKNOWN

PROV: Commissioned by the Juliana Library Company, Lancaster, Pennsylvania, in 1772, but evidently never delivered; sold by West's sons, Robins, London, 20–22 June 1829, lot 173

LIT: "Notes and Queries," *Pennsylvania Magazine of History and Biography*, XVIII, 1894, p. 514; E. V. Lamberton, "Colonial Libraries in Pennsylvania," ibid., XLII, 1918, pp. 231–32; Charles Coleman Sellers, "The Beginning: A Monument to Probity, Candor and Peace," in *Symbols of Peace: William Penn's Treaty*

681

543

with the Indians (exhibition catalogue), Pennsylvania Academy of the Fine Arts, Philadelphia, 1976

Lady Juliana Fermor (1729–1801), a daughter of the first Earl of Pomfret, married Thomas Penn (1702–1775), a son of the founder of Pennsylvania, on 22 August 1751. Thomas Penn lived in Philadelphia from 1732 to 1741. He never returned to America again, but after the death of his elder brother in 1746 he owned a three-quarter interest in the proprietary lands in Pennsylvania and was effective ruler of the state. In 1771–72 West painted *William Penn's Treaty with the Indians* (No. 85) for him.

Lady Juliana seems to have been a supporter of various cultural institutions in Pennsylvania, and her gift in 1763 of books and globes to the recently founded library in Lancaster led to the library's being renamed "The Juliana Library Company" to commemorate her benefaction. Nine years later, on 21 December 1772, the directors of the Company made the following resolution:

> *Resolved* that, in Testimony of the great Affection and Esteem which this Company bear to the Right Honourable LADY JULIANA PENN, her Ladyship be addressed and requested to permit Mr. West to take her picture to be placed in the Company's Library Room.
> *Resolved* that Benjamin West Esqʳ of Pennsylvania now resident in London, be requested to wait on Lady Penn for Permission to take her Portrait, of the Size commonly called 3/4 Size, for the Juliana Library Company at Lancaster, and at their expense. And that Edward Shippen Esqʳ the Revᵈ Mr. Barton & George Ross Esqʳ be a Committee to draw up and transmit the proper Addresses to Lady Juliana Penn and Mr. West with an Extract from the Minutes of this Meeting under the Company's Seal.

Of the committee, George Ross had been painted by West during the young artist's visit to Lancaster in the 1750s (No. 691), and Edward Shippen was the father of the Joseph Shippen with whom West had travelled to Italy in 1760. The librarian of the Juliana Library Company in 1772 was West's early patron in Lancaster, William Henry (see No. 637), in whose home the library was situated.

The painting of Lady Juliana Penn is not in Lancaster, and there is evidently no further information about the commission in the library's minutes. It has, therefore, generally been assumed that the portrait was never painted. Nevertheless, a portrait of Lady Juliana by West was sold by West's sons following his death, and that picture was presumably the work commissioned from him in 1772. It may not have been delivered because of the deteriorating relations between England and her American colonies in the years following 1772.

683 William Henry Cavendish Bentinck, Third Duke of Portland, and His Brother, Lord Edward Bentinck 1774

PRIVATE COLLECTION

Oil on canvas: 95 × 59 in. (241.5 × 150 cm.)

Signed lower left: *B. West/1774*

PROV: By family descent

EXH: RA 1775 (337) "Portrait of a nobleman and his brother; whole lengths"

ENGR: Mezzotint (16 × 10 in.) by John Raphael Smith, pub. 24 June 1780 by W. Humphrey

LIT: C. Fairfax Murray, *Catalogue of the Pictures belonging*

683

to His Grace the Duke of Portland, at Welbeck Abbey, and in London, London, 1893, p. 99 (347); Richard W. Goulding and C. K. Adams, *Catalogue of the Pictures Belonging to His Grace the Duke of Portland, K.G.*, Cambridge, England, 1936, pp. 136–37 (347)

William Henry Cavendish Bentinck (1738–1809) succeeded as third Duke of Portland in 1762. His brother, Edward Charles Bentinck, was born in 1744 and died in 1819. Their sister was the wife of the fifth Earl of Stamford, whom West painted in 1765 (No. 625). The third Duke had a distinguished political career, serving twice as Prime Minister, and West subsequently painted a second portrait of him in the role of Chancellor of Oxford University (No. 684).

In No. 683, the Duke wears ermine, and his ducal coronet is on a pedestal to the left. The social rank of the subjects made this picture the grandest portrait commission that West in 1774 had yet received. It looks forward to the double portraits of the royal princes that West was to paint in 1777 and 1778 (Nos. 564 and 568), and its appearance at the Royal Academy in 1775 may have suggested to George III the possibility of employing West for portraits of the royal family as well as for history painting.

West must have completed No. 683 almost a year

before he exhibited it, as a letter dated 17 June 1774 from a James Moray to the third Duke asks permission for "Mr. West to paint me a quarter length from the picture he has done for you."[1] Nothing further is known about this quarter length, and it may never have been painted. What appears to be a modified copy after No. 683, based probably on the J. R. Smith mezzotint, is in the National Gallery of Art in Washington and has traditionally been ascribed to Matthew Pratt.[2]

[1]Quoted by Goulding and Adams, p. 137.
[2]Oil on canvas: 30 × 25 in. (see William Sawitzky, *Matthew Pratt 1734–1805*, New York, 1942, pp. 59–60 and pl. 9. Sawitzky dates the painting *c.* 1765–66 on the assumption that Pratt painted it from life during his stay in London).

684

684 The Third Duke of Portland 1814

THE CURATORS OF THE EXAMINATION SCHOOLS, OXFORD

Oil on canvas: 96 × 72 in. (244 × 183 cm.)

Signed lower left: *B. West/1814*

PROV: Given to the University by the fourth Duke of Portland, son of the subject, in 1816

EXH: RA 1814 (103) "Portrait of His Grace the Late Duke of Portland as Chancellor of the University of Oxford"; *Loan Collection of Portraits of English Historical Personages who Died between 1714 and 1837*, Examination Schools, Oxford, 1906 (161) lent by the Curators of the Bodleian Library

LISTED: Galt, p. 234; Dillenberger, p. 190 (515)

LIT: Mrs. Reginald Poole, *Catalogue of Portraits in the Possession of the University, Colleges, City and County of Oxford*, Oxford, 1925, I, p. 143 (348)

The third Duke of Portland (for whom see also No. 683) died in 1809, five years before the date on No. 684 and before the picture was exhibited as a portrait of the "Late Duke." A view of the Radcliffe Camera through the opening on the left is consistent with the indication in the Royal Academy catalogue that the painting shows the Duke as Chancellor of the University of Oxford. He became Chancellor in 1792.

A very small and slight sketch for the composition was with the Covent Garden Gallery, London, in 1981.[1] A second version or copy was at one time in a private collection in London.[2]

[1]Pen, 2⅜ × 1¾ in.
[2]Photograph in the Witt Library, London.

685 The Reverend Samuel Preston 1797

LIBRARY COMPANY OF PHILADELPHIA

Oil on canvas: 36 × 28 in. (91.5 × 71 cm.)

Signed lower right: *B. West 1797*

PROV: Presented to the Library Company by West or Mrs. West in 1804

EXH: (?) RA 1797 (205) "Portrait of a Clergyman"; PAFA 1819 (4); *American Painting from 1700 to 1900*, Newark Museum, 1930; Philadelphia 1938 (47)

LIT: Farington Diary, 8 Feb. 1797 (Farington 1978–, III, p. 765); Tuckerman 1867, p. 101; Henderson, 1911, p. 77; George M. Abbot, *A Short History of the Library Company of Philadelphia*, Philadelphia, 1913, p. 17; Austin K. Gray, *Benjamin Franklin's Library: A Short Account of the Library Company of Philadelphia 1731–1931*, New York, 1937, p. 43; Rita Susswein Gottesman, *The Arts and Crafts in New York: 1800–1804*, New York, 1965, pp. 40–41 (76) (*Morning Chronicle*, 13 Aug. 1804)

Samuel Preston (*c.* 1717–1803) was the Rector of Chevening in Kent. Two portraits of him by West (Nos. 685 and 686) are known or recorded. The available documentation does not give any indication of which was painted first, or if the second was simply a replica of its predecessor.

On 8 February 1797, Joseph Farington recorded in his diary:

West has just finished a Head of the Revd. Mr. Preston with which he is much delighted.—He recommends a union of the two processes, the *Roman* with the *Venetian*. Smirke remarked to me that there is most of the *Roman* in this Head,—it is not a fair trial of the *Venetian*.

The two processes mentioned in this passage allude to West's experiments with the so-called Venetian Secret, with which he was occupied in the winter of 1796–97 (and for which see No. 543, etc.). The picture described by Farington in February was presumably the same work that West exhibited at the Royal Academy in the following May as a "Portrait of a Clergyman."[1]

A second reference to Preston appears in the entry in Farington's diary for 15 June 1803, written following a visit to West.[2] This records that Preston, now in his eighty-sixth year, was supposed to be dying and had directed in his will that his valuable library should go to the library at Philadelphia, with West as a trustee. Later in the same year, the Library Company of Philadelphia received notice of the bequest, and the books themselves arrived in Philadelphia between 2 and 9 August 1804. Evidently No. 685 was sent with them, but as a gift of the artist or his wife rather than as part of the bequest; the minutes of the Company for 25 August 1804 record: "The Secretary was directed to write a letter of thanks to Mr. West for the picture of Mr. Preston."[3] When and how West met Preston is not known. In 1807 West told Nicholas Biddle that it was he who induced Preston to give his library to Philadelphia, and he employed a bookseller to make the arrangements.[4] Preston seems to have had no connection with Philadelphia apart from West. He had written to the directors of the Library Company as early as 1783 congratulating them on the exploits of their fellow citizens and wishing the library well, but his interest in the library then may already have been due to West. A drawing by West of "A Christening in Chevening Church, Kent," is in the Yale Center for British Art.[5] In 1785 John Trumbull and Raphael West paid a week's visit to the Reverend Mr. Preston at Chevening.[6]

[1]The exhibited picture is identified as "Rev. Mr. Preston" in Graves 1906, VIII, p. 216.
[2]Farington 1978—, VI, p. 2056.
[3]Letter from Edwin Wolf II to Helmut von Erffa, 18 July 1962. Although the Library Company thanked West for the portrait, a notice that appeared in the New York Morning Chronicle on 13 August 1804, reporting the arrival of the portrait, states that it was presented by Mrs. Elizabeth West as "an offering of her affectionate attachment to her native city." Mrs. West was also described as the donor when No. 685 was exhibited at the Pennsylvania Academy in 1819.
[4]Wainwright 1978, p. 113.
[5]Black and white chalk on blue paper, $4\frac{5}{8} \times 7\frac{1}{2}$ in. (sold S. Leigh Sotheby, London, 1 June 1839, lot 25).
[6]Trumbull 1953, pp. 87–88.

685

686 The Reverend Samuel Preston

LOCATION UNKNOWN

PROV: Sold by West's sons, Robins, London, 20–22 June 1829, lot 93 ("Portrait of the late Mr. Preston, founder of the Prestonian Library at Philadelphia, in America")

LISTED: PC, p. 566 ("Portrait of the Rev.— Preston," West, Painting-room); UM, p. 530; BA, p. 17; Galt, p. 228; Dillenberger, p. 172 (336)

Since No. 685 was in America by the summer of 1804, the painting described in the early lists as in West's possession and sold by West's sons in 1829 must have been a separate picture. It is not known which West painted first or which he exhibited in 1797.

687 Dr. Richard Price 1788

EQUITABLE LIFE ASSURANCE SOCIETY, LONDON

Oil on canvas: 34 × 26 in. (86.5 × 66 cm.)

Signed center left: B. West

PROV: Commissioned by Dr. (? Daniel) Watkin, 1788; in the possession of the Equitable Life Assurance Society by 1868

EXH: London 1868 (915) lent by the Equitable Assurance Office

ENGR: Engraving ($12\frac{1}{16} \times 9\frac{1}{4}$ in.) by Thomas Holloway, pub. by Holloway 22 Feb. 1793

LIT: Caroline E. Williams, A Welsh Family from the Beginning of the Eighteenth Century, London, 1893, p. 61; Maurice E. Ogborn, Equitable Assurances; The Story of Life Assurance in the Experience of the Equitable Life Assurance Society, 1762–1962, London, 1962, pl. 8; "Richard Price's Journal for the Period 25 March 1787 to 6 February 1791," deciphered by Beryl Thomas with an introduction and notes by D. O. Thomas, National Library of Wales Journal, XXI, 1980, p. 384

Richard Price (1723–1791), a native of Llangeinor, Glamorganshire, was a Non-Conformist minister, and a writer on a variety of subjects including moral philosophy, government finances, and life insurance. He was a friend of Benjamin Franklin, with whom he corresponded about financial questions, and a supporter of the American cause in the revolutionary war. In 1778 the Continental Congress invited Price to take charge of the finances of the United States and offered him American citizenship. Price declined, but he retained close American ties. He was granted an honorary LL.D. from Yale in 1781 (along with George Washington), and he was elected a Fellow of the American Academy of Arts and Sciences in Boston in 1782 and a member of the American Philosophical Society of Philadelphia in 1785.[1]

In No. 687 Price holds a letter dated *Philadelphia/1784* and signed *Ben Franklin*. By his elbow in the lower right corner of the composition is a book labelled *BUTLER'S ANALOGY*; this is *The Analogy of Religion, Natural and Revealed, to the Constitution and Course of Nature* published in 1736 by Bishop Joseph Butler (1692–1756), an anti-Deist tract which had a lifelong influence on Price, and to which his own published sermons were compared in 1786.[2]

The circumstances under which West painted Price's portrait are described in a passage in Price's shorthand diary written on 4 May 1788, when Price was recuperating from a long illness:

It was my resolution to descend to the grave without consenting to sit for any picture of me. I have resisted several solicitations, but the last winter Mr. Tr(——)e overpowered me by his importunity and I consented to sit to Mr. H(——)t for a *miniature* picture. Having happened to mention this to another friend (Mr. W[——]n) he consequently observed that it was a pity that as my resolution was now broken I should not consent to have a picture of me taken in the best manner and therefore begged I would gratify him by sitting to one of the first painters. Being under great obligations to him I did not know how to refuse and I have since sat to Mr. W(——)st. This is an affair that has sorely perplexed me and I have frequently lamented my own want of firmness in this *instance*. I have vanity enough but not this sort of vanity. I have felt at the time of sitting so embarrassed and distressed that I must have been an insufferable subject. I am, however, now it is over reconciled to it and inclined to feel the vanity that I suppose is usual on such occasions. But one aspect *troubles* me exceedingly and that is the expense to which is puts Mr. W(——)n.[3]

In his notes on the diary, Dr. D. O. Thomas is unable to identify "Mr. Tr(——)e"; he identifies the painter of the miniature as probably John Hazlitt (1767–1837, the brother of William Hazlitt), "Mr. W(——)st" as West, and "Mr. W(——)n" as a Mr. Watkin, the surgeon who attended Price for several years and is mentioned in the latter's will. Watkin was possibly a Daniel Watkin, who is recorded in various medical directories of the period. In *A Welsh Family*, Caroline Williams gives a slightly different account of the picture, giving the name of Price's physician as Walker, and stating that he persuaded Price to pose while Price was recuperating from a fall from a horse. Price does write about horses in the following paragraph of his diary, but makes no mention of a fall. It, therefore, seems likely that Miss Williams confused the story (and the name of the doctor), probably because of the difficulty in deciphering Price's shorthand.

No. 687 probably was the picture painted for Dr. Watkin, but whether it remained in Dr. Watkin's possession, and when and how it became the property of the Equitable Life Assurance Society are open questions. Price was a consultant to the Society on actuarial matters from about 1768 to 1783. His nephew, William Morgan (1750–1833), who published a biography of Price in 1815, became an employee of the Society in 1774 and served as its actuary from 1775 until 1830, whereupon he was succeeded by his son, Arthur Morgan (1801–1870), who was the Society's actuary from 1830 to 1870.[4] A second version (No. 688) was presented to the Royal Society by Arthur Morgan in 1876. A copy, not by West's hand, and showing considerably less detail is in the National Museum of Wales in Cardiff,[5] and another version or copy belongs to the Society of Actuaries in London.[6]

On 13 August 1794, in the *New York Diary: or Evening Register*, Thomas Holloway advertised an engraving after a portrait of Joseph Priestley (who was a friend

687

of Price) painted by William Artaud, intended to be a companion of Holloway's engraving after No. 687.[7] Artaud exhibited a portrait of Priestley at the Royal Academy earlier that year under the title "Portrait of a Philosopher" (presumably the portrait of Priestley in Dr. Williams's Library, London), but Holloway does not seem to have produced the advertised engraving after it.

[1] For biographical details, see William Morgan, FRS, *Memoirs of the Life of the Rev. Richard Price, D.D. F.R.S.*, London, 1815; Roland Thomas, *Richard Price: Philosopher and Apostle of Liberty*, Oxford, 1924; Carl B. Cone, *Torchbearer of Freedom: The Influence of Richard Price on Eighteenth Century Thought*, Lexington, Kentucky, 1952; and D. O. Thomas, *Richard Price and America*, Aberystwyth, 1975.

[2] Cone, op. cit., pp. 11 and 164.

[3] Italicized words are in longhand in the original. We are grateful to Dr. D. O. Thomas for sending a transcription of the relevant part of the diary (which is also included in his publication of the diary) and for helpful correspondence about Price.

[4] We gratefully acknowledge two informative letters from H. W. Johnson, Deputy Manager of the Equitable Life Assurance Society, giving much information about No. 687 and about the Society.

[5] Oil on canvas, 36 × 28 in., this picture is said to have belonged to Margaret Price, a niece of Richard Price.

[6] Exhibited, *Richard Price 1723–1791*, University College of Wales, Aberystwyth, 1976 (1).

[7] Rita Susswein Gottesman, *The Arts and Crafts in New York 1777–1799*, New York, 1964, p. 39 (40).

688 Dr. Richard Price *c.* 1803

ROYAL SOCIETY, LONDON

Oil on canvas: 36½ × 28½ in. (92.7 × 72.4 cm.)

PROV: Commissioned by William Morgan (Price's nephew) *c.* 1803; presented to the Royal Society by Arthur Morgan, FRS (William Morgan's son) in 1876

LIT: Carl B. Cone, *Torchbearer of Freedom: The Influence of Richard Price on Eighteenth Century Thought*, Lexington, Kentucky, 1952, frontispiece; Norman H. Robinson and Eric G. Forbes, *The Royal Society: Catalogue of Portraits*, London, 1980, p. 242, ill. (color) opp. p. 242

No. 688 is a replica of the previous entry, and appears probably to be the work of a copyist or assistant rather than by West himself. Nevertheless, a second version of No. 687 is recorded on a bill in West's hand, dated 4 August 1803, to Wm. Morgan Esq., for "a duplicate of the picture of the late Doc^r. Price Painted by Benj. West" (private collection). As No. 688 has a Morgan provenance, it would seem to be that duplicate. It corresponds to No. 687 in all major respects, but appears thinner in handling and is less crisp in detail. Unlike No. 687, it is not signed, and the date and signature on the letter which Price holds are not legible.

Price was elected a Fellow of the Royal Society in 1765. William Morgan and Arthur Morgan were also both Fellows.

689 Thomas Robinson (later Lord Grantham) 1760

LOCATION UNKNOWN

LIT: Galt 1816, pp. 119–22, 127; Carey 1820, p. 516; Alberts 1978, pp. 38–39

Thomas Robinson (1738–1786), who succeeded his father as second Baron Grantham in 1770, was in Rome when West, his exact contemporary, arrived in July 1760. He evidently found the rumor of an American Quaker having come to Italy to study the fine arts so extraordinary that he sought West out and immediately became his friend, sponsor, interpreter, and guide. Robinson was, according to Galt, responsible for introducing West into the circle of Cardinal Albani, and he is described as West's companion in most of his early adventures in Rome.[1]

Galt states that West painted No. 689 in order to be able to show a specimen of his work to Anton Raphael Mengs, to whom he had been introduced at Cardinal Albani's villa. Mengs had asked to see a drawing by West, but,

> In returning home, our Artist mentioned to Mr. Robinson that as he had never learnt to draw, he could not produce any sketch like those made by the other students; but that he could paint a little, and if Mr. Robinson would take the trouble to sit, he would execute his portrait to shew Mengs.

The undertaking was kept secret, and the completed picture was hung, without indication of who painted it, in the house of a friend of Robinson's, Mr. Crespigné or Crispigné,[2] on the occasion of a grand assembly. There, still according to Galt, it was generally taken to be by Mengs, to whom it was known that Robinson was also sitting for a portrait, but with color superior to that usually seen in Mengs's works. Galt specifically cites the opinions of the antiquarian and dealer Thomas Jenkins and of the English painter Nathaniel Dance: the latter "thought the picture much better coloured than those usually painted by Mengs, but added that he did not think the drawing either so firm or so good as the usual style of that Artist." Mengs himself, when he saw the picture, is supposed to have told West,

"You have already sir, the mechanical part of your art," and to have advised him to set out to see and examine everything deserving his attention in Rome, Florence, Bologna, Parma, and Venice, then paint and exhibit in Rome a historical composition. Despite delays and complications caused by illness, West followed this program during the rest of his stay in Italy.

West painted No. 689 between 10 July 1760, the date of his arrival in Rome, and 20 August, when his first attack of illness forced him to go to Leghorn to recuperate. It is the first work that Galt mentions West undertaking after his departure from America, and it is specifically described by Carey as the "First specimen of his art in Rome." Galt also states that the story of the picture's success soon reached Philadelphia, where the news inspired Chief Justice Allen (see No. 581) and Governor Hamilton (No. 633) to extend financial support to the young artist.

Nothing is known about what happened to No. 689 after the summer of 1760. The circumstances under which it was painted make clear that it was not a commissioned portrait, and neither Galt nor Carey indicates that it was acquired by the sitter. In addition to posing for Mengs and West in the summer of 1760, Robinson also was painted at approximately the same time by Nathaniel Dance in a group portrait along with three other British visitors to Rome (versions in the Philadelphia Museum of Art [ill. p. 25] and the Yale Center for British Art in New Haven).[3]

For other portraits of approximately the same date by West see Nos. 582, 658, and 730. It is conceivable that Nos. 730 and 689 are the same work.

[1] See Galt 1816, pp. 101–23, passim.
[2] Both spellings are given in Galt 1816, pp. 102 and 121. He is described by Galt as "an English gentleman who had long resided at Rome," and is evidently "the good Mr. Crispin," who advised West in Rome in 1763 and was gratefully remembered by West in a letter to Joseph Shippen, written on 1 Sept. 1763 (Richardson 1978, p. 23). "Crispin" is also referred to in a letter from James Grant of Grant to Thomas Robinson, written in 1760 or 1761 shortly after both men had ended visits to Rome (Basil C. Skinner, "A Note on Four British Artists in Rome," *Burlington Magazine*, XCIX, 1957, p. 238).
[3] See *Nathaniel Dance 1735–1811*, the Iveagh Bequest, Kenwood, 1977, no. 5.

690 Sarah Ursula Rose *c.* 1756

METROPOLITAN MUSEUM OF ART, NEW YORK

Oil on canvas: 29 × 23⅜ in. (73.5 × 59.5 cm.)

PROV: By descent in the family of the sitter to Mrs. Henry Sedgwick, Stockbridge, Mass.; Edgar William and Bernice Chrysler Garbisch, by whom presented to the Metropolitan Museum of Art in 1964

EXH: *Loan Exhibition of Historical Portraits*, Pennsylvania Academy of the Fine Arts, Philadelphia, 1887–88 (367), lent by John S. Watts; *Masterpieces of American Primitive Painting from the Collection of Edgar William and Bernice Chrysler Garbisch*, Metropolitan Museum of Art, etc., 1961–64 (15); *Peintures naïves américaines: xviiie xixe Siècles: Cent onze tableaux de la Collection Edgar William et Bernice Chrysler Garbisch*, Grand Palais, Paris, 1968 (11); *American Naïve Painting of the 18th and 19th Centuries from the collection of Edgar William and Bernice Chrysler Garbisch*, Royal Academy, London, 1968 (11)

LIT: Sawitzky 1938, p. 462 (15); (?) Tinkcom 1951, p. 382 (Sir Augustus Foster)

If the subject of this portrait is correctly identified, she is Sarah Ursula Rose (1744–1823), later Mrs. Henry Miller. According to Sawitzky, she was the consider-

ably younger half-sister of Mrs. William Henry, whom West painted at roughly the same date during the visit he made to Lancaster, Pennsylvania in 1755 or 1756 (No. 638). She would have been approximately twelve years old at the time. It is possible that No. 690 was the portrait of "another Lady," which Sir Augustus Foster mentioned after No. 638 in an account of the Wests belonging to William Henry's son. Sir Augustus visited Lancaster before 1812, and the painting may have subsequently passed to the sitter, who was then still alive, or to her descendants.

The pose is virtually identical with that of Mrs. Boudé in No. 597, which West also painted in Lancaster.

691 George Ross *c.* 1755–56

See illustration p. 550

NORTH MUSEUM, FRANKLIN AND MARSHALL COLLEGE, LANCASTER, PENNSYLVANIA

Oil on canvas: 42½ × 33½ in. (108 × 85 cm.)

PROV: By descent in the family of the sitter to George Ross Eshleman, Lancaster, and given by his widow to Franklin and Marshall College

EXH: *Loan Exhibition of Historical and Contemporary Portraits*, Lancaster County Historical Society, Lancaster, 1912 (211)

ENGR: Engraving (as a half-length portrait) by Samuel Sartain, published in *Rossiana* by Major Harmon Pumpelly Read, Albany, New York, 1908, opp. p. 169

LIT: Galt 1816, pp. 34–35; Sawitzky 1938, pp. 437 and 450 (9); Flexner 1952, pp. 24–25; Alberts 1978, p. 17

George Ross (1730–1779) was an attorney in Lancaster, Pennsylvania. He was a graduate of the University of Edinburgh and was to be a member of the Continental Congress and a signatory of the Declaration of Independence.

According to Galt, West made his trip to Lancaster in order to paint portraits of the Ross family, at the instigation of Mr. Flower of Chester County, who was a fellow jurist of George Ross. Galt states that the success of these portraits greatly enlarged the sphere of West's celebrity and led to such a demand for portraits that he could hardly find time to satisfy it.

This account implies that West's Ross portraits, of which three are now known (Nos. 691–93), were the earliest of his Lancaster pictures, although, as Sawitzky points out, they seem technically more advanced and assured than West's portraits of Mr. and Mrs. William Henry, also of Lancaster (Nos. 637 and 638).

Copies of Nos. 691 and 692 are in the Lancaster Public Library. Sawitzky records an additional copy of No. 691 by Philip H. Wharton (1841–1880) in Independence Hall, Philadelphia.

Galt states that West painted portraits of the Ross children, but none of these pictures is now known.

692 Mrs. George Ross *c.* 1755–56

See color illustration, p. 5

NORTH MUSEUM, FRANKLIN AND MARSHALL COLLEGE, LANCASTER, PENNSYLVANIA

Oil on canvas: 42½ × 33½ in. (108 × 85 cm.)

PROV: As for No. 691

EXH: As for No. 691 (no. 212 in the exhibition of 1912)

LIT: As for No. 691 (Sawitzky no. 10)

See No. 691, of which No. 692 is the companion picture. Anne Lawler married George Ross on 17 August 1751. Galt writes that she "was greatly admired for her beauty."

690

691

693

Alderman John Sawbridge, mezzotint by Thomas Watson after No. 694

693 Catherine Ross c. 1755–56

PRIVATE COLLECTION

Oil on canvas: $38\frac{1}{4} \times 29\frac{1}{2}$ in. (97 × 75 cm.)

PROV: By descent in the family of the sitter

LIT: Sawitzky 1938, pp. 437 and 449 (8); Flexner 1952, pp. 24–25

Catherine Ross was the sister of George Ross of Lancaster, Pennsylvania, painted by West in No. 691. She married General William Thompson (1736–1781) of Carlisle, Pennsylvania.

694 Alderman John Sawbridge c. 1772

DESTROYED

PROV: By descent in the family of the sitter, Olantigh, Kent, until 1903, when said to have been destroyed by fire

EXH: RA 1773 (312) "Portrait of a gentleman in the character of a Roman tribune"

ENGR: Mezzotint ($24\frac{5}{16} \times 14\frac{7}{8}$ in.) by Thomas Watson, pub. 1 Nov. 1772 by S. Hooper, W. Shropshire, and T. Watson

LIT: Graves 1906, VIII, p. 213 (Horace Walpole, 1773); Sara Stevenson, "Neoclassical Dress," in *Van Dyck in Check Trousers: Fancy Dress in Art and Life 1700–1900* (exhibition catalogue), Scottish National Portrait Gallery, Edinburgh, 1978, p. 31 and ill. 30

John Sawbridge (1732–1795) of Olantigh, Kent, served as Member of Parliament for Hythe in Kent from 1768 to 1774, and for London from 1774 to 1795. He became Sheriff of London and an alderman in 1769. In 1771 he lost the election for Lord Mayor of London, but he gained that office in 1775, succeeding his quondam political ally John Wilkes in the position.

The portrait exhibited by West in 1773 as "a gentleman in the character of a Roman tribune," was identified by Horace Walpole in a marginal note to his Royal Academy catalogue as a portrait of Sawbridge, with the additional comment, "hard and heavy." Walpole's identification is confirmed by the Watson mezzotint, which shows Sawbridge in antique dress and in an antique setting, holding a scroll in his left hand and pointing to another with his right. The letters *S.P.Q.R.* on the plinth at his side, as well as the characterization of the sitter in the Academy catalogue as a Roman tribune (i.e., a protector of the rights of the plebeians against the patricians) make the painting and the print after it into explicit manifestations of Sawbridge's republican and anti-aristocratic political positions.[1]

No. 694 is the most thoroughly classicizing of all of West's portraits. It represents both an adaptation to the medium of portraiture of the celebration of Roman virtue depicted in earlier paintings such as the *Departure of Regulus* of 1769 (No. 10), and a stricter equivalent of allegorical portraits by Reynolds such as the *Lady Blake as Juno* exhibited in 1769.[2] In using Roman imagery to convey a contemporary political message West was preceded by his pupil Charles Willson Peale, whose full-length portrait of William Pitt as a Roman consul of 1768 may have been painted in West's studio (versions in the Westmoreland County Court House, Montross, Virginia, and the Maryland State House, Annapolis, Maryland).[3] The Peale portrait had an outspoken didactic message about the defense of American liberties, which would certainly have appealed to Sawbridge, and it is possible that sight of it, or, more probably, of Peale's engraving after it, inspired Sawbridge to seek an analogous portrait of himself from West. It should be noted as well that Peale based his portrait of Pitt upon a sculpture by Joseph Wilton, and, as Sara Stevenson has pointed out, sculptural portraits in classical guise were much more common in the eighteenth century than painted ones such as No. 694.

[1] See Sir Lewis Namier and John Brooke, eds., *The House of*

696

Commons 1754–1790, London, 1960, III, pp. 409–11 (entry by I. R. Christie).
²Ill. in Ellis K. Waterhouse, *Reynolds*, London, 1941, pl. 126.
³See Charles Coleman Sellers, *Portraits and Miniatures by Charles Willson Peale*, Philadelphia, 1952, pp. 1172–73 (693–95), and *Charles Willson Peale*, New York, 1969, pp. 66–67. It is unclear how much Peale may have owed to West in his conception of this portrait. It was commissioned by Edmund Jennings to be given to the gentlemen of Westmoreland County, Virginia, as a companion to a portrait that they had commissioned from West of Lord Camden. Sellers cites correspondence indicating that Camden's unwillingness to pose prevented West from completing his commission; it seems likely, nonetheless, that West may have originally intended to depict Camden in similarly classical guise.

695 John Sedley 1802

LOCATION UNKNOWN

Oil on canvas: 36 × 28 in. (91.5 × 71 cm.)

Signed lower right: *B. West, 1802*

PROV: Ehrich Galleries, New York; Walter Jennings, Cold Spring Harbor, New York (by 1918); Mrs. Jennings (in 1938); sold anonymously, Parke-Bernet, New York, 9–11 Feb. 1950, lot 217

EXH: Brooklyn 1922 (22); Philadelphia 1938 (52)

LIT: Frederic Fairchild Sherman, "The Art of Benjamin West," *Art in America*, VI, 1918, p. 156, and fig. 1; Ehrich 1918, p. 155; Dunlap 1918, I, ill. opp. p. 88; Frederic Fairchild Sherman, *Early American Painting*, New York, 1932, p. 55, ill. opp. p. 97

696 [?] The Sheridan Family *c.* 1775

WALKER ART GALLERY, LIVERPOOL

Oil on canvas: 89¾ × 63¼ in. (228 × 160.5 cm.)

PROV: (?) Sold by West's sons, Robins, London, 20–22 June 1829, lot 171 ("Portrait of a Gentleman, his Wife and Child"); bequeathed to the Walker Art Gallery in 1933 by William Hall Walker, first Baron Wavertree (1856–1933)

EXH: (?) *Exhibition of Dramatic and Musical Art*, Grafton Gallery, London, 1897 (157) as "Sheridan, his Wife and Child" by Nathaniel Dance, lent by Messrs. Turner & Horsley; Liverpool 1976 (70)

This painting has at various times been attributed to Reynolds and to Dance. Nevertheless, it, seems clearly to be a painting by West of the 1770s, as proposed in the catalogue of the exhibition *American Artists in Europe 1800–1900* in Liverpool in 1976. Traditionally, it has been said to depict Richard Brinsley Sheridan (1751–1816), his first wife, born Elizabeth Linley (1754–1792), and their son Thomas Sheridan (1775–1817). The source of these identifications is not known. Lady Wavertree was a descendant of the purported subjects of No. 696, but she is recorded in the Liverpool exhibition catalogue as having said in 1933 only that she had bought the picture many years earlier as a portrait of Sheridan with his wife and child. The Liverpool catalogue questions the identifications, but the similarity of the features of the two main sitters to those of Sheridan and his wife in other portraits would seem to support rather than contradict them.¹ If No. 696 does indeed show the Sheridan family, it must have been painted some months after 17 March 1775, the date of the birth of Thomas Sheridan. Richard Brinsley Sheridan had his first great theatrical success in 1775 with *The Rivals* and went on to succeed Garrick as the manager of the Drury Lane Theatre in the following year.

¹For Richard Brinsley Sheridan see the painting in pastel by John Russell of 1788 (National Portrait Gallery, London, ill. in *British Historical Portraiture: A Selection from the National Portrait Gallery*, Cambridge, 1957, no. 200); for his wife, see the *Linley Sisters* by Thomas Gainsborough, exhibited at the Royal Academy in 1772 (Dulwich College Picture Gallery, ill. in Ellis Waterhouse, *Gainsborough*, London, 1958, pl. 145).

697 [?] Mrs. Sheridan

LOCATION UNKNOWN

PROV: Sold by West's sons, Robins, London, 20–22 June 1829, lot 141 ("Portrait, supposed to be the late Mrs. Sheridan")

698 Sir John Sinclair of Ulbster, Bt. 1798

WICK TOWN HALL, CAITHNESS, SCOTLAND

Oil on canvas: 96 × 69½ in. (244 × 176.5 cm.)

Signed lower left: *B. West 1798*

PROV: Sold by West's sons, Robins, London, 20–22 June 1829, lot 122 ("a fine whole length Portrait of Sir John Sinclair, late President of the Agricultural Society. Painted in 1798")

LISTED: *PC*, p. 564 ("The whole length Portrait of Sir John Sinclair," under, "Various Collections"); *UM*, p. 529; *BA*, p. 16; Galt, p. 225; Dillenberger, p. 163 (248)

LIT: William Macdonald Sinclair, "Sir John Sinclair,

Founder and President of the First Board of Agriculture," *Art Journal*, LXXII, 1910, p. 34

Sir John Sinclair (1754–1835) was the heir to large estates in Caithness, in the north-east of Scotland, where he made major improvements. Among his numerous activities, he was the author of *The Statistical Account of Scotland*, published in thirty-one volumes between 1791 and 1798; the founder in 1793 and first President of the Board of Agriculture; and Colonel-in-Chief of the Rothesay and Caithness Fencibles, which he raised in 1794. In No. 698 he wears the uniform of the Fencibles, which he designed, replacing the usual kilts of Highland regiments with tartan trousers, or trews. A paper stuck in a book in the lower right is inscribed *Statistical acc*[. . .]/*of Sc*[. . .], and the charter of the Board of Agriculture lies on a table in the background along with models of a plough and a harrow. The subject holds in his right hand a letter signed *Washington*, referring to correspondence commencing in 1792 that Sinclair carried on with George Washington chiefly about agricultural matters.[1] Sheep and cattle in the background recall Sinclair's activities on his own estates, and the mountain in the distance is said to represent Morven, the highest hill and most prominent feature in the Caithness landscape.

According to William Macdonald Sinclair, writing in 1910, West painted No. 698 for the Wick Town Hall, but it seems more probable that No. 698 was the portrait of Sinclair sold by West's sons in 1829.[2] West may have painted the picture out of respect for the sitter, possibly in the hope of selling it in America. He was in contact with Sinclair by 18 September 1796, when he sent to his brother William West in Pennsylvania some volumes of the *Statistical Account* given him by Sinclair and a report that Sir John spoke highly of William's letter on the property of gypsum and of what he had heard of William's farm.[3] William's letter about gypsum had been sent to Sinclair by George Washington. The information about his farming had come from John Trumbull and from Enoch Edwards (see No. 614), who in a letter to Sinclair dated 14 September 1796, lavished extravagant praise upon William's agricultural prowess and suggested that he be made a member of Sinclair's Board of Agriculture. Edwards continued that this would be a handsome compliment to William's brother, "who has really taken it into his head to make you the greatest favorite he has in England. He is very fond of what he calls marked characters. His being surprised with a thing of that kind I know would make him grateful."[4] In 1796 Sinclair was actively considering emigrating to America, because of a falling out with Pitt, and had solicited a letter of advice from Washington about where to settle.[5] Hence, it was probably no coincidence that his friendship with Benjamin West and his interest in William's farming occurred at this time.

A drawing for No. 698 is in the British Museum.[6] The sitter was also painted by Lawrence (collection of Viscount Thurso) and on several occasions by Raeburn. In the best-known portrait by Raeburn of 1794–95 (National Gallery of Scotland, Edinburgh), he is shown in similar garb and pose as those utilized by West in No. 698.

[1] *The Correspondence of the Right Honourable Sir John Sinclair, Bart.*, London, 1831, II, pp. 4–36, contains sixteen letters from Washington to Sinclair written between 1792 and 1796.
[2] There are no records preserved in Wick about when or how the painting was acquired.
[3] Hart 1908, pp. 24–25.
[4] *The Correspondence of the Right Honourable Sir John Sinclair, Bart.*, II, pp. 68–69.
[5] Ibid., pp. 7–8.
[6] Black and white chalk on grey paper, $11\frac{5}{8} \times 8\frac{1}{2}$ in. (1920-6-15–24).

The Reverend William Smith, mezzotint by John Sartain after No. 699

699 The Reverend William Smith *c.* 1756–58

HISTORICAL SOCIETY OF PENNSYLVANIA, PHILADELPHIA

Oil on canvas: $47 \times 39\frac{1}{2}$ in. (119.5 × 100.5 cm.)

PROV: Presented by Horace Wemyss Smith, the sitter's great-grandson, to the Historical Society of Pennsylvania in 1870

EXH: *Exhibition of Historical Portraits*, Pennsylvania Academy of the Fine Arts, Philadelphia, 1887–88 (402); listed in the catalogue of Philadelphia 1938 (7), but not shown

ENGR: Mezzotint ($4\frac{3}{16} \times 3\frac{11}{16}$ in.) by John Sartain, pub. by S. A. George & Co., Philadelphia, as the frontispiece of the *Life and Correspondence of the Rev. William Smith, D.D.*, by Horace Wemyss Smith, Philadelphia, 1879

LIT: Galt 1816, pp. 71–73; Dunlap 1834, p. 44 (Dunlap 1918, I, p. 44); Horace Wemyss Smith, *Life and Correspondence of the Rev. William Smith, D.D.*, Philadelphia, 1879, I, pp. 9–10, 591–95; Sawitzky 1938, p. 456 (19); Sawitzky 1942, p. 158; Wainwright 1974, pp. 242–43; Dillenberger 1977, p. 9, pl. 5

William Smith (1727–1803), a native of Aberdeen, first came to America in 1751, and he settled in Philadelphia in 1754. In 1755 he became the first Provost of the College of Philadelphia, which he was instrumental in founding and which eventually was to become the University of Pennsylvania.

Our knowledge of Smith's relations with West comes almost entirely from Galt, who states that Smith, on a visit to Lancaster, Pennsylvania, saw West's *Death of Socrates* (No. 4) painted for William Henry.[1] Smith thereupon offered to acquaint West with classical literature and give him "such a sketch of the taste and character of the spirit of antiquity, as would have all the effect of the regular education requisite to a painter." West moved to Philadelphia to take advantage of this offer. There is no record that West was ever formally a student at the College of Philadelphia; instead Smith formed a special plan of study for him, eschewing "grammatical exercises of language" and focusing on "the picturesque circumstances" of passages from ancient history which "were likely to interest his fancy, and to furnish him at some future time with subjects for the easel." Subsequently, still according to Galt, it was Smith who heard of Chief Justice William Allen's intention to send a ship to Leghorn and who made the arrangements for West to accompany John Allen and

699

cumstance, and induced West to make an experiment by drawing his portrait in the style and attitude of the St. Ignatius.

Unfortunately neither the *St. Ignatius* nor West's copy after it is now known, and it is impossible, therefore, to determine how closely West followed his source. The animation of the pose in No. 699 is unique among West's portraits painted in America, which suggests that the pose may have been copied fairly literally from the lost model.

On a table in the lower right corner of the painting are several books, on one of which the words *POPE/ WORKS* are legible. Before them is a sheet of paper, which bears seven lines of writing. Although much of this inscription is obliterated, several words are legible, including "Britons still should" in the second line, and "To breathe Humanity" in the fifth. The compilers of this catalogue have not been able to identify the source of these lines, but the use of the word "Britons" and the hortatory tone suggested by the legible words are consistent with Smith's style in numerous sermons and pamphlets published during the 1750s.[2]

[1]Galt 1816, pp. 37–45, 68–72, and 84–85; Galt 1820, pp. 3–4 and 10.

[2]For examples, see his *Discourses on Public Occasions in America,* 2nd ed., London, 1762.

700 The Reverend William Smith 1764

LOCATION UNKNOWN

LIT: George Everett Hastings, *The Life and Works of Francis Hopkinson*, Chicago, 1926, pp. 138–39

A letter written by Smith in Philadelphia on 13 December 1766, to his former pupil Francis Hopkinson, then on a visit to England, mentions a painting by West:

The little Picture West did for me was drawn when I had just got out of an eleven Weeks Fever, & you will tell him I have now a little more Complexion, as well as Health, which I beg him to supply also to the Piece, with a Dash or two of his Brush, that I may send for it. I wrote him by his Bride & did every Thing he expected of me in that Affair; but he has never been kind enough to send me a Line.

Smith was in Britain from early in 1762 until May of 1764, and the fever referred to in the letter had been a serious illness that struck him in Ireland and forced him to remain in Dublin from September 1763 to 7 March 1764.[1] Hence, West must have begun the picture sometime between 7 March and the end of April 1764, when Smith left London for Falmouth to begin his journey back to America. What Smith did for West "in that Affair" was probably as an intermediary between the artist and Elizabeth Shewell, his bride-to-be, who sailed from Philadelphia to London on 24 June 1764, within a month of Smith's return. This activity on West's behalf is also suggested by Galt, who states that West communicated to Smith and Chief Justice Allen (who was also in England in 1763–64, cf. No. 581) his intention of returning to America to be married, and, "In consequence, an arrangement took place by which the father of Mr. West came over to this country with the bride."[2]

Nothing more is known about the painting. It was evidently not in the possession of the Smith family when Horace Wemyss Smith wrote his book about Smith in 1879, and it may never have been. Smith's letter indicates that it was in West's possession in 1766, and implies that it was there because it was still not finished.

[1]These dates are from Horace Wemyss Smith, *Life and Correspondence of the Rev. William Smith, D.D.*, Philadelphia, 1879, I, pp. 295, 330–31, 348–49, and 352.

[2]Galt 1820, p. 10.

Joseph Shippen to Italy in 1760 (see Nos. 581 and 582). In 1763, when West arrived in London, Smith was there raising money for the College of Philadelphia, and Galt records that West consulted him and Justice Allen before making his decision to remain in England in 1764. In 1766 the British edition of Smith's *Historical Account of the Expedition against the Ohio Indians in the year 1764,* which was first published in Philadelphia in 1765 without illustrations, contained two engravings after designs by West.

West evidently painted at least two portraits of Smith (Nos. 699 and 700) and one of his wife (No. 701). No. 699 is an almost complete wreck, as the illustration shows. At some time it was heavily and clumsily repainted, and a reproduction showing it in that condition accompanies Sawitzky's article published in 1938. Theodor Siegl removed the later repaintings from the canvas in 1966. An engraving by John Sartain (*above*) published in 1879 shows the painting in what appears to be an earlier condition. However, since this engraving was made some 120 years after No. 699 was painted and nine years after it had entered a public collection, it seems likely that much of the loss of original paint and consequent repainting had already occurred. Hence the differences between Sartain's engraving and

the reproduction of No. 699 published by Sawitzky may have been due to liberties taken by the engraver in attempting to make a satisfactory image out of such unpromising material. The Sartain engraving bears the legend *Aet. 30*, which would indicate that West painted No. 699 in 1757. This seems a reasonable date, but the source for it cannot be considered absolutely reliable, since it stems from over a century later. In the book by the sitter's great-grandson, in which the engraving appeared, all the information about West and about No. 699 comes from Galt.

According to Galt, West made a copy (No. 512) of the *St. Ignatius* belonging to Governor James Hamilton (for whom see No. 633). This copy suggested to Provost Smith the idea that portrait painting could do more than record physical likenesses:

he in consequence endeavoured to impress upon the mind of his pupil, that characteristic painting opened a new line in the art, only inferior in dignity to that of history, but requiring, perhaps a nicer discriminative tact of mind. This judicious reflection of Dr. Smith was however anticipated by Sir Joshua Reynolds, who had already made the discovery, and was carrying it into effect with admirable effect. The Provost, however, was unacquainted with that cir-

701

701 Mrs. William Smith (Rebecca Moore) *c.* 1758

MRS. MEYER DE SCHAUNSEE

Oil on canvas: 46 × 38 in. (117 × 96.5 cm.)

PROV: By family descent to Mr. and Mrs. George V. Smith, Ardmore, Pa.; acquired by the present owner (a descendant of the subject) in 1968

EXH: *Loan Exhibition of Historical Portraits*, Pennsylvania Academy of the Fine Arts, Philadelphia, 1887–88 (403) lent by Mrs. Thomas D. Smith; Philadelphia 1938 (8) lent by Mr. and Mrs. George V. Smith

LIT: Horace Wemyss Smith, *Life and Correspondence of the Rev. William Smith, D.D.*, Philadelphia, 1879, I, p. 595; Sawitzky 1938, pp. 443 and 456–57 (20); Albert Frank Gegenheimer, *William Smith: Educator and Churchman 1727–1803*, Philadelphia, 1943, p. 103

Rebecca Moore (1733–1784) was the daughter of William Moore, a Justice of the Peace in Chester County, Pennsylvania. She was married to the Reverend William Smith (see Nos. 699 and 700) on 3 June 1758.[1]

Albert Gegenheimer has proposed that No. 701 was "The Portrait of Miss **—** by Mr. West," which was the subject of an anonymous poem signed "Lovelace" published in the *American Magazine* in February 1758. Smith, who was the founder and editor of the *American Magazine*, was presumably responsible for a note accompanying the poem, "The lady who sat, the painter who guided the pencil, and the poet who so well described the whole are all natives of this place and very young." West was twenty years old in 1758, Rebecca Moore, twenty-five. The most likely author of the poem, Francis Hopkinson, who was a pupil of Smith's in the College of Philadelphia, was twenty-one. If this identification is correct, West painted No. 701 before the sitter became Mrs. Smith.[2]

Sawitzky, who dates No. 701 *c.* 1758, cites it and West's portrait of Elizabeth Peel (No. 681) as the two works by the artist which show the strongest influence of John Wollaston.

[1] For an account of the close relations between Smith and his wife's father, see Gegenheimer, pp. 139–45 et passim.
[2] See No. 622 for another work that has also been proposed as the painting described in the poem.

702 Sir Thomas Strange *c.* 1798

LAW COURTS, HALIFAX, NOVA SCOTIA

Oil on canvas: 94 × 58 in. (239 × 147.5 cm.)

PROV: Painted for the Halifax Town Hall

EXH: RA 1798 (144) "Portrait of Sir Thomas Strange"

LISTED: *PC*, p. 564 ("The whole length Portrait of Sir Thomas Strange—in the Town-hall of Halifax"); *UM*, p. 529; *BA*, p. 16; Galt, p. 225; Dillenberger, p. 163 (247)

Thomas Andrew Lumisden Strange (1756–1841) was a son of the engraver Sir Robert Strange (1721–1792). He was called to the Bar in 1785, and from 1789 to 1797 he was Chief Justice and President of the Council in Halifax, Nova Scotia. In 1797 he was appointed Recorder and in 1800 Chief Justice in Madras. He was knighted on 14 March 1798, before his departure from England for India.

No. 702 was evidently commissioned for Halifax on the occasion of Strange's resignation of his post there in 1797 and painted while he was in England during the following winter. The sitter had known West at least since 1784, when he called on Mr. and Mrs. West at the behest of his father.[1] His father, Sir Robert Strange, and West were friends of long standing. It was at West's suggestion that Sir Robert was knighted by George III in 1787 (see No. 575), and West exhibited a portrait of Sir Robert's widow at the Royal Academy in 1800 (No. 704).

Sir Thomas Strange was subsequently painted by Lawrence for Madras, and by Sir Martin Archer Shee for his former college, Christ Church, Oxford.

A bust-length replica is No. 703 below. Drawings, both showing the subject full length and in the pose of No. 702 but with differences in details of the judicial robes, are at Swarthmore and in the British Museum.[2]

[1] James Dennistoun, *Memoirs of Sir Robert Strange, Knt., and of His Brother-in-law Andrew Lumisden*, London, 1855, II, pp. 186–98 et passim.
[2] Black and white chalks on blue-grey paper, 15¾ × 9 in. (Swarthmore), and black and white chalks on blue-grey paper, 18¼ × 10⅞ in. (British Museum). The Swarthmore drawing is reproduced in Brooks 1925, fig. 8.

703 Sir Thomas Strange 1799

SCOTTISH NATIONAL PORTRAIT GALLERY, EDINBURGH

Oil on canvas: 36 × 28 in. (91.4 × 71.1 cm.)

Signed upper right: *B. West 1799*

PROV: By descent in the family of the sitter to Mrs. G. Beck, by whom given to the Scottish National Portrait Gallery in 1962

LIT: *Scottish National Portrait Gallery: Concise Catalogue*, Edinburgh, 1977, p. 140 (1991)

This painting is a copy of part of No. 702, purportedly painted for the Strange family. Since it is dated *1799*, the year after Sir Thomas Strange left England for India, and also the year after No. 702 was exhibited at the Royal Academy, it must have been painted from the larger picture rather than from life.

704 Lady Strange *c.* 1800

LOCATION UNKNOWN

EXH: RA 1800 (251) "The portrait of Lady Strange"

LIT: Nora K. Strange, *Jacobean Tapestry*, London, etc., [1947], p. 106

703

702

Although the compilers have not been able to locate this painting, it was evidently still in the Strange family in 1947 when Nora K. Strange, the sitter's great-great-granddaughter described it as showing the subject "as a nutcracker old lady." The Lady Strange depicted was not the wife of Sir Thomas Strange of Nos. 702 and 703, but his mother, née Isabella Lumisden (1719–1806), the widow of Sir Robert Strange (1721–1792). She was eighty-one years old in 1800, but as late as 1803 she described herself as active and in excellent health.[1] She seems to have remained friendly with West following the death of her husband, and in 1799 she wrote to her son, Sir Thomas, that she had followed West's advice in finding someone to design a coat of arms for the family.[2]

Sir Thomas Strange first married in 1797, but his wife died in the following year. He did not remarry until 1806; so his father's widow was the only Lady Strange alive in 1800.

[1] James Dennistoun, *Memoirs of Sir Robert Strange, Knt., and of His Brother-in-law Andrew Lumisden*, London, 1855, II, p. 275.
[2] Ibid., p. 212.

705 Richard Terrick, Bishop of London 1766

THE EARL OF HARROWBY

Oil on canvas: 49½ × 36 in. (125.5 × 91.5 cm.) (approx.)

Signed lower center (on the end of the small book): *B. West 1766*

PROV: By family descent via the sitter's daughter, Elizabeth, wife of the first Lord Harrowby, to the present owner

LIT: C. H. Collins Baker, *British Painting*, London, 1933, p. 116 and pl. 117; Alberts 1978, pp. 72–73

Richard Terrick (1710–1777) became Bishop of Peterborough in 1757, and Bishop of London in 1764. As Bishop of London he vetoed the proposal put forward in 1773 by several Royal Academicians including West to decorate St. Paul's Cathedral with paintings (see No. 257).

705

Although Terrick is not mentioned by Galt along with Bishops Newton, Johnson, and Drummond as one of the prelates to whom West was introduced by Dr. Markham, the Master of Westminster School, in 1765 (see Nos. 655 and 675), the date on No. 705 suggests that West must have met Terrick at much the same time.

706 John Utterson of Fareham, Hampshire 1769

ELIZABETH HOLMES FISHER GALLERY, UNIVERSITY OF SOUTHERN CALIFORNIA, LOS ANGELES

Oil on canvas: 30 × 25 in. (76 × 63.5 cm.)

Signed lower right: *B. West pinx/1769/London*

PROV: McClees Galleries, Philadelphia; Newhouse Galleries, New York; purchased by the University of Southern California in 1940

EXH: Philadelphia 1936; Philadelphia 1938 (17)

707 Mrs. Vanderwall *c.* 1766

MR. AND MRS. PHILIP I. BERMAN

Oil on canvas: oval, 32 × 42½ in. (81.5 × 108 cm.)

PROV: By descent in the family of the sitter to W. A. Willes, by whom sold, Sotheby's, London, 3 May 1961, lot 138; Julius Weitzner, London, from whom purchased by the present owners in 1962

EXH: Allentown 1962 (6)

The subject of No. 707 is said to have been the mother of Mrs. John Williams, whose portrait (No. 716) along with that of her husband (No. 715) were sold together with No. 707 in 1961. The three portraits all have the same horizontal oval shape and the same dimensions, and, hence, would seem to have been painted together at the same time. The portrait of John Williams is signed and dated *1766*. See also No. 722.

707

708 Thomas Vesey, First Viscount de Vesci, and Lady de Vesci 1776

VISCOUNT DE VESCI

Oil on canvas: 35 × 26 in. (89 × 66 cm.)

Signed lower left: *B. West/1776*

PROV: By descent in the family of the sitters

Thomas Vesey (died 1804), of Abbey Leix in Ireland, succeeded his father as Baron Knapton in 1761 and was created Viscount de Vesci in 1776, the year that West painted No. 708. He married Selina Elizabeth, the daughter of Sir Arthur Brooke, Bt., in 1769.

The subjects' kinsman, Agmondisham Vesey of Lucan, had purchased works by West by 1774 (see Nos. 37 and 131), and it is perhaps through this connection that West received the commission for No. 708. The porte-crayon and drawing (of a man's head) held by Lady de Vesci in No. 708 indicate that she had artistic interests of her own. West also painted her separately in Nos. 709 and 710.

709 Selina Elizabeth Brookes, Viscountess de Vesci *c.* 1776

VISCOUNT DE VESCI

Oil on canvas: 32½ × 25 in. (82.5 × 63.5 cm.)

PROV: Probably painted for Anne, Viscountess Northland (died 1803), sister of the first Viscount de Vesci; then by family descent to the sixth Earl of Ranfurly, by whom sold, Christie's, London, 31 July 1939, lot 12, bt. by Waley; sold anonymously, Christie's, London, 25 July 1952, lot 53, bt. by the fifth Viscount de Vesci

For the subject see No. 708. No. 709 probably dates from the same time. A second version is No. 710 below.

710 Selina Elizabeth Brookes, Viscountess de Vesci

DR. ROBERT ERWIN JONES

Oil on canvas: 34¾ × 27 in. (88.5 × 68.5 cm.)

PROV: J. MacDonell, Speanbridge, Invernesshire; Sabin Galleries, London

EXH: *English Portrait: Tudor to Georgian*, Sabin Galleries, London, 1976 (14) as "Mary Hulme"

When exhibited in London in 1976, this painting was identified as a portrait of Mary Hulme on the basis of similarity of features with those of one of the figures in No. 610 *Three Members of the Drummond Family* of 1776.[1] However, it is virtually identical in all details with No. 709 and clearly shows the same sitter.

On the reverse of the canvas is a roughly blocked in male head, possibly intended as the beginning of a portrait of the sitter's husband.[2]

[1] It should be added that the figure in No. 610 is not "Mary Hulme," who was wrongly described as a daughter of Archbishop Drummond, but the wife of one of the Archbishop's sons. Mary Hume, the wife of John Hume, Bishop of Oxford and Salisbury, was Archbishop Drummond's sister. By 1776 she would have been far too old to have been the young woman shown in No. 610.

[2] Illustrated in the 1976 exhibition catalogue.

711 George Warde 1774

J. ST. A. WARDE, SQUERRYES COURT, WESTERHAM, KENT

Oil on canvas: 15 × 18½ in. (38 × 47 cm.)

709

Signed lower left on the side of the bird cage: *B. West/1774*

PROV: Painted for the sitter's uncle, General George Warde (1725–1803); then by descent in the Warde family

LIT: Beckles Willson, "Portraits and Relics of General Wolfe," *Connoisseur*, XXIII, 1909, p. 11; Kerslake 1959, pp. 20–21

George Warde (1760–1830) who is shown as a child in No. 711, was a younger son of John Warde (1721–1775) of Squerryes Court in Kent, and the nephew of General George Warde (1725–1803), the boyhood friend of General James Wolfe. The younger George Warde was also to become a general in 1825.

Also at Squerryes Court is a portrait of Wolfe as a boy by West (No. 719), which is signed and dated *1777*

and which was painted as a companion to No. 711. Both paintings were commissioned by the uncle of the subject of No. 711, the elder General George Warde (who was unmarried). No. 711 is referred to in two documents preserved at Squerryes Court.[1] The first, which is affixed to the back of No. 719, is West's receipt addressed to General Warde and dated 21 January 1778, in which the picture of "Mr. Warde" is described as a companion to No. 719. A note on the bottom of this receipt in another hand identifies "Mr. Warde" as "Mr. Geo Warde." The other document at Squerryes Court is a note on the back of a portrait of Wolfe as a young man painted *c.* 1740 by an unknown artist; this note, which as John Kerslake has shown must have been written between 1822 and 1851, begins: "About the year 1775 this picture was sent to West to have one painted from it as a companion to the one he had painted of Geo Warde, nephew of the R^t Hon^l Genl Warde

711

the then possessor; . . ." For further discussion, see No. 719. In addition to Nos. 711 and 719, there is also a second version or copy of No. 711 at Squerryes Court.

The younger George Warde was commissioned into his uncle's regiment, the fourteenth Dragoons in 1774,[2] the year West painted No. 711, and the image of the bird being released from its cage must refer to the subject's departure from home to commence his military career.

[1]Both are quoted by Kerslake pp. 20–21, and the receipt is reproduced pl. 4.
[2]Kerslake, p. 23.

712 Dr. Warren c. 1770

LOCATION UNKNOWN

LIT: Jaffe 1975, p. 317

In a letter dated 21 July 1770, West wrote to Francis Hopkinson:

I have receved your letter with the inclosed Draft on Mr. Warren—but as he is out of Town I have not got it excepted. I can tell you a secrett I have painted a prodigious fine Portrait of him that is intended for you, but I am afraid Mrs. Warren has layed her hands on it and there will be some defeculty in getting it from her so [. . .]—don't let them rest till you get it.[1]

Irma Jaffe has equated the Mr. Warren referred to in this letter with Dr. Joseph Warren (1741–1775), who was killed in the Battle of Bunker's Hill, but that Joseph Warren is not known to have visited England or to have had any personal contact with either West or Hopkinson. Rather, the subject of West's portrait must have been a cousin of Francis Hopkinson, who is referred to several times in Hopkinson's letters as both Mr. and Dr. Warren.[2] He owned a house at Ripple, near Gloucester, where Hopkinson visited him in September 1766 and May 1767, and he appears to have given some kind of support to Hopkinson in starting a business in

Philadelphia upon the latter's return to America in the second half of 1767.

[1]Historical Society of Pennsylvania; partly quoted by Jaffe.
[2]George Everett Hastings, *The Life and Works of Francis Hopkinson*, Chicago, 1928, pp. 33, 136, 147, and 157.

713 William Wellesley (later William Wellesley-Pole, First Baron Maryborough, and Third Earl of Mornington) 1777

LORD RAGLAN

Oil on canvas: $36\frac{1}{4} \times 28\frac{1}{4}$ in. (92 × 72 cm.)

Signed bottom center: *B. West 1777*

PROV: By descent in the family of the sitter

LIT: John Steegman, *A Survey of Portraits in Welsh Houses*, Cardiff, 1962, II, p. 126.

William Wellesley (1763–1845) was the second son of the first Earl of Mornington, whose title he inherited upon the death of his elder brother in 1842. In 1778 he inherited the estates of his cousin William Pole of Ballyfin and took the additional surname of Pole. In 1821 he was created Baron Maryborough. His elder brother Richard (1760–1842) served as Governor General of India and, in addition to succeeding his father as the second Earl of Mornington, was created Marquess Wellesley in 1799. His younger brother Arthur (1769–1852) was the first Duke of Wellington. William Wellesley-Pole was active in Parliament and served, among other roles, as Chief Secretary for Ireland. He was at Eton from 1774 to 1776, the year before the date on No. 713, and he entered the Royal Navy in 1778, the year after.

In No. 713, which shows the sitter at the age of fourteen, he points with his left hand to a globe, on which can be read the words *NEW YOR[K]*, and he holds in the other a partially rolled up map inscribed *THE PROVINCES OF NEW YORK AND NEW JERSEY*. The reason for these details is not known; neither the subject nor his family is known to have had any particular connection with New York or New Jersey. It should be noted, however, that in 1776 and 1777 the chief activities of the British military forces in North America were centered in this area. Hence the map and globe may allude to William Wellesley's forthcoming commission in the Navy and his family's expectation that he would soon be sent to America.

See Nos. 711 and 719 for two other paintings of sitters the same age and with somewhat similar imagery. The latter was painted in the same year as No. 713.

713

Joseph Wilcocks, stipple engraving by S. Phillips after No. 714

714 Joseph Wilcocks *c.* 1763

LOCATION UNKNOWN

ENGR: Stipple engraving (oval, $5\frac{3}{4} \times 4\frac{9}{16}$ in.) by S. Phillips, pub. by W. Brown, 1797, as the frontispiece to the second edition of Wilcocks's *Roman Conversations*, 2 vols., London, 1797

Joseph Wilcocks (1724–1791), the son of a Bishop of Rochester, was a scholar and antiquarian. He lived much of his life in Rome and was there in 1760 when West arrived. According to Galt, West was introduced to Wilcocks by Thomas Robinson, the future Lord Grantham (No. 689),[1] and according to a letter written by West in 1795 and quoted in the preface to the second edition of Wilcocks's *Roman Conversations* in 1797:

> in company with Mr. Wilcocks, and the late Lord Grantham, Mr. West had the felicity to visit all that was great in modern elegant art, or worthy of observation in antiquity . . ., and if in a professional line my endeavours have been rendered acceptance, I do consider, and shall ever esteem myself as infinitely indebted to the honourable countenance and friendship of two such men, as Lord Grantham, and the amiable writer of the Roman Conversations.[2]

Galt mentions that West improved his knowledge of ancient costume by the study of cameos, "in which he was assisted by Mr. Wilcox, the author of the Roman Conversations . . .," during the winter and spring of 1763. In 1772 Wilcocks commissioned from West a painting of the *Angels Appearing to the Shepherds* (No. 304), which he presented anonymously to Rochester Cathedral.

No. 714 is known only via the print after it was published in the second edition of Wilcocks's book. The portrait shows Wilcocks as a relatively young man, and was probably painted before West left Rome in 1763. In the background are an obelisk and a dome surmounted by a cross, probably representing St. Peter's. The two not only situate the subject in Rome, but also reflect Wilcocks's antiquarian interests combined with Christian piety. Galt immediately follows his mention of West's studying cameos under Wilcocks's guidance with a long discussion of West's interest in the hieroglyphics on the Egyptian obelisks he saw in Rome.[3]

715

[1]Galt 1816, p. 131.

[2]Joseph Wilcocks, FSA, *Roman Conversations: or A Short Description of the Antiquities of Rome: interspersed with Characters of Eminent Romans; and Reflections, Religious and Moral, on Roman History . . . the second edition, corrected, with a proface, containing some account of the Author, . . .*, London, 1797, II, pp. xxxix–xli.

[3]Galt 1816, pp. 132–35.

715 **John Williams** 1766

ATLANTIC RICHFIELD COMPANY, CORPORATE ART COLLECTION, PHILADELPHIA

Oil on canvas: oval, $31\frac{3}{4} \times 42\frac{1}{2}$ in. (80.6 × 107.9 cm.)

Signed lower left: *B. West PINXIT/1766*

PROV: Sold by W. A. Willes (a descendant of the sitter), Sotheby's, London, 3 May 1961, lot 137 (together with No. 716); Julius Weitzner, London; Hirschl & Adler Galleries, New York, by 1967; sold anonymously, Sotheby's, London, 23 June 1971, lot 87; Hirschl & Adler Galleries, New York, 1972; Craig and Tarlton, Inc., Raleigh, North Carolina, 1974; sold anonymously, Sotheby Parke Bernet, New York, 25 April 1980, lot 4

EXH: *American Paintings for Public and Private Collections*, Hirschl & Adler Galleries, New York, 1967–68 (13)

Portraits of the sitter's wife (No. 716) and his mother-in-law (No. 707), both painted as similarly horizontal compositions the same size as No. 715, were sold by W. A. Willes along with No. 715 in 1961. This painting is the only one of the three which is signed and dated, but all three must have been painted at approximately the same time.

Since No. 715 is signed and dated *1766*, it is probably not the "Gentleman in Vandyke dress, three quarters" which West exhibited at the Society of Artists in the previous year, although it has been identified as such on several occasions. The exhibited painting may have been No. 669 above.

716 **Mrs. John Williams** *c.* 1766

LOCATION UNKNOWN

Oil on canvas: oval, $31\frac{3}{4} \times 42\frac{1}{2}$ in. (80.6 × 107.9 cm.)

PROV: Sold by W. A. Willes (a descendant of the sitter), Sotheby's, London, 3 May 1961, lot 137 (together with No. 715); Julius Weitzner, London; Hirschl & Adler Galleries, New York, by 1967; sold anonymously, Sotheby's, London, 23 June 1971, lot 88

EXH: *American Paintings for Public and Private Collections*, Hirschl & Adler Galleries, New York, 1967–68 (12)

The subject was the wife of John Williams (No. 715) and the daughter of Mrs. Vanderwall (No. 707).

716

717 Charles Willing, Jr. *c.* 1757–59
Illustrated over page

HISTORICAL SOCIETY OF PENNSYLVANIA,
PHILADELPHIA

Oil on canvas: $49\frac{1}{4} \times 39\frac{1}{4}$ in. (125 × 99.5 cm.)

PROV: Presented to the Historical Society of Pennsylvania, by St. Luke's Church, Germantown, in
1957

LIT: Wainwright 1974, p. 283 (with a tentative attribution to John Wollaston)

Charles Willing, Jr. (1738–1788), was the second son
of Charles Willing (1710–1754), a Philadelphia merchant, and his wife, the former Anne Shippen. He was
the younger brother of Thomas Willing (1731–1821),
merchant, banker, jurist, legislator, and leading citizen
of Philadelphia during the latter years of the eighteenth
century. Charles Willing, Jr., entered the family business in 1755. He spent much of his mature life as a merchant in Barbados, where he was married in 1760.

No. 717 was evidently unknown to William Sawitzky
in 1938.[1] It was brought to the authors' attention in
1978 by Gerold M. Wunderlich, who suggested the
attribution to West.[2] In pose and style it belongs with
a group of portraits generally accepted as having been
painted by West in Philadelphia between 1757 and
1759 (Nos. 622, 663, 681, and 701), and it was presumably painted during this period before the subject's
departure from Philadelphia for Barbados.

[1] A portrait of the subject's father, Charles Willing, Sr., is on
Sawitzky's list of "Portraits Erroneously Attributed to
West" (Sawitzky 1938, p. 460, no. 8).
[2] Letter of 11 August 1979.

718 John Eardley Wilmot 1812

YALE CENTER FOR BRITISH ART, NEW HAVEN, PAUL
MELLON COLLECTION

Oil on canvas: $40\frac{1}{2} \times 57\frac{1}{4}$ in. (103 × 145.5 cm.)

Signed bottom right corner: *B. West/1812*

PROV: Sold by the estate of Sir John Eardley-Wilmot,
fourth Baronet (1882–1970), Sotheby's, London, 18
Nov. 1970, lot 60; Mr. and Mrs. Paul Mellon

EXH: RA 1812 (58) "Portrait of J. E. Wilmot, Esq.,
who adjusted the losses, claims, and compensations
of the American loyalists"; New Haven 1983 (1)

ENGR: See No. 106

LIT: Courtauld Cuttings, II, p. 1 (1812); Charles
Robert Leslie, *Autobiographical Recollections*, London,
1860, II, pp. 11–12; Helmut von Erffa, "West's
Portrait of John Eardley-Wilmot," *Auction*, IV, Nov.
1970, pp. 49–50

717

LIT: Beckles Willson, "Portraits and Relics of General Wolfe," *Connoisseur*, XXIII, 1909, p. 11; Kerslake 1959, pp. 20–21, pls. 3 and 4; Kerslake 1977, p. 319

General James Wolfe (1727–1759) was the subject of West's best-known painting (No. 93), which shows his death in the hour of victory at Quebec on 13 September 1759. No. 719 is a later posthumous portrait showing him as a boy.

No. 719 was commissioned by Wolfe's boyhood friend, George Warde, who had also become a general by 1777, to be the companion of a portrait previously painted by West in 1774 of General Warde's nephew also named George Warde (No. 711). West evidently partly based the likeness of Wolfe on a small portrait by an unknown artist painted *c.* 1740–44, which is still at Squerryes Court.[1] This latter portrait has two notes attached to the stretcher, which John Kerslake has demonstrated must have been written between 1822 and 1851, and one of these notes explains the genesis of No. 719:

> About the year 1775 this picture was sent to West to have one painted from it as a companion to the one he had painted of Geo Warde, nephew of the R^t Hon^l Genl Warde the then possessor; the picture came home unlike, and was sent back to West, who returned it again still unlike, with his regrets that he had not seen the picture before he painted his large picture of the death of Wolfe, which had been engraved, that he had endeavoured to make a resemblance between them, but it would not be fair upon the engraver to paint one in which no likeness could be traced to Wolfe as represented in the engraving. The picture thus painted by West with a map of the Battle of Blenheim before him is in the Gallery at Squerryes.

The details of the commission mentioned in the above note are confirmed by West's receipt for No. 719, which is attached to the back of the painting:

> Received of Genl Warde Twenty nine pounds eight shillings—for a small picture of Genl Wolfe as a Boy—with one of Mr Warde as a companion.
>
> Jany 21st 1778—Benjn West

At the bottom of the sheet, in another hand, "Mr. Warde" is identified as "Mr. Geo Warde."

The assertion that West did not make the young Wolfe in No. 719 resemble the Squerryes portrait is somewhat puzzling, since Wolfe's features in No. 719 appear more like those in the Squerryes portrait than those in No. 93. It might be added as well that Wolfe in No. 93 does not appear to be as bad a likeness as the note quoted above suggests, and the inclusion of a "Portrait of Wolfe when a Boy, presented to West by the General's family, to assist him in forming the likeness of the hero as represented in the celebrated picture of the Death of General Wolfe. Said to be unique" in a sale of works from West's estate in 1829,[2] if correctly catalogued in that sale, suggests that West had not been entirely cavalier about Wolfe's actual appearance when painting No. 93.

In No. 719 Wolfe is seated at a table on which is unrolled a plan showing the disposition of troops labelled *BATTLE OF BLENHEIM*, and in his right hand he holds a plan of fortifications inscribed *BERGEN OP ZOOM*. Behind him, on the right are three books, one of which is entitled *HISTORY OF ENGLAND*, and on the table to the left are several pieces of armor.

Between 1731, when General Warde's father acquired Squerryes Court in Westerham, Kent, and 1738, when the Wolfe family moved from Westerham to Greenwich, Warde and Wolfe were childhood companions. Wolfe received news of his first commission in the military while on a visit to Squerryes Court in 1741, and Wolfe and Warde served together as young officers in Flanders in 1742 during the War of the Austrian Succession. It seems likely that Warde dictated the imagery

---

John Eardley Wilmot, or Eardley-Wilmot as of 1812 (1750–1815), was a barrister and politician, who from 1783 to 1788 served as commissioner to inquire into the claims of the American loyalists to compensation for their losses suffered during the American revolutionary war. No. 718 commemorates this activity. The top sheet of paper under Wilmot's right hand on the table before him is inscribed: *REPORT OF LOSSES AND COMPENSATION TO THE AMERICAN LOYAL-ISTS*, and below that is a letter addressed to *The Right Honble William Pitt*, dated *27th of Apr 1788*, and signed *John Wilmot*. The framed painting in the background shows an allegory of the *Reception of the American Loyalists by Great Britain in the Year 1783*. It is discussed separately in this catalogue in the entry for No. 106, but mention should be made here that it contains additional portraits: Sir William Pepperell and William Franklin at the head of the group of loyalists being received by Britannia, West, leaning on a cane, his palette beside him, and Mrs. West standing behind him.

Some forty-eight years previously West had painted a portrait of Eardley-Wilmot's brother-in-law, Sir Sampson Gideon, who subsequently took his wife's surname and eventually became Lord Eardley (No. 623).

719 General James Wolfe as a Boy 1777

J. ST. A. WARDE, SQUERRYES COURT, WESTERHAM, KENT

Oil on canvas: 15 × 18½ in. (38 × 47 cm.)

Signed left of center on back of armor: *B. West/1777*

PROV: Commissioned by General George Warde (1725–1803); then by descent in the Warde family

EXH: London 1868 (767) lent by Admiral Warde; *A Pageant of Canada*, National Gallery of Canada, Ottawa, 1967 (94)

718

719

of No. 719 to commemorate Wolfe's interests during this period at the beginning of his first military campaign. In 1742 Wolfe was approximately the same age as the younger George Warde at the time he entered the army in General Warde's regiment and West painted him in the companion picture (No. 711). Bergen-op-Zoom in Brabant, whose fortifications the young Wolfe is studying, is approximately forty miles from Ghent, where he was stationed in 1742.

A second version, identical with No. 719 in all significant details, is No. 720 below. What appears to be a copy by another hand, showing considerably less detail, is in a private collection in New York.

[1] See Kerslake 1959, pp. 19–24 et passim, ill. p. 24; The two notes attached to this painting's stretcher are transcribed, ibid., p. 21; the receipt on the back of No. 719 is transcribed on p. 20 and reproduced pl. 4.

[2] Robins, London, 20–22 June, 1829, lot 194. Nothing more is known about this portrait.

720 General James Wolfe as a Boy 1777

HIS GRACE THE DUKE OF WESTMINSTER

Oil on canvas: 15$\frac{1}{2}$ × 19 in. (38 × 48 cm.)

Signed left of center on back of armor: *B. West/1777*

PROV: Robert, second Earl Grosvenor, by 1804; then by family descent

EXH: BI 1833 (9) lent by the Marquess of Westminster

LISTED: *PC*, p. 562 ("A small Portrait of General Wolfe when a Boy," in the possession of the Earl Grosvenor); *UM*, p. 528; Barlow, p. 432; *BA*, p. 14; Galt, p. 220; Dillenberger, p. 152 (145)

Nos. 719 and 720 are both signed and dated *1777*. No. 720 appears on the early lists of West's works, while No. 719 does not, but the circumstances of the commission of the latter painting cited in the previous entry establish it as the first version and No. 720 as a replica, albeit a replica of equally high quality.

Although there is no documentation of No. 720 being in the Grosvenor collection prior to the autumn of 1804, when it was included in the first of the lists of West's works, West presumably painted it for Lord Grosvenor (subsequently the first Earl Grosvenor), who previously had been the purchaser of the first version of the *Death of General Wolfe* (No. 93) in 1771.

721 Mrs. Jonathan Worrell as Hebe *c.* 1775–78

TATE GALLERY, LONDON

Oil on canvas: 50 × 39$\frac{1}{2}$ in. (127 × 100 cm.)

PROV: Bequeathed by Miss Harriet Worrell (*c.* 1771–1858), a daughter of the sitter, to the National Gallery as residuary legatee after the deaths of her remaining brothers and sisters; received by the National Gallery in 1869 and transferred to the Tate Gallery in 1929

LIT: E. M. Shilstone, "The Worrell Family in Barbados," *Journal of the Barbados Museum and Historical Society*, XXIX, 1961, pp. 19–20, ill. opp. p. 19

The subject of No. 721 must be Catherine Worrell, who died in 1835 at the age of eighty-seven. She was the second wife of Jonathan Worrell (1734–1814), a wealthy landed proprietor from Barbados who came to England sometime before 1780 and died in Surrey. Jonathan Worrell married twice, and the dates of his first wife's death and of his remarriage are not known, but a description of No. 721 as a portrait of "our late mother" in a codicil of 1851 to the will of Harriet Wor-

722

rell, is hardly likely to have referred to the first wife of a man who had died almost forty years before.

The date of No. 721 appears to be *c.* 1775–78. Analogous works stylistically are Nos. 243, 247, 612, and 708. Nos. 612, 247, and probably 243 are, like No. 721, allegorical portraits, and, indeed, most of West's allegorical portraits date from these years. In depicting his sitter as Hebe, the goddess of youth and cup-bearer of the gods, West was following the example of Reynolds, who in 1772 had exhibited *A Portrait of a Young Lady in the Character of Hebe*,[1] but the composition and, particularly, the detail of the large eagle drinking from the cup, more immediately reflect the influence of the *Hebe* by Gavin Hamilton (collection of the Marquess of Exeter) which West may have known via the engraving by Domenico Cunego.[2]

Two further paintings of female subjects as Hebe are No. 613, which West probably painted *c.* 1777, and No. 733, which is signed and dated *1778*. The latter appears to have been painted as a compositional sketch for a larger portrait, and it is possible that the larger work was No. 721. If so, West completely refashioned the composition before painting the final picture. See also the *Eagle Bringing the Cup of Water to Psyche* (No. 153).

[1] Reproduced in Ellis K. Waterhouse, *Reynolds*, London, 1941, pl. 140.

[2] See Françoise Forster-Hahn, "After Guercino or After the Greeks? Gavin Hamilton's 'Hebe': Tradition and Change in the 1760s," *Burlington Magazine*, CXVII, 1975, pp. 365–71.

722 Diana Wyld 1766

MONTCLAIR ART MUSEUM, MONTCLAIR, NEW JERSEY

Oil on canvas: 33$\frac{1}{2}$ × 43 in. (85 × 109 cm.)

Signed lower left: *B. West 1766*

PROV: Sold anonymously, Sotheby's, London, 19 Dec.

1945, lot 76; E. and A. Silberman, New York; acquired by the Montclair Art Museum in 1949

The subject of this painting has been identified as the wife of Thomas Wyld of Sheen. Compare No. 707, in which the features of the sitter are remarkably similar to those of the lady in No. 722, and the dress is virtually identical. That work was identified as a portrait of a Mrs. Vanderwall when it appeared on the market in 1961.

723 Sir William Young, Bt., with His Wife Elizabeth and a Child 1767

See color illustration, p. 28

SIR WILLIAM YOUNG

Oil on canvas: 52$\frac{1}{2}$ × 67$\frac{1}{4}$ in. (133.5 × 171 cm.)

Signed lower left: *B. West/1767*

PROV: By descent in the family of the sitters

No. 723 shows Sir William Young, first Baronet (1725–1788); his second wife, née Elizabeth Taylor (1729–1801), whom he married in 1747; and one of their nine children, probably their youngest daughter, Olivia. Sir William belonged to a wealthy family who lived in the West Indies. He purchased the manor of Delaford in Buckinghamshire in 1767, was appointed Lieutenant-Governor of Dominica in 1768, and created a baronet in 1769. He was also subsequently Lieutenant-Governor of Tobago. A portrait of the entire family painted by Johann Zoffany *c.* 1766 is in the Walker Art Gallery, Liverpool.[1]

Two portraits of Sir William's eldest son are Nos. 724 and 725 below. Sir William Young was the first owner of West's *Venus Lamenting the Death of Adonis* of 1768 (No. 116).

[1] See Mary Webster, *Johann Zoffany 1733–1810*, National Portrait Gallery, London, 1976 (exhibition catalogue), p. 42 (41).

724

724 **William Young** *c.* 1767

THE PROVOST AND FELLOWS OF ETON COLLEGE

Oil on canvas: 30 × 25 in. (76 × 63.5 cm.)

PROV: Presented to the Headmaster of Eton by the
    sitter

EXH: *British Art*, Royal Academy, London, 1934 (249);
    Eton Leaving Portraits, Tate Gallery, London, 1951
    (23)

LIT: Cust 1910, p. 16 (12), pl. VIII

William Young (1750–1815) was the son of Sir William
Young, first Baronet (for whom, see No. 723). He succeeded his father as second Baronet in 1788, and, like
his father, he was to become Lieutenant-Governor of
Tobago. He entered Eton in 1758 and left in 1768.
According to a diary kept by the sitter, now in the possession of the Young family, West painted No. 724 in
1767, the same year as No. 723.

This painting is the earliest of three Eton leaving
portraits by West. The other two are Nos. 617 and 656.

725 **William Young** *c.* 1767

GEORGE C. SEYBOLT

Oil on canvas: 28¾ × 42½ in. (73 × 62 cm.)

PROV: By descent from William Young's sister, Sarah
    Elizabeth, the wife of Richard Ottley, to William
    Ottley, from whom purchased by Thos. Agnew &
    Sons, London, *c.* 1920; C. W. Kraushaar, New York,
    from whom bought by the Concord Art Association,
    Concord, Mass., in 1923; Vose Galleries, Boston,
    1975

EXH: Philadelphia 1921 (21) lent by C. W. Kraushaar;
    Brooklyn 1922 (16); Philadelphia 1938 (38)

No. 725 is a version of No. 724, and was presumably
painted at approximately the same time for the sitter's
family. It varies slightly in some details from No. 724,
notably in the lace cuffs and neckpiece.

PORTRAITS OF OTHER MISCELLANEOUS GROUPS

726 The Cricketers (?)1763
See color illustrations, pp. 15, 24

PRIVATE COLLECTION

Oil on canvas: 40 × 50 in. (101.6 × 127 cm.)

PROV: By descent in the family of Andrew Allen to the present owner

EXH: PAFA 1819 (53) "A Cricket Match"; PAFA 1832; Allentown 1962 (5); *In the Minds and Hearts of the People*, National Portrait Gallery, Washington, 1974; *1776: The British Story of the American Revolution*, National Maritime Museum, Greenwich, 1976 (336)

LIT: Lehigh 1960, pp. 11–12, ill. p. 31; Timothy Green, "The British view of 1776 and all that: Greenwich, 1976," *Smithsonian Magazine*, VII, Aug. 1976, pp. 68–69, ill. pp. 64–65

Two versions of this group portrait are known. The other version, which is No. 727 below, is signed and dated *1764*. The sitters in No. 726 have traditionally been identified as, from left to right, Ralph Wormeley (1745–1806), the brothers James Allen (1742–1778) and Andrew Allen (1740–1825), Ralph Izard (1741/42–1804), and Arthur Middleton (1742–1787). West also painted a separate portrait of Andrew Allen (No. 583) at approximately the same time, and several years later he painted a triple portrait of Arthur Middleton with his wife and baby son (No. 661). A portrait of Ralph Wormeley painted in 1763 by Robert Edge Pine belongs to the Virginia Historical Society in Richmond.

The tradition accompanying No. 727, which belonged in the nineteenth century to descendants of Ralph Izard, repeats the identification of Andrew Allen and Ralph Izard as the two men standing in the center of the group, but reverses the positions of James Allen and Ralph Wormeley, and describes the figure on the extreme right as a Mr. Beckford. This last name cannot refer to West's future patron William Beckford, who was only born in 1760; it could conceivably be William's fox-hunting cousin Peter (1740–1811). Nonetheless, the identification of this figure as Arthur Middleton seems more likely. All the other sitters were American-born—Andrew and James Allen from Philadelphia, Wormeley from Virginia, and Izard from Charleston, South Carolina—so it is probable that the fifth sitter would have been American as well. Arthur Middleton was, like Ralph Izard, whose cousin he was to marry in August 1764, a native of Charleston. And, if we allow for a difference in years, his appearance in No. 661 is reasonably consistent with that of the figure on the right in No. 726.

Izard, Middleton, and Wormeley were all students at Cambridge in the early 1760s. The Allen brothers were at the Middle Temple in London from 1761 to 1764. Arthur Middleton returned to Charleston in December 1763,[1] so if he does appear in the pictures, at least one version (presumably No. 726, which is not dated) must have been begun in that year, before his departure from England, but after West's arrival in August. Chief Justice William Allen (for whom see No. 581), the father of James and Andrew and West's early benefactor, was also in England in 1763 and 1764, and it was possibly he who commissioned No. 726.

The background has been said to be West's idea of Cambridge, which he evidently had not visited when he painted Nos. 726 and 727, although he had been to Oxford during a trip to Bath to stay with Chief Justice Allen. The bridge on the right looks remarkably like the old Walton Bridge on the Thames, which he easily could have seen on that trip, or on an earlier visit to Hampton Court.[2]

See also p. 25 above. The obvious inspiration for *The Cricketers* came from the group portraits painted by Nathaniel Dance of English visitors to Rome during the period West was in Italy.[3] Two of those portraits by Dance included sitters who were also painted by West either in Italy or shortly after coming to England (see Nos. 625 and 689). In at least one case, Dance is known to have painted repetitions for each of the sitters, and it has been suggested that West did the same with *The Cricketers*. However, only two versions are currently known, and there is no evidence to indicate that more than two ever existed.

[1] Langdon Cheves, "Middleton of South Carolina," *South Carolina Historical and Genealogical Magazine*, I, 1900, p. 243, note 1.
[2] For West's early travels in England, see Galt 1820, p. 5. For Walton Bridge see the well-known painting by Canaletto (Dulwich College Picture Gallery), reproduced in Luke Herrmann, *British Landscape Painting of the Eighteenth Century*, New York, 1974, pl. 18.
[3] *Nathaniel Dance 1735–1811* (exhibition catalogue), the Iveagh Bequest, Kenwood, 1977, nos. 4, 5, and 8.

727 The Cricketers 1764

THE BROOK CLUB, NEW YORK

Oil on canvas: 40 × 50 in. (101.6 × 127 cm.)

Signed lower right: *B. West—London/1764*

PROV: By descent in the family of Ralph Izard to Walter Izard, of Goode, Bedford County, Virginia, by whom sold to a carpet-bagger following the Civil War;[1] Ehrich Galleries, New York; purchased by the Brook Club in 1907

LIT: Ehrich 1918, p. 156; Diego Suarez, *The Collection of Portraits of American Celebrities and other Paintings belonging to the Brook*, New York, 1962, pp. 4–5

[1] Letter from George De Lancey Hanger, 7 November 1980. Mr. Hanger has also kindly sent a copy of part of the will dated 1831 of Alice De Lancey Izard, the widow of Ralph Izard, bequeathing to her grandson Walter Izard "his grand-father's picture painted by West."

728 Two Officers and a Groom in a Landscape 1777

LLOYDS BANK LIMITED, COX AND KING'S BRANCH, LONDON

Oil on canvas: 39 × 49 in. (99.1 × 124.5 cm.)

Signed lower right: *B. West 1777*

PROV: (?) Louis Ralston, 1912; sold anonymously, Christie's, London, 25 April 1913, lot 96 ("Two officers standing in a landscape conversing"), bt. by S. T. Smith; acquired by Cox and Co., London, prior to 1923, when Cox and Co. was taken over by Lloyd's Bank

728

EXH: *1776: The British Story of the American Revolution*, National Maritime Museum, Greenwich, 1976 (563) as "Francis Augustus Eliot and a Spanish officer"

Since 1952 this puzzling picture has been described as a portrait of Major Francis Augustus Eliott (1750–1813) receiving a Spanish envoy. It was, however, sold in 1913 as a picture of two unidentified officers; and it has also been described as a portrait of General Wolfe.[1] The identification of the figure on the right as Major Eliott was made by A. S. White, librarian of the War Office, on the basis of the uniform being that of the 15th Light Dragoons, in which Eliott served from 1775 to 1779, and of the similarity of the background to the background of a picture said to have been painted by George Carter in 1781 showing Major Eliott's father, Lord Heathfield, and Colonel William Green at Gibraltar, where Lord Heathfield was Governor (in the Officer's Mess, Brompton Barracks, Chatham, in 1952).[2] Unfortunately, neither of these reasons is compelling. Major Eliott was not the only officer entitled to wear the uniform shown in No. 728, and identification of either sitters or site on the basis of similarity with a work painted four years later by another, lesser artist, who could conceivably have modelled his picture on West's, is questionable. White suggested that No. 728 commemorates a stay made by Major Eliott at Gibraltar from March 1777 to March 1778, but the date of *1777* on the canvas, which must certainly have been painted in London, makes this hypothesis unlikely. Without further evidence, therefore, the identity of the sitters must be considered unknown.

The uniform of the officer on the right, identified by White as that of the 15th Light Dragoons, is red with blue facings. That of his companion is grey, with pale green collar and cuffs. As noted by White, the occasion seems to be an informal one. The officer in red is shown without his sword and sash, and he has two buttons on his waistcoat undone. Furthermore, the two men appear to have exchanged hats, presumably in a gesture of goodwill. They stand before a team of horses harnessed to a carriage, the front of which is just visible on the left edge of the painting. Before the carriage stands a groom in red leaning on a grazing horse, and the head of a second attendant is visible over his shoulder.

The landscape on the right side of the painting is reminiscent of Welsh views by Richard Wilson, such as the *Valley of the Mawddach, with Cader Idris*, possibly exhibited at the Royal Academy in 1774 (Walker Art Gallery, Liverpool). It is of course possible that Wilson provided the model for a basically imaginary landscape, which may have been intended to represent Spain, but it is also possible that the landscape represents Wales and that the painting commemorates a domestic tour made by a British officer and a visitor from abroad. There are no analogous views in the backgrounds of any other portraits by West, and since the handling, unlike that in the rest of the picture, does not appear particularly characteristic of him, it may be that the landscape is by another hand.

[1] On an old photograph in the Frick Art Reference Library, New York. This photograph evidently dates from 1912, when No. 728 was purportedly in the collection of Louis Ralston.

[2] Letter dated 8 July 1952, from A. S. White, The Library, The War Office, to R. W. Jack, Esq., Messrs. Pawsey and Payne, London. A copy of this letter was kindly sent to Helmut von Erffa by D. J. Rooke of Lloyds Bank in 1972.

729

729 The Ambassador from Tunis with His Attendants as He Appeared in England in 1781
1781

MUSEUM OF FINE ARTS, BOSTON

Oil on canvas: 28¼ × 36¼ in. (71.7 × 92.1 cm.)

Signed lower right: *B. West 1781*

PROV: Sold by West's sons, Robins, London, 22–25 May 1829, lot 115 ("Portraits of Algerines," 2 ft. 4 in. × 3 ft.), bt. by Col. d'Arcy for £23.2.0.; (?) Sortais, Paris, 1896; René Brimo, Paris by 1938; Hirschl & Adler Galleries, New York, from whom purchased by the Museum of Fine Arts in 1955 (Abraham Shulman Fund, 55.932)

LISTED: *PC*, p. 565 ("The Ambassador from Tunis, with his Attendant, as he appeared in England in 1781," West, Painting-room); *UM*, p. 530; *BA*, p. 17 ("The small picture of the Ambassador from Tunis" . . .); Galt, p. 226; Dillenberger, p. 168 (294)

LIT: René Brimo, *L'Evolution du goût aux Etats-Unis d'après l'histoire des collections*, Paris, 1938, pl. III, opp. p. 24; Boston 1969, I, p. 281 (1016), II, fig. 97; (?) Lilian M. C. Randal, ed., *The Diaries of George A. Lucas*, Princeton, 1979, II, p. 834 (entry for 18 Sept. 1896)

In the Robins sale catalogue of May 1829, the subjects of No. 729 were described as "natives of Barbary" visiting England on "some embassy from the Dey of Algiers" in the early part of the reign of George III. The castle and boat seen across the sea in the background were presumably intended by West to represent the Barbary coast. We have been unable to find record of any embassy from Tunis, Algiers, or elsewhere *c.* 1781 that No. 729 may record. West's compatriot and erstwhile pupil Mather Brown painted a comparable subject, *George III Receiving a Turkish Ambassador* (private collection), but that visit took place in 1794, considerably later than the date on No. 729.[1]

No. 729 may be the "Armenians" by West, which a Parisian art dealer named Sortais showed to George A. Lucas in 1896.

[1] Evans 1982, pp. 130–32, figs. 112 and 113.

PORTRAITS OF UNIDENTIFIED SUBJECTS

730 Unidentified Man ("The Prince of Savoy")
c. 1760–61

PRIVATE COLLECTION

Oil on canvas laid down on board: $22\frac{1}{4} \times 17\frac{3}{4}$ in. $(56.5 \times 45$ cm.)

PROV: Mrs. Edward Shippen Morris, Philadelphia (in 1962)

According to information supplied by Mrs. Edward Shippen Morris to the Frick Art Reference Library, this painting is said to show a Prince of Savoy and to have been painted in gratitude for assistance given to West by the House of Savoy. The Prince presumably would have been Victor Amadeus III (1726–1796), who succeeded his father as duke in 1773. Unfortunately, this story seems improbable. Neither West in his letters to Joseph Shippen written in 1762 and 1763,[1] nor Galt in his extended account of West's activities and friendships in Italy, nor any other source, gives any indication whatsoever that West ever had contact with any member of the House of Savoy. Yet it seems unlikely that significant assistance from such a distinguished quarter would have gone completely unrecorded.

On the other hand, since No. 730 does apparently have a Shippen family provenance, it does not seem improbable that it could have been brought back from Italy by Joseph Shippen, with whom West had travelled to Italy in 1760. Shippen returned to Philadelphia in December 1761.[2] The Van Dyck costume and the general style of No. 730 are consistent with a date of *c.* 1760–61; No. 730 is comparable to the portrait of Captain Medows which West reportedly painted in Leghorn in 1761 (No. 658), and, although on a smaller scale and with less careful finish, to West's portrait of his other travelling companion, John Allen (No. 582), which must date from the same period. The three paintings show the predominant influence of Anton Raphael Mengs, whose style West seems to have been able to emulate with remarkable success very soon after his arrival in Italy (see No. 689).[3]

Since the traditional identification of the sitter as a Savoyard prince seems unlikely, the most probable alternative is that it is a portrait of Joseph Shippen himself. Shippen (1732–1810) would have been twenty-eight years old in 1760, and his appearance in a somewhat earlier picture is reasonably similar to that of the subject of No. 730.[4] The intimacy between West and Shippen, suggested by the two long letters West wrote to Shippen after the latter's return to America, makes it seem likely that West would have painted his travelling companion's portrait. Another possibility is that No. 730 is identical with No. 689, the lost portrait of Thomas Robinson which West painted in the summer of 1760 to show to Mengs. The small scale and rather tentative and hasty execution would fit with the circumstances under which West is recorded to have undertaken that work, his first picture painted after arriving in Italy, and it is not out of the question that Shippen could have taken it back with him to Philadelphia to show to Chief Justice Allen and Governor Hamilton. But, tempting as such an identification may be, no real evidence exists to confirm it.

730

[1] Richardson 1978, pp. 16–19 and 21–25.
[2] Thomas Balch, *Letters and Papers Relating Chiefly to the Provincial History of Pennsylvania*, Philadelphia, 1855, p. lxvii.
[3] See the portrait of Robert Wood by Mengs (Bridgewater Collection, National Gallery of Scotland), reproduced in Kerslake 1977, II, pl. 915.
[4] Destroyed by fire in 1923; reproduced in Albert Cook Meyers, *Hannah Logan's Courtship*, Philadelphia, 1904, opp. p. 266. This painting was at one time ascribed to West and is discussed in Sawitzky 1938, p. 460 (7), where the attribution is rejected.

731 Unidentified Man *c.* 1764–68

WESTMORELAND COUNTY MUSEUM OF ART,
GREENSBURG, PENNSYLVANIA

Oil on canvas: $51 \times 41\frac{1}{4}$ in. (129.5 × 105 cm.)

Signed lower left: *B. West pinxit/Londinium*

PROV: Sold anonymously, Christie's, London, 25 July 1952, lot 51; Hirschl & Adler Galleries, New York, by 1954, and given by them to the Westmoreland County Museum in 1959

EXH: *250 Years of Art in Pennsylvania*, Westmoreland County Museum of Art, Greensburg, Pennsylvania, 1959 (130)

West probably painted No. 731 between 1764 and 1768. Dated portraits which are analogous in style include those of Sampson Gideon of 1764 (No. 623), the fifth Earl of Stamford of 1765 (No. 625), and Governor James Hamilton of 1767 (No. 633).

732 A Mother with Two Children *c.* 1776–78

PRIVATE COLLECTION

Oil on canvas: 49 × 39 in. (124.5 × 99 cm.)

PROV: George Henry Milles-Lade, 4th Earl Sondes (1914–1970); Leger Galleries, London, 1973; English Manor Antiques, Pride's Crossing, Mass., 1974; Old Hall Gallery, Ltd., Iden Rye, Sussex, 1977–78; sold anonymously, Christie's, London, 23 Nov. 1979, lot 169; The Art Fund, Washington, D.C., 1980; R. H. Love Galleries, Chicago, 1980

No. 732 and a second closely related painting, which shows a mother holding a child in her arms in the same pose as the corresponding figures in No. 732 but in reverse (Bayou Bend Collection, Museum of Fine Arts, Houston), appeared on the market in London, following the death of the fourth Earl Sondes in 1970. Both were credited with Sondes provenances, and both have been described as showing members of the Sondes family. Neither is signed, and neither seems to have any reliably documented history prior to 1970 or 1971.

Of the two paintings, No. 732 is more like West. In details, such as the curtain and column in the background, in style of dress, and in handling it is consistent with several other portraits by West, all from the later 1770s: notably, *Sir Thomas Beauchamp-Proctor* (No. 590), dated *1777*; *Lady Beauchamp-Proctor* (No. 591), dated *1778*; and two portraits of royal children, Nos. 570 and 573, dated *1776* and *1778* respectively. The painting in Houston is a copy of No. 732, reversed, modified in details of dress, and with the child standing on the right omitted. It does not appear to be by West's hand.

Attempts to identify the subjects of the two paintings have not been successful. It has been proposed that No. 732 shows Mary Elizabeth, wife of the second Baron Sondes, with her daughter Mary Grace and her eldest son Lewis Richard, the future third Baron Sondes (1792–1836), but since No. 732 evidently dates from the 1770s that identification is not convincing.

A drawing of a child in a similar but not identical pose to that of the child in the lower right of No. 732 and in what appears to be the same dress is in the British Museum.[1]

[1]Black chalk, 11 × 7¼ in. (1920–6–15–22).

733 Unidentified Woman as Hebe 1778
Illustrated over page

E. DEANE TURNER

Oil on canvas: 17½ × 13½ in. (44.5 × 34.3 cm.)

Signed lower left: *Benj West 1778*

PROV: Sold anonymously, Christie's East, New York, 20 March 1981, lot 48; sold anonymously, Christie's, London, 20 Nov. 1981, lot 121; Sabin Galleries, London

No. 733 is approximately the same size as Nos. 550 and 557, West's small paintings of George III and Queen Charlotte, and like those works it may have been painted as a study for a full-scale portrait. No large portrait based directly on No. 733 is now known; nevertheless, it may be an abandoned first idea for *Mrs. Jonathan Worrell as Hebe* (No. 721), which West painted at approximately the same time but with a different composition. Another portrait depicting a sitter in the guise of Hebe is No. 613. That painting shows Grizzel Dundas and is even less like No. 733, but there is some resemblance in pose and windblown hair between the lady in No. 733 and Grizzel's mother in No. 612, West's allegorical double portrait of mother and daughter dated *1777*. In addition, the ewer in No. 733 appears to be identical with one on the floor at Mrs. Dundas's feet in No. 612.

An old label attached to the stretcher of No. 733

732

identifies the work as "A Portrait of an American Lady as Hebe by West." This label was clearly not written by West, nor by someone sufficiently well informed to identify the sitter by name. Hence its description of her as American, although not impossible, may be no more than a surmise based on West's American origins. Mrs. Worrell, the subject of No. 721, was evidently from Barbados. The Dundas family seems to have had no close American connections.

734 Unidentified Man (? Dr. Homan) 1794
Illustrated over page

ART INSTITUTE OF CHICAGO

Oil on canvas: 50½ × 40 in. (128.3 × 101.7 cm.)

Signed center left (on inkstand): *Benjamin West 1794*

PROV: Ehrich Galleries, New York; gift of the family of Byron L. Smith to the Art Institute of Chicago in 1918

EXH: *Utstallning av Amerikansk Konst*, Academy of Arts, Stockholm, 1930 (110); Philadelphia 1938 (42)

LIT: Frederic Fairchild Sherman, "The Art of Benjamin West," *Art in America*, VI, 1918, p. 156 and fig. 2; Ehrich 1918, p. 154; *Paintings in the Art Institute of Chicago*, Chicago, 1961, p. 481

According to the catalogue of the West exhibition in Philadelphia in 1938 the subject of No. 734 has been said to be a "Dr. Homan, physician to George IV." Earlier published sources as well as the more recent catalogue of the Art Institute of Chicago list the subject as unidentified. The name of Dr. Homan does not appear in the published correspondence of either George III or George IV.

733

734

735 Portrait of a Gentleman in Van Dyck Dress
c. 1765

EXH : SA 1765 (154) "Portrait of a gentleman in
Vandyke dress, three quarters"

See Nos. 669 and 715.

736 Portrait of a Lady in Masquerade Dress
c. 1765

EXH : SA 1765 (153) "Portrait of a Lady in masquerade
dress, half length"

See No. 670.

737 Portraits of Two Young Gentlemen *c.* 1775

LOCATION UNKNOWN

EXH : RA 1775 (338) "Portraits of two young
gentlemen"

See No. 541.

738 Portrait of a Young Gentleman *c.* 1795

LOCATION UNKNOWN

EXH : RA 1795 (74) "Portrait of a young gentleman"

LIT : V and A Cuttings, pp. 745 and 758 (both *Morning
Chronicle*, May 1795)

In a list published in the *Morning Chronicle* identifying
the subjects of portraits in the Royal Academy exhibition of 1795, number 74 (No. 738) was listed as "A Bad
Boy." A subsequent issue of the paper discussed the
painting:

In the list of the Names of the Portraits, published
in the *Chronicle*, this is called—*a Bad Boy*, and well
is he entitled to the appellation. He is very properly
put at the top of the room, being by that means, in
a degree, out of the reach of the Critics. In his dress
he is most intolerably slovenly: his stockings are
about his heels, and one of his legs appears as crooked
as a ram's horn, though, it must be acknowledged,
that the great pillar on one side of the canvas is sufficiently straight, round, and smooth. On the whole,

if this be considered as a *Picture*, it is by no means
picturesque; and, if it is really what the Catalogue
declares—a *Portrait*, is it a very ungracious one.

Despite this intriguing discussion we have been unable
to identify the work.

739 Portraits of a Mother and Her Daughter
c. 1802

LOCATION UNKNOWN

EXH : RA 1802 (615) "Portraits of a mother and her
daughter"

No. 739 may be the same picture as No. 649, *Mrs.
Thomas Keyes and Her Daughter*, the style of which
appears compatible with a date *c.* 1802. That picture
has been said to have been painted *c.* 1806, but on stylistic grounds it would not seem impossible that West
painted it a few years before.

Appendix 1

West's Paintings for the Royal Chapel in Windsor Castle

West began the project of painting a series of pictures of biblical subjects for the Royal Chapel in Windsor Castle some time in 1779, and he worked on it until 1801. His first recorded mention of the chapel is in a letter of 15 October 1779, in which he says that his time is much taken up by the project.[1] According to William Carey, he received the commission in February 1780,[2] and he first completed and exhibited a picture for the chapel in 1781 (No. 334). In a letter written to George III on 26 September 1801, West stated that he had been instructed on the fifteenth of the previous month by the architect James Wyatt, acting on the King's behalf, to suspend work on the paintings "until further orders."[3] John Galt says that the King subsequently told West to go on with the work, and on 18 November 1803, Joseph Farington recorded that West was going on with it at his own expense.[4] In 1804, West did paint (or at least signed and dated) one oil sketch, which he later described as for a large picture for the chapel (No. 410), but he painted no full-sized pictures for the series after 1801.

Between 1781 and 1801 West completed eighteen large paintings for the chapel, and he left one unfinished (No. 236). He exhibited the completed pictures at the Royal Academy, and all but two of them (Nos. 240 and 262) were accompanied in the exhibition catalogues by lines indicating their destinations. He also exhibited nine drawings or oil sketches for chapel pictures at the Academy and identified most of them as such in the catalogues. Because plans for the chapel changed as he went along, we cannot say how many pictures he intended to paint. At its inception in 1779 the scheme may have comprised no more than sixteen paintings. After he had been told to stop work, West wrote in September 1801 that he had composed thirty-five subjects,[5] and in 1816 he told John Quincy Adams that the total number was to have been thirty-six.[6] That figure is repeated by other sources, but the various documents do not agree on what the specific subjects were to have been, and a recent article by Jerry Meyer lists forty-six titles connected to the chapel project by one source or another.[7] As Meyer notes, his list includes subjects that had been dropped from the scheme as it evolved, and others whose places in it are dubious. Among the obviously dubious are one painting and five cartoons for stained glass windows destined for St. George's Chapel at Windsor, which, somewhat confusingly, appear together with the works intended for the Royal Chapel in accounts prepared by West for the King. On other occasions as well, West does not seem to have drawn a distinction between the two chapels. When he told John Quincy Adams that he planned thirty-six subjects, he also said that he had finished twenty-five, a figure that can be explained by adding the six subjects for St. George's Chapel to the nineteen paintings that he did paint for the Royal Chapel. He worked on the projects for the two chapels, situated within a few hundreds

Benjamin West and (?) Sir William Chambers, *Design for a Side Wall of the Royal Chapel, Windsor Castle*, c. 1780. Pen, wash, and watercolor, $11\frac{7}{16} \times 18\frac{3}{8}$ in. Yale Center for British Art, New Haven

yards of each other, at the same time for the same patron. Paintings of the *Last Supper* served or were intended to serve as the altarpieces of both (Nos. 344 and 346), and West did repeat three subjects from the St. George's Chapel windows in an expanded program for the Royal Chapel shown in diagrams made in 1801, but for the Royal Chapel none of the three proceeded beyond a title inserted into a space on a rough diagram. Otherwise his work for the two chapels did not overlap, and it is reasonably easy to disentangle the two projects where they are jumbled together in the accounts and the early lists of West's works.

The first scheme for the Royal Chapel is recorded in a group of drawings evidently made in collaboration with the architect Sir William Chambers, which must represent what the artist, architect, and patron devised when the program took shape in 1779 and 1780. These drawings demonstrate that West's paintings were originally expected to go into the existing Royal Chapel designed by Hugh May in the seventeenth century, where they would replace paintings by Antonio Verrio.[8] The main side wall, depicted in three drawings showing the same arrangement of paintings, would have consisted of five large paintings of New Testament subjects, with the largest, an *Ascension* (No. 380), at the center, flanked on the left and right by slightly smaller paintings of the *Baptism, Christ Healing the Sick, St. Peter's First Sermon*, and *Paul and Barnabas Rejecting the Jews* (Nos. 316, 334, 385, and 394) (ill. p. 577). Above the four subsidiary scenes were to be four smaller horizontal compositions of Old Testament subjects. The sizes of the pictures were determined by the architecture. The *Ascension* would have risen the full height of the wall to the cornice, and the New Testament paintings on either side would have been the same size as the window bays on the wall facing them. Two drawings show the opposite wall with Hugh May's five round-headed windows left intact, but, in one of the drawings for this wall (*below*), five scenes from the Book of Revelation of the same size and proportions as the four horizontal Old Testament scenes are situated in the spaces above the windows (these spaces are left empty in the other). A drawing showing a large vertical composition of *Moses Receiving the Laws* (see No. 258) above a smaller horizontal painting of the *Last Supper* (No. 344) represents the altar wall (*opposite*), and these two paintings combined with those shown

in the aforementioned drawings for the two side walls make a total of sixteen. There is no known drawing for the fourth wall of the chapel, but as much of this wall would have been taken up by an entrance door, by the royal pew, and possibly by an organ loft, it seems unlikely that any paintings were intended for it. A drawing of a ceiling showing a large oval composition of the *Last Judgment* and smaller paintings of the four Evangelists (*opposite*) may have been for the ceiling of the chapel, and, if so, it would bring the number of paintings to twenty-one, but West seems to have done nothing about turning the sketches shown in this drawing into paintings, and there is no documentation to confirm that this ceiling was certainly intended for the Royal Chapel. All these drawings show West's compositions set into a classicizing framework designed by Chambers, or under his supervision.

The first paintings West completed, *Christ Healing the Sick*, which he exhibited in 1781 (No. 334), and the *Ascension*, which he exhibited in 1782 (No. 380), conform to the program shown in the drawings. Some modifications in this original plan appeared in 1784, when he exhibited two paintings of *Isaiah* and *Jeremiah* (Nos. 283 and 286) intended to hang on either side of *Moses Receiving the Laws*, which in the drawing shown on p. 579 is situated between two empty niches. In 1784 he also exhibited three designs for pictures for the chapel, including one of *Moses Striking the Rock* (No. 256), which is not a subject shown in the drawings, but which, as a possible substitution for one of the planned Old Testament compositions, does not disrupt the overall scheme. Much more radical departures came in 1790 and 1792, when West painted and exhibited large vertical compositions of *Moses Showing the Brazen Serpent* (No. 266) and the "Triumph of Moses over Pharaoh" (No. 254), and in 1791, when he exhibited a pair of paintings of the *Expulsion of Adam and Eve from Paradise* and the *Deluge* (Nos. 232 and 234). Three of these subjects had not been included in the earlier drawings, and the fourth, the "Triumph of Moses over Pharaoh," which had been included as a smaller horizontal composition in the drawings, was now, along with the *Brazen Serpent*, carried out on a scale proposed earlier only for four New Testament subjects. These works and others that followed indicate a substantial reorganization and expansion of the original program, but there are no known drawings or documents which explain the change.

Benjamin West and (?) Sir William Chambers, *Design for a Side Wall of the Royal Chapel, Windsor Castle, c.* 1780. Pen, wash, and watercolor, 11½ × 18⅞ in. Royal Library, Windsor Castle

Benjamin West and (?) Sir William Chambers, *Design for the Altar Wall of the Royal Chapel, Windsor Castle,* c. 1780. Pen, wash, and watercolor, heightened with white, 11 × 9¾ in. Royal Library, Windsor Castle

In a list of works prepared in June 1797 and in an accompanying letter to George III West indicated that he then intended the completed series to consist of twenty-six paintings.[9] A set of schematic diagrams made in August 1801 shows a still further expanded scheme, with walls of fourteen Old Testament and fourteen New Testament scenes facing one another, and an end wall consisting of a large *Crucifixion* (see No. 356) and spaces for three smaller paintings below (ill. p. 580). These diagrams do accommodate the increased sizes of the Old Testament subjects exhibited by West in 1790, 1792, and following years, but whether they record what he had intended as early as 1790 is questionable. In 1796 James Wyatt succeeded Chambers as the architect at Windsor. In John Galt's account of the project, Chambers does not play a role, and Wyatt is described as the architect who, upon replacing Chambers, was ordered by George III to carry the plan into effect. According to Galt, the location was not to be the old Royal Chapel, but the former Horn Court.[10] After 1796 Wyatt did work extensively at Windsor, reconstructing the state apartments in a neo-Gothic style, and in 1805–6 he converted the Horn Court into a cloister.[11] By then, however, the idea of installing West's paintings anywhere in the castle had been discarded, while in 1801 Wyatt may have contemplated turning Horn Court into a chapel. One of West's diagrams of 1801 shows his compositions set in a framework of Gothic arches and may, therefore, record an attempt to adapt the paintings to Wyatt's activity. The increase of the planned number of works to thirty-five or thirty-six may have also been in response to the increased area of wall to be covered in the proposed conversion of Horn Court. Nevertheless, significant expansion of the original program commenced in 1790, well before Wyatt came on the scene.

In 1801 Wyatt was the King's emissary who told West to suspend work on the paintings for the chapel. West told Joseph Farington on 31 May 1804, that he feared he would never finish the undertaking, "which he considered to be owing to Wyatt who wd. not proceed with the alterations in the chapel."[12] Thus it would seem that the painter fell victim to the architect, and that the paintings which were initially conceived to fit into Chambers's plans for Windsor Castle were subsequently rejected because the latter's successor would not provide a place for them. There were certainly other reasons for the termination of the project as well: among them the King's dislike of at least some of West's subjects (see No. 403), and dissatisfaction with the seemingly endless amount of time that the project was entailing,[13] as well as factors not related directly to the chapel itself.[14] Nevertheless, if Wyatt was not the sole or even the main cause of West's loss of royal patronage, his star was in the ascendant while West's was in decline, and in 1805 he temporarily replaced West as President of the Royal Academy, in part because

the Academicians believed that he rather than West had the confidence of the King. On 30 August 1804, Farington recorded a rumor that the paintings were to be installed in the Great Room at Hampton Court, but on 1 December of the same year he reported that, except for the altarpiece (presumably the *Last Supper,* No. 344), they were not to be put up at all.[15] The paintings remained in West's studio and appeared in the posthumous exhibitions organized by his sons after his death. Until 1828 they were the property of the Crown, but in that year George IV gave all but one of them back to West's sons. George IV presented that one, the *Last Supper* (No. 344), to the recently founded National Gallery, and the other eighteen paintings were sold by West's sons in 1829. Horn Court underwent another transformation under George IV to become the site of the Waterloo Chamber, where Lawrence's portraits of the leaders of the alliance against Napoleon now hang, and the original seventeenth-century chapel became part of the adjacent St. George's Hall.

Galt states that at the commencement of the project George III instructed West to draw up a list of subjects. The King then submitted the list, "which he had formed with the Artist," to a committee of eminent prelates for their approval, which they unanimously gave.[16] In 1801 West wrote to George III that the subjects had "demanded the historian, the commentator, and the accomplished painter to bring them into view."[17] Among the clerics mentioned by Galt who approved

Benjamin West and (?) Sir William Chambers, (?) *Design for the Ceiling of the Royal Chapel, Windsor Castle,* c. 1780. Pen, wash, and watercolor, heightened with white, 20¾ × 13 in. Mr. and Mrs. Erving Wolf

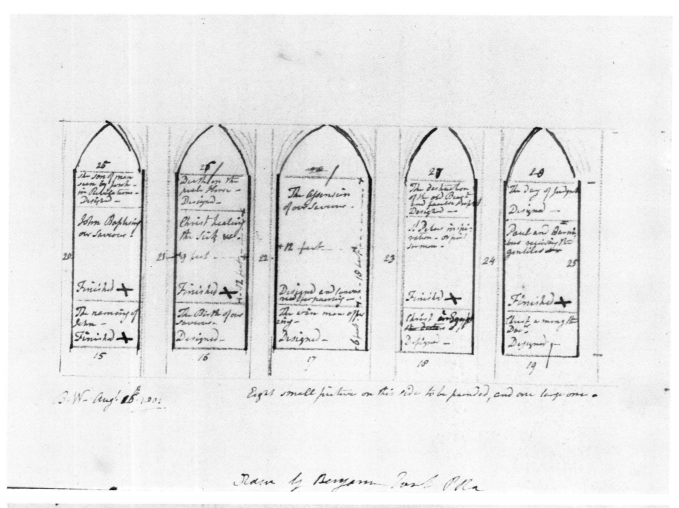

Diagram Showing an Arrangement of Pictures Intended for the Royal Chapel, Windsor Castle, 1801. Friends Historical Library, Swarthmore College, Swarthmore, Pennsylvania

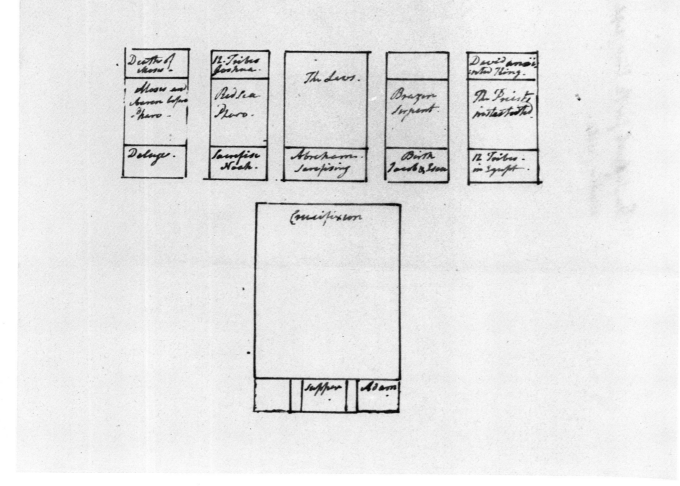

Two Diagrams Showing Arrangements of Pictures Intended for the Royal Chapel, Windsor Castle, c. 1801. Friends Historical Library, Swarthmore College, Swarthmore, Pennsylvania

the list of subjects the most prominent was Richard Hurd, Bishop of Lichfield and Coventry (and later of Worcester), Preceptor to the Prince of Wales and the Duke of York, and a favorite of the royal family. It seems likely that he played a role as historian and commentator in shaping the program, as well as in approving it.[18] West may also have been guided by the Reverend Anselm Bayly, Sub-Dean of the Chapel Royal.[19] The chief theological texts that West and his advisers probably drew upon were *The Divine Legation of Moses Demonstrated* by Hurd's patron, Bishop William Warburton, an all-encompassing treatise of which parts appeared in 1737 and 1741; and *Dissertations on the Prophecies, which have remarkably been fulfilled and at this time are fulfilling in the world*, commenced in 1754 by Bishop Thomas Newton, the erstwhile purchaser of West's paintings (see No. 675).[20] In differing ways all these men defended orthodox Anglican theology against the Deists, who accepted the existence of a God on the grounds of reason, but rejected traditional biblical testimony of a divinely revealed religion.

Writing to George III in September 1801, West called the subject of the series "the progress of Revealed Religion, from its commencement to its completion."[21] Galt termed Wyatt's proposed adaptation of Horn Court "the new chapel of Revealed Religion,"[22] and modern writers have followed Galt in applying the title to the chapel. In Royal Academy catalogues from 1781 to 1807 West described the paintings' destinations simply as "His Majesty's chapel in Windsor Castle." He prepared accounts of his work for George III in 1797 and in 1801, and in the former, as in the exhibition catalogues, the paintings were "for his Majesty's Chapel in Windsor Castle." In the latter they were for an "intended New Chapel in Windsor Castle,"[23] a slight change in wording, but one which is in accord with the suggestion made above that a plan to put the paintings in a new chapel in Horn Court rather than the existing chapel came about only after Wyatt replaced Chambers as the architect at Windsor.

In both the account drawn up in 1801 and the letter dated 26 September of the same year, West described the subjects as "from the Four Dispensations." In the account, as published by Galt, the Dispensations were "Antideluvian," "Patriarchal," "Mosaical," and "The Prophets." This seems to be an odd and unbalanced arrangement, since it lumps half the listed titles, including all the New Testament ones, under the heading of "The Prophets," and it may be due to an error in transcription either on West's part or on Galt's. Other lists of West's works, all published after 1801, provide different organizations of the Dispensations, either combining "Antideluvian" and "Patriarchal" or omitting "Antideluvian," and all of them omit "The Prophets" while adding "Gospel" and "Revelation" (or "Apocalyptic") Dispensations.[24] In the early drawings for the chapel made in conjunction with Chambers, the first subject in narrative sequence is *Moses and Aaron before Pharaoh*, and the three tiers of paintings on the two side walls represent three Dispensations: Mosaical, Gospel, and Revelation. The earliest evidence of a fourth Dispensation, Antideluvian or Patriarchal, came only in 1791 with West's exhibition of two subjects from Genesis at the Royal Academy (Nos. 232 and 234). The account of 1801 includes no subjects from Revelation, either painted or planned, and accordingly there is no Revelation Dispensation among its division of subjects. Nevertheless, subjects from Revelation do appear on the diagrams made in the same year and on all the later lists of chapel subjects; West exhibited sketches of a subject from Revelation in 1784 and 1796, identifying both as intended for the chapel (Nos. 402 and 403); and the one sketch for a chapel picture completed in 1804 (No. 410) was also of a subject from Revelation. The failure to list Revelation subjects in 1801 may have been partly due to the general confusion of Dispensations in that account, but it is also possible that West deliberately excluded this group of titles because of George III's hostility to "Bedlamite" scenes from the Revelation, which we know of from an entry in Farington's diary three years later.[25] In that case, the other oddities in the account of 1801 may have been a result of West's muddled attempt to compensate for or disguise his suppression of what had been an integral and substantial part of the program from the beginning.

COMPLETED PAINTINGS FOR THE CHAPEL

(numbers in parentheses following the titles refer to related sketches and replicas)

232 *The Expulsion of Adam and Eve from Paradise* (233)
234 *The Deluge* (235)
240 *Abraham and His Son Isaac Going to Sacrifice* (241)
245 *The Birth of Jacob and Esau* (246)
252 *Moses and Aaron before Pharaoh* (253)
254 *Pharaoh and his Host Lost in the Red Sea* (255)
258 *Moses Receiving the Laws* (259)
262 *Moses and Aaron Sacrificing* (263)
266 *Moses Showing the Brazen Serpent to the Israelites* (267)
283 *The Call of the Prophet Isaiah* (284, 285)
286 *The Call of the Prophet Jeremiah* (287)
294 *The Naming of John the Baptist* (295)
316 *The Baptism* (317)
334 *Christ Healing the Sick* (335)
344 *The Last Supper* (345)
380 *The Ascension* (381, 382, 383, 384)
385 *St. Peter's First Sermon* (386)
394 *Paul and Barnabas Rejecting the Jews and Receiving the Gentiles* (395, 396)

UNCOMPLETED PAINTING

236 *Noah Sacrificing*

SKETCHES CONNECTED TO THE PROJECT BY CONTEMPORARY DOCUMENTATION BUT NOT CARRIED OUT AS FULL-SCALE PAINTINGS FOR THE CHAPEL

256 *Moses Striking the Rock*
265 *The Death of Aaron*
269 *Moses Shown the Promised Land*
270 *Joshua Passing the River Jordan with the Ark of the Covenant*
402 *Death on the Pale Horse*
403 *Death on the Pale Horse*
410 *The Destruction of the Beast and False Prophet*

NOTES

For more extended discussions of this group of works, see Meyer 1975, Dillenberger 1977, and Pressly 1983.

1. Letter, dated London, 15 Oct. 1799, from Benjamin West to Daniel Daulby (private collection, partly quoted in Pressly 1983, p. 15).

2. Carey 1820, p. 696.

3. Galt 1820, pp. 193–94. The transcription is prefaced, "The following is the Substance of a Letter I had the honour of writing to His Majesty, when at Weymouth, by the conveyance of Mr. James Wyatt." In his accompanying text, Galt describes it as a copy of the rough draft.

4. Ibid., p. 198, and Farington 1978–, VI, p. 2166.

5. Galt 1820, p. 194.

6. Adams 1874, III, pp. 432–33.

7. Meyer 1975, pp. 264–65.

8. See H. M. Colvin, ed., *The History of the King's Works: Volume V: 1660–1782*, London, 1976, pp. 326–27; and Hope 1913, I, p. 350 and pl. XXXIX, and supplemental portfolio of plans, II (*First Floor Plan of the Upper Ward about 1790*). We are indebted to John Harris for pointing out that the schemes shown on pp. 577 and 578 were devised to fit into the seventeenth-century chapel. In addition to the drawings reproduced here, three further drawings for the two side walls are in the Royal Collection (reproduced in Meyer 1975, p. 250, figs. 1, 2, and 6). These drawings show variations in details, but repeat the overall arrangements of the walls.

9. A copy of the list is in the Historical Society of Pennsylvania, Philadelphia (see above, pp. 159–160). For the letter see A. Aspinall, ed., *The Later Correspondence of George III*, Cambridge, 1963, II, p. 593, no. 1575.

10. Galt 1820, pp. 53, 56.

11. Hope 1913, I, pp. 347–52, and Farington Diary, 2 Dec. 1806 (Farington 1978–, VIII, p. 2917).

12. Farington 1978–, VI, pp. 2336–37.

13. Farington Diary, 18 Nov. 1803 (ibid., VI, p. 2166).

14. See pp. 97–102.

15. Farington 1978–, VI, pp. 2399 and 2461.

16. Galt 1820, pp. 53–55.

17. Ibid., p. 194.

18. Meyer 1975, pp. 254–55. For Hurd, see also Millar 1969, I, p. 41, nos. 801 and 802, and Girouard 1981, pp. 21–22.

19. K. Porter Aichele, letter to the editor, *Art Bulletin*, LVIII, 1976, pp. 474–76.

20. Meyer 1975, pp. 253–55, and Dillenberger 1977, pp. 60–82.

21. Galt 1820, p. 194.

22. Ibid., p. 56.

23. Ibid., p. 209.

24. See Dillenberger 1977, p. 46. For explanation of the lists of West's works, see ibid., pp. 129–32, and above, pp. 159–162. We have noted in the entry for each relevant work (under LISTED) the Dispensation or Dispensations to which it is ascribed in the various lists.

25. Farington Diary, 1 Dec. 1804 (Farington 1978–, VI, p. 2461).

Appendix II

Transcription and translation of a note published in
Storia degli Stabilementi dell' europei in America

(Venice, 1763, I, pp. iii–viii) to accompany an engraving after West's *Savage Warrior Taking Leave of His Family* (No. 452)

La Tavola apposta per ornamento in faccia del Frontispizio è stata presa, e delineata da un Quadretto, il quale fu fatto, per dare all'Illustre Personaggio che lo bramò, un'idea degl'Indiani dell' America Settentrionale. Vedesene quì pertanto ritratta una Coppia di quelli vicino all'Provincia della Pensilvania, la di cui Capitale Filadelfia è la Patria dell'ingegnoso, ed eccellente Giovane che l'anno scorso in Livorno ne fu il Pittore. E siccome egli cercò di rappresentare ogni cosa nel vera carattere, volle poi anche, per darne ragione di ogni sua parte, accompagnare il Quadro con la seguente descrizione in iscritto; affinchè quello fosse meglio inteso, che il pennello in certi casi non puo esprimere pienamente, e che molto più poi rimaner pottrebbe da desiderarsi in una simplice stampa.

La figura principale adunque rappresenta un Guerriero Indiano, il quale uscito dalla propria capanna stà per andare ad unirsi a' compagni, e seco loro marciare ad una di quelle spedizioni militari, che dessi intraprendono per riportarne in trofeo schiavi li loro nimici, o le capigliaje che scorticano via dal cranio degli uccisi, o feriti. Egli è in equipaggio militare, con un pennacchio di piume, ornato di Guampom, cioè di pallotline, o chiocciole di varj colori infilzate, e questo attaccato ad un ciuffo di capelli, che sorgono nel vertice della testa, solo luogo su cui ve ne siano, per il costume che hanno di svellerli dalle radici in ogni altra parte. Del capo quel che nudo ne rimane è tinto di rosso, framischiato di striscie nere, come su la fronte apparisce. La faccia generalmente, e spesso ancora il petto sono lordati quasi nello stesso modo; ma ho stimato meglio di omettere questa circostanze, a fine di non sfigurar troppo le fattezze, lasciando però una de quelle striscie di color rosso sovra delle ciglia. Tutto quello che vi rimane di nudo conserva dunque il suo color naturale, il quale negl'Indiani vieppiù diventa bruno, per l'uso inveterato che ha ciascuno di loro di ungersi il corpo, fin dall'infanzia, col grasso di Orso. Quella cartilagine che separa le narici è forata, come vedesi, e da una parte all' altra penetrata da una spina d' Istrice, la quale ne diviene un ornamento costante. La strana apparenza poi delle orecchie, procede dal costume che regna fra di loro, di'inciderne intorno buona parte dell' orlo esterno, e lasciarlo così giù penzolone, ornandolo quache volta con del Guampom. Quel che a guisa di un ornamento al collo appeso ne cade su'l petto, è quel coltello, di cui essi si servono per levar crudelmente alli nemici la cotenna del capo, il capillizio, o vogliam dire la natural parrucca. Al di sotto, e da una parte, pende pur anche dal collo il cornetto, entro cui tengono la polvere d'archibugio, insieme con la saccoccia della munizione; e dall'altra parte a cintola sta l'accetta, che essi chiamano Tomahac. Lo schioppo lo portana in una mano, e questa è l'invariabile loro maniera, di giorno, e di notte, nè vanno mai senza di lui in qualunque luogo, tantocchè fin quando pigliano sonno vi si corcano sopra.

Il loro vestito è tutto di un panno ordinario, e la parte che pende giù è disposta in modo da poter tirarsela sopra il capo, e sopra le spalle, allorchè vogliono dormire, o pur quando il tempo è estremamente cattivo, sicchè, in una parola, serve a loro ancor di mantello. La parte di sotto si accomodata in modo che si adatti esattamente alle loro gambe, ed alle coscie, lungo le quali viene allacciata in guisa, che vi rimangono di quà e di là due ale, come vedesi, le quali servono a loro, passando a traverso delle macchie, a difenderli dalli rovi, e dalle spine. Le loro scarpe sono fatte ciascheduna di un solo pezzo di pelle concia di Cervo, adattate in modo che lasciano vedere la forme del piede, e vengono allacciate strette intorno alla nocca e collo del piede medesimo.

L'abito della Donna non si conforma con quello del Marito, che dalla ginocchia in giù; il di lei guarnello si allaccia su la carne, e la camiscia senza maniche vi pende su sciolta, come pur sciolto giù dalle spalle ne pende fino a'piedi il mantello. Il di lei monile, e li smanigli sono di Guampom, siccome lo sono li lavori intorno a quelli del marito. L'ornamento segnato intorno al di lei braccio sopra del gomito è una sottil piastra di argento, e per fine li capelli sono rilegati dietro con un nastro.

Il bambino che tiene alla mammella, sta legato su di una tavola, secondo il costume loro, così facendo co'loro figli fino al tempo che siano capaci di andar da se soli, nè ciò solamente con l'intenzione di formare le loro membra e tutto il corpo snello, ma per il comodo ancora di poter lasciarli presso del fuoco, senza aver da temere, che rotolando, vi abbiano da cader dentro.

Gl'Indiani non stanno tutti in Città, molte famiglie vivono solitariamente sparse quà e là ne' boschi, ove construendo le loro capanne, hanno sempre cura di situarle, come vedesi rappresentato nella stampa, vicino ad un ruscelletto di acqua, di cui essi rallentano il corso, e con de' sassi l'ingorgano per il comodo di lavarvi, e cose simili. La capanne e fatta di scorze d'alberi, sostenuta da dei rami, e piantano sempre vicino di essa delle cucuzze, le quali essi fanno in modo che vadano ad arrampicarvisi sopra, poichè fra gli altri use, il frutto serve loro per farne la tazza, e la mestola, che vedonsi disegnate vicino all'acqua.

Su l'ingresso della capanna sta un fanciulletto Indiano, il quale fa forza di trattenere il Cane, acciò no segua il suo Padrone, per dimostrare che l'Uomo va alla guerra, e non ad una partita di caccia; poichè in tal caso il fido Cane serebbeli compagno indivisibile.

E siccome è regola costante fra gl'Indiani, di non lasciar giammai la famigliuola, se nel campo della loro piccola messe il Mayz non sia talmente avanzato, che ne prometta un bastevole sostentamento, per fino al tempo del loro ritorno: così L'Uomo è rappresentato, come accennando la sua ricolta, e in atto quali che dicesse alle moglie, che siccome il Mayz è in fiore, egli con cuor più tranquillo la lascia, poichè ella può ingenarsi per sè, e per li figli, in fin ch'egli ritorni. Nè all'occasione di tali partenze fannosi più complimenti, o cerimonie di quello appunto che quì apparisce rappresentato; toltone che nelle Citta Indiane, in simiglianti congiunture, le donne si attruppano, ed escono fuori per un miglio in circa di strada, e vanno avanti degli uomini, cantando, e ballando; come appunto è accennato in questo Volume al Capitolo IV. delle Parte II. pagina 214.

La Posizione de'piedi della Donna è disegnata (potrebbe dirsi affettatamente) ma è stato fatto con l'intenzione di far vedere quanto notabilmente le Americane ne tengano rivolte le punte in dentro.

Nulla altro più rimane quì da far osservare, se non la pianta, la quale vedesi non lungi dal piede de Grano Mayz, la quale si è posta per rappresentarne una particolare all' America Settentrionale, la di cui radice è famosa tanto e mirabile per curare la morsicatura della Vipera codisona, la peripneumonia, ed altri mali, e che esser dovrebbe la

POLIGALA a foglie ovato-lanceolate, dritte, alterne, interissime; a gambo semplicissmo, il quale termina in un mazzetto di fiori ache' esso ritto. E così viene descritta dal Gronovio nella sua *Flora Virginica*.

History of the European Settlements in America

The picture facing the title page has been taken, and drawn from a small picture which was made in order to give the illustrious personage who wanted it, an idea of the Indians of North America. One sees portrayed here, therefore, a pair of them from near the Province of Pennsylvania, the capital of which, Philadelphia, is the birthplace of the talented and excellent young man who painted the picture last year in Livorno. And since he sought to represent everything in its true character, he wanted also, then, in order to explain every part of it, to accompany the picture with the following written description; so that which the brush in certain cases cannot express fully, and even more of which would be left to be desired in a simple print, would be better understood.

The principal figure represents an Indian warrior who is leaving his hut to go and join his companions, and march with them on one of those military expeditions which they undertake in order to bring back, as trophies, their enemies as slaves, or the scalps which are cut off the heads of the killed or wounded. He is in military garb, with a feather headdress, decorated with *wampum*, that is, with strings of beads or shells of various colors, and this is attached to a tuft of hair that rises above the head. That is the only place where there is any hair because of the custom they have of plucking it out everywhere else. That part of the head that remains bare is colored red intermingled with black stripes as seen on the forehead. The whole face, and often also the chest, are darkened in almost the same way. But I have considered it better to omit this circumstance so as not to disfigure the features overly, leaving, however, one of the red-colored stripes over the eyelashes. All that remains bare, therefore, keeps its natural color, which in Indians becomes much more brown from the way they have of constantly rubbing the body with bear grease. The cartilege which separates the nostrils is perforated, as you see, and from one part to the other, is penetrated by a porcupine quill which becomes a permanent ornament. The strange appearance of the ears arises from the custom that reigns among them of cutting around a good part of the outer edge and leaving it thus dangling down, sometimes decorating it with *wampum*. What seems to be an ornament hanging from the neck and falling on the chest is the knife which they use to cut the scalps—the hair, or we should say, the natural wig—cruelly off the enemy. Below and on one side, a horn, which they use to hold gunpowder, also hangs from the neck, together with an ammunition pouch. And on the other side, attached to a belt, is what they call a Tomahawk. The gun is carried in one hand; this is invariably their way, day and night, and they never go anywhere without it. Even when they go to sleep they lay down on top of it.

Their clothing is all of an ordinary cloth, and the part which hangs down is disposed in a way so that it can be pulled over the head and shoulders when they want to sleep; when the weather is bad it also serves them as a mantle. The part below is arranged to conform exactly to the legs and thighs along which it is tied so that it flaps this way and that like two wings, as you see, and serves them, passing through bushes, to protect against the brambles and thorns. Each of their shoes is made from a single piece of buckskin adapted in a way that allows the form of the foot to be seen, and each is tightly tied around the ankles.

The clothing of the woman does not conform with that of her husband; her cotton-and-flax gown is fastened to the body from the knees down, and her sleeveless blouse hangs loose in the same way as the mantle, which hangs down loosely from the shoulders to the feet. Her necklace and her bracelets are of *wampum* as is the decoration along her clothing and that of her husband as well. The ornament around her arm above the elbow is a thin band of silver, and finally, her hair is tied back with a fillet.

The child who holds her breast is tied on a board according to the custom which they maintain, until the time when the children can go about by themselves; it is not only for the purpose of making their limbs and body nimble, but for the convenience of being able to leave them near the fire without fearing that, rolling around, they will fall into the flames.

The Indians are not all in cities. Many families live in isolation, dispersed here and there in the woods where they build their huts, always taking care to situate them, as you can see represented in the print, near a little stream of water, the course of which they slow and block with stones to facilitate washing and similar things. The hut is made of bark supported by branches, and they always plant gourds near it, in such a way that they climb up, since, among other uses, the fruit serves them as cups and as ladles, which are seen indicated near the water.

In the entrance of the hut is a little Indian child who is straining to hold a dog so that it doesn't follow his master; this is to demonstrate that the man is going to war and not leaving for a hunt, since in that case the dog would be his inseparable companion.

And since it is a constant rule among the Indians never to leave their family if their little crop of maize in the field is not advanced enough to permit sufficient sustenance until the time of their return, the man is represented as if pointing to his crop. By that act he seems to say to his wife that since the maize is in flower he can leave her with a calmer heart, since she can provide for herself and the children until he returns. On the occasion of such partings they make more compliments and ceremonies than are represented here, leaving aside the fact that in Indian cities, in similar circumstances, the women throng together and go out of the city for about a mile, walking ahead of the men, singing and dancing, exactly as is indicated in this book in chapter IV of part II, p. 214.

The position of the woman's feet is designed (one could say feigned) with the intention of showing how noteworthy is the way the Americans turn the points of them inward.

Nothing more remains to be noted, except the plants which one sees not far from the maize, which have been added to represent a detail of North America and whose roots are famous as a cure for snakebite, pneumonia, and other ills, and which should be the POLIGALA with oval-lanceolate leaves, otherwise completely straight; a very simple stalk which terminates in a little bunch of flowers, which is also straight. And thus is it described by Gronovio in his *Flora Virginica*.

Translated by Lewis Andrews

Abbreviations

AAFA American Academy of Fine Arts, New York

BI British Institution, London

PAFA Pennsylvania Academy of the Fine Arts, Philadelphia

SA Society of Artists, London

SBA Society of British Artists, London

RA Royal Academy of Arts, London

125 Pall Mall The premises in Pall Mall (previously occupied by the Royal Academy) utilized by West for the private exhibitions of *Christ Rejected* (No. 353), *Death on the Pale Horse* (No. 401), and additional works.

West's Gallery West's home and studio at 14 Newman Street, converted by his sons after his death into a gallery for the display of his works.

Boston 1976 *John Singleton Copley 1738–1815, Gilbert Stuart 1755–1828, Benjamin West 1738–1820 in America and England*, Museum of Fine Arts, Boston, 1976.

Philadelphia 1976 *Symbols of Peace: William Penn's Treaty with the Indians*, Pennsylvania Academy of the Fine Arts, Philadelphia, 1976 (essays by Charles Coleman Sellers and Anthony N. B. Garvan).

Liverpool 1976 *American Artists in Europe 1800–1900*, Walker Art Gallery, Liverpool, 1976–77 (catalogue by Edward Morris).

Washington and Philadelphia 1980 *Benjamin West and His American Students*, National Portrait Gallery, Washington, 1980–81, and Pennsylvania Academy of the Fine Arts, Philadelphia, 1981 (catalogue by Dorinda Evans; see Evans 1980 under LITERATURE).

New Haven 1983 *Benjamin West's Portrait of John Eardley-Wilmot*, Yale Center for British Art, New Haven, 1983 (catalogue by Linda Landis).

San Antonio 1983 *Revealed Religion: Benjamin West's Commissions for Windsor Castle and Fonthill Abbey*, San Antonio Museum of Art, 1983 (catalogue by Nancy L. Pressly; see Pressly 1983 under LITERATURE).

Manchester 1857 *Art Treasures of the United Kingdom*, Manchester, 1857.

London 1868 *National Portrait Exhibition*, South Kensington Museum, London, 1868.

Philadelphia 1921 *Benjamin West Memorial Exhibition*, Art Alliance, Philadelphia, 1921–22.

Brooklyn 1922 *Exhibition of Paintings and Drawings by Benjamin West and of Engravings Representing His Work*, Brooklyn Museum, 1922.

Philadelphia 1936 *Benjamin West and Other Early American Painters*, McClees Galleries, Philadelphia, 1936.

Philadelphia 1938 *Benjamin West: 1738–1820*, Pennsylvania Museum of Art, Philadelphia, 1938 (catalogue by Henri Marceau; essay by Fiske Kimball).

Amherst 1950 *Benjamin West: His Times and His Influence*, Mead Art Building, Amherst College, Amherst, Mass., 1950.

Allentown 1962 *The World of Benjamin West*, Allentown Art Museum, Allentown, Pa., 1962 (catalogue by Richard Hirsch).

New York 1962 *Benjamin West*, Graham Gallery, New York, 1962 (essay by Helmut von Erffa).

London 1963 *Treasures of the Royal Academy*, Royal Academy of Arts, London, 1963.

Bregenz 1968 *Angelika Kauffmann und ihre Zeitgenossen*, Vorarlberger Landesmuseum, Bregenz, 1968, and Osterreichisches Museum für Angewandte Kunst, Vienna, 1968–69.

New York 1968 *A Benjamin West Portfolio: Drawings and Sketches*, Bernard Black Gallery, New York, 1968 (essay by E. Maurice Bloch).

New York 1975 *Drawings by Benjamin West and His Son Raphael Lamar West*, Pierpont Morgan Library; New York 1975 (catalogue by Ruth S. Kraemer; see Kraemer 1975 under LITERATURE).

PC "A Correct Catalogue of the Works of Mr. West," *Public Characters of 1805*, London, 1805 (in fact, published in 1804), pp. 559–69.

UM "A Correct List of the Works of Mr. West," *Universal Magazine*, III, 1805, pp. 527–32.

AA "An Account, delivered at the Desire of the Council of the Royal Academy, of the Great Historical Works painted for His Majesty by Benjamin West, Esq. President." *Academic Annals, published by Authority of the Royal Academy of Arts, 1804–5. Collected and Arranged by Prince Hoare, Secretary for Foreign Correspondence to the Royal Academy*, London, 1805, pp. 63–69.

Barlow Note 45 to *The Columbiad. A Poem*, by Joel Barlow, Philadelphia, 1807, pp. 430–36 (on p. 431 Barlow states that the list was given him by West in 1802).

BA "A Correct Catalogue of the Works of Benjamin West, Esq.," *La Belle Assemblée or Bell's Court and Fashionable Magazine*, IV, 1808, Supplement, pp. 13–20.

Galt "A Catalogue of the Works of Mr. West," in *The Life, Studies, and Works of Benjamin West, Esq., President of the Royal Academy of London*, by John Galt, London, 1820, Appendix II, pp. 216–34.

Dillenberger "Published Lists of West's Paintings" and "Checklist of Known Religious Works by West," in *Benjamin West: The Context of His Life's Work*, by John Dillenberger, San Antonio, 1977, Appendices I and V, pp. 129–90 and 210–15. (Dillenberger's Appendix I is a concordance of all the earlier lists cited above except that in the *Universal Magazine*, plus West's account of 1801 of his works for George III [which is cited in the PROVENANCES in this catalogue]. It is prefaced by a brief discussion of the publications in which they appeared.)

LITERATURE

Abrams 1982 Ann Uhry Abrams, "Benjamin West's Documentation of Colonial History: *William Penn's Treaty with the Indians*," *Art Bulletin*, LXIV, 1982, pp. 59–75.

Adams 1874 Charles Francis Adams, ed., *Memoirs of John Quincy Adams, Comprising Portions of His Diary from 1795 to 1848*, 12 vols., Philadelphia, 1874–77.

Alberts 1978 Robert C. Alberts, *Benjamin West: A Biography*, Boston, 1978.

Alexander 1957 Boyd Alexander, trans. and ed., *Life at Fonthill 1807–1822: with Interludes in Paris and London: from the Correspondence of William Beckford*, London, 1957.

Angelo 1830 Henry Angelo, *Reminiscences of Henry Angelo, with memoirs of his late father and friends, etc.*, 2 vols., London, 1828, 1830.

Annual Register 1820 "Memoir of Benjamin West, Esq. President of the Royal Academy," *The Annual Register: or A View of the History, Politics, and Literature of the Year 1820*, Part II, pp. 1163–74.

Barlow 1807 See under *LISTS*.

Boase 1963 T. S. R. Boase, "Macklin and Bowyer," *Journal of the Warburg and Courtauld Institutes*, XXVI, 1963, pp. 148–77.

Boston 1969 *American Paintings in the Museum of Fine Arts, Boston*, Boston, 1969.

Brayley and Britton 1801 Edward Wedlake Brayley and John Britton, *The Beauties of England and Wales: or Original Delineations, Topographical, Historical and Descriptive of Each County*, vol. I, London, 1801.

Brinton 1936 Christian Brinton et al., *Yesterday in Chester County Art*, West Chester, Pennsylvania, 1936 (Chester County Art Association and the School Board of West Chester).

Brinton 1941 Ellen Starr Brinton, "Benjamin West's Painting of Penn's Treaty with the Indians," *Bulletin of Friends' Historical Association*, XXX, no. 2, Autumn 1941, pp. 99–189.

Brooks 1925 Alfred Mansfield Brooks, "Drawings by Benjamin West," *Art Bulletin*, VIII, 1925, pp. 25–32.

Buckler 1826 J. Buckler & J. C. Buckler, *Views of Eaton Hall in Cheshire, The Seat of the Right Honourable Earl Grosvenor*, London, 1826.

Burke 1976 Joseph Burke, *English Art 1714–1800*, Oxford, 1976.

Carey 1817 William Carey, *Critical Description and Analytical Review of "Death on the Pale Horse" Painted by Benjamin West, P.R.A.: With Desultory References to the Works of Some Ancient Masters, and Living British Artists. Respectfully Addressed to the Most Noble the Marquis of Stafford*, London, 1817 (reprinted Philadelphia 1836).

Carey 1820 William Carey, "Memoirs of Benjamin West, Esq. Late President of the Royal Academy of Painting, Sculpture, and Architecture, in London," *New Monthly Magazine*, XIII, 1820, pp. 513–20, 688–97.

Collins Baker 1920 C. H. Collins Baker, *Catalogue of the Petworth Collection of Pictures in the Possession of Lord Leconfield*, London, 1920.

Comstock 1932 Helen Comstock, "American Art Notes: Benjamin West's Portraits of the Hay-Drummond Family," *Connoisseur*, XC, 1932, p. 351.

Constable 1962–68 R. B. Beckett, ed., *John Constable's Correspondence*, 6 vols., London and Ipswich, 1962–68.

Copley–Pelham 1914 *Letters and Papers of John Singleton Copley and Henry Pelham 1739–1776, Massachusetts Historical Society: Collections*, vol. 71, 1914.

Courtauld Cuttings *Courtauld Clippings File: Newspaper Cuttings, Fine Arts*, Courtauld Institute Library, London.

Croft-Murray 1970 Edward Croft-Murray, *Decorative Painting in England 1537–1837: Volume Two: The Eighteenth and Nineteenth Centuries*, Feltham, Middlesex, 1970.

Cummings 1968 Frederick Cummings, entries in *Romantic Art in Britain: Paintings and Drawings 1760–1860*, Detroit Institute of Art and Philadelphia Museum of Art, 1968, pp. 97–104.

Cunningham 1956 Charles Cunningham, "*Benjamin West's Picture Gallery* by John Pasmore," *Wadsworth Atheneum Bulletin*, 2nd series, 64, April 1956, p. 1 (reprinted in *Art Quarterly*, XIX, 1956, pp. 210–11).

Curwen 1842 *Journal and Letters of the Late Samuel Curwen . . . An American Refugee in England from 1775 to 1784*, New York and Boston, 1842.

Cust 1910 Lionel Cust, *Eton College Portraits*, London, 1910.

Dafforne 1863 James Dafforne, "British Artists: Their Style and Character: no. LXVII—Benjamin West, P.R.A.," *Art Journal*, 1863, pp. 218–20.

Devanter 1973 Ann C. Van Devanter, "Benjamin West and His Self-Portraits," *Antiques*, CIII, 1973, pp. 764–73.

Dickason 1970 David H. Dickason, "Benjamin West on William Williams: A Previously Unpublished Letter," *Winterthur Portfolio*, VI, 1970, pp. 127–33.

Dillenberger 1977 John Dillenberger, *Benjamin West: The Context of His Life's Work, with Particular Attention to Paintings with Religious Subject Matter, Including a correlated version of early nineteenth-century lists of West's paintings, exhibitions, and sales records of his works, and also a current checklist of his major religious works*, San Antonio, 1977.

Duleep Singh 1927 Prince Frederick Duleep Singh, *Portraits in Norfolk Houses*, 2 vols., Norwich, 1927.

Dunlap Diary William Dunlap, Diary kept intermittently from 1786 to 1834. Extant volumes are in the Yale University Library, New Haven, and the New-York Historical Society, New York; see Dunlap 1930.

Dunlap 1834 William Dunlap, *History of the Rise and Progress of the Arts of Design in the United States*, 2 vols., New York, 1834.

Dunlap 1918 William Dunlap, *A History of the Rise and Progress of the Arts of Design in the United States*, new edition, Frank W. Bayley and Charles E. Goodspeed, eds., 3 vols., Boston, 1918.

Dunlap 1930 William Dunlap, *Diary of William Dunlap (1766–1839)*, Dorothy C. Barck, ed., 3 vols., New York, 1930.

Edwards 1808 Edward Edwards, *Anecdotes of Painters who have resided or been born in England*, London, 1808.

Ehrich 1918 Ehrich Galleries, *One Hundred Early American Paintings*, New York, 1918.

Evans 1959 Grose Evans, *Benjamin West and the Taste of His Times*, Carbondale, Illinois, 1959.

Evans 1980 Dorinda Evans, *Benjamin West and His American Students*, Washington, 1980 (exhibition catalogue; see Washington and Philadelphia 1980).

Evans 1982 Dorinda Evans, *Mather Brown: Early American Artist in England*, Middletown, Conn., 1982.

Farington Diary Joseph Farington, Diary kept from 13 July 1793 to 30 December 1821. The original manuscript diary is in the Royal Library, Windsor Castle; a typed transcription is in the Department of Prints and Drawings, British Museum; see Farington 1978—.

Farington 1978— Joseph Farington, *The Diary of Joseph Farington*, vols. I–VI, Kenneth Garlick and Angus Macintyre, eds.; vols. VII–XVI, Kathryn Cave, ed., 16 vols., New Haven and London, 1978—.

Flexner 1939 James Thomas Flexner, *America's Old Masters: First Artists of the New World*, New York, 1939 (Viking Press), Chap. I, "'The American Raphael': Benjamin West," pp. 19–97. Paperback edition, New York 1967, with revisions, additional illustrations, and the article on "West's American Neo-Classicism" (Flexner 1952) reprinted as an appendix, pp. 315–40.

Flexner 1952 James Thomas Flexner, "Benjamin West's American Neo-Classicism," *New-York Historical Society Quarterly*, XXXVI, 1952, pp. 5–33.

Forster-Hahn 1967 Franziska Forster-Hahn, "The Source of True Taste: Benjamin West's Instructions to a Young Painter for His Studies in Italy," *Journal of the Warburg and Courtauld Institutes*, XXX, 1967, pp. 367–82.

Galt 1816 John Galt, *The Life and Studies of Benjamin West, Esq., President of the Royal Academy of London, Prior to his Arrival in England: Compiled from Materials Furnished by Himself*, London, 1816.

Galt 1820 John Galt, *The Life and Works of Benjamin West, Esq., President of the Royal Academy of London, Subsequent to his Arrival in this Country: Composed from Materials Furnished by Himself . . . Part II*, London, 1820.

Gardner 1966 Albert Ten Eyck Gardner, "West's Legacy," *Metropolitan Museum of Art Bulletin*, XXIV, 1966, pp. 225–36.

Gardner and Feld 1965 Albert Ten Eyck Gardner and Stuart P. Feld, *American Paintings: A Catalogue of the Collection of the Metropolitan Museum of Art: 1 Painters born by 1815*, New York, 1965.

Gatty 1938–39 Hugh Gatty, "Notes by Horace Walpole, Fourth Earl of Orford, on the Exhibitions of the Society of Artists & The Free Society of Artists, 1760–1791," *Walpole Society*, XXVII, 1938–39, pp. 57–88.

Gerdts 1974 William H. Gerdts, *The Great American Nude: A History in Art*, New York and Washington, 1974.

Girouard 1981 Mark Girouard, *The Return to Camelot: Chivalry and the English Gentleman*, New Haven and London, 1981.

Goodison 1977 J. W. Goodison, *Fitzwilliam Museum, Cambridge: Catalogue of Paintings III: British School*, Cambridge (England), 1977.

Grant 1958   Colonel Maurice Harold Grant, *A Chronological History of the Old English Landscape Painters*, new edition, 8 vols., Leigh-on-Sea, 1957–61 (West is in vol. III, 1958, pp. 220–22).

Graves 1906   Algernon Graves, *The Royal Academy of Arts: A Complete Dictionary of Contributors and their work from its foundation in 1769 to 1904*, 8 vols., London, 1905–6 (The entries for West are in vol. VIII, 1906, pp. 212–21).

Graves 1907   Algernon Graves, *The Society of Artists of Great Britain (1760–91); The Free Society of Artists (1761–1783)*, London, 1907.

Hall 1962   Douglas Hall, "The Tabley House Papers," *Walpole Society*, XXXVIII, 1962, pp. 59–122.

Hamilton 1831   G. Hamilton, *The English School: A Series of the Most Approved Productions in Painting and Sculpture, Executed by British Artists from the Days of Hogarth to the Present Time; Selected, Arranged and Accompanied with Descriptive and Explanatory Notices*, 4 vols., London and Paris, 1831–32.

Hamilton-Phillips 1981   Martha Hamilton-Phillips, "Benjamin West and William Beckford: Some Projects for Fonthill," *Metropolitan Museum Journal*, XV, 1981, pp. 157–74.

Hart 1908   Charles Henry Hart, "Benjamin West's Family. The American President of the Royal Academy of Arts Not a Quaker," *Pennsylvania Magazine of History and Biography*, XXXII, 1908, pp. 1–33.

Haskell and Penny 1981   Francis Haskell and Nicholas Penny, *Taste and the Antique: The Lure of Classical Sculpture 1500–1900*, New Haven and London, 1981.

Haydon 1960–63   Willard Bissell Pope, ed., *The Diary of Benjamin Robert Haydon*, 5 vols., Cambridge, Mass., 1960–63.

Hazlitt 1930–34   William Hazlitt, *Complete Works*, P. P. Howe, ed., after the edition of A. K. Waller and Arnold Glover, 21 vols., London and Toronto, 1930–34.

Henderson 1911   Helen W. Henderson, *The Pennsylvania Academy of the Fine Arts and Other Collections of Philadelphia*, Boston, 1911.

Hill 1965   Draper Hill, *Mr. Gillray The Caricaturist*, London, 1965.

Hope 1913   W. H. St. John Hope, *Windsor Castle: an Architectural History*, 2 vols., London, 1913.

Irwin 1966   David Irwin, *English Neoclassical Art*, London, 1966.

Jaffe 1975   Irma B. Jaffe, *John Trumbull: Patriot-Artist of the American Revolution*, Boston, 1975.

Jones 1963   Bob Jones, Jr., *"Revealed Religion"; A Series of Paintings by Benjamin West in the War Memorial Chapel*, Bob Jones University, Greenville, South Carolina, 1963.

Jones 1968   Beneth A. Jones, *Bob Jones University: Supplement to the Catalogue of the Art Collection: Paintings Acquired 1963–1968*, Greenville, South Carolina, 1968.

Kenin 1979   Richard Kenin, *Return to Albion: Americans in England 1760–1940* (National Portrait Gallery, Smithsonian Institution), New York, 1979.

Kerslake 1959   John Kerslake, "The Likeness of Wolfe," in *Wolfe: Portraiture & Genealogy*, Quebec House, Permanent Advisory Committee [Westerham], 1959, pp. 17–44.

Kerslake 1977   John Kerslake, *National Portrait Gallery: Georgian Portraits*, 2 vols., London, 1977.

Keyes 1973   Donald D. Keyes, "Benjamin West's Death on the Pale Horse: A Tradition's End," *Ohio State University College of the Arts: The Arts*, VII, Sept. 1973, pp. 3–6.

Kimball 1932   Fiske Kimball, "Benjamin West au Salon de 1802: La Mort sur le Cheval Pâle," *Gazette des Beaux-Arts*, VII, 1932, pp. 403–10 (expanded version of "Death on the Pale Horse," *Pennsylvania Museum Bulletin*, XXVI, no. 138, Jan. 1931, pp. 17–21).

Kraemer 1975   Ruth S. Kraemer, *Drawings by Benjamin West and His Son Raphael Lamar West*, New York, 1975 (exhibition catalogue; see New York 1975).

Landis 1925   The Hon. Charles I. Landis, "Benjamin West and His Visit to Lancaster," *Papers Read Before the Lancaster Historical Society*, XXIX, 1925, pp. 57–62.

Landis 1926   The Hon. Charles I. Landis, "Benjamin West and the Royal Academy," *Pennsylvania Magazine of History and Biography*, L, 1926, pp. 134–48, 241–53.

Lansdown 1893   Charlotte Lansdown, ed., *Recollections of the Late William Beckford, of Fonthill, Wilts. and Lansdown, Bath*, privately printed, 1893.

Lees-Milne 1976   James Lees-Milne, *William Beckford*, Tisbury, Wilts., 1976.

Lehigh 1960   "Allen Family Portraits in a Descendant's Home," *Proceedings of the Lehigh County Historical Society*, XXIII, 1960, pp. 9–31.

Leslie 1860   Charles Robert Leslie, *Autobiographical Recollections*, ed. by Tom Taylor, 2 vols., London, 1860.

Locquin 1912   Jean Locquin, *La Peinture d'histoire en France de 1747 à 1785*, Paris, 1912.

Locquin 1922   Jean Locquin, "Le Retour à l'antique dans l'école anglaise et dans l'école française avant David," *La Renaissance de l'Art Français et des Industries de Luxe*, V, 1922, pp. 473–81 (reprint, with illustrations added, of "Le Part de l'influence anglaise dans l'orientation néo-classique de la peinture française entre 1750 et 1780," *Actes du Congrès d'histoire de l'art*, 1921, II, pp. 391–99, Paris, 1924).

Marks 1965   Arthur S. Marks, "The Impact of Admiral Horatio Nelson's Death on English Art, 1805–1825," unpublished master's thesis, Columbia University, 1965.

Marks 1974   Arthur S. Marks, "Benjamin West and the American Revolution," *American Art Journal*, VI, 1974, pp. 15–35.

Mason 1879   George C. Mason, *The Life and Works of Gilbert Stuart*, New York, 1879 (reprint, New York, 1972).

Meyer 1975   Jerry D. Meyer, "Benjamin West's Chapel of Revealed Religion: A Study in Eighteenth-Century Protestant Religious Art," *Art Bulletin*, LVII, 1975, pp. 247–65.

Meyer 1979   Jerry D. Meyer, "Benjamin West's Window Designs for St. George's Chapel, Windsor," *American Art Journal*, XI, 1979, pp. 53–65.

Millar 1969   Oliver Millar, *The Later Georgian Pictures in the Collection of Her Majesty the Queen*, 2 vols., London, 1969.

Mitchell 1944   Charles Mitchell, "Benjamin West's *Death of General Wolfe* and the Popular History Piece," *Journal of the Warburg and Courtauld Institutes*, VII, 1944, pp. 20–33.

Mitchell 1967   Charles Mitchell, "Benjamin West's *Death of Nelson*," in *Essays in the History of Art Presented to Rudolf Wittkower*, London, 1967, pp. 265–73.

Montagna 1981   Dennis Montagna, "Benjamin West's *The Death of Wolfe*: A Nationalist Narrative," *American Art Journal*, XIII, 1981, pp. 72–88.

Morgan and Toole 1950   Charles H. Morgan and Margaret C. Toole, "Benjamin West: His Times and His Influence," *Art in America*, XXXVIII, 1950, pp. 205–78.

Morris 1889   Rupert H. Morris, *Guide to Eaton Hall*, Manchester, (?) 1889.

Morton and Woodbury 1895   Thomas G. Morton and Frank Woodbury, *The History of the Pennsylvania Hospital 1751–1895*, Philadelphia, 1895.

Moses 1811   Henry Moses, *The Gallery of Pictures Painted by Benjamin West Esqr., historical painter to His Majesty & President of the Royal Academy engraved in outline by Henry Moses*, London, 1811. There were at least two later editions of this work which contain additional illustrations. Internal evidence establishes that one of them appeared after 1817 and another after West's death in 1820.

Mount 1964   Charles Merrill Mount, *Gilbert Stuart: A Biography*, New York, 1964.

Neumeyer 1938   Alfred Neumeyer, "The Early Historical Paintings of Benjamin West," *Burlington Magazine*, LXXIII, 1938, pp. 162–65.

Oppé 1950   A. P. Oppé, *English Drawings: Stuart and Georgian Periods: In the Collection of His Majesty the King at Windsor Castle*, London, 1950.

Papendiek 1887   [Charlotte Louise Henrietta Papendiek], *Court and Private Life in the Time of Queen Charlotte: Being the Journals of Mrs. Papendiek, Assistant Keeper of the Wardrobe and Reader to Her Majesty. Edited by Her Grand-daughter, Mrs. Vernon Delver Broughton*, London, 1887.

Passavant 1836   M. [John David] Passavant, *Tour of a German Artist in England, with notices of private galleries, and remarks on the State of Art*, 2 vols., London, 1836 (originally published in German in 1833) (reprinted, Wakefield, 1978).

Pressly 1981   William L. Pressly, *The Life and Art of James Barry*, New Haven and London, 1981.

Pressly 1983   Nancy L. Pressly, *Revealed Religion: Benjamin West's Commissions for Windsor Castle and Fonthill Abbey*, San Antonio 1983 (exhibition catalogue: *see* San Antonio 1983).

Prown 1966   Jules David Prown, *John Singleton Copley*, 2 vols., Cambridge, Mass., 1966.

Public Characters 1805   "Benjamin West, Esq., President of the Royal Academy, etc.," *Public Characters of 1805*, London, 1805 (date on title page, but in fact published in 1804), pp. 523–69.

Pyne 1819   W. H. Pyne, *The History of the Royal Residences*, 3 vols., 1819.

Redford 1888   George Redford, *Art Sales: A History of Sales of Pictures and other Works of Art . . .*, 2 vols., London, 1888.

Richardson 1978   E. P. Richardson, "West's Voyage to Italy, 1760, and William Allen," *Pennsylvania Magazine of History and Biography*, CII, 1978, pp. 3–26.

Rogers 1966   Millard F. Rogers, Jr., "Benjamin West and the Caliph: two paintings for Fonthill Abbey," *Apollo*, LXXXIII, 1966, pp. 420–25.

Rosenblum 1960   Robert Rosenblum, review of Grose Evans, *Benjamin West and the Taste of His Times*, *Art Bulletin*, XLII, 1960, pp. 76–79.

Rosenblum 1967   Robert Rosenblum, *Transformations in Late Eighteenth-Century Art*, Princeton, 1967.

Rothenberg 1967   Jacob Rothenberg, *"Descensus ad Terram": The Acquisition and Reception of the Elgin Marbles*, doctoral dissertation, Columbia University, 1967 (Garland Press, New York and London, 1977).

Rutledge 1955   Anna Wells Rutledge, *Cumulative Record of Exhibition Catalogues: The Pennsylvania Academy of the Fine Arts 1807–1870*, Philadelphia, 1955 (*Memoirs of the American Philosophical Society*, vol. 38).

Rutter 1823   John Rutter, *An Illustrated History and Description of Fonthill Abbey*, London, 1823.

Sartain 1899   John Sartain, *The Reminiscences of a Very Old Man 1808–1897*, New York, 1899.

Sawitzky 1938   William Sawitzky, "The American Work of Benjamin West," *Pennsylvania Magazine of History and Biography*, LXII, 1938, pp. 433–62.

Sawitzky 1942   William Sawitzky, *Catalogue Descriptive and Critical of the Paintings and Miniatures in the Historical Society of Pennsylvania*, Philadelphia, 1942 (see also Wainwright, 1974).

Sellers 1939   Charles Coleman Sellers, *The Artist of the Revolution: The Early Life of Charles Willson Peale*, Hebron, Conn., 1939.

Sellers 1962   Charles Coleman Sellers, *Benjamin Franklin in Portraiture*, New Haven and London, 1962.

Shoemaker 1787   Samuel Shoemaker, "A Pennsylvania Loyalist's Interviews with George III," *Pennsylvania Magazine of History and Biography*, II, 1878, pp. 35–39.

Stacey 1966   Colonel C. P. Stacey, "Benjamin West and 'The Death of Wolfe,'" *National Gallery of Canada Bulletin*, VII, 1966, pp. 1–5.

Staley 1980   Allen Staley, "West's *Death on the Pale Horse*," *Bulletin of the Detroit Institute of Arts*, LVIII, 1980, pp. 137–49.

Storer 1812   James Storer, *A Description of Fonthill Abbey, Wiltshire*, London, 1812.

Strong 1978   Roy Strong, *Recreating the Past: British History and the Victorian Painter*, New York, 1978 (published in England as *"And When Did You Last See Your Father?" The Victorian Painter and British History*).

Tinkcom 1951   Harry M. Tinkcom, "Sir Augustus in Pennsylvania: The Travels and Observations of Sir Augustus J. Foster in Early Nineteenth-Century Pennsylvania," *Pennsylvania Magazine of History and Biography*, LXXV, 1951, pp. 369–99.

Trumbull 1953   John Trumbull, *The Autobiography of Colonel John Trumbull: Patriot-Artist, 1756–1843*, Theodore Sizer, ed., New Haven, 1953.

Tuckerman 1867   Henry T. Tuckerman, *Book of the Artists. American Artist Life, comprising biographical & critical sketches of American Artists: preceded by an Historical Account of the Rise & Progress of Art in America*, New York and London, 1867.

V and A Cuttings   *Press Cuttings from English Newspapers on Matters of Artistic Interest 1686–1835*, 3 vols., Victoria and Albert Museum Library, London.

von Erffa 1952   Helmut von Erffa, "West's 'The Washing of Sheep': Genre or Poetic Portrait? Some Lost and Some Doubtful Subjects from Thomson's 'Seasons,'" *Art Quarterly*, XV, 1952, pp. 160–65.

von Erffa 1956   Helmut von Erffa, "An Oil Sketch by Benjamin West," *Register of the Museum of Art of the University of Kansas*, VII, 1956, pp. 1–8.

von Erffa 1962   Helmut von Erffa, "Benjamin West Reinterpreted," *Antiques*, LXXXI, 1962, pp. 630–33.

von Erffa 1969   Helmut von Erffa, "Benjamin West at the Height of his Career," *American Art Journal*, I, 1969, pp. 19–33.

von Erffa 1973   Helmut von Erffa, "Benjamin West: The Early Years in London," *American Art Journal*, V, 1973, pp. 4–14.

Waagen 1854   Gustav Friedrich Waagen, *Treasures of Art in Geat Britain: being an Account of the chief collections of paintings, drawings, sculptures, illuminated MSS. &c. &c.*, 3 vols., London, 1854, and supplemental volume, London, 1857.

Wainwright 1974   Nicholas B. Wainwright, *Paintings and Miniatures at the Historical Society of Pennsylvania*, Philadelphia, 1974 (revised edition of Sawitzky 1942).

Wainwright 1978   Nicholas B. Wainwright, "Conversations with Benjamin West," *Pennsylvania Magazine of History and Biography*, CII, 1978, pp. 109–14.

Walker 1897   Lewis Burd Walker, ed., *The Burd Papers: Extracts from Chief Justice William Allen's Letter Book*, privately printed, 1897.

Waterhouse 1953   Ellis Waterhouse, *Painting in Britain 1530 to 1790*, London, 1953.

Webster 1930   J. Clarence Webster, *Wolfe and the Artists: A Study of His Portraiture*, Toronto, 1930.

Whitley 1928a   William T. Whitley, *Artists and their Friends in England, 1700–1799*, 2 vols., London, 1928.

Whitley 1928b   William T. Whitley, *Art in England, 1800–1820*, New York, 1928.

Wind 1938   Edgar Wind, "The Revolution of History Painting," *Journal of the Warburg and Courtauld Institutes*, II, 1938–39, pp. 116–27.

Wind 1947   Edgar Wind, "Penny, West & the Death of Wolfe," *Journal of the Warburg and Courtauld Institutes*, X, 1947, pp. 159–62.

Windsor Guide 1792   *The Windsor Guide; Containing a Description of the Town and Castle; the Present State of the Paintings and Curiosities in the Royal Apartments; an Account of the Monuments, Painted Windows, &c. in St. George's chapel . . .*, Windsor, 1792. We have also made reference to later editions containing additional information about works executed after 1792.

Wynne 1982   Michael Wynne, "Irish Stained and Painted Glass in the Eighteenth Century," in Peter Moore, ed., *Crown in Glory: A Celebration of Craftsmanship—Studies in Stained Glass*, Norwich, 1982, pp. 58–68.

Young 1821   John Young, *A Catalogue of the Pictures at Grosvenor House London; with Etchings from the Whole Collection*, London, 1821.

General Index

References are to page numbers unless indicated otherwise. Catalogue numbers are cited for ownership and location of works and for listings under PROV and ENGR at the beginning of entries. Any significant discussion in the text or notes to an entry is referred to by page number. Museums and other public institutions are listed under the cities in which they are situated; dealers and private collectors under their names. Individuals who appear in the catalogue solely as the subjects of portraits are recorded in the Index of Subjects and Titles. Owing to the frequency with which they appear as sources of documentation throughout the catalogue, citations of William Carey, William Dunlap, Joseph Farington, John Galt, West's sons' offer to sell works to the United States government in 1826, and the sales conducted by George Robins in 1829 are generally not indexed.

Index of Subjects and Titles

References to catalogue numbers are indicated by the abbreviations "No." and "Nos."; all other references are to page numbers. The main entry for a work or a group of works sharing the same title can be found alphabetized under the title used in this catalogue; it includes page numbers for all illustrations of and references to that work or those works in both the introductory chapters and the catalogue proper. For variant titles, alternative names of subjects of portraits, individuals who appear in pictures otherwise, topographical details, and other aspects of subject matter, catalogue numbers only are given.

Photographic
Acknowledgements

We wish to thank all those who have given permission for works in their possession to be reproduced. Most photographs and transparencies have been provided by the works' owners or, in some instances, by former owners when works have changed hands since this catalogue was begun. In addition, we should like to acknowledge the following sources (numbers in parentheses refer to pages where illustrations appear):

Ashmolean Museum (545), Borthwick Institute of Historical Research, University of York (467), Trustees of the British Museum (187, 213, 244, 253, 273, 304, 369, 404), John Brook (151), Gerald L. Carr (331), Christie's (120, 190, 285, 405, 460, 493, 576), Columbia University Libraries (19, 23, 36, 46, 47, 56, 63, 58, 59, 95, 166, 339, 352, 347, 528, 554), A. C. Cooper (326), Courtauld Institute of Art (17, 25, 167, 188, 256, 281, 327, 335, 338, 368, 381, 392, 401, 445, 480, 484, 493, 494, 497, 506, 512, 514, 526), Frick Art Reference Library (178, 250, 253, 318, 338, 392, 511, 573), Hirschl & Adler Galleries (269), A. F. Kersting (92), McCleod Photography, Inverness (76, 191), Paul Mellon Centre for Studies in British Art (177, 183, 190, 221, 231, 249, 260, 302, 319, 320, 323, 344, 353, 371, 374, 405, 416, 418, 483, 514, 518, 540, 544), Metropolitan Museum of Art (63, 150), Clichés des Musées Nationaux (83, 127), National Gallery of Art, Washington (429), National Monuments Record (224, 225), National Portrait Gallery (204, 417), New York Public Library (219, 327), Philadelphia Museum of Art (4, 8, 9, 425, 532), Cecil Reilly, (61, 216), Royal Academy of Art (37), Rutgers University Library (370), Eddie Ryle-Hodges (26, 27, 537), Scottish National Portrait Gallery (504, 509, 553), Sotheby's (185, 215, 227, 300, 537, 530, 531), STP Photography, Cardiff (563), the Revd. J. Iorworth Thomas (91), Rodney Todd-White (141), Vose Galleries (199, 202, 236, 419), Walker Art Gallery, Liverpool (185, 267, 415).

Engravings are reproduced from impressions in the Department of Prints and Drawings of the British Museum, with the following exceptions: Columbia University Libraries (47, 57, 528, 554), Courtauld Institute of Art (445, 480), Metropolitan Museum of Art (63, 150), New York Public Library (219, 327) Royal Shakespeare Gallery, Stratford-upon-Avon (275), Swarthmore College (294), Rutgers University Libraries (370, 372).

DATE DUE

GAYLORD   PRINTED IN U.S.A.